THE OXFORD HAND

THEOLOGY AND MODERN EUROPEAN THOUGHT

Edited by

NICHOLAS ADAMS,

GEORGE PATTISON,

and

GRAHAM WARD

OXFORD

UNIVERSITY PRESS

OXFORD
UNIVERSITY PRESS

Great Clarendon Street, Oxford, OX2 6DP,
United Kingdom

Oxford University Press is a department of the University of Oxford.
It furthers the University's objective of excellence in research, scholarship,
and education by publishing worldwide. Oxford is a registered trade mark of
Oxford University Press in the UK and in certain other countries

Published in the United States of America by Oxford University Press
198 Madison Avenue, New York, NY 10016, United States of America

British Library Cataloguing in Publication Data
Data available

Library of Congress Cataloging in Publication Data
Data available

ISBN 978-0-19-960199-8 (Hbk.)
ISBN 978-0-19-870980-0 (Pbk.)

THE OXFORD HANDBOOK OF

THEOLOGY AND MODERN EUROPEAN THOUGHT

ACKNOWLEDGEMENTS

The editors are grateful to Oxford University Press for their support throughout the long process of gestation of this Handbook, especially to Tom Perridge and Lizzie Robottom.

CONTENTS

PART V WAYS OF KNOWING

PART VI THEOLOGY

List of Contributors

Nicholas Adams is Senior Lecturer in Theology and Ethics at the University of Edinburgh. He is the author of *Habermas and Theology* (2006) and *The Eclipse of Grace: Divine and Human Action in Hegel* (forthcoming). He writes on German Idealism, religious public argumentation, and inter-faith engagement, with special interest in the A Common Word initiative and the philosophical aspects of the practice of Scriptural Reasoning.

Pamela Sue Anderson is Reader in Philosophy of Religion, University of Oxford, and Fellow in Philosophy, Regent's Park College, Oxford. Anderson has an MA and DPhil from the University of Oxford and an honorary doctorate from Lund University, Sweden. Anderson's publications include *Ricoeur and Kant* (1993), *A Feminist Philosophy of Religion: The Rationality and Myths of Religious Belief* (1998), *New Topics in Feminist Philosophy of Religion: Contestations and Transcendence Incarnate* (2010); and her recently completed, *Re-visioning Gender in Philosophy of Religion: Reason, Love and Epistemic Locatedness* (2012). Anderson also co-authored with Jordan Bell, *Kant and Theology: Philosophy for Theologians* (2010). Her ongoing project is *In Dialogue with Michèle Le Doeuff*.

Stephen Backhouse (DPhil, Oxford) is Lecturer in Social and Political Theology at St Mellitus College, London. He is the author of a number of books and articles on history, politics, national identity, and theology, including *Experiments in Living* (2010), *The Compact Guide to Christian History* (2011), and *Kierkegaard's Critique of Christian Nationalism* (2011).

Luke Bretherton is Associate Professor of Theological Ethics at Duke Divinity School and Senior Fellow at other Kenan Institute for ethics. He is author of *Hospitality and Holiness: Christian Witness Amid Moral Diversity* (2006) and *Christianity and Contemporary Politics: The Conditions and Possibilities of Faithful Witness* (2010). His most recent work examines the relationship between faith, democractic citizenship, and the politics of the common good through a case study of broad-based community organizing and will be published in a forthcoming book as part of the Cambridge Studies in Social Theory, Religion, and Politics series.

David Brown is Professor of Theology, Aesthetics, and Culture and Wardlaw Professor in the University of St Andrew's. His most recent work includes a series of five volumes on the relation between the wider culture and revelation and other experience of God. All are available from Oxford University Press, and include *God and the Enchantment* *of Place* (2004), *God and Grace of Body: Sacrament in Ordinary* (2007), and *God and Mystery in Words: Experience through Drama and Metaphor* (2008).

Clare Carlisle is Lecturer in Philosophy of Religion at King's College London. She is the author of *Kierkegaard's Philosophy of Becoming: Movements and Positions* (2005) and *Kierkegaard's Fear and Trembling* (2010). Her English translation of Félix Ravaisson's *De l'habitude* was published in 2008, and her next book will be *On Habit*, due to be published in 2013.

Conor Cunningham is Assistant Director of the Centre of Theology and Philosophy at the University of Nottingham. He is author of *Genealogy of Nihilism* (2002) and *Darwin's Pious Idea: Why the Ultra Darwinists and Creationists Both Get it Wrong* (2010). Cunningham also wrote and presented the acclaimed BBC documentary *Did Darwin Kill God?* aired originally in March 2009.

William Desmond is Professor of Philosophy at Katholieke Universiteit Leuven and David Cook Visiting Chair in Philosophy at Villanova University. He is the author of *Being and the Between* (winner of the Prix Cardinal Mercier and the J. N. Findlay Award for best book in metaphysics, 1995–7), *Ethics and the Between*, and *God and the Between*. He is Past President of the Hegel Society of America, the Metaphysical Society of America, and the American Catholic Philosophical Association. His most recent books are *The Intimate Strangeness of Being: Metaphysics after Dialectic* (2012) and the *William Desmond Reader* (2012).

David Fergusson is Professor of Divinity and Principal of New College at the University of Edinburgh. He is author of *Faith and Its Critics* (2009) based on the Gifford Lectures (2008).

Paul S. Fiddes is Professor of Systematic Theology in the University of Oxford and Director of Research at Regent's Park College in the University. His books include: *The Creative Suffering of God* (1988), *The Promised End. Eschatology in Theology and Literature* (2000), and *Participating in God. A Pastoral Doctrine of the Trinity* (2000).

Jim Fodor is Professor of Theology and Ethics at St. Bonaventure University in Western New York. He is author and editor of several volumes, including (with Oleg Bychkov) *Theological Aesthetics after von Balthasar* (2008), (with Frederick Christian Bauerschmidt) *Aquinas in Dialogue: Thomas for the Twenty-First Century* (2004), and *Christian Hermeneutics: Paul Ricoeur and the Refiguring of Theology* (1995). He is also editor of *Modern Theology*.

Jennifer L. Geddes is Research Associate Professor of Religious Studies at the University of Virginia, co-editor of *The Hedgehog Review: Critical Reflections on Contemporary Culture*, and a director of the Institute for Advanced Studies in Culture. She is the editor of *Evil after Postmodernism: Histories, Narratives, Ethics* and *The Double Binds of Ethics after the Holocaust: Salvaging the Fragments* (with John K. Roth and Jules Simon), and the author of over 35 articles, book chapters, reviews, and interviews. She is currently working on a book on evil, rhetoric, and ethics.

Michael Allen Gillespie is Professor of Political Science and Philosophy at Duke University. His principal focus is modern continental theory, philosophy and religion, and the history of political philosophy. He is the author of *Hegel, Heidegger and the Ground of History (Chicago, 1984), Nihilism before Nietzsche* (Chicago, 1995), and *The Theological Origins of Modernity (Chicago, 2008).* He is also co-editor of *Nietzsche's New Seas: Explorations in Philosophy, Aesthetics, and Politics (Chicago, 1988), Ratifying the Constitution* (Kansas, 1992), and *Homo Politicus, Homo Economicus (Springer, 2008).* He is the Director of the Gerst Program in Political, Economic, and Humanistic Studies.

Gordon Graham is Henry Luce III Professor of Philosophy and the Arts at Princeton Theological Seminary. He has contributed to Oxford Handbooks on Aesthetics and Systematic Theology, and his most recent books include *The Re-enchantment of the World: Art versus Religion* (2007) and *Theories of Ethics* (2010).

Arne Grøn is Professor of Ethics and Philosophy of Religion at the University of Copenhagen. He is a co-founder of, and professor at, the Danish National Research Foundation Center for Subjectivity Research. He is a member of The Royal Danish Academy of Sciences and Letters.

Daphne Hampson is Professor Emerita of Divinity at the University of St Andrews where she held a personal chair in Post-Christian Thought. She now lives in Oxford and is an Associate of the Faculty of Theology and Religion. Her publications include, *Theology and Feminism* (1990), *After Christianity* (1996/2002), and *Christian Contradictions: The Structures of Lutheran and Catholic Thought* (2001). Her *Kierkegaard: Exposition and Critique* will be published by Oxford University Press in 2013.

Stanley Hauerwas is the Gilbert T. Rowe Professor of Theological Ethics at Duke Divinity School, He was named 'America's Best Theologian' by *Time* magazine in 2001, holds a joint appointment in Duke Law School, and delivered the prestigious Gifford Lectureship at the University of St Andrews in 2001. His book, *A Community of Character: Toward a Constructive Christian Social Ethic*, was selected as one of the 100 most important books on religion of the twentieth century. More recently he has authored *Matthew: Brazos Theological Commentary on the Bible* (2006) and *The State of the University: Academic Knowledges and the Knowledge of God* (2007).

Douglas Hedley read Philosophy and Theology at the Universities of Oxford and Munich and has been lecturing in the Divinity Faculty Cambridge since 1996. He has been a visiting professor at the EPHE, Sorbonne, Paris, and has lectured in the USA, Canada, India, China, and Japan. He is the author of *Coleridge, Philosophy and Religion: Aids to Reflection and the Mirror of the Spirit* (2000), *Living Forms of the Imagination* (2008), and *Sacrifice Imagined: Violence, Atonement and the Sacred* (2011).

John Hughes was Dean and Fellow of Jesus College, Cambridge. He wrote *The End of Work: Theological Critiques of Capitalism* (2007) and edited *The Unknown God: Sermons Responding to the New Atheists* (2013).

Werner G. Jeanrond is Master of St Benet's Hall in the University of Oxford. He has previously taught systematic theology at Trinity College Dublin, Ireland, Lund University, Sweden, and the University of Glasgow. His books and articles in theology and hermeneutics have been translated into many languages, including *A Theology of Love* (2010).

David R. Law is Professor of Christian Thought and Philosophical Theology at the University of Manchester. Among his publications are two books on Kierkegaard, namely *Kierkegaard as Negative Theologian* (1993) and *Kierkegaard's Kenotic Christology* (2013). He has also published articles on Kierkegaard in the *International Kierkegaard Commentary* and in *Kierkegaard Research: Sources, Reception and Resources*.

David Lewin is Senior Lecturer in Philosophy of Education at Liverpool Hope University (UK). His research addresses the religious and philosophical implications of modern technology, as well as related philosophical issues in education. In addition to publishing several articles on the philosophy of technology and its relation to religious philosophy, he has recently published *Technology and the Philosophy of Religion* (2011) and (co-edited with Todd Mei) *From Ricoeur to Action: The Socio-Political Significance of Ricoeur's Thinking.* (Continuum, 2012).

George Pattison is 1640 Professor of Divinity at the University of Glasgow, having previously taught at Cambridge, Aarhus, and Oxford universities. His recent books include *God and Being: An Enquiry* (2011) and *Kierkegaard and the Quest for Unambiguous life* (2012). He is also co-editor with John Lippitt of *The Oxford Handbook of Kierkegaard*.

Tracey Rowland is Dean and Permanent Fellow of the John Paul II Institute for Marriage and Family, Melbourne, and Adjunct Professor, Centre for Faith Ethics and Society, University of Notre Dame, Sydney. She is the author of *Culture and the Thomist Tradition after Vatican II* (2003), *Ratzinger's Faith: the Theology of Pope Benedict XVI* (2008), and *Benedict XVI: A Guide for the Perplexed* (2010).

Steven Shakespeare is Lecturer in Philosophy at Liverpool Hope University. He is a Fellow of the Oxford Centre for Animal Ethics and co-facilitates the Association for Continental Philosophy of Religion. His published work includes *Kierkegaard, Language and the Reality of God* (2001); *Radical Orthodoxy: A Critical Introduction* (2007); *Derrida and Theology* (2009); and (co-edited with Claire Molloy and Charlie Blake) *Beyond Human: From Animality to Transhumanism* (2012).

Graham Ward is the Regius Professor Divinity at the University of Oxford. He is the author of *Balthasar at the End of Modernity* (1999), *Barth, Derrida and the Language of Theology* (1999), *Cities of God* (2000), *Theology and Contemporary Critical Theory* (2000), *True Religion* (2002), *Christ and Culture* (2005), *Cultural Transformation and*

Religious Practices (2005), and *The Politics of Discipleship* (2010). He is also the editor of *The Postmodern God* (1998), *The Certeau Reader* (1999), *Radical Orthodoxy* (1999), *The Blackwell Companion to Postmodern Theology* (2001), and, with Michael Hoelzl, *The New Visibility of Religion* (2008). He is currently working on two volumes concerned with the doctrine of God, entitled *Ethical Life.*

Merold Westphal is Distinguished Professor of Philosophy at Fordham University in New York City. The author of two books on Hegel and two on Kierkegaard, he also works on continental philosophy of religion in the contexts of existentialism, phenomenology, hermeneutics, ideology critique, and deconstruction. Recent books include *Suspicion and Faith: The Religious Uses of Modern Atheism* (1999), *Overcoming Onto-theology: Toward a Postmodern Christian Faith* (2001), *Transcendence and Self-Transcendence: An Essay on God and the Soul* (2004), *Levinas and Kierkegaard in Dialogue* (2008), and *Whose Community? Which Interpretation? Philosophical Hermeneutics for the Church* (2009).

Ross Wilson is Lecturer in Literature at the University of East Anglia. He is the author of *Theodor Adorno* (2006), *Subjective Universality in Kant's Aesthetics* (2007) and editor of *The Meaning of 'Life' in Romantic Poetry and Poetics* (2008). He is currently working on a monograph entitled *Shelley and the Apprehension of Life.*

Judith Wolfe is Lecturer in Theology & the Arts at the University of St Andrews. She is the author of *Heidegger's Secular Eschatology* (2012), *Heidegger and Theology* (2013), and a number of articles on Christian eschatology in relation to both philosophy and literature.

Johannes Zachhuber is Reader of Theology in the University of Oxford. He works on Christian theology in late antiquity and in the nineteenth and twentieth centuries. Publications include *Human Nature in Gregory of Nyssa* (2000) and *A Science of Theology? The German Debate from FC Baur to Ernst Troeltsch* (2012).

Simeon Zahl is Junior Research Fellow in Theology at St John's College, University of Oxford. He is the author of *Pneumatology and Theology of the Cross in the Preaching of Christoph Friedrich Blumhardt* (2010).

INTRODUCTION

NICHOLAS ADAMS, GEORGE PATTISON, AND GRAHAM WARD

WHAT might readers expect from a *Handbook of Theology and Modern European Thought*? For a start, they might expect a book that is ten times larger than the one now being presented. Each term of the title—'theology'; 'modern'; 'European'; and 'thought'—is eminently contestable and invites almost unlimited commentary and disagreement. Whatever the editors' sins of commission, they are therefore deeply aware of sins of omission, some of the more important of which will be addressed later in this Introduction. But whatever the details of what should or shouldn't have been included under this rubric, it seems to us clear that theology and modern European thought are not two things that might or might not be brought into relation. The chapters collected here demonstrate that they belong together in such a way that theology cannot be neatly partitioned off from the whole intellectual and cultural environment in which it is practised. Conversely, the intellectual and cultural environ-ment of modernity remains deeply entangled in theology—even (and perhaps espe-cially) when it most wants to rid itself of it. For these reasons, we shall not here attempt to narrow the definitions either of theology or of modern European thought. This does not mean that attempts to develop what has been called a properly theological theology, i.e. a theology governed by its own intrinsic sources and norms, are without value. Nor does it mean that programmes of radical secularization are meaningless. But it does mean that both the theologians' attempts to preserve the distinctiveness of their discipline and the secularists' efforts to strip society, culture, and intellectual life of what they see as its residual theological trappings never entirely escape shared—if sometimes elusive—horizons of linguistic and symbolic orders and of moral and political commitments. A greater acknowledgement of the reality of this situation will not, we believe, lead (as some might fear) to the further secularization of theology itself and its absorption into some form of cultural, anthropological, or philosophical studies. On the contrary, we suggest that such acknowledgement is likely to demonstrate how well-placed theology is to contribute—on its own terms—to the continuing debate (dispersed across a range of faculties in the university) as to what it means to be and to flourish as human beings. Conversely, descriptive and normative interpretations of the human phenomenon that simply exclude theology from the conversation will be shown to be not just self-limiting but potentially self-destructive.

In commencing with the term 'theology' we are not committing ourselves to any particular view of how theology might be more closely defined. That being said, we are broadly taking it as applying to those forms of theology that have been developed and taught in university contexts in the European world of the last two centuries. Today that includes many scholars working in faculties or departments of religion, culture, philosophy, modern languages, or other subjects, who are nevertheless heirs to many of the key texts and debates of the nineteenth and twentieth centuries. Although sharp differences may still exist between institutions committed to strong confessional identities and those that have been significantly de-confessionalized (or never were confessional in the first place), the fact is that scholars across these divides read and comment on each others' work, share in conferences, seminars, and research activities, and contribute to each others' collected volumes. Of course, edges are blurred, and there are contexts where 'theology' shades off into one or other neighbouring disciplines, but there is also a broad swathe of contemporary intellectual life where scholars take themselves to be practising Christian theology and are recognized as so doing by their fellows, including those who propose vastly different views as to just what theology is or ought to be. Recognizing this breadth, contributors to this volume are drawn from virtually the whole spectrum of theological positions widely encountered in contemporary western academic discourse and neither they nor the collection as a whole can be assigned to any particular school, movement, or tendency.

I. MODERNITY

What, then, of the term 'modern'? What is it to be modern? And who really speaks for 'modern man'—and the implied exclusion of 'modern woman' from that most ubiquitous of mid-twentieth-century jargon already indicates a major fault line in the very conception of 'modernity'! Is there in fact just 'one' modernity?

In 1979, the French philosopher, Jean-François Lyotard published a short book entitled *La Condition postmodern. Rapport sur la savoir*. It was translated into English in 1984 (Lyotard 1984). We can take the publication of this book as a convenient starting point for a critical turn within thinking about concepts that had come to dominate so much cultural and intellectual activity: the modern, modernity, modernization, and modernism. Lyotard, with his critique against what he called the 'meta-narratives of modernity' and his introduction of the term 'postmodern', opened the debate about whether modernity was over. The 1970s were a critical point in western cultural history, as the British sociologist, Daniel Bell, saw clearly in his prescient book

The Coming of Post-Industrial Society (Bell 1976). Industrialism had been almost synonymous with modernization (Kumar 1995). Now reflections upon a changed condition—primarily, economic changes associated with the oil crisis, demographic changes that emerged through increasing migration, and cultural changes with the increasing recognition of multiculturalism—began to spawn a number of socio-logical terms to describe the new situation. 'Postmodernity' was obviously one, and others followed: late capitalism (Harvey 1989; Jameson 1989), post-traditionalism (Giddens 1995), post-Fordism (Amin 2003), liquid modernity (Bauman 2000) and post-colonialism (Said 1985). What is most significant about Lyotard's volume is that the cultural hegemony of modernity, and its claim to speak to all social situations in a universal language, was now being questioned; and it is from this questioning that talk about 'modernities' emerged.

Modernity was never allergic to critique. In fact, critical thinking was exactly what modernity championed in its exultation of rationality and instrumental reasoning. Critique was one of the signs of being modern and no longer in thrall to traditional and unquestioned modes of thinking and doing. Critique was at the forefront of moder-nity's investment in the word 'progress'. Progress mapped well on to the concept of modernity, because modern is a temporal term from the Latin conjunction *modo* (meaning 'just now'). As the Latin suggests, newness is what the word is attempting to capture; change is not only what modernity announces, but what it explicitly celebrates. Modernity means going with the flow. It is committed to temporality and to contingency; as is 'postmodernity'. But, particularly in France, the intellectual climate turned from philosophies of time towards spatiality. New phenomenologies of space (LeFebrve and Bachelard) emerged and combined with the rise of structural semiotics (Levi-Strauss, Gennette, and Lacan, among others). Lyotard's thinking grew out of the structuralist tradition which began to emphasize, alongside contiguities, concepts like difference and alterity. So that when, a decade after Lyotard's thesis, David Harvey and Fredrick Jameson both proposed descriptions of the postmodern condition (1989), critics were quick to point to how their shared notion of late capitalism was in fact a modern one (a development within capitalism) and at odds with spatial differences; both their history (which was singular and in accord with Marx's view of history) and their geography (which was specifically western/USA) lacked complexity (Massey 1994; Thrift 1997). In the debates that now arose, debates which included important defenders of modernity (Habermas) and Nietzsche-inspired proponents of post-structuralism (Foucault, Deleuze, and Derrida, among others), the French sociologist and anthropologist, Bruno Latour, published his influential book *Nous n'avons jamais été modernes. Essai d'anthropologie symétrique* (1991) [*We Have Never Been Modern* (1993)].

Latour marks the next move in the development of the concept of 'modernities', in so far as his book challenged both the notions of modernity and postmodernity. Latour drew attention to the way modernity was structured according to certain fundamental dualisms (nature and culture, public and private, law and freedom, chaos and order, etc.). It structured a world view around these dualisms and the importance of keeping one from the other. Contradiction is then written into the very process of becoming modern. Latour's book is mainly concerned with the nature-culture dualism. In what was already a developing intellectual trend in the philosophy of science, the sociology of science, Latour pointed to the non-negotiable tensions, the leakages and the hybridities between the isolated notions of nature and culture that had always existed and existed still. The distinction between *Naturwissenschaft* and *Geisteswissenshaft*, central to modern thinking, was a social construction, he claimed.

The sheer ambivalence of the term modernity was now becoming obvious at a time when there was a growing reaction to 'modernization'. During the Cold War threat, when communism was an attractive option for third world countries contemplating a future, 'modernization' became a US and Western European led programme for global development. If it took place first of all among Asian societies such as India, Burma, Vietnam, and Indonesia, it soon spread to Middle Eastern countries, and finally Africa. The modernization of Latin America began much earlier. It coincided with the first wave of Western European culture to North America (under the British and French). Only the westernization of South America developed under the Spanish and Portuguese. Modernization, in which 'progress' soon became 'development' was a colonial venture. In its wake and its failure, subject also now to post-colonial criticism (from Fanon onwards), 'modernization' became synonymous with Americanization, Europeanization, and globalization (mainly spearheaded by US and European transnational corporations). But the diverse cultural conditions in these regions led not only to different programmes for modernization, and different speeds at which it could take place, but also different understandings of what being modern meant.

Modernity was splintering under the excess not only of its meaning, but the highly differentiated cultural predicaments it was trying to describe with a homogenous term and the internal critiques (of gender, race, ethnicity, and religion) it fostered. From the point of view of 'developing' countries, modernity was seen as a long list of dead, white, Christian men who had composed a history of global progress from the perspective of their own successes, and which was becoming, in fact, only a form of ideological domination as more white, Christian men now attempted to impose it upon the rest of the world. Modernity was pushed back to times prior to the Enlightenment, such as the Renaissance (Toulmin 1990); it was broken down into four major and causal social processes—the political, social, economic, and cultural—so that their different operations and interactions might be assessed (Hall 1992); its history was charted in all its hybrid complexity to trace an essential, though dialectical, character and predict its future (Touraine 1992 [1995]); and it was heralded as a victim of its own success such that a reflexive modernity, a modernizing modernity, now made possible either a new modernity (the 'risk society' according to Beck 1992) or even many (consecutive) modernities.

'Multiple modernities' is a geohistorical term coined independently but simultaneously by the British geographer, Peter J. Taylor (1999) and the German sociological historian, S. N. Eisenstadt (2000). Taylor, with whom we shall start because his is the less radical vision, proposes an historical axis along which 'primary modernities' have developed; 'primary' because they became hegemonic for the cultures they fostered and the imitation by others they inspired. This axis begins with the Dutch Republic following the Peace of Westphalia (1648) and the developments of mercantile capitalism, international law, the nation as a state, and the celebration of ordinary life. This modernity then undergoes a major shift in the late eighteenth and nineteenth centuries when Britain becomes hegemonic in a second modernity following the Congress of Vienna (1815) and with the developments of industrial capitalism, the cult of progress, and the comforts of middle class domestic life. The third modernity follows the end of the First Word War when America becomes hegemonic and benefits from a swing away from productivity to consumption, the creation of a management culture (Taylorism) and the development of suburban life. Taylor is emphatic that there is nothing necessary about the transitions from one modernity to another; there is no Hegelian *Weltgeist*. In fact, the shifts emerge when a hegemonic cycle begins to generate more complexity and uncertainty than it can control. This new situation then calls forth a new form of modernity. The world power in the best position to take advantage of this complexity and uncertainty (or find a convincing way to surmount it) steps up as the next purveyor of another hegemonic modernity that others will imitate. What is central to all modernities in this scenario is modernity's commitment to change. In the wake of a declining Americanization, morphing now into globalization, Taylor is in fact pessimistic about the future of the current world-system (Taylor 1999: 130) and the scope there is for change.

With Taylor there are multiple modernities, but they are serial. This is not the case with Eisenstadt's depiction of 'multiple modernities'. If Taylor's account is governed more by temporality (though he has a chapter on space and its colonization of place, see Taylor 1999: 95–108), Eisenstadt's is a complex geographical as well as historical account. For him, modernity is open to many interpretations and each different culture embraced and embraces its agendas (such as emancipation, collective identity, the struggle to establish the boundaries of the realm of the political, the place of reason, and emotion in social life, etc.), but they did and do so in the context of distinctive cultures, patterns of institutional life, traditions (including religious traditions), and historical experiences. They all develop distinctly modern dynamics but are pursuing different programmes reflecting different views on what makes a society modern. So, from the beginning, modernity was never one because a range of possible modernities emerged; although, through military and economic imperialism, colonialism and new diasporas the variability of modernities has much increased. This has led to the gradual and exponential decoupling of westernization from modernity. In part what fuels the distinctive character of these multiple modernities are the ways such reflexivity has to handle the antimonies within modernity itself (the dualisms we noted above with respect to Latour's work) and find ways of resolving them. To employ a metaphor used by the British sociologist, Zygmunt Bauman, modernity has now 'liquefied' (Bauman).

We might ask what binds these modernities together, such that we can still speak of modernity as an embracing concept. Both Taylor and Eisenstadt would agree that every one of their modernities is a cultural, political, social, and economic improvisation on a number of dominant modern phrases: the capacity for reflexivity or the ability for continual self-correction; a commitment to the new, to being up-to-date, and, therefore, change; and a loose ideological framework composed of certain key ideas such as freedom, the individual, economic expansion, rationality, the social, and management. Both of them end their work on the limits of modernity, particularly if modernity is so harnessed to capitalist expansion and the space for such expansion is limited. Both are aware they must raise the question, but both are also aware that they cannot answer it. After globalization, what is there? If there is such a condition as postmodernity perhaps then, and only then, will it emerge.

II. Europe

A further dimension of this multiplication of modernities is what we might call modernity's regional dimension, its topology. If the intellectual axis of modern European philosophy and theology—a big 'if', of course—lies between France and the German-speaking world, the French-German lineages are interpreted, supplemented, and controverted by other national and regional traditions. Without such supplementation and disputation our term 'European' would be significantly thinner. Nowhere is this more so than in the history of modern Russian thought, consistently haunted as it has been—and continues to be—by questions as to whether it really is European at all or in what way it is European. Perhaps, some have argued, Russia is better seen as Eurasian or as governed by a distinctive Russian idea. No topic is more fiercely contested in Russian literature, philosophy, and politics than the relationship between Russia and 'the west'. In such debates 'the west' has taken a variety of forms, including the rationalizing agendas of Russia's westernizing despots of the eighteenth century, the scientific and historicist influence of French philosophes and physiologists, the thought of English utilitarians or Left Hegelians, and the encounters displayed in industrialism, capitalism, and a succession of wars, including those of 1812, the Crimea, 1914–17, and 1941–5 (as well, of course, as the long Cold War that followed). But the debate has also—always—had a distinct theological edge, as when Dostoevsky equates Roman Catholicism with the spectre of socialism or speculates about the Slavophile vision of Russia as a 'God-bearing' nation.

Acknowledging the irony that many of the core ideas of the Slavophiles bore a striking resemblance to ideas found also in several varieties of western Romanticism (Slavophiles themselves stressed how deeply their inspirational thinkers were acquainted with early nineteenth-century German figures like Schelling and Hegel), Russia in turn has often played the role of being the west's 'significant Other'. Stravinsky's ballet score 'Rite of Spring' (1913), first performed in Paris, seemed to reveal to western audiences a previously unknown or long forgotten world of primordial energies, epitomizing a collective image of Russianness that had been formed through the early translations of Dostoevsky, Tolstoy, and other great modern Russian authors.

Thus, Barth and Thurneysen could invoke the figure of the 'Russian man' encountered in Russian literature as a counter to the rationalistic bourgeois individual of western society (and something similar can be seen in the Catholic writer Romano Guardini). After the Bolshevik Revolution, the Russian 'Other' acquired further (and for many deeply sinister) significance, conflated as it was in Nazi propaganda with international Jewry and seen as revealing the unsettling presence of the Asiatic world on Europe's own frontier. Yet, in another very different horizon, Russian religious philosophy and orthodox spirituality would be perceived as sources of renewal in western theology, with their (perceived) emphasis on apophaticism, mysticism, and a concern for the hidden depths of personal life.

Russia is not, of course, the only source of significant regional alternative to the intellectual axis. In the late nineteenth century, German versions of literary modernism were strongly impacted by a succession of influential Scandinavian authors, such as J. P. Jacobsen, Ibsen, Strindberg—and, theologians might add, Kierkegaard too belongs in part in this reception. Spain and Italy would have their own receptions and contributions, offering eloquent testimony to the singular political histories of those countries in the modern period and of the strong polarities of Catholicism and communism. Whilst this often led theology to retreat into an exclusively ecclesiastical sphere, it could also open up to moments of dialogue and convergence, that might take the form of Christian Marxisms or the kind of post-ecclesiastical and post-communist philosophies of Agamben and Vattimo that accept the unavoidability of key theological tropes.

Of course, the relation of Marxism to theology is the subject of a volume of its own. It was Marxism that was responsible for renewed engagement with Hegel's philosophy in the twentieth century, through the lectures of Alexandre Kojève (himself an emigré from Russia), whose influenced was dispersed through an audience which included Bataille, Merleau-Ponty, Sartre, and many others. It was Marxism that shaped two generations of (especially German Catholic) theologians who placed a concern with solidarity with the working class at the heart of their theologies, initially through the reception of figures like Ernst Bloch and Walter Benjamin, and then more formally through such institutions as the 'internationale Paulusgesellschaft', which included Karl Rahner and J. B. Metz. It was Marxism, mediated through this German intellectual context, which provided the basic theoretical categories for Liberation Theology in the 1970s. It was Marxism that shaped some of the leading ideas of influential late twentieth-century English-speaking theologically engaged intellectuals like Alasdair MacIntyre and Terry Eagleton, as well as theologians such as Nicholas Lash. After the crushing disappointment for many intellectuals that followed the failure of the student protests of 1968 to reshape European universities, overt rapprochements between theologians and Marxists sharply declined, and today's theological students must make a significant imaginative effort if they are to appreciate how heavily many of the core concerns of contemporary theology are dependent on Marxism for their early development.

The twentieth century has been referred to as the Jewish century, and if one thing is clear it is that modern European philosophy and theology would have been vastly different if it had not been for decisive contributions by a succession of Jewish thinkers, many of whom were also Marxists. Martin Buber, Ludwig Wittgenstein, Franz Rosenzweig, Ernst Bloch, Max Horkheimer, Walter Benjamin, Theodor Adorno, Herbert Marcuse, Lev Shestov, Emmanuel Levinas, and Jacques Derrida are only an initial selection of Jewish thinkers who have done much to shape the ideas and movements discussed in this volume. And even if, to use a distinction developed by Levinas, they are not thinkers of Judaism, they remain thinkers whose Jewish intellectual heritage contributed importantly to their thinking. But, of course, the question of Judaism is unavoidable in both theology and modern European thought for another, more terrible reason—what Jankélévitch called the 'unspeakable' event of the Shoah or Holocaust, as is especially reflected in this volume in Jennifer Geddes' chapter on 'Evil'.

Yet, ubiquitous as it has been, the significance of Jewish philosophy for theology in its relation to modern European thought has not been easy to gauge for two related reasons. The first is that many of the most significant figures were German, and in emigrating to countries like Britain and the USA, they often found they needed to re-author their theoretical apparatus in terms that were more readily intelligible in their new contexts. This process of translation has a tendency to obscure debts to this tradition's origins. The second is that these émigrés gradually formed what became the increasingly discrete discipline of Jewish Studies, which encompassed Jewish history, the study of rabbinical literature, and Jewish philosophy. That universities were hospitable to Jewish Studies meant that a (predominantly German) intellectual tradition continued to live and to develop, despite the catastrophic destruction of that heritage in mainland Europe. But the existence of a discrete discipline meant that this tradition did not so readily cross-fertilize with mainstream developments, especially in faculties of philosophy. This is now changing, as Jewish Studies becomes in some universities more dispersed across different disciplines, and it is likely that exchanges between Jewish and Christian intellectual traditions will become deeper and less of a specialist interest in the coming years. Only the surface of this cross-fertilization has been scratched in this volume, and much work remains to be done.

Much 'European' thought, like much 'continental' philosophy, does not go on in Europe, or on the continent, but is found in North America, whose university populations, and whose educational endowments, now dwarf those of the old medieval institutions. This is a relatively recent phenomenon. Theology flourishes where there are ecclesial constituencies that can afford to educate their ministers and their young people in their theological traditions. As seminaries in the USA grow in number and size, faculties of theology in Europe are shrinking, and this trend seems set to continue for the foreseeable future. This volume on theology and modern European thought thus marks a transfer of intellectual inheritance from one continent to another, or at least a significant investment in that inheritance in America that is not mirrored in Europe. This is not to say that theology has no place in Europe, so much as to register a change of geographical focus, and a shift of centres of gravity that has in many cases already taken place. Because the focus of attention here is on the nineteenth and twentieth centuries, the geographical centre of gravity of this volume is Europe; but it is clear to the editors that the development of this tradition is widely dispersed—not only in North America but in South Asia and increasingly in East Asia.

In some ways, this volume on theology and modern European thought comes at precisely the point in the history of Christianity not only when Europe has ceased to be the centre of gravity, but when the European tradition in North America itself is ceasing to be the centre. Christianity is growing fast in South America, South Asia, East Asia, and especially in Africa. What was until now been called 'non-western Christianity' and then 'world Christianity' is no longer a peripheral development stemming from the missionary endeavours of the nineteenth century and before. European Christianity has already been numerically surpassed, and it is surely only a matter of time before the intellectual centre of the tradition shifts from the great medieval European universities, and from those American universities which continue their traditions. Institutions in Africa, China, and elsewhere, which have much less continuity with the European traditions, will almost certainly take centre stage. It lies beyond the scope of this volume to chart these changes, but it needs to be acknowledged that the modern European centre of gravity which marked the twentieth-century's greatest theology—much of it in French and German—has to a significant extent come to an end, to be replaced by developments whose contours are perhaps already visible in the study of world Christianity, but which have yet to register in the core curricula of faculties of theology and of religion in Europe and North America. It is likely that this volume is a contribution to a tradition whose future will be fundamentally reshaped by a geography and by languages that only recently encountered the Bible. All this is to say that the word 'European' is a word that no longer signifies a straightforwardly delimited geographical intellectual heritage.

III. Thought

The use of the word 'thought' suggests that whilst the contributions of philosophers will certainly be an important part of the discussion, the issues are not limited to the projects of philosophers conceived in a narrowly disciplinary way. Instead, it might helpfully be taken as indicative of the kind of cultural life represented by that old phrase 'writers, artists, and intellectuals'—as well as by the professionally academic philosophers and theologians. Nevertheless, philosophy remains a central feature of modern European thought and of the chapters collected in this Handbook. The relationship between academic philosophy and modern European thought has three features that are especially relevant to this collection. First, it has often been academic philosophers who have provided the most synoptic, rigorous and generative accounts of the key issues of modern European thought. In so doing they have stimulated and provoked formative responses by those writers, artists, religious thinkers, and scholars in other disciplines and outside the academy who have both inspired and made effective the arguments of the philosophers. Kant, Hegel, Schelling, Husserl, Heidegger, and Derrida are philosophers of this kind, whose work both reflected and generated movements and counter-movements in scholarship, culture, and religious thought from Romanticism through existentialism to postmodernism.

Secondly, philosophy and theology were for much of this period pursued in a kind of symbiosis. Enemies of theology have often been the first to point out (as Nietzsche pointed out with regard to German Idealism) that many of the issues with which modern European thinkers have wrestled are, at heart, theological. Equally, from Schleiermacher to postmodernity, theology's own agenda has driven it to engage and shape philosophical investigations, as well as to participate in culture wars and political movements. 'Hermeneutics', 'existence', and 'the race' are just three of many signs of this theological contribution to the key terms of modern philosophy.

Thirdly, continental philosophy has not only taken up (however transformatively) issues of a theological provenance, but has engaged wide-ranging issues of culture and, not least, politics, and few philosophers have separated their work from the cultural and political battles of their time. Again, Kant, Hegel, Heidegger, and Derrida are the more obvious cases. But once they enter these debates, the philosophers may find themselves wrestling with intellectual challenges similar to those being addressed by many theologians. For even the most theological of theologians were driven by their own agendas to distinctive cultural and political commitments, a claim for which the history of dialectical theology provides considerable evidence. Recurrent themes in this area concern the conflicting claims of tradition, authority, autonomy, and the nature of that most modern—yet also most theological—of all modern ideas: 'freedom'.

Philosophy and philosophers will therefore play a central part in this volume. However, this is not limited to themes in the philosophy of religion, narrowly conceived, for these form only a fraction of the material in view. The volume is constantly attentive to the wider questions that many philosophers have posed, and which are also central to other 'modern European' thinkers whose work has been no less significant in shaping the intellectual culture of the last two centuries—thinkers such as Kierkegaard, Marx, Nietzsche, Freud, and Benjamin, or writers such as the great Russian novelists of the nineteenth century or Rilke, Mann, and Hesse in the twentieth (these are, of course, merely examples, and readers will readily supply their own 'canon' of culturally formative figures).

These last names indicate that literature has been an unavoidable 'tertium quid' in the relationship between 'theology' and 'philosophy' in the field of modern European thought. Like all the arts, literature is a response to the world, a world that that is already interpreted through the matrix of ideas which make up both a particular culture and a tradition. In turn, like the arts, literature fashions and impacts upon that world enabling us to see it differently; a line of hawthorn trees is never quite the same after reading the opening novel of Proust's À la recherche du temps perdu. Du côté de chez Swann just as the Brandenburg Gate is never see in the same way after Wim Wender's Der Himmel über Berlin. Without then speaking of modern literature reductively in terms of secularization, we can say that to the extent that modernity concerned itself with the significance of affairs in this world, its immanent scientific laws, its production of wealth, urban society, and the politics of the nation state, etc., then literature represented these concerns. The Enlightenment produced philosophical works about living in such a world like Voltaire's *Candide* and or Alexander Pope's *An Essay on Man*, and, indeed, the tradition of philosophers as writers of literature continued in the nineteenth century with writers such as Kierkegaard and Nietzsche and in the twentieth century with the existential novels of Jean-Paul Sartre and the semiotic novels of Umberto Eco, among others. But literature is not simply about ideas and it cannot be reduced to its contents or what it is representing. While, from the early eighteenth century onwards, novels in particular attended to social realism (Defoe, Richardson, and later George Sand and George Eliot), throughout modernity there have been writers reacting against a simple materialist view of world: some expressing longings for transcendence (like Goethe, Novalis, and the Romantic poets, and, more recently Iris Murdoch); some reflecting imaginatively within an explicitly theological world view (like Dostoevsky, T. S. Eliot, and Flannery O'Connor); and some wishing to evoke a rich aesthetic sense that was divorced from transcendence and even espoused the nihilist flux of all things (Flaubert, Baudelaire, and Rimbaud, in France, Oscar Wilde and Max Beerbohm, in Britain, and, more recently, Vladimir Nabokov). In fact, literature becomes the means for understanding the sheer cultural complexity of modernity, its restless search for the new, and its inventiveness in trying to capture that which was most authentic about the human condition. We might define modernism as an aesthetic movement in which modernity is fully conscious of itself, and in literature this entailed language being conscious of its own ability to fashion and make new. It produced works of remarkable originality which conflated any boundaries between prose, poetry, and dramaturgy—works like Joyce's *Finnegan's Wake*, Kafka's *The Trial*, and Beckett's *Waiting for Godot*.

Literature flourished in modernity, along with new technologies for the mass production and dissemination of its literary products. Increasingly, this led to the professionalism of literary criticism. If there has always been some reflection upon literature itself (Aristotle and Sir Philip Sidney), modernity greatly fostered such reflexivity with the likes of Johnson, Carlyle, and more recently Levis and Bloom becoming more important and influential than many writers of literature themselves. In fact, these people sought to raise literary criticism into an art itself. Of course, writers too became more conscious of their own artistry as a consequence of this increasing interest in the literary. In the wake of Coleridge and the rise of aesthetics in Germany, we find Henry James thinking through the poetics of the novel, Mallarmé on symbolist poetry, and Brecht on drama. Philosophers too drew on literature for developing their ideas, creating hybrid discourses between philosophy and literature: most notably Heidegger, Benjamin, Ricoeur, and Cavell. Even theologians like Hans Urs von Balthasar on Hopkins and Claudel or Rowan Williams on Dostoevsky reveal the line between literature and theology to be permeable. In modernity the Bible itself comes to be read as literature. If it becomes difficult to draw a distinction between literature and philosophy in the work of Kierkegaard and Nietzsche, then in the twentieth century we have philosophers who explicitly reject the view that philosophy is a different mode of discourse from literature: Jacques Derrida and Paul de Man, most particularly. In both philosophy and theology, important literary forms such as metaphor and narrative, generated new methods of 'doing' philosophy or theology and new lines of enquiry.

It might also be thought that space could or should have been found for exploring the ways in which the visual arts have interacted with modern European thought and theology. Painting and other visual arts have provided illustrations, points of reference, and even, arguably, extended the content of modern philosophers and theologians and in a variety of ways. We might think not only of the enormous role that expressionist painting played in the theology of Paul Tillich, but also of Barth's repeated recourse to Grünewald's *Crucifixion*, while, among the philosophers, Heidegger took a painting of some old boots by Van Gogh as a focus for his reflections on the origin of the work of art (reflections responded to, in turn, by Derrida) and Merleau-Ponty gave Cezanne's interpretation of the task of painting a pivotal role in his development of a philosophy of embodied existence. Conversely, artists have themselves responded to philosophies and theologies of art and have sometimes taken them as programmatic for their own practice, as in Eric Gill's espousal of Jacques Maritain's neo-scholastic interpretation of art and culture. In works such as 'The Ways of Worldly Wisdom' the contemporary painter Anselm Kiefer has commented on the twentieth-century crisis of German culture and ideas and his work has in turn been brought into dialogue with philosophy and theology (see, e.g. Taylor 1992; Biro 1998; Pattison 2009). Moreover, some of the great works of modern art criticism are themselves highly 'theological', as in John Ruskin's classic *Modern Painters*—perhaps the most powerful theology of art produced in modern times (see Fuller 1988; Pattison 1991).

More broadly, we may say that while 'theology and modern European thought' will inevitably involve political theory, art, and literature as well as philosophy, all of these are also affected in this period by a significant revisioning of the relationship between body and mind. Descartes's last book was entitled *The Passions of the Soul* and in it he attempts to modify the dualism between body and mind that is evident in *Meditations* and *Discourse on Method*. His attention is upon the physiology, psychology, and, to a limited extent, spirituality of the affections. This intellectual interest in the emotions was continued throughout the eighteenth century through philosophers like David Hume and Adam Smith. In *A Treatise of Human Nature*, Hume will frequently list desire (often plural) with the passions and he recognizes the important motivational functional these have upon human behaviour (and the imagination), but desire itself was not explicitly examined. It is with Kant and his *Critique of Pure Reason* that we have a named faculty of desire, and it comes very late in his thesis in relation to practical reason and freedom, and is not developed there. On the whole, during the Enlightenment, when the topic of desire arose it was treated negatively in so far as it was considered necessary to subordinate it to the Stoic primacy of the will and the intellect. When Kant relates desire to the faculty of the imagination he is following a standard association (found in Hume and Smith, for example), but for Kant desire is an intellectual property of the mind—it is the mind that desires and what it desires is the product of the higher faculties of understanding and reason. As such, desire, for Kant, is detached from passion and detached also from corporeality. Although it receives impressions of the sensuous it also announces determinative laws 'which are imperative and objectives laws of freedom and which tell us what ought to take place' (Kant 1934: 456). He goes on to inform us in the *Critique of Practical Reason* that the faculty of desire is fundamental for the production of representations of the *Ding an sich*, or what he terms (in his late definition of this faculty) the 'faculty to be by means of its representations the cause of the reality of the objects of these representations' (Kant 1996: 144). In harmony with the moral law, determined by the notion of the good and in line with the eudemonistic principle of every rational individual wanting to be happy, desire is at one point called a 'vital force' but is conflated with the will.

It is with the young F. D. E. Schleiermacher, in an essay written around 1792, never published in his lifetime and only published in the *Gesamtausgabe* in 1984, that we see the early re-establishment of the importance of desire. In *Über die Freiheit*, a reflection concerned with Kant's *Critique of Practical Reason*, Schleiermacher turns to the question of receptivity, developing Karl Leonard Reinhold's explorations of Kant, In so doing he announces a more primordial operation upon the sensuous called 'impulse' (*Trieb*) and viewed desire as an 'instinct' (*Instinkt*) which 'craves' (*gelüsten*) (Schleiermacher 1984). Desire, now closely associated with embodiment and a positive appraisal of the erotic, plays an important role in his (1799) *On Religion* and probably an even more important role in his conversations with the Schlegel brothers and the development of early Romanticism. It resonated with a new appreciation of the body, inspired by a love of all things Greek, as it found expression in the earlier work of Johann Joachim Winckelmann (see Mosse (1999) on the impact of Winckelmann on the development of the male physique, the cult of masculinity and the introduction of sport into gymnasium education). It resonated also with a rediscovery of Spinoza whose appreciation of desire (the '*conatus*' of his *Ethics*) has been a major influence on twentieth-century French philosophies of desire (most particularly Gilles Deleuze, Felix Guattari, and Luce Irigaray). Furthermore, the identification of desire as a primary human drive was complimented also by, first, new biological investigations into sexual reproduction, sexuality, and sexual difference (see Halperin 1990; Lacquer 1992; and Lloyd 1993) in which, eventually, we have to situate the work of Freud, and by the development of sexual politics (the older Wollstonecraft and late Mill). This development of modern physiology arose at the same time as the idea of the body and what Foucault called biopolitics were being expanded. In the Enlightenment, for example, the state was viewed as a machine. But, from the early nineteenth century until today, the state was being understood not mechanically but organically. Notions such as the national body, the social body, the civic body, and even the city as a body began to complement older theological construals of ecclesial and sacramental bodies (see Ward, Chapter 3 in this volume; Pile 1996; and Sheard and Power 2000).

One might best plot the philosophical history of desire in the nineteenth and twentieth centuries through the genealogy constructed by Judith Butler in her book *Subjects of Desire* (Butler 1999), since, with Butler's work, we gain entry to the contemporary concern with desire in gender and queer theory. Butler begins with an account of the ontology of desire in Hegel and then moves on to the French reception of Hegel's work in the twentieth century through Alexander Kojève and Jean Hyppolite. Two prominent figures emerge at this point: Jean-Paul Sartre who became interested in desire in his early phenomenologies of emotion and imagination and Jacques Lacan in his recasting of Freud in the wake of structuralism. Butler concludes her study with an examination of the work on desire in Deleuze and Michel Foucault. Other figures might have been named to supplement this genealogy: most notably Nietzsche and his twin interests in the body and the Dionysian, in the nineteenth century; the work of the phenomenologist Maurice Merleau-Ponty on embodied perception, in the twentieth; and the French feminists Julia Kristeva, Luce Irigaray, and Helena Cixous.

These contemporary philosophies of desire and the body have impacted considerably upon modern Christian theology. In part, they have done so by inspiring an excavation into the important role desire played in the theology of the Alexandrian and Cappadocian Fathers and Augustine, down into the Middles Ages with Bonaventure and into the Renaissance with Marsilio Ficino (see Burrus 2002 and Castelli 2007, among others). In part, they have also inspired new developments in feminist and queer theology (see Althaus-Reid 2003 and Loughlin 2007, among others).

In summary, this volume challenges and transforms certain ways of opposing, as well as fusing, 'theology and modern European thought'. We are not primarily attempting either to track the influence of modern European thought on theology or to detect the theological topics that often underlie supposedly secular forms of thought and cultural practice. Each will have its place. We have two principal aims, one positive and one negative: (1) to identify those questions and issues that have been common to and formative of both theology and modern European thought; (2) to avoid reducing the subject matter to one-sidedly theological or secular philosophical views. There will be points where it seems that theology is the driving force in a given debate, there will be other points at which theology seems more re-active. The material is complex, spanning the cross-currents of wars, revolutions, and social and cultural transformations of many nations over two centuries. Any attempt to press it into the confines of any simple narrative are likely to do poor service to the task of reflecting generatively on what it means for our contemporary theological task.

REFERENCES

Althaus-Reid, Marcella (2003). *The Queer God (God the Homosexual).* (London: Routledge).
Amin, Ash (2003). *Post-Fordism: A Reader.* (Oxford: Blackwell).
Bauman, Zygmunt (2000). *Liquid Modernity.* (Cambridge: Polity Press).
Beck, Ulrich (1992). *Risk Society: Towards a New Modernity*, trans. Mark Ritter (London: Sage).

Bell, Daniel (1976). *The Coming of Post-Industrial Society*. (New York: Basic Books).

Biro, Matthew (1998). *Anself Kiefer and the Philosophy of Martin Heidegger*. (Cambridge: Cambridge University Press).

Burrus, Virginia (2002). *Begotten, Not Made: Conceiving Manhood in Late Antiquity*. (Stanford, CA: Stanford University Press).

Butler, Judith (1999). *Subjects of Desire: Hegelian Reflections in Twentieth-Century France*. (New York: Columbia University Press).

Castelli, Elizabeth (2007). *Martyrdom and Memory: Early Christian Culture Making*. (New York: Columbia University Press).

Eisenstadt, S. N. (2000). 'Multiple Modernities', *Daedalus* (Winter) 129: 1, 1–29.

Fuller, Peter (1988). *Theoria: Act and the Absence of Grace*. (London: Chatto and Windus).

Giddens, Anthony (1995). 'Living in a Post-Traditional Society', in Ulrich Beck, Anthony Giddens, and Scott Lash (eds), *Reflexive Modernization* (Cambridge: Polity Press), 56–109.

Hall, Stuart (1992). 'Introduction', *Formations of Modernity*, ed. Stuart Hall and Bram Gieben (Cambridge: Polity Press), 1–16.

Halperin, David (1990). *One Hundred Years of Homosexuality: And Other Essays on Greek Love*. (London: Routledge).

Harvey, David (1989). *The Condition of Postmodernity: An Enquiry into the Origins Cultural Change*. (Oxford: Blackwell).

Jameson, Fredric (1989). *Postmodernism: Or, The Cultural Logic of Late Capitalism*. (London: Verso).

Kant, Immanuel (1934). *Critique of Pure Reason*, trans. J. M. D. Meikleyjohn (London: Dent).

——(1996). *Practical Philosophy*, trans. Mary J. Gregor (Cambridge: Cambridge University Press).

Kumar, Krishan (1995). *From Post-Industrial to Post-Modern Society: New Theories of the Contemporary World*. (Oxford: Blackwell).

Laqueur, Thomas (1992). *Making Sex: Body and Gender from the Greeks to Freud*. (Cambridge, MA: Harvard University Press).

Latour, Bruno (1993). *We Have Never Been Modern*, trans. Catherine Porter (London: Harvester Wheatsheaf).

Lloyd, Genevieve (1993). *Man of Reason: 'Male' and 'Female' in Western Philosophy*. (London: Routledge).

Loughlin, Gerard (ed.) (2007). *Queer Theology: Rethinking the Western Body*. (Oxford: Blackwell).

Lyotard, Jean-François (1984). *The Postmodern Condition: Report on Knowledge*, trans. Geoffrey Bennington and Brian Massumi (Manchester: Manchester University Press).

Massey, D. (1994). *Space: Place and Gender*. (Cambridge: Polity Press).

Mosse, George (1999). *The Image of Man: The Creation of Modern Masculinity*. (Oxford: Oxford University Press).

Pattison, George (1991). *Art, Modernity and Faith*. (London: Macmillan).

—— (2009). *Crucifixions and Resurrections of the Image*. (London: Student Christian Movement Press).

Pile, Steven (1996). *The Body and the City: Psychoanalysis, Space and Subjectivity*. (London: Routledge).

Said, Edward W. (1985). *Orientalism*. (Harmondsworth: Penguin Books).

Schleiermacher, F. D. E. (1984) 'Über die Freiheit', *Kritische Gesamtausgabe, I. Abt. Band 2: Schriften aus der Berliner Zeit 1796–1799*, ed. Günter Meckenstock (Berlin: de Gruyter).

Sheard, Sally and Power, Helen (eds.) (2000). *Body and City: Histories of Urban Public Health.* (Aldershot: Ashgate).

Taylor, Mark C. (1992). *Disfiguring: Art, Architecture, Religion.* (Chicago: Chicago University Press).

Taylor, Peter J. (1999). *Modernities: A Geohistorical Interpretation.* (Cambridge: Polity Press).

Thrift, N. (1997). 'Cities without Modernity, Cities with Magic', *Scottish Geographical Magazine* 113, 138–49.

Toulmin, Stephen (1990). *Cosmopolis the Hidden Agenda of Modernity.* (New York: Free Press).

Touraine, Alain (1995). *Critque of Modernity*, trans. David Macey (Oxford: Blackwell).

PART I

IDENTITY

CHAPTER 1

....

THE SELF AND THE GOOD LIFE

....

CLARE CARLISLE

'ONE swallow does not make spring, nor one fine day', said Aristotle; 'Neither does one day or a short time make someone blessed and happy' (Aristotle 2000: 12/109 8a). Likewise, one admirable action, or a brief spell of good behaviour, does not constitute a virtuous person. The self and the good life are closely connected by the fact that both are temporal phenomena, works-in-progress. In this chapter, I will not consider 'the self' by addressing metaphysical questions of personal identity, nor embark on an analysis of those virtues and values that the best human life requires. Instead, I will look at the processes that underlie and join together the concepts of selfhood and the good life: processes of development, appropriation, and acquisition through which a 'second nature' is formed. In his *Nicomachean Ethics* Aristotle quotes the poet Euanus in describing the process of acquiring certain capacities and character traits, and thereby becoming a certain sort of person: 'I tell you, my friend, it is long-lasting training | And this ends up as nature for human beings'. Here, he adds that 'the reason why habit is hard to alter is that it is like one's nature' (Aristotle 2000: 136/115 2a). This idea of second nature has remained central to our philosophical tradition. Hegel, for example, writes in the *Philosophy of Right* that,

> Just as nature has its laws, and as animals, trees and the sun fulfil their law, so custom (*Sitte*) is the law appropriate to free mind . . . Education is the art of making men ethical. It begins with pupils whose life is at the instinctive level and shows them the way to a second birth, the way to change their instinctive nature into a second, spiritual nature, and makes this spiritual level habitual to them. (Hegel 1952: 260/§151, Addition)

For Christian theology, however, it is not simply through our own experiences, actions and interactions that our lives take shape and gain meaning. The questions of who we are, and how we should live, must also be questions about our relationship to God.

Ethical questions of appropriation and acquisition become theological questions, since the processes of spiritual development are facilitated and sustained by divine grace. How, and to what extent, can God-given gifts become our own? What kind of task is receptivity to grace, if it is more passive than active? How do we understand human freedom in the context of a God-relationship? What are the differences between our original—created—nature, and the second nature that constitutes a good Christian life?

This chapter will address these questions by focusing on two nineteenth-century thinkers, Félix Ravaisson and Søren Kierkegaard, who both made original contributions to Christian thought at a time when their religious traditions were challenged by distinctively modern cultural and intellectual developments. Born just months apart in 1813, one in Catholic France and the other in Lutheran Denmark, these men were contemporaries who formulated very different responses to a common philosophical inheritance. Indeed, their views about freedom, habit, and the idea of second nature represent alternative lines of thinking that still structure the debate about how to live well in relationship to God. But in spite of their differences, Ravaisson and Kierkegaard were equally attuned to the significance of repetition in human life—and in both cases this yielded important insights into the processes through which selves develop.

I. Ravaisson on Habit, Nature, and Grace

Ravaisson's 1838 essay *De l'habitude* offers perhaps the most sustained and illuminating philosophical reflection on the concept of second nature. The text is clearly situated in the Aristotelian ethical tradition, according to which a good life consists in developing and maintaining good habits, or virtues. 'Virtue is first of all an effort and wearisome', writes Ravaisson, 'it becomes something attractive and a pleasure only through practice . . . Such is the secret of education: its art consists in attracting someone towards the good by action, thus fixing the inclination for it. In this way a *second nature* is formed' (Ravaisson 2008: 69). The similarity between this passage and the one from Hegel's *Philosophy of Right* quoted in my opening paragraph is striking, but Ravaisson is following thinkers such as Thomas Aquinas and Joseph Butler in developing Aristotle's 'virtue ethics' within a Christian theology. However, the moral and religious significance of habit is only considered some way into the second half of *De l'habitude*. The early sections of the text develop a more general analysis of habit, and it is here that Ravaisson makes a distinctive contribution to the key questions of modern philosophy. Arguing that reflection on habit challenges dualisms between the mind and the body, and between freedom and nature, he offers an account of habit that attempts to steer a middle course between rationalism and empiricism. His claim that human freedom is continuous with embodiment, inclination, and desire grounds his view of moral and spiritual life.

Ravaisson defines habit as a 'way of being' that is 'not merely a state, but a disposition, a virtue' (Ravaisson 2008: 25). Here, the term 'virtue' is metaphysical rather than moral, for it signifies a potentiality or power that underlies and facilitates particular actions. Indeed, for Ravaisson habit is not confined to human beings; it is a principle of life itself, and 'can only begin where nature itself begins' (Ravaisson 2008: 31). In the background here is Aristotle's definition of nature, in the *Physics*, as an inner principle of motion and rest, of change and remaining unchanged (see Aristotle 1970: 23/192b21-2). Central to habit is a certain relationship to change: 'from the lowest level of life, it seems that the continuity or repetition of a change modifies, relative to this change itself, the disposition of a being, and in this way modifies nature' (Ravaisson 2008: 31). In order to be capable of habit, a being must be receptive to change—otherwise repetition would make no difference to it (see Deleuze 1994: 70). Ravaisson, following Aristotle, illustrates this point with the example of a stone which, however many times it is thrown upward, does not acquire a habit of ascending rather than falling (see Aristotle 1992: 15–16/1220a38–1220b11; Ravaisson 2008: 25).[1] Unlike stones, living beings have a nature that can be modified.

However, habit involves resistance to change as well as plasticity: 'Permanence and change are the first conditions of habit' (Ravaisson 2008: 33). A habit is a more or less *settled* disposition, not a fleeting condition. Ravaisson describes habit as a 'permanent' way of being, although this permanence must surely be relative to more rapidly changing states, since we know that some habits, at least, can be broken. On this point, too, he is indebted to Aristotle, who in the *Categories* distinguishes between *hexis* (habit or disposition) and *diathesis* (state or quality) on the grounds that the former is longer-lasting than the latter. For Aristotle, a *hexis* is constitutive of a person, in so far as it has 'become through time part of a man's nature and irremediable or exceedingly hard to change' (Aristotle 1963: 24/8b28–9a4).[2] This concept of *hexis* is rooted in the Greek verb *ekhein*, 'to have', and thus it denotes a having or possessing (see Rodrigo 2011). Implicit in this idea of ownership is endurance through time: just as my belongings are kept in a place where they will be available for me to use when I need them, so my dispositions are, so to speak, 'there', ready to be exercised when the appropriate occasion arises. At both the beginning and the end of *De l'habitude*, Ravaisson connects habit with a 'tendency to persist', or to 'persevere', in being—a tendency that, he claims, constitutes the 'universal law' and 'fundamental character' of all beings (Ravaisson 2008: 27, 77). This ontological principle is repeated at the empirical level: particular habits can become like laws of nature, in so far as they give shape, order, and regularity to our acquired, 'second' natures.

So, Ravaisson's philosophy of habit turns on a certain conception of living beings as both receptive and resistant to change. This provides the basis for an account of 'having', or possession—understood as a *process* of appropriation—which is integral to the discourse of selfhood and the good life within the Aristotelian ethical tradition. Because of the influence of that tradition on Christian theology, this way of thinking

---

[1] Henri Bergson, doubtless guided by Ravaisson, repeats this point—see Bergson 1992: 268.

[2] On the role of *hexis* in Aristotle's ethics, see Burnyeat 1980; Garver 1989; Baracchi 2008: 66–73, 90–1, 112–22.

also has a crucial bearing on the relationship between human beings and God, in so far as this relationship is articulated in terms of a gift that is not only received, but appropriated, so that it effects a lasting change on the recipient. We will return to Ravaisson's theology shortly.

In *De l'habitude*, Ravaisson's preliminary ontology of habit leads to a discussion of how habit operates at different levels of organic life, from the simplest organisms to the human being. The second half of his essay then focuses on the influence of habit at different levels of human consciousness and action: the physical, the intellectual, the moral, and the spiritual. The transition between these two parts of the text consists of an important methodological claim. Ravaisson argues that he can move beyond empiricism—a stance which, as David Hume and Thomas Reid had claimed, could not yield any positive insight into the operations of habit (see Reid 1788: 120; Hume 1902: 43)—by means of a certain kind of introspection. This philosophical method bears the influence of Pierre Maine de Biran, author of an 1802 work entitled *Sur l'influence de l'habitude sur la faculté de la pensée*, but Ravaisson combines it with analogical reasoning. In fact, he deploys the analogy between nature and second nature to argue that observation of habit within the human mind reveals the hidden workings of nature that are inaccessible to empirical study. 'Up to this point, nature is a spectacle for us that we can only see from the outside', writes Ravaisson at the end of Part I:

> We see only the exteriority of the actuality of things; we do not see their dispositions or powers. In consciousness, by contrast, the same being at once acts and sees the act; or better, the act and the apprehension of the act are fused together . . . It is only in consciousness that we can aspire not just to establish [habit's] apparent law but to learn its *how* and its *why*, to illuminate its generation, and finally to understand its cause.   (Ravaisson 2008: 39)

This claim that it is possible to grasp habit not just as an effect, but as a law and a principle of nature, will allow Ravaisson to sketch a theological account of grace further on in his essay.

In the early sections of Part II of *De l'habitude*, Ravaisson presents the kernel of his argument. When we reflect on the process of habit acquisition, he suggests, we find that actions which are originally consciously chosen and directed to a goal become, by degrees, spontaneous and quasi-natural: 'habit transforms voluntary movements into instinctive movements' (Ravaisson 2008: 59). Another way of describing this process is to say that intentions, which are initially mental phenomena, come to be incorporated into the body. As habits develop, consciously-posited goals or 'ideas' increasingly become 'the form, the way of being, even the very being of [the body's] organs' (Ravaisson 2008: 57). Furthermore, habit constitutes a 'desire' for those objects and experiences to which we have become accustomed, and this desire is analogous to biological need.

This reflection on the acquisition of habits enables Ravaisson to argue that freedom and intelligence need not be regarded as distinct from the body. On the contrary, through habit these come to pervade the body and to animate it by what Ravaisson calls

'tendency'—a movement of desire that is not mechanical and blind, but not deliberative either. The 'second nature' borne of habit operates just like our original nature, and
yet this new, acquired nature is evidently imbued with freedom and intelligence. The
force of habit is 'an inclination that follows from the will . . . a law of the limbs, which
follows on from the freedom of the spirit' (Ravaisson 2008: 55–7). This suggestion that
acquired habit and skill constitute an embodied intelligence was taken up by twentieth-
century phenomenologists seeking to challenge mind–body dualism: for example, in
The Phenomenology of Perception (1945) Maurice Merleau-Ponty invokes the concept
of habit to describe the 'lived-body', whose intelligence is a 'knowledge in the hands'
(Merleau-Ponty 1962: 44, 142–4; see also Sinclair 2011).

The next step in Ravaisson's argument is to claim that, in traversing the opposition
between 'mechanical Fatality and reflective Freedom' (Ravaisson 2008: 55), habit
thereby discloses an underlying continuity. Acquired habit is 'like a spiral' (Ravaisson
2008: 77) that reaches down to the inarticulate depths of the human being. Although
we, so to speak, lose sight of habit as it descends to its vanishing point—where second
nature becomes so close to instinct as to be indistinguishable from it—we know that it
still bears the traces of its original freedom and intelligence. On this point, Ravaisson's
position is exactly opposite to that of Marcel Proust, who writes that 'if habit is a second
nature, it prevents us from knowing our first' (Proust 1996: 478). Proust here gives
eloquent expression to a pervasive interpretation of habit—one especially prevalent
among philosophers—as inhibiting reflection and obscuring the truth.[3] For Ravaisson,
however, habit as 'second nature' provides a mirror of primary nature, and thus enables
us to see what is otherwise hidden from view. When we look into this mirror, we
discover that will and instinct, desire and need, the voluntary and the involuntary, are
not dichotomous but continuous. The entire continuum of nature revealed by habit
could, in fact, be named 'freedom'.

When, towards the end of *De l'habitude*, Ravaisson discusses the religious significance of habit, it becomes clear that this continuum of nature might also be named
'grace' or 'love': 'In every thing, the Necessity of Nature is the chain on which Freedom
unfolds itself. But this is a moving and living chain: the necessity of desire, of love and
of grace' (Ravaisson 2008: 75).[4] Quoting François Fénelon, he identifies nature itself as
'prevenient grace' (Ravaisson 2008: 71)—a kind of grace that enables the will, despite its
fallen condition, to seek the good. His thought here is that, if habit is a post-reflective,
post-voluntary tendency, then nature is revealed through the mirror of habit as

---

[3] See, for example, Maine de Biran 1970: 47: 'Reflection, in the physical as well as in the moral sense,
requires a point of support, a resistance: but the most common effect of habit is to take away all
resistance, to destroy all friction . . . Reflect on what is habitual! Who could or would wish to begin such
reflection? How should one suspect some mystery in what one has always seen, done and felt? About
what should one inquire, should one be in doubt, should one be astonished? Heavy bodies fall,
movement is communicated; the stars revolve over our heads; nature spreads out before our eyes her
greatest phenomena: and what subject for wonder, what subject for inquiry could there be in such
familiar things?'

[4] On Ravaisson's interpretation of grace, see Leduc-Fayette 1993.

a pre-reflective, pre-voluntary tendency. In both cases, tendency is a form of desire. This notion of tendency bears the influence of Leibniz's interpretation of inertia as a living force that propels beings from the inside, but for Ravaisson this force 'is God within us, God hidden solely by being so far within us in this intimate source of ourselves, to whose depths we do not descend' (Ravaisson 2008: 71). God, or 'the good', is a final cause that draws beings toward itself by inciting their desire, but it is also a principle of movement within beings—what Aristotle called their 'nature' (*phusis*). By conceiving God's activity in this way, as at once transcendent and immanent, Ravaisson suggests that grace is natural as much as supernatural (see Leduc-Fayette 1993: 33–4; Janicaud 2000: 83–4). Indeed, his remarks on this issue seem to unsettle the distinction between the natural and the supernatural, just as other aspects of his analysis of habit challenge a series of philosophical distinctions and dualisms. According to Ravaisson, we desire God by nature, but this natural desire is itself a divine gift. It is very apt that the word 'love' gives expression to a divine activity both within and beyond ourselves, for love 'possesses and desires at the same time' (Ravaisson 2008: 75): as a gift, it becomes the enduring property of the human soul—its fundamental *hexis*—and yet it remains an ongoing task.

If nature-as-grace provides the impetus and the motivation to live a good life, then the development and actualization of this divinely-infused tendency is the task of human practice. Ravaisson describes this process of cultivation as follows:

> Repetition or continuity makes moral activity easier and more assured. It develops within the soul not only the disposition, but also the inclination and tendency to act, just as in the organs it develops the inclination for movement. In the end, it gradually brings the pleasure of action to replace the more transient pleasure of passive sensibility. In this way . . . the helpful activity and the inner joys of charity develop more and more in the heart of the one who does good. In this way, love is augmented by its own expressions.   (Ravaisson 2008: 69)[5]

He here blends Aristotelian ethics with Christian theology in suggesting that through the repetitions of practice and education we can acquire a virtuous 'second nature', and that we are in fact already predisposed to this, thanks to the self-giving of God within our own 'first' natures. In *De l'habitude*, it is love or charity—*caritas*—that emerges very clearly as the primary virtue, and the idea that this is both God-given and humanly cultivated is neatly expressed by Ravaisson's remark that, through habit, 'love is augmented by its own expressions'. His emphasis on Christian charity is maintained in much later works, such as the 1893 essay 'Métaphysique et Morale', written for the inaugural issue of the journal of the same name, and the posthumously-published *Testament philosophique*.

For Ravaisson, this conception of the virtuous life connects us to the whole of nature, which shares our fundamental disposition towards the good—although it is only in human beings that this becomes conscious, and is articulated intellectually as well as

---

[5] On this point, Ravaisson closely follows Bishop Butler—see Butler 1857: 108; Carlisle 2010a.

through action. On this point he differs from Aquinas, who holds that the appropri-ation accomplished by habit is confined to the rational powers of the human soul.[6] And, relatedly, while Ravaisson echoes Aquinas in making a connection between Aristotelian *hexis* (translated as *habitus* by the scholastic theologians) and grace, he departs from classical Thomism in regarding grace not just as continuing and perfect-ing nature, but as in some sense identical with nature.

An obvious question that emerges from Ravaisson's account of the good life is how it can accommodate a doctrine of sin. If love is both our origin and our goal, our nature as well as our aspiration, then what explains our frequent failures to love? And if love is an active tendency, how do we make sense of those occasions when this tendency not only fails to be actualized, but seems to be replaced by an opposing force? What would be the source of this harmful, destructive tendency? In *De l'habitude*, Ravaisson does not address these questions, nor does he mention sin or human wrongdoing. It seems that in his effort to overcome the ontological dualisms of modern thought, he overlooks the phenomenon of psychic conflict or 'double-mindedness' that preoccupies Christian writers such as Augustine, Luther, and Kierkegaard. Ravaisson is almost explicit about this, for in describing habit as 'a law of grace', 'a law of the limbs that follows on from the freedom of spirit', he provides an alternative gloss on Romans 7.

He does, however, acknowledge that habit can become pathological, since it is a principle of life that encompasses 'the abnormal and parasitic life that develops within regular life' (Ravaisson 2008: 63). The effects of habituation can entrench vicious patterns as well as virtuous ones. Although Ravaisson's discussion here focuses on physiological disease and disorder, his analysis can also apply to moral disorder:

> One becomes accustomed over time to the most violent poisons . . . Movements or situations that initially are most difficult and tiring become over time the most convenient, and end up by making themselves into indispensable conditions of the functions with which they have always been associated; in the same way, the most unhealthy air and food become the very conditions of health.   (Ravaisson 2008: 63)

This provides an illuminating account of the kind of compulsive behaviour Augustine has in mind when he writes, in his *Confessions*, that 'the rule of sin is the force of habit' (Augustine 1961: 165).[7] Nevertheless, Ravaisson remains optimistic about the good life: he indicates that, through practice, virtuous conduct becomes so natural as to approxi-mate 'the holiness of innocence' (Ravaisson 2008: 69). His apparent lack of interest in sin is mirrored by a corresponding disregard for the cardinal Christian virtues of faith and hope (although it might be argued that his moral and theological optimism is itself an expression of these virtues). Love, generosity, charity, he argues, are the substance of the good life, and this human giving is facilitated and sustained by a divine gift.

---

[6] See Thomas Aquinas, *Summa theologiae* Ia IIae, q. 50, a. 3; q. 56, a. 5; q. 58, a. 1. For an account of the concept of habit in the thought of Thomas Aquinas, see Marion 1975: 25–30; Kent 2002.

[7] For further discussion of the passage containing this quotation, see Carlisle 2010a.

From a theological point of view, Ravaisson's account of the Christian life needs to be supplemented by a discussion of how the Church, and in particular its sacraments and rituals, might provide a bridge between the 'natural' grace of 'God within us', and human efforts to exercise and cultivate this gift through their own practice. This would be a bridge between 'the voluntary and the involuntary'—terms that have shaped the analysis of habit from Maine de Biran to Paul Ricoeur. The account of habitual appropriation offered in *De l'habitude*, according to which repetition effects the gradual embodiment of ideals so as to create a spontaneously 'holy' second nature, certainly offers conceptual resources for developing a complementary account of the Christian community's role in this process. If the gift of grace is dispensed not only through the creation of each being's primary nature, but also through the sacramental practices that play a part in constituting human beings' *second* natures, then this would mediate and harmonize the two kinds of nature. Both would share in common a divine activity, which would not just be a hidden inner source proper to each individual, but a visible gift-giving that, through its repetition, binds people together.

As the chief exponent of French 'spiritualism' (see Lalande 1926)—the lesser-known cousin of German idealism that opposes 'systems that reduce everything to material elements' in holding that 'the infinite and the absolute consist in spiritual freedom' (Ravaisson 1984: 320)—Ravaisson influenced a generation of French thinkers. Among these were Emile Boutroux, Jules Lachelier, Henri Bergson, Pierre Teilhard de Chardin, and Maurice Blondel (see D'Agostino 2007). In his 1893 book *L'action*, Blondel follows Ravaisson in emphasizing a pre-reflective desire for God. At least via Blondel, Ravaisson's ideas about freedom, nature, and grace were taken up by Henri de Lubac (see Gouhier 1942: 22; Janicaud 2000: 1–6), whose contribution to some of the major documents of Vatican II cemented his influence on Catholic thought and practice. Even though Ravaisson makes little reference to Thomas Aquinas, his ideas appear to have shaped the new interpretations of Aquinas proposed by de Lubac and other Catholic thinkers associated with 'la nouvelle théologie' (see Kerr 2007: 31). This influence seems particularly significant on the question of whether there is a 'pure nature', to which divine grace is superfluous and extrinsic—something de Lubac denies, in opposition to the neoscholastic Thomists who dominated Catholic theology at the beginning of the twentieth century.[8] De Lubac understands Aquinas' account of the supernatural as insisting that 'all of spiritual nature is permeated by *freedom*, and freedom as such is a relation to divine law and the ultimate divine end' (Milbank 2005: 25). For de Lubac—as for Ravaisson—nature is always already animated and oriented by a desire for God. In an 1932 letter to Blondel, he wrote that 'This concept of a pure nature runs into great difficulties, the principal one of which seems to be the following: how can a conscious spirit be anything other than an absolute desire for God?' (cited in Feingold 2001: 628). Later, in his book on knowledge of God, *Sur les chemins de Dieu* (1956), de Lubac cites Blondel in arguing that human beings have an obscure, 'secret',

---

[8] For the neoscholastics, the doctrine of pure nature secured the gratuity of grace. For a summary of this debate, see Milbank 2005: 15–47.

preconceptual grasp of God that facilitates all thinking and willing—and again on this point there are echoes of Ravaisson's interpretation of grace as a 'secret activity' (Ravaisson 2008: 53) within nature that precedes and underlies conscious thought and deliberation. Indeed, de Lubac reads Aquinas as claiming that we can form a concept of God only if our minds already have a 'habit of God' (de Lubac 1960: 59).

II. Kierkegaard on Repetition, Freedom, and Faith

We have seen that Ravaisson develops Aristotle's ethics in placing habitual repetition at the centre of his account of the good life. Kierkegaard, however, creates an alternative concept of repetition, which corresponds to an interpretation of human freedom that breaks with the 'virtue ethics' tradition. While Ravaisson draws on Aristotelian ideas of habit and virtue to overcome the dualisms that characterize modern—and especially Kantian—philosophy, Kierkegaard echoes Kant in his negative view of habit. Kant places habit on one side of a division between freedom and necessity, will and nature, so that habit is a mere 'mechanism' which is opposed to the freedom that makes moral action possible (see Kant 1974: 148–9).[9] Similarly, Kierkegaard writes of 'the bondage of habit' (Kierkegaard 1992a: 340), and suggests that 'love is dissipated in the lukewarmness and indifference of habit' (Kierkegaard 1998: 36). Kierkegaard's willingness to remain within this Kantian framework indicates how different his intellectual project is from that shared by Ravaisson and the German Idealists.[10] His account of the good life is motivated by a concern to address the spiritual malaise that he perceived among his contemporaries, and which he diagnosed as the distinctive condition of modernity. This condition, which he sometimes describes as 'spiritlessness', consists in a religious complacency that is, in fact, the sign of a covert nihilism: confronted by a social milieu in which everyone is a Christian 'as a matter of course', Kierkegaard asks whether there exists in Christendom a single genuine Christian. He regarded the rise of the new Hegelian philosophy in Denmark as a symptom of this spiritual crisis (see Carlisle 2010b).

From this perspective, Kierkegaard challenges the idea that Christianity should, or could, become a second nature—and therefore he is critical of the Hegelian conception of *Sittlichkeit* as the substance of ethical life (see Hegel 1952: 20). In 1843, the Danish theologian Hans Lassen Martensen articulated a specifically Christian version of this Hegelian view in suggesting that in later phases of the history of Christianity, 'when the

---

[9] For a discussion of the continuities between Aristotelian and Kantian ethics, see Sherman 1997: 121–86.

[10] On Ravaisson's debt to Schelling, see Mauve 1995; Janicaud 2000: 95–100. For an account of Kierkegaard's relation to Schelling, see Hennigfeld and Stewart 2003; Olesen 2007.

Church had put out its firm roots in the world', the form of the religious life changed in so far as 'God's kingdom had become just like nature' (cited in Kierkegaard 1985: 316). For Kierkegaard, similarly, centuries of Christian practice have resulted in the 'naturalisation and domestication' (Kierkegaard 1992a: 585) of an originally scandalous, counter-cultural teaching—but unlike Martensen he regarded this as a decline rather than a progression. This theme is developed in the two books published under the pseudonym Johannes Climacus, *Philosophical Fragments* (1844) and *Concluding Unscientific Postscript* (1846). Johannes Climacus suggests that over 'eighteen centuries . . . Christianity has permeated all relations of life, reshaped the world', producing 'an illusion by which the resolving and choosing subject is trapped'. The repetitions of customary practice, he argues, 'have a diversionary power'. 'Habit and routine and lack of passion'—a sure sign of spiritlessness, for Kierkegaard—'corrupt most people, so that they become thoughtless' (Kierkegaard 1992a: 47). According to Climacus, 'the most ludicrous thing Christianity can ever become is what is called custom and habit in the banal sense' (Kierkegaard 1992a: 364). In much of his writing, Kierkegaard accentuates the paradoxical character of Christian faith, precisely in an attempt to recover the truth of this faith from the degrading forces of habit and custom. This often involves tactics of 'indirect communication' that seek to provoke the reader to question her own Christian identity, which she has hitherto taken for granted.

While habitual repetition undermines faith, Kierkegaard proposes that a different kind of repetition provides the existential basis of the Christian life. The difference between these two forms of repetition rests on the philosophical distinction between actuality and possibility. While repetition of something actual produces habit, repetition of a possibility—and by this Kierkegaard means the moment of decision, in which a person chooses between two or more possibilities—constitutes human freedom. In *Repetition* (1843), published under the pseudonym Constantin Constantius, Kierkegaard draws on the account of freedom developed by Judge William in Part II of *Either/ Or* in suggesting that the moment of decision is what Aristotle called *kinesis*: the transition from possibility to actuality (see Kierkegaard 1983: 148–9; see also Aristotle 1970: 57/201a9–11).[11] Once a choice has been made, a possibility actualized, the situation may develop in two ways: the actuality—the outward action—can be repeated, or the choice itself can be taken again, repeated qua possibility. The former case, suggests Kierkegaard, leads to the degradation of habit, and thus to a loss of freedom; in the latter case, freedom is renewed and thus preserved. It is this free relation to her existence that enables an individual to live authentically or truthfully. In *Concluding Unscientific Postscript*, Johannes Climacus invokes this kind of logic, arguing that people born into a Christian culture, who undergo the 'custom' of infant baptism, must 'transform [this] initial being-Christian into a possibility in order to become Christian in truth' (Kierkegaard 1992a: 365).

---

[11] On Kierkegaard's interest in Aristotle's concept of *kinesis*, see Stack 1974; Carlisle 2005.

In *The Concept of Anxiety* a different vocabulary is used to make a similar point. Here, Kierkegaard's pseudonym Vigilius Haufniensis writes of the 'earnestness' and 'originality' that preserve freedom in repetition: 'When the originality in earnestness is acquired and preserved, then there is succession and repetition; as soon as originality is lacking in repetition there is habit. The earnest person is earnest precisely through the originalitywith which he returns in repetition' (Kierkegaard 1981: 149). By way of illustration, we are asked to consider a clergyman who every Sunday must recite the common prayer and baptize several children. What is required of this person is not 'feeling' or 'enthusiasm', which has variable effects, but earnestness, which is 'alone capable of returning every Sunday with the same originality to the same thing'. Vigilius Haufniensis adds here that 'this same thing to which earnestness is to return is earnestness itself . . . Inwardness, certitude, *is* earnestness' (Kierkegaard 1981: 149–51). In this section of *The Concept of Anxiety*, then, earnestness comes to be synonymous with an authentic spiritual repetition.

Kierkegaard's new conception of repetition underpins an ethic of fidelity: a truth that must be lived, rather than known, since fidelity means *being true to* another person, to God, or even to oneself. This faithfulness consists of a repeatedly renewed commitment, which provides consistency through time without allowing the past to determine the future. For Kierkegaard, fidelity is an expression of passionate choice, not the dutiful or customary fulfilment of an obligation. In texts such as *Either/Or*, *Repetition* and *Stages on Life's Way*, this form of truthfulness is explored through reflection on the theme of marriage—and perhaps it was Kierkegaard's own experience of breaking an engagement that provoked these reflections. But there is evidently a conceptual connection in his work between romantic fidelity, ethical authenticity, and religious faith. As Johannes Climacus puts it, in his discussion of *Repetition*, 'a love affair . . . is always a usable theme in relation to what it means to exist' (Kierkegaard 1992a: 265).

Kierkegaard's account of freedom as repetition, with its emphasis on the individual's choice and commitment, informs the 'existentialist' ethic of decision developed in various ways by thinkers such as Jean-Paul Sartre,[12] Martin Heidegger (at least in *Being and Time*),[13] and Alain Badiou. For example, in his political philosophy Badiou draws on Kierkegaard's account of 'subjective' truth as fidelity: for Badiou, fidelity is not merely a personal ethical stance to an objective state of affairs, but is ontologically and epistemologically constitutive. He echoes Heidegger on this point, for the latter argues that 'resoluteness' is a power of disclosure, and as such is intimately related to existential truth (see Heidegger 1962: 343–6). According to Badiou, 'fidelity to an event'—whether this be a political revolution, an artistic innovation, or a romantic

[12] Sartre in *Being and Nothingness* rejects habit as a cover for 'bad faith', a flight from freedom, and therefore dismisses the very category of 'hexis': see Sartre 1969: pp. xxii–xxiii. However, in his *Critique of Dialectical Reason* Sartre discusses *hexis* more extensively, describing it as 'interiorised past', 'the sediment of praxis' (Sartre 1996: 200, 215), but still suggesting that hexis signifies a decline of free action, in so far as praxis can 'relapse into *hexis*' (Sartre 1996: 282, see also 320, 347–8).

[13] See, e.g. Heidegger 1962: 68. For a discussion of the influence on Heidegger of Kierkegaard's concept of repetition, see Carlisle 2012.

encounter—produces a stable, enduring order without undermining freedom and creativity: this fidelity is 'the opposite of repetition' considered as custom or routine (see Badiou 1984; Badiou 1993: 38–9; Hallward 2003: 128–30).

For Kierkegaard himself, however, this way of thinking—even when it is employed to clarify the task of becoming a Christian—exemplifies a humanist perspective that can only access, at best, a partial aspect of the good life. Indeed, several of his pseudonyms represent such partial perspectives in order to communicate, indirectly, their inadequacy in the absence of a deeper, religious understanding of existence. Kierkegaard's emphasis on active decision does have a positive function as a corrective against the tendency to lapse passively into *Sittlichkeit*, a customary form of Christianity. But his writing also seeks to correct a related but apparently opposing tendency: a hubristic desire to seize control of existence, which involves self-assertion at the expense of receptivity to God. This refusal of divine grace can be individual, and in this form it is analysed in great detail in *The Sickness Unto Death*, where Kierkegaard's pseudonym Anti-Climacus discusses the human condition in terms of theological concepts of despair and sin. Resistance to God can also be collective, and indeed this is how Kierkegaard interprets his own culture, which by the mid-nineteenth century was already showing signs of secularity, even though this still had an outwardly Christian form. Modern philosophy, with its emphasis on the autonomy of human reason, was for Kierkegaard one such sign (see Carlisle 2010c: 29–35).

The statement in *Repetition* that 'repetition is always a transcendence' (Kierkegaard 1983: 186) is, therefore, ambiguous. On the one hand, this means that precisely because what must be repeated is the moment of decision, repetition is open to the new and to the future; it is not—like habit—constrained by what has happened in the past. Here Kierkegaard is keen to distinguish his concept of repetition from an immanent movement in which what was already implicit is made explicit—a kind of movement that, he suggests, is common to both Socratic and Hegelian philosophy (see Kierkegaard 1983: 148–9; Kierkegaard 1985). On the other hand, the 'transcendence' of repetition refers to its divine source, and here it is a question of challenging the idea of human self-sufficiency. Although *Repetition* does not make explicit its religious orientation, the meaning of this ambiguity is clear: Christian faith is at once a decision and a gift.

The theme of the gift pervades Kierkegaard's authorship, to the extent that it is a common thread running through apparently diverse texts. The task facing the Christian is to receive the whole of her life, in its suffering as well as its joy, as a gift from God. Kierkegaard frequently emphasizes that this task is difficult, perhaps even too difficult for anyone to fulfil. Underlying his theology of the gift is an ontology of the self as a spiritual, relational being who is grounded in God, but who refuses this radical dependence (see Kierkegaard 1980: 13ff.). Paradoxically, in trying to possess itself as an autonomous being, the self fails to be who it truly is. And so the self becomes itself—gains itself as a spiritual being—by losing itself as a merely human being. In Kierkegaard's thought, the logic of the gift is founded not on a concept of possession but, on the contrary, on a concept of loss. The gift is given, but the individual cannot hold onto it—and therefore it must be repeatedly given again, 'as a blessing that the soul is constantly losing' (Kierkegaard 1992b: 127). There is an echo of this Kierkegaardian view in Karl Barth's remark, in his commentary on Romans 7, that 'we make no mention of the Spirit if we bind Him to ourselves or to our having... we should recognise that... *we* means "not we", and *have* means "not have"... *We* are "not we" and "have not"...' (Barth 1968: 273–7).

For Kierkegaard, there are two sides to the continual loss of the gift. On the one hand, human sinfulness involves a tendency to refuse God, and this tendency means that the restoration of the relationship with God—which is the content of the gift—cannot take root in a heart where sin constantly reasserts itself. This condition of the human being at once signals the *need* for grace to be 'offered anew in each moment' (Kierkegaard 1992b: 126),[14] and makes God's repeated offering entirely *gratuitous*, since it is not earned. Indeed, Kierkegaard claims that 'the need [for God] itself is a good and a perfect gift from God' (Kierkegaard 1992b: 139). On the other hand, he develops a conception of faith as the giving up of one's gifts, precisely in order to receive them back again in a new way. Both of these aspects of the loss of the gift—loss through sin, and loss through faith—are expressions of human freedom. And they both indicate that the gift never becomes one's own, a point Kierkegaard insists on in more than one religious discourse on the theme of the gift: 'the gift [does not] belong to the needy one as a possession, because he has received it as a gift' (Kierkegaard 1992b: 157); 'what earthly life does not have, what no man has, God alone has' (Kierkegaard 1992b: 134). Even the capacity to receive the gift is not a property—a *hexis*—of the human soul. 'God is the only one who gives in such a way that he gives the condition [for receiving it] along with the gift, the only one who in giving has already given. God gives both [the power] to will and to bring to completion; he begins and completes the good work in a person' (Kierkegaard 1992b: 134).

This interpretation of the gift evidently differs from the Aristotelian Catholic tradition, which as we have seen employs a concept of *hexis* or *habitus* in its doctrine of grace. If the gift is not held or possessed by the person, its repetition cannot have the cumulative effect that would facilitate a steady progress towards the good, such that we find in 'virtue ethics'. For Kierkegaard, repetition brings fresh restoration, rather than gradual improvement. On this point he echoes Luther, who contested the idea that grace can be understood in terms of the concept of *habitus* (see Lohse 2006: 47, 59–60, 72, 261). While Aquinas explained the exercise of a divinely-infused *habitus* by appealing to a natural desire for the good which, when empowered by grace, facilitates the Christian life, Luther draws a stronger contrast between grace and nature, whereby even the desire for God does not come from ourselves: 'Those who seek God, do good freely and gladly, purely for the sake of God alone... But this is the work not of our nature but of grace' (Luther 1972: 227). Our righteousness, he argues, 'comes

---

[14] The translation cited here is by George Pattison—see Kierkegaard 2010: 24.

completely from the outside' and is 'foreign' to our nature: 'God does not want to redeem us through our own, but through external, righteousness and wisdom; not through one that comes from us and grows in us, but through one that comes to us from the outside' (Luther 1972: 136). In rejecting the idea that grace is given as a *habitus*, Luther seems to suggest that even when we receive this gift it never properly belongs to us. In his lectures on Paul's Letter to the Romans, he contrasts a proud, boastful 'person of the law' who is 'confident in the righteousness which he already possesses' with the 'humble' person of faith who 'prays for the righteousness which he hopes to acquire'. According to Luther, the 'whole life' of faith 'is nothing else but prayer, seeking and begging... always seeking and striving to be made righteous... never standing still, never possessing' (Luther 1972: 251–2).[15]

Even though Kierkegaard follows Luther in denying that the gift of grace becomes one's own, he makes an idea of appropriation central to his account of the good life. This is not the appropriation of habit, which consists in the assimilation of external movements so that these become, over time, a disposition or a second nature. For Kierkegaard, faith is neither 'taught' through education, nor 'caught' through participation in communal practices. His concept of appropriation signifies a 'taking to heart'[16] or a 'making-inward' without this kind of social mediation: it happens through an individual's passionate commitment to the Christian task. This brings us back to the concept of repetition, understood both in terms of inward earnestness (or earnest inwardness), and in terms of the distinction between possibility and actuality. Kierkegaard seems to be suggesting that an authentic relation to Christian truth grasps that truth inwardly, as a pure possibility, rather than as an historical and social actuality.

All these aspects of Kierkegaard's view of the good life are brought to bear on the interpretation of the story of Abraham and Isaac presented in *Fear and Trembling* (1843). Writing under the pseudonym Johannes de silentio, Kierkegaard suggests that this biblical story subverts the idea that the life of faith, exemplified by Abraham's relationship with God, can be assimilated to the customary ethical life of a community. In deciding to obey God's command to sacrifice Isaac, Abraham relinquishes his moral duty as his son's guardian, and also the duties attending his promised role as father of the future nation of Israel. From the perspective of Hegelian ethics, Johannes de silentio argues, it is impossible to admire or even to understand Abraham's willingness to sacrifice his son. Johannes insists that the faith of Abraham cannot be mediated through his community—first, Abraham is a man in exile, and, second, he is unable to make himself understood within the nascent community represented by Sarah,

---

[15] Luther appears to qualify this statement in claiming that the grace imputed by God 'is not ours by virtue of anything in us, or in our own power' (Luther 1972: 257). This question of ownership is a matter of debate among Luther scholars: see Lohse 2006: 73; Oberman 1986: 121; Ebeling 1970: 70–1, 272.

[16] This is how Alastair Hannay translates *Inderliggjørelse*; see Kierkegaard 2009: 33. The Hongs translate *Inderliggjørelse* as 'inward deepening', while Swenson and Lowrie translate it as 'intensification of inwardness'.

Elijah, and Isaac. Abraham's relationship to God is lived out through unprecedented situations, in which there are no customs or practices to draw on. This provides the model of Kierkegaardian freedom: without the repetition of custom, there is only the repetition of choice, a perpetual 'new creation' (Kierkegaard 1983: 40). And on this point, parallels are drawn between Abraham's faith and that of Jesus' disciples, who left their families to follow a man who transgressed the ethical codes of their community (p. 66).

The theology of the gift developed in Kierkegaard's religious discourses of the 1840s illuminates the much-contested meaning of *Fear and Trembling*. Johannes de silentio insists that Abraham's 'greatness' consists not in his obedience to God in defiance of reason, but in receiving Isaac as a gift for 'a second time' (Kierkegaard 1983: 9). 'By faith I do not renounce anything; on the contrary, by faith I receive everything . . . By faith Abraham did not renounce Isaac, but by faith Abraham received Isaac' (Kierkegaard 1983: 48–9), writes the pseudonym. He describes the recipient's role in the repetition of the gift as a 'double movement' of resignation and faith, which must be made 'continually' (Kierkegaard 1983: 37), 'at every moment' (Kierkegaard 1983: 40). And the God who restores Isaac to Abraham is precisely the God who is described in an Upbuilding Discourse as 'one who, when He gives, has given already'—for Isaac was already a gift from God, given miraculously to Abraham and Sarah in their old age. The significance of Abraham's obedient surrender of his son is not, as some commentators have claimed, to advance a 'divine command' ethic, but to highlight the need for the repetition of the gift (see Carlisle 2010c: 16–19).

Kierkegaard's interpretation of Abraham emphasizes that faith is a decision as well as a gift, and that the freedom of faith consists in repeatedly choosing the possibility of obedience and trust rather than doubt and despair. Our attention is drawn to this repeated choice by Johannes de silentio's focus on the long journey to Mount Moriah (see Kierkegaard 1983: 9–14), for every step of this journey represents a renewed decision to give Isaac up and, in the same moment, a renewed expectation of receiving him back again. The four faithless Abrahams imagined in 'Exordium' remind the reader that Abraham's response of faith was one of several possibilities available to him. Through his subjective repetition, Abraham achieves a fidelity that, Johannes de silentio suggests, surpasses ordinary ethical requirements: 'he remained true to his love' (p. 120).

The literary form of *Fear and Trembling* reflects Kierkegaard's analysis of the good life in terms of a radical freedom. In each of the three 'Problems' concerning the story of Abraham, Johannes de silentio presents his readers with a dilemma that he refuses to resolve: *either* there can be a teleological suspension of the ethical, *or* Abraham—and the example of faith he provides—is lost; *either* there is an absolute duty to God, *or* Abraham and his faith are lost; *either* faith cannot be subject to the ethical requirement for disclosure, *or* Abraham and his faith are lost. These represent different aspects of a single basic dilemma: either Abraham must be condemned as a murderer—as Kant indeed argues in *The Conflict of the Faculties* (1992: 115)—or religious faith is a response to a claim from beyond the ethical sphere of familial and social duties, roles and responsibilities. The stakes of these dilemmas are high: in earlier sections of *Fear and Trembling* Johannes has urged that Abraham's faith should be regarded as the highest human possibility, and he has claimed that without faith there is only despair. In this way the reader is encouraged to make her own decision about the nature and value of faith, and to examine her own spiritual life with fresh eyes (see Carlisle 2010c: 176–81).

III. Conclusion: The Self, the Good Life, and the Question of Second Nature

Ravaisson and Kierkegaard present two very different accounts of the good life. For Ravaisson, when the Christian life becomes a virtuous 'second nature', this represents both the cultivation and the embodiment of human freedom. For Kierkegaard, however, Christianity, and the love that is at its heart, are corrupted by custom or habit, and so can never become second nature. While Ravaisson asserts that 'love is augmented by its own expressions', Kierkegaard suggests that 'love is dissipated in the indifference and lukewarmness of habit'. They thus formulate contrasting concepts of repetition, and they also offer contrasting accounts of how grace is appropriated—and for both thinkers, these are the movements through which selfhood is constituted and through which the good life is lived.

As I suggested in the introduction to this chapter, these two nineteenth-century Christian philosophers represent alternative approaches to questions of selfhood and the good life within the European tradition. Ravaisson echoes the scholastic theologians in drawing on Aristotelian conceptions of *hexis* and character—but in a way that was to provide a new impetus for Thomism. Kierkegaard echoes Luther in seeing the self as less solid, even as dispossessed, and he follows both Augustine and Kant in regarding habit as a threat to human freedom. These two lines of thought can be traced through to twentieth-century philosophy and theology.

The divergence between Ravaisson's Christian-Aristotelian 'spiritualism' and the Kierkegaardian alternative does not necessarily produce two radically different theologies. For example, John Milbank's summary of de Lubac's position vis-à-vis nature and grace might equally apply to Kierkegaard:

> Human nature in its self-exceeding seems in justice to require a gift—yet the gift of grace remains beyond all justice and all requirement. This paradox is for de Lubac only to be entertained because one must remember that the just requirement for the gift in humanity is itself a created gift.   (Milbank 2005: 30).

More generally, both Ravaisson and Kierkegaard, and the intellectual traditions they are associated with—spiritualism, existentialism, and the modern revival of virtue ethics—share in common a resistance to narrowly materialist conceptions of the human being, and to narrowly instrumentalist conceptions of goodness and value.[17] The difference between the alternative lines of thinking that I have traced in this chapter lies more in the conceptual underpinnings of these efforts to preserve the spiritual reality of human life in an increasingly technological age.[18] The difference in style and mood between Ravaisson and Kierkegaard is also instructive: for Ravaisson, the good life becomes increasingly comfortable and easy as virtue is, through practice, incorporated into a person's mind and body. The progression here is towards an ideal in which freedom and a virtuous second nature effortlessly coincide. This seems very far indeed from the anxious endless striving that characterizes the Kierkegaardian model of the good life: even those, like Abraham, who find joy in their everyday lives, or like the person of faith imagined by Anti-Climacus, who attain 'rest' in God (see Kierkegaard 1980: 14, 131), have to travel through fear and trembling, or despair. And in Kierkegaard's works, the question of *how* this spiritual movement is made remains, precisely, a question.

We have seen that questions concerning freedom and second nature underpin the debate about selfhood and the good life. Considering the contrasting views of Ravaisson and Kierkegaard on these issues can thus help to structure the debate as it continues to unfold, as well as to illuminate its historical context. For this reason, I have attempted here to distinguish, and to hold apart, two traditions which in fact intersect at various conceptual and historical moments. However, I do not mean to suggest that we are simply faced with a choice between alternative accounts of freedom, and between contrasting evaluations of habit or second nature. On the contrary, it is perhaps at the intersections of these trajectories that our thinking about the good life becomes most productive. For at these points, we confront questions that are at once ethical and ontological: Can individuals become stable, reliably virtuous selves without taking their gifts for granted? If the religious life is constituted by the repetitions of practice and custom, will it be disrupted and undermined by critical reflection? Hegel, a thinker who marks one historical intersection of the Kierkegaardian and Ravaissonian lines of thought, is one of the few philosophers to recognize the duplicity of second nature. In the *Philosophy of Mind* Hegel identifies habit as a kind of transition or articulation between freedom and necessity, between autonomy and subjection (see Hegel 1971: 140–7/§ 410).[19] 'It is the habit of living which brings on

---

[17] See Davenport 2001 for a discussion of the continuities between Kierkegaardian existentialism and virtue ethics.

[18] I am thinking of 'technology' here in the broad sense advocated by Heidegger; see, e.g. Heidegger 1993; Pattison 2007.

[19] In the *Philosophy of Right* Hegel suggests that communal ethical life (*Sittlichkeit*) is 'the concept of freedom developed into the existing world': when 'mind' or 'spirit' becomes a 'second nature', its freedom is actualized, expressed concretely out in the world (Hegel 1952: 105–9). Slavoj Zizek accentuates the ambiguity in Hegel's analysis of habit; see Gabriel and Zizek 2009: 95–121. Zizek draws heavily on Cathérine Malabou's interpretation of Hegel; see Malabou 2005: 24–38, 53–74. See also Malabou's preface to the English edition of Ravaisson's *Of Habit*, where she describes habit as an ontological principle that produces both 'grace (ease, facility, power) and addiction (machinic repetition)' (Ravaisson 2008: pp. vii–viii). Indeed, she suggests that 'it is precisely of habit as

death' (Hegel 1971: 143; see also Hegel 1952: 260) he writes, in the course of his discussion of 'subjective spirit'—and, indeed, he is referring here to spiritual life and death. Ricoeur echoes this Hegelian analysis in his 1950 work *Freedom and Nature: The Voluntary and the Involuntary*, a text which owes a great debt to Ravaisson: 'Habit is at the same time a living spontaneity *and* an imitation of the automaton, reversion to the thing. Already here there are two closely related series of facts which support two types of understanding, in terms of life *and* in terms of the machine: in terms of spontaneity *and* in terms of inertia' (Ricoeur 1966: 297; see also Ricoeur 1965: 88; Thirion 2002).

Accentuating the contrast between the two perspectives outlined in this chapter discloses an ambivalence that may never be resolved, for the development of these two perspectives within the history of philosophy and theology reflects a duplicity within the matter itself. Indeed, this is rooted in our own natures, as beings who are at once receptive and resistant to change—the twin conditions which, I have suggested, make it possible for us to develop a second nature. Our receptivity to change enables us to grow; to learn from our actions, experiences, and encounters; to respond to our world and to one another. It enables us to accept gifts when they are offered to us. But this same receptivity makes us vulnerable, inconsistent, unpredictable, and can lead to a passivity that, in succumbing to external influence, undermines moral responsibility. It is resistance to change that produces some kind of self-identity through time, conferring the benefits of reliability and order—and this also, perhaps, underlies the integrity of characters and of institutions. However, as Ricoeur notes, our conservative tendency brings with it the danger of automatism, whereby we become thoughtless and unfree. At the political level, this conservatism can entrench injustice even as it preserves order. Our capacity to develop a second nature is, then, both a blessing and a curse, for while this enables us to feel at home in the world, it can also inhibit creative change; while it brings stability to life, it can also render that life stale, to the point at which life itself declines.

Although, as I indicated in my introduction, I did not set out to define the self, receptivity and resistance to change turn out to ground a conception of selfhood as constituted by temporal processes. Perhaps what we call 'the self', or 'character', is a certain pattern of receptivity and resistance—a complex configuration of tastes and tendencies, desires and aversions—that is more or less in flux, but which maintains some shape through time. We can, then, in an Aristotelian spirit, regard the good life as a process of learning to receive and to resist in the right way, at the right time, and in the right situation. It is a question of learning, through experience, what promotes physical and spiritual health, and what undermines it, so that defending oneself against malign influences and yielding to the good becomes second nature. Practical wisdom involves knowing the difference between receiving a gift and resisting temptation—for this difference is not always obvious.

pharmakon—at once poison and remedy—that Ravaisson speaks all along' (Ravaisson 2008: p. xix). In fact, Malabou's interpretation of Ravaisson is itself somewhat ambiguous: on the one hand, she attributes to him this view of habit as *pharmakon*, but on the other hand she places him within an Aristotelian tradition that, so to speak, extols the virtue of habit, in opposition to the more modern Cartesian–Kantian view of habit as 'the disease of repetition'.

REFERENCES

Aristotle (1963). *Categories* and *De Interpretatione*, trans. J. L. Ackrill (Oxford: Clarendon Press).

—— (1970). *Physics I, II*, trans.W. Charlton (Oxford: Clarendon Press).

—— (1992). *Eudemian Ethics I, II and VIII*, trans. Michael Woods (Oxford: Clarendon Press).

—— (2000). *Nicomachean Ethics*, trans. Roger Crisp (Cambridge: Cambridge: University Press).

Augustine (1961). *Confessions*, trans. R. S. Pine-Coffin (London: Penguin).

Badiou, Alain (1984). 'Custos, quid noctis?', in *Critique* 450, 851–63.

—— (1993). *L'Ethique. Essai sur la conscience du mal.* (Paris: Hatier).

Baracchi, Claudia (2008). *Aristotle's Ethics as First Philosophy.* (Cambridge: Cambridge: University Press).

Barth, Karl (1968). *The Epistle to the Romans*, trans. Edwyn C. Hoskyns (Oxford: Oxford University Press).

Bergson, Henri (1992). *Cours II*, ed. H. Hude (Paris: Presses Universitaires de France).

Burnyeat, M. F. (1980). 'Aristotle on Learning to be Good', in Amelie Oksenberg Rorty (ed.), *Essays on Aristotle's Ethics.* (Berkeley and Los Angeles, CA: University of California Press), 69–92.

Butler, Joseph (1857). *Analogy of Religion, Natural and Revealed, to the Constitution and Course of Nature.* (London: Bell and Daldy).

Carlisle, Clare (2005). 'Kierkegaard's *Repetition*: The Possibility of Motion', *British Journal for the History of Philosophy* 13: 3, 521–41.

—— (2010a). 'Between Freedom and Necessity: Félix Ravaisson on Habit and the Moral Life', *Inquiry* 53: 2, 123–45.

—— (2010b). 'The Task of Becoming a Christian', in Rick Furtak (ed.), *Kierkegaard's Concluding Unscientific Postscript: A Critical Guide.* (Cambridge: Cambridge University Press.

—— (2010c). *Kierkegaard's Fear and Trembling.* (London: Continuum).

—— (2012). 'Kierkegaard and Heidegger', in George Pattison and John Lippitt (eds), *The Oxford Handbook of Kierkegaard.* (Oxford: Oxford University Press).

D'Agostino, Simone (2007). 'Une philosophie de l'action. L'Autre métaphysique de Félix Ravaisson', in Emmanuel Gabellieri and Pierre de Cointet (eds), *Blondel et la philosophie française.* (Les Plans: Parole et Silence), 61–77.

Davenport, John J. (2001). 'Towards an Existential Virtue Ethics: Kierkegaard and MacIntyre', in Davenport and Anthony Rudd (eds), *Kierkegaard After MacIntyre: Essays on Freedom, Narrative and Virtue.* (Chicago: Open Court), 265–330.

Deleuze, Gilles (1994). *Difference and Repetition*, trans. Paul Patton (London: Athlone).

Ebeling, Gerhard (1970). *Luther*, trans. R. A. Wilson (London: Collins).

Feingold, Lawrence (2001). *The Natural Desire to See God According to St. Thomas and His Interpreters.* (Rome: Apollinare Studi).

Gabriel, Markus and Slavoj Zizek (2009). *Mythology, Madness and Laughter: Subjectivity in German Idealism.* (London: Continuum).

Garver, E. (1989). 'Aristotle's Metaphysics of Morals', *Journal of the History of Philosophy* 27, 7–28.

Gouhier, Henri (1942). (ed.) *Oeuvres choisies de Maine de Biran.* (Paris: Aubier).

Hallward, Peter (2003). *Badiou: A Subject to Truth.* (Minneapolis: University of Minnesota Press).

Hegel G. W. F. (1952). *Hegel's Philosophy of Right*, trans. T. M. Knox (Oxford: Oxford University Press).

—— (1971). *Hegel's Philosophy of Mind: Part Three of the Encyclopaedia of the Philosophical Sciences (1830)*, trans. William Wallace and A. V. Miller (Oxford: Oxford University Press).

Heidegger, Martin (1962). *Being and Time*, trans. John Macquarrie and Edward Robinson (Oxford: Blackwell).

Heidegger, Martin (1993). 'The Question Concerning Technology', *Basic Writings*, ed. David Farrell Krell (London: Routledge).

Hennigfeld, J. and Stewart, J. (eds) (2003). *Kierkegaard und Schelling: Freiheit, Angst und Wirklichkeit.* (Berlin: Walter de Gruyter).

Hume, David (1902). *Enquiries Concerning the Human Understanding and Concerning the Principles of Morals*, ed. L. A. Selby-Bigge (Oxford: Oxford University Press).

Janicaud, Dominique (2000). *Ravaisson et la métaphysique. Une généalogie du spiritualisme français*, 2nd edn. (Paris: Vrin).

Kant, Immanuel (1974), *Anthropology from a Pragmatic Point of View*, trans. Mary Gregor (The Hague: Martinus Nijhoff).

—— (1992). *The Conflict of the Faculties*, trans. Mary Gregor (Lincoln, NE: University of Nebraska Press).

Kent, Bonnie (2002). 'Habits and Virtues (Ia IIae, qq. 49–70)', in Stephen J. Pope (ed.), *The Ethics of Aquinas.* (Washington: Georgetown University Press), 116–30.

Kerr, Fergus (2007). *Twentieth-Century Catholic Theologians.* (Oxford: Blackwell).

Kierkegaard, Søren (1980). *The Sickness Unto Death*, trans. Howard V. Hong and Edna H. Hong (Princeton, NJ: Princeton University Press).

—— (1981). *The Concept of Anxiety*, trans. Reidar Thomte (Princeton, NJ: Princeton University Press).

—— (1983). *Fear and Trembling* and *Repetition*, trans. Howard V. Hong and Edna H. Hong (Princeton, NJ: Princeton University Press).

—— (1985). *Philosophical Fragments*, trans. Howard V. Hong and Edna H. Hong (Princeton, NJ: Princeton University Press).

—— (1992a). *Concluding Unscientific Postscript to Philosophical Fragments*, vol. I, trans. Howard V. Hong and Edna H. Hong (Princeton, NJ: Princeton University Press).

—— (1992b). *Eighteen Upbuilding Discourses*, trans. Howard V. Hong and Edna H. Hong (Princeton, NJ: Princeton University Press).

—— (1998). *Works of Love*, trans. Howard V. Hong and Edna H. Hong (Princeton, NJ: Princeton University Press).

—— (2009). *Concluding Unscientific Postscript*, trans. Alastair Hannay (Cambridge: Cambridge University Press).

—— (2010). *Spiritual Writings*, trans. George Pattison (New York: HarperCollins).

Lalande, André (1926). *Vocabulaire technique et critique de la philosophie*, vol. 2. (Paris: Presses Universitaires de France).

Leduc-Fayette, Denise (1993). 'Loi de grace et liberté', *Les etudes philosophiques* 1, 25–34.

Lubac, Henri de (1960). *The Discovery of God*, trans. Alexander Dru (London: Dartman, Longman, and Todd).

Lohse, B. (2006). *Martin Luther's Theology: Its Historical and Systematic Development*, trans. Roy A. Harrisville (Minneapolis: Fortress Press).

Luther, Martin (1972). *Lectures on Romans, Luther's Works Volume 25*, ed. Hilton C. Oswald (St. Louis: Concordia).

Maine de Biran, Pierre (1970). *The Influence of Habit on the Faculty of Thinking*, trans. M. Boehm (Westport: Greenwood Press).

Malabou, Cathérine. (2005). *The Future of Hegel*. (London: Routledge).

Marion, Jean-Luc (1975). *Sur l'ontologie grise de Descartes*. (Paris: Vrin).

Mauve, Christiane (1995). 'Ravaisson. Lecteur et interprète de Schelling', *Romantisme* 88, 65–74.

Merleau-Ponty, Maurice (1962). *The Phenomenology of Perception*, trans. Colin Smith (London: Routledge).

Milbank, John (2005). *The Suspended Middle: Henri de Lubac and the Debate Concerning the Supernatural*. (London: SCM Press).

Oberman, Heiko (1986). *The Dawn of the Reformation*. (Edinburgh: T&T Clark).

Olesen, Tonny Aagaard (2007). 'Schelling: A Historical Introduction to Kierkegaard's Schelling', in Jon Stewart (ed.), *Kierkegaard's German Contemporaries, Tome I: Philosophy*. (Aldershot: Ashgate), 229–75.

Pattison, George (2007). *Thinking About God in an Age of Technology*. (Oxford: Oxford University Press).

Proust, Marcel (1996). *In Search of Lost Time*, vol. V, trans. C. K. Scott Moncrieff and Terence Kilmartin (London: Vintage).

Ravaisson, Félix (1984). *Rapport sur la philosophie en France au XIXeme siècle*. (Paris: Fayard).

—— (2008). *Of Habit*, trans. Clare Carlisle and Mark Sinclair (London: Continuum).

Reid, Thomas (1788). *Essay on the Active Powers of Man*. (Edinburgh).

Ricoeur, Paul (1965). *Fallible Man*, trans. Charles Kelby (Chicago: Henry Regnery).

—— (1966). *Freedom and Nature: The Voluntary and the Involuntary*, trans. Erazim Kohák (Evanston, IL: Northwestern University Press).

Rodrigo, Pierre (2011). 'The Dynamic of *Hexis* in Aristotle's Philosophy', trans. Clare Carlisle, *The Journal of the British Society for Phenomenology: Habit* 42: 1, 6–17.

Sartre, Jean-Paul (1969). *Being and Nothingness*, trans. Hazel Barnes (London: Methuen).

—— (1996). *Critique of Dialectical Reason*, vol. 2, trans. Quintin Hoare (London: Verso).

Sherman, Nancy (1997). *Making a Necessity of Virtue: Aristotle and Kant on Virtue*. (Cambridge: Cambridge University Press).

Sinclair, Mark (2011). 'Is Habit the Fossilised Residue of a Spiritual Activity? Ravaisson, Bergson, Merleau-Ponty', *Journal of the British Society for Phenomenology: Habit* 42: 1, 33–52.

Stack, George (1974). 'Aristotle and Kierkegaard's Existential Ethics', *Journal of the History of Philosophy* 12: 1, 1–19.

Thirion, Benoit (2002). 'La Lecture ricoeurienne de Ravaisson dans *Le Voluntaire et l'involuntaire*', *Les Études philosophiques* 3, 371–90.

Suggested Reading

Aristotle (1992).

Butler (1857).

Heidegger (1993).

Lubac (1960).

Ricoeur (1966).

Sartre (1969).

CHAPTER 2

···

NATIONALISM AND PATRIOTISM

···

STEPHEN BACKHOUSE

I. INTRODUCTION

···

WHAT kind of animal is nationalism? Commentators often assume that while nationalism is difficult to define, it is easy to know when you see it, that its expressions are overt and intermittent, that nations are synonymous with states, that nationalism is different from patriotism and that it is a distinct phenomenon from religion. Furthermore, at a popular level and among nationalists themselves, nationalism and national identity is thought to represent that which is long-standing and obvious—an inviolable brute fact of nature. Membership of a nation and allegiance to that nation is thus often assumed to be the bedrock upon which any account of personal identity or social participation must be constructed.

This chapter seeks to demonstrate how none of these notions are true. We will first consider the thorny issue of defining nationalism and describing its features. We will look at nations, states, and nation-states and from there examine the question of nationalism's relationship to patriotism. Next we will turn to the history of the nation and consider its existence as an imagined community. The narrative and liturgical nature of nationalism places it firmly in the sphere of religion. It is theology, and not race, politics, geography, or law that provides the best lens through which to critically observe nationalism. A prime example of a theological critic who is well placed to challenge nationalism's idolatrous and anti-social tendencies is Søren Kierkegaard. Kierkegaard's attack upon the self-deified establishment of Christendom contains many points of contact with theological nationalism. We will look at the outlines of his critique and then consider the positive contributions that a non-nationalistic, non-patriotic account of identity can make to a Christian theology of social life.

II. FEATURES OF NATIONALISM

'Nationalism' is notoriously difficult to define and it is therefore more useful to describe it by tracing its contours and familiar shapes. Any workable description will have to reflect the fact that 'nationalism' itself names a web of other notoriously difficult terms. Nationalisms are powerful ideologies that harness ideals of personal identity, history, race, and language, putting them to work in order to promote, at best, good citizenship and flourishing of a named people group, and, at worst, violent repression and extinction of other people-groups.

Whether they are explicitly violent or not, all nationalisms serve to underwrite the privileging of one particular cultural identity over and against other identities. Here it is important to recognize the pervasive nature of nationalism in a culture. Michael Billig helpfully uses the term 'banal nationalism' to refer to the everyday expressions of identity and affiliation, which undergird the (usually subconscious) self-understanding of members of a people-group. Instead of only paying attention to overt expressions of violent nationalism, Billig instead draws our attention to the 'ideological habits' which set the tone for daily life. 'Nationalism, far from being an intermittent mood in established nations, is the endemic condition' (Billig 1995: 6–7).[1] Here, nationalism encompasses that which establishes a 'sense of the common' in a society, including religious and generational wisdom that is privileged for racial and ethnic reasons. Nationalism contributes to the narratives by which people live their lives and base their prejudices. The kinds of people one decides are potential friends, appropriate mates, or deserving recipients of public money for healing and education (to name but a few examples) are all decisions often governed by nationalistic considerations no less then the decisions about who to deport, imprison, or kill.

Primordial and Political

In the absence of total agreement about terms, sociologist Anthony Smith has proposed some helpful working formulations. *Nationalism*, he writes, is 'an ideological movement for the attainment and maintenance of autonomy, unity and identity of a human population, some of whose members conceive it to constitute an actual or potential "nation"'. Furthermore, *nation* is defined as 'a named human population sharing an historic territory, common myths and memories, a mass, public culture, a single economy and common rights and duties for all members' (Smith 1999: 37).

With these formulations, Smith incorporates the two main forces at play in any incarnation of nationalism, namely the *primordial* and *political* (Geertz 1963).

---

[1] Following Hannah Arendt, Billig stresses that 'banal' should not be confused with 'benign'.

We are in the sphere of the primordial when we deal with that which affirms the values of heritage, blood, culture, and the like. It is therefore important to note that nations do not arise from states whose borders have been negotiated by diplomats and drawn up on a map, but from pre-rational (or a-rational) 'givens' of kin, religion, language, and custom (Geertz 1963: 109). In this way, the primordial gives life to the political. The political force describes nationalism's drive towards civic autonomy, which in turn creates various movements towards defined borders, national independence, and the relations of national groups sitting together at the world's table. A synthesis of the primordial and the political is evident in all forms of nationalism when they maintain that 'the people' must be free to pursue their own destiny. This involves fraternity, unity, the dissolving of all internal divisions, and being gathered together in a single historic territory and sharing a single public culture. In nationalism, culture and territory are determined by historic rights, heritage, and generational inheritance which together are taken to constitute 'authentic identity' (Hutchinson and Smith 1994: 4). The belief in blood ties and heritage leads to, and is in turn protected by, the political drive towards boundary identification and civil autonomy.

States and Nations

The doctrine that each nation should inhabit a territory of its own brings into view the problematic relationship between *states* and *nations*. Although the terms are commonly used interchangeably, states are not nations. Indeed, most modern countries, and certainly the countries of North America and Europe, are states hosting a multitude of nations. A state is a relatively straightforward object. It is a matter of geography, borders, and legal jurisdiction. As we have seen, the nation is much more fluid. It is detrimental to the study of nationalism then, that the term nation is often employed as a substitute for a legal, geographical unit, namely the state (or, even more misleading, the 'nation-state'). The common confusion of concepts is a problem because commentators often rightly recognized that nationalism is one of the world's most powerful socio-political forces, but then incorrectly apply and diagnose it.

Nationalism does not demand that the individual focus his loyalty upon the *state*, but upon the *nation*. As such, nationalism is a force that often works against the state, not in service to it. The point is of relevance to so-called 'nation-builders' whose business is actually in the building of stable states. With few exceptions, 'the greatest barrier to state unity has been the fact that the states each contain more than one nation, and sometimes hundreds' (Conner 1978: 383). One example can be seen in the efforts to institute new economic, political, and legal frameworks in post-invasion Iraq. In the face of constant fighting between Sunni, Shia, Kurdish, and other groups within that country, since 2003 the western allies are dealing with the fact that while Iraq might be lacking in the infrastructure of *state*, it is certainly not short of *nations*.

Patriotism and Nationalism

The confusion of states and nations is bound up with the ongoing conversation about the relationship between patriots and nationalists. Treatments of patriotism in political, theological, and popular thought tend to fall into three categories. As we have suggested, the first (and largest) belongs to those commentators who do not substantially differentiate between states, nations, patriotism, and nationalism.

The second school delineates patriots from nationalists (although not always states from nations). Here, those who wish to repudiate the vice of nationalism consider patriotism a virtue. Patriotism is seen as a middle way between bland apathy and excessive devotion: 'a particular loyalty compatible with universal reasonable values' (Vincent 2002: 111). The category covers philosophers and theologians as well as constitutional political scientists.

One theological defence of Christian patriotism can be found in the works of Dietrich Bonhoeffer, who lost his life as a result of his staunch opposition to Nazi nationalism. In a field of straw men, Bonhoeffer stands out as an example of thoughtful Christian patriotism. His works chart a Christian ethic that eschews nationalism and yet at the same time attempts to be recognizably patriotic. Here, patriotism is a positive force, distinct from the idolatry of nationalism. Bonhoeffer bases his distinction on the former's love of authentic reality as opposed to the latter's reliance on man-made and deceptive elements. Awareness and love for *reality* is an important concept for Bonhoeffer. 'Reality' is the totality of God's creation affirmed by the incarnation. To love this reality is to love the orders of preservation and purpose that God has put in place for human flourishing. For Bonhoeffer, this includes the web of tradition, relationships, religion, and history that can best be described as one's cultural heritage. Bonhoeffer's patriotism then, is love for God's order and intention for human life, and affiliation with others who share that form of life (Bonhoeffer 1955). It is significant that Bonhoeffer took pains to identify himself with Germany's plight for *Germany's* sake (Bonhoeffer 1973: 135). Bonhoeffer's private letters, journals, and books intended for publication are filled with passionate reference to the culture, inherited traditions, and land of his people. It would seem that Bonhoeffer rightly earns the sobriquet of 'true patriot' (Clements 1984: 87).

Many sociologists and political writers also assume that distinguishing patriotism from nationalism is a fairly straightforward task. Elie Kedourie defines patriotism as 'affection for one's country, or one's group, loyalty to its institutions, and zeal for its defence'. Kedourie claims that unlike nationalism, the sentiment of patriotism does not depend 'on a particular anthropology, [or] assert a particular doctrine of the state or of the individual's relation to it' (Kedourie 1960: 73–4). Jürgen Habermas compares the purely political loyalty of patriotic citizens with the focus on cultural ethnicity that manifests in nationalism (Habermas 1992). Habermas is a prime proponent of *constitutional* or *civic patriotism* defined as those movements that seek to channel nationalism's passion and make the political institutions and constitution of the state the focus of collective loyalty (Smith 1998: 211).

Constitutional patriotism is supposed to be an alternative to nationalism in certain key ways. First, it places emphasis on the intentional political identity of citizens within a free rational polity. This is opposed to the unwitting cultural and ethnic identity of some other kinds of nationalism. Secondly, where nationalism tends towards tighter conceptions of exclusivity, patriotism is thought to be more socially inclusive. Thirdly, patriotism is closely connected to the *what* of the state—its democratic form and constitutional status. Nationalism is more concerned with *who* wields power, and is ultimately indifferent to democracy or rule of law, as long as the 'right' nation runs the country. With civic patriotism, loyalty to the state is specifically set against loyalty to the nation, and it is supposed that in this way 'patriotism saves populations from nationalism' (Vincent 2002: 114). Whereas nationalism is love of nation, it is hoped that patriotism, truly, is love of country.

The third school of thought acknowledges the attempt to differentiate between patriotism and nationalism but concludes in the end that patriotism is not sufficiently distinct from nationalism to offer it a viable alternative. While the intent is to rescue populations from nationalism by focusing attention on shared and supposedly neutral symbols such as constitutions and flags, the reality is that patriotism effectively operates *as* nationalism and derives its power from the same sources. The third school of thought shares many similarities with the first, it is simply that here the synonymy of patriotism with nationalism is a conclusion rather than an assumption.

Following Margaret Canovan 'the notion that constitutional patriotism can provide a substitute for ties of birth and blood is incoherent' (Canovan 2000: 432). Patriotic language and ideas often draw from the same well as those of nationalism, despite the deliberate intention to the opposite. Commentators who wish to preserve patriotism while avoiding nationalism often unwittingly use nation language to support their cause. Bonhoeffer's 'true patriotism' relies heavily on the language of land, language, and inherited tradition. Canovan points out how even Habermas constantly betrays possessive, localized language in his discussion of supposedly supra-national identity and allegiance. Kedourie thinks it straightforward that patriotism as 'loyalty to one's group and zeal for its defence' is totally different from the outlook of nationalism. For him and other civic patriots, patriotism is not supposed to rely on a 'particular anthropology' or 'doctrine' of individual relations as nationalism does, and yet it is these very things that patriotic rhetoric manifestly *does* rely on. The reality is that patriotism, understood as allegiance to the strictly political and constitutional structures of state, still enjoys a symbiotic relationship with the nationalist ideas of particularity, sentiment, and selective memory. Furthermore, these confusions of patriotism and nationalism are inevitable, due to the foundations that patriotism and nationalism share but which many commentators do not acknowledge. Nationalism poses serious hazards for which patriotism is a well-meaning, but inadequate, solution.

Like nationalism, there is a 'theoretical cultural homogenization' and a 'moral chauvinism' implicit in patriotism (Gomberg 2002: 106; Vincent 2002: 23). This is because despite its language of rational/objective allegiance to laws and states, in practice the citizen is being asked to identify herself morally and emotionally with one particular form of life. Yet these laws and ethical rules that are the objects of patriotic affection are themselves deeply rooted in the collective (un)consciousness of an historical community. In other words, pledging allegiance to a flag is *not* simply a way to unite disparate groups around a neutral, objective symbol. It itself represents a complex web of cultural, religious, and geographical assumptions and developments.

True History?

It is often assumed, and occasionally made explicit, that patriotism names a virtue that applies to real people and concrete situations. So it is that Hegel can praise patriotism as: 'The political *disposition* [which is] certainly based on *truth* (whereas merely subjective certainty does not originate in *truth*, but is only opinion) and a volition which has become *habitual*' (Hegel 1991 [1821]: §268, p. 288).

Bonhoeffer contrasts nationalism's love of man-made concepts with patriotic allegiance to the reality of the created order. Similarly, Alasdair MacIntyre defends patriotism based on a country's 'true history' over and against the 'irrational attitude' of pledging allegiance towards those nations which have built themselves on 'largely fictitious' narratives (MacIntyre 2002: 55). Yet the assumption about the 'truth' of patriotism's love, or the assumption that there can be *any* country whose story is not largely fictitious, begs precisely the question at hand. Following George Kateb, patriotism (love of country) is 'a mistake' in large part because countries are 'best understood as an abstraction . . . a compound of a few actual and many imaginary ingredients'. Of course a country has a 'rational' place, a setting, a landscape, cities, a climate, and so on, 'but it is also constructed out of transmitted memories true and false; a history usually mostly falsely sanitized or falsely heroized; a sense of kinship of a largely invented purity' (Kateb 2006: 3, 8).

Even if patriotism is not overtly focused on race or ethnicity, it is still focused on things that are the result of selective historical memory. And any act of selection involves multiple deselections of elements that do not fit the preferred patriotic picture. By telling you *who* you are and *what* you should love, patriotic narratives make overarching identity claims along similar lines to nationalism, appealing to 'a kind of communal identity formation' that depends, in part, on a story of people and place 'to provide both identity and direction to the citizen-ideal' (Coleman 1995: 54).

American Experience

The United States of America endorses a form of civic patriotism that is, theoretically, an alternative to 'primitive' nationalism. Politicians and commentators routinely look to the USA as their positive example of a patriotic society that avoids demanding affiliation to a particular cultural or ethnic group in order to belong. Civic patriotism's hypothetical appeal is to the objective aspects of the state and its 'goods' that all people in the country can sign up to. And yet, as Charles Taylor has noted, mere appeals to democracy, justice, equality, and constitution is too 'thin' even for this country that places such a high value on the above named political goods (Taylor 1992). Almost as soon as it was introduced, the model patriotism provided by the USA has relied on the trappings of nationalism and nation-states, including appeals to founding fathers and myths, religiously endowed symbols and ideals, and references to historical, or quasi-historical narratives with ancestral/ethnic overtones. So, for example, Benjamin Franklin expressed his resentment of German immigrants in his new America. 'They will never adopt our language or customs,' he wrote, 'any more than they can acquire our complexion' (quoted in Florina 2006: 69). For Taylor, such a drift was inevitable. 'Nationalism has become the most readily available motor of patriotism.' The American Revolution was not nationalist in intent. Later, however, 'so much did nationalism become the rule, as a basis for patriotism that the original pre-nationalist societies themselves began to understand their own patriotism in something like nationalist terms' (Taylor 1997: 40–1).

The collapse of patriotism back into nationalism is also borne out in recent American experience. When American sociologist Deborah Schildkraut examined conceptions of US identity in the aftermath of the 11th September 2001 attacks she found that the most popular expressions saw American identity in the light of cultural and ethnic affiliation. Schildkraut also studied numerous reports of 'patriotically' motivated violence and disparagement of non-white, non-Christian American citizens concluding 'lingering ethnocultural conceptions of American identity have been awakened by the attacks' (Schildkraut 2002: 512). Despite the academic desire to see American patriotism as being 'decoupled from ethnicity, separated from religion and detached even from race' (Renshon 2001: 258), the reality seems to be that this decoupling exists more in theory than in practice. 'The place of race, ethnicity, and religion in determining what people think it means to be an American is still very much an active debate' (Schildkraut 2002: 514).

Modern Invention

We saw above how Taylor wrote of 'original pre-nationalist societies'. The idea of a pre-nationalist society might come as a surprise to those accustomed to the assumption that nations are as ancient as humanity itself. Yet while it is true to find affinities with tribalism, feudalism, or other iterations of local organized allegiance, nationalism proper is a relatively recent phenomenon.

Nations as we know them today are an early modern invention, with their ideology and discourse only becoming prevalent in the latter half of the eighteenth century. Habermas refers to nationalism as 'a specifically modern phenomena of cultural integration' that emerges 'at a time when people are at once both mobilised and isolated as individuals' (Habermas 1992: 3). Key dates in the growth of the idea of nationalism include: 1775 (First Partition of Poland); 1776 (American Declaration of Independence); 1784 (Herder's cultural-linguistic historical theories in *Reflections on the Philosophy of the History of Mankind*); 1789 and 1792 (the two phases of the French Revolution); and 1807 (Fichte's *Address to the German Nation* [Hutchinson and Smith 1994: 5]). The English word 'nationalism' has been traced back to occasional use in literature in 1798 and again in 1830, but it did not appear in lexicographies until the late nineteenth century (Conner 1978: 384). During the Great War of 1914–18, men fought in the name of nations that their grandparents had never heard of.

Our conception of 'the nation' is relatively new and in constant flux, its contours continuing to develop while ever-newer forms of nationalism spring up.

Because nations are continually imagined and re-imagined, nationalism requires an ambiguous relationship to history in order to thrive. It is a constantly developing construction, not simply a legal, geographic, or biological given. 'A nation must be an idea as well as a fact before it can become a dynamic force' (Barker 1927: 173).

Imagined Community

The 'nation' is an idea and consequently 'nationalism' is an act of imagination. For some, these notions are cause for righteous indignation. In her book *Londonistan*, the commentator Melanie Phillips quotes with derision a report from the Runnymede Trust which suggests that the 'nation' is an artificial construct, and that there is not a fixed conception of national identity and culture (Phillips 2006: 111).[2] In what Phillips claims is yet another example of 'British society trying to denude itself of its identity' she then attacks the Arts Council for saying 'British culture is not a single entity; we should rightly speak of British cultures' (Phillips 2006: 112). Is this, as Phillips and others suggest, an example of political correctness gone mad?

It would seem not. Quite apart from whatever recommendations they might make, the statements from the Runnymede Trust and the Arts Council regarding the reality of 'nations' and 'cultures' is straightforwardly true. There simply *is* more than one culture sheltering under the umbrella of 'Britishness'. At the very least there are four: Welsh, Northern Irish, Scottish, and English. And each of these national identities are themselves divisible into other identifiable cultures which, incidentally, have nothing to do with race. The indigenous population of Northern Ireland share the same (Caucasian) race but they are hardly one nation. Although they are both English, a Yorkshireman is not a Cornishman. A Shetland islander enjoys a different cultural identity than that of her Scottish Highlands cousin, and so on. What is more, these national identities are not part of the apparatus of the physical world like mountains or rivers—they are the psychological/cultural productions of human beings. Following Eric Hobsbawm,

---

[2] The report in question is *The Future of Multi-Ethnic Britain: Parekh Report* (Profile Books, 2001).

'nations' are sets of invented traditions comprising national symbols, mythology, and suitably tailored history (Hobsbawm 1983: ch. 1). In other words, they are artificial constructs. It is thus that Benedict Anderson can famously say of the nation that it is an 'imagined political community' (Anderson 1991: ch. 3).

The question is not whether nations are *real*, but rather *in what way* they exist. Even though they may exist only as invented constructions—kept alive by symbols, ethnic memory, myth, and common consent—it is worth emphasizing that they are still actual enough in the way they operate: 'Nations and nationalism are real and powerful sociological phenomena, even if their reality is quite different from the tale told about them by nationalists themselves' (Smith 1999: 36–7). The task for commentators is to deal with nationalism for what it is. Nations are not prehistoric, natural features of human life and the contours of nationalism are not primarily structured along racial, linguistic, legalistic, or geographic lines. Indeed, if we are to think of nationalism in terms of an analogous subject at all we would go less wrong less often if we thought of it in terms of religion.

Religious

Essence. Sacrifice. Destiny. Any student of nationalism cannot help but notice the religious flavour that nationalist narratives inevitably take. Of course, many national-isms do not attempt to hide the religious nature of their self-expression. Yet even the secular or non-religious rhetoric that accompanies some modern nationalism is, in fact, a later addition masking a foundational premiss. A common engine drives the original creation of the nation, and that engine is faith.

At nationalism's root is an explicit attempt on behalf of European nationalism's founding fathers to provide an alternative home for the passions that the people used to pour into the Christian Church. One of these threads can be traced back to 1789, when Abbé Emmanuel Sieyès published his pamphlet entitled 'What is the Third Estate?' and declared the nation to be the ground of all politics (Sieyès 1963 [1789]). Indeed, it seems that for Sieyès, the nation is more than just the ground of politics, for it is also 'the origin of all things' and it 'exists before all else', independent of 'all forms and conditions' (Schneider 1995: 38). Its law is the supreme law.

Sieyès did not produce the supposed divine attributes of the nation *ex nihilo*, for behind them lies Jean-Jacques Rousseau's doctrine of the sovereignty of the people. Rousseau is similarly a theologian in disguise with his *volonté générale*. Often understood by social historians as a political construct referring to the general will of the people, Rousseau's *volonté générale'* is, in fact, originally a theological term meaning simply the will of God.[3] In the *Social Contract*, Rousseau explicitly states his

---

[3] See especially Cavanaugh 2009. See also Riley 1986 and Viroli 1988 for an example of a more 'political' reading of *volonté générale*.

desire for a social order in which the nation, and not the (Roman Catholic) Church, attracts the fidelity of the people. Rousseau supports an inward and moralistic version of Christianity, which he calls a 'religion of man' (Rousseau 1954 [1762]: 154). Such a religion will not command the same hold over men as will his new civil religion (which, in William Cavanaugh's phrase, is 'the fully public cult of the nation-state' (Cavanaugh 2009: 114)). For Rousseau it is the people's sovereign, and not God, who 'is entitled to fix the tenets of a purely civil creed, or profession of faith'. Furthermore, any betrayal of these 'articles of faith' is to be punished by death, for such a national traitor 'has committed the greatest of all crimes' (Rousseau 1954 [1762]: 160). Is it any wonder that nationalisms encroach upon allegiances and functions normally attributed to Christianity? From the start, nationalism appropriated Christian concepts. In short, it is plausible to suggest that nationalism is essentially a reworked religious construct.

That the nation poses as a rival for individual's spiritual allegiance is not lost on sociologists or theologians. In his *Ethics*, Bonhoeffer traces the roots of nationalism back to the revolutionary age (Bonhoeffer 1955: 80). He too consistently notes the 'idolatrous' nature of nationalism. Nationalism, he concludes, is a markedly religious form of 'western godlessness' in which national affiliation forms part of the people's new 'god' (Bonhoeffer 1955: 82). The sociologist Carlton Hayes sees nationalism filling the religious vacuum left by collapsing support for Christianity in the west. Indeed, as a locus of faith nationalism is more successful—worship of the nation is more tangible than that of the Christian God, and the nation is quicker to exact violent retribution on its rivals than is the Christian Church (Hayes 1960). What humans once projected on to God, they now entrust with the nation: 'Nationalism . . . substituted the nation for the deity, the citizen body for the church and the political kingdom for the kingdom of God, but in every other respect replicated the forms and qualities of traditional religions' (Smith 1998: 98).

III. THEOLOGICAL NATIONALISM

The logic of nationalism follows contours recognizable to Christian theology. With their special days, chants, and revered cult objects, nationalisms clearly have their own liturgies. Hobsbawm is not alone in pointing out the symbolic and ritualistic life of the citizen of the modern secular nation: 'Indeed most of the occasions when people become conscious of citizenship . . . remain associated with symbols and semi-ritual practices (for instance, elections), most of which are historically novel and largely invented: flags, images, ceremonies and music' (Hobsbawm 1983: 12). But it is not only doxology that can be mapped on to the theology of nationalism.

Creation

From the theological underpinnings of nationalism naturally flow claims of providing authenticity and identity to individuals. This is nationalism's doctrine of creation: it is not God but the nation that grounds our existence and gives our lives shape.

A prime component of nationalism is that it must tell *the* story of the essential character of the people who belong to the nation. Defining the authentic identity of 'the people' involves notions of unity, dissolving all internal divisions, and subsuming the needs of the individual into the group. Such unity requires a single public culture, which in turn is determined by historic right, heritage, and generational inheritance.

As a necessary condition for authentic identity, nationalist narratives advertise themselves as historically inviolable, rooted in self-evident or common-sense truths. Only certain useful aspects of history and culture are selected for the narrative, and even then they are often radically transformed. Dead languages are revived, traditions invented and fictitious pristine purities restored. This is readily apparent, for example in N. F. S. Grundtvig's poetical and mythological project for the Norse people.[4] The same trend can also be seen in the successful reinvention of 'the Celts' in the service of Scottish nationalism. 'I believe that the whole history of Scotland has been coloured by myth; and that myth, in Scotland, is never driven out by reality, or by reason' (Trevor-Roper 2008: 1).[5] Contrary to its self-image as an 'inevitable' expression or movement of 'the people', nationalism is in fact a product of intellectual endeavour and (re)education. Nationalism is a cultural invention, indoctrinated into a people with the aim of producing *the People*.

Ecclesiology

As with Christian theology, the theology of nationalism accounts for the rightful congregation of the people. The creation of authentic life leads to the meaningful aggregation of that life. The creation of *the People* and their story also constructs an identity for the individual within the group. The story of a nation is, for nationalism, effectively the story of a 'group person' created by individuals, a factor clearly seen in Ernest Renan's influential treatise:

> A great aggregate of men, with a healthy spirit and warmth of heart, creates a moral conscience which is called a nation. When this moral conscience proves its strength by sacrifices that demand abdication of the individual for the benefit of the community, it is legitimate, and it has a right to exist.   (Renan 1882: 29)

---

[4] This nineteenth-century Danish preacher, poet, and historian was a prodigious writer and he is a highly influential figure in Scandinavian nationalism. English versions of key Grundtvig texts can be found in Broadbridge and Jensen 1984.

[5] Less polemical, but arguing a similar case, is Pittock 1991: 100ff.

The story of national identity co-opts, and claims definitive rights over, the identity of its individuals. The collective identity of the group names *the* essential component of individual identity: the collective defines the individual, and not the other way around. For example, for the Axis nations 'Japan to the Japanese [and] Germany to the Germans was something far more personal and profound than a territorial-political structure termed a state; it was an embodiment of the nation-idea and therefore an *extension of the self* (Conner 1978: 385). In nationalism's doctrine the destiny of 'the people' takes priority over that of any one individual in that group (Smith 1998: 99).

Within a social context, there are negative implications for personal identity when the national idea is taken to constitute not *part* of what goes into establishing an individual's identity, but is instead considered to account for the *whole* of who a person is. Kateb refers to 'group-sustaining fictions' which 'offer to help persons carry the burden of selfhood, of individual identity'. The greatest part of the burden is 'the quest for meaningfulness, which is tantamount to receiving definition of the self' (Kateb 2006: 4–5). Nationalisms act as group-sustaining fictions in that they provide the what, why, and wherefore for their individual adherents. Primordial appeals to ancestral culture and heritage (such as Bismarck's purported exhortation to the German people to 'think with their blood') are key elements within the construct of a nation, giving it the psychological dimension of an extended family or blood lineage when often, in fact, no such clear genetic link actually exists. These familial myths add credence to the demand that the destiny of 'the people' takes priority over that of any one individual in that group. Indeed, for nationalism, the sublimation of an individual into the group marks the highest point of authentic existence for that individual, in so far as each personal sacrifice contributes to the authentic identity of the whole (see Kedourie 1960: 81).

Soteriology

Nationalism is sometimes referred to as a 'salvation drama' (Smith 1998: 43). The Messianic ardour of nationalism is related to the national narrative that identifies and preserves 'a people' as distinct from any other 'people'. 'In order to attain the highest ideal of authentic existence, the main task of the nationalist must be to discover and discern that which is truly "oneself" and to purge the collective self of any trace of the "other"' (Smith 1998: 44). Hence the importance of having an 'authentic' history, which marks out and excludes the influence of any other culture or admits of recent, opportunistic invention on behalf of the nationalist dogma. With uniqueness comes purpose. Nationalist history reconstructs and appropriates the communal past in order to become the basis of a 'vision of collective destiny', and in so doing, it 'offers a kind of collective salvation drama derived from religious models and traditions' (Smith 1998: 90).

Nation-talk often betrays a soteriological enthusiasm that draws heavily from Judeo-Christian roots. As Max Weber notes, there is in nationalism 'a fervour of emotional influence' that does not have, in the main, a political-economic origin (Weber 1948: 171). Instead, nationalism is based upon what he calls 'sentiments of prestige' (Weber 1948: 173). The prestige of a nation is directly linked to the foundational idea (albeit not always explicitly addressed) of that nation's saving mission to the world. It is thus an idea emphasizing the notion that a particular nation's culture and spirit is set apart from other nations. Its mission provides significance to the national group and justifies sentiments of superiority, or at least the idea that the nation's culture values are irreplaceable. The nation, with its constructed culture and selective historical memory, assumes for itself an 'authentic identity', uniquely distinguished and set apart from other nations, with a divinely-sanctioned role to play in the unfolding of history and the development of humanity.

Eschatology

The Messianic fervour and sense of cultural mission is here translated into a story of the grand, inevitable, future for the chosen nation. Following closely on the heels of the story of essential identity comes nationalism's appeal to *destiny*. It was precisely the problems connected to the dogma of a nation's unique purpose that prompted Amartya Sen's concern with what he calls 'civilizational partitioning', that is, the tendency from some quarters to essentialize cultures into easily manageable, supposedly predictable, units. His target is 'the odd presumption that the people of the world can be uniquely categorized according to some *singular and overarching* system of partitioning' (Sen 2006: p. xii).[6] The process of identifying the supposed 'essence' of a unique culture inevitably leads to speculation about that culture's role and purpose on the world's stage, as well as the assumption that certain nations are destined to clash. For Sen, this is a less accurate scientific prediction than it is a self-fulfilling prophecy: 'The illusion of destiny, particularly about some singular identity or other (and their alleged implications), nurtures violence in the world through omissions as well as commissions' (Sen 2006: p. xiv).

Sen is sceptical about the way national culture is seen, rather arbitrarily, 'as the central, inexorable, and entirely independent determinant' of a society (Sen 2006: 112). Many of the conflicts of the world are sustained through the illusion of a 'unique and choiceless identity' (Sen 2006: p. xv).

Doubtless the essentialist approach is attractive for it appeals to cultural common sense while invoking the rich imagery of history. Furthermore, the appeal to 'destiny' appears to have profundity 'in a way that an immediate political analysis of the "here and now"—seen as ordinary and mundane—would seem to lack' (Sen 2006: 43). The

---

6 The main target in view is Samuel P. Huntington's *The Clash of Civilisations* (1996).

appeal is not merely confined to academics. It applies of course also to common beliefs and sentiments. Newspapers and politicians often talk of their nation's destiny and its values as opposed to others with little reflection on what these values are or how they developed. And yet the reality of the make-up and construction of cultural identity is always far more fluid and complex than an essentialized version can account for. In other words, this approach is based on an 'extraordinary descriptive crudeness and historical innocence' (Sen 2006: 58). Cultural generalizations are limited, and do not provide a good basis for predicting the future. 'When a hazy perception of culture is combined with fatalism about the dominating power of culture, we are, in effect, asked to be imaginary slaves to an illusory force' (Sen 2006: 103).

Divinization

The theological threads of nationalism are bound together to create that in which we live and move and have our being. The speculative apotheosis of national cultures has happened and is happening still within the Christianized societies of the west. Many of these, of course, are specifically Christian forms of divinization, using Christian motifs and concepts, often appropriating incarnational language to describe the divine mission of the nation itself. Behind the welter of Christianized European nationalist parties and American Christian patriotic movements lies Hegel's *Sittlichkeit* and his claim that 'the wisest of antiquity have therefore declared that wisdom and virtue consist in living in accordance with the customs of one's nation' (Hegel 1979 [1807]: 214).

Hegel's vision of social morality provides a narrative of identity that effectively confers divine legitimacy on the powers that be. If, as Hegel says, the laws of the state are the material manifestation of God's divine design on earth, then God is woven so fundamentally into the fabric of the nation and the historical development of human cultures 'that it may be legitimately assumed that he must prefer one set of people to another, he must, that is, be given to nationalistic fervor' (Dooley 2000: 15). Other nationalisms eschew overtly Christian rhetoric but, by effectively laying claim to be the source, meaning, salvation, and destiny of individuals under its aegis, they are no less absolutized for all that.

IV. TOWARDS A THEOLOGICAL CRITIQUE

The mix of politics, religion, social morality, group dynamics, individual identity, and divinization of the established order that is encompassed by nationalism renders Kierkegaard a singularly suitable interlocutor. Kierkegaard's works comprise a series of pseudonymous and eponymous books aimed at reintroducing Christianity into Christendom (Kierkegaard 1998 [1850]: 42, 123–4). His project involved close examinations of faith and knowledge, time and history, crowds and individuals, and culminated in the scathing polemics now known as the 'attack upon Christendom'.

This critique of cultural Christianity invites dialogue with modern critics of cultural nationalism. Kierkegaard can agree with Kateb's caution concerning group-sustaining fictions, or with Bonhoeffer, Smith, Weber (and others'), critical assessment of the pseudo-religious nature of nationalism. With Sen, Kierkegaard would be sceptical about the way national culture is seen, rather arbitrarily, 'as the central, inexorable, and entirely independent determinant of a society' (Sen 2006: 112). But Kierkegaard outruns these critiques, with a positive account of identity and identity formation that goes deeper than the sense of self offered by others. A Kierkegaardian assessment of the dangers of nationalistic 'group' ideology and identity politics not only anticipates critical social theorists; it also incorporates a theological impetus, which speaks directly to nationalism's pseudo-religious roots and expressions of Christianized patriotism that are alive and well (even especially) in the present age.

For Kierkegaard, the heart of the problem of post-Christian Christendom is that it fails to differentiate between quantitative information and qualitative truth: logical assent to collections of data and subscription to the sense of the common have become substituted for the demand of an individual choice of trust and love when faced with the ever-present—and potentially offensive—person of Christ. Authentic Christianity (for Kierkegaard) posits a cataclysmic decision: does the individual ground her identity in her membership of a certain civilization, abrogating all responsibility to the group, or does she orient herself before the divine as present in the God-man, with all the ethical and social consequences that follow? By contrast, Christendom takes its populations, historical maturity, and accumulation of cultural artefacts as proof of its inherent righteousness. It is not being before Christ but membership of the culture and subscription to its norms that is required for authentic existence. In other words, Kierkegaard's attack upon Christendom is an attack upon any society that deifies itself—a self-deification of the established order that can be more succinctly described as 'nationalism'.

The Social Individual

Kierkegaard is sometimes dismissed as individualistic bordering on misanthropic. However, while it remains appropriate to refer to Kierkegaard's *individualism,* he is not for that reason atomistic or antisocial. Kierkegaard's 'single individual' is inextricably intertwined with his Christological commitments and critiques of Christendom. Although he is uninterested in proving such things as the existence of God or the doctrine of the incarnation, nevertheless Kierkegaard takes them seriously. Kierkegaardian individualism assumes the priority of the divine as the ground and source of all being, and it builds from the effect of the incarnation upon human existence. As such, Kierkegaardian individualism provides an account of authentic identity that rivals commonly accepted socio-historical models. It cannot be squared with a merely socio-economic materialist view of human identity and it resists attempts to ground identity primarily in a group, class, or nation. It is precisely this theological aspect of Kierkegaard that makes him singularly well suited as a critic of nationalism. Kierkegaard's individualism offers a route to healthy interpersonal relationships and an alternative to the idolatrous deification of the nation.

Kierkegaard's single individual represents a repudiation of the wisdom of the crowd, in so far as the crowd is assumed to have a monopoly over the content and means of what a person can know. If a personal creator-God exists, then there is truth that lies at the heart of authentic human existence that cannot be accessed via social structures and congregations. A personal God relates to other persons therefore God cannot be related to *en masse*. Man is 'a synthesis of the infinite and the finite, of the temporal and the eternal' (Kierkegaard 1980 [1849]: 13). Kierkegaard's claim is that to be a human being is to have kinship with the divine, and this kinship—what each person shares with the divine—is 'the eternal'.

The radical egalitarianism implicit in Kierkegaard's anthropology of what it is to be a human being again suggests how Kierkegaardian individualism is not antisocial. His stress on the equal opportunity open to all persons bypasses absolutizing social structures in the service of authentic sociality. True relations between persons can only occur when both parties in the relationship are aware of their status as persons, rather than units in an amorphous group. If identity is wrapped up entirely within the frame of reference provided by the social web, then interpersonal relations can only be based on historically contingent factors comprised of like-for-like qualities. In short, only the person who shares your set of identity markers is 'real' to you.

Neighbourhood Not Nationhood

Kierkegaard's individualistic social contribution becomes especially apparent when we consider the moral implications of an individual-focused social ethic as worked out in *Works of Love,* an extended reflection on the biblical command to love. To this end, it is also interested in the persistent existence of the 'other' (who, of course, is always also an individual 'I who is not me'). Who or what constitutes the locus of our responsibility? Is it those who share the same social matrix, the social matrix itself or a 'person' whose definition transcends these socialized models? In other words, the 'who' of who should receive your love is affected by the 'how' of how you think that person is primarily defined.

Kierkegaard distinguishes between the love of *passionate preference* (*Elskov*) and the love of *neighbour* (*Kjerlighed*). Passionate preference is the love that is a matter for poets, of strong feelings and that which lends itself to extremes (Kierkegaard 1995 [1847]: 45). It is the sort of affection for others that is sustained through cultural similarity and shared inclinations. Set against this is *neighbour* love, a distinctly

Christian concept. Neighbour love stresses the duty towards others irrespective of shared interests or origins. Whereas the drift of love based on passionate preference is always towards 'the one', the drift of neighbour love is always towards 'the many' (Kierkegaard 1995: 49).

The one who loves only according to passionate preference must necessarily reduce his field of vision—he does not allow his range to extend to the people *near* him, but only to people *like* him. Thus, it soon becomes apparent that despite its poetic expressions or patriotic sentiment, passionate love is self-love: we desire the object of our admiration to the extent that they look like us and sound like us and share our qualities. The contrast with neighbour love is stark. Love for the neighbour does not seek to make me 'one' with the neighbour in some abstract 'united self'. Love for the neighbour is a relationship that respects the distinctions that exist between individuals, without pretending to collapse the difference (see Kierkegaard 1995: 55–6).

Neighbour love has a further advantage over preferential love in that the identification of the subject to be loved is infinitely simpler. The love of preference (as with national/patriotic affiliation) needs to draw up endless distinctions and exclusions, in order to attain the purest expression of its passion. Bookshops, libraries, and chapters in Oxford Handbooks may devote much space to the subject of describing national identity and cultural allegiance. There is no corresponding space devoted to 'neighbour'. This is because her identification is not in question. Kierkegaard remarks that when one is searching for one's neighbour, all one needs to do is open the door and go out. 'The very first person you meet is the neighbour, whom you *shall* love . . . There is not a single person in the whole world who is as surely and as easily recognised as the neighbour' (Kierkegaard 1995: 51–2).

As individuals, neighbours are real (not abstract) and their reality includes the fact that their personhood cannot be defined solely by recourse to an exhaustive inventory of cultural influences. They are in this sense objectively indefinable precisely because they are complex subjects—not simplified units defined primarily by their membership to certain groups such as nations. A social life based on selfish infatuation for the group is far less stable and useful to members of that society than one based on practical regard for others. True sociality cannot be based on affection for the compatriot, trumped up and maintained by self-serving fictions. It must be directed instead at the existing subject in the here and now. 'Love for neighbour does not want to be sung about—it wants to be accomplished' (Kierkegaard 1995: 46).

V. Conclusion

What kind of animal is nationalism? A description of its features paints a picture of a phenomenon that is abstract, fluid, and imaginatively constructed. Nationalisms appeal to primordial values of kith and kin, yet nations as we know them are relatively recent inventions. Nationalisms stake a political claim for autonomy for its distinct people, yet on closer inspection it is unclear how to define 'the people', or whether, in fact, they can be so easily delineated along racial, legal, or geographic lines.

It is the imaginative and narrative nature of patriotism and nationalism that recommends a theological critique of these powerful social forces. And they should be critiqued. The narrative of national identity is a story that focuses ever more tightly on a few core essentials, selecting sentiments and excluding facts that do not fit its desired picture of 'the people'. In modern societies where many nations inhabit one state, these narratives of nationalism lead their proponents inexorably towards isolation and alienation within the wider group. The story of the good patriot hardly fares better, drawing from the same unstable mix of self-selecting history, pseudo-religious ideas, and desire to adhere to an overarching destiny. To secularist proponents of nationalism and patriotism we wish to ask: don't you see how religious this is? And to Christian defenders of nationalism and patriotism we wish to ask: don't you see how religious this is? Casting nationalism as a primarily religious impulse is not to root it in something inviolable and ahistoric. Religions too are human constructs. The task for the theologian is to talk as excellently about the divine and the religious impulses in man as possible. Nationalism is not essentially a political movement, a legal invention, a natural feature, or a racist doctrine. It has been built from theology and it is with theology that it can best be engaged. Here Kierkegaard is offered as a fruitful guide. Not only is he the pre-eminent critic of deified establishment; he is also able to provide a positive, theological route for authentic identity that bypasses membership in the nation, country or group. Against the destabilizing and abstract nature of nationalistic fervour, Kierkegaard the individualist offers an account of social life inaccessible to the patriot in this present age.

REFERENCES

Anderson, Benedict (1991). *Imagined Communities*. (London: Verso).
Barker, Ernest (1927). *National Character and the Factors in its Formation*. (London: Methuen).
Billig, Michael (1995). *Banal Nationalism*. (London: Sage).
Bonhoeffer, Dietrich (1955). *Ethics*. (London: SCM).
—— (1973). *True Patriotism: Letters, Lectures and Notes 1939–45*. (London: Collins).
Broadbridge, Edward and Niels Lykne Jensen (1984). *A Grundtvig Anthology*. (Cambridge: James Clarke & Co).
Canovan, Margaret (2000). 'Patriotism is not Enough', *British Journal of Political Science* 30, 413–32.
Cavanaugh, William T. (2009). *The Myth of Religious Violence*. (Oxford: Oxford University Press).
Clements, Keith, W. (1984). *A Patriotism for Today: Dialogue with Dietrich Bonhoeffer*. (Bristol: Bristol Baptist College).
Coleman, John (1995). 'A Nation of Citizens', *Concilium: Religion and Nationalism*. (London: SCM).

Conner, Walker (1978). 'A Nation is a Nation, is a State, is an Ethnic Group, is a . . .', *Ethnic and Racial Studies* (October) 1: 4, 377–400.

Dooley, Mark (2000) 'The Politics of Statehood vs. a Politics of Exodus: A Critique of Levinas's Reading of Kierkegaard', *Søren Kierkegaard Newsletter* (August) 40.

Florina, Morris P. et al. (2006). *America's New Democracy*, 3rd edn. (New York: Pearson/ Longman).

Geertz, Clifford. (1963). 'The Integrative Revolution', *Old Societies and New States*. (London: Macmillan).

Gomberg, Paul (2002). 'Patriotism is like Racism', *Patriotism*. (New York: Humanity Books).

Habermas, Jürgen (1992). 'Citizenship and National Identity', *Praxis International* (April) 12: 1, 1–19.

Hayes, Carlton (1960). *Nationalism: A Religion*. (New York: Macmillan).

Hegel, G. W. F. (1979) [1807]. *Phenomenology of Spirit*. (New York: Oxford University Press).

—— (1991 [1821]). *Elements of the Philosophy of Right*. (Cambridge: Cambridge University Press).

Hobsbawm, Eric (1983). *The Invention of Tradition*. (Cambridge: Cambridge University Press).

Hutchinson, J. and Anthony D. Smith (eds) (1994). *Nationalism*. (Oxford: Oxford University Press).

Kateb, George (2006). *Patriotism and Other Mistakes*. (New Haven, CT: Yale University Press).

Kedourie, Elie (1960). *Nationalism*. (Oxford: Hutchinson).

Kierkegaard, Søren (1980 [1849]). *Sickness unto Death*. (Princeton, NJ: Princeton University Press).

—— (1995 [1847]). *Works of Love*. (Princeton, NJ: Princeton University Press).

—— (1998 [1850]). *Point of View*. (Princeton, NJ: Princeton University Press).

MacIntyre, Alasdair (2002). 'Is Patriotism a Virtue?', in *Patriotism*. (New York: Humanity Books).

Phillips, Melanie (2006). *Londonistan*. (London: Gibson Square).

Pittock, Murray (1991). *The Invention of Scotland*. (London: Routledge).

Renan, Ernest (1882). *Qu'est-ce qu'une nation?* (Paris: Calmann-Levy).

Renshon, Stanley (2001). *One America?* (Georgetown: Georgetown University Press).

Riley, Patrick (1986). *The General Will Before Rousseau: The Transformation of the Divine into the Civic*. (Princeton, NJ: Princeton University Press).

Rousseau, J.-J. (1954 [1762]). *The Social Contract*. (South Bend: Gateway).

Schildkraut, Deborah (2002). *Political Psychology* 23: 3, 511–35.

Schneider, Heinrich (1995). 'Patriotism and Nationalism', *Concilium: Religion and Nationalism*. (London SCM).

Sen, Amartya (2006). *Identity and Violence: The Illusion of Destiny*. (London: Allen and Lane).

Sieyès, Emmanuel (1963 [1789]). *What is the Third Estate?* (London: Pall Mall Press).

Smith, Anthony D. (1998). *Nationalism and Modernism*. (London: Routledge).

—— (1999). 'The Nation: Real or Imagined?', *People, Nation, State*. (London: I. B. Tauris).

Taylor, Charles (1992). *Multiculturalism and the Politics of Recognition*. (Princeton, NJ: Princeton University Press).

Taylor, Charles (1997). 'Nationalism and Modernity', *The Morality of Nationalism*. (Oxford: Oxford University Press).

Trevor-Roper, Hugh (2008). *The Invention of Scotland: Myth and History*. (London: Yale University Press).

Vincent, Andrew (2002). *Nationalism and Particularity*. (Cambridge: Cambridge University Press).

Viroli, Maurizio (1988). *Jean-Jacques Rousseau and the 'Well-Ordered Society*. (Cambridge: Cambridge University Press).

Weber, Max (1948). 'The Nation', *Essays in Sociology*. (London: Routledge).

Suggested Reading

Anderson (1991).

Backhouse, Stephen (2011). *Kierkegaard's Critique of Christian Nationalism*. (Oxford: Oxford University Press).

Billig (1995).

Cavanaugh (2009).

Gellner, Ernest (2006). *Nations and Nationalism*. (Oxford: Blackwell).

Hayes (1960).

Hobsbawm (1983).

Hutchinson and Smith (1994).

Kateb (2006).

Kedourie (1960).

Kierkegaard (1998).

Matuštík, Martin (1993). *Postnational Identity*. (New York: Guilford Press).

Sen (2006).

Tolstoy, Leo (1936). 'Christianity and Patriotism', *The Kingdom of God and Peace Essays*. (Oxford: Oxford University Press).

Viroli, Maurizio (1995). *For Love of Country*. (Oxford: Clarendon Press).

Westphal, Merold (1991). *Kierkegaard's Critique of Reason and Society*. (Pennsylvania, PA: Pennsylvania University Press).

CHAPTER 3

....

THE MAKING OF THE
MODERN METROPOLIS

....

GRAHAM WARD

There should be no fundamental difference between the way we might
orient ourselves spatially to the inside world of a great metropolis and the
inside world of a house. Both require the feeling of being bounded,
possessed, and centred... No matter how speculative the forms of the
buildings within the city may be to the eyes of its citizens, the meanings
and feelings that the buildings give will be diminished if those buildings
cannot be 'possessed'.

(Bloomer and Moore 1977: 54–5)

I. INTRODUCTION

....

OPEN the books by urban and historical geographers treating the making of the modern
European city and the facts presented are startling. If we take the years 1800 to 1910, just
over a century, then we find that the population of London grew from 1.1 to 7.3 million;
Paris from 547,000 to 2.9 million; and Berlin from 172,000 to over 2 million. In the States
figures are even more astonishing: New York grew from 60,000 to 4.8 million and
Chicago from nothing, as the land was uninhabited until the mid-nineteenth century, to
2.4 million.[1] Modernity's great symbol is the rise of the metropolis. The metropolis is
modernity materialized—for good and for evil. But despite the fact that the majority of
our greatest modern thinkers, just to limit it to philosophers and theologians, have lived
and worked in cities, there is little research on the relationship between their philosophies and theologies and the cityscapes which surrounded them, the boulevards they

---

[1] As overall guides, see Lees and Hollen (2007) and Dennis (2008).

walked down, the cafes and restaurants that fed them, the theatres, opera houses, concert halls, museums, and art galleries that entertained them and nurtured their imaginations. We need to get at how material environments furnish and figure material cultures and impact on material subjects, as individuals, groups, and classes.

There have indeed been important studies of thinkers and cities, such as the work of Lesley Chamberlain on Nietzsche and Turin or Bruno Bettelheim on Freud and Vienna. But I am considering here a closer association between cityscapes, the cultures they foster, the human subjects they form, and the intellectual productions they inform. It is the kind of association found in Walter Benjamin's essay on his early life in Berlin or his book detailing Baudelaire's association with the arcades in Paris (Benjamin 2008, 2006). But there is no comparative study for a theologian; so we have to invent something new here, establishing a different kind of theological genre that is not ecclesial history or biography or even contextual theology. We need to do this because the development of modern theology, and many of the themes that have preoccupied modern philosophy— phenomenology, hermeneutics, existentialism, utilitarianism, liberalism, dialectics, dia- logicalism, positivism, and post-structuralism, among them—are coextensive with and 'co-implicated' in the rise of the modern city. The biographical material is rich: Schleiermacher and Hegel in Berlin; Schopenhauer in Hamburg, Dresden, Berlin, and Frankfurt; Nietzsche in Turin; probably the major British theologian in the nineteenth century, F. D. Maurice, in London; Karl Marx, in London; John Stewart Mill, in London; Bertrand Russell, in London; Paul Tillich, in Berlin, Dresden, Frankfurt, and New York; Sartre, Derrida, Foucault, and Levinas, all in Paris. Kant may have lived in what was becoming a Prussian backwater, Thoreau may have retreated to Warden, Heidegger to the Bavarian forests, and their philosophies may reflect this, but so many others didn't, and the biographies do not set out to show how the theologies and philosophies of these thinkers related to the cities they inhabited; were born not just from the teaching they received but reflections on the experiences they had within the urban contexts. As the Situationist urban planner, Gilles Ivan, observes: 'Architecture is the simplest means to *articulate* time and space, to *modulate* reality, to engender dreams' (2009: 36).

The city is not just a place we live in; it is and it becomes an extension of ourselves. It is certainly not flesh of our flesh, but it is a material objectification of our souls in a manner similar to the way the body is a material objectification of our souls. If, following Aristotle, the soul is the form of the body, then in our labouring we fashion for ourselves tools and artistic fabrications (crafts) whereby we extend the physicality of our bodies. The city is both a tool and an artistic fabrication providing for human well- being through prosthetic or instrumental, and creative or aesthetic developments of our working and dwelling within the world. The traditional metaphors most descrip- tive of the city as a concept are the machine (city as tool) and the body (city as organic and artistic fabrication).[2] As both Hegel and Marx recognized, too much emphasis on

[2] Lewis Mumford, in his classic study (Mumford 1966), charts an historical shift from the organic to the technical understanding of the city. He writes so well he might be forgiven the reductive nature of such a dichotomy. Certainly, the famous expositor of the relationship between architecture and the

the instrumental productivity of tools can alienate. The city too can alienate. Witness: Jean-Paul Sartre's account of the onset of existential nausea as he wanders through the streets of an unnamed and nondescript French city (probably Le Havre, where the novel was composed) on the eve of the Second World War; or Kafka's Prague as it emerges from descriptions of Joseph K's and K's meanderings through the anonymous urban constructions of *The Trail* and *The Castle*. For Hegel the alienation issues from that necessary process of the objectification of ourselves that fashions tools in the first instance. For in that objectification the tool becomes universalized: available now to be used by anyone who sees productive advantages in employing it (Hegel 1967). And so as objectification and tool it loses its subjective and personalized meaning. The architect designs a building, an urban planner the intersection between a boulevard and an arterial road—these activities presume and conceive the need for both tools and craftsmanship. There are, of course, utilitarian specifications given to them—of function and finance—but the plans, subject to modification, are their own. That is what they are paid to do: their individual skill lies in producing such designs. The product, when constructed, belongs to everyone (and no one). Living in cities we are the inheritors of tools and craftsmanship fashioned for us; and so our creative labour can become disconnected from the ongoing productivity of the city as both a giant and

human body is, of course, Vitruvius. *De Architectura: Ten Books on Architecture*, Book III, expounds his notion of proportions. The three key elements of great architecture for Vitruvius was *firmitas, utilitas*, and *venustas* (solidity, usefulness, and beauty), but proportionality governed all three of these elements. Since architecture should imitate nature then the source of proportions should be found in nature greatest work of art: the human body. This was a microcosm for a cosmic geometry and the ideal human body gave expression to this geometry—as Leonardo Da Vinci's famous diagram reveals. According to Mumford, the body model featured particularly in the Roman conception of a city. 'Though the Romans inflated the theological currency by inventing a special god for every occasion in life, the one supreme god that they really worshipped was the body... The religion of the body was as near as the Romans ever got to religion... and the bath was its temple... The buildings themselves proclaim this fact: 'architecturally they rank among the supreme achievements of Rome; and only the Parthenon can be counted as a rival' (1966: 263). Nevertheless, the body as a civic model stills haunts the language of urban planners with their arterial roads, hard shoulders, and urban tissue as it haunts the bureaucratic language for governing civic life. One of the most influential French urban planners of the nineteenth century, Maxime du Champ, in the nine editions of his *Paris. Ses organs, ses functions et sa vie dans la seconde moitié du 19e siècle* (Paris, 1875), could still describe Paris as a vast 'body'. In fact, the city as a body became an important descriptor with the rise of concerns relating civic life to public health (see Sheard and Power 2000). Until very recently many British county councils were known as corporations. With the body, the city of stone, metal, and brick becomes an organic landscape that emphasizes civic sociality—always one of the prized values of urban living. If the British anthropologist Mary Douglas is right, the body as a model for the design of dwellings, the organization of activities that go on within such dwelling, and the designation of different activities to different spaces is an anthropological a priori. So, it might be suggested that what relates cities to human bodies is that they are the external embodiment of our own bodily sense. This organic conception of the city, in the early twentieth century, took two other forms: the notion of the garden city (which was inspired by the religious values of the garden, evident in Jewish, Christian, and Islamic figurations of paradise) and an architectural desire to express the organic relationship between urban life and the landscape (which notably appears in the utopian thinking of Frank Lloyd Wright for his project 'Broadacres').

complex machine and a body engulfing our bodies. But the fact that cities are so large means that the alienation need not be total. There may be a corner in the city—a park, a piazza, a café on a certain street—where the alienation is overcome.[3] Where there is a sense of dwelling.[4] And, in that dwelling, there is a concordance between soul, body, and civic craftsmanship; a coextensiveness that transforms the city into a body rather than a machine, an imaginative inspiration rather than an instrumental tool. The city as a body in this way is a city 'possessed' in the way Bloomer and Moore give emphasis to that word in my opening citation. The city is indwelt and its activities are creative; its labours energizing.

In understanding the city as a body made up of other embodiments (social groups, institutions, corporations, individuals) then we recognize that the body is not an object it is an event. Its reality is always emerging because it is continually in movement: relaying the internal to the external and the external to the internal, determining and being determined, informing and being formed. As such bodies are only distinguished one from another by an artificial freeze-framing which is followed by a series of separations which forgets, for its own instrumental purposes, the profound interrelationships between bodies. The room in the building where I work, the building in which that room is situated, the institution to which that building belongs, the civic location that houses that institution etc., are all bodies impacting each on the other, defining the existence of each other. Within these bodies other bodies operate: social and divisional groupings such as faculties or departments, administrations and offices. The relations between these bodies determine and regulate the qualities of life lived in and between such bodies. This does not mean the liquidation of bodies as discrete entities. There are separating surfaces and skins, even though they are each permeable. Bodies still have a unity, but it is a dynamic emerging unity that is continually under construction and under negotiation. Intercorporeality, and the affects it produces, is key to having a body sense at all (Merleau-Ponty 1999).

---

[3] In the wake of affect theory in the mid-1990s, there is a currently a revival of interest among urban geographers of the work of the mid-twentieth-century architect and planner, Gilles Ivan (a.k.a. Ivan Chtcheglov), who developed what he termed 'psychogeography'—maps of the somatic and affective interactions between bodies and urban spaces. Psychogeography was the 'study of the precise effects of the geographical environment, consciously organized or not, acting on the affective comportment of individuals' (Ivan 1989 [1958]: 45). In discussing alienation and the city, psychogeography draws attention to the way in which the city of not an homogenous and monolithic space. It becomes mythic when it is conceived as such. It is emotionally and architecturally a variegated topos.

[4] For an existential and phenomenological account of such 'dwelling', see two late essays by Martin Heidegger, 'Building Dwelling Thinking' and '. . . Poetically Man Dwells . . .' (Heidegger 1975a and b: 143–62 and 211–29, respectively). Heidegger's commitment to an anti-metaphysical philosophical project and his attention to an examination of Being's immanence, bears a patina of theological (and pagan) associations, not least in his analysis of *Ereignis* (an important word in Karl Barth's examination of revelation). I refrain from entering the debates on the possible theological use of Heidegger's work, at this point, but his analysis of dwelling as part of the human 'worlding' of the world is an important recognition of the symbiosis of dwelling and thinking.

We can take this analysis one step further. If cities are not just places of residence and work, but places in which our embodiment is enacted in ways which implode any passive-activity binary, places in which there is both withdrawal (alienation) and participation (dwelling); if the architecture and urban layouts of our cities both diminish (alienation) and enhance (possession) our creativity—then cities fashion our sentient experience and therefore our abilities to think and to imagine; they inform our capacities to desire and to believe in our possibilities. It is out of such abilities and capacities that human beings transcend their physical environments and, in doing that, transform them. Cities become places of hope, where certain imagined freedoms can be realized, where potentialities glimpsed become actualities; rather than places of despair and abjection. Either way they act upon our affectivities. In the recognition that the city can become a body in concordance with our bodies, lies the intuition of community and reciprocal relations between other human beings, other physical bodies participating in, dwelling in, the civic body. The I becomes a we—and this is now the place where *we* dwell and both an extension and an expression of our corporate body. Cities impact upon what Charles Taylor (2003) and Cornelius Castoriadis (1987) have defined our 'social imaginaries' (see also Ward 2005: 159–66).

Theologically, we have to recognize this dwelling is prior to our ecclesiologies; social bodies are prior to ecclesial bodies—both historically and phenomenologically. But if Christianity acknowledges that all things were made through Christ, then they have also to recognize that social bodies are made possible by the same Christ. And so the ecclesia which is the body of Christ, and the sacramental body that sustains its life, exists in a complex relation to the interelationality of social bodies. This is where I wish to begin exploring the relationship between Christian theology, philosophy, and the city.

Historical theology has delineated in detail the involvement of various churches (Protestant, Catholic, and Nonconformist) in urban developments that took place throughout western Europe as cities began to proliferate from the eighteenth century onwards, and major capitals like London and Paris raced beyond one million inhabitants. Much has also been done on philanthropic activities, both theologically and philosophically informed, that arose as a consequence of the industrial revolution and in response to the appalling civic conditions of the poor from the early nineteenth century up to the post-Second World War boom. Such charity work, and the progressive, enlightened philosophies behind them, built hospitals, founded public libraries, sponsored the construction of schools, supported the housing of museums and art galleries and helped established the rapid expansion of civic universities. All of which contributed enormously to transformations in the urban landscape. If much work has already been accomplished here then research has also been accumulating on the development of various urban theologies—that is, responses to the new emerging urban life since the nineteenth century by theologians wishing to marry Christian and social ethics. For example—I know the work done in Britain more than elsewhere—there has been extensive research on the Christian socialists in England (F. D. Maurice, Charles Kingsley, and Robert Ludlow), the Communion Movement, the Malvern Conferences, the theologies of William Temple and Ronald Preston, and, closer to our own time, the Church commissioned publication *Faith in the City* and the subsequent theological reflections it engendered. Most of this work was attempting to 'apply' dogmatic theology to the challenges arising in the new urban contexts: poverty, illiteracy, social atomism, etc.[5] This work led to developments in public theology, political theology, practical and contextual theology.

Historical research has also been conducted on how the city and philosophical thought, particularly social and critical theory and enlightenment rationalism, impacted upon each other. And so, we now know how early French urban planners, precursors of the great Baron Hausmann who transformed the centre of Paris, were inspired by the messianic utopianism of Henri de Saint-Simon and the egalitarian utopianism of Charles Fourrier (Papayanis 2004). The French situationists, particular Guy Debord, had considerable influence over a number of structuralist and post-structuralist thinkers such as Michel de Certeau, Michel Foucault, and Gilles Deleuze (Sadler 1998: 3, 40, 50–1, 98, 108). Charles Dicken's novel *Hard Times* reveals the ways in which Bentham's utilitarianism culturally impacted upon his thinly disguised industrial city of Manchester. When we think of some of the major movements in philosophy, they can hardly be imagined outside understanding the urban contexts to which they give expression: liberalism and John Stewart Mill's London, Freudian psychoanalysis at *fin-de-siècle* Vienna, Nietzsche's aesthetics of nihilism and bourgeois Turin, Sartre's existential alienation and Paris, Horkheimer and Adorno's critical theory and Frankfurt, then New York. In fact, could there have arisen to philosophical pre-eminence concepts like the other, dialogic (philosophical and theological) or dialectic without the rampant heterogeneity of the city? Could the importance of ethics and aesthetics in modern philosophy be conceivable outside the dense sodalities of civic living and the cultural productions and the cultural accumulations, fashioned from and for such living? Though philosophy, as an intellectual and increasingly professionalized activity, seems as though it should be divorced from the urban environments within which it was conceived, it wasn't; and it never could be.

II. BERLIN AND FRIEDRICH SCHLEIERMACHER

I could continue with generalities, but I want to focus attention on the very specific in order to depict the somatic, affective, and intellectual interactions between city

---

[5] I take seriously Brian Massumi's observation about application: 'If you apply a concept or a system of connection between concepts [dogmatic theology], it is the material you apply it to that undergoes the change, much more markedly than do the concepts. The change is imposed upon the material by the concepts' systematicity and constitutes a becoming homologous of the material to the system. This is all very grim. It has less to do with "more to the world" than "more of the same". It has less to do with invention than mastery and control' (Massumi 2002: 17).

dwelling, theology, and philosophy. The city I want to examine is Berlin and its relationship to the origins of both modern theology and certain forms of post-Kantian philosophy. I want to undertake an exploration of the work of one of the most famous Berliners, the theologian and philosopher Friedrich Schleiermacher who lived in Berlin through some of its major urban changes. It is important to understand, the development of the city to which the urban and historical geographers mainly refer is a phenomenon of the industrial revolution. This is not the case with the Berlin of either Schleiermacher or Hegel, for industrialization in Germany did not take place until the second half of the nineteenth century. What we are treating here is a city that had been developed by an absolute monarchy, inspired by that peerless example of absolute monarchy Louis XIV in his conception of Versailles. If Louis XIV was to be equated quite physically with his state ('*L'État c'est moi*'), then the urban planning of absolute monarchy was to embody this idea. So, at Versailles, the centre of his palace was his own bedchamber, and all roads from Paris and a number of other places converged on that spot (Bloomer and Moore 1977: 12). We will begin to see what this means for Berlin, and for Schleiermacher, as we proceed.

In Germany, until 1808 and the passing of the municipal ordinance (the *Städteordnung*), any urban planning and development was a ruler's initiative and prerogative (Sutcliffe 1981: 11). So, prior to this, Schleiermacher arrives at Prussia's *Kaiserstadt*. 'Before his move to Berlin, Schleiermacher's intellectual productivity was analytic and isolated. After his 1796 entry into the Berlin circle of early Romanticism, his first publications were the rhetorical fruition of his suddenly blossoming social life' (Blackwell 1982: 3). My attention here is on how the city both creates and expresses the material conditions either conducive to or constraining social life. Schleiermacher arrived in Berlin in fact in 1794, for a six-month stay as an instructor at a gymnasium. He was engaged at the time in a long treatise that was never published—*Über die Freiheit des Menschen*—which spoke of the need to appropriate and respond to the world in what is a phenomenology of human choosing and the formation of subjectivity issuing from such choosing. He was intellectually prepared then to take on the city—but he left after six months. The old city walls were still in tact—a sort of star-shaped defensive fortification crossing two tributaries of the River Spree. Within the walls were approximately 170,000 people and what drew them was the court of Friedrich Wilhelm II. In 1794, Schleiermacher kept himself to himself. To employ the language of the architects whose work I cite above—he did not 'possess' the city; he didn't engage in citizenship despite having friends like Alexander von Dohna who lived there. Most of his time until this point had been lived in either the country, for his Pietist schooling, the university township of Halle, or the country estate of the von Dohna family (where he was a tutor). When he returned in 1796, his post was as Royal Chaplain to the Charité Hospital, and we are fortunate in having a map of Berlin composed just three years prior to arrival. We can find Charité, which later formed the basis for the medical school and teaching hospital that still dominates the northern quarter of central Berlin today, outside the city wall to the north; once more surrounded by countryside. In part, this location was due to the fact that the hospital was founded following an outbreak of plague in the early eighteenth century and in Schleiermacher's time it was a military hospital. The barracks for the formidable Prussian army dominated a district to the east of the old city: König Stadt. Berlin, at this point, had grown beyond its fortified walls and although new walls and gates into the city had been created, they were to come down early in the nineteenth century.

In the 1870s, an historian of the city, Robert Springer, in his *Berlin: Die deutsche Kaiserstadt*, described the growth of the city in this way: 'There thus emerges from a fishing village an imperial city—from insignificant and scattered fishermen's cottages the capital of an internally strong, extensive, populous, politically important state, glittering with masterpieces of architecture and sculpture, distinguished for artistic zeal and intellectual culture, for academic learning, for the flowering of commerce and industry, for the higher progress of social life' (Springer 1878: 6). Most of this was to come when Schleiermacher arrived though we can see from the map the various outlying areas of the old fortified town: König Stadt where Friedrich Wilhelm I, on being crowned King of Prussia in 1701, moved his court from Königsberg and built his palace; Spandaur Vierthel and Köpnicker Viethel—two of the oldest settlements beyond the walls; then Friedrich Stadt and Neustadt to the west; and Stradauer Viethel to the east. Further south was the separate town of Potsdam, where Schleiermacher spent time as a court preacher since Friedrich the Great had built a palace there. What was most impressive was the new expansion under Friedrich the Great towards the Thiergarten, and the formation of promenades in the Thiergarten itself.

From the old castle he had created what still today is a stunning architectural panorama: the great ceremonial boulevard known as Unter den Linden, lined on either side, beyond the lime trees, by palaces, but importantly housing the Berlin Opera House and the Royal Library. This was the cultural focus of the city when Schleiermacher arrived in 1796. It was crowned by the erection of the Brandenburg gate, finished in the 1791, which led out to the Thiergarten. Commissioned by Friedrich Wilhelm II, the gate was consecrated to peace. But don't be deceived, the *Quadriga* that surmounts the gate is the goddess of victory driving her chariot before her. Nevertheless, with its Doric columns this was not an *Arc de Triomphe* like the French recapitulation of Titus's victory arch in Rome, this was a gateway to the new Athens on the River Spree. This whole concourse architecturally is designed to dwarf the human body; to immerse it in a new beauty that was both imperial and imperious.

We can see from the map that the old city of Berlin was a warren of close mediaeval streets, except for Spandaustrasse where the wealthy tended to be housed. The old city was very much the city as a fortress. But the Brandenburg gate announced a different kind of city—one that was open, fearlessly so, proud and self-confident of its power, despite the French Revolution which had toppled one of the major absolutist powers in Europe. Although Unter den Linden was constructed to allow for military parades and a demonstration of Prussian regal might, it was also constructed in terms of monumental architecture, both graceful and rational. It was an early example, the planning and architectural execution of Washington would be another, of the city as an artwork; the city as itself a new aesthetic form. Neustadt was the construction of a public space; a space for the people to be seen, meet, and congregate. So we have, in the closing years of the Prussian *ancient régime* when, due to economic pressures with respect to the rise in land and grain prices, the feudalism of the nobility was becoming increasingly unsustainable, the beginnings of a public sphere and the rise of the *Bürgertum*. 'Berlin is certainly one of the handsomest cities in Europe', George Forster declared after visiting the city in 1779 (cited in Hertz 2005: 24).

In part the expansion came with the Prussian state's administrative expansion and its choice of Berlin for its military headquarters. *Mitte*, old Berlin, housed the wealthy (bankers, jewellers, and important merchants), those whose held key offices within the royal bureaucracy, the diplomats, the homes of foreign ambassadors and landowning noblemen. Friedrich Stadt was laid out in 1688 and then extended in 1721 (Sutcliffe 1981: 10). Neustadt was developed by Friedrich the Great, and as it expanded the very wealthy began to leave the old city and move as close to the Unter den Linden as possible.

What was more, Berlin was a central European melting pot for languages and cultures. French Huguenots settled here near the Brandenburg gate in the early eighteeth century, accounting for around 20 per cent of the city's population—Friedrich the Great himself loved all things French. Here also were wealthy Jews who fled from Vienna when Austria expelled them; Jews whose historical backgrounds lay in Amsterdam and Portugal. As part of the reconstruction of the city, Friedrich the Great also built the domed Catholic cathedral of St Hedwig. Then, as the Kingdom of Poland ceased to exist, large chucks of that land were taken by the Prussians. So the city was inhabited by various peoples from Bohemia, Silesia, and even Austria. It was a place where religions met each other under enlightenment auspices of toleration; where Jews (they were not given the full rights of citizen until 1871), Protestants, and Catholics came together and lived together. The city did not have a university, but it did have the Royal Academy of Science, whose first President was Gottlieb Leibniz and it had several learned societies—like the Wednesday club—where lectures were given and academic papers discussed. It had commercial, as well as court theatres, two important and competing newspapers, lending libraries, and a private art collection open to the public.

It was then a city that buzzed with commercial, bureaucratic, and intellectual business that looked to the future, saw progress as imperative, and believed in the power of ideas. Within the confines of a traditional social hierarchy or *Stände* (nobility, peasantry, *Bürgertum*), bubbled a cultured and creative energy that pushed at the boundaries of the traditional. It was the land of the *arrivistes*: 'men who shared nothing but their aspiration to official positions and to intellectual prominence chose Berlin as the city in which to realise their dreams' (Hertz 2005: 50).

Often the originality of Schleiermacher's approach to religion and Christian theology, as expressed in his 1799 *On Religion: Speeches to Its Cultured Despisers*, is put down to sheer individual genius. No doubt there was genius or a sharp, quick-thinking intelligence. No doubt also living with Friedrich Schlegel and founding with him, his brother Augustus, and their common friend (soon to be Schlegel's wife), Dorothea Mendelssohn Viet, the journal *Athenaeum* were contributory factors. But they were factors made possible by living in the same city, meeting everyday for lunch at Dorothea's house. Even intelligence needs stimulating and nurturing. The city was now a new vibrant experience for Schleiermacher. It presented opportunities and encouragements he had not had before, most particularly an environment where dialogue and social interaction were paramount. His description of Plato's work, written just after his stay in the city, says much both about what he valued in Plato (as one of his major translators) and civic life: Plato's medium of dialogue was 'fashioned like a living being, with parts in proportion and body appropriate to mind' (cited in Blackwell 1982: 135). Berlin provided him with the material, cultural, and social conditions necessary to take his concept of freedom—as both bounded and yet infinite—and embody it. More so, because when Friedrich Wilhelm III came to power in 1797, he swept away some of the oppressive censorship of the old regime and 'raised hopes for greater freedom and constitutionalism in the German state' (Crouter 1996: p. xv).

Space is different in a city: there are modes of distance and proximity, shades of intimacy and estrangement, as buildings and streets close in upon or dwarf the urbanite. So relations between citizens are different: encountering a friend becomes easier and more regular than in the country, and one also continually encounters the stranger, the foreigner. In its turn this generates different senses of community and modifies what it is to be human, to be a social animal. The old mediaeval city emphasized familiarity (with all the paternal connotations of that term), intrigue, and insularity. Neustadt spoke of a freedom to move and so to think. Its architecture exposed the citizen to light, grand vistas, and the broad expanses of the Thiergarten. It awoke new levels of sensation, experience, and imagination; a different sense of being alive; life's boundless potential. 'Life' plays an important philosophical role in the work of Schleiermacher, as it did with Hegel and Hölderlin in their Frankfurt days.

The city created a new hunger for experience that *Bildung* disciplined and gave direction, narratives, and a teleology. The aspirations of *Bildung*, the ideal subjectivity it fashioned and promulgated, are inseparable from the growth in urban culture and modern citizenship. As we will see, the experiences of a new spatiality (modelled in terms of the finite and the infinite), new appreciation of relations and reciprocity, and a new sense of community become fundamental to understanding Schleiermacher's early writing and later theological and philosophical development.

In the city, time is different: there are appointments to make and to keep, there are invitations to events, times at which shops and libraries close and open, performances begin and end, and concerts take place. The modern city is orientated towards the future; it is this which solicits the dreams of utopians (see Pinder 2005). It is also preoccupied with the intensity of the present; *carpe diem* in the watermark inscribed in the very walls and pavements of its banking, commercial, governmental, juridical, and entertainment districts. Neustadt was an expression of the French Enlightenment view of progress and the intellectual development of European civilization; whereas Mitte and the fortified walls of the older city remained locked into a defensive past. The new city had to plan for the future of its expansion. It had to think of civic amenities (and the buildings that housed and institutionalized them). It had to think of flows of traffic, pedestrians, water, sewage, and energy supplies (see Masur 1970 and Ribbe 2002). European tourism was becoming fashionable: cities like Berlin had to prepare itself to welcome future visitors able to spread the gospel of its magnificence. There is an urgency about Schleiermacher's writings between 1796 and 1802—the urgency of a man who has to make his mark and his own future; time had become intensified.

One scholar has emphasized what in the exchanges of letters between Friedrich, Dorothea, and her childhood friend, Henrietta Herz, all remarked upon: Schleiermacher 'was a connoisseur of the art of friendship' (Richardson 2000: 828). It was the city of Berlin that provided him with the intimate friendships from which his writing and its originality sprung. In fact, it was the very *avant-garde* sense that Berliners living in the wake of enlightened monarchs had that made possible new kinds of relationship and new freedoms in relationship. As many have noted, both Schlegel and Schleiermacher enjoyed very close relationships with women who, in the early days were not their wives. In fact, both Dorothea and Henrietta were married women. Although Schleiermacher had met Henrietta earlier, when he was a teacher at the Gedike Gymnasium, they belonged to two quite different classes. She was a Jew, married to a wealthy banker and with close associations with princes, the nobility, important officials, and writers like the Humboldt brothers and Ludwig Tieck, diplomats, financiers, musicians, and artists; he was a young unknown son of a Lutheran pastor albeit with a noble patron (the Count von Dohna) and was a royal civil servant. But no one can overlook the inner connections of this crowd. Count Alexander von Dohna was the son of a very important nobleman from an old and celebrated family. He was also an influential and upwardly mobile public servant—particularly so under Friedrich Wilhelm III. Schleiermacher had worked for Alexander's father. Alexander von Dohna knew the Herzs very well indeed, in fact, when Marcus Herz died in 1803, Dohna, who was infatuated with Henrietta, proposed to her. Dohna was an important patron for Schleiermacher. It is likely that Schleiermacher first met influential people in his career like the Humboldts at Henrietta's *salon*. Dohna was a close friend of the Humboldt brothers, whose father had been a gentleman of the bedroom under Friedrich Wilhelm II.

Only the city, and the important mediatorial role *salons* played not only in the cultural and intellectual life of the city, but also in mediating across traditional social barriers, made possible not only Schleiermacher's career advancement but his self-cultivation (*Bildung* through an aestheticization of one's experience). The *salon* that met at Henrietta's house—with her husband, the doctor and 'professor', Markus, she was the first to establish *salonière* culture in Berlin—became a focus for both *Kultur* and *Bildung*. She provided the drawing-room space that could cross strongly traditional barriers with respect to gender, class, religion, and ethnicity. In fact, even in cosmopolitan Berlin, Jewish people were still socially differentiated. 'The salon, as a temporary compromise between private aspirations and public realities, was an aesthetic form since it was a means of adapting the public realm to conform to the ideal sphere of personal privacy' (Davies 1991: 29). As Schleiermacher described it in his *Monologen*, using, note, a theological term, 'where there is such a society, there is my paradise' (Schleiermacher 1988: 32). It is important to remember that remark, since redemption, for Schleiermacher—as he developed his understanding of it in his much later *Glaubenslehre*—issues from 'reciprocal relationality'.[6]

III. The City's Impact Upon Schleiermacher's Thought

The city articulated and materialized three concerns: humanity in all its heterogeneity, the freedom to make one's way, and the condition for *Bildung* or what the French called *l'éducation sentimental*—an education in the cultured ways of the world. Before then commenting more particularly on how civic living impacts upon the ideas in his ground-breaking *On Religion: Speeches to Its Cultured Despisers*, let us note that Schleiermacher's contribution to the first volume of *Athenaeum* was a fragment entitled '*Idee zu einem Katechismus der Vernuft für edle Frauen*' in which he daringly announced his own creed: 'I believe in infinite humanity [*unendliche Menschheit*], whoever they are, prior to their adopting the garments [*die Hülle*] of masculinity or femininity . . . I believe in the power of the will and education to bring me close again to the infinite and to release me from the chains of cultural ignorance [*Bildung, mich dem Unendlichen wieder zu nähern, mich aus den Fesseln der Mißbildung zu erlösen*]' (Schleiermacher 1984: 153–4). We can observe that the verb *erlösen* does mean 'to release', but it is also a theologically inflected word for 'to deliver' as used in the German rendition of the Lord's Prayer: 'deliver us from evil'. The language of the infinite bears all the traces of early Romanticism, but not when it is associated with the object 'humanity'; it is the sheer wealth of the human condition Schleiermacher is bearing witness to. Furthermore, this is not a dissolving of the finite into the infinite (as Friedrich Schlegel or Novalis described it) but a 'bring[ing] close to it'. I emphasize this because time and again Schleiermacher returns us to the material and the social; and if there is a suggestion of Romanticism's flirtation with androgeny, in other early work he is much more clear that one of the most important forms of reciprocal relationality was between man and woman. He takes up the question of sexual difference in his next piece of published work, which was explicitly on what he termed 'free sociality' [*freie Geselligkeit*], published in 1798: *Versuch einer Theorie des geselligen Bretragens* (Schleiermacher 1984: 163–84).

The essay is a sociological and anthropological reflection upon salon life or the functioning of free associations more generally, which because they are constituted between the private and public domains (in what will increasingly become established

---

[6] Schleiermacher 1989: 21 (where it describes relations between the individual and God that determine the spirituality and morality of all) and 727 (where it describes Trinitarian relations). For a more detailed analysis of this reciprocity, see Shults 1998: 177–96.

as civil society), are, Schleiermacher believes, best organized around women. In a manner that, while giving prominence to women articulates a male Romantic take which only reinforces the conventional view of women at the time, Schleiermacher views women as ideal facilitators of free sociality because, for them their public role is also their private role. '[P]recisely because women have no class in common with me besides being cultured persons, it is they who would become the founders of a better society' (Schleiermacher 1984: 178; 1995: 33).[7] The essay is then a reflection upon the role of Henrietta Hertz (and those other prominent, mainly Jewish, women who organized Berlin salon life) in the fashioning of a free society. And Schleiermacher here is already using a distinction that will be made far more famous by the German sociologist Ferdinand Tönnies in his 1887 publication: the distinction between *Gesellschaft* and *Gemeinschaft* (see Tönnies: 1957 (trans.); and Schleiermacher 1984: 169 footnote). Interestingly, he views *Gemeinschaft* as the equivalent of the Greek term *koinoniai*; *Gesellschaft* (which he associates with free sociality) is the equivalent of the Greek term *sunousiai*. He employs a distinctly theological vocabulary, but the Church for Schleiermacher is, like the state, an institution for public life (as a chaplain, he was in fact a civil servant). This is how, ecclesiologically, he understands the *koinonia* of salon life, his avowed paradise, as a *sunousiai*. This a coined term, not found either in ancient or New Testament Greek—*sun* as the prefix 'in the company of', 'together' and *ousia* as the highly metaphysical noun meaning 'being' or 'essence'. It is a coining reminiscent of several Pauline inventions to describe our condition in Christ, where he also prefixes '*sun*' to more familiar verbs and nouns to articulate the nature of our participation in Christ. Paul becomes particularly inventive with the prefix *sun* when describing the nature of the Church as the body of Christ. Witness *synekerasen* 'has composed together with' in 1 Cor. 12 and the deutro-Pauline terms *synēgeiren* (raised together with) and *synekathisen* (sit together with) in Ephesians 2:6. The Pauline association would have come easily to Schleiermacher with his profound knowledge of both Greek and the scriptures.

The essay sets out three 'laws' governing and defining 'free sociality'. These are not rules of conduct, for such would compromise any notion of 'free'. In an early adoption of a Kantian transcendental argument (which Schleiermacher will use to great effect in the Introduction to the second edition of his *Glaubenslehre*), the 'laws' are more the conditions for the possibility of free society. These are: first, everything is to be governed by reciprocal action (a formal law, in his terminology); second, all are 'to be stimulated to a free play of thoughts through the communication of what is [distinctively] mine' (Schleiermacher 1984: 170; 1995: 25) (a material law); and third, 'social activity should always remain with the boundaries within which a particular society can exist as a whole' (Schleiermacher 1984: 171; 1995: 25–6), and so each person must be governed by an overall propriety towards the others in the group

---

[7] See here also the role Ernestine plays as the *Hausfrau* preparing for the Christmas festivities in Schleiermacher's 1804 essay *Die Weihnachtsfeier*. This essay is one of the earliest explorations I know of a theology of sexual difference.

(a quantitative law). This concern for the other person is echoed throughout the writings of these early years: in a sketch entitled 'Versuch über die Schamhaftigkeit' he calls for respect for the other person (Schleiermacher 1988: 168–78). The other person always qualifies my understanding and the practice of my own freedom.[8] The primary axiom behind these three laws is that human beings are social animals; that free sociality is 'an unavoidable natural tendency' (Schleiermacher 1984: 168; 1995: 23); being human is being in relation and becoming fully human is participating in such relations. What is uppermost in the operations of these laws (besides the evident bourgeois intellectual elitism of it all) is the self-fashioning that issues from the social phenomenon of cultural exchange. And so both the self and the society become works of art in the manifestation of the operation of Bildung. Social life is construed as a work of art (Schleiermacher 1984: 167) wrought by the ongoing dialectics of the individual and society, the private and the public, receptivity and activity, feeling and doing, expressing and knowing, the personal style [Manier] and the communal tone [Ton]. It is a work of art because it has no other object or telos than itself; it transcends then Enlightenment instrumental reasoning. One becomes humanized by participation in such dialectics; and to be human is to be cultured. Life is an ongoing education; Bildung is a means both of self-transcendence and self-fulfilment. As Schleiermacher wrote to his sister Charlotte on 23rd March 1799, receiving such an education within such a forum is a moral responsibility: 'Jeder Mensch muß schlechterdings in einem Zustande moralischer Geselligkeit stehen' (Schleiermacher 1992: 49).

Now, although there are intimations of a theology here—in terms of a theological anthropology, a soteriology ('emancipation through self-cultivation' (Davies 1991: 30) in and through other people) and an ecclesiology—Schleiermacher does not develop them here. All the work that follows, from On Religion: Speeches to Its Cultured Despisers onwards, is a theological development, and modification, of what is stated here in what we might term a transcendental sociology or even an early piece of phenomenology (a phenomenology of believing). The point I wish to make is how the newly emerging city of Berlin exists like a palimpsest beneath the structure of this discourse. The city as a work of architectural art and the social body that occupies, maps, walks, and orchestrates this urban planning in the creation of its social and cultural life is the very watermark within the paper on which this reflection is written. The city as architecturally designed buildings and urban layout is experienced, and this experience is translated in various ways into the lives of the city's inhabitants. To use Schleiermacher's categories: it affects their feelings—where feelings [Gefühl] are not simply corporeal sensations and emotional affects, but also intuitions of right order or, as he puts it, 'the immediate presence of whole undivided being' (Schleiermacher 1989: 7).[9] These feelings, always qualified by the word 'intuition', which I want to gather collectively into what, existentially, after Heidegger we can call 'the feeling of dwelling',

---

[8] See also Monologen; Soloquies 79.

[9] Schleiermacher is here approving of a definition of feeling found in Steffen's Falsche Theologie, but it is a definition that accords with his own extended analysis on pp. 6–8.

are articulated (verbally, gesturally, in any number of *Gestalten*) and so become doings—and doings facilitate understanding or knowledge of the built environment and the social and cultural praxes it fosters. This is not, *pace* Hegel a subjectivist account of religion,[10] and it is not *pace* Tillich, an emotivist account of religion (Tillich 1970: 95–102). As Schleiermacher recognized, this internalization of the aesthetics of the city provoke an aestheticization of experience more generally. Following the lead of German philosopher Alexander Baumgarten who related aesthetics to the Greek *aistēsis*—'sensation'[11]—minds and bodies are thus inseparable. Thus the city as a work of art, and the moral and spiritual life of its citizens as a work of art, each impacts upon, and makes possible, the other. This dialectical activity is made possible by an anthropological a priori that Schleiermacher states quite explicitly in his *Brouillon zu Ethik*: '*alle Menschen sind Künstler*' (Schleiermacher 1998: 108).

I am aware that I have said very little so far about theology as such. Two premises are important for the steps that follow, and the interpretation of Schleiermacher's theology that they afford. First, the 'feeling of dwelling', which is the basis for our experience, means that feelings are not private, inner reflexes; they are social both in terms of source and orientation. Religion then is not a private matter either; it is not only a communal activity it issues from and maintains that community. Two words distinctively mark Schleiermacher's approach to the 1799 *On Religion*: 'experience [*Erlebnis*]' and immediate 'feeling [*Gefühl*]'. Both are words leading directly to his understanding of religion as the 'the sensibility and taste for the infinite [*Sinn und Geschmack fürs Unendliche*]' (Schleiermacher 1996: 139).[12] Second, there is no direct knowledge of God. As Schleiermacher puts it in his *Glaubenslehre*: 'we have no formula for the being of God in Himself as distinct from the being of God in the world' (Schleiermacher 1989: 748) and so 'we must declare the description of human states of mind to be the fundamental form, while propositions of the second and third forms [statements about God or the world as they appear in self-consciousness] are permissible only in so far as they can be developed out of the propositions of the first form, for only on this condition can they be authenticated as expressions of religious emotions' (Schleiermacher 1989: 125–6). Now I am not agreeing or disagreeing with either of these two premises, or the implications of Schleiermacher's theological method for various aspects of his dogmatics. What I am pointing to is the profound relationship between his experience as a Berliner and his theology. What becomes clear is the move

---

[10] For excellent analyses of the debate here between Hegel and Schleiermacher, see Nowak 1986: 288–95, and his more recent and highly readable biography 2001: 409; see also Heidegger 1975b: 19. For the role played by Hegel's student, Hermann Hinrichs, in the debate, see von der Luft 1987. The introductions to the texts are exemplary, and Luft translates (for the first time into English) important sections of the first edition of 1821/22 *Der christliche Glaube*.

[11] His two volumes of *Aesthetika* appeared between 1750 and 1759. See Schleiermacher 1989: 7.

[12] I think Crouter is spot on to translate *Sinn* as 'sensibility' rather than 'meaning' or 'sense'. He picks up Schleiermacher's emphasis in 'feeling' and 'experience' on the embodied nature of religion so unusually described as 'taste'. There is a sensuousness in Schleiermacher, which acknowledges the body's involvement in all experience.

Schleiermacher makes in his early life in Berlin for defining a *'freie Geselligkeit'* and religion with respect to experiencing such a sociality. And the move he makes towards understanding the basis of dogmatics as the feeling of absolute dependence, the consciousness of such a feeling and 'reciprocal relationality' in the *Glaubenslehre*, written following Schleiermarcher's return to Berlin in 1807, is that religion and morality are never epiphenomena of feeling and experience. That is, they are not secondary. What is both the nature of religion as a taste for the infinite and morality as a social reciprocity in pursuit of the good on the basis of understanding that all is gift in that all is absolutely dependent, are both given in experience and feeling itself. This is important to grasp for understanding Schleiermacher, and especially for understanding why he is not a liberal. For the liberal theologian, we can take Rudolph Otto as an example, the religious feeling or intuition is primary and its subsequent expression in a cultural-linguistic system secondary. Hence, then, there is no real problem with religious pluralism because at base all religions are expressions of the same fundamental experience. This is absolutely not so for Schleiermacher. Certainly, cognition and consciousness, which is only possible on the condition of the reception of what is experienced and felt, give expression to what is given *in* the experience and feeling. But the content of that feeling and intuition is its unfolding; there is no arbitrary division between the two. The feeling or intuition is the soul or form which governs the body or matter that is shaped. We move from the abstract to the more concrete accounts of experience and feeling in and through language inseparable from cognition; but the one is the direct outworking of the other. That that outworking is necessarily determined also by historical, social, and cultural conditions is accepted; but the 'also' is fundamental here—for there is that in the feeling or intuition which is universal.[13] It is an experience and feeling, as I am relating them here, to living in urban Berlin at the turn of the nineteenth century, when cities were becoming the grandiloquent stage sets for modern life as we know it. That there is no major difference between the early Schleiermacher of the *freie Geselligkeit* and the later Schleiermacher of 'reciprocal relationality' can be recognized from a statement that demonstrates the dependency of his theology upon the newly emerging urban sociality. In *On Religion* he writes: 'If there is religion at all, it must necessarily be social: this is intrinsic not only to human nature but also quite particularly to the nature of religion.... In the perpetual reciprocity in which a person stands with the rest of his species, he should express and communicate all that is in him' (Schleiermacher: 1996: 148).

As I said above, there are two sides to the Brandenburg gate. On the one hand, it is the ceremonial entrance to Berlin as the new Athens and dedicated to peace; an Athens which prided itself on its civic freedoms. On the other, it is crowned by the goddess of

---

[13] It is for this reason that Schleiermacher differs from certain early Romantics like Friedrich Schlegel: because for Schlegel the ethical (and the religious) is the aesthetic, whereas, for Schleiermacher the aesthetic is the creative activity whereby the unfolding of what is intrinsically there in the given of experience and feeling (which is moral and religious) becomes conscious in cognition (the language of thought).

victory and Prussian dominance. Only diplomats of royalty and royalty itself could use the central arch; all other ranks had to use the side arches. The city space which it opens on to, and exits from, is an urban space in which the dialectic between lordship and bondage, already articulated by Hegel in his early essay in 1798–9 'The Spirit of Christianity'—years before its famous articulation in the *Phenomenology of Spirit*. It was an urban space in which the drama of self-consciousness, subjectivity, and mutual recognition, was played out; with the potential for community and reciprocal relations. Schleiermacher as a citizen of no mean city, embodied the tension at its very entry. He was the enjoyer of civic freedoms in his attendance at salons and learned societies like the Wednesday club; he was also a civil servant paid by the crown as Chaplain of Charité. In a letter written in 1798 Schleiermacher acknowledged the tension: 'if it were to become too well known that I live so entirely among these people [his salon intimates], an unfavourable opinion would inevitably be produced by many' (Blackwell 1981: 106). The two sides of the tension became evident when his career mentor and old family friend, the Cathedral Preacher, Friedrich Samuel Gottfried Sack, worried about Schleiermacher's socializing arranged for him to spend sometime away from the city at Potsdam, where he had to preach before Friedrich Wilhelm III. The two sides collided on Schleiermacher's return with the publication, even though anonymous, of his *On Religion: Speeches to Its Cultured Despisers*. Berlin gossip easily uncovered his incognito authorship. The same Friedrich Samuel Gottfried Sack was also the Censor for the Prussian government. He sent a letter written five months earlier to Schleiermacher at the opening of 1801, castigating his friends and their 'stream of sophistry' (Blackwell 1981: 115). 'I know also that in the circle in which you live, men like me are held to be feeble-minded', he wrote. In his reply Schleiermacher acknowledged that the friends to which reference was made 'would be uncommonly glad to see me no longer a preacher' (Blackwell 1981: 119), but nevertheless he expressed the need to avoid preachers being 'outlawed in the realm of society' (Blackwell 1981: 117). But outlawed he was. In 1802, Sack arranged for Schleiermacher's departure to an obscure town on the Baltic Sea, as court chaplain. As Wilhelm Dilthey comments, in his monumental biography of Schleiermacher, this was 'a kind of exile' (Dilthey 1970: 541). And in this way Schleiermacher left Berlin . . . at least for a time.

IV. Conclusion

What I have striven to present in this chapter is how the new urban landscape provided not just a staging for the development of Schleiermacher's theology and philosophical interests in hermeneutics and dialectics; but how the city is woven into the very thought processes of Schleiermacher's work. He 'possesses' it and it 'possesses' him. In the foundational philosophical and theological process he outlines—of feeling as it issues into knowing and doing, nurtured by and fostering reciprocal relations, and informing the individual and collective notions of freedom, and aesthetic and spiritual development—the modern city's articulation of space, light, elegant proportion, social heterogeneity, and civic participation have impacted somatically, emotionally, and intellectually. The city's embodied 'psychogeography' (Gilles Ivan) is profoundly associated with his productivity. It is in this way that we can begin to think the symbiotic relationship between urban landscape and urban culture in the modern period; for, undoubtedly, this same analysis could be done for any of the theologians and philosophers I named in the Introduction. As Lewis Mumford pointed out, following a number of other scholars of cities, their planning and their architecture—cities ancient and modern: cities have always been and will always be the stuff of legends and myths. They compete for such fame. As such they have always been and always will be haunted by the religious and the metaphysical. In the twentieth and twenty-first centuries every skyscraper and every attempt to construct the tallest building in the world, provides a meditation on transcendence, utopian desires, and immortal longings. In the summer of 1951, and in response to the housing crisis in Germany that followed the end of the Second World War, Heidegger excavated some of the connections I have been examining here: 'Building and thinking are, each in its own way, inescapable for dwelling. The two, however, are also insufficient for dwelling so long as each busies itself with its own affairs in separation instead of listening to one another. They are able to listen if both— building and thinking—belong to dwelling' (Heidegger 1975a: 160–1).[14] What we think and imagine will lead to us to construct; and what we construct will inform what we think and imagine. This is foundational because we *belong* here.

References

Benjamin, Walter (2006). *The Writer on Modern Life: Essays on Charles Baudelaire.* (Cambridge, MA: Harvard University Press).

——(2008). *Berlin Childhood Around 1900: Hope in the Past.* (Cambridge, MA: Harvard University Press).

Blackwell, Albert L. (1981). 'The Antagonistic Correspondence of 1801 between Chaplain Sack and His Protégé Schleiermacher', *Harvard Theological Review* 74, 106.

——(1982). *Schleiermacher's Early Philosophy of Life: Determinism, Freedom, and Phantasy.* (Chico, CA: Scholars).

Bloomer, Kent C. and Charles W. Moore (1977). *Body, Memory, and Architecture.* (New Haven: Yale University Press).

Castoriadis, Cornelius (1987). *The Imaginary Institution of Society*, trans. Kathleen Blamey (Cambridge: Polity Press).

Crouter, Richard (ed.) (1996). 'Introduction', in Schleiermacher, Friedrich D. E. *On Religion: Speeches to its Cultured Despisers.* (Cambridge: Cambridge University Press), pp. xi–xl.

Davies, Martin (1991). 'Sociability in Practice and Theory: Henriette Herz and Friedrich Schleiermacher', *New Athenaeum/Neues Athenaeum* 2, 18–59.

---

[14] The lecture was given in August at the second Darmstadt Colloquium devoted to 'Man and Space'. It was subsequently published in Heidegger's collection of essays, *Vorträge und Aufsätze* (Pfullingen: Neske, 1954).

Dennis, Richard (2008). *Cities in Modernity: Representations and Productions of Metropolitan Space: 1840–1930.* (Cambridge: Cambridge University Press).

Dilthey, Wilhelm (1970). *Leben Schleiermachers* I/1, ed. Martin Redeker (Göttingen: Vandenhoeck & Ruprecht).

Hegel, Georg Wilhelm Friedrich (1948). *The Spirit of Christianity and Its Fate*, in Richard Kroner (ed.), *Friedrich Hegel on Christianity: Early Theological Writings*, trans. T. M. Knox (New York: Harper & Row), 182–301.

——(1967). *System der Sittlichkeit*, ed. George Lasson (Hamburg: Meiner).

Heidegger, Martin (1975a). 'Building Dwelling Thinking', *Poetry, Language, Thought*, trans. Albert Hofstadter (New York: Harper and Row).

——(1975b). '. . . Poetically Man Dwells . . .', *Poetry, Language, Thought*, trans. Albert Hofstadter (New York: Harper and Row).

Hertz, Deborah (2005). *Jewish High Society in Old Regime Berlin.* (New York: Syracuse University Press).

Ivan, Gilles (1989). 'Definitions', *Situationist International Anthology* (1958) ed. and trans. Ken Knabb (Berkeley, CA: Bureau of Public Secrets).

——(2009). 'Critique of Functionalism and Modernization', in Tom McDonough (ed.), *The Situationists and the City* (London: Verso).

Lees, Andrew and Lynn Hollen Lees (2007). *Cities and the Making of Modern Europe, 1750–1914.* (Cambridge: Cambridge University Press).

Luft, Eric von der (1987). *Hegel, Hinrichs, and Schleiermacher on Feeling and Reason in Religion: The Texts of Their 1821–22 Debate.* (Lewiston, NY: Edwin Mellen Press).

Massumi, Brian (2002). *Parable for the Virtual: Movement, Affect, Sensation.* (Durham, NC: Duke University Press).

Masur, Gerhard (1970). *Imperial Berlin.* (New York: Basic Books).

Merleau-Ponty, Maurice (1999). *The Phenomenology of Perception*, trans. C. Smith (London: Routledge).

Mumford, Lewis (1966). *The City in History.* (Harmondsworth: Penguin Books).

Nowak, Kurt (1986). *Schleiermacher und die Frühromantik: Eine literaturgeschichtliche Studie zum romantischen Religionsverständnis und Menschenbild am Ende des 18. Jahrhunderts in Deutschland.* (Göttingen: Vandenhoeck & Ruprecht).

——(2001). *Schleiermacher: Leben, Werk und Wirkung.* (Göttingen: Vandenhoeck & Ruprecht).

Papayanis, Nicholas (2004). *Planning Before Haussmann: Ideas and Proposals for a New City.* (Baltimore, MD: Johns Hopkins University Press).

Pinder, David (2005). *Visions of the City: Utopianism, Power and Politics in Twentieth-Century Urbanism.* (Edinburgh: Edinburgh University Press).

Ribbe, Wolfgang (ed.) (2002). *Geschichte Berlins.* (Berlin: Berliner Wissenschafts-Verlag).

Richardson, Ruth Drucilla (2000). 'The Berlin Circle of Contributors to "Athenaeum": Friedrich Schlegel, Dorothea Mendelssohn Viet, and Friedrich Schleiermacher', in Ulrich Barth Claus-Dieter Osthoevener (eds), *200 Jahre 'Reden über die Religion,'* (Berlin: de Gruyter), 816–58.

Sadler, Simon (1998). *The Situationist City.* (Cambridge, MA: MIT Press).

Schleiermacher, Friedrich D. E. (1926). *Schleiermacher's Soliloquies: An English Translation of the Monologen*, trans. Horace Leland Friess (Westport, NY: Hyperion).

——(1970). *Die Weihnachtsfeier: Ein Grespräch*, in *Kleine Schriften und Predigten 1800–1829* I, ed. Hayo Gerdes and Emanuel Hirsch (Berlin: de Gruyter), 226–7.

Schleiermacher, Friedrich D. E. (1983). *Über die Freiheit*, in *Kritsche Gesamtausgabe, Band I.1: Jugendschriften 1787–1796*, ed. Günter Meckenstock (Berlin: de Gruyter), 217–356.

——(1984). *Idee zu einem Katechismus der Vernuft für edle Frauen*, in *Kritsche Gesamtausgabe, Band I.2: Schriften aus der Berliner Zeit 1796–1799*, ed. Günter Meckenstock (Berlin: de Gruyter).

——(1984). *Versuch einer Theorie des geselligen Bretragens*, in *Kritsche Gesamtausgabe, Band I.2: Schriften aus der Berliner Zeit 1796–1799*, ed. Günter Meckenstock (Berlin: de Gruyter); trans. Jeffrey Hoover, 'Toward a Theory of Sociable Conduct', *New Athenaeum/ Neues Athenaeum* 6 (1995), 20–39).

——(1988). *Monologen*, in *Kritsche Gesamtausgabe, Band I.3: Schriften aus der Berliner Zeit 1800–1802*, ed. Günter Meckenstock (Berlin: de Gruyter), 6–61.

——(1988). 'Versuch über die Schamhaftigkeit', in *Vertraute Briefe über Friedrich Schlegels Lucinde*, in *Kritsche Gesamtausgabe, Band I.3: Schriften aus der Berliner Zeit 1800–1802*, ed. Günter Meckenstock (Berlin: de Gruyter), 139–216 at 168–78.

——(1989). *The Christian Faith*, trans. H. R. Mackintosh and J. S. Stewart (Edinburgh: T.& T. Clark).

——(1992). *Briefe an die Schwester* [Charlotte] 23.3.1799, in *Kritsche Gesamtausgabe, Band V.3: Briefwechsel 1799–1800*, ed. Andreas Arndt and Wolfgang Virmond (Berlin: de Gruyter).

——(1996). *On Religion: Speeches to Its Cultured Despisers*, 2nd edn. (Cambridge: Cambridge University Press).

——(1998). *Brouillon zur Ethik (1805/06)*, ed. Hans-Joachim Birkner (Hamburg: Meiner Felix).

Sheard, Sally and Power, Helen (eds) (2000). *Body and City: Histories of Urban Public Health*. (Farnham: Ashgate).

Shults, F. LeRon (1998). 'Schleiermacher's "Reciprocal Relationality": The Underlying Regulative Principle of His Theological Method', in Ruth Drucilla Richardson (ed.), *Schleiermacher on the Workings of the Knowing Mind* (Lewiston, NY: Edwin Mellen), 177–96.

Springer, Robert (1878). *Berlin: Die deutsche Kaiserstadt*. (Damstadt).

Sutcliffe, Anthony (1981). *Towards the Planned City: Germany, Britain, the United States, and France*. (Oxford: Oxford University Press).

Taylor, Charles (2003). *Modern Social Imaginaries*. (Durham, NC: Duke University Press).

Tillich, Paul (1970). *Perspectives on 19th and 20th Century Protestant Theology*. (London: SCM Press).

Tönnies, Ferdinand (1887). *Gemeinschaft und Gesellschaft: Abhandlung des Communismus und des Socialismus als empirischer Culturformen*. (Leipzig: Fues).

Ward, Graham (2005). *Cultural Transformation and Religious Practice*. (Cambridge: Cambridge University Press).

SUGGESTED READING

Benjamin (2008).
Bloomer and Moore (1977).
Dennis (2008).
Heidegger (1975a).
—— (1975b).
Lees and Lees (2007).

Mumford (1966).
Papayanis (2004).
Pile, Steven (1996). *The Body and the City: Psychoanalysis, Space and Subjectivity.* (London: Routledge).
Pinder (2005).
Sheard and Power (2000).
Sutcliffe (1981).
Taylor (2003).
Ward, Graham (2000). *Cities of God.* (London: Routledge).

CHAPTER 4

··

THE OTHER

··

PAMELA SUE ANDERSON

I. INTRODUCTION: THE OTHER

··

THE Other takes its followers on a momentous journey through modern European thought. Not long before the middle of the twentieth century, three thinkers—Jean-Paul Sartre, Simone de Beauvoir, and Emmanuel Lévinas—appear at a congested point of this journey through modern attempts to think the Other. From seventeenth-century Europe to our twenty-first-century world, a theological question persists. Is God to be replaced by the Other? An affirmative answer to this question should eventually lead to a rejection of the Other by those who have come under its subjection. Sartre, Lévinas, and Beauvoir each engage substantially and critically with the deepening of this Hegelian question of the o/Other.[1]

> Hegel's brilliant intuition is to make me depend on the Other in my being. 'I am,' he said, 'a being-for-itself which is for-itself only through another. Therefore, the Other penetrates me to the heart'. (Sartre 1981: 237)
>
> The other, absolutely other, is the Other [*l'autre, absolument autre, c'est Autrui*]. The Other is not a particular case, a species of alterity, but the original exception to the order. It is not because the Other is a novelty that it 'gives rise' [*donne lieu*] to a relationship of transcendence—it is because responsibility for the Other is transcendence that there can be something new under the sun.

---

[1] It is impossible to be completely consistent in use of the 'Other' (*l'Autre, autrui*) or 'other' (*autrui*), or, even of 'otherness' (*alterité*), in this chapter. European thinkers vary widely in their use of the o/Other with a upper case 'O' or a lower case 'o'. Often the same thinker will be inconsistent in which case is employed. Generally, I have endeavoured to follow the standard translations of the texts which are discussed. So, an upper case 'O' is given when I am discussing a text or thinker who is employing an upper case; and the same with the lower case. It should also be said that when the 'Other' starts with the upper case it is more likely, but not necessarily, the case that the thought refers to the traditional Christian or Jewish God.

> My responsibility for the other man . . . is the exceptional relationship in which the Same can be concerned by the Other without the Other being assimilated to the Same.   (Lévinas 1998: 13)

> . . . she is nothing other than what man decides; she is thus called 'the sex', meaning that the male sees her essentially as a sexed being; for him she is sex, so she is it in the absolute. She determines and differentiates herself in relation to man, and he does not in relation to her; she is the inessential in front of the essential. He is the Subject, he is the Absolute. She is the Other.   (Beauvoir 2009 [1949]: 5–6; cf. Lévinas 1987: 85 and 85 n. 69)

These statements reflect the increasingly role of the Other as (i) the one on whom '[I] depend', as (ii) 'the absolutely other', and as (iii) 'the inessential' for the retrospective narrative-journey to be unfolded here.

It is necessary to be made aware of the contested side to this narrative. Modern European thought has posed an ever-increasing threat to the underlying theological story of the Other. As a result, contemporary theology wrestles with an unresolved and, for an increasing number of thinkers, unresolvable end. Nevertheless, for an example of a self-assured and unequivocal voice concerning the nature of the Other, the twentieth-century Swiss theologian, Karl Barth, asserts that we have 'God's story' told by God himself (in the incarnation of Christ), by the Word of God (in the preaching of the Church), and by the relationality of God (in the three-in-one nature of the Christian God). Basically, for Barth, the being of God is in the act of relating. Barth uses the Trinitarian nature of the Christian God as the three-in-one for understanding that the being of the person rests in internal relations to God and to other human beings.

For the present chapter on the Other, the crucial distinctiveness of Barth's Christian conception of personal relations is that self-other relations are not (supposed to be) understood in the Hegelian sense of a foundation for self-and-other knowledge. Barth's conception of relationality is not a relating in which the other becomes mirror for the self. Instead God as the Wholly Other, in Barth's terms, 'comes to' the person, while the being of this person is in this privileged relation (Barth 1960: 55–324).

Can the Christian story of salvation, in recounting the restoration of a person's original relation to, and as created by, God continue to take precedence over the modern subject's ongoing journey of desire? The latter can be read as a personal and/or a philosophical journey of redemption. And yet, the subject of this journey will often be so close to despair that the Other never ceases to haunt the selfhood of the modern European thinker. Yet some theologians try to read this 'despair' in more positive terms: the Other ceaselessly calls the subject to responsibility and/or to love. The critical nature of this reoccurring question about the Other's relation to the subject of, on the one hand, contemporary theology and, on the other hand, modern European philosophy is ignored only at a great price.

There is a critical difference—depending upon one's conceptions of the extremes— evident in a gap between the Other in traditional Christian theology and the other in modern European philosophy. A critical question of difference should not be answered too quickly, as long as the story is worth telling and the journey is worth taking.

The heart of the theological story is captured by Paul Fiddes, when he brings Barth into conjunction with the Jewish philosopher Lévinas. In both cases, Fiddes stresses how the Other as God *comes to* mind. Each of these two European thinkers is 'called' to a 'fuller presence' of and by an Other. Fiddes's account of the presence of God in the world offers a glimpse of how God's self-revelation can become an 'event', or 'happening', taking place on 'the stage-setting of worldly objects' (Fiddes 2000). To step into this account of Barth and Lévinas, consider the following:

> '... with regard to the being of God, the word "event" or "act" is final' (Barth, *Church Dogmatics*, II/1, 1957: 263). The last word about God is that God happens. Rather than following Barth's language of God's becoming 'objective' to us through revelation, or our being granted access to the 'primary objectivity' of God's own self-knowledge (which retains Hegelian overtones), we need to reach more radically towards the language of participation in this divine Event at which Barth hints.
>
> ... Lévinas ... brings the welcome ethical emphasis that we encounter the transcendent in our infinite responsibility for the other person. He challenges the notion that the mind makes the world present through representing it accurately in thought and speech; when we attempt this, we simply make the 'the other' immanent within our own consciousness ... Rather, the otherness of other persons *enters* our world on its own account; above all the infinite (God) turns our world inside out by coming into our world and causing a rupture in our powers of representation. The 'in-finite' may be understood as that which comes 'into the finite', and it breaks in through the face of our neighbour, calling us to limitless responsibility for the other person. Thus God is not an object of the powers of correlation of our mind, but '*comes* to mind'.   (Fiddes 2000: 254–5; cf. Lévinas 1998: 62–7)

Theology and modern European thought come together (above), mutually challenging and modifying the extremes of earlier modern conceptions of objectivity and of subjectivity. The Other provides a definite focus and serves as a guide through the changing movements in modernity from early scientific objectivity to a self-consciousness which seeks to transcend any debilitating dichotomies between mind and world. Yet a closer, critical look at certain key points in modern European thought will raise serious issues about the Other.

II. A JOURNEY THROUGH KEY STAGES IN MODERN EUROPEAN THOUGHT

Arguably, nothing is more distinctive to modern European thought, especially in the twentieth century, than the question of the o/Other. Can I know the other (exists) as an independent self-consciousness? As found in the previous section, some theologians maintain that the revelation of the Christian God is the true and perfect, Wholly Other for man; this Other brings together the same and the other in an ideal union. Despite possible protestations from Barthians, such an answer to the question of the knowledge of the Other seems reminiscent of the Hegelian idealist who claims that the goal of the dialectic of the same and the other is an absolute self-consciousness. Or, in other words, the *telos* (of the human 'spirit') is absolute knowledge. A less extreme view is that twentieth-century European thinking about the Other can be read as both a form of resistance to and a series of footnotes on G. W. F. Hegel's endeavour to overcome the diremption of the self and the other in the absolute. Depending on how the Hegelian endeavour is read, key passages taken from Hegel's *Phenomenology of Spirit,* in particular, have both supported and undermined modern European theology.

The focus on the Other will draw out significant moments and salient features of the problem of the Other implicit within the history of modern European thought. First of all, the largely agreed starting point for the history of modern philosophy has been the seventeenth-century epistemological project of René Descartes. The Cartesian project pursues certain knowledge beginning with an 'indubitable', i.e. the undoubtable certainty, of thinking itself. Descartes's *cogito* becomes a pivot for both rationalist accounts of a Cartesian dualism of mind and body and empiricist appropriations of a first-person starting point—i.e. the subject 'I' of the 'I think'—for their epistemologies of perception. A logical method, a subject of thought, a clarity and distinctness of ideas prepared the way for modern philosophical discussions concerning the problem of the Other in European thought.

Second, according to the present historical sketch, the problem reaches a turning point in 1807 with the narrative of the dialectic of the other in Hegel's *Phenomenology of Spirit.* As a historical figure Hegel comes to represent both extremes of the triumphant fulfilment of a great desire (for an ideal union of self and other) and of the tragic loss of the concrete other (as it is encompassed by the absolute). Hegel as the historical representative of absolute idealism fed German Romanticism with a Romantic appropriation of a grand narrative of love as mutual recognition between self and other. This Hegelian narrative would be modified and inverted in Germany already within the course of the nineteenth century, especially but not only by the so-called 'young Hegelians', including Ludwig Feuerbach, Bruno Bauer, and Karl Marx. Much more could be said about the early Marx, Hegel's writings, and Marxist critiques of speculative thought, including critiques of Christianity.[2]

Third, this sketch focuses on those decisive years in the first half of the twentieth century, when an impressive range of thoughtful, but critical reflections on the Hegelian struggle between conflicting opposites manifests how deeply embedded the problem of the Other had become in Europe. Most notable is the manner in which the dialectic of the same and the other in Hegel's *Phenomenology of Spirit* emerges in various readings of the human struggle, especially the struggle between

[2] For a fine discussion of the young Marx's own account of Hegel's achievements and failings, which does not underestimate the critical thrust of Marx's assessment of Hegel's philosophical system, see Leopold 2007: 17–99.

the master and the slave.[3] The fundamentally *human* readings of the dialectic of subject and its other becomes the defining thread running through highly distinctive, late modern European forms of twentieth-century existentialism, phenomenology, hermeneutics, Marxism, feminism, psycholinguistics, and, most recently, of speculative realism. According to these readings, the problem of the Other exhibits clear debts to the history of interpretations both of Descartes and the Cartesians, and of Hegel and the Hegelians. An additional debt is to another philosophical figure. The ancient Greek philosopher, Plato, is recalled for his original and enduring contribution to western metaphysics. Modern European philosophy adds Plato to its list of philosophers offering an ontology of sameness and otherness. Yet an extremely serious issue will be raised over the persistence in modernity of the Platonic metaphysical categories of the same and of the other.

III. The 'French Hegel': A Divided Subject and the Unhappy Consciousness

The Cartesian legacy is eventually turned on its head in the twentieth century by a series of Parisian academics, philosophers, and critical theorists, who would carve out the 'French Hegel' and shape several generations of European thought. The momentum for this reversal of the Cartesian subject's distance from the Other begins in new readings of Hegel's narrative in the *Phenomenology of Spirit*. This narrative is creatively interpreted and appropriated from different perspectives on, and various points in, the dialectic by Jean Wahl and Jean Hyppolite at the Sorbonne, but also, by Alexandre Kojève and his followers (see Wahl 1951; Hyppolite 1974; Descombes 1980; Butler 1987; Baugh 2003; Gutting 2011). The emergence of the French Hegel meant that European thinkers were no longer content to relegate the Other to Descartes's God, to the infinite other or to the unknowable other mind.

From 1927–67, Jean Wahl lectured on the history of philosophy at the Sorbonne. In the 1950s, Wahl also gathered together—informally—a group of intellectuals forming the *Parisien Collège de Philosophie*. This group included Gabriel Marcel, Maurice Merleau-Ponty, Emmanuel Lévinas, Paul Ricoeur, and Vladimir Jankélévitch. In subsequent years, Wahl would work closely with the next generation of French philosophers, including Michel Foucault, Jacques Derrida, and Gilles Deleuze. In writing and lecturing on Hegel's *Phenomenology of Spirit*, Wahl maintains a distinctive, interpretative focus on 'the unhappy consciousness', developing Hegel's dialectic at a point

---

[3] I follow the English translations of Kojève and of Sartre in referring to 'the master and slave' rather than 'the bondsmen and the lord'; these are translations of section A, paragraphs 178–96, in Hegel's *Phenomenology of Spirit* (Hegel 1977: 111–19).

which comes immediately after the struggle of master and slave (or, 'the lord and the bondsman,' Hegel 1977: 119–39). Hegel himself explains that

> [T]he duplication which formerly was divided between two individuals, the lord and the bondsman, is now lodged in one.... the *Unhappy Consciousness* is the consciousness of self as a dual-natured, merely contradictory being.
>
> This *unhappy, inwardly disrupted* consciousness, since its essentially contradictory nature is for it a *single* consciousness, must for ever have present in the one consciousness the other also; and thus it is driven out of each in turn in the very moment when it imagines it has successfully attained to a peaceful unity with the other.   (Hegel 1977: 126)

Although Lévinas was not around when Wahl began to lecture, the former became a close philosopher-friend of the latter in 1950s Paris, developing similar, critical perspectives on history's dialectic as 'totalizing'. Both Wahl and Lévinas reject any Hegelian vision of uniting the three separate spheres of world, finite mind, and divinity through the movement of Spirit. However, Lévinas's criticisms of the dualism of the world as totality and ethical infinity seem to challenge Wahl's reinterpretation of Hegel's unhappy consciousness as largely an internal focus on self-consciousness and its own self-contradiction. While Wahl's creative reinterpretation of Hegel and of the individual's own self-image would have been attractive to the then emerging French existentialism, his account of the self's internal contradiction does not seem compatible with the external demand in Lévinas's philosophy of 'the face of the Other'. The originality in Lévinas's conception of the face of the other, or the face-to-face, is to propose that the face of the Other comes to mind, while drawing the self out of itself. In contrast, the identity of Wahl's conflicted self remains bound up with the internal activity of 'the self-same' subject.

The distinctiveness in Lévinas giving primacy to the face-to-face encounter with another person is in the Other's interruption of the subject as affectively and passively 'the same'. This decisive encounter with the face of the Other must precede and, if successful, would make redundant any Hegelian struggle for the recognition of one's own and of the other's desire (cf. Butler 1987: 5–15; Anderson 1998: 85–97, 119–21; Bergo 2011: 71). By singling out Lévinas's philosophy of the Other in its critical relation to Wahl's philosophy of the unhappy consciousness, it is possible to glimpse how radically different readings of the Other generate the lively debates of post-Hegelian philosophers. The French existentialist, the Heideggerian and the Marxist threads in the 'French Hegel' generate radical differences within the post-Hegelian debates in 1950s–1960s Paris.[4]

Wahl's contribution to the French Hegel debates engages with the dominant French neo-Kantian philosophy which had conceived the self from two points of view, i.e. the changing, empirical self and the unchanging, transcendental self. Already in the

---

[4] The roles of the other in Husserl and in Heidegger were influenced by Hegel who also influenced Sartre and Lévinas. For further background on these modern European thinkers and theology, see Joy 2011: 221–46.

interwar period Wahl's reconstruction of the conception of unhappy consciousness in his lectures on Hegel both attracted and alienated the neo-Kantian thinkers. A critical thread can be drawn from the Kantian two-aspect self to the Hegelian divided self. Although Hegel's own writing on the unhappy consciousness of the double-natured self is only a stage in the long, dialectical development of spirit, the unhappy consciousness is Hegel's version of (Kantian) self-division between the contingent, multiple, and changeable self of my experience and the essential, simple and unchanging self that I know I must be. The problem with Wahl—and possibly, with other French Kantian appropriations of Hegel's double natured self—is that unlike Hegel himself Wahl reads the unhappy consciousness as a constant condition at every stage of the dialectic, until the final synthesis in the absolute's self-knowledge. Nevertheless, this manner of creatively interpreting and appropriating the thinking of one's 'master' is one of the most distinctive ways in which modern European thought develops.

For whatever social, cultural, or political reasons, the European account(s) of the Other found in the French Hegel will reflect the crucial significance of the self's lived-experiences for modern European philosophy. As a result, the turn in European thought towards the experiences of self-division is generalized; and this must be understood in order to grasp the larger gap between what the subject experiences itself as being and an apparently unattainable other that it aspires to be. Wahl's reading of Hegel lent support to a central claim in, for example, Sartre's *Being and Nothingness* that human consciousness is not what it is and is what it is not.

With this contradictory claim about self-consciousness, the Other also comes to signify differentiation, alterity, or otherness and lack of sameness (so, ambiguity). These significations gain in importance for philosophy and theology in modern Europe and, some would say, bring in the postmodern. This changing focus is especially noticeable after centuries of philosophical theology in which a Cartesian legacy of self-sameness dominated European thought. It is in this light that the Romantic preference for (Hegel's) absolute idealism, as well as the gradually emerging, critically attractive alternatives to the absolute in Hegel's phenomenology as a perfect reciprocal union of the same and of the other, can be understood. The development of thought from Descartes's isolated indubitable to Hegel's absolute virtually eclipses the Other.

Here the European feminist voices ring clear. Under the dominance of the sameness of the abstract subject, the other becomes invisible (Irigaray 1985). The movement of modern European thought is not complete, or near its *telos*, until it manages the resurrection of the absolute Other. Raising the Other to either a highly privileged position as the absolute and/or a highly ethical manner as 'the same' becomes a no-win choice.

IV. HEGELIANISM AND MODERN ATHEISM

Due to their strong influence on a large range of European intellectuals from 1930 to 1939, Kojève's now-famous seminars at *École Pratique des Hautes Études* (in Paris) on

Hegelian idealism dramatically changed the nature of the Other, especially its implications for theology. These seminars came at the right moment, before the Second World War, when the city was full of thinkers who intended to, *and who did*, change their world by profoundly motivating the next generation of dissenting intellectuals with radical ideas. Kojève's *Introduction to Hegel* became one of the most significant political (re)readings of the *Phenomenlogy of Spirit* for both theology and modern European thought.

In part, this is significant because of the radical nature of Kojève's Hegel fitting into the thought of the time. The long period of changing cultural mood and outlook between the 1930s and 1970s supported significant transitions in liberal politics and in Christian theology. One of the arguments of Kojève's Hegel attracted positive and negative excitement: 'all that Christian theology says is absolutely true, provided it is applied not to a transcendental and imaginary God, but to Man himself, living in the world' (Kojève 1969: 571).

The reception of Kojève's seminars was groundbreaking and enduring, influencing an unusual range of thinkers, from George Bataille and Maurice Merleau-Ponty to Jacques Lacan whose teachings in turn influenced later thinkers, including Lévinas, Deleuze, Irigaray, and Kristeva. In retrospect, it is clear that the latter would read some or all of the highly distinctive writings of the original attendees who remained under the influence of Kojève's Hegel. Directly and indirectly, Kojève led more than a generation of phenomenologists, Marxists, post-structuralists, and psycholinguists to embrace an atheistic humanism. This became Europe's modern anthropology. A highly pervasive European brand of humanism would assert 'God', and then, replace it with 'Man'. Yet this atheistic form of anthropology claims a divine status for man. Essentially, Europe's modern atheistic humanism was an inverted theology.

Both Wahl and Kojève read Hegel strictly in terms of a *human* struggle. Kojève's Hegel brought the so-called French Hegel closer to the thinking of Karl Marx. This enabled a generation of existentialists—not just philosophers, but playwrights, novelists, journalists, and some religious phenomenologists—to try to bridge the gap between the German philosophies of Marx and of Heidegger on one side, and the French conception of a concrete humanism on the other side.

From 1949, Wahl's Hegel lectures provided a critical starting point—i.e. the unhappy unconsciousness—for another voice in Paris, Jean Hyppolite, who began to lecture on the history of philosophy at the Sorbonne. From 1954, Hyppolite was also the director of the *École Normale Superieure*, and remained professor at the Sorbonne and director at *ENS* until 1963. In his lectures on Hegel, Hyppolite carefully acknowledges the general validity of Wahl's interpretation, while pointing out that Hegel himself restricts the unhappy consciousness to a result of the development of self-consciousness; and this appears at a stage which makes explicit the contradiction of (the old rationalist) scepticism by bringing the conflict between finite and infinite mind into the individual's own self-image. It could be said that Hyppolite makes clear that the existentialist's reading of Hegel—for example, Sartre's reading—was not Hegel's own account but that read through Wahl's interpretation of the self and its other.

The effect of these Parisian rereadings of Hegel is to generate an almost exclusive focus on the problem of the Other. Thus, this French Hegelian shift from Cartesianism enabled more concrete philosophizing about 'man' and 'his' other in everyday life. Yet it is a philosophical issue whether French Hegelianism actually achieved this concreteness; the abstract conception of the Other continued to feed German idealism and theology. In his 1947 introduction to *La Liberté cartésienne*, Sartre aims to reclaim for 'man' what Descartes had taken away. In Sartre's words,

> It was to take two centuries of crisis —a crisis in Faith and in Science — for man to recover the creative freedom that Descartes had placed in God, and for this truth, the essential basis of humanism, to be glimpsed: man is the being whose appearance brings the world into existence. (Sartre 1947: 334)[5]

European theologians would have equally endured this twofold crisis. A rising tide of atheistic humanism in theory and in practice would be no less a threat for modern theology. Modern Europe retained strands of absolute idealism, which often supported systematic forms of modern Christian theology, not only in the form of Barth's systematics, but in Hegelian theologians as different as Dietrich Bonhoeffer (1963: 31–3) and Wolfhart Pannenberg (1985: 238–42) or, even the Jewish theist Martin Buber (1937). Each modern European theologian finds ways both to maintain religious faith and to negotiate self-other relations in theological or theistic terms.

The French hermeneutic phenomenologist Paul Ricoeur warns twentieth-century philosophers and theologians in Europe about the danger of falling prey to the 'Hegelian temptation' by developing narratives which claim to achieve the unachievable, yet deeply desired end of the Hegelian dialectic in absolute knowledge (Ricoeur 1988: 193–202). Tempting human subjects can lead to overconfidence in knowledge of the transcendent God of Christianity. Can modern theology distinguish between claims to God's knowledge and claims to human knowledge? Systematic theology might unwittingly exemplify the ultimate failure of human subjects to resist the temptation in claiming to know the other than human: the Wholly Other. Could Barth demonstrate that his theology had avoided this temptation?

Barth assumes that God is by definition other than the world. According to his *Church Dogmatics*, the distance between God and humanity is bridged by the incarnation of God in man, i.e. by Christ. Barth also assumes that humanity is taken up into 'the fullness of God' through a trinitarian doctrine in which the second 'person' of the Trinity takes on what it means to be human. As already shown, Fiddes reads Barth as claiming that knowledge of human and divine 'comes to' subjects as an event. It is something that happens to Christians.

However, the atheistic humanisms, and more or less all modern forms of anthropology, would make the strong counter-claim that absolute knowledge of God is a projection of man's own desire for knowledge and for love as a form of mutual recognition (cf. Roth 1988: 116). According to Kojève's Hegel, Christianity is the most

---

[5] This translation of Sartre is found in Descombes 1980: 30.

important form of 'slave ideology'; but it is only a stage in the evolution of the consciousness of the slave. As a slave ideology, Christianity is something that can become true by struggle and work, which will make the world conform to the ideal. Equality with the other is the ideal and, in this case, it is the slave's equality with the master. The triumph of the slave is the triumph of equality over hierarchy, the idea of equality having been introduced into history through the projections of slave ideologies. The truth of Christianity is, for Hegel, contained in its ideas of equality in a universal church and of the incarnation. These are realized when the universal and the divine take the corporal form of a particular man.

Hegel himself employs the image of heaven descending to earth to portray the incarnation. For Kojève's Hegel, love comes to man as follows:

> For Hegel, Love is mutual recognition, in opposition to the Struggle for prestige (the duel). In Love, conflicts are not essential; differences, while being marked, do not become radical oppositions. Where there is no Love, conflicts grow, the situation is untenable, everything must be destroyed. But we cannot *begin* with Love; the Master/Slave conflict is essential and primitive. Love can only exist between equals. This situation of absolute equality can occur only in the perfect (universal and homogeneous) State to which history leads.   (Kojève 1969, as cited in Ross 1988: 115–16)

V. From German Philosophy to European Anthropology and Gendered Relations

In nineteenth-century Germany, the 'Young Hegelians' included Marx, and the thinker who guided Marx's critique of religion, Ludwig Feuerbach with his distinctive anthropological critique of Christian theology (Leopold 2007: 17 and 189f.). German political critiques of Christianity played a large part in modern forms of feminism and of Marxism on the European continent and abroad. Critical responses to Hegel and Hegelians have marked modern European thought with what we have come to recognize as a series of relentless separations of the human subject and the divine other, of man and his other, of the knowing self and the external world, of the self and the other-than-self, and generally, of the same and the other.

The European feminist critique of the anthropomorphic God not only draws on Hegel in the case of Simone de Beauvoir, but on Feuerbach's critique of the male subject's 'love affair' with his God in the case of Luce Irigaray. In the trenchant words of Feuerbach:

> The Christians ... substituted for the natural love and unity immanent in man a purely religious love and unity; they rejected the real life of the family, intimate bond of love which is naturally moral, as undivine, unheavenly, i.e., in truth, a worthless thing. But in compensation they had a Father and Son in God, who

embraced each other with heartfelt love, with that intense love which natural relationship alone inspires.   (Feuerbach 1957: 70 n. 2)

Feuerbach's critique of an anthropomorphic being focuses on the perfectly loving God: natural relationships inspire this intense love of Father and Son. In turn, feminist philosophers appropriate (correctly or not) Feuerbach's critique, seeing the Christian God as the desired ego-ideal for modern European men only. Irigaray not only appropriates Feuerbach's account of the Christian God as a projection of a man's ego-ideal, but she proposes that this is a sexually specific God for men. Moreover, Irigaray contends that women also need a God for their sexually specific ego-ideal, which would allow women to 'become divine' as the ideal of the perfectly loving Mother and Daughter.

In 'Divine Women', Irigaray seeks to articulate the conditions necessary for women to develop an autonomous self-conception; a God for women is one of these necessary conditions (Irigaray 1993: 55–72). Her conception of a 'God' for women is not only premissed on a critique of the Christian God as sexually specific, but on her earlier feminist subversion of Plato's 'great kinds' of the same and the other. Her sexual subversion divides self-relations into 'the same', 'the other of the same', and 'the other of the other'. The same is what man is to man; the other of the same is what woman is to man, and the other of the other describes female relations. However, without Beauvoir's original argument concerning 'the myth of the Other' in *The Second Sex*, neither the appropriation of Hegel's problem of the Other by Sartre nor the provocation of Irigaray's claims concerning Lévinas's failure with the Other (as originally noted by Beauvoir) would have been possible. It is following after Beauvoir that Irigaray is readily able to differentiate not only the Other from the self-identical subject, i.e. the same, but distinguish the same, the other of the same and the other of the other. This progression is confirmed in Irigaray's *Speculum of the Other Woman* where the imagery in Book 7 of Plato's *Republic* is cast into same and other relations (Irigaray 1985; see Plato 1988). Plato's realm of the forms is the same, i.e. the self-identical truth; the veiled reality of the physical world is the other of the same; and the shadow world of the cave is the other of the other. The contention is that these, in Irigaray's psycholinguist terms, 'imaginary' relations to the other have divided and differentiated European thought according to various readings of social and material differences of class, of heterosexual stereotypes, and of epistemically privileged and materially dominated standpoints.

Although the different patterns of separations from the Other construed by modern European thought generally have been personified by Hegel's *Phenomenology of Spirit* in the master-slave dialectic, or the unhappy consciousness, the great kinds of same and of other are traceable to the very foundations of western thought in ancient Greece. Hegel gives various indications that Plato's metaphysical categories of same and other inform his political thinking. In turn, these become the metaphysical categories for Irigaray's feminist critique of western metaphysics. Irigaray inverts Plato's hierarchy of the intelligible world of forms and the sensible world of appearances; an invisible substratum (e.g. Plato's cave) to metaphysics is made visible in Irigaray's unpicking of the metaphysical relations of self and other. In *Speculum* Irigaray reads Hegel first and moves dialectically back to Plato, appropriating the categories of same and other for her feminism of sexual difference. In her dialectical movement from Hegel back to Plato, she maintains a fairly fixed line of distinctive appropriations of the other and the self-same subject. Her movement distinguishes, separates, and differentiates the other from the self, in order to demonstrate that there is no otherness without difference (see Anderson 1999; cf. Irigaray 1985).

It becomes evident that the Other has not simply referred to the transcendent Christian God as the Wholly Other, but refers to the Other as the woman, the neighbour, the marginalized, the outsider, the stranger, and the foreigner (Kristeva 1991: 133–63, 170f., 182–92). Yet the most problematic referent for theology and modern European thought is 'the woman' who has been universalized as the absolutely other (Lévinas 1987: 85). To repeat Beauvoir's words, '[Woman] determines and differentiates herself in relation to man, and he does not in relation to her; she is the inessential in front of the essential. He is the Subject, he is the Absolute. She is the Other' (Beauvoir 2009 [1949]: 5–6).

VI. The Other and Love/Death in Twentieth-Century French Thought

The French existential phenomenologist sought to dissolve the Cartesian problem of the other by recognizing that the Other exists when the subject experiences herself as an object of that other's consciousness; at the same time, the consciousness of the other reveals a split in her self-awareness as both subject and object. In the existentialist accounts of Beauvoir and of Sartre, an unresolvable split appears between being-for-self (*pour soi*) and being-in-self (*en soi*). This split might recall Wahl's account of the unhappy consciousness, but the unresolvable problem of the Other in existential phenomenology is determined by the external relation in which the Other becomes either a threat (of death) to, or as in Lévinas's case a responsibility of, the subject. In this context, we can recall Beauvoir's insistence that 'man' is the Subject and 'woman' is the Other; 'she is the inessential in front of the essential' (Beauvoir 2009 [1949]: 5–6).

Beauvoir gives a powerful portrait of the subject-other split in her first novel, *She Came to Stay* (*L'Invitée*), in which lived experiences of her male and female characters show the decisive failure of Hegelian mutual recognition, and, so, of love between equals (Beauvoir 1984). During the years of 1937–41, before Sartre had written *Being and Nothingness* and before Beauvoir had decided to write *The Second Sex*, Beauvoir wrote *She Came to Stay*. Writing of this novel is informed both by Beauvoir's life experiences and by her reading of Hegel. The narrative of this novel develops Hegel's claim that

'In so far as it is the Other who acts, every consciousness pursues the death of the other . . . ' The relation between the two self-consciousnesses is thus determined as follows: they test themselves and each other by a struggle to the death. They cannot avoid this struggle, since they are forced to raise this certainty of self to the level of truth.

'Every consciousness must pursue the death of the other . . . The essence of the other appears to it as another, as external, and it has to transcend that externality'. (Beauvoir 1991: 328; cf. Hegel 1977: 114)

The quotations (above) appear in Beauvoir's 14 July 1940 letter to Sartre. That letter describes the impact on Beauvoir of Hegel's claim about 'the death of the other'; and this informs the self-other relations in *She Came To Stay*.

She Came to Stay portrays the philosophical problem of 'the other'. This novel tries to resolve the problem by showing that one 'knows' that the other exists by experiencing oneself as an object of that other's consciousness. At the same time, this consciousness of the other reveals an unresolvable split in self-awareness of the self as divided by subject and object. Yet this same split shows that the self cannot be both subject and object, not *pour soi* and *en-soi*.

In psychological terms, the novel gives a concrete analysis of love and its emotional moods, especially jealousy, shame, and hate. The novel's narrative develops the impossibility of mutual relations between two subjects. In any human pair, only one subject can be *pour-soi*; the other must be thing-like, *en-soi*. Even if a couple begins united with a commitment to love as one, the two lovers will experience the inevitable failure of (this) love-commitment. So, instead of love as a reciprocal union, the heterosexual 'love'-relations explored in Beauvoir's novel oscillate between sadism and masochism (Anderson 2011: 169–84; cf. Sartre 1981: 378, 396–9, and 405; Butler 1987: 138–47).

A few years later, Sartre takes sadomasochism a step further. In Sartre, 'the paradox of determinate freedom [is] revealed in sexual life' (Butler 1987: 139; cf. Sartre 1981: 364–79). Butler argues that 'the paradox of determinate freedom, the continual problem of existing as an embodied choice, is surpassed in the Hegelian account when the body becomes the generalized body of Christ'.[6] Sartre does not follow Hegel's theological resolution of the problem of the other. Instead, for Sartre,

> . . . consciousness is always an individual consciousness, and as such is distinct from every other consciousness; nothingness persists between the partners of desire as their necessary and ineradicable difference. The interiority of the Other cannot, as Hegel occasionally appeared to think, be revealed through cognition, because the pre-reflective is the private and hidden consciousness of an agency to itself; in this sense, the pre-reflective cogito is a locus of private and inviolable freedom.   (Butler 1987: 139; cf. Sartre 1981: 241–4)

Sartre's characteristically French Cartesian assumption of a pre-reflective cogito grounds a necessary gap between self-consciousness and the other which a body

---

6 Butler 1987: 139; cf. Hegel 1977: 453–78.

mediates (Sartre 1981: 243). Sartre resists the Hegelian 'solution' to this Cartesian dualism in an idealist claim to absolute knowledge, assuming this would merely reinstate the problem of the other by reducing the other to the same. Consciousness always has its intentional object. The 'Other' is as 'original as consciousness itself'; yet it cannot be known except as mediated by bodily sensation, or emotion.

The other endangers the same. The Cartesian subject has been the absolute to which all else is relative is threatened by a second absolute, i.e. the other. To generalize, the status of the early modern subject in European thought is threatened by an intruder to the point of being overcome by its rival. It is not only that Sartre's phenomenology of the other describes the threat in a range of contradictions. The other is a phenomenon for me, but I am no less a threat 'for her'.

In the 1950–60s, European thinkers witness in Sartre the failure of a Hegelian account of love as mutual recognition. Death of the other becomes an endless pursuit of the subject under threat. Failed love and death threaten in so far as at least one of the pair must renounce the role of subject and content him/her-self with being for him/herself what s/he is for the other. This otherness as death threatens. This threat characterizes the post-Hegelian developments of modern European philosophy, political theory, psychoanalysis, and theology as evident in Feuerbach, Marx, Wahl, Kojève, Hyppolite, Beauvoir, Sartre, and Ricoeur but also, Lacan, Irigaray, Kristeva, Deleuze, and Le Doeuff.

To understand the larger European context better, one could reflect upon the fact that the neo-Kantianism which dominated French thought from the Franco-Prussian War until just before the Second World War had a strong antipathy to the absolute idealism of German thought which had grounded its *telos* in absolute knowledge. The Hegelian, all-encompassing self-knowledge would have been incompatible with the boundaries of knowledge which were fixed by Kant, but also with the concrete reality of human freedom. The salient distinction between the absolute and the individual in the neo-Kantian philosophies remains strong in the early Sartre and Beauvoir. Nevertheless, French existentialism found in Hegel its necessary premiss that the 'I [self-consciousness] pursues the death of the other' (Sartre 1981: 237; cf. Hegel 1977: 114).

The Hegelian narrative running through both theology and modern European thought focuses on the central figure of the Other. Yet with the threat of death, the non-Christian journey of desire becomes a more serious possibility for the subject haunted by the Other. In various interpretations of the dialectic of the same and the other, the Other remains ambiguous in value and meaning. It is both desired and denied. The Other can be uncanny, terrifying, and fascinating. The Other can signify differentiation, alterity, or the difference of otherness. The Other is not necessarily given a positive value, whether as the absolute, the neighbour, the stranger, or the woman/mother. Generally, it is given a range of extreme values as that which haunts or enthrals, confronting a person with what is otherwise than being the same. The modern European theologian has often toyed with and been attracted by both the absence and the full presence of God as immanent in and/or as transcendent of human reality. Does the problem of the Other become a decisive threat to human knowledge of God as the Wholly Other?

Sartre contends that Descartes's mistake robs 'Man' of his creative freedom in giving it to God. The choice had been to associate 'God' either with a Cartesian grounding of certain knowledge, or with a Hegelian version of the mutual recognition made possible by divine love. Choice of the latter led to criticism of Hegel and to the inversion of Christian theology as in the anthropology of Feuerbach or the genealogies of Irigaray. Choice of the former is in a sense 'inverted' by Beauvoir and Sartre, in so far as the o/ Other threatens the *cogito*.

In *She Came to Stay*, Beauvoir shows that bodily awareness of self and other comes through (not mental cognition, but) emotion. Sartre also responds to the Cartesian problem of other minds with an argument that only through concrete relations with others, which a subject undoubtedly has, could she or he come to the sense of self as a distinct individual. To count as a distinct 'man', Sartre reasons that self-consciousness must be more than the bare sense of being aware that it is aware of things. Without a sense of himself as an individual (person), or distinct presence in the world, that individual would be incapable of a vast array of emotions central to our sense of being a person. This sense of being an individual (person) with emotions is, according to Beauvoir and Sartre, impossible without a concomitant awareness of the other, i.e. other persons.

As in Beauvoir's novel, Sartre describes shame as an emotional state before the Other: 'I am ashamed of myself before the other'. This emotion confers on the Other an indubitable presence; 'I feel ashamed' reflecting the bodily presence of the Other replaces Descartes's indubitable. Sartre identifies this characteristically human experience of feeling shame with 'the look' (*le regard*), revealing the indubitable existence of the Other. The look both reifies and individuates me: rendering me 'an object for the Other'. The look modifies my existence: 'I now exist as myself'. This argument is not circular, since Sartre does not argue that I only become aware of myself in embarrassing or emotional experiences. Instead, the look functions whenever I am aware of myself as an object for the attention of another; and this could be the look of 'an eyeless God'. I do not first discern the presence of others and then, conclude that they look at me. Instead initially the Other is nothing more than the look, whose source may well be unknown. Becoming aware of the look is, in Sartre's terms, only the beginning of a distinctive sense of being a self.

From here, Sartre, like other French philosophers of his generation, confronts the Hegelian master-slave dialectic and the power of the negative. After the initial look as an awareness of the other which renders me an object of (his) consciousness, I engage in 'a refusal of the Other'. An ensuing battle becomes the Hegelian struggle to death whereby the 'I gains self-consciousness through negation of the Other' (Sartre 1981: 11, 241–5, 252). In the next section, this negation will be confronted in Beauvoir and other European feminists.

VII. The Absolute Other in Modern European Thought and Theology

In the first section of this chapter, Barth's doctrine of God was compared to that of Lévinas, while the American theologian Serene Jones has compared Barth to Irigaray (Jones 1993: 126–41). These comparisons both pick up on the relations of the same and the other. Both Irigaray and Barth could be said to engage in critiques of, what Irigaray names 'the logic of the same', uncovering the exclusion of otherness by the privileged identity of (male) sameness. They are each motivated by a commitment to others whose subject-hood has been colonized or distorted by a culture, which benefits from the play of a privileged (male) logic of the same. For Irigaray, the violence inherent in a male culture costs women their voices, their agency, their desires, and their relations to others of the same gender, as well as their relations to a God in their own gender (Irigaray 1993). For Barth, the violence of the self-same is implicit in what he calls 'a liberal game': he seems to equate the violence of liberal self-sameness with disinterested and apolitical projects of secular and so-called 'neutral' voices. Barth's criticism is that these voices are self-interested, political, and biased, costing those who are silenced by the fact that they do not fit the privileged identity, i.e. the logic of the same.

Barth's proposal aims to be constructive in so far as it moves beyond critiques of the secular and so-called neutral culture, seeking more positive knowledge of God and human knowledge as revealed by God. Essentially, Barth carves out a new space where 'the Word of God' could be liberated and spoken, free of its human prison. Irigaray's proposal is also constructive in so far as she aims to move beyond a critique of the masculine culture and the male (which claims to be the neutral) logic of the same, seeking to free women to create a God in their own image. Irigaray creates a new space where women could grow and discover their gender identity with a God for her, so she can become fully in becoming divine.

To present this comparison is not necessarily to advocate either Barth or Irigaray's constructive projects. There are plenty of weaknesses and disagreements between the two which could be explored. For example, Barth has God define human persons as relational, but this is not because the Other becomes a mirror for the self. In sharp contrast, a projection, or 'speculum,' of the ego-ideal for the female self is precisely what Irigaray advocates: a God is needed for women to become subjects, as much as for men, as a mirror of their sexually specific ideal. Yet the point of the comparison of Barth and Irigaray is to demonstrate how difficult it is to *think* the Other concretely. Theoretical positions and abstract arguments can be obstacles, inhibiting the nascent subjects who are unable to speak, to be heard, to become fully herself. Twentieth-century European critiques of Hegel's dialectic focus on his 'theoretical principles' and abstract account of the other. In the nineteenth and twentieth centuries, critiques of Hegel's abstract thought focus on his idea of 'a power of the negative' as a 'theoretical principle' manifested in opposition and contradiction' (Deleuze 1983: 184–5). The decisive problem is that this focus on theoretical contradictions can never alleviate real human suffering.

Being satisfied with theoretical contradiction is dangerous for Christian theology. Janet Martin Soskice finds a paradox in the Christian doctrine of 'God's otherness and nearness, the Known Unknowable, to speak in Barthian terms' (2007: 123). She acknowledges 'some of the productive current thought on a God who "relates in and through difference" coming from Lévinas'. Soskice assumes that the differences and similarities of Barth and Lévinas are manifested in contradictions of otherness and nearness, the known and the unknowable, relation and difference, Christianity and Judaism. Yet, without addressing either the contradictions or the sexism as practical issues, Soskice admits explicitly (and apparently accepts) Beauvoir's criticism of Lévinas's account of the feminine other as sexist. Soskice appears unbothered by the power of the negative in theoretical arguments. In this, she is unlike Beauvoir.

In *The Time and the Other*, Lévinas asserts that 'I think the absolutely contrary [*le contraire absolutement contraire*], whose contrariety is in no way affected by the relationship that can be established between it and its correlative, the contrariety that permits its terms to remain absolutely other, is the *feminine*' (Lévinas 1987: 83). Beauvoir's objection to, along with her fears for, 'the feminine' in Lévinas as 'absolutely other' motivate her own, if not Soskice's active concern for gender justice.

The Second Sex focuses on both the (theoretical) manner in which woman has been defined as the absolutely other and the manner in which European women have accepted in practice a role which had been assigned to them as the Other. Crucially, the French Kojèvean logic of the same and the other is broken and undermined by the 'failure' of woman to create her own other. This exception of woman is arrived at as follows:

> The category of *Other* is as original as consciousness itself. The duality between Self and Other can be found in the most primitive societies, in the most ancient mythologies; this division did not always fall into the category of the division of the sexes, it was not based on any empirical given ... Sun-Moon, Day-Night, no feminine element is involved at the outset; neither in Good-Evil, auspicious and inauspicious, left and right, God and Lucifer; *alterity is the fundamental category of human thought*. No group ever defines itself as One without immediately setting up the Other opposite itself.... For the native of a country, inhabitants of other countries are viewed as 'foreigners'; Jews are the 'others' of anti-Semites, blacks for racist Americans ... These phenomena ... become clear if, following Hegel, a fundamental hostility to any other consciousness is found in consciousness itself; the subject posits itself only in opposition; it asserts itself as the essential and sets up the other as inessential, as the object.

> But the other consciousness has an opposing reciprocal claim: travelling, a local is shocked to realise that in neighbouring countries locals view him as a foreigner: between villages, clans, nations and classes there are wars, potlatches, agreements, treaties and struggles that remove the absolute meaning from the idea of the other and bring out its relativity; whether one likes it or not, individuals and groups have no choice but to recognise the reciprocity of their relation. How is it then that

between the sexes this reciprocity has not been put forward, that one of the terms has been asserted as the only essential one, denying any relativity in regard to its correlative, defining the latter as pure alterity? Why do women not contest male sovereignty? No subject posits itself spontaneously and at once as the inessential from the outset; *it is not the Other who, defining itself as Other, defines the One; the Other is posited as Other by the One positing itself as One.* But in order for the Other not to turn into the One, the Other has to submit to this foreign point of view. Where does this submission in woman come from?

...It is often numerical inequality that confers this privilege: the majority imposes its law on or persecutes the minority. *But women* are *not a minority*... (Beauvoir 2009 [1949]: 6–7; emphasis added).

In this passage we recognize the influence of Kojèvean theoretical principles of reciprocity, of otherness and negation on Beauvoir. Nevertheless, she presents the exception of woman as the Other who is 'posited as Other by the One positing itself as One', yet she does *not* 'turn into the One' by positing an Other.

Le Doeuff reads the passage (above) denying that, 'alterity [otherness] is a funda-mental category of human thought'. Her wry criticism dismisses this category as 'a "French-style" German phenomenology [which] became a dogma' from 'Kojève's catechism... on the Left Bank of the Seine' (Le Doeuff 2007: 107). Le Doeuff also explains the practical significance of Beauvoir in recognizing an exception to Kojève's dogma:

> [Beauvoir] unhooks herself or turns away from what she nevertheless regards as an indisputable theoretical position; in this case she reintroduces an element which reopens the space of a problem: the notion of reciprocity. Granted that each consciousness regards the other as another, 'the other consciousness... sets up a reciprocal claim' [*Le Deuxième sexe*, p. 19; also see pp. 16–20] there is no Other in absolute terms. However there is one exception to this rule: between the sexes this reciprocity has not been established because women have not (yet) done the same back to those who set them up as Others.
>
> From a methodological point of view, here we can clearly see Simone de Beauvoir's technique, her *metis*, her craftiness with and towards the doctrinal philosophy she has accepted. It is a technique of reintroduction which undermines the structure.   (Le Doeuff 2007: 107–8; cf. Beauvoir 2009 [1949]: 5–11)

In the light of this Beauvoirian 'technique' of undermining the Kojèvean structure, it comes as a surprise that Soskice and many others have read the same lines of de Beauvoir as if she holds the dogma. Soskice herself embraces the logic of the dialectic theologically: 'this is precisely what God does, what God *is*: it is through being-to-other, being related, that God is one' (Soskice 2007: 123). In particular, Soskice concludes that the Christian doctrine of the Trinity, the three-in-one God, lets us 'glimpse what it is, most truly, to be: "to-be" most fully is "to-be-related" in difference' (Soskice 2007: 124). Soskice accepts the dogma of alterity, in so far as God defines himself by positing an Other, the Other in turn posits God as the Wholly Other; and so each man defines himself in relation to God. But, then, if Soskice intends woman to follow this alterity-structure, the next step would be that taken by Irigaray (1993). Each sex needs the Other of the same (as God), marking the difference between the two sexes; and so woman creates a god for her own ideal.

French Hegelianism and its critical appropriation by a range of European feminists from Beauvoir to Irigaray and, finally, to Le Doeuff takes theology and modern European thought to the heart of gender and sexual politics. When Judith Butler returns to her own post-Hegelian philosophical roots, she admits: 'the question of the "Other" seemed to me, as it did for Simone de Beauvoir, to be the point of departure for thinking politically about subordination and exclusion: . . . in asking about the Other . . . I turned to the modern source of the understanding of Otherness: Hegel himself' (Butler 2004: 240).

However, neither Beauvoir nor Butler (nor, for that matter, Le Doeuff) returns to uncover, as Irigaray does in *Speculum*, an invisible unconscious space of female *jouissance* in the struggle of the subject and his other. Irigaray's practice of disruptive mimesis of, for example, Hegel's Antigone reveals and reverses the 'eternal irony of the community' (Irigaray 1985: 214–26; cf. Anderson 1998: 194–200). With this mime, Irigaray unearths a female language of desire, constituting the invisible sub-structure, on which the social-symbolic structure, i.e. 'the male economy of the same', of exclusive relations between men still rests. Irigaray contends that women need to create their own God, in order to develop relations for the other of the same. In contrast, Le Doeuff embraces Beauvoir's exceptional woman to celebrate the diversity of women and of men, as well as to demonstrate that otherness is definitely *not* a fundamental category of *all* human thought.

The Irigarayan imperative is to become divine as male or as female. She accepts the Kojèvean catechism and extends it to women: there is not only one subject who is male, but there are two subjects; and each of the two types of subjects needs a God (as the same of the same and as the other of the same) for/in his or her own image to define two gendered subjects and their love relations. The Hegelian dialectic is resumed when women gain a place and a God of their own. But does this in fact create any transformation of the excluded and dependent other? Men need only leave women, and the other, in their separate sphere. But surely this is precisely what modern European feminism tries to abolish: a separate sphere of life where women could get on with their chores (for men) without disturbing men (Le Doeuff 2007: 227–8; cf. Whistler 2010: 128–30). For Le Doeuff, the myth of the Other is a bad (Hegelian) story. She contends that 'otherness' is not a fundamental category of all human thought. The myth of the Other, the theoretical principle (of negation) and the bad story (of endless subjection) should be given up, if women are to have the freedom to create friendships, without dependence on a male subject-God, and to have love as a relation of equals.

At the end of a momentous journey through modern European thought, this chapter lacks a happy ending. Instead it urges a new beginning. Rejecting of otherness as opens up a horizon of subjection freedom. But to achieve this it is necessary to find the point at which the slave, or female-subject, in a Hegelian dialectic scandalizes the master, or male-subject. This would be a scandal which she remembers; she will look back at him evincing a consciousness which he is not supposed to have had. The slave will show the master that he has become Other to himself. The master is, then, completely out of his own control. Yet, instead of the Other taking control, the loss of the master-self becomes the beginning of friendships in which a diversity of voices can speak and be heard. This would also mean that the modern European thinker and theologian should continue to question any self-assured and unequivocal voice concerning the nature of the Other. It would appear all together better if theologians were to reject, not assume, the pernicious category of otherness in the ongoing dialectic of the same and the other.

References

Anderson, P. S. (1998). *A Feminist Philosophy of Religion: The Rationality and Myths of Religious Belief*. (Oxford: Blackwell).

——(1999). 'Tracing Sexual Difference: Beyond the *Aporia* of the Other', *Sophia: The Journal of Philosophical Theology, Cross-cultural Philosophy of Religion and Ethics* (March–April) 38: 1, 54–73.

——(2011). 'A Story of Love and Death: Exploring Space for the Philosophical Imaginary', in Heather Walton (ed.), *Literature and Theology: New Interdisciplinary Spaces*. (Farnham, Surrey: Ashgate), 167–86.

Barth, K. (1957). *Church Dogmatics* II/1, trans. T. H. L. Parker, W. B. Johnston, H. Knight, and Haire (Edinburgh: T. & T. Clark).

——(1960). *Church Dogmatics* III/2, trans. and ed. G. W. Bromiley and T. F. Torrance (Edinburgh: T & T Clark).

Baugh, B. (2003). *French Hegel*. (London: Routledge).

Beauvoir, S. de (1984). *She Came To Stay*, trans.Yvonne Moyse and Roger Senhouse (London: Flamingo).

——(1991). *Letters to Sartre*, trans. Quintin Hoare (London: Radius).

——(2009 [1949]). *The Second Sex*, unabridged trans. Constance Borde and Sheila Malovaney-Chevallier (London: Jonathan Cape. Original edition *Le Deuxième sexe*. I–II. Paris: Éditions Gallimard).

Bergo, B. G. (2011). Lévinas' Project: An Interpretative Phenomenology of Sensibility and Intersubjectivity', in M. Joy (ed.), *Continental Philosophy and Philosophy of Religion*. (Dortrecht, London, and New York: Springer), 61–88.

Bonhoeffer, D. (1963). *Sanctorum Communio: A Dogmatic Inquiry into the Sociology of the Church*, trans. Reinhard Krauss and Nancy Lukens (London: Collins).

Buber, M. (1937). *I and Thou*, trans. R. Gregor Smith (London: T & T Clark).

Butler, J. (1987). *Subjects of Desire: Hegelian Reflections in Twentieth-Century France*. (New York: Columbia University Press).

——(2004). 'Can the Other of Philosophy Speak?', *Undoing Gender*. (London and New York: Routledge), 232–50.

Deleuze, G. (1983 [1962]). *Nietzsche and Philosophy*, trans. Hugh Tomlinson (London: Athlone Press).

Descombes, V. (1980). *Modern French Philosophy*. (Cambridge: Cambridge University Press).

Feuerbach, L. (1957). *The Essence of Christianity*, trans. George Eliot (New York and London: Harper Torchbooks).

Fiddes, P. (2000). *The Promised End: Eschatology in Theology and Literature*. (Oxford: Blackwell).

Gutting, G. (2011). *Thinking the Impossible: French Philosophy Since 1960*. (Oxford: Oxford University Press).

Hegel, G. W. F. (1977). *The Phenomenology of Spirit*, trans. A. V. Miller (Oxford: Oxford University Press).

Hyppolite, J. (1974). *Genesis and Structure of Hegel's Phenomenology of Spirit*, trans. Samuel Cherniak and John Heckman (Evanston, IL: NorthWestern University Press).

Irigaray, I. (1985). *Speculum of the Other Woman*, trans. G. C. Gill (Ithaca, NY: Cornell University Press).

——(1993). 'Divine Women,' *Genealogies and Sexes*, trans. G. C. Gill (New York: Columbia University Press), 55–72.

Jones, S. (1993). 'This God which is Not One: Irigaray and Barth on the Divine', in C. W. Maggie Kim, Susan M. St. Ville, and Susan M. Simonaitis (eds), *Transfigurations: Theology and The French Feminists*. (Minneapolis, MN: Fortress Press), 109–42.

Joy, M. (2011). 'Encountering Otherness' in M. Joy (ed.), *Continental Philosophy and Philosophy of Religion*. (Dordrecht, London, and New York: Springer), 221–46.

Kojève, A. (1969). *Introduction to the Reading of Hegel*, trans. James Nichols Jr. (New York: Basic Books).

Kristeva, J. (1991). *Strangers to Ourselves*, trans. Leon Roudiez (New York: Columbia University Press).

Le Doeuff, M. (2007). *Hipparchia's Choice: An Essay Concerning Women, Philosophy, Etc.*, 2nd edn, trans. T. Selous (New York: Columbia University Press).

Leopold, D. (2007). *The Young Karl Marx: German Philosophy, Modern Politics and Human Flourishing*. (Cambridge: Cambridge University Press).

Lévinas, E. (1987). *Time and the Other*, trans. Richard A. Cohen (Pittsburgh, PA: Duquesne University Press).

——(1998). *Of the God Who Comes to Mind*, trans. B. Bergo (Stanford, CA: Stanford University Press).

Pannenberg, W. (1985). *Anthropology in Theological Perspective*, trans. M. O'Connell (Edinburgh: T & T Clark).

Plato. (1998). *The Republic*. Oxford World's Classics, trans., introd., and notes Robin Waterfield (Oxford: Oxford University Press).

Ricoeur, P. (1988). *Time and Narrative*, vol. 3, trans. K. Blamey and D. Pellauer (Chicago: University of Chicago Press).

Roth, M. S. (1988). *Knowing and History: Appropriations of Hegel in Twentieth-Century France*. (New York: Cornell University Press).

Sartre, J. P. (1981 [1958]). *Being and Nothingness: An Essay on Phenomenological Ontology*, trans. Hazel Barnes, introd. Mary Warnock (London: Methuen & Co. Ltd).

Soskice, J. M. (2007). 'Trinity and the "Feminine Other" ', in J. M. Soskice, *The Kindness of God: Metaphor, Gender and Religious Language*. (Oxford: Oxford University Press), 100–24.

Wahl, J. (1951). *Le Malheur de la conscience dans la philosophie de Hegel*, 2nd edn. (Paris: Presses Universitaires de France).

Whistler, D. (2010). 'The Abandoned Fiancée, Against Subjection', in P. S. Anderson (ed.), *New Topics in Feminist Philosophy of Religion: Contestations and Transcendence Incarnate.* (Dordrecht, London, and New York: Springer), 127–45.

SUGGESTED READING

Anderson, P. S. (2009). 'Transcendence and Feminist Philosophy: On Avoiding Apotheosis', in G. Howie and J. Jobling (eds.), *Women and the Divine: Touching Transcendence.* (New York: Palgrave Macmillan), 27–54.

Armour, E. T. and St Ville, S. M. (eds) (2006). *Bodily Citations; Religion and Judith Butler.* (New York: Columbia University Press).

Barth, K. (1975). *Church Dogmatics* I/1, trans. G. W. Bromiley (Edinburgh: T & T Clark).

Baugh, B. (2003). *French Hegel.* (London: Routledge).

Hampson, D. (1996). *After Christianity.* (London: SCM Press).

Heidegger, M. (1962). *Being and Time*, trans. John Macquarrie (New York: Harper Press).

Husserl, E. (1960). *Cartesian Meditations*, trans. D. Cairns (The Hague: Martinous Nijhoff).

Joy, M. (ed.) (2011). *Continental Philosophy and Philosophy of Religion.* (Dordrecht, London, and New York: Springer), 61–88.

Lévinas, E. (1969). *Totality and Infinity: An Essay on Exteriority*, trans. Alphonso Lingis (Pittsburgh, PA: Duquesne University Press).

—— (1991). *Otherwise than Being or Beyond Essence*, trans. Alphons. Lingis (Dordrecht, Boston, and London : Kluwer Academic Publishers).

Ricoeur, P. (1992). *Oneself as Another*, trans. David Pellauer (Chicago: University of Chicago Press).

Romero, Joan. (1974). 'The Protestant Principle: A Woman's Eye View of Barth and Tillich', in R. Ruether (ed.), *Religion and Sexism.* (New York: Simon and Schuster), 319–40.

CHAPTER 5

....

LANGUAGE

....

STEVEN SHAKESPEARE

I. THE LINGUISTIC TURN

....

> The invisible nature of our soul is revealed by means of words —as creation is a speech whose line stretches from one end of heaven to the other . . . Between an idea in our soul and a sound produced by the lips lies the distance between spirit and body, heaven and earth. Yet what inconceivable bond unites two things which are so distant from one another? Is it not a humbling of our thoughts that they cannot, so to speak, become visible except in the crude clothing of arbitrary signs?
>
> (Gregor Smith 1960: 67)

WRITING in 1759, Johann Georg Hamann stands on the cusp of the modern European 'turn to language'. His words spin their own thread, linking the divergent scholastic inheritances of analogy and nominalism to the dawning image of language as a system of differences. Hamann reads language *both* as a theological mediation *and* as an arbitrary convention. It is this double reading which has continued to haunt, fascinate, and complicate the borderlands between theology and philosophy in the past two hundred years.

This chapter will trace some of the most important developments in this complex history. Following a brief characterization of the issues in this section, we will proceed in 'The Break with Immediacy' to examine how language became a focal point for much philosophy from the eighteenth century. The mediation of language begins to appear, not as a secondary detour from an original truth, but as a formative and deformative power in its own right. At the same time, through Hamann and others, the need for language to 'incarnate' truth still carries with it a theological resonance. In 'The Word Incarnate' this tendency is followed through idealist philosophy to debates about religious language in the twentieth century. As we move into 'The Trace of the

Other', hermeneutical, structuralist, and post-structuralist thinking is drawn upon to show that language is always referring us to an otherness, which escapes total thematic formulation, in a way that holds both promise and threat for theological projects of naming God. Finally in 'The Death and Resurrection', the way in which language (particularly as grammar and 'language-game') continues to play a key role in contemporary debates about the meaning and reference of talk about God will be examined.

It can hardly be doubted that the modern period has witnessed an intense preoccupation with language as a theme in its own right. The dispute will always be about the importance and meaning of this phenomenon. Perhaps the foremost European philosopher of the early twenty-first century, Alain Badiou, has decried the linguistic turn as an abandonment of philosophy's concern for truths (Badiou 2005; cf. Meillassoux 2008). For Badiou, the obsession with cultural mediation inaugurates a politically and ethically disabling relativism. More importantly, it is an abandonment of philosophy's ontological project. Truly to think being, for Badiou, means turning to mathematics. In its severe abstraction, mathematics can conceptualize the multiplicity of being, and the inevitably incomplete ways in which we attempt to count and classify it.

For Badiou, the turn to language remains complicit with religious mystification and elitism. It is not that language and poetry have no place in Badiou's thought, but that treating them as unavoidable mediators risks two equally fatal outcomes: being is turned into a ineffable presence, a reality in itself forever 'beyond' language, conceived as bounded discourse within which human speakers are confined; or being is evacuated as merely a conceptual construct, an effect of language. Language produces being as an acoustic illusion, an echo of its work of making meaning. In both cases, being is prejudged, whether as the correlate or creation of language. Language draws the limits of the knowable and/or the real.

On the one hand, therefore, we are witnessing a reaction to the 'turn to language' as representing a philosophical dead end, a barrier to a liberated speculative thinking. On the other, there has also been an intriguing theological attempt to claim the 'turn' as its own.

John Milbank, a pioneer and leading voice in the 'Radical Orthodoxy' trend, has argued that the linguistic turn should be interpreted as a *theological* turn (Milbank 1997: 84–120). For Milbank, it is a mistake to think that an emphasis on our linguistic access to reality inevitably entails any kind of relativistic, agnostic secularism.

Briefly, Milbank argues that it is implicit in Christian doctrine that reality is 'constituted by signs'. Modern linguistics, with its stress on the arbitrary, conventional nature of language has enabled theology to let go of its preoccupation with an ontology of fixed substances. In the process, theology is recovering a truly (radically) orthodox conception of creation. Creation is a kind of semiosis: the peaceful articulation of real differences. When theology abandons a philosophy of fixed substance, and embraces the linguistic nature of creation, it can articulate an account of meaning as 'gratuitous creation', a participation of our sign making in the gift and response of Trinitarian difference. The question for orthodoxy becomes one of finding the correct grammar for expressing and participating in divine creation.

These debates show that the question of language was never merely one about a localizable phenomenon, or a mere instrument of human knowing and communication. Rather, it invokes questions of the possible articulation of being and reality, and of what resists, subverts, or blocks that articulation. Indeed, more radically, a sense has haunted modern European thought that what language 'represents' is the complication of ontology, the ruin of any project of securing a grasp of being, which grounds itself upon an absolute point of departure or totalizing conceptual framework. Language is the articulation which *produces* the problem of inarticulation; it both precipitates and presupposes that being is always already becoming complex.

Such disturbance of simple origins might prove hostile to certain forms of theological articulation. Equally, however, it can invite different readings of the absolute other, in which the very displacement of transcendent fullness and purity becomes a theological theme in itself. The rest of this chapter will explore these possibilities under a number of headings: language as a break with immediacy; as an incarnation of ideality; as a trace of the other; as the death and resurrection of grammar.

II. THE BREAK WITH IMMEDIACY

In his journals, Kierkegaard makes a prescient comment:

> If it were the case that philosophers were presuppositionless, an account would still have to be made of language and its entire importance and relation to speculation, for here speculation does indeed have a medium which is has not provided for itself, and what the eternal secret of consciousness is for speculation as a union of a qualification of nature and a qualification of freedom, so also language is [for speculation] partly an original given and partly something freely developing. (Kierkegaard 1975: 507)

Kierkegaard's comments do not occur in a conceptual vacuum. Despite the attention given to the importance of language in twentieth-century thought, the roots of this emphasis lie in the eighteenth and nineteenth centuries. By the time Kierkegaard was writing, complex philosophical and empirical analysis of language had been well underway for some time, in both naturalistic and idealist forms distinctive from their medieval precursors.

The dream of a language perfectly transparent to conceptual thought and/or perfectly mapping on to reality had been shared in different forms by both rationalists and empiricists from the late seventeenth century (Eco 1997). For Leibniz, in a universe of monadic substances run according to a principle of sufficient reason, the abstraction and vagueness of actual language was not to be tolerated. Language could be refined, turned in to a calculus, an ideography which eliminated all equivocation and presented reality in all its rational order (Wiener 1951: 51). Locke, on the other hand, seeks to root our use of words in the chain that links complex ideas to their simple parts, and then to the always particular sense impressions which impinge upon us (Locke 1979: Book III).

In a sense, both Leibniz and Locke seek to return us to the primal scene of naming. Language is to be governed by the notion of sufficient reason. Signs must be wholly caused by and directly expressive of the discrete particulars which make up the world. There should be no ultimate division between ontology and semiology, between being or nature and signs.

However, such an ideal itself remained abstract and unfulfilled. It suggested a fundamental problem: how to account for the origin of language precisely as a distortion of natural kinds. For Locke, there are no innate ideas, and the mind is overwritten by sensory inputs. However, this leaves unexplained the mind's ability to receive these inputs, translate them into ideas, and then go on to compare and combine them into complex, hybrid forms. The mind, it seems, cannot be a blank: it is an engine for semantic thought, and even when it is idling, it bears the seeds of nature's corruption within it.

For Leibniz, the problem is related but different. If the principle of sufficient reason is universal, then the errors and ambiguities of language must also have their sufficient ground. In such a rationalist system, it is hard to avoid the conclusion that error is predetermined, a necessary articulation of reason—and therefore not error at all.

How then to account for the possibility of language in the first place, and for the reality of its going astray? The question leads to a more naturalistic and historical approach, though still haunted by some of the traits of the quest for the perfect language. Condillac and Rousseau, for example, both attempt a narrative of the origin of language, a more concrete rehearsal of its primal scene (Condillac 1971; Gourevitch 1997). Condillac in particular supplements the desire for a rigorous mathematically modelled language with a myth of creation. In an imaginary world, where only two very young children survive a flood of biblical proportions, Condillac asks what means will they find to communicate?

His answer, which shares much in common with Rousseau's, is that language emerges gradually out of instinct, as habitually repeated sounds and gestures evolve into signs. The initial language of gesture and action is supposed to avoid ambiguity, since its recipients cannot mistake its referent. Language, literally, is pointing things out. However, the tendency for linguistic signs to float free of their natural anchorage introduces an inevitable drift. Artifice replaces nature, and the only solution is the analytical one of breaking complex ideas back down into their simple parts.

At the heart of this narrative, therefore, is a desire for a simple, incorruptible origin. The problem is that this origin seems to have lent itself to corruption from the outset. The opening up of the possibility of language betrays a lack of simplicity within nature itself.

It falls to the critical philosophy of Kant to propose a radical way forward: language is merely an empirical object in the world among other empirical objects. It cannot be divested of its particularity. The Kantian effort to specify the transcendental conditions, which make knowledge possible, must bypass linguistic form, focusing on the universal forms of sensibility and the categories. In this project, language always arrives after-wards—too late to make a difference.

However, this is exactly where Hamann and other critical readers of Kant step forward. Hamann argues that the critical philosophy must fail, because it cannot account for the very medium in which it is formulated and expressed. The result of the distinctions made by philosophers (and Kant is his principal target) is that thought is left disincarnate, and worldly life is denuded of thought. Language cannot be dismissed as accidental to thought, since it is the *empirical* condition for thinking to be possible at all.

A number of corollaries should be noted. First, Hamann's point has the effect of questioning the strict division between the transcendental and the empirical. The purity of the former is always contaminated by a particularity which conditions it. The whole transcendental project, the possibility of 'drawing the limits of reason', begins to look unsteady. The self-critique of reason envisaged by Kant never quite catches itself in the act, for it must always take a detour through the maze of contingent, historical linguistic forms. For what is it that makes the transcendental structures expressible, unless those structures are not purely transparent to reason, but already have one face turned towards mediacy? If critical philosophy cannot account for the language in which it draws its distinctions, then the key distinction between appearance and the thing-in-itself becomes noumenal in its own right: unknowable and inaccess-ible to the understanding.

The second corollary of Hamann's 'metacritique' is a specific emphasis on the arbitrary nature of signs. Language is not domesticated under a principle of sufficient reason, or an empiricist fetishization of immediacy. Particular words in real languages have a contingent sound, form, and history. Their meaning is determined by usage, and by their position in relation to other words.

Such points anticipate some of the main themes of twentieth-century linguistics, especially in the wake of Saussure's structuralism, as we will see below. However, as we noted at the very beginning of this chapter, Hamann gives a surprising theological twist to his interpretation of language. It is this 'incarnational' account of the sign which constitutes the third corollary we need to draw from his opposition to Kant.

For Hamann, the 'inconceivable bond' between idea and sign links an eternal order to the contingency of embodiment. However, the imagery he uses of intuitions and concepts erotically coupled together undercuts the lingering dualism which the idea/sign distinction implies. There is a mutuality, a carnal union in which language is the becoming flesh that makes ideas possible—language as the mother, instrument and criterion of reason (Gregor Smith 1960: 252–3).

Hamann was of course an idiosyncratic thinker, but he was not alone in casting doubt on the self-contained nature of Kant's system. The debates which raged about the human or divine origin of language at this time belied a number of underlying concerns: the importance of usage, grammar, tradition, and community in establishing linguistic meaning and reference; and the problematic relationship of language to a pre-linguistic nature. Something important seemed to be at stake about the distinctiveness (or otherwise) of human reason and consciousness, and the relationship of language to an ideal order of things.

Herder, for example, saw human beings as creatures of language. Language enables us to poetize and mythologize nature, mediating between it and culture. It is not simply a set of labels applied to objects, but a dynamic of communal relationship. Herder does not advocate the more explicit incarnational approach to words of Hamann, but language still has a sacred aura for him. It animates nature; the original language is a 'pantheon', a semantic gallery of gods (Moran and Gode 1966: 134–5).

Herder's approach, at once naturalistic and mythical, can be seen as a contributing factor in the linguistic work of Wilhelm von Humboldt (von Humboldt 2000). His empirical research into languages led him to conclude that language is the 'formative organ of thought'. It does not simply express pre-existing concepts, but actively differentiates and shapes the stream of experience. Language begins to take the place of the Kantian categories, fundamentally organizing (indeed making possible) coherent experience. However, the crucial distinction is that, whereas for Kant the categories are universal conditions of human thought, for von Humboldt, differences between languages results in the formation of different world views. Language's productive capacity crosses the line between the empirical and the transcendental.

Von Humboldt's work is in part a response to the speculation about language characteristic of idealist and Romantic thought. Kant's emphasis on the active nature of the understanding in shaping our experience of the world may not have led to a deeper engagement with language in his part. Nevertheless, it opened the way to a new consideration of the relationship between language and the production of worlds. The Copernican revolution in philosophy had an unexpected semiotic dimension: the word which called creation into being out of formless chaos was now no longer attributed to God alone, but to some kind of transcendental subject, whether individual or communal.

This can be seen in its most potent form in the work of Fichte, whose own treatise 'Of Language Ability and the Origin of Language' also embraces the view that it is the '*expression of our thoughts by arbitrary signs*' (Pfefferkorn 1988: 191). Key to Fichte's approach is that language is a necessary corollary of free rationality, as we seek through signs to discover and communicate with rational agents beyond ourselves. The arbitrariness of signs is essential to their functioning as rational expression, since meaning is not rooted in natural instinct or gesture, but in the free productivity of the mind. That freedom is absolute for Fichte, as the world is itself only the product and reflection of an absolutely active, creative 'I'.

A fascinating pattern of tensions is emerging, in which language is the key site of struggle. Empiricist, naturalist, idealist, and theological accounts of language share a surprising convergence on the arbitrariness of signs and the inescapability of linguistic mediation (even if attempts to give that mediation a supplementary status are made). The age-old philosophical question of the relationship between the real and the ideal, the particular and the universal, is given a new twist. Language becomes the site of that relationship (or contradiction), and gains a peculiar status as at once empirical and transcendental, ideal and historical.

The theological implications of all of this are intriguing. There is of course the debate about the divine or human origin of language, which echoes later controversies about the nature of revelation. Do human beings have a 'natural' emergent capacity for making signs? Or is a special divine revelation or act of creation necessary in order to inaugurate the breach between human consciousness or freedom and nature? Is 'nature' itself in some sense linguistically formed, a dynamic system which already carries within itself the opening to culture? If so, is that creating word that of a transcendent God or a transcendental subject?

The Kantian turn throws up further complications. For Kant, God became a regulative ideal for investigating the order and purposiveness of the world, or for satisfying the demands of practical reason that there is a highest good, which moral agents ought to will. However, such regulative ideals cannot give us theoretical, constitutive knowledge of the objective existence of a transcendent God.

Kant arguably 'made room' for faith at the expense of any assurance that its claims were referential. Nevertheless, he still believed he had established a universal requirement for faith (once stripped of its 'positivity', its external forms and authorities, and of its speculative attempts to ground itself). When the purity of Kant's division between the empirical and the transcendental is troubled by the intervention of language, a certain externalized positivity is lodged within the presuppositions of thought. The oneness of our structures of thought is compromised, and world views proliferate. The situation which Kant wished to avoid, in which there is a relativistic war between rival empirical forms of thinking, suddenly appears endemic to thought itself.

This could be read as an opportunity for the reaffirmation of particular forms of national, racial, or institutional mythology and religion. With the wounding of self-sufficient, self-regulating reason comes a renewed need for a language grounded upon or aiming towards a transcendent ground/telos, but with the admission that such a principle could only be accessible in the guise of local, evolving, communal, traditions. Even for Fichte, the free positing of language by a rational subject had to involve reason in a kind of deception, as it was robed in sensory forms and sedimented out over time in communal forms of speech and recognition. A necessary deception, but a deception all the same.

The linguistic turn thus complicates the relationships between the natural and the cultural, between what is presupposed by knowledge and the communicable forms in which knowledge is expressed and/or created. In this way, it does strangely reflect a number of theological questions about the relationship between time and eternity, spirit and flesh, universal and particular. However, given the widespread philosophical acceptance of the arbitrariness of signs and their break with immediate certainties, such topics shift their ground. God as a regulative idea, the creator identified with an absolute subject: are we left with a thoroughly denaturalized God? Or a God who can only appear in time in the form of what Kierkegaard called a 'sign of contradiction' (Kierkegaard 1991: 124–5)?

III. WORD INCARNATE

Is a reconciliation between the empirical and the transcendental possible in the wake of this linguistic turn? And does it allow any scope for an affirmation of transcendence in anything other than a pre-critical or paradoxical mode of thinking?

These questions are clearly relevant to Hegel's speculative project. In attempting to overcome what he saw as the pernicious dualism of Kant's division between appearance and things-in-themselves, Hegel attempts to narrate the self-estrangement of Spirit, the complex necessity of its differentiation and recollection. Whether Hegel finally proposes the totalizing reconciliation of all otherness (of subject and object, finite and infinite, and so on) or maps its inevitably incomplete self-deferral is of course a disputed topic in Hegelian scholarship. However, we can say with confidence that a wholly other makes no sense in Hegel's system, since an other can only *be* an other if it is in relationship.

The labour of the negative, the forms of Spirit's incomplete reconciliation with itself, cannot simply be left behind. It would be a gross misreading of Hegel to assert that his philosophy affirms that Spirit is ultimately resolved into a timeless conceptual abstraction. Spirit is always bearing its stigmata, tarrying with the negative. To borrow Hegel's phrase, the rose must be found within the *cross* of the present, not by wishing away or superficially harmonizing its contradictions. The Christian narrative of creation, fall, incarnation, and Pentecost is therefore not simply accidental to the story Hegel tells, even if his use of it might raise orthodox hackles.

Nevertheless, the system must aim at a form of completeness, if it is not to leave a surd of unrelated, meaningless reality unaccounted for in terms of its own dialectic movement. Language plays a vital role in fulfilling this aim, since it is through signs that the split between the real and the ideal is articulated.

In the famous analysis of 'sense-certainty' at the outset of the *Phenomenology of Spirit*, Hegel argues that the most immediate knowledge is nevertheless mediated (Hegel 1977: 58–66). An awareness of the 'I' and of the object which confronts it is only possible because the immediate datum of the 'This', the 'Now' and 'Here' carries a negativity within itself. In other words, it is only possible to name an immediacy as such because we have recourse to terms which carry a universal sense beyond the particular occasion of their usage. In this strange transaction, language betrays the immediate whilst at the same time delivering us to a truer content:

> Of course, we do not envisage the universal This or Being in general, but we *utter* the universal; in other words, we do not strictly say what in this sense-certainty we *mean* to say. But language, as we see, is the more truthful; in it, we ourselves directly refute what we *mean* to say, and since the universal is the true [content] of sense-certainty and language expresses the true [content] alone, it is just not possible for us ever to say, or express in words, a sensuous being that we *mean*.   (Hegel 1977: 60)

We cannot say what we mean: the failure of signs is their paradoxical success, as they open up a realm of universality which transcends the immediate moment. In a sense, temporality only becomes possible in and through this self-deferring nature of the sign. Time can no longer be treated as a fall from truth and being; rather it is the becoming of being, the articulation of Spirit, the text and texture of the real.

Any critique of Hegel for his totalizing tendencies must take into account the complex relation of his thought to language. The sign is only possible in the shadow of its own perversion and meaninglessness. The failure is genuine, but it is Spirit's own failure, its need not to coincide with itself and be transparent to itself in order for any 'systematic' reading of the world and its history to emerge.

This needs to be kept in mind when we examine other aspects of Hegel's writing on language, such as that found in the *Encyclopedia* section on the philosophy of mind. Spirit's goal is to know itself as its own truth. In order to move away from a merely intuited union with the world, Spirit requires the externality of signs, 'to be itself in an externality of its own' (Hegel 1971: 70). A key moment arrives when mind becomes productive, learns to utter itself though creating intuitions and not merely receiving them. The sign, unlike the symbol, has no natural grounding in what it represents. It is a foreign body, and one which is paradoxically united with thought in its purest, most self-defining form. It is when words fail and thought no longer means anything that subject and object can be reconciled.

Hegel's thinking on language in many respects lays the foundations for what follows in European thinking. Language is decisively related to temporality and recognition between self and other. As we have seen, the arbitrary nature of signs had occupied thinkers before Hegel, but he was able to clarify with unprecedented rigour the necessary but precarious element of alienation necessary to language use.

Hegel's language is also intrinsically theological, even intrinsically Christian, at the same time as it opens the interiority of theological discourse to a more radical externality and a deeper immanence. The self-emptying (kenosis) of Christ, the Word of God, becomes the self-emptying of the words which define Christian doctrine, words (scriptural, dogmatic, credal) which purport to give it a secure reference and a bounded, authorized sense. Language itself becomes a self-subverting incarnation, an exposure of the absolute to and in materiality.

This simultaneous materialization and idealization of language and spirit bears an intriguing relationship to Heidegger's thought. In *Being and Time*, Heidegger had already sought to resist the reduction of language to assertive propositions (Heidegger 1962: 203–14). A mere 'philosophy of language' is not enough: the ontological significance of language has to be explored. For Heidegger at this stage, the nature of Being is approached through the specific way of being that is Dasein. Never simply identified with the human, Dasein is that being which raises the question of the meaning of Being. Ontology is therefore always bound up with questioning, care, and interpretation.

Crucial to this analysis is the conviction that interpretation is never without presuppositions. It is always already under way, much as we find ourselves 'thrown' into a world we did not choose or create. Language can take the form of idle talk, the everyday milieu which takes its world for granted; but at a deeper level, it expresses the capacity of Being to be disclosed and articulated. Being is never simply encountered as an object or a subject, but is disclosed in the dynamic acts of interpretation through which Dasein projects meaning.

In the light of this, Heidegger's later position, in which we encounter the seemingly mystical-poetic utterances that language is the 'house' or 'shepherd' of Being, becomes more intelligible. Language is not fully understood if it is treated as a merely instrumental tool for human use, something to be dominated. Rather, language as the disclosure of Being is what speaks through humans. Language itself speaks (Heidegger 1978: 411). It is the poetic word that is the paradigmatic act of language in setting beings free to disclose and fulfil their essence. Propositional language remains secondary.

Heidegger's project clearly has deep roots in pre-Socratic thinking, but also more proximate sources in a key facet of the linguistic turn, the centrality of hermeneutics. Modern theories of interpretation take their impetus from Schleiermacher and the Romantics. They are predicated upon an initial awareness of the distance that lies between the reader and the text, an awareness fuelled by Renaissance and early biblical critical textual scholarship. Ironically, it is perhaps the Protestant emphasis on scripture alone which isolates the problematic status of reading, the risk of interpretation.

Heidegger himself resisted the temptation to write a theology, but his work has clearly been hugely influential on modern theologians such as Bultmann, Tillich, and Macquarrie. The association (or equation) of God with Being in their work was, ironically, one which Heidegger himself repudiated. However, it is important to note that Being undergoes a transformation in the work of these existentialist thinkers. Being—and therefore God—is accessed in and through temporality, decision, and embodiment, not in abstraction from them. Being—and therefore God—is, in other words, accessed as articulated, in ways which call into question classical doctrines of the simplicity of God.

The tensions inherent in this approach are evident in Paul Tillich's concept of the symbol (Tillich 1951: 8–11). On the one hand, Tillich is clear that religious concepts have to take a symbolic form, by which he means images and words that direct us to a transcendent reality by participating in that reality. At the same time, there must be a grounding non-symbolic statement, which is that 'God is being-itself'. Symbols are not mere descriptors, but have a kind of sacramental power. However, they must be regulated with reference to a signifier which is ultimately direct.

It is a structure which can be compared to the seemingly very different one proposed by Karl Rahner. For Rahner there is also a sense in which language has an incarnational, sacramental, Christological, dimension. To the extent that it participates in and embodies the self-communication of the divine mystery, it can be true. However, Rahner's transcendental perspective means that such communication is received on the basis of an unthematized grasp of being, a predisposition towards transcendence which makes knowledge possible (Rahner 1982).

Clearly both Tillich and Rahner are working through the legacy of Thomistic analogy, inflected by their reception of Heidegger. The model of direct propositional language is not adequate for theological purposes, in which the very possibility of communicating about God in some way depends upon God's self-revelation. It also fails to preserve the qualitative distinction between God and creature, the mystery which is the negative face of analogical predication.

It can be (controversially) argued that, as with classical doctrines of analogy, the spectre of equivocation is only held at bay with reference to a supposed pre-symbolic, or pre-articulated grasp (or naming) of ultimate reality. In other words, analogy (or symbolism) depends on distinguishing the analogical from the univocal, by maintaining that the mode in which words are predicated of God cannot be the same as the mode in which they are predicated of creatures. The simplicity of God dictates that God is not an individual with (contingent) attributes. There cannot be a 'real' distinction between God and God's attributes, only a formal one. However, to know this distinction itself depends upon us having some kind of pre-analogical (or non-symbolic) grasp of the ground of signification. Without that, what is to prevent analogical predication descending into mere equivocation?

The linguistic turn only exacerbates this problem. If some kind of linguistic mediation is essential to the disclosure of being or the revelation of God, then do we end up losing any secure objective referent for religious language? Is it now language which is the 'ultimate' reality, or at least the inescapable horizon within which we conceive anything?

Concerns such as these are in the background of mid-twentieth-century disputes about the verification of religious truth claims. Never far from the analytical ideal inspired by Frege was the desire for a language which could be mapped on to reality, a system of one-to-one correspondences without remainder (Frege 2001). It survives even in the nuanced linguistic and interpretational theories of thinkers such as Donald Davidson. Also key to the development of this line of thinking was an emphasis on empirical observation and verification. In the hands of logical positivism, as exemplified by A. J. Ayer, this hardens into the doctrine that purported truth claims, which cannot be empirically verified, not only fail the test of what constitutes a truth claim, they are literally meaningless, since meaning is intrinsically tied to truth conditions and therefore to observations grounded in the objectivity of direct sense experience (Ayer 2001).

For some theologians, such as John Hick and Wolfhart Pannenberg, it was important to respond to this demand for verification, at least in principle (Hick 1966: 177–8; Pannenberg 2004: 48–62). However, even from within analytic philosophy, the adequacy of pure verificationism was being undermined as the century progressed. It contradicts itself by its very rigour, driven to rule its own criteria as meaningless as they are unverifiable.

One of the most interesting aspects of the complication of analytic philosophy was the recognition and theorization of the performative dimension of language, most closely associated with J. L. Austin. Language is not only descriptive; it does things, it has effects, it brings new relationships into being. In language we testify, promise, marry, order. Language is in part about its own act, its own address to the other, and the way it constitutes that address (Austin 1971).

The idea that words 'do' things evokes again the image of a creative word, a sacramental word which effects a change in the context in which it is uttered. Theological language (for example, in liturgy) can surely claim this performative dimension—but does it thereby lose its referential truth? For Austin and his heirs, the truth of performative statements had to be closely related to the speaker's intentions, to the seriousness with which they were pronounced, and to the context which defined their nature. However, such guardrails are precarious, since performative language exposes fundamental features of signification: that it always depends for its force upon norms which transcend any specific context or individual intention; and that it is always offered as an address to the other, whose reception of it cannot be fully determined.

There is, in language, no escape from the other. The weaving path we have followed from speculative idealism to logical positivism keeps reminding us that the word—even the Word incarnate—does not speak itself. As we postulated, 'language is the articulation which *produces* the problem of inarticulation'—and there is no escaping the need for interpretation, and the inevitability of its incompletion.

IV. THE TRACE OF THE OTHER

Hermeneutics has a rich history of its own, as can be gathered from both Jim Fodor's and Merold Westphal's chapters in this volume. For our purposes, it is worth recalling that, for Schleiermacher, there is an essential divinatory aspect to the interpretative act which is inseparable from reading texts grammatically and comparatively. (Schleiermacher 1998). The reader's mind must be attuned to the original motivations of the speaker or writer—an ecstatic revivification of the words before one. Words, like dry bones, need the spirit to be breathed into them once more if they are to live and speak.

The Romantic emphasis on creativity and the unique spirit of the individual genius is not far from the surface of this approach, unsurprising given Schleiermacher's closeness to that school of thought. The rational or grammatical reconstruction of meaning is not enough. There must also be feeling (not merely superficial personal emotion, but a felt attunement to a truth which surpasses direct statement) and spontaneity (for the act of interpretation is itself a creative one). This emphasis on feeling is not therefore anti-intellectual, but an attempt to do justice to the fullness of the cognitive act.

For all the dissimilarities, there is common ground here with Kierkegaard, for whom ethical and religious communication could only be indirect, poetically mediated through words and characters which demanded that the reader become self-active, creatively awakening and appropriating meaning. The reason for this is that the meaning of ethical and religious statements cannot be reduced to their cognitive or propositional content: they are essentially communications of a capability, a possibility for acting, or existing (even when the height of that possibility might be a confrontation with one's own nothingness before God, or with the sign of contradiction that is God's paradoxical appearance in time) (Kierkegaard 1991: 123).

The hermeneutical tradition remained strongly influential on twentieth-century thought. Gadamer's seminal *Truth and Method* was strongly influenced by Heidegger's work in this area, in which it is our pre-understanding of being which enables us to raise the question of its interpretation at all. A hermeneutical circle is always in motion, conditioned by the historical, finite nature of our access to Being. Gadamer proposes that 'Being that can be understood is language' (Gadamer 1979: 432).

The hermeneutical aspect of the linguistic turn thus directs our attention to questions of authorial intention and textual intelligibility. However, both of these ideas come under increasing pressure through the twentieth century, not least through the influence of Jacques Derrida.

Derrida is particularly associated with questions of language and writing, though not always for the right reasons. It is sometimes assumed that his position is that human beings are 'trapped' within language and have no access to any reality beyond it. His phrase '*il n'y a pas de hors-texte*' usually translated as 'there is nothing outside the text' can be cited to justify this interpretation (Derrida 1976: 158).

However, matters are not so simple. Derrida is reacting to two important moments in philosophical and linguistic thought, and it is worth briefly evoking these.

Structuralist linguistics is rooted in the work of Ferdinand de Saussure, and especially his *Course in General Linguistics* (Saussure 1983). For Saussure, signs could be divided into two aspects. The signifier was the physical trace or audible sound of a word. It was essentially arbitrary, its meaning given only in and through its differentiation from other signifiers. The signified was the concept to which the signifier referred, but we should note that it is the concept, not an external objective reality which is the referent here. The radical implication of Saussure's work was that signifier and signified were two sides of the same coin. In other words, signifieds were also produced and defined through differentiation: there was no fixed, Platonic or Aristotelian realm of forms of essences.

Language becomes decentred, lacking any 'master signifier' or organizing concept through which it could achieve systematic totality or correspondence to a pre-given objective reality. Language differentiates and divides up the world, and it does so in a multiplicity of ways. The idea of a perfect language or meta-language becomes a chimera.

Derrida is clearly influenced by the important of difference within structuralism. However, he resists the structuralist temptation to abstract cultural and textual structures from temporality, a move which he thought reintroduced the risk of totalization. Instead, he argued that there is always a slippage of meaning, because no structure can present its own credentials intact. In other words, no structure could wholly account for its own origin and axioms. There is an inevitable contingency (or 'play') haunting the most perfect structure, which destabilizes it from within (remember our thesis: language is the articulation which *produces* the problem of inarticulation). A system cannot articulate the possibility of its own systematicity. More radically, to articulate this possibility is already to make it impossible (Derrida 1978: 292).

Phenomenology, and particularly the work of Edmund Husserl, was a hugely influential movement in continental thinking (see Westphal, Chapter 24 in this volume). Drawing on Cartesian and Kantian roots, it advocated a bracketing out of our 'natural attitude', our assumed belief in the existence of an objective external world to which thoughts corresponded. Instead, it called for close attention to how things were given to the conscious mind, how they appeared. Such attention could discern the essences of things and the ideal structures knowledge.

Husserl sees language as the means by which ideal truths could not only originate at a certain specific time and place but also be transmitted through history; made available to those who were not their original discoverers. In a sense, the task of the recipient of this linguistic tradition was not unlike Schleiermacher's interpreter: the outer form of language was to be peeled away in order to revivify the ideal meaning contained therein.

Derrida's critique is that this view seems to presuppose an ideal point of timeless meaning, a pure fullness or presence, which can be transmitted by language and through time without its essence being affected. However, Derrida argued that the very possibility of such transmission meant that the ideal truth could not be fully and transparently present. It was always structured by the possibility of its own repetition, in contexts and times other than its own.

In a sense, there could be no pure origin of ideal meaning. Language is not just a transmission device. It is made possible by difference and temporality. Derrida coined the word *différance* to indicate this dynamic lodged in the heart of structures (Derrida 1985: 1–28). It is a combination of French words meaning difference and deferral, and it is significant that it is a word which can only be read, since when it is spoken, it cannot be distinguished from the ordinary French word for difference. For Derrida, much western philosophy has favoured speech over writing, because in speech one's intention is assumed to be more directly present in one's words. The living spirit imbues spoken utterance with its meaning. Writing, on the other hand, can be seen as the dead letter, a trace which persists even in the absence of its author, and which can become detached from its original meaning.

Derrida's point is that it is those aspects of writing which appear to make it secondary—the capacity of signs to be repeated in the absence of their author and origin—which make any language (including speech) possible. Signs are by their nature iteratable. When we combine this with Saussure's belief in the intimacy between signifiers and signified, we are drawn to the conclusion that our very conceptual schemes and ways of thinking are inescapably conditioned and ungrounded by repetition, difference, absence, dissemination, and drift.

However, this does not mean that we are simply enclosed within language, since for Derrida the 'trace' is not merely a human construct limited to words. In this context, the phrase *'il n'y a pas de hors-texte'* means that all reality is characterized by difference and temporality. The trace is everywhere at work. And rather than limiting us to a defined sphere of human projection, it opens us to a relationship with what cannot be made present: the other, the immemorial past, the future yet to come. All of these have ethical and religious overtones which are increasingly explored in Derrida's texts.

To give just one example, the 'messianic' could refer to a determinate, actual arrival of a figure who will bring history as we know it to a close, and usher in an age of truth. For Derrida, however, messianism operates without a messiah: it is an open ended affirmation, or openness to the possibility of a future which cannot be programmed or anticipated, and which demands of us a radical hospitality. Messianism exceeds determinate messianic religions, not as a more perfect realization of a messianic ideal, but as a 'weak' force, which destabilizes all fixed ideologies and scripted narratives of providence and history (Shakespeare 2009: 124–48).

Derrida's work thus connects with two of his influential contemporaries: Emmanuel Lévinas and Jacques Lacan. Despite the differences between these thinkers, all of them deal in some sense with the idea of language as an address to and from the other, rather than language as descriptive. Indeed, the priority is often given to the idea of receiving meaning from the other.

For Lévinas, the subject's self-identity is produced (in an already wounded form) by its ethical encounter with the face of the Other—a face which is both vulnerable and commanding (almost transcendent). Whereas much western philosophy places questions of being and knowledge at the centre, Lévinas insists that these are secondary to the ethical. In his distinction between the Saying and the Said, Lévinas extends this insight to language. The Said is the meaning of settled words in a codified, linguistic form; but the Saying is the dynamic, demanding act of address itself. Combined with the transcendent nature of the Other, it carries with it associations of revelation: but this is not the revelation of a 'content'. The Saying is more event than information (Lévinas 1991: 34–8, 45–50).

Lacan also emphasizes the way in which the subject is dispossessed by a language which precedes its formation. However, in contrast to Lévinas, Lacan's psychoanalytical approach claims that the subject only escapes the fluidity and narcissism of its infantile life by submitting to the 'symbolic' order. The chaotic desire of the infant needs to be regularized and channelled, and the infant separated from its fixation on the love object (the mother). The symbolic castration represents a submission of the subject to the 'law of the Father', and to the codes which structure acceptable social life. One's desire is never simply one's own; it is always received from the other. Even more radically, Lacan maintains that the unconscious itself is structured like a language (Lacan 1998: 48). It is not a merely pre-linguistic set of instinctual drives, but a complex mechanism which uses all the linguistic tropes of metaphor and metonymy before consciousness even arrives on the scene.

All of these thinkers stress a deep linguisticality, which strains our conventional definitions of language. They locate this linguistic stratum before consciousness, in the never-present experience of being addressed by the other. It is associated with themes of the other, revelation, obligation, hope, and obedience which have distinctive theological associations.

At the same time, these motifs are subverted. Derrida writes of a 'religion without religion' in which determinate doctrinal content is evacuated (Caputo 1997). This raises the possibility that the traditional God—necessary, simple, eternal—is a mirage created by the movement of language, 'an effect of the trace'. Lévinas denies direct access to God except through the trace of the sacred manifest in the face of the vulnerable finite Other. Lacan denies that there is any master signifier or big Other who can provide a reassuring foundation for our truths and perfect satisfaction for our desires.

As feminist and queer scholars have taken up and challenged these ideas, their subversive potential has deepened. Julia Kristeva, for example, draws attention to what she calls the 'semiotic' dimension of language: the embodied rhythms and cadences which bear a meaning which the symbolic and semantic cannot exhaust, For Kristeva, recovering this dimension of language is also a recovery of our relationship with the maternal, which Lacanian theory demands that we abandon and despise ('abject', to use Kristeva's term) in order to become speaking subjects. Kristeva argues that this lies at the basis of our exclusion of those parts of ourselves and our societies associated with the impurity of matter, disorder, and fluidity. Celebrating the semiotic offers an opening to view ourselves as subjects-in-process, harnessing the revolutionary potential of language in poetry and politics (Kristeva 1984).

In queer studies, the lingering attachment of psychoanalysis to norms of heterosexuality has come under more sustained attack. Judith Butler, for example, emphasizes the constructed nature of self, gender, and sex (Butler 1993). These are not natural phenomena, but are constituted by repeated performances, governed by social codes. As such, they can be repeated differently, undermining dominant norms. Repetition and performativity—key aspects of continental and analytical accounts of language—are here made central to a refusal of ideology.

Theological themes are certainly not missing in these authors, but there is wariness about attributing any objective referent to religious claims. Grace Jantzen, a feminist philosopher of religion heavily influenced by Lacan, gives the concept of God a symbolic role as an ideal which we (and she has women particularly in mind) strive to attain. The idea of an objectively existing transcendence perpetuates alienation and denigration of the material. Jantzen's alternative proposal is that religious language functions to guide and inspire its users to 'become divine' through a spiritual path which is indifferent to the independent reality of the divine (Jantzen 1998).

Jantzen shares with other feminist theologians and philosophers a commitment to expose the patriarchal, gendered nature of language. This concerns not only the prevalence of masculine language about God in the western tradition, but the pervasive philosophical and political dualisms which underlie it. Women are coded as bodily, and therefore more subject to passion and disorder, in need of the controlling, forming, normative masculine principle of reason and spirit. Kristeva and others seek to undermine this symbolic order with a different kind of language and imaginary.

Jantzen's position can arouse negative reactions, however, if it seems to make God into no more than a regulative ideal, a human projection on to the void to serve our own spiritual growth. In the desire to overcome pernicious dualisms, is the transcendence of God thrown out in the process? There is certainly a tension within recent accounts of language which echoes in some ways the debate over revelation inspired by Karl Barth. Barth rejected any analogical connection between God and humanity, which would enable a true statement about God (however qualified) to be made. Instead, foregrounding the infinite qualitative difference between God and creation, Barth insisted that only God could initiate any relationship with him. Nothing natural or human could reveal God, or even provide the condition for receiving revelation. God as wholly other must provide the content, medium, and condition for revelation as an utterly unanticipated gift (Barth 2010).

This means that, for Barth, the only words we can legitimately use about God are those elected by God to serve his purpose, for example in Scripture. It is not that these words have any natural capacity to refer to God; it is only God's free act that subordinates our words to the Word of self-revelation.

One of the issues that accompanies such a strong account of transcendence is that even to conceive of it as a possibility seems to presuppose that we possess an ability to draw such distinctions. The argument that God provides the condition for receiving revelation as well as the revelation itself lurches into an infinite regress: what gives us the condition to receive the condition to receive revelation, and so on? If God's language is to inhabit and elect ours without making our signs into pure equivocation, there must be some point of connection.

The Barthian revolution thus did not prevent the persistence of neo-Thomist accounts of analogy, and much creative work on models, metaphors, and symbols in theology (Soskice 1987). Nor could it be wholly insulated to the deconstructive approaches we have outlined above. For Derrida, the trace both subverts traditional theology and opens up a new possibility of articulating an otherness which cannot be mastered by any discourse—an otherness which, if not theological, is not simply atheistic either (Ward 1995).

Does language thus defer the death of God? Or can we say, with Hegel, that the death of God is itself prefigured in the linguistic sign as a moment of meaningless exposure to finitude, which is nevertheless the condition for the divine to be fully disseminated, and fully appropriated?

V. The Death and Resurrection of Grammar

Of course, for thinkers such as Nietzsche, the death of God cannot be recuperated by any systematic philosophy. When Nietzsche famously asserts the truth to be nothing more than 'a mobile army of metaphors, metonyms, and anthropomorphisms', the nihilistic dimensions of the linguistic turn are harshly exposed (Kaufman 1976: 46–7). Reconciliation between subject and object via the medium of language is dismissed as an illusion, for 'Every concept originates through our equating what is unequal' (Kaufman 1976: 46).

In Nietzsche's sarcastic and persuasive dismissal of the Cartesian appeal to the immediate certainty of the cogito, it is language which plays the wrecking role. The subject's inability to define its own language ex nihilo means that even those ideas which seem self-evident depend for their assertion on borrowed signs, customs, codes, and traditions. Kierkegaard's comment about language as a presupposition of philosophy is borne out here, as Nietzsche rejects any absolute beginning for thought. Language has always insinuated itself into thinking, and no firm ground is left.

In the light of this, it becomes clearer why Nietzsche claims that 'I am afraid we are not rid of God because we still have faith in grammar' . Grammar gives us the illusion of an objective order ready-made for us to occupy, an order that is not merely a human improvisation, but which is built into the order of things. As his parable of the madman in the marketplace makes plain, it was possible for people to abandon belief in God without realizing its implications: the loss of any firm anchor for morality and meaning (Nietzsche 1974: 181–2). Nietzsche's real target is not merely those who continue to believe in God, but the kind of facile atheism which claims to reject God but leave truth and ethics pretty much as they were. Once we realize the inescapable mediation of reality in language, thought can no longer claim access to any extra-linguistic referent. The death of God is an inevitable corollary of the linguistic turn, so this argument runs, because language masks or corrodes the real, constructing it according to essentially arbitrary rules whose genealogy can be unearthed.

One possible result of this trajectory of thought is the kind of a/theology practised by Mark C. Taylor, especially in his seminal text *Erring* (Taylor 1984). That book is organized around the themes of the death of God, the disappearance of the self, the end of history, and the closure of the book. In other words, what is receding in postmodernity is any defensible notion of a transcendent or transcendental ground of reality. There is no God, conceived of as a necessary being in which contingent beings find their source and telos; there is no substantial self, preserved from the changes of material embodiment and time; there is no all-encompassing story which can comprehend the beginning, course, and goal of history; and there is no encyclopaedic knowledge (or 'book') able to gather and synthesize all truths.

Instead, there is language; constantly self-deferring and self-differing, language (and particularly writing) is a play of absence and presence which never ends. The sacred is disseminated as a divine trace and milieu, making all creativity possible. Grace and salvation are refigured as the gratuity of signs and the liberation from absolutes.

In this radical reinterpretation of western salvation history, there are strange continuities. Don Cupitt, for example, proposes a non-realist philosophy of religion, in which we cannot check our representations against realities outside language. From its early Kantian phase, in which God was conceived as a guiding religious ideal, Cupitt's work has embraced a linguistic turn of its own. 'God' is now found poured out into the ever-circulating process of linguistic exchange which constitutes life for us. Our world is created as a world in and through language (Cupitt 1990).

In this image of language and thought, traditional Christian themes still emerge. The world is created from nothing by the word, but now it is created by us (not as isolated individuals, but in so far as language runs through us and makes it possible for us to articulate anything). 'God' as the name of the highest truth or ideal, is encountered as incarnate in the word, abolishing mediated religion and the two worlds dualism of much western philosophy to leave a purified affirmation of becoming and expression.

Taylor and Cupitt represent perhaps the most consistently anti-realist legacy of the linguistic turn, which finds a kind of sacred fulfilment in the death of God into the sign: an immanently secular-religious Hegelianism without guarantee or finality. They have met fierce opposition for surrendering the objective referent of religious (if not all) language, not least because it could be seen to deny theology any ability to resist the flows of contemporary secular and capitalist ideologies. Capitalism is quite comfortable with perpetual flow and the absence of fixed standards of truth and meaning.

This criticism is perhaps too easy; there is still scope for 're-imagination' and resistance of dominant norms in the work as Taylor and Cupitt, as there is in, say, Judith Butler. Nevertheless, this explicit anti-realism is not the only option for a contemporary theology steeped in linguistic analysis. A more cognitively agnostic approach is associated with the notion of language games as formulated by Ludwig Wittgenstein. Language, Wittgenstein argues, cannot be understood if it is seen only as a collection of signs or labels used to point out real objects or events. Language operates according to social rules, conventions like those which structure the playing of a game. Without such rules, even the operation of pointing out or referring would lack any meaning (Wittgenstein 1958).

This insight was further developed by Wittgenstein and others (cf. Phillips 1970) to suggest that there were different language-games, different organized areas of social discourse, which were irreducible to one another. It would be a category mistake, for example, to interpret or evaluate religious language by using the language of natural science, and vice versa. One had to enter into the logic or grammar of the game to understand how it was being used.

A related development which has been significant to theology is the emphasis on the narrative form of belief systems and identities. George Lindbeck, for example, offered an account of Christian doctrine which denied that doctrinal claims should be interpreted as straightforwardly descriptive of objective reality, or expressive of subjective ideals (Lindbeck 1984). Rather, he advocated a 'cultural-linguistic' model, in which doctrines function as the rules for Christian speech about God. Christian language does not 'correspond' to God in the abstract. Through communally repeated narrative and ritual, Christian language functions to shape people whose lives correspond to the nature and purpose of God.

There is something questionable about this attempt to make the language-game, narrative or grammar the privileged locus of truth, however (a point which applies to John Milbank's Radical Orthodoxy too). Such meta-linguistic categories presume to have a transcendental status, but the reality is that they are as compromised with the empirical as any sign or concept. From within language (taking seriously Derrida's account of the textuality of existence) we cannot draw boundaries around the limits of sense. There is no purely transcendental or transcendent perspective open to us, and communal praxis has no magical power to create in and of itself.

We began with a searching challenge to the foundations of modern critical philosophy, a challenge which was rooted in an appreciation of language as an inescapably impure presupposition of thinking. Rather than trapping us in a humanly constructed world of signs, such a perspective actually opened the way for speculative and deconstructive work to come. In the process, theology's perennial vocation to question its own possibility was given new form.

Nietzsche represents only one possible route through this new landscape. From Hamann, Kierkegaard, and Hegel onwards, we also see language interpreted through categories of incarnation, paradox, alienation, death, repetition, and temporality which open up a radical possibility of relating to non-simple otherness, to an exteriority which is never merely a correlate of human subjectivity or community. If contemporary speculative philosophy is wary of the inward-looking and pseudo-mystical undertones of the linguistic turn, it would do well to reconsider its roots and course.

In the continental tradition, philosophy of language has rarely been merely a regional application of a broader philosophical method. It is connected with fundamental questions about the nature of origins, meaning, and alterity which inevitably draw it towards the ambit of theology. To engage with this tradition, however, theology must undergo its own disarticulation: an exposure of its own logos to an unpredictable dialogue.

References

Austin, J. L. (1971). *How To Do Things With Words*. (Oxford: Oxford University Press).

Ayer, A. J. (2001). *Language, Truth and Logic*. (London: Penguin).

Badiou, Alain (2005). *Being and Event*. (London: Continuum).

Barth, Karl (2010). *Church Dogmatics I.1: The Doctrine of the Word of God*. (London: T & T Clark).

Butler, Judith (1993). *Bodies That Matter: On the Discursive Limits of Sex*. (London: Routledge).

Caputo, John (1997). *The Prayers and Tears of Jacques Derrida: Religion Without Religion*. (Bloomington, IN: Indiana University Press).

Condillac, E. B. de (1971). *An Essay on the Origin of Human Knowledge*. (Gainsville: Scholars' Facsimiles and Reprints).

Cupitt, Don (1990). *Creation Out of Nothing*. (London: SCM).

Derrida, Jacques (1976). *Of Grammatology*. (Baltimore: Johns Hopkins University Press).

——(1978). *Writing and Difference*. (London: Routledge).

——(1985). *Margins of Philosophy*. (Chicago: University of Chicago Press).

de Saussure, Ferdinand (1983). *Course in General Linguistics*. (London: Duckworth).

Eco, Umberto (1997). *The Search for the Perfect Language*. (London: Fontana).

Frege, Gottlob (2001). 'On Sense and Reference', in Martinich, Aloysius, and Sosa, E. David (eds), *Analytic Philosophy: An Anthology*. (Oxford: Blackwell), 7–18.

Gadamer, Hans Georg (1979). *Truth and Method*. (London: Sheed and Ward).

Gourevitch, Victor (1997). *Rousseau: The Discourses and Other Early Political Writings*. (Cambridge: Cambridge University Press).

Gregor Smith, R. (1960). *J. G. Hamann 1730–88: A Study of Christian Existence*. (London: Collin).

Hegel, Georg Wilhelm Friedrich (1971). *Hegel's Philosophy of Mind*. (Oxford: Clarendon).

——(1977). *Phenomenology of Spirit*. (Oxford: Oxford University Press).

Heidegger, Martin (1962). *Being and Time*. (Oxford: Blackwell).

——(1978). *Basic Writings*. (London: Routledge).

Hick, John (1966). *Faith and Knowledge*. (Ithaca: Cornell University Press).

Jantzen, Grace (1998). *Becoming Divine*. (Manchester: Manchester University Press).

Kaufmann, Walter (1976). *The Portable Nietzsche*. (New York: Viking).

Kierkegaard, Søren (1975). *Søren Kierkegaard's Journals and Papers*, vol. 3, trans. and ed. H. V. and E. H. Hong (Bloomington, IN: Indiana University Press).

——(1991). *Practice in Christianity*. (Princeton, NJ: Princeton University Press).

Kristeva, Julia (1984). *Revolution in Poetic Language*. (New York: Columbia University Press).

Lacan, Jacques (1998). *The Seminar, Book XX: Encore, On Feminine Sexuality. The Limits of Love and Knowledge*. (New York: Norton).

Lévinas, Emmanuel (1991). *Otherwise than Being or Beyond Essence*. (Dordrecht: Kluwer).

Lindbeck, George (1984). *The Nature of Doctrine: Religion and Theology in a Postliberal Age*. (London: SPCK).

Locke, John (1979). *An Essay Concerning Human Understanding*. (Oxford: Clarendon).

Meillassoux, Quentin (2008). *After Finitude: An Essay on the Necessity of Contingency*. (London: Continuum).

Milbank, John (1997). *The Word Made Strange: Theology, Language, Culture*. (Oxford: Blackwell).

Moran, John and Gode, Alexander (1966). *Rousseau-Herder: On the Origin of Language*. (New York: Frederick Unger).

Nietzche, Friedrich (1974). *The Gay Science*. (New York: Vintage).

Pannenberg, Wolfhart (2004). *Systematic Theology*, vol. 1. (London: T & T Clark).

Pfefferkorn, Kristin (1988). *Novalis: A Romantic's Theory of Language and Poetry*. (New Haven and London: Yale University Press).

Phillips, D. Z. (1970). *Faith and Philosophical Enquiry*. (London: Routledge).

Rahner, Karl (1982). *Foundations of Christian Faith: An Introduction to the Idea of Christianity*. (New York: Crossroads).

Schleiermacher, Friedrich (1998). *Hermeneutics and Criticism and Other Writings*. (Cambridge: Cambridge University Press).

Shakespeare, Steven (2009). *Derrida and Theology*. (London: T & T Clark).

Soskice, Janet Martin (1987). *Metaphor and Religious Language*. (Oxford: Clarendon).

Taylor, Mark C. (1984). *Erring: A Postmodern A/theology*. (Chicago: University of Chicago Press).

Tillich, Paul (1951). *Systematic Theology*, vol. 1. (Chicago: University of Chicago Press).

von Humboldt, Wilhelm (2000). *On Language: On the Diversity of Human Language Construction and its Influence on the Mental Development of the Human Species*. (Cambridge: Cambridge University Press).

Ward, Graham (1995). *Barth, Derrida and the Language of Theology*. (Cambridge: Cambridge University Press).

Wiener, Philip (ed.) (1951). Leibniz: Selections. (New York: Charles Scribner's Sons).
Wittgenstein, Ludwig (1958). *Philosophical Investigations.* (Oxford: Blackwell).

SUGGESTED READING

Barth (2010).
Derrida (1978).
Eco (1997).
Hegel (1977).
Heidegger (1978).
Hong, Howard and Edna (eds) (1967–78). *Søren Kierkegaard's Journals and Papers,* 7 vols. (Bloomington, IN: Indiana University Press).
Kristeva (1984).
McFague, Sallie (1982). *Metaphorical Theology: Models of God in Religious Language.* (Minneapolis: Fortress).
Milbank (1997).
Nietzsche, Friedrich (1968). *The Twilight of the Idols.* (London: Penguin).
Smith, James K. A. (2002). *Speech and Theology: Language and the Logic of Incarnation.* (London: Routledge).
Soskice (1987).
Stiver, Dan (1996). *The Philosophy of Religious Language: Sign, Symbol and Story.* (London: Routledge).
Ward (1995).
Wittgenstein (1958).

CHAPTER 6

FREEDOM AND HUMAN EMANCIPATION

DAPHNE HAMPSON

'*Freiheit is immer Freiheit der Andersdenkenden.*'
('Freedom is always freedom of the differently-thinking-one.' Or:
'Freedom is only as good as the freedom given to the one who thinks
differently.')

(Rosa Luxemburg, 1920; my translation)

THE concepts of 'freedom' and of 'human emancipation' have been central to the
project of modernity. This has had incalculable implications for the Judeo-Christian
tradition, as the inheritance of 'Athens' has vied with that of 'Jerusalem'. It is no
exaggeration to say that, within Continental Europe, the quest for individual freedom
and social emancipation was carried out in the face of the claims of transcendent
monotheism and ecclesiastical objection. But that this is the case has only made the
attempt to formulate a theological response the more interesting. In a world in which,
at the beginning of the twenty-first century, human self-actualization and liberation
have become basic ethical axioms, the question as to the place and nature of religion is
as pertinent as ever it was.

Commencing his essay of 1784, submitted for a prize, 'What is Enlightenment?', Kant
avers:

> Enlightenment is the exodus of human beings from their minority [*Minderheit*;
> minority, namely, one not yet come of age] for which they themselves must take the
> blame. This immaturity is to be equated with impotence when faced with the need
> to use one's own understanding rather than following the directions of another. It is
> blameworthy when the problem lies not in a lack of understanding, but in a lack of
> resolution and of the courage [to act] without making use of the leadership of
> another. *Sapere aude*! [Dare to know!] Have the courage to let your own reason
> serve you! is the motto of the Enlightenment.   (Kant 1996: 17; my translation)

It is hardly without significance that, in illustrating his prescript, two of the three examples that Kant adduces are ecclesiastical: 'If I have a book [the Bible] which thinks for me, a pastor who has conscience on my behalf...'. Grounded in his Lutheran heritage and addressing the question posed by his age, Kant proposes that to be enlightened is to be autonomous, unbound by authorities or powers that would cause a person to overrule his moral judgement. Autonomy is nothing less than the measure of maturity. As Alexander Pope had declared earlier in the century, the measure of man is man.

In his thinking on 'freedom' Kant betrays his native Lutheranism, transposing it into a secular key.[1] To be 'free' is for Luther, in relation to the world, to choose between alternatives. But we find ourselves bound either to the devil or to God; and to be bound to God is to be free. Luther well understands that to think that we could 'choose' God (as though God were some kind of an object) is to misunderstand that God is present as God. Behind Luther lies the Augustinian (Platonist) tradition in which to be bound to the good is to be free. Kant likewise thinks that we are only in a positive sense 'free' when our will is aligned with the good; the 'holy will' precisely has no choice, for it axiomatically does the good. To sin is for Luther to be diverted from looking to God. And again for Kant it is to be turned aside; to allow a propensity arising from what is other than the good to take precedence. Furthermore both men understand 'freedom' in terms of the will (in the case of Luther following late medieval Nominalism). For Kant it is the will that is good, or misdirected. Finally, it is for both men the internal disposition that takes priority. For Luther it is faith (the relation to God) that leads to works (serving the neighbour). It is not that, as in a Catholic system, practicing good works *leads to* the formation of a good *habitus*, an internal state.

Kant's great work on religion of 1793, *Die Religion innerhalb der Grenzen der blossen Vernunft* (Religion [as understood] Simply within the Boundaries of Reason)—as opposed to 'revelation' which, tongue in cheek, Kant says he will leave to the theologians—is the first systematic 'demythologizing'[2] (as such a hermeneutical procedure will later be termed) of Christian theology. Such a 'reading' of the myth, a translation into other terms, is in some sense present in the mid-eighteenth century in Lessing; but Kant's is the first meticulous deconstruction, showing each element to be but an externalization in mythological form of what one could arrive at 'by reason alone', that is to say quite apart from any supposed revelation. Take for example Kant's treatment of man's[3] 'redemption'. The 'Fall' has for him consisted in allowing personal inclination to take precedence over the incentive arising from the moral law. Kant then proclaims that a good principle must first be established in man (who will consequently do good works). We may note the Lutheran structure, that the revolution must come

---

[1] For the structure of Lutheran thought, see Hampson 2001: ch. 1, 'Luther's Revolution'.

[2] The German term *Entmythologisierung* simply connotes 'out of mythological [language]', lacking the derogatory connotation that 'de'mythologizing may imply.

[3] I employ 'man' as both the masculine and the generic human in which woman is 'included', for this best reflects the thought of those whom I discuss.

first; though this does not deter Kant from weaving in admonitions that may be culled from Jesuit sources as to the need for human effort!

Thus the biblical doctrine of 'Christ taking on sin' is for Kant but an externalization of that internal revolution that man *himself* must accomplish. Not least, in Kant's eyes to look to another for 'salvation' would constitute a heteronomy in which man failed in his own moral obligation. Kant writes of the 'new man':

> This moral disposition which in all its purity (like unto the purity of the Son of God) the person has made his own—or, (if we personify this idea) this Son of God himself [namely, the person of whom we are speaking!] carries for himself—and thus it is also for each person who, in a practical sense, believes in his [new] self—as the vicarious substitute the debt of sin; [i.e. the person's new self bears, as vicarious substitute, his former sin]. . . . [4] Only it must be remembered that (in this mode of representation [namely, the mythical]) the suffering which the new man, in becoming dead to the *old*, must accept throughout life is pictured as a death endured once for all by the representative of mankind.   (Kant 1960: 69; trans. adapted)

Any external saviour has become superfluous. The myth can be demythologized to reveal human acknowledgement of responsibility. Kant evaded the censor through publishing in a series of articles rather than in book form.

Freedom for Kant is transcendental, that is to say intrinsic to ourselves, part of the very structure allowing us to think or act. Seeing himself as Kant's disciple, Fichte nevertheless desired to develop Kant's thought into what he considered an integrated, 'scientific', position, a *Wissenschaftslehre*. Holding the self to be in itself freedom, such that the self posits itself (*sichselbstsetzt*), Fichte held that the self knows itself in an immediate perception. But it is also the case that the self is 'placed', coming to itself within the context of society. Wishing to see itself as limitless, the self comes up against another, who represents an *Anstoss*, a check or barrier on itself, in what is an unwelcome repulse. That other is not simply passive; rather it presents the self with an *Aufforderung*, an invitation or summons to be. In what becomes a reciprocity I likewise call forth the other into his being. It follow that, while each knows himself as limited by the social world, it is also the case—a thought that Hegel will develop—that he owes it to the other that he has the distinctive self-consciousness as a rational human being that he has.

Fichte's idealism was to spell trouble. He believed it to follow from his assumption that self is prior to knowledge of the world that the idea of God as 'objective' (for example as Creator) is, as he put it, idolatrous. Rather that which exists, the world-order, is for Fichte (or Hegel) a manifestation or exteriorization of that which most truly is; though it is yet to be fulfilled. In such an understanding, any consciousness of God must be given with consciousness itself, requiring no external God. It was a

---

[4] 'Dieser Selbst trägt für ihn, und so auch für alle, die an ihn (pracktisch) glauben, als Stellvertreter die Sünderschuld . . .'. The various English translations are far from clear.

position that the cantankerous Heinrich Jacobi declared indistinguishable from atheism, and in the ensuing fracas Fichte lost his Chair at Jena.

Kant's *Religion* made a profound impact on the young Hegel. Writing two years after its publication (in a text which, unpublished, remained unknown), 'The Positivity of the Christian Religion' (1795), Hegel discusses 'How Christianity [that is to say Jesus' religion] Became the Positive Religion of a Church' [a religion about Jesus, adhered to heteronomously] (Hegel 1948: 67.); the process which one might say Kant had reversed in his *Religion*. In his 'The Spirit of Christianity and its Fate' of 1799 (again unknown to his contemporaries), Hegel speaks of the 'obstinacy' of the Jews in clinging to their faith: 'The Romans were disappointed when they hoped that fanaticism would die down under their moderate rule, for it glowed once more and was buried under the destruction that it wrought [namely, the destruction of the Temple in AD 70].' Hegel continues:

> The great tragedy of the Jewish people is no Greek tragedy; it can rouse neither terror nor pity, for both of these arise only out of the fate which follows from the inevitable slip of a beautiful character; it can arouse horror alone. The fate of the Jewish people is the fate of Macbeth who stepped out of nature itself, clung to alien Beings, and so in their service had to trample and slay everything holy in human nature.... (Hegel 1948: 204–5)

That is to say that, through adhering to a religion of revelation 'alien' to their own being, the Jews allowed human autonomy to be subverted. Contrasting the teaching of Jesus and Kantian ethics with Judaism, Hegel writes: 'Rights which a man sacrifices if he freely recognizes and establishes powers over himself, regulations which, in the spirit of Jesus, we might recognize as grounded in the living modification of human nature [i.e. in an individual human being; a modification which Hegel thinks is fine if freely undertaken] were simply commands for the Jews and positive throughout [that is, understood heteronomously]' (Hegel 1948: 206). In Hegel, we may say, 'Athens' must reign over 'Jerusalem'.

For Kant, freedom implies the (inward) moral law (and vice versa): were I not free to obey the law, I could not be held imputable. As in the case of Kant's 'categorical imperative', that I should act according to that maxim whereby I can at the same time will that it should be a universal law, so also for Hegel I must act in accord with that which I can myself affirm as an objectively existing law; that is to say which, though subjectively derived, I set over against myself. In the case of Hegel, however, this objectivity is to be equated with institutional, public, law; that we in turn recognize to exist for our own good. If these laws—and the institutions that promulgate them—are to be recognized as promoting freedom and we are not to be alienated from them, then they must secure rights, such as freedom of conscience. Hegel's thinking is furthermore historical in that what is counted 'truth' unfolds in history. Now it will be clear that, potentially, a tension may arise between that which an individual conceives to be right (which, indeed, he or she may think it right that each should do in like circumstances) and what is public law. By contrast Kant had not perceived such a problem, having a late eighteenth-century sense of a moral outlook held in common by humanity, such that all would agree where duty lay. Illustrating this tension, Hegel sees in Sophocles' *Antigone* a clash between the earlier tribal and familiar law, so that if she is to obey her conscience and to act in accordance with tradition Antigone must bury her dead brother, and the public, state, law which Creon's prohibition represents. But it is also the case that, conservative by nature, Hegel was wary of the human caprice that taking the law into one's own hands might represent. Thus, as advanced in his *Philosophy of Right* (1820), 'freedom' is understood as the 'positive' freedom to live the fruitful life afforded by a well-ordered society. Rebellion against established laws and social traditions becomes difficult to justify.

As the eighteenth century turned into the nineteenth, the challenge to Christian theology could hardly have been greater. It fell to the theologian Friedrich Schleiermacher to make it his life's work to map out a way forward. Having spent his student years absorbing Kant and, as he put it, cleansing 'thought and feeling from the rubbish of antiquity,' presumably Christian doctrine expressed in classical terms (Schleiermacher 1958: 9), Schleiermacher took for granted the presuppositions of modernity, speaking to his contemporaries on their own terms. In what was a novel point of departure for theology, he too in an age of idealism commences from the faculties of the human mind and not from revelation or an interventionary God. Schleiermacher who came from a Pietist background was possessed of a strongly experiential theology. Addressing those whom he names 'the educated among its despisers', Schleiermacher, in his youthful *Reden* (*Speeches*) on religion (1799), writes an *apologia*. He has, he says, no quarrel with Kantian epistemology (to situate the relationship to God in the sphere of knowledge had ever been mistaken), nor with Kantian ethics (indeed chiding Kant, in saying that he finds that ethics is much more moral without the added incentive of the hope of reward, which is the basis for the postulation of 'God' in Kant's 'Second' *Critique*). Awareness of God, says Schleiermacher, should rather be placed in the realm of sensibility, akin to Kant's consideration in his 'Third' *Critique of Judgement*. Employing the language of an incipient Romanticism, Schleiermacher proclaims that we lie 'directly on the bosom of the infinite world' (Schleiermacher 1958: 43.).

Having in his early years made short shrift of Christian doctrine, but now in 1821/1822 the incumbent of the Chair of theology in Berlin, Schleiermacher published his major work *Der Christliche Glaube* (*The Christian Faith*). He attempts to rebuild what he understands as the faith of the church on the initial basis of a phenomenological depiction of the self. In relation to the world we both have a feeling of freedom (of *Sichselbstsetzen*, of having 'placed ourselves', the term employed by Fichte and Hegel), but also of dependence; both relative and hence in relation to the world a reciprocal relation. Schleiermacher then proposes that, yet more fundamentally, we sense ourselves as not-having-so-placed-ourselves, a sense of *Sichselbstnichtsogesetzthaben*; with the implication that we are 'placed'. Standing in contrast with the reciprocal relation with the world we have a *schlechthinniges Abhängigkeitsgefühl*, a sense of being simply, or totally, dependent (Schleiermacher 1928: §§3–4). It is this, says Schleiermacher, that is our relation to God.

Such a position could well be held the logical working out of the Reformation. Luther (as we have seen) is sensible of the fact that God is not to be construed as an 'other' with which we should think we inter-act. Schleiermacher came from a Reformed, not a Lutheran, background (which is significant), though he played a leading role in the creation of the *Unierte*, United, Church in Prussia. His was an adroit move in an age set on human autonomy. It did not stop him from being misconstrued by Hegel, his rival on the faculty in Berlin, who quipped (on account of Schleiermacher's talk of 'absolute dependence'), that according to Schleiermacher a dog must be the most pious of beings. Such a comment is precisely (if I read him aright) to misunderstand Schleiermacher's proposition. The point is that God is not an 'other' in the necessary sense for there to be an inter-action with God, such that the relationship with God would indeed (in the case of God) be heteronomous if depicted as an absolute dependence. Rather does Schleiermacher conceive of God as the ground of ourselves; we have, he says, a sense of *woher*, of 'whenceness'. What is clearly questionable is that a theology built on such a basis is logically, of necessity, Christian. Schleiermacher simply states that 'for the Christian' their sense of God is shaped by the mediator Jesus Christ, who himself has an unclouded God-consciousness.

The growing sense of human autonomy, together with the impossibility, post-Newton, of an interventionist God, led in the eighteenth century to a non-anthropomorphic, Deist, understanding of God as Creator; who lay behind a universe the marvels of which were increasingly becoming apparent to humankind. The stature of man entailed that he should no longer conceive of himself as in God's service. But in any case such a God posed no restrictions on human liberty. It did not follow that the dignity of man could not itself be given a theological baptism. In the words of Thomas Jefferson's 'Declaration of Independence' (1776) all men were to be deemed 'created' equal. The long shadow cast by the Thirty Years War (1618–48) having finally dispersed, by mid-century there arose in Germany a flowering of human creativity. Lessing, the foremost intellectual of those years, was working on material which was to become his profoundly tolerant and humane *Nathan der Weise* (*Nathan the Wise*), published 1779. Lessing's own religious position was something about which he kept decidedly quiet; leading after his death to public dispute as to whether he had been no more than a Spinozist, a term of disapprobation in an age in which pantheism was considered synonymous with atheism. In the next generation, Goethe could be outright hostile to religion. Meanwhile Hegel thought it circumspect to keep his scepticism hidden, that he not damage a precarious career. His *Geist* is at most an immanent unfolding of spirit as world history. Yet unlike the case of French anti-clericalism subsequent to Voltaire and the Encyclopaedists, the Germans never became volubly hostile to religion.

What exactly 'freedom' consisted in was inflected by the differing historical and social settings in which it flourished. In the Anglo-Saxon world with a rising bourgeois mercantile class and following in the footsteps of Locke, 'freedom' had 'negative' connotations, as a lack of restrictions. In stark contrast Hegel, as we have seen, conceives of 'freedom' as a 'positive' adherence to a communal ethic (with correspond-ing restrictions on individual liberty). We may also comment that the conception of freedom, whether 'negative' or 'positive', embodied the unfettered circumstances of privileged men. It was their rights and position that were to be guarded. Symbolically it could be said that the Enlightenment, followed by the revolutionary fervour of the late eighteenth century, stood for the revolt of the 'sons' against the 'father', whether that 'father' be the (sometimes enlightened) autocratic monarch, or the transcendent God of the male imagination.

Thus it was indeed a case of 'Liberté, Egalité, Fraternité'; women were excluded from its compass. In England Mary Astell had queried this as early as 1700 in her *Some Reflections upon Marriage*, writing in the preface to the third edition: 'If all Men are born free, how is it that all Women are born Slaves?' (Astell 1706: 1). When in France Olympe de Gouge had the audacity to insist that the 'rights of man' must necessarily included the 'rights of woman' she met with a short end at the scaffold. While not losing her head to a guillotine, her English contemporary Mary Wollstonecraft's *A Vindication of the Rights of Woman* (1792) was no more heeded. In conformity with Rousseau's precept, the Napoleonic Civil Code of 1804 recognized the rights of all citizens, but—again in accord with Rousseau's concept as to the near-ontological difference between men and women—it neatly solved the problem of women's suffrage by excluding them from citizenship. In Germany, Friedrich Schiller's *An die Freude* (*Ode to Joy*) (1785, revised 1803), written for a company of free-masons—that form of male bonding so characteristic of the age—set so triumphantly by Beethoven to music, advises 'Alle Menschen werden Brüder' ('All humans will be brothers'); a further line presuming a male speaker: 'Wer ein holdes Weib errungen' ('Who has won a splendid wife').

There did not lack the occasional remarkable woman who conceiving of the two sexes as a partnership aspired to equality with men. In Germany, Karoline, married successively to August Wilhelm Schlegel and to Friedrich Schelling, prior to these marriages had lived a singularly independent life as a revolutionary; indeed bearing a son to a French soldier. The young Hegel, who lodged for two years (1801–3) in the Schlegel household, evidently did not like what he saw. The 'Karoline' phenomenon represented a nightmare; possibly instrumental in his putting woman firmly back in her allotted place in household and family. On her death he wrote vituperously that 'a few here have enunciated the hypothesis that the Devil...fetched her' (Quoted Benhabib 1991: 140). In England there was Mary Wollstonecraft and her daughter Mary Shelley of *Frankenstein* fame. But such women were few and far between. Meanwhile men who in other spheres might well be progressive, when it came to gender relations were deeply conservative. Denying women an education in their own right, Rousseau notoriously prescribed for his Sophie an education such as would befit the needs of Émile (1762). Among thinkers whom we have considered, Schleiermacher deserves commendation. Not uncritical of his former flatmate Friedrich Schlegel's *Lucinde*, which portrayed the life of a liberated woman in terms generally considered notorious, his own relations with women were exemplary. Unafraid to be attracted to older women, he would have married Eleonore Grunow, thinking divorce permissible in the case of a marriage as unhappy as was hers. Schleiermacher's (1806) *Weihnachts-feier* (*Christmas Eve*) 'symposium' is a dialogue in which members of both sexes participate, while the 'Christ child' present is a little girl, Sophie (wisdom). Nor were the common people far from his mind: for his funeral cortège they lined the streets of Berlin.

The work from this age that was to prove seminal for the conception of human freedom and liberation as it developed from the mid-nineteenth century onwards was Hegel's early *Phänomenologie der Geist* (*Phenomenology of Spirit/Mind*) (1807). A unique and revolutionary work, it depicts, in allegorical terms, human winning of self-consciousness, whether individually or collectively. It was Hegel's profound insight, culled from Fichte, that human beings come into their own in relationship, as the other reflects us back to ourselves. In the work's most notable passage, two figures fight/struggle (*kampfen*) for the recognition of the other, with the outcome that one becomes 'master', the other 'slave'. Hegel then proceeds to find the 'split' (formerly characterized as between two) internal to the one individual. He writes: 'Consciousness has wrestled its Being-for-self out of itself and has had to make it into Being'; a Being which is then absolutized (Hegel 1977: §231). While our individual (or society) thinks that he/it has found a fixed point outside himself/itself, in actuality one part of what is an internal contradiction has been posited as external; the individual (or society) then postulating a relationship to this 'other'. 'The one is the actual world, that of self-estrangement, the other is that which spirit constructs for itself in the ether of pure consciousness, raising itself above the first.' This second, constructed, world 'is faith, in so far as faith is a flight from the actual world' (Hegel 1949: 513). In a process of 'diremption' the self consequently understands itself negatively, as worthless, by comparison with that which it has projected. Recognizing the contradiction between the contingent nature of the self and what Hegel names 'the universal', consciousness finds itself distraught (*unglücklich*).

Subsequent to Hegel's death in 1831, so-called 'left-wing' Hegelians of the next generation were to run with this. The son of a pastor, Ludwig Feuerbach was in 1841 to publish *Das Wesen des Christentums* (*The Essence of Christianity*), a reading of Christian theology in the light of such a projection-theory. Feuerbach, the Hegelian, writes: 'In the object which he contemplates, therefore, man becomes acquainted with himself; consciousness of the objective is the self-consciousness of man' (1957: 5). And he continues:

> Man—this is the mystery of religion—projects his being into objectivity [*vergegen-ständlicht sich*; makes an object of himself over against himself], and then makes himself an object to this projected image of himself thus converted into a subject; he thinks of himself not as an object to himself, but as the object of an object, of another being than himself.   (1957: 29–30)

That is, man accords to the projected God the 'subject' position, making himself into an 'object' in the eyes of this God, thereby undermining his sense of self. 'To enrich God, man must become poor; that God may be all, man must be nothing' (1957: 26). What is to be deduced from this is self-evident: man must reappropriate that which he has projected. Feuerbach is a materialist; man is to be brought down to earth. In what in German is a pun, Feuerbach declared in well-known words 'Der Mensch ist, was er isst', 'Man is, what he eats'. Once again—and now in more explicit form—the project of human liberation is understood as contingent upon the necessity of slaying God. The atheist George Eliot provided a translation for an English-speaking public.

The message was not lost on the young Marx. The self-estrangement that religion represented, so Marx concluded, mirrored a lack of social cohesion. Bruno Bauer had asked whether, given their religious position, Jews had the right to demand political emancipation. In his 'On the Jewish Question' (1843) Marx responds: 'We pose the question the other way round: Does the standpoint of *political* emancipation have the right to demand from the Jews the abolition of Judaism and from man the abolition of religion?'. Religion stands in the way of political emancipation. Marx continues that: 'Since the existence of religion is the existence of a defect, the source of this defect must be looked for in the *nature* of the state itself.' Citing the French constitution of the 1790s, the problem, he suggests, is that 'each man is . . . considered to be a self-sufficient monad', the only bond holding humankind together being that of natural necessity. 'It is a curious thing that a people which is just beginning to free itself, to tear down all the barriers between the different sections of the people and to found a political community, that such a people should solemnly proclaim the rights of egoistic man, separated from his fellow men and from the community' (Marx 1992: 216–217, 230). Further, in his 'Theses on Feuerbach' (1845), Marx comments that Feuerbach starts out from a *religious* self-alienation: 'His work consists in resolving the religious world into its secular basis.' Said Marx, the materialist Hegelian: 'But that the secular basis detaches itself from itself and establishes itself as an independent realm in the clouds can only be explained by the cleavages and self-contradictions within this secular basis.' And in famous words he concludes: 'The philosophers have only *interpreted* the world . . . ; the point is to *change* it' (Marx 1992: IV, XI). Were the contradictions of the secular world overcome religion would of itself fade away.

In retrospect it was a young man, writing in a minor European language and meeting with little comprehension among his compatriots, who most fully grasped the challenge that modernity represented to orthodox Christianity. Yet this is not entirely how one should describe Søren Kierkegaard's project, for he seems to have held a pre-modern understanding of history, making his Christian rebuttal more thinkable than it would otherwise be. Kierkegaard determined to free Christianity, restating it in terms narrower than had been necessary in a pre-Enlightenment world, in which the incompatibility of Christian presuppositions with what was now known had not been apparent. In his *Philosophical Fragments*, or *Crumbs* (1844)—the title is a dig at the preposterous nature of Hegelian philosophy—Kierkegaard sets up Enlightenment presuppositions, more specifically idealism, in the person of 'Socrates'. In such a world-view all knowledge is given *with* humanity; theirs to discover or elucidate.

Kierkegaard then proceeds to ask the hypothetical question: what would one have to say to escape these presuppositions? One must needs contend that something is *given* to humanity; that is to say, speak of revelation. I mention Kierkegaard's aberrant view of history as, in view of this, it is unclear how far he grasped the impossibility, as modernity presupposes, of such an interventionary act; or whether it was that he understood and rejected the post-Enlightenment consensus in this regard. But that modernity and the Christian claim to a particularity of revelation are mutually incompatible his book makes clear. In consequence, for Kierkegaard the Christian must relate to the claim that there has been such revelation through an act of faith, not assimilating it to knowledge.

As Kierkegaard well recognized, there runs in parallel an ethical incompatibility between Judeo-Christian presuppositions and modernity. In his book of the previous year, *Fear and Trembling* (1843), Kierkegaard pits the Abraham of the *akedah* (the story of the binding of Isaac, Genesis 22) against the Kantian/Hegelian presupposition that ethical behaviour entails conforming to the categorical imperative (or to the moral norms of human society), which is intrinsic to the human being himself (or to human society). By contrast the Judaeo-Christian tradition presupposes a transcendent God who, at least potentially, if the understanding of 'God' is not to be evacuated of all meaning, could command a man to do that which clashes with what humanity holds right. Abraham's willingness to obey God is nothing if not heteronomous—and Kant had precisely spoken sarcastically of Abraham's delusion. What makes Kierkegaard's writing the more interesting is that, with a part of himself, he is a child of his age. Notably in his concept of the self Kierkegaard insists that it is not that a self is, in predetermined fashion, drawn to God, but that the self must become itself in and with the drawing. Living in a pre-Enlightenment age it had not occurred to Luther (with whose thought Kierkegaard's otherwise holds so much in common) to have such emphases.

A yet further twist to the story we have told came in the early twentieth century with the work of Sigmund Freud. In his *The Future of an Illusion* (1927) Freud, too, surmises that the concept of God is a projection, in his case a wish-fulfilment grounded in the human father. Exploring this further in *Civilisation and Its Discontents* (1930) Freud allows that such a projection may serve to save people from neurosis. But this does not change the fact that religion is 'a state of psychical infantilism' (Freud 1961: 32). That evasion which is religion is thus false comfort, inhibiting human maturity. Not without sarcasm Freud writes:

> If the believer finally sees himself obliged to speak of God's 'inscrutable decrees', he is admitting that all that is left to him as a last possible consolation and source of pleasure in his suffering is an unconditional submission. And if he is prepared for that, he could probably have spared himself the *détour* he has made.   (Freud 1961: 32)

Returning again in his final year to the theme of religion in his *Moses and Monotheism* (1938), Freud pursues strange musings as to the existence of a collective memory of the 'murder' of a primeval Father by the sons to acquire access to his women. (Notice, incidentally, the conjecture that religion is the product of male desire.) Standing in a tradition that reaches back to Hegel, for Freud likewise the self is not unitary in nature. It is the tension between the super-ego (the seat of conscience, Kant's legislative reason), and an ego that wills otherwise, that gives rise to disquiet, and thus also to the projection which is religion. In Freud's case, while there may be no resolution, what freedom we may attain to is gained through self-understanding as we bring to light our conflicting drives and desires.

Without much exaggeration it could be said that, in terms of our present consideration, the watershed that was the First World War found its reflection as follows. Whereas in the period stretching from the Enlightenment to the early twentieth century man had vied with God, seeing his freedom and emancipation to be won at the expense of God, subsequent to the Great War for the most part any idea of God is simply absent from the scene. It must be an interesting question as to how far this development owed not simply to the trauma that Europeans had undergone but to social change. The 'God' whom the thinkers whom we have considered sought to slay was nothing if not the projection of the father in patriarchal society; in particular that of the nineteenth-century German *paterfamilias*—a transcendent, Hebraic, wilful, anthropomorphically conceived, God. It is notable that Kant, Fichte, Hegel, Feuerbach, Marx, Freud, and also Nietzsche without exception came from either a Jewish or a Lutheran background. Luther is of course profoundly Hebraic, setting this world of thought over-against the Latin and classical-derived, humanistic, world of Catholicism. It is this God, which these men, sought to slay to win their freedom. (Whether the 'death' of such a God rules out the possibility of a spirituality, such as Schleiermacher sought to develop, is a pregnant question we have yet to remark upon.)

By contrast with these men, the existentialists and phenomenologists of the twentieth century (if not Catholic) live in a vacant world. Meanwhile Protestant Christianity, notably as represented by the dialectical theology of Karl Barth and his disciples, in seeking the fount of theology in revelation built substantially on the heritage of Kierkegaard. Of Catholicism one might well contend that, the practical reforms of Vatican II notwithstanding, it has to this day failed to fully comprehend, let alone come to terms with, the dilemma with which Continental Protestantism has contended since the Enlightenment. Namely that, in a post-Newtonian world of cause and effect, the claim that there has been a particularity of revelation—such as that on which the Abrahamic religions are predicated—must be ruled out of court. The major thinker who, in the twentieth century, could be read as having sought a way to speak of a kind of 'spirituality' outside the Christian box (immanent, not based on revelation) is Martin Heidegger. Retaining Catholic sensibilities as to the translucence of a world that opens out onto a wider reality, the one-time Catholic seminarian who became a fine Luther scholar sought to integrate strongly Lutheran themes as to the character of human existence, while transposing the whole into a post-Christian context.

From the 1920s until well into 1960s it was the philosophical movement coined 'existentialism' which held centre stage, seeming to speak to the condition of humanity.

The nature of human freedom and responsibility proved a major theme in what were untoward circumstances. In his ground-breaking work *Sein und Zeit* (*Being and Time*) (1927) Heidegger, in the context of a phenomenological description of 'being in the world', described human *Verfallenheit*, 'fallenness', and pursued the concept of *Eigentlichkeit*, literally a coming to 'own' oneself as a discrete individual, normally rendered in English as 'authenticity'. But it was Jean-Paul Sartre who, in the midst of occupied France in 1943, in his *L'Être et le néant* (*Being and Nothingness*), as also subsequently elsewhere, majored on the question of 'choice', the corollary of human freedom, exercised in what for him was a Godless world.

Deeply Kantian, for Sartre freedom is of the very essence of the human; in his case the consequence of the fact that man is not simply inert (*en soi*) but in himself a project (*pour soi*)—terms taken, and adapted, from Hegel. Sartre is an atheist on account of the fact that (yet once again) he thinks the concept of God a projection; in his case of a desire for the fullness that a certain completion would represent. Such completion is however a state to which a human being can by definition never attain, tossed as he is between an out-going desire to fill his 'nothingness' (what it is to be *pour-soi*) and the fact that, were he ever to come to rest, he would be no more than an inanimate object (what it is to be *en-soi*). Human unrest is thus, in Sartre's case also, the consequence of a human bifurcation which is the source of both creativity and despair. As he tells us in the closing lines of *Being and Nothingness* (1943): 'A freedom which wills itself freedom is in fact a being-which-is-not-what-it-is and which-is-what-it-is-not, and which chooses as the ideal of being, being-what-it-is-not and not-being-what-it-is.' In other words: 'Man is a useless passion' (Sartre 1969: 627, 615).

What is striking about Sartre's position is that—as he explored in a public lecture subsequently published as *L'existentialisme est un humanisme* (*Existentialism and Humanism*) (1946)—far from 'freedom' in a world without God being a licence for indulgence, man is under the strictest obligation to adhere to (Kantian) moral imperatives. The difference between the two men lies in this. In the case of Kant, while it is incumbent on one to do what is right irrespective of the consequences, that good is yet chosen within the context of a thought-world in which one postulates that one's good acts conform to the nature of reality; that is to say, in which there exists a *summum bonum*, such that effort will finally be commensurately rewarded. By contrast, in the Sartrean universe not only has it become radically uncertain what the right choice may be, but the world in which one acts is no longer possessed of an ordered framework; a much more Spartan doctrine.

Thus Sartre tells of a young man who had sought his counsel as to whether he should seek to escape France and join the Free French in Britain, or remain with an elderly mother who lived only for him. Throwing him back on his own resources, but also showing him the greatness and the tragedy of what it is to be human, Sartre responded: 'You are free, therefore choose' (Sartre, 1973: 38). The young man's dilemma is incapable of resolution through Kantian universalizing, nor is it clarified by consequentialist consideration of his case—for how should one weigh the imponderable merit of embarking on a course, which might never lead to significant action of benefit to humanity, as against the only too present and pressing need of the mother? Likewise in Camus's novel *The Plague* (1947), finding himself in a world in which God is either ineffective or from which He is notably absent, and lacking any belief in recompense hereafter, the hero Dr Rieux simply does what is his duty.

An interesting engagement with existentialism, meriting consideration from a Christian perspective, is the thought of Rudolf Bultmann. A one-time colleague of Heidegger's on the faculty at Marburg, Bultmann translates the Lutheran dialectic, that we are *simul justus et peccator* (at once just and sinner) into the disparity between, on the one hand, living from a freely-given future and, on the other, the attempt to secure ourselves by reference to our past. As in the case of Luther, for Bultmann there can be no *habitus*, no way of building a future on the past, but only a purely formal continuity of person. As Bultmann puts it, provocatively, but in conformity with the structure of Lutheran thought, I relate to my past as that for which I must be forgiven. 'Future' and 'God' become synonymous as I live 'from' the future; as indeed Luther believes that we live 'from' God's acceptance of us, in what has been termed 'inverted existence'. Each day anew I am faced with the responsibility and the challenge of choosing what it is that I shall be and do. Bultmann, who would be Christian not Pelagian, conceives that it is the preaching of the resurrection of the one who died on the cross (a preaching which in itself becomes a kind of eschatological act), that delivers us into the possibility of living in faith 'from' this future, a deliverance which issues (as in Lutheranism generally) in being fully present in the service of the world.

Thus does Bultmann attempt to solve the problem that, since the Enlightenment, has plagued Continental Protestantism. While the death of Christ is a worldly event (an event of *Diesseits*) taking place in normal secular history (*Historie*), the resurrection is a proleptic event, coming from the future (*Jenseits*), an event of *Geschichte*; which in Bultmann's hands becomes the realm of meaning, to which in faith the Christian relates. While it is the resurrection of the one who died on the cross that is preached (thus tying this preaching to a particular event in history), there is no suggestion of any physical resurrection which, given the causal regularity of nature and of history, would be unthinkable. As in Kierkegaard's case, faith consists in a leap across a chasm to a realm that has been disentangled from a world in which these claims can find no basis. But to the person who doubts that the preaching of the resurrection of this man in fact so delivers one into such a freedom there lacks any answer.

It can be no chance that it was a woman, Simone de Beauvoir, the lifelong companion of Sartre, in many ways herself an existentialist, who however, challenged the Sartrean notion of radical freedom. De Beauvoir found herself strung out between, on the one hand, the aspiration that woman should, like man, become free (*pour soi*), for to rest in the complicity of being thing-like (the object that the male gaze makes of her) is simply bad faith (*mauvais fois*); while on the other hand recognizing that the circumstances in which a human life (more particularly a woman's life) is lived out, often lies outside a person's control. It was Rousseau who declared—in words that were to become programmatic for the French philosophical tradition of a free interiority—that, were he to be imprisoned in the Bastille, he would paint a picture of liberty. Sartre likewise flaunts interior freedom. But de Beauvoir knows that we are socially conditioned; that our freedom is taken from us as, in what is a 'false consciousness', we take on board the view of our selves that others reflect back to us. As she puts it in her ground-breaking work *Le Deuxième sexe* (*The Second Sex*) (1949): 'One is not born, but rather becomes, a woman' (de Beauvoir 1983: 295).

Hence de Beauvoir was riveted by Hegel's discussion of the acquisition of self-consciousness in the parable of the master and the slave. Of woman she writes: 'She is defined and differentiated with reference to man and not he with reference to her. She is the incidental, the inessential as opposed to the essential. He is the Subject, he is the Absolute—she is the Other.' Yet woman's situation is also not to be compared with that of the slave. For theoretically at least the slave can turn things around; as does indeed Hegel's slave as the parable unfolds. By contrast the problem for woman is that she is denied any kind of recognition, even as the defeated partner in what is a reciprocal relationship. Rather has she lain outside representation. Of women de Beauvoir can say: 'They have no past, no history, no religion of their own.' There is but one reality, as woman sees both the world and herself through the eyes of the master. Women 'dream through the dreams of men' (de Beauvoir 1983: 16, 19, 174).

In the mid-twentieth century the themes of freedom and human liberation were furthermore central to the thinking of a loose group of intellectuals who held in common that they were Jewish refugees from Nazi Germany; among their number Max Horkheimer, Theodor Adorno, Erich Fromm, Hannah Arendt, and Ernst Bloch. Coming from a Hegelian, Marxist background, though in Arendt's case also influenced by the thought of Heidegger, and in many cases cognizant of a psychoanalytic perspective, they sought to understand human beings with reference to their social context. The question that confronted them alike was how it could be that the country whose thinkers had proclaimed enlightenment from the rooftops could surrender to the despair of totalitarianism. As Adorno and Horkheimer comment in their famed, they discovered *Dialektik der Aufklärung* (*Dialectic of Enlightenment*) (1944) they had set [themselves] nothing less than the discovery of why mankind, instead of entering into a truly human condition, is sinking into a new kind of barbarism' (Adorno and Horkheimer 1997: p. xi). Whence had there arisen what Fromm so aptly named the 'fear' of freedom? (Fromm, 2001 [1941]).

Adorno and Horkheimer's answer to this question is, in part, that the Enlightenment itself must be judged otherwise than has commonly been the case. From Francis Bacon onwards, the movement was marked by an instrumental rationality, exercised by a rising male bourgeoisie who chose to subdue 'woman' and 'nature' (often equating the two) as 'other' to itself. If truth were told, the much-vaunted 'freedom', raised to an abstract quality of which the human person was supposedly possessed, had not issued in rights for anyone but themselves. If 'enlightenment' stood for a 'disenchantment' (as Max Weber named it) with a mythological world, it underestimated values present in the past social order and indeed (such is their thesis) was in fascism to descend into a new 'mythology'. Abjuring freedom, human beings had chosen rather conformity and submission to domination. Meanwhile technological progress had led to what Marx would have called 'alienation' from the material conditions of capitalist society. In part insightful, the problems with this book are considerable: the present author is not alone in finding it to make far-reaching generalizations when it had been better to concentrate on the peculiar circumstances pertaining in Germany and, to a lesser extent, in other European nations.

Adorno's later writing, in particular his masterly (if obscure) *Negative Dialektik* (*Negative Dialectics*) (1966) may be thought prescient to the theme of human liberation in our present and future society. Doubtless spurred on by his own experience as an 'outsider', and aghast at what could befall European Jewry, it is for Adorno a new 'categorical imperative' that human beings should 'so arrange their thought and action that Auschwitz would not repeat itself'. This necessitates what he terms a 'negative' dialectic; namely that instead of assimilating the other to self, in what he terms identity thinking (*Einheitsdenken*), the subject should grant the other precedence (*Vorrang*), honouring that other in its difference from self. For all that Hegel or Fichte grant that the self only achieves self-consciousness through the other, for Adorno idealism remains a philosophy in which the subject assimilates the object. Dialectics, he writes, consists in a 'persistent awareness of non-identity' (Adorno 1966: 365 and 5; my translations). Adorno's thought is utopian (here one thinks of his Marxist heritage), in that the call for such a negative dialectic presupposes a society riven by fundamental antagonisms. When there arrives what he names a state of 'reconciliation' its work will have been accomplished. This is clearly a political philosophy of practical import for our present conduct.

A further thinker whose work is apposite to our present situation is Arendt. For Arendt, freedom is a social concept, intimately connected with speech and action. Accordingly she finds herself at odds with much past thinking, pointing out that the association of freedom with the individual will, unknown to the ancient classical world, first came about with St Paul, followed by Augustine, as these men castigated themselves as sinners unable to do the good that they would. Arendt finds it to have had fatal consequences; the 'I-will', she writes, has become 'so power-thirsty'. Making negative reference to Rousseau, who derives sovereignty from the will, she objects that: 'If men wish to be free, it is precisely sovereignty they must renounce.' But, equally, Arendt finds herself ranged against the liberal tradition in which freedom is defined negatively as '[beginning] where men have left the realm of political life inhabited by the many'. For Arendt: 'We become aware of freedom or its opposite in our intercourse with others, not in the intercourse with ourselves' (Arendt 1954: 163, 165, 157, 148). Participation in the world of communicative and disclosive speech, the world of intersubjectivity, will involve suffering contradiction; but it is precisely this that enables our becoming unique selves.

Arendt develops what she calls a notion of 'natality', of beginning. 'Because he *is* a beginning, man can begin; to be human and to be free are one and the same. God created man in order to introduce into the world the faculty of beginning: freedom.' (Arendt 1954: 167). To be 'free' is moreover to act: 'To insert one's self into the world and begin a story of one's own', which demands courage (Arendt 1998: 186). Freedom is then not simply an inward sentiment but a political notion, requiring a public space in which a plurality of voices is not simply tolerated but encouraged. The life of the Athenian polis—her ideal situation—represented 'a kind of theatre where freedom could appear': nourished by others, human freedom and individuality could come forth (Arendt 1954: 154). Such a philosophy may be thought a pertinent comment on Arendt's native Germany, in which the right to freely express one's opinion in public space had so often been restricted and which had now descended into an abject totalitarianism in which freedom of speech and association were again disallowed.

It could thus be said that, in the twentieth century, it became ever clearer that if there was something grand about the bursting into flower of the notion of freedom and of human liberation in the European Enlightenment and its offspring the American Revolution, there was also something disingenuous about it. Slaying the father that they might have entitlement, the sons had taken care to pull the ladder up behind them. One whose thought was as seminal for political modernity as John Locke had categorized women as property; Rousseau denied them citizenship; Kant would have laughed at the idea of their enfranchisement. In these years helpless slaves in ever greater numbers were carted to the new world; a world which, destroying the native culture, white Europeans would themselves 'civilize'. The American James Campbell writes:

> I have an additional hunch about the failure of American political thinkers to conceptualize further the revolutionary experience. It is that we gave up thinking about the revolution because we knew that to do so was an exercise in delusion. It was an exercise in delusion, if not hypocrisy, because all that we said about equality, life, liberty, public happiness, freedom, the right of assembly, participation, and the other noble principles applied in fact only to the white man, not to the majority of persons in this country, who at that time were red, or to a sizable minority who were black and in chains.
>
> In a word, our racism prevented us from pursuing the profound implications of our own revolution. Our thinkers sensed this, and to avoid the issue, turned to other matters.   (Campbell 1970: 18)

A possible response to such a critique is, of course, that what is of significance is that principles were enunciated in the Enlightenment, the application of which has included an ever widening circle of persons; first all males irrespective of property qualifications, then Black males, and finally women. The order of this emancipation is not without significance, as women have been cast by men as the paradigmatic 'other'. But such a response falls short. Unless those now granted their rights are to be no more than honorary white males, the very eclecticism of persons now recognized in their full humanity must necessitate a shift in thinking. Since the ancient world when Aristotle understood *philia* as a brotherly love enabled through the fact that each saw in each another 'I', to the acclaimed fraternité of the Enlightenment and its accompanying revolutions, political society has been built on an assumed likeness. What we must now create is much more demanding: a society in which difference is both acknowledged and celebrated; what the political philosopher and feminist theorist Iris Marion Young terms a 'politics of difference' (Young 1990).

That no one shall be discriminated against on grounds of gender, race, or sexual orientation has become what we may call a 'social transcendental', an ideal with reference to which we legislate and judge. While a formal framework of laws disallowing discrimination serves an educative function and undergirds society, that in itself will not suffice to create conditions in which plurality is fostered. What is further required is a revamped praxis and renewed values.

Of recent years, some of the most interesting work here, across a range of disciplines, has been accomplished by women; perhaps unsurprisingly, given that they have been situated as outsiders. Thus the contemporary political theorist Seyla Benhabib finds herself astonished at Arendt's persistent denial of the women's issue, remarking that 'her inability to link together the exclusion of women's politics and this agonistic and male-dominated conception of public space . . . is astounding'. (One might well say that Arendt's thought is, precisely, such a fine expression of that which feminist women seek to articulate.) As have many others, Benhabib draws attention to the isolated notion of the self presupposed in early modern thought: 'The self whom Hume stumbles upon while ruminating in his consciousness or the Kantian "I" that accompanies all my representations is not the self in the human community, the acting or interacting self, but the self *qua* thinker, *qua* subject of consciousness withdrawn from the world.' By contrast, she believes: 'One needs principles, institutions and procedures to enable articulation of the voice of "others".' Following Adorno she advocates 'the model of a moral conversation in which the capacity to reverse perspectives, that is, the willingness to reason from the other's point of view, and the sensitivity to hear their voice is paramount' (Benhabib 1992: 115, n. 13, 127, 8).

Feminist academics have sought to valorize a social self; a self not simply formed within relationship, but one which thrives within the context of what the psychoanalyst and political theorist Jessica Benjamin calls 'the dance of mutual recognition' that takes place in the 'space in-between' of intersubjective relations (Benjamin 1988: 130). Such a person understands herself as set free *within* relationships, as she for her part seeks to nourish the other's self-realization. Such a notion of 'freedom' stands in stark contrast to a 'negative' concept of freedom, in which a person considers himself 'free' in so far as he is independent of the web of human relationships with its inexorable dependencies. Nor does it compare with the attempt to achieve recognition through a Hegelian agonistic struggle; nor with Fichte's knowing of the other through the fact that he limits us; nor again Sartre's argument against solipsism, that the other is known through his presence within us as 'shame'. It is of course the case that a Hegel or a Marx hope for a very different outcome; that Kant, likewise, seeks a realm in which persons treat one another as ends and not simply as means. But it must be remarked upon that major changes in the outward form of society, such as in the means of production, have not of themselves brought about true liberation. Hence the feminist slogan that 'the personal is political'. If there is to be a true flowering of freedom on the part of those who have been damaged, it will require, on the part of those who have been advantaged, a practicing of the maieutic arts of listening and receptivity, that they may put themselves in the other's shoes.

It would seem self-evidently the case that the virtues of which we are here speaking make an extraordinarily bad fit with theology as we have known it. Not least has 'God' Himself been cast as the incarnation of what must be the apogee of the male's wildest imagination as to what it is to be 'free': one and alone, all-sufficient (possessed of aseity), omnipotent, having the first word and the last. Indeed, transcendent monotheism in any form would seem singularly inapposite, its singularity and implied separation standing in stark contrast to the eclecticism and interrelational equality that our society values. Recognizing that the male God has acted as a transcendental which has allowed of men's self-actualization, feminist thinkers have questioned whether it may not be that women are in need of a 'transcendental'; an image which, if the projection of human subjectivity, acts through its very articulation as a transformative ideal. Thus the Feuerbachian Luce Irigaray has proposed that, in place of the dichotomy that we have known in which, given God-like powers, man is associated with 'the spiritual' while woman is associated with the material, we need a sensible or embodied transcendental which acknowledges two sexes in their interrelational equality.

As in Schleiermacher's revolutionary age it would seem that, through the profound revolution in normative ideals that we have undergone, the plank has been kicked from under religion as we have inherited it. A religion of the father and the sons, or the Father and the Son, which cast woman as the 'other', will be seen as politically problematic. Such ideologies have been instrumental in legitimizing social hierarchy, in particular (given their gendered nature) gender hierarchy. Any conception of God must needs be non-anthropomorphic and thereby gender inclusive. Such a revolution is not something that the Abrahamic religions can undergo, given their claims to a historical particularity of revelation which serves to root them in the outlook and symbolism of a past society. But (as I have argued elsewhere) a notion of God as not foreign to us but rather as moving between us fits well with an understanding of the self as having porous ego boundaries and a praxis which focuses on attending. Not least is Schleiermacher's thought suggestive here.

If, as Rosa Luxemburg recognized, the measure of the presence of freedom is whether the one who *thinks* differently has freedom, we must say that today the litmus test as to the presence of 'freedom' has become whether the one who is otherwise *embodied* than white, male, and heterosexual is granted the recognition and respect that alone will allow her or him to flourish. As post-Hegelian thought has recognized, we are ourselves only genuinely free when the other be accorded their full humanity. An honouring of the eclecticism of humanity will entail that inherited myths are judged unacceptably partial. But it does not follow that we cannot find another way to articulate an understanding of that which is God. If such a conception is both commensurate with our ethics and thinkable in terms of a post-Enlightenment epistemology, theology will enter into its maturity. Or will it be that, while one part of humanity reverts to pre-Enlightenment tribal Gods who demand allegiance and fetishistic rituals, the rest of us must make do with what is little more than a materialistic secularity? They are stark choices that lie before us.

REFERENCES

Adorno, Theodor (1990 [1966]). *Negative Dialektics*, trans. E. B. Ashton (London: Routledge).
——and Horkheimer, Max (1997 [1944]). *Dialectic of Enlightenment*, trans. J. Cumming (London and New York: Verso).
Arendt, Hannah (1954). 'What is Freedom', *Between Past and Future: Six Exercises in Political Thought*. (London: Faber & Faber).
——(1998). *The Human Condition*. (Chicago and London: University of Chicago Press).
Astell, Mary (1706). 'Preface', *Some Reflections on Marriage*, 3rd edn. (London: printed for R. Wilkin).
Benhabib, Seyla (1991). 'On Hegel, Women and Irony', in M. L. Shanley and C. Pateman (eds), *Feminist Interpretations and Political Theory*. (Cambridge: Polity Press).
——(1992). *Situating the Self: Gender, Community and Postmodernism in Contemporary Ethics*. (Cambridge: Polity Press).
Benjamin, Jessica (1988). *The Bonds of Love: Psychoanalysis, Feminism and the Problem of Domination*. (New York: Pantheon).
Campbell, James (1970). *Hannah Arendt Prophet for our Time*, Detroit Industrial Mission Pamphlet, 18 (http://www.religion-online.org/showchapter.asp?title=2074&C=1913).
De Beauvoir, Simone (1983 [1949]). *The Second Sex*, trans. H. M. Parchley (Harmondsworth: Penguin).
Feuerbach, Ludwig. (1957 [1841]). *The Essence of Christianity*, trans. G. Eliot (New York: Harper Torchbooks).
Freud, Sigmund (1961 [1930]). *Civilisation and Its Discontents*, trans. J. Strachley (New York and London: W. W. Norton).
Fromm, Erich (2001 [1942]). *The Fear of Freedom*. (London and New York: Routledge).
Hampson, D. (2001). *Christian Contradictions: The Structures of Lutheran and Catholic Thought*. (Cambridge: Cambridge University Press).
Hegel, G. W. F (1948 [1795]). 'The Positivity of the Christian Religion'; 'The Spirit of Christianity and its Fate' [1799], in trans. T. M. Knox, *Hegel's Early Theological Writings* (Chicago: University of Chicago Press).
——(1949 [1807]). *The Phenomenology of Mind*, trans. J. B. Baillie (London: Allen & Unwin);
——(1977 [1807]). *The Phenomenology of Spirit*, trans. A.V. Miller (Oxford, New York, Toronto, and Melbourne: Oxford University Press).
——1984). *The Letters*, trans. Clark Butler and Christiane Seiler (quoted by Benhabib 1991) (Bloomington, IN: Indiana University Press).
Kant, Immanuel (1996 [1784]) 'What is Enlightenment?', in *Practical Philosophy*, ed. and trans. M. J. Gregor and A. Wood (Cambridge: Cambridge University Press).
——(1960 [1793]). *Religion within the Limits of Reason Alone*, trans. T. M. Greene and H. H. Hudson (New York: Harper Torchbooks).
Luxemburg, Rosa (1983 [1920]). 'Die russische Revolution: Eine kritische Würdigung', *Gesammelte Werke*. (Berlin: Dietz).
Marx, Karl (1992). 'On the Jewish Question' [1843] and 'Theses on Feuerbach' [1845], in *Karl Marx: Early Writings*, trans. R. Livingstone and G. Benton (Harmondsworth: Penguin).
Sartre, Jean-Paul (1969). *Being and Nothingness: An Essay on Phenomenological Ontology*, trans. H. Barnes (London: Routledge & Kegan Paul).
——(1973). *Existentialism and Humanism*, trans. P. Mairet (London: Methuen, 1973).

Schleiermacher, Friedrich (1928 [1821/2]). *The Christian Faith*, ed. H. R. Mackintosh and
J. S. Stewart (Edinburgh: T & T Clark).
——(1958 [1799]). *Friedrich Schleiermacher on Religion: Speeches to its Cultured Despisers*,
trans. J. Oman (New York: Harper and Row).
Young, Iris Marion (1990 [1986]). 'The Ideal of Community and the Politics of Difference', in
L. J. Nicholson (ed.), *Feminism, Postmodernism* (New York and London: Routledge).

Suggested Reading

Arendt (1954).
Berlin, Isaiah (1969 [1958]). 'Two Concepts of Liberty', in *Four Essays on Liberty*. (Oxford:
Oxford University Press).
Bultmann, Rudolf (1962). *History and Eschatology: The Presence of Eternity*. (New York and
Evanston: Harper Torchbooks).
De Beauvoir (1983 [1949]).
Feuerbach (1957 [1841]).
Hegel (1977 [1807]).
Kant, Immanuel (1956 [1788]).*Critique of Practical Reason* ('Second' *Critique*), trans. L. White
Beck (Indianapolis and New York: The Bobbs-Merrill).
——(1985 [1784]).
——(1998 [1793]). *Religion within the Boundaries of Mere Reason*, trans. A. Wood (Cam-
bridge University Press).
Luther, Martin (1961 [1520]). 'The Freedom of a Christian', in ed. J. Dillenberger, *Martin
Luther: Selections from His Writings*. (Garden City, New York: Doubleday Anchor).
Sartre, Jean-Paul (1973). *Existentialism and Humanism*, trans. P. Mairet (London: Methuen).
Schleiermacher, Friedrich (1988 [1799]). *On Religion: Speeches to its Cultured Despisers*, trans.
Richard Crouter (Cambridge: Cambridge University Press).

PART II

THE HUMAN CONDITION

CHAPTER 7

....

WORK AND LABOUR

....

JOHN HUGHES

THE 'question of labour' is a peculiarly modern one, describing a set of connected concerns, which arose in Europe through the processes of the industrial revolutions of the eighteenth and nineteenth centuries. The rapid changes in working conditions, due to new technologies, which encouraged mechanization and urbanization, led to the foregrounding of this question of labour, particularly in the thought of radical and progressive figures in Britain, France, and Germany. For these thinkers, traditional ways of thinking about human work were too aristocratic and agrarian to make sense of the new realities of work, while these realities, the conditions of the newly emergent 'working classes', were the key to the future of Europe. Initially this debate happened largely outside of specifically theological discourse and was often quite anti-theological in its desire to cast off more traditional ways of thinking (even if it was still shaped by earlier theological ideas). However, by the end of the nineteenth century, theologians had begun to engage directly with the question of labour, which, with the rise of Marxism in the East, became a key philosophical concern in the early and mid-twentieth century. This theological engagement may be thought to have reached its high point in the various activities of liberation theologians, industrial missions, and Christian labour movements, and the development of normative principles for the ethics of work by ecclesiastical reports and other teaching documents. The discussion of labour in theological circles has quietened somewhat in the last twenty years, which some would attribute to the apparent triumph of capitalism since the fall of Communism in the USSR and the decline of manufacturing in the 'post-industrial' west. However, arguably, globalization and the ever-increasing virtualization of economic activity in contemporary capitalism can be seen as a fulfilment rather than refutation of some of the most important elements of the nineteenth-century 'critiques' of labour, which are thus as relevant today as ever. Rather than confining myself to the narrowly and self-consciously theological, I will be drawing out some of the theological ideas implicit in or raised by the more mainstream approaches to the question of labour, before considering some of the explicitly theological responses. The discussion will be structured around the three headings of 'Utility', 'Politics', and 'Ontology'.

I. Utility: Political Economy and 'Natural' Labour

The British political economists of the late eighteenth and early nineteenth centuries, such as Adam Smith (1723–90), David Ricardo (1772–1823), Jeremy Bentham (1748–1832), Thomas Malthus (1766–1834), James Mill (1773–1836), and John Stuart Mill (1806–73), were the first significant modern theorists of labour. In differing ways, they shared a theory of labour as the principle source of the value of things, based upon a model of human labour in the supposed 'state of nature'. Behind them stood the 'labour theory of property and value' developed by John Locke in his *Two Treatises of Government* (1690). For medieval Christian thought, as can be seen for example in Thomas Aquinas (ST IIa IIae, q. 66, a. 2), it was generally believed that *communal* ownership is natural and aligned with the use of things, while private ownership is secondary, concerns the management of things, and is only established by positive human law. Locke introduced a radically new way of thinking centred on a theory of labour, for which private property is something natural, linked with the appropriative usage of things. Locke argued that

> every Man has a *Property* in his own *Person* . . . . The *Labour* of his Body, and the *Work* of his Hands, we may say, are properly his. Whatsoever then he removes out of the State that Nature hath provided, and left it in, he hath mixed his *Labour* with, and joyned to it something that is his own, and thereby makes it his *Property*. (Locke 1988: II, 27)

Locke's repeated references to the situation in the New World ('Thus in the beginning all the World was *America*' (Locke 1988: II, 49)) indicate that it is the contrast between property rights in the Old World and the apparent lack of any formal division of ownership in the Native American societies which leads him to conceive of labour, in terms of appropriation-for-use, as the 'primitive' origin of ownership. Locke goes on to suggest that labour is not merely the origin of private ownership, but also, more radically, the origin of *value*: 'For 'tis *Labour* indeed that *puts the difference of value on every thing*' (Locke 1988: II, 40). While he admits that there may be some other element to value, with most things he claims it will be less than one hundredth part of that value. Locke's theory of labour as oriented to use and the principle natural source of value is still framed in the traditional Christian context of reflection on the divine command and cursing of work in the story of Adam and Eve, but it is these other novel elements which make it particularly suited to the rising bourgeoisie, and which will be taken up without the theological context by the political economists. On the one hand this theory of labour has the radical quality of challenging all inherited and unequal claims to ownership, because if labour is the source of value then the world belongs to the 'use of the industrious and rational' not the idle (Locke 1988: II, 34). On the other hand, it also reflects the bourgeois desire for expansionist appropriation of supposedly 'idle' land, whether the enclosure of common land in England or the claiming of 'virgin' land in the New World. Beyond this, it embodies an elevation of individualistic private ownership over common ownership, as something more fundamental and natural, rather than merely artificial and secondary. Even more crucially, the claim that labour is the principle source of value has a curious twofold effect, which is particularly significant from a theological perspective: value is at one and the same time immanentized and paradoxically rendered pre-cultural. The value of things is no longer primarily something to be discovered, given by God in the ungraspable mysterious teleology of all things which establishes their right relations; rather it is something arbitrarily 'put into' things by human labour. Yet this sense of value as entirely man-made does not issue in a sense of the cultural mediation of value. Rather because this is presented in the context of the fictional pre-cultural 'state of nature', value is not something negotiated by the cultural processes of exchange. Instead the 'natural' processes of labour and consumption aim to provide an apparently fixed, universal, quantifiable, and morally neutral measure of the 'value' of things. Qualitative distinctions are flattened into one common quantitative scale. The Lockean theory of labour thus contributes to an anti-theological immanentizing and naturalizing of value, which will find its fullest expression in utilitarianism and free market economics. Labour is reduced to a matter of mere utility, an expression of our animal necessities.

With Adam Smith's *The Wealth of Nations* (1776), Locke's revolutionary theory of labour found its way into the heart of the founding text of political economy, which was also the birth of classical economics as a modern, ostensibly neutral, descriptive 'science'. 'Labour' says Smith, the Professor of Moral Philosophy and friend of David Hume, 'is the real measure of the exchangeable value of all commodities . . . Labour was the first price, the original purchase-money that was paid for all things' (Smith 1991: 26). Smith qualifies this account of the state of nature somewhat when it comes to modern civil society where value in exchange, or 'price', consists of wages, profit, and rent, but labour in the state of nature remains foundational for him. As for the later political economists, more complex civil societies are viewed as arising out of the state of nature for purely rational reasons of efficiency, such as increasing the capacity for production and consumption through the division of labour. The division of labour is celebrated not as in classical authors for its ability to bind humans together through their diverse needs, but rather through its capacity to increase productivity. The financial speculator David Ricardo, in his *On the Principles of Political Economy and Taxation* (1817), continued this way of thinking, insisting that 'The value of a commodity . . . depends on the relative quantity of labour which is necessary for its production'. With Jeremy Bentham this emphasis on labour and production as the source of value shifts to a focus on utility as consumption, although this is now conceived not in terms of the right use of things, according to a received teleological perspective, but the immanent, naturalized and self-justifying utility of pleasure or pain.

Criticisms: The Neglect of the Soul, Morality, and History

This labour theory developed by the political economists took various forms, but all of its proponents shared an immanentizing, naturalist perspective, viewing labour as an essentially morally neutral, quantifiable force, on the model of Newtonian physics. From this they manifest a sympathy for laissez faire economics as leaving these forces to balance themselves out without intervention. These views were not without significant theological opposition, for their apparent 'egoism' and 'materialism', from the Cambridge Platonists, through William Law and Bishop George Horne's 'Letter to Adam Smith', to Samuel Taylor Coleridge's Platonic-Kantian rejection of 'corpuscularism'. Yet it should be recognized that in addition to Hobbes and Locke, there were other Christian thinkers who paved the way for political economy, such as Dean Josiah Tucker of Gloucester, and many who wholeheartedly embraced it. The most notable of these was Thomas Malthus, a Church of England priest and the first professor of political economy, who rejected the perfectibilism of other Enlightenment figures while providing a theological gloss upon the egoism and agonism of political economy in terms of sin and theodicy: 'If Locke's idea be just, and there is great reason to think that it is, evil seems to be necessary to create exertion; and exertion seems evidently necessary to create mind' (Malthus 1993: 145).

Beyond theological opposition, the most penetrating criticisms of the political economists concerned their neglect of the element of historical contingency in the organization of labour and exchange so that bourgeois society and economy is made to seem the most superior and rational system. The desire to discover a rational science of political economy, comparable to the natural sciences, led to a neglect of the cultural and moral elements which shape the decisions as to what to produce and what to consume, making economics seem like a science of necessity. It was Marx who, following the more historical methods of German Idealism, made the claim that it is precisely because humans are *homo faber* that our socio-economic life has a history and is never just 'natural'. Arguably however, as we shall see later, even Marx held to a Whiggish naturalized view of history as having its own single rational immanent necessity which could be scientifically described. In this sense, it is perhaps Max Weber (1864–1920) whose greater emphasis on the sheer historical contingency of culture in shaping patterns of economics provided the more penetrating analysis of the relationship of political economy to modern capitalism. Weber's account in *The Protestant Ethic and the Spirit of Capitalism* famously linked the spirit of modern capitalism to specifically religious causes in the puritan ethos of work as proof of one's election combined with suspicion of luxury and consumption: 'Labour came to be considered in itself the end of life, ordained as such by God' (Weber 2001: 105). Far from being rooted in greed and gambling, specifically *modern* capitalism, according to Weber, derives from an ascetic and highly rationalized work ethos: 'Now [Christian asceticism] strode into the market place of life, slammed the door of the monastery behind it, and undertook to penetrate just that daily routine of life with its methodicalness' (Weber 2001: 101). Weber also drew attention to how the anti-traditionalism and disenchantment of the world (*Entzauberung der Welt*) in Puritanism contributed to the pursuit of profit becoming the end in itself, sundered from traditional accounts of human flourishing or of the intrinsic and just value of things. 'The radical elimination of magic from the world', he claimed 'allowed no other psychological course than the practise of worldly asceticism' (Weber 2001: 97). If Weber is correct, the exclusion of moral concerns from political economy is not necessary at all, but is part of a particular theology of disenchantment. The spirit of utility which shapes modern working (the instrumental, rational, anti-traditional pursuit of profit, regardless of means) is the product of a particular theology, even if that theology generally no longer provides even the minimal restraint upon it which it once did.

II. Politics: Society, Labour, and Cooperation

We have already seen that the theory of labour developed within the tradition of political economy was not without political consequences. The essentially bourgeois view of human nature which it embodies encourages a strong view of private ownership and a minimal role for the intervention of the state, although it can also as we have seen support a critique of 'idle' historic monopolies of land and capital. The primacy of the 'state of nature' in this view encouraged however a marginalizing of the social and political dimensions to work in favour of the paradigm of the solitary hunter-gatherer as more fundamental. Yet there were other traditions of reflecting on work, normally grouped together as 'socialist', for which the cooperative, social, and political dimensions were in no way secondary. In France, arising partly out of the experience of the Revolution and the subsequent re-imagining of the body politic, the utopian socialists such as Henri, Comte de Saint-Simon (1760–1825), Charles Fourier (1772–1837), and Pierre-Joseph Proudhon (1809–65) all stressed the cooperative, collective element to human labouring, even if they differed over whether this should be centrally organized or more genuinely democratic and anarchic. The most significant philosopher of labour in the nineteenth century, who certainly developed the socialist, political dimension of the question was Karl Marx (1818–83), who with Friedrich Engels (1820–95), combined elements of the French radical political tradition with the economic analysis of the British Political Economists and the historical perspective of German Idealism to produce a synthesis which, at least on the surface, was hostile to religion and would dominate twentieth-century discussions of labour. In Britain, coming out of the literary Romantic hostility to the conditions of the working classes under industrial capitalism, there was another more cultural-literary tradition of Romantic critics of capitalism, including Thomas Carlyle (1795–1881), John Ruskin (1819–1900), and William Morris (1834–96), who were not so anti-theological. These British authors shared sympathies for pre-modern traditional artisanal models of labour, encouraging freedom and responsibility among workers and patterns of co-operative labour oriented to real social and human goods rather than abstract profit.

These three traditions are characterized, in contrast with the political economists, by a newly critical perspective on the situation of industrial manual labour in the nineteenth century and a more or less utopian imagining of how things might be organized differently. This was primarily at the level of the political questions of the unjust distribution of wealth, which divided Europe into those who had no assets and had to work and those who had assets and did not, but it also extended to the very nature and quality of work itself, as we will see in the final section.

The French 'Utopian' Socialists

The theological dimension was more marked among some of the earlier French utopian socialists, even if it often took heterodox forms or was mixed up with positivistic elements. Saint-Simon illustrates this well, embracing science and industrialization as the greatest hope for the future well-being of humanity, but also affected by counter-revolutionary Catholic thought in rejecting the agonistic individualism of the Enlightenment and stressing that any social transformation will only be achieved by moral education and the rational coordination of industry and society by meritocratic leadership. Saint-Simon was influenced by political economy via Jean-Baptiste Say, and shared its suspicion of idleness. Despite his aristocratic background, his journal *Industrie* drew attention to the unjust situation of the working classes, although he believed that the interests of different classes were not essentially in opposition and so could be overcome by peaceful means of the reorganization of industry and society, rather than by violent revolution, for which view he earned Marx's scorn. In *Le Nouveau christianisme*, written in 1825 just before his death, Saint-Simon finally broke with Comte's positivism and his earlier more cynical use of religion to make his call for social reform explicitly Christian, identifying the heart of Christianity with fraternal affection and the obligation to help the poor, while also looking for a renewed Church, purged of corruption. Saint-Simon's followers generally took a more Comtean, positivist approach than their master, with some even forming their own quasi-religious cult, while retaining the stress on the collectivization and central coordination of industry and society. Similar emphases were found in the writings of Charles Fourier, who also rejected the political economists' ideas of trade, the division of labour, and competition, in favour of the organization of society into cooperative 'phalanxes', living in *phalanstéres*. He believed that organized cooperation would increase productivity and ensure a decent minimum standard of living for all. Fourier looked for a more explicitly utopian future, in which humanity's natural desires were set free from oppressive codes of sexual morality, and our relations with nature were transformed beyond industrialism, when work itself would become pleasurable and like play. After his death there were a number of attempts to put some of his ideas into practice in communities in America, characterized by Marx as 'small experiments, necessarily doomed to failure'. A more significant legacy was Fourier's influence upon the *oeuvriers* and their demands for the right to work, which led to the establishment of state cooperatives for the unemployed after the Revolution of 1848. These movements were also influenced by Pierre-Joseph Proudhon's *What is Property?* (1840), which gave the famous answer: 'theft'. Proudhon shared the social analysis of other French socialists, looking to labour as the basis for the redistribution of wealth to create a more just society. In contrast to Saint-Simon however, he possessed a deep suspicion of government and so took the cooperative thought of his predecessors in a more radically democratic and mutualist direction, tending at times towards anarcho-syndicalism. Together, these three French thinkers, with their stress upon cooperation rather than competition in labour and an egalitarian society with justice for the propertyless workers, influenced Marx and the British socialist tradition. Nevertheless, questions remain concerning the ultimate grounds of their critique and utopian visions, questions which are manifest in their ambiguous relation to the theological on the one hand, and which were articulated by Marx in his accusation that they were 'unscientific', on the other.

Karl Marx: Alienated Labour

It was the aim of the German thinker Karl Marx to overcome this deficiency by providing an account of labour which would be thoroughly 'scientific'. Marx became the most significant modern philosopher of labour, despite his limited recognition during his lifetime, when his ideas were taken up by various revolutionary workers' movements in the late nineteenth century, and then particularly when, following the Russian Revolution of 1917, 'Marxism' was made the official view of the USSR, and subsequently of China and eastern Europe. This 'canonization' and systematization of Marx's thought, begun by his friend Engels who published many of his writings posthumously, generates its own problems with interpretation. Marx's originality and significance come partly from his innovative synthesis of apparently conflicting traditions: German Idealism, French political thought, and British political economy. While at university he had been influenced by the thought of the Young Hegelians, such as Feuerbach, who offered a materialist account of history in which religious and metaphysical thought is seen as mere shadows of reality to be overcome. During the revolutionary 1840s he combined this with the French socialist concern for social and political justice, writing for a number of radical journals. At about the same time he began seriously to read the British political economists, in order to give his thought a more solidly 'scientific', economic foundation than his predecessors.

The foundation of Marx's thought was his labour theory which constituted his anthropology: '*labour* is the *essence* of man' (Marx 1988: 50). Here he synthesized Hegelian ideas with political economy, enabling him at the same time to criticize both. Adam Smith's labour theory is accepted, but used to develop a radical historicist critique of Smith's naturalism. There is no state of nature, because humanity is irreducibly historical; our labour does not merely produce things, we also 'make' our world and ourselves. This sounds like a Hegelian account of history as auto-genesis, but it is important to notice that political economy has enabled Marx to transform this from a theory of intellectual history into socio-economic history, or historical materialism, beyond Hegel. The history of ideas is not, as for so many previous writers in the idealist tradition, the substance of human progress; rather it is epiphenomenal, the ideological 'superstructure' which merely expresses the material 'base' of real, socio-economic history. It is 'not consciousness that determines life', Marx argues, 'but life that determines consciousness' (Marx 1998: 101).

Marx develops this labour theory into a critique of capitalism through his account of alienation (*Entaeussern*), which blends insights from Hegelianism and political economy to describe how the 'surplus value' generated in all labour is not enjoyed by the labourer under capitalism, but rather is taken away to generate profit for someone else. The worker is alienated from his labour, and thus from himself. This alienation takes place because of the unjust distribution of capital within society, as the French socialists had claimed, with those who own assets (capitalists) using their capital to control and extract labour from the workers who do not (the proletariat). There is a genuine conflict of interests, competition, between these classes which cannot simply be harmonized through organization, as the utopian socialists had thought. Yet this class conflict is not eternal, but rather the product of a particular phase of history (capitalism) and will work itself out through the processes of history (dialectical materialism), which will lead to violent revolution and the establishment by the proletariat of the communist society, where the alienation of labour under capitalism will be overcome. For Marx this is not just a description of a necessary historical process, it is also, paradoxically, a call to action: 'The philosophers have only interpreted the world, in various ways; the point is to change it', 'The Proletarians have nothing to lose but their chains; they have a world to win. Workers of the world, unite!' (Marx 1998: 571; 1996: 30).

Two related questions occur about Marx's project: just how 'scientific' is his method? And, what is the real role of religion in his thought? Marx is famously an atheist materialist; religion, for him, is part of the superstructural realm of 'ideology', concealing the real truth of material relations, and to be left behind in the true communist society. More than this, Marx's account of the alienating surplus of labour began as an extension of the Young Hegelian critique of religion to intellectual production as such. Religion is the archetypical form of intellectual production for him, the original idolatrous 'fetishism' which precedes capitalist commodity fetishism. All ideology, it seems, is 'priestly'. Marx turns on the philosophy which had seemed to be the tool for critiquing religion and accuses it of being an equally alienating abstraction. Does this mean that thought itself is alienating and deceptive, and all ideas are ideology? Apparently not; *science* is Marx's preferred term for genuine knowledge as opposed to ideology: 'consistent naturalism', 'real, positive science'. At times this sounds like a crude scientistic positivism, as when Marx expects his historical claims to be 'verified in a purely empirical way', 'with the accuracy of physical science'. But at other moments, his historicism drives him towards a more pragmatist view of truth as realized in critical action, where it seems that the only thing that distinguishes proletarian truth from bourgeois falsehood is its capacity to bring its own predictions to pass. In this ambiguity we see Marx's rejection of any transcendent notion of truth, as much as any transcendent notion of ethics. His analysis claims to be thoroughly materialist and the rejection of the residual 'theology' even of metaphysics is part of this. Here it seems Marx is not so far from the naturalism of the political economists after all, despite his historicism. Utility has been smuggled in through the back door. Yet, given that his 'predictions' have not apparently been vindicated by empirical observation, it is far from clear whether Marx can actually sustain the critical political heart of his entire project on this purely immanent basis. Why should we be dissatisfied with alienated labour at all; and what possible ground could we have for hoping this might be overcome? Marx's determination to found his political critique on immanent, 'scientific' principles is problematic and involves a deliberate repression of theological-ethical aspects of his thought, such as the utopian vision of unalienated labour and the protest at social injustice, which may actually be more fundamental. As Benjamin famously suggested, drawing upon the image of a 'robot' playing chess which was actually operated by a hidden dwarf, it may be that there is a theological dwarf operating the supposedly automatic Marxian puppet.

British Romantic Views of Labour

In Britain in the nineteenth century there was another tradition of cultural-literary critiques of capitalism, which did not attempt to justify themselves on purely immanent, scientistic grounds, but had more in common with the French socialists, including a more positive, though still not unambiguous relation to theology. This tradition grew out of the Romantic rejection of industrial utilitarianism and materialism. This found literary expression in William Blake's contempt for the 'dark Satanic mills' and in Dickens's character Mr Gradgrind, but took more precise form in Coleridge's Platonist hostility to the egoism of political economy, which denied the soul and any transcendent truth or goodness. After Coleridge it was Thomas Carlyle who became one of the most prominent spokesmen for this more Romantic criticism of capitalism.

Carlyle drew upon the Gothic sympathies developed by Scott and Pugin to contrast the avaricious pursuit of profit for its own sake without regard for the human or environmental costs in modern industry and trade ('mammonism') with the well-ordered society of the medieval monastery in *Past and Present*. Influenced by German Romantic thought, Carlyle claimed that 'there is a perennial nobleness, and even sacredness, in Work'; for him, the monastic tradition was correct to think that *laborare est orare*, work is worship, because 'man perfects himself by working' and 'Labour is Life' (Carlyle 1909: 202–3). He railed against the idleness of the leisured classes who lived off their capital, and idolized the 'Hero' or strong and virtuous leader who took courageous decisions for the sake of the common good. Following from this, Carlyle called for a new 'chivalry of labour' and a new 'aristocracy' of the captains of industry, admiring humane employers such as the great Quaker businesses. The example of the monastery obviously suggested a form of collective cooperation rather than individual competition, but Carlyle went further in insisting upon the need for an explicitly transcendent vision of the just society, such as that upon which the monastery was founded. Carlyle was not an apologist for Roman Catholicism (although even the choice of example was controversial in Protestant circles) and spoke warmly, for example, of Islam and Confucianism, as if the specificities of claims of revelation were largely a matter of indifference to him; but he clearly identified the egoism of mammonism with 'practical atheism' and the alternative hope for a renewed society with submission to divine justice and the restoration of the primacy of the soul over the stomach. Carlyle presents a critique of nineteenth-century capitalism on the basis of a theological natural law view, combined with a remarkably strong account of the sacred dignity of labour, understood as heroic Herculean struggle.

Similar emphases can be seen in the art critic and social essayist John Ruskin. In *Unto this Last* (1860) Ruskin follows Carlyle in developing a very similar critique of political economy as a false 'science' which denies the soul and morality, reducing humanity to a 'covetous machine', constantly at war with itself. Likewise his solution is essentially the same as Carlyle: we must recover virtue and sacrifice and nobility in our working life, through the proper exercise of judgement in accordance with the divine law. The medievalist sympathy for the Gothic is developed by Ruskin in *The Stones of Venice* (1853), building upon Pugin, into an account of the medieval artisan as the exemplar of unalienated labour: labour that is free, responsible, creative, intelligent as well as practical, and enjoying the fruits of its work. According to this view, beauty and pleasure are signs of just working conditions, while ugliness is a sign of enslaved labour. More than this, artisanal labour is not simply the highest form of human work; it is also the one that most properly resembles God's work: free, creative, delighting in its creation. Although Ruskin's own religious views were complex, moving from Evangelicalism, through phases of Biblical scepticism and spiritualism, towards a tentative return to a more open Christian faith, his social criticism was always expressed in Christian terms. More practically, Ruskin was involved in some of the beginnings of the cooperative movement and the working men's educational movement, and was connected with early Christian socialists such as F. D. Maurice.

William Morris developed Ruskin's account of the medieval artisan as the ideal of emancipated labour, overcoming the separation of beauty and usefulness and the division of labour into intellectual (free, responsible) work and manual (servile) work. Art, for Morris, was not about decadent ornament, but the 'element of sensuous pleasure' in the work itself, which is its only true reward (Morris 1993: 368). Following Ruskin, the ugliness of contemporary art was seen as reflecting the social injustices of its production. Morris combined this aesthetic account of true work with an analysis of history influenced by Marx, so that he looked for its realization through a revolution rather than education and moral transformation and regarded religion as part of the old order that would be swept away. Nevertheless, his aestheticism and medievalism saved him from the cruder positivism and hostility towards theology of other strands of atheist Marxism. Morris put his theories into practice with his own design firm which played a key role in the development of the arts and crafts movement, and also through his involvement in the nascent British socialist movement. Through his youthful involvement with the pre-Raphaelites he exercised a considerable influence upon British ecclesiastical tastes, while his later writings were formative for what would become the British Labour party. One of his indirect disciples was the Roman Catholic artist and essayist Eric Gill, who would develop Morris's social criticism in a much more explicitly theological direction.

The Christian Socialists

Although, as we have seen, many of the early nineteenth-century writers about the question of labour employed theological frameworks of thought, whether consciously or not, it was not until the mid-nineteenth century that more explicitly *Christian* responses began to be developed. In France certain strands within the followers of Saint-Simon, such as Philippe Buchez, who was briefly president of the French Constituent National Assembly in 1848 and one of the founders of the worker-owned journal *L'Atelier*, held 'socialist' views clearly derived from Christian principles. This tradition of Christian 'socialism' migrated to Britain partly through the influence of John Ludlow, who with the theologian F. D. Maurice, and the authors Charles Kingsley and Thomas Hughes, formed the first significant group within the Anglo-Saxon theological world to identify themselves as 'Christian socialists' in the 1840s. They were responding to the rise of a mass workers' movement in Chartism in the United Kingdom and the influence of cooperativist views of labour deriving from the utilitarian factory reformer Robert Owen and his 'Owenite' followers. Theologically however the Christian socialists were more indebted to the Coleridgean Romantic rejection of utilitarianism. These Christian socialists were active in the early labour and cooperative movements and in promoting education among the working classes, establishing the Working Men's College in 1854 in London. Their vision of Christianity as essentially social against all forms of egotistical individualism and their refusal of the separation between the sacred and the secular led them to call for mutual collaboration rather than competition: 'by labouring strenuously in God's strength, that we may realise the true

Fraternity of which this age has dreamed' (Morris 2005: 149). It is worth noting in passing that the dismissal of these more ethical and frequently Christian forms of socialism as 'utopian', purely derivative, bourgeois, and essentially quietist is due to the dominance of the self-proclaimed 'scientific' Marxist socialism in the twentieth century. If the 'scientific' nature of this perspective is called into question, particularly in relation to its view of history, then these alternative repressed socialist traditions emerge as at least as significant.

The Social Teaching of the Churches

The institutional churches in Europe, with some exceptions, were initially suspicious of the revolutionary and sometimes anti-Christian intentions of the working-class political movements in mid-nineteenth-century Europe, with the inclusion of 'socialism' and 'communism' among Pius IX's 1864 'syllabus of errors' being an extreme, but not unrepresentative example. By the late nineteenth century however this situation had shifted significantly, with moves which would mark the beginning of the modern development of the Church's tradition of social teaching. Pope Leo XIII's encyclical *Rerum Novarum* on the condition of labour (1891) continued to reject the atheism, materialism, class warfare, and revolutionary intentions of much of modern socialism and to insist on the necessity of private property, but it also applied traditional Catholic teaching on economic justice to the contemporary situation of the working classes in such a way as to draw some radical conclusions. The pope rejected the free market view that the supply and demand of labour should determine wages purely through the free contracting of employers and employees. Instead he pointed to concerns of natural justice to insist upon decent working conditions, just wages, and the duties of employers towards their employees: 'Workers are not to be treated as slaves' (Leo XIII 1983: 20). The encyclical insisted upon the duty of the state to intervene to protect the vulnerable and encouraged the organization of workers to defend their rights, although it looked for more corporatist models of collaboration between the state, employers, and employees, rather than the confrontational model more common within the trade union movement. The encyclical had a wide influence and contributed to the development of Catholic workers' movements and political parties in Europe and elsewhere. This magisterial tradition of reflection upon social concerns continued in the Roman Catholic Church with *Quadragesimo Anno* (1931), the Second Vatican Council's document *Gaudium et Spes* (1965), *Populorum Progressio* (1967), and particularly with the encyclicals of John Paul II, who had spent most of his ministry in an officially communist country: *Solicitudo Rei Socialis* (1987), *Centisimus Anno* (1991), and *Laborem Exercens* (1981). The latter encyclical provides the most sustained account of labour within this tradition. The three objects of labour which John Paul II lists include the traditional production for self-preservation, but also the more modern concerns of the societal transformation of nature through technology and the transformation of self and society through cultural production. These two concerns indicate how much official Catholic teaching has been influenced by the more general discussion of the problem of labour. This does not mean that the pope succumbs to a relativizing progressivism, nor a naïvely uncritical attitude to modern technology. He insists that even the rapidly changing situation of modern labour 'remains within the Creator's original ordering' (John Paul II 1981: 4) and expresses concern that the increasing role of technology requires responsible ethical handling in order to avoid becoming dehumanizing. The pope sees this neglect of the human subjective dimension to work in both the free market ideology of the Right and the centralist collectivism of the Left, which are equally 'materialist' (John Paul II 1981: 7). We can see the familiar natural law emphasis on just wages and conditions of employment, complemented by the pope's own personalist philosophy. The generally positive Catholic view of natural human agency as a created good even after the Fall is extended through a more unusual account of the cooperation of human labour with divine labour in the building of the Kingdom. This is combined with a spirituality of work, looking back to Christ the carpenter of Nazareth and suggesting that Christianity was responsible for a radical revaluation of manual labour in the ancient world. Again here we can see the influence of particularly modern views of labour as at least potentially salvific. These views had already been accepted by the magisterium at the Second Vatican Council, where *Gaudium et Spes* declared: 'By their work people ordinarily provide for themselves and their family, associate with others as their brothers and sisters, and serve them; they can exercise genuine charity and be partners in the work of bringing God's creation to perfection.' Beyond this, 'through the homage of work offered to God humanity is associated with the redemptive work of Jesus Christ, whose labour with his hands at Nazareth greatly added to the dignity of human work' (Flannery 1996: 246). We will return to these more ontological questions in the final section. While the Roman Catholic Church has offered the most developed ecclesial reflection upon labour, we can see similar approaches taken by other Churches, as in the report *Unemployment and the Future of Work*, produced by the Council of Churches for Britain and Ireland in 1997.

Liberation Theologies

Parallel to the official teaching of the Churches, during the last fifty years movements characterizing themselves as 'Liberation Theology' have arisen in academic circles and at more popular levels within the Churches, initially in Latin America, but spreading to the rest of the world, including Europe. These movements share a common sense of understanding the Christian message in terms of radical identification with the cause of the oppressed alongside the proclamation and practice of the gospel in terms of total liberation, including liberation from injustice, material poverty, and oppression. Drawing upon earlier traditions of Christian social thought and arising out of the social and political upheavals of the 1960s and the *aggiornamento* in the Roman Catholic Church associated with the Second Vatican Council, the manifesto for 'Liberation Theology' was formulated by the Peruvian Dominican priest Gustavo Gutiérrez in Chimbote, Peru, in 1968, and developed into his seminal study *A Theology of Liberation* (1971). In this work Gutiérrez claimed that theology should be 'critical reflection on praxis', that 'liberation' should be the paradigm for contemporary understandings of salvation, and that the Church should stand in radical social and political solidarity with the poor and oppressed. Liberation theology found expression not only in academic and popular circles but also within the ecclesiastical hierarchy, especially at the Latin American episcopal conferences at Medellin, Colombia, in 1968, which spoke of the 'preferential option for the poor', and at Puebla, Mexico, in 1979. Some have seen Liberation Theology as in opposition to the social teaching of the Roman hierarchy, and it is certainly true that there have been points of friction such as the instructions from the Congregation for the Doctrine of the Faith in 1984 and 1986 and the censuring of some of the teachings of Leonardo Boff and Jon Sobrino, among others. Liberation theologians have at times accused the ecclesiastical hierarchy of being complicit with oppressive regimes and neglectful of the concrete realities of the poor; while the CDF claimed that some liberation theologians had compromised the faith through adopting an essentially Marxist analysis of the social situation, which led to an excessively materialist and immanentist account of salvation and an overly conflictual view of class warfare, encouraging Christians to be dangerously politically partisan and even caught up in violent revolution. Despite these genuine instances of tension, it would perhaps be more plausible to follow Gutiérrez himself in seeing liberation theology and the Church's social tradition as not so far removed from one another and mutually informing. The original analysis of liberation theology arose out of the application of the Church's social teaching to the situation of Latin America and avoided the reduction of salvation to material prosperity and class warfare; while, as we have indicated, the liberation theologians' 'preference for the poor' and expectation of salvation as including real material transformation in this life seem to have been taken up by the magisterial tradition, particularly in the writings of Paul VI and John Paul II. Likewise, Gutiérrez and other liberation theologians have insisted that the preferential option for the poor does not exclude the universal nature of the Christian hope of salvation; while conversely papal teaching has affirmed the priority of labour over capital and reiterated the classical principle articulated by Aquinas and others that the rights of private property are secondary to the right to life, so that there are circumstances in which redistribution by expropriation is permissible. The view of labour at the heart of liberation theology is very similar to the post-Vatican II magisterial tradition, seen in *Laborem Exercens*, as in Gutiérrez's view that 'humanity fulfils itself by continuing the work of creation by means of its labour' or that 'to work, to transform the world, is to become a man and to build the human community; it is also to save', which he sees evident in the biblical narrative of the Exodus from slavery into the promised land (Gutiérrez 2001: 158). Although at times this can sound as if humanity immanently saves itself through labour, as when he claims that 'faith "desacralises" creation, making it the area proper for human work', at other times he is careful to set this human labour within more participatory accounts of sharing in God's work: 'Salvation, totally and freely given by God . . . —is the inner force and the fullness of this movement of human self-generation initiated by the work of creation' (Gutiérrez 2001: 157–8).

III. Ontology: Human and Divine Work and Rest

We have seen how the economic and political views of labour raise more fundamental ontological questions about human labour: Is labour the source of value or should it seek to correspond to the true value of things? Does labour operate according to morally neutral, quantifiable laws of necessity, like other physical forces, or is it always hermeneutical, cultural, and moral? Is human labour naturally self-interested and competitive, or can it be organized cooperatively? Are its ends purely material or are they also more spiritual? Is labour oriented towards the purely mundane ends of subsistence or to more ultimate ends such as human salvation? These last questions raise the possibility of some sort of analogy or participatory relationship between human and divine work and the relation of human work to rest, which has traditionally been seen within the Christian tradition as more 'divine' than labour, while the latter has been associated with the curse of the Fall.

Ontologies of Labour

As we have seen, behind the Marxist categories, which have dominated so much political and economic discussion of labour, stand the philosophy of Hegel and German Idealism and Romanticism more generally. The question of action and practice had dominated these philosophical movements as they sought ways to develop more holistic philosophical systems on the basis of Kant's practical philosophy in the second critique, in order to overcome the dualism of the epistemological approach of the first critique and the tradition of Cartesian rationalism before that. Whether this was through Goethe's assertion that 'In the beginning was the Act', or the philosophies of will in Fichte or Schopenhauer, or more significantly the aesthetic philosophy of creation in Schelling and the philosophy of freedom in Hegel, there was an attempt among these philosophers to elevate *praxis* to the essence of humanity. These were *ontologies* of labour. Activity, labour, creation, were seen as essentially human: humans make themselves and their world. From these beginnings there has been a crucial ambiguity over this turn to the act: whether it should be conceived in a Promethean, nihilistic fashion as if humans have usurped God as the author of reality (as in Fichte and Schopenhauer), or whether this emphasis on *homo faber* should be seen as part of the *imago dei* by which humanity reflects, shares in, and continues the work of its Maker who is Pure Act (as perhaps is more the case with Schelling and Hegel). The former ontological position has, as we have seen, frequently coincided with a more materialist account of the ends of labour and a more agonistic account of the social relations implicit in labour. These ways of thinking about labour as ontological, rather than purely economic or political, more obviously connect directly with fundamental theological questions such as what it is to be human, and these quasi-theological debates were very much part of the milieu from which they emerged. However it was not until the twentieth century that explicitly *theological* ontologies of labour emerged (although we have noted traces of such a development in earlier strands of nineteenth-century thought). These twentieth-century 'theologies of work' were a significant influence on the development of the Church's social teaching and of liberation theologies in the last century. They embodied a transition from a purely justice-based concern with securing the minimum conditions for workers, towards a more potentially open-ended and qualitative transformation of the nature of human labour, so as more fully to participate in the divine labour of salvation.

Theologies of Work: Chenu and Volf

Whether from a Catholic perspective, such as the Dominican Marie-Dominique Chenu writing in 1950, or from a Protestant background, such as Miroslav Volf, these theologies of labour share a desire to respond to the challenge of Marxism and to offer a positive account of human labour within the economy of salvation. Both move beyond natural law theologies of creation with their concern for justice, towards more Christological and pneumatological views of human labour as sharing in the building of God's kingdom on earth. Chenu was part of the *ressourcement* movement in Catholic thought and looked to Maximus the Confessor to support a positive account of human activity transforming nature in cooperation with God. Despite some criticism at the time, Chenu's views were vindicated at the Second Vatican Council, where they found expression in *Gaudium et Spes*, as we saw previously. He also wrote at the time of the Dominican 'worker-priests' experiment, where French priests were exempted from parochial responsibilities and sent to work in the factories in order to reach the working classes who had become alienated from the Church. Chenu's desire to give a positive theological account of the dignity of human labour beyond mere subsistence and his sense of the radically changing nature of labour in modernity, leads him to make some very large claims for human work, perhaps influenced by the evolutionary thought of Teilhard de Chardin, such as that work achieves the 'synthesis of man and nature' which will lead to the 'complete assumption of the universe by man' (Chenu 1963: 26, 73). Alongside Chenu and the French worker-priests, there were other movements and writers within the Roman Catholic Church which contributed to the development of a spirituality of work in the mid-twentieth century, from Dorothy Day and the Catholic

Worker Movement in the United States, which combined the promotion of distribu-
tivist political thought with direct action to help the poor, to the more conservative St
Josemaria Escrivá, the Spanish priest who founded *Opus Dei* as a movement for the
sanctification of the ordinary life of the laity. Within the Church of England, and from
a more literary-aesthetic perspective, Dorothy L. Sayers developed an account of
human creative work as analogous to the creative action of the Holy Trinity.

A similarly high view of human labour and its relation to salvation is found in
Miroslav Volf's *Work in the Spirit*. Coming from a Croatian Pentecostalist background,
Volf is influenced by the political emphasis on eschatology in Jürgen Moltmann's
Theology of Hope (itself influenced by the Marxist Ernst Bloch). Responding to
Marxism, Volf sees the priority of contemplation over action in traditional Christian
thought as an alien Greek philosophical denigration of labour, while he believes that
the traditional Protestant theologies of work in terms of vocation (*Beruf*) are unsuited
to the contemporary realities of labour. He would replace these ideas of vocation, which
he claims are founded upon a backward-looking theology of creation, with an account
of the gifts of the Spirit, which sets human labour in the context of collaborating with
God in building the Kingdom through the eschatological *transformatio mundi*. This
enables him to speak of a judgement of works ('All work that contradicts the new
creation is meaningless; all work that corresponds to the new creation is ultimately
meaningful' Volf 1991: 121) while also insisting that good work is so integral to our
salvation that it follows us into the eschaton (appealing to Revelations 14:13, Ephesians
6:8, and 1 Corinthians 3:12).

The idolatry of work and the theology of rest? Barth and Pieper

If twentieth-century theologies of work have generally held these high views of human
labour in relation to salvation and divine labour, the theological adoption of ontologies
of labour has not been without its critics. Two of the most important have been the
Reformed Swiss theologian Karl Barth (1886–1968) and the German Roman Catholic
Thomist Josef Pieper (1904–97), who both criticized the modern idolatry of work as
Promethean, against which they sought to recall the scriptural command to rest and
the traditional priority of contemplation over action and divine action over entirely
non-commensurate human responses. For Barth, work is essentially 'this worldly'
(Barth 1961: 471) while the Sabbath commandment 'points [man] away from everything
that he himself can will and achieve' (Barth 1961: 53). Pieper reiterates the Aristotelian
principle that 'we work in order to be at leisure', while he sees the modern world of
'total work' as embodying the opposite ordering (Pieper 1998: 4). For Pieper 'the festival
is the origin of leisure' and 'there is no festival that does not get its life from ... worship'
(Pieper 1998: 34, 51). While both Barth and Pieper argue from traditional premises for
this caution towards idealizing views of labour, it is not insignificant that they wrote out
of a wider cultural and philosophical context, which was more sceptical than the

nineteenth century about human scientific and technological capacities to resolve all problems and establish the Kingdom of Heaven on Earth. These mid-twentieth-century critiques of technocratic societies and instrumental and utilitarian modes of reasoning were themselves indebted to earlier strands of Romantic thinking which ran parallel with the more positive views expressed in Hegel and Marx. In Barth's case this meant that his commitment to socialism was closer to the spirit of Kierkegaard and the cultural pessimism of the West German socialists of the 1930s such as Theodor Adorno and the Frankfurt School rather than the naïvely optimistic view of science and progress expressed in Soviet Marxism. For Pieper, his Thomist concern with the classical hierarchical ordering of leisure and labour in Plato and Aristotle was sympathetic to the critique of technology found in Martin Heidegger's phenomenological analysis. For Heidegger, western thought has been dominated by the 'equipmental' relation of *techne* which reduces things to tools to be used, as opposed to the organic shining forth of things which he sees in the work of art and other ways of relating to Being less concerned with mastery. This phenomenological approach to the question of work has been developed subsequently by Hannah Arendt and more explicitly theologically by Jean-Yves Lacoste.

IV. Concluding Remarks

The theologies of work, deriving from nineteenth-century ontologies of labour, can be seen not simply as a theological response to a new social situation and developments in secular thought, but rather as a genuine outworking of radical elements of the Christian gospel itself. Leaving aside the somewhat sentimental question of Christ's occupation as a carpenter in Nazareth, within the New Testament, particularly St John and St Paul, we can see how theurgic and liturgical elements of the Jewish Wisdom tradition are developed to speak of the collaboration of human works with the work of God. Such a collaboration can be seen as implicit in the logic of Chalcedonian Christology, while the divine kenosis and exaltation of human nature in the incarnation could encourage the anti-hierarchical elevation of traditionally servile activities. Such a view would fit with the apparent eschatological suspension of the opposition between work and rest on the Sabbath through the advent of the Christ: the eternal Sabbath has arrived in which all time and space is sacred and all work can become liturgy. At the very least, the New Testament could be said to problematize the conventional opposition between work and rest, work and worship, and slavery and freedom; while more fundamentally, its suggestion of an analogy of participatory cooperation between divine and human work points towards a possible *ultimate* convergence, beyond our temporal horizon, between work and rest, work and worship, human work and divine work. If this is so, then the exalted view of the dignity of human labour and creativity which has developed throughout the Christian tradition, from the early ascetic and monastic movements, through the Renaissance and into modernity, seems not just an accident, but rather an authentic outworking of these revolutionary insights. To situate work within this theological teleology, against secularizing tendencies within and without the Church, so that it can be *more or less* worshipful, *more or less* participatory in God's work, provides the basis for Christian critical judgement of work, as we have seen.

However, we have seen a number of possible difficulties with this 'convergence' perspective on work, worship, and rest, most obviously in its more extreme Romantic forms: such a position has been accused of encouraging an idolatry of work embodying the Promethean temptation to see human value as self-made rather than a gift of grace; it can also lead to an over-realized eschatology, which thinks it can live beyond the diurnal rhythms of work and rest, but which in effect simply loses any sense of the value and meaning of rest; finally, it can also produce a spiritualizing idealization of work, which abolishes all proximate, this-worldly ends for working with the insistence that all work must be directly *for* God and like God's work, and is thus incapable of comprehending the necessary toil of subsistence, the post-lapsarian character of human work which continues to separate it from rest and worship. These problems can become particularly acute when these ontologies of labour are secularized, as in Marxism for example. In such cases there is no sense of this idealization being kept in check by a more ultimate, as yet unattainable horizon, and the ultimate goal of work is immanentized as simply working for work's sake, or abstract profit, personal pleasure or something similar.

REFERENCES

Adorno, Theodor and Max Horkheimer (1997). *The Dialectic of Enlightenment.* (London: Verso).

Arendt, Hannah (1998). *The Human Condition.* (Chicago: Chicago University Press).

Barth, Karl (1961). *Church Dogmatics* III:4. (Edinburgh: T. and T. Clark).

Benjamin, Walter (1999). *Illuminations.* (London: Pimlico).

Carlyle, Thomas (1909). *Past and Present.* (London: Oxford University Press).

Chenu, Marie-Dominique (1963). *The Theology of Work: An Exploration.* (Dublin: Gill and Son).

Flannery, Austin (1996). *Vatican Council II: Constitutions, Decrees, Declarations.* (Dublin: Dominican Publications).

Gill, Eric (1983). *A Holy Tradition of Working.* (Ipswich: Golgonooza Press).

Gutiérrez, Gustavo (2001). *A Theology of Liberation.* (London: SCM).

Heidegger, Martin (1993). *Basic Writings.* (London: Routledge).

John Paul II (1981). *Laborem Exercens.* (London: Catholic Truth Society).

Lacoste, Jean-Yves (2000). *Le Monde et l'absence d'oeuvre.* (Paris: Presses Universitaires de France).

Leo XIII (1983). *Rerum Novarum.* (London: Catholic Truth Society).

Locke, John (1988). *Two Treatises of Government.* (Cambridge: Cambridge University Press).

Malthus, Thomas (1993). *An Essay on the Principle of Population.* (Oxford: Oxford University Press).

Marx, Karl (1988). *Economic and Philosophical Manuscripts of 1844.* (New York: Prometheus Books).

—— (1996). *Later Political Writings.* (Cambridge: Cambridge University Press).

Marx, Karl (1998). *The German Ideology.* (New York: Prometheus Books).
Moltmann, Jurgen (1969). *Theology of Hope.* (London: SCM).
Morris, Jeremy (2005). *F. D. Maurice and the Crisis of Christian Authority.* (Oxford: Oxford University Press).
Morris, William (1993). *News from Nowhere and Other Writings.* (London: Penguin).
Pieper, Josef (1998). *Leisure as the Basis of Culture.* (South Bend, IN: St Augustine's Press).
Ruskin, John (1911). *Unto this Last and Munera Pulveris.* (London: George Allen and Sons).
Sayers, Dorothy L. (2002). *The Mind of the Maker.* (London: Continuum).
Smith, Adam (1991). *The Wealth of Nations.* (London: David Campbell Publishing).
Volf, Miroslav (1991). *Work in the Spirit.* (Oxford: Oxford University Press).
Weber, Max (2001). *The Protestant Ethic and the Spirit of Capitalism.* (London: Routledge).

SUGGESTED READING

Arendt (1998).
Arnal, Oscar (1986). *Priests in Working-class Blue: The History of the Worker Priests (1943–1954).* (New York: Paulist Press).
Chenu (1963).
Gutiérrez (2001).
Hughes, John (2007). *The End of Work: Theological Critiques of Capitalism.* (Oxford: Blackwell).
John Paul II (1981).
Lash, Nicholas (1981). *A Matter of Hope.* (London: Darton, Longman, and Todd).
Löwy, Michael and Robert Sayre (2001). *Romanticism against the Tide of Modernity.* (London: Duke University Press).
Marx (1996).
Pieper (1998).
Pontifical Council for Justice and Peace (2002). *Work as Key to the Social Question: The Great Social and Economic Transformations and the Subjective Dimension of Work.* (Vatican City: Libreria Editrice Vaticana).
Reed, Esther (2010). *Work, for God's Sake: Christian Ethics in the Workplace.* (London: Darton, Longman, and Todd).
Turner, Denys (1983). *Marxism and Christianity.* (Oxford: Blackwell).
Volf (1991).
Weber (2001).

CHAPTER 8

....

SUFFERING IN THEOLOGY AND MODERN EUROPEAN THOUGHT

....

PAUL S. FIDDES

I. Forms of Thought about Suffering

....

From the late eighteenth century onwards, theological and philosophical reflection on the phenomenon of suffering has taken three main forms, usually interlinked. First, it has been associated with the status of evil in the universe, where suffering has been seen as a manifestation of evil, or caused by evil, or as a consequence of moral evil. This approach has often taken the particular form of 'theodicy', or the attempt to reconcile the presence of evil and suffering in the world with an omnipotent, good, and loving creator. Second, the pressing question has appeared to be how to live authentically in the face of suffering, to avoid being destroyed by it, and if possible to overcome it. Third, human suffering has been placed in the context of tragedy, in both its literary genre and in the derivative sense of 'the tragic aspects of life'. We might call these three forms of thought about suffering 'theoretical', 'practical', and 'aesthetic', while taking care not to regard them as mutually exclusive.

In this account we shall be tracing the interweaving of these three forms of thought during the modern European era, and noticing the shift of emphasis in different times and in different thinkers. As, on our course, we approach the latter part of the twentieth century, moving into the shadow of two world wars and the Holocaust, we shall find a marked shift from theory to practice, witnessing to a growing impatience with the search for abstract explanations of suffering, and a new stress on the practical issues of how to cope with it. In Christian theology, this shift has been marked by an increasing interest in the relevance of the crucifixion of Jesus for the problems of human suffering, rather than for traditional doctrines of atonement, and this in turn has led back to a kind of theodicy, though with a more practical weight than earlier attempts. Central to this new theodicy has been an affirmation of the suffering of God, overturning centuries of orthodoxy which had insisted on divine passibility and immutability, but following a track marked out already by Hegel and Schelling in the nineteenth century.

Suffering is both an inner feeling and the result of impact from causes that may be within or beyond our bodies; many medical authorities thus distinguish between the 'pain experience' and the 'pain sensation', the first being a matter of state of mind and the second a matter of the bodily senses (Hick 1968: 329; cf. Scarry 1985: 161–76). On the one hand suffering is a movement within the psyche, an emotion or troubling of equanimity; on the other hand it is an injury we receive from circumstances and causes which are often beyond our control. The link between *physical* pain and inward suffering is a variable one; people in certain psychological states of mind can make light of the sensation of physical pain: soldiers in the excitement of battle, accident victims in shock, even victims of torture in a state of religious exaltation can suffer pain without great inner feeling of distress. Conversely, people can experience considerable stress of mind while in physical safety. Nor should we suppose that an injury inflicted even from outside is always a matter of physical sensation; we may forget that such causes of suffering as bad housing conditions, the threat of poverty, and psychological warfare are also painful impacts on us. Much suffering is caused today by conditions which promote isolation and loss of meaning. Despite the complexity of the phenomenon of suffering, however, we may describe it as both what we feel and what is inflicted upon us.

II. The Making and Remaking of a Theodicy: The Theoretical Approach

Beginning with 'theoretical' approaches, we observe that the scene was set for discussion of suffering in modern European thought by Gottfried Leibniz in his *Theodicy* (1710), surveying what he diagnosed as the 'best of all possible worlds'. Influenced by an older contemporary, Nicolas Malebranche, Leibniz argued that theodicy should be based not only on the *effects* of God's work in the universe, its visible details, but on the *means* God may be presumed to employ to bring about his works. God will be justified as a good God in a world of suffering if God has chosen the one world out of an infinite number of possible worlds in which two principles are combined: laws which are the most beautiful, simple, and harmonious possible, and phenomena that are rich in diversity and plenitude (Leibniz 1990: 254–7). The point of Leibniz's theodicy is to make clear that a world that is simplest in laws and richest in effects will be the best of all possible worlds, but not necessarily a world in which each individual being enjoys the perfection that is actually there. What makes this world best is obviously not the total absence of pain and other evils. But God is like an excellent architect who knows that a beautiful building will not always be 'convenient' for everyone (Leibniz 1990: 262). Evil and suffering are not positively willed by God, but they belong to the course of nature as determined by its laws, laws which are themselves simple, universal, and fecund (Leibniz 1990: 140, 255).

Such a theodicy would have no claim, of course, unless goodness does preponderate over evil. Leibniz is not disturbed when he observes that miseries befall the best people, as well as innocent animals. The world only appears at first sight to be a confused chaos, for when we look more carefully, the opposite can be established (Leibniz 1990: 99, 130–2, 281–3). Leibniz argues that the limited scope of our experience of the world means that we will be unaware of the whole picture—a claim held up mercilessly to satire in Voltaire's play *Candide*, which makes clear that the more experience one gains the worse things actually appear. Though Leibniz's approach to suffering is highly theoretical, it does have practical implications, at least in terms of an optimistic attitude: while Leibniz is not maintaining that any particular evil event will finally result in the good, he does encourage a positive response to suffering based on the will of God as the supreme strategist. All evils will work towards the good of the *whole*, and dissonance will ultimately be resolved in harmony.

As the eighteenth century progressed, the attack on Leibnizian types of theodicy came from several quarters. In the first place, a more secular optimism developed in the later years of the Enlightenment period, apparently undermining the need for any religious optimism at all; progress in empirical science, technology, and medicine, together with legislative reforms raised hopes that sickness, hunger, and civil disturbance would soon disappear and so the problem of suffering would vanish with it, making all theodicy redundant. We shall see a similar mood re-emerging in the twentieth century between two world wars. From a different angle, there was the negative impact upon religious faith of the horrifying earthquake in the city of Lisbon (1755), which seemed too huge a disaster to be accommodated within a theory of divine teleology. Finally, Kant—who had abandoned an attempt to create a theodicy based on a dynamic and developmental process of creation when he heard the news from Lisbon—formulated a philosophy of human perception in which a theodicy such as that of Leibniz is ruled out.

According to Kant, human minds, constructed as they are, can only know phenomena in the world, and cannot know the noumenal reality that the mind postulates as transcending the realm of appearances (Kant 1933: 290–4). A Leibnizian theodicy cannot then be valid since the reason is incapable of knowing what the relationship might be between the world which is experienced and any highest or divine wisdom that the reason conceives in its drive towards an idea of unity and harmony. Experience can *prove* nothing about the moral wisdom of God. It cannot prove that suffering in the world belongs in a teleological scheme designed by a God who is supremely wise and good, although in its investigation of the world the reason *proposes* an idea of a higher law and higher purposes to which nature is subject, and this concept 'regulates' its discoveries. We cannot then read the final aim of God from the book of the world. (Kant 1998a: 23–4) However, we *can* vindicate the wisdom of God in a suffering world, not from experience of the world, but from our own human moral concept of how a God would act. This is what Kant calls an 'authentic theodicy', based on the moral reason in which God 'announces' the divine will, and Kant finds it 'expressed allegorically in an ancient holy book'—the Book of Job (Kant 1998a: 24–5).

For Kant, a Leibnizian type of theodicy ('doctrinal' rather than 'authentic') asserts a metaphysical knowledge of divine agency which cannot in fact be known. The friends typify this error, when they insist that the suffering of Job must be an outworking of the justice of God in punishing Job's supposed crimes. In contrast to their philosophical flattery of God, not to speak of their confusion about the limits of reason, Job maintains a sincerity of heart and moral integrity of conscience, not pretending to certainty when in doubt, that wins God's approval. The result is that Job is allowed by God to see the 'the wisdom of his creation, especially its inscrutability'. He has a glimpse in chapters 38–41 of the 'beautiful side of creation' and also 'the horrible side...counterpurposive, and incompatible with a universal plan established with goodness and wisdom' (Kant 1998a: 26). The point is that the ways of God are inscrutable and hidden to the understanding. It is only faith that assures us that there is 'an order and maintenance of the whole which proclaims a wise creator', and this faith is rooted in morality rather than the other way around. It is finally our own moral integrity that assures us of the wisdom of the Creator whom our reason postulates.

Kant opposes Leibniz's theodicy because he denies his metaphysic, and offers an alternative 'authentic theodicy', with the practical implication that we should live with integrity in face of the demands of our moral reason. F. W. J. Schelling agrees at least so far with Leibniz, that it *is* possible to know the wisdom of God in nature. Against Kant's intention, Schelling with other German Idealists (and the English Romantic poet S. T. Coleridge) ironically finds the clue to this very capacity in Kant's own system. Kant had directed attention to the human reason that had *ideas* of a transcendent and noumenal reality—ideas of the unity of the self, the wholeness of the world, and God as creator and lawgiver of all—while insisting that only the phenomenal could be *known* through the categories of the understanding; now the Idealists affirmed knowledge of the noumenal through participation of the human mind in a transcendent and Absolute Idea.

Schelling, however, modifies Leibniz's theodicy. On the one hand, evil cannot be considered as a merely negative reality or defect of being (as Leibniz had proposed, following Augustine's notion of evil as *deprivatio boni*). On the other, the best of all possible worlds cannot include, as an unavoidable condition, the realization of some evil with its attendant suffering. All this means that the 'best world' that God creates is a 'system of freedom' in which evil is both a possibility of freedom and a positive reality, though not a direct intention of God (Schelling 2006: 18–25). If God's moral excellence is to be maintained, however, God must recognize himself as willing and able to turn around, through cooperation with free created persons in history, all the consequences of a free human choice of evil (Schelling 2006: 50–1, 72–4). This, we notice, is a theodicy that depends on a vulnerable and suffering God, foreshadowing the trend in theodicy in the late twentieth century. Kierkegaard criticizes the 'strange' way that Schelling applies psychological concepts such as anxiety, anger, and suffering to God and the cosmos as well as to the individual mind (Kierkegaard 1980: 59), but Schelling's use depends on his principle of affinity between individual consciousness, the Absolute Idea and a natural world which is suffused by the *Logos* or idea (or law) which the Absolute produces in birth pangs of 'yearning' (Schelling 2006: 29–30).

For Schelling, evil and suffering as positive realities have their root in the 'ground' which is one pole of the being of God, the other being 'existence'. The divine ground of existence, symbolized as 'darkness', 'disorder', and 'chaos' has an unconscious will which is a yearning for unfathomable unity, and which is the abysmal matrix from which the radiance of God's existence is eternally begotten. The divine existence, symbolized as 'order', 'form', and 'rule' has a conscious will, a will of understanding set against the will of desire in the ground. The whole of created nature is characterized by a reflection of these two forces, which reach an intensity in the human consciousness: there is an original darkness which is rooted in the divine ground, and a regularity of law brought by the logos from the divine existence (Schelling 2006: 27–32). Evil is not actualized in God, but appears both in nature ('natural evil') and in its most malicious form in human life ('moral evil'). Evil, understood as Augustine's 'privation' appears as the meaningless brutality of nature, the nameless and purposeless suffering of animals without mind. Against this Schelling sets the particular, determinate evil of mankind, the 'radical evil' identified by Kant (1998b: 52–61), which is more than mere 'privation' (Schelling 2006: 32–7).

Moral evil is more terrifying than natural evil, and creates a deeper suffering, as it involves purpose; the individual human will, which is an image of the will of the absolute, raises itself in pride to the status of universal will which belongs only to God. Evil, though rooted in the divine ground, is not Actualized in God since there is an inseparable unity between ground and existence in the Absolute. Evil emerges in the assertion of human will when the two forces of nature, 'the eternal bond of forces', are torn apart. The most harmful kind of suffering thus springs from the dark recess of God's being, but only when it is ripped from its eternal unity with the light of existence by the human spirit (Schelling 2006: 41–4). Schelling hopes to make evil and suffering more conceivable by having the world derive from God as ground, according to an image of birth, rather than from a divine act.

Schelling's theodicy may be briefly compared with that of his contemporary Hegel. For Schelling, the Absolute Idea penetrates a nature which is generated from the dark ground of God. For Hegel, the Absolute Idea takes a *relative* form in nature, exposing itself to its opposite (Hegel 1979: 38–9, 69–73). For Schelling, the polar forces are ground and existence, darkness and light: for Hegel they are self and its other. For Hegel, evil and suffering are thus a necessary part of the coming of the Idea to itself; the Idea can only come to full self-consciousness through immersion into what is totally other, which means a created consciousness separated from God and experiencing the most awful death of God-forsakenness (Hegel 1979: 153–61). For Schelling, evil emerges from a basic darkness and from the freedom of the cosmos. For Hegel, the first moment of being negates itself, cancelling identity, and opening up a movement of return towards new unity. For Schelling, the first moment produces or 'doubles' itself in the birth of logos, intensifying the unity. For Hegel, the process is one of inner logic, with implicit content unfolding by necessity. For Schelling, the process is a procreation, the procreative striving of a purposeful will, in which the procreated has some freedom and independence of its own. Schelling takes the image of divine begetting more seriously than Hegel, for whom it is equivalent to self-negation. However, for both thinkers, in order to reveal God's self and be the living God, God must risk God's self in suffering the impact of evil.

Perhaps this is what leads Schelling finally to a theodicy in which the making of personality through struggle, both human and divine, is the final good: 'God, that is the person of God, is the general law, and everything that happens, happens by virtue of the personality of God.' The sufficient reason for suffering and the unfolding of the whole through the pain of history is the furtherance of personal life, but there can be no sufficient reason for life itself: 'God himself is not a system, but rather a life: and the answer to the question as to the possibility of evil in regard to God . . . also lies in this fact alone' (Schelling 2006: 61–2). Schelling is claiming an irreducible and unaccountable value for personal life. If the making of persons is worth all the suffering, then we can take an optimistic attitude towards progress in history despite its counter-purposive elements. This is not quite a Leibnizian theodicy which thinks the harmony of the whole is a rational deduction; theodicy has been remade as a step of faith in the value of personality, and it has a metaphysical basis that is missing in Kant's theodicy of moral reason.

III. Resignation and Active Suffering: Practical Approaches

Alongside theoretical approaches to suffering that have practical implications, the nineteenth century shows us practical approaches to suffering which imply some theory about the world, but in which the presenting problem is how to deal with suffering rather than explain it. We may find three key examples of this: one from a non-theistic standpoint (Schopenhauer), one from within the circle of faith (Kierkegaard), and one from a believer who is in protest against God (Dostoevsky). They have a common viewpoint against Leibniz's confidence in the beauty and goodness of the universe as a whole, despite their differences. Schopenhauer declares: 'that thousands have lived in happiness and joy would never do away with the anguish and death-agony of one individual' (Schopenhauer 1969: ii. 576); Kierkegaard declares: 'if there is just one individual man who has valid reason to complain, then the universe does not help' (Kierkegaard 1999: i.18 [41]); Dostoevsky's character Ivan Karamazov exclaims: 'is the

whole universe worth the tears of one tortured child?' (Dostoyevsky 1982: 287). The
question, then, is how the individual, in his or her inwardness, is to face suffering.

Schopenhauer generally showed respect for Kant (with an exception over the value
of compassion), and professed the greatest contempt for Schelling and Hegel. While he
took Kant's thought in his own idealist direction, he strongly rejected the optimism of
his idealist contemporaries which was based on the progress of the idea through nature
and history towards reconciliation of opposites. In Schopenhauer's view, 'all life is
suffering', and no human resources will ever overcome it (Schopenhauer 1969: i. 310).
His metaphysic thus seems to be formulated with a practical end—to understand and
justify a pessimistic world view. His basis thesis is that the 'world is idea and will'. From
Kant's epistemology, in which sense impressions from the phenomenal world are
shaped by categories in the understanding, he drew the conclusion that the world as
perceived is simply a creation of the mind: 'the world is my idea'. The real world is the
inner and subjective 'I' that perceives, and this is the 'I' that we know as *will*: our will is
'the thing in itself' (Schopenhauer 1969: i. 110). For Schopenhauer, this must be true of
every other body or phenomenon—everything in the world is a duality of will and idea,
although only human beings are *aware* of themselves in this way. Unlike Schelling's
view of the distinctive quality of will in human reason, the will in the stone and the will
in a person is the same will.

This metaphysic supports a view of universal and inevitable suffering, so that
'nothing else can be stated as the aim of our existence except the knowledge that it
would be better for us not to exist' (Schopenhauer 1969: ii. 605). On the one hand the
nature of will is to strive to live at the expense of others, so that the outcome is universal
conflict. Suffering engendered by this conflict is the normal and inescapable condition
of life. On the other hand, suffering is 'the hindrance of the will through an obstacle
placed between it and its temporary goal'; to creatures who will, suffering is caused by
dissatisfaction of their own state or condition, 'and is therefore suffering so long as it is
not satisfied' (Schopenhauer 1969: ii. 309). Through this life of suffering, Schopenhauer
proposes from reading Hindu texts, each of us is being punished for our existence in a
particular way. No theodicy can succeed, for even if Leibniz were correct that this is 'the
best of all possible worlds', a Creator would have created not only the world but
possibility itself, and 'therefore he should have created the possibility of a better
world than this one' (Schopenhauer 2004: 48). Each act of suffering drains away
value from the universe as a whole and evil can never be balanced by the good that
exists along with or after it.

In the face of all this, Schopenhauer has practical recommendations. The only way
out of the circle of suffering consists in loss of the will. In a few 'saints', the conscious
intellect can gain 'insight' into the nature of the will and so learn to refuse to enter the
contest of wills, allowing individuality to wither away in the manner of Buddhist
'detachment' (Schopenhauer 1969: i. 378–9). Or the will might, spontaneously, just
disengage *itself* from the world in a kind of act of grace. Or suffering may be so severe
that the will to life within us is broken. More proactively, one might resort to *the arts* in
the face of suffering (Schopenhauer himself went to a concert or play nearly every

night) as the will can momentarily cease to act when absorbed in aesthetic contemplation (Schopenhauer 1969: i. 390). Pessimism is thus expressed in a mood of resignation, tolerance, and compassion. We must be resigned to the world as 'a place of atonement, a sort of penal colony'; in deliberate reference to the Hindu concept of *karma*, Schopenhauer urges that 'you will no longer regard the calamities, sufferings, torments and miseries of life as something irregular and not to be expected, but will find them entirely in order, knowing ourselves to be punished . . . .' (Schopenhauer 2004: 49). Since every person's life is 'expiating the crime of being born', we shall show tolerance and patience in regarding each other as fellow-sufferers. We shall exercise pity and compassion for others, which alone gives our actions moral value; here Schopenhauer takes issue severely with Kant, who discouraged pity on the grounds that it gives those pitied a power over one's own moral autonomy (Schopenhauer 1965: 144; see also Kant 1956: 123). Finally, urges Schopenhauer, we shall accept the prospect of annihilation or extinction as the only true cure for the sickness of life.

Kierkegaard judged that Schopenhauer's practical pessimism was a useful antidote to the optimistic view of human progress in contemporary Lutheranism, influenced as it was by Hegel (Kierkegaard 1999: iv. 31 [3881]). Like Schopenhauer also, Kierkegaard turns to inwardness in the face of suffering, to the subjectivity of an 'existential thinker' rather than seeking an objective system of theodicy. But unlike Schopenhauer, his subjectivity is not a form of anthropocentric idealism; the truth to be found in inwardness is a passionate commitment to the paradox of Christianity, that with Christ eternity has come into time. As a 'knight of faith', with a stance that he admits will seem absurd to the mere rationalist or moralist, his practical approach to suffering is not resignation but affirmation. Through his pseudonym Johannes Climacus, Kierkegaard advocates an 'active' suffering, urging that 'the highest action in the inner world is to suffer'. This is taking hold of the suffering that befalls us, accepting it for ourselves and doing something with it, 'coming to an understanding with misfortune' and so 'acting to transform existence' (Kierkegaard 1992: 431–4). The 'pathos-filled actuality of suffering' is not present as long as a person understands suffering as 'accidental' or 'alien'; the actuality of suffering consists in understanding suffering as 'essential'. This is a new way of seeing, a shift of 'life view' or 'seeing as', rooted in a subjectivity which is a passion for what is ultimate, transcending a mere act of will.

Active suffering is then a feature of the 'religious' stage of life, a relation to final and eternal concerns. Kierkegaard here dissents from Schopenhauer: 'if to exist at all, to be a human being, is to suffer, then Christianity is robbed of its dialectic . . . Christianity becomes a pleonasm, a superfluous comment, chit-chat, for if to be a human being is to suffer, then it is certainly ludicrous to advance a doctrine with the formulation: to be a Christian is to suffer' (Kierkegaard 1999: iv. 31–2 [3881]). In *The Gospel of Sufferings* Kierkegaard asserts that joy in suffering is possible because of Christian teaching that 'hardship is the road' to enter eternal life (Kierkegaard 1993: 292–3, 301–5). Ideas shape emotions, especially ideas about our *telos* or goal, and religious thoughts are the basis for a configuration of emotions of suffering very different from natural ones (Kierkegaard 1992: 443–7). Where the secular person responds to suffering with anxiety, the

Christian responds with calm trust. Kierkegaard hastens to assure us, however, that faith is not masochism: we should not think that 'sorrow is more meritorious than joy' (Kierkegaard 1990: ii.493 [2178–9]). The inevitability of suffering is no justification for thinking of suffering instrumentally as having some God-designed purpose within an economy of salvation. Suffering is not *necessary* to reach one's goal and enter the Kingdom, but as a matter of fact it is inescapable. It will be inflicted on us, and we can 'see it as' a passage-way to the Kingdom and eternal happiness. Quite the contrary to what is generally believed, suffering is definitely not a threat to human existence. Unlike sin, which is a real threat, suffering can restore in us the balance of our true self by awakening the eternal within us. It is, conversely, the presence of the eternal in history that enables all of life's suffering to become a moment when compared with the eternal joy of the Kingdom.

For the novelist Dostoevsky, the suffering which is voluntarily undertaken awakens a will to freedom within us. Raskolnikov (in *Crime and Punishment*) and Dmitri Karamazov (in *The Brothers Karamazov*) gain this sense of freedom in the end because they seek suffering. Father Zossima considers that anguish is so valuable that he sends Alyosha Karamazov away from the monastery with the order that he should first suffer with and among people before taking his final vows. Dostoevsky affirms the will as the primary factor of existence. As with Kant, the laws of nature are constructions of the human mind, and thus predictable, while the will is unpredictable and so inhabits a realm of freedom. According to Dostoevsky, laws and ideas are created for the sake of human beings, and for their sake they must be eternally re-created. Consequently, the rebellion of Dostoevsky's heroes consists in acting in complete indifference to nature (1993: 14, 24–5).

However, Dostoevsky perceives the danger inherent in absolute freedom. Human free will, when set loose from any moral or guiding principle, is at liberty to perpetrate the most monstrous acts, especially domination of others. For Raskolnikov, if God is dead then 'all things are lawful'; for Ivan Karamazov, in a world without God 'everything is permitted'. As with Schopenhauer, the exercise of the will leads to conflict and so suffering. But through the suffering of guilt and remorse, and the voluntary facing of even greater suffering to make atonement for oneself as well as for others, true freedom can be gained. Sonia points the way to Raskolnikov's redemption. He must go and stand at the crossroads, bow down, kiss the earth which he has defiled, and then bow down to all the world and say that he is a murderer: 'Suffer and expiate your sin by it, that's what you must do' (Dostoevsky 1950: 401). So Dostoevsky states: 'I believe that the main and most fundamental spiritual quest of the Russian people is their craving for suffering—perpetual and unquenchable suffering' (Dostoevsky 1949: 36). Like Kierkegaard, Dostoevsky's view of suffering is Christological, but in this case a mystical identification with the suffering Christ. He echoes the deep-seated Russian conviction that the weak, the unjustly injured, and those enduring martyrdom for Christianity will, at the Last Judgment, be exalted above the rich and powerful aristocracy: 'the meek shall inherit the earth'.

Not all this suffering is voluntary. When Dostoevsky's Ivan Karamazov tells of the torment of children, and then concludes that one must reject the world of divine creation ('I hasten to return my ticket of admission') what Ivan doubts is not God's existence, but any demonstration that God's benevolence is effective in a world of stark evil. Ivan accepts there may be a Leibnizian 'harmony' in eternity, but there is no harmony in the actual universe here and now, and no future harmony can justify the unjust suffering of the present (Dostoevsky 1982: 287). In Ivan's subsequent parable about Christ, 'The Legend of the Grand Inquisitor', the ultimate aim of Christ's life and death is the revelation of the great truth of human freedom, but history shows that freedom leads to moral chaos and to brutal suffering; this, we may say, is the lesson of Schopenhauer. So human beings have renounced their freedom and agreed to submit to the social and legal authority of the state which guarantees security by despotic rule, as personified in the 'Grand Inquisitor'. In the parable, Christ responds to the accusation that his mission has failed by silently kissing the Grand Inquisitor, and Alyosha responds to the parable by kissing Ivan (Dostoevsky 1982: 309). There is ambiguity here: Ivan is exhilarated because for him the human kiss (love) *replaces* the presence and providence of God, while for Alyosha, the kiss *represents* the active love of God. For Alyosha and for Dostoevsky the question 'is the universe worth the tears of one tortured child?' cannot be answered by a rational theodicy; worth can only be *shown* through the kiss of suffering love. The kiss is the unexpected gesture—'the miraculous breaks in'—establishing the true freedom of Christ (Williams 2008: 31). Voluntary, suffering love is thus a means of acquiring the freedom over law that Dostoevsky desires, without dominating others; it is also a practical means of coping with a situation of unjust suffering.

For Schopenhauer, the practical response to inescapable suffering is resignation (with compassion for others); for Kierkegaard and Dostoevsky it is active suffering, though Dostoevsky shows a deeper mysticism of suffering and an even stronger emphasis on human will than is present in Kierkegaard.

IV. THE TRAGIC SENSE OF LIFE:
THE AESTHETIC APPROACH TO SUFFERING

Nietzsche inherits this stress on the will from both Schopenhauer and Dostoevsky (both of whom he revered as his teachers), their own thought stemming from the moral will in Kant, but he replaces the resignation of Schopenhauer with an active affirming of suffering and life. Though this may seem Dostoevskian, for Nietzsche the 'Super-man' (*Übermensch*) first evoked by Dostoevsky now imposes a totally human value on life, and so one might say that Nietzsche stands more on the side of the Grand Inquisitor than of Christ, coping with human suffering by creating an elite who can bear the horrid truth of existence, in order to control others and benevolently decrease their misery. This philosophy of life is expressed in a theory of tragedy, so that Nietzsche overtly places an aesthetic approach to suffering alongside the theoretical and practical approaches already developed. The *Übermensch* of Nietzsche's later work is foreshadowed by the 'Dionysian man' of the *Birth of Tragedy*, that is the person who has experienced the suffering of the human condition and who overcomes it by embracing it.

For Nietzsche, art must be a mirror of the painful reality of life. Greek tragedy is the truest art form because the destruction of the tragic hero is the paradigm of human suffering. Nietzsche proposes that tragedy combines two moods—the Apollonian and the Dionysian: the first offers attractive images of individual characters in the drama, expressing the drive of life towards distinction and individuality, while the second is embodied in the chorus, expressing the horror of existence and the drive towards loss of individuality in a primal unity. The Dionysian mood encapsulates the awful truth of human life, that all persons are destined for dissolution of their identity, a metaphysical pessimism at odds with both the Socratic and Christian tradition (Nietzsche 1999: 25–8, 39–41). We enjoy watching tragedy, Nietzsche proposes, because we understand that in watching a ritual self-destruction we are gaining insight into own condition. We enjoy recognizing this truth because the dissolution of our identity and individuality is both what we fear most and also what gives us the most intense pleasure. There is pleasure because in self-dissolution we both return to our original state (as Schopenhauer proposed) and are also returning from a world of illusions, individuality being the highest illusion (Nietzsche 1999: 101–5). Nietzsche thus offers a kind of secular 'theodicy' based on tragic theory: the world is seen to be worthwhile by contemplating it as an aesthetic phenomenon. The putative spectator of this drama of life is the non-individuated reality behind all appearances, the Primordial Unity (*das Ur-Eine*); this reality is not God, but can be imagined to be like a child playing in the sand on the beach, haphazardly creating and destroying individual forms. The world will seem 'justified' to us to the extent to which we can, through various aesthetic experiences, come close to identifying ourselves with the primordial child and seeing the beauty of the play (Nietzsche 1999: 105, 114).

Tragedy, bringing Dionysus and Apollo together, thus transforms pessimism into affirmation. We can replace a pessimism that saps the will with a pessimism that is life-enhancing. Schopenhauer's pessimism is a 'pessimism of weakness', avers Nietzsche, while the Greek and his own is a 'pessimism of strength' (Nietzsche 1999: 4, 10). Just as pain and pleasure belong together in dramatic tragedy, so they belong together in the tragedy of life: suffering is a necessary companion to creative living, so that we can tolerate 'as much displeasure as possible as the price for the growth of an abundance of subtle pleasure and joys' (Nietzsche 1957: 86). To the degree to which one suffers, so one can be part of the elite that surpasses itself (the *Übermensch*): 'How deeply one can suffer almost determines the order of rank' (Nietzsche 1954: 679). In the face of suffering, the self-surpassing person will recognize the illusion of the individual self, affirm life, exercise the will to power and so join the audience which views the tragedy of the world.

Such a person will also abjure all pity for the suffering of others, since Nietzsche agrees with Kant that one who pities is susceptible to control and manipulation by those pitied, and so loses moral autonomy. The cross of Jesus thus epitomizes for Nietzsche the decline of life: 'is it true, what they say, that pity choked him ?' (Nietzsche 2005: 227). While Nietzsche objects to the traditional notion of a God of infinity and immutability because this concept denigrates humans who suffer, he also objects to the idea of a suffering God since worship of this God would sap the nerve of the will to power. Nietzsche has borrowed his own catchword 'God is dead' from a Lutheran phrase about the God who 'lies dead' in the cross. But, he thinks, a suffering and compassionate God would sanction mere resignation to suffering and the fostering of an enervating pity. It has taken recent theology to assert that a suffering God would join Ivan Karamazov's protest *against* suffering inflicted on life's victims.

For Nietzsche, suffering in everyday life can be called a 'tragedy' because the dramatic form of tragedy reflects this suffering and strengthens the will to face it. If daily suffering can be imaged as a tragedy, then its 'spectators' can find the same resistance to despair. The Spanish philosopher, novelist, and dramatist Miguel de Unamuno, writing just before the First World War, follows Nietzsche in linking the 'tragedy' of life to the tragedy of the theatre. Like Nietzsche, he thinks that the *corporate* experience of a tragic play will enable the audience to sharpen its self-awareness and face sufferings with a new affirmation of life. However, opposing Nietzsche, Unamuno finds the practice of pity and compassion to be fundamental in coping with 'the tragic sense of life' in everyday existence and in the theatre. We must practice 'weeping in common' and the sympathy of daily life is intensified in the ritual space of the theatre, giving us hope: 'I am convinced that we should solve many things if we all went out into the streets and uncovered our griefs, which perhaps would prove to be one sole grief' (Unamuno 1921: 17). Viewing a tragic drama with others enables us to share our sorrows in suffering the human tragedy, to recognize the universality of the human condition, and so reach out with hope despite the doubts of reason.

Hope is possible because sympathy and pity are at the heart of Unamuno's metaphysic of a universal consciousness, just as they are in his theory of tragedy. Unamuno follows Schopenhauer in finding suffering to be inescapable: there is a 'tragic sense' to life because human beings possess consciousness, and this inevitably involves suffering, since self-consciousness means an awareness of our limits. 'The evolution of organic beings is simply a struggle to realize fullness of consciousness through suffering' (Unamuno 1921: 140–1); this is the only way that human beings can attain a moral personality, since 'pain, which is a kind of dissolution, makes us discover our internal core' (Unamuno 1921: 212). Unamuno notes that Schopenhauer's view of a universal will in humanity and nature led him to a view of universal suffering, since 'the will is a force that feels itself—that is, which suffers'; Unamuno approves of Schopenhauer's conclusion that compassion must be the foundation of all morals. However, he judges that Schopenhauer was unnecessarily brought to unrelieved pessimism by his lack of a 'social and historical sense, his inability to feel that humanity also is a person, although a collective one'. In short, Schopenhauer's egoism 'prevented him from . . . personalizing the Will of the universe' and so 'feeling God' (Unamuno 1921: 147).

Sympathy in suffering, for Unamuno, teaches us to know God as the supreme suffering personality. We pity what is like ourselves and so love reaches out to others in compassion; as it reaches out universally it

> discovers that the total All, the Universe, is also Person possessing a Consciousness, a Consciousness which in its turn suffers, pities, and loves and therefore is consciousness. And this Consciousness of the Universe, which love discovers, personalizing all that it loves, is what we call God. And thus the soul pities God and feels itself pitied by Him.   (Unamuno 1921: 139)

This results in an optimistic view of the universe, explaining not 'the *why*, but . . . . the ultimate *wherefore*', giving a meaning to the whole. As we 'live and love—that is, suffer and pity—in this all-enveloping supreme Person', we have the assurance that we are 'enriching' a God who creates God's self in us (Unamuno 1921: 152–3).

Taking his departure from a theatrical analogy, Unamuno has arrived at a theodicy reminiscent of Schelling and Hegel, and he shows a similar tendency towards determinism in so far as suffering appears to be a cosmic necessity for moral progress. But his stress on sympathy brings him close, as he claims, to Kierkegaard's leap of 'passionate' faith over against mere rationalism (Unamuno 1921: 115), and a renewed stress on love as compassion has been a key part of recent theologies of suffering.

V. Newer Practical Approaches

In the aftermath of the slaughter of the First World War and the growing storm-clouds of the rise of National Socialism in Germany, two divergent attitudes to suffering can be perceived in the European tradition. Both represent a continuity with trends of thought in the previous century. In the first place there is a strain of optimism, based on a Marxist analysis of the dialectical process of history. It seemed that humankind had learnt its lesson through the First World War, and this catastrophe need never be repeated. Suffering would cease to be a problem, since it would be abolished through progress towards a new humanity. This might be seen as an extension of the trajectory sketched by Hegel and Schelling, though now with a Marxist flavour. It is represented by the early work of the Frankfurt school, in the work of Theodor Adorno and Max Horkheimer. While the early Horkheimer, for instance, denounces the utopia of the Romantics as a hopeless attempt to return to a golden age, he commends attempts to shape the future in concrete ways. Writing in 1933, in the face of the 'suffering of past generations' which can 'receive no compensation', he urges that dialectical materialism is 'concerned with changing the concrete conditions under which men suffer'; thus he calls for a 'struggle for a better order of things', finding confidence in 'developmental tendencies which point beyond the immediate present' (Horkheimer 1982: 22–6, 32).

On the other hand, there is a pessimistic, negative strain more reminiscent of Schopenhauer which is represented by a figure who haunted the margins of the same Frankfurt School, Walter Benjamin. For Benjamin, in the light of the suffering of history, any confidence in progress is futile. There *is* a hope for utopia (and here he parts company with Schopenhauer), but only in the end of history. Writing in 1940, he denies that history represents progress, and describes it as 'one single catastrophe which keeps piling wreckage upon wreckage' (Benjamin 1969: 257). Drawing on Jewish messianism and the Jewish mysticism of Gerschom Scholem, Benjamin proposes that we must await an inbreaking of something new from the future which will redeem all the suffering of the past: 'The Messiah himself consummates all history, in the sense that he alone redeems, completes, creates its relation to the Messianic. For this reason nothing historical can relate itself on its own account to anything Messianic' (Benjamin 1986: 312). Since for Benjamin history is essentially a history of suffering, it cannot itself give birth to a different future. The messianic history of life runs counter to the history of the suffering of the world which leads only to death; but on its counter-course it offers something redemptive to the whole history of suffering.

In recent years the Reformed theologian Jürgen Moltmann has greeted Benjamin's perception as a foreshadowing of his own Christian eschatology: the resurrection of the Christ who, in his death participated in the suffering of the world, promises a future event when his coming will reverse the suffering caused by evolution and so-called 'progress' in history (Moltmann 1974: 165). Moltmann is clearly taking a more literal view of a 'last day' of judgement, where Benjamin is concerned only with the way that the 'now-time' can be changed by a messianic perspective which can never be objectified in a particular event. They both, however, see the conditions of suffering in the present as capable of being transformed by hope.

From 1940 onwards, influenced by the experience of the Holocaust, Horkheimer increasingly takes up the approach of Benjamin: in the face of human suffering we have a 'longing for the totally other', though (unlike Benjamin) he is agnostic about whether to call this other 'God', since we do not know what God is (Horkheimer 1978: 239). This 'wholly other' is a universal righteousness into which the subjects of society can enter without compulsion. There is a longing for 'perfect righteousness' which can never be realized during the course of secular history, for even if a better society were to bring the present disorder into harmony, 'it could not make good past misery, nor assume past distress into some all-embracing reality' (Horkheimer 1970: 69). Echoes of Schopenhauer are evident here, in the insistence that there can be no compensation for suffering, although Benjamin and Horkheimer go beyond the earlier thinker in their hope for something 'other' to come that exceeds human possibilities, even though it is unthinkable and unspeakable.

Moltmann finds in the later Horkheimer, as in Benjamin, a resonance with his own theology of the 'crucified God' (Moltmann 1974: 223–7). He identifies a kind of 'protest atheism', which he also discerns in Dostoevsky's character Ivan, protesting against the God of conventional metaphysical theism who supports a theodicy which either tolerates suffering or offers compensation for it. He agrees with Horkheimer that belief in such a God is idolatry. A suffering God, Moltmann proposes, is on the side of protest, objecting out of a divine experience of pain to human suffering, and promising a new creation in which righteousness will be established for all the oppressed. Like Benjamin and Horkheimer he proposes a practical approach to suffering arising from orientation to the future: for Moltmann, hope in a future which is still outstanding for God, but which God will bring, gives incentive for change in contemporary society, arousing a discontent with the *status quo* and attacking causes of suffering out of a kind of permanent 'revolutionary consciousness' (Moltmann 1979: 8–12). Practical strategies for facing suffering in the twentieth century have thus, in contrast to those of the previous century, been marked by eschatologies which are either religious or secular.

A similar messianism to that of Benjamin and Horkheimer is to be found in Emmanuel Levinas, who laments that no rational meaning is to be discerned in history itself (Levinas 1990: 95). Deeply affected by the Holocaust, of which he had personal experience, Levinas asserts that we are living in a time 'after the end of theodicy'. Theodicy is a 'temptation' which consists in 'finding God innocent . . . or in making suffering bearable' (Levinas 1988a: 161). The phenomenon of Auschwitz demands that we conceive of 'the moral law independently of a Happy End'. Moral behaviour springs from the recognition that the 'other' makes an infinite demand on us; indeed, living before the face of the other establishes us as personal subjects in the first place. Referring to our utter responsibility for the other which is not a reciprocal relationship, he often quotes Dostoevsky's Father Zossima: 'Each of us is guilty before everyone for everyone, and I more than the others' (Levinas 1998a: 146; Dostoevsky 1982: 339). 'That', he comments, 'is the idea of dissymmetry. The relationship between me and the other is unsurpassable' (Levinas 1988b: 179). Levinas's practical response to 'useless suffering', a suffering which is completely senseless, is, in effect, the 'active suffering' commended by Dostoevsky and Kierkegaard. But this takes the form of an asymmetrical, non-mutual responsibility for the other: 'the very phenomenon of suffering in its uselessness is, in principle, the pain of the Other' (Levinas 1988a: 163). Suffering eludes comprehension, and cannot be integrated into any rational scheme of explanation. Suffering and evil are not just excessive because suffering 'can go beyond what is bearable'; they are 'not only non-integratable', but also show 'the non-integratability of the non-integratable' (Levinas 1998b: 128). Suffering cannot be justified by a theoretical theodicy, but it does have a quality of malignant transcendence that opens us up to the 'infinite' demand of the Other. For Levinas, this is the infinity of the other person, but behind and beyond this he also recognizes a God, or a 'Good beyond Being', who is never present but has always 'just passed by', as Moses in a story in the Torah catches only a glimpse of the retreating back of God (Levinas 1996: 63–4). A relationship with God is entangled in the responsibility we bear for the other person and in the justice we work with others to achieve, but the horror of Auschwitz tells us that God has withdrawn from the scene to leave room for human, adult responsibility. This leads Levinas to make a twist on the messianic theme. The 'Other' that comes to disturb us with eschatological urgency is embodied here and now in the suffering neighbour. Yet also in Jewish Rabbinic texts, the Messiah who breaks into history is the suffering man who does not evade the burden of others' suffering, who carries the responsibility of the world: 'Who finally takes on the suffering of others if not the being who says "Me" (*Moi*)?' While we wait for the coming of something which cannot be objectified, which transcends and unsettles history, everyone can nevertheless act *as if* they were themselves the Messiah (Levinas 1990: 88–95).

VI. NEW PERSPECTIVES ON TRAGEDY

We have seen that the kind of 'practical approach' to suffering that is characteristic of the twentieth century has been, like that of the previous century, marked by 'active suffering'; however, in comparison with the earlier period, a stress on the exercise of the will has been modified by an openness to something 'new' in the future, often expressed in messianic symbolism, and so tending towards theology. In this approach there is a blending of pessimism and hope, although more overtly optimistic views of history have also persisted in some quarters. Indeed, manifestations of this optimism have prompted one influential literary theorist to reassert the Nietzschian view of tragedy, underlining the approach to suffering we have called 'aesthetic'. As Nietzsche had blamed the decline of tragedy in the Hellenistic period on Socratic confidence in theoretical reason, and on Enlightenment optimism in his own time, so George Steiner claims that tragedy is not possible today because of optimism generated by Marxist views of history, by the Christian story of resurrection and eternal life, and by scientific confidence in progress. In *The Death of Tragedy*, Steiner writes that 'tragedy would have us know that there is in the very fact of human existence a provocation or a paradox; it tells us that the purposes of men (sic) sometimes run against the grain of inexplicable and destructive forces.' It teaches us 'of the unfaltering bias toward inhumanity and destruction in the drift of the world'. As in Nietzsche, tragedy offers no compensation for this: 'the wounds are not healed and the broken spirit is not mended' (Steiner 1961: 128–9, 291). Tragedy, he asserts, offers only a controlled *repetition* of suffering.

However, with particular reference to Chekhov, Steiner also hints at the possibility of a unity between tragic and comic drama (Steiner 1961: 301–2), and it might be claimed against his general argument that the genre of tragi-comedy supplies us with no less of a radical sense of insecurity than tragedy, as well as a glimpse of hope. Here is a discernible parallel between 'practical' and 'aesthetic' approaches to suffering. Just as pessimism about suffering has been blended with (non-objectifiable) messianism, so tragedy has characteristically taken the form of tragi-comedy in the latter part of the last century and still does today. On the one hand, practitioners have claimed that it deepens the sense of the intractability of evil and the inexplicable nature of suffering. Comedy can be anarchic, disruptive, and threatening. As the playwright Eugene Ionesco puts it:

> For my part I have never understood the difference people make between the comic and the tragic. As the 'comic' is an intuitive perception of the absurd, it seem to me more hopeless than the 'tragic' . . . . it seems to me that the comic is tragic, and that the tragedy of man is pure derision.

On the other hand, as Ionesco also perceives, humour offers a kind of freedom, liberating the imagination to wander where it will, releasing the mind from the constraints of rationality. So Ionesco writes: 'the comic alone is able to give us the strength to bear the tragedy of existence' (Ionesco 1984: 26–7).

Samuel Beckett's humour, as a master of tragi-comedy offers a realistic vision of human suffering, which can neither be explained nor excused. His tramps, or clowns, in *Waiting for Godot* speak the truth, through their absurd dialogue, about the unremitting nature of their suffering, endured in a slow crucifixion of boredom. Vladimir protests to Estragon 'You're not going to compare yourself to Christ!' and Estragon replies, 'All my life I've compared myself to him'. Vladimir objects, 'But where he lived it was warm, it was dry!' and Estragon adds, 'Yes. And they crucified quick' (Beckett 1965: 52). At the same time, the humour raises just the possibility of renewal in the life of repetitive misery portrayed in *Godot* and *Endgame*. As Jeffrey Nealon has argued from a postmodern perspective, the plays are not a modernist lament for the *loss* of meaning in our present age; rather they show an '*excess* of meaning and possibility', which is brought about by the liberating notion of play (Nealon 1992: 51). In decentring the self the language games break old structures of thinking, so that there is just a hint of truth in the tramps' celebration of 'the beauty of the way and the goodness of wayfarers' (Beckett 1965: 16).

The cinema in the late twentieth century has certainly shown the tendency to alleviate tragedy with a note of hope, and in this sense has preferred the genre of tragi-comedy, though the 'comedic' element (or a movement towards resolution) is not always humorous. The director Andrei Tarkovsky has been deeply influenced by Dostoevsky, as is evident in his comment that 'there has to be suffering, because it's through suffering, in the struggle between good and evil, that the spirit is forged' (Tarkovsky 1994: 297). In the film *Andrei Rublev*, the fifteen-century Russian monk and icon painter Andrei Rublev renounces his art, unable to make sense of the deep suffering of the population around him. However, years later, upon watching a young boy masterfully crafting a giant bell, Rublev's creative flame is rekindled, and the scenes change suddenly from black and white to colour as he returns to his canvas.

Ingmar Bergman's films explore the suffering of abandonment, the experience of being betrayed and left alone. All sources of security—other people, the family, social institutions, and especially God—are withdrawn, and the world becomes silent and the landscape like a desert. In *The Seventh Seal*, for instance, characters and audience travel through a barren land devastated by plague; Jöns says of the suffering of the fourteen year-old child burnt as a witch, that there is 'emptiness under the moon'. Bergman shows that suffering is intensified as a sense of abandonment modulates into self-destructive emotions, as with Karin in *Wild Strawberries*. But if characters can face their darkness honestly, the spiritual desert that seems endless can become a place of rebirth in which the soul may be nourished again. Suffering can be a passion that, like Christ's, ends in resurrection. But, as Jesse Kalin (2003: 11) suggests, for Bergman this is never a justification of suffering, a good that excuses suffering and gives it a meaning. There is no theodicy in Bergman, only a vivid sense of what Bergman in *Winter Night* has named 'the silence of God'; yet healing and nourishment do exist as real possibilities in the world, and suffering keeps them open.

These new perspectives on suffering within the art form of 'tragedy' bring us, like 'practical' approaches, to theological reflection. We recall Steiner's critique that the Christian vision of the world is 'anti-tragic', since the shape of the story of Christ is a 'divine comedy' (in Dante's sense of *commedia*), 'leading the soul towards justice and resurrection' (Steiner 1961: 331–2). The implication is that this story prevents us from taking suffering and dissolution as seriously as tragedy does. Yet we have seen that tragedy in our age expresses human disintegration while hinting that the loss does not have to be total. For their part, theologians have replied to Steiner that the resurrection of Christ does not cancel the suffering of the cross and so undermine the desolation of human suffering (MacKinnon 1968: 96–103; Lash 1979: 214–15). The cross remains tragic since the resurrection does not reverse it, being an event of a completely different order. Death is not overcome by some inner meaning of the event of suffering, making it less final, but by new creation. It is just because death is final within this old order of creation, and Christ meets its finality head on, that God has to do something new in the face of death. The suffering of the cross has no intrinsic meaning, but it can *acquire* meaning. With regard to eschatology, theologians influenced by process theology have urged that it is possible to conceive of final consummation and final tragedy together, in the reaping of a harvest of what A. N. Whitehead called a 'tragic beauty' (Whitehead 1939: 356, 380–1). *Apokotastasis* need not exclude elements of tragedy, as one can envisage that there are values and experiences which have tragically not been actualized, and even in bringing about a new creation the God who feels and values the worth of every life will be open to 'the tragedy of unfulfilled desire' (Fiddes 1988: 105–6).

VII. A New Kind of Theodicy

We have been tracing the afterlife in recent years of 'practical' and 'aesthetic' responses to suffering which were developed earlier in the nineteenth century, and have observed the way that they have been adopted in theological reflection It seems, however, that theology 'after Auschwitz' has abandoned the quest for the *first* form of response we considered, a 'theoretical' theodicy of a Leibnizian kind (Rubenstein 1992: 293–6). It is clear that Ivan's question, 'is the universe worth the tears of one tortured child?' cannot be answered positively in any way that is rationally convincing, and it is better to let theology be 'ruptured' by the stories of victims (Surin 1986: 149). But there is, nevertheless, a widespread conviction that some affirming of divine passibility may provide a basis for a leap of faith that asserts 'it *is* worth it', taking Schelling's step of belief in the worth of personality. There has been, for instance, a resurgence of Schelling's perception that only divine suffering begins to make credible any 'free-will' defence of the existence of evil and suffering in the world. If a creator is to take the risk of suffering appearing in a free world, then such a god must run the risk of suffering in god's own self. Such an argument has undeniable aspects of a theodicy about it, though it remains fragmentary.

Suffering, it was observed at the beginning of this article, involves feeling and injury. On both grounds suffering was traditionally denied to God. The first seemed to destroy God's bliss, and the second God's aseity, or the belief that that God held existence only from God's self (*a se*). Both seemed to imply change in God. These philosophical arguments have, in much recent theology, been outweighed by the conviction that any talk about love implies that the lover suffers in sympathy with the beloved, and is affected and conditioned by the contribution that the other makes to the relationship (Jüngel 1983: 320, 325–8). While all talk about God must be metaphorical, even to apply love analogically to God seems to require the language of suffering, and this is even more appropriate in circumstances of extraordinary human suffering such as the Holocaust. Aseity, it has been argued, need not mean self-sufficiency (Fiddes 1988: 67–8) and change in God can mean having new experience rather than moral decline (Moltmann 1977: 62–4). While some theologians have maintained the impassibility and immutability of God, it is notable that they have generally also wanted to ascribe 'intense concern for the world', grief and sorrow to God in a way that was not typical of mediaeval philosophy (Weinandy 2000: 168–70). All this results in a 'practical' approach to suffering, which is marked by reassurances of God's presence and empathy with those who are suffering. In European theological thought, affirmations of the suffering of God were in fact strengthened during the twentieth century by scholars of the Hebrew Bible, both Jewish and Christian, who observed that the prophets expressed the pathos of God in sympathy with the suffering people of Israel (Robinson 1955: 184–5; Heschel 1962: 223–6).

In accord with this practical approach to suffering, theology of the death of Christ has increasingly been focused on the transformative effect in human life of the engagement of God in human suffering and forsakenness. The event of the cross is seen to make an impact on the whole triune being of God, and this in turn enables human participation in God. Moltmann lays stress on 'division' and 'disruption' in the communion of the Trinity for the sake of solidarity with humanity (Moltmann 1974: 207), while the Catholic Hans Urs von Balthasar (holding to a modified view of impassibility) finds that the 'otherness' and difference that exists eternally between the persons of the Trinity has room within it to embrace the separation at the heart of human suffering (Balthasar 1994: 323–5). Echoes of Hegel can be detected in these accounts, but essentially practical approaches are being supported by a more modest and more humble theodicy.

It seems that an attempt at a more thorough-going theodicy has nevertheless been made by the Reformed theologian Karl Barth, for whom evil is a 'nothingness' which owes its 'reality as non-reality' to God's rejection of it—it is that to which God says 'no' at the beginning. This nothingness casts its shadow into creation: the 'shadow-side' of creation which includes suffering is on the borders of nothingness, but is not nothingness itself. The shadow has been assumed by Christ along with the positive side of existence, and so the shadow together with the light can praise God (Barth 1961: 289–312). Barth is offering a partial explanation of suffering, but it is not of a Leibnizian kind, based on a world view of the harmony of creation. It is based instead on the creative will of God and on the assumption of the shadow by Christ in his life and the encounter of Christ with nothingness in his death. While the theory might be judged to diminish the sheer intractability of evil to which Levinas draws attention, it does belong to the modern assertion of the engagement of God with human suffering; Barth stresses that God is free to be 'conditioned as well as unconditioned' by the world (Barth 1957: 303).

One strain of Christian theology has, it is true, denied any aspect of theodicy to the suffering of God, finding it to be a symbol of the *absence* of God, in a similar way to Levinas' notion of divine withdrawal. Dorothee Soelle, for example, finds that the only effective presence of God is in human beings who suffer, as the representatives of the suffering but absent God. They do God's work by affecting us and moving us towards true humanity. The suffering of Christ, she thinks, cannot be claimed to be more intense than the suffering of others; unwittingly echoing Beckett's Estragon she judges that 'A fifty-year old woman piece worker hangs on the cross no less than Jesus—only longer' (Soelle 1975: 146). But Christ helps us to keep a kind of doubting faith in the absent God as he stands in for him in the world: 'He comforts those whom, up to now, God has left in the lurch . . .' (Soelle 1967: 137). Echoing Kierkegaard's view of suffering as 'the highest action in inwardness', Soelle urges us to 'choose' the suffering that befalls us, for 'what I take belongs to me in a differing sense from something I only bear' (Soelle 1975: 103); but this choice is made, unlike Kierkegaard, in the courageous acknowledgement of God's absence.

Most modern theologians, however, portray God as *hidden* in a suffering world rather than absent from it. Modern theology has thus shown its own kind of integration of theoretical, practical, and aesthetic forms of thought about suffering that have been inherited from the nineteenth century. Generally in modern culture 'practical' responses to suffering have taken up the earlier emphasis on 'active suffering', while being shaped by a new openness to the future. 'Aesthetic' responses have absorbed the blend of pessimism and optimism embodied in tragi-comedy. 'Theoretical' accounts of suffering, however, as developed earlier by Leibniz and then by German Idealism, are usually met with suspicion today. In this cultural context theology has taken a predominantly 'practical' approach, which is characterized both by protest against suffering in the light of future hope, and by assurance of God's presence in suffering. This is supported by the 'aesthetic' element of finding tragic dimensions in the story of the crucified and resurrected Christ, and is often accompanied by fragmentary 'theory' in the form of a modest theodicy of a suffering God.

REFERENCES

Balthasar, Hans Urs von (1994). *Theo-Drama. Theological Dramatic Theory*, vol. iv, *The Action*, trans. G. Harrison (San Francisco: Ignatius Press).

Barth, Karl (1957). *Church Dogmatics*, vol. ii, *The Doctrine of God*, Part 1, trans. G. W. Bromiley and T. F. Torrance (Edinburgh: T. & T. Clark).

——(1961). *Church Dogmatics*, vol. iii, *The Doctrine of Creation*, Part 3, trans. G. W. Bromiley and T. F. Torrance (Edinburgh: T. & T. Clark).

Beckett, Samuel (1965). *Waiting for Godot*. (London: Faber and Faber).

Benjamin, Walter (1969). 'Theses on the Philosophy of History', *Illuminations*, trans. Harry Zohn (New York: Schocken Books).

——(1986). 'Theological Political Fragment', *Reflections: Essays, Aphorisms, Autobiographical Writings*, trans. E. Jephcott (New York: Schocken Books).

Dostoevsky, Fyodor (1949). *The Diary of a Writer*, trans. Boris Brasol (London: Cassell).

——(1950). *Crime and Punishment*, trans. C. Garnett (New York: Dutton).

——(1982). *The Brothers Karamazov*, trans. D. Magarshack (Harmondsworth: Penguin).

——(1993). *Notes from Underground*, trans. R. Pevear and L. Volokhonsky (New York: Knopf).

Fiddes, Paul S. (1988). *The Creative Suffering of God*. (Oxford: Oxford University Press).

Hegel, G. W. F. (1979). *The Christian Religion: Lectures on the Philosophy of Religion, Part III*, trans. P. C. Hodgson (Missoula: Scholars Press).

Heschel, Abraham (1962). *The Prophets*. (New York: Harper & Row).

Hick, John (1968). *Evil and the God of Love*. (London: Collins/Fontana).

Horkheimer, Max (1970). *Die Sehnsucht nach dem ganz Anderen*, Ein Interview mit Kommentar von H. Gumnior (Hamburg: Furche-Verlag).

——(1978). *Dawn & Decline: Notes 1926–1931 and 1950–1969*, trans. M. Shaw (New York: Seabury Press).

——(1982). 'Materialism and Metaphysics' [1933], repr. in *Critical Theory. Selected Essays*, trans. M. J. O'Connell et al. (New York: Continuum).

Ionesco, Eugene (1984). *Notes and Counter Notes: Writings on the Theatre*, trans. D. Watson (London: John Calder).

Jüngel, Eberhard (1983). *God as the Mystery of the World*, trans. D. L. Guder (Edinburgh: T. & T. Clark).

Kalin, Jesse (2003). *The Films of Ingmar Bergman*. (Cambridge: Cambridge University Press).

Kant, Immanuel (1933). *Critique of Pure Reason*, trans. N. K. Smith (London: Macmillan).

——(1956). *Critique of Practical Reason*, trans. L. Beck (Indianapolis: Bobbs-Merrill).

——(1998a). 'On the Miscarriage of All Philosophical Trials in Theodicy', in A. Wood and G. Di Giovanni (eds), *Religion Within the Bounds of Mere Reason and Other Writings*. (Cambridge: Cambridge University Press).

——(1998b). *Religion Within the Boundaries of Mere Reason*, trans. A. Wood and G. Di Giovanni (Cambridge: Cambridge University Press).

Kierkegaard, Søren (1980). *The Concept of Anxiety*, trans. R. Thomte and A. B. Anderson (Princeton, NJ: Princeton University Press).

——(1992). *Concluding Unscientific Postscript*, trans. H. V. Hong and E. H. Hong (Princeton, NJ: Princeton University Press).

——(1993). *The Gospel of Sufferings*, in *Upbuilding Discourses in Various Spirits*, trans. H. V. Hong and E. H. Hong (Princeton, NJ: Princeton University Press).

Kierkegaard, Søren (1999). *Søren Kierkegaard's Journals and Papers*, 2nd edn., 7 vols., ed. and trans. H. V. Hong and E. H. Hong (Bloomington, IN: Indiana University Press).

Lash, Nicholas (1979). *Theology on Dover Beach.* (London: Darton, Longman, and Todd).

Leibniz, G. W. (1990). *Theodicy: Essays on the Goodness of God, the Freedom of Man and the Origin of Evil*, trans. E. M. Huggard (Chicago: Open Court).

Levinas, Emmanuel (1988a). 'Useless Suffering', in R. Bernasconi D. Wood (eds.), *The Provocation of Levinas: Re-thinking the Other.* (London: Routledge).

——(1988b). 'The Paradox of Morality', in R. Bernasconi and D. Wood (eds), *The Provocation of Levinas.* (London: Routledge).

——(1990). Difficult Freedom. *Essays on Judaism*, trans. Seán Hand (Baltimore, MD: Johns Hopkins University Press).

——(1996). 'Meaning and Sense', in A. Peperzak, S. Critchely, R. Bernasconi (eds), *Emmanuel Levinas: Basic Philosophical Writings.* (Bloomington, IN: Indiana University Press).

——(1998a). *Otherwise Than Being, or, Beyond Essence*, trans. A. Lingis (Pittsburgh: Duquesne University Press).

——(1998b). *Of God who Comes to Mind*, trans. B. Bergo (Stanford, CA: Stanford University Press).

MacKinnon, Donald (1968). *Borderlands of Theology and Other Essays*, ed. G. W. Roberts and D. E. Smucker (London: Lutterworth Press).

Moltmann, Jürgen (1974). *The Crucified God*, trans. R. A. Wilson and John Bowden (London: SCM Press).

——(1977). *The Church in the Power of the Spirit*, trans. M. Kohl (London: SCM Press).

——(1979). *The Future of Creation*, trans. M. Kohl (London: SCM Press).

Nealon, Jeffrey (1992). 'Samuel Beckett and the Postmodern: Language Games, Play and Waiting for Godot', in Steven Connor (ed.), *Waiting for Godot* and *Endgame.* (London: Methuen).

Nietzsche, Friedrich (1954). *The Portable Nietzsche*, selected and trans. W. Kaufmann (New York: Viking Press).

——(1957). *The Gay Science*, trans. W. Kaufmann (New York: Vintage Books).

——(1999). *The Birth of Tragedy and Other Writings*, ed. R. Geuss and R. Speirs, trans. R. Speirs (Cambridge: Cambridge University Press).

——(2005). *Thus Spoke Zarathustra: A Book for Everyone and Nobody*, trans. G. Parkes (Oxford: Oxford University Press).

Robinson, H. Wheeler (1955). 'The Cross of Jeremiah' (1925), repr. in *The Cross in the Old Testament.* (London: SCM Press).

Rubenstein, Richard (1992). *After Auschwitz. History, Theology and Contemporary Judaism*, 2nd edn. (Baltimore, MD: Johns Hopkins University Press).

Scarry, Elaine (1985). *The Body in Pain: The Making and Unmaking of the World.* (New York: Oxford University Press).

Schelling, F.W.G. (2006). *Philosophical Investigations into the Essence of Human Freedom*, trans. J. Love and J. Schmidt (New York: SUNY Press).

Schopenhauer, Arthur (1965). *On the Basis of Morality*, trans. E. F. J. Payne (Indianapolis: Bobbs-Merrill).

——(1969). *The World as Will and Representation*, 2 vols, trans. E. F. J. Payne (New York: Dover).

——(2004). *Essays and Aphorisms*, trans. R. J. Hollingdale (Harmondsworth: Penguin).

Soelle, Dorothee (1967). *Christ the Representative: An Essay in Theology after the 'Death of God'*, trans. D. Lewis (London: SCM Press).

——(1975). *Suffering*, trans. E. R. Kalin (London: Darton, Longman, and Todd).

Steiner, George (1961). *The Death of Tragedy*. (London: Faber and Faber).

Surin, Kenneth (1986). *Theology and the Problem of Evil*. (Oxford: Blackwell).

Tarkovsky, Andrei (1994). *Time Within Time: The Diaries 1970–1986*, trans. K. Hunter-Blair (London: Faber and Faber).

Unanumo, Miguel de (1921). *The Tragic Sense of Life in Men and in Peoples*, trans. J. E. Crawford Flitch (London: Macmillan).

Weinandy, Thomas (2000). *Does God Suffer?* (Edinburgh: T & T Clark).

Whitehead, A. N (1939). *Adventures of Ideas*. (London: Cambridge University Press).

Williams, Rowan (2008). *Dostoevsky: Language, Faith and Fiction*. (Waco: Baylor University Press).

SUGGESTED READING

Bernstein, Richard (2002). *Radical Evil: A Philosophical Investigation*. (Cambridge: Polity).

Fiddes, Paul S. (1988). *The Creative Suffering of God*. (Oxford: Oxford University Press).

Levinas, Emmanuel (1988a). 'Useless Suffering', in R. Bernasconi and D. Wood (eds), *The Provocation of Levinas: Re-thinking the Other* (London: Routledge).

Moltmann, Jürgen (1974). *The Crucified God*, trans. R. A. Wilson and John Bowden (London: SCM Press).

Rubenstein, Richard (1992). *After Auschwitz. History, Theology and Contemporary Judaism*, 2nd edn. (Baltimore, MD: Johns Hopkins University Press).

Soelle, Dorothee (1975). *Suffering*, trans. E. R. Kalin (London: Darton, Longman, and Todd).

Steiner, George (1961). *The Death of Tragedy*. (London: Faber and Faber).

Surin, Kenneth (1986). *Theology and the Problem of Evil*. (Oxford: Blackwell).

CHAPTER 9

DEATH

GEORGE PATTISON

En effet, il est toujours extraordinaire de mourir.

(Vladimir Jankélévitch)

I. INTRODUCTION

DEATH and religion have been associated throughout recorded history and archaeology suggests that this association goes back into the prehistorical era. Remembrance of death, its certainty, pain, and implications for living are frequently central to religious practice, in Christianity as in other religious traditions. Religion for its part has provided the metaphysical and mythical context in which death could be experienced as humanly meaningful. And perhaps death remains a focus or spur to religious feelings, speculations, and reflections even in a post-religious secular age. Philosophy too, since at least Plato's *Phaedo*, has been associated with death—although the Platonic prescription that the task of philosophy is to prepare for dying has been challenged by those, like Spinoza, who think that the philosopher should think of nothing as little as he thinks of death. And, predictably, the respective contributions of religion and philosophy to the general understanding of death in western societies are hard to disentangle. If the understanding of death we find in Plato was in part formed by the beliefs and practices of ancient Greek religion, Platonic ideas of the soul's immortality became in turn woven into the fabric of subsequent Christian teaching. By the commencement of the early modern period, a broad amalgam of Platonic, Stoic, biblical, and ecclesiastical teachings provided an accommodating framework for understanding death and for instructing individuals in how to prepare for it and how to mark it, whether and when to weep, and whether and when and for what to express hope. The immortality of the individual soul and Christian teaching on a general resurrection combined and recombined in a variety of ways, no matter how theoretically problematic or even, at times, incoherent this amalgam actually was.

Yet whilst fragments of this once-dominant paradigm doubtless linger on in the popular understanding of Christian teaching, this chapter will explore how it has been dissolved and effectively sidelined in mainstream modern theological and philosophical thought. This, I suggest, also significantly weakens the complex bonds linking philosophical and Christian views of death.[1] In this situation, it is to Christian theology's advantage to reopen the dialogue with philosophy—not, in the first instance with the presumption that some common message might be hammered out but that philosophy and theology alike share the need to rethink this most unthinkable yet thought-provoking topic.[2]

II. A CHANGING VIEW OF DEATH
AND IMMORTALITY

Already in the seventeenth and early eighteenth centuries a combination of new scientific knowledge and approaches to the Bible rendered previous assumptions about the immortality of the human soul questionable.[3] Nevertheless, by the later eighteenth century, insistence on the immortality of the soul had become one of the lynchpins of Christian apologetics. Joseph Butler declared that 'whether we are to live in a future state . . . is the most important question which can possibly be asked' (Butler 1906: 257). He also states that the belief that God 'will finally judge mankind in righteousness, and render to all according to their works in a future state' is one of the defining features of Christianity (Butler 1906: 121). The implications of such belief for the eighteenth-century's conception of social order are nicely summarized in the anecdote concerning the deist Anthony Collins who, when asked why he insisted on his servants attending church despite arguing for freedom in matters of religious belief, answered, 'I do it that they may neither rob nor murder me'.

But the doctrine of future rewards and punishments was also seen as integral to the grounds of morality in more philosophically defensible formulations. Kant grouped immortality with God and freedom as one of the three metaphysical assumptions that were needed in order to underwrite belief in morality—even if this was, of course, in a

---

[1] A 1998 collection of essays *Death and Philosophy* takes virtually no account of any Christian teaching on the subject. Aquinas, Kierkegaard, and Jesus Christ get respectively one, two, and three mentions, but that's about it. See Malpas and Solomon 1998.

[2] In addressing the question within a history of ideas perspective, I am far from denying the validity of other approaches. One might, for example, look more closely at the changing rituals associated with death—including, for example, the impact of cremation as a relatively new cultural practice in the west, new modes of memorialization, the growth of memorial services, and the widespread abandonment of preaching judgement in favour of eulogizing the dead.

[3] See Thomson 2008.

purely regulative mode. Kant argued that although—or precisely because—the supreme object of moral striving is the attainment of a holiness that is not possible in this sensuous world, practical reason must conceive of itself as proceeding along a progressive approximation towards this ideal and that, given the unattainability of the object, this process will also be conceived of as infinite. However, such an infinite process 'is only possible if this same rational being has an infinitely abiding existence and personality (which is what is called the immortality of the soul)' (Kant 1974: 252).[4] Kant's view may not of itself be 'the' Christian view and is also compatible with some versions of reincarnation or what Hick calls 'pareschatologies', that is, post-mortem states of consciousness that precede the final fulfilment of the soul in God (see Hick 1976). Nevertheless, Christian theologians readily incorporated it into their own teaching.

In the decades following the French Revolution, however, the doctrine of immortality found itself on the back foot. In 1828, David Friedrich Strauss wrote a prize essay on the resurrection of the flesh of which he wrote that 'as soon as I made the last full-stop, it was clear to me that there was nothing in the whole idea of resurrection' (Harris 1973: 19). The Danish theologian H. L. Martensen reported Strauss as saying 'I had scarcely finished reading Hegel's *Phenomenology of Spirit*, before that belief [immortality] fell away from me like a dead leaf' (Martensen 1882: 131). That the *Phenomenology* did indeed internalize a radical sense of the finitude and unqualified mortality of the human subject and that this was both absolutely integral to Hegel's whole philosophical programme as well as being a point at which Hegel distanced himself from the Judaeo-Christian tradition would be forcefully argued in the twentieth century by Alexandre Kojève. According to Kojève, Hegel sees consciousness of death as the necessary point of transition from a purely natural to a spiritual life. Spiritual life is precisely life that has incorporated this consciousness into itself: not in the sense of its going beyond nature into an eternal world existing objectively and independently of human beings but as consciousness of its own temporality and finitude. This denial of post-mortem survival is seen by Kojève as equivalent also to the denial of God or of any reality beyond the world of nature. The subject that knows its own mortality in the Hegelian manner knows it solely as an event within nature or within immanence.[5]

Whether this is a correct interpretation of the *Phenomenology*, Hegelianism certainly provided a powerful impetus to those younger thinkers minded to deny the possibility of any future life. Ludwig Feuerbach's *Thoughts on Death and Immortality* (1830), according to a recent translator, 'is a straightforward denial of the Christian belief in personal immortality, a plea for recognition of the inexhaustible quality of the only life we have, and a derisive assault on the posturing and hypocrisies of the professional theologians of nineteenth-century Germany' (Feuerbach 1980: p. ix). Feuerbach argues

---

[4] First edition |A 220. More recently the links between the doctrine of immortality and ethical responsibility have been explored in a rather different vein by J. Derrida, in dialogue with Jan Patočka, in Derrida 1995.

[5] See Kojève 1947.

that since the religious person speaks of God as infinite and human beings as finite, and since 'nothingness and death' are inherently characteristic of finitude, it follows that the very existence of an infinite God itself demands recognition of the finite human being's 'nothingness and death'. Yet we finite, temporal, and individual beings nevertheless also participate in the infinite, the eternal, and divine, which, as his concluding paragraph states, is 'life, consciousness, Spirit, nature, time, space, everything, in both its unity and its distinction...immortal'. We are not to judge the value of our individual life by its short temporal span but are to immerse ourselves in life and by doing so participate in the universal flow of divine love (Feuerbach 1980: 172–3). In *The Essence of Christianity* (1841), Feuerbach sums up: 'Faith in a future life is therefore only faith in the true life of the present; the essential elements of this life are also the essential elements of the other: accordingly, faith in a future life is not faith in another unknown life; but in the truth and infinitude, and consequently in the perpetuity, of that life which already here below is regarded as the authentic life' (Feuerbach 1989: 181). Yet in projecting this authentic life beyond the present into a future world, human beings manifest and reinforce their self-estrangement: 'The future life is the present in the mirror of imagination' (Feuerbach 1989: 182). Later, in *The Essence of Faith according to Luther*, he will say that 'death ... is the only ultimate basis of religion. And the abolition of death, immortality, is the only ultimate goal of religion, at least of the Christian religion, and the means of this abolition is God' (Feuerbach 1967: 126).

But it was not only the anti-Christians who were turning away from ideas of the immortality of the soul. In the *Speeches on Religion* Schleiermacher laments in demythologizing terms how 'most people' understand immortality in an essentially 'irreligious' manner:

> [T]hey resist the infinite and do not wish to get beyond themselves and they are anxiously concerned about their individuality . . . they do not want to seize the sole opportunity death affords them to transcend humanity; they are anxious about how they will take it with them beyond this world, and their highest endeavour is for further sight and better limbs. But the universe speaks to them, as it stands written: 'Whoever loses his life for my sake, will find it, and whoever would save it will lose it' . . . In search of an immortality, which is none, and over which they are not masters, they lose the immortality that they could have, and in addition their mortal life with thoughts that vainly distress and torment them. But try to yield up your life out of love for the universe. Strive here already to annihilate your individuality and to live in the one and all . . . .   (Schleiermacher 1988: 139)

As he sums up, 'To be one with the infinite in the midst of the finite and to be eternal in a moment, that is the immortality of religion' (Schleiermacher 1988: 140).[6]

---

[6] In *The Christian Faith*, Schleiermacher will affirm a bodily resurrection involving 'a renovation of organic life which has links of attachment to our present state' (Schleiermacher 1989: 713), but he resolutely declines to give any specific content to this statement: 'we therefore always remain uncertain how the state which is the Church's highest consummation can be gained or possessed in this form by individual personalities emerging into immortality' (Schleiermacher 1989: 720).

Schleiermacher writes to defend 'religion' but his position nevertheless has significant analogies with that of Feuerbach. They both reject what they see as vulgar misconceptions and recommend identification of the self with 'undying' universal life or will. This blurring of the boundaries between Christian and non- or anti-Christian revisions of the traditional amalgam is well-evidenced in Ralph Waldo Emerson's essay 'Immortality' (1876), in which he suggests that 'the real evidence [for immortality] is too subtle, or is higher than we can write down in propositions . . . We cannot prove our faith by syllogisms' (Emerson 1893: 504). Yet, claiming to be offering an interpretation of (among others) Jesus and Augustine, Emerson states that 'Future state is an illusion for the ever-present state. It is not length of life, but depth of life. It is not duration, but a taking of the soul out of time . . .' The person who experiences this 'is rising to greater heights, but also rising to realities; the outer relations and circumstances dying out, he entering deeper into God, God into him, until the last garment of egotism falls, and he is with God,—shares the will and the immensity of the First Cause' (Emerson 1893: 504).[7] It is a matter of debate whether or how such passages might still be read as 'religious' and Emerson might plausibly be read—as Nietzsche himself read him—as closer to Nietzsche than to Schleiermacher.

Here, then, we see the emergence of a basic conceptual paradigm shared by radical atheists, Christian apologists, and post-Christian advocates of a spiritual life. This paradigm, we may add, continued to be an influential current both in popular piety and in theological and philosophical reflection on into the late twentieth century, as in D. Z. Phillips's 1970 essay on *Death and Immortality*, where he argues that belief in post-mortem survival is not integral to Christian belief in immortality, since 'For the believer, his death, like his life, is to be in God. For him, this is the life eternal which death cannot touch; the immortality which finally places the soul beyond the reach of the snares and temptations of this mortal life' (Phillips 1970: 60).[8]

Naturally the picture is complicated if we then also take into account popular piety. Victorian hymn books and graveyards will remind us that the rhetoric of heaven as 'another place' where souls dwell in immortal light remained powerful. Nor should we forget that the nineteenth century would produce that most literalist of approaches to the 'afterlife', namely, spiritualism, often claiming for itself the status of a properly modern, scientific world view. For any individual, perhaps especially for any educated but not philosophically or theologically specialist person, several of these resources might be more or less seamlessly combined and in such a way that it is not always easy for those who come after to disentangle the threads.[9] How far various mixtures of pre-modern and revisionist views of immortality continue to be effective in the popular

[7] It is striking that Emerson illustrates this with a story drawn from Hindu tradition. See also Poe 1976: 205–309.

[8] Don Cupitt puts it more bluntly: 'It is spiritually important that one should not believe in life after death but should instead strive to attain the goal of spiritual life in history' (Cupitt 1980: 10).

[9] In the twentieth century, Karl Rahner attempted to integrate what he called the 'all-cosmic relationship' into Catholic theology in a formalized manner. See Rahner 1961: 25–33.

imagination today lies beyond the scope of this chapter, but we should not assume that they are entirely exhausted.

III. INCOMPREHENSIBLE DEATH

If the early nineteenth century saw the gradual emergence of a new paradigm focused on the fusion of the individual with cosmic life, Kierkegaard would pioneer a rather different rewriting of the Christian heritage. Kierkegaard rejects any theoretical, objective, or 'speculative' approach and in his *Concluding Unscientific Postscript* he reflects on 'what it means to die' as illustrative of what is involved in 'becoming subjective' (Kierkegaard 1991: 165). In relation to death, he knows 'what people ordinarily know' about the causes of death and is also familiar with what both poets and clergy have to say about it. But the real issue is not death in general but '*my dying*'. To think about that is not merely a speculative exercise but 'an act', 'because the development of subjectivity consists precisely in this, that he, acting, works through himself in his thinking about his own existence, consequently that he actually thinks what is thought by actualizing it, consequently that he does not think for a moment: Now, you must keep watch every moment—but that he keeps watch every moment' (Kierkegaard 1991: 169). In relation to a question such as that of my own death I am essentially an interested party, and my 'interest' (or, as he elsewhere puts it, 'concern') is integral to what the question means. So too in relation to immortality. Kierkegaard's mentor Poul Martin Møller had wryly noted that a royal ordinance of 1799 had forbidden the publication in Denmark of any work calling into question the immortality of the human soul and that this might preclude the publishing of Hegel's works. Nevertheless, by 1837, when Møller published his own essay on the topic, the issue was openly debated. Referring to Møller, Kierkegaard observes that 'I know some have found immortality in Hegel; others have not. I know that I have not found it in the system, since it is unreasonable to look for it there anyway, because in a fantastical sense all systematic thinking is *sub specie aeterni* and to that extent immortality is there as eternity'—which might be said to be close to the view we have already encountered in Feuerbach. 'But this immortality is not at all the one enquired about, since the question is about the immortality of a mortal, and that question is not answered by showing that the eternal is immortal, because the eternal is, after all, not the mortal, and the immortality of the eternal is a tautology and a misuse of words' (Kierkegaard 1991: 171). The point is not about 'the eternal' or humanity in general but about actual individuals having to decide whether they themselves are or are not immortal. The question cannot therefore be answered in a purely disinterested scholarly or objective way. As Kierkegaard puts it, 'essentially the question of immortality is not a learned question; it is a question belonging to inwardness, which the subject by becoming subjective must ask himself'—that is, the question is 'Do *I* become immortal or am *I* immortal?' (Kierkegaard 1991: 173). Against the kind of metaphysical reasoning indulged by the early Feuerbach, Kierkegaard asks 'where is the place that is the unity of the infinite and finite, where he, who is simultaneously infinite and finite, can speak simultaneously of his infinitude and his finitude, and whether it is indeed possible to find this dialectically difficult place, which is nevertheless requisite?' (Kierkegaard 1991: 175).

This insistence on the need for an 'interested' or 'concerned' subjective approach is taken up in Kierkegaard's upbuilding discourse, 'At a Graveside', published under his own name in the collection *Upbuilding Discourses on Imagined Occasions*. The first section is put in the mouth of a priest, speaking at a graveside. It is very brief, only three pages, beginning and ending with the words 'it is over'. This, Kierkegaard suggests, epitomizes how to speak seriously of death: briefly and to the point and, above all, in the very presence of death. The purely literary discourse that now follows cannot speak in that way, since it doesn't speak about just one particular person but about death in general. Yet, he says, because it concerns death it can, after all, be serious in its own way. In fact, 'seriousness' emerges as a major theme, and is contrasted with what he calls 'mood' or, as it might be translated, 'whimsy'. He dismisses the Epicurean saying that one should not fear death since where death is, I am not and where I am, death is not. This is precisely what, in the *Postscript*, he speaks of as the knowledge '*that* one must keep watch' as distinct from actually '*keeping* watch'. It is playing at seriousness, but is not itself serious. Both seriousness and whimsy know the same things about death and can say the same things about death—but how they say what they know is completely different. Both recognize that life is over in death, but where whimsy speaks of falling asleep or muses on the infinitely various ways in which neither the hour nor the manner of death can be anticipated, the serious person holds fast to the insight that death can only ever concern him fully as his unique, ineluctable death. The hallmarks of such a serious attitude to death are the recognition that death is decisive, indefinable, and inexplicable. This last, as Kierkegaard emphasizes, is to be taken literally. Meditating on death does not make us expert in the art of dying, i.e. it yields neither theoretical nor practical consolation. Rather it unsettles our whole manner of living and reveals the questionableness of our lives: 'the inexplicability is not a request to solve enigmas, an invitation to be ingenious, but is death's earnest warning to the living: I need no explanation; but bear in mind, you yourself, that with this decision all is over and that this decision can at any moment be at hand; see, it is very advisable for you to bear this in mind' (Kierkegaard 1993: 101).

Another discourse, 'There will be the resurrection of the Dead, of the Righteous— and of the Unrighteous', comes at the question from another angle. Here, Kierkegaard says, the Christian position assumes immortality, but not in order to 'console': The Christian effectively says, '"Nothing is more certain than immortality; you are not to worry about, nor to waste your time on, not to seek an escape by—wanting to demonstrate it or wishing to have it demonstrated. Fear it, it is only all too certain; do not doubt whether you are immortal—tremble, because you are immortal."' (Kierkegaard 1997: 203). Why: tremble? Because the resurrection is a resurrection to judgement: 'Immortality is not a continued life, a continued life as such in perpetuity, but immortality is the eternal separation between the righteous and the unrighteous . . . immortality and judgment are one and the same' (Kierkegaard 1997: 205). The outcome of preaching immortality, then, is the same as the outcome of meditating on the inexplicability of death: it is to direct the question back to the whole manner of a person's life. In this regard, although interpretable as a radical counter-move to 'Left' and 'Right' speculative revisions of traditional teaching on immortality, Kierkegaard repeats in modern form the teaching of *The Imitation of Christ*: 'Very soon the end of your life will be at hand: consider, therefore, the state of your soul' (à Kempis 1952: 57).[10]

Michael Theunissen has argued that it was Kierkegaard's discourse 'At a Graveside' to which Heidegger especially refers when, in *Being and Time*, he remarks that there is more to be learned philosophically from Kierkegaard's upbuilding works than from his more strictly philosophical ones. In any case, the convergence of content with Heidegger's own meditation on human being-towards-death seems striking (Theunissen 2006: 328–9). However, before returning to Heidegger, a further feature of the nineteenth-century discussion should be noted: that this was by no means a debate confined to philosophers and theologians but deeply engaged poets, novelists, painters, and musicians. It is clearly impossible even to list all the relevant examples that might be called on in support of this comment, but it is perhaps not entirely arbitrary to give special weight to the nineteenth-century Russian novel and to the theme of death in German music, from Schubert to Mahler. However, for reasons of space, it is only the former I shall consider here.

IV. Death in Tolstoy and Dostoevsky

Although important treatments of death are found in many Russian writers, it was especially Tolstoy and Dostoevsky who would have the greatest influence on the twentieth-century discussion. Although they did not know Kierkegaard, they would give dramatic portrayals of the terrifying unthinkability of death that he too had spoken about.

Whilst death stalks the pages of a novel such as *War and Peace*, from Princess Marie's death in childbirth, through the deaths of thousands on the battlefield of Borodino, and on to Prince André's gradual surrender to the all-encompassing life of the cosmos, it is *The Death of Ivan Ilych* that has played a particularly important role in the modern discussion. Tolstoy's tale opens with Ivan Ilych's colleagues learning of his death, which ' . . . aroused, as usual, in all who heard of it the complacent feeling that, "it is he who is dead and not I"' (Tolstoy 1960: 96). Ivan Ilych is a successful lawyer, who has lived in conformity with what might be expected of a successful lawyer.

---

[10] Thomas also emphasizes the link between 'immortality' and responsibility.

But then he becomes terminally ill. 'The syllogism he had learned from Kiezewetter's Logic: "Caius is a man, men are mortal, therefore Caius is mortal," had always seemed to him correct as applied to Caius, but certainly not as applied to himself' (Tolstoy 1960: 131). Notionally, he now acknowledges its truth, but he cannot make sense of what this incomprehensible 'It' means:

> And what was worst of all was that *It* drew his attention to itself not in order to make him take some action but only that he should look at *It*, look it straight in the face: look at it and without doing anything, suffer inexpressibly. And to save himself from this condition Ivan Ilyich looked for consolations—new screens—and new screens were found, and for a while seemed to save him, but then they immediately fell to pieces or rather became transparent, as if *It* penetrated them and nothing could veil *It*'. (Tolstoy 1960: 133)

Increasingly aware that he had not, in fact, lived as he ought to have done, Ivan Ilych attempts to evade, deny, or resist the shattering knowledge of his impending death and to cling on to his imperilled ego. It is only at the end of the last three days of his life that a moment of compassion for his son takes him outside himself and although he is no longer capable of communicating this insight to those around him 'it was revealed to him that though his life had not been as it should have been, this could still be rectified' (Tolstoy 1960: 155).

> 'And death . . . where is it?'
> He sought his former accustomed fear of death and did not find it. 'Where is it? What death?' There was no fear because there was no death.
> In place of death there was light.
> 'So that's what it is!'he suddenly exclaimed aloud. 'What joy!'
> To him all this happened in a single instant, and the meaning of that instant did not change.
> For those present his agony continued for another two hours. Something rattled in his throat, his emaciated body twitched, then the gasping and the rattle became less frequent. 'It is finished!' said someone near him.
> He heard these words and repeated them in his soul.
> 'Death is finished,' he said to himself. 'It is no more!'
> He drew in a breath, stopped in the midst of a sigh, stretched out, and died.
> (Tolstoy 1960: 155–6)

Tolstoy has unforgettably portrayed death's terrors, but, in the end, there is consolation, there is light and joy—although the text leaves open whether this is simply the experience of the man who is dying or whether it also points to something 'beyond' the threshold.[11]

Dostoevsky too, draws attention to the terror of death. When the eponymous hero of *The Idiot*, Prince Myshkin, is introduced to the daughters of the Epanchin family, he rather inappropriately turns to the subject of death. Reflecting Dostoevsky's own

---

[11] However, it seems clear from other writings that Tolstoy did not believe in any 'afterlife'.

experience of having been sentenced to death by firing squad, the Prince tells the story of 'a certain man' who was awaiting execution. 'He said those five minutes seemed like an endless time to him, an enormous wealth. It seemed to him that in those five minutes he would live so many lives that there was no point yet in thinking about his last moment . . .' (Dostoevsky 2001: 60), and so, the Prince continues, the man made arrangements to say good bye to his friends and to reserve just two minutes for thinking about himself and looking around for the last time. When those two minutes came, 'He knew beforehand what he was going to think about: he wanted to picture to himself as quickly and vividly as possible how it could be like this: now he exists and lives, and in three minutes there would be *something*, some person or thing—but who?' (Dostoevsky 2001: 60–1). Seeing the sunlight shining off the gilded dome of a nearby Cathedral 'it seemed to him that those rays were his new nature and in three minutes he would somehow merge with them . . .' (Dostoevsky 2001: 61). The worst feature of this situation, we are told, was the 'constant thought': 'What if I were not to die! What if life were given back to me—what infinity! And it would all be mine! Then I'd turn each minute into a whole age, I'd lose nothing, I'd reckon up every minute separately, I'd let nothing be wasted!' (Dostoevsky 2001: 61). Eventually, this thought so fills him with anger that he starts to wish they'd hurry up and shoot him. At which point the Prince breaks off. Here it is not simply the terror of death, but also its absurdity, its sheer unthinkability in relation to life, that Dostoevsky emphasizes.

But the Prince doesn't stop there. Asked by the girls to give them a subject for their painting, he recalls an execution by guillotine he had witnessed in Lyons. His narrative emphasizes the relentless organization and channelling of time, the isolation, confusion, and terror of the condemned man, describing ever more intensely the 'unthinkability' of death. The Prince vividly portrays the condemned man's nausea, how he greedily kisses the cross and how his head throbs with all he is remembering and thinking, including arbitrary and absurd details, such as the rusty bottom button on the executioner's jacket.

> And to think it will be so till the last quarter of a second, when his head is already lying on the block, and he waits, and . . . knows, and suddenly above him he hears the iron screech! You're bound to hear it! It may only be one tenth of an instant, but you're bound to hear it! If I were lying there, I'd listen on purpose and hear it! It may be only one tenth of an instant, but you're bound to hear it! And imagine, to this day they still argue that, as the head is being cut off, it may know for a second that it has been cut off—quite a notion! And what if it's five seconds!   (Dostoevsky 2001: 65)

The Prince's recommendation for the young ladies' art class is therefore the face of a condemned man kissing the cross instants before his death!

In the course of his story, the Prince alludes to Holbein's painting of the dead Christ that he (like Dostoevsky) had seen in Basel. This picture reappears at several important moments later in the novel. The Prince himself says of it that '"A man could lose his faith from that painting!"' (Dostoevsky 2001: 218). Why? Because, as another character, the young nihilist and consumptive Ippolit explains, it portrays even the Saviour of the world as a corpse like any other, devoid of any beautiful or consoling features. As Ippolit says

> Nature appears to the viewer of this painting . . . in the shape of some huge machine of the most modern construction, which has senselessly seized, crushed, and swallowed up, blankly and unfeelingly, a great and priceless being—such a being as by himself was worth the whole of nature and all its laws, the whole earth, which was perhaps created solely for the appearance of this being alone! (Dostoevsky 2001: 408)

Even the one who was able to call Lazarus forth from the grave must also submit to annihilation. How, in the face of such an image can one go on believing in any resurrection? How can one even believe in the light and joy experienced by an Ivan Ilych?

Dostoevsky has his own answers to these questions, although they are presented in his novels under the self-imposed rules of authorial irony, dialogical polyphony, and unfinalizability, so we can never say, simply, that Dostoevsky 'teaches' the power of resurrection to overcome even the annihilation figured in Holbein's painter.[12] Whatever it may involve, the passage from this life to eternal bliss in the 'beyond' cannot be assumed as occurring as a simple matter of fact, without the terror of death having been first confronted.

V. Being-Towards Death

Paul Tillich would identify the First World War as the moment when 'the lid was torn off' the cultural evasion of death, adding that 'The picture of Death appeared, unveiled, in a thousand forms. As in the late Middle Ages the figure of Death appeared in pictures and poetry, and the Dance of Death with every living being was painted and sung, so our generation—the generation of world wars, revolutions, and mass migrations—rediscovered the reality of death' (Tillich 1955: 171).

Perhaps the fin-de-siècle and the first decade of the twentieth century were not so oblivious of death as this comment suggests, but it is unsurprising that the decade after the First World War would see the publication of one of modern philosophy's most influential contributions to the subject of death, namely Heidegger's *Being and Time*.[13]

---

[12] For further discussion, see Pattison 2001: 193–203.

[13] One might also think here of Franz Rosenzweig's *Star of Redemption*, a work of philosophy that opens with the words 'from death' and concludes with the words 'into life' and that was begun while the author was serving as a front-line soldier. Tillich's remark might also occasion us to think about the impact of mass death and, in religious contexts, examples of martyrdom and sacrificial death on the modern interpretation of death. In a sense, everything said by, e.g. Heidegger, Sartre, and Lévinas, presupposes those historical experiences of death they lived through. However, there is not space here separately to thematize these important issues.

Here, having to die is not just one feature of Dasein alongside others such as 'idle talk' or 'curiosity'. Death is what Dasein must face if it is to come into an authentic relation to its own being and this existential 'anticipation' of death is therefore the condition for being able to understand the meaning of Being as such. It seems to be precisely in relation to death that the many threads of this dense work come together. In now focusing on chapters I and II of Division Two, where the treatment of death is most explicit, we are therefore inevitably going to make many shortcuts. Nevertheless, I hope to say enough to show something of the originality of Heidegger's contribution and how the theme of death relates to the larger whole of *Being and Time*.

By the start of Division II, Heidegger has already established that a basic feature of Dasein's being-in-the-world is that it is always 'ahead of itself' in care, always relating itself to some project, task, or obligation, something still to be done or still to be thought. Even more basically, Dasein, the human self as 'being-there', is not from the outset a conscious, centred ego but a being-in-the-world, i.e. a being that exists and can know itself only in the context of its manifold involvements in its world. It only becomes a 'subject' in and by the process of distinguishing itself from these involvements and determining its relations to them and it is only in the course of this process that it comes to learn its specific 'existentiell' possibilities. These possibilities accrue to it on the basis of what Heidegger calls its 'thrownness'—I did not choose to be born an English-speaking male in the year 1950, but since that is what, by virtue of my thrownness, I am, particular possibilities become open or closed to me as a result. Yet that I avow these possibilities as my own and that I chose, e.g. to make the most of the educational opportunities that my time and place and social origin gave me, is down to me, that is, I project myself upon them and incorporate them into my personal identity. Thus, Heidegger says, Dasein is a 'thrown project'. The condition of being such a 'thrown project' is clearly a highly dynamic and open one. Such a being— Dasein—will never be knowable for what it is in terms of some universal or trans-temporal essence since it becomes what it is through its unique and dynamic relation to its distinctive possibilities nor will it ever coincide with itself in an absolute sense, as in the German Idealists' beloved formula of A = A.

Never? Perhaps if Dasein could look forward to an infinite expanse of time it would indeed be able to discover, to choose, and to live to the full each of the life possibilities into which it is thrown. Then, perhaps, we could make ourselves whole and go to our deaths in the spirit of 'ripeness is all', like fruit, falling from the bough under the weight of its own plenitude. But that, of course, is not how it is. Death as we know it cuts each of us short. Some are able to live in such a way as to fulfil sufficient of their possibilities to be able to go towards death as if to completion, but few can really do so. And, certainly none can count on being able to do so. No matter how robust my health, the drunken motorist, the failed aircraft engine, or the mystery virus can bring my life to an end—just like that. Even in relation to the life possibilities I want to fulfil and believe myself capable of fulfilling, I can never know whether I will, in fact, have time to fulfil them. That is to say death sets an unanswerable question mark against the basic possibility of my being-a-whole. It is therefore unlike any other life possibility, and, in Heidegger's formulation, it is therefore 'that possibility which is one's ownmost, which is non-relational [i.e. it is distinct from all other possibilities], and which is not to be outstripped [i.e. overtaken—I cannot set myself a project that would take me beyond my own death]' (Heidegger 1962: 251/295).[14] I can, to some extent, answer for a relatively limited project such as passing an exam, but I cannot answer for the achievability of the whole ensemble of my life projects because they are all bounded by a possibility—my 'ownmost'—they can never incorporate. But that means that I cannot answer for being who I want to be, I cannot answer for myself. Having to die throws my whole existence—my existence as a whole, as a unitary, centred self—into question.

All of this is concealed by the way in which people mostly talk about death. In our average everyday way of living and talking about ourselves, death is simply one event or happenstance among others, 'a mishap which is constantly occurring—as a "case of death". Someone or other dies, be he neighbour or stranger . . . "One of these days one will die too, in the end; but right now it has nothing to do with us."' (Heidegger 1962: 253–4/296–7). In keeping with the general characteristics of 'idle talk' that he has already examined, death is so far from being a unique, all-encompassing event that it is spoken about as an event or occurrence like any other, something which has no definite meaning but is swathed in ambiguity, and, above all, something which always happens only to 'one', not to me: 'In Dasein's public way of interpreting, it is said that "one dies", because everyone else and oneself can talk himself into saying that "in no case is it I myself", for this "one" is the "nobody"' (Heidegger 1962: 253/297). Even in dealing with those who are dying, we comfort them by assurances that it'll be alright and that things will soon return to normal: 'In this manner the "they" provides a constant tranquillization about death. At bottom, however, this is a tranquillization not only for him who is "dying" but just as much for those who "console" him' (Heidegger 1962: 254/298). If we are in any doubt about the kind of thing Heidegger is talking about, he refers us to Tolstoy's *Ivan Ilych*. We can never really experience the death of others and the possibility of doing so is constantly pre-empted by the distracting, tranquillizing ways in which 'one' talks about it.

Ivan Ilych, we recall, found a moment of illumination in—and only in—the very moment of death, but he was no longer able to communicate that insight to others. Jankélévitch has such deathbed scenes in mind when he writes of the human fascination with the last words of the dying, as if the dying person is perhaps afforded a glimpse into the beyond that can be relayed back to the living. However, it is not just that we cannot experience what is happening in others' deaths, but even for the dying the instant of death is such that 'it is not possible to grasp it in that very moment itself' (Jankélévitch 1977: 359). No matter how near the end, the dying person is, after all, still living, and in the moment of death itself, is already dead. There is no mediating term. For those not yet in that moment and who are therefore not in a position to be

---

[14] The first number here and subsequently refers to the first German edition.

vouchsafed the indisputable evidence of a vision such as that of Ivan Ilych, is there anything left but despair? Heidegger thinks there is.

Although death faces us with a possibility that is non-relational and not to be outstripped, a possibility that, as it were, eviscerates all our other life possibilities, it is nevertheless a possibility towards which we, in our thrownness, are thrown and, to that extent, analogous to our other possibilities. And, just as we can choose to affirm or to neglect these other possibilities, so too in the case of death, we can neglect it (as 'one' does), or we can choose it—to use Heidegger's expression 'run towards it' (translated as 'anticipation' by Macquarrie and Robinson). In resolutely running towards it we allow death to be seen for what it is and we see ourselves in the light that our ineluctable mortality throws retrospectively upon the rest of our lives. As Heidegger puts it,

> anticipation [running towards] reveals to Dasein its lostness in the they-self, and brings it face to face with the possibility of being itself, primarily unsupported by concernful solicitude, but of being itself, rather, in an impassioned freedom towards death—a freedom which has been released from the illusions of the 'they', and which is factical, certain of itself, and anxious.   (Heidegger 1962: 266/311)

In such anticipation—and in such anticipation alone—Dasein finds the wholeness that none of its other possibilities, alone or together, are able to give it.

All of this is said at the level of what Heidegger calls 'existential' analysis, that is, as belonging to the structures of human existence as such. How it might work out at the level of what he calls the 'existentiell', that is, in an individual's life, is another matter. Heidegger himself admits that from the existentiell point of view having to live in the light of such an ontological possibility of authentic being-towards-death might seem like 'a fantastical exaction'. That it is, in fact, liveable is the burden of the following chapter, in which he explores what he calls the existentiell 'attestation' of authentic being-towards-death. To this end, he explains conscience as a 'call' experienced by Dasein to be true to itself and to accept responsibility ('being guilty') for itself as thrown towards its own death.

Heidegger's presentation is both bold and subtle. But it is also exposed both to misunderstandings and to criticisms and has provoked alternative accounts that build on but also qualify his account.

Sartre, for example, dismissed Heidegger's claim that death uniquely individuates.

> 'It is,' he says, 'perfectly gratuitous to say that "to die is the only thing which nobody can do for me". Or rather there is here an evident bad faith in the reasoning... [since] the *my* here has nothing to do with a personality won by overcoming everyday banality... it refers simply to that selfness which Heidegger expressly recognizes in every Dasein—whether it exists in the authentic or inauthentic mode—when he declares that "Dasein ist je meines". Thus from this point of view the most commonplace love is, like death, irreplaceable and unique; nobody can love for me'.   (Sartre 1969: 534)

But has Sartre understood Heidegger correctly? It seems not, since whilst an authentic running towards the possibility of death does indeed liberate Dasein from the distractedness of average, everyday existence, the claim that dying 'is the only thing which nobody can do for me' is not quite Heidegger's point in *Being and Time*. Part of the problem of average everydayness and the idle talk in which it encompasses our attempts to think about our lives is that not only in relation to death but in relation to anything whatsoever the essential 'mineness' of existence is dissipated and covered over. But death does not, as it were, impose this mineness on us in a way that other experiences or situations do not (perhaps by virtue of its emotional pressure or physical pain), but is distinctive because, long before we find ourselves on our deathbeds, it raises the question as to the wholeness of our lives. The driving force of Heidegger's argument is not to do with cultivating 'a personality' that has overcome banality but with the problem of Dasein being unable to constitute itself as a whole on the basis of the life possibilities into which it is thrown by birth and circumstances. Moreover, as we have seen Heidegger make clear, he only subsequently addresses the question as to how this might work out or be attested in the case of an individual life.

In fact, the hinge of Sartre's own account is essentially akin to Heidegger's argument about Dasein's relation to its possibilities. As Sartre puts it, 'death is not *my* possibility of no longer realizing a presence in the world but rather *an always possible nihilation of my possible which is outside my possibilities*' (Sartre 1969: 537). For both Heidegger and Sartre the challenge of death is precisely the way in which, given that 'to be oneself is to come to oneself' (Sartre 1969: 538), death suspends the possibility of ever arriving definitively at the self that one is striving to become. This is why, in Heidegger's argument, the discussion of death is followed by an examination of conscience, guilt, and responsibility. Death is not an external power that has any meaning outside the question of our own defining self-relationship. But whereas Heidegger appears to maintain that it *is* possible to reach the point of coinciding with oneself and taking back into one's existentiell life a resolute openness to the truth revealed in death, Sartre regards such claims as epitomizing bad faith. For Sartre we are an unhappy consciousness that can never coincide with itself.

Perhaps related to this last point is Theunissen's objection that—in contrast to Kierkegaard—Heidegger *does* finally make death conceivable, conflating the inconceivable and unrepresentable reality of death with the process of dying which thus emerges as what being-towards-death actually means. In this sense, Heidegger essentially returns to the position of Feuerbach: that to relate authentically to death is really to commit oneself without reserve to living. Thus, Theunissen says, Heidegger 'volatilizes [death] by dissolving it into life and therewith dissolving it into possibility . . .' (Theunissen 2006: 340).

Lévinas too challenges what he sees as Heidegger's framing of the question of death in terms of the subjectivity of individuals confronting their own death. His own privileging of the ethical demand over whatever a general philosophical ontology might be able to achieve is clearly visible in his comment that that 'for Heidegger . . . the fear of becoming a murderer would not be able to surpass [i.e. in existential seriousness] the fear of dying' (Lévinas 1993: 107). If we are to think death, there may be more to think of than our own future decease. As an alternative to Heidegger (whose work he nevertheless calls an 'obligatory passage') Lévinas turns to the Marxist thinker Ernst Bloch. For Bloch, as summarized by Lévinas, the starting point for understanding history is human beings' common concern to overcome the concrete forms of historical suffering. In the history of humanity's journey towards a definitive surmounting of such suffering, the true being of human beings emerges most clearly in work and in hope. The relationship between work and hope can in turn be seen in terms of an interplay between fulfilment and non-fulfilment: human beings' life in the world is always incomplete as long as there is still work to be done, while the summons to work is itself motivated by the unconditional hope of a future and common fulfilment. The spirit of utopia thus drives human beings to work for each others' betterment and to exist in a genuinely historical way. To Heidegger's analysis of Dasein as a nullity that consistently fails to realize itself as a whole, Bloch opposes the role of all the work that is still to be done in the world, and to Heidegger's anticipatory resoluteness in the face of death he opposes the spirit of utopia. From which Lévinas concludes that time is not defined by death, but by hope (Lévinas 1993: 109–11). Ultimately this means that far from thinking of time in the singular light cast by death, death itself is to be thought in the perspective of utopistic time—i.e. an envisaged redemption not just of the individual, but of humanity (Lévinas 1993: 122). Of course, there is nothing in *Being and Time* to make us suppose that someone who had fulfilled the demand of authentic resoluteness would be *pessimistic*, but we would have to say that their good cheer in the face of life's challenges was self-generated rather than grounded in hope or, to be perhaps more precise, in a basic hopefulness. For hope and hopefulness, as understood by Lévinas and Bloch do not depend solely on the decisions we ourselves take vis-à-vis our possibilities but are themselves central to those possibilities. As such, hope certainly needs to be chosen and affirmed, but the possibility of hope is given.

And note a further implication of this. For if hope is understood as a basic possibility that is *given* to us, then the burden placed upon each individual of having to choose him- or herself authentically in relation to death is significantly alleviated. Here we might oppose Dostoevsky to Tolstoy. Whereas the latter, despite repudiating any idea of the afterlife, nevertheless affirmed a moment of vision into an all-reconciling light being revealed to the dying, Dostoevsky's 'idiot' reminds us of the impossibility of actually living with the hyper-consciousness of those who know they are about to die. Such hyper-consciousness inevitably perishes in the day to day. Therefore—and the whole sequence of Dostoevsky's mature novels bears this out—living with an honest and unrestricted recognition of death cannot be grounded solely on the confrontation with death itself. There is another perspective to be taken into account, and one that we have not ourselves constructed.

VI. Towards a Theological Approach

If at this point we turn to the question of hope, is it in order to reintroduce a supernaturalistic conception of immortality? By no means, if we do so in the spirit of

Gabriel Marcel's comment that 'to hope is not essentially to hope that' (Marcel 1951: 162), construing hope instead as a basic orientation towards existence. Or, as Janké-lévitch (with some inspiration from Shestov) puts it, there is a difference between *'espoir'*, 'hoping that', and *'espérance'* (which he also calls *'l'espérance désespérée'*) or being infinitely or 'optatively' hopeful, even when there is nothing left to hope for (Jankélévitch 1977: 380–3).[15] But how might we recognize and lay hold of such a possibility if we have to reckon with the fact that our lives all end in death and if death is a final cessation of consciousness?

A theological answer to that question might seem to be found in the kind of insistence on the Lordship of God found in Barth's lectures on 1 Corinthians, *The Resurrection of the Dead.* As in Kierkegaard's discourse on the resurrection, Barth resists all temptations to speculate on possible post-mortem states of the departed. The point of Paul's message is not here, but in the affirmation of God's supreme and unquestionable Lordship, in relation to death as to life (Barth 1933). However, before moving to a directly theological comment on the grounds for hope, let us first consider one more issue and do so in critical conversation with Heidegger.

Lévinas's objection to Heidegger was not simply that his treatment of death led to the depletion of hope, but also that it remained focused on the individual rather than on humanity. As we have seen, even if Sartre is wrong in the way in which he makes the unsubstitutability of the individual pivotal to Heidegger's argument, Heidegger does insist on the impossibility of experiencing the deaths of others and those who have become authentically resolute are said to confront their death as their ownmost and inalienably individual possibility. The 'mineness' of death is not so much a mechanism by which to break free from the banality of the everyday but the first-fruits of our having committed ourselves to living conscientiously and responsibly (in the specific senses of these words that Heidegger gives them). But what if death is not essentially characterized by 'mineness'? What if death is a point—or even the pre-eminent point—at which the general structure of the 'mineness' of experience breaks down?

Heidegger reminds us of the false consolations so frequently offered to the dying, but is there not also powerful 'existentiell' attestation to the lived power of love in the words of the dying and those who will soon mourn them? Death may not take away the lives of the bereaved, it may not even ruin their lives (except in pathological cases), but it can and often does change their lives profoundly. And it does so not only because it is arguably the clearest reminder we can have of our own death ('Ask not for whom the bell tolls . . .'), but also because the very structure of our lives is a being-in-the-world that includes our being-with-others, as Heidegger himself has helped us to see. We are not who we are other than in our relations to others and therefore the death of a loved one (who is also, actively, a loving one) has the potential radically to reorientate our very existence.

---

[15] An analogous idea has recently been discussed by Jonathan Lear under the rubric 'radical hope'. See Lear 2008.

It would go far beyond the scope of this chapter to justify the claim that this being-with-others is most appropriately understood as placing us under the exigency of love, but if that were once allowed, then we could see a serious alternative both to the Heideggerian and to the Sartrean meditations on death. For Sartre, death means that the meaning of our lives, passes into the hand of the Other,

> like a coat which I leave him after my disappearance . . . Richelieu, Louis XV, my grandfather are by no means the simple sum of my memories, nor even the sum of the memories or the pieces of knowledge of all those who have heard of them; they are objective and opaque beings which are reduced to the single dimension of exteriority. In this capacity they will pursue their history in the human world, but they will never be more than transcendences-transcended in the midst of the world. (Sartre 1969: 544).

Death deprives the subject of all its subjective meaning 'in order to hand it over to any objective meaning which the Other is pleased to give to it' (Sartre 1969: 544). And, as Sartre adds, since this process of reception is itself unfinished, I am in the end handed over to a contingent and indeterminate future. It is 'the triumph of the Other over me' (Sartre 1969: 545), but even as such it does not issue in any 'final judgement' on who I am but will always be revisable. Thus all the possible meanings of my life remain forever in contingency.

Against this, stands Marcel's claim that 'the consideration of one's own death is surpassed by the consideration of the death of a loved one'. Commenting on a remark by Léon Brunschvig 'that the death of Gabriel Marcel seemed to preoccupy Gabriel Marcel much more than the death of Léon Brunschvig preoccupied Léon Brunschvig', Marcel added that 'the only thing worth preoccupying either of us was the death of someone we loved' (Marcel 1973: 131). In Marcel's perspective, the reality of love means that Sartre's foreboding about the 'triumph' of the Other inherent in the Other's power to memorialize my life in a manner dissociated from my own subjectivity is misplaced. 'Loving memory'—where there has really been love—does not reduce me to an object but precisely recognizes me as subject and, therewith, summons the one remembering to be faithful to me in their love. As Jankélévitch put it, death not only marks life as both irreversible and irrevocable, which, among other things, means that death can never undo the reality of 'having loved' (Jankélévitch 1977: 465–7).[16] Whether there is such a reality is another matter—but this is a matter of creative fidelity to life itself and not a matter of 'objective' judgement.

All of these reflections are possible within an essentially humanistic framework. What, then, might distinguish a theological approach? Let us think again about the suggestion that hope was a *given* possibility and not simply the reflex of heroically resoluteness in the face of death: hope—and, we might now add, the claim of love. Where Heidegger's 'conscience' in the end speaks, as he himself says, by 'keeping silent' and thus reminding

---

[16] Cf. Berdyaev's idea of the creative memory of the dead as a participation in the divine life of heaven—Berdyaev 1943: 111.

us of the silence to which our entire chattering existence will one day—and perhaps sooner than we think—be reduced, a religious conscience will understand itself as called, addressed, claimed by a Word that, even if we have no human words adequate to speaking it, is not silence. Such a Word both grants and summons us to be faithful to possibilities of hope and love.[17] Both the more specific content of that Word and how it relates to such theological topics as creation (the original gift of the possibility of hope) and redemption (the renewal of that gift in a situation of individual and collective sin) are other matters. For now it is enough to have arrived at a point at which philosophers in the modern European tradition might understand why theologians might want to speak as they do, and theologians recognize the essential commonality of their concern with that of the philosophers. For what, after all, is more a matter not of hyper-individualized care but of common concern than death?

REFERENCES

Barth, Karl (1933). *The Resurrection of the Dead*, trans. H. J. Stanning (London: Hodder and Stoughton).

Berdyaev, N. A. (1943). *Slavery and Freedom*, trans. R. M. French (London: Geoffrey Bles).

Butler, Joseph (1906). *The Analogy of Religion, Natural and Revealed*. (London: Dent Dutton).

Cupitt, Don (1980). *Taking Leave of God*. (London: SCM Press, 1980).

Derrida, J. (1995). *The Gift of Death*, trans. D. Wills (Chicago: Chicago University Press).

Dostoevsky, F. M. (2001). *The Idiot*, trans. R. Pevear and L. Volokhonsky (London: Granta Books).

Emerson, Ralph Waldo (1893). *Works of Ralph Waldo Emerson*. (London: George Routledge).

Feuerbach, Ludwig (1967). *The Essence of Faith According to Luther*, trans. M. Cherno (New York: Harper and Row).

——(1980). *Thoughts on Death and Immortality: From the Papers of a Thinker, along with an Appendix of Theological-Satirical Epigrams, Edited by One of His Friends*, ed. and trans. J. Massey (Berkeley, CA: University of California Press).

——(1989). *The Essence of Christianity*, trans. George Eliot (New York: Prometheus).

Harris, H. (1973). *David Friedrich Strauss and his Theology*. (Cambridge: Cambridge University Press).

Heidegger, Martin (1962). *Being and Time*, trans. J. Macquarrie and E. Robinson (Oxford: Blackwell).

Hick, John (1976). *Death and Eternal Life*. (London: Collins).

Jankélévitch, Vladimir (1977). *La Mort*. (Paris: Flammarion).

Kant, Immanuel (1974). *Kritik der praktischen Vernunft*. (Frankfurt am Main: Suhrkamp).

Kierkegaard, Søren, (1991). *Concluding Unscientific Postscript*, trans. H. V. Hong and E. H. Hong (Princeton, NJ: Princeton University Press).

——(1993). *Three Discourses on Imagined Occasions*, trans. H. V. Hong and E. H. Hong (Princeton, NJ: Princeton University Press).

---

[17] On the difference between the 'silence' of the Heideggerian conscience and the voice that is able to speak 'the gift of death', see Derrida 1995: 31–3.

Kierkegaard, Søren (1997). *Christian Discourses*, trans. H. V. Hong and E. H. Hong (Princeton, NJ: Princeton University Press).

Kojève, Alexandre (1947). *Introduction à la lecture de Hegel. Leçons sur la phenomenologie de l'esprit*. (Paris: Gallimard).

Lear, Jonathan (2008). *Radical Hope: Ethics in the Face of Cultural Devastation*. (Cambridge, MA: Harvard University Press).

Lévinas, E. (1993). *Dieu, la mort et le temps*. (Paris: Grasset).

Malpas, Jeff and Solomon, Robert C. (1998). *Death and Philosophy*. (London: Routledge).

Marcel, Gabriel (1951). *The Mystery of Being, II: Faith & Reality*, trans. R. Hague (London: Harvill).

——(1973). *Tragic Wisdom and Beyond*, trans. S. Jolin and P. McCormick (Evanston: Northwestern Universities Press).

Martensen, H. L. (1882). *Af mit Levnet*. (Copenhagen: Gyldendal).

Pattison, G. (2001). *A Short Course in the Philosophy of Religion*. (London: SCM Press).

Phillips, D. Z. (1970). *Death and Immortality*. (London: Macmillan).

Rahner, Karl, (1961). *On the Theology of Death*, trans. C. H. Henkey (London: Burns and Oates).

Sartre, Jean-Paul, (1969). *Being and Nothingness*, trans. H. Barnes (London: Methuen).

Schleiermacher, F. D. E. (1988). *Speeches on Religion*, trans. R. Crouter (Cambridge: Cambridge University Press).

——(1989). *The Christian Faith*, eds. H. R. Mackintosh and J. S. Stewart (Edinburgh: T. & T. Clark).

Theunissen, Michael, (2006). 'The Upbuilding in the Thought of Death: Traditional Elements, Innovative Ideas, and Unexhausted Possibilities in Kierkegaard's "At a Graveside"', in Robert L. Perkins (ed.), *International Kierkegaard Commentary, Vols. 9 & 10: Prefaces and Writing Sampler and Three Discourses on Imagined Occasions*, trans. G. Pattison (Macon, GA: Mercer University Press).

à Kempis, Thomas (1952). *The Imitation of Christ*, tran. L. Sherley-Price (Harmondsworth: Penguin).

Thomson, Ann (2008). *Bodies of Thought: Science, Religion, and the Soul in the Early Enlightenment*. (Oxford: Oxford University Press).

Tillich, Paul (1955). *The New Being*. (New York: Scribner).

Tolstoy, Leo, trans. A. Maude (1960). *The Death of Ivan Ilych and Other Stories* (New York: New American Library).

Suggested Reading

Ariès, P. (1981). *The Hour of our Death*. (London: Allen Lane).

Barth (1933).

Becker, E. (1973). *The Denial of Death*. (New York: Free Press).

Derrida (1995).

Heidegger (1962).

Hick (1976).

Kierkegaard (1993).

Nadas, Peter (2004). *Own Death*. (Göttingen: Steidl).

Stokes, P. and Buben, A. J. (eds) (2011). *Kierkegaard and Death*. (Bloomington, IN: Indiana University Press).

CHAPTER 10

EVIL

JENNIFER L. GEDDES

I. INTRODUCTION

ONE usually begins chapters of this sort with a definition of the topic under discussion. However, in the case of a chapter on evil, this is problematic since the definition of evil and the uses to which such a definition are put are two major points of discussion and disagreement. While there might be widespread consensus about certain things that should be labelled evil—for example, the events of the Holocaust or torturing a child—what we are saying when we call these things evil is far from clear. As Richard Bernstein notes, 'there is a disparity between the intense moral passion that we feel in condemning something as evil and our ability to give a conceptual account of what we mean by evil' (Bernstein 2002: p. ix). He continues, 'we lack a discourse that is deep, rich, and subtle enough to capture what has been experienced' (Bernstein 2002: 3).

In fact, writing on evil is sometimes so abstract it is easy to forget that it is one of the most vexing, distressing, and persistent issues in human life. The online *Stanford Encyclopedia of Philosophy* entry on the problem of evil, for example, begins with this statement: 'The epistemic question posed by evil is whether the world contains undesirable states of affairs that provide the basis for an argument that makes it unreasonable for anyone to believe in the existence of God'[1]

At one end of the spectrum are statements like this, in which evils become 'undesirable states of affairs' that pose epistemic questions; at the other end is the wailing of a mother beside the body of her dead child. The hyper-rational articulation of the former discourse belies an effort to tame the horror of evil; the visceral outcry of the latter silences efforts at articulation and rationality itself. Thus, writing about evil faces at least two temptations: the temptation to try to domesticate or tame evil with theorizing,

---

[1] http://plato.stanford.edu/entries/evil/

on the one hand, and the temptation to despair in the face of it, which leaves us paralysed with nothing to say. Evil calls forth deep desires for understanding, while simultaneously constraining or damaging our capacities for so doing.

In attempting to offer a broad but useful mapping of the ways in which theology and modern European thought have grappled with evil, this chapter is organized into three sections, each of which addresses a fundamental question about evil: Why is evil? Who is evil? and What is evil? As it turns out, these most basic questions concerning evil are the most difficult, the most hotly contested, and involve the highest stakes. Each question locates an identifiable conversation on evil, though almost no major thinker confines his or her work to just one of them. One could argue that in modernity the emphasis moves from why to who to what, though the discussions about why evil is and who does evil are far from over and continue vigorously into the present moment. Rather than offering a strict chronology, then, what is presented here is more of a mapping of some major conversations about evil that take place in the modern period, with a few key voices representing each conversation.

There is nothing close to coverage here—a topic as vast and persistent as this could never be 'covered', even if this chapter extended into a multiple volume set—and certainly each reader will see gaping holes, key figures who should have had their place in these pages, and glaring simplifications of complex ideas. The goal here, however, is to outline one path through the terrain marked 'Evil in Modern European Thought' (with theology itself understood as one mode of European thought); point out a few key sites along the way—sites of deep thinking, moral grappling, and long-reaching influence; and offer a narrative that distinguishes and connects some distinct strands of conversation about evil.

Before moving into a discussion of evil as constituted by these three questions about evil, it is worthwhile to take a step back for a moment to ask: just how important is the topic of evil in the work of theologians, philosophers, social theorists, novelists, poets, and the like in the modern period? It is a subject of some debate. Focusing on post-war Europe, many scholars cite Hannah Arendt's statement that 'the problem of evil will be the fundamental question of postwar intellectual life in Europe' in the context of showing how clearly wrong she was. Terry Eagleton argues that 'On the whole, postmodern cultures, despite their fascination with ghouls and vampires, have had little to say about evil' (Eagleton 2010: 15). In contrast to these scholars, Susan Neiman, in her important book *Evil in Modern Thought: An Alternative History of Philosophy*, suggests that 'the problem of evil is the guiding force of modern thought' (Neiman, 2002: 2–3), despite the fact that in the post-war period 'no major philosophical work but [Hannah] Arendt's own appeared on the subject in English, and German and French texts were remarkably oblique' (Neiman 2002: 2).

Whether evil is the fundamental question, on the one hand, or merely an oblique subject in modern European thought, on the other, depends on where and how one looks when thinking about evil. This chapter sides with those who see it as the former, or rather, as a set of questions driving modern European thought, whether visible within those texts, or haunting them more invisibly. The questions—Why is there evil in the world? Who is the person who does evil? and What is evil?—take up fundamental questions about God, the world, humans, and moral life. The section 'Why is Evil?' focuses on the ways that people have grappled with their understandings of God and the world in the face of their experience of, or exposure to, evil. I look at works that ask why evil happens in this world, with particular attention to theodicy, tracing discussions of theodicy from Leibniz's coinage of the term to Levinas's call for its end. The section 'Who is Evil?' probes the nature of humans and the agency of the individual subject, asking what kind of beings we are and why some of us do evil things. I look at those thinkers, such as Kant, Freud, and Arendt, who move from investigating the world to investigating the human subject, as evil-doer, evil-sufferer, or evil one. The section 'What is "Evil"?' explores the nature of evil—just what do we mean when we use the word 'evil' and what are the implications its use has for moral thought? I outline two major, but contradictory shifts in thinking about evil in the modern period: the relativization of evil, on the one hand, and the absolutizing of it, on the other.

II. Why is Evil? Theodicy from Leibniz to Levinas

As a response to evil, the question 'Why?' is as old as recorded human history. In the Hebrew scriptures, Job asks the question over and over again, once his sufferings reach a certain point. When events we deem evil happen, they confound our understanding of the world, and for religious believers, they call into question the nature of God as creator and sustainer of the world. Theology has sought to answer the questions: Why is there evil in the world? Why did God create the world such that it included the possibility of evil? Why does God allow extreme suffering? Is this suffering punishment for our sins? Why does God allow some people to suffer who seem least to deserve it, while allowing others to do evil with seemingly no punishment? David Hume states the problem of evil for belief in God succinctly: 'Is he willing to prevent evil, but not able? then he is impotent. Is he able, but not willing? then he is malevolent. Is he both able and willing? whence then is evil?' (Hume 2007: 74). Theodicy has been a major genre of response to these questions, in its effort to defend the goodness and justness of God despite the presence of evil in the world.

The Rise of Theodicy

Gottfried Leibniz coined the term 'theodicy' from the Greek words *theos* (God) and *dike* (justice), describing the defence of the goodness and justice of God in the face of the presence of evil in the world. In 1710, he published *Essais de Théodicée sur la bonté de Dieu, la liberté de l'homme et l'origine du mal*, arguing that despite the presence of evil in the world, Christians believe in a good and just God. This is, he argued, the best of all possible worlds: 'if there were not the best (optimum) among all possible worlds, God would not have produced any ... there is an infinitude of possible worlds among which God must needs have chosen the best, since he does nothing without acting in accordance with supreme reason' (Leibniz 1985: 128). So sure was Leibniz that this was the best possible world that he argued that 'if the smallest evil that comes to pass in the world were missing in it, it would no longer be this world; which, with nothing omitted and all allowance made, was found the best by the Creator who chose it' (Leibniz 1985: 128–9).

The 1755 Lisbon earthquake, and the fires and tsunami that followed it, caused people throughout Europe to question the nature of the world they lived in. Walter Benjamin, trying to communicate the theological and intellectual shock waves this event caused in the European world, wrote: 'it was one of the largest and most destructive earthquakes of all times. Yet it was not for this reason alone that it excited and preoccupied the entire world like few other events in that century. The destruction of Lisbon in 1755 was roughly the equivalent to the destruction of London or Chicago today' (Benjamin 2005: 536).[2] In responding to the Lisbon earthquake, much philosophical thinking about evil moved from wondering why God allows such things to happen, to wondering about the very character and existence of God. Might God have an evil streak? Has God abandoned the world, and thus allowed something like this to happen? Might it be possible that there is no God at all?

In the wake of the Lisbon earthquake, Voltaire argued that theodicies are useless, or, even worse, they are theories that distract us from our obligations to help those who are suffering. In his poem 'The Lisbon Earthquake: An Inquiry into the Maxim "Whatever is, is Right"', he denounced efforts to justify God, while such suffering occurs in the world:

> Oh wretched man, earth-fated to be cursed;
> Abyss of plagues, and miseries the worst!
> . . . .
> Say, when you hear their piteous, half-formed cries,
> Or from their ashes see the smoke arise,
> Say, will you then eternal laws maintain,
> Which God to cruelties like these constrain?
> . . . .
> Was then more vice in fallen Lisbon found,
> Than Paris, where voluptuous joys abound?
> Was less debauchery to London known,
> Where opulence luxurious holds her throne?
>
> (Voltaire 1977: 560–1)

---

[2] My thanks to colleague Chad Wellmon for introducing me to Benjamin's essay on the Lisbon earthquake.

Others found Voltaire's view heartless. For example, in his 'Letter to Voltaire on Optimism' (18 August 1756), Rousseau countered that such an approach to suffering actually makes things worse, increasing suffering, rather than helping it. He wrote: 'Pope's poem ["Essay on Man"] alleviates my sufferings and encourages me to be patient; yours increases my sufferings, incites me to complain, and, taking from me everything but a shattered hope, it reduces me to despair' (as quoted in Voltaire 2000: 109). For Rousseau, humans are meaning-seeking creatures, who need to look for reasons and find hope; theodicy is a natural form of response to evil and suffering, not a theoretical imposition on to it.

The Leibniz–Voltaire–Rousseau exchange reveals a set of conflicting concerns related to the presence of evil in the world, the goodness of God, and the proper human response to those who suffer. On the one hand is the effort to show the presence of a meaning or a purpose behind things, even though the occurrence of horrendous events seems to suggest otherwise to us. This desire for meaning, it is argued, is a genuinely human desire, not one limited to the theological and philosophical specula-tors among us. On the other hand is the argument that all our theoretical speculation actually serves to distance us from—and sometimes keep us safe from—the actual suffering and sufferers that result from evil. This evasion of suffering is also an evasion of responsibility, it is argued, and one that makes us guilty of not helping those in need.

The debate about theodicy has continued into the contemporary period. In analytic philosophy the problem of evil is posed in the form of three seemingly contradictory propositions when taken as a trio: God is all-good, God is all-powerful, and there is evil in the world. Analytic philosophers like Richard Swinburne and John Hick, among others, have all engaged in different forms of theodicy that seek to prove the goodness of God in the face of evil. Others, like J. L. Mackie, have argued that their efforts fail. Some theodicists have emphasized the conditions necessary for the human exercise of free will or for the development of our souls. The free will defence argues that, in order for humans to be able to freely choose to do good, they need to have the capacity to choose not to do good. The possibility of evil in the world is the cost of creating free beings who can freely choose to love God and each other. That humans have chosen to make that possibility an actuality is our fault, not that of God. This way of responding to evil seeks to preserve the character of God as all-good and all-powerful, while trying not to diminish the reality of evil in the world, moving the blame for evil from God to humans.

Some Christian theologians have rejected the very formulation of the problem of evil, arguing that the characterization of God that it contains is inaccurate or simplistic. Often the focus here is on the suffering of Christ as a counter to the suggestion that God is out there watching humans inflict and suffer evil. Karl Barth focuses on a God who is judged and rejected in our place, rather than one who has abandoned us to our suffering. In *The Crucified God*, Jürgen Moltmann argues against the depiction of God as omnipotent: 'a God who cannot suffer is poorer than any man. For a God who is incapable of suffering is a being who cannot be involved.... a God who is only omnipotent is in himself an incomplete being, for he cannot experience helplessness and powerlessness' (Moltmann 1974: 222–3). Instead, Moltmann builds a theology around the hope that the crucified and resurrected Christ brings to those who suffer and to the healing and redemption that will come in the eschaton, the end times. Marilyn McCord Adams, in *Horrendous Evils and the Goodness of God*, moves away from discussion of evil in general to look at the particular suffering of individuals and argues that, in the end, God is able to make each individual's life a greater good than the evils he or she has suffered and is able to 'defeat' those evils (Adams 1999). In the most successful of these theodicies is the recognition that the problem of evil is not one that can be solved once and for all, neatly or fully. Rather there are ways to respond theologically to suffering in this world that do not preclude the existence of God, but rather require the vision of a God who cares even more deeply than we do about alleviating and overcoming it.

The End of Theodicy

While analytic philosophy and theology have continued to engage in theodicy, the horrendous evils of the last century have certainly contributed to the growth of the 'anti-theodicy' camp. The arguments against theodicy are as varied as the kinds of theodicies, and the charges against theodicy include that it ignores the limits of human knowledge, forgets the suffering of the victim, justifies the suffering of others, and collapses under the weight of the evils of the twentieth century, particularly the Holocaust.

  While most of our discussion of Immanuel Kant will take place in the next section, he is also an important voice in this conversation. He argues against theodicy because he thinks it makes morality impossible. Kant sees the question of why God allows evil both as outside the realm of human understanding and as damaging to morality. If we were assured that all our good actions would, in the end, bring us eternal joy and happiness, despite what seemed to be evidence to the contrary in this world, we could never freely choose the good. In order for humans to be able to freely choose to do their duty, they cannot know that their virtuous actions will lead to good ends or rewards. If we did know this, we would begin to do things for instrumental reasons, to get the good reward, rather than for the sake of duty itself. Instead, Kant argues, we must choose the good, choose to do our duty, without any certainty that it will bring us a reward in the end. Those who claim certainty about the meaningfulness of our suffering in this world and God's purposes for evil, Kant argues, are actually involved in the destruction of the conditions necessary for morality and for faith.

  A more common reason behind rejecting theodicy has to do with the rejection of any attempt to justify the suffering that happens in this world. A strong fictional voice in this camp is Ivan Karamazov in Fyodor Dostoevsky's *Brothers Karamazov*, who argues forcefully not against the existence of God, but against the justice of the world as created by God and against any theology that proposes that 'it all works for good in the end'.

And if the suffering of children goes to make up the sum of suffering needed to buy truth, then I assert beforehand that the whole of truth is not worth such a price. I do not, finally, want the mother to embrace the tormentor who let his dogs tear her son to pieces! . . . they have put too high a price on harmony; we can't afford to pay so much for admission. And therefore I hasten to return my ticket. And it is my duty, if only as an honest man, to return it as far ahead of time as possible. Which is what I am doing. It's not that I don't accept God, Alyosha, I just most respectfully return him the ticket.   (Dostoevsky 2002: 239)

Ivan goes further than calling into question the goodness of God. He also condemns even those who agree to participate in this vision of the world. Speaking to his brother Alyosha, he asks:

'answer me: imagine that you yourself are building the edifice of human destiny with the object of making people happy in the finale, of giving them peace and rest at last, but for that you must inevitably and unavoidably torture just one tiny creature, that same child who was beating her chest with her little fist, and raise your edifice on the foundation of her unrequited tear—would you agree to be the architect on such conditions? Tell me the truth.'
    'No I would not agree,' Alyosha said softly.   (Dostoevsky 2002: 239)

Some who argue against theodicy point to the Holocaust as a major turning point in the history of its very possibility. Pre-eminent among these is Emmanuel Levinas, who states that the atrocities of the twentieth century, and in particular the Holocaust, mark the end of theodicy. He writes:

Perhaps the most revolutionary fact of our twentieth-century consciousness—but it is also an event in Sacred History—is that of the destruction of all balance between Western thought's explicit and implicit theodicy and the forms that suffering and its evil are taking in the very unfolding of this century . . . suffering and evil inflicted deliberately, but in a manner no reason set limits to, in the exasperation of a reason become political and detached from all ethics.   (Levinas 1998: 97)

He concludes that 'the disproportion between suffering and every theodicy was shown at Auschwitz with a glaring, obvious clarity. Its possibility puts into question the multimillennial traditional faith' (Levinas 1998: 97). For Levinas, even asking the question 'Why?' in relation to suffering that is not one's own becomes a culpable question, since it suggests the effort to justify the others' suffering. Theodicy proceeds, he argues, by justifying the suffering of others for some higher purpose, but 'the justification of the neighbor's pain is certainly the source of all immorality' (Levinas 1998: 99). He proposes that we must not try to explain or justify others' suffering, but rather see it as, in his term, 'useless' and as something to be prevented or stopped.

A Secular Theodicy?

More recent grapplings with evil have sought to revitalize the notion of theodicy not as a defence of the goodness or justice of God, but rather as a defence of the worthiness of the world. Larry Bouchard suggests that we think of theodicy as 'any endeavor, theological or otherwise, to bring coherence to the problems of evil and thereby justify humanity to itself' (Bouchard 1989: 1–2). In *Evil in Modern Thought*, Susan Neiman describes theodicy as a necessary effort to continue to believe in the world. The problem of evil, according to Neiman, is 'fundamentally a problem about the intelligibility of the world as a whole' (Neiman 2002: 7–8). Whenever we think, 'that ought not to have happened', we are, she argues, engaged in theodicy. This secular theodicy is not about justifying God, but rather about the belief that the world should be a certain way and that when it is not that way, something is wrong, and wrong in a way that demands a response. In this version of theodicy, the question 'Why?' is not aimed at explaining the evils in the world but about registering a protest that this is not the way things should be and about attempting to change the world to make it better, so that it more resembles the way we think it should be.

III. Who is Evil? The Evil-Doer in Kant, Freud, and Arendt

The question 'Why is there evil in the world?' remains a pressing question for many. However, another major conversation about evil in the modern period does not focus on the world or on God's role in making or intervening in it, but rather on the individual subject as doer and sufferer of evil. Hence it moves from thinking about the world to thinking about the internal workings of the human subject and to what evil says about who we are as humans. Immanuel Kant is a key figure for moving thinking about evil into the murky depths of the human will as he seeks to describe how someone becomes evil. Sigmund Freud moves thinking about the evil-doer from the realm of will and choice to that of instincts and drives. Both he and Kant propose a universal picture of the structure of the human subject that describes, even though it cannot explain, how he or she comes to do evil. Contextualizing the evil-doer in the conditions of modern life, Hannah Arendt claims that in the modern period, there is a new kind of evil-doer—one who has no evil intentions, yet is still responsible for evil, and further whose lack of evil intentions does not lessen his guilt, but rather increases it. While concern with human sin, fallibility, guilt, wrongdoing, and the like runs throughout the history of European thought, there is a strong emphasis in modernity on explaining human action not by recourse to sin, but by a more secular description of human agency.

One strand in this conversation about who is evil moves between the monstrous and the demonic, on one end, and the human, on the other. Those who do the things we deem evil are seen to have moved outside the realm of the human. Either their actions belie their demonic nature or the actions transform and distort their agents beyond the limits of humanity. Much of popular culture displays an aesthetic fascination with this kind of depiction of evil, whether in the form of vampires, zombies, demons, or monsters.

There are two main criticisms of this view of evil: first, that characterizing anyone who does something we deem evil as a monster suggests that evil is beyond the scope of humanity. If this is so, people who do evil cannot be held accountable to the rules of humanity, since they are no longer part of humanity. Declare someone a monster, and, the argument goes, you can no longer try him in a court of law, you can no longer reasonably expect him to follow the laws of humanity. The second major criticism of this view is the aestheticization that seems to follow, particularly in popular culture representations, such that evil becomes an object of fascination, rather than something to be prevented or resisted. The suffering of the victims of these 'monsters and demons' is eclipsed by the intriguing otherness of the evil-doer. A similar aestheticization occurs in the depiction of evil-doers as 'evil geniuses', such that they have a kind of heroic glory that makes them glamorous, larger than life. There is a sense in which these evil-doers are pushed to the extremes of humanity, though not pushed beyond its boundary.

In her novel *Frankenstein*, Mary Shelley plays with this at times fluid borderline between the monster and human as agent of evil. Just who is the agent of evil in the story: the human creator of the monster, or the monster himself? There is much in the story that draws our sympathy towards the creature and much that draws our judgement of the creator. The popular mistaking of the title as referring to the monster, rather than his creator, is one small example of this confusion between the two.

Demonizing perpetrators registers the extremity of the event, but does so at the cost of any possibility of accountability. We also distance the perpetrators from ourselves in such a way as to render ourselves safe from any possible accountability. Tzvetan Todorov warns against this kind of move: 'the perpetrators of this evil were neither monsters or beasts but ordinary people, rather like us.... First of all, we must not abandon the principles of justice, the guilty must be judged, each according to his precise acts and responsibilities.... Second, we must refuse to establish a radical discontinuity between "them" and "us," to demonize the guilty' (Todorov 1996: 229). The discussions of Kant, Freud, and Arendt below reveal three major thinkers who show the radical continuities between those who do evil and ourselves, offering important, but different, counters to the propensity to demonize evil-doers such that they are beyond the realm of the human.

Immanuel Kant and the Will

It would be hard to overestimate Kant's influence on modern European thought, and more specifically, on the trajectory of work on evil within it. In *Religion within the Limits of Reason Alone*, Kant moved deep within the human psyche, as he explored the foundational maxims of the individual subject's will. By moving our attention from the world out there to ourselves, to the limits of our knowledge and hence the limits on what questions it makes sense to ask, Kant reframed the ways to approach and even pose the question of evil.

Rather than looking for an explanation as to why a good, all-powerful god allowed evil to exist in the world, Kant declared answers to such questions beyond the limits of human understanding. The reason for this was not the traditional Christian view that 'God's ways are not our ways and that therefore we cannot understand them in this life, but will one day.' Kant argued that we cannot know there is an answer we will one day discover. Instead, we can only hope and have faith that such is the case—it is precisely certainty that makes morality impossible.

Rather than focusing on the goodness and justice of God, or even of the world, Kant moved the discussion of evil to an internal stage, describing the ways in which someone becomes an evil person. He moved the question from a 'Why?' to a 'Who?'—not 'Why is there evil in the world?' or 'Why does God allow evil to happen?' but, rather, 'Who is the person who does evil?' 'How does a person become evil?'

Kant's answer depends on his moral psychology. Kant affirms the goodness of our predispositions, while arguing that we have an innate propensity for evil—not in the sense of it being inevitable that we will do evil but in the sense of it always being a possibility. If we put self-love above concern for the general good as the general maxim of our will, then we are evil, says Kant. Evil is not a matter of wicked intentions, but of misordered priorities.

Though Kant describes the ways in which someone becomes evil, and stresses the individual's responsibility for whomever he or she becomes, whether good or evil, he also stresses the inscrutability of why someone might become evil: 'But the rational origin of this perversion of the will whereby it makes lower incentives supreme among its maxims, that is, of the propensity to evil, remains inscrutable to us' (Kant 1960: 38). We can know how someone becomes evil, but never the why, precisely because a free will can never be determined nor its actions fully explained.

Sigmund Freud and the Death Drive

While the language of evil may seem foreign to Freud's oeuvre, his work has been a key moment in the move to understand the world through intense focus on the interior architecture of the human person. More than any other thinker in the modern period, his work has shaped the ways in which we understand human motives and desires, and hence human actions. The questions 'Who is evil?' and 'Who is the person who does evil?' are questions that emerge from this intense focus, and if Freud seems less interested in the moral register that such questions might seem to suggest, he is deeply interested in why humans do seemingly irrational but deeply destructive things.

Like Kant, he finds the 'propensity' for evil—for sheer destruction of either our selves or others—inscrutable, but that mystery does not reside in the nature of the freedom of the will. Rather, the mystery is rooted in the drives that propel us—namely the death drive and the love drive. These drives cannot be completely controlled or tamed, and certainly not eradicated, only suppressed, sublimated, or redirected. Which drive will have the upper hand at any one time cannot be predicted with any certainty.

Rather than free beings who are good, but with a propensity for evil and the freedom to act on that propensity, we are, in Freud's view, beings who are at war within ourselves, slaves of our drives. Some of us have some means for shaping the direction and impact of those drives, but we cannot escape them. In this view, evil is the ever-present possibility that may erupt at any time, despite our vigilance. Civilization seeks to keep it in check, but as even the events of the last years of Freud's life showed, this can sometimes seem like a feeble attempt to suppress a sporadically and chaotically erupting volcano.

Hannah Arendt and the Banality of Evil

Like Kant and Freud, Arendt's focus is fixed firmly on human individuals, rather than on God or the transcendent realm. In her (in)famous book *Eichmann in Jerusalem: A Report on the Banality of Evil*, Arendt did not propose a theory of evil, but rather presented a description of a new kind of person who does evil. The book was initially a series of reports she wrote for *The New Yorker* on the trial of Nazi official Adolph Eichmann. A German Jew born in 1906, Arendt fled Nazi Germany in 1933 after being arrested, worked for Jewish organizations in France, and finally settled in the United States, where she lived out the rest of her life as a public intellectual, teacher, and writer. Arendt tells us that she went to Jerusalem expecting to meet a monster, but instead encountered a clown. To her, Eichmann did not seem to have any strong motives of hatred, deep anti-Semitism, or psychopathic sadism that would have explained his high-level participation in the murder of millions of Jewish children, women, and men. Rather, he seemed to have organized their murder without any apparent motivations other than advancing in his career and carrying out Hitler's orders. He was, Arendt tells us, thoughtless. By thoughtless, she did not mean that he was unkind nor that he was stupid. Rather, he never thought about what he was doing; he never reflected on the meaning of his actions. He was unable to think otherwise than from a very narrow, self-absorbed perspective.

Arendt discovered a new kind of evil-doer in Eichmann—a person who could send thousands to their deaths all in a day's work, without a thought. Contrary to what some of her critics charged, Arendt was in no way excusing Eichmann. Rather than diminishing his culpability, Eichmann's thoughtlessness actually increased his responsibility in Arendt's eyes. In fact, in thinking through the implications of this failure of reflection, Arendt writes: 'That such remoteness from reality and such thoughtlessness can wreak more havoc than all the evil instincts taken together which, perhaps are inherent in man—that was, in fact, the lesson one could learn from Jerusalem' (Arendt 1964: 287–8).

In her essay, 'Thinking and Moral Considerations', written several years after *Eichmann in Jerusalem*, Arendt writes that by the book's subtitle *The Banality of Evil* she

> meant no theory or doctrine but something quite factual, the phenomenon of evil deeds, committed on a gigantic scale, which could not be traced to any particularity of wickedness, pathology, or ideological conviction in the doer, whose only personal distinction was a perhaps extraordinary shallowness. However monstrous the deeds were, the doer was neither monstrous nor demonic, and the only specific characteristic one could detect in his past as well as in his behavior during the trial and the preceding police examination was something entirely negative: it was not stupidity but a curious, quite authentic inability to think.   (Arendt 2003: 159)

Arendt explored the question of whether engaging in thinking could be a means to resist evil. Whereas Kant pointed to the will to explain who is evil and Freud pointed to the death drive to explain why we are all potential evil-doers, both of them thus implying a universal structure of the human subject, Arendt implied a more pluralistic picture of those who do evil. By describing Eichmann as a new kind of evil-doer, Arendt implicitly suggested that we cannot once and for all describe and thereby recognize the evil-doer in our midst. New cultural configurations, technological advances, and the like create new possibilities not only for human flourishing, but also for new forms of evil. Surprisingly, Arendt's view of the evil-doer may be the most terrifying of the three, for it suggests that we may even now be moving along the path towards doing evil that we don't recognize—or that we may already be there.

IV. WHAT IS 'EVIL'?

In discussions of the questions 'Why is evil?' and 'Who is evil?', there is often an unstated assumption that we all agree on what evil is. However, this question is perhaps the most difficult of the three. Just what do we mean when we call something or someone evil? Most writers on evil note that there is some general, if not universal, agreement on certain things that are evil, but what we mean by calling those things evil is not clear. 'Evil' is a powerful yet often vague term.

The Ontological Status of Evil

Traditionally, in European thought, different kinds of evil have been identified. Premodern thinkers saw a range of evils, including supernatural evils (for example, evil beings like demons or destructive events caused by the anger of the gods or God), natural evils (such as earthquakes and epidemics), and human or moral evils (such as murder or treachery). Moving into modernity, discussions of evil began to be less about supernatural or natural evils, and more about human or moral evils, thus moving responsibility from the transcendent realm to humans themselves.

Related to the division of evils into kinds is the question of what one might call the ontological status of evil. Is evil something, for example, a being, like Satan, or a force in the world battling against good? Or is evil somehow negative, a lack or distortion of good, that is, something that has no ontological standing on its own? The idea of evil as privation, as a lack of the good, as having no being and substance of its own, runs at least as far back as Augustine, with emphasis on the pathetic, paltry, or banal character of evil. This view of evil can take at least three forms: evil as the absence of good, evil as parasitic on the good, and evil as the perversion of the good—and sometimes some combination of the three. In each of these, evil is defined by a lacking ontology that cannot or does not sustain itself.

Others argue that this view of evil fails to acknowledge the powerful suffering that evil inflicts, and we must, instead, focus on it as a destructive force, an agent of suffering, not merely a lack. Jean Améry, in his essay 'Torture', notes that 'there is no "banality of evil," and Hannah Arendt who wrote about it in her Eichmann book, knew the enemy of mankind only from hearsay, saw him only though the glass cage [referring to the glass shield that protected Eichmann during his trial]. When an event places the most extreme demands on us, one ought not to speak of banality' (Améry 1986: 25). While Améry misreads what Arendt is referring to with her subtitle 'the banality of evil', his critique is an important caution against any theorizing that loses sight of the real experiences of evil and the sufferings that result from it.

Theologians have traditionally responded to the question 'What is evil?' by recourse to original sin, but many have explored the ontological status of evil, trying to account for its powerful destruction but limiting its force in relation to the power and purposes of God. For example, Kierkegaard finds the source of evil in boredom, and Barth's theology locates evil in nothingness, or *das Nichtige*; while Paul Tillich focuses on the demonic as a force in the world. A more popular presentation of this view comes in BBC Special Correspondent Fergal Keane's writing about his experiences in Rwanda:

> I am conscious that my words will always be unequal to the task of conveying the full horror of the crime of genocide. For what I encountered was evil in a form that frequently rendered me inarticulate. This was evil as a presence, not as a word or concept.   (Keane 1997: 4)

In *The Symbolism of Evil*, Paul Ricoeur tried to dialectically bridge these views, bringing the positive and negative aspects together, with the negative never able to overcome the positive:

> evil, however positive, however seductive, however affective and infective it may be, cannot make a defection, in the sense that the dispositions and functions that make the humanity of man might be unmade, undone, to the point where a reality other than the human reality would be produced.   (Ricoeur 1967: 156)

Further he suggests that 'evil is not symmetrical with the good, wickedness is not something that replaces the goodness of a man; it is the staining, the darkening, the disfiguring of an innocence, a light, a beauty that remain. However *radical* evil may be, it cannot be as *primordial* as goodness' (Ricoeur 1967: 156). Whether grappling with a positive or negative view of evil, these theologians are far away from the radical relativization of evil effected by Nietzsche.

Friedrich Nietzsche and the Origins of 'Evil'

Whether theological or not, all modern thought has had to contend with the radical reorientation of thinking about evil issued by Nietzsche. By focusing on the origins of the word 'evil' and the rhetorical work that it does, he moves discussion of evil from an empirical fact about the world or human nature, to a constructed category and a linguistic tool created as a means of gaining power. Nietzsche tells us that 'at the age of thirteen I was exercised by the problem of evil' until he learned 'no longer to seek the origin of evil *behind* the world' (Nietzsche 1956: 151). Instead he claims to approach evil as a philologist, looking at the word's origins and evaluating it in pragmatic terms— what use did such a term have for human life? He asks:

> Under what conditions did man construct the value judgments *good* and *evil*? And what is their intrinsic worth? Have they thus far benefited or retarded mankind? Do they betoken misery, curtailment, degeneracy, or, on the contrary, power, fullness of being energy, courage in the face of life, and confidence in the future?   (Nietzsche 1956: 151)

In *Beyond Good and Evil*, he proposes that 'what one age perceives as evil is usually an untimely echo of something that was once perceived as good—the atavism of an older ideal' (Nietzsche 1998: 69).

Nietzsche reconceives morality as a human tool, rather than an innate structure of the universe or of human nature, and he approaches the problem of evil from the question of what value the language of good and evil has, or more crassly, to what uses it has been put, and to what uses, if any, it should be put in the current moment. Here the ontological status of evil—is evil a being like the devil or a force at work in the universe or a propensity within human nature?—drops from view, and evil becomes part of the linguistic/conceptual toolbox in service to the will to power.

Specifically, Nietzsche traces the movement from an aristocratic or noble master morality, which was, he proposes, structured by the binary good-bad, to the slave morality ascetic priests created by overturning that binary, such that all that was considered good—nobility, courage, pride—took on the negative pole in the new binary good-evil. This good-evil binary, Nietzsche argues, has been used to de-enervate humans, particularly the best and strongest humans, such that they are losing their will, their energies, their passions, and their strength. These passions and energies are constricted by the rule of guilt and the desire to avoid it. The language of evil, according to Nietzsche, keeps us looking for a world beyond or behind our own. Nietzsche calls for moving beyond this good-evil binary, not in a return to the good-bad binary, but to a new one—one that recognizes that morality is merely a set of categories we use to order the world and our place in it, rather than a description of the way the world is. Instead of the language of good and evil, and the guilt that follows it, Nietzsche suggests a language of human prosperity, flourishing, and health.

In Nietzsche's work, evil moves out of the world, out of human nature, and into language, becoming a word that can be applied to certain people or phenomena to achieve certain outcomes. This radical relativization of the concept of evil renders it a malleable tool rather than a fact about the world.

The Holocaust and Evil

While Nietzsche radically relativized evil by reconceiving of it as merely a humanly created concept, rather than a fact about the world or about human nature, the events of the Holocaust have, in contrast, come to be seen as a new moral absolute. In a pluralistic world, there seems to be less and less that we can agree on, but the Holocaust stands as a paradigm of evil and as a 'negative absolute', to use a term coined by Michael Berenbaum. Discussions of evil often take the Holocaust as the paradigm of evil or as an undisputed example of evil.

And yet, this absolutizing of the evil of the Holocaust has not enabled a clear and certain theorizing about evil or answer to the question 'What is evil?'—rather, quite the opposite has been the result. Even while the Holocaust has become the most docu-mented, studied, and discussed atrocity in human history, the efforts to grapple with it, speak about it, and understand its evil are unendingly fraught with stumblings, stutterings, and silences.

In fact, writing about the Holocaust has often theorized the inadequacies of language to articulate the evils of the Holocaust. The philosopher Sarah Kofman, writing of the impossibilities of speaking about the Holocaust while finding herself compelled to do so, asks:

> How then can one tell that which cannot, without delusion be 'communicated'? That for which there are no words—or too many—and not only because the 'limit experience' of infinite privation, like all other experiences, cannot be transmitted? How is it possible to speak when you feel a 'frenzied desire' to perform an impossible task—to convey the experience just as it was, to explain everything to the other, when you are seized by a veritable delirium of words—and yet, at the same time, it is impossible for you to speak. Impossible, without *choking* . . . a strange *double bind*: an infinite claim to speak, *a duty to speak infinitely*, imposing itself with irresistible force, and at the same time, an almost physical impossibility to speak, a *choking* feeling. Knotted words, demanded and yet forbidden. . . .   (Kofman 1998: 38–9)

The question 'What is evil?' becomes the question 'How can I speak of this and how can I not speak of it?' As Primo Levi writes: 'The need to tell our story to "the rest," to make "the rest" participate in it, had taken on for us, before our liberation and after, the character of an immediate and violent impulse, to the point of competing with our other elementary needs' (Levi 1993: 9). Moving closer to the end of the spectrum in which words become cries, writing about the evil of the Holocaust is often about the ways the Holocaust has broken down interpretive frameworks, conceptual tools, and language itself. Rather than the malleability of the language of evil suggested by Nietzsche, Holocaust survivors note the inadequacy of language to communicate the evils they suffered.

Even those who are not survivors, but rather are scholars of the Holocaust, express concern about the adequacy and moral appropriateness of language to engage with the evil of the Holocaust. Theodor Adorno famously claimed that it was barbaric to write poetry after Auschwitz (though he not so famously revised that claim). Historian Raul Hilberg takes that one step further when he asks about scholarly writing on the Holocaust: 'You all remember Adorno's dictum that it is barbaric to write poetry after Auschwitz. I am no poet, but the thought occurred to me that if the statement is true, then is it not equally barbaric to write footnotes after Auschwitz?' (Lang 1988: 25).

Like Arendt's implicit claim that the face of evil-doers changes through time, that new kinds of evil-doers come into being as culture changes and technologies advance, writing on the Holocaust suggests that new answers to the question 'What is evil?' become necessary, and that at the same time they seem unavailable. Many scholars see the Holocaust as an unprecedented event that issues in a new possibility for evil in the future. Because it happened once, it is now possible for similar forms of evil to happen again in the world. Zygmunt Bauman registers a caution: 'To put it bluntly, there are reasons to be worried because we know now *that we live in a type of society that made the Holocaust possible, and that contained nothing which could stop the Holocaust from happening*' (Bauman 1989: 88). While we should quarrel with the determinism present in his suggestion that nothing could have stopped the Holocaust from happening, it is striking that nothing did.

Implications

In the modern period, discussion of the question 'what is evil' oscillates between a relativism that avoids all moral judgements—which, ironically, Nietzsche would denounce as nihilism—and a fundamentalism, inhabited by both the religious and secularists alike, that uses moral judgements like an axe to destroy all who are different. In one, there is no fundamental answer to the question—'evil' is just a word that it might be time to discard—and in the other, there is one fundamental answer to that question—and that answer is the other who is our/my enemy.

Nietzsche moves the discussion of evil to the realm of philology and rhetoric, and away from theology, epistemology, or psychology, reorienting us away from thinking about 'evil' as an empirical fact about the world and/or human nature to viewing it as a linguistic structure. Others have followed in his wake suggesting that the word is so theologically weighted that it should be abandoned. The word, it is argued, distracts us from action—from responding to real suffering and preventing future injustices—by the theological and theoretical questions it raises. Further, the word 'evil' has so often been used to label one's enemies and then justify horrific action against them that, it is argued, we would have less suffering and a more humane world without its use. Others see this utilitarian view of 'evil' as nihilistic, leading to a relativism that offers us no grounds for making moral judgements in the face of evils. Unless we have some way to name and judge the worst sorts of things that people do to one another, we will have no way to identify evils and reduce suffering.

The effort to grapple with the events of the Holocaust has shown aspects of both sides of this debate. On the one hand, the Nazis used the language of evil to label the Jews and then justify their actions against them. When someone or some group is labelled 'evil', the limitations about what can and cannot be done to them start to fall away, often in the minds of both perpetrators and bystanders. The power of the word to do this is part of its danger. But, on the other hand, the Holocaust calls for outrage, for a clear judgement that this is evil; there is a clear and immense need to be able to judge as more than just wrong the horrors that the Nazis inflicted. Thus, there is a need for careful study of the rhetorical uses to which the word 'evil' is put, such that it is not wielded as a weapon to justify destruction of one's enemies, but also so that it is used responsibly as part of the moral vocabulary we need to navigate the world.

Likewise, in thinking further about evil in modern European thought, we need to keep in mind the range of responses to evil with which we alluded at the beginning of this chapter—the intellectual evasion of the realities of evil and the suffering it causes that can tempt us away from responsible action, on the one hand, and the paralysing despair that can engulf us while seeking to engage them, on the other. We must not abandon our thinking, despite its frustrations, and we must not forget our bodies, lived experiences, and actual sufferings of evil, despite the discomforts that attention to suffering brings to our thinking and conceptual schema.

References

Adams, Marilyn McCord (1999). *Horrendous Evils and the Goodness of God*. (Ithaca: Cornell University Press).

Améry, Jean (1986). *At the Mind's Limits: Contemplations by a Survivor on Auschwitz and Its Realities*, trans. Sidney and Stella P. Rosenfeld (New York: Schocken Books).

Arendt, Hannah (1964). *Eichmann in Jerusalem: A Report on the Banality of Evil*. (New York: Penguin).

——(2003). *Responsibility and Judgment*, ed. Jerome Kohn (New York: Schocken).

Bauman, Zygmunt (1989). *Modernity and the Holocaust*. (Ithaca: Cornell University Press).

Benjamin, Walter (2005). *Selected Writings 1931–1934*, vol. 2, part 2, ed. Michael W. Jennings, Howard Eiland, and Gary Smith (Cambridge, MA: Harvard University Press).

Bernstein, Richard J. (2002). *Radical Evil: A Philosophical Interrogation.* (Cambridge: Polity Press).

Bouchard, Larry D. (1989). *Tragic Method and Tragic Theology: Evil in Contemporary Drama and Religious Thought.* (University Park, PA: Pennsylvania State University Press).

Dostoevsky, Fyodor (2002). *The Brothers Karamazov*, trans. and anno. Richard Pevear and Larissa Volokhonsky (New York: Farrar, Strauss, and Giroux).

Eagleton, Terry (2010). *On Evil.* (New Haven: Yale University Press).

Freud, Sigmund (1961). *Civilization and Its Discontents*, trans. James Strachey (New York: Norton).

Hick, John (1978). *Evil and the God of Love*, rev. edn. (San Francisco: Harper & Row).

Hume, David (2007). *Dialogues Concerning Natural Religion and Other Writings*, ed. Dorothy Coleman (Cambridge: Cambridge University Press).

Kant, Immanuel (1960). *Religion within the Limits of Reason Alone*, trans. Theodore M. Greene and Hoyt H. Hudson (New York: Harper & Row).

Keane, Fergal (1997). *Season of Blood: A Rwandan Journey.* (New York: Penguin).

Kofman, Sarah (1998). *Smothered Words*, trans. Madeleine Dobie (Evanston, IL: Northwestern University Press).

Lang, Berel (ed.) (1988). *Writing and the Holocaust.* (New York: Holmes & Meier).

Leibniz, G. W. (1985). *Theodicy: Essays on the Goodness of God, the Freedom of Man, and the Origin of Evil*, ed. Austin Marsden Farrer, trans. E. M. Huggard (La Salle: Open Court Publishing).

Levi, Primo (1993). *Survival in Auschwitz: The Nazi Assault on Humanity*, trans. Stuart Woolf (New York: Collier).

Levinas, Emmanuel (1998). 'Useless Suffering', *Entre Nous: On Thinking-of-the-Other*, trans. Michael B. Smith and Barbara Harshav (New York: Columbia University Press).

Moltmann, Jürgen (1974). *The Crucified God: The Cross of Christ as the Foundation and Criticism of Christian Theology.* (New York: Harper & Row).

Neiman, Susan (2002). *Evil in Modern Thought: An Alternative History of Philosophy.* (Princeton, NJ: Princeton University Press).

Nietzsche, Friedrich (1956). *The Birth of Tragedy and the Genealogy of Morals*, trans. Francis Golffing (New York: Doubleday Anchor Books).

——(1998). *Beyond Good and Evil*, trans. Marion Faber (Oxford: Oxford University Press).

Ricoeur, Paul (1967). *The Symbolism of Evil*, trans. Emerson Buchanan (Boston: Beacon Press, 1967).

Swinburne, Richard (1998). *Providence and the Problem of Evil.* (Oxford: Clarendon).

Todorov, Tzvetan (1996). *Facing the Extreme: Moral Life in the Concentration Camps*, trans. Arthur Denner and Abigail Pollak (New York: Metropolitan Books).

Voltaire (1977). *The Portable Voltaire*, ed. Ben Ray Redman (New York: Penguin).

——(2000). *Candide and Related Writings*, trans. David Wootton (Indianapolis: Hackett).

Suggested Reading

Adams (1999).

Arendt (1964).

Bernstein (2002).

Dostoevsky (2002).
Hick (1978).
Hume (2007).
Kant (1960).
Leibniz (1985).
Levi (1993).
Neiman (2002).
Nietzsche (1956).
Ricoeur (1967).

CHAPTER 11

....

LOVE

....

WERNER G. JEANROND

I. THE CENTRAL PLACE OF LOVE IN CHRISTIAN TRADITION

....

THE arrival of modernity has challenged many traditional paradigms of thinking about the nature, place, and vocation of human beings in this universe. Although richly contributing to the different discourses on divine and human love and questioning many of their traditional assumptions, modern European thought—Christian and secular—continued to confirm the centrality of love in the lives of women, men, and children. Disagreement on the origin of love—is it divine, human, evolutionary, biological, or cultural?—did not affect the general consensus that all human beings need love to develop their personalities, relational capacities, and ways to happiness.

Thus, the concern with love in modernity has not experienced the radical ruptures and discontinuities generally associated with the breakthrough of modern and post-modern ways of thinking. In spite of shifting contexts and perspectives, modern reflections on the praxis of love in religion, literature, the arts, philosophy, theology, sociology, psychology, etc., continue to be influenced, albeit in different ways, by classical Hebrew, Greek, and Roman as well as medieval, Renaissance, Reformation and early modern concepts of love. The desire for love has characterized human beings in all known cultures past and present and has invited comparisons between the different conceptualizations and expressions of love. Hence, there seems to be a universal dimension in love that transcends its particular shapes and manifestations beyond differences in time, place, and language.

Christian approaches to love share with other religious and non-religious ap-proaches the understanding that love seeks the other, desires to be with the other, and wishes to relate to the other in different degrees of intimacy. The Bible confronts Jews and Christians with the divine command to love God, their fellow human beings, and their own selves (Deut. 6:5; Lev. 19:18 and 33; Matt. 22:37–40, etc.). Here love is more than feeling, emotion, sex, sensation, attitude of mind, behaviour, and morality, though all of these aspects are important for a more comprehensive concept of love. Jewish, Christian, and Muslim theologies of love reflect on the particular requirement of relating in love to God, the radical other, who has endowed human beings with the gift of love, and whose very being, according to Christian expression, is love (1 John 4:8 and 16). Hence, love invites Christians into a dynamic network of relationships that includes God. Biblical love involves the acceptance of God's gift of loving relationship and covenant; a willingness to develop faithful and forgiving relations with God, other people, God's creation, and one's own emerging self; and a passionate desire for transcendence and transformation of both self and other.

Does adequate reflection on love, therefore, demand specific discourses for neighbourly love, love for the universe, love for God, and love for my own emerging self? Or should love be approached as fundamentally one—exploring how all our 'loves' together contribute to the dynamic network of transformative relationships? Or should love be discussed most appropriately in terms of its respective agent: God and the human being—either as radically different or as intimately related agents of love?

Before we explore approaches to love in modern European thought, however, and examine how they differ from one another and from previous approaches we need first to discuss briefly the biblical, patristic, and medieval heritage.

II. Pre-Modern Christian Thoughts on Love

Christian concepts of love have emerged in response both to particular interpretations of biblical notions and traditions and to changing spiritual, cultural, and intellectual views of human nature. The Hebrew scriptures record a number of expressions for God's love and care for people and in turn their relationship to the God of Israel, to friends, and strangers. Forced to find suitable Greek equivalents, the translators of the Septuagint and the authors and compilers of the emerging New Testament chose *agape* and *philia* as the principal terms for divine and human love. *Eros* was not used in order to avoid possible confusion with Eros, the Greek god of love, and associated notions of cosmic power, fertility, lust, and temptation. This linguistic predicament illustrates the contextuality of all human approaches to love.

Greek philosophy provided a significant context for evolving Christian notions of love. For Plato the ultimate object of love was the transcendent God. Eros is the force that moves souls to the search for the good, the beautiful, and the true. Love allows human beings to transcend themselves; human nature is thus essentially a striving for the soul's knowledge and possession of the good. Aristotle approached human love in terms of friendship (*philia*) as benevolence rather than desire (Lindberg 2008: 8).

Understanding God as the unmoved mover, he argued that God is loved by all, but loves only himself.

The Synoptic Gospels stress Jesus' citation of the Torah's double love commandment (Deut. 6:5–6; Lev. 19:18) and thus confirm that his own proclamation of the command to love God, neighbour, and enemy was firmly in line with Jewish tradition (Matt. 22:37–40 and par.). However, the gospels differ in their definition of the horizon of love. In Luke's Gospel Jesus admonishes everybody to become a neighbour to persons in need (cf. the story of the Good Samaritan in Luke 10). The Johannine community restricts the horizon of love to members of this embattled community itself. Paul recommends love as the way of tackling conflict and otherness in the church at Corinth (1 Cor. 13) and shows it to be the most appropriate way for Christians to respond to the Spirit of Christ (Romans). Thus, although New Testament texts agree on the centrality of love, they conceptualize love differently.

Influenced by Neoplatonist anthropology and in contrast to Gnostic anthropology, many early Church theologians understood love as the God-given eternal fulfilment beyond bodily constraints, cosmic limitations, and human sinfulness. God is the only subject and agent of love. Human beings are called to love God. He alone is worthy of love.

Augustine identified God's love as the only genuine form of love. It alone deserves our full praise and passionate desire. God alone can love. When human beings love each other, it is in reality God who loves in them. Union with God must be the goal of the life of the elect. This goal was not seen as somehow competing with the Synoptic Gospels' proclamation of God's reign or the Johannine focus on eternal life. On the contrary, the desire for union with God was understood to flow from the divine love, which the gospels present as the essence of Jesus' proclamation, ministry, sacrificial death, and resurrection.

Augustine followed the apostle Paul in setting love (in Latin *caritas* and occasionally *dilectio*) as the highest of the virtues—besides faith and hope, culminating in his famous dictum 'Love and do what you will' (Augustine 1955: 316). However, Augustine must not be misread along the lines of 'love is all you need'. Rather he stresses the rootedness of all good intentions in love. The love of God and of fellow humans must always be seen as God's gift. Augustine distinguished between egocentric self-love (*cupititas*) and self-less love (*caritas*). *Caritas* is the motion of the soul towards the enjoyment of God for God's sake, and the enjoyment of one's neighbour and one's own self for God's sake. *Cupititas* is the motion of the soul towards the enjoyment of one's self, one's neighbour, or any corporal thing for the sake of something other than God (Augustine 1958: 88). Hence, all true love is directed to God from whom it comes in the first place.

Augustine exerted an enormous influence on all subsequent western theologies of love. His spiritual and theological attention to human desire for God and God's love supported the development of Christian mysticism and its approach to the vision of God (McGinn 1991: 228–62). Moreover, Augustine's exploration of the inner life of the self, i.e. the soul, notably in his *Confessions*, extended the horizon of human love to include a new and spiritual interface for the intimate encounter between God and the human being. However, according to Augustine, any mystical vision must be brief and imperfect since the soul is 'a fallen creature, bound by both original and individual sin, and hence any such elevation is always a result of God's action in us' (McGinn 1991: 233).

The philosophical framework in which Augustine developed his concept of love as the highest good (*summum bonum*) was Platonic. However, unlike Plato, Augustine identified the *summum bonum* with the personal God. For Plato, all human beings love the good, whereas for Augustine, all human beings love God who is love. Johannine theology provided the biblical framework for this fusion of the highest good with God who is love (1 John 4:8 and 16). In Johannine spirit, Augustine conceived of the unity of love in terms of a theological unity. Here, a Platonic heritage, a particular biblical tradition, and a mentality seeking unity and stability beyond all worldly divisions and conflicts merged. For Augustine, God is love—its origin, goal, and sole subject (Jeanrond 2010a: 53–4).

Augustine's theology of love centres around what God can do for fallen humanity. Important issues in our contemporary debates on love, e.g. embodiment, gender, subjectivity, autonomy, emancipation, relational choice, the desire for and the recognition of otherness, had no great significance for him. Longing, bodies, images of the self, all of these are subjected to change in time; they are not eternal. Augustine was of course concerned with his fellow human beings and their specific needs. Yet he approached human beings in respect of that which lives inside them as their interior source of being. No individual self means anything in comparison with this eternal source.

While Augustine had identified God's love as the ontological goal of and spiritual motivation for the human journey, the rediscovery of human subjectivity and agency in the high Middle Ages reclaimed love now as the *human* way towards the eternal goal. This anthropological revolution, still unfolding today, has brought a new dynamics to the exploration of human love. Not only God was to be respected as a loving subject, but also women and men. The rediscovery of Aristotle's philosophy thanks to the fruitful encounter between Christian, Jewish, and Muslim thinkers, an emerging new approach to biblical hermeneutics, a radical shift in the sociology of knowledge from a monastic monopoly of education now to the establishment of ever new centres of learning (i.e. the university movement in many parts of Europe), the foundation of new monastic movements increasingly concerned with the formation of individual human lives according to new social paradigms, and a related interest in new forms of group formation in medieval society, all of these factors impacted strongly on the emergence of new concepts of love.

Although these philosophical, anthropological, theological, and cultural departures have unleashed a radical rethinking of the role of human beings in this universe, this process was first more devoted to how human behaviour conformed to social models than to the emancipation of the individual and autonomous self and the ensuing pluralism of subjective projects, which have characterized modern and postmodern approaches both to the self and to human love (Bynum 1982: 85). In any case, for many theological voices in the twelfth and thirteenth centuries human beings were capable of love thanks to their likeness to God. God has created men and women in His image (*imago dei*). The divine origin of love was thus reconfirmed, but new conclusions were drawn: God has enabled human beings to love because they bear God's image within themselves. Compared to Augustine's concept of love, a radically new anthropological orientation begins to affirm the human capacity to love, to explore what this capacity entails, and how it can be developed and improved in the respective orders of life. Three resulting developments in particular have influenced future discussions of love in Europe: The mystics' rediscovery and refiguration of the loving relationship between the human self and God; the scholarly study of love especially in Thomas Aquinas's systematic theology; and the emergence of romantic love at the medieval courts in southern France and in related literature.

Medieval mysticism combines—in differing weights—Platonic concerns with interiority and transcendence as mediated by Augustine and further shaped by the work of Pseudo-Dionysius, hermeneutical preferences for allegorical readings of biblical texts (notably of the Song of Songs and the Psalms), and a new appreciation of the human capacity to enter into a relationship that opens the prospect of a mystical union with God. Medieval mysticism thus stands at the interface between the older paradigm of concentrating totally on God's love and the emerging new paradigm of exploring human love in its own right, though intrinsically related to divine love. There are many different strands, however, within this rich and fluid field. Bernard of Clairvaux, for example, encouraged his readers (mostly fellow monks) to explore human experience and to read in the book of their hearts, thus opening the way for a retrieval of both subjectivity and embodiment—to be sure not yet in any modern sense, but in a sense which helped to pave the way for further examinations of their role for human love.

Also Thomas Aquinas's systematic study of love in his *Summa Theologiae* illustrates at once respect for and a radical departure from central aspects of the Augustinian approach to love. Using Aristotle's concept of friendship, Thomas suggested that human beings were created to become friends with God. Moreover, he argued that love was not the union with the desired object itself; rather the union was the result of love. Hence, love (*caritas*) is now presented as a praxis in response to the infusion of the virtue of love into the human being by God. Love, the highest among the three theological virtues, denotes union with God, whereas faith and hope do not. Moreover, love is an act of will made possible by God's sharing of himself with us human beings— God who is love (Thomas Aquinas 1975: 37 and 69). Therefore, love can grow in depth and intensity in the life of the human subject. Thomas can distinguish but not separate the love of God and the love of neighbour. Hence, he treats of love as one single concept comprising many dimensions (Thomas Aquinas 1975: 117). Love as the habit infused by God into our souls always includes a co-orientation to love's creator.

Thomas also formulated an intriguing distinction between 'love' and 'like'. He considered it absurd to command persons to like their enemies. Rather, he argued, the point was to *love* our enemies as fellow human beings who like the rest of us carry God's image in them, though not to *like* their evil deeds and intentions (Thomas Aquinas 1975: 105).

Thomas further extended the horizon of love: Love is a universal gift from God that calls for human response, discernment, and moral development. In spite of the universalizing and totalizing claims of medieval scholastic theology and its intimate connection with a patriarchal and hierarchical ecclesiastical imagination and the resulting exclusions of erotic consideration of love, Thomas's approach to love represents a significant move towards a new conceptualization of human love and agency on the way to modern concepts of love and subjectivity.

The emergence of such a new understanding of human love and subjectivity can also be studied in the development of courtly love, which quickly spread from the Provençal courts to other courts in Europe. Hence, at this period in time, love was reclaimed and refigured in a number of social locations at once: in monastic life and mystical thought, in academic reflection on Church and theology, and in courtly contexts. It was expressed in different forms of discourse, including mystical contemplation on biblical texts, theoretical reflections on Christian praxis, and poetic songs about love and associated feelings, devotions, and desires. Such songs and related literary texts were directed at the venerated lady in the case of the male Troubadours, or at the beloved friend in the case of the female Troubadours (cf. Jeanrond 2010a: 83–9). This intensification of love discourses and the broad focus on human experience as the centre of loving activity besides divine love (expressed in the different communicative genres of Church, court, and university) continued uninterrupted throughout Renaissance and Reformation.

Although the horizon of love widened all the time to encompass ever more aspects of nature, universe, body, beauty, and mind, the spiritual link between human love and God remained unbroken. However, sexuality was not yet at the forefront of such discourses on love. The Augustinian heritage still prevailed with its deep seated suspicion of the erotic body—'the obstacle to apprehending the body as spiritual' (May 2011: 138). The erotic was of course present in prayer, art, and literature though in 'Platonic' forms and in the service of the spiritual network of divine-human relationships.

Martin Luther brought the two major strands in the Christian tradition of love together: the Platonically inspired Augustinian heritage of seeing human life as captivated by sin and imperfection and the Aristotelian inspired affirmation of the human capacity to love. Luther distinguished sharply between divine and human love. While the former is perfect, the latter is deficient because it always includes egoistic dimensions. Our love always seeks our own benefits and follows our own desires. God's love creates the good. 'For the sinners are beautiful, because they are loved; but they are not loved because they are beautiful. That is why human love shuns the sinners, the evil doers' (Luther 1883: 365; my translation). However, Luther did not look down on human love; nor did he deny that the objects of human love were part of God's good gifts. Rather, right human love of God acknowledges and praises God for these precious gifts of divine creation.

While Thomas Aquinas defended the unity of love, Luther contrasted divine and human love. Thanks to the work of Christ both loves can be reunited afresh. Hence, according to Luther faith in divine justification through Christ allows this new unity of love to come about. Faith shapes human love and thus makes good works possible. In Luther we see one of the first references to 'Christian love'. Hitherto, love was considered as a gift from God, a theological virtue. Now love is either united with God's love in Christ, i.e. Christian love, or it remains a non-Christian, i.e. sinful and imperfect, love. Once a universal gift, love has now become an object of confessional dispute.

III. Love With or Without God

Enlightenment thinking on love did not at first dismiss all reference to God from the network of loving relationships. However, attention shifted further towards the exploration of the human capacity to love. Human love was now considered as an affect of the human soul rather than as a transformative gift from God. Michel de Montaigne approached love with the help of Aristotle's concept of friendship as an essential aspect of human nature. The transformative potential of love became here an aspect of true humanity, which human beings should critically and self-critically know and enjoy (May 2011: 141). René Descartes replaced the traditional metaphysics of love with a psychological definition: Love is an emotion of the soul, caused by the movement of minds which motivates the soul to unite itself willingly with objects which appear suitable to her (Meckenstock 1991: 159). Love was now treated as a dimension of human nature and life and, as a result, of ethics.

In Baruch Spinoza's *Ethics* the link between love and nature was further strengthened. Whereas Descartes had distinguished between mental and physical dimensions of reality, Spinoza rejected any such dichotomy with significant consequences for his understanding of love. Love was no longer expected to offer a way out of this reality in terms of transcending it to a higher, divine level. Instead love was to affirm nature as a whole—and God is nature conceived as an intelligible whole. Hence, understanding nature taken as a whole is the highest form of love: *amor intellectualis Dei*—the intellectual love of God. Within the orbit of his immanentist and transpersonal approach to God, Spinoza distinguished between true love of God and passionate human love (*amor est laetitia*) that seeks union with the other. The wise person should concentrate on the former. Thus, in Spinoza's thought we see an attempt to overcome the traditional theology of love where human love is to be transcended towards divine love, and a renewed effort to split this refigured intellectual love from human passion and sexual expression. Genuine love continues to relate everything to God, now understood as nature as a whole. This conflation between God and nature as a whole allowed two different conclusions: Either the entire universe is a mystical whole in which eternal love manifests itself, as in various expressions of Romanticism, or it is the only place in which enlightened human love as a social phenomenon can authentically flourish, as in different forms of Enlightenment thinking (May 2011: 151).

Jean-Jacques Rousseau developed certain Romantic lines of thought within his overall Enlightenment project—notably with regard to his understanding of love. Moreover, he introduced a genuinely modern concern into the discourse of love, namely the pursuit of personal identity. Distinguishing clearly between love of the self (*amour de soi*) and love for the self (*amour propre*), Rousseau continued the exploration of the potential of human nature for genuine goodness. Sexuality and pleasure are not bad, they are part of our nature, and spiritual perfection will intensify physical satisfaction. Rousseau analysed and praised love's higher possibilities though always respecting love's natural conditions. However, Rousseau was aware of 'the struggle between the good and the corrupt in love, and especially of how easily love can be hijacked by pride and vanity. He wants love to explore our innermost impulses, and also to uphold a wider natural order binding human beings, to which he sees the marriage bond as central' (May 2011: 163). The human being needs love, is capable of love, and becomes a self through love.

Immanuel Kant did not directly contribute to the study of love. However, his philosophical reflection on God destroyed the foundation of the concept of love as a predicate of God. Moreover, Kant considered his ethics firmly in line with the double love command in the Bible. He was interested in a concept of practical love which concerned the will, yet not with 'pathological love' which had to do with sympathy and inclination. The young Hegel criticized Kant's focus on the will in love. He emphasized instead that law and inclination are no longer separate in love. In religion, love is not only subjective feeling (*Empfindung*) but at the same time also objective image and representation (*Vorstellung*) (Hegel 1986: 250–1).

Unlike Rousseau, Romantic writers, such as Friedrich Schlegel, Novalis, and others, attended to the mysterious nature of love as well as to its formative power (*Liebe als Bildung*) and prepared the way for a movement—still continuing today—which has promoted some sort of religion of love: love proclaimed as either the return or the path to paradise. Love unites body and soul; it is the solution to all human desires, searches, and aspirations. It is truly salvific. Through love human beings reach their full humanity. *All you need is love.* Love reunites human beings with nature, the universe, the innermost self, the beloved self, and the infinite. In Schlegel's words, it is only now that a feeling for the world has really dawned on us. This concept of love combines the erotic and the spiritual; it seeks to overcome all divisions and dualities; it divinizes human nature. Various elements from traditional theological discourses of love are regrouped here in order to generate a fully human way to reach divine status. Divinization, once proclaimed by Christian theologians as the way to salvation given by God to humanity in Jesus Christ and his Church, is now refigured to manifest an authentically human praxis of love. No longer is God love, but now human love is God.

'It is itself the supreme Good; the creative source of all things; absolute Being; immortal; true; nameless' (May 2011: 169).

Human love creates a new union between selves, nature, and the universe. European literature has been exploring this theme, its potential and its ambiguities in all its genres ever since. The modern experience of an at times painfully experienced individuality has found its equally modern remedy: human love. It alone builds the bridge between the individual and the human other and it alone promises a blissful union. Hence, transcendence through love has now become a fully human religion with its own priests and rituals—and sacrifices. Giuseppe Verdi's Violetta in *La Traviata* and Richard Wagner's *Liebestod* in *Tristan und Isolde*—to name just two examples— orchestrate the ultimate human sacrifice on stage: death for one's love's sake (cf. de Rougemont 1983: 230–1).

Although Enlightenment and Romanticism approaches to human love still displayed some of their Christian roots, they increasingly concentrated on the particular relationship between friends and couples. The love of God and the love of neighbour—in the sense of becoming a neighbour to other human beings—increasingly disappeared from these discourses.

Paradoxically, modern atheist philosophers reclaimed some of the Jewish and Christian heritage of attending to others and their needs while at the same time renouncing any remaining theological reference in love. Arthur Schopenhauer, Ludwig Feuerbach, Karl Marx, Friedrich Nietzsche, Sigmund Freud, and others have wrestled with human love—with its potential and its distortions. Their contributions to critical thinking have had a great impact—even if not always explicitly acknowledged—on emerging theologies of love. In different ways they have helped to widen the horizon of love again beyond the intimate orbit of the love of a couple.

In Schopenhauer's thinking the old Christian distinction between selfish love (*eros*) and selfless love (*agape*) reappears now in secular discourse. Only agape, that says no to all selfish desires for sexual union and satisfaction in an individual-centred world and that leads even to the surrender of human willing, is hailed as pure and ultimately 'salvific'. Such compassionate and giving love reflects the love of neighbour shown by the Good Samaritan (May 2011: 177). As we shall see in the subsequent section, a similar dichotomy between eros and agape will resurface in some twentieth-century Christian discourses on love. However, Schopenhauer did not deny eros or the human sexual drive related with it; rather he argued for a larger horizon in which love in all its aspects comes to its own: the will-to-life (*Wille zum Leben*) and, associated with it, the procreation of our species. 'Sex is a voice of the will-to-life of the species that speaks through each of us. And that will-to-life, in turn, manifests the cosmic Will that is the innermost essence of everything' (May 2011: 185).

In line with the anthropological turn in modern philosophy, Feuerbach saw love as the primary concept of a realized humanity. Love is not a predicate of God; rather it was falsely attributed to God because it is divine in itself. Affirming the foundation of all thinking in human sensual experience and embodiment, he argued that love discloses the concrete nature of a person, her infinite depth in the finite, and her absolute value. Hence, love offers the authentic way to understanding the human other. Marx shared Feuerbach's affirmation of sensuality. Moreover, he understood human self-realization as the development of the senses—not only of the bodily but also of the spiritual (*geistige*) senses. Among the latter we find will and love as practical senses. Marx's critique of the exploitative nature of bourgeois marriage led him to proclaim a new form of love, which was to transcend the narrow boundaries of the family and manifest itself in the solidarity of the working classes.

Nietzsche challenged traditional Christian love discourses on two accounts: Firstly, he denounced the validity of the entire western moral system in which love had played a major part. Secondly, he exposed the theological underpinnings of this system and introduced the thought intended to shatter it completely: God is dead. Hence, all discourses on love emerging from such a false system must be perverse. What Christians call love of neighbour reveals in fact the thinly masked attempt to hide the inability to love one's own self and the desire to possess the other. Hence, what Christians understand as love has in reality to do with hatred. Against the bourgeois desire to control and to own Nietzsche recommended a positive affirmation of human destiny. 'Amor fati: let that be my love henceforth!' (Nietzsche 1974: 223). Hence, for him, genuine love affirms everything and the eternal return of everything. Nietzsche recognized the potential of transcendence in love, however not a transcendence towards some God, but a desire for and transcendence towards the *Übermensch*. Love means to love existence. The personal love of a couple was of no interest to Nietzsche. His critique of both Christian and Romantic approaches to love has had a greater impact on subsequent philosophical and theological concepts of love than his attempts to replace them with a mere love of existence. By challenging the religious, cultural, social, political, and bourgeois interests invested in love as deplorable efforts to protect life from its uncertainties, ambiguities, escapism, and wrapping it in the sweetness of latter day Valentine Day celebrations, Nietzsche's hermeneutics of suspicion has helped the modern discourse of love to face up to love's particular predicaments, vested interests, and unreasonable expectations.

Freud further developed the hermeneutics of suspicion directed at all discourses on love. Throughout his career Freud remained committed to explore and expose love's many shadows and its tragic nature. While the early Freud considered life to be 'an unrelenting contest between the needs of self-preservation, driven by what he called "ego-instincts", and the insistent demand of the libido for sexual gratification', the later Freud examined 'how love and its loss forge our sense of selfhood: how they enable us to recognise our independent existence as individuals, separate from others' (May 2011: 201–3). Especially Freud's study of the impact of our earliest (parental, etc.) loves in life on our adult loves has focused much attention to the possible interdependence of the different stages of love in our lives. For Freud, the overall aim in love was integration. However, in his late writings he not only analysed libido and integration but also the human drive towards disintegration, the death instinct, which includes aggression and an inclination to murder. Through his lifelong studies of sexuality and love, Freud—combining biological, psychological, and philosophical reflections—helped significantly to widen the horizon and deepen the critical attention to different dimensions of human loving (cf. Heine 2008). Moreover, he carried on Nietzsche's line of thinking by dismantling the idea that any stage in human desire for love could ever be considered innocent. Not even the most 'natural' love of children for their parents is free from interests, fears, and projections. Notwithstanding the scientific accuracy of his theories, Freud demonstrated the need for a hermeneutics of suspicion to accompany any critical discourse on love.

IV. AGAPE AS AUTHENTIC CHRISTIAN LOVE

Christian thinkers have reacted in different ways to the philosophical, cultural-critical, anthropological, sociological, psychological, and literary approaches to love in modernity. Some Christian concepts of love were developed directly in opposition to such discourses; others resulted from a more critical conversation with the discussion of love in modernity. Christian thinkers have attempted either to separate genuine 'Christian love' from other forms of human love (discussed in this section) or to develop a more comprehensive notion of love in critical and self-critical conversation with the wider debate on love in western culture (discussed in the following section).

Søren Kierkegaard distinguished sharply between natural or human love and genuinely Christian love of God and of neighbour. In *Works of Love* he argued that Christian love was not interested in understanding love as such but concerned with the works of love; the mystery of love cannot be exhaustively described; all genuine love comes from God and is dynamic and eternal. Thus, the point of Christian faith is not just to proclaim love, but to love. Kierkegaard's discussion is explicitly related to New Testament concepts of love, notably the Johannine approach (see Jeanrond 2010a: 108–9). He acknowledged that love may of course be found in all kinds of traditions. However, Christian love differs radically from natural human love, from any feeling of being or falling in love, from any appeal to lasting friendship, from any romantic love explored in fiction, from any preferential love, in short from any ordinary human endeavour. Kierkegaard distinguished between love (*Kjerlighed*) and erotic love (*Elskov*), between love oriented towards its depth in God and love rooted in human desires, choices, and projects. Christian love demands that God be loved unconditionally. Only such love is eternal. As far as our neighbour is concerned, he must not be confused with any object of preferential love—erotic love and friendship are instances of preferential love. Rather the human being is called to becoming a neighbour to the other human being. To love God and the neighbour is a commandment, a duty, and only if it is recognized as such is love theologically relevant. Only in the unconditional love for the neighbour is God the 'middle term' (Kierkegaard 1995: 58). However closely related, the love of God, on the one hand, and the love of neighbour and of self, on the other, must be clearly distinguished. Adequate self-love is completely determined by one's love for the other: 'To love yourself in the right way and to love the neighbor correspond perfectly to one another; fundamentally they are one and the same thing' (Kierkegaard 1995: 22). The loving person is called to surrender his or her subjectivity in love and in praise of love for God: 'Through self-denial a human being gains the ability to be an instrument by inwardly making himself into nothing before God. Through self-sacrificing unselfishness he outwardly makes himself into nothing, an unworthy servant' (Kierkegaard 1995: 365).

Anders Nygren continued (though without explicit reference to Kierkegaard) this dichotomy between authentic Christian and other forms of love. Nygren's magnum opus *Agape and Eros: The Christian Idea of Love* was to have a great impact on twentieth-century theology. Nygren aimed at rehabilitating a Lutheran theology of God's love, firmly based on divine grace and in stark opposition to any modern (religious or non-religious) concept of love, which he denounced for being grounded in human desire or romantic sentiment. The latter he called 'eros-love'; divine love he named 'agape-love'. Here eros stands for that human form of egocentric and desiring love which strives to reach the divine sphere by its own strength, whereas agape stands for that love which originates in God and requires a human attitude of receptivity and passivity accordingly. An erotic attitude (Nygren traced it back to Plato) focuses on something that is of great attraction and value to human beings and thus causes desires in them, whereas agape is addressed to every human being and as such creates a value in that being (Nygren 1982: 78). Agape is God's way to humankind. It is the chief enemy of human self-love. Eros and agape 'belong to two entirely separate spiritual worlds, between which no direct communication is possible' (Nygren 1982: 31). In traditional Christian approaches to love, e.g. Augustine's, Nygren diagnosed a problematic mixture, or synthesis, of eros-religion and agape-religion. He felt called to restore a thoroughly purified Christian understanding of love. Moreover, he contrasted his pure and universal Christian love also with classical Greek and Jewish concepts of love in order to demonstrate their inadequacy. He acknowledged that Jesus took over the commandment to love from the Old Testament, 'but He fills it with new content by setting it in relation to the new fellowship with God which He has brought' (Nygren 1982: 92). Christian universal love, Nygren argued, transcends the boundaries of Jewish legal righteousness in two ways: it now includes all human beings, even the sinner. This Christian love is presented here as 'completely revolutionary' and 'entirely new' (Nygren 1982: 53), whereas the eros-motif is shown to be old.

Neither Kierkegaard nor Nygren wished to condemn human sexuality and embodied sensuality. Rather both, though in different way, challenged any human effort to master divine love. Both chose a theocentric approach to love. According to Nygren, God comes to us from outside; only God and the neighbour can be loved with the love that is given to us by God; an autonomous human self-love is ruled out (Nygren 1982: 710).

In spite of his critique of Augustine's theology of love and desire, Nygren remained indebted to central aspects of the Augustinian heritage. Like Augustine and Luther, Nygren approached love from anthropological and theological presuppositions that considered the human being first of all in terms of sin, guilt, and damnation, i.e. as radically alienated from God and therefore at best as a channel of God's gracious love. Moreover, for Nygren the human being was not a divinely empowered agent or subject of love, but a mere instrument of God's love. Nygren's implicit reaction to any anthropologically based, modern discourse on love was totally negative.

Karl Barth and his theological followers agree with Nygren and Kierkegaard that Christian love comes from God through Jesus Christ. Barth's strong Christological focus left no room for considering either God's history of love with Israel or the presence of love in God's creation. However, unlike Nygren, Barth affirmed the human potential to love, i.e. human subjectivity in love, as the work of the Holy Spirit (Barth 1956: 103). Whereas Nygren understood love in terms of God's action over against human passivity, Barth introduced love as a human response to God's love of humanity in Christ. Both theologians acknowledged fellowship with God as the proper horizon of Christian love, though only Barth explicitly discussed this ecclesiological framework for Christian love in his *Church Dogmatics*. Barth agreed with Nygren's dualism between self-giving, sacrificial agape-love, and possessive, autonomous eros-love. 'Erotic love is a denial of humanity' (Barth 1958: 738). But unlike Nygren, he acknowledged the ongoing mixture of both loves in the one human being. For Barth Christian love is and remains ambiguous.

Barth understood divine and human love to be related acts. God's love moves human beings to act accordingly. Love is act (*Tat*) and not feeling. 'Christian love is the response of love based on the electing, purifying and creative love of God. It is thus love for God as the One by whom the Christian is first loved' (Barth 1958: 790). Barth identified the reconciliation between God and humankind achieved in Jesus Christ as the qualitative difference between Christian love and other forms of love. Thus, Barth's theology of love is a function of his particular Christology and soteriology.

Barth differs from Kierkegaard also with regard to preferential love. Kierkegaard had rejected any form of preferential love and argued that the Christian was called to become a neighbour to anybody requiring so, whereas Barth affirmed that the Christian chooses and differentiates in correspondence to the love of God (Barth 1958: 803). Like Nygren, Barth saw the originality of Christian love anchored in the mystery of Jesus Christ. However, unlike Nygren, Barth kept insisting that, as a result of Christ's love, the human being is now enabled to love. Love is a human act made possible by the Holy Spirit.

The three theologies of love considered here have remained very influential in contemporary theology. They continue to be adopted by Christians who approach the gift of God's love in Christ against the background of fallen humanity and the resulting hope in God's salvation. Every approach to love is conditioned by its starting point. If the starting point is characterized predominantly by sin, guilt, and damnation, the related theology of love will respond to this human condition accordingly. If, however, the starting point is both theological and anthropological, i.e. reflects faith in God's ongoing good creation and critically and self-critically examines the subjectivity and ambiguity of human love, different kinds of discourses on love are likely to emerge.

Each of these three modern discourses on Christian love witnesses also to the larger spectrum within such a cluster of theologies. Barth and Kierkegaard affirm human subjectivity in love. Human beings are co-workers with God. Yet their selfhood is given in order to be given away again in perfect sacrifice. Nygren does not affirm any subjective agency in love; rather he defends Christian passivity: God loves *through* the human being. At best, the human being can be said to be a channel of God's love. Barth affirms the action-character of human love, though not as strongly as Kierkegaard who insists on the total praxis-nature of human love. Moreover, Kierkegaard's horizon of love, mediated through Christ, is universal: Everybody is called to become a neighbour to the others. Finally, while Kierkegaard and Nygren denounced human eros or desire in love (though not sexuality), Barth tried somewhat to overcome the sharp dichotomy by acknowledging the ambiguity of all human love. At least a hand is stretched out here to those modern thinkers whose discourse on love has been both firmly grounded in anthropology and in an awareness of the possible and at times tragic distortion of human love relationships.

V. Towards a Comprehensive Theology of Love

In this section four approaches are discussed that have attempted to overcome the separation between divine and human love and to explore the potential of human love within the dynamic and transformative divine-human network of love. They not only affirm that genuine love originates in God, but also that the human vocation to develop loving relationships with the respective others and to accept human desire as a divine gift draws human beings more deeply into the overall mystery of love.

Friedrich Schleiermacher developed his integrative theology of love in critical reaction to the different love discourses of his time. For him, as for the young Hegel, religion and love were inseparably linked. Love mediates between the individual and the group, between the particular and the universal. Hence, the concept of love allows the appropriate articulation of individuality, integrity, and relationality of human life. In his *Speeches* Schleiermacher presented love and joyful contemplation of the universal spirit (*Weltgeist*) as the aim of religion—a religion free from fear (Schleiermacher 1988: 115). Against Schlegel he argued that love represented a form of interaction in which the communal process of formation (*Bildungsprozess*) between irrevocably individual persons occurs (Stock 2000: 65). In *The Christian Faith* he developed his theology of love more systematically. Beginning with the Johannine statement 'God is love', Schleiermacher unfolded his doctrine of God both with respect to God's essence and to human subjectivity. Although all human beings are capable of being addressed by God's love, it is first through the effect of salvation in Christ that God's love is realized in human beings and that they can have knowledge of this love. Hence, love is central for human sanctification. Love of other human beings and love of God are inseparable and intrinsically linked to the manifestation of the kingdom of God (Meckenstock 1991: 163–4).

Paul Tillich explored both the ontological and the ethical nature of love. In *Love, Power, and Justice* he stressed the uniting power of love. Human beings experience a strong desire to overcome their alienation from one another, but also from their own self. 'Love is the drive towards unity of the separated' (Tillich 1960: 25). Love is more than emotion. However, as an emotion it anticipates the reunion (neither unity nor identity!) which takes place in every love relation. Love is more than passion and pleasure; it is union with that which fulfils the desire. Ultimately, love links human beings to the ground of being, God. However, human love is not called to copy divine love but to explore human freedom and its relation to the divine depth of love. Implicitly, Tillich rejected Nygren's dichotomy and resumed Plato's understanding according to which love draws human beings to union. Explicitly, he rejected the attacks on eros by those theologians who depreciate culture and by those 'who deny a mystical element in man's relation to God' (Tillich 1960: 30).

Tillich paid particular attention to the loving subject and the issue of self-love. He called for a clarification of the often confused notions of self-affirmation, selfishness, and self-acceptance and then went on to consider the question of justice towards one's own self. Any love that does not include justice is 'chaotic self-surrender, destroying him who loves as well as him who accepts such love' (Tillich 1960: 68). As self-control highlights the dimension of power in love, so justice towards oneself stresses the necessary dimension of justice in love. He recognized the dangers associated with an estranged view of the self in love. 'Love reunites; justice preserves what is to be united' (Tillich 1960: 71). Accordingly, Tillich reflected also on the impact of love on the Christian community of love, i.e. the Church. Love under the conditions of the ambiguities of life must not be seen as a way out of life, rather it remains the most promising approach to the vicissitudes of life in spite of the conditions, precisely when there is faith in the Spirit's presence 'which judges the church's judging and struggles against its distortions' (Tillich 1963: 179). The intimate relationship between love and faith as well as their ultimate goal in the life of persons and of the community of love are thus clear: 'Whereas faith is the state of being grasped by the Spiritual Presence, love is the state of being taken by the Spiritual Presence into the transcendent unity of unambiguous life' (Tillich 1963: 134).

Tillich did not develop a theology of love against, but in critical and self-critical conversation with modern thinking. His theology pursues a unifying concept of love according to which divine love (agape) is not understood as the opposite of human forms of love, but as the perfecting power of all human love to which it has always already been related.

Karl Rahner too explored a unitary concept of love (i.e. love of God, of neighbour, and of self may be distinguished, but not separated), while emphasizing both human freedom and the continuing development of the human self. Rahner understood love as the only virtue that challenges the human being to be fully him- or herself, totally self.

In love, human beings must risk themselves without assurances, without guarantees. Therefore, the essence of love cannot ever be fully grasped. Love is marked by an eschatological dimension. It is the eternal connecting point between God and human beings. Genuine love constitutes a radically new community of human beings. This new community allows the reign of God to begin in secret; it is the miracle of the birth of eternity in our midst (Rahner 1969a: 231). However, this miracle of love must not be confused with social planning; love cannot be produced or 'made'. Within the framework of his transcendental approach to theology, Rahner distinguished between love as reflected and explicit mode of action, on the one hand, and love as an as yet not conceptualized transcendental horizon of action, on the other—mirroring to some extent Tillich's ontological and ethical dimensions of love (Jeanrond 2010b). Rahner affirmed human agency and subjectivity: we are able to love our neighbour as our neighbour, and not just as an instantiation of our love for God. However, that we can love our neighbour is already a result of God's gift of love, and thus never separated from God's love and from God's gracious self-communication in Jesus Christ in our universe. Rahner knew that love was not a Christian invention or possession. However, he identified in every genuine act of love of neighbour, anonymously as it were, the presence of Jesus Christ. Moreover, Rahner explicitly affirmed the erotic, desiring nature of human love. All genuine love is always grace, and genuine grace is love.

Rahner appreciated the difficulties of proclaiming God's love in our world stigmatized by experiences of God's absence, of horrendous evil, of Auschwitz. Hence, he argued that only on the basis of an ultimate solidarity with the condemned of this earth (*mit den 'Verdammten dieser Erde'*) may the word of the love of God for human beings be risked (Rahner 1969b: 245). God's love, like God self, remains a radical mystery.

The focus of Rahner's theology of love was the whole human person as the divinely empowered subject of love. Hence, he reflected also on the significance of the human body in the order of salvation and on human sexuality and its significance for understanding Christian marriage. He regretted the Manichean, body-denigrating, Platonist tendencies in the Christian tradition that all too often had bedevilled human sexuality, and he welcomed the Second Vatican Council's reappraisal of marriage in terms of partnership. But he also questioned distortions of human sexuality in modern culture and called for a proper approach to the ambiguity of human sexuality in Church and society.

In his first encyclical letter *Deus Caritas Est*, Pope Benedict XVI joined in the ongoing theological attempt to explore a unitary concept of love which distinguishes but does not separate God's love and human love. Moreover, Benedict accepts eros as a necessary ingredient in all love, including God's own love (*Deus Caritas Est* 7). Human eros, however, is always in need of purification. Like Rahner, Benedict both regrets past denigrations of the body and criticizes contemporary trends of divinizing the human body.

The first part of the encyclical stresses the unity of love in creation and salvation history—both integrated aspects of God's loving action, and the second part is devoted to the practice of love by the Church, understood here as a community of love, and to the issue of social love. In addition to affirming the subjectivity of individual Christians as agents of love (although reflections on human self-love are missing), the pope attributes even to the Church the status of an agent of love (*Deus Caritas Est* 32).

The question of the nature and possible role of institutions of love, e.g. family, friendship, marriage, school, Church etc., and of the appropriate horizon of love which ought to include social love (i.e. love committed to freedom, justice, and peace) that seeks to transform alienating, oppressive, and exploitative structures into emancipatory structures has been widely discussed in recent political, liberation, feminist, gender-conscious, ecological, and post-colonial theologies (cf. Jeanrond 2010a: 173–237).

VI. Contemporary Challenges to a Theology of Love

In conclusion, seven among the emerging challenges to contemporary theologies of love will be briefly identified.

First, the ongoing process of globalization has also intensified the encounter between different religions and their respective theologies of love (cf. Greenberg 2008). An inter-religious hermeneutics of love that discusses the potential of love for this complex encounter of religions and cultures and resulting conversations has become necessary. Thus, 'conversations of charity' ought not to be understood as the desired result of human encounter and dialogue, but as the way to approach otherness and to promote mutual understanding in encounter and dialogue (Williams 2003: 98; and Jeanrond 2010c).

Second, compared with medieval and early modern Europe, fewer people today are supported by firmly structured communities, associations, or groups; the power of the social group into which one is born has diminished if not disappeared altogether. In modern and postmodern Europe the individual human being has emerged as the primary and autonomous agent of life, emancipation, choice, and happiness. Thus, while the burden on the individual to shape her or his life has grown, support by social and religious groups and structures has weakened. The individual subject of love has now reached full autonomy with total responsibility for his or her love. Thus love is now often regarded as a project to design and shape one's own life, one's own children, one's own religion, one's own relations, one's own God, one's own culture and destiny. As a result, love relationships, mostly reduced to the mere horizon of a couple, are not so much threatened by assaults from outside than by implosion.

Third, love now often appears as the only escape from loneliness. Hence, love has become a carrier of many new weights on her increasingly unsupported wings. 'People seek partners and "enter relationships" in order to escape the vexation of frailty, only to find that frailty yet more vexing and painful than before. What was meant/hoped/expected to be a shelter (perhaps *the* shelter) against fragility proves time and again to be its hothouse' (Bauman 2003: 25).

Fourth, the present generation is inclined to consider children as the ultimate and purest project of human love (Beck and Beck-Gernsheim 1995: 102–39). Nevertheless, every child, however much designed and planned, however purely desired, adopted, accepted, and loved, will eventually need to develop into his or her own self. Every love of a child will sooner or later become aware of its asymmetrical character: Children demand to be loved for their own sake, loved 'away' from their parents and guardians. They will resist being mere objects of love and care. They will demand to be respected as emerging subjects in their own right. Thus, they will have to disappoint their parents' plans, hopes, and desires. Eventually, they will test the true extent of parental love. They demand from their parents a sacrifice in love. Hence, even the 'purest' projects of our loves confront us with their otherness. There is no love without otherness. And the praxis of love may demand sacrifices.

Fifth, sociologists have been discussing the contemporary desire for the pure relationship whose feature it is 'that it can be terminated, more or less at will, by either partner at any particular point. For a relationship to stand a chance of lasting, commitment is necessary; yet anyone who commits herself without reservations risks great hurt in the future, should the relationship become dissolved' (Giddens 1993: 137). That is why so many contemporaries would wish to keep their love 'liquid' (Bauman 2003): They are prepared to invest some of their energies for a shorter period of time without any lasting commitment to a relationship with the other. However, the other's real otherness, and indeed one's own otherness, can hardly come into full play in such short-cut relationships.

Sixth, the desire for pure relationships shares an important feature with romantic love. In both instances, love is reduced to a myth, amputated of its full force of otherness, and elevated to an object of belief—love is being objectified. However, the sweet and threatening otherness of both the other and the self as well as the radical otherness of God can only be explored in the actual praxis of love—involving action and critical contemplation. However, this exploration will unavoidably transform all subjects involved in this praxis. Therefore, it makes no sense both to desire to love and to wish to remain unchanged.

Seventh, Christian theology is committed to reflect on the centrality of love in Christian religion and in the world at large. Hence, it must never cease to explore past, present, and potentially new and better approaches to the dynamic and transformative network of loving relationships, i.e. my relationship to other human beings, to God, to the created universe, and to my own emerging self. This network includes all divine-human relationships and must therefore not be reduced to only the life and horizon of a loving couple. Christian theologies of love are challenged to consider the always greater horizon of love because they know that the virtue of love desires the sanctification of all human relations, political, social, cultural, religious, ecological, etc. According to Christian faith, the God-given virtue of love promotes a human praxis of love which is attentive and forgiving, desiring and reconciling, community building and transformative, emancipatory and eschatological.

References

Aquinas, Thomas (1975). *Summa Theologiae*, vol. 34: *Charity*, trans. R. J. Batten, OP (London: Eyre & Spottiswoode).

Augustine, Saint (1955). *Augustine: Later Works*, trans. John Burnaby (Philadelphia: Westminster Press).

——(1958). *On Christian Doctrine*, trans. D. W. Robertson, Jr (New York: Macmillan and London: Collier Macmillan).

——(2008). *Confessions*, trans. Henry Chadwick (Oxford: Oxford University Press).

Barth, Karl (1956). *Church Dogmatics*, vol. IV: 'The Doctrine of Reconciliation', Part I, eds. G. W. Bromiley and T. F. Torrance, trans. G. W. Bromiley (Edinburgh: T & T Clark).

——(1958). *Church Dogmatics*, vol. IV: 'The Doctrine of Reconciliation', Part II, eds. G. W. Bromiley and T. F. Torrance, trans. G. W. Bromiley (Edinburgh: T & T Clark).

Bauman, Zygmunt (2003). *Liquid Love: On the Frailty of Human Bonds*. (Cambridge: Polity Press).

Beck, Ulrich and Beck-Gernsheim, Elisabeth (1995). *The Normal Chaos of Love*, trans. Mark Ritter and Jane Wiebel (Cambridge: Polity Press).

Benedict XVI (2005). *Encyclical Letter Deus Caritas Est*. (Vatican City: Libreria Editrice Vaticana).

Bynum, Caroline Walker (1982). *Jesus as Mother: Studies in the Spirituality of the High Middle Ages*. (Berkeley, CA: University of California Press).

De Rougemont, Denis (1983). *Love in the Western World*, trans. Montgomery Belgion (Princeton, NJ: Princeton University Press).

Giddens, Anthony (1993). *The Transformation of Intimacy: Sexuality, Love and Eroticism in Modern Societies*. (Cambridge: Polity Press).

Greenberg, Yudit Kornberg (2008). *Encyclopedia of Love in World Religions*, 2 vols. (Santa Barbara: ABC Clio).

Hegel, Georg Wilhelm Friedrich (1986). *Frühe Schriften*, Werke, vol. 1. (Frankfurt am Main: Suhrkamp).

Heine, Susanne (2008). 'Lieben = Leben/Leben = Lieben', *Lieben: Provokationen*. (Innsbruck-Wien: Salzburger Hochschulwochen), 106–23.

Jeanrond, Werner G. (2010a). *A Theology of Love*. (London and New York: T & T Clark).

——(2010b). 'Rahner's Theological Method and a Theology of Love', in Pádraic Conway and Fáinche Ryan (eds), *Karl Rahner: Theologian for the Twenty-first Century*. (Oxford and Bern: Peter Lang), 103–19.

——(2010c). 'Toward an Interreligious Hermeneutics of Love', in Catherine Cornille and Christopher Conway (eds), *Interreligious Hermeneutics*. (Eugene, Oregon: Cascade Books), 44–60.

Kierkegaard, Søren (1995). *Works of Love*, trans. Howard V. Hong and Edna H. Hong (Princeton, NJ: Princeton University Press).

Lindberg, Carter (2008). *Love: A Brief History through Western Christianity*. (Malden, MA, and Oxford: Blackwell).

Luther, Martin (1883). 'Disputatio Heidelbergae habita. 1518', in *D. Martin Luthers Werke. Kritische Gesamtausgabe*, vol. 1. (Weimar: Böhlau), 353–74.

McGinn, Bernard (1991). *The Foundations of Mysticism. The Presence of God: A History of Western Christian Mysticism*, vol. 1. (London: SCM Press).

May, Simon (2011). *Love: A History*. (New Haven and London: Yale University Press).

Meckenstock, Günter (1991). 'Liebe VII. Neuzeit', in *Theologische Realenzyklopädie*, ed. Gerhard Müller, vol. XXI (Berlin and New York: Walter de Gruyter), 156–70.

Nietzsche, Friedrich (1974). *The Gay Science*, trans. Walter Kaufmann (New York: Vintage).

Nygren, Anders (1982). *Agape and Eros: The Christian Idea of Love*, trans. Philip S. Watson (Chicago: University of Chicago Press).

Rahner, Karl (1969a). *Theological Investigations*, vol. 6, trans. Karl-H. and Boniface Kruger (London: Darton, Longman and Todd).

——(1969b). 'Liebe'. In *Sacramentum Mundi: Theologisches Lexikon für die Praxis*, vol. 3. (Freiburg: Herder), 234–52.

Schleiermacher, Friedrich (1988). *On Religion: Speeches to Its Cultured Despisers*, trans. Richard Crouter (Cambridge: Cambridge University Press).

Stock, Konrad (2000). *Gottes wahre Liebe: Theologische Phänomenologie der Liebe.* (Tübingen: Mohr Siebeck).

Tillich, Paul (1960). *Love, Power, and Justice: Ontological Analyses and Ethical Applications.* (Oxford: Oxford University Press).

——(1963). *Systematic Theology*, vol. 3. (Chicago: University of Chicago Press).

Williams, Rowan (2003). *Lost Icons: Reflections on Cultural Bereavement.* (London and New York: Continuum).

SUGGESTED READING

Bauman (2003).

Brady, Bernard V. (2003). *Christian Love.* (Washington, DC: Georgetown University Press).

Brümmer, Vincent (1993). *The Model of Love: A Study in Philosophical Theology.* (Cambridge: Cambridge University Press).

De Rougemont (1983).

Jeanrond (2010a).

Lindberg (2008).

May (2011).

Oord, Thomas Jay (2010). *Defining Love: A Philosophical, Scientific, and Theological Engagement.* (Grand Rapids, MI: Brazos Press).

Tillich (1960).

Williams (2003).

PART III

THE AGE OF REVOLUTION

CHAPTER 12

....

SOVEREIGNTY

....

LUKE BRETHERTON

THE analogy between soul, polity, and universe is a leitmotif in reflections on political order. While exemplified in Plato's *Republic*, it is an analogy that is common within the Christian tradition, one often derived from a doctrine of God that emphasizes the oneness, omnipotence, sovereignty, and transcendent lordship of God over the universe. By extension there is said to be but one king governing the polity, one father governing the family, and each human governing his or her own actions. God is the archetypal sovereign and human sovereignty—in all its forms—takes on the various attributes ascribed to God's nature. Eusebius, in his panegyric to Constantine articulates this theo-political logic. He envisages the emperor as an icon of the divine sovereign and government as a reflection of the divine order:

> Invested as [the emperor] is with a semblance of heavenly sovereignty, he directs his gaze above, and frames his earthly government according to the pattern of that Divine original, feeling strength in its conformity to the monarchy of God. And this conformity is granted by the universal Sovereign to man alone of the creatures of this earth: for he only is the author of sovereign power, who decrees that all should be subject to the rule of one. (*Oration in Praise of the Emperor Constantine*, 3. 5)

On one reading, modernity is a revolution against this way of conceptualizing sovereignty and the hierarchal schema supposedly legitimized by it. Modernity is said to represent the dethronement of God, kings, and all patriarchal and patrician authorities, replacing them by human reason, constitutional democracy, and an egalitarian social structure in which power rises from the bottom up. On this reading of history it is assumed that the further back in time one goes the greater the unconstrained power of rulers. This chapter examines a number of counter-intuitive suggestions that contest the idea that modernity represents a revolution against top down, hierarchal schemas of sovereignty previously legitimized by Christianity. The first contention is that the modern period witnessed an untrammelled centralization and expansion of political sovereignty, both conceptually and in practice. This centralization was largely premissed on the notion that divine sovereignty is indivisible—a notion that comes to prominence in early modern theological and political thought and which in turn provoked various counter-reactions. The second contention is that far from rejecting theological notions of sovereignty, modern notions of sovereignty have a theological pedigree that in turn produces a theological counter-reaction.

Modern European thought on sovereignty is a palimpsest that sees itself as painted over and replacing earlier medieval understandings of political authority. On closer inspection, however, modern conceptions of sovereignty trace over and reproduce many aspects of these earlier conceptions. Against overly disjunctive readings of the relationship, Quentin Skinner and other historians of political thought have prevailed in their arguments that we cannot understand modern political concepts without understanding their foundations in the medieval and early modern period. Carl Schmitt goes beyond making a point about intellectual history contending that all modern political concepts are secularized theological concepts and so continue to carry a trace of their original imprint. In the wake of Schmitt, Continental Philosophers, in particular Jacques Derrida and Georgio Agamben, have done much to trace this theological imprint in modern notions of political sovereignty. For Derrida there is always 'some unavowed theologeme' at work in even the most secularized societies, and when it comes to claims to sovereignty, we cannot escape the inherently theological dimension to such claims (Borradori 2003: 113; Derrida 2003: 155). Derrida's insight is not without precedent in the modern period. For example, Proudhon remarks in his *Confessions of a Revolutionary* (1849) 'at the basis of our politics we always find theology'. On Derrida's account we have not replaced God with something new. Rather we have simply displaced God but left the structural analogy intact so that in God's place is put an autonomous, sovereign individual with an indivisible will who issues laws to him- or herself. Parallel to notions of God's sovereignty and nature, what is sovereign is taken to be what is legitimate and moral. Yet the paradox is that at the very point at which the supreme sovereignty of the self-governing individual is posited, the individual is increasingly seen to be 'bare life' who is subject to what Michel Foucault calls 'biopower': the control of entire populations through numerous and diverse techniques for achieving the subjugation of bodies. Building on and responding to these insights, theologians offer theological critiques of modern liberalism. For example, Oliver O'Donovan sees liberalism as doomed to incoherence unless it understands itself as the apostate child of Christianity, repents, and re-grounds its claims in the Christ-event (O'Donovan 1996: 275). In the spirit of such concerns we need to see the relationship between theology and modern conceptions of political sovereignty not as a wholly new relationship but as an iteration of earlier developments.

The first section of this chapter excavates the pre- and early modern developments out of which modern notions of political sovereignty emerge. The second examines the intertwined theological and philosophical development of a view of sovereignty as indivisible in dialogue with the work of Hobbes, Rousseau, and Hegel and their modern reception. This section ends by mapping the counter-movement in modern theology that critiques indivisible notions of sovereignty by drawing on a Trinitarian doctrine of

God and Pauline and Augustinian eschatology. Interwoven with the first and second sections are assessments of the alternative political imaginaries inherent in such notions as a messianic age, Cockaigne, Arcadia, and utopia—all of which dissolve any need of a single sovereign power. Correlations are drawn between these alternative political imaginaries and modern attempts to conceptualize a social order that has no need of a single sovereign power: namely, Marxism, anarchism, and technocracy. The last section sketches a counter-tradition of thinking about sovereignty as neither indivisible nor in need of dissolution but as inherently distributed through various powers. This counter-tradition is given voice in the work of Althusius, Otto von Gierke, the English Pluralists, notions of sphere sovereignty, and Catholic Social Teaching and involves the recovery of a chastened Aristotelian conception of humans as political animals.

I. MEDIEVAL AND EARLY MODERN TRAJECTORIES

To make sense of the continuing theological imprint in modern conceptions of sovereignty we must begin with the emergence of voluntarism and nominalism. John Duns Scotus (c.1265–1308) and William of Ockham (c.1288–1348) are central to the shift from a participatory metaphysics to one in which God's sovereign will is the ultimate principle of being (voluntarism) and the separation of being and thinking such that mental concepts are not taken to directly refer to real things (nominalism). A number of modern theologians, most notably John Milbank, identify Scotus and Ockham as the beginning point of a genealogy of modern notions of individual and state sovereignty. The shift to voluntarism and nominalism is a shift from seeing God as Logos (that is, as a loving, relational, and Trinitarian divine presence in whose order humans can participate creatively through reason) to seeing God primarily as a sovereign whose omnipotent will is unbounded, absolute, and indivisible (Elshtain 2008). In the former, good order comes through right participation within the limits of creation and patterns of social relations the *telos* of which are communion with God mediated through participation in Christ's body, the Church. In the latter view, order and social peace comes through obedience and subordination to the sovereign and indivisible will of God and those who represent God on earth, whether as pope or emperor. The latter view also gives rise to a conflict between ecclesial and political authority over who is the true Vicar of Christ on earth, a conflict that shapes profoundly subsequent conceptions of sovereignty (Kantorowicz 1957).

When God is primarily understood as a willing agent who delegates his authority to a human representative, various solutions present themselves as to how to resolve the conflict between ecclesial and political authorities over whose sovereignty is supreme. One solution was to create not two swords, each of which has a co-equal and reciprocal role in shaping the political order, but two distinct domains—'spiritual' and 'secular'—

within which ecclesial and political authorities exercise sovereign power without threatening each other. This solution was not without precedent. In *The Bond of Anathema*, Pope Gelasius I (492–6) distinguishes between a realm of 'spiritual' activity governed by the Church and a realm of 'secular' affairs' over which the Church had no control. However, for Gelasius what was envisaged was the independence of the Church to decide its own affairs within what Augustine called the *saeculum*: the non-eschatological, historical order that exists between Christ's ascension and *parousia*. The dual responsibility and division between the two authorities was to safeguard the modesty of both: only Christ could be both priest and king. In the modern period, however, the 'spiritual' becomes private and interiorized while the 'secular' pertains to what is public and material (i.e. social, economic, and political) such that the body is ruled by the state while what happens to the soul is a 'religious' and thereby immaterial matter.

Coming in the wake of the shift towards nominalism and voluntarism is the shift from complex or gothic space to simple space (Milbank 1997: 268–92). After the French Revolution, the paradigmatic modern polity is taken to be the republican nation-state whose citizens determine their own laws. This paradigm itself has its origin in the conception of the ideal polity being constituted by one people, one religion, and one law under God (Hastings 1997). This conception came to pre-eminence among Protestant political thinkers partly influenced by their engagement with Talmudic scholarship (Nelson 2010). The bounded nation-state with a single law and indivisible source of rule, which at the same time is unbounded in the exercise of its sovereign will within its own borders, contrasts with the complex and overlapping jurisdictions of Christendom in which the sovereign authorities of the pope, emperor, kings, abbots, bishops, dukes, doges, and various forms of self-governing corporations were interwoven with each other and spanned disjunctive spaces. Prior to Rousseau, Thomas Paine, and Thomas Jefferson were John Milton, James Harrington, and a host of Protestant polemicists who viewed monarchy in particular as idolatrous and sinful. This republican position was in turn opposed by the assertion of the divine right of kings: an equally simple and singular early modern conception of political space. For both republicans and the proponents of absolute monarchy, the key texts were Deuteronomy 17:14 and I Samuel 8 and the question of whether scripture marks kingship as inherently wicked or positively required (Nelson 2010: 23–56).

In the shift to the nation-state as a singular and simple space with an indivisible sovereign authority (whether monarchical or democratic) a key debating point was the legitimacy or otherwise of constitutional pluralism. Of particular concern in these debates was the status of the Holy Roman Empire, formed from the late tenth century onwards, but which, after the Diet of Cologne in 1512, became the Holy Roman Empire of the Germanic Nation and consisted of most of central Europe. As commitment to singular constitutional forms gained pre-eminence the Germanic Imperial Constitution—the vestigial form of Christendom's complex space—came to be seen as a problematic exception rather than a norm. Behind this shift lies the rejection of Aristotelian political thought, which saw constitutional pluralism as the ideal: the idea that the best form of government involved monarchical, aristocratic, and democratic elements. Jean Bodin's *Les Six livres de la République* (1578) is the prototype and catalyst for a rejection of Aristotle and a conception of sovereignty as indivisible and singular (Franklin 1991: 298–344). Bodin directly attacks the Germanic Imperial Constitution. For Bodin, sovereignty is absolute and means that the sovereign must not be subject in any way to the commands of someone else (Bodin 1992: 11). Bodin can locate sovereignty in a single person, in the people, or in a faction of the people. However, to combine these elements in a mixed constitution is 'impossible and contradictory, and cannot even be imagined. For if sovereignty is indivisible...how could it be shared by a prince, the nobles, and the people at the same time' (Bodin 1992: 92). As the Roman Catholic philosopher Jacques Maritain noted, in his critique of modern conceptions of sovereignty:

> When Jean Bodin says that the sovereign Prince is the image of God, this phrase must be understood in its full force, and means that the Sovereign— submitted to God, but accountable only to Him—transcends the political whole just as God transcends the cosmos. Either Sovereignty means nothing, or it means supreme power separate and transcendent—not at the peak but above the peak...—and ruling the entire body politic *from above*. That is why this power is absolute (ab-solute, that is non-bound, separate) and consequently unlimited, as to its extension as well as to its duration, and unaccountable to anything on earth.   (Maritain 1950: 346)

For Carl Schmitt, this conception of sovereignty is to be celebrated not decried (2007).

A counter-voice to Bodin is that of Johannes Althusius (1563–1638). Althusius systemizes the medieval constitutional view and catalyzes the emergence of modern federal and consociational views of sovereignty as distributed and shared (Hueglin 1999; Black 2003). However, with the defeat of absolutist monarchies and the passing of the *ancien régime*, republican and democratic self-government increasingly comes to be seen as the only form of legitimate (and God-given) rule. Such a form of rule could involve a separation of legislative, judicial, and executive elements but sovereignty is still taken to be indivisible and derived from a single source. Bodin rather than Althusius sets the course. The theory of sovereignty and the political form of the nation-state come to mirror and justify each other. By contrast, for medieval constitutionalists, sovereignty was divided and shared among all the estates in proportion to their contribution to the body politic, which as a body was necessarily made up of many parts and could be one and many or, echoing the Eucharistic body, catholic and distributed simultaneously.

Another shift is the eclipse of Trinitarian theology and the emergence of Deist, Unitarian, and rationalist conceptions of God. Immanuel Kant (1724–1804) both exemplifies and intensifies the marginalization of Trinitarian theology. For Kant, the right political order of perpetual peace is the analogue of the right ontological order of a rule governed, rational deity. The Church, its liturgies, rituals, and institutional form is to be tolerated but can have no public presence in the rationally administered state. In the move away from Trinitarian to more monarchical, voluntarist, and rationalist doctrines of God, there is an almost inescapable process of mimesis whereby sovereignty itself takes on the pattern of being indivisible, set apart, non-participative, and defined by the exercise of a single will, the sole function of which is to secure an immanent rational mechanism.

A sensibility we inherit not only from the Marxist historiographical concern for 'people's' history, but also from Freud and Foucault, is how attention to what is repressed or marginal unveils key aspects of a culture's self-understanding. So alongside the formal inheritance of medieval and early modern political thought we must attend to the informal legacy of popular piety in which millennialism, Cockaigne, and Arcadia suggested alternative visions of political order. For Renaissance Humanist and Puritan republicans the well-ordered commonwealth required the overcoming of sin and the vicissitudes of *fortuna* through the exercise of personal virtue, a disciplined society, well crafted laws, and strong government. However, from the Brethren of the Free Spirit and the Taborites through to the Anabaptists of Münster, those seized with expectation of an immanent millennium rejected programmes of reform (Cohn 1970). For example, the millenarian Anabaptist Thomas Müntzer (1489–1525) understood that he and his followers were already living in the end of days when earthly sovereigns were overthrown and all things were to be held in common.

The trace of millennial expectations is also echoed in numerous modern revolutionary programmes that reject the existing liberal capitalist system *tout court* and envisage themselves as vanguards ushering in a new time. For some the connection is explicit: in *The Peasant's War in Germany* (1850) Friedrich Engels interprets Müntzer as a proto-Communist revolutionary; likewise in *Thomas Müntzer als Theologe der Revolution* (1921), Ernst Bloch envisages Müntzer as embodying an anticipatory utopian consciousness that finally comes to expression in Marxism. An alternative form of millennial expectation can be overheard in Walter Benjamin (1892–1940), who combined Marxism with Jewish mysticism and for whom the messianic provides a critical horizon that interrupts and calls into question all historical political programmes. These appropriations provoked their own theological response. Martin Buber saw them as forms of 'dispossessed Messianism' (Buber 1950), while Henri de Lubac, in his two-volume work *La Posterité Spirituelle de Joachim de Flore* (1979–1981), explored in detail the connections between medieval millennialism and modern political thought. De Lubac's study points to a key theological issue at stake in the modern appropriation of millennialism: that is, is the Church the primary mediator of divine revelation or can it be superseded in a new age of the spirit by a revolutionary social movement.

The zealous fervour of reform and millennial movements, which at times converge and then separate like cross-cutting tidal flows, must be set against those who dreamed of Cockaigne. Cockaigne was a paradisiacal land in which all social, political, and economic problems dissolved because every individual was satisfied and every need was met (Pleij 2001). Pieter Bruegel the Elder's *Land of Cockaigne* (1567) depicts such a dreamworld in which eggs have legs and walk to you, roasted pigs amble around with carving knives strapped to their backs, and fowl lie down on a silver platter ready to be eaten. In relation to our concerns here the point of interest is not that Cockaigne is a land without labour, production, or conflict, but that it requires no governing authority: it is a spontaneous order of plenty. The notion that the best of all possible worlds is an apolitical socio-economic realm that spontaneously organizes itself is of course echoed in neo-liberal economics, which postulate material prosperity flowing spontaneously out of the free decisions of individuals. Theoretical exploration of these themes are found in the work of Johann Kaspar Schmidt (whose *nom de plum* was Max Stirner; 1806–56), a one-time associate of Engels and so-called 'individualist anarchist', and the former student of Ludwig von Mises, the American Murray Rothbard (1926–95), who coined the term 'anarcho-capitalism'. This pro-capitalist, anti-statist vision has an analogue in an anti-capitalist and anti-statist vision that rested on a parallel voluntaristic anthropology and notion of spontaneous order. It is a position exemplified in the anarcho-syndicalism of Pierre-Joseph Proudhon (1809–65) and Georges Sorel (1847–1922). They looked to the abolition of the state as any need for coercive power and centralized coordination would disappear within a decentralized and federal organization of *syndicats* or occupational associations, which in turn would give rise to a spontaneous order of transactions and exchanges. The government of persons would be replaced by the administration of things and a new polity, one founded on the workshop not the state, would be created, a polity in which the need for political order was eradicated through the advent of technocratic self-government.

Cockaigne, Arcadia, and millennialism are pre- or post-political visions. The negotiation of a common life in the face of immorality, competing and conflicting interests, profound differences of world view, and the unequal distribution of resources are dissolved because either all needs are satisfied (Cockaigne); all citizens exist in a state of pastoral innocence uncorrupted by civilization (Arcadia/noble savage); or justice is achieved through the return of the true king who vindicates the virtuous and removes the vicious, turning the existent world upside down in order to establish what is true and good (millennialism). However, these forms of spontaneous order are not ones we have the agency to achieve and they exist beyond any actual spatio-temporal realm. They are either a golden age that cannot be recovered, a result of an apocalyptic event, or sheer fantasy. What changes in the modern period is the emergence of a revolutionary ideal whereby humans believe they can remake the world. As Charles Taylor notes, a key feature of the modern period was the loss of a sense of what it meant to participate in and collaborate with a pre-existing order, understood theologically or otherwise, and the emergence of a view of order as imposed *ab extra* on nature by the human will (Taylor 2007: 123–30). John Milbank sees nominalism and voluntarism as the fissure out of which such a shift crawls (Milbank 1990: 12–17). Taylor names the shift in how the world is imagined as the move from cosmos to universe (Taylor 2007: 323). Most Christian and Platonic conceptions of order entail a sense that the cosmos provides meaning to those who participate in it and a sense of this meaning can be discerned through right participation, political or otherwise. This is the basic architecture on which conceptions of natural law depend. Part of the shift into the modern period, however, is a move to disengagement and disenchantment such that the cosmic order comes to be understood as mechanistic and morally neutral: it cannot disclose to us any sense of how we should live. Thus, in the shift from cosmos to universe, political sovereignty becomes unbounded by moral limits while sovereign individuals can remake the world as they please.

This shift to the centrality of the unbounded sovereign will is reflected in Thomas More's *Utopia* (1516), which is premised neither on a notion of spontaneous order irrupting through an apocalyptic event nor an alternative reality through which to render contingent and satirize present conditions. More's utopia does not exist outside of or beyond history. It is designed as a blueprint and intended as a guide to action in history. Unlike his republican peers, More's ideal commonwealth issued not from the actions of a prince or parliament but from technocratic procedures. Its founder, Utopus is not a lawgiver after the model of Solon or Moses, but a systems designer and bureaucrat. His laws are not based on revelation, nature, or immemorial custom. They are a work of artifice. More's utopia is entirely different in kind to an Arcadia or a Cockaigne where the lawgiver is unnecessary because everyone is a law unto themselves; or the millennium, where the law is divinely inspired and written on the heart rather than externally imposed (Davies 1991: 341–2). *Utopia* presents a post-political regime in which we see foreshadowed all attempts to supersede the need for a sovereign political ruler through a rationally and scientifically administered state.

II. HOBBES AND THE INDIVISIBLE SOVEREIGNTY OF THE ONE

As we move past the French Revolution we see the inheritance sketched above play out and developed in new ways. The concept that comes to the fore in modern notions of sovereignty is its indivisibility. It is derived from a view of God's sovereignty yet is asserted as a reaction against the ways in which the authority of Revelation is taken to threaten the unity of the political order. To understand this paradox it is useful to focus on conceptions of sovereignty in Hobbes, Rousseau, and Hegel. Modern discussions of sovereignty operate in the shadow of Hobbes (1588–1679). While debates about the exegesis and context of Hobbes's own writing continue, given the nature of the volume, I will focus less on the specifics of what Hobbes did or did not say and its context in the seventeenth century and more on the contemporary reception of Hobbes. For this purpose the work of Carl Schmitt (1888–1985) stands as a crucial figure. Schmitt looks back both to the constitutional debates of the sixteenth and seventeenth centuries, out of which Hobbes emerged, and stimulates a renewed attention to Hobbes in Continental Philosophy.

On Schmitt's reading the core purpose of the state for Hobbes is to protect its citizens. Conversely, the primary duty of the citizen is to obey the sovereign. As Schmitt puts it: 'The *protego ergo obligo* is the *cogito ergo sum* of the state.... [H]uman nature as well as divine right demands its inviolable observation' (Schmitt 2007: 52). However, the relationship between citizens and the sovereign is a reciprocal one: the citizen gives obedience and receives protection in return. However, the obedience is given to an abstract sovereign who can be monarchical, democratic, or aristocratic in form but whose sovereignty is absolute and indivisible and transcends the immanent political order. Thus the mark of sovereignty is the ability to decide the exception. Unlike in the divine right of king's theory, for Hobbes, sovereignty is not derived from God above but flows up and is authorized from below via a covenant entered into between individuals (Schmitt 2007: 52).

Here we encounter the anti-Aristotelian element of Hobbes. Humans are not inherently political animals and there are no 'natural' intermediate elements between the individual and the sovereign. All groups, especially the Church, must be made to serve the state and are subsidiary or incorporated under state sovereignty. In Rousseau's estimation:

> Of all Christian Authors the philosopher Hobbes is the only one who clearly saw the evil and the remedy, who dared to propose reuniting the two heads of the eagle, and to return everything to political unity, without which no State or Government will ever be well constituted.   (Rousseau 1997: 146)

In individualist-contractualist theories of sovereignty, from Hobbes onwards, the Church is the primal enemy as it is the paradigmatic form of an alternative source of sovereign power that relativizes the claims of the political sovereign. For all his espoused Catholicism, Schmitt sees this clearly and is adamant about the need to 'de-anarchize' Christianity.

Yet obedience to the sovereign is conditional. For Hobbes, if the sovereign does not protect citizens then any duty to obey is dissolved: citizens cannot swap the fear of the state of nature for the fear of a 'Moloch'. It is the latent right of resistance in Hobbes's account of sovereignty, combined with Hobbes's distinction between public and private belief that led Leo Strauss to postulate against Schmitt that Hobbes vindicated limited government and should be seen as a liberal rather than the prophet of authoritarianism. Schmitt agreed, but for Schmitt this was the pathos of Hobbes. For Schmitt, Hobbes fatally undermined his own political philosophy by incorporating the right of freedom of thought and belief into his political system. As Schmitt puts it: 'This contained the seed of death that destroyed the mighty leviathan from within and brought about the end of the mortal god' because it created a whole area of independent activity over which state had no authority (Schmitt 1996: 57). Schmitt objected to the distinction between inner freedom of faith and outer conformity of confession and behaviour. But while this may be the conceptual objection he cites as undermining Hobbes's theory of state, it is the 'indirect' powers of the Church and of interest groups, which in Schmitt's view are re-iterated in the nineteenth century as modern political parties, trade unions, and social organizations, acting independently of the state under the banner of freedom of conscience, that Schmitt points to as the primary problem.

These 'forces of society' threaten the indivisible and transcendent sovereignty of the state (Schmitt 1996: 73). By way of contrast, where Schmitt sees the emasculation of Leviathan, Foucault and Agamben see its triumph. On their account, the constitutional liberal state turns out to be the bio-political state. It no longer needs external threats because far from conscience constituting a realm set apart from state power, it constitutes the extension of state power into the hearts, mind, and habits of citizens. We no longer need a sovereign Leviathan because we have internalized its ways.

For Schmitt there is a paradoxical relationship between the mythic symbol of the leviathan and its relationship to what he sees as the Prussian and French process of state building. Hobbes's sea monster becomes the trope for European land powers whose absolutist monarchies, positivist law state, standing army and bureaucracy, contrast with the seafaring, mercantilist power, and mixed, parliamentary constitution of England. For Schmitt: '[Hobbes's] concepts contradicted England's concrete political reality' (Schmitt 1996: 85). Like Schmitt, Karl Barth also sees Hobbes's leviathan as the mythic embodiment of modern European 'political absolutism', from the sun-king Louis XIV to the Fascism and Stalinism of his own day (Barth 1981: 221). In contrast, C. B. MacPherson (1911–87), who connects the reception of Hobbes with post-Second World War developments in European Marxism, takes exactly the opposite view. For Macpherson, Hobbes's political philosophy was the ideological articulation of England's seafaring, proto-capitalist state. On Macpherson's reading Hobbes is observing the emergence of a 'possessive market society' where everyone is taken to be an autonomous, self-directing individual and not as Aristotle would have it, a socio-political animal. The need for society only arises so as to secure one's individual self-interest and not to realize one's freedom and potential through relationships.

MacPherson was frequently accused of giving an anachronistic reading of Hobbes. However, whatever his failings as an interpreter of Hobbes, MacPherson anticipates the connection between centralized political sovereignty and the re-emergence of laissez-faire economics with Reagan, Thatcher, and Sarkozy. MacPherson draws on Marx to point to how the state, far from being opposed to the market, is used to buttress property relations and serves the interests of capital. Conversely, he draws on Hobbes to unveil the need capitalism has for a strong sovereign authority, something Marx viewed as epiphenomenal.

III. ROUSSEAU AND THE INDIVISIBLE SOVEREIGNTY OF THE MANY

Affected by a different set of theological disputes within a different context we find in Rousseau (1712–88) an alternative to Hobbes's attempt to resolve the question of sovereignty. Rather than resolve the rivalry of independent, individual wills by postulating the renunciation of their independence in order to be directed by the one indivisible will of the sovereign, for Rousseau, each indivisible will is directed to choose the general will. Rousseau rejected Hobbes because for him Hobbes's conception of the protection-obligation of the social contract does not lead to sovereignty but despotism. In his view, just because the Leviathan produces peace, that does not make it legitimate. For Rousseau: 'To renounce one's freedom is to renounce one's quality as man, the rights of humanity, and even its duties . . . . Such a renunciation is incompatible with the nature of man, and to deprive one's will of all freedom is to deprive one's actions of all morality' (Rousseau 1997: 45). While Rousseau shared Hobbes's conception of sovereignty as inherently indivisible, he sought an account of sovereignty that maintained the freedom of the individual and provided a foundation for political order on something other than egoistic self-interest. Rousseau conceived of sovereignty as a property of a people rather than as an aggregate of individual wills. The sovereignty of the many is expressed through the unified *volonté générale*: each one becomes subsumed within the singular will of the many.

To make sense of the general will it is necessary to locate it within a specific set of theological debates. Rousseau, drawing on a distinctively French contribution to moral and political thought, developed the notion of 'generality' as a point midway between particularity and universality. The general interest is good whereas particular interests are sectional and therefore bad. Justice is linked to generality and opposed to 'particular' exceptions and interests. Patrick Riley argues that Rousseau's notion of generality arises out of seventeenth-century debates about predestination (1986). The theological debate, one that began with the dispute between Augustine and Pelagius, was about how a general will for universal salvation could be related to the election of particular humans for salvation. Riley argues that in the seventeenth century the Jansenist Arnaud 'invented' the idea of the general will for examining this question. The notion of the general will was subsequently developed as a moral philosophical category by Pascal, for whom the particular will leads to disorder and self-love (*amour propre*). On this account, not to be directed toward *le general* is 'unjust' and 'depraved'. Rousseau transmutes a theological and then moral distinction into a political one: the general will of the citizen to place the good of the republic above his or her particular will becomes not only the basis of the political order but also the 'salvation' of egoistic individuals through converting *amour propre* into *amour de soi*. In the process, the Church comes to be seen as a particular interest that threatens to divide the sovereign, general will of the people. For Rousseau, what must be promoted instead is some form of civil religion that bolsters the general will. However, as Ronald Beiner notes, Rousseau's advocacy of civil religion was itself deeply ambiguous and contradictory (Beiner 2011: 73–83). Yet as with Hobbes, what threatened the indivisibility of sovereignty was the public pursuit of private interests, and this is exactly the danger 'religion' represented when conceptualized as a private and particularistic interest.

IV. Hegel and the Indivisible Sovereignty of the Rational State

Hegel (1770–1831) was an avid reader of Rousseau when attending the seminary at Tübingen. Question about the unity of the political order, the role of religion in causing political divisions, and how to overcome such divisions haunted Hegel as it did Hobbes and Rousseau. Like Rousseau, Hegel found Christianity problematic. In his early writings he contrasts Christianity, which he saw as creating a disjuncture between a private, otherworldly, and individualistic belief and practice and the obligations of citizenship, with an idealized Greek *Volksreligion* that he saw as harmoniously integrating political, cultural, and religious life. For the young Hegel the Christianity he saw, and what he took to be its politically enervating effects, was a symptom of the more fundamental lack of freedom that could only be overcome through the formation of a rationally administered and socially unified nation-state.

In Hegel's early work Christianity teaches people to look to heaven for their fulfilment and this in turn trains them to accommodate themselves to their political and economic alienation. Thus an otherworldly eschatology is the enemy of political and economic freedom: a theme picked up by Marx. Hegel blamed religion for the rupture of the Holy Roman Empire of the Germanic Nation and this itself was a manifestation of the broader problem of the assertion of particularity against universality. In contrast to France and Britain, the Holy Roman Empire of Hegel's day was a mosaic of three hundred more-or-less sovereign territories: there were the monarchies of Prussia and Austria; several Prince-Electors; ninety-four princes, both ecclesiastical and secular; one hundred and three barons and forty prelates; and fifty-one free towns (Cullen 1979: 42). The Gothic constitution that so troubled Bodin and other early modern constitutionalists was still in operation. Only now, these overlapping and intersecting sites of sovereignty were not viewed by Hegel as a constitutional anomaly, but as an anomaly to the spirit of the age. The problem was not conceptual and legal but absolute: it should no longer exist, it was an obstacle to the realization of human freedom, and what was needed was a unified nation under a supreme sovereign. In Hegel's work the state, as a unity, is alone the bearer of sovereignty. While he does not completely reject the medieval inheritance, for Hegel, medieval society, as a mere conglomeration of factions, does not possess the harmony and unity of functions characteristic of the state (Nederman 1987: 500–20).

By way of contrast, those contemporary thinkers who advocate complex space over simple space take a very different view to Hegel. After the historical experience of totalitarianism, the complex sovereignty of the Holy Roman Empire, where ecclesial and secular rulers had to negotiate and limited each other's sovereignty, looks very attractive. It is the unified and sacralized nation-state that appears the problem not the solution. In the wake of gulags and death camps the concerns of Hobbes, Rousseau, and Hegel for a unitary sovereign power able to secure and guarantee order against the disorder and chaos of particular interests whether of the individual or the group have been reversed. The indivisible sovereign is now the wolf from whom we need protection. Agamben's work illustrates this inversion. He turns Schmitt on his head so that far from the sovereign deciding the exception being the answer to the problem of lawlessness, the lawless state of exception—the paradigmatic form of which is the death camp—has become the true *nomos* of the modern state (Agamben 2005). Given a state where this kind of exception is the norm, multiplicity and diversity are no longer the problem but the solution.

For Hegel different constitutional forms—monarchy, aristocracy, and democracy—must be understood as historically contingent (Hegel 1967: 177). Given the evolution of history, these forms are inevitably subsumed within and superseded by the modern state which is the realization of universality in historical existence. All division is converted into internal differentiation rather than substantive difference. Hegel divides the powers of the state into three: legislature, executive, and crown. However, these divisions are one of functional differentiation and do not represent any division of sovereignty. It is not so much a separation of powers as a division of labour (Hegel 1967: 188). The state is now the substantive unity and all particular powers are simply moments and different manifestations of its univocal nature.

Hegel envisages the hereditary monarch to be the personification of the constitutional state's indivisible and organic unity. Hegel's account of hereditary monarchy is Christological in shape and origin: the idea of the unity of the state has to be realized in a particular individual in order to manifest its universal presence in history and move beyond being an abstract idea to objective realization (Hegel 1967: 185). The monarch is a kind of God-man: through the monarch, the implicit unity of the universal spirit and particular natures and interests of civil society becomes real and assumes a definite existence. The monarch being hereditary had an unfounded, non-contractual basis to his sovereignty and so the authority of the sovereign transcended the immanent political order.

If the monarch is the personification of the divine will, it is the nation-state that sublates (*aufheben*) religion because it becomes the vehicle for fulfilling the universal element in the human spirit. Within Hegel's overall schema, the state replaces the Church as the bearer of salvation wherein a people can realize their freedom and catholicity. As Hegel puts it: 'The state is the divine will' (Hegel 1967: 166). Christianity is but one stage along the way in the realization of freedom in history. The organic unity of the state and its actualization of freedom is the fulfilment of the divine will. It is a manifestation of the kingdom of God within history as opposed to an eschatological kingdom that interrupts history (Lakeland 1984: 53; O'Regan 1994). Rejecting the two swords tradition that stems from Gelasius, Hegel is highly critical of the view of the Church as the vestibule of the kingdom of God and the state as representing the earthly kingdom. Hegel sees this as a false dichotomy. Church and state should not stand in opposition to each other. While there is a proper difference of form, truth and rationality are the content of both (Hegel 1967: 170–1). The state, of which the Church is a part, is not a mere 'mechanism' or means to an end. Rather, to participate in the state is to participate in the rational life of self-conscious freedom. Beyond Hegel stands the political theology of Johann Baptist Metz (b. 1928), Jürgen Moltmann (b. 1926), and Dorothee Sölle (1929–2003), and thence Liberation Theology, and a commitment to praxis within history as a means of salvation and the historical anticipation of the universal kingdom of God in particular social, economic, and political forms of order, a commitment that owes as much to Hegel as it does to Marx and Ernst Bloch.

In terms of political theory, Hegel is Janus-faced. He looks back towards Hobbes and Rousseau and the assertion of the indivisibility of sovereignty and forwards towards the dissolution and distribution of sovereignty. For Hegel, the state is both one and sovereign, with each part contributing to the whole. Rather than a single sovereign figure or will being needed in order to hold together particular interests as was the case for Hobbes, particular interests are transcended through the rationally and juridically administered state. Yet Hegel anticipates in some ways what Hannah Arendt seeks: that is, the re-establishment of space and time for political judgement and the move away from the Kantian procedural state. The political system Hegel envisages builds in and accepts a plurality of interests and a unified public sphere that is not subordinated to economic and social life but represents the arena of free and universal action in which human being is realized. But as a vision of a sovereign state exercising its authority over a whole population and every aspect of life, Hegel's sovereign political system can also be seen to contain the seeds of what Foucault identifies as the panoptical state in which the sovereignty of a single public authority such as a monarch remains but at the same time is superseded by and dispersed within a field of relations, discourses, and technologies that habituate those within the state to conform to its order. Power is no longer exercised over the body by an external authority but becomes 'bio-power' exercised within, through, and around the body such that sovereignty becomes an internalized and self-administered regime of 'governmentality'.

V. Trinitarian and Augustinian Responses

Hegel's use of the doctrine of the Trinity as a way of developing a framework for the meaning of time, and his transmutation of Salvation history into salvation through the processes of history, inspired and provoked a theological counter-reaction. The theological recovery of the finitude of time and space, the alterity of the divine, and therefore the creaturely limits of human action within history came to focus on a restatement of Trinitarian theology. In Protestant theology, the work of Karl Barth (1886–1968) is central to this restatement. In Roman Catholic theology, alongside Henri de Lubac (1896–1991) and Hans Urs von Balthasar (1905–88), it is the work of Karl Rahner and Catherine LaCugna that sparked renewed attention to the Trinity. The intellectual *ressourcement* of modern theology these theologians catalyzed through their engagements with scripture, patristic thought, and the development of a constructive Trinitarian theology enabled the legacy of nominalism and voluntarism to be challenged.

With the recovery of a Trinitarian theology, good order comes to be seen not as the result of the exercise of sovereign will. Instead, good order is constituted through participation in right relationships as encountered and empowered through participation in the perichoretic communion of Father, Son, and Holy Spirit. In place of images of political rulers (emperors, kings, or lords), music, drama, and dance become more common analogies for the nature of God. In such accounts God is no distant sovereign but both loving Creator and intimately and vulnerably involved in creation through the ongoing work of the Son and the Spirit. In the light of this kind of God, monarchical, absolute, and indivisible claims to political sovereignty that over-ride the freedom and dignity of the one, the few, or the many are revealed as in opposition to the divine nature and the true order of being, which is one of harmonious difference in relation. Likewise, humans are not monadic individuals but persons in relation with a status above and beyond any immanent social, economic, or political claims upon them.

The supposed link between monotheism and authoritarianism gave a particular impetus to the felt need for a restatement of Trinitarian theology. For example, Moltmann sees a direct link between Trinitarian conceptions of God and the legitimization and sacralization of dominatory forms of rule. By contrast, he states: 'The doctrine of the Trinity which, on the contrary, is developed as a theological doctrine of freedom must for its part point towards a community of men and women without supremacy and without subjection' (1981: 192). Key in directing attention to the Trinity as a way of countering political absolutism was Erik Peterson's response to Carl Schmitt's 1922 essay *Political Theology*. In his *Monotheism as a Political Problem* (1935) Peterson sought to counter Schmitt's theory of sovereignty by attacking its theological roots, in particular Schmitt's claim that sovereignty was defined—in a way that was structurally analogous to God—by the sovereign's location within and outside the law, and so, like God, the sovereign possessed the power to decide the exception to the rule of law. Following Peterson, a social model of the Trinity came to be seen as a way to counter domination and violence justified on the grounds of monotheism. Some went so far as to see the Trinity as itself the basis for a social programme (Volf 1998: 403–23). For example, Moltmann saw a personalism grounded in the doctrine of the Trinity as providing a middle way between the collectivism of communism and the individualism of liberal capitalism (Moltmann 1981: 199–200). However, such a sentiment can be as theologically problematic as that which it replaces, for it simply replicates the problem of presuming a mimesis between the divine nature and particular forms of social and political life, albeit more egalitarian and less oppressive ones. Here we encounter the question of whether we can ever legitimately draw direct correlations between divine and human nature.

The emphasis on the Trinity as the basis for a social programme is theological naïve. On the one hand, as Hegel's appropriation of the Trinity illustrates, the doctrine of the Trinity itself has been aligned with numerous forms of absolutism. On the other hand, monotheism can be used as a way to resist political absolutism. As exemplified in the

Barmen Declaration, Karl Barth's emphasis on the sovereignty of God as mediated through the lordship of Christ provided the basis for challenging the totalitarian claims of the Nazis. The lordship of Christ relativized all other claims to sovereignty. For Barth, it is the vocation of the Church, as the community of faithful witness, to say 'yes' to that which affirms, renews, and anticipates the fulfilment of the order revealed by the life, death, and resurrection of Jesus Christ, and in saying yes to that, it must say 'no', in both belief and practice, to those forms of rule and patterns of life that disorientate and destroy the created order as recapitulated in the Christ-event. The problem is not monotheism per se, but the nature and orientation of the rule one serves. By serving themselves and not Christ, humans become subject to what Barth called the 'lordless powers' (Barth 1981: 213–33). For Barth, the primary embodiments of the lordless powers were Leviathan (all forms of political absolutism) and Mammon (the idolatry of money, material possessions, property, and resources) (Barth 1981: 233). Against the disorder produced by the lordless powers stands the rule (*basileia*) of divine order.

The fundamental theological challenge Hegel posed, and beyond Hegel, all immanent claims to ground sovereignty, is one of time. The real challenge is the refusal of eschatology or rather the historicization of eschatology and thence the absolutization and divinization of the finite. If this time is all there is, then politics has no limits as it has to bear the full weight of human meaning and possibilities. The problem is not totalitarianism but the totalization of politics as such which leads either to an over-investment in political projects as programmes of salvation or an under-investment that despairs of any meaningful political activity being possible. In contrast, when politics is understood to be an activity in the *saeculum*—that time between Christ's ascension and his return—it is freed to bring about a limited but nevertheless meaningful peaceableness. As Sheldon Wolin recognized, the great gift of Christianity to politics is time and in particular, the relativization of historical time (Wolin 2004: 111–15). Christians have time to hope and live in a time when change is possible and in which past and present are connected in the communion of saints (Hauerwas 2007: 147–64). At the same time, as Stanley Hauerwas has forcefully argued, Christians do not have to establish regimes to control the time so as to determine the outcome of history, rather, they can live out of control because the fulfilment of history is already inaugurated in the resurrection of Jesus Christ. A Christian vision of time as history, as open to redemption and as fulfilled in the eschaton undergirds the possibility of politics as a finite and contingent activity that has limits, but also significance beyond the immediate needs and vicissitudes of the moment. Eschatology disqualifies any absolute claims of a political sovereign to shape human life and reasserts the need for the pluralization of political space as reflective of the complex nature of this time between Christ's ascension and *parousia*. The complexification of political space is theologically necessary so as to hold open the existence of times and spaces that are not subject to political control. On this account, the status of the Church as a *res publica* is based on its vocation to bear witness within the political order to an order and rule that is over and beyond this or that spatio-temporal order.

Within the kind of 'Augustinian' vision of politics that has come to pre-eminence in modern Christian political thought, politics is about negotiating what is necessary for a tolerable earthly peace. It is not an end in itself, but serves an end—communion with God—beyond itself. Any idea that there can be a Christian society or nation needs to be treated with suspicion, as is any project of salvation or human fulfilment through politics. A theological politics, as distinct from a project of political theology that instrumentalizes the theological in the service of the political, must resist the temptation to render the prevailing hegemony as 'natural' or ontologically foundational. All political formations and structures of governance are provisional and tend towards oppression, while at the same time, whether it be a democracy or a monarchy, any political formation may display just judgements and enable the limited good of an earthly peace through the pursuit of common objects of love.

VI. Sovereignty Distributed

If the recovery of Trinitarian theology represents one counter-voluntarist stream of theology, there is also another counter-movement. This other stream of Christian reflection begins not with the doctrine of God but with human nature and more specifically, the recovery of an Aristotelian sense of humans as political animals and attention to customary practices and tradition as constitutive of securing a common life. Such a beginning point is in stark contrast to most modern political thought—even in its conservative strands—that not only begins with the individual as the primary point of reference but also sees tradition (even if it wants to preserve it) as of the past and in conflict with what is new or modern. The Weberian rationalist-legal order that is the dominant political imaginary shaping both left and right banishes custom to the realm of the private. By contrast, for medieval constitutionalists, custom mediated consent and established historical practices, such as use of common land, set limits on what could or could not be done. These limits were not set in stone: they constituted arenas of negotiation and enabled discretionary judgements built on apprenticeship into particular habits of action. The counter-tradition that takes time, social life, and customary practice as having public force is best identified as consociational. However, it should be noted that my use of the term 'consociational' differs considerably from its more technical use in political science to describe particular constitutional and power sharing arrangements. The primary advocate of this use of the term is Arend Lijphart (1980).

On the kind of consociational account envisaged here, to arrive at *good* political judgements requires *phronesis* and to acquire *phronesis* requires training in the virtues. The arenas through which we come to be formed in the virtues are schools, forms of craft production, congregations, or any form of local society that aspires, as Alasdair MacIntyre puts it: 'to achieve some relatively self-sufficient and independent form of participatory practice-based community and that therefore need to protect themselves from the corrosive effects of capitalism and the depredations of state power' (MacIntyre 2006: 155). On this account, the pursuit of the virtues through forms of institutionally mediated practices with substantive goods is a prerequisite for being a good citizen: that is, being one who has the understanding and the ability to rule and be ruled and so is able to make good political judgements. The sense of what it means to be a *zoon politikon* developed here is better described as Althusian rather than Aristotelian (Hueglin 1999: 56–82). Althusius rejected Aristotle's distinction between natural domestic rule and the political rule among free and equal citizens. For Althusius, all forms of social life, whether in the family or the guild, may participate in the formation of political life. However, this does not mean that Althusius totalizes the political sphere so that every aspect of life is subsumed within it. Rather, as Thomas Hueglin clarifies:

> For Althusius, each consociation or political community is determined by the same principles of communication of goods, services, and rights. The essence of politics is the organization of this process of communication. Therefore, families and professional colleges are as much political communities as cities, provinces, or realms insofar as they participate in this political process through their activities. (Hueglin 1999: 95–6)

In contrast to Aristotle who overly separates public and private, and most modern conceptions that separate social plurality from the public sphere in order to maintain political unity, Althusius allows for the pluralization of the political in order to accommodate and coordinate the diversity of associational life, whether economic, familial, or religious. To be a political animal is not to be a citizen of a unitary, hierarchically determined political society. Nor is it to participate in a polity in which all authority is derived from a single point of sovereignty. Rather, it is to be a participant in a plurality of interdependent, self-organized associations that together constitute a consociational polity. In such a compound commonwealth, federalism is societal and political rather than simply administrative (Hueglin 1999: 113). In contrast to constitutional federalism as a way in which to limit sovereignty, as exemplified in the American constitution, which, *pace* Hegel, leaves undisturbed the indivisibility of political sovereignty, consociationalism envisages a full-orbed federalism whereby sovereignty is distributed across distinct corporate entities. Sovereignty emerges through a process of mutual communication between consociations and their reciprocal pursuit of common ends. Unity is premised on the quality of cooperation and relationship building and is not secured through either legislative procedure, the singular nature of sovereignty, or the formation of a unitary public sphere premissed on a homogeneous rational discourse.

It is as a provider of various consociational conceptions of sovereignty that we can make sense of a theologically diverse, yet interlinked tradition of political reflection. If Althusius is its progenitor, a key mediator is Otto von Gierke, who along with those he influenced, notably the English Pluralists (John Neville Figgis, and the early work of G. D. H. Cole and Harold Laski), is directly criticized by Schmitt. Schmitt sees them as the alternative and a threat to the position he is trying to establish (Schmitt 2007: 40–5).

While there were substantive differences between them (unlike Figgis, Cole and Laski had a decidedly voluntaristic anthropology), up to 1920 the English Pluralists advocated a decentralized economy based on the non-capitalistic principles of cooperation and mutuality and proposed a radically federalist conception of the state (Hirst 1993; Runciman 1997; Laborde 2000: 45–100). In their view sovereignty was not something that could be appropriated by a single agency or institution. Rather it emanated from the complex and divided governing powers that compose the body politic. In distinction from anarcho-syndicalists such as Proudhon, the Pluralists thought there was still a need for a public power but its role was severely circumscribed. A key concern of the Pluralists was the question of how to maintain the freedom and self-development of all forms of association, particularly the churches and trade unions.

A further strand of consociationalist thought can be identified in the sphere sovereignty of the Dutch Neo-Calvinists, Abraham Kuyper (1837–1920) and Herman Dooyeweerd (1894–1977). For them, the sovereignty of independent spheres such as the family, schools, and workplaces are expressions of the sovereign will of God. Each sphere has a relative autonomy and specific character that needs to be respected. Government has a role in ordering and protecting the general good but it does not have the authority to interfere with or determine the character or *telos* of each sphere (Chaplin 2011). In turn, the state is bounded by the sovereignty of other spheres. It was in the Netherlands that notions of sphere sovereignty overlapped with and found a parallel expression in the emergence of Roman Catholic Christian Democratic thinking. Central to this were Jacques Maritain and the development, from *Rerum Novarum* (1891) onwards, of Catholic Social Teaching, with its advocacy of principles of subsidiarity and a form of constitutional corporatism.

Maritain argues for a genuine plurality and a corporatist conception of civil society whereby there are multiple yet overlapping 'political fraternities' that are independent of the state (Maritain 1968: 163). He distinguishes his account from fascist and communist ones that collapse market, state, and civil society into a single entity *and* from collectivist and individualistic conceptions of economic relations (169–71, 186–95). A parallel distinction is made by Pius XI in *Quadragesimo Anno* (1931) as a way of distinguishing a Christian corporatist vision of politics from fascist ones. On this account corporatist and personalist forms of civic association and economic organization are precisely a means of preventing the subsuming of all social relations to the political order. Within the sphere of civil society there can exist multiple and overlapping and, on the basis of subsidiarity, autonomous forms of institutional life, forms that are not reducible to either a private or voluntary association.

A variety of criticisms are made of the approach Maritain and Catholic Social Teaching developed. Milbank criticizes *Quadragesimo Anno* as giving too much ground to fascism and calls on Catholic Social Teaching to pay far closer attention both to socialism and medieval forms of gothic space (Milbank 1997: 268–92). O'Donovan goes further and criticizes the very concept of subsidiarity. He argues that when it is understood as a way of protecting the integrity and relative autonomy of parts in relation to an overarching and integrating whole, then the totality of the whole always assumes an over-riding, or even totalizing claim in its movement towards an all-embracing unity (O'Donovan 2005: 259). Thus, the need for Maritain and Catholic social thought more generally to distinguish itself from fascism on this score is not incidental, but a problem intrinsic to the conceptualization of subsidiarity itself.

William Cavanaugh criticizes Maritain's conception of the relationship between the Church and state. Cavanaugh contends that Maritain spiritualizes the Church as a social body and thereby underemphasizes the extent to which the Church is itself a polity or *res publica* that forms and socializes human bodies in ways that are very different to those of the modern nation-state. As Cavanaugh puts it:

> [T]he key difficulty with Maritain's project is that he makes the Christian community the repository of purely supernatural virtues which stands outside of time, and thus interiorizes and individualizes the Gospel. Because he has sequestered political virtue from any direct habituation in Christian community, the state becomes that community of habituation, the pedagogue of virtue.   (Cavanaugh 1998: 195)

In the light of this critique it is perhaps not surprising how Christian Democratic parties developed in Europe after the Second World War. They became aligned with a turn to the state as both the sole keeper of the common good and as the primary or only means of addressing social and economic ills via legal regulation and welfare programmes. In short, they swapped a consociationalist vision for a Hegelian one.

Central to the Christian consociationalist tradition is the sense in which we do participate in a cosmic order than can disclose to us some measure of meaning and purpose. It is this cosmic social imaginary that distinguishes the theological consociationalism of Figgis, Kuyper, and Maritain et al. from their secularist counterparts, notably Emile Durkheim (1984) and Paul Hirst (1994). This consociational tradition, with its distributive and federal conception of sovereignty, offers a rich yet under-explored thickening of more Trinitarian and Augustinian responses to political and economic absolutism. It is the combination of one or more strands of consociational thought with a Trinitarian theological anthropology and an Augustinian eschatology that needs to frame contemporary theological accounts of sovereignty if they are to move beyond critique to constructive conception.

REFERENCES

Agamben, Giorgio (2005). *State of Exception*, trans. Kevin Attell (Chicago: University of Chicago Press).

Barth, Karl (1981). *The Christian Life: Church Dogmatics IV.4 Lecture Fragments*, trans. Geoffrey Bromiley (Edinburgh: T & T Clark).

Beiner, Ronald (2011). *Civil Religion: A Dialogue in the History of Political Philosophy.* (Cambridge: Cambridge University Press).

Black, Antony (2003). *Guild and State: European Political Thought from the Twelfth Century to the Present.* (London: Transaction Publishers).

Bodin, Jean (1992). *On Sovereignty: Four Chapters from 'The Six Books of the Commonwealth'*, trans. Julian Franklin (Cambridge: Cambridge University Press).

Borradori, Giovanna (2003). *Philosophy in a Time of Terror: Dialogues with Jürgen Habermas and Jacques Derrida.* (Chicago: Chicago University Press).

Buber, Martin (1950). *Paths in Utopia.* (New York: Macmillan).

Cavanaugh, William (1998). *Torture and Eucharist: Theology, Politics, and the Body of Christ.* (Oxford: Blackwell Publishers).

Chaplin, Jonathan (2011). *Herman Dooyeweerd: Christian Philosopher of State and Civil Society.* (Notre Dame, IN: University of Notre Dame Press).

Cohn, Norman (1970). *The Pursuit of the Millennium: Revolutionary Millenarians and Mystical Anarchists of the Middle Ages.* (Oxford: Oxford University Press).

Cullen, Bernard (1979). *Hegel's Social and Political Thought.* (Dublin: Gill and Macmillan).

Davies, J. C. (1991). 'Utopianism', in J. H. Burns and Mark Goldie (eds), *The Cambridge History of Political Thought: 1450–1700.* (Cambridge: Cambridge University Press).

Derrida, Jacques (2003). *Voyous.* (Paris: Galilée).

Durkheim, Emile (1984). *The Division of Labour in Society*, trans. W. D. Halls (Basingstoke: Palgrave).

Elshtain, Jean Bethke (2008). *Sovereignty: God, State, and Self.* (New York: Basic Books).

Franklin, Julian (1991). 'Sovereignty and the Mixed Constitution: Bodin and his Critics', in J. H. Burns and Mark Goldie (eds), *The Cambridge History of Political Thought: 1450–1700.* (Cambridge: Cambridge University Press).

Hastings, Adrian (1997). *The Construction of Nationhood: Ethnicity, Religion, and Nationalism.* (Cambridge: Cambridge University Press).

Hauerwas, Stanley (2007). 'Democratic Time: Lessons Learned from Yoder and Wolin', *The State of the University: Academic Knowledges and the Knowledge of God.* (Oxford: Blackwell Publishing).

Hegel, Georg W. F. (1967). *Hegel's Philosophy of Right*, trans. T. M. Knox (Oxford: Oxford University Press).

Hirst, Paul (1993). *The Pluralist Theory of the State: Selected Writings of G. D. H. Cole, J. N. Figgis and H. J. Laski.* (London: Routledge).

——(1994). *Associative Democracy: New Forms of Economic and Social Governance.* (Cambridge: Polity).

Hueglin, Thomas (1999). *Early Modern Concepts for a Late Modern World: Althusius on Community and Federalism.* (Waterloo, ON: Wilfrid Laurier University Press).

Kantorowicz, Ernst (1957). *The King's Two Bodies: A Study in Mediaeval Political Theology.* (Princeton, NJ: Princeton University Press).

Laborde, Cécile (2000). *Pluralist Thought and the State in Britain and France, 1900–25.* (Basingstoke: Macmillan Press).

Lakeland, Paul (1984). *The Politics of Salvation: The Hegelian Idea of the State.* (Albany: State University of New York Press).

Lijphart, Arend (1980). *Democracy in Plural Societies: A Comparative Exploration.* (New Haven, CT: Yale University Press).

MacIntyre, Alasdair (2006). 'Three Perspectives on Marxism: 1953, 1968, 1995', *Ethics and Politics, Selected Essays*, vol. 2. (Cambridge: Cambridge University Press).

Maritain, Jacques (1950). 'The Concept of Sovereignty', *The American Political Science Review* 44: 2, 343–57.

——(1968). *Integral Humanism: Temporal and Spiritual Problems of the New Christendom*, trans. Joseph Evans (New York: Charles Scribner's Sons).

Milbank, John (1990). *Theology and Social Theory: Beyond Secular Reason*. (Oxford: Basil Blackwell).

——(1997). 'On Complex Space', *The Word Made Strange: Theory, Language, Culture*. (Oxford: Blackwell Publishers, 1997).

Moltmann, Jürgen (1981). *The Trinity and the Kingdom of God*, trans. Margaret Kohl (London: SCM).

Nederman, Cary (1987). 'Sovereignty, War and the Corporation: Hegel on the Medieval Foundations of the Modern State', *The Journal of Politics* 49: 2, 500–20.

Nelson, Eric (2010). *The Hebrew Republic: Jewish Sources and the Transformation of European Political Thought*. (Cambridge, MA: Harvard University Press).

O'Donovan, Oliver (1996). *The Desire of the Nations: Rediscovering the Roots of Political Theory*. (Cambridge: Cambridge University Press).

——(2005). *The Ways of Judgment*. (Grand Rapids, MI: Eerdmans).

O'Regan, Cyril (1994). *The Heterodox Hegel*. (Albany: State University of New York Press).

Pleij, Herman (2001). *Dreaming of Cockaigne: Medieval Fantasies of the Perfect Life*, trans. Diane Webb (New York: Columbia University Press).

Riley, Patrick (1986). *The General Will Before Rousseau: The Transformation of the Divine into the Civic*. (Princeton, NJ: Princeton University Press).

Rousseau, Jean Jacques (1997). *The Social Contract and Other Later Political Writings*. (Cambridge: Cambridge University Press).

Runciman, David (1997). *Pluralism and the Personality of the State*. (Cambridge: Cambridge University Press).

Schmitt, Carl (1996). *The Leviathan in the State Theory of Thomas Hobbes: Meaning and Failure of a Political Symbol*, trans. George Schwab and Erna Hilfstein (Westport, CT: Greenwood Press).

——(2007). *The Concept of the Political*, trans. George Schwab (Chicago: University of Chicago Press).

Taylor, Charles (2007). *A Secular Age*. (Cambridge, MA: Belknap).

Volf, Miroslav (1998). ' "The Trinity is Our Social Program": The Doctrine of the Trinity and the Shape of Social Engagement', *Modern Theology* 14: 3, 403–23.

Wolin, Sheldon (2004). *Politics and Vision: Continuity and Innovation in Western Political Thought*. (Princeton, NJ: Princeton University Press).

CHAPTER 13

....

TRADITION

....

TRACEY ROWLAND

TRADITION (in Latin *Traditio* and Greek *Paradosis* or παραδοσις) has been a key concept in Christian theology since the times of Clement of Alexandria (*c*.150–*c*.215), Irenaeus of Lyon (*c*.130–202) and Vincent of Lérins (d. *c*.445). In his famous *Commonitorium* of 434, Lérins set out criteria for distinguishing between authentic tradition and heresy. At a time when Christological heresies proliferated the need for such principles was clear and urgent. However in the early to high Middle Ages as the Church became more established the emphasis was not so much on the nature of tradition vis-à-vis heresy, but on ancillary questions about the authority of the scriptural commentaries of Early Church Fathers and the Conciliar creeds in their relation to scripture. Material of this nature can be found, for example, in the works of Hugh of St Victor (1091–41), St Bonaventure (1221–74), and William of Ockham (1288–1348). Henry of Ghent (1217–93) also anticipated the Reformation issue of whether members of the hierarchy might go off the rails and start raising to the status of tradition ideas which were merely matters of private judgement and custom (Nichols 1991: 173). One might say that there was a steady build up in the high medieval period to the problem that burst forth in the sixteenth century. The nature of tradition and its relationship to scripture emerged as such hotly disputed theological territory that it led to war, another schism within the Christian realm and the publication of 35 new editions of the *Commonitorium* in one century. The modern history of the theological treatment of tradition is therefore usually taken to begin with the Reformation and in particular with the Council of Trent's decree *De canonicis Scripturis* in 1546.

I. REFORMERS AND COUNTER-REFORMERS
....

Whereas the Protestant Reformers emphasized the *sola scriptura* principle, treating the many Catholic religious traditions or customs as mere human constructions and often abuses of the faith, the Catholic Counter-Reformers fostered the idea that the deposit of the faith is to be found in both scripture and tradition. Tradition itself, however, was left undefined by the Council of Trent, though its polyvalent character was not lost on Martin Chemnitz—the 'Prince of the Theologians of the Augsburg Confession'—who identified no fewer than eight different types of tradition in his four volume magnum opus, *Examen Concilii Tridentini* (1566–75). The most significant distinction is between upper case T Tradition understood as something like 'the deposit of the faith' and lower case t traditions understood as pious practices. Kevin J. Vanhoozer has argued that 'the Reformers did not object to the use of the church fathers or deny that the Bible ought to be interpreted in the context of the life of the ongoing church. What they rejected was rather the elevation of non-canonical, and hence human traditions, that were thought to supplement the revelation given in Scripture' (Vanhoozer 2003: 149).

Prominent among the Counter-Reformers was Melchior Cano (1525–60) whose publication of *De locis theologicis* in 1563 fostered the notion of tradition as a 'container of doctrine'. As Peter Candler summarizes his influence:

> What becomes of scripture in Melanchthon becomes of tradition in Cano: both are now thought of primarily as sources, containers of doctrine, *instrumenta doctrinae*, from which one can compose an argument, or even a body of teaching which corresponds to the text, whether the text in question is 'scripture' or 'tradition'. For the two have now been so thoroughly divorced that it is impossible for either Protestants or Catholics, in this period, to imagine their 'sources' as anything but 'books' ... Tradition now becomes a *thing to be interpreted* rather than the act of interpretation itself.   (Candler 2006: 29)

A parallel development was the treatment of revelation in the works of Francisco Suárez (1548–1617). Suárez fostered a propositional account of revelation by which revelation does not disclose God himself so much as pieces of information about God. This was fundamentally different from the account of Thomas Aquinas (1225–74) and was to have far-reaching consequences for the Catholic understanding of tradition:

> Thomas never had cause to reify the mediation into words or propositions through which God hands over 'things to be believed'. Nor does Thomas separate the moment of belief or assent from some prior moment of apprehension ... [F]or Thomas, revelation takes place in the judgment and understanding, as part of the assent of faith. Revelation does not occur 'on its own', as if it were a thing apart, before becoming part of human thought and experience.   (Montag 1999: 57)

The effect of the Suárezian revision was that revelation was no longer understood as an illumination of the soul. Instead, as John Montag and John Milbank, among others, have argued, it morphed into an additional package of information to top up a rationalist metaphysics, which claimed to be able to comprehend being without any reference to God. This account of revelation neatly dovetailed with Cano's 'doctrinal-container' theory of tradition.

II. Dei Verbum

The Suárezian account of revelation, along with variations on Cano's account of tradition, was widely taught in Catholic academies up until the Second Vatican Council (1962–5) and its promulgation of *Dei Verbum* (*The Dogmatic Constitution on Divine Revelation*) in 1965. This document sought to overcome the scripture-tradition dualism by recognizing that both scripture and tradition flow from the same revelation of Christ (anticipated in the Old Testament) and merge into a unity. According to *Dei Verbum* the plan of revelation is realized by *deeds and words* having an inner unity: the deeds wrought by God in the history of salvation manifest and confirm the teaching and realities signified by the words, while the words proclaim the deeds and clarify the mystery contained in them.

Dei Verbum can therefore be read as a rejection of the Suárezian account of revelation as well as a response to issues thrown up by the scholarship of Josef Rupert Geiselmann (1890–1970). Geiselmann had noted that while the draft of the Tridentine decree *De canonicis Scripturis* originally contained the statement that the truth of the gospel is contained 'partly in the Sacred Scriptures, and partly in the unwritten traditions' the final decree stated that the truth of the gospel is contained in scripture and tradition. The use of 'and' made the decree ambiguous. Did it mean that tradition refers to those doctrines not found in scripture or did it mean that tradition is an expansion of what was already latent in scripture? On this basis Geiselmann claimed that the issue of the relation of scripture to tradition had been left unresolved by the Council of Trent and he personally favoured an approach whereby tradition makes explicit what is already latently present in scripture. Such an interpretation has the merit of assuaging Protestant suspicions that Catholic dogma is created in the imaginations of members of the hierarchy in their search for solutions to political problems.

In 1963, Joseph Ratzinger argued that both Geiselmann and *sola scriptura* Protestants tend to overlook the relationship of scripture and tradition to revelation—the larger context in which it belongs. For Ratzinger, revelation is more than scripture. He spoke of a 'pneumatic surplus' of revelation which cannot be reduced to writing and *pace* Suárez, he stated that revelation cannot be pocketed like a book one carries around. According to Ratzinger, scripture is not synonymous with revelation but is only a part of revelation's greater reality. He praised the Protestant scholars Karl Barth (1886–1968) and Emile Brunner (1889–1966) for understanding this fact. As he was later to emphasize, for Christians, truth is a person. In a redaction of this paper published in 1966, he (1966: 46) summarized his own account of tradition in the following list of propositions:

(i) At the beginning of all tradition stands the fact that the Father gives the Son over to the world and that the Son for his part allows himself to be given over to the 'nations', as a sign. This original *paradosis*, in its character as judgment and gift of salvation, is continued in the abiding presence of Christ in his Body, the Church. To that extent the whole mystery of Christ's continuing presence is

primarily the whole reality which is transmitted in tradition, the decisive fundamental reality which is antecedent to all particular explicit expressions of it, even
those of scripture, and which represents what has in fact to be handed down.

(ii) Tradition then exists concretely as presence in faith, which again, as the indwelling of Christ, is antecedent to all its particular explicit formulations and is
fertile and living, thus developing and unfolding throughout the ages.

(iii) the organ of tradition is the authority of the Church, that is, those who have
authority in it.

(iv) Tradition also exists, however, as actually expressed in what has already become
a rule of faith (creed, *fides quae*), by the authority of faith. The question whether
certain express affirmations were transmitted from the beginning side by side
with scripture, whether, therefore, there is a second material principle besides
scripture, independent from the beginning, becomes quite secondary in comparison, but it would probably have to be answered negatively.

The final clause of this list amounts to an acknowledgment that the Protestant side of
the debate does have some merit. In the same paper Ratzinger noted that the quintes-
sentially Protestant question is: 'can the word be given over to the Church without fear
that it will forfeit its own power and vitality under the shears of the magisterium or in
the rank growth of the *sensus fidelium*?'; while the Catholic question to the Protestants
is: 'Can the word be posited as independent without thereby delivering it up to the
caprice of exegetes, evacuating it of meaning in the controversies of historians and so
robbing it entirely of binding force?' (Ratzinger 1966: 31). Against the Protestants,
Ratzinger clearly sees a rôle for the sacred hierarchy as 'operation ground-control', as
he described it in *Principles of Catholic Theology* (1982), but with the Protestants he is
wary of the Suárezian tendency to raise ecclesial doctrines to the status of revelation.

The treatment of revelation, scripture, and tradition in *Dei Verbum* bears strong
resonances to the work of the Swiss Lutheran theologian Oscar Cullmann (1902–99)
who was a Protestant observer at the Second Vatican Council. Karl Barth joked that
such was Cullmann's influence his tombstone would carry the inscription 'advisor to
three popes'. Cullmann made a study of the word *Paradosis* as it appears in the New
Testament, especially in St Paul's *First Letter to the Corinthians*. He argued that 'The
formula of I Cor. 11:23 refers to the Christ who is present, in that he stands behind the
transmission of the tradition, that is, he works *in it*'. 'The *Kyrios* appears as the content
of the *Paradosis*, but he is at one and the same time *its content and its author*'
(Cullmann 1956: 68). As with *Dei Verbum*, Christ is presented as himself the revelation
of the Father, and the apostles are charged with the transmission of this *Paradosis*
under the guidance of the Holy Spirit. Cullmann however rejected the notion, central to
Catholic ecclesiology, that the sacred hierarchy and in particular the papacy continues
to do the same work as the Apostles throughout the *saeculum* until the end of time.

The gulf between Protestant and Catholic understandings of the relationship between scripture and tradition has been far less wide in the post *Dei Verbum* era, though

scholars influenced by Karl Barth's criticism of the Catholic account of tradition in the first volume of his *Church Dogmatics* do continue to keep the sixteenth-century debates alive. With reference to Vincent of Lérins, Barth noted that the standard Catholic conception of tradition was 'composed by a professed semi-Pelagian and, in the first instance, obliquely directed against the Augustinian doctrines of predestination and grace' (Barth 1956: 550). Barth read Trent's *De canonicis Scripturis* as a magisterial endorsement of Lérins's account of tradition. In general however, the promulgation of *Dei Verbum* (which conspicuously failed to invoke the authority of Lérins) and the Christocentric thrust of other Conciliar documents, has helped to displace the standard Protestant caricature of a Catholic as someone who is likely to know more about Stoic philosophy than the writings of St Paul and be more interested in Aristotle than Christ. From the Protestant side there has been a move to recognize that their typically sixteenth-century understandings of tradition were often myopic, and in particular there has been a recognition that traditions with a lower case t (mostly cultural practices) are not what the Early Church Fathers understood by tradition. Nonetheless, another problematic has risen causing divisions as much within as across denominational boundaries. This is the relationship between History and Tradition.

The Tübingen School

The issue of how history might influence the development of tradition has been a dominant theme in theological scholarship since the early nineteenth century and was particularly strong in the works of the Tübingen scholars Johann Adam Möhler (1796–1838), Johann Sebastian von Drey (1777–1853), and Johannes von Kuhn (1806–87). Grant Kaplan encapsulated the spirit of the Tübingen scholarship in the following paragraph:

> Through Romantic and Idealist lenses, the Tübingen School re-envisioned tradition as a living truth instead of the transmission of old ideas, the church as an organism instead of a *societas perfecta*, Christ as the incarnate *logos* rather than a mere teacher, and the Holy Spirit as an active participant in human life instead of a departed entity who last engaged in the world's affairs during Pentecost. (Kaplan 2006: 99)

Möhler was influenced by von Drey's notion of an organic development of tradition and the rôle of the Holy Spirit animating the life of the Church and by G. W. F. Hegel's notion of dialectical development. Combining these two insights Möhler emphasized tradition's living or dynamic nature and suggested that the development of the faithful's understanding of tradition occurs through the resolution of conflicting interpretations. Consistent with the anti-Kantian thrust of the Romantic scholarship of the era, the Tübingen theologians emphasized that the reception of the Christian tradition amounted to a personal participation in the life of the Trinity and not the adoption of some higher moral teaching (Kaplan 2006: 80). They stood opposed to the Kantian project of reducing Christianity to the level of an ethical framework and they approached the Catholic faith as a religion of sentiment (*Gemüth*) and well as of reason (*Verstand*). In this latter sense they anticipated some of the seminal themes in early mid-twentieth-century personalist philosophy. They also emphasized the historical nature of revelation while, nonetheless, retaining a role for dogma. Though not strictly speaking as a Tübingen scholar, the works of Matthias Joseph Scheeben (1835–88) of Cologne have also been described as offering a 'combination of romance and system: a lyrical appeal to the imagination, [consistent with the interests of the Romantics] and a virile challenge to the intellect [typical of scholasticism], the inspiration of metaphor and the conceptual power of an architectonic account of the revelation carried by the Church' (Nichols 2010: p. ix).

III. John Henry Newman and the Oxford Movement

At the same time as the Tübingen scholars were working on the history and tradition problematic against the background of German Romantic philosophy, High Church Anglicans in Oxford were dealing with a similar set of issues as they attempted to historically position the Church of England vis-à-vis other denominations and validate its claim to orthodoxy. Many in this milieu were influenced by the ideas of Richard Hooker (1554–1600). In *The Laws of Ecclesiastical Polity* published in several volumes, Hooker advanced the thesis that scripture was properly interpreted by the tradition of the early Greek Fathers and that the early creeds based on scripture were consistent with reason (Prickett: 2009: 106–7). Hooker's retention of a rôle for tradition and reason in the interpretation of scripture placed him closer to the positions of the theologians of Trent than to the anti-tradition and anti-reason orientation of the Continental Reformers. The most significant member of the Oxford Movement to work in this area was John Henry Newman (1801–90) whose studies led to his conversion to the Catholic faith in 1845.

In his *Essay on the Development of Christian Doctrine* Newman noted, as Möhler had earlier done, that doctrinal development usually occurs when some element of the tradition is the subject of controversy and conflicting interpretations which require a higher resolution. He affirmed the need for a sacred hierarchy to act as the final organ of authority in the resolution of such conflicts, but he also emphasized that the faithful who are not members of the magisterium are also a locus of the living tradition. In the fifth chapter of the work he set out a list of seven criteria by which one might discern true developments from corruptions:

(i) Preservation of Type. (Here Newman refers to an organic metaphor earlier used by Vincent of Lérins. A baby's limbs grow and develop but they are still the same limbs);

(ii) Continuity of principles. (The life of doctrines may be said to consist in the law or principle which they embody);

(iii) Power to assimilate alien matter to the original idea. (The harder it is to assimilate an idea the more likely it is to represent a corrupting influence).

(iv) Logical Sequence. (A doctrine is likely to be a true development, not a corruption, in proportion as it seems to be the *logical issue* of its original teaching);

(v)   Anticipation of its Future. (The fact of early and recurring intimations of tendencies which afterwards are fully realized, is evidence that those later and more systematic fulfilments are in accordance with the original idea);

(vi) A conservative action upon its past. (A true development illustrates, not obscures, corroborates, not corrects, the body of thought from which it proceeds);

(vii) Chronic vigour. (Corruption is distinguished from development by its transitory character). (Newman 1903: 169–208)

Newman's ideas began to penetrate German scholarship in the 1920s when his works were translated by Erich Przywara (1889–1972), editor of the influential *Stimmen der Zeit*, by Edith Stein (1891–1942) a Jewish-convert philosopher, and by the cultural critic Theodor Haecker (1879–1945). Newman's *Essay on the Development of Doctrine* and *Grammar of Assent* were also taught to the post-Second World War generation of German seminarians by Gottlieb Söhngen (1892–1971) and Newman scholarship in general was fostered by Heinrich Fries SJ (1911–98) who was a professor of fundamental and ecumenical theology in Munich. By the time of the Second Vatican Council the German theologians, Ratzinger included, were well versed in the ideas of Newman.

IV. ALASDAIR MACINTYRE: TRADITION AND INSTITUTIONAL STRUCTURES

Newman's notion of the rôle of historical crises in the development of doctrine and his emphasis on the organic nature of the unfolding of tradition mirrored the conclusions of Adam Möhler and foreshadowed the late twentieth-century scholarship of Alasdair MacIntyre whose debt to Newman in this context is acknowledged. MacIntyre writes as a philosopher so his account of upper case T tradition is an account of tradition understood as any intellectual framework, not exclusively one associated with the Catholic tradition. His scholarship has offered insights into how lower case t traditions assist in the mediation of upper case T tradition as well as accounts of how such upper case T traditions develop through the resolution of crises. One of MacIntyre's central arguments is that ideas are not merely transmitted in books and learned lectures, they can also be transmitted through social practices. MacIntyre also concurs with the conclusions of contemporary hermeneutical scholarship that thinking always involves thinking in the context of some particular and specific public, which will normally have its own institutional structure. In each of these structures there will be:

(i)   A conception of truth beyond and ordering particular truths;
(ii) A conception of a range of senses in the light of which utterances to be judged true or false and so placed within that ordering are to be construed;
(iii) A conception of a range of genres of utterance, dramatic, lyrical, historical and the like, by reference to which utterances may be classified so that we may then proceed to identify their senses; and
(iv) A contrast between those uses of genres in which in one way or another truth is at stake and those governed only by standards of rhetorical effectiveness. (MacIntyre 1990: 200–1)

Similarly, Hans Georg Gadamer argued in *Truth and Method* that human beings always operate from within the horizons of particular languages and traditions and thus that meaning is not an objective property of the text which can be extracted from a position of complete neutrality. Rather the act of understanding a text requires a 'fusion of horizons' (Gadamer 1975: 305). When applied to the scriptures this means that they must be interpreted from within the horizon of faith itself and, from the perspective of Catholic theology; the institution of the Church and her interpretations of the passages, forms part of that horizon. Ratzinger, for example, has written that 'the exegete must realise that he does not occupy a neutral position above or outside Church history and he must acknowledge that the faith is the hermeneutic, the locus of understanding, which does not dogmatically force itself upon the Bible, but is the only way of letting it be itself in' (Granados 2008: 29).

The same recognition of faith as a necessary *preambula* to exegesis was defended by Hans Urs von Balthasar (1905–88) in the following terms:

Christ's divinity cannot be wholly comprehended through his humanity, and no more can the divine sense of Scripture ever be fully plumbed through the letter. It can only be grasped in the setting of faith, that is to say, in a mode of hearing that never issues in final vision, but in a profession without end, a progression ultimately dependent, in its scope, on the Holy Spirit. Faith, the foundation of all our understanding of revelation, expands our created minds by making them participate in the mind of God, disclosing the inward divine meaning of the words through a kind of co-working of God (I Cor. 2: 9–16).   (von Balthasar 1989: 21)

This is not an exclusively Catholic principle but one shared with many Protestant scholars who take their cue from St Paul. As Kevin Vanhoozer expresses the principle: 'Scripture is not merely "writing" but rather a key instrument in the communicative economy of the triune God in which the Father is revealed, the Son reveals, and the Spirit is the agent of revelation's perfection' (Vanhoozer 2003: 165).

Protestant theologians associated with the Post-Liberal theology of the Yale Divinity School, such as George Lindbeck, Hans Wilhelm Frei, and Stanley Hauerwas have also emphasized the hermeneutical importance of their Christian communities as providers of their own 'depth grammars' and linguistic frameworks. With reference to the work of T. S. Kuhn (1922–96) in the philosophy of science and Ludwig Wittgenstein (1889–1951) in the philosophy of language, Lindbeck rejected the suggestion that such an approach to scriptural interpretation results in an extreme relativism but he nonetheless acknowledged that reasonableness in theology has something of an aesthetic rather than scientific-empirical character (Lindbeck 1984: 130). This theme was taken up by Kevin J. Vanhoozer in his work on the *Drama of Doctrine* in which the gospel is presented as a theo-drama and doctrine is treated as a necessary interpretative tool to direct the Church to participate rightly in the drama of redemption (Vanhoozer 2005: 77).

Lindbeck also distinguished between three fundamental theological styles: the cognitivist-propositionalist, the experiential-expressivist and the cultural-linguistic. Vanhoozer has suggested that these three styles could more or less be classified as: epic, lyric, and dramatic. The cognitivist-propositionalist is archetypical of scholasticism with its emphasis on doctrinal propositions. The theology of Friedrich Schleiermacher (1768–1834), the Moravian Pietist who rejected the *sola scriptura* principle and replaced it with religious experience, is taken as prototypical of the experiential-expressivist style. The cultural-linguistic or dramatic seeks to link the interior religious experiences to the beliefs and practices of a given ecclesial community. It represents a fusion of what Nichols calls 'romance' and 'system' and it makes the traditions (upper and lower case) of a given ecclesial community of central importance. According to Vanhoozer, drama combines the inner subjectivity of lyric with the external objectivity of epic: it 'preserves the cognitive, truth-telling drama, though its exhibit of the truth in the language of actions is richer than the merely propositional' (Vanhoozer 2005: 100–1).

V. The Roman School

In contrast to the Oxford and Tübingen projects not all nineteenth- and twentieth-century Catholic scholars were enthusiastic about examining the relationship between history and dogma and appropriating elements of German Romantic philosophy for theological ends. A number associated with the revival of scholastic thought regarded the notion that history might play a rôle in the development of tradition as extremely dangerous. They especially feared any ideas that might send Catholic theology in the same direction as that taken by Schleiermacher.

In contrast to the Tübingen scholars, who might be described as looking for a way of making a place for history within theology without going down the path of Schleiermacher-style subjectivism, scholars of the Roman School emphasized the immutability of doctrine, and thus a static notion of tradition, tied tightly to the decrees of the magisterium or sacred hierarchy. The First Vatican Council (1869–70) defined tradition as a 'divine deposit, delivered to the Spouse of Christ, to be kept faithfully and declared infallibly'. The rôle of the magisterium was to define the traditional belief, most usually by promulgating it in the form of a dogma. The major figure of the Roman School was Johannes Baptist Franzelin (1816–86), a Jesuit Cardinal prominent in the pontificate of Pius IX. He was a papal theologian during the First Vatican Council and published *Tractatus de divina traditione et scriptura* in 1870. He tied tradition closely to the teachings of the magisterium and he distinguished between active and objective tradition. The objective tradition referred to that which is handed down, the active tradition to the process of the transfer.

The Roman School's concern about historical relativism reached its peak at the turn of the twentieth century. In the encyclical *Pascendi Dominici Gregis* published in 1907, Pius X condemned a cluster of ideas under the banner of the heresy of 'Modernism'. Although difficult to define precisely, Modernism has been described as a tendency 'to rely exclusively on historical science so as to determine the theological meaning of biblical and other texts, without acknowledging any rôle for tradition in the hermeneutical process' (Nichols 1998: 84). The works of Alfred Loisy (1857–1940) and George Tyrell (1861–1909) were treated as prototypical of this heretical orientation. Consistent with the sense of alarm sounded in *Pascendi*, in *De immutabilitate traditonis contra modernam haeresim evolutionismi* published in 1929, Louis Billot (1846–1931) argued that tradition has no independent existence outside the Church's contemporary teaching. As a caricature one may argue that the Modernists wanted history without tradition and that the Roman School wanted tradition without history.

Notwithstanding the anxiety about the relativizing propensity of concepts like historical development, the issue of the tradition-history relationship would not go away. It became a central theme in the discussions around the declaration of the doctrine of the Assumption of Our Lady by Pius XII in 1950 (there being little documentary evidence of the doctrine's existence in the Early Church) and it was an even greater issue for the generation of theologians coming to maturity in the 1960s. The Church's engagement with the cultures of modernity and postmodernity demanded an understanding of the mediation of history in the realm of ontology and the relationship between salvation history and secular history, where secular refers not to an ontological space, but to the period between Christ's ascension and his return in glory. Whereas the Council of Trent was focused on the scripture-tradition relationship, and the warring factions were Protestant and Catholic, by the late nineteenth and early twentieth centuries, the dominant problematic had become the history-tradition relationship and the warring factions have become the proponents of modernization and an evolutionary ontology against those who regard the biblical teachings as normative for all times.

VI. Maurice Blondel

One of the first to directly address this problematic was Maurice Blondel (1861–1949) who published an essay on history and dogma in 1903. Blondel sought to overcome the dualism by developing a notion of the incarnation of dogma *within* history and he argued that the synthesis of dogma and history lies 'neither in the facts alone, nor in the ideas alone, but in the Tradition which embraces within it the facts of history, the efforts of reason and the accumulated experience of the faithful' (Blondel 1994: 257). With reference to this 'accumulated experience' he further argued:

> Christian practice nourishes man's knowledge of the divine and bears within its action what is progressively discerned by the theologian's initiative. The synthesis of dogma and facts is scientifically effected because there is a synthesis of thought and grace in the life of the believer, a union of man and God, reproducing in the individual consciousness the history of Christianity itself.   (Blondel 1994: 287)

Yves Congar (1904–95) summarized Blondel's attempt at a *via media* in these terms:

> Over against these two opposing caricatures [the hostile to history stance of the Roman School and the historical relativism of the Modernists] Blondel set tradition, in which history and dogmas are united by a live current passing in both directions — from the facts to the dogma, and from faith to the facts. To oppose the data of history and the statements of dogma was to make an unwarranted separation between the two elements of a single reality with an essentially religious nature.   (Congar 1960–3: 215–16)

A more recent appraisal of the contribution of Blondel has been offered by Oliva Blanchette (2010: 746–7). He notes that for Blondel the term tradition has a far stronger meaning than in ordinary discourse. It does not mean the accumulation of the wisdom of the ages, it is something totally different from a Burkean sense of tradition. The events narrated in the scriptures are not 'pastiches that one relegates to a past all bandaged up and left behind'—rather 'the narration of them is the beginning of a new supernatural stage in the spiritual life of humanity'. Thus, tradition is 'a continuous flow of the supernatural experience of faith and practice', requiring the authority of the magisterium to 'assure fidelity to the original endowment in its movement of unceasing innovation'.

Blondel's account of tradition as presented in *History and Dogma* influenced Henri de Lubac (1896–1991), one of the most significant *periti* at the Second Vatican Council, and de Lubac in turn was a major influence on the theological formation of Joseph Ratzinger. Working backwards, Blondel had been influenced by Newman who had been introduced to French readers by Henri Bremond. Blondel also came to know of the Tübingen school through Georges Goyau, who was an author of an important study on Johann Adam Möhler. The very first edition of Blondel's journal *Annales de Philosophie Chrétienne* made reference to the significance of the German Catholic writers of the Romantic period.

VII. The Criticism of Vincent of Lérins

In a move that ran parallel to the rejection of the Suárezian account of revelation in *Dei Verbum*, scholars from the mid-twentieth century and onwards began to criticize

Lérins's test to distinguish authentic elements of tradition from those that were heretical. According to Lérins for a particular idea to be an authentic component of the tradition it had to have been held by everyone, everywhere, in the Church from the earliest times. The principle is summarized in the phrase *Quod ubique, quod semper, quod ab omnibus*. In his essay on the Transmission of Divine Revelation, Ratzinger wrote (1969: 187):

> He [Lérins] no longer appears an authentic representative of the Catholic idea of tradition, but outlines a canon of tradition based on a semi-Pelagian idea . . . The rejection [by the fathers of the Second Vatican Council] of the suggestion to include again Vincent de Lérins's well known text, more or less canonized by two councils, is again a step beyond Trent and Vatican I . . . It is not that Vatican II is taking back what was intended in those quotations: the rejection of a modernistic evolutionism, an affirmation of the definitive character of the revelation of Christ and the apostolic tradition, to which the Church has nothing to add, but which is its yardstick, but it has another conception of the nature of historical identity and continuity. Vincent de Lérins's static *semper* no longer seems the right way of expressing the problem.

According to Cyril O'Regan, von Balthasar was also persuaded that Lérins's 'univocal and static view of tradition does not correspond to the palpable fact of the development of doctrine' and was 'in danger of denying the symbolic nature of all language with respect to the divine and promoting the view that doctrine is adequate to the mystery to which it refers' (O'Regan 1998: 330). O'Regan summarized von Balthasar's account of tradition with the statement: 'truth is objective, yet refracted over time through Christian communities, and exemplary members of these communities' (O'Regan 1998: 337). Von Balthasar endorsed the notion of the development of tradition but stated that it is wrong to think of this process as something like filling in pieces of a jigsaw puzzle, 'as though "progress" consisted in first of all establishing the main outlines of the faith, and then proceeding to the more and more detailed work required to complete the edifice' (von Balthasar 1963: 102–3).

The Russian Orthodox theologian Vladimir Lossky (1903–58) was also critical of Lérins's formula for distinguishing authentic tradition from heresy. He noted that the maxim '*quod semper, quod ubique, quod ab omnibus*' can be applied in full only to those apostolic traditions which were orally transmitted during two or three centuries. The New Testament scriptures already fall outside this rule, for they were neither 'always', nor 'everywhere', nor 'received by all' before the definitive establishment of the scriptural canon. In a statement which resonates with von Balthasar's opposition to the 'jigsaw' theory of the development of tradition, Lossky wrote:

> If one can still speak of development, it is not knowledge of revelation in the church which progresses or is developed with each dogmatic definition. If one were to embrace the whole account of doctrinal history from its beginnings down to our own day by reading the *Enchiridion* of Heinrich Denzinger or the fifty in-folio volumes of Giovanni Mansi, the knowledge that one would thus have of the mystery

of the Trinity would be no more perfect than was that of a father of the fourth century... A doctrine is traitor to tradition when it seeks to take its place... As an expression of truth, a dogma of faith belongs to tradition without all the same constituting one of its 'parts'. It is a means, an intelligible instrument, which makes for adherence to the tradition of the church. It is a witness of tradition, its external limit or, rather, the narrow door which leads to knowledge of truth in the tradition. (Lossky 1995: 141)

For Lossky dogmas are thus a clarification of tradition but the tradition is not constituted by a collection of doctrinal propositions. Such propositions operate to steer people clear of heretical icebergs but they cannot ever be added up one to another to constitute the tradition. With reference to the inadequacies of both the Tridentine and Protestant treatment of tradition, Lossky concluded:

Tradition is not the content of revelation, but the light that reveals it; it is not the word, but the living breath which makes the words heard at the same time as the silence from which it came, it is not the truth, but a communication of the Spirit of truth, outside which the truth cannot be received... The pure notion of tradition can then be defined by saying that it is the life of the Holy Spirit in the church, communicating to each member of the body of Christ the faculty of hearing, of receiving, of knowing the truth in the light which belongs to it, and not according to the natural light of reason. (Lossky 1995: 113–34)

Notwithstanding all the above criticisms of Lérins, Thomas Guarino has argued that while it is fashionable to be critical of Lérins and ponder how a professed semi-Pelagian could have come to hold so much influence, and while his maxim *Quod ubique, quod semper, quod ab omnibus* clearly has its limitations, one should pay attention to his less well-known second limb or second maxim, that any kind of growth or development needs to be '*eodem sensu eademque sententia*'. In other words, development must be a *perfectus* rather than a *permutatio* of what went before. Guarino claims that this second maxim of Lérins influenced Newman, Möhler, and Kuhn's idea of an organic development and that it remains a valid and useful principle (Guarino 2006: 34–72).

VIII. THE FRENCH TRADITIONALISTS

The criticisms of Suárez and Lérins, which one finds in the works of scholars such as Lossky, Ratzinger, and von Balthasar, or at least, the suggestion that revelation is not primarily propositional and that capital T tradition is something deeper than a compilation of dogmas, is one of the points of conflict between the 'Traditionalists', mostly followers of Archbishop Marcel Lefebrve, and those who gave their assent to documents such as *Dei Verbum* of the Second Vatican Council. The *Motu Proprio Ecclesia Dei Adflicta* of John Paul II, published in 1988, accused followers of Archbishop Lefebrve of holding to an incomplete and contradictory notion of tradition, especially in so far as it does not take sufficiently into account the living character of tradition. One might say that the Lefebrvists strongly prefer Lérins, Suárez, and Billot to Newman, Möhler, Blondel, Lossky, Ratzinger, or von Balthasar. The Traditionalist movement is strongest in France and at least one reason for this may be gleaned from the following observation of Alexander Dru in his preface to Maurice Blondel's *History and Dogma*. Speaking of the treatment of tradition in French intellectual life after the Revolution, Dru concluded:

> Tradition was viewed in a political light and, regardless of what it was applied to, came to mean the conservation of a heritage, of an object, and in Christianity of a clearly defined object, 'the deposit of the faith'. The handing down of the 'deposit' was looked upon as an impersonal process; the whole emphasis fell on *what* was handed down, and no thought was given to *how* it was handed down. The common view of Tradition was mechanical, and it would hardly be a caricature to say that it was so objective as not to imply any believers to hand down the deposit. This impersonal way of conceiving Tradition led inevitably to what Blondel calls *fixisme*, the notion that nothing whatsoever should change and therefore in practice to *un rétrogradisme meurtrier*, a fatally retrograde attitude towards intellectual questions. (in Blondel 1994: 214)

Added to this dimension of the problem is the fact that the Traditionalists are not only concerned about upper case T tradition but they are also concerned about lower case t traditions, and in this context they do receive a sympathetic hearing from Ratzinger/ Benedict XVI who has been critical of the post-Conciliar pastoral strategy of marketing the Catholic faith in the idioms of contemporary popular culture and accommodating her liturgical culture to the same. This strategy of 'correlating' Catholic tradition to the trends in contemporary culture and intellectual life was promoted by the Flemish Dominican Edward Schillebeeckx (1914–2009) in a series of essays published in the late 1960s at the height of the post-Conciliar enthusiasm for all things *moderne*. Ratzinger has compared such strategies to those of the owner of a haberdashery shop who updates his stock with every passing fashion season and he has been particularly sensitive to the Traditionalist's claim that the liturgical revolution of the late 1960s and 1970s, promoted as a necessary pastoral reform for 'modern man', has adversely affected the transmission of upper case T tradition.

IX. Tradition and Liturgy

There is a wealth of scholarly material on the way in which tradition is transmitted through rituals, particularly through the Mass. Contemporary scholars who have contributed to this field include: David Torevell, Jean Borella, Aidan Nichols, and Catherine Pickstock. Yves Congar, the author of the two volume *La Tradition et les traditions* concluded that if 'tradition in its dogmatic foundation is an interpretation of scripture continuing that of Christ and his apostles, the liturgy is truly the holy ark containing sacred tradition at its most intense' (Congar 2004: 142). In a passage written between the years 1960–3, Congar rhetorically asked how tradition could possibly be transmitted to new generations after successive centuries of 'demolition work' (the theological misadventures of at least four centuries) and in a passage which now reads as poignant, he concluded:

> But we need only step into an old church, taking holy water, as Pascal and Serapion did before us, in order to follow a Mass which has scarcely changed, even in externals, since St. Gregory the Great . . . Everything has been preserved for us, and we can enter into a heritage which we may easily transmit in our turn, to those coming after us. Ritual, as a means of communication and of victory over devouring time, is also seen to be a powerful means for communion in the same reality between men separated by centuries of change and affected by very different influences.   (Congar 1960–3: 429)

A rather complex aspect of the Traditionalist problem is thus that there is a difference between pre-Conciliar traditions (solemn liturgies, processions, devotions to the saints, etc.) and pre-Conciliar theology, principally a Suárezian-infused scholasticism, which is often equated with upper case T tradition. Whereas the Traditionalists want a restoration of both lower case t traditions and pre-Conciliar theology, those who support the Conciliar renewal, especially as it is presented in *Dei Verbum*, want to separate the two. For example, Ratzinger/Benedict XVI believes that liturgy should be solemn and theocentric and he has complained that the Traditionalists who prefer the Missal of John XXIII to the Missal of Paul VI have been unjustly treated like 'lepers'. Nonetheless, as a theology professor he was highly critical of baroque-era scholasticism, which represented the high point of the 'container of doctrine' theory of tradition, and he specifically stated that he did not regard belief in limbo to be a part of the Church's tradition. He claimed that limbo was simply a theological hypothesis which enjoyed a certain popularity for a time but he would not raise it to the status of tradition. For many Traditionalists however, the issue of whether or not a person believes in limbo has become a litmus test for an orthodoxy even more narrowly drawn than anything conceived by Lérins.

Congar's observation above is particularly significant because in it he recognizes that he was dealing with a theological establishment, which had been subjected to centuries of demolition work, but he thought that notwithstanding the pitiful condition in which the tradition was being *intellectually* mediated, at least *liturgically* it was being mediated in a pristine form. Paradoxically, after 1968, at a time when work had begun on the theological renewal, the liturgical mediation of tradition began to rapidly decline. Congar concluded that the Reformers were the heirs to an unhealthy separation of scripture, Church and tradition and that this pre-Reformation split was further exacerbated by the post-Tridentine tendency to separate theology from spirituality. By the seventeenth century, tradition had come to be associated with the doctrinal decrees of the magisterium, and while 'life's spiritual conditions were doubtless presupposed, they did not enter into the epistemological structure of tradition' (Congar: 1960–3: 397). The head-heart division of the seventeenth century was followed by the head-centred rationalism of the eighteenth century and the heart-centred romantic historicism of the nineteenth century, at least one branch of which fed into the correlationist projects of the 1960s. For Congar, the current need was to restore an appreciation of the relationships between scripture, Church and tradition, and within all three, to acknowledge a place for the Holy Spirit. This would in turn require a renewal of theological anthropology in such a way that no single faculty of the human soul was either excluded, eclipsed, or made to carry the whole weight of the communication between God and the human person.

X. LIEVEN BOEVE AND RE-CONTEXTUALIZING TRADITION

With reference to the conflict between the correlationists of the 1960s and 1970s and the stance of the Traditionalists, Lieven Boeve of Leuven offers the principle that those who inherit a tradition are not only its heirs but also its testators, and that tradition develops when there has been a change in context by those who receive it (Boeve 2003: 24). Boeve argues that both the correlation-to-modernity theorists and the Traditionalists generate problems because they only adhere to a single pole of the relationship with tradition—either to the pole of being an heir, or to the pole of being a testator (Boeve 2003: 49). Whereas the correlationists were seeking to correlate the Catholic faith and modernity, Boeve's project is one of *re-contextualizing* the Catholic faith with reference to postmodernity. According to Boeve the 'Christian faith and tradition are not only contained in a specific historico-cultural context, but are also co-constituted by this context' (Boeve 2006: 31–7). Precisely what Boeve means by 'co-constituted' and by 're-contextualise' is yet to be fully elaborated but his work appears to be taking a very different trajectory from Ratzinger. With reference to St Basil the Great's botanical metaphor of grafting a tree, Ratzinger has written that when Christianity meets a pre-Christian culture it needs to make a wound in that culture, a slit, as it were, in which to graft a new tree. Though postmodernity represents more of a post-Christian than a pre-Christian culture, it is probable that Ratzinger would apply the same principle of making a slit or wound in the culture, in particular one that takes the form of pruning back certain growths which represent heretical mutations of the earlier Christian 'sap' or 'tradition'. While a culture which has rejected Christ is not in the same position as one that has never received him, in both cases Ratzinger would see the need for a kind of medicinal wounding to precede any evangelization.

Ratzinger's own understanding of tradition appears to be closer to the work of Josef Pieper (1904–97). Although Pieper died before Boeve's recontextualization project began, he anticipated the use of the testator-beneficiary metaphor. Contrary to the position now taken by Boeve, Pieper argued that what a student learns through her own efforts is her own property, but what she receives from tradition is something more like the loan of a gift. Pieper also endorsed St Augustine's maxim *quod a patribus acceperunt, hoc filiis tradiderunt*. This means that the last child in line receives from his father exactly the same thing as the first in line handed over to his 'son'. The *traditum* is something that in the accomplishment of the process of tradition does *not* grow. (Pieper 2008: 21).

Within the territory of contemporary Catholic theology there appears to be emerging a fault line between those who regard the Christian tradition as itself providing all the elements needed for the Church's mission in the world and those who speak of Christianity as an 'open narrative' where the openness is to an incorporation of elements external to the tradition, albeit elements sensitive to the postmodern criticisms of the culture of modernity. For one group the metaphors are mostly borrowed from the health industry, for example, removing mutations and inflicting surgical wounds, for the others the metaphors are mostly borrowed from the hospitality industry, such as openness, welcoming, accepting, dialoguing, and conversing. The scholarship in this area however is yet to reach maturity.

XI. The Rahner-Küng Debate

In 1973, the Congregation for the Doctrine of the Faith issued the *Declaratio circa Catholicam Doctrinam de Ecclesia contra nonnullos errores hodiernos tuendam* in which it recognized that 'even though the truths which the Church intends to teach through her dogmatic formulas are distinct from the changeable conceptions of a given epoch and can be expressed without them, nevertheless it can sometimes happen that these truths may be enunciated by the Sacred Magisterium in terms that bear traces of such conceptions'. In this statement there is acknowledged that the historical context in which doctrines are formulated can in some sense influence the formulations. This is especially true of the philosophical language which has been used.

While this Declaration of the Congregation for the Doctrine of the Faith came out in June 1973, a month earlier Hans Küng and Karl Rahner had considered the issue of whether papal or Conciliar decrees could be so thoroughly determined by historical factors as to be completely erroneous. The two corresponded over this theoretical issue of the difference between mere historical influence and strong historical determination. In the first volume of his *Theological Investigations*, Rahner had noted that the history of theology is by no means to be equated with the progress of doctrine, because it is also a history of forgetting. (Rahner 1964: 151). Sometimes there is a deepening of the understanding of various elements of tradition, but at times there can also be an eclipse of some important element. Nonetheless, while acknowledging this, Rahner wrote that his conscience would never allow him to admit that 'a solemn papal or Conciliar definition could in principle be not merely historically restricted, limited, open to correction, but measured against the Gospel itself—downright erroneous'. Küng however was of the view that a solemn papal or Conciliar definition could indeed turn out to be downright erroneous (Peter 1978: 159–69).

In the fourth volume of his *Theological Investigations* Rahner observed that the problem of the development of doctrine, as a subtheme of the whole issue of the nature of tradition, is very difficult because it 'ultimately reaches down to the obscure depths of a general ontology of being and becoming, of the persistence of identity in change—and also comprises the general metaphysics of knowledge and mind, which frames the same questions in searching for truth, with regard to its identity and real historical development' (Rahner 1966: 5). In the final years of his life he came to the conclusion that the development of doctrine was not merely a difficult task but one that in the post-Conciliar era was near impossible given the plethora of new theological frameworks and philosophical movements. A common theological vocabulary was becoming increasingly difficult to identify.

XII. Georges Florovsky and the Transposition of Doctrine

This issue of the rise of new philosophical vocabularies was addressed by the Russian Orthodox scholar Georges Florovsky (1893–1979) who, taking up a position at polar ends of the spectrum from Rahner, argued that it was no historical accident that the gospel was given to the world in the Greek language. He emphatically stated that 'in the religious destiny of man there are no accidents' and he believed that when divine truth is expressed in a human language, the words themselves are transformed and sanctified. Therefore the words of dogmatic definitions should not be criticized as historically imprisoned or otherwise limited but should be received as 'eternal words, incapable of being replaced' (Florovsky 2004: 23). Nonetheless, consistent with Lossky and Ratzinger, among others, Florovsky emphasized that revelation is not exhausted in 'words' or in the 'letter' of scripture and further, he noted that tradition is best known and understood by participation in the life of the Church, not by genealogical research. Like the Tübingen scholars and Blondel and those influenced by them, Florovsky insisted upon the living nature of tradition.

The issue of the viability of projects designed to transpose doctrines into new philosophical idioms and the related subject of whether or not liturgical language should be 'updated' is often analysed in the context of linguistic philosophy. At the time of the Second Vatican Council, John XXIII was of the view that it is possible to distinguish 'between the substance of the ancient doctrine of the *depositum fidei* and the formulation of its presentation'. This was also the view of Karl Rahner. Fergus Kerr has observed that Rahner's assumption was that communication comes after language and that language comes after having concepts. This is now regarded as highly problematic. As Cardinal Francis George has explained:

> Implicitly, Pope John's statement seems to support an instrumental view of language, regarding language as the means whereby a speaker gives expression to thoughts which exist independently of language, through the employment of words whose meanings are the object of explicit agreement between prospective speakers. By contrast, an expressivist view of language holds that thought has no determinate content until it is expressed in a shared language. (George 1990: 88)

Francis George argues that cultural forms and linguistic expressions are not in fact able to be distinguished from one another as accidents were distinguished from substance in classical philosophy: 'a change in form inevitably entails also some change in content. A change in words changes in some fashion the way that we think' (George 1990: 47).

The kinds of insights to be found in the philosophical works of MacIntyre, Gadamer, and Wittgenstein and contemporary linguistic philosophers are therefore highly relevant to the theological treatment of tradition, including notions like the organic development of doctrine and liturgical language. The history and tradition problematic can be broken down into the subfields of hermeneutics and issues in linguistic philosophy.

XIII. Romantic versus Classical Orthodoxy

While the names of Schillebeeckx, Rahner, and Küng came to be associated with post-Conciliar theological liberalism, with Ratzinger, de Lubac, and von Balthasar being the leading names associated with theological orthodoxy, John Milbank has identified a new divide within the orthodox camp between those whom he classifies as Romantically and classically orthodox. He referred to the placement of something like Wordsworth's 'feeling intellect' at the heart of theology as the hallmark of the Romantically orthodox, while the hallmark of the classically orthodox is a focus upon objective reason, almost to the exclusion of everything else, certainly anything relating to the human heart. In the following paragraph Milbank offers a caricature of the two positions which can be construed as contemporary variations on the earlier nineteenth-century distinctions between the Roman School and the Oxford-Tübingen Schools:

> The 'romantics' think that the collapse of a reason linked to the higher *eros* led to the debasement of scholasticism and then to secular modernity. Resistance to the latter had therefore to oppose rationalism and even to insist more upon the role of the 'erotic' – the passions, the imagination, art, *ethos* etc. than had been the case up

till and including Aquinas. The exponents of 'classicism' on the other hand (largely located in the United States) trace secularity simply to a poor use of reason and regard the scholastic legacy, mainly in its 'Thomistic' form, as sustaining a true use of reason to this very day.... The conflict between these two parties is therefore one between opposed metanarratives.   (Milbank 2010: 26).

Not only are these two camps defined by their different accounts of the rise of secularism, and their different understandings of the relationship between objectivity and affectivity but they also subscribe to different understandings of the notion of upper case T tradition and different judgements about the importance of lower case t traditions in the meditation of upper case T tradition. For the 'romantics' upper case T tradition cannot be reduced to Cano's 'container of doctrines', and the lower case t traditions are vitally important for the transmission of upper case T tradition and indeed the liturgical life of the Church is the place where the tradition understood in something like Möhler or Lossky's sense is most powerfully mediated. For the classically orthodox however the tradition is defined by the catalogue of doctrines and lower case t traditions are of little interest since these are usually of their nature historically or culturally relative, and thus not easily amenable to being the subject of doctrinal formulations. As MacIntyre observed in an article on his debt to Gadamer, 'modern Thomism only exhibited an awareness of the import-ance of the historical turn and the hermeneutical turn in philosophy relatively late in its history'. He also noted that even today there are Thomists who 'regard any acknow-ledgment of the historically conditioned character of philosophical—or for that matter of scientific or historical—inquiry as making a certain kind of relativism inescapable' (MacIntyre 2002: 157). MacIntyre believes that it was one of Gadamer's achievements to have demonstrated that this is not so and Milbank similarly credits Blondel with such an achievement.

Milbank cites Romanus Cessario OP, Steven A. Long, and proponents of the Thomism of the late Ralph McInerny as exemplary of the classically orthodox position, suspicious of any entanglements with history and hermeneutics. Among the Roman-tically orthodox he lists scholars associated with both the Radical Orthodoxy and *Communio* journals, including in the latter case, Benedict XVI, as well as 'neo-patristic and sophiological currents of Orthodox thought' and 'various maverick Catholic intellectuals', namely William Desmond, Philipp Rosemann, Johannes Hoff, and Olivier-Thomas Venard OP. In the idiom of Lindbeck one could say that the 'classically orthodox' exemplify the cognitivist-propositionalist approach. In contrast, the Radical Orthodox scholars and the *Communio* scholars are more likely to follow a cultural-linguistic or dramatic approach to the whole theme of tradition. Within this, there is a place for doctrine, and certainly the *Communio* scholars are influenced by ideas about the organic development of doctrine which flow from Newman and Möhler, but their understanding of 'tradition' is much more multifaceted, broader, and deeper, than a pocket book of doctrines. They follow Blondel in seeing history and dogma as two aspects of a single reality.

In the final analysis, contemporary theology bears some of the hallmarks of the Reformation era in the sense that there is a crisis within the tradition about the very nature of tradition. While centuries of scholarship and ecumenical endeavours have narrowed the divisions over the scripture-tradition relationship, the contemporary divisions over the history-tradition relationship and subsidiary issues within the fields of hermeneutics and linguistic philosophy are generating new alignments across denominational boundaries and new divisions within both the Catholic community and the communities which trace their origins to the Reformation.

REFERENCES

Bainvel, J. V. (1905). *De Magisterio vivo et traditione*. (Paris: Gabriel Beauchesne et Cie).

Balthasar, Hans Urs von (1963). *On Theology of Revelation: A Theology of History*. (New York: Sheed and Ward).

——(1989). *Explorations in Theology, Vol. I: The Word Made Flesh*. (San Francisco: Ignatius).

Barth, K. (1956). *Church Dogmatics, Vol. 1: The Doctrine of the Word of God*. (Edinburgh: T & T Clark).

Beaumer, J. (1959). 'Die Frage nach Schrift und Tradition bei Robert Bellarmin', *Scholastik* 34, 1–22.

Billot, L. (1929). *De immutabilitate traditionis contra modernam haerim evolutionismi*. (Rome: Gregorianum).

Blanchette, O. (2010). *Maurice Blondel: A Philosophical Life*. (Grand Rapids, MI: Eerdmans).

Blondel, M. (1994). *The Letter on Apologetics and History and Dogma*, trans. Alexander Dru and Illtyd Trethowan (Grand Rapids, MI: Eerdmans).

Boeve, L. (2003). *Interrupting Tradition: An Essay on Christian Faith in a Postmodern Context*. (Louvain: Peeters Press).

Bouillard, H. (1970). *Blondel and Christianity*, trans. James M. Somerville (Washington, DC: Corpus Books).

Candler, P. (2006). *Theology, Rhetoric, Manuduction, or Reading Scripture Together on the Path to God*. (Grand Rapids, MI: Eerdmans).

Chadwick, O. (1957). *From Bossuet to Newman: The Idea of Doctrinal Development*. (Cambridge: Cambridge University Press).

Chemnitz, M. (1971). *Examination of the Council of Trent*. (St Louis: Concordia).

Congar, Y. (1960–3) *La Tradition et les traditions*, 2 vols. (Paris: Librairie Arthème Fayard).

——(2004). *The Meaning of Tradition*. (San Francisco: Ignatiu).

Cullmann, O. (1953). *La Tradition. Problème exegetique, historique et theologique*. (Neuchâtel: Cahiers Theologiques).

——(1956). 'The Tradition', *The Early Church*, ed. A. J. B. Higgins (London: SCM).

Deneffe, A. (1931). *Der Traditionsbegriff: Studie zur Theologie*. (Münster in Westfalen: Aschendorff).

Dietrich, D. J. and Himes, M. J. (1997). *The Legacy of the Tübingen School: The Relevance of Nineteenth-Century Theology for the Twenty-First*. (New York: Crossroad).

Franzelin, J. B. (1870). *Tractatus de divina traditione et scriptura*. (Rome: Sacred Congregation for the Propagation of the Faith Press).

Florovsky, G. (2004). *On Church and Tradition: An Eastern Orthodox View*. (La Canada: Holy Trinity Orthodox Mission).

Gadamer, H.-G. (1975). *Truth and Method*. (New York: Seabury).

Geenan, G. (1952). 'The Place of Tradition in the Theology of St. Thomas', *The Thomist* 15: 110–35.

Geiselmann, J. R. (1966). *The Meaning of Tradition*. (New York: Herder and Herder).

George, F. (1990). *Inculturation and Ecclesial Communion*. (Rome: Urbaniana University Press).

Granados, J. (2008). *Opening up the Scriptures: Joseph Ratzinger and Biblical Interpretation*. (Grand Rapids, MI: Eerdmans).

Guarino, T. G. (2006). 'Tradition and Doctrinal Development: Can Vincent of Lérins still Teach the Church?', *Theological Studies* 67: 34–72.

Kaplan, G. (2006). *Answering the Enlightenment: The Catholic Recovery of Historical Revelation*. (New York: Herder and Herder).

Kasper, W. (1962). *Die Lehre von der Tradition in der Römischen Schule (Giovanni Perrone, Carlo Passaglia, Clemens Schrader)*. (Freiburg: Herder).

——(1975). 'Tradition als Erkenntnisprinzip Systematische Überlegungen zur theologischen Relevanz der Geschichte', *Theologische Quartalschrift* 155: 198–215.

Lerinensis, V. (1985). *Commonitorium pro catholicae fidei antiquitate et universitate adversus profanas omnium haereticorum novitates*, in *Corpus Christianorum*, Ser. Lat. 64 (Turnhol).

Lindbeck, G. (1984). *The Nature of Doctrine: Religion and Theology in a Postliberal Age*. (Philadelphia: Westminster Press).

Lossky, V. (1995). 'Tradition and Traditions', in Daniel R. Clendenin (ed.) *Eastern Orthodox Theology*. (Grand Rapids, MI: Baker Books), 125–46.

Louth, A. (1983). *Discerning the Mystery: An Essay on the Nature of Theology*. (Oxford: Clarendon Press).

Lubac, H. De (1968). *The Sources of Revelation*, trans. Luke O'Neill (New York: Herder and Herder).

Macintyre, A. (1984). 'The Virtues, the Unity of a Human Life and the Concept of a Tradition', in Michael Sandel, (ed.), *Liberalism and its Critics*. (Oxford: Basil Blackwell), 125–48.

——(1990). *Three Rival Versions of Moral Enquiry*. (London: Duckworth).

——(2002). 'On Not Having the Last Word: Thoughts on our Debts to Gadamer', in J. Malpas, et al. (eds), *Gadamer's Century: Essays in Honour of Hans-Georg Gadamer*. (Boston: MIT Press).

Mackey, J. P. (1963). *The Modern Theology of Tradition*. (New York: Herder and Herder).

Marot, H. (1960). 'Aux origines de la théologie anglicane. Écriture et tradition chez Richard Hooker', *Irénikon* 33, 321–43.

Milbank, J. (2010). 'The New Divide: Romantic versus Classical Orthodoxy', *Modern Theology* 26: 26, 38.

Montag, J. (1999). 'The False Legacy of Suárez', in John Milbank et al. (eds), *Radical Orthodoxy*. (London: Routledge), 38–64.

Newman, J. H. (1903). *An Essay on the Development of Christian Doctrine*. (London: Longmans, Green and Co).

Nichols, A. (1990). *From Newman to Congar: The Idea of Doctrinal Development from the Victorians to the Second Vatican Council*. (Edinburgh: T & T Clark).

——(1991). *The Shape of Catholic Theology*. (Edinburgh: T & T Clark).

——(1998). *Catholic Thought Since the Enlightenment*. (Leominster: Gracewing).

——(2010). *System and Romance: The Theological Synthesis of Matthias Joseph Scheeben*. (Denver: Augustine Institute).

O'Regan, C. (1998). 'Balthasar: Between Tübingen and Postmodernity', *Modern Theology* 14: 3 (July), 325–53.

Peter, C. J. (1978). 'The Rahner-Küng Debate and Ecumenical Possibilities', in Paul C. Empie et al. (eds), *Teaching Authority and Infallibility in the Church: Lutheran and Catholics in Dialogue*. (Minneapolis: Augsburg Publishing).

Pieper, J. (2008). *Tradition: Concept and Claim*, trans. E. Christian Kopff (Wilmington: ISI).

Prickett, S. (2009). *Modernity and the Reinvention of Tradition: Backing into the Future*. (Cambridge: Cambridge University Press).

Rahner, K. (1964). *Theological Investigations*, vol. 1 (Baltimore, MD: Helicon Press).

——(1966). *Theological Investigations*, vol. 4 (Baltimore, MD: Helicon Press).

——and Ratzinger, J. (1966). *Revelation and Tradition*. (New York: Herder and Herder).

Ratzinger, J. (1969). 'Commentary on the Dogmatic Constitution on Divine Revelation', in H. Vorgrimler (ed.), *Commentary on the Documents of Vatican II*, vol. 3 (New York: Herder and Herder).

——(2007). *Jesus, the Apostles and the Early Church*. (San Francisco: Ignatius).

Rüstow, A. (1951). 'Kulturtradition und Kulturkritik', *Studium Generale* 4: 307–11.

Schumacher, B. N. (2009). *A Cosmopolitan Hermit: Modernity and Tradition in the Philosophy of Josef Pieper*. (Washington, DC: Catholic University of America Press).

Taylor, C. (2005). 'Geschlossene Weltstrukturen in der Moderne', *Wissen und Weisheit* (Münster: Dokumentation der Josef Pieper Stiftung, Band 6), 137–69.

Vanhoozer, K. J. (2003). 'Scripture and Tradition', *The Cambridge Companion to Postmodern Theology*. (Cambridge: Cambridge University Press).

——(2005). *The Drama of Doctrine: A Canonical-Linguistic Approach to Christian Theology*. (Louisville: Westminster John Knox Press).

Ward, G. (1995). *Barth, Derrida and the Language of Theology*. (Cambridge: Cambridge University Press).

SUGGESTED READING

Blondel (1994).

Candler (2006).

Congar (2004).

Cullmann (1956).

Florovsky (2004).

Geenan, G. (1952). 'The Place of Tradition in the Theology of St. Thomas', *The Thomist* 15, 110–35.

Geiselmann (1966).

Lindbeck (1984).

Lossky (1995).

Lubac, De (1968).

Montag (1999).
Newman (1903).
Nichols (1990).
Pieper (2008).
Rahner and Ratzinger (1966).
Vanhoozer (2003).

CHAPTER 14

···

MESSIANISM

···

JUDITH WOLFE

I. INTRODUCTION

···

MODERN European thought in all its aspects has been shaped and permeated by ideas and visions that first consolidated in religious or theological contexts. Of those ideas and visions, messianism—the expectation of a Messiah—is among both the most potent and the most adaptable, inflecting a wide variety of attitudes to history, politics, and anthropology in post- (as it had in pre-) Napoleonic Europe.

A latent theme of this volume as a whole is the question how the relationship between its two title terms—*theology* and *modern European thought*—is to be configured. Two possible paradigms present themselves: Either it is a matter of influence (whether by the first on the second or by the second on the first), or it turns out to be impossible to draw the clear lines that would be required to speak of the influence of one entity on another at all—impossible because ideas and visions traditionally brandmarked as specifically theological are (as Heidegger, for example, would argue) more properly analysed as existential categories rustled by religion.

The case of messianism displays the full complexity of this contest of paradigms. On the one hand, careful analysis makes clear that 'messianism' is a concept that is not unproblematically reducible to 'existentialia' in the Heideggerian sense; in other words, it does not merely point to some immanent feature of human existence whose philosophical value can be understood equally well, or better, without reference to any religious content. On the contrary, messianism is originally (and aboriginally) the fruit of revealed religion, originating in the irreducible difference, even opposition, between the divine and human realms, which the divine takes the initiative to bridge. On the other hand, the most interesting aspect of messianism in modern European thought is precisely the transposition of revelation into reason, and of the meta-historical into the intra-historical—transpositions implicitly suggesting that this immanent realm was always the true home of messianic expectation. The sometimes disastrous political and military consequences of this assumption constitute important evidence in the analysis of this concept.

The religious provenance and dimension of messianism can be focused through a juxtaposition with utopianism, with which it is often conflated. Both concepts—'messianism' and 'utopianism'—describe attitudes towards the future that are characterized by hope that a perfect society is possible and, often, imminent. But they sharply diverge in their understanding of 'possibility'. Broadly speaking, utopianism regards the perfection of human society as possible within the parameters of human nature and capability: It projects no ontological discontinuity between present and perfect humanity, but rather expects the latter to be achievable by the efforts of the former. Messianism in its pure form, by contrast, is founded on the conviction of a radical discontinuity between present human existence and the possibility of a perfect society, and consequently on the need for a Messiah: a Saviour 'anointed' by God. In bringing about a better society—a 'messianic age' of peace and joy—the Messiah is expected radically to change the present constitution of humanity, perhaps violently and to the express exclusion of parts of the human population.

Utopianism, then, has traditionally been the fruit or by-product of 'philosophies of glory', to adapt Luther's phrase: philosophies of the perfectibility of man, whether through reason or work. Plato's Republic is the earliest and most magnificent example of such a utopia of rational man. Its criticism by later generations, and the expressly satirical construction of literary 'utopias' ranging from Aristophanes' cloud cuckoo land and More's Utopia to the societies of *Gulliver's Travels* and *Brave New World*, may be taken precisely as anti-utopian professions of the imperfectability of man.

Messianism, by contrast, is the characteristic outlook of revealed religion, passed on from Judaism to Christianity and (in less strong form) to Islam. That it emerges, in the Hebrew Bible, as the hope of an oppressed people is unsurprising; what is startling and distinctive is that this people believes in the sovereignty of a God whose commands and claims not only the surrounding (enemy) peoples but also the Israelites themselves are constitutively incapable of following. Consequently, the order revealed or prophesied by this God requires a radical reversal both of collective fortunes and of the human heart.

> I will give you a new heart and put a new spirit in you; I will remove from you your heart of stone and give you a heart of flesh. And I will put my Spirit in you and move you to follow my decrees and be careful to keep my laws. Then you will live in the land I gave your ancestors; you will be my people, and I will be your God. (Ezekiel 36:26–8)

Christianity (from the word *christos*, which is the Grecization of the Hebrew *mashiach*, 'anointed') began as a Jewish movement, soon incorporating Gentiles, that distinguished itself from other forms of Judaism by the proclamation that the Messiah expected by Israel had come in the person of Jesus of Nazareth. Though messianic professions were not uncommon among Jewish sects, the claim for Jesus proved extraordinarily divisive because it drastically modified the messianic profile projected in the Hebrew Bible. Rather than merely a divinely appointed leader, the Messiah was here identified with God himself, 'made flesh and dwel[ling] among us' (John 1:14). Jesus' arrogation of the power to forgive sins, culminating in a death expressly undergone—in reference to Jewish ritual sacrifices—'for the forgiveness of sins' (Matthew 26:28), and vindicated by his resurrection from the dead, was a striking and pivotal development of the Israelite expectation of a Messiah.

Apart from its specifically theological and soteriological consequences, this Christian proclamation also had profound implications for understanding human history. Most immediately, it consolidated and radicalized the dialectical structure of promise and fulfilment governing ancient Israelite historiography. Not merely was there, now, the promise of a Messiah to come at the end of history; God himself had already come as the saviour, and by his resurrection and ascension promised a second coming at which he would raise the dead to life:

> Christ has been raised from the dead, the first fruits of those who have fallen asleep. For as by a man came death, by a man has come also the resurrection of the dead. For as in Adam all die, so also in Christ shall all be made alive. But each in his own order: Christ the first fruits, then at his coming those who belong to Christ. (1 Corinthians 15:20–3)

Among other things, this implied that God had, in a certain sense, a history: He had entered the world as a man and would enter it again. Historical existence, both of the individual and of the world as a whole, was no longer something radically dividing the created from the eternal order, but had been entered and recapitulated by God himself (see, e.g., Irenaeus of Lyons, *Against Heresies* 3). This also meant that history had a meaning: it was a 'history of salvation' that would culminate in the Second Coming of Christ, at which 'books [would be] opened' (Revelation 20:12) and the significance of all that had gone before would be revealed (see esp. Augustine, *The City of God*).

This messianic understanding of history profoundly shaped European thought both pre-modern and modern. And always, history could have two senses: collective and individual. In modernity, the archetypal collective variety has been messianic nationalism; the archetypal individual variety has been eschatological existentialism. In both areas, German culture and thought has been both paradigmatic and, perhaps, most influential. It is therefore on modern German thought that this chapter will focus.

II. Messianic Nationalism: The Example of Germany

The Christian understanding of the Messiah as God incarnate—and, consequently, of God as Spirit enfleshed (John 1:1–14, 4:24)—was profoundly influential on early modern conceptions of personhood and, perhaps more importantly, nationhood. In prominent German thinkers such as E. M. Arndt, J. G. Fichte, and G. W. F. Hegel, this metaphysical aspect of Christianity combined with its more general apocalyptic aspect into a Romantic nationalist vision of Germany.

It has been shown by Klaus Vondung and other historians that an apocalyptic imagination suffused and shaped German nationalism from its beginnings in the Napoleonic Wars. Napoleon's reign itself was interpreted apocalyptically by German writers as prominent as Johann Gottlieb Fichte, Friedrich Schlegel, and Heinrich von Kleist (see Richter 1909). At first glance, their response resembled the outbreaks of apocalyptic fervour that had accompanied so many political and social upheavals in medieval and Reformation Europe (see esp. Cohn 1972). Seen as events so terrible and incomprehensible that they could only be contained in an apocalyptic vision, Napoleon's defeat of Austria and Prussia in 1805 and 1806 led to visionary proclamations of the coming turn of the age:

> Indeed, if just beings animate and judge the world, then there is now more hope than ever, seeing how thick a cloud of presumption and iniquity, of lies and injustice, the most ruinous of goddesses, the beguiling ancient one, has gathered over the head of the great slayer. This will, indeed it must, erupt in thunder and lightning, and devastate him and the world together.   (Arndt 1910a: 83, cited in Vondung 1988: 158)[1]

But although simple, biblicist millenarian interpretations of the events—already familiar from the Turkish invasions, the Peasant Wars, the Siege of Muenster, and so forth—were advanced by some, a new, 'Romantic' nationalist eschatological narrative was developed alongside this more familiar one; it was the latter which came to define German nationalism from the Rhine Confederation to the world wars.

In the second and third volumes of his influential pamphlet collection *Spirit of the Age* (1809–14), Ernst Moritz Arndt developed an apocalyptic account of the Napoleonic age as the 'Last Holy War' against the 'Prince of Darkness and Enemy of the Sons of Light' (Arndt 1910a: 128). Although clearly influenced by earlier millenarian tracts, Arndt here facilitates a substantially different vision by shifting the traditional biblical vocabulary of a judging God to one of 'Spirit': the 'judging Spirit that moves through history'; 'the gigantic spirit that . . . rides through time' (Arndt 1910b: 111, 127–8, cited in Vondung 1988: 160). This shift enables him to identify this quasi-divine Spirit, entrusted with world judgement, with the national spirit of the Germans: 'Believe', Arndt exhorts Germany, 'this time is your time, its God and its Spirit are your God and your Spirit, and you will lead the radiant round dance of the new century.... You are the Spirit and Soul of the new history' (Arndt 1910b: 303, 305, cited in Vondung 1988: 160). This 'new century', rising from the turmoil of the French Revolution, is to be a 'third epoch of Christianity', under the rule of God as a national, 'German' deity (Ennen 1968: 15–16). Germany has here become God incarnate.

---

[1] This and all further quotations from German language sources are my own translations.

This conflation of divine 'Spirit' and German national 'spirit' had been prepared (though by no means intended for nationalist aims) by the philosophy of language of Hamann and Herder. Their conception of language was modelled on the Johannine *logos* as the creative Word of God, here associated not with the Son but with the Spirit (see Herder 1985: 104). Hamann regarded language as the expression of the soul not only of the individual but, more fundamentally, of the nation (Hamann 1821: 449; see also Vondung 1988: 170). Herder, more didactically, suggested that each language expresses or 'realizes' the 'spirit' of a people, and shapes individuals into a nation: Language 'is a divine organ of instruction, punishment and direction for everyone who has sense and ear for it.... Whoever has been educated [*erzogen*] in the same language, whoever can pour his heart into it, express his soul in it, belongs to the *people* [*Volk*] of *this language*' (Herder 1881: 287; see also Vondung 1988: 171).

Fichte—who became a defining influence on Arndt during his studies in Jena from 1793–5—echoes the claim that 'not man speaks, but human nature speaks in him, and proclaims itself to those like him' (Fichte 1912: 426). Similarly, a language develops through the fortunes and encounters of a people, and is so 'necessarily' what it is; 'not the people expresses its knowledge [*Erkenntnis*], but its knowledge itself expresses itself in them' (Herder 1881: 287). The German people is superior to other Germanic tribes because it alone, among them, has retained its primordial, 'necessary', organic language, whose acquisition educates or forms all Germans in the spirit of the German nation, which is a manifestation of spirit as such (Herder 1881: 422–5). Like its language, so the German people are pure and primordial—'a primordial people, *the* people as such' (Fichte 1912: 470). The Slavs and other 'tribes', by contrast, have adopted the language of another people (Fichte 1912: 423). The difference is absolute: 'the German speaks a language which is alive right down to its emergence from the power of nature'; the 'other Germanic tribes', by contrast, speak a language which 'stirs on the surface, but is dead at its root' (Fichte 1912: 436). In practice, this means that among Germans, all communal (that is, lingual) life is already 'intellectual formation [*Geistesbildung*]', and is, accordingly, saturated by a sense of purpose, seriousness, and diligent labour. Among other Germanic tribes, by contrast, life and intellectual formation remain separate, and its members 'drift through life unawares [*sich ... gehen lassen*]' (Fichte 1912: 438).

This primordial relation to Spirit singles out the German people for a historical destiny: 'to found the kingdom of Spirit and reason as such' (Fichte 1912: 607). Only in Fichte's time, in the depth of despair and disintegration after Prussia's defeat by Napoleon, has this Spirit revealed itself to the people. The 'forefathers' who fought in the wars of the Reformation 'did not quite know what [they] were fighting for': in addition to their own conscience, a 'higher Spirit compelled [them], which never fully revealed itself to [them]'. It is for the self-realization, the growth to 'independent existence [*eigenständiges Dasein*]' of this Spirit that German 'blood has flown' throughout history. 'It is up to you', Fichte exhorts his compatriots, 'to justify this sacrifice and realise its meaning by instating this Spirit in the world dominion destined for it' (Fichte 1912: 607). This is the *telos* of the entire history of the German people.

Again and again, Fichte describes this task in deliberately messianic language, e.g. as the resurrection of a 'glorious form' from the corpse of Germany, stepping into the 'dawn of the new world' which has already risen, and which Fichte, in his speeches—in other words, through the skilled shaping of the language that itself embodies this new spirit—will focus as in a 'mirror', to bring 'courage and hope to the weary, joy to those in deep sorrow' (Fichte 1912: 390; alluding to Jesus' messianic proclamation in Luke 4:16–20). The conclusion to his *Speeches to the German Nation* is equally explicitly messianic: To the Germans it is given 'to pass Last Judgement' on the question whether man is called to 'rise up to higher worlds' or to 'continue to slumber in a mere animal or plant-life' (Fichte 1912: 609).

> Among all the newer people it is you in whom the seed of human perfection is most decisively planted, and to whom progress in this development is entrusted. If you perish in this your essence, then all hope of the entire human race for salvation from the depths of its evils perishes with you.   (Fichte 1912: 609)

A decade later, G. W. F. Hegel develops a more systematic, detailed and wide-ranging version of the idea of national spirits. In the *Philosophy of Right* (1821), Hegel defines world history as the 'interpretation and actualization of the universal spirit' (Hegel 1942: §342). This happens through the dialectic interplay of the several 'national spirits'. Interpreting Schiller's line '*Die Weltgeschichte ist das Weltgericht*' (Schiller 1965: 133), Hegel postulates that this dialectic actualizes 'the universal spirit, the spirit of the world, free from all restriction, producing itself as that which exercises its right—and its right is the highest right of all—over these finite spirits in "world history, which is world judgement [or 'Last Judgement']" ' (Hegel 1942: §340).

In each age, one national spirit is the vehicle of that moment of the world spirit. During its epoch, 'that nation *rules* in world history', exercising the 'absolute right' of the world spirit, while 'the spirits of the other nations are without rights, and . . . count no longer in world history' (Hegel 1942: §347). The last and highest of these vehicles, for Hegel, is the 'Germanic empire' [*das Germanische Reich*], which completes the realization of the world spirit, so fulfilling the 'Last Judgement' or 'judgement of the world' (Hegel 1942: §352).

This vision was immediately absorbed into the prevailing eschatological nationalism of the German Romantics. In 1848, quoting Schiller via Hegel, Arndt writes (1912: 127–8, cited in Vondung 1988: 139), 'World history is the Last Judgement *of the peoples*'. Knowing himself an exponent of the dominant power of this last age of the history of the world spirit, and therefore as holding the interpretative key of history, he continues: 'With the judge, world history, I declare at the outset [of this tract]: the Poles and the whole Slavonic tribe are inferior to [*geringhaltiger als*] the Germans' (pp. 127–8).

Like Fichte, Arndt holds it as central that the national spirit must be realized or fulfilled through political action; in an 1810 speech, he exhorts the German people, 'You must lend this Spirit a body' (Arndt 1921: 55, cited in Vondung 1988: 175). Even F. W. J. Schelling, who emphasizes that the aspiration for an ideal state within history must end in 'apocalyptic enthusiasm' (Schelling 1958: 734), nevertheless maintains that it is the 'historical destiny of the Germans' to realize a 'true theocracy' beyond clerical government [*Priesterherrschaft*], founded on the 'reign of the known divine Spirit itself' (Schelling 1958: 728; see also Vondung 1988: 166).

III. MESSIANIC SUFFERING: POETRY AND POLITICS

The poetry of Friedrich Hölderlin, the most influential German Romantic poet, is impelled by a vision of history which is both distinctive and recognizable. In 'Brod und Wein' (1800), Hölderlin divides time into two past and one projected era: the golden age of ancient Greece, when the gods were present on earth, raising man to an almost divine height of artistic and cultural achievement; the night following the departure of the gods; and their anticipated return. The pivotal stanzas are VII and VIII.

> VII
> But friend! we come too late. The gods do live,
> But above our heads, up in another world.
> Eternally they act there, and seem to care little
> Whether we live, so much do the heavenly ones spare us.
> For not always is a weak vessel capable of containing them,
> Only sometimes does man endure divine fullness.
> Thereupon, life is a dream of them. But errancy
> Helps, like slumber, and strong make need and night,
> Until enough heroes have grown in the iron cradle,
> Hearts which resemble the gods in strength and otherwise.
> Thundering, they realize it. In the meantime, I often think it
> Better to sleep than to be thus without companions,
> To wait thus; and what to do and to say in the meantime
> I don't know, and wherefore poets in time of scarcity?
> But they are, you say, like the holy priests of the wine-god,
> Who travelled from land to land in holy night.

> VIII
> For when some time ago now—to us it seems long—
> Up rose all those whom life had made glad,
> When the Father had turned his face from us mortals
> And mourning began, rightly, all over the earth,
> When, last, a silent genius appeared, comforting
> Divinely, who announced the end of the day and left,
> Then as a sign that he had once been there and would come
> Again, the heavenly choir left several gifts,
> In which we may, as always, rejoice in humanly fashion,
> Since for spiritual joy greater things had grown too great
> Among humans, and still, still we lack those strong for highest

Joys, but silently some thanks do live on.
Bread is the fruit of the earth, but it is blessed by light,
And from the thundering god issues the joy of wine.
Therefore do we think of those in heaven when we eat and drink,
Who were here and shall return in due time,
Therefore do the singers sing earnestly of the wine-god
And not vainly invented sounds the Old One's praise.[2]

One of the striking features of this as of many Hölderlinian poems is its transposition of the Judeo-Christian idea of the suffering that the Messiah has (or had) to undergo into a destiny for Germany and the German poet. This suffering, which in the Biblical books of Isaiah and the New Testament was the result of the Messiah's rejection by his people, is here the fate of the few who are conscious enough to notice the absence of the gods.[3] This painful consciousness, for Hölderlin, is itself a quasi-messianic task; for here and elsewhere in his poetry, the return of the god is predicated precisely on the human realization of his absence. This, indeed, is the role of the poet 'in time of scarcity': to expose himself to the darkness of the present night and proclaim that darkness to his fellow men. This role is fraught with pain and risk. It requires the poet to sustain a mood of 'holy mourning' about what can no longer be invoked, leading to the 'overwhelming affliction' of needing to name what is to come. The urge is distressing because it involves the awareness that he must open himself to a darkness or emptiness which—even if his naming of them achieves its goal of hastening the coming of god— may overpower the poet (see e.g. Heidegger 1980: 18, 62–3).

Hegel, too, presents suffering as both the initial condition and the continuing character of Germany's realization of spirit. After rehearsing three previous stages in world history—those of the 'Oriental', 'Greek', and 'Roman' empires—Hegel, in the last part of his *Philosophy of Right*, turns to the final phase of the self-realization of spirit, the age of the 'Germanic empire':

> [With the disintegration of the Roman empire,] spirit and its world are . . . both alike lost and plunged into . . . infinite pain . . . . At this point, spirit is pressed back upon itself in the extreme of its absolute *negativity*. This is the absolute *turning point*; spirit rises out of this situation and grasps the *infinite positivity* of this its inward character, i.e. it grasps the principle of the unity of the divine nature and the human, the reconciliation of objective truth and freedom as the truth and freedom appearing within self-consciousness and subjectivity, a reconciliation with the fulfilment of which the Nordic principle . . . of the Germanic peoples, has been entrusted.   (Hegel 1942: §358; translation emended)

This fulfilment comes about only through a struggle (*Kampf*) between spiritual and worldly forms of the realm, culminating in the establishment of the state.

---

[2] For the German text see, e.g. Hölderlin (1970: 293–4).

[3] It is also linked by the poet to the sufferings of Dionysos, as hinted at 'Bread and Wine' itself, a link that raises issues that go far beyond the scope of this article and can only be noted here.

These two realms stand distinguished from one another, though at the same time they are rooted in a *single* unity and Idea. Here their distinction is intensified to absolute opposition, and a stern struggle [*Kampf*] ensues, in the course of which the realm of spirit lowers the place of its heaven to an earthly here and now, to a common worldliness of fact and idea. The mundane realm, on the other hand, builds up its abstract independence into thought and the principle of rational being and knowing, i.e. into the rationality of right and law. In this way, their opposition *as such* loses its marrow and disappears. The realm of fact has discarded its barbarity and unrighteous caprice, while the realm of truth has abandoned the world of beyond and its arbitrary force, so that the true reconciliation which discloses the *state* as the image and actuality of reason has become objective. (Hegel 1942: §360; trans. emended)

The suffering involved in the realization of spirit is a necessary concomitant of the struggle of welding together the spiritual and the worldly.

In some sense dormant during the time of the German Confederation and much of the German Empire, this apocalyptic vision—centred on the German national spirit as that which will, in its political self-fulfilment, bring salvation to the whole world (see Schenkendorf 1815: 6, cited in Vondung 1988: 189; Fichte 1911: 568)—was revived during the First World War. Hundreds of war poems, sermons, and lectures invoked it, frequently with reference to Fichte, Hegel, and Arndt (see Vondung 1988: 197). However, an important shift had occurred: What was required to bring the German spirit to fulfilment, now, was not merely educational or even political action, but military action; the suffering exacted was death on the battlefield.

Friedrich Gogarten described the German national spirit as bearer of revelation and so agent of salvation: 'To our highest thoughts, the German people and the German spirit are the revelation of eternity' (Gogarten 1915: col. 55, cited in Vondung 1988: 191). Sociologist Johann Plenge described the war as a 'crusade in the service of World Spirit', whose highest developmental stage was represented by Germany—for which reason the German crusade would 'redound to the salvation of the world' (Plenge 1915: 200). Pastor Karl König, having equated 'the history of the divine spirit [*göttliche Geistesgeschichte*]' with 'the history of the human spirit', states his conviction that the latter would find its fulfilment in the German spirit. Germany, consequently, *had to* win the apocalyptically interpreted war, 'simply because this is a necessity of the history of the human and divine spirit on this earth' (König 1915: 6). Philosopher Rudolf Eucken, too, insisted that Germany must win the war, as a defeat would 'rob world history of its deepest meaning' and 'signify the downfall of human history' (Eucken 1914: 22). Adolf Lasson, another philosopher, concurred in this spiritual interpretation of Germany's military power: 'Our army and navy too are a spiritual power' (Lasson 1914). And König again: 'This army is an embodiment of our national spirit' (König 1915: 15, cited in Vondung 1988: 204). Indeed, the attitude is so common as to be satirized in Karl Kraus' *Last Days of Mankind*, in whose epilogue 'Dr.-Ing. Abendrot from Berlin' appears as a self-declared 'knight of the Spirit' ('Ritter vom Geist'), who concocts lethal gas '[u]m endlich den endlichen Endsieg zu kriegen, und dann also endlich unendlich zu siegen' ('to finally gain the final final victory, and therefore finally infinitely to triumph') (Kraus 1992: 278).

This is the quasi-religious nationalist imagination which educated National Socialist leaders such as Arthur Moeller van den Bruck, Adolf Hitler, Alfred Rosenberg, and Joseph Goebbels received and refashioned.

IV. National Socialism as a Messianic Ideology

The National Socialist development of German apocalyptic nationalism was defined by a persistent tension between opposing definitions of the German *Volk*. Leading Nazi thinkers such as Adolf Hitler, Joseph Goebbels, and Alfred Rosenberg described the *Volk* not as a spiritual entity but as a body defined by 'blood and soil', a 'race' (see esp. Darré 1943). Other voices, often associated with the university, such as the student poets Gerhard Schumann and Herbert Böhme and the philosopher Martin Heidegger, persisted in an older understanding of the *Volk* as an entity of spirit called to a spiritual destiny. Although in practice and for the most part, this understanding of the *Volk* was successfully integrated into the politics and culture of the *Reich*, it nevertheless stood in marked contrast to the dominant ideology informing that system—an ideology encapsulated in Hitler's definition of 'the people as such as a substance of flesh and blood' (Hitler 1938b, cited in Vondung 1988: 208). The seminal work of this religio-racial approach to nationalism is Alfred Rosenberg's programmatic *Myth of the Twentieth Century* (1930). In this extremely influential historical-philosophical study, Rosenberg—an early member and intellectual leader of the NSDAP and editor of the *Völkische Beobachter* from 1921—propounds a 'religion of blood', replete with a 'metaphysics' of 'race', to supersede Christianity (Rosenberg 1930: 23). Rosenberg writes:

> Humanity, universal church, and the autocratic 'I' detached from blood relations, are to us no longer absolute values, but desperate, already decaying principles introduced by a polarity-less rape of nature for the sake of abstractions. The flight of the nineteenth century into Darwinism and positivism was the first great, though merely brutish protest against the ideals of powers that had become void of life and air, powers that had once swept over us from Syria and Asia Minor and prepared an intellectual degeneration. What was disregarded by this Christianness and *humanitas*, constantly dissolving into the All, was the stream of blood-red, real life, which rushes through the veins of all true peoples and every culture; or else, blood was desouled into a chemical formula and so 'explained'. But today, an entire race is beginning to sense that values can only be created and sustained where the law of blood determines the ideas and deeds of man, whether consciously or unconsciously.   (Rosenberg 1930: 22)

Rosenberg's conclusion echoes, in its apocalyptic fervour, that of Fichte's *Reden an die deutsche Nation*, but shifts Fichte's focus from a regime of spirit to one of blood. What the study of history in the context of racial theory [*Rassenkunde*] reveals, Rosenberg claims, is

> the terrible consciousness that today we are faced with a final decision. Either we will, through the renewed experience and cultivation [*Hochzucht*] of the ancient blood, together with a heightened will to fight [*Kampfwillen*], rise to a purifying achievement, or even the last Germanic-occidental values of civilisation and national breeding [*Staatenzucht*] will sink into the dirty floods of people of the world cities, will be stunted on the blistering, infertile asphalt of a bestializing inhumanity, or will drain away as infectious germs in the form of self-bastardizing emigrants to South America, China, Dutch India, Africa.   (Rosenberg 1930: 82)

Apocalyptic nationalism—whether focused on national spirit or blood—typically involves a conceptual replacement of the millennial reign of the Church by that of the nation; often, as in both the Fichtean and the Hitlerite variants, it insists on a realization of this reign through political and military action. This apocalyptic fervour for the forceful realization of the kingdom comes to stirring expression in the poetry of Böhme and Schumann. Böhme, later *Reichsfachschaftsleiter* (leader of the Reich's professional association) for poetry, writes in *Bekenntnisse eines jungen Deutschen* (1935): 'We believe in the vocation of our people, and in the living sacrifice of our dead for the immortal greatness of our work, the Germans' desire, the eternal *Reich*' (Boehme 1935: 28). And again: 'This faith means nothing other than: Germany.|Germany, understood celestially, a people in all its infinity, that is the *Reich*' (Boehme 1935: 32).

This identification of eschatological kingdom with earthly *Reich*, and the consequent need for its political and military realization, is a foundation stone of National Socialist ideology. In some cases, this appropriation seems quite unconscious. Goebbels, for example, naturally uses religiously inflected language to express his nationalist sentiments. On 16 October 1925, upon the passing of the Locarno Treaties, he notes angrily in his diary:

> I'm about to lose faith in humanity! Why were these peoples given Christianity? Only to play fast and loose with it! Where is the man who will drive these hucksters with a whip out of the temple Nation! Is the whole world destined for downfall? If it weren't for us, despair . . . .   (Goebbels 1960: 35)

But more often, the programme is explicit. Thus, the title of Arthur Moeller van den Bruck's programmatic *Das dritte Reich* (1923) is chosen not only by analogy to the two preceding 'German' empires, but also in explicit reference to the 'Third Reich' prophesied by the twelfth-century Christian apocalypticist Joachim of Fiore—the millennial kingdom of Christ (see Bärsch 1998: B. I.1–2). The Christian press did not miss the challenge implied in this claim: The Catholic journal *Hochland* publically criticized Moeller van den Bruck and the NSDAP as early as 1931 for applying a term properly belonging to a truly universal Christian kingdom to a secular political 'Ersatzreich' (see Rosenstock-Huessy 1931).

In his prefatory letter to Heinrich von Gleichen, Moeller van den Bruck describes his vision in greater detail, picking up the entire tradition of apocalyptic nationalism:

> Instead of government by party we offer the ideal of the THIRD EMPIRE. It is an old German conception and a great one. It arose when our First Empire fell; it was early quickened by the thought of a millennium; but its underlying thought has always been a future which should be not the end of all things but the dawn of a German Age in which the German People would for the first time fulfil their destiny on earth . . . .
>
> We must be careful to remember that the thought of the Third Empire is a philosophical idea; that the conceptions which the words 'Third Empire' arouse— and the book that bears the title—are misty, indeterminate, charged with feeling; not of this world but of the next . . . . This dream would be lethal to the Germans if they contented themselves with merely day-dreaming about it . . .
>
> Let us [therefore] be perfectly explicit: the thought of the Third Empire—to which we must cling as our last and highest philosophy—can only bear fruit if it is translated into concrete reality. It must quit the world of dreams and step into the political world. It must be as realist as the problems of our constitutional and national life; it must be as sceptical and pessimistic as beseems the times.   (Moeller van den Bruck 1934: 13–14)

The Antichrist of this national apocalypse is not now Napoleon but the Jew, deploying Marxism as his tool of deception and domination. In his tellingly titled speech *Der entscheidende Weltkampf* ('The decisive world struggle'), given at the Party Congress in Nuremberg in 1936, then-*Reichsleiter* Alfred Rosenberg characteristically refers to the Soviet Union as 'Sowjet-Judäa' (Rosenberg 1936: 2; see also Bärsch 1998: B. I.2.c, B. I.3.c). Similarly, Goebbels writes in praise of Nashivin's *Rasputin*, 'A grandiose portrait of Russian Bolshevism . . . but oppressive in its cruelty. Thus may the devil rage when he rules the world. The Jew must be the Antichrist of world history' (Goebbels 1960: 85). And Hitler declares in *Mein Kampf*:

> If the Jew, with the aid of his Marxist creed, should triumph over the peoples of this world, then his crown will be the dance of death of humanity, then this planet will once again, as millions of years ago, move through the ether devoid of human life.
>
> Eternal nature mercilessly avenges the violation of her laws.
>
> Thus I believe myself to be acting on behalf of the almighty Creator: By resisting the Jew, I fight [*kämpfe*] for the work of the Lord.   (Hitler 1938a: 69-70; see also Kurz 2002: 134)

While in this passage, Hitler portrays the *Reich* as the realization of Judeo-Christian aspiration, it is more typical of *Mein Kampf* to call for a conscious replacement of Christian hope by nationalist fervour—a harnessing of the emotional power of religious faith for a decidedly different object.

> At a time, however, at which one side, equipped with all the weapons of a *Weltanschauung* (albeit an infinitely criminal one), forms up to fight against the prevailing order, the other can resist for good only if its resistance clothes itself in the forms of a new, in our case political faith, and exchanges the shibboleths of a weak

and cowardly defence for the battle cry of courageous and brutal attack.   (Hitler 1938a: 414)

And more fully:

> The term 'völkisch' functions similarly as the term 'religious'. Both already imply some few fundamental insights. But both, even if eminently significant, are so indeterminate in their form that they rise above the value of mere opinion, to be accepted or rejected at will, only by being incorporated, as basic elements, into the framework of a political party. For the realisation of visionary [weltanschauungs-mäßiger] ideals and the demands they entail are no more achieved through the mere feelings or inner wishes of the people than the attainment of freedom is achieved through mere desire for it. No: only when the ideal urge for independence is organised for battle [kampfesmäßig] by military means of power can the urgent wish of a people be transformed into glorious reality.   (Hitler 1938a: 417–18)

It is noteworthy that this apocalypse is motivated not teleologically, but genealogically: Rather than moving towards a previously revealed eschatological kingdom, as in Christian apocalypticism, or a dialectically projected self-realization of spirit, as in Hegelian nationalism, Hitlerite nationalism has a *source*—the right to *Lebensraum* inscribed in the *völkisch* blood—, but no clear *goal*. Symptomatically, then, National Socialist rhetoric is suffused by the idea of 'wresting' or 'hoicking' the people from 'the depths' (*aus der Tiefe reissen*)—not by that (characteristic of Herder, Hegel, and Fichte) of 'raising them to the heights'. This emphasis on the depths from which, rather than the heights to which, the German people must heroically rise, are all apparent in Hitler's *Mein Kampf*:

> Germany is, today, the next great strategic goal [Kampfziel] of Bolshevism. It requires all the energy of a young, missionary-style [missionshaften] idea to hoick our people, wresting them from the coils of this international serpent and arresting the contamination of our blood from within. The powers of the nation thus released may then be used for the safeguarding of our peoplehood [Sicherung unseres Volkstum], which may, until time everlasting, prevent a repetition of recent catastrophes.   (Hitler 1938a: 751–2)

Most explicit about the replacement of Christianity with an apocalyptically motivated nationalism is Heinrich Himmler. The Reich Security Head Office, which he created in 1939 as a merger of the *SD*, the *Gestapo* and the Criminal Police, included a department concerned with the churches (*Kirchenabteilung*). Here, as Wolfgang Dierker describes, 'the abolition of the Christian churches was seen merely as part of an entire transformation of man and society, which was pressed ahead with in the consciousness of knowing the laws of historical development *and its final state*'. (Dierker 2002: 538). Thus, Himmler's SS-*Sturmbannführer* and head of department IV B for 'Political Catholicism' in the Reich Security Head Office quite consistently demanded in 1940 a 'final solution of the religious question' (cited from MS in Dierker 2002: 547).

Hitlerite apocalyptic nationalism also incorporates the idea of suffering in both its aspects: that of the 'infinite pain' out of which the German spirit wrests its identity, and that of the 'struggle' [Kampf] involved in this wresting—an agonizing struggle to weld together spirit and political reality. Moeller van den Bruck describes the condition from which this *Reich* will be born as one of pain and mourning:

> Over Germany, to-day only one flag is flying, the token of mourning and the symbol of our life: one only flag, which tolerates no colour near it, and robs the people who move below its sable folds of all their joy in merry pennons and in gaudy standards: only the black flag of need, humiliation and an utter bitterness—a bitterness which clothes itself in self-control lest it should pass into despair. (Moeller van den Bruck 1934: 242–3)

Hitler and Goebbels concretized this idea of the birth of an eschatological kingdom from suffering (symbolized, for van den Bruck, by the 'sable flag'), in the ritual celebration of the (failed) Beer Hall Putsch of November 1923, presented as the birth pangs or messianic woes of the coming kingdom. Only at these celebrations was the 'banner of blood' (*Blutfahne*) carried at the putsch displayed to the public (see Vondung 2005: 88), and the quasi-liturgical texts accompanying them presented the death of sixteen of Hitler's followers as a sacrifice necessary for the subsequent victory. In correspondence with the 'sacral event' of 1923, Vondung argues, 'Hitler's seizure of power was interpreted as a second sacral event which made true the revelation of 9 November. The content of this revelation was the *Reich* under National Socialist rule.... As an eternal *Reich* it was considered to be the final period of the National Socialist "history of salvation" ' (Vondung 2005: 92).

A similar message was conveyed by the poetic centrepiece of the great festival meeting of the Reich Culture Chamber, staged by Goebbels at the National Opera in Berlin in May 1936. 'Heldische Feier' was a long liturgical poem by Gerhard Schumann (1911–95), who was active in the National Socialist student government, and was awarded the *Deutsche Buchpreis* for the collection in which it appeared. The poem, full of eschatological language, concludes:

> The cathedral rises to stupendous heights . . .
> For all the world a never-resting monument to the dead.—
>
> And suddenly there arises over the cacophony . . .
> Alone and grand in the sky that opened for it,
> The image of the *Feldherrnhalle* bathed in red.
>
> We build the eternal *Feldherrnhallen* of the *Reich*,
> The steps into eternity,
> Until the hammers slip from our fists.
> Then immure us in the altars.   (Schumann 1935: 77; see also Baird 1990: 141–3)

The vision of the nation as both the subject and the object of an eschatological faith, born from, and in, suffering and struggle, pervades Schumann's poetry, often focused emblematically in Hitler as the suffering Messiah. The seventh sonnet of Schumann's cycle *Die Lieder vom Reich* (1935) places Hitler in the Garden of Gethsemane:

> Then night came. The one stood, wrestling in mortal agony.
> Blood flowed from the eyes which, seeing,

Died in the face of the terror
That rose from the valleys to the peak.

Cry of agony arose and broke harshly and anxiously.
Despair, at the end of its strength, grasped at nothing.
He reared, trembling in fear of the heaviness –
Until the command forced him to his knees.

But as he rose the firelight
of the chosen one shone round his head. And descending
He carried the torch into the night.
The millions bowed to him in silence,

Delivered. The heavens flamed with the pale flame of morning.
The sun rose. And with it rose the Reich.   (Schumann 1936: 20)

V. Jewish Messianism

The triumphalist messianism of the German nationalists both in the era of the First World War and during the National Socialist regime stood in stark contrast to the largely pessimistic messianism of prominent Jewish thinkers. Although this chapter is not the place examine modern Jewish messianism per se, a generalization of the import of a handful of influential Jewish writers and philosophers will be instructive.

In 1885, the official platform of Reformed Jews changed the hope expressed in the Amidah (Judaism's daily office of prayers) for a *go-el*, a redeemer, to *geulah*, redemption—a change expressly linked to Hegel's vision of an 'ever more enlightened' society (see CCAR 2004). The Central Conference of American Rabbis, in its Commentary on the Principles for Reform Judaism, signals retrospective reservations about this decision, whose optimism was 'smashed' by the '[t]he cataclysmic events of the first half of the 20th century' (CCAR 2004).

In Ernst Bloch's Marxist utopianism, the Hegelian hope for progress is still apparent. Bloch regarded religious messianic language as the husk of an elaboration of human possibility which it was his task to uncover and recast in the language of utopianism (see esp. Geoghegan 1996: ch. 3). Particularly in the revolutionary apocalyptic rhetoric and action of Joachim of Fiore and Thomas Müntzer did Bloch see the beginnings of such a (re-)translation of messianism into utopianism, and so models for his own and Marxism's work (see Bloch 1977).

> Man still lives everywhere in his pre-history; indeed, everything is still poised before the creation of the world as a just and right one. True genesis occurs not in the beginning but in the end, and it only begins to begin when society and existence are radicalized, i.e. grasp themselves by the root. But the root of history is man, working, creating, changing and outstripping his conditions. When man grasps himself and roots that which is his without self-renunciation and -alienation in real democracy, something emerges in the world which radiates into everyone's childhood and where no one yet has been: home.   (Bloch 1985: 1628)

Walter Benjamin (1892–1940), by contrast, fiercely contests any continuity between 'profane' history and the coming of the Messiah:

> Only the Messiah himself completes all historical occurrences, namely in the sense that he first redeems, fulfils, and creates the relation of the latter to the Messianic. This is why nothing historical can attempt to relate itself to the Messianic. This is why the kingdom of God is not the *telos* of the historical *dynamis*; it cannot be posited as the latter's goal. From the perspective of history, it is not goal but end. (Benjamin 1977: 203)

This impossibility of anticipating the Messiah in history leads, for Benjamin, to the necessity of viewing history as both doomed to catastrophe and tragically unable to end. In the ninth thesis of 'On the Concept of History', Benjamin expresses this pessimism in quasi-religious language:

> There is a picture by Klee called Angelus Novus. It depicts an angel who seems to be about to depart from something at which he stares. His eyes and mouth are wide open and his wings unfurled. The angel of history must look like that. His face is turned towards the past. Where a chain of events appears before *us*, *he* sees one enormous catastrophe incessantly heaping ruins on ruins and flinging them at his feet. Fain would he tarry, rouse the dead, and join what is broken. But a storm blows from Paradise, which has been caught in his wings and is so strong that the angel can no longer furl them. This storm drives him relentlessly into the future, to which his back is turned, while the heap of ruins before him mounts up to heaven. What we call progress is this storm.   (Benjamin 2007: 317)

Hannah Arendt gives this a specifically anti-Hegelian reading: the 'angel of history' does not 'dialectically advance, his face facing forward to the future', but faces the past. But his wish to tarry, rouse the dead, and join what is broken ('which would supposedly bring the end of history') is denied him by the guardians of Paradise, who repel intruders not only by the sword but by a stormy headwind (Arendt and Benjamin 2006: 59).

This is a distinctively Jewish vision, in which the 'transcendent' element of a Messiah has been separated from the expectation of apocalyptic cataclysm. Because only the Messiah, who cannot be anticipated from within history, could redeem history, history is forced to undergo apocalypse after apocalypse without thereby being ended.

> . . . I hardly feel the need to make sense of the state of the world in general. A great many cultures have already perished in blood and horror on this planet. Of course one must wish that it will one day experience one that has left both behind — indeed, I am inclined to assume that it waits for one such. But whether *we* are capable of laying such a gift on its three hundred- or four hundred-millionth birthday table is, alas, very questionable.   (Letter to Werner Kraft, 28 October 1935; Benjamin 1999: 193)

Karl Kraus (1874–1936), like so many Jewish writers and artists after him, is another German-speaking Jew who turns the Jewish messianic sensibility towards the apocalyptic rather than the redemptive. Kraus's satirical play *The Last Days of Mankind* depicts the First World War, and ends with an apocalyptic scenario. Over a grotesque battlefield, on which the 'lord of hyenas' has led his pack in a waltz among the corpses, the apocalypse descends: A meteor shower is followed by flames, 'world thunder', and finally 'doom'. The last words are the voice of God: 'I did not want this' (Kraus 1992: 280). This chillingly ambiguous statement, ironically echoing Kaiser Wilhelm, is equally an apology to the world and a repudiation of it—God is unwilling to take the world home, and it is doomed to go on by itself.

VI. Messianism and Philosophy: The Case of Martin Heidegger

The perpetuation of apocalyptic anxiety or even horror without any clear hope of an inbreaking of God to end or vindicate it is a characteristic of much modern Jewish (anti-)messianism: Outside the German boundaries of the present chapter, it also appears in Jacques Derrida's work, where messianism becomes a version of *différance*—one more sign in whose nature it is to project a *telos* which, contrary to appearances, is nevertheless not the origin but merely an effect of the sign, and so can be neither reached nor eliminated.

But perhaps the philosophical figure who represents the most interesting crossroads between nationalist messianism, 'existential' and deconstructionist anti-messianism, and a residual religious messianism, is Martin Heidegger.[4] Recent research into Heidegger's early theological training and work has made it clear that his earliest attempts to formulate a phenomenological account of human existence are both motivated and fuelled by religious—including eschatological—interests and ideas (see esp. Wolfe 2012). In his endeavour to give a phenomenological account of human existence, Heidegger turned to the discovery of eschatology as a central preoccupation of the Early Church by A. Schweitzer, the 'History of Doctrine' school, and especially Franz Overbeck.

Some of Heidegger's earliest phenomenological investigations were devoted to the eschatology of St Paul and of Augustine (see Heidegger 2011). In these investigations, Heidegger arrived at the postulation of an existential sense of eschatological unrest as the central characteristic of authentic Christian experience, and so of authentic existence in general. In his lecture series *Introduction to the Phenomenology of Religion*, Heidegger takes the fifth chapter of Paul's Epistle to the Thessalonians as his text: '[You] know very well that the day of the Lord will come like a thief in the night.... But you, beloved, are not in darkness, for that day to surprise you like a thief.... So then, let us not fall asleep as others do, but let us keep awake and sober' (1 Thessalonians 5:1–5).

---

[4] See Michael Gillespie, chapter 18 in this volume, for another view of Heidegger's political messianism.

For Heidegger, the phenomenological significance of this passage lies in the fact that Paul's expectation of the *parousia* is not controlled by speculation about the exact time of Christ's return but, on the contrary, effects a complete transformation of his experience of time or temporality as such. It calls forth a subjective experience of time 'without order and fixed spots, which cannot be grasped by any objective notion of time', and thus gives rise to eschatological 'affliction' (*Bedrängnis*), characterized by an existential insecurity or uncertainty that arouses an intense 'watchfulness' that cannot be delegated to any third party (Heidegger 2011: 98, 104).

Heidegger's description of this expectant restlessness, however, is inescapably at odds with its Christian sources, since the philosopher's commitment to a phenomenological (i.e. immanent) description of the human situation leads him to abstract the 'existential' experience of expectation from its traditional object: the 'blessed hope' for the Kingdom of God. The object of eschatological 'care' or 'affliction' is now no longer (as for Paul) the dark and death-filled world *inflected by* its imminent 'solicitation' by Christ, but only that world in its transience. Against the Christian vision, Heidegger in the mid- to late 1920s thus develops a systematic 'eschatology without eschaton' that finds paradigmatic expression in his account of being-unto-death, and underlies both his critique of theology and his reconception of metaphysics. On this account, the Being of *Dasein* is, at its most authentic, a *question* for each *Dasein*. This question cannot be answered or resolved in any traditional sense, because the consummation of Dasein—death—is at the same time its negation. Authentic existence (paradigmatically exhibited by the early Christians) is the resolute living of this perpetual, inavertible, and inescapably personal (*eigentlich*) possibility—it is *Sein zum Tode* (being-unto-death).

One of the most controversial aspects of Heidegger's thought is his temporary espousal, not long after the publication of *Being and Time*, of elements of National Socialist ideology, and his membership in the NSDAP. There is a persistent worry among Heidegger's readers that his phenomenology is intrinsically related to his Nazism. The eschatological dimension of his early thought reveals both that there is a connection and that it is by no means necessary.

Heidegger's National Socialist ideas are developed primarily in speeches (most famously his inaugural lecture upon accession to the rectorate of the University of Freiburg, 'The Self-Assertion of the German University', 1933) and in his lectures on Hölderlin (1934–6). Heidegger embraces Hölderlin's description of the poet's (and philosopher's) task of embattled anticipation of what is to come, and consolidates his own move, towards the end of *Being and Time*, away from a focus on the individual's future to a focus on the destiny of the people (*Volk*). Thus, in his inaugural address, he transposes his earlier juxtaposition of authentic existence and dispersion in the crowd into a collective register: In 1933, is it no longer an orientation towards one's individual future (with its inavertible end) that enables authentic existence, but a quasi-Fichtean concentration of life in the service of a higher law, given to the people by its own spirit. This vision of a national spirit focused in the messianic figure of the *Führer* is even clearer in Heidegger's 'Exhortation to the German Students' the same year:

May the courage to sacrifice [yourselves] for the salvation of the essence and the exaltation of the innermost power of our people in its state grow in you unceasingly. Not theorems or 'ideas' should be the rules of your being. Rather, the *Führer* himself and alone *is* the present and future German reality and its law .... *Heil Hitler*. (Martin 1989: 177)

It is clear from the opening and closing paragraphs of the inaugural address that Heidegger does not adopt the identification of the *Volk* by blood of Rosenberg and Hitler, but an identification by spirit familiar from Romantic nationalism. 'The assumption of the rectorate', he writes, 'is the commitment to the spiritual leadership of this institution of higher learning'. But this spiritual leadership requires that 'the leaders, first and foremost and at any time, are themselves led—led by the relentlessness of that spiritual mission [*geistiger Auftrag*] that forces the destiny of the German people into the shape of its history' (Neske and Kettering 1990: 5).

Herman Philipse argues in *Heidegger's Philosophy of Being* that Heidegger's turn from his call to authenticity in *Being and Time* to his exhortation to faith in Hitler in 1932–3 is explicable 'psychologically' if we understand the account of authenticity as the first step of a 'Pascalian strategy' according to which 'an analysis of the human condition should reveal that authentic existence is an unbearable burden, from which we try to escape into forms of inauthenticity or diversion' (Philipse 1998: 266). The only alternative (and this is the second step of this alleged Pascalian and/or Kierkegaardian strategy) is a 'leap to faith'. 'The lectures on the fundamental concepts of metaphysics of 1929–30 aim at preparing us for a religious conversion, as did *Was ist Metaphysik?* and Kierkegaard's *The Present Age*' (Philipse 1998: 268). Philipse claims that the years 1930–2 brought the disappointing realization that grace was not forthcoming. The result, he claims, was a turn to Nazism as an alternative 'salvation'.

Though superficially attractive, this explanation is implausible. In fact, it is the prior rejection of the necessary or even possible irruption of a transcendent God which made Heidegger's belief in Hitler as *Führer* ('guide'/'leader') into a new, metaphysical age possible, though by no means necessary.

Heidegger's actual movement is inverse to that which Philipse suggests. Rather than embracing Nazism out of disappointment with an absconded God, Heidegger develops, in the late 1930s and beyond, a future eschatology out of disappointment with Hitler. In his 1946 talk on Hölderlin and Rilke, 'Wherefore Poets?', Heidegger no longer argues, as he had done in the early and mid-1930s, that the eschatology articulated by Hölderlin has been (or is about to be) realized. But what has been given up is only the identification of Hölderlin's coming god with the Third *Reich*, not the messianic orientation as such:

'And wherefore poets in time of scarcity?' The word 'time' here means the world age to which we ourselves still belong. The appearance and sacrificial death of Christ ushered in, for Hölderlin's experience of history, the end of the day of the gods [*das Ende des Göttertages*]. Evening falls. Since the 'united/agreeing/few three' ['*einigen drei*'], Heracles, Dionysius and Christ, have left the world, the evening of world time is descending into its night. The night of the world is spreading its darkness. The world age is determined by the staying-away of God, by the 'absconsion of God'. (Heidegger 1950: 269)

What is required, in this time, is holiness, not as an end in itself but as a preparation for a god who can only come from without:

> The turn of the age does not happen by a new god, or the old one anew, bursting from his ambush. Where should he turn upon his return, if no dwelling has been prepared for him by mankind? How could there be a god-fitting dwelling for the god if a glow of divinity has not first begun to shine in all that is?   (Heidegger 1950: 270)

This enigmatic stance is vigorously repeated in the interview given to *Spiegel* in 1963, published shortly after his death in 1976; an interview which, in its attempted rehabilitation of Heidegger's National Socialist phase, insists on precisely this need for openness to a god who must come from without, or doom humankind by remaining absent:

> HEIDEGGER: Those questions bring us back to the beginning of our conversation. If I may answer quickly and perhaps somewhat vehemently, but from long reflection: Philosophy will not be able to bring about a direct change of the present state of the world. This is true not only of philosophy but of all merely human meditations and endeavours. Only a god can still save us. I think the only possibility of salvation left to us is to prepare readiness, through thinking and poetry, for the appearance of the god or for the absence of the god in our downfall; so that we do not, crudely put, 'croak', but that if we perish, we perish in the face of the absent god.
> ... [Philosophy and the individual can do nothing except] this preparation of the readiness to keep oneself open to the arrival or absence of the god. Even the experience of this absence is not nothing, but rather a liberation of human beings from what I called the 'fallenness into what is' in *Being and Time*. A contemplation of what *is* today is part of a preparation of the readiness we have been talking about.
> SPIEGEL: But then there really would have to be the famous impetus from outside, from a god or whomever. So thinking, of its own accord and self-sufficiently, can no longer be effective today? It was, in the opinion of people in the past, and even, I believe, in our opinion.
> HEIDEGGER: But not directly. (Heidegger 1988: 100–1)

VII. CONCLUSION

The role of messianism in modern German thought and culture has been both pervasive and diverse, and research into its sources, forms, and implications is still in its early stages. Among the necessary tasks of further research are comparative studies of messianism and utopianism (as exemplified, most influentially, in Marxist ideologies), and of the messianic nationalisms of the great European nations, including France and, perhaps most importantly, Russia. The interplay of Russia's nationalist messianism (centred on the kenotic peasant Christ and belief in a future as the 'Third Rome') and its utopian communism deserves full-length study.

Amid the appropriation of messianism in 'secular' European thought and culture, it is also important to remember that a simple, devotional anticipation of Christ's second coming, though waxing and waning, has never died in the Christian west, and is shared (though in the context of a different understanding of Jesus) by Islam. Neither has Judaism surrendered belief in the coming of the Messiah as a central tenet of its religion; in its morning prayer, it professes according to Maimonides' thirteen principles of faith: 'I believe with perfect faith in the coming of the Messiah. And though he may tarry, yet I will wait for him every day till he comes'. Amid and alongside historiographical, political, and philosophical accounts of modern messianism, theology has its own task in speaking for and about such religious hope.

REFERENCES

Arendt, H. and Benjamin, W. (2006). *Arendt und Benjamin: Texte, Briefe, Dokumente*, ed. D. Schöttker (Frankfurt: Suhrkamp).

Arndt, E. M. (1910a). *Ernst Moritz Arndts Sämtliche Werke, vol. 9: Geist der Zeit 2*, ed. E. Schirmer (Magdeburg: Magdeburger Verlagsanstalt).

——(1910b). *Ernst Moritz Arndts Sämtliche Werke, vol. 10: Geist der Zeit 3*, ed. E. Schirmer (Magdeburg: Magdeburger Verlagsanstalt).

——(1912). *Werke: Auswahl in Zwölf Teilen*, vol. 12, ed. W. Steffens (Berlin: Bong).

——(1921). *Hoffnungsrede vom Jahre 1810*, ed. E. Gülzow (Greifswald: Verlag Dr K. Moninger).

Baird, J. W. (1990). *To Die for Germany: Heroes in the Nazi Pantheon*. (Bloomington, IN: Indiana University Press).

Bärsch, C. (1998). *Die politische Religion des Nationalsozialismus*. (Munich: W. Fink).

Benjamin, W. (1977). *Gesammelte Schriften*, vol. 11:1, ed. R. Tiedermann and H. Schweppenhäuser, (Frankfurt: Suhrkamp).

——(1999). *Gesammelte Briefe*, vol. 5: 1935-7, ed. C. Gödde and H. Lonitz (Frankfurt: Suhrkamp),

——(2007). *Kairos: Schriften zur Philosophie*, ed. R. Konersmann (Frankfurt: Suhrkamp).

Bloch, E. (1968). *Atheismus im Christentum*. (Frankfurt: Suhrkamp).

——(1977). *Thomas Müntzer als Theologe der Revolution*. (Frankfurt: Suhrkamp).

——(1985). *Das Prinzip Hoffnung*. (Frankfurt: Suhrkamp).

Böhme, H. (1935). *Bekenntnisse eines Jungen Deutschen*. (Munich: Eher).

CCAR (2004). 'Commentary on the Principles for Reform Judaism'. http://ccarnet.org/ Articles/index.cfm?id=45&pge_prg_id=4687&pge_id=1656 accessed 27 October 2011.

Cohn, N. R. C. (1972). *The Pursuit of the Millennium*. (New York: Oxford University Press).

Darré, W. R. (1943). *Neuadel aus Blut und Boden*. (Berlin: J. F. Lehmanns Verlag).

Dierker, W. (2002). *Himmlers Glaubenskrieger: Der Sicherheitsdienst der SS und seine Religionspolitik, 1933-1941*. (Paderborn: Schöningh).

Ennen, E. (1968). 'Ernst Moritz Arndt: 1769-1860', *Bonner Gelehrte: Beiträge zur Geschichte der Wissenschaften in Bonn*. (Bonn: H. Bouvier), 9-35.

Eucken, R. (1914). *Die weltgeschichtliche Bedeutung des deutschen Geistes*. (Stuttgart: Deutsche Verlags-Anstalt).

Fichte, J. G. (1911). *Reden an die deutsche Nation. Werke: Auswahl in sechs Bänden,* vol. 5, ed. F. Medicus (Leipzig: F. Meiner).

Geoghegan, V. (1996). *Ernst Bloch*. (London: Routledge).

——(1960). *Das Tagebuch von Joseph Goebbels, 1925/26,* ed. H. Heiber (Stuttgart: Deutsche Verlags-Anstalt).

Gogarten, F. (1915). 'Volk und Schöpfung', *Protestantenblatt* 48.

Hamann, J. G. (1821). *Hamann's Schriften,* vol. 1, ed. F. Roth (Leipzig: G. Reimer).

Hegel, G. W. F. (1942). *Hegel's Philosophy of Right,* ed. and trans. T. M. Knox. (Oxford: Clarendon Press).

Heidegger, M. (1934). *Die Selbstbehauptung der deutschen Universität.* (Breslau: Verlag Wilh. Gottl. Korn).

——(1950). *Holzwege.* (Frankfurt: Klostermann).

——(1980). *Hölderlins Hymnen 'Germanien' und 'Der Rhein',* ed. S. Ziegler (Frankfurt: Klostermann).

——(1988). 'Spiegel-Gespräch mit Martin Heidegger', *Antwort: Martin Heidegger im Gespräch,* ed. G. Neske and E. Kettering (Pfüllingen: Neske), 81–114.

——(2011). *Phänomenologie des Religiösen Lebens,* ed. M. Jung, T. Regehly, and C. Strube (Frankfurt: Klostermann).

Herder, J. G. (1881). 'Haben wir noch das Publicum und Vaterland der Alten: Eine Abhandlung', *Herders Sämmtliche Werke,* vol. 17, ed. B. L. Suphan (Berlin: Weidmann).

——(1985). *Frühe Schriften 1764–1772,* ed. U. Gaier (Frankfurt: Deutscher Klassiker Verlag).

Hitler, A. (1938a). *Mein Kampf.* (Munich: Eher).

——(1938b). *Das dichterische Wort im Werk Adolf Hitlers.* (Berlin: Eher).

Hölderlin, Friedrich (1970). *Sämtliche Gedichte,* vol. 1, ed. D. Lüders (Bad Homburg: Athenäum).

König, K. (1915). *Sechs Kriegspredigten.* (Jena: Diederichs).

Kraus, K. (1992). *Die letzten Tage der Menschheit,* ed. E. Früh (Frankfurt: Suhrkamp).

Kurz, G. (2002). 'Braune Apokalypse', in J. Brokoff and J. Jacob, *Apokalypse und Erinnerung in der deutsch-jüdischen Kultur des frühen 20. Jahrhunderts.* (Göttingen: Vandenhoeck and Ruprecht), 131–46.

Lasson, A. (1914). *Deutsche Art und deutsche Bildung.* (Berlin: Carl Heymann).

Martin, B. (1989). *Martin Heidegger und das 'Dritte Reich': Ein Kompendium.* (Darmstadt: Wissenschaftliche Buchgesellschaft).

Moeller van den Bruck, A. (1934). *Germany's Third Empire,* ed. and trans. E. O. Lorimer (London: Allen & Unwin).

Neske, G. and Kettering, E. (1990). *Martin Heidegger and National Socialism: Questions and Answers.* (New York: Paragon House).

Philipse, H. (1998). *Heidegger's Philosophy of Being: A Critical Interpretation.* (Princeton, NJ: Princeton University Press).

Plenge, J. (1915). *Der Krieg und die Volkswirtschaft.* (Münster: Borgmener).

Richter, O. (1909). *Die Lieblingsvorstellungen der Dichter des deutschen Befreiungskrieges.* (Leipzig: Seele).

Rosenberg, A. (1930). *Der Mythus des 20. Jahrhunderts: Eine Wertung der seelisch-geistigen Gestaltenkämpfe unserer Zeit.* (Munich: Hoheneichen-Verlag).

——(1936). *Der entscheidende Weltkampf: Rede des Reichsleiters Alfred Rosenberg auf dem Parteikongress in Nürnberg 1936.* (Munich: M. Müller & Sohn).

Rosenstock-Huessy, E. (1931). 'Das Dritte Reich und die Sturmvögel des Nationalsozialismus', *Hochland* 28, 193–211.

Schelling, F. W. J. von (1958). *Philosophie der Mythologie. Schellings Werke*, vol. 5, ed. M. Schröter (Munich: Beck).

Schenkendorf, M. von (1815). *Gedichte.* (Stuttgart: Cotta).

Schiller, F. (1965). 'Thalia', *Sämtliche Werke*, vol. 1, ed. G. Fricke and H. G. Göpfert (Munich: Hanser).

Schumann, G. (1935). *Die Lieder vom Reich.* (Munich: Langen, Müller).

——(1936). *Wir aber sind das Korn: Gedichte.* (Munich: Langen, Müller).

Vondung, K. (1988). *Die Apokalypse in Deutschland.* (Munich: Deutscher Taschenbuch Verlag).

——(2005). 'National Socialism as a Political Religion: Potentials and Limits of an Analytical Concept', *Totalitarian Movements and Political Religions* 6: 1, 87–95.

Wolfe, J. (2012). *Heidegger's Secular Eschatology.* (Oxford: Oxford University Press).

SUGGESTED READING

Bärsch, C. (1998). *Die politische Religion des Nationalsozialismus.* (Munich: W. Fink).

Bloch, E. (1986). *The Principle of Hope*, trans. N. Plaice, S. Plaice, and P. Knight (Cambridge, MA: MIT Press).

Cohn (1972).

Dostoevsky, F. M. (1907). *Politische Schriften*, ed. and trans. A. Moeller van den Bruck (Munich: Pieper).

Fichte, J. G. (1968). *Addresses to the German Nation*, trans. G. Moore (New York: Harper & Row).

Hegel (1942).

Heidegger, M. (2004). *Phenomenology of Religious Life*, trans. M. Fritsch and A. Gosetti-Ferencei (Bloomington, IN: Indiana University Press).

Loewith, K. (1949). *Meaning in History: The Theological Implications of the Philosophy of History.* Chicago: University of Chicago Press.

Moeller van den Bruck, A. (1934). *Germany's Third Empire*, ed. and trans. E. O. Lorimer (London: Allen & Unwin).

Vondung, K. (2000). *The Apocalypse in Germany*, trans. S. D. Ricks (Columbia: University of Missouri Press).

Wolfe (2012).

CHAPTER 15

NIHILISM AND THEOLOGY: WHO STANDS AT THE DOOR?

CONOR CUNNINGHAM

Nihilism stands at the door; whence comes to us this uncanniest of all guests?

(Friedrich Nietzsche 1968: 7)

Behold I stand at the door, and knock. If any man shall hear my voice, and open to me the door, I will come in to him, and will sup with him and he with me.

(Rev 3:20)

Man has this choice, however, and this alone: Nothingness or a God.

(F. H. Jacobi, 1994: 534)

I. INTRODUCTION

THERE have always been nihilists. Hegesias, a rhetor of the third century BC, was known as the 'death persuader', because after people listened to him they would commit suicide. Ptolemy II banished him from Egypt. But if there have always been nihilists, has there always been nihilism? And crucially, how does it relate to theology?

Jean-Baptiste Louis Crevier seems to have been the first to use the term nihilist in 1761. He employed the term to describe the 'disciples' of Peter Lombard. He pointed out that in *Libri Sententiarum*, Lombard argues that 'in as much as he is a man, Jesus Christ is not something, or, in other words, is nothing. This proposition is scandalous, and yet some of his disciples supported it and formed the heresy of the nihilists.' (Crevier 1761 and Weller 2011: 19) In the sense in which it is generally used today, the term 'nihilism' was introduced by F. H. Jacobi in an open letter to Fichte (1799), in which he described the philosophy that followed in the wake of Kant as *Nihilismus*. The term did not enter common usage, however, and it was not until the writings of Nietzsche that nihilism came to prominence. Nietzsche diagnosed Europe as having fallen into nihilism for the simple but dramatic reason that, he said, God is now dead, and we have killed him by way of our incredulity, apathy, and *ressentiment*. Confronting such nihilism, which he saw as degenerate, it is generally agreed that Nietzsche endeavoured to overcome (*überwinden*) it, by constructing an entirely new way of looking at existence, employing concepts such as the 'Overman' (*Übermensch*) and the 'eternal return'. In later sections we shall discuss those philosophers who were influenced and inspired by the claim that God is dead. One wider consequence of the advent of nihilism was a severe disenchantment of the world (described by Max Weber) and the rise of an all-encompassing materialism (nihilism's great progeny), which sought to consummate the death of God (proposed in various forms within Marxism).

In many a trendy Parisian café, and in many an austere Anglo-Saxon philosophy lecture hall, there has for some time been a rumour afoot, uttered in conspiratorial tones: *there is nothing but matter*. Like some scary bedtime story, we are supposed both to enjoy this story and to be fearful of it. We are to enjoy it, because it is supposed to be radical, emancipatory even. Such materialism is thought to topple every church and make a mockery of all religions? Where would you locate the soul or even the mind? We are to fear it, because for materialists, all culture skates on very thin ice: love, poetry, literature, intercourse, they are each but a façade, behind which lies the truth, the truth about us all, and about everything, the *réel* hiding behind every face, our closest yet most foreign neighbour:

> What we see in there, these turbinate bones covered by a whitish membrane, is a horrendous sight... there's a horrendous discovery there, that of the flesh one never sees, the foundation of things, the other side of the head, of the face... the flesh from which everything exudes, at the very heart of the mystery... formless... Spectre of anxiety... the final revelation, you're this—You are this, which is so far from you, this which is ultimate formlessness.   (Lacan 1991: 154–5)

Without any solid reference points (a sense of self, a soul), disorientated, material man, stumbles around the rooms of his own house—his own body, and his life—as if it were someone else's home. What was once familiar seems strange, odd, and threatening. Sigmund Freud refers to this as the Uncanny [*Unheimlich* (eerie, or strange)] which still bears the trace of *Heimlich* (home like, or familiar).

According, then, to those who spread the rumour of materialism (and thus nihilism), the truth of our situation can be compared to Magritte's *La Reproduction Interdite* of 1937 in which the man looking in the mirror sees only the back of his head. In other words, the face as some sort of special, iconic site is only a material fiction. It is a fiction generated by the nominal play of language; for it is language which fools us into thinking we exist; it seduces us into a sense of our being. Behind the grammar of such conjurations lies the *réel*, namely, matter. And matter is always threatening to reveal itself: sometimes in a stain, or a corpse, or disease, or a smell, breaking out of all contrived vessels. This reveals a nominalism in our pretence to order and classify. On such a view, concepts are not real: they display merely arbitrary human invention. Words are no more than fictions: 'the conceptual understanding of empirical reality is equivalent to murder' (Kojève 1963: 140; see also Blanchot 1995: 323). He gives the example of the concept 'dog'. In order for such a concept to work it must be something of a lie, in so far as the concept 'dog' is not itself a dog, and in truth, any actual dog is not identical with the concept. So, every time we say 'dog' we betray reality, we betray, and therefore violate the entity which we are forcing to fall under the concept's explanatory power. This is what Lacan referred to as—*manque-à-être* (Lacan 1992: 294). Furthermore, in order for the concept 'dog' to work all dogs must be mortal, otherwise we could not detach the concept from any particular dog—they would be eternally the same, and in so being would be unthinkable. We require finitude, or mortality, just to be able to think at all: you are thinkable only because you will die. For Hegel this seems to be true of God also, and maybe that is why he tells us that 'God cannot be god without the world'. This infamous phrase is ambiguous, but some take it to mean that God, in being infinite and therefore in a sense everything, would be unthinkable and therefore equivalent to nothing, because without a contrast, without the mediation provided by the finite, God would be unintelligible as a concept. To some degree, this was partly what Hume (or at least Philo) was arguing in the *Dialogues Concerning Natural Religion*. There, Hume makes the point that if God were unique, a singularity, so to speak, then God would be beyond all analogical thinking. That is, God would be unthinkable. This also stands for the concept 'universe', and here Hume anticipates Alain Badiou: if the universe is everything, and is real, it cannot be thought, for if it were, it would not be everything. Therefore 'universe' is not a legitimate concept. Jean-Paul Sartre had already called this idea a 'detotalized totality'. Badiou will define this as the One that is not and Lacan as, *'L'Une-en-moins'* (Lacan 1998: 129; Sartre 2000: 623). The same might be said for Hegel's concept of God, or at least Kojève's Hegel: if God were real, that is, if God were truly infinite and eternal, then God would in effect be dead, since God would be unintelligible. Here then, atheism and theism (or nihilism and theology) begin to look very similar, even exchangeable. Sartre had already spoken about a 'missing God', and this crucial ambiguity between nihilism and theology will be built upon by figures such as Alain Badiou, Gianni Vattimo, Jean-Luc Nancy, and Giorgio Agamben (see below). Alas, forms, essences, and natural kinds all fade away. In their wake is the now ubiquitous threat of dust, pure matter, merely arranged maybe thus rather than so. As Badiou says, 'The void proper to life, as death shows, is matter.' (Badiou 2004: 99) In other words: 'everything that is bound testifies that it is unbound in its being' (quoted in Brassier 2004: 50). This unboundedness is what Sartre called 'the being of the slimy' (Sartre 2000: 610).

In light of the above, we ought to heed the words of Robert Spaemann, who seeks to develop ways of thinking that offers 'resistance against this oblivion' (quoted in

Zaborowski 2010: 118). But does nihilism offer an opportunity for theology? Does it not free us from many idols, or indeed does it not once again help reveal the *ex nihilo* from whence all came? Maybe then, it is fair to say that the overcoming (*Überwindung*) of nihilism is its consummation (*Vollendung*): in the 'first step toward the true overcoming of nihilism. . . . we need to go expressly up to the limit of nothing' (Heidegger 2000: 217–18). Yet this, no doubt, is the danger of dangers (*die Gefahr der Gefahr*), both for nihilism and for theology (Nietzsche 1968: 44–5). Nietzsche spoke about those 'supreme values in whose service man should live, especially when they were hard on him and exacted a high price' and how that now 'the shabby origin of these values is becoming clear, the universe seems to have lost value, seems meaningless—*that is only transitional*' (Nietzsche 1968: 10). Maybe this is why Maurice Blanchot reluctantly concludes that 'Nihilism tells us its final and rather grim truth: it tells us of the impossibility of nihilism' (Blanchot 1993: 149).

II. Nihilism's Needs: Badiou, Vattimo, Nancy, and Agamben

Nihilism has many needs, as we will see, but the most serious, essential need is that it must not simply be nihilistic; that is, it cannot be mere lack. This fundamental need is witnessed in the necessary move to colonize theology, as when we see advocates of nihilism appropriating religious terms and concepts in an effort to remove any residual dualism between atheism and theism, and to ward off any sense of limit or absence. The first person to be examined here is Badiou. His main need will be to rid himself of finitude, so that the notion of a *beyond* is nonsensical. But that will come at a cost, for in losing any sense of a beyond, we will see that it is not transcendence that suffers, but immanence, in other words, it is the natural (and not the supernatural) that is lost in the flux of mere history. Vattimo, Nancy, and Agamben will each be even more explicit in their attempt to colonize religion by setting up counterfeit theologies, in the hope of saving nihilism.

Badiou

In his typically brazen manner, Badiou tells us 'I take the formula "God is dead" literally. It has happened. Or, as Rimbaud said, it has passed. God is finished. And religion is finished, too' (Badiou 2006: 23). One might respond that, contra Badiou, there does seem to be a great deal of religion around, indeed, more than one might expect if God is dead. But Badiou responds that 'What subsists is no longer religion, but its theatre' (Badiou 2006: 24). That is to say, we may well go to church, sing hymns, participate in rituals, but deep in the night we know that we believe more in stones than we do God. We are incredulous, in fact; that's why God is elsewhere—in Heaven, because He certainly isn't here. According to Badiou, there are three forms that God, so-called, takes. The first is that of religion, which he argues involves an encounter. For example, it is always someone's God—Abraham's, Isaac's, Jacob's, Jesus', and so on (Badiou 2006: 26).Then there is the God of metaphysics, and this God involves philosophical proofs, none of which are convincing. Lastly, there is the God of the Romantics, the God of the poem, and this God is the only one that, in a sense, remains today. In fact, this is the one that Badiou sets out to destroy. Badiou warns us that 'What still maintains a power of promising nowadays, and the poetic and political disposition of the return of the gods or re-enchantment of the world, is the consensual motif of finitude' (Badiou 2006: 29). He continues, 'Finitude is like the trace of an afterlife in the moment that entrusts the overcoming of the religion-God and the metaphysics-God to the poem-God' (Badiou 2006: 29). The point is that finitude accommodates, if not invites, a thinking of that which is not finite, namely, the infinite, a beyond that may or may not promise more. We do not know, but we can hope. Moreover, in not being finite it must in a sense be better, because unlimited, divine even. Badiou has a solution to this: be done with finitude, by domesticating or laicizing the infinite: 'As for philosophy, the aim is to finish up with the motif of finitude and its hermeneutical escort. The key point is to unseal the infinite from its millenary collusion with the One. It is to restitute the infinite to the banality of the manifold-being, as mathematics has invited us to so since Cantor' (Badiou 2006: 30). Put differently, the infinite is not beyond. It cannot be because there is no finitude beyond which it could go. The reason that there is no finitude is because the infinite is here, it is everywhere and everything—it is in fact everyday banality. If that is the case, then all three forms God may take are now meaningless, and the third one, that of the poem has nothing to lament about, because it has nowhere to lament about: 'That is because we have lost nothing and nothing returns' (Badiou 2006, 31).

According to Badiou, 'There is no God. Which also means: the One (l'Un) is not. The multiple "without one"—every multiple being in its turn is nothing other than a multiple of multiples—is the law of being' (Badiou 2001: 25). How, we might ask, can that be a *law*, without re-invoking the One? Invoking Cantorian set theory, Badiou argues that the One is not, because there can be no set of all sets; that is, there are no paradoxical sets. This decision, because that is what it is, is based on what is called the 'axiom of foundation', which rules out a completed actual infinity, instead only permitting finite iterations. However, Badiou is only speaking about the (apparently) Romantic notion of the infinite, and not the Christian one. Moreover, he merely elects to present us with (i.e. merely asserts) a diabolic counterfeit double of the Absolute. In his case the Absolute is nothingness, the abyss, since being is merely multiples of multiples, all the way down. But there is a cost, one that does not obtain for the Absolute: quite simply Badiou's abyss must produce, it must create, for lack of a better word, otherwise once again a banal contrast governs—in other words, if the abyss is not productive, then a definite article is possible—*the* abyss, or even merely the abyss, and if that obtains it accommodates the possibility of its opposite. Put differently, the abyss must be nothing *and* something.

For Badiou, being is neither one nor multiple; rather it is a 'multiple of multiples' (Badiou 1988: 24). Badiou denounces the One through an act of pure faith (Badiou 2009: 108), but in so doing, he does not want it, the denounced One, to reappear as 'the' pure flux. That is why the flux must be impure, that is, it must produce 'ones'—it must count for something, something must count. So he advocates a 'subtractive ontology': Badiou can only present Being if it is nothing, yet in being nothing it must still be something. Put differently, if Being is mere nothingness, then, again, we could imagine it full—but what if it is full, and yet remains nothingness, this then is complete nihilism (Cunningham 2002). Indeed this is why Badiou argues that Being is 'neither one. . . . nor multiple' (Badiou 1988: 24). It is simply a matter of the presentation of presentation. But here, for Badiou, to notice inconsistency requires consistency, and vice versa. In the same way, the uncountable, the non-One is only possible if something counts. Put another way: being is never presented yet it is subtracted from presentations in so far as we realize that every presentation is not really real. It is rather a nominal conjuration of meaning; one that arises from corralling the stuff of being, which is nothingness, into pretend situations, objects, meanings, events, situations, and so on. This is what Badiou calls the 'without-place of every place' (Badiou 1998: 200). This, he claims, is the sole truth of Capitalism, because Capitalism posits things, but assigns them no intrinsic value (Badiou 1988: 25).

What Badiou terms 'events' are possible because there is a situation, but also the crucial dualism of *belonging* and *inclusion*. Within any situation something belongs. Some things count, they are noticed, they have a sort of suffrage, but within the set of any such situation there are subsets which are included even though they do not belong. These subsets offer an excess, which, on the one hand, reveal the meta-truth—all is inconsistency, nothing is—while, on the other hand, the possibility of an event remains. It remains because that which is *included* but does not *belong* becomes the fuel for something approaching an escape, or a reconfiguration—for example negroes in the US in the last century were included—they were American, but they did not belong, and this difference fuelled the Civil Rights movement. More importantly, there is always a base element to which no other element belongs. Badiou offers his cat as an example: it is

> an element of the set of living beings, and it is composed of cells that are in turn elements of this set, if one grants that they are living organisms. But if we decompose a cell into molecules, then into atoms, we eventually reach purely physical elements that don't belong to the set of living beings. There is a certain term (perhaps the cell, in fact) which belongs to the set of living beings, because those elements all involve only 'inert' Physico-chemical materiality.   (Badiou 2008: 71)

Now, none of the above makes much sense, at least without begging a handful of questions. For example, the process of the gradual reduction to the base element relies on terms (cat, living, inert, chemicals, etc.), even to get going, or to be noticed. At the same time such terms lie outside Badiou's philosophy, because according to him, everything is merely multiples of multiples, therefore there are no natural kinds, categories, and so on. Moreover, once again, the state of the situation (Badiou's own phrase, meaning the governing identity of a multiple—call it democracy, racism, left or right wing politics, etc.) of his philosophy (let us call it materialism) dictates, a priori, the logic of the analysis. Why, after all, can it not be the other way around? That is, why can the living cat not itself be the base element, so to speak, of the inert chemicals? Indeed, surely life is an event that cannot be counted by the situation of inert chemicals. So why then discount it, that is, why think you can reduce the cat for that very reason (Cunningham 2010)?

A crucial point to be made here is that Badiou's understanding of Being rests on his use of the empty set—the set with no members. But the empty set is only possible because there are actual sets—that is, sets with members. Moreover a set can only exist in a possible world if its members exist (Lewis 1991: 13; Lowe 2001: 254). The inference is that the empty is barred from all possible worlds (Baldwin 1996). This argument links with the so-called *argument against nihilism*, which attacks what is called the 'subtraction argument'. Very briefly, the subtraction argument asks us to realize that we have no problem imagining any particular object not existing, so why not go the whole way and imagine a possible world with no concrete objects (Lowe 2002). One issue we should bear in mind here is that there are those, like Badiou, who would argue that such a possible world is in fact the world 'we' inhabit right now. That is to say: there are no concrete objects. Badiou calls this 'the destitution of the category object' (Badiou 1999: 72). But surely if mereological nihilism obtains so too would logical nihilism: how could any single thought form an intelligible utterance? Opponents of the subtraction argument argue from 'the necessary truth of mathematical claims to the necessary existence of abstract objects' (Lowe 2001: 254). But according to these opponents of metaphysical nihilism (that is, a world without any concrete objects), abstract objects cannot exist in a world without concrete objects. Therefore, every possible world contains concrete objects (But if that is indeed the case, then surely there is no such thing as a possible world, there's just this world.) One wonders whether, in a manner analogous to Badiou's championing of the empty set, the motive here is to relativize the importance of existence; to deflate its worth.

One other problem with Badiou's veneration of sets is that in the real world objects are essentially related to each other, while members in a set bear no substantive relations because sets are not concrete. Sets are merely abstract objects, and as such are dependent on concrete objects, not the other way around. Badiou's argument is self-defeating: if sets were all there was, there is nothing, and so there would be no sets, nor any 'thought' about a set, as the thought of sets cannot itself be a set—here the paradoxes upon which Badiou's notion of inconsistent multiplicity trades come back to bite (Coggins 2010: 42). To conclude our discussion of Badiou: his nihilism is unsuccessful as it is trapped by a *constitutive necessity* of which it can give no account. In short, this nihilism cannot be done with the One, nor can it eradicate finitude. Finally, his understanding of the infinite has nothing to with Christianity's understanding of transcendence. In sum, Badiou's nihilism is a Pelagian atheism as it must work perpetually to achieve its own salvation, that is, to save itself from not being nihilism. This manifests itself in its endless need to keep counting ones so that nihilism results, or arrives, and the One does not. But like Godot, this nihilism never turns up. Badiou's nihilism is in the end too needy.

Vattimo and Nancy

> Nietzsche's idea that God is dead is already contained in the Christian idea of the death of God.
>
> (Maurice Merleau-Ponty 1964: 27)

When he engages with Christianity, Vattimo employs the word *Verwindung* rather than *Überwindung*; that is, he seeks not to surpass it, but somehow to twist it, or assume an ironic acceptance of it (Vattimo 2004: 27–8). And he does not seek to surpass Christianity because of the truth it bears: 'The real passage into postmodernity is the event that Nietzsche called "the death of God". In Christian doctrine this death is that of Christ on the cross, and it is not out of the question that in his proclamation Nietzsche was taking on the role of secularized interpreter of this event' (Vattimo 2004: 51). In this way, the death of God is not the death of Christianity and a lapse into banal nihilism; rather the death of God is Christianity. 'The Nietzsche of the death of God and the Heidegger of *Ereignis* [the Event of Being] are the most radical heirs of the anti-metaphysical principle that Christ brought into the world' (Vattimo 2002: 109). Crucially, this so-called anti-metaphysical principle is made manifest in Vattimo's distinction between *pensiero debole* (weak thought) and *pensiero forte* (strong thought):

> The Kenosis that occurs as the incarnation of God and most recently as seculariza-tion and the weakening of Being and its strong structures (to the point of dissol-ution of the ideal of truth as objectivity) takes place in accordance with a 'law'of religion, at least in the sense that it is not by its own decision that the subject is committed to a process of ruin, for one finds oneself called to such a commitment by the thing itself.   (Vattimo 1996: 22)

Christianity, in light of divine kenosis, is a weakening of thought, and therefore if we are to be Christian, or if we are to imitate Christianity, we should likewise weaken our thought, which means to abandon any notion of absolute objectivity.

Vattimo tells us: 'In short I have begun to take Christianity seriously again because I have constructed a philosophy inspired by Nietzsche and Heidegger, and have inter-preted my experience in the contemporary world in light of it' (Vattimo 1999: 33). This is what Vattimo calls a nihilistic rediscovery of Christianity, one made possible by what he also terms the 'weakening of Being', not just a weakening of thought. In other words, Being is not to be thought of as a metaphysically self-evident objectivity, but instead is indirectly communicated through countless images and perspectives, and this involves the 'fabulization' of the world. As he says, 'The images of the world we receive from the media and the human sciences, albeit on different levels, are not simply different interpretations of a reality that is "given" regardless, but rather constitute the very objectivity of the world' (Vattimo 1992: 24–5). According to Vattimo, there is an ethical import to this weakening of thought, this fabulization, because it renders it impossible to use truth as a weapon. In this way nihilism is ethical, whilst the idea of transcendence accommodates if not encourages violence. For this reason, '[t]he weakening of God, through Kenosis, is the dissolution of divine transcendence' (Vattimo 2002: 27). But any such dissolution is no loss but a gain; nor does it betray Christianity, rather it is to live it, to fulfil it.

Moreover, there is, according to Vattimo, a somewhat natural link, or a certain fittingness, between nihilism, the weakening of Being, of thought, and Christianity (Vattimo 1999: 34–5). The God of violence, the God who demands violence, He who comports a strong sense of Being, rather than a weak one, is the God of metaphysics. But that God is now dead, as Nietzsche told us. By contrast, 'the incarnation, that is God's abasement to the level of humanity (the kenosis of Philippians) will be interpreted as the sign of a non-violent and non-absolute God of the post-metaphysical epoch' (Vattimo 1999: 39). This kenosis leads Vattimo to suggest that in Christianity we can discern the original 'text of which weak ontology is the transcription' (Vattimo 1999: 70). Indeed, he goes so far as to say that 'postmodern nihilism constitutes the actual truth of Christianity' (Vattimo and Rorty 2005: 47). One sure sign of the kenosis, according to Vattimo, is secularization itself. In other words, rather than interpret this phenomenon as an enemy of Christianity, it is instead a true fruit of Christianity: God became man, and then Christianity, imitating Christ, emptied itself of divinity too, and in so doing stayed true to God by staying true to the Earth. As John Gray points out, 'the chief significance of evangelical atheism is in demonstrating the unreality of secularism' (Gray 2007: 267); 'secular thinking is a legacy of Christianity and has no meaning except in a context of monotheism' (Gray 2007: 268). Indeed, 'Post-Christian secular societies are formed by the beliefs they reject, whereas a society that had truly left Christianity behind would lack the concepts that shaped secular thought' (Gray 2007: 268). In short, atheism, or secularism is not an opponent of Christianity but its progeny, even its truth. And this secularization is constitutive for the identity of the west. As Nancy says, '[n]ot only is atheism an invention specific to the West, but it must also be considered the element in which the West invented itself' (Nancy 2008: 14).

Like Vattimo, Nancy claims to be faithful to Christianity, or rather faithful to the truth of Christianity; a truth Christianity is as yet unaware of (Nancy 2010: 40). This is to go beyond the binary opposition of atheism and theism, for it is to argue that the truth of theism, or rather of Christianity, is a certain atheism; likewise, atheism only becomes true by way of religion, or by way of a certain grace, because if it lacks grace and is merely natural, it remains trapped in the bind of lack, and therefore remains reactively dualistic. And this is the case because 'Christianity became, by itself, a humanism, an atheism, and a nihilism' (Nancy 2008: 23).

One way to think of this weakening of religion, is to view Christianity as giving up its claim to transcendence. This surrender realizes or reveals the truth of creation *ex nihilo*—it does come from nothing. If there is a God, then, on the one hand, creation has not truly come from nothing and, on the other, such a God's presence would mean that creation is not really real –it would only be a phantasm, a mere suburb of Heaven. Therefore, atheism is the truth of creation. As Vattimo says, 'Christianity's vocation consists in deepening its own physiognomy as source and condition for the possibility of secularity' (Vattimo 2002: 20). According to Nancy, the true genius of Christianity is that the word became flesh (*logos sarx egeneto*), which means for him that in some sense there is what he calls a spacing in flesh, in the body. This is a spacing which opens up the body, offering an interval that suggests a certain sense of possibility (Nancy 2010: 78).

> The opening of the world in the world is the result of a destitution or a decon-struction of Christianity, which goes back or which advances in it all the way to the extremity at which nihilism breaks up the presence and the value of God, breaks up the sense of salvation as an escape from the world, erases all value inscribed upon a heaven, erases heaven itself, and leaves the world intact and touched by a strange gaping that is grace and wound at the same time.   (Nancy 2008: 78)

Here Nancy is saying much the same as Vattimo, at least in his understanding of kenosis: atheism is the truth of Christianity, that is, it is Good News. Similarly for Nancy, 'Christianity is accomplished in nihilism and as nihilism' (Nancy 2008: 147). For Nancy, monotheism actually introduces the *deus absconditus*, for monotheism is an absencing (*l'absentement*) of presence; unlike polytheism which is the presence of absence. If one thinks about it for a moment, it is not until the advent of monotheism, that is, of a truly transcendent God, that absence is possible, that atheism is possible. On the one hand, God by definition is beyond comprehension and, on the other, we now have 'someone' who accommodates absence. That is to say, is not this unknown/unknowable God true atheism (Nancy 1997a: 69)? To repeat: we now have a 'proper' understanding of God, so now the absence of this true God's presence is possible. Indeed, Nancy goes so far as to argue that Christianity 'self-atheises' (*s'athéise*) (Nancy 2008: 82). From the belief in a transcendent God to the kenosis of that God and then this god's eventual death—this is atheism as has never before been possible. Indeed, if Lacan is correct and God is unconscious (this unconscious God is the true atheism), why would a religion invent a transcendent God, have that God self-empty, and then die? Surely there must be an unconscious confession of atheism here. 'We are not yet atheists' (Nancy 1997b: 158). Nancy tells us that we can only become atheists when we open the *sense of the world*. That is, if we do not limit the world, that which is immanent or, again, if we can be surprised by it. But we leave finitude behind only by opening it up (Nancy) or rendering it non-existent (Badiou). 'This is what is at stake in an "atheism" that owes it to itself to deny itself the position of the negation it proffers, and the assurance of every sort of presence that could substitute for that of God' (Nancy 2008: 86). In other words, atheism, like nihilism, cannot know itself, cannot be sure of what it stands for, what it offers, for if it is simply a denial then it remains beholden to the very thing that it thought it had defeated. Atheism cannot be atheistic. Again, the same can be said of nihilism, only then does nihilism attain truth or accomplish what it means to signal. In light of nihilism's need not to be nihilistic, a simple sense, this is why we witness so many materialists writing on St Paul, lauding his universalism. In so doing they are not simply rejecting him, they colonize him; they colonize that which we would have presumed to be beyond the ken of nihilism. But any such demarcation of a beyond does, by definition, limit nihilism, and therefore nihilism cannot be the whole truth. As Watkin says, 'What post-theological integration attempts is not to oppose theism but to occupy it, not expel theism but to ingest it, taking terms and patterns of thought previously associated with theism and reinscribing them' (Watkins 2011: 14).

There is a worrisome element in this nihilistic embrace of Christianity: it seems to be motivated by a concern about authority (univocally construed, which is to say, that authority can only have *one* meaning, one form, or one mode of manifestation, and that mode is always to be rejected: authority is *always* an imposition, and offence). As Vattimo says, if objective truth really exists, then 'there will always be someone who is more in possession of it than I and is thereby authorized to impose its law/obligation on me' (Vattimo and Caputo 2007: 37). But how then can we speak of 'crimes against humanity' and any attendant court? Any such court will inevitably issue judgements and any such judgements must surely be examples of strong thinking. Yes, of course there is the potential abuse of power, authority, and so on, but surely, even if we don't care about losing both the baby and the bathwater, we must at least keep the bath, otherwise prisons are a complete (not a partial) offence and so we can release the rapists, the paedophiles, those who have committed genocide. We can go and have a latte whilst we observe them heading for the hills, ever so calmly, and no doubt eventually entering into our own houses. The kenosis of God, the condescension or debasement, is surely done for *a reason*, and, after all, this weak Christ informs us that no one gets to the Father except through him, which is surely very strong thinking, to say the least. Is it not, therefore, that we should resist falling into a dualism of weak/ strong thinking, but rather understand instead that there is always a paradoxical link between them both? For example, Christian creedal orthodoxy argues that Christ had two natures but only one person (a single *esse*). Is such a model not a far more satisfactory model of how we are to approach Being than that offered by Vattimo or, for that matter, Nancy? And we must remember that according to many from the Christian tradition, union differentiates, while Vattimo appears to want to begin with distinction. But distinction always seems to leave those (positive) nihilists who would deconstruct Christianity, Being or 'strong thought' with an unknown, yet employed third thing or term (*tertium quid*). It is a term which invisibly and indeed *strongly*, nay, tyrannically governs the whole show—for it goes unchallenged. Christ in his person reveals that there is always crib and throne, and that our understanding of the latter is mediated by the former. But, crucially, vice versa: we don't understand a crib unless there is a throne. Arguably then, Vattimo's nihilism is not weak enough, and Nancy's deconstruction is too parasitic on Christianity. As Watkins says, 'In deconstructing Christianity Nancy imitates Christianity' (Watkins 2011: 39).

Agamben

According to Agamben the road to redemption lies in the 'definitive profanity of the profane' (Agamben 1993b: 102). That is, like Vattimo and Nancy, we must use Christianity to enable a true, pure, and indeed profound atheism. As he says, this vision is based on a possibility; one that leads to 'A new and more blessed life, one that is neither animal nor human' (Agamben 2004: 87). Following Michel Foucault's assertion that 'man' is a recent invention, one that is 'neither a clearly defined species nor a substance; it is rather a machine or device for producing the recognition of the human' (Foucault, 1970: 387), Agamben seeks to bring to the fore this idea of 'anthropological machinery'. That is, the idea that we are made (not created). Put differently: we are an outcome of contingent forces or regimes (Foucault 1970: 26). As Agamben puts it, 'The transformation of the species into a principle of identity and classification is the original sin of our culture' (Agamben 2007: 59). But again, and indeed as we shall see further, this is just one more 'adolescent' rebellion against being told what to do. Of course, I'm all for rebellion, but one has to be careful, since *someone* needs to be emancipated from *something*. And, ontologically speaking, that is very expensive.

Again, like Vattimo, and Nancy, Agamben tells us that

> If theological tradition has therefore always understood revelation as something that human reason cannot know on its own, this can only mean the following: the content of revelation is not truth that can be expressed in the form of linguistic propositions about a being (even about a supreme being) but is, instead, a truth that concerns language itself, the very fact that language (and therefore knowledge) exists.   (Agamben 1999: 40)

Moreover, for Agamben, it is the Trinity that is the true and utter expression of language's existence, because, we must remember, as a phenomenon, language cannot speak. Language is a sort of silent substance that accompanies or lies within all speech, and therefore every utterance, but it does so as its very possibility and yet as its complete impossibility. Language speaks—that is the miracle—but in so doing, in the end, all speech says nothing: 'Trinitarian structure is nothing other than the movement of its own self-revelation. And this revelation of the word, this presupposition of nothing, which is the sole presupposition, is God: "and the Word was God"' (Agamben 1999: 41). Put differently, if the Word is God, if the Word is the revelation of God, even if the Word was God, somehow this means that God is dumb, that language is dumb. Yet it is all the more extraordinary if that being the case: for how does silence speak if that is what language is? The Word was God, but God still needed a Word. The Word is, Agamben tells us, the voice that 'signifies signification itself' (Agamben 1999: 42). Or again, 'The name of God, that is, the name that names language is, therefore, a word without meaning, the place of pure signification without anything being signified' (Agamben 1999: 42). This sounds gnomic, but is really very simple: A word must be in language so that it can be the Word or, rather, the Word must be the possibility of words without being a word itself. This being the case, the Word of God is the absence and yet possibility of all words. The implication of this is, as said, that all words are a loud silence full of empty saying. This is true nihilism, but Agamben does not stop there. This is not the night in which all cows are black, or at least it is a different variation of it. This is a night in which all sound is silent; all lives are dead, even though breathing. In short, this is a demonic abyss, and not even that. Agamben seeks to develop his constructive, demonic, nihilism (after all, the Devil wants a kingdom, so there is no point in going all napalm on us), by way of reinterpreting Aristotle's division of actuality and potentiality. He does this in a bid to 'decreate' us.

'The only way to be truly "ethical" is to simply be one's ownmost potentiality' (Agamben 1993: 44). Notice that Agamben has to put the ethical in quotation marks because, of course, to be consistent 'the ethical' has also to be in its ownmost potentiality if it, too, is to be 'ethical', And so continues the regress (Agamben 1993: 44). This potentiality is our potentiality, one that is 'beyond any vocational actuality' (Agamben 1993a: 44). This appears to be a move towards emancipation, but, once again, it is merely utter catastrophe. If we accept Agamben's position, then all the actual is somehow potential, and the potential is actual. In other words, that which *is*, is, in a sense, illegal, therefore it is a lie, a pretence, ontologically speaking—it hides that which could be otherwise (counterfactually), like some parsimonious ontological menu (here is where the serial killers live). In other words, any entity that exists, any behaviour that is recommended, does so only at the expense of other entities or behaviours that could exist, and whose potential rummages around beneath the skin of that which is threatening to be born, and any prohibition of birth is in a sense wholly illegitimate, as this is radical democracy, truly universal suffrage– radical to the point that democracy is also under threat. But we are then in a whole nest of atrocious difficulties; for cancer, as an example, begins to get equal rights. It is, therefore, no longer 'cancer' but instead a new and valid realization or suggestion of potentiality. The same would occur with the Holocaust.

Agamben tells us that the 'unprecedented violence of human power has its deepest roots in the structure of language' (Agamben 1993b: 7). Here we must ask, in the wake of Primo Levi—*if this is a man?* Certainly, we need to have a sense that in defining something or someone we have reduced them or it to that definition. But in defining things (not because we think we have captured them), the things themselves have captured our attention precisely because of their excess. Again, this is an example of Agamben's demonic catastrophe: I name the rose, even if, like Celan, it is 'no one's rose'. I only know that because it is, still, a rose. Otherwise who cares? Throw it on the fire! Agamben like Giles Deleuze, has a hero in Hermann Melville's Bartleby, he who would, famously, 'prefer not to'. The point of this 'I would prefer not to' is that it opens a space of total ambiguity. He does not, after all, say 'no I won't', which any system can easily accommodate. Rather he loosens the chains of the system's logic, sending it into a sort of fibrillation—*does not compute*, as the Daleks would most likely say. In so doing, the contingency of that system, or indeed of any system, is revealed. The possibility of a new world, a Badiouian event, if you will, becomes possible—and so Potentiality raises its emancipatory head. But does it? The problem is, once more, that Bartleby's 'I'd prefer not to' becomes 'I can't', or even 'it can't'.

Agamben tells us that 'potentiality and actuality are simply the two faces of the sovereign self-grounding of Being' (Agamben 1999: 18). But for ethics, this is a disaster since it evacuates ethics of all content. Indeed, the irony here is that Agamben actually comes to exemplify an instance of his account of how the law works: 'Not only does necessity ultimately come down to a decision, but that on which it decides is, in truth, something undecidable in fact and law' (Agamben 2005b: 30). In other words, Agamben, in most of his writings, is actually providing an account, if not a critique, of his own work.

Agamben argues that the human is the species that lies somewhere between bare life (*nuda vita*), or sheer physicality or animality, and the world of the symbolic, of language. That is: humans exclude bare life, but such exclusion is constitutive, therefore it is included—'I am not that'. *Zoē*, for Agamben is pre-linguistic life, whilst *bios* is political and linguistic. Bare life lies between, like *zoē*, but a crucial difference remains: for it is *zoē* as political, in other words, it is the inclusion/exclusion of *zoē*—*zoē* on its own cannot enter the political as it is essentially and forever pre-linguistic, but it can, unwittingly, be co-opted, that is, pre-linguistic life can at times be made to operate within a mode of thought: 'you are *only* matter', for example. The realm of bare life offers a site of potentiality that presents a source of radical change, because in bare life we are and we are not; that is, we are animals, human, and neither. Like Bartleby, bare life says 'I'd prefer not to'—it says something without saying anything in particular; sees something, without seeing anything in particular. In other words, it is not merely that our concept ('dog', to use a previous example) fails the object or the entity, which is to say, it falls short, and therefore betrays reality, it is, put differently, inadequate, inherently so. But that could suggest another concept might be possible that would not fail, it would be adequate—an illusion we tend to suffer. No, the point of Bartleby, the point of bare life, is potentiality. Whatever suffers description merely presents itself as a 'preference' and, in so doing, it lies between a yes and a no, a right and a wrong, a man and an animal, a language and the pre-linguistic.

One crucial example of the 'Bartleby' logic, for Agamben, is Christ; for Christ, in being God but also being man, suspends the dualism of the sacred and the profane. As Chalcedon has it, Christ has two natures and therefore he is fully human and fully divine, yet these two natures reside in one person (one *esse*). That makes it impossible now to locate the divine, on its own, or to locate the human. 'In Christianity, with the entrance of God as the victim of sacrifice and with the strong presence of messianic tendencies that put the distinction between the sacred and profane into a crisis, the religious machine seems to reach a limit point or zone of undecidability, where the divine sphere is always in the process of collapsing into the human sphere and man always already passes over into the divine' (Agamben 2007: 79).

With Agamben, we now live in world we no longer understand. Indeed we can never understand it. It is as if we resided perpetually in the moment before Adam names the animals—we are no longer at home, but live in the world of the uncanny (*Unheimlich*), of potentiality, or what Agamben also calls infancy and halo.[1] 'The world of the happy and that of the unhappy, the world of the good and that of the evil contain the same states of things; with respect to their being-thus they are perfectly identical. Neither just have matter but spirit too—for that is to remain in the previous economy. That the just person does not reside in another world. The one who is saved and the one who is lost have the same arms and legs. The glorious body cannot but be the mortal body itself. What changes are not the things but their limits. It is as if there hovered over them something like a halo, a glory' (Agamben 1993a: 92). Maybe because we can no longer discern the divine from the human, the sacred from the profane, and maybe even the human from the animal (in relation to bare life), then we can no longer limit what may have termed at one point, the material. Indeed, we know that God became man. Moreover, we cannot now say how things are different—since we have no loss, you can't look for a difference as such, as that is to remain trapped by an outmoded dualism. In short, we cannot separate or discern, in a non-questioning begging manner, the divine from the mundane—both suffer a radical and perpetual *epoché*.

Agamben tell us that 'In pushing each thing toward itself through the as not, the messianic does not simply cancel out this figure, but makes it pass, it prepares the end. This is not another figure or another world: it is the passing of the figure of this world' (Agamben 2005a: 25). If that is the case then we cannot juxtapose the world here that has now passed with some world beyond—in other words, this world is no longer locatable (it is no longer *here*, as there is no here), and if that is the case how can we, legitimately, speak of another to come, one that may lie beyond. What Agamben sees in the messianic and in Christianity is a potential to go beyond all dualisms: jew/nonjew, man/woman, and so on. According to Agamben, Christianity divides the division (Agamben 2005a: 49). Paradoxically, Agamben sees in this the ultimate profanation of religion, while also, in some sense, the profane itself. For example, it becomes meaningless to contrast the atheist with the theist. We have, or so it would seem, passed through a radical process of *epoché*. That is, we have at last suspended our natural attitude, and that goes for both atheist and theist: we no longer know what it means to be an atheist or a theist—we reside between in the swamp of potentiality. We are now 'at the end of all days that is every day' (Agamben 2007: 27). This is creation, not from nothing but, as nothing. There, in the between of potentiality, lies a new, revolutionary (and dare we say, diabolic) view of the world. The figure that perhaps most encompasses this condition is that of the unbaptized infants who die, but do not go to Hell. They appear, at least in the writings of Thomas Aquinas (debatably, to say the least, see Bonino 2001; and Oakes 2008); they enjoy something of a natural beatitude, in so far as they are happy and, therefore, do not miss Heaven: 'Neither

[1] It is not that these can all be equated, exactly, but there is a family resemblance.

blessed like the elected, nor hopeless like the damned, they are infused with joy with no outlet' (Agamben 1993a: 6). And Bartleby signifies this natural beatitude, as he 'dwells so obstinately in the abyss of potentiality' (Agamben 1993a: 254). Here Agamben is playing on the notion of *de potentia absoluta*. Indeed, Agamben argues that Bartleby comes, unlike Christ, not to redeem what was, but 'to save what was not' (Agamben 1993a: 270). In so doing, he affects an act of 'decreation'. But in the end, this is wholly question begging, and seems, as said, to be demonic.

III. Conclusion

Let us conclude with some final reflections about nihilism and creation *ex nihilo*. There is, according to Augustine, no before or after to Creation, for all temporal terms are a fruit of creation, an effect of creation, and not a framework within which Creation is to be understood. In other words, for Augustine, time itself was created, and thus we creatures see things in temporal terms but these are inappropriate to God. If they were, in fact, appropriate then Creation would not be *ex nihilo*, but would arise once again from the structuring of pre-existent material. Thus as Augustine tell us, 'When a builder puts up a house and departs, his work remains in spite of the fact he is no longer there. But the universe will pass away in the twinkling of an eye if God withdraws his ruling hand' (Augustine 1982: 117). In other words, just as Creation does not have a beginning, it is, in a sense, never over (ontologically speaking). Aquinas, picking up on Augustine's thinking nearly a thousand years later, makes clear 'God's relation to the creation is understood as a purely conceptual relation, while the creature's relation to God is real' (Aquinas, *STh* I q.45. a.3. ad.1); or again, 'Every relation which we consider between God and the creature is really in the creature, by whose change the relation is brought into being; whereas it is not really in God, but only in our way of thinking, since it does not arise from any change in God' (Aquinas, *STh* III, q.2. a.7; see also *STh* I q.28. a.1. ad.3; STh I q.6. a.2. ad.1). With regard to the question of change, Aquinas expands on this elsewhere, saying,

> Creation is not a true change, but is rather a certain relation of the created thing, as a being that is dependent on the Creator for its existence and that connotes succession to previous non-existence. In every change there must be something that remains the same although it undergoes alteration in its manner of being . . . In creation this does not take place in objective reality, but only in our imagination.' (Aquinas, *Comp. Theol.*, 99; see also; ScG, II, c.18, n. 952)

This means that for us creatures, for all that is created the temporal is a result of our createdness.

For Augustine, and even more so for Aquinas, our existence is not essential to us (what Aquinas calls the real distinction between our essence and our existence). Because we are created, because all we have is received, it is perpetually the case that in a sense our being is always naked. As Anselm says to God 'You are in no way less, even if they should return to nothing' (Anselm 1979: ch. 20). Eckhart echoes this: 'He could add the entire world to God and would have nothing more than if he had God alone' (Eckhart 1974–8: 65). This means that creatures are in a sense nothing, and both Eckhart and Aquinas concur: 'All creatures are one pure nothing. I do not say that they are a little something or anything, but that they are pure nothing' (McGinn 2001: 66; Eckhart sometimes terms this nothingness of the creature—*nullitas*, but for Aquinas to be a creature means to be an actual being)—'each created thing, in that it does not have existence save from another, taken in itself, is nothing' (Aquinas: *STh*1a, 2ae, q.109, a2). As St Augustine said of God; 'But you are deeper than my inmost being and higher than my own height' (Augustine 1991: 43). This intimacy, this non-invasive, divine concurrence, informs the world. Here we see in the starkest possible terms the non-dualism of Christian theology: God cannot be something alien to immanence, something simply different. Maybe then, it is better to conclude that we would rather answer the door to Christ, who is, in the end, a more 'uncanny' guest than nihilism, with all its needs, and its diabolic destruction of the world. In this way, we must understand that nihilism is not the truth of Christianity, but, if anything, Christianity is the truth of nihilism. If, that is, there is any truth to nihilism. That possibility makes me pause to think that maybe Fyodor Dostoevsky is correct, 'Nihilism isn't even worth talking about' (Dostoevsky 1987: 333).

References

Agamben, Giorgio (1993a). *The Coming Community*, trans. M. Hardt (Minneapolis, MN: University of Minnesota Press).

—— (1993b). *Infancy and History: The Destruction of Experience* Verso. (London).

—— (1998). *Homo Sacer: Sovereign Power and Bare Life*, trans. D. Heller-Roazen (Stanford, CA: Stanford University Press).

—— (1999). *Potentialities*, trans. D Heller-Roazen (Stanford, CA: Stanford University Press).

—— (2004). *The Open: Man and Animal*, trans. K. Attell (Stanford, CA: Stanford University Press).

—— (2005a). *The Time that Remains*, trans. P Dailey (Stanford, CA: Stanford University Press).

—— (2005b). *State of Exception: Homo Sacer II*, trans. K. Atell (Chicago: University of Chicago Press).

—— (2007). *Profanations*, trans. J. Fort (New York: Zone Books).

Anselm, St (1979). *Proslogion*, trans. M. J. Charlesworth (Oxford: Clarendon Press, 1965; reprinted 1979, Notre Dame, IN: University of Notre Dame Press)

Augustine, St (1982). *The Literal Meaning of Genesis*, eds. J Quasten, Walter Bughardt, and Thomas, Lawler, 3 vols. (Mahweh, NJ: Paulist Press).

—— (1992). *Confessions*, trans. H. Chadwick (Oxford: Oxford University Press).

Badiou, Alain (1988). *L'Être et l'événement*. (Paris: Seuil).

—— (1998). *Court traité d'ontologie transitoire*. (Paris: Seuil).

Badiou, Alain (1999). *Manifesto for Philosophy: Followed by Two Essays*. (New York: State University of New York Press).

—— (2001). *Ethics: An Essay in Understanding Evil*, trans. Peter Hallward (London: Verso).

—— (2004). 'The Event as Trans-Being,' *Theoretical Writings*, trans. Ray Brassier and Alberto Toscano (London: Continuum).

—— (2006). *Briefings on Existence*, trans. N. Madarasz (New York: SUNY Press).

—— (2008). *Number and Numbers*, trans. R. McKay (Cambridge: Polity Press).

—— (2009). *Conditions*, trans. S Corcoran (London: Continuum).

Baldwin, T. (1996). 'There Might be Nothing', *Analysis* 56: 4, 231–8.

Benjamin, Walter (1999). *Selected Writings*, vol. 2, trans. R. Livingstone (Cambridge, MA: Belknap Press).

Blanchot, Maurice (1993). *The Infinite Conversation*, trans. S Hanson (Minneapolis, MN: University of Minnesota Press).

—— (1995). 'Literature and the Right to Death', *The Work of Fire*. (Stanford, CA: Stanford University Press).

Bonino Serge-Thomas, O. P. (2001). 'La Théorie des limbes et le mystère du surnaturel chez saint Thomas d'Aquin', *Revue thomiste* 101, 131–66.

Brassier, Ray (2004). 'Nihil Unbound: Remarks on Subtractive Ontology and Thinking Capitalism', in *Peter Hallward*, ed. *Thinking Again: Alain Badiou and the Future of Philosophy*. (London: Continuum).

Cantor, G. (1980). *Gesammelte Abhandlungen Mathematischen und Philosophischen Inhalts*. (Berlin: Springer).

Coggins, Geraldine (2010). *Could There Have Been Nothing?* (New York: Palgrave).

Crevier, Jean-Baptiste (1761). *Historie de l'université de Paris, depuis sonorigine jusqu'en l'année 1600*. (Paris: Desaint et Saillant).

Cunningham, Conor (2002). *Genealogy of Nihilism*. (London and New York: Routledge).

—— (2010). *Darwin's Pious Idea* (Grand Rapids, MI: Eerdmans).

Dostoevsky, Fyodor (1987). *Selected Letters*, trans. A. MacAndrew (New Brunswick: Rutgers University Press).

Eckhart, Meister (1974–8). 'Omne datum optimum', *Sermons*, vol. 1, trans. Jeanne Ancelet-Hustache (Paris: Éditions du Seuil).

Foucault, Michel (1970). *The Order of Things: An Archaeology of the Human Sciences*. (New York: Vintage Press).

Gray, John (2007). *Black Mass: Apocalyptic Religion and the Death of Utopia*. (New York: Farrar, Straus, and Giroux).

Heidegger, Martin (2000). *Introduction to Metaphysics*, trans. G. Fried and R. Polt (New Haven, CT: Yale University Press).

Jacobi, F. H. (1994). 'Open Letter to Fichte', *The Main Philosophical Writings and the Novel Allwill*, trans. G. di Giovanni (Montreal and Kingston: McGill-Queen's Press).

Kojève, Alexandre (1963). *Introduction to the Reading of Hegel*, trans. James Nichols (Cornell University Press: New York).

Lacan, Jacques (1991). *The Seminar of Jacques Lacan, II: The Ego in Freud's Theory and in the Technique of Psychoanalysis, 1954–1955*, ed. Jacques Alain-Miller, trans. Sylvana Tomaselli (London and New York: W. W. Norton & Company).

—— (1992). *The Seminar of Jacques Lacan, Book VII: The Ethics of Psychoanalysis*, trans. D. Potter (London: Routledge).

—— (1998). *Seminar XX: On Feminine Sexuality: The Limits of Love and Knowledge*, trans. B. Fink (New York: Norton).

Lewis, David (1991). *Parts of Classes*. (Oxford: Oxford University Press).

Lowe, E. J. (2001). *The Possibility of Metaphysics*. (Oxford: Oxford University Press).

—— (2002). 'Metaphysical Nihilism and the Subtraction Argument', *Analysis* 62, 62–73.

McGinn, Bernard (2001). *The Mystical Union of Meister Eckhart*. (New York: Crossroad Books).

Maurice Merleau-Ponty, Maurice (1964). *The Primacy of Perception*, trans. J. Edie (Evanston, IL: Northwestern University Press).

Milbank, John (2007). 'The Return of Mediation, Or the Ambivalence of Alain Badiou', *Angelaki: Journal of the Theoretical Humanities* 12: 1, 127–43.

Nancy, Jean-Luc (1997a). *Creation of the World*, trans. F. Raffoul (Atlantic Highlands, NJ: Humanities Press).

—— (1997b). *The Sense of the World*, trans. J. Librett (Minneapolis, MN: University of Minnesota Press).

—— (2008). *Dis-Enclosure: The Deconstruction of Christianity*, trans. B. Bergo, G. Malaenfant, and M. B. Smith (New York: Fordham University Press).

—— (2010). *L'Adoration: Déconstruction du christianisme 2* (Paris: Galilée).

Nietzsche, Friedrich (1968). *The Will to Power*, trans. W. Kauffmann and R. J. Hollingdale (New York: Vintage).

—— (1972). *The Gay Science: With a Prelude in Rhymes and an Appendix of Songs*, trans. Walter Kaufmann (New York: Vintage).

—— (1997). 'On the Use and Abuse of History for Life', *Untimely Meditations*, trans. R. J. Holingdale (Cambridge: Cambridge University Press).

Oakes, Edward (2008). 'Catholic Eschatology and the Development of Doctrine', *Nova et Vetera* 6, 419–46.

Sartre, Jean-Paul (2000). *Being and Nothingness*, trans. H. Barnes (London: Routledge).

Vattimo, Gianni (1992). The *Transparent Society*, trans. David Webb (Cambridge: Polity Press).

—— (1996). *Beyond Interpretation: The Meaning of Hermeneutics for Philosophy*, trans. David Webb (Cambridge: Polity Press).

—— (1999). *Belief*, trans. Luca D'Isanto and David Webb (Cambridge: Polity Press).

—— (2002). *After Christianity*, trans. Luca D'Isanto (New York: Columbia University Press).

—— (2004). *Nihilism and Emancipation*, trans. W. McCuaig (New York: Columbia University Press).

—— and Caputo, John (2007). *After the Death of God*, ed. Jeffrey Robbins (New York: Columbia University Press).

—— and Rorty, Richard (2005). *The Future of Religion*. (New York: Columbia University Press).

Watkin, Christopher (2011). *Difficult Atheism*. (Edinburgh: Edinburgh University Press).

Weller, Shane (2011). *Modernism and Nihilism*. (London: Palgrave Macmillan).

Zaborowski, Holger (2010). *Robert Spaemann's Philosophy of the Human Person*. (Oxford: Oxford University Press).

Suggested Reading

Agamben (1998).
Badiou (2001).
Cunningham (2002).
Gray, John (2007).
Jacobi (1994).
Kojève (1963).
Lowe (2001).
Meillassoux (2008a).
Nancy (1997a).
Vattimo (1999).
—— (2004).
Watkin (2011).
Weller (2011).

CHAPTER 16

SACRIFICE

DOUGLAS HEDLEY

The question you raise next
Is one that is a common concern for virtually all humans,
Both those who have given time to education
And those relatively lacking in experience of philosophical reasoning;
I mean the question of sacrifice.

(Iamblichus 2003: 5.1 199.5–7)

THE concept of 'sacrifice', as Iamblichus remarks, is puzzling. It is a deeply rooted and pervasive aspect of human culture. Some, like René Girard, employ sacrifice as a central motif in their work. Other scholars, like Détienne, regard the category of sacrifice in much scholarly work as an artificial Christian prejudice. In this chapter we shall bracket the question of the status of the concept of sacrifice and consider how the idea has been employed. We shall venture a schematic division between three general types of constructive theory of sacrifice in the modern period: the spiritual, the economic-pragmatic, and the aesthetic. The first belongs to the mainstream Christian inheritance but we can find instances beyond theology proper. Here sacrifice betokens the necessary battle between the lower and the higher self in an axiological universe. Maistre and Weil are representatives of this form of thinking about sacrifice. The economic view of sacrifice is most obviously associated with the Durkheimian conception of religion, where the sacred becomes a function of society and where sacrifice is a means to an end. Finally, we have the aesthetizisation of the violence of sacrifice in Nietzsche and Bataille. Sacrifice for these authors becomes an image of a Dionysian affirmation of life itself, with it dark and violent aspect included, and the vehement repudiation of both any higher Divine telos to sacrifice and some merely functional-prudent construal of 'making sacred'. Yet before we can appreciate the Christian development, it is necessary to examine the context from which it emerged.

'Religion' as a term is notoriously difficult to define. It is often observed that sacrifice expresses the kernel of the religious phenomenon. It is certainly striking how closely the same word is applied for worship and sacrifice in Indo-European. The Sanskrit verb *yaj yajati* or the noun *yajna* connote both worship and sacrifice. *Ta hiera* the sacred rites in Greek mean equally the sacrifices. The noun *sacrum* in Latin is a holy thing or a sacrificial object. There is clearly some deeply rooted link between the ancient language of worship (at least among Indo-Europeans) and sacrifice. The origins of the English 'devotion' in the Latin to sacrifice, 'devovere', is a striking instance of this. Why is the cultural phenomenon of religion so closely linked to practices of offering, oblation, or propitiation?

Yet, of course, the term 'sacrifice' itself is problematic. The German word *Opfer* contains the various senses of the Latin for sacrifice: *sacrificio*, victim: *victima* and offering: *oblatio*. The English term sacrifice bears much ambiguity. The meaning of sacrifice of self or sacrifice of others is unclear from common usage. If we speak of the sacrifice of young men and women in war, say, it is not clear whether they are sacrificial victims of the body politic/military or whether they acting in readiness to sacrifice *themselves*. The horrors of the last century caused by the willingness of totalitarian regimes to glorify violence in quasi-sacral terms has made such language problematic as well as ambiguous. Moreover, if ritual killing is a central aspect of sacrifice, does this not suggest that religion is deeply, if not exhaustively, violent? This is a question that has fascinated leading modern Continental thinkers on sacrifice from the Savoyard counter-revolutionary apologist Joseph de Maistre (1753–1821) up to the French-American thinker René Girard (b. 1923). One can read in the twenty-first century reports of tribal sacrifices of young women in tribal south Asia or Voodoo corpses found in London. Does the spectre of Iphigenia in Aulis or Isaac on Mont Moriah still haunt the human psyche? Has the horror of human sacrifice been carefully disguised and transformed into secular forms?

The etymology of the word sacrifice is 'making sacred': the paradigm act of consecration. The basic ritual form of sacrifice appears in various cultures without relatively minor variations (Henninger 1987). Its figurative form obviously presupposes some grasp the ritual version.

As a ritual, sacrifice presents an immediate problem for reductionistic modes of thought. Given our evolutionary development where scarcity is crucial, it is odd that an activity as conspicuously wasteful as sacrifice should be so universal. The power of figurative or spiritualized sacrifice in many traditions is equally hard to square with such reductive accounts of human behaviour.

One common explanation is that sacrifices are attempts to bribe the gods. Much depends here upon how the sacrifice is conceived: as a prudential instrument of control (however ill-conceived or misguided) or a means of deliberate annihilation. Theories of sacrifice often depend upon background hypotheses in anthropology or theology.

A common theme among commentators is the ambivalence of the sacred in western thought. The 'Holy' is a source of terror as well as comfort or consolation and Maistre and Girard in their reflections on sacrifice reinforce this profound aspect of the ambivalence of the holy. In this way they avoid the crude dichotomies of good or bad in much of the Anglo-Saxon discussion of religion.

Another point is the centrality of Francophone thought on sacrifice from Maistre to Bataille and Girard. This characteristically Gallic interest and obsession may be explained both by the intense sacrificial spirituality of the Counter-Reformation and also the pivotal experience of the French Revolution. Writers as diverse as Maistre or Robespierre viewed the great events of the French Revolution: the insurrection of August 10, the September Massacres, the Terror, and the reaction against the Jacobins on 9 Thermidor as sacrificial events (Goldhammer 2005: 1–26).

I. Sacrifice in Ancient Philosophy

One commonly imagines sacrifice as belong to an archaic pre-philosophical period. Indeed, ancient philosophy might be said to have started with the critique of bloody sacrifices. The philosophical monotheism of Xenophanes, Empedocles, or Plato evolved out of a critique of the crude anthropomorphism of much popular religion. The supreme, transcendent philosophical *arche* developed by the philosophers, whether Plato's Good, 'Thought thinking Itself' in Aristotle, or the One of Plotinus, was not a crude projection of human fears. Nor was the reverence of this supreme being part of a quasi-economic *do ut des* (Young 1975: 37–42).

The end of ancient Greek philosophy saw a revival of the idea of sacrifice in the attempt of pagans of late antiquity to justify the ritual practices of Graeco-Roman piety against the Christians. By the end of antiquity, the dominant philosophical schools, Platonism and Stoicism, were monotheistic. The rise of Christianity did ignite the desire to provide a justification for the tradition of Graeco-Roman rituals against the imported Semitic religion. This was facilitated by a non-literal interpretation of the Hellenic myths and by a prioritizing of ritual practices in later Neoplatonism. Plotinus seems to have had little interest in religious practice and sees salvation or *soteria* as attained through contemplation (*theoria*) of and union (*henosis*) with the transcendent source, not through ceremonial or sacrificial rituals. The vegetarian Porphyry wrote extensively on sacrifice (Porphyry 2000). Iamblichus insists that rituals and sacrifices are legitimate forms of theurgy or divine work. This Neoplatonic rehabilitation of ritual was the model for a pagan Renaissance in late antiquity, briefly realized by the Emperor Julian the Apostate. Iamblichus died in 325, the year of the Synod of Nicea, when Christian Orthodoxy was promulgated.

Christianity had an ambivalent relationship to sacrifice. The emergence of the religion out of Post-exilic Judaism was closely linked to questions surrounding the validity of the Temple in post-exilic Jerusalem and, indeed, the destruction of the Jerusalem Temple in AD 70. Hosea 66 'I desire mercy not sacrifice' is taken up by Jesus

Christ in Matthew 9:9–13. In Romans 12:1 St Paul speaks of Christians 'offering their bodies as living sacrifices'. This reflects a general tendency within Christianity to spiritualize the notion of sacrifice as a practice of renunciation.

The sacrifice of self preached by Christ and Paul is closely linked to the doctrine of the sacrifice of the incarnate Son by the Father. On the full Nicene Trinitarian theology, Christ is atoning for humanity through his sacrificial and priestly activity. The mercy of the Father is tempered by his demand for Justice which can only be fulfilled by the sacrifice of Christ. Here the Christian model of the death of Christ as sacrificial is modelled on the Old Testament paradigm of Abraham and Isaac on Mount Moriah.

The parallels between the death of Christ as a sacrifice and images and practices of sacrifice among Hebrews and pagans can be interestingly observed in Christian art and architecture. The remarkable Basilica of San Clemente in Rome is situated about three hundred yards from the Coliseum. The church has richly symbolic decorations, in particular a twelfth-century mosaic of the sacrificial cross of Christ as the tree of life. There is a fourth century basilica and an underground Mithraic Temple from the end of the 2nd century AD, the latter containing an altar in which the figure of Mithras is depicted slaying a bull. The construction of a Christian church on the site of a Mithras Temple is a striking instance of a Christian church incorporating a pagan pre-structure.

Two aspects of the Christian view of sacrifice are worth mentioning. The fact that Christ is presented as the priest and the sacrificial lamb. Furthermore, the sacrifice of his death is 'once for all'. Thus the peculiarity of the Christian legacy resides in the fact that it was never a sacrificial religion per se and yet its theology has been so deeply shaped by symbols and metaphors of sacrifice.

II. Sacrifice in the Modern Period

The influence of the Christian theology upon modern thought and culture scarcely needs any emphasis. The convulsion of the Reformation and the Renaissance generated furious and erudite debates about the efficacy and nature of the Eucharist. The leading French Oratorian Pierre de Bérulle (1575–1629) was the proponent of an intense theology of sacrifice of the Counter-Reformation (Strenski 2002). The God of Abraham and Isaac and the God of Jesus is a God of sacrifice and mainstream Christianity, Catholic or Protestant upheld resolutely the sense of Christ's death being a sacrificial act and thereby reconciling God and humanity. It was the impact of the radical anti-Trinitarian movement known as Socinianism that did most to sustain a critique of the very principle of sacrifice. The main doctrinal document of Socinianism, the Racovian Catechism of 1602, explicitly repudiates substitutionary atonement. Socinian critiques within Christianity clearly reinforced the fiercely *ethical* criticism of Christian doctrine that emerged with such force in the Enlightenment. How can a good God demand cruel punishment for a frail humanity? Much of this debate about the questionable goodness of the Christian God concentrated upon the story of Abraham and Isaac, which Christians traditionally saw as a typological prefiguring of the death of Christ.

The modern period is also one of colonial expansion and the discovery of cultures where Spanish accounts of human sacrifice as practiced by the Aztecs and Mayans exercised a great influence (Hughes 2007: 53–66). The great critique of the French Revolution, the Savoyard thinker Joseph de Maistre (1753–1821) placed sacrifice at the centre of his thought. De Maistre discusses such phenomena alongside practices such as the Sati or widow burning in nineteenth-century India.

The ideals of the Enlightenment generated the French Revolution with its ideals of liberty, equality, and fraternity. Although a secular, if not atheist, state, the ideologues of the Revolution, especially Robespierre, were quite happy to enlist the language of sacrifice to help the cause. A lawyer by training, Maistre was a voracious scholar with a deep knowledge of ancient, particularly Platonic, thought. Plato, Plutarch and Origen play a central role in his philosophical and theological reflections.

The centrality of the idea of sacrifice enables him to dwell on the enigmatic nature of warfare and punishment, in opposition to secular, economic, and utilitarian values. The absurd and cruel violence of warfare and capital punishment belies the breezy anthropological optimism of the Enlightenment:

> The entire earth, perpetually steeped in blood, is nothing but an immense altar on which every living thing must be immolated without end, without restraint, without respite, until the consummation of the world, until the extinction of evil, until the death of death.   (Maistre 1993: 381–2)

Maistre was trained by the Jesuits and had a strong aversion to the Jansenists, whom he blamed in part for the French Revolution. Behind the theology of Jansenism lies the predestinarian thought of Augustine. The problem of evil and suffering in the world was ultimately explained in terms of the inscrutable will of the Deity. Maistre was also a great admirer of the great Alexandrian Origen. Freedom is at the heart of Origen's theology: divine judgement must be just and applied to responsible creatures. Responsibility presupposes freedom. Maistre shares this emphasis upon freedom and responsibility but the price he pays for this Origenistic avowal of human freedom is an unflinching depiction of the return to God, salvation itself, as a process of sacrificial purgation. Sacrifice becomes a key to the entire cosmos: the world is an altar of bloodletting which at the same time is a means of grace. Providence, in Maistre's view, is guiding all history towards the end of suffering and death, but the redemptive process is necessarily enigmatic and troubling in this finite state. Salvation for Maistre, as for Origen, is a *paideia* through Christ. Here Maistre works with a deeply cosmological paradigm rather than a more forensic/Anselmian readjustment of the relation between man and God. Human life is all subject to process of terrible sacrificial purgation, of which the death of Christ is the recapitulation.

According to Maistre, it is not religion that is the cause of conflict but rather mankind's fallen nature and sacrifice is the attempt to stem it. Suffering is purgative as well as punitive. It can only be expiated by sacrifice, which is *vicaria anima*, a substitute soul. Maistre sees instances of this practice throughout the heathen world. Ancient pagans did not sacrifice wild or useless animals. But 'the most valuable because of their utility, the gentlest, the most innocent, those nearest to man because of their instincts and habits (. . .) the most *human* victims in the animal kingdom were chosen, if I may express it that way' (Maistre 1995: 35–9). Before Christ a sacrificial victim was anthropomorphic. After Christ, the paradigmatically human is the willing self-sacrifice. Christianity is distinctive because for it sacrifice is ethical: as self-renunciation. The Christian aims to be Christ-like in self-abnegation: 'under the empire of this divine law, the just man (who never believes himself to be such) nevertheless tries to come up to his model through suffering. He examines himself, he purifies himself, he works on himself with efforts that seem to surpass humanity to obtain finally the grace of being able to return what has not be stolen' (Maistre 1995: 381–2).

Maistre is fascinated by the ethical ambivalence of warfare and punishment and its relation to society. Perhaps the primary shock of Maistre's mediations upon war is the product of our contemporary anaesthetic civilization. Perhaps Maistre is scandalous to the contemporary mind because of the remarkable capacity of a highly developed technological society not merely to prevent pain for its own members, but also to hide suffering. One does not have to be an adherent of Foucault to see the craving for comfort and security as part of an attempt to administrating life and eradicate the unsightly and troubling: avoiding confrontation with the old and the sick. For democratic politicians understandably worried about votes the dead and the wounded of wars are to be rendered, as far as possible, invisible.

Consider the paradoxical claim that 'war is divine'. It is typical of his provocative rhetoric. In fact, Maistre refers again to the 'horrible enigma', that is anomalous status of war: *'Rien n'est plus contraire à sa nature, et rien ne lui répugne moins: il fait avec enthusiasme ce qu'il a en horreur'*[1] (Maistre 1993: 660). His own life had been violently disrupted by the revolutionary wars and much of his adult life was spent in sad exile from family and home.

A thinker who is surprisingly close to Maistre is Simone Weil, as can be seen in her idea of decreation. Like Maistre, Weil was fascinated by intimations of Christianity in Indic and Hellenic sources. Like Maistre, Weil draws upon a tradition of mystical cosmogony. For Weil, God created the world through an act of sacrifice. It was through the divine contraction that finite being could be. And yet the most profound human vocation is to find union with God by renouncing this God given independence. The dark and troubling aspects of human existence become for Weil, the fuel for the process of decreation. Her own ultimate sacrifice of self, in refusing any more than the rations of those suffering on the Continent, was shaped by this vision: the false God changes suffering into violence, the true God changes violence into suffering (Weil 1995: 65).

---

[1] 'Nothing is more contrary to his nature, and nothing is less repugnant to him: he enthusiastically performs that which fills him with horror.'

III. The Anthropological Theories and the 'Data' of Sacrifice

Maistre's or Weil's explicitly theological account of sacrifice can be contrasted with the Durkheimian tradition of sociological explanation of sacrifice. This strand of reflection upon sacrifice was based in the religion section of the *École pratique des hautes études*, 1886. It was here that French anthropological theorizing about sacrifice developed intensely, often drawing upon British anthropologists.

Durkheim (1858–1917) was the founding father of sociology and Henri Hubert (1872–1927) and Marcel Mauss (1872–1950) were among his most distinguished and influential protégés. The phenomenon of religion, according to the Durkheim school, is explained as the cohesive power of the social body, which in turn is experienced as the sacred. For Durkheim, Hubert, and Mauss, sacrifice is viewed in terms of ritual gifts, as a part of human society and as public and observable. Sacrifice in this strand of thought is value neutral but could conceivably be valuable as a mechanism of social cohesion: the object of sacrificial activity is ultimately the projection of society itself. Religious ideas are, for them, social facts. Religion is thus a particular imaginative reification of social bonds and sacrifice is the symbolic means by which the individual acknowledges the communal force embodied by the deities.

One might expect anthropology to provide raw data, empirical evidence about sacrifice of an incontrovertibly empirical kind. And yet the anthropological theories are theory soaked. The main source of 'gift' theories of sacrifice is the English anthropologist Edward Burnett Tylor in his *Primitive Culture: Researches in the Development of Mythology, Philosophy, Religion, Language, Arts and Custom* (1871). Tylor defines sacrifice as 'a gift made to a deity as if he were a man' (Tylor 2010: II, 328). This most primitive level of sacrifice looks like a bribe. However, Tylor believes that sacrifice evolves to higher stages. The second stage is that of the homage, in which there is often a shared meal. The third stage is one of 'abnegation'. Notwithstanding this evolutionary modification, the core paradigm of sacrifice in Tylor is utilitarian. The sacrificer offers a gift for a favour from the god: sacrifice is a form of a crude or even economic '*do ut des*'. Marcel Mauss's observation is that the gift paradoxically entails obligation. A gift seems freely given; the value of the gift seems based upon the benefit accrued. However, Mauss notes that in human societies a gift generates a reciprocal relationship between giver and receiver: there are 'no free gifts' and he employed as an illustration of this the intense rivalry induced by gift exchange in Pygmy groups in the Andaman islands.

William Robertson Smith in his *Religion of the Semites* of 1889 attacked this idea of sacrifice as gift and replaced it with the idea of sacrifice as primarily the sacrificial meal as an 'act of communion'. He argues that sacrifice is prior to any idea of property. The item, animal, or victim sacrificed was already deemed holy and not the property of the sacrificer. The sacrificial act was not the offering of a gift to the god or gods but primarily a mystical meal that cemented the communion between the worshippers and the unseen divine realm.

Many commentators have objected to any strict opposition between gift and communion theories of sacrifice. H. Hubert and M. Mauss in their great work *Sacrifice: Its Nature and Function* view sacrifice as the means of *mediation* between the profane and the sacred. Drawing upon Hebraic and Vedic materials, they do not investigate the origins of sacrifice (Hubert and Mauss 1964). Sacrifice is explained as complex process of substitution. The victim of the sacrifice can become an instrument of divine power by taking the place of the sacrificer and thus absolving the sacrificer from guilt and death. This explains the complex rites of sacralization and desacralization. Sacrifice, on this view, does not emerge from the pre-existent sacred. Rather, the social practice of sacrifice becomes a way of defining the sacred in relation to the profane.

IV. OEDIPAL VIOLENCE? FROM FREUD TO GIRARD

Much Continental thought is deeply dependent upon the thought of Freud. Freud's reflections upon religion emerge out of the works of anthropological exploration of religion through theories of sacrifice, exemplified by Robertson Smith or the French anthropologists. Freud provides an explanation of the origins of sacrifice in his comparison of savage and contemporary society in *Totem and Taboo* in 1913: 'the beginnings of religion, morals, society and art converge in the Oedipus complex.' (Freud 1961: 156). It is here that Freud elaborates his highly speculative theory of the death of the primordial father by the horde. All religion is grounded in the guilt generated by this highly ambivalent relation to the primal father. The totem is a surrogate for the primal horde father and the sacrificial killing of the totem constitutes a repetition of the primal killing.

The totemic system was, according to Freud, a covenant with the father-figure, who bestows protection, care, and indulgence upon the worshippers. The practitioners of the system undertook to respect his life, that is to say, not to repeat the deed which had brought destruction on their real father (Freud 1961: 144). The two cardinal injunctions of totemism: slaying the totem and copulating within the tribe correspond to the Oedipal acts of patricide and incest. Hence Freud thinks that he has a psychological and historical explanation (i.e. the original criminal deed of slaying the primal father) for the emergence of religion as exemplified by totemism.

Freud draws explicitly upon Robertson Smith: The holy mystery of sacrificial death 'is justified by the consideration that only in this way can the sacred cement be procured which creates or keeps alive a living bond between worshippers and their god' (Freud 1961: 137). God is the projection of the father image of an individual, and this God is both oppressor and victim. The killing of the totemic animal and the meal is the repetition and celebration of the original primal murder. The meal is in part a celebration but also a purgation from the guilt of the killing.

In his recent book, *Battling to the End*, René Girard accuses anthropologists in general of colluding with psychoanalysis (Girard 2010: 62). They view prohibitions as directing against sex. The real problem, according to Girard is not sex but violence. Prohibitions are best seen as directed against mimetic rivalries, within which sexuality often plays a role. The core problem, in Girard's eyes, lies in the mimetic rivalry that is a relentless mechanism of violence. For Girard, the lack of sacrifice in contemporary culture is a kind of problem: without this mechanism societies are much more susceptible to violence. Girard thinks he has discovered the origins of sacrifice in relation to the mechanism of violence. Like Freud, he is offering a grand theory of the origins of sacrifice, which draws upon anthropology but which attempts to provide an account of the origins of sacrifice. He agrees with Freud that communal murder is key to religion, but Girard denies the parricide.

Girard is a literary scholar by training and his core anthropological theory of 'mimetic desire' seems to have been derived from literary research into Dostoevsky and Proust rather than from anthropology. In *Deceit, Desire and the Novel* he explores the process by which the desires of agents are mediated by the desires of others. The model of human desires, for Girard, is the desire of another. Hence human appetites are not unmediated desires for specific objects but always mediated by a model. One might say we actually desire what we imagine the other desiring. Girard sees an inherently violent component to this 'mimetic desire' since it is inherently competitive. The model quickly becomes a rival and a bar to the fulfilment of desire. This competition generates violence. Thus conflict is a fundamental part of Girard's apocalyptic vision of human life.

Girard sees sacrifice in archaic societies as a method for diffusing inherent violence. He interprets sacrifice as essential scapegoating, in which the escalating societal violence generated by mimetic rivalry is deflected upon an arbitrary victim. However, though the sacrificial victim is subject to arbitrary violence, it thereby attains a sacral status. The sacrificial victim is the source of the resolution of conflict and is revered as such. Hence Girard sees the ambivalence of the sacrifice—the victim is both guilty and yet holy. Many religious rites articulate this primordial experience of the resolution of conflict through scapegoating and the judicial system is a modern version of an essential sacrificial structure.

Girard presents a profound critique of the Durkheimian tradition of viewing the 'sacred' as constituted by social relations and structures. For Girard, the truth is precisely the opposite. Society is generated by the sacred violence of ritual sacrifice.

The final aspect of Girard's Christian vision is his view of the Bible as a critique of the scapegoat mechanism. The particular genius of Christianity, in Girard's view, is the vision of the world from the perspective of the victim, i.e. from Christ. This is the unique revelation of the violence that has been camouflaged by human society through the scapegoating mechanism. Girard, although very different from Maistre in his estimate of sacrifice and his identification of sacrifice with the scapegoat, is akin to

Maistre in seeing sacrifice as a key to human history. He is quite different from the value neutral approach of Mauss and Hubert. Just as Maistre saw the execution of Louise XVI at the French Revolution as a sacrificial death, Girard sees political and social events as profoundly sacrificial (Girard 2001: 93). Equally, both Maistre and Girard see violence as an inescapable and terrifying dimension of human life and one to which only Christianity can offer an antidote (Girard 2001: 137ff.). René Girard places the emphasis upon the victim and the process of scapegoating: Pogroms, lynching, and genocide become thus forms of persisting human sacrifice (Girard 2001: 64). It is striking that the sacrificial term 'holocaust' is generally employed for the Nazi genocide of European Jewry during the Second World War. The Nazi term 'Final Solution' or *Endlösung* was clearly a euphemism, and Shoah (meaning 'catastrophe') is preferred by Jews.

V. FROM HEGEL TO KIERKEGAARD: THE SACRIFICIAL SUSPENSION OF THE ETHICAL

Freud's theories are based upon the idea of the son killing the Father. But in an important sense the story of the Father killing the son is more prominent in the western tradition, especially through the Akedah and Christian Theology (Pailin 1981: 10–42). How could a good God demand something so terrible of his son? Voltaire thought that the story revealed the customary nature of human sacrifice among the ancient Hebrews. What of the terrifying God who demands blood in various religions? Is the Christian God not simply a more sophisticated variant of this widespread theological Moloch?

Nietzsche famously dismissed German Idealism as the product of the Protestant parsonage (Nietzsche 1968: 121). Hegel, though not himself a child of the parsonage, did study theology and his idea of the speculative Golgotha constitutes a high point in western theorizing about sacrifice. What Christian theology depicts as the self-sacrifice of God and resurrection is the dramatic-poetic representation of a key feature of mind or Geist. The nature of spirit/mind or Geist is constituted through the process of negation. In a famous line from the end of the *Phenomenology*, Hegel presents the imposition of form and order as the 'sacrifice' of the spirit: '*Seine Grenze wissen, heisst sich aufzuopfern wissen*' (Hegel 1983: 763) 'To know its limits is to know how to sacrifice itself'. For spirit that is conscious of itself as spirit, the path to self-consciousness is through the *sacrifice* of the natural and immediate life of the self whereby it is in opposition to the not-self. Self-conscious or spiritual life is not the development and then cessation of energy but a continual shattering of the immediate self and renewal and realization of that self in and through the not-self. This is the key to the Master-Slave dialectic: self-consciousness is constituted by its relation to the other. There is no authentic recognition of another self without sacrificing one's own absoluteness.

This fact at the level of personal selfhood is also a truth at the level of 'absolute spirit'—the divine mind. In making that which seems, prima facie, a *limit* a very part of itself, spirit or self-relection has no absolute limit. Spirit knows its own limit, can integrate and thus transcends it. Self-conscious life is properly a continual dying to live. Sacrifice of self, paradoxically, becomes its means of self-realization. The imagery of Golgotha is closely linked to what Hegel calls the 'Bacchanalian revel': the dismemberment of Dionysus. Spirit is not that realm of splendid detachment from reality but the truth that emerges from the 'tremendous power of negativity' and engagement with death.

The great theme of Hegel's philosophical theology is the ultimate unity of philosophy and theology. The picture language of the religious imagination is a representation of truth that can be understood in purely conceptual terms. Thus the imagery (*Vorstellung*) of sacrifice is a way of representing the conceptual truth of the Idea (*Begriff*) that must face and overcome negation. In knowing its limits, spirit transcends them. If Hegel's metaphysical bias is for the absolute over the temporary and the contingent, it is also the case that *only* through the sacrifice in the finite and contingent realm—the cup of history in Hegel's poetic imagery taken from Schiller's *Die Freundschaft*—that the infinity of spirit foams forth:

> *Aus dem Kelche dieses Geisterreiches*
> *Schäumt ihm seine Unendlichkeit.*

The eternal idea is not a refuge from, but is to be grasped within, the real conflicts and limitations of actual history. Sacrificial mediation is the very centre of Hegel's speculative dialectic. The vehemence of Kierkegaard's critique of Hegel is not appreciated by those who fail to recognize Hegel's deep and elective affinity to the *Stirb und Werde!* ('Die and become!') mystical death of Christian theological tradition. Christianity is the absolute religion for Hegel in so far as God surrenders himself in Christ and this sacrificial surrender is self conscious and leads to the emergence of spirit. This reflects the generic and philosophical dialectic of spirit as a dying to live and the attainment of a higher identity through the sublimation of negation.

Kierkegaard attacks precisely this identification of faith and reason in Hegel's speculative theology in his exploration of paradox. One of Kierkegaard's most striking contributions to his critique of Hegel's theological rationalism is through a controversial reading of Genesis 22 where Abraham is asked to sacrifice his son on Mount Moriah and is then stopped from killing his son by an angel. The boy is then substituted by a ram caught in the thicket. Kierkegaard interprets this story through the pseudonym of Johannes de Silentio who is astonished by and cannot understand Abraham. What looks, from the perspective of ethics like attempted murder, is presented to the religious mind in the story of Abraham as true sacrifice and an exemplar of piety.

Kierkegaard (or at least Johannes de Silentio) presents Abraham and Isaac on Mount Moriah as a tale of the limits of the ethical phase of life. It should be said that Kierkegaard does not offer a univocal interpretation of Genesis 22. Instead he presents a series of reflections upon, and re-imaginings of the narrative. His main concern is with the primacy of faith rather than presenting a doctrine about the relationship of religion to ethics. However, the text suggests a number of implications for any serious consideration of the limits of the ethical and its relation to faith. If the 'ethical' in Kantian/Hegelian terms is the domain of the universal, Abraham represents the Knight of Faith: the resolute believer who has utter faith in God and thereby in himself. That Abraham was prepared to obey God even in the command to murder his son is a sign of his complete commitment. This freedom is unmediated. The Knight of Faith is unlike the 'knight of infinite resignation'. Kierkegaard contrasts Abraham with the tragic hero Agamemnon. Agamemnon is called to sacrifice his daughter Iphigenia. In so doing, Agamemnon at least gains the recognition of his men who know *why* he made the sacrifice. Abraham, however, stands completely alone before God, with no human recognition of his plight. Rather than Hegelian mediation, it is his 'unmediated' faith that is evinced by Abraham's teleological suspension of the ethical. This is the suspension of ethical norms for a higher, i.e. religious goal. Abraham's fear and trembling in the face of his terrible unmediated sacrifice is Kierkegaard's strident repudiation of the Hegelian domestication of sacrifice through his theory of dialectical mediation of the spirit.

Kierkegaard's reading of Genesis 22 has had an enormous impact on twentieth-century Continental thought: especially Levinas and Derrida. Both philosophers had a particular interest in the sacrifice of Abraham. Levinas criticizes the 'transcendence of the ethical' in *Fear and Trembling* (Levinas 1998: 26–38). Kierkegaard is espousing violence when existence goes beyond both the aesthetic and the ethical stages. Levinas has been criticized for attributing the position of Johannes to Kierkegaard and for a simplistic reading of the negation of the ethical. (Levinas 1996: 76). The responsibility of Abraham is dreadful and Johannes is hardly guilty of contempt for the ethical with the notion of teleological suspension. For Derrida, by way of contrast, Moriah is our ethical 'habitat every day' (Derrida 1995: 69). The dilemma of Abraham shows how our incapacity to 'respond to ... the love of another without sacrificing the other other'. It reveals the fact that Abraham's dilemma is the problem of ethics. Any case of responsibility is a betrayal and sacrifice of other responsibilities. The application of responsibility is in fact 'absolute treachery' (Derrida 1995: 68). This is the gift of death (Derrida 1995: 96). Abraham's dilemma thus becomes the normal state of humanity. But this is an equally extreme misreading of *Fear and Trembling* because Derrida does not take seriously the aspect of faith in the text. How can such a reading distinguish between the terrible responsibility of the Knight of Faith and that of the tragic hero? Derrida's denial of the coherence of the idea of responsibility is in opposition to the teleological suspension of the ethical in Kierkegaard's work. There may be a dimension of Lutheran critique of works in the idea of the teleological suspension of the ethical, in that faith involves the sacrifice of autonomy. The idea of the suspension of the ethical, however, requires the very coherence of the ethical.

VI. From Nietzsche to Bataille

Nietzsche dismisses the servile spirit of Christianity with its glorification of death and suffering. His critique of altruism and egalitarianism and his rejection of the validity of remorse is based upon a critique of the Christian model of self-sacrifice and self-abnegation and the virtues of sympathy and humility as symptoms of a life-denying sickness (Nietzsche 2002: 50). Nietzsche's counter-deity is a sacrificial god: Dionysus and the self-overcoming of the superman is a form of sacrifice. In the later period of his thought, the association of Dionysus with violence and the sacrifice of the weak becomes increasingly pronounced. In *Beyond Good and Evil* Nietzsche insists that a healthy aristocracy understands its role as the 'sacrifice of countless people who have to be pushed down and shrunk into incomplete human beings, into slaves, into tools, all *for the sake of the aristocracy*' (Nietzsche 2002: 152).

Here we return to basic questions about the nature of sacrifice: Is it a form of abandonment or annihilation? Or is sacrifice an archaic and camouflaged form of prudence? For the followers of Durkheim, Hubert, and Mauss, sacrifice is essentially prudential. But for Roman Catholic Counter-Reformation spirituality or the neo-Nietzschean Bataille, sacrifice is a riposte to prudence. Its hallmark is destruction.

In striking contrast to Maistre, Georges Bataille (1897–1962) denied any providential or productive force to sacrifice. Bataille was deeply influenced by Nietzsche. Sacrifice is ritual violence: a transgressive and disruptive force that is at odds with bourgeois values. In this sense, Bataille is an inheritor of Kierkegaard and Nietzsche, especially the Nietzsche of his *The Genealogy of Morality*.

Bataille is deliberately (one might add perversely) championing the recovery of the intimacy of animal/instinctual through sacrifice: this Bataille's version of the Dionysiac triumphing through sacrifice over against instrumental rationality. Sacrifice is an outlet for excess energy that characterizes living organisms: a 'prodigious effervescence of life' (Bataille 1992: 53). Through sacrificial violence the individual overcomes individuality and experiences the primordial unity of existence. The pointless violence of sacrifice becomes a celebration of life. Whereas Durkheim and Girard are supporting peace and order, Bataille's is an avowal of violent, profligate, and ecstatic destruction. Such a view obviously leaves the political realm in a most precarious position. He also reverses the traditional western conception of sacrifice as an image of the victory of the spiritual over the animal in mankind. Man is unique as the animal that has been degraded by a utilitarian relation to plants or animals through pastoral civilization. Humanity is thus alienated from its environment as a world of objects. Religion qua sacrifice 'is the search for lost intimacy' (Bataille 1992: 57). Sacrifice is the returning of things to an order of intimacy between sacrifice and world: hence destruction and consecration become the same. The animal self, which Maistre views as the source of discontent of mankind in so far as it conflicts with conscience, becomes a creative telos for Bataille as for Nietzsche.

VII. Conclusion

One might imagine that sacrifice is a concept that resists any philosophical explication. It seems to belong to an archaic pre-philosophical and pre-scientific domain of human culture. Yet when we consider the philosophical tradition in the more narrow sense, we find that sacrifice often plays a central role in questions such as punishment, evil, remorse, war, altruism, forgiveness, personal identity. The strongly hermeneutical dimension of Continental philosophy has disposed many philosophers in this tradition to explore the legacy of sacrifice as it has emerged within the philosophical milieu. Not merely those philosophers who have been concerned with the hermeneutical legacy of Christianity or classical antiquity, aspects of anthropology and psychology, but within a central strand of reflection from Hegel, Kierkegaard, and Nietzsche. Modern European thought has been shaped by the most archaic of all religious problems, the problem of sacrifice.

REFERENCES

Bataille, G. (1992). *Theory of Religion*. (New York: Zone).

Derrida, J. (1995). *The Gift of Death*, trans. D. Wills (Chicago: Chicago University Press).

Durkheim, D. É. (2001). *The Elementary Forms of Religious Life*. (Oxford: Oxford University Press).

Freud, S. (1961). *Totem and Taboo*, trans. Strachey (London: Routledge & Kegan Paul).

Girard, R. (2001). *I See Satan Fall Like Lightening*. (Leominster: Gracewing).

——(2005). *Violence and the Sacred*. (New York: Continuum).

——(2010). *Battling to the End: Conversations with Benoit Chantre*, trans. Mary Baker (East Lansing: Michigan State University Press).

Goldhammer, J. (2005). *The Headless Republic: Sacrificial Violence in Modern French Thought*. (Ithaca: Cornell University Press).

Hedley, Douglas (2011). *Sacrifice Imagined: Violence, Atonement and the Sacred*. (New York: Continuum).

Hegel, G. W. F. (1977). *Phenomenology of Spirit*, trans. A. V. Miller (Oxford: Oxford University Press).

——(1983). *Phänomenologie des Geistes*, ed. Göhler (Frankfurt: Ullstein).

Henninger, J. (1987). 'Sacrifice', trans. M. J. O'Connell, in M. Eliade (ed.), *The Encylopedia of Religion*, vol. 11. (New York: Macmillan), 544–57.

Hubert, H. and Mauss, M. (1964). *Sacrifice: Its Nature and Function*, trans. W. D. Halls (Chicago: University of Chicago Press).

Hughes, Derek (2007) *Culture and Sacrifice: Ritual Death in Literature and Opera*. (Cambridge: Cambridge University Press).

Iamblichus. (2003). *On the Mysteries (De Mysteriis)*, trans. E. Clarke, J. Dillon, and J. P. Hershbell (Atlanta: Society of Biblical Literature).

Kierkegaard, S. (1974). *Fear and Trembling*, trans. W. Lowrie (Princeton, NJ: Princeton University Press).

Levinas, E. (1996). 'A Propos of "Kierkegaard vivant"', *Proper Names*. (London: Athlone Press), 66–79 at 76.

——(1998). 'Existence and Ethics', in J. Rée and J. Chamberlain (eds). *Kierkegaard, A Critical Reader*, (Oxford: Blackwell), 26–38.

Maistre, J. de (1993). *St Petersburg Dialogues or Conversations on the temporal Government of Providence*, trans. Richard Lebrun (Montreal: McGill).

Nietzsche, F. (2002). *Beyond Good and Evil*, ed. R. P. Hortsmann and J. Norman (Cambridge: Cambridge University Press).

Pailin, D. A. (1981). 'Abraham and Isaac: A Hermeneutical Problem before Kierkegaard', in R. L. Perkins, (ed.) *Kierkegaard's* Fear and Trembling: *Critical Appraisals*. (Alabama: University of Alabama Press), 10–42.

Porphyry (2000). *De Abstinentia*, trans. G. Clark, *Porphyry: On Abstinence from Killing Animals*. (London: Duckworth).

Robertson Smith, W. (1889). *The Religion of the Semites*. (London: A. and C. Black)

Strenski, Ivan (2002). *Contesting Sacrifice*. (Chicago: Chicago University Press).

Tylor, E. (2010 [1871]). *Primitive Culture*. (Cambridge: Cambridge University Press).

Weil, S. (1995). *Gravity and Grace*. (London: Routledge).

Young, F. (1975). *Sacrifice and the Death of Christ*. (London: SPCK).

SUGGESTED READING

Armenteros, C. (2011). *The French Idea of History: Joseph de Maistre and his Heirs, 1794–1854*. (Ithaca: Cornell University Press).

Bataille (1992).

Bradley, O. (1999). *A Modern Maistre: The Social and Political Thought of Joseph de Maistre*. (Lincoln and London: Nebraska).

Bubbio, D. (2008). 'The Sacrifice of the Overman as an Expression of the Will to Power: Anti-Political Consequences and Contributions to Democracy', in eds. Herman, Siemens and Vasti, Roodt (eds), *Nietzsche, Power and Politics Rethinking Nietzsche's Legacy for Political Thought*. (Berlin: Walter de Gruyter), 269–98.

Burkert, W. (1979). *Homo Necans: The Anthropology of Ancient Greek Sacrificial Ritual and Myth*. (Berkeley, CA: University of California Press).

Carter, J. (2003). *Understanding Religious Sacrifice: A Reader*. (London: Continuum).

Daly, R. J. (2009). *Sacrifice Unveiled*. (London: T & T Clark).

Girard (2005).

Heesterman, J. C. (2003). *The Broken World of Sacrifice: An Essay in Ancient Indian Ritual*. (Chicago: Chicago University Press).

Hedley (2011).

Hegel (1977).

Henrichs, A. (1984). 'Loss of Self, Suffering, Violence: The Modern View of Dionysus from Nietzsche to Girard', *Harvard Studies in Classical Philology* 88, 205–240.

Hubert and Mauss (1964).

Keenan, D. K. (2005). *The Question of Sacrifice*. (Indiana: Indiana University Press).

Kierkegaard (1974).

Maistre, de (1993).

Sarineen, R. (2005). *God and the Gift: An Ecumenical Theology of Giving*. (Minnesota: Liturgical Press).

Scruton, R. (2004). *Death-Devoted Heart: Sex and the Sacred in Wager's Tristan and Isolde*. (Oxford: Oxford University Press).

Tylor (2010 [1871]).

CHAPTER 17

···

WAR AND PEACE

···

STANLEY HAUERWAS

I. EUROPE AND WAR

···

In his *Confessions* Augustine asks, 'What, then, is time?' He responds observing, 'I know well enough what it is, provided that nobody asks me; but if I am asked what it is and try to explain, I am baffled' (Augustine 1970: 264). Odd though it may seem, I suspect the same is true if we ask, 'What, then, is war?' There is little reason to think we do not know what war looks like. After all unlike time we assume we can 'see' war. Yet if we are asked why we do not describe a conflict between mafia families, a conflict in which organized groups of people kill and are killed, as 'war' we may well discover that war like time is not easily explained.

John Keegan has even written a book entitled, *A History of Warfare* (Keegan 1994). If you can write a history of a subject then it would seem you must know what makes a war a war. Yet Keegan wisely disavows any attempt to distinguish in a decisive fashion war from other forms of killing. He does so because he thinks war is an 'essentially contested concept'. The best he can do, the best anyone can do, is to stipulate what they understand war to name. Though many assume that they know a war when they see one, they may well miss the fact that what they have come to 'see' is in service to a particular ideology.[1]

For example, Michael Howard worries that how war is understood by 'liberal intellectuals', that is, as a pathological aberration from the norm of peace, does not

···

[1] The subject I was given was 'war and peace'. I have assumed my primary responsibility was to write about war and I have done so. However the very presumption that war is to be treated before peace can give the impression that 'peace' is but the absence of war. Such a presumption, however, is surely a mistake if peace both ontologically and morally is a more determinative reality than violence. That does not mean that 'peace' is no less a 'contested concept' than war. These are matters I unfortunately must leave aside given the more historical work that seems appropriate to this volume.

do justice to the reality that war names. The problem, according to Howard, is if war is assumed to be pathological and abnormal then all conflict must be similarly regarded. But from Howard's perspective war is a particular kind of conflict between a very specific kind of social groups, namely, sovereign states. Howard draws on Clausewitz's and Rousseau's argument that if one had no sovereign states you would not have wars. 'As states acquire a monopoly of violence, war becomes the only remaining form of conflict that may legitimately be settled by physical force' (Howard 1983: 11).

Howard's claim that war is only properly so called after the creation of sovereign states is a strikingly modern presumption. To so understand war reflects a construal of war that goes hand and hand with the creation of that entity we now call modern Europe. How one determines when 'modern Europe' begins is a matter of dispute, but at the very least 'modern' indicates the loss of Christendom. That loss had deep implications for how war and the justification of war and peace was and is to be understood. When Christendom was presupposed, those at war with one another had a sense they were part of a wider civilization. Accordingly a conflict between two princes could be mediated by a king or a bishop because both sides assumed they shared the same standards. That was not true when war was against the 'infidels' (Yoder 2009: 11).

After the Reformation bishops no longer were political actors. They no longer had the power to restrain the use of war by kings and princes as an expression of political interest. That did not mean, however, that some did not try to establish grounds for understanding as well as limiting war between the emerging political realities. Hugo Grotius is rightly given credit for first expressing the significance of this new reality, that is, how a legal order between sovereign states might be possible as a way to limit war. His *De Jure Belli ac Paci* (1619) presumed that there exists a common human nature that makes possible cooperative agreements between states. Grotius, therefore, represents the attempt to develop an ethics of war after the loss of Christendom.

To ask what makes a war a war, therefore, turns out to be extremely important for how the ethics of war is to be understood. The ethics of war does not begin with the question of whether a particular war can or cannot be justified on just war grounds. For example it is instructive to ask: 'If a war is not just what is it?' The question is instructive because many assume even if a war cannot be justified on just war grounds it nonetheless may be necessary and therefore an obligation for the citizens of a particular state. This position is often identified as a form of 'realism' that presumes the development of the nation-state system of Europe.

To so understand war as the expression of the reality of Europe may seem arbitrary but Howard's position is widely shared by some of the most thoughtful work on war and peace. For example W. B. Gallie argues in his extremely important book, *Philosophers of Peace and War: Kant, Clausewitz, Marx, Engels and Tolstoy*, that the very idea of international politics—that is, the systematic study of the use of the threat of war and expansion of commercial and cultural contacts—awaited developments in the eighteenth century that recognized that to establish a civil constitution was dependent on a law-governed relation between states (Gallie 1978: 1).

Philip Bobbitt complicates Howard's and Gallie's account by suggesting that the development of what we now call war must begin with a history of the evolution of the modern state from the princely states of the fifteenth century, to the kingly states of the seventeenth century, that climax in the development of the nation-states from the state-nations of the eighteenth century (Bobbitt 2002: 69–213). The most important difference between these states for understanding war as a correlative of European developments is that transition from the state-nation to the nation-state. The former, according to Bobbitt, is a state that mobilizes a national, ethnocultural group to act on behalf of the state whereas a nation-state creates a state to benefit the nation it governs (Bobbitt 2002: 146). Bobbitt argues the state-nation was Napoleon's great creation through the military innovation of universal conscription (Bobbitt 2002: 151). Even though Napoleon lost he had insured the triumph of the state-nation as those who had beaten him had to mirror his achievement.

Bobbitt's account of the development of the states that comprised Europe is the background necessary to justify his contention that the very character of the states so conceived was 'a by-product of ruler's effort to acquire the means of war' (Bobbitt 2002: 174, quoting Charles Tilly). Such a state is the consequence of the necessities required to sustain the military expenditures necessary to insure the support of the administrative professionals that commanded the battle fleets to control the seas. But it is also the case that the democratic revolution of these states brought about a bureaucratization of force structures that changed the character of war itself (Bobbitt 2002: 174). As a result the wars of the state-nations were wars of the state that were made into wars of the peoples whereas the wars of the nation-states were wars that championed causes that had popular support by being fought for popular ideals (Bobbitt 2002: 204).[2]

Though Bobbitt thickens Howard's and Gallie's understanding of the relation of war and the state he is in fundamental agreement with their contention that war is constitutive of the development of international constitutional orders. From such a perspective war is not good or bad. Rather war simply 'is'. In a series of lectures at the *College De* France in 1975 through 1976 entitled, *Society Much be Defended*, Michel Foucault argued in a similar fashion that Clausewitz's famous proposition, 'War is the continuation of politics by other means' should be inverted. Foucault observed 'the role of political power is perpetually to use a sort of silent war to reinscribe that relationship of force, and to reinscribe it in institutions, economic inequalities, language, and even the bodies of individuals. This is the initial meaning of our inversion of Clausewitz's aphorism—politics is the continuation of war by other means. Politics, in other words, sanctions and reproduces the disequilibrium of forces manifested in war' (Foucault 2003: 15–16).

---

[2] Bobbitt observes that the nation-state gains its legitimacy from the claim that it is doing something unique in history, that is, maintaining, nurturing, and improving the conditions of its citizens (p. 177). That is why the nation-state, unlike the state-nation, depends on the success of maintaining modern life. Thus a severe economic depression undermines the legitimacy of those that would govern such states in a way the state-nation is not delegitimated.

According to Foucault, the inversion of Clausewitz's proposition helps us see that a crucial transition in the practices and institutions of war, which were initially concentrated in the hands of a central power, became associated both in *de facto* and *de jure* terms with emerging state power. 'The State acquired a monopoly on war' which had the effect of making war seem to exist only on the outer limits of the great state units. War became the technical and professional prerogative of a carefully defined and controlled military apparatus. The army now becomes an institution. This means, Foucault argues, that we cannot assume that society, the law, and the state are like armistices that put an end to wars. Beneath the law, war continues to rage. 'War is the motor behind institutions and order. In the smallest of its cogs, peace is waging a secret war. To put it another way, we have to interpret the war that is going on beneath peace; peace itself is a coded war. We are all inevitably someone's adversary' Foucault 2003: 50–1). Contrary to Hobbes, sovereignty is not the result of the war of all against all, but rather what we should learn from Hobbes is that it is not that war gives birth to states but rather sovereignty is always shaped from below by those who are afraid (Foucault 2003: 96).[3]

II. Kant on War

It is extremely important that the account of war correlative to the institution of an international order exemplified by the development of the nation-states of Europe not be seen as antithetical to the rule of law. For as Foucault implies the developments in international law worked to legitimate war as an essential function of the state. Paul Kahn observes that law and war are

> common expressions of the modern political culture of the sovereign nation-state. The state writes itself into existence by drafting a constitution. It expresses the historical permanence of that law by defending it at all costs. It demonstrates its own ultimate significance in the life of the individual citizen through the act of sacrifice that war entails.... All citizens become appropriate subjects of sacrifice and all history becomes coterminous with the continuation of the state.   (Kahn 2005: 279)

The connection between law and war W. B. Gallie argues was given its strongest theoretical justification by Kant in his pamphlet, *Perpetual Peace*, written in 1795. In that pamphlet Kant was intent to provide an account of the emerging order he thought might create a more lasting peace (Kant 1970).[4] Though often identified as a pacifist Kant, like Howard and Bobbitt, thought war could not be abolished though he sought to make war less likely. By so doing he made articulate the presuppositions that

---

[3] Foucault seems to echo themes from the word of Carl Schmitt.
[4] I will be referencing Gallie's account of this important work.

continue to shape modern assumptions about war and peace. If we are to understand where we are today it is, therefore, necessary to understand Kant, or at least Gallie's account of Kant, because few have seen as clearly as Kant how the attempt to establish political order by reason ironically results in the making war inevitable and, thereby, morally necessary.[5]

Kant begins *Perpetual Peace* by putting forward the conditions he thinks nations must adhere to maintain peace between themselves. Nations must pledge not to enter into secret treaties; they must refuse to acquire other states through inheritance, purchase, or gift; they cannot have standing armies though they can create citizen militias for defence; they cannot go into debt to sustain the military; they must not interfere with the internal constitution of another state; nor can they use assassins or try to subvert other governments. Those that can sign a treaty so conceived must be constituted by representative government because Kant knew such a treaty would only be the beginning of the process of peace.

Gallie rightly argues that Kant thought his understanding of the conditions necessary to sustain a more lasting peace between nations to be an expression of his central philosophical ideas. He sought to show how reason could lead to the formation of the relation between nations that could result in unity and peace. In particular Kant's project in *Perpetual Peace* was 'to construct a framework of ideas within which the generally acknowledged rights and duties of states vis-à-vis their *own* citizens can be shown to require, logically, acknowledgement of certain equally important rights and duties towards each other (and each other's citizens) if their traditionally recognized tasks are ever to be effectively discharged' (Gallie 1978: 13–14). In effect Kant gave a philosophical defence of Grotius's presumption that a common humanity exists sufficient to sustain a law-like relation between nation-states.

Like Rousseau, whom Kant admired, Kant wrote of international relations assuming the arrangements of eighteenth-century Europe. Kant thought that European states represented an advanced stage of development because they shared the inheritance of a common civilization. Kant, therefore, believed that even though wars continued to break out the greatest threat to civilization, that is, the overthrow of established political units within their own borders, was made less likely by the equilibrium between states in the nation-state system (Gallie 1978: 18). It was, thus, assumed that if a European power threatened its neighbor an alliance of powers would oppose it. 'War, therefore, was not simply a necessary evil within the European system, it was also the indispensible safeguard of the survival and independence of the different European states' (Gallie 1978: 18).

---

[5] I draw on Gallie's account of *Perpetual Peace* because, as Gallie notes, Kant's pamphlet, which Kant wrote in a 'popular' style in the hopes it might be widely read has led to a mass of contradictory interpretations many of which can be justified by the text. I use Gallie not only because I think his reading to be right, but because how he reads Kant also makes clear Kant's relevancy for the subject of this chapter.

Kant, of course, did not think that war was a 'good thing'. Rather he thought war to be one of the greatest evils humans endure. Yet he also thought that an international order must have as its task to keep the peace between like-minded states. Accordingly Kant thought an essential precondition of an international order is the non-interference in the internal affairs of other states. He assumed that the task of creating such an order would take many years. Though he thought that like-minded states could sign a non-aggression treaty he nonetheless assumed that every citizen 'should be prepared to defend his country from foreign invasion' (Gallie 1978: 21).

Kant knew that various philosophers and political leaders had sought to escape war by two means: (1) by imagining a vast empire which could control all subject people; (2) or by creating a strong federation of sovereign states united by their mutual defence. The latter was Rousseau's position yet Kant rejected it as well as the presumption of peace through empire. He rejected empire as a solution to the problem of inter-state relations because an empire would only substitute one form of tyranny for another. On the other hand, federations are not strong enough to enforce peace which meant he thought any attempt to enforce peace between sovereign states to be delusion (Gallie 1978: 24).

Thus Kant's belief that until there is asymmetry between establishing and maintaining just constitutions and maintaining a relationship between states the use of force in self-defence could not be ruled out. Gallie summarizes Kant's position noting that for Kant 'an act of defensive war may be justified as preserving a (relatively) just state in existence; but it cannot be justified in respect of that kind of relation between states which Reason positively requires that all states should strive to bring into being' (Gallie 1978: 24). Kant recommended, therefore, that states form confederations so that the 'peace' between them could be extended to like-minded powers.

Gallie notes that Kant's 'cosmopolitan ideal' is neither a world state nor an anarchistic utopia, but rather the hope of a world in which the rights of individuals can transcend the boundaries of their own nations. Peace would be secured not by a supernational authority, but by the mutual recognition of states constituted by citizens who recognize the rights and duties incumbent on rational beings to respect other nationals who are also so constituted (Gallie 1978: 27). Kant in *Perpetual Peace* expresses, therefore, his commitment to the rational consciousness of the free individual who too often is tragically blind and wayward. Thus he took the task of 'perpetual peace-*making* as, like all the other major tasks of mankind, essentially a matter of man's remaking of himself' (Gallie 1978: 35).

Kant's position has been endlessly critiqued and qualified but his fundamental perspective continues to shape how war has been understood by those committed to maintaining the nation-state system. Kant was the ultimate liberal if liberal names the attempt to create a politics of reason enshrined in law. Yet the question remains whether the liberal state so conceived can comprehend the reality of war. Gallie suggest the reality of war received its most determinative expression in the work of Tolstoy and Clausewitz.

Tolstoy's great work, *War and Peace*, a work that like *Perpetual Peace*, was a response to the Napoleonic wars, is Tolstoy's attempt to show how little wars can be understood (Gallie 1978: 101). That is why in *War and Peace* the most coherent units of action is relatively small groups of men who share the demands of war. They do not nor can they experience the battle as a whole. Yet Tolstoy is at pains in his great novel to show that neither do those who are in command of the armies have control or knowledge of the total action of the armies in battle. According to Gallie, however, what most bothered Tolstoy was not the killing itself, but rather the progressive dominance of life by 'the anonymous, irresistible, seemingly irreversible-bureaucratic state machines' (Gallie 1978: 125).

Though Tolstoy and Clausewitz seem to represent antithetical positions in a quite remarkable way how they understood war is quite similar. In particular Clausewitz understanding of Absolute War, that is, war fought for the complete destruction of the enemy no matter what the cost, cannot be comprehended by 'reason' is not that different from Tolstoy (Gallie 1978: 5–52). Clausewitz and Tolstoy, in quite different but complementary ways, support Paul Kahn's claim that the sacrifice that war requires cannot 'find a moral foundation in a theory of the democratic legitimacy of law' (Kahn 2008: 103).

According to Kahn the fundamental feature of war is killing and being killed. War is not about the life and death of individuals who participate in war, but rather war is about the existence of 'the sovereign as an imagined reality of transcendent value' (Kahn 2008: 150). In short Kahn suggests that war is the way states sanctify their existence. An ironic result given the widespread presumption that the creation of the modern nation-state system was necessary to stop Catholics and Protestants after the Reformation from killing one another. It is to that presumption that I must now turn.

III. THE MYTH OF RELIGIOUS VIOLENCE

In *The Myth of Religious Violence* William Cavanaugh challenges the widespread presumption that religions promote violence (Cavanaugh 2009). The presumption that religious violence is uncontrollable reflects Kantian-like justifications of the nation-state system of Europe. From such a perspective religion is identified with transhistorical and transcultural aspects of human life that are allegedly not subject to rational control. Accordingly religion must be restricted to the 'private' region of our lives and prohibited from having a public role. In contrast to religious communities the secular nation-state represents universal and timeless truth making possible the resolution of differences short of war (Cavanaugh 2009: 3).

Cavanaugh explores the historical record used to justify the presumption that religious violence cannot be controlled because religions are not subject to reason. Thus it is alleged that in the aftermath of the Protestant Reformation, in which Christendom was divided between Catholics and Protestants, the 'wars of religion' devastated Europe. Because Catholics and Protestants were unable to settle their doctrinal differences they embarked on a century of chaos and bloodletting that ravaged Europe. Peace between the warring religious communities was only made possible by the rise of the secular nation-state. The Peace of Westphalia in 1648 was the expression of this new reality. The state now had a monopoly on use of violence requiring Protestants and Catholics to submit to the religiously neutral sovereign state (Cavanaugh 2009: 123).

The power of this story, a story in which the state becomes the principal agent, is evident by the role the story plays in the thought of Spinoza, Hobbes, Locke, Rousseau, Gibbon, and Voltaire. The story is repeated endlessly, moreover, by contemporary political theorist such as Skinner, Stout, Shklar, Rawls, and Pocock. Thus Pocock's characterization of the Enlightenment as

> the emergence of a system of states, founded in civil and commercial society and culture, which might enable Europe to escape from the wars of religion without falling under the hegemony of a single monarchy; second, as a series of programmes for reducing the power of either churches or congregations to disturb the peace of civil society by challenging its authority.   (Quoted by Cavanaugh 2009: 139)

The only problem with this story, according to Cavanaugh, is it is not true. Cavanaugh observes that if it were true one would expect to find that Catholics killed Protestants and not fellow Catholics. Likewise one would think that Protestants killed Catholics but not necessarily other Protestants. Moreover if the story is true then the wars named the wars of religion must have had as their primary cause the cause of religion rather than political, economic, or social purpose.

Yet Cavanaugh argues that it is simply impossible to isolate something called religion from politics and economics. That Catholics killed Catholics and Protestants killed Protestants in the so-called religious wars is sufficient to suggest that more was at stake than being Catholic or Protestant. At the very least what was at stake was the beginnings of the development of the modern state system which had begun, as we now can see, prior to the Reformation. For what is clear is that the political actors that represented the beginnings of such states used antagonism between Catholics and Protestants to legitimate the growth of the state (Cavanaugh 2009: 142).

The historical record simply does not support the story of the 'religious wars'. Cavanaugh points out that Charles V spent much of the decade following Luther's excommunication fighting the pope even sacking Rome in 1527. Charles was also more frequently at war with France rather than the Protestants in Germany. In the Schmalk-aldic War of 1546–7 the Protestant princes supported the Catholic emperor in the wars against France. In 1552 the Catholic king, Henry II of France, attacked the emperors army while the Catholic princes of the empire took a position of neutrality. In 1583, the Protestant Jan Casimir of the Palatinate joined the Catholic duke of Larraine to fight against Henry III. In 1631, Cardinal Richelieu of France made a treaty with Sweden to subsidize the Swedish war effort. Indeed in the latter half of what we now call the Thirty

Years' War the battle was largely between Catholic France and Catholic Habsburgs (Cavanaugh 2009: 142–50).

These examples, and Cavanaugh provides many more, make clear that any attempt to isolate 'religion' from social, economic, and political realities cannot be sustained. Indeed it is crucial for Cavanaugh that the very creation of the category 'religion' is a correlative of the attempt to legitimate state control of the Church. For as Cavanaugh observes the creation of the category, 'religion', has a history. In the pre-modern west it would have never occurred to Christians that their faith might be a species of a more universal category called religion. To be sure religion in the Middle Ages was associated with bodily disciplines of 'the religious' but that use of the term meant that what it meant to be 'religious' was a concrete expression of a set of practices (Cavanaugh 2009: 81).

It may seem a small point to argue, as Cavanaugh does, that the very category of 'religion' is a construct. But he suggests, rightly, when religion became a description of an alleged reality more comprehensive than a specific faith it served as an ideological justification of the nation-state. In other words the creation of 'religion' went hand in hand with the growth of the nation-state which was justified as necessary to save Europe and later the whole world from religious violence. From Cavanaugh's perspective the state so understood, moreover, is not a secularized state, but rather one that is sacralized. For in the name of controlling religious violence the nation state 'replaced the church in its role as the primary cultural institution that deals with death. Christianity's decline in the West necessitated another way of dealing with the arbitrariness of death. Nations provide a new kind of salvation; my death is not in vain if it is for the nation, which lives on into a limitless future' (Cavanaugh 2009: 114).[6]

The myth of religious violence is, therefore, anything but innocent. Cavanaugh characterizes the myth as part of the folklore of western societies that has no basis in reality other than the reality it creates by its constant repetition. The repetitive character of the story, however, is necessary just to the extent the story legitimates the power of the nation-state in the west to wage war. It is a story of salvation in which the nation-state claims a monopoly on legitimate violence to save us from the violence of religion. The story is used to foster the idea, particularly in the United States, that secular social orders are inherently peaceful. The power of the story is evident just to the extent that a nation that spends more on military than all the nations of the world combined prides itself on being a peace loving country (Cavanaugh 2009: 127).

IV. The Ethics of War and Peace

I began observing that to know what makes war a war is not obvious. I have tried to elaborate that claim by suggesting how the development of the modern state system of

---

[6] Cavanaugh is here characterizing Benedict Anderson's views.

Europe produced an account of war that made war unavoidable but hopefully seldom necessary. The irony, however, of war so understood was subsequent wars were 'total' in a manner that made it impossible for those who were not in the military to be protected from the war. Equally ironic was the use of the 'Enlightened' ideology of the European powers to justify their imperial ambitions in wars against people who were not advanced enough to be 'nations'.

The reality of war, particularly the war described as the First World War, seemed so senseless and the loss of life so massive and purposeless that it led many to conclude that war could not be justified. The 'pacifism' that followed in the wake of that war was a 'liberal' position that assumed that war simply was 'irrational'. A pacifism so conceived reflected some of the rationalist presumptions Kant had developed in *Perpetual Peace*. Indeed many read Kant as an advocate of pacifism. Though to so read Kant was a mistake, such a reading did suggest how difficult it was to try to think ethically about war.

In 1960, a church historian, Roland Bainton, at Yale Divinity School wrote *Christian Attitudes Toward War and Peace: A Historical Survey and Critical Re-Evaluation*, in which he provided a typology that determined for many what they took to be the ethical alternatives for how war should be understood (Bainton 1960). Bainton identified three stances Christians have taken toward war: pacifism, just war, and crusade. It is important to remember that Bainton understood these to be 'types', that is, they are characterizations that in reality might be more complex. For example a crusade—that is a war fought for a cause that is so important the means used to achieve victory cannot be limited—was often thought to be just in the Middle Ages.[7]

By contrast a just war is a war fought to accomplish a limited end. This requires that the means used must be appropriate to the end. Though Bainton named just war as historically one of the major Christian options in truth the use of just war criteria for justifying or critiquing war was largely absent from Christian and non-Christian reflection on war after the Reformation. It was only with the work of Paul Ramsey that just war again became a viable way to think about the ethics of war. In particular Ramsey in 1961 published, *War and the Christian Conscience: How Shall Modern War be Conducted Justly?* (Ramsey 1961). In the book Ramsey drew on Augustine to suggest that just war is best understood as a response to an unjust attack on the innocent rather than an act of self-defence. Therefore those that would defend the innocent should seek only to use as much violence as necessary to deter the attack on the innocent. For a war to be just, therefore, a declaration of war is required by the legitimate authority to make clear to the enemy the limited nature of the war and the conditions for surrendering.

---

[7] This way of putting the matter can be misleading because the Crusades for the Holy Land were often fought as 'just' requiring knights to distinguish between combatants and non-combatants. Though this was often thought to be a matter of honour required of knights it nonetheless suggested that a war whose end was 'religious' was still assumed to be just. All of which is a reminder that the just war criteria were developed over many centuries and could appear quite different at different times.

The war once begun must, moreover, if it is to be just, be fought in a manner that the intention for going to war is no different than the reason declared for the war. A legitimate authority is, therefore, required to insure that the war is a public matter. The war must be fought, moreover, in a manner that clearly distinguishes the killing in war from murder. That is why the principle of discrimination was so important for Ramsey because it requires that non-combatants be distinguished from combatants.

Ramsey was deeply influenced by the 'realism' of Reinhold Niebuhr. Niebuhr justified the Christian participation in war by arguing that the relative justice between nations was only possible if war was not disavowed. Crucial for maintaining justice (and peace) within as well as between nations was the establishment as near as possible of a more or less equal balance of power. Accordingly, Niebuhr was a sworn enemy of all attempts by Christians to think that war might be avoided. The question for Niebuhr was never whether war could be justified, but how soon a war might need to be or avoid being fought to make less likely a larger or destructive war (Niebuhr 1932). Though he would be critical of Kant's 'rationalism' Niebuhr assumed a world not unlike the one Kant tried to justify in *Perpetual Peace*.

Ramsey was deeply appreciative of Niebuhr's perspective, but worried that there was inadequate control on Niebuhr's justification of war as crucial for securing justice in a nation-state system lacking any legitimate authority. Ramsey, therefore, attempted to show how just war could be understood as an expression of the kind of realism represented by Niebuhr. Such a view of just war has been questioned by Daniel Bell for failing to see that just war is not, as Ramsey sometimes seemed to suggest, a checklist to see if a war passes the just war criteria, but rather just war is a way that the Church discerned whether Christian participation in war can be understood as a form of discipleship (Bell 2009).

Though Bainton made reference to the Anabaptist understanding of Christological pacifism in his book, he seems to have thought that some form of liberal Protestant understanding of non-violence to be the most persuasive. It was the kind of liberal pacifism John Howard Yoder associated with secular humanism, which is based on the presumption that humankind names a sufficient community to make possible an appeal across differences that can secure agreements short of war (Yoder 2009).[8] As an alternative to secular pacifism Yoder, drawing on his Anabaptist tradition, developed an account of Christological pacifism that was political exactly because it is non-coercive. Pacifism, according to Yoder, is required by the cross of Christ for it is in the cross that God refuses to save coercively. Jesus, therefore, does not fit the Kantian mould because he is not commending his ethic for anyone, but for those that would be disciples (Yoder 2009: 316).

---

[8] Though Yoder used Bainton's typology he argued that the 'blank cheque' needed to be added to Bainton's three. For as Yoder argued, in fact most Christians, particularly after the Reformation, were schooled not to call into question those that ruled them. Accordingly they simply killed who their ruler asked them to kill. In short they simply gave a 'blank cheque' to war.

Yoder represents a form of pacifism that assumes that a Christian understanding of war draws on an eschatological perspective unavailable to those that do not share the Christian worship of Christ. Accordingly, he is not convinced that questions about effectiveness, which can be quite important, should determine how the Christian is to think about war. He puts it this way: 'Jesus was not successful. Jesus did not promise his followers that if they did things right, they would conquer with time. The non-coerciveness of agape includes renouncing the promise of power; it includes renouncing the mechanical model of how to move history. Yet that acknowledgement does not mean simple despair or unconcern. It rather means a promise of victory, the paradigm of which is the Resurrection' (Yoder 2009: 359).

Yoder's arguments for Christian non-violence are clearly dependent on theological claims and, in particular, an understanding of the priority of the Church to the world. Accordingly he represents an alternative to the Christendom assumptions that shaped how Christians understood war in inner war Europe. For Yoder the primary agent is not the emerging nation-states or the international system, but the Church. That does not mean he would fail to recognize the world that has developed, a world that the Howards and the Bobbitts describe, but he refuses to believe that world must be assumed as necessary. At the very least Yoder represents a challenge to the role war too often plays in providing the sacrifices thought necessary to justify the ethos of the modern state.

I referred above to Paul Kahn's contention that the political meaning of the modern state, the state created by European thought, is sustained by the practice of sacrifice, of killing and being killed. It is hard to see how that claim can be denied after the wars of the twentieth century (see, for example, Allen Frantzen 2004 and Ivan Strenski 2002). Through sacrifice, and in particular, the sacrifice of war citizens are created just to the extent they are subjects who can be called on to make the sacrifices war demands (Kahn 2008: 35). That is why the Christian alternative to war is best thought of not as an 'ethic', but the Christian alternative to war is Eucharist (Hauerwas and Wells 2011: 415–26). Christ is the end of all sacrifices not determined by his cross.

REFERENCES

Augustine (1970). *Confessions*, trans. R. S. Pine-Coffin (Harmondsworth: Penguin).

Bainton, Roland (1960). *Christian Attitudes Toward War and Peace: A Historical Survey and Critical Re-Evaluation*. (Nashville: Abingdon Press).

Bell, Daniel (2009). *Just War as Christian Discipleship: Recentering the Tradition in the Church Rather Than the State*. (Grand Rapids, MI: Brazos Press).

Bobbitt, Phillip (2002). *The Shield of Achilles: War, Peace and the Course of History*. (New York: Anchor Books).

Cavanaugh, William (2009). *The Myth of Religious Violence: Secular Ideology and the Roots of Modern Conflict*. (New York: Oxford University Press).

Foucault, Michael (2003). *Society Must Be Defended*, eds. Mauro Bertani and Alessandro Fontana, trans. David Macey (New York: Picador).

Frantzen, Allen (2004). *Bloody Good: Chivalry, Sacrifice, and the Great War*. (Chicago: University of Chicago Press).

Gallie, W. B. (1978). *Philosophers of Peace and War: Kant, Clausewitz, Marx, Engels and Tolstoy*. (Cambridge: Cambridge University Press).

Hauerwas, Stanley (2011). *War and the American Difference: Theological Reflections on Violence and National Identity*. (Grand Rapids, MI: Baker).

Howard, Michael (1983). *The Causes of War*. (Cambridge, MA: Harvard University Press).

Kahn, Paul (2005). *Putting Liberalism In Its Place*. (Princeton, NJ: Princeton University Press).

——(2008). *Sacred Violence: Torture, Terror, and Sovereignty*. (Ann Arbor: University of Michigan Press).

Kant, Immanuel (1970). *Perpetual Peace* in *Kant's Political Writings*, ed. H. Reiss, trans. H. Nisbit (Cambridge: Cambridge University Press).

Keegan, John (1994). *A History of Warfare*. (New York: Vintage).

Niebuhr, Reinhold (1932). *Moral Man and Immoral Society*. (New York: Scribner's Sons).

Ramsey, Paul (1961). *War and the Christian Conscience: How Shall Modern War Be Conducted Justly?* (Durham, NC: Duke University Press).

Strenski, Ivan (2002). *Contesting Sacrifice: Religion, Nationalism, and Social Thought in France*. (Chicago: University of Chicago Press).

Yoder, John Howard (2009). *Christian Attitudes to War, Peace, and Revolution*, ed. Theodore Koontz and Andy Alexis-Baker (Grand Rapids, MI: Brazos Press).

Suggested Reading

Bainton (1960).

Bell (2009).

Cavanaugh (2009).

Kahn (2005).

Hauerwas, Stanley (1985). *Against the Nations: War and Survival in a Liberal Society*. (Minneapolis: Winston).

——(2011).

Ramsey (1961).

Yoder (2009).

CHAPTER 18

....

RADICAL PHILOSOPHY AND POLITICAL THEOLOGY

....

MICHAEL ALLEN GILLESPIE

TWENTIETH-CENTURY continental philosophy developed within the horizon of Nietzsche's claim that God is dead. This claim is often interpreted as a post-Darwinian proclamation of atheism. Nietzsche's claim, however, is not that there is no God but that God, by which he means the Christian God, is dead, and that we thus no longer have anything to believe in. Or to put the matter in slightly different terms, we no longer live in a world infused by divine will but in a world in which God has died, a world determined and shaped by this death, a world in continual mourning for this God and the meaning and purpose that he gave to existence.

For Nietzsche, the solution to this problem lay in the creation of new gods, new values, meanings, and purposes. Nietzsche believed, however, that this could only be attained if man were first hardened by a long period of war and destruction. The path that led through this abyss, however, promised the epiphany of the superman who, he believed, would institute a thousand-year Dionysian Empire (Kuhn 1992: 237). The apocalyptic and messianic elements in his thought are unmistakable and have exercised a profound influence on many of his twentieth- and twenty-first century successors who have followed a path from radical nihilism/scepticism/atheism to new forms of religiosity that underpin new political theologies. This essay explores the interplay of radical philosophy and political theology by examining the path that Martin Heidegger followed from Catholicism through philosophical atheism to a new religion of Being and the connection of this understanding of Being to his messianic political theology.[1] In so doing, I will show how the trajectory inaugurated by Heidegger's theological starting point led through a seemingly abstract concern with issues of fundamental ontology to a fatal political commitment; the withdrawal from which in turn further impacted his later vision of both religion and philosophy.

---

[1] See Judith Wolfe, chapter 14 in this volume, for further contextualization of Heidegger's thought in relation to 20th century messianism.

Heidegger is of particular interest in this context since, having begun his career as a theological thinker, he developed a radical version of philosophy that was significantly influenced by his theological sources. The political implications of this philosophy came into the open with his commitment to National Socialism in 1933, thus illustrating the appeal of National Socialism to mystical, apocalyptic, and messianic elements in religion. With his withdrawal from Nazism into a more poetic world view Heidegger did not renounce these elements, but rather sublimated them to the necessity of a prior poetic reconstitution of thinking. Yet even this poetic turn does not obviate the dangers of applying these kinds of religious sources too directly to philosophical work and political life. Post-Nietzschean continental philosophy sought to reground human life and morality without reference to God. Indeed, it sought to radically separate itself from anything that played a role even vaguely related to the metaphysical role played by the Christian God, but, as we see in the case of Heidegger, the more radically philosophy sought to separate itself from God, the more likely it was to succumb to new forms of political theology and religion that provided little moral direction and even fewer constraints on human action.

On the surface, Heidegger seems very distant from any kind of theological commitment. Perhaps more than any thinker of the twentieth century, Heidegger sought to root his thinking in radical questioning. Indeed, he developed his vision of philosophy in opposition to western metaphysical and theological doctrine and dogma, rejecting all systematic accounts of man and the world or what he later came to call all 'onto-theological' metaphysics (See, for example, Heidegger 1988b: 1; Heidegger 1949: 1) Beginning in the 1930s, however, Heidegger defended National Socialism as at least in some ways compatible with his thought. On the surface his support for Nazism seems to be a denial of his anti-metaphysical and anti-theological views, since it tied his thinking to a specific world view rooted in a naturalistic metaphysics. In attempting to explain this deviation, Jacques Derrida and others have portrayed this support for National Socialism as a manifestation of a lingering humanism in Heidegger's thought (Derrida 1991). I want to suggest that this reading presents a mistaken picture of the relationship between philosophy and politics that Heidegger describes. The path of radical questioning leads Heidegger to Nazism not because it is humanistic or metaphysical, but because it rejects all rational grounds for action in favour of a revelatory or mystical intuitionism that is in fact a reversion to a radically nominalist and voluntarist religiosity.[2] It is this form of religious worship of a hidden or unknown God that lies at the heart of his messianic political theology and thus is the basis for his attachment to and support of National Socialism. We see this borne out not only in his stance and statements in the 1930s but also in the new notion of thinking as poetic (or oracular) utterance (which can guide us to a different future) that he develops in the aftermath of the Nazi period. He argues in the final period of his thought that poets alone can

---

[2] On Heidegger's attempt to regain the immediacy that he believed characterized the mystical relationship to God, see Kisiel 1996: 71, 81, 84, 108, 114. I use 'mystical' in this sense throughout the essay. By 'voluntarist' here (and throughout) I refer to the doctrine of divine and not human freedom.

provide us with the oracular guidance we need to lead us through and beyond the technological wilderness of the modern world.

Following Nietzsche and many other nineteenth-century thinkers, Heidegger believed that the structures of modern life failed to provide the possibility for a meaningful human existence. In Heidegger's view, modern man like Nietzsche's last man is mired in the mundane concerns of everyday life, lost in a world of beings without any connection to the whole, to God, or to Being. In contrast to medieval man whose activities were connected in multiple ways to a transcendent reality, modern man lives in a disenchanted world, surrounded and dominated by a realm of objects that neither connect him to nor point him towards anything beyond himself.

In his earliest thought, Heidegger developed this account of the hollowness of modern life in an explicitly Catholic context, and he apparently believed that it could be overcome by a more ardent adherence to his religion. He even sought for a time to become a priest, although this attempt was derailed by ill health. However, a brief experience at the front during the First World War and a crisis of faith in 1917–19, led him to move away from the regnant Thomism of his time (Kisiel 1993: 72–3). Already in his *Habilitationsschrift*, he had looked to Duns Scotus in opposition to Aquinas, and his crisis of faith led him down an ever more 'Protestant' path, towards a conception of religiosity based on the thought of Ockham, drawing explicitly on Eckhart, Luther, Schleiermacher, and Kierkegaard (Safranski 1994:14).[3] During the period after 1918, he sought a relationship to his own life that was akin, as Theodore Kisiel point out, to the relationship the mystic had to God (Kisiel 1993: 107–8). Building on Husserl and Dilthey, he attempted to conceptualize this 'life' as the 'primal something,' 'life in and for itself' , the 'historical or situated I', 'factical life experience', '*Dasein*', and ultimately as 'Being' (Kisiel 1993: 16–17). Heidegger's movement away from theology culminated with his decision that there could be no theological philosophy and his declaration that he was a philosophical (although not a personal) atheist (Kisiel1993: 113; see also Heidegger 1988b: 197, and Heidegger 1988: 30). Although he abandoned traditional theology, Heidegger did not abandon religion. Indeed, like Luther he believed that philosophy had to separate itself from theology in order to break through to the immediate experience of primal life, because it was only on this basis that the realm of true religiosity, the realm of the holy, could be opened up. Such a goal, he believed, could be attained only through the most radical philosophical questioning that shattered the theoretical and theological overlay that separated modern human beings from reality.

---

[3] His marriage to a Protestant and their common reading of Luther may also have played a role in this transformation. Kierkegaard exercised an important influence for Heidegger but his impact is generally overrated, in part due to the early misinterpretation of the treatment of death in Being and Time as Kierkegaardian. Such a reading that focused on the radically individualizing character of death in large part explains the surprise of so many of his students at his affiliation with the Nazis. His lectures on Aristotle from the first half of the 1920s, however, point to the collectivist character of Dasein. On this point see Gillespie 2000. Heidegger himself repeatedly makes this clear in his 1934 lecture series on 'Logic as the Question of the Essence of Language' that was originally titled 'State and Science' (Heidegger 1998: 42–70).

In this period Heidegger conceptualized this new way of thinking within the framework of phenomenology as 'primordial science' (Heidegger 1987: 24; Heidegger 1993: 1). As he first envisioned such philosophizing, it was to be based on a radical questioning that led to answers and ultimately world views (Heidegger 1993: 5; Heidegger 1988b: 3, 43). This primordial science was in his view the thinking that grounds the rest of science, opening up actuality as it is given prior to scientific questioning (Heidegger 1995: 3, 9; Heidegger 1988b: 43; Heidegger 1994b: 2). It begins without definitions, deflating all scientific claims to certainty, and does not aim at a final theoretical answer but at the revelation of the mysterious source of questions and thinking in practical life experience (Heidegger 1988b: 13, 18; Heidegger 1994a: 76).

While this conception of thinking seems to have much in common with traditional philosophy, it is actually anti-theoretical and anti-conceptual. During the period after the First World War through the mid-1920s, Heidegger gradually became convinced of the necessity of uncovering what had remained concealed in philosophy since the time of Plato and Aristotle through a radical questioning not merely of beings but of Being itself, of the 'is' that is at the basis of all thinking, acting, and being. He hoped, as he put it in *Being and Time,* to pose anew the question of Being (Heidegger 1953: 23). In confronting the question, 'What is being?' previous philosophy in Heidegger's view turned to the Being of beings. While Being was thus revealed as the origin of beings, it was also concealed, since it was understood in terms of beings as if it were just another being. Traditional western philosophy thus left Being itself unthought. It is this ultimate question, the question of Being itself that Heidegger believed was most pressing (Heidegger 1994b: 158. See also Heidegger 1997a: 42; Heidegger, 1959a: 201, and Heidegger 1988b: 37).

The necessity for a more radical questioning was already clear to Heidegger in 1919. He was convinced that asking *what* something is in the manner of traditional philosophy never comes to the concrete individual thing but only to the species, the ineffable universal (Heidegger 1994b: 149). The first question that must be posed by philosophy is thus not the question of *what*-Being but of *that*-Being; not the question of the qualities of a being but the question of existence itself (Heidegger 1994b: 152). At this time Heidegger attempted to raise this question within the framework of Husserlian phenomenology but in contrast to Husserl who sought to determine the structures of Being (*Sein*) through an analysis of forms of consciousness (*Bewusstsein*), Heidegger focused not on consciousness but on an analysis of historical human Being-in-the-world or what he called there-Being (*Dasein*). In Heidegger's view, I do not experience my 'I' by itself but always embedded in an environment (Heidegger 1995: 13). The 'I am' was as crucial for Heidegger as it was for Husserl, but he focused on the 'am' rather than the 'I', on Being rather than consciousness (Heidegger 1988b: 172–3). This is a crucial difference, for philosophy thereby ceases to be an egological reflection and becomes an examination of the factical life experience (Heidegger 1988b: 168) .

Heidegger's attempt to raise the question of Being begins with an analysis of *Dasein* because man is the only being who has his own Being as a question. Stones and trees *are* and 'have' Being, but they do not 'have' it as an issue or question. Whether they are or what they are or what they are to be is indifferent to them. They are not concerned. They do not care. They are merely beings. *Dasein*, by contrast, is more than a being because it is a question to itself, because it is concerned with what it is and is to be.

Humans in Heidegger's view become the beings they are as a result of this connection to Being, by being struck or overpowered by Being. Like Luther, Heidegger attributes very little to human will. Humans become *Dasein* and enter into a connection with Being in Heidegger's view only 'because *Dasein* stands in a special relation to Being'(Heidegger 1959: 140). Without an understanding of Being, man could not relate to himself as a being, could not say I and thou, could not be a person, could not be a self (Heidegger 1959: 144). Thus an understanding of Being is the ground of the possibility of being human (Heidegger 1982: 25; Heidegger 1997a: 45). Heidegger's thought is thus not humanistic or anthropocentric but ontocentric, centred around a hidden Being that is strongly reminiscent of the *deus absconditus* of the late Middle Ages and the Reformation.[4]

Humans can question only because they stand within the question of Being. This question is not a question *about* Being. Being is not something that we ask about or describe. Nor is this exactly a question posed by Being. Rather Being itself *is* only *as* a question, and all beings are, in a manner of speaking, answers to it. Being is this fundamental question because it is radically other than beings. This difference between Being and beings is what Heidegger calls 'ontological difference'. Being (like the post-scholastic God) is not anything categorical. Heidegger thus rejects all attempts to define Being as the most general concept or the highest or supreme being as insufficiently attentive to ontological difference.

While Heidegger grants priority to Being, Being is in the world always only through *Dasein*. The world thus comes to be *as it is* only through *Dasein*, which is the place (*Da-*) at which Being (*Sein*) manifests itself. In its radical otherness Being cannot appear among beings as just another being, but only as nothing (Heidegger 1959: 24).[5] *Dasein* as the site of the epiphany of Being is therefore 'the place-holder of the nothing' (Heidegger 1949: 15; see also 18; and Heidegger 1969: 44). To philosophize we must stand in the midst of this nothingness and allow ourselves to be drawn into the radical questioning that it engenders. Concretely, this experience of Being as nothing is the experience of death, as he puts it in *Being and Time*, or more generally of human finitude (Heidegger 1953: 231–67; Heidegger 1997a: 43; Heidegger, 1965: 200). It is the hurly-burly in which man is caught up and in which he seeks to grasp his own being without employing imaginative constructions (Heidegger 1983: 28).[6] Heidegger suggests that this is the experience of anxiety, despair, rejoicing, or boredom (Heidegger 1959: 1).

---

    [4] This is the meaning of Heidegger's claim that man is a who not a what (Heidegger 1959: 144; Heidegger 1989: 245).
    [5] Heidegger here accepts Meister Eckhart's claim that God and nothing are the same (Safranski 1994: 496).
    [6] Heidegger's path is different than that of Nietzsche who was convinced of the need to employ images and metaphors to make sense out of the inexpressible.

All of these reveal the meaninglessness of beings individually and as a whole. Radical philosophical questioning thus puts one's entire inner and outer existence at risk (Heidegger 1983: 139; Heidegger 1988a: 17). To come to experience reality for Heidegger, one must pass through despair, through the dark night of the soul so well known to mystics such as St John of the Cross as well as Luther, and dwell in terrifying uncertainty, giving up all hope of an ultimate answer (Heidegger 1994a: 3; Heidegger 1959: 30).

This radically unsettling experience besets everyone from time to time, but most run away from it or repress it, since it places a painful question mark over existence. This retreat into the realm of prevailing answers or what Heidegger calls everydayness in *Being and Time* is the source of fallenenss and inauthenticity (Heidegger 1953: 173–80). Heidegger believes for us to lead an authentic communal life, it must become a more general experience. The philosopher (like Luther's evangelical Christian) thus must chase human beings out of the contentment of everyday existence and into the abyss of Being (Heidegger 1983: 31). Philosophy must bring humans to confront their own finitude and compel them to face anxiety, boredom, and meaninglessness. Only in this way will it be possible for *Dasein* to re-establish an authentic relationship to Being, as the place (the *Da*) of Being (*Sein*). Moreover, because we exist always in a world with others, what is necessary is not merely an individual, Kierkegaardian leap but the committed leap of a whole people, into nothingness. Heidegger's goal is thus to bring about a revolution not merely in the self-understanding of the philosopher but in our very Being-together-in-the-world as a people and a community, to prepare for a messianic transformation of human life (Heidegger 1998; Sheehan 1993: 91).

The presupposition of this notion, according to Heidegger, is the recognition that Being is time. This was one of the principal goals of *Being and Time* (Heidegger 1953: 39).[7] Philosophy, since Plato, understood Being only in terms of one mode of time, the mode of presence. The necessary corollary of this idea is that what *does* change is not Being. In opposition to this core metaphysical idea, Heidegger argues that Being includes coming to be and passing away and thus is essentially historical. Consequently, it is crucial to know not *what* is but *how* Being reveals itself, In so far as we are the place Being comes to be, what is decisive is understanding how to be in our time, i.e. how to live within the prevailing revelation of Being (Heidegger 1976: 131).

Heidegger argues repeatedly that for the Greek the word for revealing was *alêtheuein* that means to bring-into-unforgetfulness, or out of concealment. He analyses this Aristotelian notion of truth most fully in the first section of his lecture on Plato's *Sophist* in 1924–5 (Heidegger 1992: 10–231). He argues there that Aristotle recognized five modes of *alêtheuein* in and through which we open up the world: *sophia* or wisdom, *episteme* or science, *technê* or the know-how of making, *phronêsis* or the know-how of acting, and *nous* or intuition of first principles. *Sophia, epistêmê,* and

---

[7] I do not mean to suggest in this discussion that *Being and Time* and many of Heidegger's other works were *only* concerned with the questions I deal with here or that they were not concerned with deep philosophical questions that are in some sense separable from the theological elements in his thought.

nous, Aristotle argues, are concerned with the unchanging, *technê* and *phronêsis* with the changing. The process of opening up the world through *sophia* is *philosophia* and its practitioner is the *philosophos.* The process of opening up the world through *phronêsis* is praxis, and especially politics, and its practitioner is the *phronimos.*

While Heidegger draws on Aristotle, he rejects the idea that anything is unchanging and thus denies the superiority Aristotle attributed to wisdom. All wisdom or theory is in his view merely a form of technical knowledge. The question is then not whether *sophia* is superior to *phronêsis* but whether *technê* is superior to *phronêsis,* or to put it in more familiar language, whether economic and technical know-how is superior to ethical and political judgement. Heidegger believed that modernity had come to be dominated by the universal technical organization of everyday life, and *Dasein* had come to be treated as if it were just another being to be produced, ordered, and controlled. This issue appears in *Being and Time* as the question of the role of equipmentality and then appears in his later thought as the question of technology (Heidegger 1953: 66–72). Technology seeks to convert everything, including humanity itself, into a raw material that can be exploited and used up in the production of the means of production, that is, in the service of further technology.[8] Technology in this sense is not a tool in the hands of a self-conscious humanity, but the destiny of the West. This question is latent but not yet explicit in the first section of *Being and Time,* which is much more concerned with demonstrating the primordial character of the practical (the ready-to-hand) and the derivative character of the theoretical (the present-at-hand). But it becomes more explicit in the later discussion of historicity as the way in which one form of the practical, i.e. *phronēsis,* is shown to be essential to the authentic being of *Dasein,* in contrast to more technical explanations that depend upon a traditional or scientific understanding of time and efficient causality.

Heidegger argued that the pre-eminent and most dangerous forms of this techno-logical impulse were the metaphysically identical twins Americanism and Marxism which he believed were squeezing Europe from both sides (Heidegger 1984: 86; Sluga 1993: 236). The salvation of the West thus depended on establishing a new relationship to technology and this required raising the question of Being *as* the question of technology. Heidegger's goal was thus to reveal technology as a revelation of Being and to demonstrate the necessity for technology to be guided not by *technê* or by *sophia* but by *phronêsis.*

Heidegger agrees with Aristotle that *phronêsis* aims not at the good as such but at what is good in the circumstances peculiar to this time and place (Heidegger 1992: 135; Marcuse 1924: 125). In contrast to Aristotle, however, Heidegger abandons the trad-itional notion of *phronêsis* as everyday practical reason, moving in a revelatory and messianic direction.[9] For Heidegger *phronêsis* is the recognition of what is called for

---

[8] Richard Bernstein has pointed out the similarity of Heidegger, Marx, Weber, and Lukács on the role of technology (Bernstein 1992: 100. See also Wolin 1993: 210).

[9] In *Being and Time* Heidegger characterizes this moment as a 'resolute rapture' in which *Dasein* is 'carried away' (Heidegger 1953: 338).

historically, what is fated or destined by the revelation of Being (Marcuse 1924: 12). This is understood not by comparison to previous experience but by what becomes apparent in a 'moment of vision'. He thus sees *phronêsis* not as practical wisdom but as the moment of supreme spiritual revelation and decision that holds open the possibility of breaking out of the mundane present into a different reality by establishing a new relationship to Being (Safranski 1994: 207–10).

Each moment of vision, according to Heidegger, is rooted in an intuition into the possibilities for the future opened up by the prevailing revelation of Being within a particular tradition with its unique heritage. What is seen in this moment is not what has been and therefore must be, but how we are projected towards the future by the particular character of the question of Being as it strikes us concretely here and now and the resources in our past that enable us to construct an answer to it (Heidegger 1953: 338–9; Kisiel 1995: 245). Each moment of vision thus provides a range of answers to the question of what one ought to do. There is no fixed notion of the human good that it reveals. Indeed, for Heidegger the human good varies according to the moment or *kairos* (Kisiel 1993: 299).[10] It is thus necessary to be open to this moment and its demands. Heidegger assigns the task of making this decision about the good and thus about action not to the philosopher but to the *phronimos*. '*Phronêsis* makes the location of the one who performs the action accessible: in securing the Why, in making available the particular Whither, in apprehending the Now, and in stretching out the How' (Heidegger 1988b: 381). The *phronimos* in messianic fashion has a unique revelatory insight into the particular historicity of the situation because of his openness to Being. He or she is thus able to reveal what is to be done.

In the chaos of the early 1930s Heidegger became convinced that a pivotal moment had arrived. 'Everywhere', he wrote, 'there are tumults, crises, catastrophe, suffering: the current social misery, the political hurly-burly, the impotence of science, the weakness of religion' (Heidegger 1983: 243). He believed that this apocalyptic chaos could only be dealt with through a primordial confrontation with the question of Being and the leadership of someone with the phronetic vision to guide the German people to a better future. It was in this context and with this goal in mind that Heidegger understood and promoted the National Socialist movement. Hitler and the leadership of the Nazi Party seemed to Heidegger to be the only hope for such leadership and thus offered the best chance of a meaningful existence for Germany and Europe as a whole (Safranski 1994: 198).

Phronêsis is typically thought of as practical wisdom or deliberative judgement in an Aristotelian sense, but, as Heidegger conceives it, it is closer to a Christian conversion experience brought about by something akin to divine grace and enlightenment. Thus, while Heidegger here works within an Aristotelian framework, he is deeply indebted to

[10] We should note the importance of Heidegger's understanding of the kairos for the Lutheran theologian Paul Tillich, who argued that there are various kairoi or crises in history that open up the possibility of an existential decision by human beings. Pre-eminent among them in his view was the appearance of Christ.

Paul, Augustine, Eckhart, Luther, and Kierkegaard. The moment of vision is understood less in a philosophic than in a poetic or religious fashion. Drawing on Augustine's kairetic account of time as stretching itself backwards to creation and forwards to the apocalypse, Heidegger sees each moment of vision as revealing a new world, both forward and backwards in time (Gillespie 1989: 33–51).

This moment of vision brings about a transformation of *Dasein* as Being-in-the-world (Heidegger 1998: 120, 160). Following Paul and Luther, Heidegger sees this moment as an absolute affliction in which one faces the possibility of one's own death and thus the possibility of nothingness. This moment of despair, however, is also the moment of total commitment (Heidegger 1953: 338; Kisiel 436–7). As Heidegger puts it in *Being and Time*, it is thus the call of conscience, the call to face and accept the fact that one is thrown into this world (and not some other) and that one's future is set by the destining of Being and not by one's free will (Heidegger 1953: 267–301; Kisiel 1995: 306; Brogran 1995: 278). Since the content of the revelation in the moment of vision is not set in advance, it is necessary to hold oneself open to this moment (Kisiel 1993: 299). Given the human tendency to flee the anguish of this openness, the moment can only be successfully traversed if one pre-commits oneself to endure it. For Aristotle such a holding-oneself-ready is *hexis*, which we typically translate as 'habit' (Marcuse 1924: 71). Heidegger, however, understands it in a more Augustinian fashion as preparation for a turning around, i.e. for conversion (Kisiel 1993: 438).[11]

In contrast to many of his contemporaries, Heidegger saw the crisis of the 1930s as a valuable shock that might stimulate a communal confrontation with the question of Being. Not surprisingly, he was disappointed by the response of the liberal and left-wing parties which were unwilling to face what he saw as the true question, and sought instead only to repair the system and make it work better, i.e. more productively. As a result, Heidegger looked elsewhere for the kind of phronetic leadership he believed was necessary and became convinced that the best chance of renewal and salvation lay in the social and political programme of Hitler and the National Socialist movement. They seemed to offer the possibility of a confrontation with what Heidegger thought of at the time as the dominance of *technē*, and the chance of subordinating it to the rule of *phronêsis*; of establishing what Heidegger was later to call a free relationship to technology. Heidegger did not believe that every Nazi had this goal in mind or even that the Nazi movement would inevitably bring this about, but he was convinced that the possibility for such a revolution only existed within this movement. What was necessary to bring this revolution about was a commitment by the positive intellectual forces in Germany to support this movement and Hitler in particular. He saw himself playing a leading role in this effort.[12]

[11] This notion of turning around is also central to his analysis of Plato's allegory of the cave in *Plato's Doctrine of Truth*.

[12] Heidegger to Jaspers 3 Apr. 1933: 'As dark and questionable as everything is, so I sense ever more, that we are growing into a new actuality and that a time is becoming old. Everything depends upon whether we prepare the right point of attack for philosophy and help it come to its task' (Heidegger/Jaspers 1990: 152).

Despite his grave concerns about the role that technology played in the modern world, Heidegger was never simply an opponent of technology and never sought its destruction. The problem, as he saw it, was not technology per se but the hegemony that technology had come to exercise over human action. *Technê* as a form of uncovering reveals the world as a process of production. Everything within the world is thus seen as merely the equipment with which this productive enterprise is carried out. Modern man imagines that technology produces goods to satisfy his wants and desires, but technology can only serve human beings if they act untechnologically, i.e. only if they live according to something other than technical (and that includes economic) imperatives. Only if distinctively human action is placed at the centre of our concern will technology serve our ends. We thus can only become active (as opposed to productive) if we are guided by *phronêsis,* which means for Heidegger, if we are guided by the intuition of a *phronimos.* We can only be active if we resolutely face the possibility of our own death and accept the destiny that is revealed to us by the *phronimos* in the moment of vision. Without such resolve, we lose the capacity for action and become mere cogs in the equipment that constitutes the world uncovered by *technê* that produces the 'unrestricted organization of the average man' (Heidegger 1959: 37). It was this resolve that Heidegger saw in the Nazi movement.

The Nazis, Heidegger believed, were resolutely opposed to both Americanism and communism. They also despised high theory, experts, and intellectuals, trusting instead to the feelings and sensibilities of the *Volk.* They accepted the need for machine technology and technical expertise, but believed it had to be subordinated to the good of the *Volk.* They also recognized the necessity of leaders who posed the deepest questions and acted resolutely on their insight into the necessities of the moment.

Central to Heidegger's support of the Nazis was his belief that they might make possible a widespread confrontation with Being. If leaders posed the question of Being radically enough, a common questioning would pervade the community (Ott 1988: 34). Thereby, the *Volk* could play 'an active role in shaping its fate by placing its history into the openness of the overpowering might of all the world-shaping forces of human existence and by struggling ever anew to secure its spiritual world' (Ott 1988: 35). This, however, could not be achieved by a merely theoretical engagement (Wolin 1993: 45). Germans, according to Heidegger, had to be 'forced out into the uncertainty of all things, in which the necessity of engagement is grounded' (Wolin 1993: 45). Such a profound questioning, especially in the universities, might provide the foundation of a science of the *Volk,* and serve as the foundation for a truly spiritual world.

Heidegger believed that there was evidence that such a spirit pervaded the National Socialist movement. In his view the young nationalist Schlageter who was executed by the French for sabotage in 1923 (and held by the Nazis to be a martyred national hero) exemplified the kind of courage that was necessary. Heidegger believed such courage characterized many Nazis (Wolin 1993: 45, 51). We know from letters and personal accounts that he believed Hitler was committed to facing the deepest and most troubling questions, and his inspirational example, Heidegger hoped, would evoke a communal reflection on the question of Being. In effect, Hitler in messianic fashion would turn men around and lead them out of the Platonic cave into the light of reality (Safranski 1994: 266).[13] It was with a view to assisting in this project that Heidegger joined the party.

The Nazis, according to Heidegger, understood that knowledge was fundamentally rooted in praxis and thus were reunifying life in a way unknown since the time of the early Greeks. These Greeks understood theory as the highest mode of human activity, but only as the supreme realization of practice, the innermost determining core of their existence as a people (Wolin 1993: 31–2). The new way of knowing that Heidegger believed was awakening in the Nazi movement and that was exemplified in his own thinking could similarly root human beings in practice (Wolin 1993: 58). Thus, in thinking about education in the National Socialist state, Heidegger wanted to train students not merely in intellectual disciplines but in practical ways as well. He thus recommended training in labour service, military service, and knowledge service in order to perfect this growing unity of acting and knowing (Wolin 1993: 37).[14]

Heidegger was convinced that such a re-establishment of *praxis* guided by *phronêsis* would subordinate technology to human ends, i.e. to the realization of the *Volk* as a manifestation of the revelation of Being. He suggests that this is particularly evident in the Nazi conceptualization of the role of labour. Technology under the rule of *phronêsis* roots production in the purposes of the *Volk*. Thus, Heidegger argues that 'every worker of our people must know why and to what end he stands there, where he stands', for it is only in this way that the individual is rooted in the *Volk* and their fate (Safranski 1994: 305). 'Labour is also not simply the production of goods for others. Nor is labour simply the occasion and the means to earn a living. Rather: *For us, "work" is the title of every well-ordered action that is borne by the responsibility of the individual, the group, and the State and which is thus of service to the Volk*' (Wolin 1993: 59; see also Heidegger 1998: 57).[15] Under Nazi leadership, workers will not simply labour for an hourly wage but for a higher national purpose made evident to them by inspirational leadership. Like the stone mason working on a cathedral in the Middle Ages their work will have a transcendent purpose.

While Heidegger saw all of these developments as hopeful, he recognized that they were ultimately dependent on the self-assertion of the *Volk* through an act of founding in which it wills itself as the end of its activity. For Heidegger, this is the supreme

[13] This Platonic imagery is not ad hoc, but corresponds to Heidegger's reading of and reflection on Plato's *Republic* at the time. Heidegger's leader in contrast to Plato's philosopher-king, however, is guided not by the rational comprehension of the unchanging idea of the good, but by an inspired intuition into what is necessary here and now, by what he characterized in *Being and Time* as the moment of vision and historicity. (Heidegger 1953: 338).

[14] Heidegger's knowledge service was consciously in opposition to Jünger's focus on a labour front and a war front. Otto Pöggeler, 'Heidegger's Political Self-Understanding', in Wolin 1993: 212.

[15] Heidegger describes the importance of labour in this lecture course. Labour for him is an authentic concretization of the task of the *Volk*, and it is only through such labour with the *Volk* that one is able to be *Dasein* (Heidegger 1998: 129, 154). Labour is thus the basic connection of man to man, the foundation of one's possibility of being with others (Heidegger 1998: 156). To be unemployed is thus to be alienated from things and the world as such; it is a form of spiritual destruction (Heidegger 1998:154).

practical task that he believed the Nazis led by Hitler were carrying out. A people or *Volk*, as Heidegger understands it, is not based upon blood but upon a common feeling or mood that comes from its attunement to the prevailing revelation of Being (Heidegger 1998: 153). The various individuals become a people through their faith in the 'divine will' revealed by their leader.[16] In his view, a mood or feeling is not an expression of an individual soul but a fundamental occurrence of the temporality in which *Dasein* primordially is (Heidegger 1998: 130). We wrongly denigrate feelings because we do not see how they connect us to beings as a whole (Heidegger 1998: 150). The egocentric world of liberalism is thus overcome and disappears, according to Heidegger, when we immerse ourselves in the feelings or mood of the people (Heidegger 1998: 151, 155). The self-assertion and creation of a *Volk* thus depends upon the emotional submersion of the individual in the *Volk* as a manifestation of the prevailing revelation of Being. To submit to this mood in Heidegger's view is thus the highest form of self-responsibility. Indeed, it is only in this way that one can authentically become oneself.

The successful establishment of the *Volk*, its self-governance, the freedom it affords, and the elimination of class differences all depend on *phronêsis*. The problem, however, is that *phronêsis* is rare, since human beings are generally lost in their everyday concerns. Only those few individuals who are resolute in their questioning and courageous in the face of death and nothingness can possibly have phronetic insight. Liberal democracy in Heidegger's view is highly unlikely to attract or elect such leaders and is therefore unlikely to succeed in overturning the dominance of technical rationality. The people need leaders who have peered into the abyss and have the inspired knowledge necessary to lead the *Volk* and without such leaders a free community cannot sustain itself.[17] Successful leadership, however, depends upon others being willing to follow. 'Loyalty and the will to follow [must thus] be daily and hourly strengthened' (Wolin 1993: 47). Success thus depends on the recognition and acceptance of the fact that 'the Führer alone *is* the present and future German reality and its law' (Wolin 1993: 47). For National Socialism to be successful, both the leader and the people must share the same fundamental feeling or mood, for it is only the basis of such feeling that great things become possible (Heidegger 1998: 130). An authentic leader thus cannot merely command but must convince and inspire by directing individuals according to the fundamental mood through which they are a *Volk*.

Heidegger played an important role in the early 1930s in promoting such a National Socialist future. He joined the party and became Rector of Freiburg University. He also spoke out publicly in support of Hitler and the restructuring of German politics and society. At the local level in Freiburg, he tried to institute changes in the structure of the

---

[16] As harsh as this might sound to us, Heidegger in this way does distance himself here from the explicitly racist elements in the National Socialist movement.

[17] Heidegger remarked in 1934 that the authentic community does not have unconditional precedence because there are many decisive things that come from the ruling force and solitude of a single man (Heidegger 1998: 51. He apparently is thinking here not merely of Hitler but of the Greeks who used violence to create and found cities and who thereby became *apolis* (Heidegger 1959: 152–3).

university. To provide a more practical orientation, Heidegger ran re-education camps for faculty, trying to reorient them according to the *Führerprinzip*. Not surprisingly, he met with widespread resistance within the professoriat. He also laid out plans for a new academy in Berlin that he hoped to found and lead in order to train all future German university instructors in this new leadership style. His plans give us some concrete indications of what he thought might be done on a National Socialist foundation to transform Germany. This academy was to be a philosophic community, akin to the cloister of a holy order. Teachers and students would live together and perform their academic work in common. They would also labour together at various jobs. In their free time there would be common recreational activities, including martial exercises, marching, and celebrations. However, not all activities would be in common. There would also be time for solitary work and reflection and for gathering together in small groups for conversation. Furthermore, every individual would have his own cell (Safranski 1994: 325–6). This vision of National Socialism is reminiscent of monasticism. Indeed, the Nazi movement in Heidegger's imagination seems to have been a cross between the Greek polis and the Christian monastery. All of this, however, was to be centred not around a traditional God or Church, but around the hidden or absent god revealed in the question of Being. Similarly, the head of this new religion was not a man of God steeped in established rituals and traditions, but a messianic leader guided by his intuitions and feelings about the common destiny to which he and his *Volk* are called.

All of Heidegger's efforts to facilitate and spiritualize the Nazi project failed. After a few months he resigned as Rector and was increasingly deprived of all positions of responsibility. The regime was suspicious that his private ('Freiburgian') National Socialism was not expressly wedded to the principles of the regime, and particularly to its anti-Semitism. The party leaders also had little desire to be spiritualized by a recondite professor. Moreover, his connections to the Church raised many suspicions. In any case he spent the remainder of the Nazi period teaching and writing, but with no administrative authority. This notwithstanding, he was never willing to explicitly dissociate himself from the regime, and even as late as his *Spiegel* interview in 1964 suggested that the Nazi movement might have been successful if properly led and guided.

The failure of the Nazi movement to bring about the transformation of German life Heidegger longed for led him to re-evaluate his notion of the role of philosopher and the *phronimos*. Why had the Nazi movement failed? The easy answer that Heidegger at times gave was that the Nazis had not listened to him, that Hitler and his followers had been too crude and uneducated to understand the necessity for a philosophical revolution of the sort Heidegger had in mind. At other times he suggested that his plan for spiritualizing the Nazi movement would have succeeded if the rest of the German spiritual elite had risen above narrow self-interest and followed his lead (Heidegger 1990: 25). He ultimately seems to have concluded, however, that the failure of the movement had more to do with the strength of traditional metaphysics, which was much greater than he had imagined. Even his probing questions and the crisis of the time had been unable to shake belief in the prevailing metaphysical answers to the question of Being. He concluded that unless the West was liberated from the hegemony of metaphysics that now manifested itself in the unparalleled sway of technology it would be impossible to hear the question of Being.[18] While Heidegger was disappointed by the Nazis, he did not abandon his core project. Instead he became convinced that its successful completion would require a more thorough preparation.

In his thought of the 1920s and early 1930s, Heidegger had imagined in Nietzschean fashion that powerful men, drawing what he calls the overpowering power of Being, could bring about a transformation of human life (Heidegger 1959: 152). In the later 1930s, he became increasing sceptical that this transformation could be achieved. On the surface, he thus seemed to turn away from a messianic politics. The principal problem, as he saw it at that time, was not that man had forgotten or neglected the question of Being, but that Being itself had withdrawn and concealed the fact of this withdrawal, effacing its very absence. Here he made a decisive turn away from the notion that the problem lies in the failure of human beings to a view that the problem originates in Being itself. This turn is strongly reminiscent of the turn within Christian thought that characterized the Reformation. Like Luther, Heidegger concluded that man cannot save himself. He can be saved only by 'grace' alone. Modern man cannot force open the question of Being, he can only wait to be struck by it when and if Being turns its face back to man. While Heidegger believed that such a turn was under way and that we had to prepare ourselves to receive it, he also became convinced that this turn depended on Being and not on us. Thus, he concluded in a manner reminiscent of Luther that, 'only a God can save us' (Wolin 1993: 209). Philosophy's role is to prepare us for the arrival of this 'God'. We thus see a shift not away from messianism per se but away from the notion that such a leader and such a transformation were imminent. Thus rather than proclaiming the arrival of a new messiah, Heidegger increasingly comes to see himself (drawing increasingly on poetry) as a prophetic voice for a future transformation.

Written in the period of his growing disillusionment with the Nazi movement, the *Beiträge zur Philosophie* is a first step along this path.[19] Here Heidegger, attempts to make a new beginning, parallel to the beginning of the presocratics by turning the focus from *Dasein* to Being itself. Central to his thought during this period is a notion of questioning not as the activity of man coming to terms with his relation to Being, but as a gesture of Being itself. Heidegger here thus sees himself not as someone knocking on the door of Being, but as the spokesman or shepherd of Being (Heidegger 1989: 4).

---

[18] It is important to note that Heidegger did not abandon the idea of the *phronimos*, although it is clear that philosophers must clear the ground for him more completely.

[19] The *Beiträge* often seems to be more an organized collection of notes that a completed work, but many scholars, following Pöggeler, have long considered it the foremost expressions of Heidegger's teaching (Pöggeler 1963: 254–80).

Heidegger in this context turns back to the necessity of questioning as the act most necessary in our time. He believes that such a turn is necessary because we find ourselves in the age of complete 'questionlessness' (Heidegger 1989: 110). We cannot even bear questions—if one 'philosophical' medicine man cannot answer them for us, we run to another. Why is this? All of the answers to the question of Being, beginning with those of the presocratics were necessarily and inevitably inadequate to Being itself. Thales, for example, tried to come to terms with the awesome mystery of Being by naming it, but by characterizing it as water he interpreted it in terms of a being (Heidegger 1975: 453). Such an answer could not tame the overwhelming power of Being. With Plato and Aristotle, however, answers came to predominate over questions, not so much because their answers were more correct, but because Being itself withdrew and ceased to appear in all of its questionableness. The history of metaphysics is characterized by the ever increasing withdrawal and forgetfulness of Being, and the growing dominion of answers over questions. In our time, according to Heidegger, we have forgotten that there even is a question of Being. Thinking for us has become science and calculation. In place of wonder we have curiosity; in place of questions we have problems (Heidegger 1988b: 195; Heiddeger 1988a: 5; Heidegger 1994a: 73, 78–9).

The end of philosophy is thus not due to spiritual enervation, as Nietzsche suggested, but to the exhaustion of the question that originally animated philosophy, the question of the whatness of beings. In Heidegger's view we must now turn from the investigation of the Being of beings to Being itself. Such thinking begins, Heidegger suggests, not with the experience of wonder (*Erstaunen*) but with an experience of terror (*Erschrecken*) (Heidegger 1989: 15, 20, 46). True philosophy is not just empty scepticism or rhetoric that conceals a determinate answer, but opening oneself up to the complete sweep of the fundamental questions (Heidegger 1994b: 186; Heidegger 1988b: 197). Only in this way can one come to live authentically. 'In the age of complete questionlessness of everyone it is sufficient first once to ask the question of all questions' (Heidegger 1989: 11).

The task of philosophy as Heidegger saw it during this period of his thought thus was more an individual than a communal activity (Heidegger 1998: 42–70). As he put it in a remark reminiscent of the early Christians, 'We must go into the catacombs'. He had little hope that a *phronetic* leader could make a substantive difference, since the reign of technology was too well established to allow room for *phronêsis*. His goal was thus to prepare for future thinkers (and leaders) by fostering a faith in the revelatory power of the questionable (Heidegger 1989: 11).

> The questioning ones . . . are the authentic *believing ones*, because they—opening the essence of truth—hold to the ground. The questioning ones—alone and without the help of an enchantment—set the new and highest level of standing in the middle of Being, in the Occurrence (*das Ereignis*) as the middle. The questioning ones have set aside all curiosity; their seeking loves the abyss, in which they know the oldest ground. (Heidegger 1989: 12)

Heidegger here sees himself following Hölderlin and Nietzsche who had the courage to stand in the region of Being, the region of the most questionable that is used by the gods and forgotten by men (Heidegger 1989: 432). Like them Heidegger does not seek an answer, only an ever deeper questioning, an ever deeper penetration into Being (Heidegger 1989: 362). He remarks in a manner worthy of Meister Eckhart that 'the grounding of the ground must, however, dare the leap into the abyss and measure and endure the abyss itself' (Heidegger 1989: 380). His connection to the mystical tradition is evident, although there are also significant differences.[20]

Posing the question of Being more profoundly requires the deconstruction of western metaphysics. The failure of Nazism revealed the need to deal with the deeper question of the withdrawal and forgetfulness of Being. This in turn engendered the question of the history of Being. This question has three parts. The first is the guiding question of metaphysics, 'What is the Being of beings?' (Heidegger 1989: 76). This question characterized metaphysics and led to the (mis)interpretation of Being as a mere being. This notion of Being, however, was not the result of human error, but the consequence of the withdrawal of Being. In coming to terms with this question within the history of western metaphysics we are thus coming to terms with Being itself in the process of withdrawing and effacing its withdrawal. The task of philosophy in coming to terms with this history of Being is thus hermeneutic. On the surface this activity resembles scholarly interpretation of texts, but the goal is not to explain what the thinkers thought but to reveal what they left unthought, i.e. the question of Being. Heidegger thus seeks to uncover the questionableness of the guiding question (Heidegger 1982: 116). In this way what was unthought can be thought (Heidegger 1997b: 72). In working out the guiding question of metaphysics, he argues, we are thus already asking the fundamental question of the truth of Being (Heidegger 1982: 113, 123).

The passage from the guiding question to the fundamental question occurs by means of what Heidegger calls the transitional question, 'Why is there being rather than nothing?' (Heidegger 1989: 509). The history of metaphysics culminates in the question of the nothing, which is the unrecognized question of Being. Out of this question arises first the question of the meaning of Being and then the question of the truth of Being, the unconcealment of Being itself (Heidegger 1988c: 30). This revelation of Being Heidegger calls the Occurrence (*Ereignis*).[21] Heidegger's goal is thus not to present a history of western thought but to penetrate to the most questionable, the mystery of Being. In the language of the *Beiträge*, this means moving ever closer to the last god

---

[20] Perhaps the strongest argument for the impact of mysticism on Heidegger's thought is Caputo 1986. His position has been called into question by both Gall 1986 and Pezze 2009. For a more traditional scholarly consideration see Sikka 1997 and Rosenstein 1978.

[21] This key term is translated in a variety of ways: as 'event'; or as 'coming into view'; 'things coming into themselves by belonging together'; 'enowing'; and 'appropriation' or 'propriation'. It is clearly built on the term *eigen* which means 'own' as in 'one's own'. It is also related to *eigentlich*, 'ownmost', and *Eigentlichkeit*, 'authenticity'. It is the event by which the truth of Being is manifest; the event in which Being reveals itself.

(Heidegger 1989: 409–17, 508–9).[22] The deconstruction of metaphysics that takes place in the work of the middle period of Heidegger's thought thus has the identical messianic goal as his earlier work, the salvation of humanity and a reconstitution of *Dasein* through the re-establishment of the rule of Being in human life. In Heidegger's work, philosophy thus continues to play a peculiarly religious role.

On the surface, Heidegger's path of radical questioning seems to have little in common with theology, which Heidegger sees as a form of metaphysics. Religion itself, however, is often anti-theological. Late medieval nominalism, for example, argued that theology had too low an idea of God, that instead of treating him as radically omnipotent and thus radically other, it treated him as a being, seeking to understand him by analogy to beings. The true God as they saw him was incomprehensible, subject neither to nature nor to logic. Such a God could only appear as a question to man, unfathomable, unthinkable, unnameable. Indeed, human beings could only 'know' such a God through revelation or mystical intuition (See Gillespie 2008: 19–43).

In his late thought Heidegger's approach to Being and thus to God does not follow the path of assertions or syllogisms but questions, and in this respect has much in common with radical versions of apophatic theology. Heidegger had already remarked in *An Introduction to Metaphysics* that 'questioning is the authentic and proper and only way of appreciating what by its supreme rank holds our existence in its power' (Heidegger 1959: 83). It is a short step from this view, to Heidegger's more explicit later claim that 'questioning is the piety of thinking'.[23] Even in his ostensibly most radical philosophical moment, Heidegger's thought in important ways is still shaped by religion. Moreover, he also laid the ground for a new theology, based not on metaphysics but on the poetic revelation of the truth of Being. This theological focus on the poetic revelation of Being becomes increasingly explicit in his late thought and eventually supplants the radical philosophical position he had earlier defended.

Heidegger argues in *An Introduction to Metaphysics* that there can be no language without a determinate meaning of Being and that language thus has its origin in man's departure into Being (Heidegger 1959: 82, 171). In this departure, he suggests, language was the primordial poetry in which a people spoke the question of Being (Heidegger 1959: 171). In his late thought, by contrast, he seems to reverse this order. He argues that, 'the hearing of the promise is the authentic gesture of that which currently needs thinking, not questioning. Because the listening is a listening for the responsive word, hearing unfolds itself on the promise of the to-be-thought always in a questioning about the answer' (Heidegger 1959b: 180). Underlying this claim is the notion that it is actually language, or to put it theologically, the 'Word,' that speaks and not man, that 'man speaks only insofar as he always responds (*ent-spricht*) to language' (Heidegger

---

[22] Safranski argues that in the *Beiträge* Heidegger speaks of God not as a what but as a how (Safranski 1994: 358–9).

[23] Heidegger 1954: 35. Kisiel sees Heidegger's questioning is a kind of piety (Kisiel 1993: 80).

1957: 34; see also Heidegger, 1959b: 32). In his earlier thought Heidegger argued (following Novalis) that philosophy was homesickness (Heidegger 1983: 7). Questioning in this sense arises out of our sense of being strangers, out of place and/or out of time. Philosophic questioning is an investigation of this strangeness, a pathway ever deeper into this abyss. Heidegger's later thought is less devoted to such radical interrogation. Instead, he seeks to learn how to dwell, to be at home: 'everything rests on this, to learn dwelling in the speaking of language' (Heidegger 1959b: 32). The underlying importance of living in the Word that Luther proclaimed lies just beneath the surface here, although for Heidegger the Word has become separated from a personal, incarnate God.

Questioning does not disappear in Heidegger's late thought as an element of philosophic activity but it is clearly demoted in importance. In *The Essence of Language*, he argues that when we ask about the essence of language, it always already has spoken to us. Each question holds itself within the promise of that which is put into question. When we think this through sufficiently, he claims, we inevitably come to the conclusion that questioning is not the authentic gesture of thinking, but hearing the promise of that which come forth in the question. Questioning, he still maintains, is the piety of thinking, but only because it asks about the essence, seeks to reveal the truth of the essence (Heidegger 1959b: 175).

While it is true that the late Heidegger seeks a kind of *Gelassenheit*, it would be a mistake to conclude that this is a form of contentment. It is rather a rejection of the wilful path of self-assertion. In the years during and after the Nazi period he focused on the history of the withdrawal of Being in western metaphysics. This history, he concluded, ended with the triumph of a philosophy of will and the nihilistic will to will first in Schelling and German idealism but then finally and fully in Nietzsche. In this way, Heidegger came to see his own earlier emphasis on questioning as entwined with subjectivity and will. He thus concluded that we cannot come to Being by willing. The rejection of willing, however, is not a rejection of questioning as such. The will to know, he argues, is not thinking, but the arrogance of self-consciousness that does not want to be dominated by the questionable, that does not want to hear the word of Being. In place of the will to know Heidegger seeks to engender a willingness to listen to the question and to what speaks out it as the essence of thinking. What is crucial is not that we will but that Being turn towards us. We can only prepare ourselves to accept such a revelation and live in the hope it will occur.

In Heidegger's view we must cultivate listening to the word of Being and by this he means a careful listening and attending to those who use language most deeply, that is, to the poets. They stand nearest and in greatest thrall to Being and are our principal access to what Being sends us as our destiny. They serve in this sense as the prophets of Being, standing in its abyss more resolutely than any others. In his late thought Heidegger thus increasingly turns to Hölderlin, George, Trakl, Rilke, and other poetic voices for guidance. While his concern with questions continues, he no longer defines philosophizing as a form of homesickness. Indeed, he asserts that, 'wandering in the direction of the questionable is not an adventure but a return home'.[24]

Heidegger's late thought is thus in a sense more preparatory. Thinking and philosophizing continue to be important but they are both subordinate to oracular poetry. Transfiguring our age in his view requires coming to terms with the essence of technology, which he believes lies in *poiesis*, making in the most fundamental sense. Dealing with technology is thus an essentially poetic task, for only the poet can show us *how* technology is a revelation of Being. While Heidegger does place great emphasis on these poetic voices during this period of his thought, it would be a mistake to believe that he has abandoned his earlier messianic vision of a phronetic leader. If we were to describe the arc of Heidegger's thought with a Greek analogy, we might say that he moves from Socrates to Oedipus and then finally to Teiresias, from radical questioning as primordial science, to questioning as the preparation for *phronêsis*, to questioning as the piety of thinking that looks to oracular poetry for guidance in preparing for the arrival of a new God. All three, the philosopher, the leader, and the poet, however, remain essential to the transfiguration of our Being-in-the-world that he imagines. In the 1930s he imagined that the philosopher and the leader acting in tandem could in Promethean fashion wrest fire from the gods. In his later thought he came to realize that they could only succeed if God were willing to grant what was needed and that only the poet could show them the way to the altar of such a distant divinity.

In the end and throughout his life, I thus want to argue, Heidegger like many of those who followed in Nietzsche's wake continued to worship at the altar of the hidden or unknown God. At his core Heidegger was thus not a humanist or metaphysician in any traditional sense but a millenarian thinker who hoped to prepare the ground for the arrival of a new messiah who would lead his age and people to a new and if not better then certainly more authentic way of life.

While Heidegger's example points towards the dangers of a messianic political theology, such an ideology remains attractive because it promises a revolutionary transformation of existing circumstances. Such a rapid transformation is particularly seductive because it seems to liberate us from the 'slow boring of hard boards' that Weber maintained was the essence of modern political life. Such slow and deliberate reform seems impossible to those who adopt such a radical perspective, because, as they see it, we live under the universal hegemony of some dark power whether it is called 'world technology', or 'global capital'. Unless and until this this dominating power is eliminated nothing of significance can be accomplished. From such a perspective the differences between, for example, the production of corpses in a concentration camp and the production of fertilizer in a fertilizer plant, to use a Heideggerian example, are insignificant. From this perspective only a total change of direction can restore value to human life. The immoderate pursuit of the good, however, often ends up producing evil.

---

[24] Heidegger 1954: 60.

Moreover, the reliance in such circumstances upon the special revelation of messianic leaders and the communal enthusiasm they generate is always fraught with danger especially when it seeks to cast aside and replace all institutions, practices, and ways of thinking that have hitherto provided stability and order to human life. We may imagine as Heidegger does (paraphrasing Hölderlin), that 'where the danger is, the saving power grows', but an analysis of the great crises in human history suggests that the saving power is most often absent or distant in such times of need, and that most often civilizations and cultures are thus not renewed or transfigured but simply come apart at the seams. Heidegger's example shows us how easy it is for those who choose to act on such hopes to end up supporting moral monstrosity.

REFERENCES

Bernstein, Richard (1992). *The New Constellation: The Ethical-Political Horizons of Modernity and Postmodernity.* (Cambridge, MA: MIT Press).

Brogran, Walter (1995). 'Heidegger's Aristotelian Reading of Plato: The Discovery of the Philosopher', in *Research in Phenomenology 25.*

Caputo, John (1986). *Mystical Element in Heidegger's Thought.* (New York: Fordham University Press).

Derrida, Jacques (1991). *Of Spirit: Heidegger and the Question,* trans. G. Bennington and R. Bowlby (Chicago: University of Chicago Press).

Gall, Robert (1986). 'Mysticism and Ontology: A Heideggerian Critique of Caputo', *The Southern Journal of Philosophy* 24, 463–75.

Gillespie, Michael Allen (1989). 'History and Temporality in the Thought of Heidegger', *Revue Internationale de Philosophie* 43, 33–51.

—— (2000). 'Martin Heidegger's Aristotelian National Socialism', *Political Theory* 28, no. 2, 140–66.

—— (2008). *The Theological Origins of Modernity.* (Chicago: University of Chicago Press).

Heidegger, Martin (1949). *Was ist Metaphysik?* (Frankfurt am Main: Klostermann).

—— (1953). *Sein und Zeit.* (Tübingen: Niemeyer).

—— (1954). *Vorträge und Aufsätze.* (Pfullingen, Neske).

—— 1957) *Hebel, der Hausfreund.* (Pfullingen: Neske).

—— (1959). *An Introduction to Metaphysics,* trans. Ralph Manheim (New Haven, CT: Yale University Press).

—— (1959b). 'Das Wesen der Sprache', in *Unterwegs zur Sprache.* (Pfullingen: Neske).

—— (1965). *Kant und das Problem der Metaphysik.* (Frankfurt am Main: Klostermann).

—— (1969). *Seminaire tenu au Thor en septembre 1969 par le Professeur Martin Heidegger.* (Paris: by Roger Munier. Thor 1969).

—— (1975). *Die Grundprobleme der Phänomenologie.* (Frankfurt am Main: Klostermann).

—— (1976). *Wegmarken.* (Frankfurt am Main: Klostermann).

—— (1982). *Vom Wesen der Menschlichen Freiheit: Einleitung in die Philosophie.* (Frankfurt am Main: Klostermann).

—— (1983). *Die Grundbegriffe der Metaphysik: Welt—Endlichkeit—Einsamkeit.* (Frankfurt am Main: Klostermann. GBM).

—— (1984). *Hölderlins Hymne 'Der Ister'.* (Frankfurt am Main: Klostermann).

—— (1987). *Zur Bestimmung der Philosophie: Die Idee der Philosophie und das Weltanschauungsproblem (Kriegsnotsemester 1919).* (Frankfurt am Main: Klostermann. ZBP)

—— (1988a). *Ontologie (Hermeneutik der Faktizität).* (Frankfurt am Main: Klostermann).

—— (1988b). *Phänomenologische Interpretationen zu Aristotles: Einführung in die Phänomenologische Forschung.* (Frankfurt am Main: Klostermann).

—— (1988c). *Zur Sache des Denkens.* (Tübingen: Niemeyer).

—— (1989). *Beiträge zur Philosophie (Vom Ereignis).* (Frankfurt am Main: Klostermann).

—— (1990). 'Das Rektorat, 1933–1934', in *Martin Heidegger and National Socialism: Questions and Answers,* eds. Günther Neske and Emil Kettering (New York: Paragon).

—— (1992). Platon: *Sophistes.* (Frankfurt am Main: Klostermann).

—— (1993). *Grundprobleme der Phänomenologie (1919/20).* (Frankfurt am Main: Klostermann). GP).

—— (1994a). *Einführung in die Phänomenologische Forschung.* (Frankfurt am Main: Klostermann).

—— (1994b). *Prolegomena zur Geschichte des Zeitbegriffs.* (Frankfurt am Main: Klostermann).

—— (1995). *Phänomenologie des Religiösen Lebens.* (Frankfurt am Main: Klostermann).

—— (1997a). *Der Deutsche Idealismus (Fichte, Schelling, Hegel) und die Philosophische Problemlage der Gegenwart.* (Frankfurt am Main: Klostermann).

—— (1997b). *Was Heisst Denken?* (Tübingen: Niemeyer).

—— (1998). *Logik als die Frage nach dem Wesen der Sprache.* (Frankfurt a Main: Klostermann).

—— and Jaspers, Karl (1990) *Briefwechsel. 1920-1963.* eds. Walter Beimel and Hans Saner (Frankfurt am Main: Klostermann).

Kisiel, Theodore, (1993). *The Genesis of Heidegger's Being and Time.* (Berkeley, CA: University of California Press).

—— (1995). 'Genealogical Supplements: A Reply of Sorts', *Research in Phenomenology* 25, 245.

Kuhn, Elisabth (1992). *Friedrich Nietzsches Philosophie des europäischen Nihilismus.* (Berlin, De Gruyter).

Marcuse, Herbert (1924). *Heidegger Lecture Transcript: Grundbegriffe der aristotelischen Philosophie* (manuscript in Marcuse Archive).

Ott, Hugo (1988). *Martin Heidegger Unterwegs zu seiner Biographie.* (Frankfurt am Main: Campus).

Pezze, Barbara Dalle (2009). *Martin Heidegger and Meister Eckhardt: A Path Towards Gelassenheit.* (London: Edwin Mellen Press).

Pöggeler, Otto (1963). *Der Denkweg Martin Heideggers.* (Pfullingen: Neske).

—— 'Heidegger's Political Self-Understanding', in Richard Wolin, *Heidegger Controversy.* (Cambridge, MA: MIT Press).

Rosenstein, Leon (1978). 'Mysticism as Preontology: A Note on the Heideggerian Connection', *Philosophy and Phenomenological Research* 39 no.1, 57–73.

Safranski, Rüdiger, (1994). *Ein Meister aus Deutschland. Heidegger und seine Zeit.* (Munich: Hanser).

Sheehan, Thomas, (1993). 'Reading a Life: Heidegger and Hard Times', in Charles Guigmon (ed.), *The Cambridge to Heidegger*. (Cambridge: Cambridge University Press).

Sikka, Sonya (1997). *Forms of Transcendence: Heidegger and Medieval Mystical Theology*. (Albany, NY: State University of New York Press).

Sluga, Hans (1993). *Heidegger's Crisis: Philosophy and Politics in Nazi Germany*. (Cambridge, MA: Harvard University Press).

PART IV

··

THE WORLD

··

CHAPTER 19

···

NATURE

···

GORDON GRAHAM

I. CONCEPTIONS OF NATURE
···

HANDEL's *Messiah* was first performed in 1742. Its setting of texts from the King James Bible is so memorable that many of them are now indelibly associated with the musical accompaniment Handel gave them. One of these is the opening aria for Tenor, a setting of words from the prophet Isaiah 'Every valley shall be exalted, and every mountain and hill laid low, the crooked straight and the rough places plain'. The power and familiarity of the music easily leads us to overlook this important fact: the vision of the perfect world that it describes is one in which all geographical features are eliminated entirely, in favour of a featureless plain. This is an ideal so at odds with the modern emphasis on admiring wilderness and preserving landscapes, that it is difficult for us to take it seriously, or even understand how anyone might do so. Yet the mere fact that this familiar passage expresses a highly unfamiliar view of the natural world should alert us to the possibility that nature can figure in moral and religious thought in radically different ways—as something to be feared and placated, manipulated and exploited, admired and emulated, or respected and preserved.

These alternative sets of attitudes are both parts of, and reflective of, alternative conceptions of nature. The purpose of this chapter is to articulate four such conceptions as they have figured in (broadly) European thought over several centuries. Although historical generalization is always a danger, and stadial accounts of history are unfashionable, it is plausible to think of these four conceptions as following in an historic sequence, from the early modern period to the present day, and to label them premodern, Enlightenment, Romantic and environmental ideas of nature. For purposes of exposition it is helpful to list them in this way, but we cannot assume that the sequence is a progressive one. While it is commonly supposed that advances in natural science, together with a greater human sensibility to the non-human world, has led to nature being conceived in better ways than in times past, this is by no means indisputable.

A second aim of this chapter, therefore, is to offer some critical assessment of these different conceptions, and thus illuminate, at least to some degree, the difficult philosophical issue of how we *ought* to think about nature.

II. The Pre-Modern

Isaiah's vision of a perfect world lacking valleys or hills arises from a perception of 'the wilderness' as a dangerous and deeply inhospitable place. Among its many dangers, of course, are the 'wild' animals, with which (on this conception) human beings are inevitably at enmity. Accordingly, in a perfect world, this too would be amended. The 'holy mountain' is one in which dangerous creatures have lost their natural instincts—the lion shall eat straw like the ox, the wolf shall live with the lamb, the cow and the bear shall graze, and it will be possible for small children to play in close proximity to poisonous snakes (Isaiah 11). This ideal contrasts sharply with the real world, where, of course, there is a conflict between nature and humanity. Even those who stay well away from wilderness cannot escape this conflict since they remain at the mercy of the elements, the seasons, and natural calamities such as floods and earthquakes.

The writers of the Hebrew scriptures firmly believed that nature was God's creation and thus ultimately under His control. However, since none of us was present when God laid the foundations of the earth and fixed its dimensions (Job 38), the inner workings of the natural world must ultimately remain a mystery. At the same time, natural forces are used by God for the purposes of warning and chastising, and (as in the case of the rainbow), making promises. It is in this way that the non-human world takes on human meaning. We can 'read' natural events for signs of God's intentions for humanity (as represented by the Children of Israel), so even if 'the foundations of the earth' pass our comprehension, nature is still purposefully animated. That is to say, it is not simply an inanimate backdrop to human life, but a sphere of agency, and while the fact that it is independent of humanity means that its workings will sometimes be indifferent to human welfare, the natural world can also have implications for the conduct of human life.

A belief in the animation of the world does not require monotheism, however. The Jews were unusual. In ancient, and more modern times, and across a number of otherwise rather disparate cultures, polytheism—a belief in many gods—appears to be much more common. For polytheists the natural world is the theatre of operation for a large array of spirits. Some control natural processes– fertility in the case of the Ceres, the Roman goddess of agriculture, for example—others animate general natural phenomena—thunder in the case of the Norse god Thor—and still others are to be found in highly specific locations—as the Greek Dryads dwelt in trees. From a human point of view, the actions of any of these spirits can be both positive and negative—friendly or hostile, beneficial or detrimental, nurturing or malicious. Their actions are detected sometimes in the effects they have, and sometimes in the behaviour (normal and abnormal) of different animals, plants, rivers, hills, and so on. Those who know how, can placate such spirits, so that they do not thwart human purposes, or call upon them (manipulate them even) in order to assist humanity.

Among the philosophers of ancient Greece and Rome we can find a related conception of nature as animated—'ensoulment'—that is neither monotheistic nor polytheistic. Plato's dialogue *Timaeus* draws a distinction between 'the father and maker of all this universe' who is 'past finding out' (28c) and the universe, which is itself 'a living creature truly endowed with soul' (30b). This soul 'contains within itself all intelligible beings' and so the various operations of the natural world are manifestations of it. Plato reasons about nature 'from the top down', so to speak, but in *The Nature of the Gods* Cicero (106–43 BCE) reports Zeno as arguing 'from the bottom up' to a similar conception: 'If well-tuned pipes should spring out of the olive, would you have the slightest doubt that there was in the olive-tree some kind of skill or knowledge? . . . Why then should we not believe that the world is a living and wise being, since it produces living and wise beings out of itself?' (Bk. II, ch. VIII)

In Ovid's *Metamorphoses* this living and wise being is identified as female—Mother Earth. The expression still has currency, of course, which is testimony to the many centuries over which it held sway. More especially the Earth was to be thought of as a nursing mother, for these obvious reasons—biologically speaking birth and death are natural events and it is the natural world that provides us with nutrition and shelter. The image is no doubt strengthened by the ease with which it works both ways—the womb has often been described as fertile ground in which male seed is planted—but the intuitive appeal of Mother Earth is also revealed in the revulsion that the search for precious metals sometimes prompted. Milton's *Paradise Lost* (1667), for example, shares Ovid's deep distaste for men who 'with impious hands, Rifld the bowels of thir mother Earth, for Treasures better hid' (Bk. I, 684–90).

Nevertheless, the image of the Earth as a nursing Mother is inherently unstable. Its one-sidedness was plain in even the most animistic world of thought. In the first place, this 'mother' did not merely nurture; she presided over devastating famines, plagues and natural disasters. In the second place, while the suckling child is essentially a passive recipient of maternal care, for the most part, food and shelter have to be wrung from 'mother' nature, and this requires the steady application of human effort and, more importantly, inventiveness. Consider bread, the 'staff of life'. Without plant life, certainly, there would be no bread, but this most basic foodstuff is the outcome of a quite remarkable and complex manipulation of the natural world—sowing, reaping, grinding, mixing, fermenting, proving, baking, not to mention the artificial selection of types of grain. The earth may give the birds and the beast 'their food in due season' (Psalm 145), but for the most part human beings have had to learn, not just how to take it, but how to make it.

It is true that both these undeniable aspects of nature—the danger it poses and the obstacles it presents to extracting benefits from it—are compatible with attributing agency to the natural world, and so continuing to regard it as a sphere in which one or more spiritual powers are at work. Furthermore, it is intelligible to suppose that there are spiritual ways in which the threat that such powers present to human welfare can be averted or their aid invoked. The aim of both magic spells and religious rituals can be thought of in this way—though the medieval Church long waged a war against magic as the enemy of true religion (see Thomas 1991). Still, recourse to these methods is in large part a confession of ignorance, and at best their efficacy must prove sporadic; the spirits can be wilful. So it can hardly come as a surprise that people were inevitably pressured into conceiving the natural world differently—namely, as something to be *mastered*. This is a pressure all the more difficult to resist once science and technology begin to make serious advances.

III. The Enlightenment

In his exploration of the sources of religion, David Hume (1711–76) writes:

> We are placed in this world, as in a great theatre, where the true springs and causes of every event are entirely concealed from us; nor have we either sufficient wisdom to foresee, or power to prevent those ills, with which we are continually threatened. We hang in perpetual suspense between life and death, health and sickness, plenty and want, which are distributed amongst the human species by secret and unknown causes, whose operation is oft unexpected, and always unaccountable.   (Hume 1993 [1757]: 140)

Hume here identifies ignorance as the main driver in the growth of superstition. 'Could men anatomize nature', he continues, they would come to see that all the events are produced by 'a regular and constant machinery' (Hume 1993 [1757]: 141). In these few sentences Hume encapsulates a major shift that took place in the course of the seventeenth and eighteenth centuries. Nature came to be conceived neither as a vast array of spiritual powers nor as an organism with a life and purpose of its own, but as a machine whose workings were waiting to be discovered. Once understood, they could then be manipulated to human ends.

To think of nature in this mechanistic way remains compatible with a belief in divine creation. Indeed most of its chief protagonists were believing Christians. But the theology with which it was most easily combined was deistic rather than theistic. The 'great watchmaker' sets the machine going but does not act directly in its operation. Even Hume, who was thought by his contemporaries to be some sort of infidel, seems to affirm a very thin version of deism. In his *Dialogues Concerning Natural Religion*, the character of Philo (widely regarded as Hume's own mouthpiece) declares that when we look around the world 'a purpose, an intention, a design strikes everywhere the most careless, the most stupid thinker, and no man can be so hardened in absurd systems, as at all times to reject it' (Hume 1948 [1776]: 82).

If the final break with creationism was yet to be made, the mechanistic conception of nature was nevertheless a very great change in thinking. It was owed, many held at the time, to the experimental methods extolled by Francis Bacon (1561–1626) and especially the extraordinary scientific advances that were made by Isaac Newton (1643–1727). There is reason to wonder whether such a huge—and widespread—shift in conception can plausibly be attributed to the writings of just two men, however brilliant or innovative. And indeed it is not hard to find other influences at work. The eighteenth century saw the advent of an Agricultural Revolution, in which Britain took the lead. Farm machinery, land reforms, crop rotation, and animal husbandry hugely increased agricultural production. Though often described as 'scientific' farming, this is science in only a very broad sense. Neither a systematic approach to planting nor technical invention requires major theoretical advances in physics or chemistry of the kind that were made by Newton and Robert Boyle (1627–91). Nor is any sustained philosophical reflection required to arrive at the conclusion that there is good reason to abandon molly dances (for instance), whose impact is uncertain, when the use of seed drills, iron ploughs, and threshing machines and so on, results in greatly increased yields, while reducing costs at the same.

Still, it is true that these practically valuable outcomes were allied with, or at least accompanied by, deep changes in the way that people came to conceive of nature. The best known philosophers of the seventeenth century—Thomas Hobbes, René Descartes, Gottfried Leibniz, for example—laid the foundations for a mechanistic conception of the world that steadily gathered pace over the course of the seventeenth century. Natural philosophy came to be displaced by natural science, and by the eighteenth century Hume's conception of nature as a complex system of regular and constant machinery whose workings could be rationally investigated was widely shared.

The rise of the mechanical conception of nature led, among other things, to that radical dualism between mind and body which is a characteristic of the Cartesian philosophy. Thinking of nature as a machine places it in a quite different relation to human thought and desire than thinking of it as a nurturing mother, or any other sort of 'soul'. With radical dualism in place, however, a question arises as to what exactly falls each side of the division. The human mind, it seems, must be constituted by a metaphysically different substance than is the human body. Notoriously, this led Descartes to the belief that other animals must be machines incapable of feeling pain—a truth that their apparent pain-behaviour disguises from us, presumably.

Radical dualism between the natural and human worlds is hard to sustain. In many respects, animals are very *unlike* machines, while we ourselves appear to be subject to the very same natural processes as (other) animals—birth, growth, ageing, death. Hume held 'that no truth appears to me more evident, than that beasts are endowed with thought and reason' (*Treatise* Bk I/Part III/Sect. XVI). Even if it is true that the human mind in some sense transcends these processes, there must nonetheless be some connection or other between the physical and the mental. Famously, Descartes found it in the pineal gland, which lies at the base of the brain. It is hard not to regard this as a quite arbitrary choice—especially since he revised his view after discovering that the higher animals also have this gland. But in truth, no such entity could do the work required of it, since it would have to have precisely the twofold character of body *and* mind that metaphysical dualism makes impossible.

An alternative response, of course, is to forswear dualism and encompass the human within the natural. This is the strategy enthusiastically adopted by the philosophers of the Scottish Enlightenment. It is not just plants and animals, or physical and cosmological systems that can be subjected to and illuminated by the methods of Bacon and Newton. So too can humanity itself. Francis Hutcheson (1694–1746), widely hailed as 'Father' of the Scottish Enlightenment, roundly declares at the outset of his *Inquiry in the Original of Our Ideas of Beauty and Virtue* that 'there is no part of Philosophy of more importance, than a just Knowledge of Human Nature' (Hutcheson 2008 [1725]: 7). His use of the expression 'human nature' precisely captures the unity which Cartesian dualism denies. As its title makes plain, David Hume's first philosophical work—*A Treatise of Human Nature*—is a sustained endeavour of this kind, an application of the experimental philosophy to moral subjects that will place 'the science of man' on 'a solid foundation', as he tells us in the introduction (Hume 1967 [1739]: p. xvi).

The science of man was taken up with remarkable energy, not least because most of its exponents believed, with Hutcheson, that 'the Importance of Truth is nothing else than its . . . Efficacy to make Men happy' (Hutcheson 2008 [1725]: 7). By an interesting route this generated a new, and rather different, orientation to the non-human world, namely an aesthetic one. Over the course of the seventeenth century, Italian, and especially Dutch painters, brought naturalistic landscape painting to increasing prominence, a development that met with both popular acclaim and commercial success. In accordance with the principles of the new science of man, writers on aesthetics (like Hutcheson) located the origins of aesthetic pleasure in human nature. This neatly explains how landscapes, and other natural objects not of human making, take on aesthetic value for human beings; their natural beauty finds a natural response in human pleasure. Moreover, the transience and degeneration to which the beauty of landscapes, sunsets and the like is inevitably subject, can be transcended without aesthetic loss—and even improved a little, perhaps—when it is captured within an enduring work of art—a painting.

By the late eighteenth century this trend culminated in the dominance of the 'picturesque' in landscape painting. The term acts as a kind of halfway between the 'beautiful' and the 'sublime' (a distinction there will be occasion to return to). That is to say, the 'picturesque' constitutes a harmonious unity of art and nature. This conception of nature as a rational order within which the human and the non-human may be encompassed, also finds expression in landscape gardening, another notable feature of the eighteenth century. Two dimensions of this development are of special interest. First, the harmonious relation of human art to natural process takes on the form of a cooperative collaboration between the two. The aim is not to extract from a recalcitrant nature something especially beneficial to human beings, but to bring the natural order to a greater degree of perfection. Second, what is aimed for has no immediately utilitarian value. In gardening we pass beyond the search for food and shelter, and look to nature for the enriching ornamentation of life. Gardening on this grand scale implies that while the wildness of nature holds no terrors, neither is it there simply to be controlled or mastered. It can also be transformed, and in its turn it can transform us.

This new 'science', then, in both its theoretical and practical applications seems to promise an enlightened unity of man and nature in place of both pre-modern super-stition and Cartesian dualism. Yet Hume's investigations in the first part of the *Treatise*, as he himself admits, do not proceed as smoothly as one might hope. They generate a kind of 'philosophical melancholy and delirium' and lead him into 'dreary solitudes and rough passages'. Even the new philosophy, it seems, is 'incapable of dispelling these clouds'. Happily, though 'nature herself suffices to that purpose'. And so, he says, after a game of backgammon, or dining with friends, 'I find myself absolutely and necessarily determined to live, and talk, and act like other people in the common affairs of life' (Hume 1967 [1739]: 269).

There is something of a paradox here, however. If Hume is right, human *nature* functions in ways that *reasoning about* human nature cannot capture, with the inescap-able implication that there is some element in our humanity which inevitably escapes the science of man. It appears to follow that even the most sustained attempt to locate human beings within nature has to acknowledge a radical gulf between the human and non-human worlds. A science of human nature cannot, in the end, be modelled on a science of sticks and stones.

Where does the difference lie? The experimental method requires that knowledge be based upon observation. Observation requires a subject (the one who observes) and an object (the thing observed). A 'science of man' conceived along these lines thus requires us to be *both* subject *and* object at one and the same time. But this is impossible. What is possible, certainly, is that human beings can be studied as objects, can be treated, that is to say, like sticks and stones. This can only be done, however, if we exclude the very thing that distinguishes human beings from inanimate objects—namely subjective consciousness. In short, the Enlightenment conception of 'human nature'—despite its humanistic tone—is actually de-humanizing. Such, at any rate, people came to think, a conclusion that played its part in the rise of yet another conception of nature.

IV. ROMANTICISM

If the eighteenth century can be described as the era of rational enlightenment, the nineteenth century witnessed a rejection of rationalism, a revolt against 'Reason' that generally falls under the name of 'Romanticism'. Romanticism is not easily character-ized. While it finds unmistakable expression in literature, politics, music, painting, philosophy, and theology, it is impossible to specify any one concept or principle that underlies all these manifestations. There is evidently the same spirit, we might say, behind the philosophical writings of Jean-Jacques Rousseau (1712–78), the nationalism of Mazzini, the music of Tchaikovsky, the novels of Emily Bronte, and the paintings of

Eugene Delacroix, and yet it does not seem to distil this common 'spirit' into a single idea. In their different ways, the philosophy, music, literature, painting, and politics of the Romantic period may all be said to be reactions to the implications, and the effect of, enlightenment 'science'. They all arise from a sense that the objective inquiry characteristic of the natural sciences somehow results in a 'disenchantment of the world' (to employ the expression that Max Weber later coined), and all of them respond by privileging 'feeling' over 'reason'.

In his contribution to this volume, David Brown charts this widespread search for 'The Sacramental in Modern European Thought' (one aspect of his more wide ranging exploration begun in *God and the Enchantment of Place*). For present purposes, it is only Romanticism's relation to nature with which we are concerned. Here, arguably, a key concept is that of the 'noble savage'. Book I, chapter I of Rousseau's *Social Contract* begins with this famous assertion: 'Man was born free, and everywhere he is in chains' (Rousseau 1994 [1762]: 45). The *Social Contract* takes up a theme which made its first appearance in Rousseau's *Discourse on Inequality*, namely the enmity between nature and society. Our natural condition is one of freedom, but over the ages the pressures and institutions of social life have confined us more and more. The philosophers of the Scottish Enlightenment like Hume, Smith, and Ferguson understood the history of humanity to be one of general, if not always steady, improvement, a move, that is to say, from barbarity to civilization, Rousseau offers us a quite different trajectory—from noble savagery to desiccated conformity.

Rousseau thought that social organization could be made compatible with our nature, and that education had a key role to play in this. Others were less sanguine, perhaps, and with Rousseau's picture as background, conceived of the philosopher's and the artist's task as one of recovery—stripping away the thick veneer of cultural accumulation in order to liberate once more the true impulses which ought to animate the human heart. The implications for our concept of nature are not hard to detect. Romanticism rejects any radical dualism between 'nature' and 'man', but in contrast to the enlightenment thinkers it does not seek to find unity in a rational order that encompasses the human and the non-human, so much as in a common natural energy that enlivens human beings, as it does the non-human world, when it has not been cramped and confined by custom, convention, or control. The underlying thought is one to which the poet Dylan Thomas (1914–53) gives powerful expression—'The force that through the green fuse drives the flower, drives my green age . . . The force that drives the water through the rocks, Drives my red blood' (Thomas 2003: 90).

This alternative conception of nature and our relation to it had an important impact on aesthetic understanding. In 1756, Edmund Burke (1729–97) published *A Philosophical Inquiry into our Ideas of the Sublime and the Beautiful*. His account of the distinction incorporated in the title proved to be very influential. Like Hume, Hutcheson and others, Burke believes beauty gives us a special kind of pleasure. There is a delight to be experienced in the sensual apprehension of fine china, gold filigree, elegant dress, or lyric poetry which cannot be explained by their utility. It is their style and appearance, not their usefulness, that pleases us, and so gives them aesthetic value. By contrast, the 'sublime', if properly understood, prompts a radically different kind of response, a reaction closer to horror than delight. 'Horror' is not quite right, however, since we are not repelled by the sublime. Rather, it exercises a certain fascination over us; we are attracted by it despite ourselves, so to speak. The words 'pleasant' or 'pleasurable' seem altogether inadequate, though. The strange allure that people experience when out in the midst of thunderstorm, on the edge of a vast precipice, beside a cataract, or on the highest peak of a mountain range, is not 'pleasure', but something more akin to religious awe; we are at one and the same time alarmed and thrilled.

If this is correct, we can see just how erroneous it is to suppose that 'the picturesque' stands somewhere between the beautiful and the sublime. Rather, the picturesque, whether in landscape painting or in landscape gardening, is a domestication of nature that destroys its sublimity. The raging cataract that is depicted in a beautiful picture no longer threatens us; the mysterious forest track that is landscaped into a charming woodland walk is a place where we wander contentedly. No doubt the 'picturesque' aims at being an almost mirror-like representation of nature's ordered beauty. In reality, it eliminates the natural, or at least places nature 'everywhere in chains', as political society does to Rousseau's noble savage.

The eighteenth-century Enlightenment ideal aimed to explain the human mind in terms of laws applicable to all of nature, while at the same time displaying an 'artistry' in nature that gives human beings aesthetic pleasure. The Romantic ideal works in the opposite direction we might say. It strives to reveal behind the order of civility the natural endowments of the 'untamed' human spirit, to set the noble savage free, as it were. This altered way of thinking set a new agenda for painters, writers, and composers, whose aim was no longer to beautify nature, but to capture something of the sublime in art. It is easy to find contrasting examples between eighteenth-century aestheticism and nineteenth-century Romanticism—Gainsborough's portraits of well-dressed landowners against rural backdrops *versus* the ominous landscapes of Caspar David Friedrich, Jane Austen's eponymous *Emma* picnicking in sunshine on Box Hill *versus* Emily Bronte's Catherine, blown by the winds on Yorkshire's *Wuthering Heights*, Haydn's elegant string quartets *versus* Tchaikovsky's powerful symphonies, Pope's mannered 'Essay on Man' *versus* Wordsworth's quasi-mystical 'Prelude'.

The philosopher who may be said to have pursued this new naturalism to its logical limits was Friedrich Nietzsche (1844–1900). For Nietzsche, the human spirit has been held captive for two millennia or more, by the Christian religion. Its key concept, original sin, is a 'dangerous and disastrous trick' (Nietzsche 1994 [1887]: 95), the product of a 'conspiracy of those who suffer against those who are successful and victorious', exploited by wily priest-craft and aided and abetted by the institutions of state, 'a gruesome hybrid of sickness and the will to power'. The result is that:

> all those instincts of the wild, free, roving man were turned backwards against man himself. Animosity, cruelty, the pleasure of pursuing, raiding, changing and destroying—all this was pitted against the person who had such instincts: *that* is the origin of 'bad conscience'.   (Nietzsche 1994 [1887]: 61)

Since 'God is dead' (Nietzsche's famous declaration in *The Gay Science*, 1882) the task is first, to accept that along with the rest of nature, we ourselves are simply the outcome of an evolutionary process, and second, to acknowledge that our human nature is as it is, and not as religion has falsely construed it—or as post-Christian morality idealizes it. If we open our eyes to the facts of our nature, we have to acknowledge that being *truly* human includes a proclivity for mastery, for sexual prowess, for cruel pleasures. 'Morality' bids us shun these proclivities as 'wrong', but this, Nietzsche says, is like making 'the birds of prey *responsible* for being birds of prey'. Like them, we are as nature made us—'Human, all too Human', the title of a book of aphorisms he published in 1878. Human life lived to the full lends no credence to the mortifications of religion or the conventions of morality. Rather, it joyfully pursues these natural desires, and does so, moreover, in clear recognition of the fact that in the end, the future promises nothing more than death.

Nietzsche's naturalism conflicts with very many of the values that underlie contemporary ways of thinking. This conflict is one that he readily acknowledged. The radically different understanding of human existence that he advocated, he firmly believed, would not and could not take hold until such time as people not only came out from the long shadow of the Christian religion, and also abandoned the moralizing anti-naturalism that is its secular residue. It is easy to criticize Nietzsche on the grounds that his views do not accord with (for example) the morality of human rights and social welfare. But this is question begging, and simply more evidence (for the Nietzschean) that secular moralists are still held captive by a view from which they have not yet found the strength to free themselves.

The issue of interest for the topic under discussion, though, is whether Romantic naturalism as espoused by Nietzsche offers us a more satisfactory way of relating the human and the non-human worlds, more satisfactory that is to say, than either of those that preceded it—the pre-modern conception of a sometimes open, sometimes hidden hostility between the two, or the Enlightenment's unhappy combination of the disenchantment of humanity and the domestication of nature.

It is not difficult to construct an argument that suggests it does not. Consider Nietzsche's parallel with the birds of prey.

> There is nothing strange about the fact that lambs bear a grudge towards large birds of prey; but that is no reason to blame the large birds of prey for carrying off little lambs. And if little lambs say to each other, 'These birds of prey are evil; and whoever is least like a bird of prey and most like its opposite, a lamb, is good isn't he? then there is no reason to raise objections to this setting up of an ideal, beyond the fact that the birds of prey will view it somewhat derisively, and will perhaps say, 'We don't bear any grudge at all against these good lambs, in fact we love them, nothing is tastier than a tender lamb'.   (Nietzsche 1994 [1887]: 13/28)

In drawing this parallel, Nietzsche is chiefly interested in saying something about relations between strong and weak human beings. In point of fact, though, his example of birds and the lambs they prey on suggests a much broader application—namely *between,* and not merely *within* species, and especially between *homo sapiens* and the rest.

The nineteenth-century poet Gerard Manley Hopkins was a Romantic poet of sorts. Though a convert to Roman Catholicism, his poem 'As kingfishers catch fire' captures something of the picture that Nietzsche's parallel.

> Each mortal thing does one thing and the same:
> Deals out that being indoors each one dwells;
> Selves—goes itself; myself it speaks and spells,
> Crying Whát I do is me: for that I came.   (Hopkins 1996: 129)

Nietzsche's naturalism appears to urge humanity to 'deal out the being' that dwells within, to abandon both religious constraints and moral scruples in order to cry 'what I do is me', and thus claim its place in the vast evolved contingency that is the world of nature. Yet history provides ample evidence for the contention that when *homo sapiens* 'selves—goes itself', the result is domination of the rest of nature. Human beings have proved cleverer, more adaptable and more fecund than any other species. We have no natural competitors, and consequently, as a species we face no 'higher' constraint on the fullest expression of our 'nature'. Romanticism is certainly a notable feature of the nineteenth century, but so is urbanization and industrialization. Indeed, to some extent these were the very things that Romantics aimed to protest against—though sometimes with uncertain voices. Rousseau's naturalistic attack on the destructive forces of civilization—*The Discourse on Inequality*—is nonetheless dedicated to the city of Geneva of which he was proud to be a citizen.

Nietzsche saw more clearly than others perhaps that Romantic naturalism cannot generate constraints of a certain kind. The flowering of the human spirit cannot be guaranteed to leave the beauty of 'nature' just as it is. Landscapes made up of coal-mines, quarries, and slums, species driven to extinction, ancient forests felled for timber, these are also manifestations of the 'human, all too human'. Yet if they are, then, by a somewhat circuitous route, we have returned to a position in which man is often in conflict, and sometimes at war, with the rest of nature. Now for the first time Isaiah's vision of the earth as a featureless plane filled with tamed animals is a serious prospect, though no longer one to be brought about by divine fiat, but by the collective impact of human activity.

V. ENVIRONMENTALISM

Nietzsche, I have suggested, takes Romantic naturalism to its logical, if unwelcome, conclusion, a conclusion especially unwelcome to Romantics since it was in the nineteenth century that increasing sensitivity to the non-human world gathered pace. The clearest manifestation of this was the animal welfare movement. Towards the end of the preceding century, the English philosopher Jeremy Bentham had made the important observation that if morality is (in part at any rate) concerned with the prevention of unnecessary suffering, then the crucial question about animals is not whether they can speak or reason, but whether they can suffer (Bentham 1960 [1823]: ch.17 footnote). The evident truth of this explains the fact that as the century proceeded a great many organizations sprang into existence that were expressly committed to, for instance, the promotion of more humane farming methods, or the abolition of vivisection, or the ending of cruel sports like cock-fighting and bear baiting. Alongside this practical development, the moral importance of animal welfare figured evermore prominently in ethics and political philosophy. Animal welfare was eventually elevated to the level of 'animal rights', not least as a result of an influential book with that title published by the activist Henry Salt in 1892.

As Bentham's famous remark implies, ethical concern with the welfare of animals is easily explained in terms of an extension of the moral principles that we apply to fellow human beings. The extension of rights to animals is more questionable, but not nearly as problematic as a more dramatic development, namely the extension of a moral or ethical concern to the inanimate non-human world. Neither the concept of 'welfare' nor 'rights' is easily applied to rivers, forests, mountain ranges, or tracts of wilderness. Can landscapes suffer, or rivers have rights? And yet, the line of argument that began with animal welfare did seem to launch ethics on a trajectory that sought to invest the whole of the natural world with a special kind of value, one that implied something like moral constraint on the part of human beings.

The key figures in the articulation of this new conception of nature are American. In 1836, Ralph Waldo Emerson (1803–82) published an essay entitled 'Nature'. Though published anonymously, Emerson soon came to be recognized as its author, and in the following year he gave a speech at Harvard on a similar theme. Both works are regarded as foundational in the philosophical movement known as Transcendentalism, and both marked the development of a distinctively American school of thought. This was made possible in large part because of the contrast between the vast virgin territories of the United States on the one hand, and the densely populated, heavily urbanized countries of Europe on the other. Emerson travelled in Europe and met many of the people associated with European Romanticism, including William Wordsworth, Samuel Taylor Coleridge, and Thomas Carlyle. For most of the Romantics—of whom these may be said to be three—there was an inevitable tension between human civilization and the natural world. Their perception of this tension was sustained by the fact that the marks of European civilization are deeply engraved on the European landscape, so deeply engrained in fact that anything plausibly called 'nature' is at best only dimly discernable. Emerson, by contrast, had come from a huge continent in which the impact of industry and civilization was (at that point) minimal. In the essay *Nature*, accordingly, he advances a view of nature rather different to that of the European thinkers, one derived from the sense that anyone travelling in North America could hardly fail to view human beings as just one small part of a vastly greater whole. From the 'transcendentalist' point of view, nature we might say is a Garden of Eden without God, a place in which our task is to make a home that is in harmony with the whole. The label 'transcendental' is in fact a little misleading. It might be more accurate to say that this conception of nature is based on the idea that that which is most deeply in accord with the human spirit is immanent in the natural world. Here, perhaps, we can detect a final break with the idea that nature's spirituality derives from divine creation.

Nature's inherent spirituality is an idea made more explicit in another 'transcendentalist' figure, Henry David Thoreau (1817–62). Thoreau read Emerson's *Nature* as a student at Harvard College. He too published an immensely influential book—*Walden; or Life in the Woods*. His book was the outcome of a two year experiment in 'simple living' in a cabin built by Thoreau in woods that Emerson owned around Walden Pond in Concord, Massachusetts. 'I went to the woods because I wished to live deliberately, to front only the essential facts of life, and see if I could not learn what it had to teach, and not, when I came to die, discover that I had not lived.', he writes (Thoreau 1995 [1854]: 25). As this sentence reveals, Thoreau was not simply in pursuit of novel experience but of something more like 'the meaning of life', and this in turn shows that Transcendentalism has a quasi-religious character. This is no accident. Before he set off on his European travels, Emerson had been a Christian minister in Boston where, along with many others, he experienced a growing sense of the need for a new, post-Christian spirituality. It was this development that eventually led him to resign his charge, and his 'Transcendentalist' philosophy was an attempt to secure an alternative spiritual dimension to human life, one stripped of outdated historical and theological ideas.

This quasi-religious conception of nature as a source of spiritual nourishment for the human soul, has proved very influential in the environmental movement, even if this has not always been acknowledged. It received partial expression in the poetry of Walt Whitman (1819–92), which Emerson admired and commended, but more importantly came to be allied with a love of and concern for wilderness. A key figure in this development was the Scottish born American naturalist John Muir (1838–1914), identified by an admirer as 'one of the patron saints' of twentieth-century environmentalism, a description that further confirms the implicit religious dimension.

This dimension is evident in Muir's attitude to nature. His upbringing was Christian and his knowledge of the Bible extensive. He admired the writings of Carlyle, Emerson, and Thoreau, and with them he came to think of the wilderness as a new Bible, a 'Book of Nature' in which the divine could be directly apprehended and through which the forests and sierras were revealed as our true 'home'. Emerson anticipated the same idea, writing in an early lecture that 'Nature is a language and every new fact one learns is a new word; . . . I wish to learn this language, not that I may know a new grammar, but that I may read the great book that is written in that tongue' (Emerson 1959: 50). Though by preference a naturalist and practical explorer, with considerable personal effort Muir also became a prolific writer. Much of his writing is descriptive, but it also represents a vision of nature diametrically opposed to Isaiah's. The wild fastnesses of hills and valleys are not to be feared, but to be valued, admired and above all, preserved from human depredation.

In accordance with this vision Muir became a key figure in the movement to save wilderness, notably in California, as well as a founder of the Sierra Club, which remains one of the most prominent environmental organizations in the United States. The environmental movement of the twentieth century owes more to Muir than to Emerson or Thoreau, as is shown by two key texts that stand out in its development. One is *Sand County Almanack*, a collection of posthumously published essays by Aldo Leopold (1887–1948) of which 'The Land Ethic' is perhaps the best known. Leopold's essays are very much more, in the spirit of Thoreau and Muir than of Emerson, and he expressly undertakes to explain and defend the value of wilderness. The second key text—*Silent Spring* by another naturalist, Rachel Carson (1907–64)—appeared in 1962 and took the environmental conception of nature an important step further by introducing an ecological dimension.

This was not an entirely unprecedented development. On his trip to Europe in 1832, Emerson had been powerfully impressed by recent advances in zoology, botany, and geology and in particular by new systems of classification which displayed the intricate interconnection between the different parts of nature. The term 'ecology' was coined thirty years later by a German biologist as the name for the scientific study of this interconnectedness. Though 'ecology' and 'environmentalism' are often used interchangeably they have importantly different meanings. The study of ecology, we might say, uncovers phenomena that call for greater environmental responsibility. This is true of *Silent Spring*. Its title brilliantly conveys the warning of a future in which birds no longer sing, and identifies this as a devastating outcome of the widespread agricultural use of chemicals, by humans—and for humans of course. Whereas the biologists who impressed Emerson demonstrated a connection between plants and animals, Carson's book aimed to show that the human world was no less interconnected with all the inhabitants of the earth. As a result, since human actions could not be isolated in their effects, seemingly innocent, or even beneficial practices, could have disastrous results in far off times and places.

Ecology employs the concept of an ecosystem—a set of connections that makes the flourishing of each part of the system mutually interdependent. It is not difficult to see that inanimate elements—rivers, soils, terrains—can form important parts of the system. In this way, ecology forges a link with nature writ large that no ethic based upon welfare or rights could do. And thereby it provides the essential basis for a very wide-ranging conception of environmental responsibility.

VI. Religious Naturalism

Environmentalism, aided by ecological study, invokes a concept of nature that does not stand in opposition to humanity, but encompasses it. Indeed, the fundamental contention is that humanity needs to learn this lesson: we are just one part of a far larger interconnected ecosystem, and we disregard this interconnectedness at our peril. That is why environmental awareness calls for environmental responsibility. This way of stating the matter, however, has prompted a line of thought which pushes the conception of nature in a more explicitly religious direction.

In a short but very influential paper published in 1973, the Norwegian philosopher Arne Naess (1912–2009) drew a distinction between 'deep' and 'shallow' ecology. Shallow ecology he characterizes as any view that bases environmental responsibility on the implications for future human welfare. Deep ecology, by contrast, takes the detrimental impact of human beings on the larger environment to matter in itself, regardless of what it might mean for human health or prosperity. Naess thinks that only deep ecological views are ultimately defensible because they alone meet this fundamental requirement: a true concern for nature must shift the focus of attention away from human beings entirely.

Rather obviously, by this criterion most environmental campaigns are either shallow, or at best, a mix of the shallow and the deep. It is the economic and medical implications of global warming, ozone depletion, soil erosion, river pollution and so on, that most easily and frequently command moral and political support, and the associated practices of 'reduce, reuse, recycle' are plainly meant to have material benefits. To classify all this as 'shallow', however, overlooks the fact that finding a properly 'deep' explanation for environmental responsibility is very difficult. Appeals to biodiversity, or natural beauty, for example, very easily turn out to rest upon human values. Diversity is often defended in terms of their potential medical or other benefits that cannot currently be anticipated. The preservation of natural beauty, too, seems inescapably human, since 'aesthetic pleasure' is not something (almost all) other animals experience. Even Leopold in his eloquent essay on 'Wilderness', ultimately rests its significance on value to humans. For while he wants to exclude the coach tours, motorboats, and campgrounds that turn wilderness into a human recreation facility, he still makes its value to science and to the individual explorer key elements in his case.

The point to emphasize is that 'shallow' ecology is hard to avoid. The only way of doing so is to reverse a common way of thinking that makes nature subservient to humanity, and instead make human values completely subservient to nature. We must come to see the natural world in a way that 'changes the role of Homo sapiens from conqueror of the land-community to plain member and citizen of it' (Leopold 1970 [1949]: 240). But what conception of the 'land-community' or the biotic-community (as he elsewhere puts it) can secure this attitude? The answer has proved to be a religious one—the Earth as sacred.

As the title of her book reveals, it is just such a conception that another American writer aims to provide. In *The Sacred Depths of Nature* Ursula Goodenough says that the goal of her book 'is to present an accessible account of our scientific understanding of nature and then suggest ways that this account can call forth appealing and abiding religious responses—an approach that can be called religious naturalism' (Goodenough 1998: pp. xvi–xvii). Religious naturalism of this kind can be seen to be the result of Emerson's Transcendentalism taken to its logical conclusion. To describe it as 'naturalism' is to disavow any theological conception that seeks the ultimate explanation of existence outside the natural world, and to call it religious is to affirm that it can meaningfully describe the world that science discloses to us as sacred. Religious naturalism so conceived is thus at the polar opposite of the ancient conception of physical nature animated by spirits, while at the same time distinguished from the Enlightenment's conception of the world as a disenchanted 'Machine'.

It can reasonably be held, of course, that given what has been said so far, all that religious naturalism amounts to is an aspiration to have the best of both worlds. It has still to be shown how this is possible. One interesting and influential author who has been thought to provide the sort of conception that religious naturalism requires is the biologist James Lovelock. Lovelock first formulated the 'Gaia hypothesis' in 1979. The hypothesis takes its name from the Greek supreme goddess of Earth, but though the name might suggest some sort of neo-nature mysticism, the Gaia hypothesis is a strictly scientific explanation of the history of the Earth. In his most recent version (2006) Lovelock explains it as follows.

> Going outwards from the centre, the Earth is almost entirely made of hot or molten rock and metal. Gaia is a thin spherical shell of matter that surrounds the incandescent interior; it begins where the crustal rocks meet the magma of the Earth's hot interior, about 100 miles below the surface, and proceeds another 100 miles outwards through the ocean and air to the even hotter thermosphere at the edge of space. It includes the biosphere and is a dynamic physiological system that has kept our planet fit for life for over three billion years. I call Gaia a physiological system because it appears to have the unconscious goal of regulating the climate and chemistry at a comfortable state for life.   (Lovelock 2006: 15)

Lovelock thinks that the hypothesis that the Earth is a dynamic physiological system has a direct bearing on human behaviour since he thinks that environmental problems such as global warming require us 'to know the true nature of the Earth and imagine it as the largest living thing in the solar system, not something inanimate like that disreputable contraption "spaceship Earth" ' and that this calls for a 'change of heart and mind' (Lovelock 2006: 17).

Lovelock expressly endorses 'respect for Gaia' as the true and adequate ground of deep ecology. If Lovelock is right, Gaia is more important than we are. In *The Revenge of Gaia* he warns of a cataclysmic future for human civilization, one possibly quite close at hand. However, to fear for the future of human life as we currently know it does not imply that we need be fearful for the future of Gaia,

> The Earth has recovered after fevers . . . and there are no grounds for thinking that what we are doing will destroy Gaia; . . . humans are tough enough for breeding pairs to survive, and Gaia is the toughest of all. What we are doing weakens her but is unlikely to destroy her. She has survived numerous catastrophes in her three billion years or more.   (Lovelock 2006: 60)

The pattern exhibited in this way of thinking is an ancient one. It is to be found in the Old Testament, for example, where the prophets warn that failure to acknowledge the Most High and to walk in the paths He has prescribed will lead to terrible results.

Though some of these will be natural disasters, it is plainly absurd to think that God is damaged by these. In a strikingly similar fashion, Lovelock tells us to 'plan our own destiny within Gaia' (Lovelock 2006: 141). He speaks of combating the 'hubris' (spiritual pride) that prompts the 'sin' of environmental recklessness. In keeping with this religious language, his autobiography is called *Homage to Gaia*.

Religious naturalism that makes the Earth its focus does mark a move beyond the ethical principles and political campaigns of 'shallow' ecology. To characterize the Earth as the Being to which humanity owes its existence makes it a direct rival to the 'One True God' of the Abrahamic faiths of Judaism, Christianity, and Islam. There is this crucial difference, though: God is personal; Gaia is not. It is the personhood of God (however that is to be understood exactly) that makes the practices of prayer and worship intelligible. We acknowledge God's sovereignty, respond to God's gifts, follow God's will, ask for God's assistance. These only make sense if God is an intentional agent. Gaia on the other hand is not an agent, but 'a physiological system [which] appears to have the unconscious goal of regulating the climate and chemistry at a comfortable state for life' (Lovelock 2006: 15). If Lovelock is right, we have reason to be fearful of the working of Gaia, and this accords with Goodenough's contention in *The Sacred Depths of Nature* that 'religious emotions can be elicited by natural reality'. Even if this is true, and we have good reason to call these emotions 'religious', it makes Nature fall far short of the divine.

VII. Taking Stock

The purpose of this chapter has been to survey the alternative conceptions of nature that over a long period have underlain the ways in which people have understood nature's relation to human life. Depending on how we think of nature, we will understand this relationship differently—as one of conflict, harmony, or subservience. The impulse to reflection here comes from the necessary recognition of duality. It is incontestable that there is some way in which humanity is to be contrasted with nature. It is true that we are biologically evolved entities, and that natural science has shown this. Yet we do not stand in the same relation to our biological origins as other entities do. No other animals have speech and writing, live under complex legal systems, devise pharmaceutically based remedies to illnesses, or invent sophisticated methods of transport and communication. These differences, and their significance can be mistakenly identified and misunderstood, of course. For most of history people have denied what Hume thought to be evident, that other animals have the ability to reason and communicate, and have even denied what seems to be incontestable, that other animals suffer. Yet for all this between the weakest human intellect and the cleverest animal there remains a huge gulf.

It is no less incontestable, on the other hand, that human beings engage in sexual reproduction, need nutrition, require protection from extremes of heat and cold, are prone to illness, and subject to aging and death. Facts like these demonstrate that human beings belong to a much larger natural world, and constitute an insurmountable obstacle to Cartesian substance dualism.

The upshot seems paradoxical: we can neither assert nor deny the duality of nature and civilization. Similarly, we cannot affirm or deny their identity. The mechanical conception of some of the philosophers of the Enlightenment cannot properly accommodate the distinctiveness of humanity; the Romantic attempt to re-enchant the world generates a conflict between civilization and nature in one way or another. It seems that what is required is an overarching frame which can exhibit the common origin of nature and civilization in a way that preserves their differentiation. On this score, perhaps, the pre-modern conception has something to teach us. The ancients tended to see everything as spiritually animated. For polytheists there were many separate spirits, ordered perhaps in hierarchies, but all independent of the nature they animated. For monotheists, these spiritual beings, like the material things they animated, were under the sovereignty of God and subject to his purposes. The world of contemporary thought has difficulty with the idea of 'spirits', and yet cannot dispense with some idea of 'the human spirit'. One way of relating people and nature is to see them as beings in which the spiritual and the material are united in being distinct expressions of the creative activity of God.

REFERENCES

Bentham, J. (1960 [1823]). *A Fragment of Government and Introduction to the Principles of Morals and Legislation*, ed. Wilfred Harrison (Oxford: Basil Blackwell).

Brown, David (2004). *God and Enchantment of Place.* (Oxford: Oxford University Press).

Burke, E. (2009 [1757]). *A Philosophical Enquiry into the Origin of our Ideas of the Sublime and Beautiful.* (Oxford: Oxford University Press).

Carson, R. (1962). *Silent Spring.* (Boston: Houghton Mifflin).

Cicero, Marcus Tullius (1997). *The Nature of the Gods*, trans. C. D. Yonge (Amherst NY: Prometheus Books).

Emerson, Ralph Waldo (1959). *Early Lectures 1833–36*, ed. Stephen Whicher (Cambridge, MA: Harvard University Press).

Goodenough, U. (1998). *The Sacred Depths of Nature.* (New York and Oxford: Oxford University Press).

Hopkins, Gerard Manley (1996). *Gerard Manley Hopkins The Major Works*, ed. Catherine Phillips (Oxford: Oxford World's Classics).

Hume, D (1967 [1739]). *A Treatise of Human Nature.* (Oxford: Clarendon Press; reprinted from the original edition in three volumes and edited with an analytical index by L. A. Selby-Bigge).

—— (1993 [1757]). *The Natural History of Religion*, ed. J. A. C. Gaskin (Oxford: Oxford University Press).

—— (1948 [1776]). *Dialogues concerning Natural Religion*, ed. H. D. Aiken (New York: Hafner).

Hutcheson, F. (2008 [1725]). *Inquiry into the Original of Our Ideas of Beauty and Virtue*, ed. Wolfgang Leidhold (Indianapolis: Liberty Fund).

Leopold, A. (1969 [1946]). *A Sand County Almanack: With Other Essays on Conservation from Round River*. (Oxford: Oxford University Press).

Lovelock, J. (2000). *Homage to Gaia: The Life of an Independent Scientist*. (Oxford: Oxford University Press).

—— (2006). *The Revenge of Gaia: Earth's Climate Crisis and the Fate of Humanity*. (New York: Basic Books).

Naess, Arne (1973). 'The Shallow and the Deep, Long Range Ecology Movement', *Inquiry* 16, 95–100.

Nietzsche, F. (1968 [1895 and 1889]). *Twilight of the Idols and The Anti-Christ*, trans. R. J. Hollingdale (London: Penguin Classics).

—— (1994 [1887]). *On the Genealogy of Morality*, ed. Keith Ansell-Pearson (Cambridge: Cambridge University Press).

—— (2001 [1887]). *The Gay Science*, ed. Bernard Williams (Cambridge: Cambridge University Press).

Plato (1961). *The Collected Dialogues*, ed. Hamilton and Cairns (Princeton, NJ: Princeton University Press).

Rousseau, J. J. (1994 [1762]). *The Social Contract*, trans. Christopher Betts (Oxford: Oxford University Press).

—— (1997). *'The Discourses' and Other Early Political Writings*, trans. Victor Gourevitch (Cambridge: Cambridge University Press).

Thomas, Dylan (2003). *The Poems of Dylan Thomas*, new rev. edn., ed. Daniel Jones (New York: New Directions Publishing).

Thomas, Keith (1991). *Religion and the Decline of Magic: Studies in Popular Beliefs in Sixteenth and Seventeenth-Century England*. (London: Penguin).

Thoreau, Henry David (1995 [1854]). *Walden; Or, Life in the Woods*. (New York: Dover Books).

Suggested Reading

Brown (2004).

Burke (2009 [1757]).

Collingwood, R. G. (1945). *The Idea of Nature*. (Oxford: Oxford University Press).

Leopold, A. (1969 [1946]).

Lovelock (2000).

Merchant, Carolyn (1980). *The Death of Nature: Women, Ecology and the Scientific Revolution*. (New York: HarperCollins).

Mill, J. S. (1874). 'Nature', *Three Essays on Religion*. (London: Longmans Green).

Thomas (1991).

Thoreau (1995 [1854]).

CHAPTER 20

BEAUTY AND SUBLIMITY

ROSS WILSON

I. THE INVENTION OF AESTHETICS

THE philosophical discipline dedicated to the investigation of beauty and sublimity in nature and art, the discipline of aesthetics, is often spoken of as having been at some point, like the internal combustion engine, or the telephone, 'invented' (cf. Caygill 2001). Given that there has been reflection on the beauty and, if not sublimity, then certainly the grandeur both of nature and the results of human creativity for, as far as it is possible to tell, ever, why is it that *aesthetics* is thus imagined as having been invented? One answer to this question is that the invention of aesthetics does in fact mark a radical break with earlier thought about beautiful nature, sublimity, and art by instantiating a distinct regime according to which these are to be considered without, as previously required, reference to questions of moral or conceptual judgement. Whereas, so this answer proceeds, for earlier thinkers concerned with questions that aesthetics would come to claim as its own, beauty was to be considered as participating in both truth and goodness (see e.g. Eco 1988), for thinkers after the aesthetic turn, beauty was freed from moral and epistemological considerations altogether or, to put this another way, bereft of its traditional association with truth and goodness. But putting it both of these ways at once suggests that aesthetics is a very peculiar regime of thought indeed: it is an invention or innovation, while, on the other hand, it is a bereavement or a rending of a prior unity.

What effected this innovation and rending? Here is one answer:

> Modernity is the separation of spheres, the becoming autonomous of truth, beauty and goodness from one another, and their developing into self-sufficient forms of practice: modern science and technology, private morality and modern legal forms, and modern art. This categorical separation of domains represents the dissolution of the metaphysical totalities of the pre-modern age. (Bernstein 1992: 5–6)

As Bernstein acknowledges, this disentangling of truth, goodness, and beauty from each other—or, indeed, their opposition to one another—is not exactly exclusive to what we might want to call 'modernity': Plato, famously, opposed the philosophically constituted city, founded on the love of truth, to the dangerously beguiling blandishments of the poets. But the implication of Bernstein's necessarily abbreviated characterization given above is that modernity is chiefly typified by the fact that the effect of this separation of spheres is the dissolution of prior 'metaphysical totalities'. The project of categorical separation as a pre-condition of the development of the autonomy of those categories is, that is to say, the project of secularization.

Mention of modernity's characteristically secular nature hardly clears up the difficulties with the concept of modernity; if there is a more questionable and contentious term than 'modernity' it may very well be 'secularity'. On the one hand, modernity's keenness to trumpet its secularity as central to its very modernity often seems to be in inverse proportion to the degree to which modernization and secularization have been fulfilled (if 'fulfilled' is the right word here). We may rightly ask if society has ever been either modern or secular (cf. Cannell 2010). This question is, of course, too large to be tackled here, and so I want in this chapter to focus in particular on the relation of 'modern' and 'secular' aesthetics to the theological forebears from which it is apparently radically distinct. To be clear, I am not concerned here with examining 'modern' attempts to formulate a theological aesthetics, such as that by Hans Urs von Balthasar (von Balthasar 1982–9)—interesting, of course, as this would be; rather, I want to investigate instead the lingering inheritance of and antagonism toward theology in some instances of reflection on the beauty of nature and art, and on the sublime, in modern thought. Modern aesthetic thought is engaged, in Coleridge's taut phrase, in a 'war embrace' with the theological inheritance it would at once disavow and preserve (Coleridge 1983: II, 26; 1997: 330).

Of course, it might justly be claimed, especially by those given to suspect the claims of 'modernity' to be 'secular', that the entire tradition of modern western aesthetics can be characterized in this way. That entire tradition, regrettably, does not lie within the purview of this chapter, and a number of important figures will not receive the attention they would otherwise merit here. Chief among them, perhaps, is G. W. F. Hegel, whose aesthetics insistently impinge on theological questions (or vice versa). It is important to Hegel early on in his lecture course on fine art, for instance, to show how the products of human art are effectively a work of the divine—which does not, therefore, make its appearance in natural beauty alone, but which, in fact, establishes for itself a more 'suitable thoroughfare' in artworks (Hegel 1975: I, 29–30). Hegel and a range of writers within and beyond the tradition of German Idealism pose crucial questions for thinking about the relation between theology and modern aesthetics. But rather than offer a broad and rather brisk conspectus of those questions, I focus instead on two examples of the relation between aesthetics and the theological. In turning to Kant's *Critique of Judgement* I examine the text often credited if not with inventing the aesthetic then with elaborating one of its earliest systematic formulations. The reason Kant's third *Critique* has been credited with this status is that its explicit aim is to carve out a space for aesthetic judgement that would, first, separate it from cognitive and moral judgement, and, second, establish it as a distinctively human (and thus neither animal nor, crucially, divine) capacity. Part of the work of Kant's founding of aesthetics, therefore, involves the attempt to clear the ground of inherited theology. I will investigate how thoroughgoing that clearance really is.

If Kant's is in some sense an attempt to evade the theological inheritance of aesthetics, Theodor Adorno's work represents a confrontation with it. This is a confrontation not in the sense that Adorno wishes to purge aesthetics of theology—a task left undone from the outset of modern aesthetics—but rather to argue that aesthetics both is and is not cryptically theological. Adorno is usefully paired with Kant here, not so much because of his deep engagement with Kant's aesthetics, but rather because he sets the specifically tense relationship with theology that secretly characterizes aesthetics from its inception in a historical context that is not merely invoked but is rather made to do important explanatory work.

It is useful, in order to get more fully underway this specific investigation into Kant's apparent initiation of the separation of the aesthetic from the theological, to return briefly to Bernstein's elaboration of the specific status of modern aesthetics. I mentioned above that aesthetics is on the one hand an invention and, on the other, a work of mourning in response to a bereavement. This is how Bernstein articulates the bereavement that it is at the heart of modern aesthetic thought:

> [E]very conception of the alienation of art from truth is simultaneously a work of remembrance, a work of mourning and grief, even for those philosophers who doubt that such an 'original' state of union ever existed. In modernity beauty is not only alienated from truth, but grieves its loss; modernity is the site of beauty bereaved—bereaved of truth.   (Bernstein 1992: 4)

Were this not bleak enough, we might add that beauty is also bereaved of goodness. However, a number of important qualifications need to be reiterated at this point. First, in so far as the 'mourning and grief' that Bernstein describes is also 'a work of remembrance', the loss that beauty has suffered is not a total loss. Second, even were this loss, so to speak, total, it is a loss, it is well to recall, by which something is gained. That 'something' is the autonomy of the aesthetic. If the characteristic mode of modern art (with which Bernstein is primarily concerned here and elsewhere in his work) is then both morally and cognitively dirempt, it is also free. This freedom or, indeed, emancipation is emphasized, for example, by Jürgen Habermas in his response to what he sees as the narrowness of Adorno and Max Horkheimer's critique of instrumental reason in their early *Dialectic of Enlightenment* (Habermas 1987: 112–13). There are many questions to be asked about Habermas's defence of what he calls 'modernity's specific dignity', the emergence in modernity, that is, of distinct spheres of expertise, but rather than going into them here I want instead to focus on another, more fugitive qualification that needs to be emphasized here and which is the focus of this chapter. The separation of goodness, truth, and beauty—or the three transcendentals (see Lotz 1975)—'represents,' as Bernstein puts it 'the dissolution of the metaphysical totalities of the pre-modern age'. But that dissolution is, as I have been stressing, at the same time a 'remembrance', a 'mourning', and not an obliteration or forgetting. In fact, 'dissolution' is a happy term for the investigation I want to conduct today: has the apparently superseded assumption of 'metaphysical totality' been obliterated in 'modernity', or do fragments and traces of it float instead in a seemingly alien medium?

II. All the Beauty in the World

Before turning to Kant's third *Critique* in detail, a possible objection to the account of the aesthetic that I have been sketching needs first to be addressed. It might be argued that it is a mistake to emphasize the significance of the distinctiveness of the aesthetic in particular as characteristic of modern philosophy: what is characteristically modern, that is to say, is not so much the emergence of the aesthetic as such, but the emphatic rather than provisional distinction drawn between goodness, truth, and beauty. So, in an account such as Habermas's, for instance, there is as much emphasis on the distinctness and autonomy of the regimes and practices of knowledge and morals as there is on beauty; beauty, therefore, is no more characteristically bereft of metaphysical unity than are truth and goodness. And after all, the simple fact that the *Critique* of Kant's that I want to address here was his *third* reminds us that there are another two, dealing just as autonomously with knowledge, on the one hand, and morals, on the other.

This is a powerful objection, but I want to maintain nonetheless that, for Kant at least, beauty has become distinct in a way that truth and goodness have not. Beauty is distinct because it is only discernible by human beings, as Kant makes quite explicit: 'beauty has purport and significance only for human beings, i.e. for beings at once animal and rational (but not merely for them as rational beings—as spirits for example—but only for them as both animal and rational)' (Kant 2007: 41). This is emphatic in its disenfranchisement of animals and, more importantly for my purposes here, purely spiritual beings as judges of beauty. Elsewhere in his philosophy, Kant does examine other, non-aesthetic, kinds of judgement that are only available to human beings. So, for instance, human beings make singular empirical judgements of the kind that God need not make because, given His intuitive rather than discursive understanding, He already knows everything in advance of its actual instantiation. Similarly, only human beings are subject to duty, because acting out of properly moral motivations is for them a struggle, whereas for God it is, as it were, automatic (cf. Wilson 2007: 140–1). This differentiation of human dutiful action from divine moral conformity is especially notable because Kant appears provocatively to suggest in the opening statement of the *Groundwork for the Metaphysics of Morals* that the human will that performs its duty, namely, the good will, is better than the morally untroubled will of God, that is, the holy will: 'It is impossible to think of anything at all in the world, or indeed even beyond it, that could be considered good without limitation except a good will' (Kant 1996: 49).

Far-reaching as the consequences of this suggestion from the beginning of Kant's *Groundwork* may be, it is still worth stressing that aesthetic judgement presents a special case: while spiritual beings are capable of kinds of judgement analogous with human empirical judging and moral judging, judging the beautiful is wholly closed to them, because there is no conceptual or rational ground on which the specific sensual singularity of aesthetic judgement may, so to speak, be circumvented.

This entails, then, that beauty and sublimity, discernible by aesthetic judgement, are decisively closed off, by Kant, from theological consideration, at least in so far as aesthetic judgement is the exclusive preserve of beings that are at once animal and rational, that is, human beings. In judging beauty and sublimity, so he implies, we are alone.

What we might term the humanization of aesthetic judgement has two further significant features. First, upon human beings is bestowed the freedom to think of anything as beautiful, without reference to any imaginable higher court of appeal. Unconstrained by standards of beauty that transcend humanity, we are free, Kant strikingly states, 'to turn anything into an object of pleasure' (Kant 2007: 41). This freedom is the basis for Kant's discrimination of the pleasure in the beautiful from the gratification of the agreeable and the esteem of the good, because both of those, in their different ways, dictate what we are to take delight in, whereas the beautiful is not dictated to us at all. This freedom for human beings to 'turn anything' into the beautiful has rightly been viewed as fundamental to Kant's status as, in fundamental ways, anticipating the developments of both Romantic and, indeed, Modernist artistic practice (cf. De Duve 1999).

What I want to focus on here, though, is another consequence of this remarkable human freedom. The world on this account would seem to be wholly devoid of beauty without the intervention of human judging. In §9 of the *Critique of Judgement*, Kant aims to decide whether pleasure precedes or follows the judging of the object in an aesthetic judgement, and thus to answer the question as to whether we first feel pleasure in an object which we then communicate to others, or rather whether we first judge an object in a way that is communicable and then for that reason feel pleasure. According to Kant, 'it is the universal capacity for being communicated incident to the state of the mind in the given representation [that is, the representation judged beautiful] which, as the subjective condition of the judgement of taste, must underlie the latter, with the pleasure in the object as its consequence.' (Kant 2007: 48) The crucial point of this argument is that the pleasure felt in judging beauty is dependent upon some feature of the human mind—its 'capacity for being communicated'—rather than some feature of the object judged—indeed, were the latter the case, the feeling involved would be one 'of mere agreeableness to the senses' and thus only private (Kant 2007: 48), an option that Kant has rejected. Beauty is then, for Kant, in a fundamental way dependent upon the human mind rather than on objects in the world. Indeed, he asserts later in §9 that 'beauty is for itself, apart from any reference to the feeling of the subject, nothing' (Kant 2007: 49).

It seems that Kant's aesthetics is based on a thoroughgoing humanizing of the beautiful. Of course, this contrasts starkly with a host of both pagan and Christian thinkers for whom the appreciation of beauty, so to speak, is a significant capacity of God's as well: after all, the goodness that the God of Genesis sees in the light that He brings into being is not only an instrumental or moral but an aesthetic one: God sees that the light is beautiful. One way of reading Kant's asseveration that 'beauty is . . . in itself nothing', by contrast, would be to say that at the moment of the emancipation of beauty from goodness and truth, and hence the freedom of human beings to find anything beautiful, it is annihilated.

On closer inspection of Kant's aesthetics, however, that humanizing of the beautiful is not as thoroughgoing as it might at first seem. Indeed, the articulation of the precise nature of the 'purport and significance' that beauty has, so Kant claims, only for humans is in fact indebted to the, according to Kant, unavoidable reference to an understanding that transcends our own. This reference first comes into view in Kant's introduction to the *Critique* where he is explaining why, although the *Critique of Pure Reason* had established the possibility of the experience of nature in general, that investigation did not exhaust the laws actually obtaining in nature in its particularity. This is a long, but revealing passage:

> But there are such manifold forms of nature, so many modifications, as it were, of the universal transcendental concepts of nature, left undetermined by the laws furnished by the pure understanding a priori . . . , and for the reason that these laws only touch the general possibility of a nature (as an object of the senses), that there must also be laws in this regard. These laws, being empirical, may be contingent as far as the light of our understanding goes, but still, if they are to be called laws (as the concept of nature requires), they must be regarded as necessary on a principle, unknown though it be to us, of the unity of the manifold. Reflective judgement which is compelled to ascend from the particular in nature to the universal, stands, therefore, in need of a principle. This principle it cannot borrow from experience, because what it has to do is to establish just the unity of all empirical principles under higher, though likewise empirical, principles, and thence the possibility of the systematic subordination of higher and lower principles. Such a transcendental principle, therefore, reflective judgement can only give as a law from and to itself.   (Kant 2007: 15)

Kant is explaining here the problem that one may very well be in possession of the laws of nature in general (and Kant had outlined these in the first *Critique*), but their application to this particular nature that we experience is still, as it were, an open question. The role that beauty plays in answering this question is that it shows that nature in its particular existence is amenable to our cognitive faculties in general, even though it does not engage them in specific cognitive judgements. But the point I wish to emphasis here is that Kant casts the contingency of empirical laws as quite possibly contingent on the specific character of '*our* understanding' (his emphasis). Indeed, only slightly further on in §IV of the introduction, he offers the following solution to the gap between the general laws of nature that originate in our cognitive faculties and the specific laws of nature:

> [A]s universal laws of nature have their ground in our understanding, which prescribes them to nature (though only according to the universal concept of it as nature), particular empirical laws must be regarded, in respect of that which is left undetermined in them by these universal laws, according to a unity such as they would have if an understanding (though it be not ours) had supplied them for the benefit of our cognitive faculties, so as to render possible a system of experience according to particular natural laws.   (Kant 2007: 16)

Thus, we cannot but invoke an understanding quite distinct from ours in order to explain the lawfulness of particular nature, or, as Kant puts it a bit further on in the introduction,

> judgement is compelled . . . to adopt it as an a priori principle, that what is for human insight contingent in the particular (empirical) laws of nature contains nevertheless unity of law in the synthesis of its manifold in an intrinsically possible experience—unfathomable, though still thinkable, as such unity may, no doubt, be for us.   (Kant 2007: 19)

Now, it is important to note—as Kant does, of course—that what is at work here is simply an assumption that human beings cannot help making, and not, therefore, anything like an insight into nature's actual constitution by a superhuman and supernatural understanding, such as God's: we 'read [unity] into' nature.

At issue throughout the third *Critique*'s treatment of beauty is, then, the degree to which we can allow ourselves to think of beauty as subsisting in the world at all and how, furthermore, we might assume it got there. As we have seen, on the one hand, Kant declares that human beings are free to turn anything whatever into the beautiful, the implication of which is that there is nothing already beautiful anywhere to be found in nature. But on the other hand, and as I have just been outlining, in so far as we do come to see anything as beautiful, by the same token we cannot but invoke an understanding that transcends ours as its source. (This invocation need not, of course, be precisely conscious in any individual judgement of beauty.) The tension between these two claims is keenly felt throughout the *Critique of Judgement*, even (or especially) where Kant is staking out the territory of his own particular contribution to aesthetics:

> [T]aste may be said invariably to judge on empirical grounds of determination and such, therefore, as are only given *a posteriori* through the senses, or else it may be allowed to judge on an *a priori* ground. The former would be the *empiricism* of the critique of taste, the latter its *rationalism*. The first would obliterate the distinction that marks off the object of our delight from the *agreeable*; the second, supposing the judgement rested upon determinate concepts, would obliterate its distinction from the *good*. In this way beauty would find itself utterly banished from the world, and nothing but the dignity of a separate name, betokening, maybe, a certain blend of both the above-named kinds of delight, would be left in its stead.   (Kant 2007: 174)

In general, this passage is a fairly typical example of Kant's discrimination of his point of view from established empiricist and rationalist positions. What the passage claims is that, were either of the rival positions regarding beauty admitted, then beauty would disappear and what would remain would be the agreeable and good, perhaps sometimes mixed together and given the name of beauty—a name which would not itself refer to anything 'in the world'. This way of putting it does, however, differ subtly but significantly from the straightforward statement that beauty is 'nothing in itself' apart from human judging. To say that beauty is nothing in itself prior to human judgement does imply an aesthetic nominalism: it is to say that, in fact, 'beauty' is indeed a special name, albeit one that is distinct from 'good' and 'agreeable'. Here, however, that nominalism is taken to be a bad consequence of conflating the beautiful with the good and the agreeable; rather, beauty exists 'in the world'.

This apparent equivocation might be explained by saying that beauty is 'in the world' once it has been seen there by human beings, and not before. That kind of explanation is, of course, a key move in Kant's philosophy as a whole, and it is, in fact, the move that he thinks he is making here. So, for example, later in §58, he cautions against getting carried away with the idea that beauty really can be found in nature, where 'really' means not as a consequence of human judging. This is how he puts it: 'For nature to have fashioned its forms for our delight would inevitably imply an objective purposiveness on the part of nature, instead of a subjective purposiveness resting on the play of imagination in its freedom, where it is we who receive nature with favour, and not nature that does us a favour' (Kant 2007: 177). The subtlety of that distinction between receiving nature with favour and nature doing us a favour is instructive. It is especially instructive because Kant is seeking to situate here a kind of agency or activity: it is we who view nature in such a way, rather than nature presenting itself in such a way. But the terms of this distinction are equivocal with regard to activity. For Kant, it is crucial that humans are active and nature is passive, but what we do is 'receive nature', which is a markedly passive activity. Furthermore, while it might justly be argued that the whole point of this distinction is to show that it is our receiving that is favourable to nature, nonetheless the phrase 'we . . . receive nature with favour' harbours an ambiguity in that it might be taken either that we favourably receive nature or that we receive something that we cannot but imagine as nature-with-favour, even if we acknowledge that we cannot say that nature does us that favour. In any case, Kant's argument here is spoken in a middle, rather than active or passive, voice—so long as we understand that middle not as a happy medium, nor, to borrow Kant's term, 'a certain blend', but rather as the site of painful indecision, an open wound.

And that wound can be opened in different ways. So, whereas we have been examining the ways in which Kant's protestations that beauty is nothing apart from human judgement are compromised, he remarks elsewhere that 'To say: This flower is beautiful, is tantamount to repeating its own proper claim to the delight of everyone' (Kant 2007: 111). For sure, Kant goes on here diligently to remind the reader that, although we might 'suppose from this . . . that its beauty is to be taken for a property of the flower itself', in fact 'the judgement of taste consists precisely in a thing being called beautiful solely in respect of that quality in which it adapts itself to our mode of receiving it' (Kant 2007: 111–12). But the difference between a 'property' and a 'quality' of an object, it might be suspected, carries more weight than it can properly bear here, and, moreover, even if an object cannot be beautiful in respect of one of its own properties, it is nevertheless capable of adapting itself to human sensible capacities. The central paradox of the humanization of the beautiful in Kant's aesthetics is that with their new freedom to judge any object at all beautiful—as it were, to bestow beauty on any object they choose—human beings inescapably cannot but have recourse to taking that beauty as the cipher of something that transcends their own powers of judgement, and that betokens an understanding and will quite other than their own.

III. Grace and Favour

Perhaps it is needless to say that theologians wishing to show that modern thought is far from having separated itself from theological conceptions of beauty have found rich pickings in Kant. In a historically informed and finely argued essay, for instance, John Milbank, whose project in general is concerned to question the secularizing presumptions of *soi-dissant* modern thought (Milbank 2006), has argued that Kant's aesthetics is exemplary of the unavoidably theological nature of the aesthetic in modernity, all disavowals notwithstanding (Milbank 2004). In particular, Milbank stresses the importance of the sublime as the concept that 'came to dominate modern aesthetic theory', and he claims that the sublime functions as the tacit persistence of transcendence in a modernity that would otherwise flaunt its 'simple rejection of transcendence in favour of immanence' (Milbank 2004: 211).

Although any straightforward presumption of the sublime over the beautiful in modernity might be arguable, Milbank wants rather to emphasize two important points. First, the beautiful and the sublime are sundered in modern aesthetic thought, with the consequence that the sublime is identified chiefly by its moment of displeasure, with, that is, the mortification of what at one point Kant calls 'those things of which we are inclined to be solicitous (worldly goods, health, and life)' (Kant 2007: 92). Second, the sublime played a crucial role in the shift away from older theological to modern modes of thinking. This might sound surprising, because the latter, as I have indeed suggested here, rest on immanent assumptions, foregoing reference to transcendence beyond the human and secular context, whereas the sublime seems precisely to insist on the significance of concerns beyond the proliferation of worldly goods and the preservation of health and life. Milbank's main contribution, however, is to show in detail how the transcendence imagined in the sublime is an ersatz transcendence, a dummy for the transcendence is has succeeded. Far from involving the dismissal of transcendence, the sublime is its radical revision, as Milbank outlines:

At its heart lay a new thinking of the transcendent as the absolutely unknowable void, upon whose brink we finite beings must dizzily hover, as opposed to an older notion of a supra-hierarchical summit which we may gradually hope to scale. (Milbank 2004: 211)

It is this aspect of the sublime—which Milbank reads as the consequence not of the heroic wish of modernity to divest itself of theological ways of thinking but rather of a perverted theological understanding of the human relation to God—that has, of course, played a major role in the late twentieth-century recuperation of the sublime from an aesthetic tradition which had otherwise come to be viewed with a certain degree of suspicion. For instance, Jean-François Lyotard and others have seen in the sublime the most radical challenge anywhere in Kant's philosophy to the dominance of rationality and the concomitant assumption of the comprehensibility of the world (Lyotard 1994). The work of Lyotard on this topic clearly lends strong support to Milbank's interpretation of the stark difference between the sublime and the 'older notion of a supra-hierarchical summit' that it comes to replace, given that the latter is an eventually (hopefully) reachable source of ultimate reason.

It might legitimately be objected, as, for example, Paul Guyer does, to readings of the kind advanced by Lyotard and, albeit to different ends, Milbank that their version of Kant's sublime is only half the story (Guyer 2000: pp. xxxi–xxxii). Dizzy hovering would, for Kant, be merely bewildering, embarrassing, or horrible (all terms he uses to describe the moment of displeasure in the sublime). But that moment is just a moment, and the account of the sublime goes on to posit a more fundamental rationality than that based on our sensible capacity to apprehend the world. Thus Kant states, for example, that *'The sublime is that, the mere capacity of thinking which evidences a faculty of mind transcending every standard of the senses'* (Kant 2007: 81). Displeasure is the sublime's Good Friday—the mortification of our sensible faculties—to be followed surely enough by its Easter Morning, in the inevitable recognition of our super-sensible rational capacity—inevitable because, so Kant argues, it is we ourselves that issue the demand that sensibility grasp something that exceeds its capacities. The objection to reading the sublime as tacitly modelled upon Easter is, of course, that the sensible, so to speak, stays mortified, and is not recovered on a higher plane, but simply superseded.

IV. History of Art

To give a fully adequate account of the exact theological resonances and sources of Kant's account of the sublime would require much more discussion that I have space to engage in here. The point I want to take from Milbank is, in fact, a more general one: modern aesthetics is unavoidably predicated upon theological assumptions and habits of thought, which are nevertheless variously diluted, deformed, and deflected. Thus late in the first part of the *Critique of Judgement*, for instance, Kant remarks that because we judge empirically in aesthetic judgement without, however, being subjected to empirical laws, then, as he tellingly puts it, judgement 'finds a reference in itself to something in the subject itself and outside it, and which is not nature, nor yet freedom, but still is connected with the ground of the latter, i.e. the supersensible—a something in which the theoretical faculty is combined with the practical in a shared and unknown manner' (Kant 2007: 181). Milbank comments:

> Since aesthetic judgment is here construed as participating in a divine coordination of nature and freedom which is unknowable, it is clearly like an event of grace. Likewise it tends to encourage in us a belief in an orderdness of nature that goes beyond mere means-end relation as a 'purposiveness without purpose,' yet this is not apodictically provable and so requires *faith*.   (Milbank 2004: 233, n. 43)

Thus, Milbank is able to claim that '[t]he aesthetic is here no "modern equivalent for the religious," but rather in its integrity bears the theological ineliminably within its heart, remembering that the aesthetic is only judged with a kind of *faith*, and unpredictably arrives through a kind of *grace*' (Milbank 2004: 225). But, as Milbank's own language—in spite of the urging of those italics—hints, beauty for Kant is only 'a kind of' grace or 'like' it, and only 'tends' to encourage a belief in a divinely ordered nature— a belief that Kant hedges around with multiple qualifications as soon as ever it is announced; even if the theological has not been eliminated, it has been diluted or altered. Thus Milbank is also able to complain that Kant does not consistently develop these hints that run counter to the departure of aesthetics from theology.

It should have at least become clear that these problems with either viewing aesthetics as a modern, secular, and autonomous discipline, or an inalienably theological one, do not admit of straightforward solution. This may be a matter of regret for some (and rejoicing for others), but the at once ineliminable and undeveloped theology at the heart of modern aesthetics is a matter for interpretative responses other than regret at the neglect of an opportunity or rejoicing at the avoidance of an error. Rather, as I intimated above, Kant's aesthetics occupies a site that is not so much a centre-ground between theological and modern thought but a no-man's land. Its inheritance of theology is not such as simply to smuggle the theological into the apparently secular but rather to submit it to the stress of the process of a secularization that, despite its self-image, is neither fulfilled nor free-standing.

I want to turn now to Adorno's consideration of this situation, but first it must be noted that this turn also involves a transition from what has been a discussion of natural beauty and sublimity to a discussion of art. Two points in particular need to be made here. First, I began this chapter by reflecting on the emergence of the category of the aesthetic as a category distinct from morals and epistemology. A comparable account may also be given of art, such that distinctively artistic practices and works develop in so far as those practices are distinguished from ritual and those works no longer serve as objects of religious devotion. Again, the completion of this process of distinction is deeply contestable, with some commentators willing to claim that aesthetic appreciation just is a form of religious observance, even if it is not properly or always recognized as such (see e.g. Gell 1998). Second, the judge's apparent independence from pre-ordained standards in Kant's account of aesthetic judgement—his or her freedom to 'turn anything' into an object of the beautiful—is echoed and, in fact, deepened by the modern artist's freedom of creation. The modern artist is a creator out of nothing in the sense that his or her creation fulfils no standing criterion. The statement attributed to Torquato Tasso that 'no-one [sic] deserves the name of creator except God and the poet' is an early encapsulation of what is at stake here (Serassi 1858: I, 316), in its suggestion of a Promethean creativity that is in fact in competition with, rather than easily subsisting alongside, God's exclusive status as creator of everything.

But although it may seem that since the Renaissance, western art has progressively freed itself from vassalage to religious and theological precedent, Adorno emphasizes instead that the final expunging of art's theological heritage would in many ways be an expunging of art itself. Adorno's distinctive contribution to this debate is that he grasps the relation between art and theology not as competitive straightforwardly, but much rather as a fraught interaction of antagonistic but mutually dependent elements whose specific contours are historically shaped. This is clear from the following passage of *Aesthetic Theory*, for example:

> What radiates wordlessly from artworks is that *it is*, thrown into relief by *it*—the unlocatable grammatical subject—*is not*; it cannot be referred demonstratively to anything in the world that previously exists. In the utopia of its form, art bends under the burdensome weight of the empirical world from which, as art, it steps away.... The theological heritage of art is the secularization of revelation, which defines the ideal and limit of every work. The contamination of art with revelation would amount to the unreflective repetition of its fetish character on the level of theory. The eradication of every trace of revelation from art would, however, degrade it to the undifferentiated repetition of the status quo. (Adorno 1997: 105–6; cf. Brändle 1984: 150, 153)

Art is revelation because it shows to be existing something that is not at all deducible from anything already existing in the world. But this theological moment is not simply adopted in art; rather, it is secularized. It is important to emphasize, however, that secularization is not imagined by Adorno here as a completed (or even complete-able) process, if what secularization means is anything like the gradual obliteration of the theological. (Indeed, something of this is noticeable in the oddly juxtapositional phrase '[t]he theological heritage of art is the secularization of revelation' itself, which does not imagine the theological heritage as being secularized but as secularization itself.)

What Adorno attempts to describe is a situation in which an unapologetically theological reading would be fetishistic and a bluntly secular account would be basely conservative. Much earlier in his career than the late and unfinished *Aesthetic Theory*, Adorno had addressed this situation quite explicitly in his set of reflections, 'Theses on Art and Religion Today'. The 'today' of this title is significant because in these theses Adorno had argued that the kind of willed reunification of art and religion, canvassed by some, would be unhistorical, for '[t]his unity [between art and religion] was not a matter of purposeful cooperation, but resulted from the whole objective structure of society during certain phases of history, so the break is objectively conditioned and irreversible. Unity of art and religion', he went on, 'is not simply due to subjective convictions and decisions but to the underlying social reality and its objective trend' (Adorno 1992: II, 292–8). Crucially, moreover, Adorno even doubts that the vaunted unity of art and religion ever existed at all, not least because art 'in the proper sense of freedom of human expression' that is not separated from religion is not really art at all. In view of this definition, art 'always was, and is, a force of protest of the humane against the pressure of domineering institutions, religious and others, no less than it reflects their objective substance' (Adorno 1992: II, 293).

This might be taken to imply that the opposition of art to religion could be fitted into a celebratory narrative of modernity's emancipation from ecclesiastical coercion, and that Adorno's account as a whole seeks simply to point out the historical crassness of any attempt to ally art and religion. First, though, modernity is not entitled to celebrate the opposition of art to repressive institutions as one of its achievements because the modern world is precisely characterized, for Adorno, by the entrenchment of repressive, if often unnoticed, administration. Second, while Adorno is keen to emphasize the problems afflicting wilful attempts to reunify art and religion, he also wishes to argue that the tense opposition that subsists between them is matched by a 'productive interaction' (Adorno 1992: II, 296). In keeping with the emphasis that his work as a whole evinces, Adorno envisages this 'interaction' not as the deployment in artistic works of theological concepts or motifs, but rather, as we saw above in *Aesthetic Theory*, in the mode of a work of art's being, 'the halo of its uniqueness, its inherent claim to represent something absolute' (Adorno 1992: II, 296). Thus it is, for Adorno, who is drawing on Walter Benjamin's investigations into the archaic anticipations of modern artistic work, that '[e]very work of art still bears the imprint of its magical origin' (Adorno 1992: II, 296).

When this last claim is placed in the context of the 'Theses' as a whole, a difficulty with Adorno's attempt to grasp the relationship between religion and art comes into view. Adorno once remarked that Karl Marx rampaged among epistemological categories like a bull in a china shop (Adorno 1973: 206), and it is tempting to level a similar criticism at Adorno here: the 'Theses' seem to speak more or less interchangeably of 'magic', the 'theological', 'religion', and 'spirit', with apparently little acknowledgement that these terms are quite different, and thus, it might be argued, Adorno's treatment of the relation between art and religion in fact suffers from the ahistorical lack of specificity with which he charges those who would posit their unity.

In response, it is fair to point out that Adorno does clearly distinguish between what he calls in the 'Theses' the 'archaic unity between imagery and concept' (Adorno 1992: II, 293) and a time at which this unity has broken down into religion, on the one hand, and art, on the other. And, moreover, *Aesthetic Theory* envisages the difference of artworks from 'cultic images' as following from the fact that '[b]y the autonomy of their form, artworks forbid the incorporation of the absolute as if they were symbols. Aesthetic images stand under the prohibition on graven images' (Adorno 1997: 104;

cf. Koch 1989). Thus, on the one hand, works of art distinguish themselves from one form of religious practice, but precisely in so doing share in another theologically motivated prescription. Most importantly, however, 'Theses' concludes by thinking through the relation of art to religion in a particular example, that of Marcel Proust. What emerges from this is that the relation of art to religion that most interests Adorno is not, in fact, vague, but is rather focused on the artistic recuperation of a specific theological doctrine, namely, the doctrine of immortality. Adorno writes:

> It is [Proust] who, in a nonreligious world, took the phrase of immortality literally and tried to salvage life, as an image, from the throes of death. But he did so by giving himself up to the most futile, the most insignificant, the most fugitive traces of memory. By concentrating on the utterly mortal, he converted his novel, blamed today for self-indulgence and decadence, into a hieroglyph of 'O death, where is thy sting? O grave, where is thy victory?'   (Adorno 1992: II, 298)

It is crucial that this takes place 'in a nonreligious world' because that fact suggests that Proust's insistence on immortality is an act of resistance to a world that, as Adorno argues throughout his work, would liquidate the unique, concrete detail in the service of total fungibility. And is it an accident that Proust's novel, in doing this, was 'converted'?

But the point to be maintained despite the more theologically conducive conclusion to Adorno's 'Theses' is, nonetheless, that the unity of art and religion be not simply posited; indeed, this would be implied, for Adorno, in the fact that it is only by means of a focus on the most worldly experience that Proust is able, as Adorno says, to 'materialize' the theological notion of immortality—somewhat in keeping, in fact, with religious tradition in Adorno's view, since 'The great religions have either, like Judaism after the ban on graven images, veiled the redemption of the dead in silence, or preached the resurrection of the flesh. They take the inseparability of the spiritual and physical seriously' (Adorno 1974: 242). It is worth returning very briefly, in conclusion, to one of the quotations from Jay Bernstein with which I began. 'Every conception of the alienation of art from truth is simultaneously a work of remembrance, a work of mourning and grief, even for those philosophers who doubt that such an "original" state of union ever existed.' It can seem like what is being remembered and mourned here is something that, as Adorno suggests, may never have existed in the first place—but we must not rush to consign what has never existed to the dustbin of non-entity. In Samuel Beckett's *Endgame*, Clov responds to Hamm's frustrated outburst that God is a bastard who does not exist, 'Not yet'. For Adorno, as for Bernstein, the theological aspect of art is not only an inheritance from the past, even if it is also that, but a bequest to the future, the realization of whose promise is hardly guaranteed.

The discipline of aesthetics may only be viewed as a modern invention once modernity itself is understood as deeply implicated in the theological inheritance that it would seek to disavow. The severance of beauty from truth and goodness, and its establishment as an exclusively human capacity, is not as complete as, at the initiation of modern aesthetics, Kant, for one, might sometimes have thought or, in fact, wished. But to point this out is not to insist that an 'authentic' aesthetics ought simply to have that inheritance fully and explicitly restored to it, as if the aesthetic had never at all strained at, even if it never slipped, its theological moorings. It is perhaps only when the bonds between the aesthetic and the theological are most stretched that they are at their tightest.

References

Adorno, Theodor (1973). *Negative Dialectics*, trans. E. B. Ashton (London: Routledge & Kegan Paul).

—— (1974). *Minima Moralia: Reflections from Damaged Life*, trans. E. F. N. Jephcott (London: Verso).

—— (1992). 'Theses Upon Art and Religion Today', *Notes to Literature*, trans. Shierry Weber Nicholsen, 2 vols. (New York: Columbia University Press).

—— (1997). *Aesthetic Theory*, trans. Robert Hullot-Kentor (London: Athlone Press).

Bernstein, J. M. (1992). *The Fate of Art: Aesthetic Alienation from Kant to Derrida and Adorno.* (Cambridge: Polity Press).

Brändle, Werner (1992). *Rettung des Hoffnungslosen: Die theologischen Implikationen der Philosophie Theodor W. Adornos. Forschungen zur systematischen und ökumenischen Theologie*, 47 (Göttingen: Vandenhoeck & Ruprecht).

Cannell, Fennella (2010). 'The Anthropology of Secularism', *Annual Review of Anthropology* 39, 85–100.

Caygill, Howard (2001). 'Über Erfindung und Neuerfindungen der Ästhetik', *Deutsche Zeitschrift für Philosophie* 49, 233–41.

Coleridge, Samuel Taylor (1983). *Biographia Literaria*, eds. James Engell and W. Jackson Bate, 2 vols. (London: Routledge & Kegan Paul; Princeton, NJ: Princeton University Press).

—— (1997). 'What is Life?', in William Keach (ed.) *The Complete Poems*. (London: Penguin).

De Duve, Thierry (1999). *Kant after Duchamp.* (Cambridge, MA: MIT Press).

Eco, Umberto (1988). *The Aesthetics of Thomas Aquinas*, trans. Hugh Bredin (London: Radius).

Gell, Alfred (1998). *Art and Agency.* (Oxford: Oxford University Press).

Guyer, Paul (2000). 'Editor's Introduction', in Paul Guyer (ed.) *Critique of the Power of Judgement*, trans. Paul Guyer and Eric Matthews (Cambridge: Cambridge University Press), pp. xiii–l.

Habermas, Jürgen (1987). *The Philosophical Discourse of Modernity*, trans. Frederick Lawrence (Cambridge: Polity Press).

Hegel, G. W. F. (1975). *Aesthetics: Lectures on Fine Art*, trans. T. M. Knox, 2 vols. (Oxford: Clarendon Presso.

Kant, Immanuel (1996). *Groundwork of the Metaphysics of Morals*, in Mary Gregor (ed.), *Practical Philosophy*, trans. Mary Gregor (Cambridge: Cambridge University Press), 37–108.

—— (2007). *Critique of Judgement*, tr. James Creed Meredith, rev. edn. Nicholas Walker (Oxford: Oxford University Press).

Koch, Gertrud (1989). 'Mimesis und Bilderverbot in Adornos Ästhetik: Ästhetische Dauer als Revolte gegen den Tod', *Babylon* 6, 36–45.

Lotz, Johannes Baptist (1975). 'Transcendentals', in Karl Rahner (ed.) *Encyclopedia of Theology: A Concise Sacramentum Mundi.* (London: Burns & Oates), 1746–8.

Lyotard, Jean-François (1994). *Lessons on the Analytic of the Sublime*, trans. Elizabeth Rottenberg (Stanford, CA: Stanford University Press).

Milbank, John (2004). 'Sublimity: The Modern Transcendent', in Regina Schwartz (ed.) *Transcendence: Philosophy, Literature, and Theology Approach the Beyond.* (New York: Routledge), 211–34.

—— (2006 [1990]). *Theology and Social Theory*, 2nd edn. (Oxford: Blackwell).

Serassi, Pierantonio (1858). *La vita di Torquato Tasso.* (Florence: Barbera, Bianchi).

Von Balthasar, Hans Urs (1982–9). *The Glory of the Lord*, trans. Erasmo Leivà-Merikakis et al., ed. John Riches et al., 7 vols (Edinburgh: T & T Clark).

Wilson, Ross (2007). *Subjective Universality in Kant's Aesthetics.* (Oxford: Lang).

Further Reading

Adorno (1997).
Bernstein (1992).
Habermas (1987).
Hegel (1975).
Kant (2007).
Milbank (2004).
Wilson (2007).

CHAPTER 21

....

TIME AND HISTORY

....

ARNE GRØN

Whatever happens, every individual is a *child of his time*; so philosophy
too is *its own time apprehended in thoughts.*   (Hegel 2008: 15)

Such responsibility does not give one time, a present for recollection or
coming back to oneself; it makes one always late. Before the neighbour
I am summoned and do not just appear.   (Levinas 1989: 180)

PRELUDE

....

TIME and history are prominent but also ambiguous themes in modern western
thought. They even concern the character of contemporary thought itself. If it is to
be contemporary it must reflect on its own historical condition. But this requirement
rests on a universal claim that humans are situated beings. While metaphysics arguably
saw the world from a perspective beyond time and history, we are now supposed to live
in a post-metaphysical age. This chapter critically reviews this common understanding.
It argues that the underlying scheme of immanence vs. transcendence must be questioned if we take seriously that humans are situated in time and history. Instead of
thinking of theology in 'post-' terms, e.g. in a post-metaphysical age, I suggest that we
look at ways in which time and history become questions to us, and at movements
humans perform, not least in religion, in relating to time and history. Taking its point
of departure in the question of the human condition, the chapter focuses on the tension
between two claims: humans are what they are *in* time, and they are humans *in relating
to* time. This tension comes to the fore when we address the time of the different times:
past, present, and future. What it means to be situated, as humans, in time as the time
of different times, is discussed through two leitmotifs: ethics and infinity. Both motifs
are seen through the question of human history as the history of difficult freedom.

Autonomy and ambiguity go together. We can be entangled by our own projects of freedom. This forms the background for reconsidering the temporality of faith and love.

I. Time, History, and the Human Condition

When Kant in 1784 wrote 'What is Enlightenment?' he asked, 'in a very precise moment of history': 'What are we?' He proposed 'as a philosophical task to investigate not only the metaphysical system or the foundations of scientific knowledge but a historical event—a recent, even a contemporary event' (Foucault 2002: 335). The implication is that even philosophical thinking aiming at what is universal is contemporary in the intensified sense that it must reflect on its own historical condition: even as we philosophize we are *situated* beings. But this means that the awareness of being contemporary or modern is supported by the *universal* claim that, as humans, we are temporal and historical beings.

Modernity implies a sense of historical time. Distinguishing the present from what has been is not something new, but the modern claim that we live in a changed world, in conditions which set us apart from pre-modern times, does reflect a dramatic change in world view, involving a changed sense of time. This is apparent when time and history become questions concerning contemporary thought: what does it mean to think in the present situation? But what is then called 'our age' is distinguished from other epochs by the claim that 'we' have come to understand that humans are historically situated beings.

A common way of formulating this claim is that we now live in a post-metaphysical age. Thinking in contemporary terms, then, is defined in opposition to a metaphysical tradition, which arguably sees human life in a perspective from beyond time and history. But the very claim that the situation in which we now live and think has changed, implies that time and history belong to the human condition.

How can time and history become a matter of what it is to be human? Human existence as we know it is not only an existence in time—it also involves reflections on the fact that our existence is temporal. Even before explicit philosophical reflection, human forms of life are already ways of dealing with time. Human beings form their lives in responding to changes in time, for example to the hours of the day, seasons of the year, and the ages of a human life. Furthermore, the natural and cultural conditions in which we live may also change to the point that a form of life is irretrievably lost. Time has then changed. Such a change *of* time which is not captured within a pre-given rhythm of changes *in* time becomes a matter of history.

Time is experienced in various ways and poses different questions, but changes of time may bring humans to ask the further question: what their existence is like, as a human existence. Such experiences of time affecting human existence are articulated and reflected in religion, art, and philosophy. What is important here is the intertwining of two processes: (1) coming to ask not only questions that relate to time but *the* question of time itself, and (2) being brought to reflect on the character of human existence. The question of time becomes part of human temporality which gives a clue to what it is to be human.

But if time belongs to the human condition, is the human condition itself a matter of time and history? It may be argued that this is the implication of much of western thought since the beginning of the twentieth century: moving from the claim that time is the condition of possibility of human existence to the claim that the human condition itself is subject to change in time and history. In order to capture the significance of time and history we need a notion of what it is to be human—which at the same time is called into question by the claim that we are historical beings. This *aporia* invites us to ask once more what it means to be human in time and history.

II. After Metaphysics?

What is meant by metaphysics when speaking of a post-metaphysical age? In the tradition from Parmenides, metaphysics appears to be bound to a claim of timelessness (Theunissen 1991: 89ff.). Two moves seem to be decisive. First, the world of time and change is only to be understood by recourse to a world beyond time—in Plato the world of ideas. Second, Christian theology, formed through Greek metaphysics, views the world of time and history from an ultimate point of orientation beyond, God as the highest being. It is against this double move that time is accentuated as the condition of human existence. Thus, when Nietzsche lets his 'mad man' declare the death of God, it is a historical move in more than one sense (Nietzsche 1988a: § 125). The 'death of God' traces the historical event that the double move of metaphysics now belongs to the past. God is dead in and through the way 'we' live, the mad man claims, but he realizes that he is 'too early': the people at the marketplace, his addressees, do not understand him. 'We' still live in the shadows of the past metaphysics. But Nietzsche's move is also historical in a further sense. The death of God is not only a matter of interpreting a history not fully realized, but also a matter of opening the world as a world of change to be reinterpreted.

However, the idea that we live in a post-metaphysical age may mirror what it criticizes: the certainty offered by metaphysics. We may overlook how metaphysics also harbours a sense of the questions to which it offers answers. Let me briefly indicate two arguments for hesitating here. Firstly, in Plato, the world of time and change is not simply contrasted to an eternal, timeless world. Rather, time imitates eternity in that it has form, there being a *world* of time and change (cf. *Timaios* 37c–d). Secondly, metaphysics begins with the question of how to orient oneself in a world of time and change, and the answer that this world has form in participating in eternal forms testifies to the problem of time as the constant possibility of change.

In order to give a more nuanced picture, then, let me outline three motifs, associated with Hegel, Nietzsche, and Kierkegaard, respectively. Firstly, in Hegel we can discern the following argument (see e.g. Hegel 1977: 46ff.): If the finite and the infinite are seen as two worlds which we can relate to each other, the infinite is turned into a finite entity; it is infinite over and against the finite. Instead, true infinity comprises the finite. The absolute shows itself to be absolute in time and history. But does this argument against the conception of two worlds—this world of time and change and a world beyond—amount to a claim to immanence without transcendence? This question which sets the agenda after Hegel seems to find an answer in Nietzsche's diagnosis of nihilism pervading the metaphysical tradition from Plato, which constitutes the second motif: placing the true world beyond the world of becoming and perishing empties this world of truth.[1] Thirdly, the claim to immanence without transcendence depends on the point of departure, the division between two worlds. Maybe the very schema—immanence vs. transcendence—must be questioned. Thus, in Kierkegaard we find the argument that genuine transcendence interrupts a purely *human* transcendence, which we see in, e.g., the tendency to idealize and idolize love (Kierkegaard 1995: 154ff.).

III. Beyond Time?

What about religion? If it is to give orientation for leading a life in a world of time and change, must religion operate with an ultimate instance, a god, beyond time? Does talk of God lend itself to metaphysics? Especially twentieth-century Protestant theology seeks to avoid a metaphysical notion of God as beyond time and the representation of time and eternity as two worlds. Sources of inspiration are not least Hegel, Kierkegaard, and Nietzsche. Hegel breaks up the metaphysical point of orientation: God as the absolute is not simply beyond time, but opens towards human history, to the point at which history becomes the history of the absolute. This forms the background for different answers in the twentieth century to the question of time and God (e.g. Pannenberg 1988: 440ff.

In contrast, Nietzsche and in particular Kierkegaard have inspired attempts to reformulate God's transcendence through a critique of human, all too human, conceptions of God. God reveals himself in contradiction to and as withdrawn from humans seeking to master their own history. How, then, is the relation between God and human history to be thought? One answer is to insist that the biblical God is not the God of metaphysics. The God of both the Hebrew and the Christian Bible is a god of history, while the God of metaphysics is without history. Another answer is to turn the notion

---

[1] Cf. for example Nietzsche 1988b: 80f.: 'Wie die "wahre" Welt zur Fabel wurde'.

of God as the Lord of history around in the concept of a god who, in suffering and weakness, takes part in human history.

Again, the prevailing contrast to metaphysics may be questioned in two respects. Firstly, although the historical condition is changed so that a metaphysical position appears impossible, articulating this condition still seems to presuppose metaphysics. Secondly, before operating with two worlds, metaphysics can be seen as the movement of transcendence in which the human subject itself is transcended. In that sense, metaphysics is more an opening of questions than an answer.

This last approach—looking at the movements performed in relating to time—is even more fruitful when reconsidering religion. At first, religion may seem to lead away from an existence bound up with time and history, but how can a move *beyond* time be decisive for a human existence *in* time?[2] The move beyond time is motivated by experiences of time to which humans are subjected, but the move itself can deal with time and human concerns. Furthermore, through the movement 'beyond time' the *question* of time can appear—precisely as a question about what it means to be situated as humans. In the movement 'beyond', human finitude can enter the picture in the perspective of an ultimate concern; in religious terms: salvation.

When, for example, religious traditions view the world of time and change as a world of trial and transition, this is a way of living in this world of time and change. This life is to be lived as if we were already 'beyond' (cf. Nietzsche 1988c: § 43). Moreover, seeing this life as a trial may be challenged from within religion. Operating with God as the anchor-point of orientation also opens the question as to what this ultimate point means.

Consider the following passage from one of Kierkegaard's upbuilding discourses:

> When the sailor is out on the ocean, when everything is changing all around him, when the waves are born and die, he does not stare down into the waves, because they are changing. He looks up ... By the eternal, one can conquer the future, because the eternal is the ground of the future, and therefore through it the future can be fathomed.   (Kierkegaard 1990: 19)

Apparently, the line of orientation runs straightforward (or upwards), but a twofold critical turn is possible. Firstly, in orienting ourselves by the eternal, we remain on the ocean. Being situated in time is the condition for orientation. Secondly, the one asking for orientation may herself be brought into question, as the one being thus situated.

In this reflective turn, the question of God opens up questions concerning how the one asking is situated and how she situates herself. Instead of an apparently straightforward line of orientation—orienting ourselves by a point beyond time—a reversal takes place: God is not simply the anchor-point beyond time; before God, we are turned into a question for ourselves (Augustine 2008: Book X, xxxiii (50)). In orienting ourselves, we place ourselves *in relation to* the point of orientation, thereby resituating

---

[2] Karl Marx's theses on Feuerbach (Marx 1973: 5–7) could be taken in this direction: even as an escape, religion testifies to the social and historical conditions in which humans live.

ourselves in the world of time and history. If we could place ourselves *in* the point of orientation, it would not be ultimate.

Religions are human phenomena also in the sense that they can both point to and cover up how humans are situated in time. They testify to human temporality. It is becoming clear that time as a human condition does not mean that we are simply subjected to time. Rather, the move 'beyond time' taking place in time shows that humans are situated in time *relating to* time. Humans exist temporally as reflecting that they are temporal beings. This is not self-reflection, but the way in which we exist: anticipating, remembering, judging, forgiving, etc. Religious notions such as faith, hope, concern, and salvation, all testify to time as human condition. Therefore, a philosophical reflection on religion may rediscover human temporality. In fact, the modern 'turn' to time and history not only contrasts religious ways of opposing time and eternity; it also draws on experiences articulated and reflected in religion.[3]

Time affects us in what we are so that we may be led to ask whether we can be reduced to the time to which we are subjected. The movement beyond time can be seen as a countermove which shows that, in time, humans are more than time. We are not simply changed by being subjected to time, but are able to ask what happens to us in time, and whether we can preserve ourselves in time, even as we are being changed by it.

Instead of thinking of theology in 'post-' terms, e.g. in a post-metaphysical age, I suggest that we look at ways of dealing with time in which time is in question and that we focus on the following tension: we are subjected to time; yet, in being subjected to time, the question is how we ourselves relate to time. My suggestion is to take *infinitude* and *ethics* as leitmotifs in addressing this issue. In seeking to orient ourselves in time, our finite existence is placed in an infinite perspective, both in the sense that it is a matter of what matters to us, and that it is an open question as to what the significance is of what happens to us and what we ourselves do. Situated in time, we face the question what we do ourselves. This means that ethics is already implied in our relation to time. This comes to the fore not only in being concerned about the future, but also in dealing with the past.

IV. Concern, Memory, and Forgetting

For humans qua temporal beings time is a matter of concern. Asking what will happen to us and what to do in response we articulate questions that concern how we live our life. We experience time as concerned beings. Time, then, can be taken as a matter of what happens to us in time and what we are to do in response: time is 'time for . . .' (cf. *Ecclesiastes* 3:1–8). But if time comes to us as a matter of what we are to do, the implicit question is what we use time for. These two aspects—time as coming to us and time as a matter of what to do—are intertwined and irreducible.

---

[3] A major example is the early Martin Heidegger, see esp. Heidegger 2004.

Obviously, concern 'concerns' the future. Accounting for human temporality, it seems natural to emphasize the primacy of the future, as Heidegger does in *Being and Time*. But how do we then account for the remarkable feature that humans are concerned not only with the time to come, but also with what is history, despite the fact that we cannot change the past, and that there is still a life to live? Can the concern for the past be accounted for in terms of the concern for the future?

Although the future is a matter of human concern, it will also disappear in time. Yet time which means something to us does not simply disappear in time. It leaves traces, at least in us. This indicates that humans have history not only in the sense of experiencing and 'making' history. They also seek to keep the past in mind, telling and preserving history. Thus we have history in the twofold sense of making and telling history (cf. Ricoeur 2004). But remembering is not only a matter of effort. The past can return against our effort to let it be. This suggests that the past 'has' us before we 'have' it. Although it is past, it still means something to us, but not simply in the sense that we give meaning to it. Rather, we may ourselves be called into question.

A further aspect of humans' temporal nature is that they can take an attitude towards time, and become concerned about time itself. Telling or writing history shows that humans are in time as 'more than time'. They are situated in time by relating to time and can paradoxically put up resistance to what seems irresistible, the passing of time. 'Writing down' what has passed is a move against the annihilation of time. But the enemy is not just that time appears to change everything in time. Rather, we are telling and preserving history against forgetting, both others' and our own. Again, this shows that, as subjects, we are ourselves involved in time passing: letting time go, we ourselves are changed and may even forget what once meant something to us.

Remembrance, then, can be understood as the effort to preserve what has been important to the ways humans have understood themselves. Apparently, what humans want to remember are great deeds and events—to the point of doing what they do *in order to* be remembered; also in this sense they can want to 'write' history. Yet humans manifest themselves not only in their actions, but also in their sufferings. This suggests that what we seek to remember is not so much what has happened or what has been done, but the persons who have lived through what happened. But what then when we move from remembering individual histories to a shared or common history? World history seems more likely to be nameless, but this confirms that it is a history not only of deeds, but also of sufferings.

In remembering, something is at stake for us. This can be seen in both individual and collective struggles about the power to write the history in question—and thereby to be able to consign something to history. Remembering and forgetting are ways of dealing with what is—or should be—important to us. If we are in a position to write the history in question it seems that it is up to us to decide what should be remembered. If we also are the ones to remember, it is a matter of what matters to us, and this we decide ourselves. But if this were all there is to memory, it would be difficult to account for the problem of dealing with past wrongs. Although we are to decide for ourselves, history involves others. It is remarkable how the past plays into the ways humans interact with each other. How to deal with the past may even concern *the conditions* that make human coexistence possible. This is in particular the case in the aftermath of mass atrocities. Although ethics concerns what Jean Améry calls the future as the genuine human time (Améry 1980: 68), the past becomes an ethical issue in terms of past wrongs. We may even argue that our moral sensibility is at stake in dealing with past wrongs. Is there an obligation to remember?

In the preface to *The Ethics of Memory*, Avishai Margalit reconstructs his parents' debate on memory, starting at the end of the war in British-ruled Palestine: 'The only honorable role for the Jews that remain is to form communities of memory—to serve as "soul candles" like the candles that are ritually kindled in memory of the dead,' his mother claims. His father's response is:

> We, the remaining Jews, are people, not candles. It is a horrible prospect for anyone to live just for the sake of retaining the memory of the dead. That is what the Armenians opted to do. And they made a terrible mistake. We should avoid it at all cost. Better to create a community that thinks predominantly about the future and reacts to the present, not a community that is governed from mass graves. (Margalit 2004: p. viii f.)

Forgetting may be a way of taking upon us the time to come, if memory has turned the past into a monument or if the present is turned into memory of the dead. But even if memory does not lead directly into the future, what is at issue in memory is still how to deal with the time to come. Past history opens a space of remembering in the form of reminding us about what is important to us in relation to the future.

It is noteworthy how, in the beginning of twentieth-century German and French philosophy, remembering and forgetting become motifs inscribed in philosophical reflection itself. Bergson (1950) and Heidegger (1962) share the insight that prevailing forms of understanding time actually distort and conceal time in an original sense, turning time into something other than the time we live. Therefore, philosophical reflection should form a countermove that uncovers and reminds us of what is forgotten. According to Heidegger, this requires that we re-appropriate questions which have both been opened and covered up in history. We are to begin radically by learning to question what is worth questioning (*fragwürdig*).

But the motif of forgetting also indicates ambiguities of human history reflected in the history of modernity. According to Kierkegaard, it is possible to forget what it means to exist—while existing (1992: 249). It may be more difficult to avoid this kind of forgetting when living in an age proclaimed to be an age of reason and progress. Yet when modernity invites us to think of history in these terms it may also provoke a sense of the dialectics of Enlightenment (Horkheimer and Adorno 1994).

If it is possible to forget what is important to us as human beings, it is of critical importance to remember in order not to forget. In this vein we may speak of an ethics of memory: the obligation to remember what has been of human concern in the past. Remembering then is not just put in the service of concern for the future, but becomes a matter of maintaining a sense of humanity. What is at stake is not only a past more or less shared, but also a sense of the condition we share as humans. What we share is already the temporal and historical character of existence. To remember and to forget are not just something we do, as we undertake an action. They are ways of existing, dealing with what is important to us. Rediscovering time as the time we live is about understanding what it means to be what we are. The question of time becomes a matter of human self-understanding.

V. Existence and Nature

We have access to time as temporal beings. The temporality of human existence makes it possible for us to ask the question of time. Yet this does not mean that time can be reduced to the time of human existence. Rather, the time of human life appears as a disturbing episode in the time of the world (Blumenberg 2001: 73). The time of human existence is itself determined by another time, the time of nature, between birth and death, time passing and changing without our making. Furthermore, although human time is about what matters to us and what we make out of time, the time of human existence itself shows that there is a nature or character in human existence. The structures of human existence are not of our making but make our making possible. More than that, remembering cannot catch up with the past; rather, the past withdraws itself, to the point of being presupposed and immemorial (Levinas 1969; Rosenzweig 2005).

Understanding the time of human existence is therefore about the character of existence. Time is inscribed into the classical definition of existence in Kierkegaard's *Concluding Unscientific Postscript*: 'to exist is to become' (Kierkegaard 1992: 199). Furthermore, human existence is an existence *'in between'*: it is a synthesis of the infinite and the finite, 'situated in time' (Kierkegaard 1992: 221). This implies that a human being is 'in becoming' in the sense that we are 'on our way' in life, between birth and death. We are, each of us, in the middle of life in such a way that we cannot place ourselves at the point of beginning (birth) or at the point of the end (death). Being ourselves in becoming means that each of us has our own way to go. We may travel together through life, but this is only possible because we cannot 'stand in' for each other. Thus, we are 'in between' in the double sense: being ourselves finite and infinite situated in time, and being caught between birth and death.

This existence 'in between' is rephrased by Heidegger in terms of being 'thrown into' existence and projecting oneself towards the future (Heidegger 1962: §§ 29, 31, 57f., 68). 'Thrownness' belongs to the way we exist. Yet the notion of 'thrownness' may be misleading: we are 'born into' a human history, and this 'natality' implies that we are to begin ourselves, Hannah Arendt claims in reinterpreting Augustine (Arendt 1998: 8f., 176f.). This is more in line with the motif of beginning in Kierkegaard. While beginning in Heidegger is, in a critical sense, the beginning of questioning, in Kierkegaard it is rather a matter of beginning with oneself in the sense of coming to have one's own history.

We are not simply projecting ourselves towards the future but are also 'thrown back'. Anticipating death as the possibility which gives us nothing to 'actualize', we are disclosed to ourselves: our 'kind of Being is anticipation itself' (Heidegger 1962: 307). Is anticipation (*Vorlaufen*) a way of re-appropriating passivity and time? Or is it a way of rediscovering time as the time to come to us? The latter seems to be the case in Kierkegaard's discourse 'At a Graveside'. Anticipating, it is difficult to think in earnestness what death means for one's life. The challenge is to think that there *comes a time* when there is no more time. This is difficult because it runs counter to our natural propensity to think that there is still time; thus, in delaying we give ourselves time. But if we can endure thinking that there comes a time when there is no more time, we can let the thought of death have 'retroactive power' and let it be 'impelling in life' (Kierkegaard 1993: 100). Thinking that all is over, we can be struck by the thought that all is not yet over. That is, we can come to receive time as a gift. Thinking the thought of death, then, is a countermove. To forget what it means to exist is implied in forgetting to ask what it means to die (Kierkegaard 1992: 165ff.).[4] We know that we are going to die and yet we forget, through our ways of knowing, what this means. The motif of forgetting and remembering is thus intensified. The very 'act' of existing is temporal, and yet we can, while existing, forget what it means to exist. Consequently, we face the task of having to remind ourselves: concern, memory, and forgetting are ways of existing, and, notably, ways of existing that concern our existence.

Existing 'in between' implies that the one's existing is distended in time. In *Confessions* Book XI Augustine notes: 'Perhaps it would be exact to say: there are three times, a present of things past, a present of things present, a present of things to come. In the soul are these three aspects of time, and I do not see them anywhere else. The present considering the past is memory, the present considering the present is immediate awareness, the present considering the future is expectation' (xx (26)). Yet time also manifests itself in and through what we are doing, even while talking about time: 'I confess to you, Lord, that I still do not know what time is, and I further confess to you, Lord, that as I say this I know myself to be conditioned by time. For a long period already I have been speaking about time, and that long period can only be an interval of time' (xxv (32)). Times are measured by me, Augustine continues and asks: 'Then am I not measuring time itself?' I do so by measuring how long it takes, for example, to recite a poem. 'That is why I have come to think that time is simply a distension. But of what is it a distension? I do not know, but it would be surprising if it is not that of the mind itself' (xxvi (33)).

Heidegger places Augustine within the horizon of the ordinary time experience. By contrast, '*temporality is the primordial 'outside-of-itself in and for itself*', he claims, and continues: 'We therefore call the phenomena of the future, the character of having been, and the Present, the "*ecstases*" of temporality' (Heidegger 1962: 377). What is the difference between 'distension' and 'ecstasis'? Both appear to indicate that we exist outside of ourselves. But dis-tension leaves open the problem about the unity of

---

[4] For further discussion, see Chapter 9 by Pattison in this volume.

existence. How do we come back to ourselves when being distended? The answer indicated by Heidegger is that temporality is 'a process of temporalizing in the unity of the ecstases' (Heidegger 1962: 377). This makes possible human ways of being concerned. But how is the unity of the ecstases to be understood? The primary phenomenon of authentic temporality is the future, Heidegger claims (1962: 378), and 'the primordial phenomenon of the *future as coming towards* [*Zu-kunft*]' is Dasein's 'letting-itself-*come-towards*-itself' (Heidegger 1962: 372).

But maybe there is more to be found in Augustine's remark on distension than Heidegger allows. If time is the distension of the mind or soul, the mind itself is distended in time. 'In time' could be taken as time coming to us, passing with us, and changing us while we are concerned about or doing something, or interrupting us in the moment. But is time not turned into something subjective when defined as the distension *of the soul*? My suggestion is that we reverse the direction of questioning. What is in question here is the nature of subjectivity. Instead of time being reduced to the mind, subjectivity is intrinsically temporal. We are not what we are, and then temporal. We are not, as subjects, inserted in time. Being situated in time is how we are subjects.

If ecstatical temporality is primordial time, what about the time of nature? If the time of narration links the time of cosmos and the time of existence (cf. Ricoeur 1985), how do we account for the limits of narrative in terms of existence? Existing 'in between', we cannot take beginning (birth) and end (death) into the account we seek to give of ourselves. Although we come to have our own history within the history into which we are born, we can only tell our story in virtue of the limits to our narrative. Seeking to narrate our life we face the difficulty of putting life to words. While we narrate or remember, time happens to us. Nature is not merely a constraint on our choices. The time of nature also plays into the time of existence. This comes to the fore in the very nature of human existence as an existence between birth and death. The fact that this is turned into a question of beginning a history on our own shows that humans take part in nature *as humans*.

The time of existence—as the time of concern—makes it possible for us to ask about the time of nature. At the same time, we can experience that time goes on, 'unconcerned' about our concern, and that human history only appears as an episode in the history of cosmos. Our time disappears in the time of the world. This tension, however, also bears human traces. Religions may be understood as human ways of dealing with the tension between time without our concern and concerned time.

VI. THE MOMENT AND WORLD HISTORY: DIFFICULT FREEDOM

Time is not only 'tensed' as the time of different times: future, present, past. The time of existence is also in tension with the time of nature playing into existence. But within human time there is a further tension: how does ecstatical temporality relate to the time of a shared world history? Can we understand this in terms of the moment of time in contrast to a history taking place between individuals? The Kierkegaardian model of accentuating the moment of decision and the Hegelian model of having history as a whole in view are often contrasted. However, both in individual lives and in a common history time can be compressed into decisive moments that separate before and after. Such moments can be described by saying that the world is no longer the same, but it takes time to find out how it is changed.

Human history testifies to the fact that human existence is a concerned existence. We are affected by what happens to us because something matters to us. Yet individual histories of human concern can disappear in what is supposed to be a shared human history. At the same time humans only come to have their own history within a common history. But is this common history in fact shared? Does human history 'add up'? Viewing history as a totality changes history as it is lived; it turns history into past, but past history was also history taking place. Understanding past history requires a sense of history as not yet concluded.

Modernity cultivates a sense of historical time by turning history into a matter of freedom, affirming that humans should be the subjects of their own history. History is something we make. But precisely in these terms, the history of modernity is deeply ambiguous. We are also victims of the history we are supposed to make. As a history *about* making history it testifies to the difficulty of human freedom. Our freedom is not only threatened by what happens to us but also by our own responses. We can be entangled by our own projects of freedom. Human history then is the history of difficult freedom. Autonomy is not simply the power to carry out our own projects; we are ourselves brought into question: how do we live with our own doings?

How can the notion of the decisive moment of time play into an account of the history of difficult freedom? Following Kierkegaard's *The Concept of Anxiety*, let us try to reformulate the notion of sin as an attempt to capture the difficulty of freedom. Kierkegaard claims that sin only enters the world through the individual who fails, and each time it is something new. This is not to deny that humans have failed before. On the contrary, ethical faults committed by humans accumulate in the history humans share, but this is the history of sinfulness, not sin. Each individual begins on her own in that she is to account for herself. This is how she gains her own history, yet beginning in a history already begun and shared with others. Beginning on one's own takes place in the decisive moment when one discovers oneself as guilty, Kierkegaard claims. But 'he who becomes guilty in anxiety becomes as ambiguously guilty as it is possible to become', he continues (Kierkegaard 1980: 61). Due to this ambiguity it is difficult to describe the decisive moment as a moment of decision. The implied passivity is crucial: one *becomes* guilty. This means that one is to live with one's own actions. But the further implication is that the decisive moment concerns the life which is decided in the moment. Therefore, there can be a 'take' on 'the whole' of one's history in the moment of decision.

The difficulty of freedom lies in the intensified ambiguity that we can make ourselves unfree. The history which is supposed to be one's own is a history in which freedom can both be lost and lose itself. Modern ways of thinking of history in terms of human self-determination easily overlook the complicating feature that autonomy is not simply a goal to be realized but is already a matter of *how* this is done. A *history* of freedom is not freedom unfolding or realizing itself. Rather, it is the history of the adventures of freedom, and, as such, a drama of which the end is not yet written. Recognizing this is not only difficult for modern ways of dealing with history in terms of human projects, it is also a challenge to theology in rethinking God and human history. Taking leave of the notion of God as Lord of history does not in itself solve the problems we face; rather it leaves open the problem implied in theodicy. The problem of moral evil is just as radical as before. Precisely on these terms the significance of the past is open for the future. This leads us back to the ethics of memory.

VII. Ethics, Time, and History

Time is passing without our doing. It changes us without and often despite our will. Yet time is a matter of what we do and how we relate to time. Before asking about time we are questioned about it: what do we use the time passing for? Situated 'in time', we cannot extract ourselves from time, which means that time becomes a matter of being a self. Subjected to time we are also subjects. Although time passes without our doing, letting time go is already doing something. Time does not become an ethical issue only when we decide that it should.

Yet ethics is not a natural relation to time. Rather, it reverses historical time. Consider memory again. Remembering takes time but it also deals with time. 'Memory recaptures and reverses and suspends what is already accomplished in birth—in nature,' Levinas claims and adds: memory is 'an inversion of historical time' and as such 'the essence of interiority' (Levinas 1969: 56). Remembering, we show ourselves to be temporal beings who are not absorbed in time. While time is passing we make a countermove, not only against time passing but also against ways of dealing with history. Time as life from birth to death is not the same as history, Levinas argues. While the former can question what we make out of time, the latter is written by the survivors. But history as the more or less totalizing view on history is problematic precisely due to the history which is subjected to this view. If ethics and history seem to fall apart, it is because of the intrinsic link between the time of human existence and ethics. Ethically speaking, history is 'too much'. An ethics of memory concerns a history which bears witness to what has been a matter of concern for those whose history it is.

The ethical 'reversal' of historical time therefore concerns history. Accentuating the ethical countermove, Jean Améry notes that 'resentment is not only an unnatural but also a logically inconsistent condition. It nails every one of us onto the cross of his ruined past. Absurdly, it demands that the irreversible be turned around, that the event be undone. Resentment blocks the exit to the genuine human dimension, the future'

(Améry 1980: 68). Yet Améry insists on his resentment. Why? Writing his essay in the mid-1960s, seeking to clarify the victim's condition, Améry faces a culture that encourages acting as if nothing has happened and letting what has happened—the catastrophe, the Holocaust—remain in the past. But the time-sense of the one who lets what has happened remain what it was, who lets time heal his wounds, 'has not moved out of the biological and social sphere into the moral sphere' (Améry 1980: 71). The absurd demand that the irreversible be turned around is a countermove against the tendency to live as if nothing has happened. While the first is naturally impossible, the second is morally impossible.

Although remembering counteracts the kind of forgetting that lets the past be past, it does not solve the 'dark riddle' of evil: 'there is really nothing that provides enlightenment on the eruption of radical Evil in Germany,' Améry maintains (1980: p. viii). He does not aim at explaining this evil but insists on its moral nature. The evil to which he, as a victim, bears witness is not banal but radical (Améry 1980: 35f.). Writing his reflections on his own history, Améry counters the indifference which turns radical evil into something that had also happened in the world. Yet the point in speaking of the banality of evil (Arendt 1994) may be that this banality is horrifying. In this infinite perspective in which the human condition is at stake, the concern of an ethics of memory is to preserve a sense of the humanity at issue in a history of inhumanity. Remembering past wrongs is about moral sensibility. The ethics of memory therefore is not so much a matter of us choosing to remember; rather it is about us being obligated to remember.

The ethics of memory turns on the intricate relationship between ethics and time. Although ethics concerns what we choose to do, it is not of our making and choice but places us in the accusative before we can place ourselves in the nominative. Responsibility for another does not proceed from freedom, but 'comes from what is prior to my freedom'. 'Such responsibility does not give one time, a present for recollection or coming back to oneself; it makes one always late. Before the neighbour I am summoned and do not just appear' Levinas claims (1989: 180). Consequently, the implications of being situated in time before we situate ourselves concern the *sense* of ethics. Being responsible 'before the neighbour' is not first a matter of making ourselves responsible. Rather, responsibility always makes one late. Apparently, this move points backwards, but on a closer reflection it moves us forwards: it is the condition on which we are to respond to the other.

Although we are committed before committing ourselves, we can only respond to the ethical demand by committing ourselves. When we commit ourselves, we make ourselves responsible. We are to answer for ourselves. Thus, when we make promises, we bind ourselves for the time to come (Arendt 1998: 243ff.; Ricoeur 2004: 486ff.). We point to ourselves as the one to keep the promise. We may fail to keep our promises, but we can also fail to answer for ourselves. Yet there is an even more radical possibility implied here—that of making ourselves indifferent to what we have done. This is the possibility of losing one's 'soul'—to speak in an almost forgotten language. One loses one's soul in giving up on oneself. This is of infinite significance in that it affects the condition for being oneself in relating to others. This again shows how our two leitmotifs—infinity and ethics—are intertwined. To reformulate one aspect of the notion of eternity: losing one's soul is an eternal loss in the sense that it affects the character of our existence in time since it concerns how we are situated in comporting ourselves in time. Although this is a matter of what we do, it is not a result of what we decide. Rather, the question is whether we can ourselves endure what we do, that is: preserve ourselves in time. Making ourselves more or less indifferent to what we do shows that we cannot carry the weight of our own actions. In this sense, 'the eternal' concerns our relation to time.

VIII. The Temporality of Faith, Hope, and Love

If faith shows the temporality of human existence (cf. 1 Cor. 13:12), what is the temporality of faith? Faith is about what one has set one's heart on (Luther). Faith and hope concern what we are concerned or care about. But this is not simply to be seen from what we invest our time in. Rather, faith is more about redirecting one's vision as one is oneself transformed. Again, this is not simply a matter of different priorities. It involves a passivity of the self in that it makes demands on the self and takes time. It is about coming to see one's life in a different light, realizing what ultimately matters. This 'ultimately' is not a point of orientation beyond time, but concerns the time to come. In this sense, future is the 'incognito' of eternity, as it is put in Kierkegaard's *The Concept of Anxiety* (1980: 89). The moment of decision concerns one's life as a whole, but towards the future as the time to come.

Faith and hope respond to another human possibility, despair. The possibility of despairing or giving up hope testifies to human temporality: we are exposed to time in that we can be affected in what concerns us. Suffering a loss, we can be brought to despair. Yet, in despairing, the individual despairs. The temporalities of faith and hope accentuate the intertwinement of passivity and activity. They too show that humans are exposed to time as concerned beings, but they also harbour the courage to carry the burden of time. In faith one may go 'beyond time' in the sense that one puts up resistance towards what one experiences. Faith is both about receiving the time to come and opening up the future where despair closes it.

How then should we understand the temporality of love? Love binds itself to what it cares about, but this means that in love one becomes vulnerable. But if we seek to redirect our concern, for example in love of ideals, this is still an answer in time to time: How can one remain faithful in time? How can love be a way of dealing with time in time, thus 'living time'? Let us follow the lead indicated above, namely, that what is at issue is how we preserve ourselves in time, which requires of us that we carry the burden of time and even counteract the force of time.

Time is not only passing by, but also *changing*—to the point of changing us. It is important to bear in mind that the possibility of changing is crucial in order to stay human. But possibility is not simply possibility we dispose of, but also possibility we face. Thus, experiences of love harbour the difficult insight that *love* can change. Something can happen that brings love to be changed, or it can change 'over the years'. But 'Love is not love|Which alters when it alteration finds' (Shakespeare: Sonnet 116). Although it responds to what happens, love does not just go along with time's changes; rather it is supposed to put up resistance to change. Why? If love means binding oneself to what one cares about, it is a matter of a defining commitment.

If, then, love is a matter of binding and commitment, the burden of time to be carried is also that of carrying oneself. Facing the power of time to change, our attention is first drawn to what can happen to us. In terms of love, we are vulnerable first and foremost in that we can be deceived. But maybe the picture should be reversed: 'To defraud oneself of love is the most terrible, is an eternal loss, for which there is no compensation either in time or in eternity', Kierkegaard writes in *Works of Love* (1995: 5f.). The question is not only what can happen to us, but also what we can do in being subjected to what happens to us. Precisely because being deceived by others would affect us in our ways of finding ourselves in the world, it is all the more important to point to the danger hidden in this: that of despairing or giving up on ourselves. As already indicated, 'eternal loss' is about the point on which everything hinges: the attitude in which the world is open to us. This is not an attitude which we can pick and choose and dispose of. Rather it is the attitude in which one chooses attitudes. What we have here is not a point of orientation beyond time, but the radical possibility of giving up in time. Despairing, or renouncing hope, has an infinite significance.

At this point we can see how time and ethics, and time and the other, are intertwined. This is indicated in Kierkegaard's distinction between sorrow and despair: I do not have the right to despair, because I *shall* sorrow. So it is with love. 'You shall preserve love, and you shall preserve yourself and by and in preserving yourself preserve love' (Kierkegaard 1995: 43). The distinction between despair and sorrow is about relating to the future even in dealing with the past. In despair we close ourselves in upon ourselves, shutting off the time to come, but sorrow slowly opens us up, thereby preserving love.

This intertwining of self-relation, time and the other means that the line of orientation is once more broken: first we are led back to being situated in time, second we find ourselves in the ethical relation implied in time. Searching for the answer to the problem of time in eternity, like a sailor who looks up into the heaven in order to find his point of orientation in the stars, may ignore the possibility of an eternal loss in time. The broken line of orientation is to be seen in Kierkegaard's accentuating the duty in the commandment: You shall love your neighbour as yourself (Matt. 22:39). Love here undergoes 'the change of eternity', Kierkegaard claims (1995: 32). What does this mean? If we read 'the change of eternity' as a second change *against* the change which time seems to induce, eternity is not just beyond time; rather eternity's change takes place *in time*, as a change *of time*. But this requires that time is not one thing; rather, temporality 'divides within itself': 'Only the eternal can be and become and remain contemporary with every age; in contrast, temporality divides within itself, and the present cannot become contemporary with the future, or the future with the past, or the past with the present' (Kierkegaard 1995: 31f.). The eternal is *present* in a sense in which time is not, but this presence of the eternal is accounted for in terms of the temporal. What this implies is then to be explained in terms of selfhood and temporality: the eternal 'redoubles' in that it is 'in an outward direction and in an inward direction back into itself' at the same time (Kierkegaard 1995: 280). What does this mean?

Our two leitmotifs, infinity and ethics, once again show themselves to be intertwined. Firstly, duty as 'eternity's change' deals with ways in which we use time. Asking about what love is and who one's neighbour is takes time and is already a matter of ethics since we are called to account for the time used. Opening up an interval, a spare moment, 'a concession is made to curiosity and idleness and selfishness' (Kierkegaard 1995: 97). Even the act of making a promise falls under suspicion. What is put into the foreground is not the act of commitment, but the act of delaying or postponing. Being in the accusative, addressed by the commandment to love one's neighbour, the moment in which we begin is not at our disposal, but carries a history of time wasted: 'God is an eternity ahead—that is how far the human being is behind. So it is with every one of eternity's tasks. When a person at long last starts to begin, how infinitely much was wasted beforehand, even if for a moment we would forget all the deficiencies, all the imperfections of the effort that at long last had its beginning!' (Kierkegaard 1995: 102). We are always late, but that is how we begin. Secondly, the commandment is 'eternity's change' in that it transforms the way we *see the other*: we are to see the other beyond 'the world' of differences and changes by which humans judge each other. This change is infinite in that duty turns the addressee towards herself: as the one who has to fulfil the commandment. 'Eternity's change' then is a change of time, the time in which relating to the other takes place. How humans relate to time becomes a matter of the eternal. When we engage in settling an account of love, comparing our own and the other's doings, we lose 'the moment, the moment that ought to have been filled with an expression of love's life...A moment lost, then the chain of eternity is broken' (Kierkegaard 1995: 183).

How is this also about preserving ourselves in time? As we are already situated in time, we are placed before the other, prior to situating ourselves. The other has already broken into our self-relation. But this means that our self-relation is at stake in relating to the other. The danger against which we are to preserve ourselves concerns *ourselves*: it is our possibility of betraying ourselves and of giving up on ourselves. Being situated in time is accentuated ethically as being in the accusative. Conversely, when, in love, there is no account to be settled, time can be received as a gift, in doing the works of love. Time then receives 'infinite worth' (Kierkegaard 1993: 84).

Is time received as a gift to be given to the other? Is this an impossible gift? (Derrida 1992: 6ff.) The question is how we place ourselves. In giving time, as appreciation, we are in danger of pointing towards ourselves as the giver. This shows the ethical relation implied in relating to time. We do not master the ethical significance of what we do.

IX. Time, History, and Transcendence

Modernity cultivates a sense of historical time not least in terms of immanence and autonomy. However, taking leave of the notion of two worlds—this world of time and change, on the one hand, and a world beyond, on the other—leaves us with a notion of immanence which is itself questionable. It draws upon ideas about transcendence that some claim to have left behind. Time can appear as immanence when we contrast time and eternity. But the notion of time as immanence is misleading for at least two reasons. Firstly, we are not simply 'in time' but we also relate to time. In this sense, human existence is to be understood in terms of transcendence. There is human transcendence in imagining what is not and saying no to what is, as Sartre emphasizes (2003). Secondly, this transcendence from within takes place in time. Relating to time we are still situated in time. 'Situated in time' does not imply time as immanence, but rather time as transcendence: although time is 'time for' and opens up the question what we make out of time, time *comes to us*. Before being an empty time to be filled with expectations and plans, the future is time coming (*avenir: à venir, Zu-kunft*). No matter how much we seek to transcend time towards the future, we are ourselves transcended in time. We can only transcend time as beings situated in time in such a way that time comes to us. If we are to describe the human condition in terms of time, then, the intertwining of relating to time and being situated in time is crucial. Put differently, if we are to speak of immanence, we need a complex notion of transcendence.

This applies even more to the notion of history as immanence. No matter how much we seek to 'make' history, we are subjected to history, including the history that we make. If the guiding idea of history-as-immanence is that human history becomes more and more human, as the history of freedom, the history of modernity reminds us of human ambiguities. Ironically, history is only turned into immanence, the history of human freedom, if it is subjected to a total view on human history. If we are to describe the human condition in terms of history, the complication of autonomy and ambiguity is crucial. In order to describe experiences of time coming to us, demanding us to respond, and the history of human ambiguities, we need to reconsider the question of ethical and religious transcendence. Can human history be understood as immanence—as the history of humans acting and suffering—in a perspective of redemption? If religion points to an ultimate perspective beyond the history humans make, maybe this perspective concerns the fullness of history to which humans have been subjected. Such a reversal of the ultimate perspective must be thought as the opposite of a totalizing view on human history. Maybe that is what is indicated in Benjamin's thesis on history as citable:

> A chronicler who recites events without distinguishing between major and minor ones acts in accordance with the following truth: nothing that has ever happened should be regarded as lost for history. To be sure, only a redeemed mankind receives the fullness of its past—which is to say, only for a redeemed mankind has its past

become citable in all its moments. Each moment it has lived becomes a *citation à l'ordre du jour*—and this day is Judgement Day.   (Benjamin 1999: 246).

In concluding, let me summarize two lines of argument, corresponding to the two leitmotifs: infinity and ethics. Firstly, as humans we transcend time in relating to time, but we only do so situated in time as time coming to us. In transcending time we are ourselves transcended in time. Situated in time, we may experience a turn of time, as an inversion of transcendence (Theunissen 2000: 922, 969f.): time experienced as new. Rather than speaking of the immanence of time we should speak of time in terms of transcendence: the transcendence of time takes place in time coming to us. Secondly, reconsidering transcendence must be linked to the question: what is the time of the different 'times': past, present, future? Time *as* the time of the other is diachronic and precedes our response (Levinas 1987). It is the time of the other to come and the time of our being already responsible.

REFERENCES

Améry, Jean (1980). *At the Mind's Limits*, trans. Sidney Rosenfeld and Stella P. Rosenfeld (Bloomington, IN: Indiana University Press).

Arendt, Hannah (1994). *Eichmann in Jerusalem: A Report on the Banality of Evil*. (New York: Penguin).

—— (1998). *The Human Condition*. (Chicago: University of Chicago Press).

Augustine (2008). *Confessions*, trans. Henry Chadwick (Oxford: Oxford University Press).

Benjamin, Walter (1999). 'Theses on the Philosophy of History', *Illuminations*, introd. Hannah Arendt, trans. Harry Zorn (London: Pimlico).

Bergson, Henri (1950). *Matter and Memory*, trans. Nancy M. Paul and W. Scott Palmer (London: Allen and Unwin).

Blumenberg, Hans (2001). *Lebenszeit und Weltzeit*. (Frankfurt am Main: Suhrkamp).

Derrida, Jacques (1992). *Given Time: I. Counterfeit Money*, trans. Peggy Kamuf (Chicago: Chicago University Press).

Foucault, Michel (2002). 'The Subject and the Power', *Power: Essential Works* 3 (London: Penguin).

Hegel, G. W. F. (1977). *Phenomenology of Spirit*, trans. A. V. Miller (Oxford: Oxford University Press).

—— (2008). *Outlines of the Philosophy of Right*, trans. T. M. Knox (Oxford: Oxford University Press).

Heidegger, Martin (1962). *Being and Time*, trans. John Macquarrie and Edward Robinson (Oxford: Blackwell).

—— (2004). *The Phenomenology of Religious Life*, trans. Matthias Frisch and Jennifer Anna Gosetti-Ferencei (Bloomington, IN: Indiana University Press).

Horkheimer, Max and Adorno, Theodor W. (1994). *Dialectic of Enlightenment*, trans. J. Cumming (New York: Continuum).

Kierkegaard, Søren (1980). *The Concept of Anxiety*, trans. Reidar Thomte and Albert A. Anderson, *Kierkegaard's Writings* VIII. (Princeton, NJ: Princeton University Press).

—— (1990). *Eighteen Upbuilding Discourses*, trans. Howard V. Hong and Edna H. Hong, *Kierkegaard's Writings* V. (Princeton, NJ: Princeton University Press).

—— (1992). *Concluding Unscientific Postscript*, trans. Howard V. Hong and Edna H. Hong, *Kierkegaard's Writings* XII.1. (Princeton, NJ: Princeton University Press).

—— (1993). *Three Discourses on Imagined Occasions*, trans. Howard V. Hong and Edna H. Hong, *Kierkegaard's Writings* X. (Princeton, NJ: Princeton University Press).

—— (1995). *Works of Love*, trans. Howard V. Hong and Edna H. Hong, *Kierkegaard's Writings* XVI. (Princeton, NJ: Princeton University Press).

Levinas, Emmanuel (1969). *Totality and Infinity: An Essay on Exteriority*, trans. Alphonso Lingis (Pittsburgh: Duquesne University Press).

—— (1987). *Time and the Other*, trans. Richard A. Cohen (Pittsburgh: Duquesne University Press).

—— (1989). 'God and Philosophy', trans. Richard A. Cohen and Alphonso Lingis, in Seán Hand (ed.), *The Levinas Reader*. (Oxford: Blackwell), 166–89.

Margalit, Avishai (2004). *The Ethics of Memory*. (Cambridge, MA: Harvard University Press).

Marx, Karl (1973). 'Thesen über Feuerbach', *Marx-Engels Werke* 3. (Berlin: Dietz Verlag).

Nietzsche, Friedrich (1988a). *Die fröhliche Wissenschaft, Kritische Studienausgabe* 3, ed. Giorgio Colli and Mazzino Montinari (Berlin: de Gruyter).

—— (1988b). *Götzen-Dämmerung, Kritische Studienausgabe* 6, ed. Giorgio Colli and Mazzino Montinari (Berlin: de Gruyter).

—— (1988c). *Der Antichrist. Kritische Studienausgabe* 6, ed. Giorgio Colli and Mazzino Montinari (Berlin: de Gruyter).

Pannenberg, Wolfhart (1988). *Systematische Theologie* 1. (Göttingen: Vandenhoeck &Ruprecht).

Ricoeur, Paul (1985). *Temps et récit III: Le temps raconté*. (Paris: Seuil).

—— (2004). *Memory, History, Forgetting*, trans. Kathleen Blamey and David Pellauer (Chicago: University of Chicago Press).

Rosenzweig, Franz (2005). *The Star of Redemption*, trans. Barbara E. Galli (Madison: University of Wisconsin Press).

Sartre, Jean-Paul (2003). *Being and Nothingness: An Essay on Phenomenological Ontology*, trans. Hazel E. Barnes (London and New York: Routledge).

Shakespeare, William (1973). *Complete Works*, ed. Peter Alexander (London and Glasgow: Collins).

Theunissen, Michael (1991). *Negative Theologie der Zeit*. (Frankfurt am Main: Suhrkamp).

—— (2000). *Pindar. Menschenlos und Wende der Zeit*. (München: C. H. Beck).

Suggested Reading

Brudholm, Thomas and Cushman, Thomas (eds) (2009). *The Religious in Responses to Mass Atrocity: Interdisciplinary Perspectives*. (Cambridge: Cambridge University Press).

Dalferth, Ingolf U. (1997). *Gedeutete Gegenwart. Zur Wahrnehmung Gottes in den Erfahrungen der Zeit*. (Tübingen: Mohr Siebeck).

—— (2003). *Die Wirklichkeit des Möglichen. Hermeneutische Religionsphilosophie*. (Tübingen: Mohr Siebeck).

Flasch, Kurt (1993). *Was ist Zeit? Augustinus von Hippo. Das XI. Buch der Confessiones. Historisch-philosophie Studie. Text—Übersetzung—Kommentar*. (Frankfurt am Main: Klostermann).

Grøn, Arne, Damgaard, Iben, and Overgaard, Søren (eds.) (2007). *Subjectivity and Transcendence*. (Tübingen: Mohr Siebeck).

Heidegger, Martin (1992). *History of the Concept of Time: Prolegomena*, trans. Theodore Kisiel (Bloomington, IN: Indiana University Press).

Kosselleck, Reinhart (1985). *Futures Past: On the Semantics of Historical Time*, trans. Keith Tribe (Cambridge, MA: MIT Press).

Levinas, Emmanuel (2000). *God, Death, and Time*, trans. Bettina Bergo (Stanford, CA: Stanford University Press).

Schulz, Walter (1972). *Philosophie in der veränderten Welt*. (Pfullingen: Neske).

Theunissen, Michael (2001). *Reichweite und Grenzen der Erinnerung/Scope and Limits of Recollection*, trans. Bruce Allen (Tübingen: Mohr Siebeck).

Welz, Claudia (2008). *Love's Transcendence and the Problem of Theodicy*. (Tübingen: Mohr Siebeck).

CHAPTER 22

....

TECHNOLOGY

....

DAVID LEWIN

'My God, what have we done?'—
Robert Lewis, the co-pilot of the Enola Gay, the B-29 bomber that
dropped the first atomic bomb.

(Thomas 1978: 326)

I. INTRODUCTION
....

ON 2nd August 1939, thirty days before Germany's invasion of Poland, Albert Einstein, along with several other scientists, wrote to President Franklin D. Roosevelt about the efforts being made by the Nazis towards the purification of uranium for the development of nuclear weapons technology. Soon afterward the US government initiated a covert research operation called 'The Manhattan Project'. Six years and two billion dollars later, the first atomic bomb, code-named 'the gadget', was detonated in Los Alamos, New Mexico.

This defining moment in human history has received significant reflection, and, perhaps more than any other event, signalled the birth of serious and systematic reflection upon technology. What might theologians contribute to this debate?

This chapter will argue that modern theology provides a distinctive contribution to understanding technology, not least because theology, like technology is concerned with the future. I argue that the newly formed paths within the philosophy of technology have generally failed to engage with the theological tradition, a failure which accounts, in no small part, to the ecological, social, and existential crises of the technological age. More than any other, nuclear technology has drawn the world's attention to these crises, but even prior to this, Ernst Kapp, Oswald Spengler, Ernst Jünger, and many others had already raised concerns about the direction of western technological culture, with the First World War providing a profound and terrifying stimulus. The bombings of

Hiroshima and Nagasaki further established an age of apocalyptic fear expressed by many philosophers and critics, Günther Anders and Karl Jaspers in Germany, and Albert Camus and Georges Bataille in France, to name a few. Even Einstein, a key figure in the development of the nuclear age, became a leader in the peace movement and eventual disarmament following the catastrophic events in Japan.

But where there is fear, hope is also close at hand as scientists and politicians saw the enormous potential of nuclear technology. As Martin Heidegger noted, in the 1950s Franz Joseph Strauss could wax lyrical about the possibilities of the atomic age: 'The atomic age can become a prosperous, happy age full of hope, an age in which we live through atoms. It all depends on us!' (Heidegger 1996: 122). As early as September 1946, Pierre Teilhard de Chardin went even further in his essay 'Some Reflections on the Spiritual Repercussions of the Atomic Bomb', stating that the 'brief flash of an explosion of matter, has made of [human beings] . . . a new being hitherto unknown to themselves' (Teilhard 1964: 146). For Teilhard this moment represented the dawning of a new phase of consciousness upon the earth.

The reflective sentiment expressed in the opening quote might seem impressive until we realize that Robert Lewis is actually reported to have said to his crewmates, 'My God, look at that son-of-a-bitch go!' (Thomas 1978: 326) as the atom bomb was released over Hiroshima. Only later is his narrative constituted in more 'philosophical' terms when he comes to write of the events in his notebook. But in his more philosophical mood, Lewis captures our ambivalence to modern technology, both as a destructive force of unprecedented proportion, and as something somehow beyond human control. The recurring question of who is responsible, both for the progress of modern technology and the destructive consequences, is central to this chapter. An important component of the ambivalence that has animated much of the discussion and literature about technology is that the freedom of human beings is profoundly curtailed by technology; that we are at the mercy of unprecedented and unnatural forces that have been unleashed by our hubris, or simply by a lack of care. This crisis in capability is expressed in the pilot's question: what have we done? From the theological point of view, we can ask for forgiveness on the basis that in a more general sense *we know not what we do*, as Christ does on our behalf on the cross (Luke 23:34). What makes this general appeal on our behalf specific to the age of technology? It is nothing less than the recognition that we are entering a new historical phase in which our ability to understand the world seems unable to keep pace with the effectiveness or impact of our actions within it. As Günther Anders puts it, there is an uncanny incapacity to conceive of what technology can produce or do:

> As engineers, at least as engineers of nuclear weapons, we have become omnipotent— an expression that is little more than a metaphor. But as intellectual beings we do not measure up to this omnipotence of ours. In other words: by way of our technology we have gotten ourselves into a situation in which we can no longer conceive (*vorstellen*) what we can produce (*herstellen*) and do (*anstellen*). What does this discrepancy between conception (*Vorstellung*) and production (*Herstellung*) signify? It signifies that in a new and terrible sense we 'know no longer what we do'. (Nordmann 2005)

That we 'know not what we do' raises the question of our responsibility, for clearly our ignorance would seem to mitigate that responsibility. But we cannot be excused from our responsibilities firstly because technical actions are, in some sense, *our* actions, and secondly, because we have become aware, however dimly, of the disproportion between our technical production and our conception. Our task, then, is to understand what it is that we are doing, which begins with clarifying the sense in which we know not what we do. More than any other, theological discourse is equipped to clarify our dependence, fragility, and finitude in ways that seem consistent with the task just outlined. It is for this reason that theologians have much to offer contemporary debates about technology. And there are additional reasons to suppose that theologians have a unique contribution to make, in particular an orientation to the future.

II. THE FUTURE

We have always been interested in the future, perhaps, as Criswell remarks in the infamous movie *Plan 9 from Outer Space*, because that is where we are to spend the rest of our lives. But our interest in the future also reflects a particularly theological orientation, to do with an ontological priority that the future appears to take, from Wolfhart Pannenberg's future orientation expressed in *prolepsis* (Pannenberg 1996), to Jürgen Moltmann's theology of hope (Moltmann 1967), to Teilhard's faith in the future (Teilhard 1964, 1975). A cluster of ideas evokes that temporal priority which sees *Omega* as the fulfilment of time and history: progress; destiny; eschatology; parousia; hope; these ideas depend upon a sense of the promise of things to come. The narratives of human history witness to this temporal directionality, often located within an explicitly theological context. From the promises of God to Abraham, to Christ's anticipated return, the great western religions consistently speak of a Kingdom yet to be realized.

This interest in the future is reinforced in the present age by the advance of modern technology. Not surprisingly, it has been tempting to identify the extraordinary developments of technological societies with the establishment of the Kingdom of God. As Paul Tillich puts it, 'technology can liberate from the bounds that space and time set to the human community. Without it the great idea of all eschatological hope—the idea of *one* community—could never be realised' (Tillich 1988: 60). That technology might be the means by which human community is realized flies in the face of so many theological and cultural assumptions, not least that technical utopias can only be what Paul Ricoeur called 'a rationalist corruption of Christian eschatology' (Ricoeur 1965: 81). It is hard to imagine that the infinite promise of technology could ever quench the spiritual thirst that animates our deeper nature. Moreover, the quest for infinite technology seems indicative of a secular culture having vanquished or simply lost the spiritual depth of religious life. Thus Josef Pieper supposes that the utopian-millenarian hope for an intra-historical salvation can only occur in the context of a secular historicism (Pieper 1999: 24–8). For Pieper, the irreducibly religious character of history cannot be translated into a secular narrative, for any such narrative assumes an ultimate fulfilment.

While technology seems animated by future possibilities, those visions are, for the most part, cast within a more mundane context. In many cases, the progress that engineers dream of has seemed basically reducible to technical improvements to material conditions. The radical ideas espoused by Ray Kurzweil, Hans Moravec, and others, that human finitude will be overcome by future technical achievements through the development of artificial intelligence—that, for example, our identities can be uploaded to eternally maintained supercomputers—remains a distinctly marginal prospect (Moravec 1988; Kurzweil 1999; Kurzweil and Grossman 2004; DeLashmutt 2006). The mainstream of technical activity does not pursue this infinite post-human agenda, but modestly settles for 'improving standards', or even simply providing the engineers with a well-paid job to do (DeLashmutt 2009). The extraordinary success of modern technology in providing circumscribed improvements can seem in stark contrast to the shameful lack of progress within the history of philosophy and theology. And we do not have to look too hard to find voices asserting that where philosophy and religion have failed to eradicate the problems of the world, modern technology promises to do so (Bacon 1994; Mitcham 1996: 83).

But surely the more radical polarizations between salvation in the next life, and happiness in this, are as much a legacy of over-determined Platonism as they are characteristic of Christian theology. The division between nature and grace is pertinent inasmuch as the history of Christendom has reinforced this dualism between technical and spiritual endeavours (Dupre 1993: 167–89). Yet the picture is complicated by the observation that Reformed theology also included 'worldly' activities as a part of religious ascetics, thereby inviting industrial and technical activities into spiritual life (Weber 2003; Szersyznski 2005: 51–64). Indeed the notion that post-Reformation European culture created an environment in which science and technology could flourish has been a popular thesis for some time (White 1964; Fudpucker 1984; Weber 2003). Furthermore, it is important to recognize that certain theologians such as Teilhard de Chardin and Philip Hefner (Hefner 2003), and some engineers, such as Friedrich Dessauer (Dessauer 1972), have, in their enthusiasm for technological development, sought to overcome the dualistic tendencies that have persistently animated the theological tradition. The degree to which any nature/ grace dualism is an essential aspect of the theological tradition remains a deeply contentious issue for contemporary theology (Milbank 1990). Wherever one comes down on this central issue, the effects of this dualism can be felt in the ways theologians have tended to regard questions of technology as somehow lacking in the dignity and significance of more universal theological themes. By contrast, many philosophers have addressed the problem of technology somewhat thematically, though, in general, they have remained resolutely silent on any contribution that theology might make.

III. Towards a Theology of Technology

During the twentieth century, a number of philosophers developed a distinctive philosophy of technology (Mitcham and Mackey 1973, 1983). Many of the philosophers who are regarded as founders of this sub-discipline, such as John Dewey and Martin Heidegger, have resisted separating the questions raised by technology from deeper metaphysical questions. Nevertheless, the philosophy of technology as a distinct sub-discipline continues to gather interest, particularly in North America and the Netherlands with the work of figures such as Albert Borgmann, Langdon Winner, Don Ihde, Hans Achterhuis, and many others (Higgs, Light, and Strong 2000; Achterhuis 2001). In general, the approach of these thinkers has been to focus on secular philosophical themes, tending to leave any theological responses to technology well alone. Consequently, a fissure has opened up between philosophers who reflect on technology, and theologians who develop their own questions about the religious and ethical implications of technology. Apart from certain notable exceptions (Borgmann 1984; Mitcham and Grote 1984) recent philosophy of technology has tended to reinforce this gulf, the so-called 'empirical turn' in the philosophy of technology being characteristic of this isolationism (Achterhuis 2001). For some, this strategy of pursuing a secular philosophy of technology may simply reflect the spirit of disenchantment that has engulfed the modern world, but as we awaken to the 'post-secular' world from the dream of the rationalist elimination of religion, we must recognize that a secular narrative of technology is not sufficient to account for the *meaning* of modern technology. Whatever the reasons for this fissure, theologians have a distinctive and vital contribution to make in thinking through technology even though surprisingly few have directly considered these relations (Pattison 2005: 1). This remarkable lacuna is most likely accounted for by the fact that there appears to be nothing at stake in the relation between technology and theology.

By contrast, the history of the relation between science and religion is well documented (Brooke 1991; Barbour 1998), a relation in which the very truth of things has been at stake. Regardless of the numerous ways in which theologians have sought to reconcile scientific discoveries with the theological tradition, what is important is that science raised questions that theologians could not ignore: the theory of evolution, to take one contentious example, continues to demand theological responses, if only in that theologians have been concerned to justify their existence in the face of the explanatory powers of modern science. Technology, on the other hand, seems to present no direct challenge to the authority of scripture or tradition. Consequently there has been no reason for theologians to address the question of technology beyond the specific details of particular problems raised by this or that technological device. In short, technology itself has seemed epistemically neutral, and in so far as modern theology is regarded as an epistemic discipline (itself a highly contentious issue), then there appears to be no question concerning technology. From this point of view, the development of technology remains a neutral activity that calls for ethical deliberation only to determine the appropriate usage of what that development offers. Having split the atom, the technicians call on politicians, philosophers, and theologians to consider the appropriate context in which such a device might be put to use. Here it is all too easy to isolate the technical domain from the ethical in a way in which the question of technology is not really raised at all. In contrast to this, the first step to questioning technology is to acknowledge that technology is not neutral, that, as George Pattison puts it in his seminal study *Thinking About God in the Age of Technology*, 'technology is not just something that mediates between our mental intentions and the physical world about us, technology gets inside our heads and affects the way in which we conceive reality' (2005: 3). But we must be aware that there is something uncanny about the way technology affects us at this deep level, an uncanniness that, I argue, is expressed through a general but deep ambivalence towards technology.

IV. TECHNOLOGICAL AMBIVALENCE

It is important to understand just how ambivalent towards technology modern culture has become. In general we can appreciate the many advances of this age, but our appreciation is often attenuated by an irrepressible disquiet about our capacity to sustain the present rate of development. The mechanization of food production, for example, has brought great capacity for food manufacture but at what environmental cost? Will nuclear technology ever deliver on its promise of virtually unlimited energy without threatening future generations? Do online environments and virtual networks support or displace those direct human relationships that sustain and nourish our human identity? Are we able to maintain some measure of control over the development of the many self-regulating technologies that exist beyond the capacity of human senses, in the tiny world of nano devices? As numerous and overwhelming as such questions are, they do not represent a real challenge to technology itself, rather, these questions are addressed only to specific problems for which specific solutions can be sought. Consequently there is no problem with technology per se, only with pollution resulting from certain modern forms of transportation, with forms of alienation characteristic of certain modern work practices, and so on. Occasionally social theorists and philosophers raise deeper issues by questioning whether, for example, the lifestyles of the technically affluent regions coincide with the fulfilment of human nature. Herbert Marcuse is one such theorist.

What Marcuse famously called our one-dimensional society (Marcuse 1991) seems to have grown accustomed to the general sensibility that all is not well with technological progress. Despite the celebration of many technical achievements, there exist too many unknowns for anything more than a muted ambivalence expressed both by a confidence in humanity's power, and a passionate though often inarticulate resistance to overzealous manipulation of the given patterns of nature formulated, for example, as the 'wisdom of repugnance', or the 'yuk factor' (Kass 1997; Midgley 2000). The philosophical responses to this sensibility have been varied, but in so far as they have adhered to the approaches of critical theory, they have consistently failed to address the theological depth the question of technology calls for. In particular philosophers do not address the question of the ultimate concern of technology.

Many philosophers would immediately point out the fallacious assumption within this question. For technology, being neutral, is concerned with nothing at all (Feenberg 1991). Human beings have concerns; technology is simply the means to some end expressed by a human agent. As I have already indicated, those familiar with the philosophy of technology might not fall into the common error of assuming that technology is simply a neutral tool (Heidegger 1977: 4–6). But surely, it could be argued, I am projecting a human attribute (having concerns) on to technology. Even if we could agree upon a general definition of technology, and even if we could grant that technology is not simply neutral, that does not mean that it has concerns or designs for the future. While it must be admitted that the technical device does not directly have intentions, our human concerns are mediated, augmented, and modified by the plethora of devices that surround us. In other words, the kinds of concerns with which technology tends to engage us, may be less than ultimate in nature, a point I shall elaborate when I come to discuss Tillich. Certain critical theorists have been keen to explore how technical and bureaucratic processes diminish freedom and human capability, and one clear way in which this is achieved has been through the manipulation of needs and desires (Mumford 1940; Marcuse 1991; Feenberg 1999). However, any simply neo-Marxist analysis of technological society is in danger of raising more questions than answers: in particular, to what end is technological society manipulating human desires? From a theological point of view, any critical theory of technology limits itself by its refusal to engage in what we can call *teleological* questions—questions addressing the ultimate concern of technology.

Those theologians who have attempted to address technology more thematically have tended to reinforce the kind of general ambivalence which we have just seen. I will sketch out the theological responses of two major twentieth-century French thinkers whose attitudes to technology could scarcely be more distinct, Teilhard de Chardin and Jacques Ellul. One thing Teilhard and Ellul do share is the distinctly theological concern of the ultimate trajectory within technology. As Ellul laments on the closing page of his influential study *The Technological Society*, '[n]one of our wise men ever pose the question of the end of all their marvels', his analysis drawing out the implications of the omission of this question. After looking at the dichotomy between the negativity of Ellul and the positivity of Teilhard, I will introduce the more circumspect (or simply more ambiguous) treatments of technology reflected in the theologies of Tillich, Berdyaev, and others. This mediated view will direct our attention to the influence of Martin Heidegger, whose impact on this area is unparalleled.

V. TECHNOLOGY: GOOD OR EVIL?

Out of the chaos of the First World War, Teilhard de Chardin sensed 'an impending cosmic birth' (Shafer 2002: 826), foreseeable, in large part, through the extraordinary progress of modern technology. Teilhard is known for writings that develop a radical synthesis of his scientific work as an evolutionary biologist and palaeontologist, with spiritual insights that remained firmly rooted in Catholic Christian soil. Despite the reticence and resistance of his Jesuit superiors to some of his more developed ideas, (which resulted in an ecclesiastical ban on certain writings) Teilhard remained committed to a grand unification that has been variously called poetry, mysticism, natural theology, and process metaphysics (Barbour 1969: 136). Teilhard's vision is rooted in a faith in the future that cannot be extricated from his radical extrapolations of evolutionary theory. His attitude to technology also reflects a profound faith in the capacity of human beings to 'build the earth' (1969: 37). At the present time, this capacity finds its form in the technical activities of human beings that seem, in Teilhard's view, organized by the convergent energy of love: 'The day will come when, after harnessing space, the winds, the tides, gravitation, we shall harness for God the energies of love. And, on that day, for the second time in the history of the world, humankind will have discovered fire' (1975: 86–7).

The unprecedented detonation of the atom bomb in the 'bad-lands' of Arizona, represented, for Teilhard, the birth of a new human being, new because aware of the tremendous possibilities as well as responsibilities that were opening up: 'the final effect of the light cast by the atomic fire into the spiritual depths of the earth is to illumine within them the over-riding question of the ultimate end of Evolution' (Teilhard 1964: 153). Although this ultimate end is hardly drawn out by Teilhard, he clearly saw great reason to hope that all technical activities were part of a great enfolding energy towards Omega point. Undoubtedly, the structure of linear time, and the theology of hope which it supports, allows Teilhard to develop this extraordinary synthesis of theology with science and technology. It must be said, though, that Teilhard's interpretation of time and history are by no means universally shared within modern Christian thought.

In contrast to the comedy of technological progress characterized by Teilhard, we must place the tragic narrative of technological determinism, most eloquently formulated by 'the founding father of the anti-technological movement' (Florman 1994: 46), Jacques Ellul. In the 1950s, Ellul developed an influential critique of modern technology, the dominant theme of which was the emergence of a 'technological tyranny' that was overtaking human freedom. For Ellul, technology—which he called *la Technique*—is defined as a self-perpetuating 'cult of efficiency' (Christians 2002), as 'the *totality of methods rationally arrived at and having absolute efficiency* (for a given stage of development) in *every* field of human activity' (Ellul 1964: p. xxv). While individual freedoms appear efficacious, they are contained within the context of a 'rigorous determinism' (p. xxviii) unique to the technological age—basically reducible to the rule of efficiency. The predominance of *technique* results in a litany of now common-place woes: the homogenization of global culture; the increasingly stressful pace of life; the disappearance of nature; the meaninglessness of modern work practices; the mantra of improved standards of education amounting to little more than social integration; performance management across all domains of public life defined, of course, by determinable attributes; and so on.

More than any other theologian, Ellul has developed a systematic attitude to modern technology in a sequence of books and articles which have come to typify the pessimism characteristic of the modern age (Ellul 1980, 1983, 1990). But Ellul's analysis cannot simply be called a theology of technology largely because of its sociological character. To some extent it is possible to associate his negativity with his profession as sociologist since, in contrast to the simply empirical analysis of the 'science of society' (which is, of course, at least as theory-laden as any other empirical endeavour), the disposition of theological discourse is guided by hope. What certainly *is* theologically driven within Ellul's analysis is the assumption that any and all efforts to liberate the human condition from its postlapsarian labours are hopeless without the intervention of grace, which, as Pattison observes and Ellul himself acknowledged, reflects the Kierke-gaardian and Barthian influence (Ellul 1990; Pattison 2005: 52).

Ellul's dualism between the prelapsarian world in which the artifice of technology is redundant because labour is unnecessary, and our fallen state in which aberrant technologies are developed to mitigate our finite condition, seems also to reflect Kierkegaardian and Barthian influence. It is a dualism that can bind us to the false choice between the secular atheism of modernity, which often, but by no means always, embraces modern technology, and a state of radical dependence on God in which our technical endeavours only obscure the fundamental relation of finitude and transcendence.

Teilhard seems to effortlessly work through this false choice by seeing no real dualism at play, which some theologians have regarded as evidence of Teilhard's lapse into pantheism despite the fact that Teilhard repeatedly identifies his view in contrast to any form of pantheism (de Lubac 1965).

VI. TECHNOLOGY AND MEDIATION

Modern theology has had to respond not only to the extraordinary success of modern science and technology, but even more directly to the rise of secularism and the death of God. Of course, from a thematic perspective one can hardly distinguish these aspects of modernity since scientific discoveries are certainly an essential element of the secular narrative. Apart from these general associations, I suggest it might be more illuminating to understand modern technology as a pragmatic (non-thematic) expression of secularism. I have already noted that theologians are reticent to engage in questions concerning technology because at root it is commonly believed that 'Christianity is something utterly other than technique; it involves a way of looking at things which is foreign to the way in which the technical mentality views things' (Blair 1984: 45). And there is a corresponding notion that the use of certain devices will erode religious faith, that the online world, to take one example, will displace the possibility of encounter that defines the religious dimension of life. Is this because there is a sense in which technological power is a form of hubris? The postlapsarian state is one in which to labour is to be human, and so labour-saving techniques and devices might seem to recall the arrogance of Prometheus or the presumptuousness of Adam and Eve eating the fruit from the tree of the knowledge of good and evil. In addition we might wonder whether our new found technical capacities encourage a sense of autonomy, undermining the fundamental religious awareness that Friedrich Schleiermacher identified as a feeling of absolute dependence (Schleiermacher 1976: 132). Similarly, Rudolf Otto's account of numinous experience may be something increasingly scarce in the urban environments of the technological age—the cathedral vaulted ceilings now brought closer by good lighting for the new aesthetic, may no longer hold quite the sense of *Mysterium Tremendum* they once did (Otto 1950: 12–24). Or theologians may simply be still reconciling themselves to the stark fact famously announced by Rudolf Bultmann, that the use of modern technologies precludes us from a genuine belief in the New Testament world of spirits and demons (Bultmann 1984: 4). Of course theology has gone a long way in accommodating itself to the modern world, passing through a series of theologies of culture that have engaged with our new contexts, Paul Tillich's method of correlation being exemplary in this regard (Tillich 1951: 59–66).

Although Tillich did not develop a systematic or even very consistent view of modern technology and its relation to theology, his writings on the subject have been significant enough for J. Mark Thomas to have gathered them together in a volume entitled *The Spiritual Situation in Our Technical Society* (Tillich 1988). What is characteristic of Tillich's engagement with technology is an ambiguity concerning its creative and destructive possibilities (Tillich 1988: p. xiv; Pattison 2005: 47). So long as our technical capacities are located within the larger context in which human nature and its ultimate destiny take priority over technological ends, then technology can grant us the power to do great things. However, the technological age (what Tillich refers to as the second period of modern society in the following quote) seems preoccupied with means. Where we were once utopian in seeking the perfect world, we now seek only the perfect means and forget to contemplate the ultimate orientation of those means. As Tillich puts it,

> Technical reason provides means for ends, but offers no guidance in the determination of ends. Reason in the first period [of early Bourgeois revolution] had been concerned with ends beyond the existing order. Technical reason became concerned with means to stabilize the existing order. Revolutionary reason had been conservative with respect to means but 'utopian' with respect to ends. Technical reason is conservative with respect to ends and revolutionary with respect to means. It can be used for any purposes dictated by the will, including those that deny reason in the sense of truth and justice. The transformation of *revolutionary reason* into *technical reason* was the decisive feature of the transition from the first to the second period of modern society. (Tillich 1988: 6)

Today we are so distracted by the pursuit of ever more effective means, that any contemplative mood that might provide a space in which those means can find a deeper ordering structure, has no opportunity to arise. Our ability to bring about all that we desire tends to have the unfortunate effect of deafening us to our ultimate concern: 'As long as the preliminary, transitory concerns are not silenced, no matter how interesting and valuable and important they may be, the voice of ultimate concern cannot be heard' (Tillich 1988: 44). In so far as technology is able to displace or conceal the depth dimension involved in our ultimate concern then modern technology is in danger of being only 'a telos that negates a telos' (Tillich 1988: 80), which is really a means that negates an end. The question hinges again upon the ultimate concern of technology, which for Tillich must be located within the larger narrative of human civilization rather than usurping that narrative by its own effectiveness at delivering preliminary goods. The good life is in danger of being circumscribed in technical terms as constituted by those goods that are definable, measurable, and consumable. The main problem with defining the good life in terms accessible to technological advance, is the tendency to reduce the depth dimension of things and experiences to coherent deliverables and circumscribed attributes (See Higgs, Light, and Strong 2000). The same idea is illustrated by the technical metaphor that in the digital age the infinite variety of human speech is transformed/reduced into binary code.

Nicholas Berdyaev also addressed the question of technology in a piecemeal fashion. Like Tillich, Berdyaev saw technological society as reversing the relation between means and ends such that what I call an *ontological inversion* seems to have taken place: 'Technique, organization and the productive processes are a reality while spiritual culture is unreal, a mere instrument of technique. The relation between end and means is reversed and perverted' (Berdyaev 2006: 217). The rush of technological advance gives only a stronger impression of this inversion as society seems increasingly dominated by the development of ever-more ingenious means of production, alongside an ever-deeper erosion of our ability to conceive the meaning of technology. And, as we saw earlier, this is reflected in the disproportion between production and conception, with the result that we know not what we do.

The varied theological responses to technology that we have considered are broadly unanimous in arguing for the need to establish a proper relation between means and ends; that technology needs to be located within a greater (vertical) context. If this is agreed then we must ask how we are to ensure that right relationship? Who exactly is in a position to determine this relationship and ensure that the pursuit of genetically modified crops, to take just one example, is placed within a larger teleological context? It is at this point that Heidegger offers a particularly interesting analysis.

Among Heidegger's many controversial statements is his apparent denial of human capability and responsibility where he says that no political, scientific, or technical group can slow the progress of technology. Indeed he goes further by saying that, '[n]o merely human organisation is capable of gaining dominion over it' (Heidegger 1966: 52). This statement has been controversial within the philosophy of technology for some time, particularly in reference to the implied technological determinism in statements such as this (Feenberg 1999: 15–17, Thomson 2005: 44–78). But this criticism of Heidegger really misses the point of his work as a whole. Anyone familiar with Heidegger's broader oeuvre will appreciate his general suspicion of any form of autonomous subjectivity such as is developed in the Cartesian and Kantian philosophical tradition. Thus his attenuation of capability and responsibility in relation to technology must be understood in the light of his general deconstruction of the agency and the will (Davis 2007).

So the fact that 'no merely human organization' can properly locate technology suggests that human capability alone is not enough. It is part of the story, but not sufficient in itself. Clearly Heidegger does not want to invoke the traditional idea of God—the God of onto-theology as Heidegger puts it (Wrathall 2003; Thomson 2005)— as the supreme agency in control of technology, and yet he believes that something 'other' is part of the ordering of technological activity. It is no coincidence that Heidegger's turn to poetics coincides with the later considerations of technology. For Heidegger, only the poetic imagination radically disrupts the ubiquitous coupling between human activity and the quest for ever-greater efficiency, because only the work of art is not reducible to human values. Only a poetic turn is radical enough to break the grip of technological thinking.

Despite the fact that from time to time Heidegger betrays a critical, if not quite contemptuous, attitude towards theological thought, he remained what I would call *theologically ambiguous* throughout his long career, often suggesting that some higher agency must visit us, or that we must patiently wait for something to be disclosed. As Iain Thomson has shown (2005: chs 1 and 2), this theological ambiguity is deeply related to Heidegger's view of technology since our ability to attend to the depth and givenness of things in the world is displaced by an essentially technological understanding of reality. In order to clarify Heidegger's view and its theological significance, I will discuss a distinction at the heart of understanding technology, the distinction between what is natural and what is artificial.

VII. Natural and Artificial

For most theologians who consider the issue, modern culture has become too identified with technological devices and processes to allow for any larger narrative. There remains a persistent concern that the technical mediations with which devices surround us, disengage us from the sacred centre of religious truth. Some thinkers, who might hesitate to call their work *theology*, take a distinctly religious approach in expressing this danger, for example Albert Borgmann, Jerry Mander, and others (Borgmann 1984; Mander 1991; Guardini 1994). As Borgmann would say, the technical device disburdens and disengages in equal measure (Borgmann 1984: 61ff.). The Internet, already a classic example of the two faces of technology, seems to facilitate communications and relations, and we could not entirely deny that even in its brief life it has ameliorated many tedious activities. Yet many people find its scope overwhelming, and the proliferation of opinions and perspectives undermining of deep engagement. Social networking can likewise appear superficial or fetishistic. Although the technology is new, the general structure of these concerns is not. Kierkegaard had similar concerns about the popular press of his day that seemed to encourage a similarly disengaged chatter (see Dreyfus 2004).

In broad terms the general assumption behind these kinds of concern seems to be that there is a state of nature in which technical devices do not figure. This view assumes that we begin as creatures naked before God, a condition that finds its secular form in the concept of the noble savage; that we are essentially independent creatures who construct social and technical relations through expediency rather than any essential or natural proclivity. The technical devices and processes that are later constructed (not created) are not really part of true human identity, but are artificial overlays upon what is first given in the created order of things. Alternative narratives of human identity recognize a fundamental coherence, even causality, between the evolution of technological tools and devices, and the cortical development associated with the emergence of human beings, raising the question of what came first, the human mind or the technological device (see Stiegler 1998).

As informal, or even just vague, as the distinction between the natural and the artificial can often seem to be, it is remarkably persistent, particularly because the ambivalence people feel about technology needs some theoretical anchorage. The preference for the natural over the artificial, expresses the enduring anthropology in which human being is located within a natural order, whether in its theological, or secular form. This purity of human nature has an enduring relevance in the modern age, with the ecological movement reasserting a sense of a dualism between the natural state of humanity, in contrast to the excesses of the technological age. Furthermore, it is hard to imagine any ancient society that does not express a sense of natural order, whether explicitly or implicitly, but the technological age takes the significance of the natural/artificial distinction to a new level. This assumption of a natural order does much to define how it is that beings, in their essence, should be. Crucially, this state of nature appears *given* to us rather than determined by us. Of course the conception of the givenness of nature has not gone untouched by modernity, but, certainly within religious discourse, it has proved remarkably resilient, even enjoying a resurgence within contemporary philosophy of religion (see Janicaud 2000; Marion 2002; Wrathall 2003). Scientific method has all but displaced teleology by its identification of causality in purely 'efficient' terms, and yet the deeper sense in which things have a *telos*, an inner movement towards their own fulfilment, suggests that things are organized by an order that is both immanent (within the thing) and transcendent (drawing the thing to it teleological fulfilment). A sense of our general harmony with natural law, or what might simply be called *being*, is often part of the reflection upon technology, and provides us with a way of developing the analysis of Heidegger.

Although Heidegger's long career involved a wide range of approaches, his later work very often returns to questions of being in the technological age. Among his best-known essays is his *The Question Concerning Technology*, in which, among other themes, he explores the different ways in which the Rhine River is made present, an example we shall consider in some detail. For Heidegger there is an essential distinction to be made between the kind of technology that adheres to the patterns of a natural order, and those that do not. This distinction is famously illustrated in the following passage:

> The hydroelectric plant is set into the current of the Rhine. It sets the Rhine to supplying its hydraulic pressure, which then sets the turbines turning. This turning sets those machines in motion whose thrust sets going the electric current for which the long distance power station and its network of cables are set up to dispatch electricity. In the context of the interlocking processes pertaining to the orderly disposition of electrical energy, even the Rhine itself appears to be something at our command. The hydroelectric plant is not built into the Rhine River as was the old wooden bridge that joined bank with bank for hundreds of years. Rather, the river is dammed up into the power plant. What the river is now, namely, a water-power supplier, derives from the essence of the power station. In order that we may even remotely consider the monstrousness that reigns here, let us ponder for a moment the contrast that is spoken by the two titles: 'The Rhine,' as dammed up into the power works, and 'The Rhine,' as uttered by the artwork, in Hölderlin's hymn by that name. But, it will be replied, the Rhine is still a river in the landscape, is it not? Perhaps. But how? In no other way than as an object on call for inspection by a tour group ordered there by the vacation industry.   (Heidegger 1977: 16)

In this provocative passage Heidegger contrasts the way the Rhine appears either as something ready to provide human beings with electricity, or as something to be contemplated through the poetic word. Whether or not we agree with Heidegger that the poetic word offers a more authentic or natural experience of the Rhine (an implied view which, significantly, Heidegger does not directly state), the point is to see the relation behind the specific example: that there exists a *manner of revealing things that expresses only the projections of human will* (what we would call *artificial*), and there is a *manner of revealing things that adheres to their own essential nature* (what we would call *natural*). The former shows the river to be subject to the command of technology since it has become subservient to the needs and operations of the power station. The latter allows what is built into the river to be subject to its flow and current. The former does not pay heed to what is given in the presence of the river, while the latter pays attention to its presence. The poetic word further acknowledges the gift of the presence of the river by the simple celebration of what is given without any reference to what may be of value to us, the utility of that presence.

But isn't Heidegger's distinction here conditioned by his own romanticized view of pre-industrial rural life? Heidegger can surely be criticized since his examples often appeal to an intuitive or heuristic sense that might not stand formal scrutiny. I have argued elsewhere that this criticism is not really fair, since Heidegger is well aware that the kinds of argumentation that do stand up to formal analysis are themselves reflective of a fundamentally technological orientation, and he is quite deliberate in his use of an informal manner of expression (see Lewin 2011). In the context of the essay as a whole—or as Heidegger would say, within the path of his thought—Heidegger's argument works to illustrate, or witness to a situation rather than express an indefatigable logic, and despite the clear ambivalence with which the philosophy of technology regards Heidegger's contributions, not least because of this methodological nuance, he remains a foundational figure within this domain.

So what conclusions are we to draw from Heidegger's illustrative account? Why are such reflections important for theologians to consider? We might draw from this a general sense that what is natural corresponds to what is given in being, while what is artificial does not. But even if we can accept such a general distinction, what does it tell us about the appropriateness of specific technologies? Do we suppose that genetic modification or nuclear technology are artificial in a negative sense since they do not accept things in their givenness? In principle this argument can hardly be distinguished from the statement that if God had wanted us to fly he would have given us wings! Sensitivity to what is given should not preclude human creativity, not least because human creativity is itself given. In this sense we cannot define any human activity as simply an imposition upon being. There is a sense in which all human activity belongs to being, and so the natural/artificial distinction crumbles before us. This cul-de-sac exists because the terms in which human activity is understood places it in opposition to divine grace, or what is (naturally) given. The need to establish clarity of agency and responsibility encourages us to locate agency either with human beings or with God: either we are active and God is passive, or God is active and so we are passive. As orthodox theology, in particular neo-orthodoxy, has opposed finitude with transcendence, so human and divine agency have been seen as wholly discontinuous. Of course human beings can be inspired and enthused by God, but, in the final analysis, my will must always submit to Thy will. The ability of human beings to conceal their own value-structure from themselves, and to call their own will divinely inspired is perhaps too well known to recount here. Just as atheists have been keen to point out the tendency of human beings to project finite understandings on to a transcendent order, so theologians have understood the capacity of human beings to project human desires from the finite to the infinite realm, and have often warned against such idolatry. But, in fact, this danger exists *because* the divine and human agencies are not quite as discontinuous as some neo-orthodox theologies might argue. The danger of misperception of human desire is predicated upon the ability to act with and for God, to act on the basis of a more originary apprehension of God (Aquinas 2007: 92–112). There can, in this domain, be no absolute division, a lack which does not deny a relation of difference or deference, but only of absolute incongruity. Consequently, the religious subject remains in constant dialogue with the theological basis that motivates the specific form of religious life. From a Heideggerian point of view, this is significant because the distinction between the natural disclosure of being through the example of the mill only works to nourish a dialectical understanding of a necessarily informal distinction between the natural and the artificial. As we saw, the distinction seems vulnerable to attack: it may simply reflect our own prejudices about what pays heed to what is given in being—or by God—and what does not. It is important to note, as Teilhard does, that human creativity cannot be dismissed as aberrant, not even to the extent seen in Ellul. On the other hand, this does not simply affirm any and all human activities as reflecting the given capacities of the human spirit. And so perhaps we are called to adhere to a subtle (or vulnerable, fragile) faculty that might guide us in marking out the infinite line that describes human action in concert with divine action. Clearly this is no easy task, just as the unity of desire that defines an action that fulfils the will of God cannot be derived by a methodological approach. On the contrary, this kind of dialogical theology is a spiritual discipline that calls us to listen and attend to what is called for. But it is a theology, albeit dialogical, and as such it provides an approach of sorts to understanding—or at least, 'thinking about'—a distinction critical to the philosophy of technology, the distinction that concerns the actions of human beings that are appropriate and those that are not.

Theologians are right to point out that technological action encounters the same ultimate dilemmas that are faced by all kinds of individual and social action, and where a theological approach is relevant, then that dilemma seems best expressed by theologians who wonder how the agency of God and of the human agent can be related. On the other hand, philosophers of technology are correct to point out that the range of human action requires us to be particularly attentive. As Hans Jonas has said, the range of technological action has awakened us to an unprecedented imperative of responsibility (Jonas 1984: 1–24).

One must wonder, then, whether the approach that recognizes the fragility of our ultimate concern is adequate to take on the new context of the technological age. In other words, because our actions have such dramatic consequences, do we not need to be absolutely sure of the direction we are taking and the commitments we are making? Now more than ever do we not need to insure ourselves against the fragilities and contingencies of human nature?

While this continues to be the great temptation, it is also true that the more ultimate our concern, the more elusive it is. This is not a technical problem to be resolved by greater social resources, but is an essential element of human existence. It is only the technological age that demands we cipher all needs and hopes through the funnel of an entirely measurable, scalable, and secure plan of action.

The proper response to this aporia seems to come from the 'way of negation' characteristic of mystical theology. From Dionysius the Areopagite to Meister Eckhart, from St Augustine to St John of the Cross, the theological tradition suggests, time and again, that we come to know ourselves, and God, to the extent that we are able to accept that we 'know not what we do'. The disproportion between production and conception calls us ever more urgently towards a way of negation. But what is to be negated? Are we to abandon our technological environment? My suggestion has been, rather, that we adhere to the sense of our own finitude, that we recognize in the urgent demand to subdue the earth a failure to understand that we have already accomplished this act. As Tillich says, 'The words "subdue the earth" are fulfilled by technology' (Tillich 1988: 59), and yet the disproportion between conception and production widens. In the end we are called to recognize the fragility of the good, a recognition which makes an infinite demand upon us that we attend to what gives itself. This attention makes possible the proper synthesis between nature and culture, between technology and theology.

VIII. Conclusion

In this chapter we have recognized that a number of theologians have not been prepared to accept the secular narrative of technology, namely, that technology amounts to the neutral activity of human beings that we can safely leave to technicians and politicians. Theologians have sought to establish a proper relation between the development of technological means, and the *meaning* of human action. It is because theology addresses itself to what is ultimate, that it can be aware of its contingency, which, I argued, is a vital ingredient in understanding our relation to technology. A recognition of contingency is a presupposition of theology. But so also is an orientation to the future. In the final analysis, the extraordinary symbiosis between the hope implied in the work of theology, and the hope implicit in technical innovation locates technological action in the domain of the theological.

References

Achterhuis, Hans (ed.) (2001). *American Philosophy of Technology: The Empirical Turn*, trans. Robert Crease, *Indiana Series in the Philosophy of Technology*. (Bloomington, IN: Indiana University Press).

Aquinas, St Thomas (2007). *Summa Theologica Vol 1 of 10* (Hong Kong: Forgotten Books).

Bacon, Francis (1994). *Novum Organum*. (Chicago: Open Court).

Barbour, Ian (1969). 'Teilhard's Process Metaphysics', *The Journal of Religion* 49: 2, 136–59.

——(1998). *Religion and Science: Historical and Contemporary Issues*. (London: SCM Press).

Berdyaev, Nikolai (2006). *The Meaning of History*. (New Jersey: Transaction Publishers).

Blair, George (1984). 'Faith Outside Technique', in Carl Mitcham and Jim Grote (eds.), *Theology and Technology: Essays in Christian Analysis and Exegesis*. (Lanham, MD: University of America), 45–51.

Borgmann, Albert (1984). *Technology and the Character of Contemporary Life: A Philosophical Inquiry*. (Chicago: University of Chicago Press).

Brooke, John Hedley (1991). *Science and Religion: Some Historical Perspectives*. (Cambridge: Cambridge University Press).

Bultmann, Rudolf (1984). *New Testament and Mythology*, trans. S. Ogden (Philadephia: Fortress Press).

Christians, Clifford (2002). 'Religious Perspectives on Communications Technology', *Journal of Media and Religion* 1: 1, 37–47.

Davis, Bret W. (2007). *Heidegger and the Will: On the Way to Gelassenheit*. (Evanston, IL: Northwestern University Press).

De Lubac, Henri (1965). *The Faith of Teilhard de Chardin*. (London: Burnes and Oates).

DeLashmutt, Michael (2006). 'A Better Life Through Information Technology? The Techno-Theological Eschatology of Posthuman Speculative Science', *Zygon* 41: 2, 267–88.

——(2009). 'Religionless in Seattle', in Chris Deacy and Elisabeth Arwect (eds), *Exploring Religion and the Sacred in a Media Age*. (Farnham: Ashgate), 85–102.

Dessauer, Friedrich (1972). 'Technology and Its Proper Sphere', in Carl Mitcham and Robert Mackey (eds), *Philosophy and Technology*. (New York: Free Press).

Dreyfus, Hubert (2004). 'Nihilism on the Information Highway: Anonymity versus Commitment in the Present Age', in Andrew Feenberg and Darin Barney (eds), *Community and the Digital Age*. (Oxford: Rowman and Littlefield), 69–81.

Dupre, Louis (1993). *Passage to Modernity: An Essay in the Hermeneutics of Nature and Culture*. (New Haven, CT: Yale University Press).

Ellul, Jacques (1964). *The Technological Society*, trans. J. Wilkinson (London: Jonathan Cape).

——(1980). *The Technological System*, trans. J. Neugroschel (New York: Continuum).

——(1983). *Living Faith: Belief and Doubt in a Perilous World*, trans. P. Heinegg (New York: Harper and Row), 1983.

——(1990). *The Technological Bluff*, trans. G. W. Bromiley (Grand Rapids, MI: Eerdmans).

Feenberg, Andrew (1999). *Questioning Technology*. (New York; London: Routledge).

Florman, Samuel (1994). *The Existential Pleasures of Engineering*, 2nd edn. (New York: St Martin's Griffin).

Fudpucker, Wilhelm (1984). 'Through Christian Technology to Technological Christianity', in Carl Mitcham and Jim Grote (eds), *Theology and Technology: Essays in Christian Analysis and Exegesis*. (Lanham, MD: University Press of America), 317–34.

Guardini, Romano (1994). *Letters from Lake Como: Explorations in Technology and the Human Race*, trans. G. W. Bromiley (Grand Rapids, MI: Eerdmans).

Hefner, Philip (2003). *Technology and Human Becoming*. (Minneapolis: Fortress Press).

Heidegger, Martin, (1966). *Discourse on Thinking: A Translation of Gelassenheit*, trans. John M. Anderson and E. Hans Freund (New York and London: Harper & Row).

——(1977). *The Question Concerning Technology*, trans. W. Lovitt (New York: Harper and Row).

——(1996). *The Principle of Reason*, trans. R. Lilly (Bloomington, IN: Indiana. University Press).

Higgs, Eric, Light, Andrew, and Strong, David (eds) (2000). *Technology and the Good Life?* (Chicago and London: University of Chicago Press).

Janicaud, Dominique (ed.) (2000). *Phenomenology and the Theological Turn: The French Debate*. (New York: Fordham University Press).

Jonas, Hans (1984). *The Imperative of Responsibility: In Search of an Ethics for the Technological Age*, trans. Hans Jonas and David Herr (Chicago and London: University of Chicago Press).

Kass, Leon (1997). 'The Wisdom of Repugnance: Why We Should Ban the Cloning of Humans', *The New Republic* 216: 22, 17–26.

Kurzweil, Ray (1999). *The Age of Spiritual Machines*. (Cambridge, MA: MIT Press).

——and Terry Grossman (2004). *The Fantastic Voyage: Live Long Enough to Live Forever*. (New York: Rodale).

Lewin, David (2011). *Technology and the Philosophy of Religion*. (Newcastle upon Tyne: Cambridge Scholars Publishing).

Mander, Jerry (1991). *In the Absence of the Sacred: The Failure of Technology and the Survival of the Indian Nations.* (San Francisco: Sierra Club Books).

Marcuse, Herbert (1991). *One-Dimensional Man: Studies in the Ideology of Advanced Industrial Society.* (London: Routledge).

Marion, Jean-Luc (2002). *Being Given: Towards a Phenomenology of Givenness.* (Stanford, CA: Stanford University Press).

Midgley, Mary (2000). 'Biotechnology and Monstrosity: Why We Should Pay Attention to the "Yuk Factor" ', *Hastings Center Report 30.*

Milbank, John (1990). *Theology and Social Theory: Beyond Secular Reason.* (Oxford: Blackwell).

Mitcham, Carl (1996). *Thinking Through Technology: The Path between Engineering and Philosophy.* (Chicago: University of Chicago Press).

——and Mackey, Robert (eds) (1973). *Bibliography of the Philosophy of Technology.* (Chicago: University of Chicago Press).

——(1983). *Philosophy and Technology: Readings in the Philosophical Problems of Technology.* (New York: Collier Macmillan).

Mitcham, Carl and Grote, Jim (eds) (1984). *Theology and Technology: Essays in Christian Analysis and Exegesis.* (Lanham, MD: University Press of America).

Moltmann, Jürgen (1967). *The Theology of Hope.* (London: SCM Press).

Moravec, Hans (1988). *Mind Children: The Future of Robot and Human Intelligence.* (London: Harvard University Press).

Mumford, Lewis (1940). *Technics and Civilisation.* (New York: Harcourt, Brace and Co).

Nordmann, Alfred (2005). 'Noumenal Technology: Reflections on the Incredible Tininess of Nano', *Techné: Research in Philosophy and Technology* 8: 3, 3–23.

Otto, Rudolf (1950). *The Idea of the Holy.* (Oxford: Oxford University Press).

Pannenberg, Wolfhart (1996). *Systematic Theology: Vol. 2*, trans. Geoffrey Bromiley (Grand Rapids, MI: Eerdmans).

Pattison, George (2005). *Thinking About God in an Age of Technology.* (Oxford: Oxford University Press).

Pieper, Josef (1999). *The End of Time.* (San Francisco: Ignatius Press).

Ricoeur, Paul (1965). *History and Truth.* (Evanston, IL: Northwestern University Press).

Schleiermacher, Friedrich (1976). *The Christian Faith*, trans. H. R. MacKintosh and J. S. Stewart (Philadelphia: Fortress Press).

Shafer, Ingrid (2002). 'From Noosphere to Theosphere: Cyclotrons, Cyberspace and Teilhard's Vision of Cosmic Love', *Zygon* 37: 4, 825–52.

Stiegler, Bernard (1998). *Technics and Time, vol. 1: The Fault of Epimetheus*, trans. George Collins and Richard Beardsworth (Stanford, CA: Stanford University Press).

Szerszynski, Bronislaw (2005). *Nature, Technology, and the Sacred.* (Malden, MA, and Oxford: Blackwells).

Teilhard de Chardin, Pierre (1964). *The Future of Man*, trans. Norman George Denny (London: Collins).

——(1969). *Human Energy.* (New York: Harcourt Brace Jovanovich).

——(1975). *Towards the Future.* (London: Collins).

Thomas, Gordon, and Max Morgan-Witts (1978). *Ruin from the Air: The Atomic Mission to Hiroshima.* (London: Sphere).

Thomson, Iain (2005). *Heidegger on Ontotheology: Technology and the Politics of Education.* (Cambridge: Cambridge University Press).

Tillich, Paul (1951). *Systematic Theology, Vol. I.* (Chicago: University of Chicago Press).
—— (1988). *The Spiritual Situation in Our Technical Society*, ed. J. Mark Thomas (Macon, GA: Mercer University Press).
Weber, Max (2003). *The Protestant Ethic and the Spirit of Capitalism*, trans. Talcott Parsons (New York: Dover Publications).
White, Lynn Townsend (1964). *Medieval Technology and Social Change.* (London: Oxford University Press).
Wrathall, Mark A. (ed.) (2003). *Religion after Metaphysics.* (Cambridge: Cambridge University Press).

Suggested Reading

Arendt, Hannah (2003). 'The "Vita Activa" and the Modern Age', in Robert Scharff and Val Dusek (eds), *Philosophy of Technology: The Technological Condition: An Anthology.* (Oxford: Blackwell), 352–68.
Borgmann, Albert (2003). *Power Failure: Christianity in the Culture of Technology.* (Grand Rapids, MI: Brazos Press).
Feenberg (1999).
Guardini (1994).
Hefner (2003).
Heidegger (1977).
Kroker, Arthur (2004). *The Will to Technology and the Culture of Nihilism: Heidegger, Nietzsche and Marx.* (Toronto: University of Toronto Press).
Pattison (2005).
Stiegler (1998).
Szerszynski (2005).
Tillich (1988).
Ward, Graham (ed.) (1997). 'Introduction, or, A Guide to Theological Thinking in Cyberspace', *The Postmodern God: A Theological Reader.* (Oxford: Blackwell), pp. xv–xlvii.

PART V

WAYS OF KNOWING

CHAPTER 23

···

WISSENSCHAFT

···

JOHANNES ZACHHUBER

OVER the past two hundred years, few theological issues have been debated with as much academic and, more than occasionally ideological, fervour as the status of theology as science or *Wissenschaft*. Advocates of this epithet have sometimes treated it as a modern day shibboleth whose enunciation alone would grant theologians, and their work, admission into intellectually respectable places of learning (Harnack in Rumscheidt 1989: 91). This attitude, unsurprisingly perhaps, has then provoked the opposite view, according to which modern ideas of *Wissenschaft* are fundamentally incompatible with theology and their adoption, consequently, a grave danger to the proper pursuit of the discipline (Vilmar 1874: 38). I shall argue here, however, that a closer look at some of the most formative debates suggests a more nuanced picture. The topic may be best described as an overlap of two very different problems. The first is the justification of modern theology as a critical discourse whose parameters are not automatically set by Church doctrine or tradition. The second is the need to classify theology within an overall system of knowledge institutionalized in the university. While the former originated in seventeenth-century England and Holland, the latter is an inheritance from the high Middle Ages. Both inform nineteenth- and twentieth-century debates about theology as *Wissenschaft*, but whereas the more spectacular issues and controversies are products of modern criticism, the underlying questions are often better explained by reference to its institutional context. In the following, I shall therefore start from some considerations seeking to clarify the precise scope of the problem and its emergence (I). Their results will serve as a template for the exposition and evaluation of the two major conceptions of *Wissenschaft* developed in the former half of the nineteenth century and discuss their impact on theology (II, III). In a final part, I offer some reflections about their legacy today (IV).

I. A SCIENCE OF THEOLOGY?

It is often said, in the words of Anselm of Canterbury, that theology is 'faith seeking understanding' (Anselm of Canterbury 1998: 87). From its origins Christianity has consistently acknowledged the need to engage in rational reflection about its beliefs and practices, the interpretation of its scriptures, its forms of organization and governance, events in its history, and its relation to rival accounts of reality. Beyond this very general and inevitably vague sketch of what would constitute such a rational discourse, or what it should cover, however, very little has ever enjoyed universal consensus. Do all these diverse problems provide the material for a single discipline? How should investigation and debate about them be conducted? Where do its insights originate? What are the sources and what are the criteria to distinguish right from wrong, the appropriate from the less appropriate, in this process of reflection? Is there, or should there be, a final arbiter on issues arising within this reflective enterprise and, if so, by virtue of what competence would this person or group of persons make their decisions binding?

None of these questions allows for a straightforward answer, and all of them have provoked strikingly divergent replies over the centuries. It is, for example, easy to forget that the name theology itself as a disciplinary term came to prominence only in the western Middle Ages (Pannenberg 1973: 11–12). While it is a matter of convenience for us to refer to Patristic thought as 'theology', one must keep in mind that the Fathers would never have dreamt of describing the distinction between their own pursuit and that of Platonists or Stoics in terms of 'sciences' or 'disciplines'. The thirteenth-century settlement of theology as the 'queen of sciences' and of philosophy as its 'handmaiden', which so easily appears to us as the classical backdrop to more recent controversies, would have seemed counter-intuitive to Origen or Augustine. Things began to change from about the sixth century with the development of what might be called early scholasticism, which saw more systematic use of elementary philosophical texts by Christian authors (Grabmann 1909–11: vol. 1, 92–116), but the emergence of the idea of theology as a separate area of study, as one kind of *scientia* next to others, follows both intellectually and institutionally the establishment of the medieval university (Geyer 1964: 143).

The latter observation is no coincidence. Theological reflection always happens within an institutional context of which the university is only one and, historically speaking, not necessarily the most enduring nor the most prominent one. Yet extended and sustained reflection about the place of theology within a broader system of learning and knowledge has hardly ever taken place outside of this particular environment. This is true for the Middle Ages (Köpf 1974) as much as it is for the nineteenth and twentieth centuries, where the *locus* of debates about theology as *Wissenschaft* is the modern (and originally German) university (Howard 2006).

This latter debate, which stands at the centre of the present chapter, has inevitably been informed and shaped by issues arising from the specifically modern transformation of Christian theology: the rise of biblical criticism, Kantian and post-Kantian philosophy and history of dogma to name but a few. Yet while the two sets of problems overlap, they are by no means coextensive. On the contrary, for rather obvious reasons modern theology was originally spearheaded by individuals without institutional dependence on either the Church or the university, such as Toland, Spinoza, or Reimarus. For none of these authors, however, was the problem of whether or in what sense theology was a science or *Wissenschaft* paramount. It became an issue precisely with thinkers whose activity was directly related to the organization of theology within the academy. This is true for Friedrich Schleiermacher, whose reflections on the topic result directly from his involvement in the foundation of the University of Berlin in 1812, but also for John Henry Newman who lectured on *The Idea of a University* as rector of the newly established Catholic University at Dublin in the 1850s, and even for Wolfhart Pannenberg's extended reflections on *Theology and the Philosophy of Science* (a rather misleading rendering of *Wissenschaftstheorie und Theologie*), which were written at the height of institutional controversies about the German university in the early 1970s.

Why is the university context crucial? Part of the answer surely relates to the pedagogical dimension of theology. The aggregate of Christian teaching and learning needs to be passed on from generation to generation, and the university has always been primarily a place to facilitate such intergenerational transmission of knowledge through teaching and study. In order for this to succeed, however, questions concerning the delimitation and organization of the material as well as its rhetorical and didactic presentation become paramount. Within theology, one may identify here a second-order discourse whose primary subject is no longer the actual content of the doctrine of faith, but its structure, the relationships between individual theories or dogmas, and the method of their investigation.

Theology has been taught and studied, however, in places other than the university and a didactic concern is not, therefore, limited to this particular environment. Thus, while the tendency to organize doctrinal, ethical, and practical elements of the Christian tradition into a coherent whole was in many ways driven by the requirements of catechesis and, by extension, by the need to train those who are to catechize, this in itself does not yet engender the question of theology's status as a science. The latter only arises from an attempt to situate theology within the totality of human knowledge, and this precisely is necessitated by its integration into an institution that aims to embrace and cultivate human learning in its entirety. As its very name suggests, this is what the university has, since its inception, intended to achieve. The question, then, whether theology is *scientia*, science, or *Wissenschaft*, while ultimately striving to give something like a self-definition of theology as an intellectual enterprise, has had, historically, its primary purpose in the need to justify and explain the logic of its inclusion, as a discipline, within this very institution.

The precise idea of the university, and the understanding of science, of knowledge and of theology have, of course, changed dramatically over the centuries. Yet it is instructive to note that the question of whether theology is *scientia* was by no means rhetorical when it was first raised in the thirteenth century (Köpf 1974: 125–54); in fact, the caveats and reservations expressed by those who discussed it back then in many ways anticipate later controversies and may thus indicate problems transcending the specific parameters of *Wissenschaft* as conducted within the modern academy. Without going into the details of the medieval debate, it may be useful to summarize some key problems as a heuristic starting point to the more detailed analysis of the modern discussion. It will turn out that all the fundamental problems recur; modern theories, which will be discussed in the remainder of the text, can be understood as seeking to address one or more of them within their specific historical and intellectual environment.

First, how can a field of study be a science if it relies for its premises or principles on revelation? According to Aristotle, demonstration is only possible from principles that can either be demonstrated or are self-evidently known (Aristotle 1964: 115 [71^b 19–25]). While we can make deductions from information we gain from others, those will never be known by us with certainty. Aquinas argued such knowledge was possible as long as the principles were known to God and to the saints and accepted as revelation by everyone else (Thomas Aquinas 1926: 15 [q. 1, art. 2, resp.]), but William of Ockham strongly disagreed:

> It is absurd to claim that *I* have scientific knowledge with respect to this or that conclusion by reason of the fact that *you* know principles which I accept on faith because you tell them to me. And, in the same way, it is silly to claim that *I* have scientific knowledge of the conclusions of theology by reason of the fact that *God* knows principles which I accept on faith because he reveals them.   (William of Ockham 1967: 199; Eng. trans. Freddoso 2000: 334)

This problem lingers in the modern debate primarily in a historicist transformation, famously formulated by Lessing: 'accidental truths of history can never become the proof of necessary truths of reason' (Lessing 1956: 53).

Second, how do the various parts of theology form a unity? The problem is illustrated by the ambiguous use of the term theology itself, which is sometimes employed more narrowly for the speculative reflection about Christian doctrine, but in the academic context usually denotes the ensemble of exegetical, historical, doctrinal, and practical disciplines. What unites them, and how are they in this form distinct from, and yet analogous to, subjects like philosophy, history, physics, or linguistics? In the German tradition, this problem is usually referred to as 'theological encyclopaedia', and its treatment is closely related to the discussion about theology as *Wissenschaft*.

Third, what methodologies ought to be used in its pursuit and what criteria are acceptable in adjudicating conflicting judgements? As will be seen, from the middle of the nineteenth century, conceptions of science or *Wissenschaft* increasingly emphasize its procedural aspect thus bringing this particular problem to prominence. Frequently now, the question of theology's character as *Wissenschaft* is all but identified with its willingness to succumb to rational enquiry and a readiness to accept whichever conclusion is best supported by argument. At the same time, of course, rationality itself was increasingly subject to critical questioning, and this debate too has had its impact on theology.

Fourth, how precisely is theology related to Christian faith and practice? Is faith merely a motivating factor for intellectual interest in theological enquiry or does it, in its own specific structure, influence the actual operation and practice of theology? If the former, theology can easily appear indifferent or even implicitly hostile to faith; in fact, the most impressive academic and public prestige of certain theologians has, not only in modernity, often provoked the most sustained criticism from within the Church. Yet if theology is in any more specific way beholden to its basis in Christian faith, this might appear in tension with, or even in contradiction to, the detached and impartial attitude required of the 'scientist' with regard to their object of study.

II. Friedrich Schleiermacher's Concept of Theology as 'Positive Science'

None of these questions is new to modernity, but it is, nevertheless, the case that developments from the late eighteenth century created conditions provoking new answers to most or all of them. These changing conditions can be described in various ways; they are related to all the fundamental transformations happening in European societies during those decades. As far as theology's academic status is concerned, however, debates about university reform are crucial.

At the end of the eighteenth century, the university was considered by many as one of those institutions founded in the Middle Ages that had outlived their sell-by date (Howard 2006: 1–4). Few if any of the major intellectual and scientific advances of the Age of the Enlightenment originated in universities, and it seemed only consequent that modernizing regimes, such as those installed subsequent to the French Revolution, would seek to promote higher education through different institutions. The initiative by leading Prussian intellectuals to found a new university in Berlin, following their country's military defeat against Napoleon in 1806, happened in the teeth of this development and is, for this reason, often regarded as a watershed in the history of the western university. Remarkably, this political initiative called forth significant contributions from some of the most distinguished public intellectuals of the age, weighing in on the idea and the purpose of such an institution (Crouter 2005: 142–50; Howard 2006: 130–211).

The memoranda, written in the main by Johann Gottlieb Fichte, Wilhelm von Humboldt, Friedrich Wilhelm Joseph Schelling, and Friedrich Schleiermacher, sought to address the structure of the university, its appropriate educational ethos, and its overall place within the polity. They all share certain premisses, the first of which is that *Wissenschaft* in the true sense is philosophy. This, of course, had been Aristotle's position, and it is indeed remarkable how traditional in this regard all these reformers are. Philosophy is the science's science, the discipline whose task it is to organize knowledge and this property predisposes it to its place at the heart of an institution aiming to embrace knowledge in its entirety. Philosophy contains within itself the principles both of science's diversity and of its unity; it explains and justifies which disciplines are needed systematically to cover any potential aspect of human knowledge and learning. This notion of science, or *Wissenschaft*, combines the Aristotelian tradition of philosophy as the systematic organization of knowledge with more Romantic ideas of an organic unity-in-multiplicity. Yet while all participants in this debate more or less agreed on this foundation, the consequences they drew from it for the actual constitution of the ideal university differed considerably. For the present purpose, it is most instructive to contrast Johann Gottlieb Fichte's and Friedrich Schleiermacher's positions. Both have something to say about the place of theology within the university, but it is important to perceive this as part of broader attempts to define this institution as a place for *Wissenschaft*.

Fichte's approach, in line with his overall philosophy, is starkly deductive (Anrich 1956: 150–1). It is also, in practical terms, the most innovative, even revolutionary in character as it suggests disposing of three of the four traditional faculties (Law, Medicine, Theology) whose need had not arisen from systematic reflections but from the state's practical need to train lawyers, doctors, and priests. Fichte is willing to recognize this kind of practical concern, but suggests it ought to happen outside the university, in institutions cultivating subject-specific combinations of theoretical and practical principles—not unlike, one might say, divinity, medical, and law schools in today's American system (Anrich 1956: 155). By contrast, the university was to be the place founded on pure principles of theoretical knowledge and therefore in its entirety, so to speak, philosophical.

It is well known that Fichte saw no place for theology in his university; it is less well known that he gives two very different reasons for this exclusion. The first is that theology, or at least traditional theology, makes use of insights and principles that are not generally shared knowledge. This, Fichte argues, was incompatible with a public institution of universal learning (Anrich 1956: 154–5). In the vein of Kant's argument in *The Conflict of Faculties*, Fichte demands of theology that it open itself up to critical enquiry if it wishes to retain a place within academic debate. It is easy to perceive behind this line of thought a typically modern rejection of the supernatural following in the wake of Kant's demolition of philosophical theology. Yet while it is true that Fichte's concept of reason owes much to the philosophical development that flows from Descartes to Kant, the historical antecedents of his argument go back to the medieval controversy, mentioned above, concerning theology's ability to justify its insights as knowledge (*scientia*) on the basis of Aristotle's notion of science.

Yet even without any reference to authoritative revelation, theology could not have a place in Fichte's university. This is because, much like law and medicine, it does not constitute its own field of enquiry; that it exists as a discipline in the traditional university is on account of practical needs, not systematic reflection. As far as the latter is concerned, it would appear that, according to Fichte, what theologians study—to the extent that it deserves the name of *Wissenschaft*—would fall under either metaphysics (where it is about the existence and the nature of God), ethics, history, or languages. In particular, he accepts that Old Testament studies make important contributions to oriental studies, but by the same token they would be better off if regrouped within a department studying the languages and the culture of the Ancient Near East (Anrich 1956: 161–2).

To get a sense of the force of Fichte's argument, it may be useful to compare it to John Henry Newman's justification of theology within his university. Such a comparison is instructive because both thinkers argue in some ways very similarly. Both deduce the idea of a university from the principle of universal knowledge (Newman 1996: 3). Yet Newman, unlike Fichte, maintains that, on this basis, theology must be part of such a university because without it, knowledge would not be complete (Newman 1996: 25). Nowhere in his celebrated essay, however, is he on shakier ground than where he tries to give examples of what the subject matter is that only the theologian can work on. Thus he cites the example of the historian Henry Hart Milman who in 1829 caused a scandal at Oxford by writing a *History of the Jews* from a secular perspective. Newman's comment is this:

> I must conclude that he was betrayed into a false step by the treacherous fascination of what is called the Philosophy of History, which is good in its place, but can scarcely be applied in cases where the Almighty has superseded the natural laws of society and history.   (Newman 1996: 67)

Yet from Newman's own (or indeed from Aristotle's) principles it is unclear how a division into secular and sacred history could obtain within a 'scientific' context thus illustrating, against his apparent intentions, precisely the difficulty entailed by any attempt to claim for theology its own separate field of investigation.

Unlike Newman, Schleiermacher does not dispute Fichte's argument that theology cannot lay claim to its own systematic niche within the totality of human knowledge. His justification of its presence in the university, consequently, proceeds in a rather different way. In order to appreciate it, his understanding of *Wissenschaft* must be considered. It would be mistaken to see the latter only as a proxy for the establishment of the right of theology within the university. Rather, Schleiermacher's opposition to Fichte's view of *Wissenschaft* is deeply rooted in his own philosophical concept of knowledge and communication, which he developed extensively in his lectures on *Dialectics* and on *Paedagogik* (Crouter 2005: 150).

Occasional Thoughts on Universities in the German Sense is the treatise Schleiermacher wrote specifically as part of the intellectual debate surrounding the foundation of the University of Berlin. He starts by observing in good Aristotelian fashion that *Wissenschaft* is something human beings desire (Anrich 1956: 223). This goal, however, cannot be achieved by even the most gifted individual, but needs the collaboration of many. *Wissenschaft* is not therefore an individual but a social pursuit, more specifically it is the pursuit of the group united by a common language, the nation (Anrich 1956: 225–6). This makes it similar to the state, but while the latter in order to act must be able to subjugate individual wills, *Wissenschaft* can thrive only under the condition of freedom. There is therefore reason for the state to support *Wissenschaft*, but equally, for both sides to mind their respective differences (Anrich 1956: 228–32).

Since *Wissenschaft* needs to be both taught and practiced, it is cultivated in several different institutions: schools have the primary purpose of educating and forming young people; academies on the other hand exist as the republic of letters seeking to unite those who are masters of their fields (Anrich 1956: 233). Characteristically, the university for Schleiermacher is a third in between these two; it must exist due to the dynamic nature of the system: *Wissenschaft*, in order to be advanced by the leading lights in their respective disciplines, needs to be initiated, and this has to happen in a place dedicated to its principles. The purpose of the university, then, is to impart to young people the very idea of *Wissenschaft*, the notion of the unity of knowledge in all its diversity (Anrich 1956: 237–41).

Politically, Schleiermacher's argument is evidently pitched against the contemporary French model, which had discarded the university in favour of a dual system of schools and academies (Howards 2006: 2). His conception of the university as primarily responsible for the *idea* of *Wissenschaft* means that, as in Fichte's plan, philosophy is at its heart (Anrich 1956: 258–9). More to the point, however, Schleiermacher's concept of philosophy, and thus his idea of *Wissenschaft*, is different from Fichte's in that he sees it as always embedded in the cultural contexts from which such practice emerges. The centre of his philosophy is ethics, but ethics as understood as a system of goods (Schleiermacher 1992). It is for this reason that he can defend the traditional structure of the university: theology, law, and medicine all benefit from regular exchange with philosophy, but philosophy itself would be incomplete without those extensions. Not in the sense that theology ultimately is philosophy of religion—if anything, Schleiermacher tends to the opposite view—but because philosophical reflection cannot ever be conducted in abstraction from the concrete realities of nature and culture. Schleiermacher is deeply sceptical about the ability of the human mind to construct a system of thought capable of explaining reality in its fullness—hence his opposition to Fichte and Hegel and his advocacy of a dialogical epistemology as first philosophy. Knowledge and hence *Wissenschaft* are fundamentally dependent on communication and exchange; they are always perfectible and never complete.

It is this open system of *Wissenschaft* that facilitates theology's inclusion in the university. Schleiermacher does not claim that theology is an indispensable part of a system of knowledge, as both Fichte and Newman do, nor accept for theology any narrow definition of science as normative. In fact, his argument for the retention of the traditional 'higher faculties' is remarkably conservative: this particular structure has emerged 'naturally' (Anrich 1956: 257) and for this reason continued for such a long period of time. The Faculty of Theology, in particular, was founded by the Church

> . . . in order to preserve the wisdom of the Fathers; not to lose for the future what in the past had been achieved in discerning truth from error; to give a historical basis,

a sure and certain direction and a common spirit to the further development of doctrine and Church.   (Anrich 1956: 258)

In other words, theology exists because the Church needs clarity about its doctrines and practices, and such clarity is achieved by permitting these issues to be openly debated in permanent exchange with all other areas of human knowledge. Theology is taught in the university because the public has an interest that this is done well and that church ministers are appropriately trained in the same way that it wants doctors with a good medical education and judges with a proper understanding of the law. This is what Schleiermacher calls 'positive science' (*positive Wissenschaft*), a discipline that is not constituted by systematic deduction from the idea of knowledge, but by a practical requirement. Yet it is not a trade, since a solid and permanent exchange with *Wissenschaft* proper, that is, with philosophy, is vital for its proper exercise. A professor of law or of theology therefore, according to Schleiermacher, who does not make an effort to contribute actively to philosophy—in the wide sense in which it includes not only metaphysics and ethics but also philology and history—deserves to be ridiculed, even excluded from the university (Anrich 1956: 261). This does not mean that all theologians have to be polymaths, but that students of theology must be allowed to expect from their teachers the ability and the willingness to traverse the distance between their theological area of expertise and related philosophical fields: the moral theologian must be conversant in ethics, the New Testament scholar in classics, the Systematic Theologian in logic and metaphysics and so forth.

It is this same conception that underlies Schleiermacher's *Brief Outline of the Study of Theology* (Schleiermacher 1850). If this writing has less to say about the relationship of theology to other academic disciplines and is instead focused more on the inner structure of the discipline, this does not reduce its relevance for the problem of theology as *Wissenschaft*. Already in Aquinas the question of whether theology is *scientia* is immediately followed by the question whether it is *one* science, and Fichte, as has been seen, rejects theology from the university largely because he denies its internal coherence. Schleiermacher's own line of argument is that as a 'positive science', theology derives its unity not from its place within a system of *Wissenschaft*, but from the practical need of the Church to have appropriately trained leaders (Schleiermacher 1850: 93, § 5). Schleiermacher in fact acknowledges the force of Fichte's argument where he concedes that theology without its practical purpose of Church government would disintegrate (Schleiermacher 1850: 93).

It is this purpose, then, that serves as the organizing centre of theology as *Wissenschaft* for Schleiermacher, and philosophical and historical parts of the discipline are instrumental to this ultimate goal. What exactly does this mean for theology as *Wissenschaft*? It may be useful at this point to come back to the four questions that were earlier shown to be at the heart of the debate about theology as science. Looking at Schleiermacher's concept against this background yields interesting results.

First, like Thomas Aquinas, Schleiermacher accepts that theology is based on principles that are not themselves part of science. For Aquinas, these principles had been revealed and passed down to us through the authority of the teaching magister-ium of the Church; the theologian thus relies on somebody else's knowledge for his work. Schleiermacher does not appeal to supernatural facts, but in his theory too the theologian is dependent for his work on something external to scientific rationality, the existence of the Church as a historical and social reality. One might say that in practice the difference between the two is small; after all, revelation is always (or almost always) accessible only as historical information whether contained in biblical texts or in authoritative writings of the ecclesiastical tradition. Yet it seems clear that, nevertheless, something fundamental is at stake here, which may be called the historicization of religion. In *The Christian Faith* Schleiermacher argues that utter novelty of a historical movement, which cannot be deduced from previous events, is the only reasonable meaning the word 'revelation' could possibly have (Schleiermacher 1999: 50). It is precisely this inscrutable reality of Christianity as a historical and social formation (which Schleiermacher calls the Church) that provides an extra-philosophical focal point of reference for theology in Schleiermacher's theory.

It is then evident, second, that this same historical and social reality of Christianity is also the principle that unites the various philosophical, historical, and practical fields pertaining to it. This, precisely, was Schleiermacher's argument in the *Brief Outline*.

As for methodology, thirdly, this is where Schleiermacher's concept is perhaps most evidently *wissenschaftlich*. All theological work must not only be conducted in ways that can stand up to the highest standards of academic enquiry, they must also be constantly aware of possible cross-references and interferences between their theo-logical and related non-theological work. This sounds innocent enough, but one wonders whether Schleiermacher was aware of the enormous ramifications this principle could and would cause for theological work. Did he realize that application of those methods was most likely to yield results different from, if not in outright contradiction to, traditional Christian views? It appears that he thought (much like his idealist contemporaries) that historicism could be contained by proper philosophical reflection, and while he himself, more than Hegel, engaged in exegetical and historical work, its results soon became the butt of ridicule because of their lack of critical edge. Decades later, commenting on Schleiermacher's lectures on the life of Jesus, Albert Schweitzer comes to a similarly devastating conclusion: 'Nowhere indeed is it more clear that the great dialectician had not really a historical mind than precisely in his treatment of the history of Jesus' (Schweitzer 1910: 62).

What, finally, about the relationship between theology and faith? Schleiermacher draws a clear distinction between religion and theology. The former is a fundamental dimension of human nature, the latter a second-order discourse about it. Thus theology as *Wissenschaft* would seem to be primarily a historical and philosophical interpret-ation of the faith that exists within the Christian community at a given time together with its historical emergence. Schleiermacher's references to Church governance in the *Short Outline*, however, indicate that its task is not merely descriptive. Theology can and indeed has to be critical, separating what is 'healthy' within the body of the Church from heretical or schismatic aberrations (Schleiermacher 1850: 105). Even so, it is needed by the few who have responsibility for shepherding the flock, not by the individual believer. While Schleiermacher chose Anselm's motto *credo ut intelligam* to adorn the title page of *The Christian Faith*, his view clearly was that individual faith, or religion, does not need theological reflection, but only its social and historical manifestation as an increasingly extended group (Schleiermacher 1850: 91–2).

Schleiermacher's view of theology as *Wissenschaft* combines a concept of science as philosophy whose Aristotelian pedigree is still clearly recognizable with a moderately historicist perception of religion. By opting for an open philosophy of *Wissenschaft* that situates the university within the context of a society's cultivation of learning, he creates a space for theology without either forcing it into the straightjacket of a deductive system of universal knowledge or assigning to it a place merely in the domain of private opinion. Accepting theology's function for the Church as its organizing principle, he offers a powerful model for its disciplinary unity. Yet he seems in an odd way unconcerned about the consequences of accepting *wissenschaftlich* methodology for theological work; occasionally he seems to hint that the ecclesiastical pole would serve to mitigate potentially critical conclusions, for example about the canon (Schleiermacher 1850: 146), but overall he seems to have underestimated the enduring force of historicism in the undoing of all traditional belief claims.

III. Theology as the Science of Religion

Schleiermacher may have classified theology as 'positive science'; he certainly never used *wissenschaftlich* as an epithet for a particular kind or type of theology. *Wissenschaft* is not, for him, a polemical term to be employed against theological opponents; it does not designate a school. Among the younger members of the Tübingen School, however, such use becomes currency from the late 1830s. Writing in the editorial of the newly established *Theologische Jahrbücher*, F. C. Baur's son in law, Eduard Zeller, states in 1841 that this journal 'starts from the idea of free *Wissenschaft*'. The primary imperative of the yearbook, he continues, is 'to accept freedom and consistency of thought as necessary and justified even within theology' (Zeller 1842: p. v).

Zeller's language strikes a note that is very different from anything to be found in Schleiermacher. Yet it would be mistaken to find the difference only in the more animated temper of public debates shaping up for the storms of 1848. Zeller and his colleagues argue on the basis of a new understanding of *Wissenschaft*, which at that time was about to take over as the dominant model heavily informing all public perceptions and expectations of academic work. This development happened largely outside theology; it also seems to have taken hold, at least initially, without great fanfare simply by being accepted by an increasing number of academic specialists. The philosopher Adolf Trendelenburg observes in 1840 that 'the sciences (*Wissenschaften*) happily try out their own particular ways but often without reflection about their method, as they are interested in their object, not in their procedures' (Trendelenburg

1840: vol. 1, p. vi). He thinks this is the fault of philosophers like Hegel, who neglected empirical work and induction, and he attempts to remedy the situation by offering, in his *Logical Investigations*, a more suitable philosophy of science. Yet crucially, his own attempt follows after the event and thus recognizes, at least implicitly, that successful historians, linguists, or scientists no longer wait for the philosopher to take the lead, but proceed self-confidently with their own research. This is a far cry from the situation at the beginning of the century, when Fichte, Schelling, Humboldt, and Schleiermacher, in spite of their disagreements, took for granted the identity of philosophy and *Wissenschaft*. A quarter of a century later, all that remains for Trendelenburg and others is to take note of an emerging consensus about the practice of *Wissenschaft* across various disciplines.

Due to the intellectual clamour surrounding the foundation of the University of Berlin, this date is often associated with the shift to modern notions of *Wissenschaft*, but, as has been seen, the conceptions proffered by the protagonists of that debate were not revolutionary. The revolution happened more silently: by 1840 it was clear that *Wissenschaft* was in practice no longer defined with reference to the universality of knowledge, but to the formal rules of a particular procedure. This makes *Wissenschaft* dynamic and open, geared towards progressive discovery of new knowledge, which however can never be more than provisional. It rules out, on the other hand, any firm adherence to philosophical or religious principles; in fact, any predisposition of the individual academic is considered at best indifferent and, more often than not, problematic with regard to the scientific goal. In this transformation, *Wissenschaft*, in the words of Herbert Schnädelbach,

> ... was constituted as research-science, that is, as empirical science .... It became an open and changeable system of knowledge, indeed one committed to change, in which systematization was subordinated to the ideal of innovation. It was a totality, the identity of which came principally from rules of procedure and standards of testing .... (Schnädelbach 1984: 91)

It is easy to see that Zeller's emphatic affirmation of theology as *Wissenschaft*, committed to research that is free and unconstrained by political and religious preconceptions, corresponds to this new idea. Yet he was by no means the first to espouse this as an ideal. If it is the case that the broader transformation of the notion of *Wissenschaft* during this time happened silently and gradually, the situation in theology was very different indeed as the normative claim of the new ideal was enunciated with the loudest and shrillest fanfare possible in the one book which captured, and divided, public attention as few others had done before or after, David Friedrich Strauss's *Life of Jesus*. In the preface to the first edition of 1835, the author, who had just turned 27, concedes that there may have been others more qualified to write a book like this in terms of their erudition. He goes on, however, to defend his undertaking with the following argument:

> The majority of the most learned and acute theologians of the present day fail in the main requirement for such a work, a requirement without which no amount of learning will suffice to achieve anything in the domain of criticism, namely, the

internal liberation of the feelings and intellect from certain religious and dogmatical presuppositions; and this the author early attained by means of philosophical studies. If theologians regard this absence of presupposition from his work, as unchristian: he regards the believing presuppositions of theirs as unscientific. (Strauss 1860: 4)

It is likely that this passage offers the first use ever of the term *Voraussetzungslosigkeit* ('absence of presuppositions') in the context of modern debates about *Wissenschaft*. In any case, it is evident how Strauss with his notorious gift for polarization sets up a contrast between the old-fashioned, albeit erudite, theologian and himself as a representative of a modern, scientific mindset. This intention to provoke, to indicate irreconcilable differences between the old and the new is even more marked in his *Glaubenslehre*, published in 1840–1, which in its subtitle promises to describe the Christian doctrine of faith 'in its historical development and in its struggle with modern *Wissenschaft*' (Strauss 1840–1).

Strauss then soon came to the conclusion that 'modern' science left no room for theology. Yet Zeller's example shows that other members of the same school did not want to go that far. Rather, they stipulated a theology willing to accept the challenge posed by the new standard of *Wissenschaft*. What did this mean in practice? It certainly is no coincidence that the major proponents of this move were, broadly speaking, historical theologians. Thus, for them working *wissenschaftlich* primarily meant to conform to the critical standards developed and accepted by contemporary historiography and related disciplines. As the special place of *The Life of Jesus* in this debate indicates, the primary battleground on which this controversy was fought was biblical exegesis with its potential to demolish long cherished and even at the time widely held Christian assumptions and beliefs.

This focus on method, on open-endedness, and absence of dogmatic presuppositions is in line with the general ethos of *Wissenschaft* that had come to prominence at the time. With regard to the older debate about theology as science, this brings about, at the very least, a shift of emphasis. The question of how far theology ought to adopt the methodology accepted by other disciplines had always been contentious. Schleiermacher had unequivocally affirmed it as a sign of theology's integration into *Wissenschaft* but evidently believed that its responsibility to the Church could contain the more destructive consequences potentially engendered by this decision. Strauss and Zeller, in slightly different ways, push this principle to its extreme and make its acceptance the criterion of *wissenschaftlich* work.

Yet it would be simplistic to reduce their position to an accommodation of theology to a current intellectual trend. In the case of Strauss an early interest in the theological encyclopaedia is documented, and its traces are evident in *The Life of Jesus* itself. One of his earliest published writings was a lengthy review of the *Encyclopaedia of the Theological Sciences* (sic!) by the Hegelian Karl Rosenkranz (Strauss 1839: 213–34). From this writing it is evident that Strauss assigned to the exegetical subjects the task critically to undo the seeming historicity of the biblical narrative in order to prepare for its restoration by the more speculative disciplines. The same logic underlies his advocacy of what he calls the 'mythical interpretation' of the gospel in the *Life of Jesus*. As the long final chapter on Christology makes clear, Strauss hoped to show that the truth of the Christological dogma would become apparent after all erroneous attempts to tie it to the historical Jesus had been rejected (Strauss 1860: 896).

Strauss, then, has an answer to the question how theology as *Wissenschaft* can be one, and this answer is very different from Schleiermacher's. The goal of theology is speculative knowledge; theology is thus—to use the traditional terminology—a theoretical not a practical science. This knowledge can only be attained, however, after the illusion that historical knowledge could have religious significance has been undone, and this is achieved by critical exegesis. Its function within theology is thus negative; it does not yield historical knowledge but destroys the deceptive certainty created by the narrative spell of the biblical stories.

Strauss also has an answer to give to the two remaining questions at the centre of traditional debates about theology's status as a science. In so far as he finds its purpose in the elevation of historical faith to speculative knowledge, theology is, in principle, relevant for every believer (Strauss 1860: 899–900). It is faith seeking understanding, more precisely faith being transformed into understanding or knowledge. And to the extent that it aims at a virtual transformation of faith into knowledge, it should also be clear that its principles are ultimately derived from speculative philosophy. At this point at the latest it should be evident that, in spite of his rhetorical appeal to modern *Wissenschaft*, Strauss's conception of theology is deeply indebted to German Idealism, especially to Hegel's philosophy. Strauss himself admits this freely (Strauss 1860: 4), but more important is something else: what is true for Strauss, who arguably is an extreme and also a very early representative of new *Wissenschaft*, is true also for the much broader mainstream of German theology in the latter half of the nineteenth century, which, behind the ostentatious affirmation of the new paradigm of *Wissenschaft*, often hides a debt to the same Romantic-idealistic resources that had inspired an earlier generation but was publicly disowned at least from the 1840s. It is this clandestine perseverance of an idealistic legacy, which relied on the possibility of a philosophical interpretation of the results of historical criticism that facilitated the adoption of the new standard of *Wissenschaft* in German university theology until the end of the long nineteenth century. It helped that the situation was not much different in the wider German academy where all major philosophical schools had equally strong idealist leanings (Köhnke 1991), but at the same time this practice has, arguably, been the source of considerable misunderstanding and confusion outside Germany where the creed of *Wissenschaft* was, understandably, taken more at face value.

Not all theologians, to be sure, followed in the wake of Strauss. On the contrary, he soon became an outcast from the academic community and apparent or real closeness to his views for a long time was enough to stymie any theologian's career. Quite apart from his personal standing, however, it seems evident why his particular concept of theology as *Wissenschaft* could not inspire academic work in the long term. If the exegetical and historical subjects really contributed to theology only or primarily by undermining traditional assumptions, their job would be complete fairly soon; in fact, it would not seem that much could be done beyond what Strauss had already achieved in his own work. Much more influential, therefore, was the view according to which biblical and historical theology contributed positively to theology by reconstructing the history behind the available textual sources. This, strictly historicist, conception of theology as *Wissenschaft*, in fact is the second major theory of the nineteenth century. In terms of the research it inspired it has been, arguably, even more influential than the one espoused by Schleiermacher as it underlies in different ways the work of the two foremost theological schools, the Tübingen and the Ritschl School.

The origins of this alternative conception can be traced back to Friedrich Wilhelm Joseph Schelling's lectures *On University Studies*, written in 1803 and thus part of the same debate that had also produced Fichte's and Schleiermacher's programmatic treatises. Schelling suggests an outlook for theology that is strongly informed by history and justified by Christianity's influence on historicization:

> This is the great historical thrust of Christianity; this is the reason for which a Christian science of religion must be inseparable from, indeed wholly one with history. But this synthesis with history, without which theology itself could not be thought, in turn requires as its condition a higher Christian view of history. (Schelling 1857: 291)

A 'higher Christian view of history' is here explicitly enlisted to justify Schelling's own, idealist philosophy of history. At the same time, his formulation contains a methodical demand for the thorough historicization of theology. In the context of Christianity, a 'science of religion' must not only be 'inseparable' from, but 'wholly one' with history. Christian theology, in other words, not merely has a historical component, but is, strictly speaking, its own history. Such an ideal form of historical theology is, however, only possible on the soil of Christianity—just like Schelling's philosophy, which reaches this insight.

Schelling's intuition is developed into a veritable theory by Ferdinand Christian Baur, founder of the Tübingen School and teacher of both Strauss and Zeller. For him, theology is *Wissenschaft* by offering a full integration of philosophy and history centred on the notion of the Incarnation (Zachhuber 2011: 58–64). The idea, as well as the reality, of God's becoming, in Christ, part of human history transforms the latter from an arbitrary sequence of isolated events into an orderly whole which in its entirety conforms to and reveals the divine plan. Yet if history is thus endowed with meaning and significance, it also and by the same token becomes the primary source of religious insight and truth. Only Christianity enables such historicism, which is far from relativist, but the product of this new perception of humankind's development in its turn takes on a normative role for Christian theology as well. Theology in its entirety, then, becomes something like a philosophy of the history of religion that develops its truth claims through historical analysis and, concurrently, allows the result of its historical work to be interpreted in light of philosophical insights.

In practical terms this means that the argument for the absoluteness of Christianity becomes the lynchpin for this understanding of theology. Absoluteness does not signify here the broader assumption that Christianity is set apart from other religions as the full and ultimate revelation of truth, but refers to the more specific idea that historical work is able to establish absolute value judgements. If considered properly, the study of the history of religions, then, proves not merely that Christianity is the highest or the most advanced of them; it reveals the religion of the Incarnation as the 'religion of religions' as religion in itself and thus qualitatively different from all others.

Ernst Troeltsch recognized the centrality of this argument when, at the turn of the century, he argued that the impossibility of establishing this kind of absoluteness within a historicist framework pulled the rug from underneath all those attempts. This makes his book on *The Absoluteness of Christianity and the History of Religion*, published in 1902, a milestone in this debate (Troeltsch 1971). Yet in pointing out the failure of this project, Troeltsch was not triumphalist. He himself strongly sympathized with an approach to theology that started from the historicist turn, which he saw as irrevocable, a point he might have seen confirmed by the fact that Wolfhart Pannenberg's extensive argument for theology's character as *Wissenschaft* in 1973 essentially still draws on the same pattern (Pannenberg 1973: 349–61).

How does this model reply to the questions standing in the background of the whole debate? In response to the first question about the principles that determine theological work, the possibility that these could be inaccessible to general knowledge is emphatically excluded. We have seen Strauss and Zeller express this through the use of the word 'absence of presuppositions' (*Voraussetzungslosigkeit*). Later on, Heinrich Scholz and Pannenberg argue that the alternative to accepting this premiss would be to reduce theology to *private* opinion and thus take away precisely what it is meant to achieve, public justification of the tenets of the Christian faith (Pannenberg 1973: 333–4). Aquinas' (and later Barth's) view that theology is based on revealed principles is thus excluded as is Schleiermacher's affirmation of theology's dependence on the faith of historical Christianity (Pannenberg 1973: 299).

The unity of theology as one science, secondly, within this model is tantamount to the unity of historical and systematic theology. As such, it is much more rigorously conceived than in Schleiermacher's theory, which had been willing to allow for a variety of disciplines within theology bound together through their common purpose with regard to Church governance. Ultimately, the unity of the discipline is guaranteed by its common object or field of research that is, religion (Pannenberg wants it to be God, but God *as revealed through the entirety of world history*: Pannenberg 1971). Historical and systematic interpretations go hand in hand in its elucidation aimed at justifying the claims of Christianity to be the true religion which enables full knowledge of God.

It is evident, thirdly, that issues of procedure or method are central to the present model. Theology is *Wissenschaft* in so far as it is willing to adopt the same standards of rational, intellectual investigation that are accepted in other disciplines, certainly in philosophy or history, but possibly also in the sciences. Here, the procedural emphasis of the 'new' conception of *Wissenschaft* from the 1830s makes itself felt. Yet as has become increasingly clear, this affirmation has as a tacit premiss, which is shared, interestingly, by all proponents of this model, from F. C. Baur to Ernst Troeltsch to

Wolfhart Pannenberg, an idealist philosophy of history. Only the adoption of such a philosophical framework assuages the worry that the acceptance of empirical and open-ended methods of research in theology could ultimately lead to results incompatible with the fundamental tenets of Christianity. In practice, of course, this presupposition has frequently been shaken, and it is for this reason that over the 180 years of its existence this model has regularly given way to the variety encountered in Strauss and Zeller (or indeed in Bultmann), who admit or even expect critical results from historical and exegetical studies as a cathartic corrective of a naïve, literalist faith as (seemingly) suggested by 2 Corinthians 3:6.

What, finally, is the consequence the adoption of this model has for the relationship between faith and theology? It might appear to be a largely negative or at least critical one; after all, proponents of this model have been the most willing to employ the word *wissenschaftlich* with a normative emphasis in the direction of those seemingly less willing to adopt a critical stance towards traditional faith. Yet things are not quite so simple and straightforward. In fact, individual proponents of this model can be theologically rather conservative, as is Pannenberg. What unites them is the view that faith in itself is cognitive and therefore can but also ought to be theologically elucidated. This is in stark contrast to Schleiermacher for whom individual faith does not need theological reflection. Baur, Troeltsch, and Pannenberg all agree that this quasi-Kantian attempt to 'annul reason to make room for faith' (Kant 1996: 31) was essentially a disingenuous pseudo-intellectual trick.

This last consideration ought to prove, if proof still be needed, that this model far from being a sell-out of theology to the principles of modern *Wissenschaft*, is based on a robust affirmation of theology's commitment to the truth of Christianity. How far it has succeeded with its task is quite another matter. Its twin presuppositions of theology's need to establish a cognitive core of true propositions at the heart of the Christian faith and of the imperative of doing this on the basis of the same methods or standards of investigation used and accepted throughout the academy have, without a doubt, inspired some of the most impressive work of theological scholarship over the past two centuries.

IV. CONCLUSION

Nineteenth-century debates about theology as *Wissenschaft* can seem outdated for several reasons. With hindsight it is apparent how much—in spite of all controversy—they are predicated on a lingering sense that Christianity is an intellectually dominant factor in western culture. The fate of theology consequently mattered to the public in a way hardly imaginable today when the role and significance of religion is assessed, if at all, in ethical and aesthetic terms. This increasing detachment of Christian ideas from the mainstream of western intellectual life has, at the same time, encouraged theologians throughout the twentieth century to take a more consciously distanced if not outright confrontational attitude to the prevailing ideals of their cultural environment. This development begins in earnest with the emergence of dialectical theology after the First World War and has since found expression in various theological movements across national and denominational boundaries. This is not to deny that these developments coincided with debates in the wider academy and beyond, which, in their turn, questioned the validity of nineteenth-century ideals of scientific enquiry. The decades since the early twentieth century have seen such a quick succession of various theories of science, of cognition, of language, and knowledge, put forth by philosophers, sociologists, literary critics, and others, that few would today be willing to stand up and identify one or the other as dominant in the way this might perhaps still be possible for much of the previous century. Indeed, this pluralization of approaches has been perceived by some as a new opportunity for theology which might regain intellectual prestige and, at the same time, realign itself to a more traditional mode of operation by searching self-confidently for its own proper self-definition.

In a way the observations made in the course of this chapter would appear to confirm and even strengthen this perception. Being *wissenschaftlich*, it has been shown, always was a particular concern of university theologians. Even in the nineteenth and early twentieth century there were others, outside the academy, who made memorable contributions to theology, some of them, like Kierkegaard, insisting on the *unscientific* character of their work. Theology as *Wissenschaft* is not, emphatically, the same as modern theology; to understand itself, and function, as *Wissenschaft* is a 'discipline' imposed on theology by virtue of its integration into the university as an institution. These findings imply, at the same time, that it is unwarranted to expect from a repudiation of *Wissenschaftlichkeit* a return to more traditional or more dogmatic forms of theology (Webster 2005: 12–13); conservative and liberal theologians coexisted and coexist within the academy as well as outside it.

Being *Wissenschaft*, and being recognized as *Wissenschaft*, for theology, then, is neither indispensable nor inherently dangerous. It has been, and for many still is, one way of situating the rational reflection of the Christian faith within the horizon of contemporary conceptions of knowledge, its acquisition, justification, and presentation, and to defend its legitimacy against this background. That modern conceptions of *Wissenschaft* can themselves be seen as contingent products of particular historical developments is true, but does not mitigate their factual sway over intellectual discourse in nineteenth- and twentieth-century western societies. Theology may well have a contribution to make to the criticism of those paradigms—though theologians have by no means been alone in critically questioning their validity—but as an intellectual pursuit it is *willy nilly* subject to its formative powers. Reflection about theology's character as *Wissenschaft* has therefore, in the nineteenth and twentieth centuries as much as in the thirteenth century, primarily served to relate the analysis of its factual operation to its ideal. Its measure of success is not, therefore, whether or not it accepted this task, but how convincing it has been able to respond to the questions which, as we have seen, lie at its heart.

References

Anrich, Ernst (1956). *Die Idee der deutschen Universität. Die fünf Grundschriften aus der Zeit ihrer Neubegründung durch klassischen Idealismus und romantischen Realismus.* (Darmstadt: Wissenschaftliche Buchgesellschaft).

Anselm of Canterbury (1998). *The Major Works.* (Oxford: Oxford University Press).

Aristotle (1964). *Analytica Priora et Posteriora*, ed. W. D. Ross (Oxford: Oxford University Press).

Crouter, Richard (2005). *Friedrich Schleiermacher: Between Enlightenment and Romanticism.* (Cambridge: Cambridge University Press).

Freddoso, Alfred J. (2000), 'Ockham on Faith and Reason', in P. V. Spade (ed.), *The Cambridge Companion to Ockham.* (Cambridge: Cambridge University Press), 326–49.

Geyer, Bernhard (1964). 'Facultas theologica. Eine bedeutungsgeschichtliche Untersuchung', *Zeitschrift für katholische Theologie* 75, 133–45.

Grabmann, Martin (1909–11). *Die Geschichte der scholastischen Methode*, 2 vols. (Freiburg: Herder).

Howard, Thomas Albert (2006). *Protestant Theology and the Making of the Modern German University.* (Oxford: Oxford University Press).

Kant, Immanuel (1979). *The Conflict of the Faculties*, English/German parallel text, ed., trans, and intro. M. J. Gregor (Lincoln and London: University of Nebraska Press).

——(1996). *Critique of Pure Reason*, trans. W. Pluhar (Indianapolis: Hackett).

Köhnke, Klaus Christian (1991). *The Rise of Neo-Kantianism: German Academic Philosophy between Idealism and Positivism*, trans. R. J. Hollingdale (Cambridge: Cambridge University Press).

Köpf, Ulrich (1974). *Die Anfänge der theologischen Wissenschaftstheorie im 13. Jahrhundert.* (Tübingen: Mohr and Siebeck).

Lessing, Gotthold Ephraim (1956). *Lessing's Theological Writings*, selected and trans. H. Chadwick (Stanford, CA: Stanford University Press).

Pannenberg, Wolfhart (1971). *Revelation as History*, trans. D. Granskov (London: Collier Macmillan).

——(1973). *Wissenschaftstheorie und Theologie.* (Frankfurt am Main: Suhrkamp).

Rumscheidt, Martin (ed.) (1989). *Adolf von Harnack: Liberal Theology at its Height.* (London: Collins).

Schelling, Joseph (1857). *Sämmtliche Werke*, ed. K. F.A. Schelling, vol. I: 5. (Stuttgart/Augsburg: Cotta).

Schleiermacher, Friedrich (1850). *Brief Outline of the Study of Theology*, trans. W. Farrer (Edinburgh: T & T Clark).

——(1992). *On the Highest Good*, ed. H. V. Froese (Lewiston and New York: Edwin Mellen Press).

——(1999). *The Christian Faith*, trans. H. R. Mackintosh and J. S. Stewart (Edinburgh: T & T Clark).

Schnädelbach, Herbert (1984). *Philosophy in Germany, 1831–1933*, trans. E. Matthews (Cambridge: Cambridge University Press).

Schweitzer, Albert (1910). *The Quest for the Historical Jesus: A Critical Study about its Progress from Reimarus to Wrede*, trans. W. Montgomery and F. C. Burkitt (London: Adam and Charles Black).

Strauss, David Friedrich (1839). *Charakteristiken und Kritiken. Eine Sammlung zerstreuter Aufsätze aus den Gebieten der Theologie, Anthropologie und Ästhetik.* (Leipzig: Wigand).
——(1840–1). *Die christliche Glaubenslehre,* 2 vols. (Tübingen: Osiander).
——(1860). *The Life of Jesus Critically Examined,* trans. M. Evans (New York: Calvin Blanchard).
Thomas, Aquinas (1926). *Summa Theologica,* ed. P. Faucher, vol. 1, 4th edn. (Paris: Lethielleux).
Trendelenburg, Adolf (1840). *Logische Untersuchungen,* 2 vols. (Berlin: Bethge).
Troeltsch, Ernst (1971). *The Absoluteness of Christianity and the History of Religions,* trans. D. Reid (Louisville: John Knox Press).
Vilmar, August (1874). *Dogmatik,* ed. K. W. Piderit (Gütersloh: Bertelsmann).
Webster, John (2005). *Confessing God: Essays in Christian Dogmatics II.* (London: T & T Clark International).
William of Ockham (1967). *Opera Theologica,* vol. 1 (St. Bonaventure, NY: Franciscan University Press).
Zachhuber, Johannes (2011). 'Albrecht Ritschl and the Tübingen School. A Neglected Link in the History of Nineteenth Century Theology', *Journal of the History of Modern Theology* 18, 51–70.
Zeller, Eduard (1842). 'Vorwort' *Theologische Jahrbücher,* vol. 1. (Tübingen: Fues), pp. iv–viii.

SUGGESTED READING

Crouter (2005).
Diemer, Alwin (1968). *Beiträge zur Entwicklung der Wissenschaftstheorie im 19. Jahrhundert.* (Meisenheim: Hain).
Harris, Horton (1976). *The Tübingen School.* (Oxford: Oxford University Press).
Howard (2006).
Kant (1979).
MacIntyre, Alasdair (1990). *Three Rival Versions of Moral Enquiry: Encyclopaedia, Genealogy and Tradition.* (London: Duckworth).
Newman (1996).
Pannenberg, Wolfhart (1976). *Theology and the Philosophy of Science.* (Eng. trans of Pannenberg 1973), trans. F. McDonagh (Louisville: John Knox Press).
Schleiermacher (1850).
Schnädelbach (1984).
Webster, John (2005a). 'Theological Theology', in Webster (2005), 11–31.

CHAPTER 24

....

HERMENEUTICS

....

JIM FODOR

I. INTRODUCTION

....

HERMENEUTICS, in its modern philosophical sense, names a set of inquiries into the fundamental relation between being, language, and human understanding. This peculiar usage of the term 'hermeneutics' has achieved currency only relatively recently. Prior to the nineteenth century there was no such thing as 'universal hermeneutics'. Rather, in its earlier idiomatic usages, 'hermeneutics' referred to an 'auxiliary art' situated within established disciplines (e.g. law, theology, and philology) and whose primary purpose was to set forth rules governing the interpretation of texts that enjoyed canonical authority for a historical community. The aim of explicitly formulating and codifying interpretive rules, techniques (*techné*), and procedures in each of these areas was essentially practical and pragmatic: to promote sound interpretive practice, especially concerned with but not exclusively limited to difficult or problematic texts, and also indirectly to mitigate misunderstanding, avoid arbitrariness in interpretation as much as possible, and to thwart needless disagreements and disputes about the meanings of texts. Consequently, those who had an interest and proficiency in hermeneutics were, by and large, specialists or other professionals (theologians, jurists, philologists, and historians).

In the nineteenth century, however, the scope of hermeneutics not only widened considerably but transformed itself from a sub-discipline into a mode of philosophizing itself. 'Philosophical hermeneutics', as the expression is used today, does not mean the interpretation of philosophical texts, or any canonical texts, but the establishing of interpretation as the central, fundamental problem of philosophy.

Hermeneutics has undergone a sea change, from a regional, context-specific subsidiary art into a universal mode of philosophizing that has come to dominate European thought for the last two centuries.[1] Contemporary hermeneutics emerged from Romanticism, German Idealism, and the phenomenology of Husserl and Heidegger, as well as French structuralism and post-structuralism. The present account will focus on four primary figures instrumental in this revolution of hermeneutics from the regional to the universal: Schleiermacher, Dilthey, Gadamer, and Ricoeur. Heidegger is also briefly discussed because of his influence on Gadamer. There are others, to be sure, who with justification could be added to the list, including: Bultmann, Ebeling, Caputo, and Vattimo. But these four exemplars are chosen because they best exhibit the intellectual issues that have been common to and formative of both theology and modern European thought. Moreover, although religious and theological considerations are never absent from their hermeneutical reflections, none of these four (with the exception of Schleiermacher) have been regarded or identified exclusively as a theologian. It is important to register the significance of this fact. What accounts for the wide appeal of these four thinkers is their ability to transcend disciplinary boundaries. Their work demonstrates that it is impossible to separate out the theological from other intellectual currents that have informed modern western societies and which are now shaping present global cultures. These thinkers challenge the conventional wisdom that discrete disciplines occupy independent territories governed by separate logics and intellectual agendas. Their cross-fertilization suggests new ways of contrasting, as well as fusing, theology and modern European thought. This chapter seeks to describe and contribute to that cross-fertilization.

II. Elements of Continuity Between 'Classical' and 'Contemporary' Hermeneutics

While hermeneutics in its modern sense as first philosophy is qualitatively different than its ancillary disciplines, there are elements of continuity between the two. One of these elements of continuity is the breadth or reach that the practice claimed. Like their contemporary counterparts, classical hermeneutical theorists presumed that their work had a general validity if not universal bearing. Because of the normative role of the canonical texts that were interpreted, such as the Homeric poems or sacred texts, exegesis of those texts was relevant to a broad community (Ferraris 1996: 2–3). Moreover, until the end of the eighteenth century, it was not uncommon to find hermeneutical theories

---

[1] Perhaps the most significant overview of the history of hermeneutics, in terms of its influence in shaping subsequent thought and development in this area, is that offered by Wilhelm Dilthey, 'The Rise of Hermeneutics (1900)', in Dilthey (1996). Other more recent accounts that trace this history post-Dilthey include Ricoeur (1981); Grondin (1994); and Ferraris (1996).

promulgating rules governing the interpretation of written texts, discourses, and linguistic signs in the strict sense, but also rules for interpreting any and all kinds of signs, including natural ones (e.g. the so-called book of nature). Thus, classical theorists too, claimed or explored the idea that methods of interpretation might be widely or even universally applied.

A second element of connection or continuity between pre-modern and contemporary hermeneutics is that both have a distinctively practical orientation or political/pragmatic interest. This is true not simply in the obvious sense that there are inextricably concrete, real life consequences concomitant with any specific interpretative outlook. Legal hermeneutics, for example, concern not only judges but all legal subjects. But it is also true in a more fundamental, organic sense. The hermeneutical style of philosophizing is a practical engagement of the world in which praxis precedes any theoretical determination.[2] Hermeneutics, in other words, is a practical philosophy, involved intrinsically and unavoidably with social and political transformation, not mere speculative theory or private contemplation.

A third similarity between classical and contemporary hermeneutics is its mediatory or reparatory function. The root of the term 'hermeneutics' is the Greek expression *hermēneuein*. *Hermeios* is the name given to the priest at the Delphic oracle and Hermes, the wing-footed messenger god whom the Greeks credited with the discovery of language and writing, and who plays an important mediating role by 'transmuting what is beyond human understanding into a form that human intelligence can grasp' (Palmer 1969: 13). Whether concerned with communication between the gods and the mortals, or linguistic exchanges among humans themselves, three distinct albeit intersecting interests inhere in hermeneutics: (1) 'expression' (utterance, speaking) or to express aloud in words, that is, 'to say'; (2), 'explication' (interpretation, explanation), that is, 'to explain' or make clear what is hidden or obscure or implicit; and (3) 'translation' (acting as an interpreter) or 'to translate', as in rendering a foreign tongue into the 'home' language of the translator's audience (Palmer 1969: 12–32). All three interests interweave to constitute the 'Hermes process' such that 'something foreign, strange, separated in time, space or experience is made familiar, present, comprehensible; something requiring representation, explanation, or translation is somehow "brought to understanding"—is "interpreted"' (Palmer 1969: 14).

Despite strong connections with certain concerns of classical hermeneutics, philosophical hermeneutics cannot be regarded as the prolongation or mere 'extension of originally regional practices but rather as a move to a different level' (Ferraris 1996: 3).[3]

---

[2] On this point especially, see the work of Andrew Bowie, e.g. Bowie 1990.

[3] See also Gadamer 1993: 178: 'Thus the science of hermeneutics—as developed by Schleiermacher . . . — is not, then, just one more stage in the history of the art of understanding.'

Friedrich Schleiermacher (1768–1834) is widely regarded as the 'transitional' or 'hinge' figure marking the shift from classical to modern hermeneutics.

III. Schleiermacher and the Inception of Modern Hermeneutics

Schleiermacher is viewed as the founder of modern hermeneutics principally because of his attempts to 'universalize' hermeneutics or to develop a philosophical interpretive method that accounts for the manifold regional interpretive strategies and techniques employed in various areas of humanistic study and inquiry. Prior to Schleiermacher, the work of interpretation varied according to the different aims of the respective disciplines (e.g. philological methods are applied to classical texts of Greco-Roman antiquity and exegetical methods are applied to the sacred texts of Christian scripture). What is yet needed, Schleiermacher believes, is a proper method that is able to rise above 'regional' variations in hermeneutical practices by virtue of its ability to subsume their diverse operations in light of an overarching intelligibility. In short, his aim is to subordinate the indigenous rules of exegesis and philology to the general problematic of understanding. Like Kant, who sought to set forth the conditions of the possibility of understanding for the natural sciences, Schleiermacher wishes to outline the conditions of the possibility of understanding for the human sciences—to spell out the universally valid rules of understanding. The effect would be to unify all regional hermeneutics.[4] By 'deregionalizing' (Ricoeur 1981: 44) hermeneutics or shifting the focus from the meaning of specific texts to the conditions of the possibility of all understanding, Schleiermacher effectively elevates hermeneutics to a genuinely philosophical enterprise. Along with this 'elevation' of hermeneutics to the level of understanding generally comes an expansion of hermeneutics beyond the domain of written texts to include all significant manifestations of human spirit and life.

The Grammatical (Objective) and the Technical (Psychological) Moments of Interpretation

In developing his philosophical hermeneutics, Schleiermacher was keen to do justice to both the objective dimensions of language (evident in its impersonal structures of grammar, syntax, morphology, phonetics, etc.) and to its distinctively subjective side

---

[4] As Ricoeur aptly puts it, 'Hermeneutics was born with the attempt to raise exegesis and philology to the level of a *Kunstlehre*, a "technology" which is not restricted to a mere collection of unconnected operations' Ricoeur 1981: 45.

(the unique, original utterances and expressions of individual language users). The task of the former 'moment'—which he labelled the grammatical side of interpretation—is to elucidate an expression by reference to the total context constituted by the possibilities of a natural language. 'Language is the embodiment of everything that can be thought in it . . . Everything particular in it must be able to be understood from out of the totality' (Schleiermacher 1998: 229). The task of the latter 'moment' of interpretation—which he termed subjective or technical-psychological[5]—is to account for the spontaneous and original expressions, the creative and 'poetic' utterances, of individual language users that are irreducible to the rules of the language. According to Schleiermacher, '*Understanding is only a being-in-one-another of these two moments (of the grammatical and the psychological)*' (Schleiermacher 1998: 9).[6] Each moment depends on the other for its own realization, which means that neither side is ever in play without some degree of the other side also being in play. There is, in other words, a sort of interpenetration and reciprocal dependence of the grammatical and the technical-psychological 'moments'.

On the one hand, the individual language user 'is determined in his thought by the (common) language and can think only the thoughts which already have their designation in his language' (Schleiermacher 1998: 9). That is, every intelligible expression or utterance is but an instance of the overall pattern characteristic of a natural language, and to that extent is already determined, operating at a supra-individual level. The individual speaker/writer is thus 'subjected' to the constraints (the rules of usage) of a language over which that person has no fundamental power. Stated otherwise, the relation of the language user (the individual subject) to language is 'receptive' in so far as 'language is received from the external world and the subject has no significant effect on the meanings it conveys' (Bowie 2005: 73). On the other hand, language is the means by which an individual mind manifests itself. The author 'collaborates in the language: for in part he produces something new in it . . . in part he preserves what he repeats and reproduces' (Schleiermacher 1998: 91). In a true sense, the author or utterer is the source of authority over whatever linguistic expression she or he produces—which is another way of indicating the 'spontaneous' relationship a subject has with language: 'meaning relies on the mental acts of the producer of the text' or utterance (Bowie 2005:

---

[5] Schleiermacher's terminology is difficult to pin down here in part because of a) the incomplete, unpublished nature of his writings on hermeneutics and b) because of the fluid and evolving character of his hermeneutics as evidenced in various editions and versions of his manuscripts on the subject. 'Schleiermacher poses certain problems for both translators and readers because he does not always sustain a consistent terminology.' See Bowie's remarks in 'Note on the text and translation', in Schleiermacher 1997: p. xxxix.

[6] The characterization of the second moment as either 'technical' or 'psychological' is problematic for different reasons. 'Technical' suggests, misleadingly, a form of specialization—usually scientific or technological in nature. This is not Schleiermacher's meaning here. Rather, Schleiermacher names the second moment of interpretation 'technical' (although in his later writings he does use the term 'psychological') because he sees his overall project as a *Kunstlehre*, a 'technology'. Similarly, to specify it as 'psychological' is misleading in so far as it suggests a focus on the inner thoughts, intentions, and desires of the speaker/writer. Schleiermacher does not believe that the primary task of an interpreter is to exercise a sort of 'empathy'.

73). While the grammatical side of interpretation relegates the author/utterer to the background and 'regards him as just an organ of the language', on the technical side the speaker/author is valorized and regarded as 'the real-ground of the utterance and the language merely as the negative limiting principle' (Schleiermacher 1998: 230). The speaker or writer, in other words, employs language for his or her own individual purpose such that language becomes the instrument by and through which a soul discloses itself to itself and to others. And because utterances express the *self*, clearly part of the interpreter's objective is to understand the meaning of that utterance as the expression or thought of another *person*. Language, construed in its technical-psychological 'moment', requires the interpreter to go behind each utterance to reach 'the inner recesses of thought' (Grondin 1994: 72). This is the reconstructive task of interpretation.

Another way to articulate these two sides or aspects of language is as a relationship between part (individual meaning) and whole (the structure of a given language). The interplay between the whole and the part is the 'hermeneutic circle' or the mutual dependence of 'intentionalism' and 'structuralism'. Schleiermacher draws from both structuralism and intentionalism-psychologism. The former holds that the formal structures of language are the true bearers of meaning, not the expressions of individual language users or the contingent biographical, cultural, or historical circumstances of their utterances. The latter claims that true understanding is achieved whenever one can transpose oneself, through an act of empathy or identification, into the mind of the speaker or author. Separately these two doctrines are each limited and incomplete. Together they more nearly approach Schleiermacher's universal hermeneutics. Schleiermacher writes, 'understanding has a dual direction, towards the language and towards the thought'. There are not two different kinds of interpretation only one, which means that 'every explication must completely achieve both' the grammatical and the technical-psychological (Schleiermacher 1998: 229). There is, then this dialectical or circular movement between part and whole that informs Schleiermacher's hermeneutics.

The Hermeneutic Circle: Dialectic of Part and Whole

In addition to the twofold operation of the grammatical and the psychological 'moments' of interpretation, Schleiermacher emphasizes the interpretive interplay between the parts of a text and the whole. He writes, 'on the one hand the whole [of the text] can only be understood via the particulars, and on the other hand...the particular can only be understood via the whole' (Schleiermacher 1998: 148). Thus, within a single sentence there are the subject and the predicate, 'which mutually determine each other' (Schleiermacher 1998: 61). Each provides the context for the other. 'The subject must receive its final determinacy via the predicate and the predicate via the subject' (Schleiermacher 1998: 239). But that is only the initial level, for a sentence—the smallest unit of understanding—is but the first of many wholes. In order for understanding to advance to a higher level, the sentence must be understood not just in terms of the relations of its own internal parts to the whole, but also in combination with other sentences (and their parts). These together constitute a yet larger, second whole: a text. And texts, in turn, must be understood in light of even grander (third-level) wholes; namely, a genre, and vice versa. Sometimes, as in the case of the Christian scriptures, there is also a canonical whole which is comprised of various books each of which contain multiple genres. This is yet a wider (fourth-level) whole that comes into play where particulars and totalities mutually interpret one another in ever greater degrees of complexity and interrelation. Finally, the fifth-level whole within which to understand multiple genres (but also canons) would be that of a language itself. In each case and at every level, a provisional anticipation of the meaning of the whole is projected or ventured, which is then tested, revised, corrected, and adjusted in light of a consideration of its individual parts, and vice versa. This continual back-and-forth between parts and the whole generates a series of revised understandings, each of which provides some guidance or a basis for yet further and more refined, albeit still provisional, anticipations of the meaning of the whole, followed by still subsequent revisions. And so on and so forth.[7]

Consideration of ever-widening concentric circles of meaning with their relative parts and wholes in continuous mutual relations of anticipation and re-adjustment or self-correction is a daunting task. And this is only the grammatical side or 'moment' of the interpretative enterprise! Schleiermacher's technical-psychological 'moment' must also be included. The second pole of the hermeneutical task entails a comprehensive appreciation of the author's or utterer's biography and indeed their history: 'all the moments of their life, and this only from the totality of their environments . . . via their nationality and their era' (Schleiermacher 1998: 9).[8] Here, too, a parallel set of ever-widening circles is at play: the immediate occasion of the text or utterance; the relation of this episode to other life-moments in the author/utterer's life; the relations between the life of the author/utterer and the lives of others (e.g. family, neighbourhood, community, country); and the relations of the author's life to other significant authors, living and deceased, who have influenced the author in question. In sum, the part/whole dialectic occurs *within* each of these two hermeneutical 'moments' as well *between* them. As Schleiermacher puts it, 'every utterance has a dual relationship, to the totality of language and to the whole thought of its originator' (Schleiermacher 1998: 8). Every utterance must therefore be understood 'via the whole life to which it belongs'—where 'the whole life' means not only the totality of language as a set of impersonal structures (the grammatical side) but also the totality of the person's life (the technical-psychological side) who

---

[7] For an extended and detailed description of this process using the scriptures as an example, see Westphal 2001: 112–14.

[8] 'The vocabulary and history of the era of the author relate as the whole from which his writings must be understood as the part, and the whole must, in turn, be understood from the part' (Schleiermacher 1998: 24).

is the originator of that particular utterance or text. The prospect of mastering this ever-expanding compass of knowledge is overwhelming. And perhaps that is precisely Schleiermacher's intent: to underscore the fact that the task of interpretation is an infinite one, never exhausted, always provisional. Schleiermacher conceives the interpretive process—both in terms of the subject matter and of the speaker/writer—as an asymptote which is always approached but never reached.

Misunderstanding and the Refusal of Absolute Knowledge: The Condition of Human Finitude

In classical hermeneutics, the presumption was that understanding occurs more or less of its own accord, naturally. Traditional hermeneutics assumed that people generally understood language quickly and easily, until they encountered some obstacle or impediment—say a contradiction or puzzle or enigma. It was at these points where hermeneutical assistance was needed. Formerly, the state of understanding—in an artless, ordinary sense—was considered normal and natural; non-understanding, confusion, or misunderstanding was the exception. Consequently, classical hermeneutics largely limited itself to specific problematic passages in a text, offering directions that would shed light on obscurities or clarify problems. Schleiermacher, however, inverts this supposition: the 'normal' state of human being is misunderstanding not understanding. Hermeneutics is thus applicable not only occasionally and restricted to 'difficult cases' (problem areas in the text) but 'understanding must be desired and sought *at every point*' (Schleiermacher 1998: 22; my emphasis). Hermeneutics, then, is involved *from the onset* of the endeavour to understand any utterance and not only when obstacles are encountered in problematic cases. Because of the universality of the need for interpretation, understanding needs to proceed methodologically, according to a 'technology' or art (*Kuntslehre*).

Schleiermacher further contends that misunderstanding (or, perhaps better worded, non-understanding) can never completely be eliminated because one can never claim to have thought something through to the end. 'In every attempt at understanding—even one that appears to succeed—the possibility of some last vestige of misunderstanding cannot be ruled out' (Grondin 1994: 70). Schleiermacher never speaks of 'complete' understanding in the sense of something total, definitive, or absolute. Understanding is always and only provisional. Again, the interpretive task is an infinite one.

Schleiermacher rejects the Hegelian ideal of complete philosophical knowledge. Indeed, one of the fundamental assumptions of Schleiermacher's hermeneutics is that reason cannot escape from its location within a historically specific language. This does not mean that reason becomes impossible, only that it cannot make absolute claims, nor can it achieve complete consensus. We must always 'begin in the middle' of our history and language, which entails an orientation to praxis, making practical wisdom and judgement in interpretation inescapable.

Hermeneutics and the Praxis of Communication

Schleiermacher's 'praxical' orientation to hermeneutics is evident in his use of the term *Kunstlehre*. The word *Kunst* can mean either 'craft' or a technical skill that requires tacit knowledge and is not reducible to rules. By referring to the hermeneutical method as a *Kunstlehre* Schleiermacher implies that the method requires practical wisdom or judgement. *Kunstlehre* entails 'an irreducible sense of contextuality' that cannot be transcended (and thereby fixed) by an overall concept. That is, context alone clarifies specific utterances or expressions. But of course contextual interpretations, given that they are endlessly expandable, can never finally yield an unambiguous meaning. Hence, interpretation 'requires one to make ungroundable, fallible judgements about what is the real matter in hand' (Bowie 1990: 149). There is no absolute court of judgement. Invoking language as a whole will not serve this grounding function for the simple reason that 'no language is totally available to us, not even one's own mother-tongue' (Schleiermacher 1977: 84, in Bowie 1990: 160). The grammar or rules of language, in other words, cannot fully account for the creative, novel, or productive use of language by its individual users.[9]

One of the distinctively Romantic themes informing Schleiermacher's hermeneutics is the inherent and irreducible individuality of human beings. Individuality is expressed in the activity of the will, the 'free productivity' of language which is not reducible to the way in which it is subsequently theorized. For Schleiermacher, the singularity of the individual is neither subsumable by the concept nor reducible to a set of rules of language use. This is Schleiermacher's technical-psychological side of interpretation. Once more, practical wisdom, judgement, and discernment are necessary.

In addition to the dialectical movement back and forth between the grammatical and the technical-psychological, Schleiermacher's hermeneutics involve pairing other contrasting concepts in a part/whole scheme. One central pair is the interplay between 'divination' and 'comparison'. This duality, just like the first pair, is also interpenetrating and mutually implicating. The divinatory method is an attempt to walk holistically in another person's shoes. The comparative method, by contrast, understands the person as a particular example of a more general type. Schleiermacher explains:

> The divinatory method is the one in which one, so to speak, transforms oneself into the other person and tries to understand the individual element directly. The comparative method first of all posits the person to be understood as something universal and then finds the individual aspect by comparison with other things included under the same universal. (Schleiermacher 1998: 92–3)

Both implicate, refer back to each other, and are thus inseparable. Without comparison, divination would lack credibility and absent divination comparison would lead to infinite regress.

---

[9] Even postulating the notion of the totality of a language (like Saussure's *langue*) will not do precisely because linguistic rules do not carry the certainty of their application with them. In other words, stipulating the agreed rules of usage, the 'code' that makes intersubjective communication possible, cannot provide the basis for implementing those rules.

It is tempting, in light of Schleiermacher's unmistakable Romantic proclivities, to construe the act of 'divination' as some sort of mystical act of identification with the speaker or written text rather than as one aspect of the mundane, always incomplete, praxis of understanding one another and the world. But if one takes seriously what Schleiermacher says about how the grammatical and the technical-psychological 'moments' of interpretation are mutually activating, as well as the divinatory and the comparative poles of interpretation, then it is clear that Schleiermacher is not espousing a form of intentionalism or psychologism. Interpretation does not mean, for him, a kind of empathy whereby one 'feels one's way into' another person's thoughts via their writings. Yet, thanks to his famous pupil and biographer, Wilhelm Dilthey (1833–1911), this feature of Schleiermacher's legacy has become rather more pronounced in the subsequent reception and development of modern hermeneutics.

IV. Wilhelm Dilthey's Hermeneutical Project: From Text to History

Perhaps the most important legacy of Dilthey's hermeneutical project is his effort to establish the epistemological foundations of the human sciences (*Geisteswissenschaften*) on equal footing with the natural sciences (*Naturwissenschaften*). Dilthey differentiated between the natural sciences and the human sciences on two grounds. First the two domains have different objects of investigation. The natural sciences investigate phenomena 'external' to humans, whereas the area of most interest for the human sciences is the human being. They also have different modes of knowing. Knowledge in the natural sciences is derived from observation of the outside world, whereas in the human sciences it is derived from a 'lived experience' (*Erlebnis*), in which the act of knowing is inextricably linked to, and hence inseparable from, the object known. In the positivistic age of the late nineteenth century, the paradigm of sure, certain knowledge was the natural sciences. Dilthey challenged the fundamental positivistic assumption that there is a single model of intelligibility and that all knowledge is grounded on the form of empirical explanation exemplified by the natural sciences. He contended that the human sciences also exhibit a legitimate form of knowing, albeit using different categories such as meaning, purpose, and value. What is distinctive about the type of knowing that prevails in the human sciences is that the understanding of meaning touches and transforms the 'object' under investigation—the human being—whereas in the natural sciences a causal explanation does not modify or change the substance of the phenomenon.

Dilthey attempts to relate, in a coherent and satisfactory way, explanation (*Erklärung*), the dominant epistemological mode of the natural sciences, with its counterpart, understanding (*Verstehen*), the characteristic epistemological method of the human sciences. Like Schleiermacher, Dilthey associates understanding with the knowledge of agency—the ability to disclose the reason or motivation behind human action. To be sure, human actions may also be explained in terms of physical forces, but this only provides knowledge of their effects. Physical explanations do not address the individual nature of agency as the source of human action. The focus of all human sciences is the individual. Dilthey's fundamental project is to relate 'external experience' and 'internal experience'. He contends that the latter, the psychic act, with its attendant feelings, affects, passions, processes of thought, and acts of the will, may be carried over on to external objects. For example, we express ourselves by writing. The core project of the human sciences is to understand inner experiences not as discrete, isolated facts that can be explained scientifically, but as a 'living nexus' (*Zusammenhang*) or a means of insight into the human experience. According to Dilthey's maxim, 'We explain nature, we understand mental life' (Grondin 1994: 86), for only what the mind has created it understands.

In order to avoid a reversion to psychologism, Dilthey invokes the notion of 'experience' (*Erlebnis*). Experience, in this sense, is generally conceived of in pre-propositional terms. Every subject knows immediately, from its own *Erlebnis*, that it is part of a course of life and that within that life it encounters not only its own inner world but also an external, 'objective' set of manifestations of the spirit instantiated in various cultural forms and societal structures. One cannot directly grasp mental life itself, but one can grasp what it intends through its expressions: it signs and works. According to Dilthey, understanding is achieved only by way of mediation. Knowledge of oneself, of others and the world is always and everywhere mediated through signs and works. There is no direct route to the mind. Instead we have to investigate the mind through the detour of human activities and the manifestations of the human spirit.[10]

Dilthey's advance on Schleiermacher is to broaden hermeneutics from the science of interpreting texts to the science of interpreting all historical expressions. After Dilthey, 'the text to be interpreted [is] reality itself and its *interconnection* (*Zusammenhang*)' (Ricoeur 1981: 48). The broadest canvas of all, the most fundamental expression of life, is not writing and texts but the entire panoply of human history. 'Before the coherence of the text comes the coherence of history, considered as the great document of mankind' (Ricoeur 1981: 48). Dilthey's ability to establish a pact between history and hermeneutics is clearly his signature mark and lasting contribution.

Dilthey made a valiant effort to interrelate on the widest possible frame, universal history, the dynamism of human life, its spontaneity and individuality, within the formal structures of its concrete life expressions, its objective, and impersonal filaments. However, it is not quite clear that he succeeded. Instead, Dilthey leaves one with a fascinating ambiguity emerging from his insight that the 'psychic state' is not understood from within but only on the basis of 'the external stimuli that aroused it' (Dilthey 1996: 253). The observation that understanding requires consideration of external contextual factors is nothing new, of course. This has already been explicated with nuance and sophistication in Schleiermacher. Also, an appeal to physical context using Dilthey's categories may fall under 'explanation'—a form of knowing more appropriate to the natural sciences.

---

[10] 'I understand myself only by means of the signs which I give of my own life and which are returned to me via others' (Ricoeur 1981: 51).

Perhaps Dilthey is postulating a mode of explanation unique to the human sciences whereby 'explanation' would amount to the knower reflecting on external factors in order better to grasp the inner processes to be understood.[11] For Dilthey, the appeal to objective externalities satisfies his concern for the equal scientific status of understanding vis-à-vis explanation. It is not clear, however, that this finally escapes a fundamental opposition between explanation and understanding. To anticipate a future hermeneutical development discussed below, Ricoeur proposes an alternative mode of explanation to Dilthey that does not require appeal to universal laws. Here the particular is not subsumed in the universal in a way that Dilthey feared but was not able to articulate. Yet at the same time Rioceur's way of articulating the objective operations that constitute the explanatory moment of interpretation allow for what is contextual—'external' to the author—to enter into the very process of understanding itself in a manner that is integral, rather than opposed, to understanding.

The fundamental unresolved question in Dilthey is whether the task of understanding the mind of another in his or her irreducible singularity finally eclipses that of understanding the text. For if 'the object of interpretation is constantly shifted away from the text . . . towards the lived experience which is expressed therein', then the ultimate aim of interpretation appears to be 'not *what* a text says, but *who* says it' (Ricoeur 1981: 52). What is gained in the vastly increased scope of the hermeneutical project from the realm of written texts to all human activity is offset by the interpreter's apparent inability or refusal to relinquish the psychological goal of 'transference into another mental life' (Ricoeur 1981: 53). In the end, Dilthey's hermeneutics remains an epistemology and arguably a problematic one because grounded in the immediacy and self-transparency of the cogito. Thus, Dilthey remains trapped within the irresolvable debates between objectivism and relativism (Bernstein 1983). What can be said for his efforts, however, is that by aligning the hermeneutical enterprise with history itself rather than any of its individual authors and actors, hermeneutics acquires greater universality. In that respect Dilthey prepares the way for the displacement of epistemology towards an ontology of interpretation.

V. HEIDEGGER: THE SHIFT FROM EPISTEMOLOGY TO ONTOLOGY

With the philosophy of Martin Heidegger (1889–1976) comes a shift away from epistemology to ontology. Heidegger de-couples the hermeneutical question from its presumed home within theories of knowledge. He 'de-psychologizes' understanding by making it 'worldly,' effectively displacing Dilthey's presupposition that understanding

---

[11] This is something that Ricoeur later takes up, albeit in a modified way, in his own hermeneutics; namely, the adoption of a 'new attitude' towards explanation displayed along the lines of Saussure's structuralist model.

is primarily a matter of understanding the mind of another person. Under Heidegger's scheme, the ontology of understanding constitutes the very condition of the possibility of discourse. He posits a mode of inhabiting the world that is logically prior to, and not itself part of, the phenomenal world. This shift to uncovering the ontological conditions of understanding brings to the fore a new question: 'instead of asking "how do we know?" ' it will be asked 'what is the mode of being who exists only in his understanding?' (Ricoeur 1981: 54). In short, the epistemological question is eclipsed by a more primordial interrogation regarding the way a being encounters being even before it confronts the world as a possible object of knowledge.

Heidegger's ontological project, as commonly understood, does not arise from an interest in language. Indeed, in Heidegger understanding becomes entirely severed from the problem of communication—which, in relation to a more elemental ontology of being, can only be seen as a derivative question of merely secondary interest. 'Being-in' (the world) rather than 'being-with' (others) is primordial. In so far as the question of the world takes precedence over the question of the relation of self to other, understanding is effectively 'de-psychologized'. Heidegger's contribution to hermeneutics, then, is to 'clarify' 'a link to reality more fundamental than the subject-object relation' (Ricoeur 1981: 56). This pre-epistemological way of being in the world manifests itself as 'feeling' or 'orientation' that has not yet risen to a level of conceptual thematization. 'In knowledge, we posit objects in front of us; but our feeling of the situation precedes this vis-à-vis by placing us in a world' (Ricoeur 1981: 56). According to Heidegger, we must 'have an ontological *pre-understanding* of being' (Ricoeur 1981: 54). It is this ontological sense of being 'which anchors the whole linguistic system' (Ricoeur 1981: 56).

The leading figure in modern hermeneutics, Hans-Georg Gadamer, adopts and expands upon Heidegger's shift towards an ontological, rather than an epistemological, conception of understanding.

VI. Gadamer and the Ontological Deepening of Hermeneutics

Hans-Georg Gadamer (1900–2002) is widely regarded as one of the leading contemporary advocates of philosophical hermeneutics. He develops and deepens a number of themes adumbrated in Heidegger's philosophy. But in doing so Gadamer makes his own contributions. He rehabilitates the concept of prejudice from its castigation and dismissal by Enlightenment thinkers. He explains the generative importance of pre-understanding in interpretation as well as the inescapable influence of tradition. He introduces concepts such as 'historically effected consciousness'; the 'fusion of horizons', and the operative dynamics of 'play' (*Spiel*) in understanding and conversation. Through the latter idea he emphasizes the central role of *phronēsis* (practical judgement/wisdom) in interpretation.

Gadamer picks up where Heidegger left off: namely, with Heidegger's uncovering of the fore-structure of understanding (Gadamer 1993: 265 ff.). In true hermeneutical fashion, Gadamer appropriates these insights by elaborating and modifying them. Gadamer refers to 'facticity' as a kind of opaque, inscrutable ground of human existence which eludes, and to some extent resists, comprehension and understanding. And yet at the same time, somewhat paradoxically, 'facticity' constitutes the very basis of understanding. For Gadamer the task or project of understanding, *Verstehen*, is to move from a state of private isolation, which in a sense pre-exists understanding, into a community or tradition of understanding. Gadamer describes a dialectical oscillation between one's having always already been thrust into a situation (*Geworfenheit*), and one's thrusting or projection of oneself forward (*Entwurf*)—understanding is 'a *projection* within a prior *being-thrown*' (Ricoeur 1981: 56). The nature of human existence is one of actively seeking understanding even while being borne along by it. There is an 'always already' feature to understanding that preconditions the understanding any being will have. This is what Gadamer means by the term 'effective historical consciousness'.

Being situated, saturated, and history-laden is the condition of human existence. Human beings are embedded within history in a pre-reflective or pre-rational sense. To be immersed in history means that there can be no 'original,' unmediated starting point, no self-grounded beginning to the kind of certain knowledge that Descartes dreamed of. Gadamer exposes as fantasy the notion of 'sheer objectivity' wherein one would see, with no expectations or anticipations, what is simply there—'the facts'. Projections of the past on to the future are inescapable when coming to understand anything. This deep, pre-thematic sense of belonging to history and to the world means that 'my consciousness is not a transparent, self-grounding vehicle that puts me in immediate contact with its "object" but is rather a grounded opacity (or at best a translucency) that enables a richly mediated contact with its "object" ' (Westphal 2009: 74).

The Hermeneutical Circle on the Ontological Plane

Gadamer's account of 'effective historical consciousness' casts important light on the ontological structure of circularity (the hermeneutical circle) that leads to understanding. Understanding has the same self-reflective configuration as 'effective-historical consciousness', whereby 'the subject itself enters into the knowledge of the object; and in turn, the former is determined . . . by the hold which the object has upon it, even before the subject comes to know the object' (Ricoeur 1981: 57). The circularity between subject and object is not vicious because the object as a whole is not fully disclosed at the beginning of the process. The common experience of reading a text provides a case in point. 'A person who is trying to understand a text is always projecting [anticipating]. He projects a meaning for the text as a whole as soon as some initial meaning emerges in the text. Again, the initial meaning emerges only because he is reading the text with particular expectations in regard to a certain meaning' (Gadamer 1993: 267).

What these expectations are and where they come from is not, however, entirely up to the reader to decide. They are not explicitly or fully under the reader's self-conscious awareness or control in so far as they operate at a subconscious level. The reader is ensconced within them due to his or her place in time, history, and language. In the same way that one first belongs to history before it belongs to the subject, so too the subject is first a dweller in language before he or she becomes a self-aware and self-conscious user of it. Being discloses itself in language, to be sure, but it also conceals itself—which means that consciousness inexorably affected by history is more being in its opaque profundity and depth than it is raised to explicit awareness in consciousness. Interpretation is thus an ongoing, infinite task. 'Hermeneutical reflection...brings before me something that otherwise happens behind my back. Something—*but not everything*, for...being is never fully manifest' (Gadamer 1967: 38; my emphasis).

The hermeneutical circle, explicated ontologically, means that some degree of understanding is achieved prior to the emergence of the subject/object differentiation. The anticipation of meaning that governs our understanding of a text is not an act of pure subjectivity, but proceeds from our immersion in a tradition. Conversely, '[t]radition is not simply a permanent precondition; rather, we produce it ourselves inasmuch as we understand' and participate in its evolution. 'Thus the circle of understanding is not a "methodological" circle, but describes an element of the ontological structure of understanding' (Gadamer 1993: 293). Gadamer, influenced by Heidegger, raises to an ontological level Dilthey's insight that there is no identifiable point of origin for the task of understanding.

Prejudgement/Prejudice

The Enlightenment idealized true knowledge as a form of knowing that is completely free of prejudices. According to Kant, for instance, in order to think autonomously, i.e. in a mature way, an individual must sever all his or her allegiances with tradition and all forms of authority. By contrast Gadamer contends, in his rehabilitation of the notion of prejudice, that a pure unencumbered knowledge, from nowhere, is impossible. Prejudices or prejudgments actually enable understanding rather than foreclosing or distorting it; that is, they positively condition understanding. They act almost like transcendental conditions of understanding. Pre-understandings, of course, do not often survive intact when subjected to scrutiny and testing and when situated in a wider circle of knowledge. Almost invariably, prejudices are amended and adjusted upon further engagement with the subject matter. Rather than getting beyond or outside prejudices, one learns instead to recognize prejudices by working them out interpretively. The trick is not to escape the hermeneutical circle of understanding and assume an unprejudiced view from no particular place whatsoever; the trick rather is ever to strive at becoming more conscious of our particular hermeneutical situatedness so that new and more appropriate judgements can eclipse the role of older and less appropriate prejudgements in conditioning our understanding. The first task in interpretation consists in a reflexively critical understanding that is concerned 'not merely to form anticipatory ideas, but to make them conscious, so as to monitor them and thus acquire right understanding from the things themselves' (Gadamer 1993: 269). That is, judgement has a reflexive quality: to the extent that one makes a judgement on what is being understood, the subject matter also calls the interpreter's self-understanding into question/judgement. The back and forth between the one and the other 'works out' the true character of the matter. There is no single criterion by which an interpreter can know in advance what 'appropriate' prejudices will permit the 'thing itself' to speak; however, there are more or less trustworthy indicators. For example, temporary distance may allow the interpreter to see—with the benefit of hindsight—which prejudgements more adequately do justice to the subject matter. That said, no one interpretive rule is sufficient, for, as Gadamer explains, 'history very often has a concealing effect, and interpretive approaches often block access to the very things they mean to reveal' (Grondin 1994: 113). The best one can do is to commit to an ongoing dialectical process of anticipation and correction.

Fusion of Horizons

From the foregoing analysis of prejudice and the dialectical/dialogical interaction between the interpreter and the text/other, one of the hallmarks of a philosophical or ontological hermeneutics becomes evident: its fallibility. Hermeneutical understanding is continually open to revision; it displays a readiness to alter its judgements in favour of better insight. This stands in sharp contrast to the Enlightenment ideal of philosophy as absolute knowing. Philosophical hermeneutics is committed to the irreducibly temporal and historical 'situatedness' of human being. Compared to the goals of the Enlightenment, its claims are rather more reserved, modest and, in an important sense, chastened.

A helpful metaphor Gadamer uses to express this genuine but limited way of being and knowing is 'horizon' (borrowed from Husserl). In one regard, the spatial image of horizon is just another way of describing context. But in a deeper sense it points to the way in which our situation is always more extensive than we might at first appreciate, precisely because a horizon includes things of which we are not immediately aware. Horizon speaks to 'the way in which thought is tied to its finite determinacy, and to the way one's range of vision is gradually expanded. A person who has no horizon does not see far enough and hence overvalues what is nearest to him. On the other hand, "to have a horizon" means not being limited to what is nearby but being able to see beyond it' (Gadamer 1993: 302). To have a horizon, therefore, is not to be confined or restricted in a debilitating sense, but to be positioned in an appropriately human way. It enables access to certain views on the world even as it sets a limit beyond which we cannot see. While perpetually being bounded by a horizon in no way precludes movement and expansion, it does suggest that we must let go of the epistemological fantasy of 'a view from nowhere'.

The Absorption of 'Play' (Spiel) as Game, Performance, and Conversation

Gadamer sometimes speaks of hermeneutics as a *Gespräch*, or conversation. He believes that 'reaching' or 'attaining' an understanding is intrinsically communal. However, as conceived by Gadamer the interest or emphasis of the conversation is not so much on the interlocutors themselves, but rather on the subject matter (*Sache*) about which they cooperatively seek greater clarity. Because of their focus on the subject matter the interlocutors can experience a sort of self-forgetting that comes with losing oneself in the experience of where the conversation is leading or taking the interlocutors. One might think of this on analogy with a musical performance, a drama or an athletic contest, a game, where 'the players', to the extent that they enter into the play, might be said to experience a vanishing of self-consciousness. That is, the players/performers do not attend at all on 'making an impression' on the audience, or 'playing to the crowd', for to do so is precisely to lose the subject matter. Good players or performers (interlocutors) instead 'yield' to the music or the drama or the game (conversation) of which they are now a part or into which they have now been 'absorbed'.

The concept of play reinforces again the practical orientation of hermeneutics. Negotiating the world, learning what it means to play its various language games, requires a form of practical judgement (*phronēsis*) that is acquired through formation and apprenticeship to a sociality and to a language more so than to a method that stands above and thus immune from that formative sociality and by means of which a true interpretation is guaranteed.

Gadamer's contributions to the development of hermeneutics as a first philosophy are several. First, he appropriates the ontology of Heidegger to suggest that the task of understanding involves bringing human beings more fully into being as well as the act of knowing or interpreting human texts and actions. Second, Gadamer provides a corrective to the Enlightenment project of pure unbiased knowledge, to suggest that all knowledge is mediated and there is no 'bird's eye' view from which to understand human action. Finally, he introduces key metaphors including the fusion of horizons and the concept of play that articulate dimensions of the hermeneutical project that demonstrate both its infinite scope and its practical orientation.

VII. Paul Ricoeur: A Post-Ontological Hermeneutical Return to Schleiermacher

Paul Ricoeur (1913–2005) builds on the sophistication of Gadamer's hermeneutical project, corroborating and extending Gadamer but also taking hermeneutics into new areas of inquiry. Ricoeur's hermeneutical engagements are too vast and wide-ranging to allow easy summary. At best a few key emphases can be highlighted. Two in particular are noteworthy: his reorientation of hermeneutics as a critical discipline and his expansive understanding of interpretation as a poetic enterprise.

Hermeneutics as a Critical Discipline after the Disavowal of the Cogito

Ricoeur enters the hermeneutical conversation through Husserl and phenomenological tradition. Phenomenology emphasized the importance of intentionality for meaning. It also sought, following Descartes, to discover an originary experience wherein consciousness is fully present to itself. This is a futile misadventure according to Ricoeur. For the thinking self cannot intuit immediate self-transparency by virtue of the fact that the self always already exists within an immeasurable universe of signs that constitutes its life-world. The self inescapably finds itself mediated to itself, through the vast array of signs which it strives to figure out, to interpret. We indwell a life-world before we are able to attain self-conscious understanding of it—which rules out intuition or intentionality as the origin of meaning. Because there can be no pure unmediated intention for an interpreting subject, Ricoeur rejects phenomenology's starting point. He does not jettison the notion of a self or an ego altogether but rehabilitates it in a more nuanced and mediated form (see Ricoeur 1992).

Ricoeur's hermeneutical project thus amounts to an ambitious quest for meaning via an extended detour through the world of signs. The cultural works and signs that he draws upon include myths, symbols, desires, actions, and stories. These artefacts are pre-philosophical modes of expression saturated with ambiguity, opacity, and hidden depths. From the archaic symbolic forms of evil to the irreducible polesemy of metaphor, Ricoeur patiently explores the mechanisms whereby cultural signs continually generate and regenerate meaning (see Ricoeur 1967; and Ricoeur 1977). In this Ricoeur extends the notion of 'text' beyond the written word to include the whole domain of meaningful actions. Moreover, to the extent that human thought and action are determined by powers and forces other than the conscious intentions of agency—individual or communal—the demand for a critical hermeneutics, meaning a hermeneutics that can test its own validity, is inescapable.[12]

Ricoeur's hermeneutics becomes a *critical* theory in so far as his project is committed to both explanation and understanding. Unlike previous hermeneutical accounts, such as Dilthey's, where the explanatory model is borrowed from the empirical sciences, Ricoeur derives explanatory methods from within the field of signs and language itself (e.g. linguistics, structuralism, semiology). This is a key move in two ways. First, it

---

[12] Ricoeur eschews the idea of *total* reflection: ' . . . it is impossible for an individual, and still more for a group to formulate everything, schematize everything, pose everything as an object of thought . . . ' (Ricoeur 1991: 251).

means that 'explanation' no longer functions as a concept borrowed from the natural sciences. Instead, explanation in Ricoeur's sense names 'a model of intelligibility that belongs, from its birth so to speak, to the domain of the human sciences' (Ricoeur 1981: 157). Because explanation is native to language itself it is capable of being integrated with understanding in a reciprocal and complementary way. From its inception, therefore, hermeneutics contains within itself an explanatory 'moment' that gives it critical leverage to determine validity in interpretation according to its own standards and criteria without the need to appeal to external epistemological frameworks.

The second consequence of Ricoeur deriving explanatory models from within the domain of signs and language is that the notion of understanding is also significantly modified; it ceases to be a psychological one and becomes instead an 'intra-textual concept' (Ricoeur 1981: 162). From the Romantics through Dilthey and beyond, hermeneutics has operated with an overly subjective idea of understanding according to which the aim of interpretation was 'to coincide with the inner life of the author' (Ricoeur 1981: 150). By contrast, Ricoeur seeks to follow the intention *of the text* and not 'the presumed intention of the author [or] the lived experience of the writer' (Ricoeur 1981: 161). The reader of the text is 'addressed' not by another subject or person but by 'the situation created or instituted by the work itself' (Ricoeur 1981: 143). Interpretation thus becomes an objective process that is the act *of* the text before it is an act *on* the text.

The Poetic Reconstitution of the Self in Light of the Text

Ricoeur's hermeneutics has an unmistakable critical dimension. But it is also evinces an equally important *poetic* quality. According to Ricoeur, the interpretive process cannot be reduced to specifying the objective interrelations among the components of a work or a text. In addition to an explanatory and critical 'moment', there is a second, complementary 'moment' of understanding wherein a reader or interpreter appropriates the work to him or herself. Appropriation links the reader to 'the world of the text' such that the everyday trajectory of first-order reference is intercepted and suspended in order that a second-order reference might be freed up or disclosed. 'The world of the text' constitutes a new sort of distanciation—a distanciation of the real from itself, so to speak—with its imaginative variations on the real. The world of the text introduces a fictive dimension into our apprehension of reality, generating and opening up new possibilities, within everyday reality, of being-in-the-world.

What the world of the text intends is not the mental life of another—a world '*behind* the text'—but rather it is a world '*in front of* the text' which the work unfolds or reveals. 'It is not a question of imposing upon the text our finite capacity of understanding, but of exposing ourselves to the text and receiving from it an enlarged self . . .' (Ricoeur 1981: 143). The *what* to be appropriated is the matter proposed or projected by the text or work in accordance with which the interpreter is invited to project, to realize, one of her or his ownmost possibilities.

This dialectical relationship between explanation and understanding effects a movement that Ricoeur calls 'a hermeneutical arc'. This movement tracks from a stage of initial naïveté (first-order belongingness), through a phase of critical distanciation, to a recovery of meaning in a second naïveté (higher level belongingness). But even in the recovery phase distanciation plays a role. Understanding always remains understanding at and through distance. Distanciation is productive in that it enriches understanding by incorporating varying levels of textuality within it. 'To explain more is to understand better' is Ricoeur's motto (Ricoeur 1985: 5).

Interpretation, moreover, is as productive as it is reproductive. The meaning generated through the hermeneutic process is at once invented and discovered—in a double sense that pertains both to the 'subject matter' and to the 'self'. That is, the matter of the text and the matter of the self emerge concurrently in the hermeneutical process. Understanding is always and at the same time self-understanding: 'the constitution of the *self* is contemporaneous with the constitution of *meaning*' (Ricoeur 1981: 159). As the interpreter arrives at meaning, she also discovers that she has come to be herself in yet another, ever richer, fuller way.

Finally, for Ricoeur, there is no end to the activity of interpretation. Interpretation is as perpetual as life; each reading, each attainment of meaning, is always provisional, revisable, open, and continuously fecund in light of further possibilities. Realizing, actualizing possibilities, necessarily involve action, will, choice—a practical and political dimension. Hermeneutics engages the self it generates, and vice versa: the self reflects on the process by which it interprets the world and through which it arrives at its self-understanding which, in other words, is a realization of one of its ownmost possibilities in the world 'in front of the text'. Like his predecessors, Ricoeur envisions hermeneutics as a practical philosophy—inseparable from the political, the social, and the ethical, a facet of human will and desire, an ineludible dimension of freedom and nature, action and suffering.

VIII. THEOLOGICAL IMPLICATIONS

From this brief overview of modern hermeneutics, five central implications pertinent to theology stand out. First, hermeneutics exposes foundationalist epistemology as illusory. Transparent self-knowledge cannot be obtained with absolute certainty either through method or through strategies of immediate intuition. Instead, theology, like other disciplines that explore meaning in human action, must interpret language and signs. Interpretation's unendingly provisional (because historically and temporally contingent) character contributes constructively to theology. The inescapability of the hermeneutical circle—the dialectical, mutually reciprocal relation of part and whole—illuminates the kind of 'systematicity' intrinsic to theology. Rather than a static, inert and abstract 'system' of ideas, theology is more appropriately characterized as a dynamic, temporally unfolding series of negotiated settlements, interruptions, and resettlements. The dynamic process presupposes human fallibility and finitude, acknowledges its historical situatedness, yet is informed by an eschatological reserve. The 'already' is never separated from the 'not yet'. Hermeneutics helps foster a theology of hope chastened by time and tempered by human limitation.

Second, by elucidating the manifold ways in which all human actions and works are infused with multiple meanings, which transcend the intent of the author, hermeneutics supports a sacramental sensibility that views created, finite, material reality as communicative and disclosive of God's presence. A hermeneutically-informed sacramental sensibility resonates with theology's concern with incarnation—i.e. how the Word (the logos of God) is intensively and extensively enfleshed and living. The Word of God is inscribed in written texts and in the human heart, which means that the task of correctly interpreting the Word of God arises wherever shared forms of religious life are performed and practiced: in liturgy, in the reading and exposition of scripture in preaching, in prayer, in practices of hospitality and friendship.

Third, hermeneutics focuses attention on tradition, an issue of long-standing interest to theology. Our human condition is that we are immersed in and formed by a set of forces we have not chosen and over which we do not exercise mastery. On the positive side, this gives human beings orientation and a sense of bearing by virtue of deep, pre-reflective belongingness. But our immersion in tradition also has a darker side. It means that the search for self-understanding must expose and acknowledge both cultural contingencies and more dangerous desires: sin, self-deception, and the 'will to power'. Theology, then, cannot finally be separated from ideology critique.

Fourth, according to hermeneutical theory, 'figuring out' the meaning of work or text is not merely deciphering the author's intent, but a productive activity as well (realizing one's ownmost possibilities in front of the text). It follows that understanding is intrinsic to application because concurrent with it. That is to say, hermeneutics reminds theology that the application or appropriation of meaning is always integral to theological understanding, not its optional addendum. Theology is inescapably a practical and political undertaking.

Fifth, hermeneutics emphasizes *phronēsis* (practical judgement or 'the wisdom of judgement in situation') (Ricoeur 1992: 249). *Phronēsis*, along with its attendant virtues of listening, courtesy and attention, can be incorporated into theology. Even as the self is interpreted into being via the mediation of signs and works, so too the aim of theological hermeneutics is continually to open itself to the solicitation of the other whose claim upon us has already been made and to whom we feel compelled to respond. Indeed, theological wisdom is often disclosed in contexts of disruption and suffering, where we are 'brought up short' by the text, where we are made aware just how much the world eludes our definition or control, where 'limit experiences' confound our best efforts at comprehension. Hermeneutical theology is less about conceptual closure and more a way of responding to the other in all their as-yet-to-be-realized depth and excess. In so doing we are drawn ever more fully into an expansive and productive dialogue.

The evolution of hermeneutics from disciplinary-specific rules of interpretation to a first philosophy in the last century has contributed significantly to modern theology. Hermeneutics has influenced theology's methods, its goals and the epistemological assumptions that guide the theologian. The cross-fertilization may just be beginning. Theology in the twenty-first century has much to gain through an ongoing dialogue with hermeneutical philosophy.

REFERENCES

Bernstein, Richard (1983). *Beyond Objectivism and Relativism: Science, Hermeneutics, and Practice*. (Philadelphia, PA: University of Pennsylvania Press).

Bowie, Andrew (1990). *Aesthetics and Subjectivity: From Kant to Nietzsche*. (Manchester: Manchester University Press).

——(1997). *From Romanticism to Critical Theory: The Philosophy of German Literary Theory*. (London and New York: Routledge).

——(2005). 'The Philosophical Significance of Schleiermacher's Hermeneutics', in Jacqueline Mariña (ed.), *The Cambridge Companion to Friedrich Schleiermacher*, (Cambridge: Cambridge University Press), 73–90.

Dilthey, Wilhelm (1996). *Hermeneutics and the Study of History*, selected works, vol. iv, ed. and intro. Rudolf A. Makkreel and Frithjof Rodi (Princeton, NJ: Princeton University Press).

Ferraris, Maurizio (1996). *History of Hermeneutics*, trans. Luca Somigli (Atlantic Highlands, NJ: Humanities Press, 1996).

Gadamer, Hans-Georg (1967). *Philosophical Hermeneutics*, trans. and ed. David E. Linge (Berkeley, CA: University of California Press).

——(1993). *Truth and Method*, 2nd rev. edn, trans. Joel Weinsheimer and Donald G. Marshall (New York, NY: Continuum Publishing House).

Grondin, Jean (1990). 'Hermeneutics and Relativism', in Kathleen Wright (ed.), *Festivals of Interpretation: Essays on Hans-Georg Gadamer's Work*, (Albany, NY: SUNY Press).

——(1994). *Introduction to Philosophical Hermeneutics*, trans. Joel Weinsheimer (New Haven and London: Yale University Press), 42–62.

Palmer, Richard (1969). *Hermeneutics*. (Evanston, IL: Northwestern University Press).

Ricoeur, Paul (1966). *Freedom and Nature: The Voluntary and the Involuntary*, trans. Erazim V. Kohak (Evanston, IL: Northwestern University Press).

——(1967). *The Symbolism of Evil*, trans. Emerson Buchanan (New York: Harper and Row).

——(1970). *Freedom and Nature: An Essay on Interpretation*, trans. Denis Savage (New Haven, CT: Yale University Press).

——(1977). *The Rule of Metaphor: Multi-disciplinary Studies in the Creation of Meaning in Language*, trans. Robert Czerny, Kathleen McLaughlin, and John Costello (Toronto: University of Toronto Press).

——(1980). 'L'Originaire et la question-en-retour dans la Crisis de Husserl', in François Laruelle (ed.), *Textes pour Emmanuel Levinas*, (Paris: J-M Place).

——(1981). *Hermeneutics & the Human Sciences*, ed. and trans. John B. Thompson (Cambridge: Cambridge University Press).

——(1985). *Time and Narrative*, vol. 2, trans. Kathleen McLaughlin and David Pellauer (Chicago: University of Chicago Press).

——(1991). *From Text to Action*, trans. John B. Thompson and Kathleen Blamey (Evanston, IL: Northwestern University Press).

——(1992). *Oneself as Another*, trans. Kathleen Blamey (Chicago: University of Chicago Press).

Schleiermacher, Friedrich (1977). *Hermeneutik und Kritik*, ed. Manfred Frank (Frankfurt am Main: Suhrkamp).

——(1998). *Hermeneutics and Criticism and Other Writings*, ed. and trans. Andrew Bowie (Cambridge: Cambridge University Press).

Westphal, Merold (2001). *Overcoming Onto-theology: Toward a Postmodern Christian Faith*. (New York: Fordham University Press).

——(2009). *Whose Community? Which Interpretation? Philosophical Hermeneutics for the Church*. (Grand Rapids, MI: Baker Academic).

SUGGESTED READING

Arthos, John (2009). *The Inner Word in Gadamer's Hermeneutics*. (Notre Dame, IN: University of Notre Dame Press).

Caputo, John D. (1987). *Radical Hermeneutics: Repetition, Deconstruction, and the Hermeneutic Project*. (Bloomington, IN: Indiana University Press).

Frei, Hans W. (1974). *The Eclipse of Biblical Narrative: A Study in Eighteenth and Nineteenth Century Hermeneutics*. (New Haven, CT: Yale University Press).

Fodor, James (1995). *Christian Hermeneutics: Paul Ricoeur and the Refiguring of Theology*. (Oxford: Clarendon Press).

Kearney, Richard (2001). *The God Who May Be: A Hermeneutics of Religion*. (Bloomington, IN: Indiana University Press).

Louth, Andrew (1983). *Discerning the Mystery: An Essay on the Nature of Theology*. (Oxford: Clarendon Press).

Malpas, Jeff and Satiago Zabala (eds) (2010). *Consequences of Hermeneutics: Fifty Years After Gadamer's* Truth and Method. (Evanston, IL: Northwestern University Press).

——Ulrich Arnswald, and Jens Kertscher (eds) (2002). *Gadamer's Century: Essays in Honor of Hans-Georg Gadamer*. (Cambridge, MA: MIT Press).

Mueller-Vollmer, Kurt (ed., intro., and notes) (1988). *The Hermeneutics Reader: Texts of the German Tradition from the Enlightenment to the Present*. (New York: Continuum Publishing Company).

Risser, James C. (1997). *Hermeneutics and the Voice of the Other: Re-reading Hans-Georg Gadamer's Philosophical Hermeneutics*. (Albany, NY: State University of New York Press).

Thiselton, Anthony C. (2006). *Thiselton on Hermeneutics: Collected Works with New Essays*. (Grand Rapids, MI: Eerdmans Publishing Company).

Tracy, David (1987). *Plurality and Ambiguity: Hermeneutics, Religion, Hope*. (San Francisco, CA: Harper and Row, Publishers).

Vattimo, Gianni (1997). *Beyond Interpretation: The Meaning of Hermeneutics for Philosophy*, trans. David Webb (Stanford, CA: Stanford University Press).

Westphal (2001).

——(2009).

CHAPTER 25

....

PHENOMENOLOGY

....

MEROLD WESTPHAL

PHENOMENOLOGY is a descriptive empiricism that seeks carefully to describe human experience in all of its various modes. It is an epistemology that seeks to understand the nature and limits of human understanding; or rather, it is a series of diverse accounts of what human knowledge is and can be. In Hegel and Husserl we find two exemplars of the Cartesian quest for certainty, either on a foundationalist model (Husserl) or a holistic model (Hegel). If these two represent major moments in modern philosophy, post-Husserlian phenomenology is a series of departures from Husserl (heresies, one might call them) that represent various ways of making the transition to postmodern philosophy. We will examine the contributions of Heidegger, Gadamer, Ricoeur, Lévinas, and Marion, and do so with particular regard to how phenomenology impacts the question of God.

I. HEGEL AND HUSSERL

....

While one can trace the origins of phenomenology back almost as far as one wishes, the term was introduced into European culture primarily by Hegel and then, a century later, by Husserl. Central to both thinkers is the primary concern of modern philosophy, knowledge, its nature and limits. Both thinkers belong to the rationalist tradition stemming especially from Descartes according to which, when the nature of knowledge is properly grasped, its limits will tend to disappear. It will not be the task of philosophy to know particular details about the world, but its general structure and meaning will be comprehensively and definitively known.

These phenomenologies belong to 'modern' philosophy, sometimes referred to as the Enlightenment Project. They phenomenologically describe the path by which philosophy comes to possess knowledge that is

1) Clear and distinct—nothing ambiguous, nothing hidden, everything fully present to consciousness.

2) Certain—beyond doubt and the challenge of various scepticisms and thereby final.

3) Universal and objective—free from presuppositions and perspectives, not relative to anything particular or contingent.

For Hegel, phenomenology is the 'Science of the *experience of consciousness*' (Hegel 1977: 56). Each of the three terms is key. By science Hegel does not mean physics and chemistry, but systematic, comprehensive knowledge as just described. By experience he does not mean the reception of sensory input, as the empiricists would have it, but two quite different themes. First, philosophy will deal with the familiar, what ordinary, pre-philosophical life presents to us, including but not limited to sense experience, which turns out to be the poorest anticipation of genuine knowledge. It will be the task of philosophy to render experience in this sense scientific by putting it in its place, showing the nature and limits of its various forms until it reaches a place where it no longer needs to transcend itself and is infinite, unlimited. Second, experience signifies the ordered journey, partly structural, partly historical, through the various inadequate forms of supposed knowing until that unsurpassable stage is reached (Hegel 1977: Preface and Introduction).

Hegel does not define consciousness as Husserl will, namely as intentionality (consciousness of . . .), but he might well have. The various stages or forms of consciousness are diverse modes in which we and the world in which we find ourselves are given to us and taken by us. (Hegel and Husserl are both idealists in the sense that nothing is given cognitively to us apart from the way it is taken by us.) But Hegel's goal is not to map and classify the rich fields of consciousness, though he does this. It is rather to tell the story of how consciousness is ultimately transformed into self-consciousness, how all modes of consciousness can ultimately be seen as modes or embodiments of ourselves as mind or spirit (*Geist*). Religion and Philosophy are the two final stages on the journey. What religion experiences as consciousness, awareness of something other than itself (God), philosophy experiences as self-consciousness, full and final awareness of human subjectivity itself, both individually and especially collectively. This is 'the point where knowledge no longer needs to go beyond itself' (Hegel 1977: 51), for it has become the human spirit fully present to itself and as such is absolute spirit and absolute knowing at once (Westphal 1998: chs 7–8). Postmodern critiques of presence and of totalizing thought always have Hegel as a major target.

The religious significance of Hegel's *Phenomenology* continues to be debated. Whether it is read as a rationalized theism or as pantheistic humanism, Marx sees it as hopelessly religious, since it appeals to a 'spiritual' principle, spirit in its necessary historical unfolding, as the ultimate ground and explanation of the real rather than to a 'materialist' principle, economic and technological forces. In the process, it legitimates the historical status quo instead of providing the much needed critique of both capitalism and religion. Some later readings share Marx's view that Hegel is a genuinely religious thinker but welcome him on just that ground. Still other readings see Hegel's thought as a pantheism of the historical, human spirit anticipating, Feuerbach's theory that theology is anthropology, that what religion takes to be a transcendent God is only the projection of an ideal image of the human. Thus, instead of 'God is love' we get 'human love is divine, the highest thing there is'. Here Hegel's pantheism is seen as a thinly disguised atheism. Hegel resisted being called a pantheist, since he did not want to be called an atheist and have the same trouble as Fichte before him—Fichte lost his job in the university—but his texts give considerable evidence for this reading. As we learn from Spinoza, one can talk endlessly about God while being an a-theist.

However construed, Hegel's project belongs to the larger Enlightenment project that can carry the name of one of Kant's books—religion within the limits of reason alone. The basic idea is that religion on its own is insufficiently rational and needs to be purified by philosophical reason either a) by keeping the kernels while throwing away the husks (Deism, Spinoza, Lessing) or b) by reinterpreting religious beliefs in the light of a purportedly autonomous philosophy, thereby bringing to light their incipient rationality (Kant, Hegel). For Hegel this translation means converting the language of religion, representations (*Vorstellungen*), the conceptual tools of everyday experience and the pre-philosophical sciences, including theology, into genuinely philosophical concepts (*Begriffe*). Hegel sees this as giving us a new, improved version of Christianity, while his critics see it as distorting religion in general and Christianity in particular beyond recognition.

Whether scholars today use Hegel as a whipping boy (along with Descartes) for what philosophy should never try to become or continue to find stimulating and challenging ideas in his work, his phenomenological project as a journey to the absolute knowing of absolute spirit and the larger system to which it serves as a kind of introduction cannot be said to be alive today. For that reason the term 'phenomenology' today draws its meanings almost exclusively from Husserl and the revisions (heresies, one might say) that have arisen out of his thought.

Husserl shares with Hegel the ideal of philosophy as absolute knowing—1) clear and distinct, 2) certain and final, and 3) objective and universal. Two slogans express this ambition. The first is the title of a crucial essay, 'Philosophy as Rigorous Science' (Husserl 1981: 159–97). It is a critique of philosophies in the naturalist or historicist mode. The critique of naturalism is a brief recap, in essence, of his extended critique of psychologism in *Logical Investigations* (Husserl 1970, vol. I). What psychologism, naturalism, and historicism have in common is placing the foundations of human thought in the real world of particularity and contingency, thereby making thought relative to conditions that are not universal and objective. In other words, they make philosophy as a genuine science impossible. Philosophy must extract itself from the world of nature, the world of history, and the human psyche as an entity part natural and part historical.

The other slogan is 'Back to the things themselves' (an obvious dig at the neo-Kantian slogan, 'Back to Kant'). Philosophy must be grounded in an 'ideational intuition' that retains its identity throughout the worlds of change, and thus of particularity and contingency. Accordingly, 'we can absolutely not rest content with "mere words", i.e. with a merely symbolic understanding of words . . . Meanings inspired only by remote, confused, inauthentic intuitions—if by any intuitions at all—are not enough: we must go back to the "things themselves" ' (Husserl 1970: I, 252). In a critique of empiricist naturalism, he similarly writes,

> But to judge rationally or scientifically about things signifies to conform *to the things themselves* or to go from words and opinions back to the things themselves, to consult them in their self-givenness and to set aside all prejudices alien to them . . . all science must proceed from *experience*, must *ground* its mediate cognition on immediate experience.   (Husserl 1983: 35)

In other words, language drags thought down out of the sunlight into the cave when it is not itself grounded in immediate experience. So far as it is but the bearer of sedimented, traditional interpretations whose intuitional bona fides are not evident, language itself, beginning with the language of logic, must be purified and regrounded. Whereas Hegel's project is teleological, moving towards a goal, Husserl's is archaeological, working back to authentic origins.

Heidegger captures nicely the thrust of these two slogans when he defines phenomenology as the task 'to let that which shows itself be seen from itself in the very way in which it shows itself from itself' (Heidegger 1962: 58).

Husserl develops his programme around three key notions. The first of these is intentionality. Consciousness is unique in that unlike everything else it is *about* something. Consciousness is always consciousness *of* . . . If language is about something it is not as marks on a page or sounds in the air but as inhabited by and expressive of consciousness. Any mode of consciousness can be analysed in terms of the intentional act (*noēsis*) and intentional object (*noēma*), the meaning or sense that is correlative to the act.

The second notion is that of the phenomenological reduction, a.k.a. the *epochē*. If the intentional object were thought of as something real in the world of nature or history, the intentional act would have to be a real relation between an ego or psyche, equally embedded in the worlds of nature and history and that object; then the relativity that keeps philosophy from being scientific would prevail. The *epochē* does not deny or doubt the worldly reality of subject and object but abstracts from this aspect of the situation, bracketing the realism of the 'natural attitude' in order to attend to the correlation of act (the how of givenness, *noēsis*) and object (the what of givenness, *noēma*) in consciousness. The knower becomes, not in actual fact but *as attended to*, the transcendental ego, purified of anything empirical and thus contingent. It is a subjectivity for which there is the world but which is not itself in the world. In parallel, the object becomes the meaning or content of the act, wholly immanent to that act. This immanence does not mean that I am looking at my representation or idea of the object but rather that I am attending *to the object as intended*, as given to an ideal, unworldly consciousness and as taken by that consciousness.

The third notion is that of the eidetic reduction, the reduction to essence. The object (my telephone, say) may still seem to be too particular to be the content of universal knowledge, and its particularity is all too easily traced to its location in nature and history, or, more abstractly, in space and time. So the second abstraction or reduction is to move from fact to essence, to *attend* to the universal features of objects and the modes of their givenness so as to generate meanings not tied to any particular natural or historical situation. Only with the help of such meanings can the other sciences be truly scientific, so in this way philosophy can be the rigorous science that gives to the other sciences their status as truly scientific.

The whole of the Husserlian project is more complex than this. The notion of immediate presence in intuition raises the question of time consciousness; the notion of a transcendental ego raises the question of intersubjectivity; and the flight from nature and history raises the question of what a phenomenological approach to nature and to history might look at. Husserl addresses all these questions and others as well. But the three notions briefly described above are the basic building blocks of his project of making philosophy a rigorous science, something he takes none of his predecessors to have accomplished. In his later works he expresses doubts himself.

The theological significance of strictly Husserlian phenomenology is minimal. Little has been done and little attention paid to what has been done within purely Husserlian horizons, whether it involves phenomenological approaches to God or to religion itself. To do either of these has seemed to require deviations from Husserlian orthodoxy— hence the reference above to phenomenological heresies. Before turning to these we can ask why Husserlian phenomenology has not in itself proven fruitful for theology or philosophy of religion.

The simplest answer, which doesn't take us very far, is that Husserl himself wasn't much interested in matters theological and, unlike Hegel, did not point the way to developing his project in relation to God or to religion. A possibly more basic answer is that Husserl's project represents a methodological prejudice against the proposed subject matter, God as the religious 'object' or religion as the modes of human subjectivity in relation to God or the Holy. The transcendental ego is too pure, too abstract, not human enough to be religious itself. God, at least the God of the Abrahamic monotheisms, is not encountered in the ethereal spaces in which the transcendental ego dwells; and the ideal meanings it constitutes are not the meanings of actual human religion, which takes place in the world. To assume that the intentional acts that constitute religion and the noematic senses or meanings correlative to them by which God or the Holy is understood are best understood by removing oneself from the world in which they occur may well be arbitrary and self-defeating. To cut oneself off from religious life may be to cut oneself off from understanding religious life. This is not to say that one must be religious to understand religion, a believer in order to understand God, even if there is a sense in which this is true. For the real world in which God is encountered and religion is practised is inhabited not only by believers of many different types, but also by unbelievers. It may be that in that world rigorous science with theological import is not possible, religion being very different from, say, mathematics. It is not unimportant that Husserl's phenomenology developed out of his concern for mathematics and logic.

II. THE HERMENEUTIC TURN[1]

It is just the assumption that human understanding requires genuinely human thinkers that is made by the turn to hermeneutical phenomenology, with respect not just to religion but also to the subject matter of the humanities, the social sciences, and at times even the natural sciences. This is the first of the 'heresies' mentioned above, revisionist versions of the Husserlian project that abandon the ideal of rigorous science shared, at least in general, by Hegel and Husserl. The main figures are Heidegger (1962), Ricoeur (1981), and Gadamer (1989/2004[2]). Together they represent a turn from 'modern' to 'postmodern' philosophy in so far as they abandon as unnecessary and unavailable the ideals of knowledge described above.

Hermeneutics is the theory of interpretation, and hermeneutical phenomenology, also known as philosophical hermeneutics, interprets intentionality as interpretation rather than as intuition. What is given underdetermines what is taken or how it is construed, and this requires an act of interpretation or seeing-as where more than one such construal is compatible with what is given to intuition. The famous duck-rabbit figure cited by Wittgenstein exhibits this structure (Westphal 2009a: 24). Heidegger presents all human cognitive acts as interpretations, so hermeneutics is epistemology (Westphal 2001: ch. 3). Gadamer focuses on texts and text-like works of art. Ricoeur focuses on texts and text-like human action. All three share Schleiermacher's desire to extend interpretation theory beyond any particular discipline such as law, literary criticism, or theology (Westphal 2001: chs 6 and 8); none focuses primarily on religion; all three are highly relevant to religion as various interpretations of self and world and to theology as scriptural interpretation whether academic, ecclesial, or laic.

Hermeneutical phenomenology represents a double turn away from the ideal of absolute knowing. First, it shifts the goal of reflection or thought from knowledge to understanding. This is a subtle shift that involves at least two elements: a) a move away from primary preoccupation with how to identify what propositions are true and when true beliefs deserve the honorific title of knowledge, and b) a move towards interpreting the 'object' of cognition as more nearly like a subject than like an object such as a tree or a computer. A text 'speaks' to me in a more nearly literal sense than, say, a beautiful bird song or sunset. There is quite literally a human speaker behind the text, possibly of unknown identity, whereas this is not true of the bird song or sunset. In this way texts claim us and address us in the way in which mere objects do not. What is given for interpretation is already an interpretation of its own subject matter.

Second, whether cognition is thought of in terms of knowledge or understanding, the idea of a neutral, presuppositionless and thus a universal and objective result is

---

[1] See also Chapter 23 by Fodor in this volume.

[2] These two versions of the second revised edition inexcusably have different pagination and will be cited as 1989/2004.

abandoned. In its place is the theory of the hermeneutical circle (Westphal 2009a: ch. 7). When we come to interpret any phenomenon we come with prior expectations, presuppositions, what Gadamer will call prejudices (pre-judice, pre-judgement). We always interpret from some situation, some standpoint, some horizon. We are always somewhere (particular and contingent) and never nowhere. The hermeneutical inter-pretation of interpretation sees it as perspectival cognition. There are four things to notice here:

1) These presuppositions or prejudices function as a priori elements of understanding. We bring them with us to the task, and our interpretations are guided and shaped by them. As in Kant's *Critique of Pure Reason*, they are the conditions for the possibility of experience (as interpretation). But unlike the a priori elements of Kant's First Critique, these are not universal and necessary, ahistorically unchanging. They are revisable and revised in the course of using them—hence the circle. In the movement from twelve to six o'clock, interpretations are guided by a priori horizons of expectation; in the movement back from six to twelve, those presuppositions are revised in the light of what is learned from actually using them. Neither the presuppositions nor the inter-pretations to which they give rise are independent variables (Gadamer 1989/2004: 265–77/268–78). Each is conditioned by the other, just as the basketball player with the ball and the defender are mutually conditioned by each other. What the player with the ball does depends significantly on what the defender does, shooting if the defender drops off and driving to the basket if the defender plays too tight. But at the same time, the defender's actions are conditioned by the action of the offensive player, playing loosely if the latter is quick and eager to drive and more closely if the latter is 'hot' from the outside.

2) Presuppositions or prejudices are sometimes 'true' and sometimes 'false', which means that some help us better to understand the phenomenon in question while others lead to misunderstanding (Gadamer 1989/2004: 298–9/298). The process of interpretation is the ongoing revision not only of interpretations but also of the presuppositions (principles, criteria) that guide them. There is no method that can render this project neutral and objective, since the employment of any method is itself the presupposition that it will best illuminate the subject matter, a presupposition open to challenge and revision. Nor can this process be brought to a close. The history of the interpretation of Shakespeare, the American Constitution, and the Bible shows this clearly enough. Individuals or schools of interpretation may claim finality for them-selves, but history rudely ignores such claims and continues to produce new interpret-ations, new methods, new presuppositions.

3) However presuppositions are born, they are borne, sustained, and disseminated by traditions (*traditio*, transferring, handing over, giving over by means of words). Individual interpreters, even geniuses, do not create *ex nihilo*; their presuppositions (perspectives, situations, horizons) are rather to a very large extent the product of the traditions by which they have been shaped and thus of the communities, actual or virtual, to which they belong or have belonged (Gadamer 1989/2004: 276–85/277–85).

Consciousness is always historically effected consciousness (*wirkungsgeschichtliches Bewusstsein*). It is in every case to a dramatic degree the product of its own history (Gadamer 1989/ 2004: 300–7/299–306; 341–79/336–71). Over against Husserl, the claim is that we understand better when we acknowledge our immersion in the world rather than trying to abstract from it or extract ourselves out of it; and over against Hegel, the claim is that, short of the eschaton, which we are not, we can never bring closure or totality to our historically shaped plurality—different interpretations from different perspectives.

4) If interpretation is inherently perspectival, the path to an 'objectivity' that will challenge the absoluteness and finality of any particular (and in that sense 'subjective') interpretation or tradition of interpretation might well be not to flee perspectives but to multiply them. That is the assumption of Ricoeur's suggestion that the path 'to the things themselves' needs to take place by means of 'the detour through the contingency of cultures, though an incurably equivocal language, and through the conflict of interpretations' (1970: 42). It requires 'the long detour of the signs of humanity deposited in cultural works' and of 'the detour of understanding the cultural signs in which the self documents and form itself . . . [so that] reflection is nothing without the mediation of signs and works' (1981: 143, 158–9). In other words, instead of fleeing prior interpretations and the words in which they are expressed, as suggested by Husserl's version of the slogan 'Back to the things themselves', Ricoeur makes a virtue of necessity in arguing that our interpretations are and ought to be mediated by the rich variety of prior interpretations. Since we cannot terminate the 'conflict of interpretations', we might as well try to learn from it. We might call this epistemic ecumenism.

If we look at the history of the interpretation of, say, Shakespeare, the American Constitution, and the Bible, we cannot fail to notice that philosophical hermeneutics predicts just what we find: a rich and unending variety of interpretations bearing the marks of the traditions by which their presuppositions have been transmitted to the interpreters. This easily gives rise to what Berger and Luckmann call 'the vertigo of relativity' (1967: 5). It is eloquently expressed by Dilthey, for whom 'the relativity of every kind of human apprehension of the totality of things is the last word of the historical world-view . . . But where are the means to overcome the anarchy of opinions that then threatens to befall us?' (1996: 389). Have we fallen into a different-strokes-for-different-folks world in which 'anything goes'?

One answer to this haunting question is to appeal to some method in terms of which interpretation can at least approach universal and objective validity. But, as already noted, this is not presuppositionless thought but the presupposition that the method will get us to the things themselves But such presuppositions may be 'true' or 'false' in Gadamer's sense. To adopt the microscope as the means of studying the moon (from earth) won't help. We can't even see the moon through a microscope. The choice of a telescope will be a 'truer' presupposition, for it will help us see much that is hidden from the naked eye. But it will also hide the aesthetic and romantic aspects of a full moon, especially over water, which can be seen from the perspective of the naked eye.

We will be located in a historical tradition (natural science) in terms of which our vision will be perspectival.

Another attempt to escape the vertigo of relativity is to insist, in the case of texts at least, that the meaning is precisely the original meaning intended by the author for the original readers. At least in this case the text will be seen as having a fixed and determinate meaning at which to aim. Gadamer and Ricoeur refuse to equate a text's meaning with the *mens auctoris*, mind of the author. But even if we assume that a text has only a single meaning unilaterally determined by the author, it does not follow that we can access this in an objective and universally valid manner. We read the author's language in the light of our own language or, in other words, we read the text from the perspective(s) which we occupy; so it should not be surprising if there are vigorous disputes among highly qualified interpreters over just what that original authorial meaning was.

'Was' signifies another problem. The reduction of interpretation to the recovery of an original meaning requires interpreters to pretend to live in a different world, possibly very different, from the one they actually inhabit, to be what they are not, contemporaries of Amos, or Paul, or Shakespeare, or the Founding Fathers. This makes of the text an artifact we observe rather than a voice by which we are addressed. Or, as LaCocque and Ricoeur put it, 'Cut off from its ties to a living community, the text gets reduced to a cadaver handed over for autopsy . . . It is almost as though one were to give the funeral eulogy of someone yet alive' (1998: p. xii). If texts from the past are able to speak to us today it is over the time span that separates us from them, not by pretending to have abolished that distance. This means that our own perspective is not irrelevant to interpretation.

The suggestion here is that our libraries are not museums, much less cemeteries. Classic texts, those that have played a founding role for the cultures to whose canon they belong, continue to instruct and inspire those cultures. As Gadamer's references to the claims texts make on us or the way in which we are addressed by them suggest, the goal is to learn from them, to listen to what they have to say to us now. This is to say that the epistemic goal is deeper than mere knowledge in the sense of sorting out the true propositions from the false ones. It is rather understanding, the self-understanding that is closer to what we mean by wisdom than what we have come to mean by science. It is about *knowing-who* we are and *knowing-how* to live, not just about *knowing-that* certain facts obtain.

This is why Ricoeur says

> the text must be unfolded, no longer towards its author, but towards its immanent sense and toward the world which it opens up and discloses . . . the essential question is not to recover, behind the text, the lost intention, but to unfold, in front of the text, the 'world' which it opens up and discloses . . . what must be interpreted in a text is a *proposed world* which I could inhabit and wherein I could project one of my ownmost possibilities.   (Ricoeur 1981: 47, 53, 111, 141–2; cf. 93, 218)

This is also why Gadamer insists that application is an essential part of interpretation, bridging, not abolishing the historical gap between the then of the text and the now of our own lives by seeing that then from our now (Gadamer 1989/2004: 307–41/306–36).

It is enough to say that we understand in a *different* way, *if we understand at all*... It is part of the historical finitude of our being that we are aware that others after us will understand in a different way. And yet it is equally that it remains the same work whose fullness of meaning is realized in the changing process of understanding, just as it is the same history whose meaning is constantly in the process of being defined. The hermeneutical reduction to the author's meaning is just as inappropriate as the reduction of historical events to the intentions of their protagonists.   (Gadamer 1989/2004: 296–7, 373/296, 366)

Gadamer draws the conclusion that hermeneutics is a double task. 'Not just occasionally but always, the meaning of a text goes beyond its author. That is why understanding is not merely a reproductive but always a productive activity as well' (Gadamer 1989/2004: 296/296). E. D. Hirsch, Jr, a major defender of hermeneutical objectivism, has allowed the vertigo of relativity to leave him so dizzy that he cannot even read this passage straight. He leaves out the 'merely' and the 'as well' and attributes the following quotation to Gadamer: 'Understanding is not a reproductive but always a productive activity.' Then he concludes that for Gadamer a text 'means whatever we take it to mean' and that he denies 'that the text has *any* determinate meaning' (Hirsch 1967: 249). One expects better reading from undergraduates.

What Gadamer actually says is that hermeneutics is both reproductive and productive. It is reproductive in that it seeks to discover the original, authorial meaning, to reproduce it as faithfully as possible. It is productive in that it seeks to hear what that original meaning might have to say to us in a situation very different from that of the author and the original readers, one the author could not even have imagined. The double task is quite direct: what *did* the text mean then (the reproductive task) and what *does* it say to us now (the productive task). In a theological context, Nicholas Wolterstorff puts it this way: what *was* the human author of a particular scriptural text saying to his original readers back then, and what *is* God saying to us through the same inscriptions now? (Wolterstorff 1995: 56.)

Legal and literary hermeneutics do not presuppose a living speaker now addressing us through a text in this way as its ultimate author. But with or without the theological claim, the double task of exegesis and application remains: what did it mean then and what does it mean now? Jacques Derrida expresses it nicely, defending, as it were, Gadamer against Hirsch (neither of whom he mentions):

To produce this signifying structure [an interpretation] cannot consist of reproducing, by the effaced and respectful doubling of commentary, the conscious, voluntary, intentional relationship that the writer institutes in his exchanges with the history to which he belongs thanks to the element of language. This moment of doubling commentary should no doubt have its place in a critical reading. To recognize and respect all its classical exigencies is not easy and requires all the instruments of traditional criticism. Without this recognition and this respect, critical production would risk developing in a direction at all and authorize itself to say almost anything. But this indispensable guardrail has always only *protected*, it has never *opened* a reading.   (Derrida 1976: 158)

Hirsch's stark either/or—either the author unilaterally determines the meaning or else anything goes—is a false one. The reproductive task (doubling commentary) places constraints on interpretation, but differences of context will take new readers to new readings (the productive task) beyond the horizons of the original meaning. Given the multiplicity of situations in which new readers find themselves, there will be a multiplicity of interpretations that remain within the constraints of the guard rail.

Gadamer gives two examples: performing a play or musical piece and translating a text. There are real constraints and one can simply get it wrong. While playing Hamlet one cannot say, 'To fish or not to fish'. Similarly, one just gets it wrong if one plays a C# where the score has an F or translates *Leid* as harm, hurt, injury, wrong, pain, sorrow, grief, or mourning, though one can translate *Leid* as any of these, depending on context, without violating the guard rail. Those who use different translations of Homer or the Bible may well have a favourite, just as music lovers may prefer Gould's 1981 version of the Goldberg Variations to the famous 1955 version. But it does not follow that only my favourite is right and the others all wrong. The conflict of interpretations referred to by Ricoeur is between those that are right as distinct from those that are wrong (guard rail violators), but also among those that are right but simply different from each other.

Wolterstorff gives another example that emphasizes the interpreter's context. Mom says, 'Only two more days till Christmas.' To the children, these are words of comfort, to her husband words of challenge and exhortation—'It's time to get your shopping done.' (Wolterstorff 1995: 55). Two very different speech acts. If we suppose that she is unaware of being overheard by her husband, we have the typical situation of a writer and readers other than the originally intended ones. In such cases it is not strange at all if (same text) + (different context) = (different interpretation). But this does not mean that the text can mean just anything we want it to. The husband would just be wrong to take his wife's statement as the suggestion that he buy that Porsche he has always wanted.

The moral of the story is quite simple. Interpretations are relative to contexts (traditions, cultures, languages, presuppositions) because as interpreters we are relative to contexts, inextricably embedded in perspectives that shape our interpretations. We can move from one situation to another, but we are always somewhere and never nowhere. Theologically speaking, this is the reminder that only God is absolute and we are not God. In a more secular language, this relativity simply expresses 'the historical finitude of our being' (Gadamer 1989/2004: 373/366). It is no license for an 'anything goes' free for all. But it means that it is neither likely nor desirable that the 'conflict of interpretations' will soon or easily terminated. The hard work will remain of sorting out those differences that can be celebrated, from those than can only be tolerated, and from those that must be opposed.

We are a long way from Husserl's project of philosophy as rigorous science. In what sense, then, are we still doing phenomenology? Four points.

1) We are still working with the concept of intentionality, now redefined as interpretation rather than intuition.

2) The phenomenological reduction is correspondingly redefined in that the subject of experience is an in-the-world interpreter rather than a transcendental ego. The empirical particularities of any given interpreter are bracketed in favour of an eidetic structure, the general form of a historically effected interpreter.

3) The intentional act (*noēsis*)—intentional object (noema) structure is similarly redefined as the act of interpretation and the 'object' as interpreted.

4) The goal of getting 'to the things themselves' is retained, not as a flight from words and prior interpretations, but via the detour through other interpretations. It is this conversation among conflicting interpretations that is given the task of keeping our own from becoming sedimented, stale, and dogmatic, putting us in touch more with ourselves than with the things themselves.

III. INVERTED INTENTIONALITY

Emmanuel Lévinas is a main figure in another revisionist version (heresy) of Husserlian phenomenology. He sees the mainstream of the western philosophical tradition as the systematic 'reduction of the other to the same'. This does not mean a solipsistic denial of anything real other than oneself but the absorption without remainder of the meaning of anything other into one's own horizons of possible meaning. Nothing can be permanently surprising or incomprehensible. Hegel is all too good an example in so far as he makes it the goal of philosophy to convert consciousness into self-consciousness. This does not mean that I see nothing but myself in the mirror but that I see everything 'other' than myself as mirroring and embodying the structures of my own thought. Just as for many theists the ideas in the mind of God are the archetypes of the particular things that imitate them by participating in them, so for Hegel this eternal logos is found in human thought at the level of speculative philosophy and articulated in his logic.

Lévinas sees this tendency in its many forms as failing to take seriously enough the phenomenological slogan, 'To the things themselves' as articulated by Heidegger, according to whom the task is 'to let that which shows itself be seen from itself in the very way in which it shows itself from itself' (Heidegger 1962: 58). That which is other than oneself must be allowed to be the agent, showing itself, and it must be allowed to do so on its own terms, from itself, or, in Lévinas' phrase, *kath'aútó*. 'Manifestation *kath'aútó* consists in a being telling itself to us independently of every position we would have taken in its regard, *expressing itself*' (Lévinas 1969: 65). The 'object' must be given primacy over the 'subject' of experience and what counts for the latter as reason and intelligibility.

For Lévinas, Husserl's phenomenology remains too 'Hegelian' in this respect. The intentional act is an act of *Sinngebung* or meaning conferral. The subject, in the mode of the transcendental ego, remains the agent, the origin, the source of meaning, not in the sense that the world is a fiction that we create but that it can be given to us only as we take it, only within our own horizons of expectations (Lévinas 1998: ch. 4). This is why Lévinas seeks 'the possibility of *signification without a context*' (Lévinas 1969: 23). This does not mean that the subject has ceased to live within determinate horizons of meaning but rather than the 'other' needs to be able to penetrate these defences and present itself in its own terms, *kath'aúto*. In other words, 'not every transcendent intention has the noesis-noema structure' and 'language institutes a relation irreducible to the subject-object relation' (Lévinas 1969: 29, 73).

Heidegger's revisions of Husserl represent progress, but are not radical enough for Lévinas (Lévinas 1996: ch. 1). Heidegger replaces the transcendental ego with Dasein (an attempt to free reflection from the conceptual baggage associated with such terms as self, person, subject, ego, soul, etc.); and he emphasizes that Dasein is by its very essence in-the-world, not uncontaminated by its particularities and contingencies. One implication of the worldliness of Dasein is the hermeneutical turn. (Heidegger eventually realized that this includes the philosopher whose interpretations of interpretation are not themselves historically and culturally unsituated). But the *noesis-noēma* structure remains. The intentional act is now the interpretation given by Dasein and within the horizon of Dasein's world. As the object of Dasein' interpretive intentionality, the other remains reduced to the same.

Lévinas gives us three formulas for what is needed here but lacking. The first is 'the overflowing of objectifying thought by a forgotten experience from which it lives'. Second, with reference to Heidegger's account of experience as disclosure, '*The absolute experience is not disclosure but revelation*'. Finally, one experiences the other as truly other 'only on call from the Other. *Revelation* constitutes a veritable inversion [of] *objectifying cognition*' (Lévinas 1969: 28, 65–7).

In this inversion the arrows of intentionality (consciousness of . . . interpretation of . . .) flow towards me from the other rather than emanating from myself. The act of *Sinngebung* is performed by the other who is now more a subject than an object and more the agent than I myself. I and my world are interpreted by the other, who sets my agenda for me and gives my identity to me. 'The Other measures me with a gaze incomparable to the gaze by which I discover him' (Lévinas 1969: 86).

Of course, the other involved here is not some physical object other than myself, my telephone, say, but a human other. Lévinas identifies this other as the face, not an object that I see but the source from which another sees and addresses me. The linguistic element is very important. 'The face speaks' (Lévinas 1969: 66), which is why I encounter the other as such 'only on call from the Other'. This call is a call to ethical responsibility, to justice, and eventually to love. The agenda set for me by the mere presence of the face of the other, whether or not it actually says anything and regardless of what it may say, is an ethical responsibility. This ethical call is the 'forgotten experience' that underlies all other human experience, and this is why ethics and not ontology or epistemology is first philosophy for Lévinas. That ethics if first philosophy means that the question of justice is prior to the question of truth, 'that truth is founded on my relationship with the other, or justice. To put speech [being addressed] at the origin of truth is to abandon the thesis that disclosure, which implies the solitude of vision, is the first work of truth' (Lévinas 1969: 99).

By calling this event revelation, and using a lot of other religious language in connection with it (height, glory, holiness, goodness), Lévinas seeks to make clear that the authority undergirding inverted intentionality comes from the human other only in so far as that other is in some sense the bearer of something divine. As with Kant, ethics is autonomous and prior to religion, whose status is somewhat ambiguous. Often Lévinas sounds as if 'God' is just the name for the depth dimension of the human self that is the foundation of ethics (Westphal 2008: especially chs 3–4). God is not presented as another other who calls me to responsibility (or graciously grants forgiveness and reconciliation). But Lévinas assumes that religion and ethics are deeply intertwined and that the two together presuppose inverted intentionality, being called by a voice not my own to a mission and identity not grounded in my autonomy.

Lévinas insists that he is a phenomenologist, but only with reference to 'an intentionality of a wholly different type' (Lévinas 1969: 23). This turns out to be the inverted intentionality we have just encountered. Neither Hegel, nor Husserl, nor Heidegger (as developed by Gadamer and Ricoeur) give us a phenomenology with transparent access to the ethical-religious dimensions of experience and thus to the things themselves. Gadamer, indeed, speaks of the claims made on us by the texts we interpret, and Ricoeur interprets a variety of religious texts and phenomena; but neither, from a Lévinasian perspective, thematizes the inverted intentionality required by these aspects of their thought.

Lévinas has two important predecessors. Jean-Paul Sartre is a phenomenologist working within a revisionist Husserlian framework. His goal is not rigorous science but the clarification of the existential predicaments that make up human life. One of these is the 'Look'. Philosophers have often discussed 'the problem of other minds'. How do we know that there are other persons or selves, that those animals that look a lot like ourselves (when seen in a mirror or photograph) have an inner consciousness like our own? Sartre puts the question in phenomenological terms: how is the other person given to me as a subject and not just an object? He rejects all views for which the other is first given as an animal object and then by inference or interpretation with the help of analogy is taken to be another self. Phenomenologically speaking, the problem of other minds is no problem at all. The other person or self is given to me as such in the experience of being seen. This is a fundamental experience as direct and immediate as the experience of my own body.

The Look is obviously a case of inverted intentionality. The 'consciousness of . . .', the act of *Sinngebung* that defines me and my world is not my own but that of the other whose 'object' I have become. The Look generates three emotional responses: fear, shame, and pride. Fear because as embodied I can be hurt by the other. Shame and pride refer not to physical interaction but to evaluative judgement, moral or otherwise (I can be ashamed of my clothes, for example). It might seem that I would welcome the Look that evokes pride and resist the Look that evokes shame. But that is not the case. Either way, my autonomy has been compromised and it is the other who gets to define me and my world. So I resist the Look of the other by either looking back so as to objectify the other or by manipulating the other's subjectivity so that it only seems to be another's but is really my own (Sartre 1956: Part 3, chs 1 and 3). This objectification and this manipulating are violence as much as the physical violence that is feared.

There is an ethical and religious signification to inverted intentionality for Sartre. Because we see the other who sees and judges us as a threat, our 'concrete relations with others' turn out to be the war of all against all. Echoing Hegel's famous discussion of lordship and bondage, Sartre sees each of us as trying to escape existential slavery by becoming master of the other. It is my Look that must neutralize and prevail over the other's Look. This is very different from Lévinas' account, according to which I desire the presence of the other and can respond with welcome and hospitality. Sartre is aware of the ugliness of the scene he paints, but has only this to say about it. 'These considerations do not exclude the possibility of an ethics of deliverance and salvation. But this can be achieved only after a radical conversion which we can not discuss here' (Sartre 1956: 412, n.14).

The language of salvation and conversion has religious overtones and suggests that the underlying problem could also be described as sin. Sartre does not use that language, but in a section entitled 'Existential Psychoanalysis' he diagnoses the fundamental problem in overtly theological language. Each of us wants to be

> a consciousness which would be the foundation of its own being-in-itself by the pure consciousness which it would have of itself. It is this ideal which can be called God. Thus the best way to conceive of the fundamental project of human reality is to say that man is the being whose project is to be God . . . man fundamentally is the desire to be God.   (Sartre 1956: 566)

In his phenomenology of inverted intentionality Sartre is one of the great secular theologians of original sin, the refusal to accept finitude and responsibility and the attempt to be absolute lord and master of oneself and of everyone else.

Søren Kierkegaard is another precursor of Lévinas (Westphal 2008: 2010). In order to illuminate the nature of faith, in *Fear and Trembling* he retells (through a pseudonym) the story of Abraham's near sacrifice of Isaac in Genesis 22. The God of Abraham, and thus the biblical God of Jews and Christians, is a personal God in the quite specific sense of being a performer of speech acts. Phenomenologically speaking, God is given to us when we find ourselves addressed, spoken to by a voice not our own.

In the story of Abraham, which begins in Genesis 12, the divine speech acts are of two types, inseparably intertwined: promises and commands. God promises certain blessings to Abraham and at the same time commands him to act in certain ways (initially to leave his homeland and eventually to sacrifice his son, Isaac, a command cancelled only at the last minute). Abraham is a knight of faith not by virtue of some creedal affirmation but by the double act of trusting in the promises of God and obeying the commands of God.

In contrast to the Sartrean self, Abraham does not see inverted intentionality (being addressed, called to an identity and a responsibility given by another) as to be escaped no matter what. The divine call is a gift, a scary one, to be sure, and not a threat. Like the Lévinasian self, Abraham welcomes the other into his life in ways that sacrifice his own autonomy. Unlike the Lévinasian self, Abraham recognizes God to be a voice not only other than his own but also other than any human voice, individual or collective.

In all three phenomenologies (Lévinas, Sartre, Kierkegaard), the self is given to itself in an inverted intentionality, and where the self does not insist on being God itself, God (whatever or whoever is genuinely divine) is also given to the self in 'an intentionality of a wholly different type'.

IV. GIVENNESS WITHOUT RESTRICTION:
THE SATURATED PHENOMENON

The phenomenology of Jean-Luc Marion is another departure from the Husserlian project in order to be more faithful to its aims, especially as defined by Heidegger: 'to let that which shows itself be seen from itself in the very way in which it shows itself from itself' (Heidegger 1962: 58). Like the phenomenologists of inverted intentionality, with whom he could easily be classified, he thinks it necessary to go beyond the phenomenologies of Husserl and Heidegger in order to let phenomena show themselves in their own terms (Marion 1998). That is his first goal. In order to accomplish it he extends inverted intentionality, as it were, by treating every phenomenon as a kind of subject or agent, taking as seriously as possible the notion that it shows itself (Heidegger), expresses itself (Lévinas), or, in Marion's own preferred language, derived from Husserl, gives itself.

His second goal is to develop a phenomenology that will be a valuable tool for theology and philosophy of religion. When he speaks of revelation or epiphany, using biblical examples, he has been accused of smuggling theology into phenomenology. His reply is that as a phenomenologist he describes various *possible* modes of experience without committing himself to their *actuality*. Whereas faith and theology affirm that revelation has occurred, that God has spoken, that God has appeared, phenomenology only describes the form of givenness such events would have to have, whether illusory or veridical. It neither affirms nor denies what faith and theology affirm (Marion 2002: 4–5, 235–6, 242).

Marion begins with a negative task, to show the limitations of the phenomenologies of Husserl and Heidegger. His claim is that in each case they arbitrarily restrict what can be given, what can become a phenomenon. They do this by making the subject (ego or Dasein) and its horizons or world, the conditions of the possibility of appearing, precluding the possibility of what doesn't fit within that *noēsis-noēma* framework. To say that they forbid certain types of phenomena is not to say that they keep them from appearing but rather than they are unable to give a cogent account of such phenomena (Marion 1998; 2002: §§19–22).

What sort of phenomena might this be? It includes all the phenomena that exceed and overwhelm the ego and its horizons, not just momentarily but permanently. To say that they give rise to an infinite hermeneutic is to say that the other is never reducible to the same, that no language or conceptuality can ever do full justice to what is given. The telling always falls short of what is to be told (Marion 2002: 211, 228–9, 239–40).

Marion calls such phenomena saturated because they give more to intuition than conceptuality can capture or language express. He distinguishes four types: the historical event; the idol, by which he curiously means the work of art, painting in particular; the flesh, by which he means feelings such as agony, suffering, grief, desire, and orgasm, affective immediacies that may or may not have a primarily bodily origin; and the icon, by which he means essentially what Lévinas means by the face.

From his earlier contrast between the idol and the icon (Marion 1991: chs 1–2), Marion retains the notion that the icon 'no longer offers any spectacle to the gaze and tolerates no gaze from any spectator, but rather exerts its own gaze over that which it meets. The gazer becomes the gazed upon' (Marion 2002: 232).This originally referred to the icon in the literal sense, a religious picture used for devotional, almost sacramental purposes such that 'in a nearly perfect inversion . . . the icon opens in a face that gazes at our gazes in order to summon them to its depth' (Marion 1991: 19). But whereas in the earlier contrast the idol signified any sensible or conceptuality that cut us off from the things themselves by simply mirroring ourselves to ourselves (Marion 1991: 11–17), in the later usage it signifies something visible (or audible if one wanted to take music instead of painting as the example) that in giving itself to us exceeds and overwhelms our capacity to receive (Marion 2002: 229–31).

Marion calls attention first to the fact that there is nothing religious or theological about this category of phenomena. The argument that phenomenology must decentre the ego and its horizons in order to take account of them is a purely phenomenological argument. But in the second place, he argues that only such a phenomenology can do descriptive justice to the experiences that faith takes to be revelation or epiphany. In fact, he says that phenomena of revelation involve all four basic categories of saturated phenomena: historical events whose significance can never be adequately and definitively expressed; scenes that bedazzle and exceed the grasp of all our conceptual tools; feelings, the names of which fall woefully short of the affections signified; and the personal other by whom we are called to responsibility and given an identity and agenda beyond our own choices.

Who, then, is the 'subject' to whom this givenness is given? Not the transcendental ego, nor Dasein, but 'the Gifted' (Marion 2002: Book V). While for theology this might imply a Giver, for phenomenology it does not. It only implies that every phenomenon gives itself and that some phenomena give themselves to us in ways that disorient and reorient ourselves. We are 'the Gifted' in so far as such givenness gives us to ourselves.

V. Summary

The story of phenomenology is, of course, much richer and complex than this. But these vignettes enable us to trace a movement from modern to postmodern philosophy and from epistemology in quest of certainty to a more nearly existential understanding of who we are, of what it means to be a human self. In this latter part of the story the epistemological dimension does not disappear. Phenomenology is always an account of the nature and limits of human knowledge. But in the hermeneutical turn the understanding self is embedded in the world, immersed in history, and subject to the theoretical and practical claims of traditions, which embody earlier interpretations and become internalized as the presuppositions of our own construals. In inverted intentionality the alterity of these claims is intensified in so far as we are addressed by other persons and not just by impersonal traditions. In saturated phenomena we learn the limits of our understanding as qualitative and not just quantitative (as if it consisted simply in the propositions we don't yet know). That such phenomena generate an infinite hermeneutic means that our knowledge is never final and exhaustive but always penultimate and incomplete. How far this leaves open the question of God remains, predictably, a matter of debate.

References

Berger, Peter and Luckmann, Thomas (1967). *The Social Construction of Reality: A Treatise in the Sociology of Knowledge*. (Garden City: Doubleday).

Derrida, Jacques (1976). *Of Grammatology*. (Baltimore, MD: Johns Hopkins University Press).

Dilthey, Wilhelm (1996). 'Reminiscences on Historical Studies at the University of Berlin', in Rudolf A. Makkreel and Frithjof Rodi (eds), *Hermeneutics and the Study of History*, vol. 4: *Selected Works*. (Princeton, NJ: Princeton University Press).

Gadamer, Hans-Georg (1989/ 2004). *Truth and Method*. (New York: Continuum).

Hanson, Jeffrey (ed.) (2010). *Kierkegaard as Phenomenologist: An Experiment*. (Evanston, IL: Northwestern University Press).

Hegel, G. W. F. (1977). *Phenomenology of Spirit*. (Oxford: Clarendon).

Heidegger, Martin (1962). *Being and Time*. (New York: Harper & Row).

Hirsch, E. D., JR (1967). *Validity of Interpretation*. (New Haven, CT: Yale University Press).

Husserl, Edmund (1911). *Philosophy as Rigorous Science: Shorter Works*.

——(1970). *Logical Investigations*. (London: Routledge & Kegan Paul).

——(1981). *Shorter Works*. (Notre Dame: University of Notre Dame Press).

——(1983). *Ideas Pertaining to a Pure Phenomenology and to a Phenomenological Philosophy: First Book, General Introduction to a Pure Phenomenology*. (The Hague: Martinus Nijhoff).

Kierkegaard, Søren (1983). *Fear and Trembling/Repetition*. (Princeton, NJ: Princeton University Press).

LaCocque, André and Ricoeur, Paul (1998). *Thinking Biblically: Exegetical and Hermeneutical Studies*. (Chicago: University of Chicago Press).

Lévinas, Emmanuel (1969). *Totality and Infinity*. (Pittsburgh: Duquesne University Press).

——(1996). *Basic Philosophical Writings*. (Bloomington, IN: Indiana University Press).

——(1998). *Discovering Existence with Husserl*. (Evanston, IL: Northwestern University Press).

Marion, Jean-Luc (1991). *God Without Being*. (Chicago: University of Chicago Press).

——(1998). *Reduction and Givenness: Investigations of Husserl, Heidegger, and Phenomenology*. (Evanston, IL: Northwestern University Press).

——(2002). *Being Given: Toward a Phenomenology of Givenness*. (Stanford, CA: Stanford University Press).

Ricoeur, Paul (1970). *Freud and Philosophy: An Essay on Interpretation*. (New Haven, CT: Yale University Press).

——(1981). *Hermeneutics and the Human Sciences*. (New York: Cambridge University Press).

Sartre, Jean-Paul (1956). *Being and Nothingness: An Essay on Phenomenological Ontology*. (New York: Philosophical Library).

WestphaL, Merold (1998). *History and Truth in Hegel's Phenomenology*. (Bloomington, IN: Indiana University Press).

——(2001). *Overcoming Onto-Theology: Toward a Postmodern Christian Faith*. (New York: Fordham University Press).

——(2008). *Lévinas and Kierkegaard in Dialogue*. (Bloomington, IN: Indiana University Press).

——(2009a). *Whose Community? Which Interpretation? Philosophical Hermeneutics for the Church*. (Grand Rapids, MI: Baker Academic).

——(2010). 'Divine Givenness and Self-Givenness in Kierkegaard', in Jeffrey Hanson (ed.), *Kierkegaard as Phenomenologist: An Experiment*. (Evanston, IL: Northwestern University Press).

Wolterstorff, Nicholas (1995). *Divine Discourse: Philosophical Reflections on the Claim that God Speaks*. (New York: Cambridge University Press).

Suggested Reading

Blundell, Boyd (2010). *Paul Ricoeur between Theology and Philosophy: Detour and Return*. (Bloomington, IN: Indiana University Press).

Hart, Kevin and Michael A. Singer (eds) (2010). *The Exorbitant: Lévinas Between Jews and Christians*. (New York: Fordham University Press).

Ricoeur, Paul (1967). *Husserl: An Analysis of His Phenomenology*. (Evanston, IL: Northwestern University Press).

Risser, James (1997). *Hermeneutics and the Voice of the Other: Re-Reading Gadamer's Philosophical Hermeneutics*. (Albany, NY: SUNY Press).

Westphal (2001), especially chs 3, 6, 7, and 8.

——(2006). 'Vision and Voice: Phenomenology and Theology in the Work of Jean-Luc Marion', in *International Journal for Philosophy of Religion* 60: 1–3.

——(2009a).

——(2009b). 'Inverted Intentionality: On Being Seen and Being Addressed', *Faith and Philosophy* 26: 3.

CHAPTER 26

THE METAPHYSICS OF MODERNITY

WILLIAM DESMOND

I. THE PLURIVOCITY OF BEING AND MODERN METAPHYSICS

THE sources of metaphysical thinking are in an original astonishment before being in its being there at all. There is something 'too much' about this being there; it is overdeterminate in the sense of exceeding our determination. As such it arouses our perplexity, a troubled and indeterminate restlessness of mind seeking to make intelligible sense of it. Perplexity, in turn, yields to a curiosity that is zoned in on more determinate beings, and the determinable dimensions of happenings. I would like to suggest that metaphysics in modernity has focused very strongly on the determinability of being, and with bringing being from a perplexing and equivocal indeterminacy towards more and more univocal determination. We look to overtake conceptually the original overdeterminacy, and to that degree the project is also the overcoming of metaphysical astonishment. To this end we reconfigure the given ethos of being in a variety of univocal figurations. The end of metaphysics seems to lie in the absolute determinability of being, and with this the dissolution of the original astonishment. The doing of metaphysics is its undoing.

Is there more to be said? Recalcitrant equivocities keep coming back, something with which we are only too familiar in postmodernity. I want to look at how an unrelenting stress on determinability yields the inverse result, namely, an indeterminacy verging on the voiding of being. We encounter a paradoxical coupling of determinable fixing and indeterminate voiding. Our reflections here will lead to Kant and Hegel as hugely significant for metaphysics in modernity, and indeed for what comes after modernity. But Kant and Hegel are as much inheritors of older patterns of thinking already in train in modernity as well as initiators of newer patterns whose implications still challenge us. A certain dialectic of univocal fixations and equivocal recalcitrances reaches a high point in Hegel's speculative philosophy, after which modern metaphysics seems fated to fall back into a deeper post-idealist, post-rationalist equivocity in which we still seek orientation. In all of this there is a certain dearth of ontological astonishment and a kind of evacuation of the overdeterminacy of being. The question this poses for us is whether there is a post-dialectical metaphysics wherein fidelity to ontological astonishment lives on and seeds new thought.

My approach will be both historical and systematic: historical in touching on some major thinkers in modernity; systematic in that how metaphysics has been understood itself reflects a constellation of senses of being, which are not always laid out with systematic clarity. It is important to bear in mind the plural nature of the practices of metaphysical thinking. Sometimes the critique of metaphysics is done in a certain shadow of scholasticism, and this is true of Heidegger even and those influenced by him. Modern rationalism is not devoid of connection to the earlier scholasticism, while the reaction of Kant and Hegel to rationalism is important. In the twentieth century, Heidegger had huge influence and he is to be honoured for trying to resurrect the question of being. One worries about a second forgetfulness of being, since many of those indebted to him speak more about him than about being. Rather than a univocal totalization of 'metaphysics', we should focus both on the plurivocity of being, beyond all totalization, and the plurality of practices of metaphysics.[1]

II. THE DOUBLING OF BEING AND METAPHYSICS

In the popular mind metaphysics has to do with what lies beyond our ordinary experience, with things of a higher, perhaps spiritual nature, such as the soul and God. It often seems defined by certain binary conceptions such as appearance and reality, the sensible and the spiritual, the visible and the intelligible. The result is said to be a doubling of being, a two-world picture: the 'here and now' and the 'beyond', the aesthetic and the noetic, time and eternity. This concept of metaphysics has especially

---

[1] We should not forget thinkers like Gabriel Marcel (1951); Karl Jaspers (1969–71); and A. N. Whitehead (1978), and, in the USA, figures like Paul Weiss (1995) and others who do not fit into the divide between Continental and analytic philosophy. There is a tradition variously indebted to Aquinas, whether these be more traditional Thomists, transcendental Thomists, or others again like Jacques Maritain (1948). One thinks of Edith Stein (2002) and her attempted dialogue between phenomenology and mediaeval thought. Latterly, Continental philosophy figures like Giles Deleuze (1994) and Alain Badiou (2005) remind us of metaphysics as a living option. There is much fresh openness to metaphysics coexisting with much talk about our being post-metaphysical. Given my brief in this chapter, I will not be addressing analytic metaphysics, which thrives largely outside of the shadows of the perplexing equivocities Continental metaphysics has undergone since Kant and Hegel. Analytic metaphysics is driven to seek a kind of dianoetic univocity.

been attacked at the latter end of modernity, not least by Nietzsche (Nietzsche 1968). Metaphysics avoids life here and now, voids immanent being as aesthetic happening. There is something at work overall in modernity that can be taken to end here and I will return to this. We are dealing with still living questions. If we have been touched by Nietzsche, we will also be tender to the claimed connection of metaphysics and religion: Christianity is Platonism for the people, he famously said—though Schopenhauer (1966: vol. 2, ch. XVII) all but said as much in his earlier essay on our need for metaphysics. The issue of divine transcendence is often taken to be closely aligned with this binary conception. I will touch on this issue, since there is more at stake with transcendence, religious or metaphysical, than allowed for by binary ways of thinking.

It would be misleading, however, to fixate on this binary conception. In the ancient world what came to be called metaphysics was simply called 'first philosophy' and first philosophy claimed to deal with the most ultimate sources of intelligibility, the most original sense(s) of being, and not necessarily in separation from concern with different domains of beings wherein in life we find ourselves diversely. Plato draws our attention to our renewed perplexity about the 'to be' in the *Sophist* (244a), and Heidegger recalls this perplexity at the beginning of *Being and Time* (2010). But one might think of Aristotle, in the work that historically came to be known as the *Metaphysics*, who explicitly posed the questions of first philosophy as being bound up with the idea that being is said in many senses (*to on legetai pollachōs, Metaphysics* 1003b5).

I would formulate this as the question: what does 'to be' mean, what is it 'to be', what is the sense or senses of the 'to be'? The first nature of this has to do with the fact that all beings, events, processes are, or happen to be. That they are at all is something that exceeds what they are. There seems a universality that is more than a mere generality, more than a specific universality, a kind of hyper-universality—'transcendental' is the traditional word for this. While we might think of this as merely abstract and indeterminate—for it is not anything in particular, nor is it any kind of being or process—it might be said to be intimate to all beings and processes as such. I would call it an intimate universal. We should bear this in mind when later we see the tendency in modernity to render being as an empty indeterminacy, hence not only weakening or losing the concrete universality, but also the intimacy. We will come to this emptying out or voiding of being.

We can take Aristotle's view of the plurivocity of being as fruitful for our purposes. The senses of being he outlines—and Aquinas concurs (Aquinas 1995)—are the univocal, equivocal, and the analogical. Very generally, the univocal sense puts the stress on sameness; the equivocal puts the stress on difference, a difference sometimes dissimulated by our ways of speaking; the analogical somehow mixes the same and the different, being partly one and partly the other, and with reference to the relation of the sameness and difference to something shared by both. Aristotle, it is true, talks of a primary sense of being, which is *ousia* (sometimes translated as 'substance'), and difficulties with what is called a substance metaphysics are part of the controversies of modern thought. The question of the highest being, *ho theos*, in Aristotle's conception of first philosophy, is also replete with questions—not only whether God is to be described as the highest being (*ens supremum*) but whether there is something to God not to be confined to the terms of metaphysics, a God beyond metaphysics, and beyond, just because God is God, and nothing but God is God. What I have called the intimate universality of being is very suggestive about the being of the divine as no being, in one sense nothing at all and yet enigmatically intimate to all beings as their always companioning, enabling source of being. These issues continue to haunt metaphysical perplexity.

This plurivocity can be helpful for getting a hold of crucial dimensions of modern metaphysics. I suggest a quest for supreme univocity, with a recurrent oscillation with equivocity. On one side, this leads to the weakening of the analogical sense of being, and on the other, to the emergence of a more dialectical sense, which tries to mediate univocity and equivocity. Nevertheless, the quest for univocity still persists and equivocations in modern dialectic inevitably raise questions about a post-dialectical or trans-dialectical way of philosophizing. In the aftermath of idealistic dialectic, metaphysics has often been condemned in terms of a post-dialectical equivocity, but one might ask if something more is possible. My suggestion is that at the end of modernity we need to reformulate the plurivocity in a fourfold way, adding to univocity, equivocity, and dialectic what I call the 'metaxological' sense of being. What of the analogical sense? The metaxological might be aligned with the analogous in this regard—an analogy is always *between* one thing and an other. The nature of that between or *metaxu* is at issue for metaphysical thinking. I think this fourfold sense of being can both take us back behind modernity and point us forward to postmodernity and beyond. This fourfold way can help us see some of the major episodes of modern metaphysics in an illuminating light (Desmond 1995).

Metaphysics as *ta meta ta physika* has been taken to mean the things beyond the physical,[2] and the word seems to direct us away from the 'here and now'. But there is a significant double sense to the word '*meta*': '*meta*' can mean both 'in the midst' but also 'over and above', 'beyond'. This double sense defines something of what metaphysics might mean: thought concerning both the immanent and the transcendent, thought immanently self-surpassing, yet thought surpassed by what is not determined purely immanently. The *metaxu* as immanence is a given porosity of being, already in relation to what is beyond itself. This means it is impossible to fixate univocally an immanent side and a transcendent side, a 'here and now' and a 'beyond'. There is thinking that passes between them—on an ontological boundary we cannot absolutely fix.

I suggest that this double sense of '*meta*' can be taken to correspond to the difference of *ontology* and *metaphysics*. Ontology (as a *logos* of *to on*) can be taken as an exploration of given being as immanent; metaphysics can be seen as opening a self-surpassing movement of thought that points us to the porous boundary between immanence and what cannot be determined entirely in immanent terms. Pre-modern metaphysics is

---

[2] It has been suggested that the word derives from the classification of an Alexandrian librarian: *ta meta ta physika*, the texts lying next to the texts dealing with *ta physika*, the physical things.

sometimes taken to opt for the *meta* as 'above', while modern philosophy generally has opted for the *meta* as immanent. In modernity any such doubleness tends to be seen as an equivocity to be overcome or replaced by a more immanently inclusive univocity. This turn away from the *'meta'* as 'above' stretches from the beginnings of modernity to significant currents that proclaim themselves to be postmodern and post-metaphysical. If the doubleness of the *'meta'* suggests a porous boundary between immanence and what is not determined entirely in immanent terms, we will have to demur in the face of modern and postmodern efforts to postulate finite immanence as the absolute horizon of significance, greater than which none can be thought (Desmond 2012).

III. The Devaluation of Being: Between Autonomous Thought and Religion

Here it is relevant to recall a 'between space' connected with this doubleness of the 'meta', that is, the space between philosophy and religion. One might connect a reconfiguration of this 'between space' with the devaluation or voiding of being. Being religious is perhaps our most ultimate way of addressing the ultimate equivocities of being, and indeed of our being addressed by the ultimate mystery itself. In premodern metaphysics what seems evident is a certain porosity of religion and philosophy. In modernity the putative hegemony of theology is progressively eschewed, as the autonomy of philosophy is more and more asserted. It is still possible in such a development for the ethos of being to be religiously inflected, and for the practice of philosophy to be either secretly or overtly porous to what the religious communicates. One could suggest, however, that in modern metaphysics this relation to theology is haunted by equivocity, going hand in hand with a certain mutation in religious porosity. Some might attribute this to the legacy of a univocalization of being and the divine in the late Middle Ages—and there is something to this—but if this is so, what is perhaps more significant is the emergence of an orientation of mind that would univocalize all being in a more immanently active sense. I am thinking of modernity, early modernity especially, as marked by a kind of epistemic irritability with the equivocity of being. This equivocity is a perplexing ambiguity in things whose significance often eludes us. Of this we are tempted to think we ought to be master. The drive to be the determining measure and a kind of ontological irritation and impatience go hand in hand. We must construct modes of knowing and active interventions that make us the measure of what is other to us, especially as so elusively equivocal.

One thinks of the modern mathematization of nature and the hope of empowering technological interventions. One thinks of how in the scientific objectification of nature, externality is stripped of all its qualitative textures, these being consigned to mere secondary qualities—bare being is little more than a devalued thereness. Also the uncoupling of autonomous thinking from religion is connected with a loss of the good of the 'to be'. Every 'to be' is just there neutrally, and not marked with a worth that is both endowed and inherent to it. In the modern frame there is a repudiation of the Aristotelian fourfold causality. Ends or final causes will always be marked by some equivocity; there is no mathematical univocity about them. But their exclusion from the scheme of intelligibility yields a *purposeless process*, ongoing from nothing to nothing. There is an evaporation of the sense of the good as defining the teleology of being. The good of the whole is no longer there, and in its place we find ontologically devalued thereness.

Here the pre-modern hospitality of being and good, signalled in the old doctrine of the transcendental concepts, is replaced by the divorce of being and good. The worth of being is not for itself. It is for us to determine what it is. There is a reconfiguration of the ethos of being in terms of valueless objectivity and a subjectivity said to be the source of all value. There is not an acknowledgement of an ontological porosity between being and us, a porosity, moreover, marked by the texture of qualitative value, understood first in an ontological and not a moral sense. Irritation with equivocity also goes with a lessened appreciation for the figurative, for the fact that we figure our sense of being. One might argue that the analogical sense allowed a figuration of the world replete with signs of the divine, a figuration that allowed a feel for the intimate strangeness of being, and a poised living with equivocity. A dominating univocity loses this poise. The poise of finesse for the figurative now yields to a different figuring power, the determining power of geometry.

The devaluation of being goes with a diminution of our original receptivity to being, and the substitution of doubt for wonder. What we doubt we no longer love with a native ontological affirmation. We retract from that, we retract it, and given being appears as a valueless other over against us—an object—something thrown over against us. If being religious helps in keeping open porosity between the human and divine, our original mindfulness to being as other is a porosity in rapport with what is there, in wonder and astonishment. With doubt that porosity mutates into a suspicion of the other, and a suspicion of ourselves as unable to know that other. True, this can be a productive suspicion in that it breeds a new endeavour to be, in which we project our determining power over the whole of the otherwise valueless thereness. We see this relative to science and technology as reductive of the equivocal otherness to objects that are to be subject to the measure of a univocalizing science. We see this also as relative to philosophy, now proclaiming itself as autonomous knowing. One thinks of Descartes and hydra-like doubt—doubt about historical traditions, expressed in cautious diffidence in relation to theological authority, methodical doubt diversely expressed in the practice of a philosophy half in and half out of older forms—half in terms of the older scholastic concepts, half out in plotting the new science.

Is the autonomous philosopher then a friend or a foe of metaphysics and the divine? Is a metaphysics possible that in the long run does not prove to be godless? For we can so emphasize autonomy that we inevitably have metaphysical cramps in dealing with anything heteronomous. If it is in the nature of metaphysics to be 'meta', it always has to come to terms with the heteronomous. But the autonomization of thinking goes with a reconfiguration of the ethos of being, since in the light of a *nomos* of *to auto*, *to heteros* is less to be immediately denied as mediately reconfigured. Added to the devaluation of given being as other, the structural effect of this reconfiguration in the patterns of thinking is that the previous pre-modern porosity to the religious must be closed off. One could claim that religion is porous to the most radical of heteronomies, and this not necessarily in the mode of binary opposition mentioned earlier, but even in the very richness of immanence itself. The richest sense of the 'to be' tells us of what cannot be delimited to immanence only. But this autonomy, whether affirmed in rational form, or deconstructed into more irrational energies, is shadowed by an ontological allergy to the 'above'.

What about the release of immanent transcending beyond immanence? If autonomy is in the ascendant, this immanent transcending bends back to itself, that is, to immanence again. If there is a porosity of metaphysics to religion in pre-modern thinkers, modernity is the epoch in which this porosity is at best viewed as equivocal in light of a more conceptual univocity; at worst it is closed off entirely, since anything communicated through that porosity not only reeks of equivocity but threatens to mutilate the self-proclaimed autonomy of immanent thought. This passage in the porosity cannot be let be.

And yet we must ask again: Is modernity, in the configuration at issue, an *interim* from which we are now emerging? There are signs that this may be the case, but these signs are themselves equivocal and need discernment in terms other than autonomous immanence. If this is true, part of what comes after modernity—and if metaphysics is to continue—is a new porosity to the religious.

IV. RATIONALIST AND EMPIRICIST VOIDINGS: DIANOETIC AND AESTHETIC UNIVOCITY

Turning back to an earlier phase of modernity, I want briefly to call to mind two dominant pursuits of the determinability of being, namely, rationalism and empiricism, both of which have contributed to the voiding of being and the undoing of metaphysics. While empiricism sought aesthetic univocity in grounding sense-impressions, rationalism was in search of a dianoetic univocity. By the latter I mean to recall the quasi-mathematical kind of thinking of *dianoia* we find on the third level of Plato's divided line. In modernity this can be connected with what Pascal calls *l'esprit de géométrie*. Rationalism is bound up with the self-assertion of autonomous thinking and its uncoupling from the equivocities of the religious. Reason turns to itself as its own and only standard, claiming to be sufficient for itself. It turns towards given creation so as to be reconceptualized in the univocities of scientific and mathematical exactitudes. It turns to the human being as its own measure of self-determination, uncoupled from any mysterious God who cannot be quite univocally factored in any equation of immanent autonomy. Overall reigns the conviction that purely on the basis of a priori reasoning we can have certain and universal knowing of the most ultimate things. It is not coincidental that the gods produced by this way of thinking should be what elsewhere I call the Gods of geometry (Desmond 2008: ch. 3). This is most evident in figures like Spinoza and Leibniz. *L'esprit de finesse* risks being replaced by *l'esprit de géométrie*. Pascal already suspected this in relation to Descartes, realizing that without finesse, there is no religion, and perhaps also no true metaphysics. The Gods of geometry seem to produce rational certainty about the ultimate but they rouse scepticism as to their compatibility with the living God of religion. Geometry without life itself dies, for there is more to life than geometry—and a God of geometry alone, without finesse, is not far off from the death of God later proclaimed with existential pathos.

The ascendant professorial rationalists of the eighteenth century are not now widely studied but thinkers like Wolff and Baumgarten were to shape the mind of Kant importantly, with consequences for succeeding practices of metaphysics. Eighteenth-century rationalism is not unconnected with the heritage of scholasticism. One thinks of how the scheme of general and special metaphysics was to shape the pedagogy of the schools for centuries, general metaphysics dealing with *ens*, special metaphysics with the soul, God, and the world. This scholastic, rationalistic scheme lies in the background of Kant, and it is a shadow behind Hegel. Indeed it has continued to influence scholastic philosophy claiming a debt to Thomas right into the twentieth century. It is a shadow that also lies at the back of the Heideggerian critique of 'metaphysics'. The quest of dianoetic univocity puts me also in mind of Badiou's (2005) claim that ontology is mathematics, though significantly from the present point of view he claims that 'the void' is 'the proper name of being'.

The dianoetic univocity we are dealing with here leads to an evacuation of being, not unrelated to the previously mentioned devaluation of being. We are certainly not talking about the 'too muchness' of being in its given overdeterminacy. Being becomes little more than the most indeterminate of universal concepts, and because it is indeterminate it is empty of the determinate contents that we know from the ordinary engagements of the world in everyday experience. As we know from the history books, the twin of rationalism is said to be empiricism, as the twin of the a priori is the a posteriori. Not surprisingly with empiricism, the search for determinable univocity is aesthetic, in the sense of deriving from the senses and sensible being. The world is as it appears to our senses, and in this appearance we find the point of true contact with concrete being. The search for grounding impressions is at the origin of determination and determinability.

Can we connect the aesthetic univocity of empiricism with the fundamental porosity of the human being to what gives itself? But of this porosity no absolute univocalization is possible, since every univocalization presupposes it. I would argue that without the porosity the receptivity of metaphysical mindfulness to being makes no sense, but while this porosity is presupposed by all determinate cognitive activities, it is easily misunderstood or distorted. Our sensuousness, our incarnate being, our flesh is itself an ontological porosity, but it is not free of the saturated equivocity, which to escape from or overcome is part of the project of modernity. To dwell in this saturated equivocity of the flesh asks for finesse not just geometry, and without the finesse the metaphysical significance of the flesh itself is not going to be understood. (Merleau-Ponty had finesse in this equivocal matter of flesh.) The empiricists tend to be the twins of the rationalists, but just as there is no self-contained dianoetic univocity, so is there also no such aesthetic univocity. All univocities taken as yielding certainty and universality seem to be dissolved by Hume. We end here with the sceptical inversion of the certitudes of the rationalists. This is not much help to metaphysics and contributes to its undoing, especially of the rationalistic sort; nor indeed does it contribute to any kind of cognitive claim, even as the world goes on and Hume can enjoy backgammon and a glass of claret. How to bring geometry and finesse together in proper poise continues to be a great question for modern metaphysics.

V. Voiding Being and Transcendental Positing: the Kantian Equivocation

We reach one of the watersheds of metaphysics in modernity, namely the work of Kant. He was called the 'All-destroyer' by Mendelssohn, and many see him as a revolutionary turning point in modern thought. Without denying his importance, in truth he is the inheritor of a certain reconfiguration of the ethos of being in train since the onset of modernity, and to a degree he is asleep to some of the deeper metaphysical presuppositions of this reconfiguration, even while he expressed something of their essence, and imposed on them a modified reconfiguration. In some ways, he is more an end than a beginning—an end that begins something which, in due course, will call the frame of modernity into account.

Adapting one of Kant's famous sayings, dianoetic concepts without aesthetic intuitions are empty, aesthetic intuitions without dianoetic concepts are blind. His way between these two and beyond them he calls transcendental. Philosophy as transcendental is contrasted with traditional metaphysics which is transcendent, that is, dealing with realities beyond the boundaries of experience. Kant is still driven by a fundamental commitment to univocity in the determination of being. This is evident in his acceptance of Newtonian science and its world picture, in his architectonic ambitions in philosophy, in his desire to put metaphysics on the secure path of science, and in his stress on rational necessity and universality as the only marks of true scientific cognition. He is heir to the dualism of modernity in this sense: we are not to try to bridge the dualism of subject and object in a naïve realist or purely objective manner, but must take the transcendental turn that supposes we think objects as conforming to our knowing rather than our knowing conforming to objects. 'Transcendental' in his usage refers to the conditions of the possibility of knowing, not as with the pre-modern usage referring to the (hyper)universality of being, truth, one, good, universals applicable to all being, beyond the generic universals applicable to kinds of being. In addition, Kant's transcendental ego might be seen as pointing towards a kind of metaphysics of subjectivity. Transcendental subjectivity is the most necessary principle of unity redefining the space between subject and object, reconfiguring their relation through its immanent synthesising power.

Kant speaks of a Copernican revolution, and one takes Copernicanism to be *heliocentric*. But where or what is the sun in Kant's way of thinking, if the knowing subject stands at the centre of the constellation of intelligibilities? Plato is heliocentric, one might say. In his figuring, the sun refers us away from ourselves to the Good as transcendent. Since 'transcendental' for Kant is not 'transcendent', we are referred back to one side of the *meta*, namely, the immanent side, understood in terms of the transcendental ego, the ultimate point of unity in the synthetic activity of knowing. We might talk even about a transcendental univocity. The point is that it is not being as being that interests Kant but our knowing of beings. Being is nothing for itself, being does not stun mindfulness with the 'too muchness' of the overdeterminate. Being as determinable must be referred to transcendental positing—with a little supplementary help from the otherwise formless flux of aesthetic happening.

Kant presents us with a contrast between dogmatism and scepticism. He rejects the dogmatic metaphysicians, and sometimes this is taken to be a rejection *tout court* of all-pre-critical metaphysics. But who are the dogmatic metaphysicians? Plato or Aristotle? Surely not. For Kant they are the rationalists of which he himself was earlier one. Kant was in revolt against his own scholastic rationalism—though he produces a transcendental version of scholastic rationalism. What of the sceptics? Kant was their opponent, though he confesses to being awakened from his own dogmatic slumbers by Hume and his scepticism. But his version of 'critique' is rather like a Trojan horse from this standpoint. There may be a more insidious scepticism hidden in the thing, and it is brought into the centre of all knowing under the seeming respectable name of 'critique'. 'Our age is an age of critique' he tells us, and we suspect he is advertising an epistemic superiority over the naïve realists. This self-congratulation might well be one of the bewitchments of the age. In the name of reason, critique itself becomes a new idol of scepticism that cannot see the beam in its own eye for all its rooting out of the specks in the old eyes of traditional philosophy, morality, and religion. The secret complicity of scepticism and critique returns in dialectic in its negative form, and also in more deconstructive thinking.

We should be hesitant about acceding to Kant's insinuation that the whole of traditional metaphysics is dogmatic. Of course, the sceptic seems to win at least an indirect victory, since it turns out we are incapable of knowing the thing itself. We are urged to dare to know, but what starts with a hortatory bang ends with an epistemic whimper, since we can't know anything in itself. While this whimper is disheartening for metaphysics as a theoretical discipline, metaphysics can be heartened again if we shift to practical reason, and the moral sphere (Kant 1997a). This, our re-location to a non-cognitive space, can seem hugely liberating. Indeed one might applaud it for enriching the sense of what it is to be—unknowingly; nevertheless, it produces a downgrading of claims of philosophical reason in the long run. It opens the gates to the others of theoretical reason, but this turn to morality as other will be followed by more irrational others as time goes on. Kant would not approve of the latter, of course, but he does contribute to a flattening of the doubleness of the 'meta'. Our epistemic confinement to what is immanent in the domain of experience becomes a principle of immanence that rejects knowledge of the transcendent. This is equivocal, since there is a kind of beyondness to his moral God. It is questionable if Kant maintains a poise between immanent ontological reflection and metaphysical thinking about what is more than immanent.

What are some of the theological or religious consequences to which one might pay attention? There is especially what I call the antinomy of autonomy and transcendence as other. Kant's philosophy is one of autonomy, but where does transcendence have a place? The transcendence of nature is hard to distinguish from the valueless mechanism of Newtonianism. This is the deterministic nature of the *Critique of Pure Reason* (Kant 1989), though in his *Critique of the Power of Judgement* (Kant 2000) he tries to restore something of its life as 'purposive'. This is an 'as if' restoration, and is still framed transcendentally. Going with the weakened 'is', we are allowed to look at nature 'as if' it were purposive. We cannot say: it *is*. The transcendence of the human being is reconfigured as moral autonomy set in opposition to heteronomy. God is the greatest of heteronomies, and hence we must defend morality without religion. God has to be brought back by Kant to deal with the antinomy of pure practical reason, in reconciling virtue and happiness (Kant 1997a). The suspicion is aroused that this is a moral *usage* of God, echoing an epistemic usage we find in Descartes. God allows us to deal with an antinomy in the immanent system of moral autonomy, but that is it, really. We think we close a gap but we don't of course. If God entails a transcendence greater than which none can be conceived, Kant has no way to handle the living God. God is folded back into morality, and we seem to have protected immanence from any intrusion from what is beyond itself.

In style of thinking Kant is still quite scholastic and his sense of being is quite anorexic. His withered sense of ontological astonishment is typically rationalist, even though he is tortured by worries that he might be overshooting the mark in his trust in *ratio*. His moral philosophy is at the centre. It is the only place where a kind of metaphysics might come to be—as we see from the title of one of his most famous books, *Groundwork of a Metaphysics of Morals* (Kant 1997b). Only morality reveals something unconditional, and hence here there is some opening possible to the ultimate metaphysical perplexities. Interestingly, while there are little touches of a more ontological porosity in Kant's *Critique of the Power of Judgment*, in the final accounting he reiterates his rejection of all theology, and explicitly natural theology, except for a moral theology. In the end this is just morality, and not a lot of theology. You might as well drop the word 'theology'—it is just morality. Admittedly, Kant had something of a bad conscience, since there are troubling antinomies within moral autonomy that autonomy does not seem quite able to handle. A 'supplementary' appeal to a moral God is not entirely closed off. We see this not only in Kant's dealing with happiness, which moral virtue cannot guarantee, but also in his dealing with radical evil which shows an inner debility, even perversion, in the root of our moral being.

Overall then dianoetic univocity gives way to transcendental univocity, which gives way to moral autonomy, even as the Gods of geometry are replaced by the moral God. There is something metaphysical about this in reference to the doubleness of the *meta*, since we move from the immanence of autonomy to the 'beyond' of the moral God. Of course, this 'beyond' was said by some not to be able to hold its ground. Already in Kant there is the equivocity as to whether it compromised the immanent autonomy he would absolutize, were it possible. But those who were to come later were much less polite with any 'beyond', and in the name of immanent autonomy, or indeed the autonomy of the immanent as such. The first sense of the *meta*—the sense of being 'in the midst'—closes itself off from the second sense as referring to the 'beyond', and the result is the changing of the nature of metaphysics entirely in the direction of an immanent ontology.

Today we think of Heidegger when we hear the term 'ontotheology', and he uses it to describe a certain way in which philosophy brings God into thought. A charge is directed at the *causa sui* of Spinoza or Hegel, and the charge sometimes seeps beyond these two towards the entire tradition of metaphysics. We should remember the term is Kant's from the *Critique of Pure Reason* (A632, B660), and is mentioned in connection with the ontological argument. This is the proof of God by a priori reason, indicating that reason through itself alone can establish the existence of God. Kant is famous for his reputed demolition of the argument, and in that sense he is a foe of ontotheology. The demolition is resisted by reserves of complexity and nuance on less simplistic interpretations of the argument. But that aside, the purported demolition is a sign of the loss of faith in the strategies of a rationalistic metaphysics. Moreover, one can see more perspicuously some of the issues at stake if we grant this connection with Kant vis-à-vis ontotheology. Not least, the matter reveals how hesitant we should be in letting this term 'ontotheology' be a weapon against the entire tradition of metaphysics. If we connect ontotheology with the ontological argument, clearly Aquinas has already criticized that as a way to God. And even in the Anselmian version, and the prefiguration of it in Augustine, there is the porosity of religion and thought which insists again and again that *Deus semper maior*. It is a question whether this is only just a way of bringing God into philosophy. It could rather be seen as an opening in immanent thought that explodes the pretension of immanent thought to close in on itself entirely. That is to say, the hyperbolic nature of God beyond all conceptualization is at issue when we think the thought of that greater than which none can be thought. This is not at all ontotheology in the bad sense, and indeed it overlaps with Kant's own mission against the conceptual idols of the uncritical rationalists.

I said there was an anorexic quality to the ontological attunement of Kant. This dearth of ontological astonishment is not greatly overcome in his metaphysics of morals. The starry skies above could be the opening to robust ontological astonishment in the aesthetics of happening, but there is not more than a flash, even at that an 'as if' flash, and then the devalued thereness reigns again. Even with the moral law, Kant drags his feet with anything 'more', and we feel that he has not been taken beyond a cramped rationalism by these hyperbolic happenings. He is always trying to rein in the native self-transcending of the human spirit, confining us to the cramped little island of his truth, surrounded by the ocean of error and its deceitful mist banks and shifting shapes (*Critique of Pure Reason*, A 235, B 294–5). Confined to the island of his truth, the rest of being is full of threat and anxiety and even terror. We fear a quasi-Pascalian terror in hiding from itself, holding in check its ontological alarm within the architectonic structures of transcendental scholasticism.

VI. Being Nothing and the Whole: Hegel's Speculative Completion

Hegel, like Kant, is a hugely influential thinker in connection with modern metaphysics and the voiding of being. Kant's transcendental response goes with an evacuation of the overdeterminacy of being, an anorexia of metaphysics whose yet undying impulse he still tries to nourish morally. Metaphysics clings to life, fed by a separation of theoretical and practical reason, hard to disentangle from a kind of laming of reason's confidence, and paradoxically twinned with a mutation of the sceptical impulse in critique tempted to a hubris in its own debunking powers. That debility of reason Hegel rejected. In his thought one can discover much of a recapitulation of modernity and its reconfiguration. He was attuned to how the modern struggle with the duplicity of equivocity produces in univocity its own doubleness, evident in the form of binary thinking: object versus subject, determinism versus freedom, the dianoetic versus the aesthetic, rationalism versus empiricism, Enlightenment versus faith. Such binary thinking divides the whole, though it presupposes the whole. Hegel, by contrast, insists on the unity of reason in a speculative philosophy claiming to transcend such binary thinking, and their unexpurgated contamination of Kantian dualisms. The dualistic mode of thinking is the problem rather than the solution. To think the separation we must presuppose the togetherness. Hegel draws our attention to the self-surpassing character of thinking which cannot be separated from being. How being and thinking are together is the question.

There is a continuation and critique of Kant and a claim to complete him. Even though Hegel's speculative confidence is not now fashionable and something of Kant's critical caution is more to contemporary tastes, the fact is that Hegel asked many of the right questions about Kant, even if perhaps his answers still raise our eyebrows. Metaphysics seems finished after Kant—theoretical metaphysics anyway. Hegel agrees: something revolutionary happens in Kant, but he and Schelling claimed to complete the revolution. They felt that Kantian critique was not thorough enough. There was too much of simply accepting as given the already laid out tablet of categories, more or less taken over from traditional Aristotelian scholasticism.

Notice the stress on categories. There is a turn to the immanences of thought, yes, but the question of the priority of thought or being is important. If our primary stress is on categories, then we take knowing to be the measure of being, not being as the measure of knowing. This stress on the categories is continuous with a turn to the immanence of thought, and the belief that a fuller unfolding of that immanence will yet yield the systematic completeness that Kant held to as a desideratum, even if the realization was not always what was desired. The immanence of thought can be seen as in agreement with Kant's prioritizing of the transcendental ego, even if this gets reinterpreted in directions Kant would not approve. It provides philosophy with access to the source whence are generated the diversity of fundamental categories we need to make being intelligible. A determining source is required of the diverse categories needed for the determinability of being and the determination of its intelligibility. Accounting for this determining source will show it ultimately, for Hegel, to be self-determining. The doubleness of the *meta* will be collapsed into the immanence of self-determining thought. Logic and metaphysics will be the same in a post-transcendental ontology of the categories—Hegel's (1969) own *Science of Logic.*

For Hegel there is a *determination process* more ultimate than *determinate products.* The dynamism of thinking is self-transcending and more than a series of fixed determinations, more than even the formal rules governing their connections. More than a formal logic we need a new logic, a logic that reveals as much a dialectic of being as of thought, since being and thought cannot be fixed as determinacies on two sides of a dualism. Dialectic deconstructs the dualism, overcoming the limits of binary thinking of the older metaphysics. Thus Hegel claimed that Kant's understanding of the antinomic character of reason is ripe with a speculative significance we now need to harvest. What looks like an impasse for reason rather opens a space for a true speculative deployment of reason as ultimately *self-determining.* Hegel is still Kantian in taking over and speculatively transforming Kant's transcendental unity of apperception, and thus continues the modern stress on the self-determination of thinking rather than on being as such.

All of being—nature, history, God—will be said to be dialectically determinable in accord with reason's self-determination. Speculative dialectic will claim to offer the self-determining *logos* of the whole. We are to move beyond the fixed univocal determinacies of the analytic understanding, beyond the equivocities of the merely indeterminate, and this in order to complete metaphysics in a logic that shows thought to be immanently self-determining. Take note of how in this grand project, the over-determinacy of being is evacuated from the outset in the direction of the most indeterminate, that is, empty concept, which is all but nothing, and must give way via becoming to more determinate being. One could see in all this a continuation of the voiding of being in the direction of an empty indeterminacy.

Consider the question: How does being come to be determinately intelligible? Hegel connects thinking with determinate negation, or more generally with subjectivity as self-relating negativity. What is simply given to be is not intelligible as such; it is a mere immediacy till rendered intelligible, either through its own becoming intelligible, or through being made intelligible by thinking. Thinking as negativity moves us from the simple givenness of the 'to be' to the more determinately intelligible. The 'to be' is no more than an indeterminacy, and hence deficient in true intelligibility, till this further development of determination has been made by thinking as negativity. Thinking as a process of negation is in process towards knowing itself as a process of self-determining. There is a logic overall that governs the movement: from indeterminacy to determination to self-determination. There is no overdeterminacy of being. Given being can barely be said to be, and even less can it be said to be intelligible till rendered so by determining thinking. Hence, being becomes the most indigent of the categories that is all but nothing, till thought understands that it has already passed over into becoming. If we refer to the famous opening of Hegel's *Logic*, one could suggest, among other things, that Hegelian negativity, via a logic of self-determining thought, is born of and leads to a dearth of ontological astonishment. Instead of mindful porosity to being as the marvel of the 'too much', we find rather the 'nothing' of an empty indeterminacy.

There is here a certain apotheosis of the previously mentioned immanence of thought. The older metaphysics is criticized by a post-transcendental ontology of categories, all governed by the immanence of autonomous thought whose consummation Hegel's logical unfolding seeks to accomplish. I mention this connection with rationalism: in his *Encyclopaedia*, in treating of different attitudes of thought to objectivity, Hegel first directs himself to 'metaphysics' (Hegel 1991: §§26–83), by which he means, in fact, the rationalism of the eighteenth century, noted earlier in connection with Kant. Hegel is not simply hostile but rather endorses the philosophical thinking of the things of reason, though now we must meet the standard Kantian requirement of subjecting the categories to critical reflection. Hegel sought a rethinking of these same matters in a post-Kantian perspective. The spirit of genuine speculative philosophy has not been 'demolished' by the critique of Kant. Hegel's logic reminds us of a dialectical Wolffian rationalism set in dialectical motion; the static categories of rationalism are reorganized and set in motion, all on the way to the complete system of categories of his *Science of Logic*.

While the resources of dialectical thinking are rich, paradoxically Hegel's efforts to 'complete' metaphysics may have done more to 'demolish' it than Kant's more scholastically cautious critique and his more overt intent to put metaphysics in its place. Once again surfaces the worry about a dearth of ontological astonishment about such a system. Our ontological attunement to the mystery of being is weakened. Being is both strange and intimate, and rationalism might be too callow to address it, but a dialectically dynamized transformation of rationalism might also be lacking in metaphysical finesse for it. The consummation of metaphysics in speculative dialectic, sometimes attributed to Hegel, wherein is developed a post-transcendental identity of being and thinking, may well contribute more to the sickening of the metaphysical impulse. The doubleness of the *meta* is collapsed into the dialectical univocity of immanence. One major theological consequence is the claim to speculatively surpass the transcendence of God. God too is made entirely immanent, and religious seeds are sown that in post-Hegelian thought will spring up and bloom as atheist darnel.

VII. THE OVERDETERMINACY OF BEING AND TRANS-DIALECTICAL METAPHYSICS

In a last reflection on post-dialectic metaphysics I want to say that since Hegel we can see a continuing wrestling with the voiding of being, often accompanied by the belief that 'metaphysics' is behind us. I would say that perhaps certain practices of metaphysics are behind us, but that metaphysics as concerned with the fundamental senses of the 'to be' is not and cannot ever be behind us. Sometimes the voiding of being takes on sombre colours, not only in more nihilistic currents, but even in a darkening of devalued being into a kind of evil of being (such as we find with Schopenhauer and Nietzsche). In focusing on post-dialectic metaphysics, I will be concerned to stress the move from the voiding of being to a rethinking of the recessed overdeterminacy of being. This is the 'too muchness' of being for thought that thinks thought alone, that is, thought defining itself by the immanence of its own autonomy.

Hegel's speculative high noon was seen by some as the consummation of metaphysics but its aftermath was, paradoxically, less jubilation in mission accomplished as a malaise with rational philosophy itself, and the outbreak of a rash of anti-metaphysical tics. To many, Hegel's confidence in speculative reason appeared as an overconfidence, producing a kind of metaphysical bubble, the deflation of which seems more true to immanence. Instead of the absolutely self-sublating univocity of Hegel, we must de-sublate the absolute and bring it more truly back to the human source, said to be its *incognito* producer. In Feuerbach, Marx, and others the God-man becomes the Man-God. While this signals a hyperbolic self-assertion on the part of humanity, by contrast, speculative reason is stripped of its metaphysical pretensions, loses its self-confidence, and turns the negating power of thinking even against philosophy itself. The de-sublation of idealistic metaphysics can also be infiltrated by a recessed belief in the evil of being, and in the face of this the modern subject can become the abject non-self of some postmodern expurgations. The hubris of the ascendant subject and the dejection of the abject non-self vie with each other, but for both the 'big other' of traditional metaphysics and religion is dead.

It is worth noting that the question of the end of metaphysics is not a first for twentieth-century thought but is seeded in Hegel and extensively shapes those coming after him, such as Kierkegaard, Marx, Schopenhauer, or Nietzsche. The 'overcoming of metaphysics' with Heidegger, or the excoriation of meaningless metaphysics with more positivistically-inclined philosophy (Comte, Carnap, and others), or the deconstruction of metaphysics with Derridean thought, all seem to lie along the line of this deflation of confidence in philosophical reason that we have diversely witnessed since Kant's critique of pure reason, and Hegel's reconfiguration of transcendental philosophy in terms of speculative dialectics. One could argue, however, that Hegel's system is not at all the consummation of metaphysics but the systematic completion of a project of being as determinability, culminating in a self-determining process, which in the beginning and in the end hides the overdeterminacy of being. This overdeterminacy is not the indeterminate; it exceeds determination and self-determination, and always calls for thought—thought in which some form of metaphysics is not only necessary but unavoidable.

Such a form might be called *trans-dialectical metaphysics*. One might speak of post-dialectical metaphysics, but the word 'post' is perhaps too much of a temporal qualifier and there is here a *systematic issue* at stake as well as an historical. Historically, post-Hegelian philosophy has huge investments in trying to revolt against, or outlive, or modify that Hegelian practice of dialectic. This is true of both Continental philosophy as well as analytic. Merleau-Ponty in the 1950s speaks of a debt to Hegel incurred by almost all the strands of contemporary philosophy—he mentions, for instance, Marx, Nietzsche, phenomenology, existentialism, and psychoanalysis (Merleau-Ponty 1964: 63). Likewise, the historical narrative that plots the identity of analytic philosophy starts with Moore and Russell and is hugely defined by their turn against idealism and Hegelianism generally (Hylton 1990). Systematically, trans-dialectical thinking better expresses the point in terms of the philosophical issues at stake. 'Trans' indicates a beyond or a going beyond, and the question is whether dialectic does justice to both the going beyond of thinking as well as the beyond of thinking. It is important to note these two, since there *is* a going beyond of thinking in Hegel, but it is an immanent one, and hence there is, in the end, no beyond in a sense other to, or more robust than, an immanent transcending, the immanent transcending of thinking. There is no stronger sense of otherness and transcendence that finally does not submit without remainder to the appropriating power of immanent dialectical thought, as Hegel conceives this. Once again we return to the doubleness of the *meta*: in the midst and yet also beyond. Can these two be held together? How can we hold them together? Are we somewhere between these two?

To speak of the 'trans' might remind some more of a Platonic dialectic than a Hegelian in respect of keeping open the porosity of philosophical eros to transcendence as other. Interestingly, many anti-Hegelian post-Hegelians are often deeply in agreement with Hegel on this score. They are anti-Platonic, in claiming to be entirely immanent in their view or in their practice of philosophy. They may deconstruct the Hegelian totality but they share with Hegel the finally non-negotiable commitment to immanence as such. Deleuze is a clear example of this. Loud critic of Hegel though he is from a Nietzschean point of view, yet he is in complete agreement with Hegel as a philosopher of immanence—and not surprisingly, since for Hegel, as much as for Nietzsche and Deleuze, Spinoza is the founding father, if not heroic figure of modern philosophy—the 'Christ of philosophers', as Deleuze puts it (Deleuze 1994: 60). The impulse to absolutize a certain univocity of immanence can take different forms, other to the immanence of Hegel's self-determining system. I think of the immanence of a postulatory finitism such as informs the fundamental ontology of Heidegger; or the immanence of the scientistic univocity informing many projects of science and technology; or the form that tries to break out of all form in the rhapsodic univocity of Dionysian immanence, whether Nietzschean or postmodern; or a naturalizing pragmatism devoid of any suggestion of mystery at the heart of the intimate strangeness of given being.

Thought thinking itself reaches a kind of acme in Hegel's idealistic form of dialectic, but what emerges at this high noon is the need for thought thinking *the other of thought thinking itself*. We can see this in many figures—Marx, Kierkegaard, Schopenhauer, Nietzsche, Heidegger—and well into the twentieth century. This other to thought thinking itself is at issue in many thinkers in the line of inheritance from post-Hegelian dialectic. Of course, there is nothing that entirely escapes controversy here. Moreover, one might suspect that not a few proposed candidates for this otherness are far from being post-dialectical, and even less trans-dialectical, in so far as they embody a recurrence of deep equivocity, or an oscillation of univocity and equivocity. (One could see analytic philosophy in a similar light.) It is interesting on this score to see something of a revival of the study of Schelling among postmodern thinkers. The other to thought thinking itself is at stake. Schelling sought to offer a positive philosophy (dealing with the 'that' of existence) to balance and complete the negative philosophy (dealing with the 'what' of things) whose impulse he shared with Hegel (Schelling 2008). That his search already occurs from *within* idealism I take to be a sign of the 'trans' as therein hidden or covered over by the immanent practices of idealistic dialectic. These signs may indicate what kind of mindfulness is to be sought to think the 'trans' better or more truly. Some recent commentators make Schelling much more non-Hegelian than he is; after all, Hegel was himself a Schellingian and the two cannot be so simply uncoupled from each other. One of the things binding them still is the canonical status of Spinoza. They both are in love with an immanent God—even if there is more darkness and recalcitrance and otherness to Schelling's version of that immanent God.

There is a 'trans' of thinking in the middle, a passage in the between, but in intermediation with what is other to thought thinking itself. The 'trans' opens a plurivocal intermediation with the other to thought thinking itself. It opens up what I call metaxological metaphysics, in answer to the 'after' of Hegel, both in the sense of the 'post' and in the sense of the 'trans'. Nevertheless, the 'trans' is more important than the 'post', and indeed in metaxological form it is able to rejoin earlier practices of philosophical dialectic, where finesse for the 'more' of the beyond is less domesticated than in the immanent categories of a modern rationalistic system. Beyond the geometrical God, beyond the moralized God, beyond the immanent God of the whole, beyond the new pagan gods of Nietzsche and Heidegger, there is the God of the *metaxu*.

Heidegger is not wrong to talk about a forgetfulness of being, even if one hesitates at his epochal framing of such a claim and its own univocalizing of the plurivocal practices of metaphysical thinking. One wonders about his implication in the voiding of being in so far as he (certainly in his earlier work) seems to ontologically privilege anxiety before the nothing. One wonders about his later gesture of crossing out being, a gesture saturated with equivocities asking further thought. Yet he does offer, among other things, important reflections on truth as *aletheia* as more primordial than determinate truths that can be given more univocal propositional form. There is an interplay between determinacy and something more indeterminate. While not lacking ontological attunement to the over-determinate, one worries if the shadow of the modern devaluation of being falls over his thought, in so far as we seem to have being without the good—just as with Levinas (1968) we seem to have good without being. Beyond the voiding of being, metaphysical finesse asks new thought on the togetherness of the 'to be' and the 'to be good'. One might think of the earlier Marion trying to escape the vice of Heideggerian being with a God without being (Marion 1991). But does this escape the devaluation if it means ending with being without God? In the later Marion we have the 'saturated phenomenon', and while this is suggestive for something beyond the voiding of being, the stress seems more on the inverse of transcendental positing (Marion 2002). It remains in the frame of phenomenology rather than in the trans-dialectical *metaxu*. This *metaxu* is more fully an ontological-metaphysical space wherein we meet what I call the *hyperboles of being* (Desmond 2008).

One could say that the forgetfulnesss of being is as much elemental as epochal. It is our nature to forget being in determining its overdeterminacy, as we reconfigure our constitutive participation in the intimate strangeness of being. We determine its over-determinacy in pursuit of a cognitive mastery that just in its mode of knowing produces an unknowing of being as always more than us, as endowing and enabling us, even as we try to overtake it. A metaxological metaphysics can be seen as a systematic and trans-systematic response to this recurrent slippage into a loss of mindfulness of being, into even a second forgetfulness of being. The overdeterminacy is not univocal determinability, not equivocal indetermination, not dialectical self-determination. It calls for an opening of thought to the other of thought thinking itself, and in compan-ionship with some post-Hegelian signs that have been noted.

The voiding of being, while not devoid of nihilistic implications, might also be said to lead to a kind of 'return to zero' in which a new interface with the overdeterminacy of being becomes possible. The original porosity to being that we see in ontological astonishment may open metaphysically to an effort to think anew the overdeterminacy of being. There is here something like a paradoxical conjunction of seeming opposites in bringing together this porosity and overdeter-minacy: the first looks like 'almost nothing', the second like something 'all but too much'. And yet this doubleness is truer to being and void: an original porosity of philosophy to being as given, undergone in the ontological astonishment that finds itself in receipt of communication from the overdeterminacy of being. This double-ness is also truer to the twofold *meta* of metaphysics. The excessive self-confidence of modern rationalism and idealism is over; the studied over-caution of analytic ordinariness is not fully true to the robust eros of philosophical mindfulness; the postulatory finitude of much recent Continental philosophy is too self-insistently immanent; the abjection of postmodern anti-rationalism saws the branch of being on which it is unhappily sitting. One might speak of a new, endowed poverty of philosophy in which fresh porosity to the overdeterminacy of being can be opened. In a field long lying fallow, in the midst even of the darnel, new shoots of promise can show in, can grow out of, postmodern perplexity.

References

Aquinas, St. Thomas (1995). *Commentary on Aristotle's Metaphysics*, rev. edn., intro. and trans. John P. Rowan, Preface by Ralph McInerny (South Bend, IN: Dumb Ox Press).

Badiou, A. (2005). *Being and Event*, trans. O. Feltham (London: Continuum).

Deleuze, G. and Guattari, F. (1994). *What is Philosophy?* trans. H. Tomlinson and G. Burchell (New York: Columbia University Press).

Desmond, William (1995). *Being and the Between*. (Albany, NY: State University of New York Press).

—— (2008). *God and the Between*. (Oxford: Blackwell).

—— (2012). *The Intimate Strangeness of Being: Metaphysics after Dialectic*. (Washington, DC: Catholic University of America Press).

Hegel, G. W. F. (1969). *Science of Logic*, trans. A. V. Miller (New York: Humanities Press).

—— (1991). *The Encyclopaedia Logic (with the Zusätze): Part 1 of the Encyclopaedia of Philosophical Science with the Zusätze*, trans. T. F. Geraets, W. A. Suchting, and H. S. Harris (Indianapolis, IN: Hackett).

Heidegger, M. (2010). *Being and Time*, trans. Joan Stambaugh, revised with a foreword D. J. Schmidt (Albany, NY: State University of New York Press).

Hylton, Peter (1990). *Russell, Idealism, and the Origins of Analytical Philosophy*. (Oxford: Clarendon Press).

Jaspers, Kart (1969–71). *Philosophy*, 3 vols., trans. E. B. Ashton (Chicago: University of Chicago Press).

Kant, Immanuel (1989). *Critique of Pure Reason*, trans. and eds. Paul Guyer et al. (Cambridge: Cambridge University Press).

—— (1997a). *Critique of Practical Reason*, trans. and ed. Mary Gregor, intro. Andrews Reath (Cambridge: Cambridge University Press).

—— (1997b). *Groundwork of a Metaphysics of Morals*, trans. and ed. Mary Gregor, intro. Christine Korsgard (Cambridge: Cambridge University Press).

(2000). *Critique of the Power of Judgment*, ed. Paul Guyer, trans. Eric Matthews (Cambridge: Cambridge University Press, 2000).

Levinas, Emmanuel (1968). *Totality and Infinity*, trans. A. Lingis (Pittsburg: Duquesne University Press).

Marcel, Gabriel (1951). *The Mystery of Being*. 2 vols. (London: Harvill Press).

Marion, Jean-Luc (1991). *God without Being*, trans. Thomas A. Carlson, foreword David Tracy (Chicago: University of Chicago Press).

—— (2002). *In Excess: Studies of Saturated Phenomena*, trans. R. Horner and V. Berraud (New York: Fordham University Press).

Maritain, Jacques (1948). *A Preface to Metaphysics*. (New York: Sheed and Ward).

Merleau-Ponty, Maurice (1964). *Signs*, trans. H. Dreyfus and P. Dreyfus (Evanston, IL: Northwestern University Press).

Nietzsche, Friedrich. (1968). *Twilight of the Idols and the Anti-Christ*, trans. R. J. Hollingdale (Harmondsworth: Penguin).

Schelling, F. W. J. (2008). *The Grounding of Positive Philosophy: The Berlin Lectures*, trans., intro., and notes Bruce Matthews (Albany, NY: State University of New York Press).

Schopenhauer, Arthur (1966). *The World as Will and Representation*, 2 vols., trans. E. F. J. Payne (New York: Dover Books).

Stein, Edith (2002). *Finite and Eternal Being*, trans. K. F. Reinhardt (Washington, DC: ICS Publications).

Weiss, Paul (1995). *Being and Other Realities*. (Chicago and La Salle: Open Court).

Whitehead, A. N. (1978). *Process and Reality: An Essay in Cosmology*, corrected edn. with comparative readings and detailed index, D. R. Griffin and D. W. Sherburne (New York: The Free Press).

Suggested Reading

Deleuze, G. and Guattari, F. (1994).

Desmond (1995).

Hegel (1969).

Heidegger (2010).

Kant (1989).

Levinas (1968).

Marion (1991).

Schelling (2008).

Whitehead (1978).

PART VI

THEOLOGY

CHAPTER 27

···

THE BIBLE

···

NICHOLAS ADAMS

THE period from 1800 to 1945 saw some of the most turbulent changes to approaches to the Bible in modern European thought. It is a period of dramatic contrasts and unresolved contradictions. The contrasts arise because of the increasing divergence between experts and lay persons: the historical and philological studies of biblical scholars contrasted more and more strongly with performative and traditional figural reading of the Bible in Christian worship. Contradictions arise as a consequence of this. The question of whether and to what extent the Bible is like other books invites new, distinctively modern, attempts to account for the Bible's status—and these attempts appeal to a broad range of criteria which are not necessarily in harmony with each other, such as the quality of the text, the use of the text in communities, and understandings of divine revelation. There is one repeated failed attempt to resolve the contradictions thrown up by competing criteria: the quest for a single framework within which to place the practices of expert biblical scholarship and the practices of worshippers in churches—the most famous of these attempts being the quest for the historical Jesus. This chapter approaches these issues by engaging with a series of classic texts, taking them chronologically, in three sections.

Please note: the following abbrevations are used throught this chapter.

ER: Karl Barth, *The Epistle to the Romans* (1921)
HC: F. D. E. Schleiermacher, *Hemeneutics and Criticism*, (1805–33)
IS: Benjamin Jowett, 'The Interpretation of Scripture' (1860)
LJ: David Strauss, *Life of Jesus Critically Examined* (1835)
NTM: Rudolf Bultmann, 'New Testament and Mythology' 1948)
PS: G. W. F. Hegel, *Phenomenology of Spirit* (1807)
VJ: Ernest Renan, *The Life of Jesus* (1863)

The first section considers the work of Hegel and Schleiermacher, and connects aspects of their philosophies to issues in biblical interpretation. Hegel's contribution to a range of topics is vast: here one small part will be treated, namely, the relation between 'representation' and 'conceptual thinking'. Schleiermacher's development of hermeneutics deserves its own essay as a contribution to theology and modern European thought. The remarks here will be restricted to the relation between the rule-bound nature of language and the spontaneous nature of the language-user, which come together in style and interpretation. The second section considers three classic essays on the Bible (one German, one French, and one English) by Strauss, Renan, and Jowett. These essays articulate significant nineteenth-century cultural contradictions vis-à-vis the Bible, many of which persist in our own time. These include the increasing specialization and professional expertise that is brought to bear on the Bible by scholars, and the increasing distance between scholars and laypersons that is a consequence of this; it also includes various failed attempts to find a single intellectual framework within which to place historical-critical inquiries into the plain sense of scripture, on the one hand, and into habitable narratives for worship, on the other—usually with the consequence that narrative is eclipsed (to echo Hans Frei's felicitous phrase) in favour of the plain sense. The third section considers two contrasting influential twentieth-century approaches to the Bible: Barth's expressionist commentary on Romans and Bultmann's existentialist programme of 'demythologization'.

The earlier part of the period saw the ballooning of translations of the Bible into the world's vernaculars, often serving the needs of missionaries, in languages as varied as Persian (1838), Urdu (1843), Xhosa (1859), Tongan (1862), Maori (1868), and, surprisingly late, Russian (1876). William Robertson Smith's article 'The Bible' for the ninth edition of the Encyclopedia Britannica (1875) brought issues of the authorship and dating of the Old Testament to a wide public, cementing developments (to be surveyed in the second section) in which scholarly research increasingly challenged, and then transformed, popular conceptions of the Bible. The reaction from his own Free Church of Scotland tradition was so severe that a heresy trial was brought against him, the outcome of which was Robertson Smith's departure from Scotland for a readership in Arabic in Cambridge. The strong reaction to the encyclopaedia entry was caused not by any new arguments it contained, but by the emphatically public character of the work and the consequent public confrontation of the contradictions it displayed. Chief among these was the challenge to literal interpretations of the Bible caused by the dating of the Pentateuch to a period after Moses's death, thus ruling out Mosaic authorship. The latter part of the period saw the stabilization of scholarly editions of the Hebrew and Greek texts on which translations of the Bible came to be based, with the first editions of Eberhard Nestle's *Novum Testamentum Graece* in 1898 and Rudolf Kittel's *Biblia Hebraica* in 1906. These editions, with their detailed apparatus and self-conscious handling of variant manuscript sources, transformed scholarly study of the Bible, and ensured that from the end of the nineteenth century onwards the 'Bible' read by scholars was different from that read by ordinary worshippers.

I. HEGEL AND SCHLEIERMACHER

Hegel's *Phenomenology of Spirit* (1807) does not concern the Bible directly, but it had a significant effect on biblical interpretation. Hegel's philosophy was a major influence on his junior Tübingen alumnus David Strauss, but it had a wider impact through the distinction Hegel made between 'representation' (*Vorstellung*, also translated as 'picture-thinking') and 'the concept' (*Begriff*). What the Bible presents representationally, philosophy presents conceptually. The relation between the two terms is often misunderstood. For Hegel, philosophy is able to 'think' what religion is able to 'picture'. This is often taken to mean that, for Hegel, philosophy 'overcomes' or even 'supersedes' religion (or indeed any representational activity). This is not true. One of the remarkable aspects of Hegel's thought is that alongside a formidably sophisticated account of philosophy he takes serious what we might call the 'common-sense' point of view and affirms that it produces valid judgements given its limited sphere of operation [*eingeschloßne Wirklichkeit*], namely, everyday life. Common sense (in this case in the sphere of religion) genuinely apprehends reality [*Wirklichkeit*]; but in representational thinking, reality fails to 'receive its perfect due' (PS: 412).

How are these distinct practices to be handled? The answer to the question mirrors the central claim of this chapter: different practices call for, but often do not receive, different frameworks of interpretation. Phrased rather less compactly, the practices of everyday life are distinct from the specialized practices of scholars. There is no single framework of meanings, significance, and interpretation that can encompass everything. Consider a choir singing Psalm 51 ('Miserere mei') on Ash Wednesday and an Old Testament scholar studying Psalm 51 as part of her research into a monograph on *The Meaning of the Psalms*. These are both practices: one is the practice of worship, the other is the practice of scholarship. They are each oriented to the same object, in this case Psalm 51. Yet the practices are distinct. Interpreting the practices of worship requires an approach that is oriented to performance or ritual, while what is needed to interpret the practices of scholarship will be more focused on the discursive. The tools suitable to interpret the practices of scholars may not be suitable for interpreting the practices of worshippers, and vice versa.

Hegel is one of the first major modern philosophers to insist that different spheres of activity, including those of everyday life, have their own integrity. More specifically, he insists that philosophical activity does not compete with the practices of everyday life. The practices of everyday life are not as 'complete' a self-conscious activity as fully conceptual philosophical thinking, for Hegel, but they are compelling and valid: philosophical thinking does not replace the practices of everyday life: 'the witness of spirit can be present in manifold and various ways; it is not required that for all of humanity the truth be brought forth in a philosophical way' (Hegel 1985: 256).

The philosophical task is one of distinguishing different spheres of activity and preserving a sense of their integrity. It is thus striking that many influential nineteenth-century thinkers who consider the interpretation of the Bible—including the three figures in the next section—do not distinguish different practices in relation to the Bible. The contrasts are much more between 'ancient' and 'modern', 'mythical' and 'historical', 'unscientific' and 'critical'—together with a narrative of the inevitable displacement of the 'old' by the 'new'. Instead of Hegel's subtle account of the simultaneity of everyday and specialist practices, and of the relation between them, one sees an insistence that sophisticated 'scientific' approaches simply supplant more traditional practices.

Practices may be distinct. But they are often related to each other. Hegel saw clearly that the specialist practices that accompany a turn to 'the concept' have an effect on everyday life. It becomes possible to make sense of the settlements of previous eras in new ways. One can (and Hegel does) recount the struggles of the past as the working-out of contradictions. For example, he interprets Sophocles' *Antigone* as a struggle between two rival moral imperatives: submission to the sovereign, defended by Creon, and submission to the Gods, defended by Antigone. There is, however, a crucial qualification in Hegel's account: as he says famously in the preface to the *Philosophy of Right* (1821), 'the owl of Minerva begins its flight only with the onset of dusk' (Hegel 1991: 23). In other words, it is possible to understand events and their relation only after the fact; and the way the contradictions expressed in the struggles of an age play out is only visible after they have played out. As we shall see, some of the leading intellectuals who followed Hegel were far more confident of their ability to resolve the contradictions of their own time decisively in favour of 'scientific' or 'modern' perspectives. Instead of finding themselves in the middle of complex sets of contradictions, brought on by changes in scholarly activity, many figures of the nineteenth century and beyond simply suppose that older everyday practices are defunct, and that some new approach (happily, their own) is needed.

Hegel is important for us not only because of his attention to different practices of thinking, and their relation to each other: he also made a significant contribution to interpretation of texts, including the Bible, although this contribution is not widely known, and it was only with Gadamer's *Truth and Method* of 1960 that it fed back into the mainstream of hermeneutics. Hegel's main argument about interpretation of scripture in the *Lectures on the Philosophy of Religion*, delivered five times in Berlin between 1821 and 1831, is that such interpretation is a 'witness of the spirit'. By this he means that it is an activity of the church, pursued according to the canons of doctrine. His corollary argument is that scholarly focus on purely 'historical' questions is not really interpretation of scripture, and makes no contribution to 'truth'. In other words, Hegel refuses to acknowledge the relevance for Christian life of interpretation of the Bible that is divorced from its location in worship, guided by the tradition of doctrinal development that marks the character of the church.

F. D. E. Schleiermacher's *Hermeneutics and Criticism* is directly concerned with interpretation of the Bible. It was written in notes between 1805 and 1833, with the majority of the work from 1819 onwards (Scheleiermacher 1998).[1] Of all the modern

---

[1] This edition translates and abridges Schleiermacher 1977.

texts that consider interpretation of the Bible, *Hermeneutics and Criticism* is probably the most philosophically significant. Schleiermacher is interested in two aspects of interpretation: the technical and the artistic. He also attempts to show how the interpreter acts in ways that are both spontaneous and receptive. Unlike many modern philosophers' attempts to reduce complex acts to one foundational concept (e.g. Fichte's 'I') Schleiermacher is interested in pairs of terms that persist in relation to each other, and are not reducible one to the other.

Interpretation is technical for Schleiermacher because it involves mastery of grammar, i.e. a fixed system of rules that precedes any act of reading or writing. It is also an art (*Kunst*) because no system of rules can specify how its rules are to be applied. For related reasons, interpretation is both spontaneous and receptive. It is spontaneous because the act of interpretation is free and undetermined; and it is receptive because its material, and the structure which governs it, is given. Accounts of interpretation require both terms, in relation to each other, without reducing to the one or the other.

Hermeneutics and Criticism lays out a vision and a rationale for reading the Bible in the same way as one reads other texts: there is no difference, in principle, between secular or sacred textual interpretation:

> ...the question now imposes itself...whether the Holy Books ought to be dealt with differently because of the Holy Spirit? We cannot expect a dogmatic decision about inspiration because this must depend upon the explication. We must *first of all* not make a difference between the speaking and the writing of the Apostles. For the future church had to be built on the first of these. But precisely for this reason we also must, *second*, not believe that in the Scriptures the whole of Christianity was the immediate object. For they are all directed at specific people and could not be correctly understood even in the future if they had not been correctly understood by these people. But the people could not wish to seek anything but determinate individual things in the [Scriptures], because for them the totality had to result from the mass of particulars. We must therefore explicate them in the same way and thus assume that, even if the writers were dead tools, the Holy Spirit could only have spoken through them in the way they themselves would have spoken. (HC: 16–17)

This extraordinary paragraph contains *in nuce* an entire philosophy of interpretation. It advances seven claims.

(1) Dogmatic decisions about inspiration will rest upon interpretation of the Bible. One has to interpret the Bible first before one formulates any doctrines. For that reason, one cannot appeal to doctrine to know how to interpret the Bible.

(2 implied) The question of whether to read the Bible differently from other books cannot be prejudged by appeal to doctrine, because there must have been *some* interpretation—prior to any doctrines—that led to those same doctrines.

(3) One cannot distinguish between what the earliest figures wrote and what they said. This is because the Church's written text is based on Apostolic oral tradition.

(4) The New Testament is not about 'Christianity'. Its texts are occasional and oriented to specific groups. It is because these original addressees were able to understand these occasional texts that their successors (i.e. the Church, and the 'Christianity' which developed) were able to understand them.

(5) The original addressees looked for particular things in those texts: if they came to have any sense of the whole, it was because they had a sense of the parts.

(6) We modern readers must approach the Bible in the same way.

(7) Even if the original authors were passive recipients of divinely inspired scripture, it is still the case that what they wrote was ordinary language, [and not some special language, which they would not have understood].

The basic thrust of this argument is nicely summarized by Andrew Bowie in his introduction: '...we assume that knowledge is constituted in the same way for everyone for there to be knowledge at all' (Bowie in Schleiermacher 1998: p. xxviii). In other words, we must assume that the New Testament writers thought in ways that resemble our own: otherwise understanding is impossible. And that means we must learn their languages, master the grammars that structure them, and gain our sense of the whole by understanding the parts.

Later basic categories such as 'inspiration' and 'Christianity' and even the 'whole' of scripture are historical products that developed through reading the Bible. One cannot make them conditions for reading the Bible because they are themselves the result of reading the Bible. This is Schleiermacher's basic argument for reading the Bible in the same way that we read any text. It is important to recognize that this does not entail a denial of divine inspiration, nor does it undermine doctrines or claim that the Bible is like any other book. *The thing that is the same is our reading.* It is crucial to grasp this, because devout defenders of orthodox belief who came after Schleiermacher tended to claim that certain theories about *how we read* entailed heretical views about *what the Bible is.* Schleiermacher here makes only one claim about what kind of thing the Bible is: it was written in human languages, and we have only one method of interpreting human languages, regardless of what is written. In summary, there is no 'special hermeneutics' for revelation. A 'general hermeneutics' will serve quite adequately, and indeed is the only approach that can, quite literally, make any sense.

II. Strauss, Renan, and Jowett

Over the middle part of the nineteenth century, the reading public became more and more interested in debates about the Bible, signalled by intense interest in books such as Strauss' *Das Leben Jesu* (1835) and Renan's *Vie de Jésus* (1863), and celebrated articles such as Jowett's 'On the Interpretation of Scripture' (in *Essays and Reviews*, 1860). One of the most striking developments, especially during the nineteenth century, is a new set of categories within which to make sense of the Bible, and which are set before the public. A concern with genre comes to the fore, as well as a new and intense interest in such things as 'myth' (Strauss) and 'legend' (Renan).

Strauss's monumental *The Life of Jesus Critically Examined* (*Das Leben Jesu, kritisch bearbeitet*) of 1835 nicely expresses the widening gap between the reading practices of professional theologians and the religious practices of worshipping Christians. Strauss himself points out this gap: 'the present work is so framed, that at least the unlearned among [the laity] will quickly and often perceive that the book is not destined for them' (LJ: p. xxx). (He changed his mind about this in 1864 however when he published a book with similar aims entitled *Das Leben Jesu für das deutsche Volk.*)

Strauss engages in a self-consciously 'modern' endeavour. His aim is explicitly to offer a new approach to the Bible, better suited to a period satisfied neither by the 'supernatural' interpretations of the older tradition (represented by Origen) nor by the 'natural' interpretations of rationalist commentators (represented by J. G. Eichhorn and H. E. G. Paulus). This new approach he names the 'mythical'. Strauss states his aim in the opening lines of the preface to the first edition: '. . . it was time to substitute a new mode of considering the life of Jesus, in the place of the antiquated systems of supranaturalism and naturalism (LJ: 3).

The book is structured in three parts: a short introduction, which presents the different modes of Biblical interpretation, a long second part (many hundreds of pages), with each chapter devoted to one episode in the life of Jesus, and a final short '*Schlußabhandlung*' or closing essay, whose purpose is to argue that the demolition of the historicity of the accounts of the life of Jesus does not touch the 'eternally true Christian faith'. The 'critically annihilated', he says with typical drama, must be 'dogmatically re-established' (LJ: 867; translation amended).

Strauss' work is polemical, and his rhetorical aims in the introduction are served by strong contrasts between competing categories. The most significant categories are 'scientific' [*wissenschaftlich*] versus 'unscientific', 'modern' versus 'ancient', 'myth' [*Mythos*] versus 'history', and 'supernatural' versus 'natural'.[2] These contrasts remain to this day the principal building blocks in many polemical attacks on 'religion'. By 'scientific' (we might say 'scholarly' for the German *wissenschaftlich*) he means 'the absence of presuppositions', which is contrasted with the unscientific presence of 'believing presuppositions' in the work of religious scholars (LJ: p. xxx).

The main argument of *The Life of Jesus* is that previous 'supernatural' and 'natural' interpretations of the New Testament must give way today (i.e. in 1835) to a new modern interpretation called the 'mythical'. The main problem, which he identifies at the start, is that 'the fundamental ideas and opinions in . . . early writings fail to be commensurate with a more advanced civilization' (LJ: 11). This incommensurability leads to contradictions in the self-consciousness of believing Christians, which are displayed in attempts to reconcile these ancient and modern fundamental ideas and

---

[2] The English noun 'myth' was not in common use when Eliot was translating in the 1860s, and she uses 'mythus' throughout. The short word 'myth', so redolent of the ancient and the mysterious, is very modern. Its common use today is substantially due to Strauss.

opinions through forms of biblical interpretation. These contradictions eventually reach a crisis point, Strauss says, where the believer faces a choice when confronting a problematic event in scripture which is attributed to God. Either he must say, 'It did not happen that way', or he must say, 'If it happened that way it was not divine'. This is a familiar rhetorical move, and also one of the classic formal fallacies, the false dichotomy. Strauss presents two choices, implies they are exclusive and refuses to consider alternatives. Strauss is thus able to draw his fallacious conclusion: the believer must in the first case deny the event's historicity, or in the second case deny its divinity.

Strauss then offers a fascinating taxonomy of responses to this intolerable contradiction. He divides responses into 'biased' and 'unbiased' (befangen/unbefangen). A biased response blinds itself to consciousness of the difference between the achievements of modern education and what one finds in ancient records. A biased interpretation imagines that it presents nothing but the 'original meaning'. An unbiased response clearly acknowledges and openly admits that one must view what the old authors recount in a way that is different from how they viewed it. Strauss's point is that those who present the 'original meaning' of the text are, as we might say today, in denial.

Strauss's final point is one that will resonate thereafter. 'The [unbiased] standpoint, however, in no way entails rejection of the old religious writings; holding fast to the essential, the unessential can be boldly abandoned' (LJ: 12; translation amended). This distinction, between the essential and the unessential, together with the project of disentangling them, later became one of the hallmarks of classical nineteenth-century German liberalism, as well as of some reactions against it, such as Bultmann's.

Strauss does not reflect deeply upon his categories. He uses them to great rhetorical effect, but he does not discuss them much. The reader will look in vain to discover what is meant by 'supernatural' and 'supernaturalist', or by 'historical' and 'mythical'. There are two observations to make about Strauss's binary oppositions (myth/history, scholarly/unscholarly, biased/unbiased, ancient/modern, essential/unessential). The first is that they are properties of reading rather than properties of the text. Even the genre oppositions—myth/history—which might be thought to be properties of the text are more properly thought of as elements in a system of classification, and systems of classification are not properties of objects, but are produced by those who study them. The second is that they are not as opposed as they seem. We should distinguish 'scientific' from 'philosophical' systems of classification (see Collingwood 2008). For binary oppositions to function adequately in a 'scientific' system of classification (e.g. air-breathing/water-breathing for animals, or 'colour/black and white' for photography), they need to be well-formed oppositions which more or less exhaust the possibilities. The existence of exceptional cases (e.g. amphibians or sepia photographs) does not ruin the type of classification in play: it presents no threat to it and plays a quite normal role within it, because it is limited in extent. If one is working with a philosophical system of classification, by contrast, the classes overlap. They do so not primarily in exceptional cases but in general and in principle. Strauss's binary opposition 'myth/history' is a nice example. If Strauss means to use a 'scientific' system of classification, the contrast between the terms is strong, and any exceptions will be merely limited in extent and significance. Most objects will be either 'mythical' or 'historical'. It is, however, obvious that this is not so for Strauss. The 'historical' can include the 'mythical', as in the historical study of mythology. And the 'mythical' can include the 'historical', as in the study of propaganda. It is also obvious that something considered 'historical' in one sphere of practice or at a particular time, may become considered 'mythical' in or at another. The Bible is not *either* 'mythical' *or* 'historical' as a whole; and neither are *some* elements 'mythical' while *others* are 'historical'. The classes include each other all the way down. This is a sign that we are dealing with a philosophical and not a scientific system of classification.

The greatness of Strauss is that he recognizes a problem. He notes that the attempts of previous scholars to pry apart the 'historical' and the 'mythical' material fail because one only has the text (LJ: 30). Strauss insists on taking texts *as a whole*, and argues that one can only distinguish 'authentic' and 'inauthentic' or 'historical' and 'mythical' portions if one has criteria for such division. Just as we lack 'purely historical' accounts with which to compare the Bible narratives, so any criteria brought to bear on the text are, precisely, *brought to bear* and are not properties of the text but of the reader's practice.

The problem Strauss presented (and continues to present) is that the mythical 'representational' quality of the text is opposed to the philosophical 'idea' presented in the text. This contrast funds his distinction between 'the essential' and 'the unessential' in the text. Unlike Hegel, who insists on doing justice to a variety of practices of reading, Strauss thinks that only one is acceptable for 'modern' readers. Consequently a whole variety of practices of reading (especially in worship) disappear from view and no longer need to be interpreted. The only practice that Strauss considers is the scholarly study of the Bible. If one asks the question, what is the relation and interconnection between scholarly and ecclesial practices of reading, Strauss's text yields only confusion and contradiction. He seems to suppose (but never outright claims) that the practices of reading the Bible that one finds in worship are ripe for replacement: his new 'mythical' approach is not merely an account of scholarly practices but of all 'modern' practices of reading. This problem persists and the confusions intensify after Strauss.

Renan's *Life of Jesus* (*Vie de Jésus*, 1863, translated immediately into English) carries a title similar to Strauss's long work, but is quite different in length, style, and intent. At around 460 short and generously spaced pages (311 in English), it is a fraction of the length of *Das Leben Jesu*. It is written for the general public and engages with almost no scholarship on the Bible: the footnotes are a mixture of Biblical citation and references to ancient authorities which supplement the scriptural narratives. Renan offers a brief contemporary literature review in his introduction, and then lays the secondary sources aside. The text itself is a composite of the four gospels, enriched by material from the apocrypha, Philo, Josephus, the Talmud, and the Church Fathers. The book tells the story of the life of Jesus, and offers description of the history and culture in which he lived. Renan refers to Strauss's work and suggests that where *Das Leben Jesu* is a work concerned to debate the theological issues, his own attempt will concentrate more narrowly on the historical. It aims, as he says, to be a 'biography' or a 'history', and he draws an analogy with 'the Legends of the Saints, the Lives of Plotinus, Proclus, Isodore, and other writings of the same kind' (VJ: 25).

His approach yields a short, highly readable text. It is self-consciously selective from among the gospels, producing as uninterrupted a narrative as possible. The most obvious analogue to Renan's book is not Strauss's *Life*, but the myriad of Renaissance paintings of scenes from Jesus' life whose painters faced similar challenges: the need to choose between sources (favouring some and ignoring others), and to present a confident and easily understood picture in which no trace of the difficulties remains. The tone of Renan's work is effortlessly confident. Its pages read much more like descriptions of works by Titian than of the gospels. Although there is discussion in the introduction of the uncertainties and difficulties surrounding the composition of a biography of Jesus, these do not obtrude in the text itself, which is fluent and assured. It is no surprise that the book was an enormous success.

Renan's implied reader has a great interest in history, geography, psychology, and culture, and is not (and does not wish to be) distracted by doctrine or theology. This is particularly nicely expressed in the final three chapters. 'Jesus in the Tomb' deletes the resurrection thus:

> For the historian, the life of Jesus finishes with his last sigh. But such was the impression he had left in the heart of his disciples and of a few devoted women, that during some weeks more it was as if he were living and consoling them.   (VJ: 296)

For those interested in the relation of theology and modern European thought the most striking aspect is Renan's emphatic refusal to consider doctrine or theology. The prose is pious, in a strongly anti-institutional way, painting Jesus as a wonderful and extraordinary man. At the same time, it ruthlessly excises any trace of those later ecclesial developments which make Jesus a subject for study in the first place. Such throwaway comments as 'Men did not become his disciples by believing this thing or that thing, but in being attached to his person and in loving him' (VJ: 302) are typical. A thick and uncompromising wedge is driven between the person of Jesus and the Christ of the Church.

Renan's *Life of Jesus* is an intimate book, addressing the reader in a style that foreshadows later radio broadcasts. It sold well: *Vie de Jésus* had sold 60,000 copies by November of 1863, and was translated into over a dozen languages (Mott 1921: 236).

There is, however, a dark side to Renan's text in material relating to Jews. Consider the following observation from early on in the text:

> In Jesus' time, [Galilee] counted among its inhabitants many non-Jews (Phoen-icians, Syrians, Arabs and even Greeks). Conversions to Judaism were not at all rare in these kinds of mixed areas. It is thus impossible to raise here any question about

race or to explore what blood flowed in the veins of the one who contributed most to erasing distinctions of blood in humanity. (VJ: 22)[3]

The claim is extraordinary. We cannot say whether Jesus was Jewish or not, Renan says, and in any case, it does not matter. No evidence is offered to support this bizarre claim. This attempt to play down the Jewishness of Jesus was of course by no means the last in late modern European scholarship and itself influenced later anti-Semitic approaches in Germany (Heschel: 30–8). Renan produced one of the most successful atheist readings of the Bible and it is uncompromisingly chauvinist: ' "Christianity" has thus become almost a synonym of "religion." All that is done outside of this great and good Christian tradition is barren' (VJ: 303).

Jowett's 'On the Interpretation of Scripture' is the final and longest contribution to *Essays and Reviews* (1860). The volume sold over 20,000 copies in its first months and generated public controversy. Jowett's famous claim—'to read Scripture like any other book'—is often mistakenly taken to mean that, in his view, there is no difference between the Bible and other books. This is not true. Jowett's essay is more about the interpreter than the text. More particularly it is about the qualities that an interpreter should possess and display. It is attentive to genres of interpretation—and this predominates in his preamble much more than the issue to which he later turns, namely the genres of the scriptural texts. Jowett makes an emphatic distinction between the interpretative stance of the preacher and that of the scholar. 'Anyone who has ever written sermons is aware how hard it is to apply Scripture to the wants of his hearers and at the same time to preserve its meaning' (IS: 333–4). One of the trends set in the early nineteenth century is the increasing use of methods developed in the interpretation of classical Greek and Latin texts in biblical scholarship. Jowett presents a mature phase in this development when he observes parallels between how one tackles problems in interpretation in the two literary corpora. With respect to the classical authors, there are numerous difficulties to be confronted:

> our imperfect acquaintance with the meaning of words, or the defectiveness of copies, or the want of some historical or geographical information which is required to present an event or character in its true bearing. (IS: 334)

The difficulties are compounded when it comes to scripture. There are received interpretations which have the full weight of traditions (worse: traditions that contradict each other), and which cause interpreters not to notice that their own interpretations almost automatically harmonize the meanings of the gospel writers with the doctrines of later creeds, controversies, and circumstances. Jowett summarizes this as 'fear of disturbing the critical canons which have come down from former ages' (IS: 335). Imagine, he says, how absurd it would be to read Sophocles with the same unquestioned faith in distinct (and incompatible) schools of interpretation, implausible attempts to prefer later manuscripts

---

[3] Renan returns to this theme—in which he explicitly dismisses the idea of Jesus' Jewishness—at the end. See VJ: 309.

over earlier, and contempt for scholars who insist on interpreting Sophocles with reference to the ideas and beliefs of his age, rather than those of the interpreter's own time. What struck Jowett's contemporaries about this comparison, which guides the whole of his essay, is the suggestion that the Bible has the same status for the reader as works of classical antiquity. Yet Jowett displays contrary tendencies:

> No one who has a Christian feeling would place classical on a level with sacred literature; and there are other particulars in which the preceding comparison fails, as, for example, the style and subject, although the interpretation of Scripture requires 'a vision and faculty divine' [Coleridge], or at least a moral and religious interest which is not needed in the study of a Greek poet or philosopher, yet in what may be termed the externals of interpretation, that is to say, the meaning of words, the connexion of sentences, the settlement of the text, the evidence of facts, the same rules apply to the Old and New Testaments as to other books.   (IS: 337)

It is not clear what is meant by 'style and subject' as opposed to 'externals of interpretation', nor why one would not need a moral and religious interest in the study of Greek poets or philosophers. Jowett articulates two things which sit uneasily with each other. First, classical literature is 'not on a level' with the Bible; second 'the same rules apply' to the Bible as to classical literature. The difficulties were not only Jowett's: he expresses the contradictions and uncertainties of his age.

Having catalogued the ills that befall interpretations of scripture that are guided by theology, Jowett proceeds to sketch the ideal scholarly critic.

> All the after-thoughts of theology are nothing to him [the interpreter]; they are not the true lights which light him in difficult places. His concern is with a book in which as in other ancient writings are some things of which we are ignorant; which defect of our knowledge cannot however be supplied by the conjectures of fathers or divines.   (IS: 338)

A studied naïveté is encapsulated in his deceptively simple claim about the proper orientation of the scholar:

> The greater part of his learning is a knowledge of the text itself; he has no delight in the voluminous literature which has overgrown it. He has no theory of interpretation; a few rules guarding against common errors are enough for him. His object is to read Scripture like any other book, with a real interest and not merely a conventional one. He wants to be able to open his eyes and see or imagine things as they truly are.   (IS: 338)

Jowett's is no unthinking denial of the history of interpretation. On the contrary, he urges his readers to consider that history, in detail, and to observe how interpretations down the ages have tended to conform to doctrinal orthodoxies, and particularly to note that as these doctrines change, interpretations of scripture change with them. Jowett suggests that the history of doctrine is simultaneously the history of the interpretation of scripture. Against this, he discerns a shift in his own time: 'Educated persons are beginning to ask, not what Scripture may be made to mean, but what it does' (IS: 340). The method for discovering the latter is, typically for Jowett, disarmingly simple:

> He who in the present state of knowledge will confine himself to the plain meaning of words and the study of their context may know more of the original spirit and intention of the authors of the New Testament than all the controversial writers of former ages put together.   (IS: 340–1)

Jowett argues for an interpretation of the plain sense of scripture, together with historical study of words' contexts. Put differently, against the variety of interpretative approaches of previous ages he recommends a narrowing of focus, and a flattening of the texture of interpretation. For Jowett, the plain sense has two notable surface features, which he does not spell out. First, there is but one single plain sense; second, as a corollary of this, no disagreements about plain sense are envisaged. The problems, as Jowett sees them, arise when more theologically imaginative readings come into view, particularly when such readings contradict the plain sense.

The focus is on 'rule'-bound inquiry into 'words' with fixed 'meanings'. For Jowett, words have meanings. And if they have meanings for communities, which he acknowledges in a limited way, the only community that counts for the scholar is the community which produced the text. Why this should be is not explained. Jowett does not consider the contemporary worshipping community that reads the text, for example, beyond his references to the preacher.

The activity of the interpreter, for Jowett, is not a practice embedded in an economy of other practices such as producing, consuming, marrying, educating, negotiating, bearing responsibility, and dying. Interpreting does not show up as a 'practice' in this sense at all: it is presented rather as a series of disinterested acts of cataloguing. The business of the interpreter is explanation of phrases rather than shaping and expressing the imaginations of those who act in the world. The price Jowett pays for ridding scripture of theological infestation is the abolition of scripture's significance for any living community other than the community of scholars.

Jowett's rhetoric and its influence derives its force from strong contrasts between theology, on the one side, and natural science, history, and mathematics on the other. The principal contrast concerns facts and fallacies.

> In natural science it is felt to be useless to build on assumptions; in history we look with suspicion on *a priori* ideas of what ought to have been; in mathematics, when a step is wrong, we pull the house down until we reach the point at which the error is discovered. But in theology it is otherwise. . . .   (IS: 342)

Before considering the contrast with theology, some repair of this argument is needed Natural science plainly does revise assumptions; history does call into question claims that do not rest on evidence; and mathematics does reconfigure itself systematically. But Jowett fails to specify *under what conditions* these radical forms of inquiry are initiated. Jowett has no account of the logic of inquiry. Rather than noticing the occasions which prompt scientific, historical, and mathematical inquiry to place the current state of play in question, he implies a permanent state of revolution.

Strengthening Jowett's description of these sciences is necessary if one is to feel the full impact of his contrast between science and theology. The principal claim is that *theology is peculiarly resistant to initiating radical inquiry as such*. It preserves the majesty of the edifice even when its foundations are plainly rotten; it defends agreeable conclusions even when the reasonings that lead to them are plainly fallacious; discrepancies in the text are obscured by appeals to God's inscrutable action, and so forth, he says. One can see why these arguments should prove so influential: to an extent they are true. Theological edifices persist long after the conditions which produced them have ceased to exist; doctrinal claims are often defended without regard for the strength or weakness of any arguments which were originally offered in their support; difficulties in interpreting scripture are often treated as tasks for the interpreter rather than as outright discrepancies between texts.

Jowett (and many after him) takes this as evidence of the intellectual dishonesty of theology vis-à-vis the Bible: it is undoubtedly one of the most rhetorically devastating attacks mounted against theology as a discipline. This is, however, because Jowett does not investigate *why* theology displays these characteristics. He does not consider theology as a social practice.

Jowett does not consider scripture as texts to live by. He thus does not consider what is at stake in theology: the identity of a community, the narrative by which it lives, the pattern of worship by which its moral vision is formed and sustained. To refuse *immediately* to question basic axioms when disagreements break out in the community is not necessarily bad theology, although absolute refusal in the face of persistent problems might well be. On the contrary: the distinctive mark of poor theology in the modern period might be described as excessive haste and premature willingness to call fundamental axioms into question. Jowett's attack on theology is devastating, but this is due in part to the failure of key social categories—tradition, community, narrative—to show up in his analyses.

III. BARTH AND BULTMANN

Karl Barth's *The Epistle to the Romans* (1918, second substantially revised edition 1921, translated into English 1932) was a milestone in theological interpretation of the Bible. Its purpose was to challenge contemporary Christians, including scholars, to take seriously the claim that 'our problems are the problems of Paul; and if we be enlightened by the brightness of his answers, those answers must be ours' (ER: 1).

The Epistle to the Romans was widely viewed at the time as an assault on academic historical-critical scholarship of the Bible. Barth denied this. He says mildly that the 'historical-critical method of Biblical investigation has its rightful place; it is concerned with the preparation of the intelligence—and this can never be superfluous.' He goes on to say that if faced with a straight choice between the historical-critical method and 'the venerable doctrine of Inspiration' he would choose the latter. 'Fortunately, I am not compelled to choose between the two,' he says. He states his aim as a contribution to a 'conversation between the wisdom of yesterday and the wisdom of tomorrow' (ER: 1).

That is not how the book was received. It was widely supposed by figures such as Adolf Jülicher (famous for his work on the 'messianic secret' in Mark) and Eberhard Vischer (who had just, in 1917, published the second edition of a book on Paul's letters) that Barth was dismissing the entire enterprise of historical-critical scholarship. Vischer's book had been published as part of a newly-commissioned collection of 'popular books in the history of religions for German Christians today', by leading scholars, all of which were historical-critical in method. It was not so much the claims Barth made in his commentary that excited criticism. It was the genre in which it was composed: it did not resemble anything a respectable scholar would produce. It opens with the first verse of Romans: 'Paul, a servant of Jesus Christ, called to be an apostle...' and dives straight into theological commentary:

> Here is no 'genius rejoicing in his own creative ability' (Zündel). The man who is now speaking is an emissary, bound to perform his duty; the minister of his King; a servant, not a master. However great and important a man Paul may have been, the essential theme of his mission is not within him but above him – unapproachably distant and unutterably strange.   (ER: 27)

And it ends, commenting on Romans 16:17–20 ('Now I beseech you, brethren, mark them which are causing divisions and occasions of stumbling, contrary to the teaching which ye learned: and turn away from them!),

> Tale care lest ye be deceived, especially by those who are nearest to you and most plausible! Beware of the annual market of religious goods with its many, busy, glittering stalls! Be especially careful, because ye are yourselves in the midst of it all, and because ye have no criterion by which ye are able to distinguish yourselves from those who – **serve not our Lord Christ, but their own belly,** save the *putting again in remembrance* (xv. 15). Beware – of yourselves! ... *He that hath ears to hear, let him hear.*   (ER: 536–7; emphasis in original)

Barth's voice is not the voice of the detached scholar, weighing evidence. Unlike Friedrich Zündel, quoted at the start, who wrote books *about* figures (including Christoph Blumhardt) and about the time of the Apostles, Barth attempts to re-present Paul's voice to a contemporary readership. Barth's voice is Paul's voice. It directly addresses the reader. It calls the reader's life into question. It polemicizes against the dangers of the surrounding society. It says, 'Be different!'.

The Epistle to the Romans is not a book *about* the Epistle to the Romans. It aims to *be* the Epistle to the Romans in the form of an epistle to contemporary German-speaking Christians. It is exciting, challenging, bold, and extreme. (Much like the text on which it is a commentary.)

The principal scholarly antagonism to Barth's commentary stemmed from Barth's refusal to contextualize Paul's voice, Paul's concerns, Paul's anger. The tools developed by historical-critics were often used by Barth's predecessors to show how different Biblical times were from modern times. This, indeed, is the premiss from which Strauss's *Life of Jesus* proceeds, as we have seen. The task of understanding the Bible was—for the biblical critics—one of discovering how strange it was, how alien its mode of thinking and—as we shall see in the case of Bultmann—how implausible its cosmology was. Barth's performance of an alternative (a *performance* because he does not discuss his alternative: he simply executes it) refuses to shield the reader from the force of Paul's voice by historicizing it. Quite the reverse: Barth's purpose is to bring Paul into arresting conversation with the contemporary reader. There is no denial that there is an interpretive task, and no claim that St Paul can speak immediately to a contemporary readership. (Clearly no commentary would be needed were this the case.) Rather, there is an explicit obstruction to the idea that historical and critical scholarly methods can de-claw the text and render its claim harmless, accompanied by a firm intention to bring the text to life in a way that renews its strongest claims on future generations of Christians, and not just the Christians in Rome in the first century.

The important aspect of Barth's book for our purposes here is the way it dramatizes the seeming contradiction between the practices of scholars and those of worshippers. This is only an apparent contradiction: it arises when errant attempts are made to find a single intellectual framework in which to locate these distinct practices. Yet Barth too, in his preface, offers a single framework to make sense of various approaches to the interpretation of the Bible. He shows an awareness that these are distinct practices when he contrasts historical-critical research with the doctrine of inspiration, thus suggesting a difference between the discursive character of the one and the performative character of the other. But in deciding not to be compelled to choose between them, this distinction blurs somewhat, and Barth offers no account of how the two practices might be related to each other. His own text is the fruit of such a relation, but it is left to the reader to determine its implications.

What *The Epistle to the Romans* clearly displays is that the practices of scholarly investigation and the practices of worshippers are in a relation of some kind, and that Barth's decision to prioritize the practices of worship was perceived as a rejection of scholarly practice, rather than a qualification of it. Any serious analysis of *The Epistle to the Romans* must thus engage the issue of the relation between discursive and performative interpretations of the Bible, and the problem of the contradictions that arise when a single framework within which to place them is imposed. We shall return to this issue at the end.

Rudolf Bultmann's essay 'New Testament and Mythology' (1948, translated into English in 1953) is the last of the classic texts on the Bible to be considered here. It has a similar purpose to Barth's commentary on Romans, namely to enable modern readers to engage existentially with the Bible or, put differently, to enable the Bible to speak meaningfully to contemporary readers. Barth and Bultmann are often seen as competing figures, with Bultmann cutting a 'liberal' figure on the stage, and Barth playing the role of 'neo-orthodox (and anti-liberal) antagonist. Matters are not quite so simple. There are certainly stark differences between them, and the genres of their texts are utterly unlike each other. But the fundamental orientation of both figures is to cause the text to address the contemporary reader, against a background acknowledgement that there are obstacles to its so doing.

Bultmann's essay is discursive where Barth's is performative and it offers an account of the specific problem that confronts the modern reader of the New Testament, together with a review of recent relevant scholarship and the dominant positions in the field. Like my earlier discussion of mythology, Strauss's *Life of Jesus*, Bultmann's essay starts with the problem of the modern reader. Recalling Strauss's remarks on 'antiquated systems' that require substitution with an up-to-date framework, Bultmann opens with a dramatic presentation of the antiquated cosmology of the New Testament and states the problem: '*the kerygma is incredible to modern man, for he is convinced that the mythical view of the world is obsolete*' (NTM: 3; original emphasis).

Like Strauss, Bultmann's solution to this problem is characterized by strong contrasts. Strauss's contrasts were scientific/unscientific, modern/ancient, myth/history, supernatural/natural. Bultmann's are the 'modern' versus 'primitive' world view and, 'scientific' versus 'mythological' cosmologies. Like Strauss, Bultmann has a strong historical sense, and sees clearly that to affirm the truth of ancient cosmologies in modern times is to do something quite different from what the inhabitants of such ancient cosmologies did. Christians in the first two centuries *anno domini* did not consider their cosmologies and affirm them. They inhabited them. Bultmann points out, with exemplary clarity, that modern persons do not inhabit them. They have been rendered obsolete, over several centuries, by transformations in modern physics and biology: 'all our thinking today is shaped irrevocably by modern science' (NTM: 3). Because of this, any attempt to bypass such developments and to affirm the truth of biblical cosmologies is a distinctly modern and woefully voluntarist strategy. As Bultmann nicely puts it, 'it is impossible to revive an obsolete view of the world by a mere fiat' (NTM: 3). And there is, he says, no reason to try, because there is nothing specifically Christian about the cosmology of the New Testament: it is the world view in which the gospel is articulated, but the world view is not what the gospel announces.

The task Bultmann sets before his readers is therefore to ask, what does the gospel announce, and can it be articulated independently of the mythological cosmology which characterizes the New Testament? Or, in his own words:

> The only honest way of reciting the creeds is to strip the mythological framework from the truth they enshrine—that is, assuming that they contain any truth at all, which is just the question that theology has to ask.   (NTM: 4)

It is at this point that Bultmann parts company with Strauss. Strauss had devoted hundreds of pages to demonstrating that it is impossible to extract a historical deposit from the New Testament: it is mythological through and through, and must be interpreted as an integral whole in the form it takes. There are no reliable criteria, he says, for distinguishing true kernel from mythic shell: the whole is mythological. Bultmann takes this for granted and takes up the positive task Strauss had relegated to his final concluding essay : to show what can be recovered as doctrinally 'essential' when one discards the 'inessential' form in which it is clothed. Bultmann places this task to the fore: 'If the truth of the New Testament proclamation is to be preserved, the only way is to demythologize it' (NTM: 10).

It is here that Bultmann's difficulties become intense. The principal difficulty is how reliably to draw the distinction between 'myth' and 'truth'. He begins by attempting to define myth, and he does so by distinguishing two kinds of description: 'an objective picture of the world as it is' and 'man's understanding of himself in the world in which he lives' (NTM: 10). This resembles the well-known troubled distinction between 'fact' and 'value'. Alternatively, it might be viewed as a distinction between 'theoretical' and 'practical' knowledge, or between 'information' and 'identity' or between 'how things are' and 'who we are, and what we should do'. The problem with this distinction is that practical projects are often articulated in descriptions of the world (descriptions are often 'theories to live by'), and that descriptions of the world are always products of social and moral practices, including the social and moral practices of natural science. In common with most thinkers who make this kind of distinction, Bultmann makes no investigation into the categories in play. Instead, he offers a schematic and brief list of features that myth displays. They are four. Myth articulates (1) the ground and limitation of human action, (2) the conviction that the origin and purpose of the world lies beyond it, (3) human consciousness of being dependent on external forces, (4) the conviction that by being dependent on transcendent forces, we can be freed from worldly forces. He concludes, 'The real purpose of myth is to speak of a transcendent power which controls the world and man, but that purpose is impeded and obscured by the terms in which it is expressed' (NTM: 11).

This is a curious explanation of myth. It makes no reference to social practices. Bultmann's account focuses on what is said, and wholly ignores who says it, and how or when it is said. In terms familiar from social anthropology, it is an account of myth divorced from an account of ritual. Given the undoubted and emphatically ritual character of the kinds of Christian speech in which Bultmann is interested this is probably a ruinous move. This observation offers a clue to a puzzle I will return to at the end, namely the recurrence of attempts to demythologize the Bible in each generation.

Bultmann's solution to the problem of 'modern' readers is to interpret the New Testament as proclamation which confronts the reader with an existential claim. The task is to articulate that claim, and the understanding of 'who we are', in ways that are unencumbered by the ancient cosmology in which the New Testament proclamation is clothed.

The final two-thirds of Bultmann's essay are devoted to articulating this understanding. The most interesting problem Bultmann confronts is the question of whether one needs the New Testament in order to confront and address questions about human existence, given that modern philosophy seems to do quite well (Bultmann thinks) without it. There is, Bultmann observes, a remarkable convergence between existential philosophy and the claims of theology, a convergence partly explicable, he observes, because of the importance of Luther and Kierkegaard for that existential philosophy.

Let us return to Bultmann's initial claim that 'the mythical view of the world is obsolete'. Something about this claim should strike the contemporary reader. Strauss made an identical claim in 1835. Bultmann's essay states the same problem in 1948 (and it would be restated again by J. A. T. Robinson in *Honest to God*, citing Bultmann, in 1963, with even greater public sensation). It is striking because it seems evident that if these essays are intended to transform 'modern' understandings of the Bible, they repeatedly fail, and indeed need to be endlessly repeated. This is not because of a lack of exposure. Strauss was translated by George Eliot, in a volume that sold well and became a classic. Bultmann's programme of demythologization caused a big stir beyond the confines of scholarly journals. It is tempting to wonder if the problem of 'modern man' has been falsely stated, or if it exists at all, given that attempts to produce 'convincing' frameworks for modern readers fail to 'take' in each generation and require restatement every few years, these days by the 'new atheists' who address the modern reader with an up-to-date 'scientific' framework. If past performance is any guide, they too—like Strauss and Bultmann before them—will fail. An attempt to explain why is offered in the conclusion to this chapter.

Bultmann himself acknowledges this problem: he notes that his attempt at demythologization is not the first, and that many of his observations about the problems and tasks are repetitions of approaches undertaken thirty or forty years previously: 'it is a sign of the bankruptcy of contemporary theology that it has been necessary to go all over the same ground again' (NTM: 12). Bultmann suggests that the problem relates to the failure of nineteenth-century liberal theology, which he characterizes as jettisoning the kerygma along with the mythology and, especially in Harnack, of harvesting 'broad, basic principles of religion and ethics'. Bultmann is emphatic that such liberal theology is 'no longer the proclamation of the decisive act of God in Christ' (NTM: 13). Bultmann has a secondary target in view, however: contemporary reactions against liberal theology, which display 'a return to a naïve acceptance of the kerygma', which is accompanied by 'uncritical resuscitation of the New Testament mythology', and which runs the risk of making 'the Gospel message unintelligible to the modern world' (NTM: 12).

Barth and Bultmann are remarkably close in their fundamental orientation, which is to interpret the Bible in such a way as to proclaim Jesus Christ and, through that proclamation, to disclose to modern readers the decision with which the gospel confronts them. The difference lies in the relation between text and practice, between myth and ritual, between discursive and performative interpretation.

IV. Conclusion

The common thread through the work of Strauss, Renan, and Jowett is an exposition of the Bible in which worship fails to appear. By contrast, the work of Hegel, Schleiermacher, and Barth is marked by an account of religious practice, in which reading the Bible takes its primary place. Similar considerations apply to the 'new atheists' who scoff at the ridiculous beliefs Christians have, especially their ridiculous beliefs about the Bible: worship fails to appear in these accounts too. Bultmann presents an interesting case, and displays contrary tendencies. For long stretches of his discussion of mythology, worship fails to appear, and his account suffers accordingly. Yet at arguably the most important point, in a discussion of demythologizing the cross, worship unexpectedly appears centre-stage:

> The cross becomes a present reality first of all in the sacraments. In baptism men and women are baptized into Christ's death (Rom. 6.3) and crucified with him (Rom. 6.6). At every celebration of the Lord's Supper the death of Christ is proclaimed (1 Cor. 11.26). The communicants thereby partake of his crucified body and his blood outpoured (1 Cor. 10.16). Again, the cross of Christ is an ever-present reality in the everyday life of the Christians.   (NTM: 36–7)

These contrary tendencies—excluding ritual from playing a structurally significant role, and yet including it at certain moments—are left unresolved in Bultmann's essay, and they exemplify the contrary tendencies displayed in approaches to the Bible in the period considered in this article.

My concluding observations about the Bible in modern European thought return to where the argument began. The history of approaches to the Bible is in part the history of a failure to reach the level of insight reached by Hegel and Schleiermacher. The two earlier figures acknowledge that practices of interpretation are aspects of wider and more complex social practices, and insist that the practices of scholarship are distinct from, but in relation to, practices of worship. Attempts to confront the problem of 'modern' readers are doomed to failure if they do not consider the place of the text in worship, or (to use social anthropological categories) the inextricability of myth from ritual. Any successful attempt, by contrast, will take seriously the distinction between different kinds of practice (in this case the practices of scholarship and of worship) and will not attempt to force both into the same interpretative framework. Hegel is superb on this question. His *Phenomenology* is a *tour de force* of insistence that philosophy may articulate self-consciously and conceptually what religious life performs implicitly and representationally, but relies on it and can never replace it. This is true *a fortiori* of biblical scholarship: we read the Bible with such attention to detail only because of its primary location in ritual. Hegel's successors fail to achieve this level of insight, generally preferring to describe the text, or methods of interpretation. Instead of sustained engagement with the practices of worship, which produce those practices of reading and interpretation, the practices of scholarship are falsely pitted against practices of worship, as if they are the same kind of thing. Hegel is also exemplary in his insistence that the practices of natural science and the practices of religious life are, alike, social practices, which are not only distinct but constantly in relation to each other. The attempts of Strauss and Bultmann, in particular, to pit the 'objectivity' of science against the 'naïveté' of religion fail, like many accounts of science and religion, because they do not take the social-practical character of science seriously. The story of the Bible in modern European thought can in part be described as the story of failed attempts to isolate the Bible from its ritual context, accompanied by attempts, like Hegel's and Barth's (and at times Bultmann), to refuse this isolation.

The implications this struggle has for the study of the Bible in the contemporary university seem relatively clear: there is a struggle in the university itself over whether to isolate biblical interpretation from practices of worship (including the theology that derives from such practices) or to integrate it with the study of ritual (including the ethics which derives from such ritual). That struggle is far from over.

References

Barth, Karl (1933). *The Epistle to the Romans*, trans. E. Hoskyns (Oxford: Oxford University Press).

Bultmann, Rudolf (1972). 'New Testament and Mythology', in H.-W. Bartsch (ed.), *Kerygma and Myth: A Theological Debate*, trans. R. Fuller (London: SPCK).

Collingwood, R. G. (2008). *An Essay on Philosophical Method*. (Oxford: Oxford University Press).

Hegel, G. W. F. (1977). *Phenomenology of Spirit*, trans. A. V. Miller (Oxford: Clarendon).

—— (1985). *Lectures on the Philosophy of Religion, Vol. III: The Consummate Religion*, ed. Peter Hodgson, trans. R. Brown and Stewart J. Hodgson (Berkeley, CA: University of California Press).

—— (1991). *Elements of the Philosophy of Right*, ed. Allen Wood, trans. H. B. Nisbet (Cambridge: Cambridge University Press).

Heschel, Susannah (2008). *The Aryan Jesus*. (Princeton, NJ: Princeton University Press).

Jowett, Benjamin (1860). 'On the Interpretation of Scripture', *Essays and Reviews*. (London: Parker and Son).

Mott, Lewis (1921). *Ernest Renan*. (New York: Appleton).

Renan, Ernest (1864). *The Life of Jesus*, trans. E. Wilbour (London: Trübner and Co).

Schleiermacher, F. D. E. (1977). *Hermeneutic und Kritik*, ed. Manfred Frank (Frankfurt: Suhrkamp).

—— (1998). *Hermeneutics and Criticism*, trans. A. Bowie (Cambridge: Cambridge University Press).

Strauss, D. F. (1846). *The Life of Jesus Critically Examined*, trans. M. Evans (London: Chapman Brothers).

Suggested Reading

Barth (1933).
Bultmann (1972).
Hegel (1977).
Jowett (1860).
Renan (1864).
Schleiermacher (1998).
Strauss (1846).

CHAPTER 28

··

INCARNATION

··

DAVID R. LAW

THE doctrine of the incarnation has its biblical basis in such passages as Jn. 1:1–18 and Phil. 2:6–11, which affirm that Christ, though equal with God, became flesh, assumed a human form, and dwelled among human beings. The doctrine acquired its classical formulation at the first four ecumenical councils. The Councils of Nicea (325) and Constantinople (381) fixed in the Nicene Creed the affirmation that Christ is 'of one being with the Father' (*homoousion*), while the Councils of Ephesus (431) and Chalcedon (451) resulted in the 'two-natures' doctrine, which in the words of the Chalcedonian Definition, affirms that Christ must be confessed as one person in two natures, unconfusedly, immutably, indivisibly, inseparably. The divine and human natures in Christ are united in a 'hypostatic union', the coherence of which was secured by the *communicatio idiomatum*, the doctrine that Christ's divine attributes were communicated to his human nature.

The eighteenth-century revolution in European thought known as the Enlightenment set in train modes of thinking which profoundly affected the understanding of the incarnation. The Enlightenment emphasis on reason as the bar at which all truth claims must justify themselves led some to reject the incarnation because it was incapable of rational justification. Further blows to the classical doctrine were dealt by the rise of the natural sciences and the development of historical criticism of the Bible. Scientific advances placed in question the truth of Christ's miracles, thereby undermining one of the traditional proofs of his divinity. Historical criticism uncovered Jesus' relationship to his surrounding culture, thereby creating a greater consciousness of Jesus as a historical individual, which intensified the problems of the relationship between Jesus' divinity and humanity. Historical criticism also raised questions concerning the historicity of the accounts upon which the classical doctrine of the incarnation was based. The growing awareness of the divergence between the Christ of classical Christianity and the Jesus revealed by historical criticism created the problem of the relationship between 'the Christ of faith' and 'the Jesus of history'.

The Enlightenment period was characterized also by the search for an identity of religions. Underlying the historical or 'positive' religions is a 'natural religion' common to all religions, which are merely local manifestations of this common, underlying 'natural religion'. The individual characteristics of Judaism, Christianity, and Islam, are due merely to prejudice or custom and do not arise from reason, as G. E. Lessing (1729–81) portrayed in his play *Nathan the Wise* (1779). On this reckoning the incarnation is merely a Christian idiosyncrasy, a view which was intensified by the increasing contact between Christianity and other faiths brought about by European colonialism. The availability of the sacred literature of non-Christian religions as a result of the work of Max Müller (1823–1900) made possible the comparative study of religion, while the History of Religions School, the leading representative of which was Ernst Troeltsch (1865–1923), showed how early Christianity had been conditioned by the religious beliefs circulating in its cultural milieu. The effect of these developments has been to weaken absolutist claims for Christianity and to bring about a shift from exclusivism to pluralism, i.e. from the view that salvation is to be found only in Christ to the recognition that other faiths are independent but equally valid encounters with the divine.

The Enlightenment critique of Christian doctrine was intensified by Kant's *Critique of Pure Reason* (Kant 1990), which criticized metaphysics for pressing beyond the limitations of experience. Kant differentiated between phenomena, which are how things present themselves to the perceiver, and noumena, which are what things are in themselves. For Kant, while phenomena can be verified by experience, noumena are inaccessible to the human mind and are as such unverifiable. The difficulty for metaphysics is that many of its propositions fall into the category of noumena. Consequently, they are unverifiable by experience and therefore cannot count as knowledge. Kant's rejection of the epistemological status of metaphysical statements together with his critique of the traditional proofs of God's existence undermined the metaphysical foundations upon which the doctrine of the incarnation was based. His 'Copernican revolution', which shifted the criterion for the validity of epistemological claims from the object known to the *knower*, led him to re-conceive metaphysics in terms of the mapping out of the a priori structures that allow human beings to make sense of their experience and construct it into knowledge of the world, a form of philosophy he described as 'transcendental idealism'. Kant himself addressed the theological crisis he had created by substituting ethics for metaphysics and advancing a moral interpretation of religion in his *Critique of Practical Reason* (Kant 1997) and *Religion within the Limits of Reason Alone* (Kant 1934). Although such notions as God, freedom, and immortality cannot be empirically verified, they are justifiable on the basis of the support they give to the practical reason or conscience. In order to lead moral lives, human beings act as if these notions were true, even though they are impossible to verify empirically.

The Enlightenment critique of Christian doctrine and Kant's critique of metaphysics resulted in a shift in the direction in which Christology was carried out. From the early Church until the Enlightenment the dominant trend was to do Christology 'from above'. That is, the starting point for reflecting on Jesus of Nazareth was to begin with his divinity and then consider in what sense such a divine being could be said to be human. The impossibility of providing a rational justification of Christ's divinity in light of the Enlightenment and Kantian critique, however, prompted the reversal of the direction of Christological reflection. Despite some notable exceptions, the dominant trend in Christology since the Enlightenment has been to do Christology 'from below'. That is, the starting point for Christological reflection is the humanity of Jesus and the problem is to establish in what sense it is possible to speak of this human being as divine.

The philosophy of G. W. F. Hegel (1770–1831) can be read as an attempt to recover metaphysics after Kant's critique. Kant's transcendental idealism had created a series of dualisms: phenomena and noumena, knowledge and faith, subject and object, the theoretical and the practical, God and the world. Hegel sought to overcome these dichotomies by understanding history as a dialectical process in which ideas manifested themselves in ever fuller and richer forms. Hegel achieves this by distinguishing between *Vorstellungen* or 'representations' and *Begriffe* or concepts. Progression towards the truth consists of a dialectical relationship between representation and concept, in which an initial representation gives way in a historical process to subsequent representations, which express more adequately the concept articulated by the original representation. Hegel interprets this process not only in terms of human beings' progression towards higher forms of conceptuality, but also in terms of a philosophy of development according to which *Geist*, Spirit or Mind, comes to know itself by unfolding itself in history in ever higher forms. For Hegel, this self-knowledge comes about through absolute spirit manifesting itself in what is other than itself. To know itself in its other, the spirit creates the world, in which it alienates itself from itself by objectifying itself in its other and yet simultaneously embarks on the process of overcoming this alienation by relating itself to its other in historical forms such as political institutions, art, culture, and religion.

The conceptual content of philosophy and religion is the same, namely spirit. The key difference between them is that they express this common content in different forms. Whereas religion employs representations, philosophy brings to expression the conceptual content intuitively grasped but inadequately articulated in the representations employed by religion. On this understanding, Christ is the representation of the idea of divine-human unity and is the most extreme point of the spirit's procession into its other.

After Hegel's death Hegelianism moved in two distinct directions known loosely as right-wing and left-wing Hegelianism. 'Right-wing Hegelianism' denotes such thinkers as Philipp Marheineke (1780–1846), who employed Hegel's thought in a politically and theologically conservative way and who affirmed the compatibility of Hegelianism and Christianity. It was, however, the left-wing Hegelians who were historically of greater significance, above all Ludwig Feuerbach (1804–72) and Karl Marx (1818–83).

Feuerbach employs his 'transformative method' to transpose Hegel's philosophy of spirit onto the human being. For Feuerbach, it is not Hegel's absolute spirit but the individual human spirit which comes to self-knowledge through objectifying itself in its other. It achieves this by externalizing human attributes and projecting them in an abstract and idealized form on to the concept of God. As Feuerbach puts it, 'God is the idea of the [human] species as an individual—the idea or essence of the species . . . freed from all the limits which exist in the consciousness and feeling of the individual' (Feuerbach 1854: 152). In short, human beings create God in their own image. An important feature of Feuerbach's treatment of Christianity is his application of the Hegelian notion of alienation to human beings. Whereas for Hegel it is the spirit which alienates itself from itself in objectifying itself in its other, for Feuerbach it is human beings who suffer alienation. In projecting their attributes on to the concept of God, human beings alienate themselves from their own human nature. Christian doctrines are the result of this objectification of human attributes and are expressions of the alienation of human beings from their essential nature.

For Marx, the weakness in Feuerbach's analysis is that he failed to recognize the role of economic factors in human beings' self-objectification and alienation. Without identifying these factors it is impossible to liberate human beings from the alienating effects of self-objectification, hence Marx's famous comment in the eleventh of his *Theses on Feuerbach* that, 'the philosophers have only interpreted the world in various ways; the point, however, is to change it'. Marx transfers Hegel's philosophy to the economic sphere and interprets religion as a superstructure arising from the conditions of economic exploitation. Once these conditions have been removed, the need for religion will fall away.

The third of the great nineteenth-century critics of Hegelianism was the Dane Søren Kierkegaard (1813–55). For Kierkegaard, each human being is a unique, irreducible, free individual who posits himself as a self though his existential decisions and his choice of life-view. By subsuming human beings into an all-embracing philosophy of spirit Hegel annihilates precisely those features of human existence that make human beings human. Kierkegaard was particularly critical of Hegel's reduction of Christianity to the status of an inferior form of thought destined to be superseded by philosophy. For Kierkegaard, faith and knowledge, religion and philosophy belong in two distinct spheres. Consequently, Hegel's attempt to translate religious concepts into a supposedly more adequate philosophical terminology constitute a fundamental misunderstanding of the nature of Christianity. As he puts it in *Concluding Unscientific Postscript*, 'Christianity is not a doctrine, but . . . is an existence-communication' (Kierkegaard 1992: 379–80). Despite his critique, Kierkegaard drew on insights from Hegel's thought. Like Feuerbach, Kierkegaard transposes Hegelian dialectic from absolute spirit to the human spirit. In contrast to Feuerbach, however, Kierkegaard understands the human spirit not in terms of 'species-being' but as 'the single individual', a key notion in Kierkegaard's thought. As Hannay succinctly puts it, Kierkegaard has turned Hegel 'outside-in' (Hannay 1982: 19–53), by exploiting Hegel's philosophy of spirit to construct an analysis of the human self. It is the existential analysis of such phenomena as anxiety and despair that Kierkegaard develops on the basis of this creative appropriation of Hegelianism that has led to his being widely regarded as the father of existentialism.

The critique of metaphysics initiated by Kant reached its nineteenth-century apogee in the announcement of the 'death of God' made by Friedrich Nietzsche (1844–1900), a phrase which refers not only to the end of the metaphysical God who had for so long dominated western thought, but also to the impossibility of arriving at universal principles and stable values. 'Universal' values are nothing of the kind but are cultural constructs of the society in which they are held. Nietzsche describes this new situation as 'nihilism'.

The seemingly insuperable problems faced by metaphysics led to a return to Kant's critical idealism and to 'neo-Kantianism', a collective term for several philosophical movements inspired by Kant's critical method which flourished between c.1870 and 1920. The neo-Kantians conceived of philosophy as a science of values, which are understood not as facts but as norms. Truth is not intrinsic to facts but is a value human beings impose upon them. The return to Kant was emulated by theologians, above all by the Ritschlians, who interpreted doctrines not as factual statements but as value judgements. This approach provided the philosophical basis of 'liberal Protestantism', a movement which held that by recovering an account of the historical Jesus freed from the Church's dogmatizing it became possible to reinterpret Christianity in moral terms.

In the 1920s, neo-Kantianism gave way to phenomenology and existentialism. In *Logical Investigations* (1901–2) and *Ideas* (1913) Edmund Husserl (1859–1938) developed phenomenology—the study of the structures of human consciousness—by investigating 'phenomena', i.e. the way things appear to the human consciousness. Husserl took up Bretano's concept of intentionality and supplemented it with his notion of *epoché* or 'bracketing'. Intentionality denotes the fact that the consciousness is always *directed towards* something. The character of this 'something', however, is 'bracketed' in order to focus on the consciousness that is directed towards the object rather than on the object towards which the consciousness is directed. This method enables Husserl to describe the categories the human consciousness employs in its engagement with the world and to map out their interconnections.

The attraction of Husserl's philosophy to other philosophers, notably the existentialists, was that it offered an alternative to Cartesian dualism. Husserl's treatment of intentionality in terms of directedness towards an object seemed to provide a way of overcoming the subject-object dichotomy by interpreting the relationship with the world as something given in the categorial structure of consciousness. Theologians, too, drew on insights from phenomenology. Tillich, for example, held that, 'Theology must apply the phenomenological approach to all its basic concepts' (Tillich 1953: 106).

Martin Heidegger (1889–1976), however, held that Husserl had failed to deal with a still more fundamental question, namely with the *meaning of being*. In his *Being and Time* (1927) Heidegger takes up this question but draws on impulses from phenomenology as a means of posing it. In raising the question of being Heidegger takes as his starting point the concrete individual existence of the human being or *Dasein*. Posing the question of being means first achieving clarity about the being who poses the question.

Heidegger explores the distinctiveness of *Dasein* by considering the different modes of being-in-the-world which *Dasein* can sustain. Because the categories inherited from the philosophical tradition have ignored these modes of *Dasein*'s being-in-the-world Heidegger draws on phenomenology to develop the categories or rather 'existentialia' appropriate to the human being's being-in-the-world. It is this that prompts his existential analytic and his focus on such modes or 'moods' of being as anxiety, guilt, and being-towards-death.

Heidegger's philosophy had a major influence on the development of existentialism. Karl Jaspers (1883–1969) developed his existentialist philosophy independently of Heidegger, but Jean-Paul Sartre (1905–80), Maurice Merleau-Ponty (1908–61), and others drew on Heidegger's *Being in Time* in the development of their own thought. Existentialism is in part a reaction against the abstract, rational, scientific world view and the impact this world view has had on the human being. It emphasizes the dynamism of human being and stresses engagement, commitment, action, choice, and responsibility. The centre of existentialist thought is the human individual in the concrete situations and crises of everyday existence.

Heidegger is important also for his critique of ontotheology, a term denoting the tendency of western thought to conceive of being as a pre-eminent entity such as God or consciousness. Such a notion of being is the result of the abstraction of individual instances of being and ignores being's temporal character.

Nietzsche and Heidegger's critique of metaphysics has been highly influential on late twentieth and early twenty-first-century European thought. Postmodernist thinkers have taken up the notion that metaphysics has run its course and employed it as the basis of their philosophizing. Jean-François Lyotard (1924–98) claims that, 'The ideas of western civilization issuing from the ancient, Christian and modern traditions are bankrupt' (Lyotard 1999: 37), and defines postmodernism as 'incredulity toward meta-narratives' (Lyotard 1989: p. xxiv). Emanuel Levinas (1906–95) employs the term 'totality' to critique philosophies which undermine the difference, distinctiveness, and particularity of the other by interpreting reality on the basis of a single, all-encompassing concept (Levinas 1969). For Levinas, atheism acts as a counterforce to the totalizing tendency of metaphysics, for it protects the difference of the other by refusing to allow selves to be subsumed into the totality of being.

Drawing on Levinas' notion of alterity, Jacques Derrida (1930–2004) interprets metaphysics as an act of violence by which one seeks to subsume the other completely into one's self (Derrida 1978). Derrida's deconstruction of the metaphysics of presence and his critique of logocentrism, with its rejection of the notion of a universal logos, raise questions concerning the conception of Christ as the incarnation of the divine Word. For Derrida, language is characterized by ambiguity. There is a mismatch between language and that about which language speaks. This mismatch is called *différance* by Derrida, a term based on the French word *différer*, meaning both 'to differ' and 'to defer'. The ambiguity of texts means that their meaning is constantly deferred. Consequently, there can be no closure, but only a constant flow of meanings (Derrida 1974).

The critique of metaphysics stretching from Kant through Nietzsche and Heidegger to the postmodernists raises radical questions concerning the status of the incarnation. If, as the classical doctrine appears to assume, the incarnation is dependent on substance ontology and a metaphysics of presence, then the doctrine would seem to be undermined by the critique of its metaphysical underpinnings.

One of the impacts of modern European thought, then, has been to knock out the foundations upon which the doctrine of the incarnation has traditionally been based. This metaphysical critique has been compounded by the feminist critique of the Father-Son terminology of the Trinity and incarnation as deeply harmful to women, for they hypostatize Jesus' maleness into an ontological characteristic of God's being. The feminist critique of patriarchy places in question a religion which holds that the divine Logos has incarnated himself as a man.

Theologians have reacted to the impact of modern European thought on the incarnation by creatively transforming the figure of Jesus. In so doing, they have drawn on different strands of European thought as resources for reconstructing the doctrine of the incarnation. Since the Enlightenment, this has led to a plethora of new Christologies attempting to adjust the doctrine of the incarnation in the light of new ways of thinking, while still remaining true to the Christian conviction that God was in Christ.

I. THE ETHICAL CHRIST

A major response to the crisis faced by the classical doctrine of the incarnation in modernity has been to interpret Christ in *ethical* terms. This was a strategy adopted by Lessing, who at the conclusion of 'On the Proof of the Spirit and of Power' asks what binds us to Christ's teaching if we can no longer have confidence in the dogmatic claims made about him. Lessing answers his own question with the comment that it is the *teachings themselves* that bind us (Chadwick 1956: 55).

A similar strategy is adopted by Kant, who rethinks the two-natures doctrine in moral terms. In *Religion within the Limits of Reason Alone* Kant interprets the Gospel of John's Logos theology as a reference to the rational and moral principle that resides in every human being (Kant 1934). In the 'godly-minded teacher', i.e. Christ, this idea of complete moral perfection was expressed in a human individual. Christ is not unique in this respect, however, for all human beings possess within them the idea of complete moral perfection. There is consequently no need for a unique empirical actualization of moral perfection, for we all possess it and have the capacity to actualize it. Nevertheless, despite a moral example being strictly speaking unnecessary, Christ's life provides human beings with a useful, concrete example of a human being who has actively lived a life of moral perfection. As such Christ is the archetype (*Urbild*). Consequently, he is a source of encouragement and hope that all human beings can attain to complete moral perfection.

For nineteenth-century liberal Protestantism, Kant provided the basis for interpreting the person of Christ in a way which avoided the pitfalls of the Chalcedonian

Definition. Albrecht Ritschl (1822–89) follows Kant in rejecting metaphysics and develops an ethical interpretation of Christ. Drawing on the neo-Kantian distinction between fact and value, Ritschl argues that, 'Every cognition of a religious sort is a direct judgement of value' (Ritschl 1966: 398). For Ritschl, the starting point for Christology is Christ's moral impact and the Church through which Christ's moral impact is mediated. Christ's uniqueness consists in his introduction of the consciousness of a new type of relationship with God into history and in his founding of the Christian community, while his divinity resides in our acknowledgement of the meaning he imparts to our lives. If we honour Christ as God, 'then that is a value-judgement of a direct kind. It is not a judgement which belongs to the sphere of disinterested scientific knowledge, like the formula of Chalcedon' (Ritschl 1966: 398).

Willibald Hermann (1846–1922) rejects the Chalcedonian definition because of its metaphysical character and its inability to express the inward nature of the believer's relation to Christ (Herrmann 1895). For Herrmann, Christian doctrines are expressions of the new personal life brought about by Christianity. This new personal life is faith, which Herrmann understands as a revelation in which the human being experiences communion with God. For Herrmann, this revelation is expressed above all in the 'inner life' of the historical Jesus, which stamps its 'impression' (*Eindruck*) on human beings and brings us into communion with God. Furthermore, the moral consciousness which resides in human beings' conscience finds its expression in Christ, who as such is the founder of the ethical community called in biblical terms the kingdom of God. In Christ and the community he founded we encounter the historical embodiment of moral value. It is the capacity of Jesus' inner life to impress itself upon us and his embodiment of the moral law that make it appropriate to describe him as divine.

Adolf von Harnack (1851–1930) followed the anti-metaphysical trend in nineteenth-century theology by attempting to identify the essence of Christianity not by distilling it from the doctrines of Christianity but by means of historical analysis. For Harnack, dogma is the result of 'the work of the Hellenic spirit upon the Gospel soil' (Harnack 1893: 5). Harnack regards Logos Christology, the doctrine of the incarnation, the understanding of salvation as deification and the two-natures doctrine as examples of the activity of this Hellenic spirit. These doctrines played an important role in the early Church, for they provided the means of maintaining Christian identity against the threat posed by Roman and Hellenistic culture. Since this threat no longer exists, traditional Christological dogma is redundant, and we must return to the foundations of Christology by means of historical criticism. According to Harnack, historical study reveals that Christology was not part of Jesus' message, for 'The Gospel, as Jesus proclaimed it, has to do with the Father only and not the Son' (Harnack 1901: 144). It is thus not Jesus that is the message of the gospel but the human being's relationship to God the Father. This is the essence of the gospel that Jesus preached, which must be recovered as the basis of a modern Christology.

Ethical Christologies solve the Christological problem created by modern European thought by interpreting Christ as the teacher, exemplar, and embodiment of moral values. In so far as Christ expresses these more fully than other human beings, he can be described as 'divine'. Ethical Christologies thus detach the two-natures doctrine from its metaphysical moorings and interpret it as a metaphor for Jesus' moral character and the exemplary way he has fulfilled the moral law.

The success of this solution was placed in question by several factors. Neo-Kantianism and its theological counterpart liberal Protestantism are based on a dichotomy between facts and values. It is questionable, however, whether they can be so easily detached from each other. Furthermore, the success of liberal Protestant attempts to ground the ethical notion of Christ on the historical Jesus was threatened by advances in New Testament scholarship, which showed that the gospels do not provide a historical account of Jesus and his 'inner life', but are themselves coloured by a theological agenda. Johannes Weiss (1863–1914) and Albert Schweitzer (1875–1965) drew attention to the eschatological character of Jesus' ministry and to the fact that the kingdom of God was for Jesus not only a moral notion but also an apocalyptic event in which God was expected to intervene directly in history (Schweitzer 1914, 2000; Weiss 1971). A further problem with ethical Christologies is the danger of so humanizing Christ that he becomes merely an embodiment of human values. As Tyrell famously put it, 'The Christ that Harnack sees, looking back through nineteen centuries of Catholic darkness, is only the reflection of a Liberal Protestant face, seen at the bottom of a deep well' (Tyrell 1913: 44).

II. THE CHRIST OF RELIGIOUS EXPERIENCE

The Christology of Friedrich Schleiermacher (1768–1834) was motivated by his concern to avoid the ahistorical, supernatural approach of orthodox Christology, which was no longer tenable after Kant's critique of metaphysics, while circumventing the 'empirical' Christologies of the rationalists, which reduce Christ to merely a teacher of moral values.

Schleiermacher was influenced not only by Kant's critique of metaphysics but also by the Romantic movement, which was a reaction to the Enlightenment's overemphasis on rationality. Works such as *The Outpourings of an Art-Loving Monk* by W. H. Wackenroder (1773–98) and the poetry of Novalis (1772–1801) attempted to recover the *sense* for the infinite, a sense that was mediated not merely through the reason, but above all through feeling and imagination. This notion of feeling as a sense or taste for the infinite was taken up by Schleiermacher in his *On Religion: Speeches to its Cultured Despisers* (Schleiermacher 1988) and in a reworked form in his later *Christian Faith* (Schleiermacher 1989), where he formulates the religious consciousness in terms of a 'feeling of absolute dependence'. This notion provides Schleiermacher with the key to reinterpreting Christian doctrines as expressions of the contents of the believer's consciousness. Sin, for example, is interpreted as resistance to God-consciousness.

The strategy Schleiermacher employs to anchor Christ to the Christian's religious consciousness is, like Kant, to interpret Christ as the *archetype* of God-consciousness. Like all human beings Christ possessed God-consciousness. In contrast to other human beings, however, Christ's God-consciousness was dominant and undistorted. He possessed an absolutely powerful God-consciousness. As such, Christ is the archetype (*Urbild*) and historical manifestation of perfect and complete God-consciousness.

This notion of Christ as the archetype of God-consciousness allows Schleiermacher to rework the two-natures doctrine. It is the absoluteness of Christ's God-consciousness that constitutes his divinity, while Christ's humanity consists in his objectively exhibiting the God-consciousness that all human beings have the potential to achieve. Schleiermacher sums up the similarity and difference between Christ and other human beings in the following way: 'The Redeemer, then, is like all men in virtue of the identity of human nature, but distinguished from them all by the constant potency of his God-consciousness, which was a veritable existence of God in him' (Schleiermacher 1989: 385).

Schleiermacher, then, found a way of emphasizing Christ's uniqueness that avoided treating Christ as a supernatural being or reducing him to a teacher or a prophet. The difference between the ordinary human being and Christ is not qualitative but quantitative. They both possess God-consciousness, the difference being that in Christ the God-consciousness is dominant, whereas in other human beings it exists in a weak and distorted form. It is the dominance of Christ's God-consciousness that allows us to speak of Christ as divine. Schleiermacher's Christology thus seemed to offer a way of affirming the two-natures doctrines that avoided the metaphysical problems of the Chalcedonian Definition.

III. THE IDEALIST CHRIST

Hegel's interpretation of history as a dialectical process in which ideas actualize themselves in progressively higher forms was seen both by Hegel himself and his theological followers as a means of recovering Christ's significance after Kant's critique of metaphysics. Hegel integrates Christ into his philosophy of spirit as a turning point in the spirit's process of coming to know itself in history. Christ's role is twofold. Firstly, by uniting the divine and the human, or rather, in making explicit the previously implicit divine-human unity, Christ brings about reconciliation between spirit and its other. In Christ God knows himself in human consciousness, and the human being knows himself in God. Secondly, Christ's death constitutes both the spirit's most extreme self-alienation into its other and the point at which this alienation is overcome in the spirit's new and now explicit self-unity. Christ's death is also important because it enables Christ's transition from representation to concept. Through his death Christ sheds the sensuous and the particular. Thereby Christ becomes a memory (*Erinnerung*), with the result that interiorization (*ErInnerung*) of spirit can begin. This occurs when the life of God passes beyond Jesus to the third moment in the divine life, symbolized by the Holy Spirit. The Church itself begins this process, albeit in inadequate form, in its development of doctrine, for in doctrine the meaning of the divine-human unity Jesus represents is expressed *for the present*.

By integrating Jesus into his philosophy of spirit Hegel is able to solve two Christo-logical problems. Firstly, he bridges Lessing's ugly ditch between historical events and religious truths by interpreting Christ as the historical realization of the idea of divine-human unity. The scandal of particularity is overcome by integrating Christ into a broader scheme of historical development. Secondly, Hegel is able to retain the language of the two-natures doctrine. Christ is both divine and human in the sense that it is in the person of Christ that an awareness of divine-human identity between God and humankind is achieved.

Hegel's influence on subsequent Christology was profound. David Strauss (1808–74) took up Hegel's distinction between representation and concept and made it the basis of his notion of myth, which he employed as the hermeneutical key for interpreting the gospels in terms of Christ's representation of the concept of divine-human unity (Strauss 1846). Hegel also sparked a debate on the *necessity* of the incarnation and the question of sin. Was the incarnation a necessary stage in the life of absolute spirit or was it God's free response to the fall?

In twentieth-century Christology Hegel's influence is evident in the Christologies of Jürgen Moltmann (b. 1926), Hans Küng (b. 1928), and Wolfhart Pannenberg (b. 1928). Pannenberg's understanding of revelation as the process of God's indirect self-revelation in history echoes Hegel's understanding of history in terms of the spirit's coming to know itself through its self-manifestation in the historical process (Pannenberg 1968, 1969). Küng accepts Hegel's critique of the static God of conventional metaphysics and employs Hegel as a resource for thinking through the relation between God and history in terms of God's self-manifestation as the source, centre, and goal of the world process (Küng 1980, 1987). Moltmann's interpretation of history as the Trinitarian history of God owes much to Hegel (Moltmann 1974).

Hegelianism not only provided resources for rethinking the incarnation, but also stimulated Christological thinking by prompting a backlash against his thought. For his critics Hegel's philosophy of spirit threatens divine transcendence by dissolving the distinction between God and humankind and undermines the centrality of the incar-nation, which is not a unique event, but is a manifestation of the universal truth of the identity of God and humankind. The whole of history is a process of the spirit's incarnation of itself in ever higher forms. Jesus Christ is merely a special instance of this process. Such criticisms prompted Hegel's opponents to seek more adequate ways of conceptualizing the incarnation.

IV. The Kenotic Christ

The resurgence of kenotic Christology in the nineteenth and early twentieth centuries was an attempt to refine the metaphysics of the incarnation in response to the historical and metaphysical problems caused to classical Christology by historical criticism and the critique of metaphysics. These problems were compounded by the development of the new discipline of psychology and the increasing importance of the notion of personality. Increasing knowledge about the workings of the human mind confronted theologians with the problem of how the Logos and Jesus' human psychology could coexist. Kenotic theologians addressed these problems by arguing that on becoming incarnate Christ divested himself of his divine attributes or prerogatives.

In developing the notion of kenosis the kenotic theologians engaged with contemporary idealist philosophy either as a resource for the construction of their Christologies or as the philosophical position which their Christologies were intended to refute. Idealist philosophy also provided some of the terminology upon which theologians would draw in the construction of kenotic Christology. Of particular importance was Schelling's concept of 'potency', a term which Schelling employs to denote the powers of being that bring about and structure reality. Some kenotic theologians employed this notion to conceive of the entry of the Logos into existence as the actualization of a potency within the Godhead (Thomasius 1845, 1856–63), while others made use of it to interpret the incarnate life of the Logos as the depotentiation of his divine nature (Liebner 1849; Frank 1885–6). Other kenotic theologians turned to Hegel for inspiration, as is evident in J. L. König's notion of kenosis as God's self-finitization (*Selbstverendlichung*) into his other (König 1844).

The negative influence of idealist philosophy on kenotic Christology consisted in the threat some theologians believed Hegel posed to the classical doctrine of the incarnation, which prompted them to develop their kenotic Christologies as an alternative to Hegel. This was the case with the most influential of the kenotic theologians, namely, Wolfgang Gess (1819–91), who constructed a kenotic Christology based solely on the biblical witness, and Gottfried Thomasius (1802–75), who reworked the Lutheran doctrine of the *communicatio idiomatum* to restate the two-natures doctrine in a way that met contemporary criticisms. The problem with the Lutheran treatment of the *communicatio idiomatum* was that it was not carried through fully enough, a weakness Thomasius corrects by supplementing the Lutheran doctrine with the concept of the *genus tapeinoticum*, which affirms that the divine nature undergoes self-limitation during the incarnation. Thomasius develops this notion of divine limitation by distinguishing between two types of attribute possessed by the Logos, namely the 'essential' or 'immanent' attributes of truth, holiness, love, and absolute power, and the 'relative' attributes of omnipotence, omnipresence, and omniscience. It is this latter type of attribute that the Incarnate Logos lays aside for the duration of the incarnation in order to live a genuinely limited life as a human being.

The notion of Christ renouncing divine attributes in order to become incarnate led to a backlash, notably from Isaak Dorner (1809–84), who rejected kenotic Christology for undermining the doctrine of immutability (Dorner 1994). Twentieth-century theologians have found it less difficult to part company with the strong notion of immutability advanced by Dorner. This is the consequence not only of the continuation of certain strands of nineteenth-century thought but above all of the effect of two world wars. The notion of God as co-sufferer, the paramount expression of which is the suffering and death of Jesus Christ, has become firmly entrenched in twentieth-century theology (e.g. Moltmann 1974).

V. THE DIALECTICAL CHRIST

The rationalist and humanist Christologies that dominated much of nineteenth- and early twentieth-century thought were challenged by thinkers who believed that such Christologies omitted something essential from the Christian faith. The reduction of Christ to a moral teacher or the embodiment of a philosophical idea failed to do justice both to the Bible and to the person of Christ. Thinkers who took this line saw contemporary European thought not as a resource for reconstituting Christology on a supposedly more adequate basis but as a threat to the believer's relation to Jesus Christ. The task was thus to draw up the battle lines between Christianity and contemporary thought in order to prevent the incarnation from being subsumed into moral, historicist, and philosophical categories. Kierkegaard and the dialectical theologians of the twentieth century advance a notion of what we might call the 'dialectical Christ'. Christ is dialectical because there exists an 'infinite qualitative difference' between God and humankind, and yet despite this God paradoxically enters human history in the person of his Son Jesus Christ.

Kierkegaard argues that the incarnation is a paradox that cannot be dissolved by thought, nor can it be subordinated to a theory of historical development. In Jesus Christ God has entered time and become a human being, something which in Kierkegaard's eyes is a contradiction, since time and eternity, humanity and divinity, are mutually exclusive opposites (Kierkegaard 1985, 1991, 1992). Despite their opposition, however, they have nevertheless been united in Jesus Christ, a fact which makes Christ the 'absolute paradox'. As Kierkegaard puts it, 'The thesis that God has existed in human form, was born, grew up, etc., is certainly the paradox *sensu strictissimo*, the absolute paradox' (Kierkegaard 1992: 217).

The incarnation is a paradox not only to the contemporaries who encountered Jesus in person but to all subsequent generations, since God's presence in time as a human being is a contradiction whether we live in the first or twenty-first century. The only way the individual can become 'contemporary with Christ' is by faith. But the individual cannot attain faith by means of his/her own powers but requires divine assistance. God gives this assistance by providing the human being with the condition of faith. In providing this condition, God is restricted neither by time nor by place. He can grant it to the contemporary and the non-contemporary alike. Consequently, one's position in history is irrelevant. Immediate contemporaneity and historical reports at best serve only as the *occasion* by which the human being may be prompted to think about Christ (Kierkegaard 1985: 100). But whatever the source of their confrontation with the Christ-event, whether through first-hand experience or through the reports of others, both are confronted with the Christ's question to Peter at Caesarea Philippi: 'Who do you say that I am?' (Matt. 16:15). If Christ provides the condition, then both the contemporary and the non-contemporary can reply, 'You are the Christ. I believe in you.'

Kierkegaard's emphasis on the paradoxical character of the incarnation was an important factor in the development of the 'dialectical theology' or 'theology of crisis' of the early twentieth century, the main representatives of which were Rudolf Bultmann (1884–1976), Karl Barth (1886–1968), Friedrich Gogarten (1887–1967), Eduard Thurneysen (1888–1974), Emil Brunner (1889–1966), and to a lesser extent Paul Tillich (1886–1965). A further influence on dialectical theology was the rediscovery by Weiss and Schweitzer of the eschatological character of Jesus' ministry, which took on new relevance in the crisis of western civilization brought about by the First World War and the pessimistic post-war *Zeitgeist* epitomized by Oswald Spengler's *Decline of the West*. Dialectical theology also drew on insights from Dostoevsky and Feuerbach. Dostoevsky's novels provided a profound analysis of human existence, in particular human beings' rebellion against their limitations and their lust to usurp the place of God (Thurneysen 2010), while Feuerbach had correctly identified the anthropocentric character of nineteenth-century theology. For the dialectical theologians anthropocentric theologies failed to take into account that human beings are in sin and that therefore moral consciousness, religious experience, and God-consciousness cannot provide the basis for talking about God. This critique of anthropocentric theology was accompanied by a critique of 'religion', understood as human beings' attempt to construct a relationship with God on their terms. Such attempts, however, lead to human beings constructing idols based on the projection of their own desires. A viable theology must put aside anthropocentricism and make not the human being but God its point of departure.

In the second edition of his *Epistle to the Romans* Barth argues that God is not revealed in nature, history, or in human consciousness or experience, not even in Jesus' human life. Divine revelation cannot be identified with anything in this world, nor can God be known directly. God's revelation is thus the 'most complete veiling of his incomprehensibility' (Barth 1968: 98). Brunner makes a similar point, describing God's revelation of himself in Christ as 'a form of the presence of God which it is possible to mistake for the exact opposite, as his complete absence' (Brunner 1952: 441). God is the Unknown God who is at the boundary of this world of sin and death. Despite this, the Unknown God is not unknowable, for in Christ God touches our world 'as a tangent touches a circle, that is, without touching it. And, precisely because it does not touch it, it touches it as its frontier, as the new world' (Barth 1968: 30). In Christ the wholly other intersects reality 'vertically, from above'. But this vertical intersection has no horizontal dimension. Christ does not extend into history as a stage in the historical process or in the religious consciousness of subsequent human beings. The incarnation is not a historical event alongside other historical events, but is of a completely different order from all other events in history. What we observe in the life of Jesus is not the historical manifestation of God, but rather 'bomb-craters' caused by the unknown reality of God (Barth 1968: 30). But we do not have the reality of God himself. God remains hidden even in the revelation of the new world in Christ's resurrection.

In his *Church Dogmatics* Barth endeavoured to develop a wholly Christocentric theology that excluded all non-theological justification of Christianity. Theology is possible only because God speaks, and does so in his Word in Jesus Christ. Consequently, it is God's Word in Jesus Christ that is the only legitimate starting point for theology. From God's uttering of his Word the Trinitarian relations can be derived, for in his Word God reveals himself in a threefold way, namely as revealer, revelation, and revealedness. Barth's most sustained treatment of Christology occurs in volume IV of *Church Dogmatics*, where he takes as his point of departure 'the way of the Son of God into the far country', a poetical expression for the descent of the Logos into human existence and his incarnation among human beings in humility and weakness (Barth 1956: 192). The Son not only goes into the far country, but also returns as 'the royal man' through his exaltation. Barth sums up these two movements with the statement that, 'It was God who went into the far country, and it was man who came home' (Barth 1958: 21). Christ is thus both the revelation of God in the world and the perfecting of the human being in a relation to God.

Dialectical theology disintegrated as a coherent movement in the early 1930s over the question of natural theology and role of philosophy in theology. While Barth stove to 'exclude ... to the very best of my ability anything that might appear to find for theology a foundation, support, or justification in philosophical existentialism' (Barth 1975: p. xiii), Bultmann turned Heidegger as a resource for doing theology. Gogarten also turned to existentialism and developed a post-metaphysical interpretation of Christianity in terms of secularization (Gogarten 1970). Brunner and Barth fell out over the role of a 'point of contact' between God and human beings (Brunner-Barth 1946), a division which was accentuated still further by Brunner's turn to the personalism or 'I-Thou' philosophy of Martin Buber (1878–1965) and Ferdinand Ebner (1882–1931). Dialectical theology was thus unable to sustain its rejection of non-theological modes of thought. As the respective theologians began to reflect on how to communicate the gospel to twentieth-century human beings they drew on the resources of contemporary thought, notably on existentialism.

VI. THE EXISTENTIALIST CHRIST

Existentialist philosophy provided resources for thinking through the incarnation in terms of Christ's meaning for the concrete, personal existence of modern human beings. The focus in such Christologies is on Christ's existential impact on the life of the believer. Christological dogma is understood not as an objective statement about Christ's nature but as a statement of *Christus pro me*, what Christ means to me. An early version of existentialist Christology can be found in Kierkegaard's thought, whose paradox Christology is accompanied by a emphasis on Christ's existential significance to the believer, who comes into a relationship with the paradox of the God-man not by intellectual means but only by a paradoxical leap of faith. In the twentieth century, impulses were taken up from Kierkegaard, but above all from Heidegger to develop an existential interpretation of Christ by Bultmann, Tillich, and others.

Bultmann's historical studies had convinced him of the impossibility of basing faith on the historical Jesus. Although a historical kernel underlies the gospels, it has been obscured by such mythological terms as incarnation and atonement. He exclaims, 'What a primitive mythology it is that a divine being should be incarnate, and atone for the sins of men through his own blood!' (Bartsch 1953: 7). Neither liberal Protestantism nor Chalcedonian Christology provide a solution to this problem, for both have made the same mistake of objectifying Christ. Bultmann writes: 'The formula "Christ is God" is false in every sense in which God can be understood as an entity which can objectivised, whether it is understood in an Arian or a Nicene, an orthodox or a liberal sense' (Bultmann 1955: 287). To avoid the impasse of liberal Protestantism and orthodox Christianity Bultmann turns to the 'kerygma', i.e. the core preaching or proclamation of the Church concerning Christ's significance. What is significant is only 'the That' (*das Dass*) of Jesus, that is, the fact that he has existed. The history of the individual, Jesus of Nazareth, is not significant. What is significant is the fact that he has been, and the faith elicited by the individual's encounter with the kerygma.

The kerygma, however, is clothed in mythological language and, furthermore, the twentieth-century view of the world is radically different from that of the first century. If the New Testament is to be intelligible and accessible to modern human beings, it must be 'demythologized' or translated into a language intelligible to modern human beings. To achieve this, Bultmann draws on Heidegger's existential analytic and interprets the kerygma in terms of an encounter with an existence-possibility, which demands a decision from the individual for or against authentic existence. When demythologized, the mythological language of the kerygma can be read as the representation of the new life that emerges when human beings renounce their attachment to worldly things and live their lives in the presence of transcendence.

For Tillich, 'theology has received tremendous gifts from existentialism, gifts not dreamed of fifty years ago or even thirty years ago' (Tillich 1959: 126). Tillich draws on existentialist philosophy in the development of his 'method of correlation', which consists in articulating the existential questions thrown up by the situation in which human beings find themselves and showing how the Christian message can address these questions (Tillich 1953: 8). For Tillich, human beings' experience of finitude implies the notion of the infinite and prompts the search for the 'ground of being' or 'being itself' which transcends finitude. This analysis of the human situation allows Tillich to reintroduce such theological concepts as God, which is the theological term for the ground of being which transcends finitude, and to conceive of Christ as the New Being that resolves human beings' existential crisis by enabling them to overcome estrangement.

For Tillich, the weakness of the Chalcedonian Definition stems from the inadequacy of the terms 'human nature' and 'divine nature', which are conceived as lying 'beside each other like blocks and whose unity cannot be understood at all' (Tillich 1957: 148). The term 'human nature' fails to do justice to the dynamic character of Christ's life, while 'divine nature' denotes that God is beyond essence and existence and is therefore inapplicable to Christ, who is situated *within* and not beyond existence. Consequently, Tillich calls for the replacement of the Chalcedonian language of two natures with the concepts of 'eternal God-man-unity' or 'Eternal God-Manhood'. These terms are to be preferred because they 'replace a static essence by a dynamic relation' (Tillich 1959: 148).

Heidegger's philosophy has also been drawn upon by Anglophone theologians as a resource for thinking through Christ's significance, notably by John Macquarrie (1919–2007). Macquarrie understands God as 'absolute letting-be', which he defines as 'the ontological foundation of love' (Macquarrie 1977: 302). This loving letting-be manifests itself in Christ, in whom 'selfhood passes into Christhood', the result of which is that 'the human Jesus becomes the Christ of faith, [and] there is convergence of the human and divine "natures" in the one person' (Macquarrie 1977: 302–3).

Existentialist motifs have been taken up by some Roman Catholic theologians, notably by Karl Rahner (1904–84), who combines transcendental Thomism with an existentialist understanding of the human person. For Rahner, the problem with the two-natures doctrine is that it treats Christ in isolation from human history and consequently fails to do justice to 'the contemporary mentality which sees the world from an evolutionary point of view' (Rahner 1978: 206). Furthermore, the Chalcedonian terminology of *nature* and *hypostatic union* no longer speaks to modern human beings. In order to recover the underlying intention of Chalcedon while reformulating it in a more adequate language, Rahner develops what he calls *transcendental Christology*. This entails interpreting Christ in relation to the existential structure of the human being and showing how that structure points beyond itself towards the transcendent.

VII. The Political Christ

An early example of the political interpretation of the incarnation is provided by Hermann Reimarus (1694–1768), for whom the incarnation is a fiction created by Jesus' disciples to secure their political and economic status after Jesus' death (Talbert 1971). The Jesus of liberal Protestantism was also implicitly political in that he was understood to embody the values of contemporary bourgeois society. In the 1920s and 1930s Nazi theologians constructed an 'Aryan Jesus' stripped of his Jewish identity, who embodied the values of National Socialism (Heschel 2008). Arguably the most influential political conception of Christ, however, has been that developed by theologians who have drawn on Marxism for their inspiration.

The political theologies developed by the German Protestant theologian Jürgen Moltmann and the Roman Catholic theologian Johann Baptist Metz (b. 1928) owe something to Marxism. Moltmann draws on Bloch's Marxist inspired *Principle of*

Hope, while Metz's engagement with the Frankfurt School, particularly Walter Benjamin, has influenced his critique of the conflation of Christianity with the values of bourgeois society. To recover the counter-cultural force of Christianity Metz interprets Jesus in terms of his concept of 'dangerous memory', speaking of 'the dangerous memory of Jesus Christ' and 'the dangerous memory of freedom (in Jesus Christ)' (Metz 1981, 2007).

Marxism has had its greatest influence on Christology, however, in South American liberation theology, where it has provided Gustavo Gutiérrez (b. 1928), Rubem Alves (b. 1933), Leonardo Boff (b. 1938), and Jon Sobrino (b. 1938) with the basis for analysing structures of oppression and recovering the relationship between faith and *praxis*, which they hold have been neglected by European theology.

In 1972, Boff published his *Jesus Christ Liberator: A Critical Christology of Our Time*. Boff accepts the Chalcedonian Definition, which was composed 'when orthodoxy formulated with full lucidity the fundamental truth that Jesus is wholly and simultaneously true man and true God' (Boff 1980: 183). He takes as his Christological starting point, however, the historical Jesus, for 'the historical Jesus puts us in direct contact with his liberative programme and the practices with which he implements it' (Boff 1980: 279). It is in the life of Jesus that we see God's solidarity with the poor, his exposure of the structures of oppression, and his opening up of a new, liberated history.

An influential liberation Christology was Sobrino's *Christology at the Crossroads*. In this work Sobrino identifies two developments in Enlightenment thought, the first of which was brought about by Kant, whose emphasis on human autonomy played an important role in freeing human reason from theological hegemony. The second development was brought about by Marx, who 'championed the liberation of the whole person from a religious outlook that supported, or at least permitted, economic and political alienation' (Sobrino 1978: 348). According to Sobrino, 'Christological reflection in Latin America seeks to respond to the second phase of the Enlightenment. It seeks to show how the truth of Christ is capable of transforming a sinful world into the kingdom of God' (Sobrino 1978: 349). To this end, Sobrino draws on Marxism to interpret Christ in terms of *political love*, which expresses itself in different ways towards different human beings: 'Out of love for the poor, he took his stand *with* them; out of love for the rich, he took his stand *against* them. In both cases, however, he was interested in something more than retributive justice. He wanted renewal and re-creation' (Sobrino 1978: 369–70).

The liberating character of Jesus' ministry prompts Sobrino to call for 'liberator' to be added to the descriptions of Jesus, since, 'There is no reason why Christological titles should be the exclusive prerogative of one particular culture, even that of the New Testament writers.' Consequently, 'Today Jesus could quite rightly be called the liberator', since 'it is through Jesus that we learn what liberation really is and how it is to be achieved' (Sobrino 1978: 379). In becoming a lowly human being God showed his solidarity with the oppressed and in so doing opened up the possibility of a new, liberated history.

VIII. The Eschatological Christ

The rediscovery in the late nineteenth and early twentieth centuries of the apocalyptic character of Jesus' ministry was seen by some theologians as presenting the opportunity for integrating the figure of Christ into contemporary developments in evolutionary biology and into a dynamic conception of history.

The Jesuit priest and scientist Pierre Teilhard de Chardin (1881–1955) attempted to overcome the gulf that had opened up between the natural sciences and Christianity in the modern era. In support of this aim he drew on Henri Bergson's *Creative Evolution* (1907), but reinterprets in Christian terms Bergson's pantheistic notion of a creative force underlying the evolutionary process. Teilhard understands evolution to be a process by which ever more complex entities emerge from less complex entities. In this evolutionary process there are critical thresholds at which qualitatively new and higher realities come into existence. In the history of evolution there have been two such critical thresholds, namely, the emergence of life itself and 'hominization', i.e. the evolution of human beings and with them the emergence of self-consciousness in the evolutionary process. Teilhard projects this evolutionary process into the future and speculates that the self-consciousness that has emerged with human beings will continue to develop towards ever higher forms, ultimately culminating in the 'omega point' at which all things are united in God. The role of Christ in this evolutionary process is that he expresses the omega point before it has been achieved. Christ is the proleptic incarnation of the omega point and as such is the guarantor of its reality. Teilhard thus extends Christ's significance to the entire universe, which is destined to be drawn ever more fully into and become the body of Christ (Teilhard 1965: 13). Such considerations lead Teilhard to attribute to Christ a third, 'cosmic', nature alongside his human and divine natures.

Pannenberg criticizes existentialist interpretations of Christianity and rejects the demythologization of eschatology, for 'when one is dealing with the truth of the apocalyptic expectation of a future judgment or a resurrection of the dead, one is dealing with the basis of Christian faith' (Pannenberg 1968: 83). Pannenberg's notion of eschatology is grounded in the notion of 'universal history', the underlying principle of which is God (Pannenberg 1968, 1969). Pannenberg argues that God discloses himself indirectly through his acts in history. The revelatory character of these acts resides not in themselves, however, but is derived from the goal towards which history is tending. It is from the *end of history* that historical acts receive their revelatory force. This eschatological fulfilment of history has been proleptically realized in Christ, above all in his resurrection.

Christ's status, however, cannot be assumed a priori but must be established on the basis of the history of the man Jesus by showing 'how Jesus' appearance in history led to the recognition of his divinity' (Pannenberg 1968: 17). For Pannenberg, the ground of Jesus' unity with God is the resurrection, the significance of which was then projected back onto Jesus' earthly life. From this unity the doctrine of the incarnation can be derived, since 'Jesus' unity with God in the revelatory event of his resurrection from the dead can be understood only as his unity with God's eternal essence, so that the eternal divinity of God cannot be appropriately conceived except in relation to Jesus of Nazareth' (Pannenberg 1968: 158). The resurrection is also the basis for the affirmation of Christ's true humanity, for 'In Jesus himself the ultimate destiny of man for God, man's destiny to be raised from the dead to new life, had been fulfilled' (Pannenberg 1968: 210). In order to remain true to his Christology from below, Pannenberg attempts to establish the historical probability of the resurrection (Pannenberg 1968: 83–104).

In *Theology of Hope* Moltmann takes up Bloch's concept of 'the not-yet', according to which the entire universe is in a process of becoming, and applies it to the biblical notion of promise. For Moltmann, eschatology is 'not one element of Christian theology, but it is the medium of Christian faith as such, the key in which everything in it is set' (Moltmann 1993: 16). Indeed, for Moltmann, 'From first to last, and not merely in the epilogue, Christianity is eschatology, is hope, forward looking and forward moving, and therefore also revolutionizing and transforming the present' (Moltmann 1993: 16). The basis of this hope is a definite reality, namely the crucifixion and resurrection of Jesus Christ, which gives Christian hope a grounding in history which distinguishes it from mere utopianism.

In *The Crucified God* Moltmann moves from 'the remembrance of Christ in the form of the hope of his future' to 'hope in the form of the remembrance of his death' (Moltmann 1974: p. xxi). This shift in emphasis takes the form of reflecting on God's solidarity in the crucified Christ with 'the godless and the godforsaken'. The problem with the two-natures doctrine is that it 'must understand the event of the cross statically as a reciprocal relationship between two qualitatively different natures, the divine nature which is incapable of suffering and the human nature which is capable of suffering' (Moltmann 1974: 253). Such a Christology, however, 'will "evacuate" the cross of deity' (Moltmann 1974: 253). In place of this static Christology Moltmann interprets the cross as a Trinitarian event between the Son and the Father in which the Son undergoes the experience of being abandoned by the Father, while the Father undergoes the experience of grief at the death of his Son (Moltmann 1974: 251). Yet in this experience the Father and Son 'at the same time are most inwardly one in their surrender' (Moltmann 1974: 252). From this dialectical relationship of separation and inward surrender between Father and Son, there proceeds the spirit, 'which justifies the godless, fills the forsaken with love and even brings the dead alive' (Moltmann 1974: 252). In this way the cross is taken up into the Trinitarian God and 'integrated into the future of the "history of God"' (Moltmann 1974: 255). This history of God 'contains within itself all the depths and abysses of human history' and because there is therefore 'no suffering which in this history of God is not God's suffering', there is also 'no life, no future, and no joy which have not been integrated by his history into eternal life, the eternal joy of God' (Moltmann 1974: 255).

IX. THE POST-METAPHYSICAL CHRIST

The Nietzschean-Heideggerian critique of metaphysics and the awareness of the historically conditioned character of theological assertions led in the twentieth century to a movement away from metaphysical conceptions of Christ. If the incarnation is understood as dependent on a particular type of metaphysics, such as the substance ontology of the early Church, then it would seem destined to die with the death of metaphysics. There have been some thinkers, however, who have attempted to rescue the incarnation from its metaphysical heritage.

Conscious of living in a world 'come of age', Bonhoeffer holds that the Christian faith needs to be rethought in light of the world's maturity. This leads Bonhoeffer to introduce the idea of the 'religionless', 'non-religious', or secular interpretation of biblical concepts. 'Religion' is characterized by 'inwardness', i.e. the concern with individual religious needs, and 'metaphysics', i.e. that which is unworldly, transcendent, and beyond our world. The biblical message, however, is intended for *this* world (Bonhoeffer 1981: 92). 'Religion' is thus for Bonhoeffer an abdication of responsibility. It is inward looking and retreats from the world rather than engaging in it. In place of such 'religion', the human being must live and make decisions *etsi deus non daretur*, even if there were no God. It is God himself who compels us to do this, for 'The God who is with us is the God who forsakes us', something which is expressed above all by God's allowing himself to be pushed out of the world on to the cross. It is precisely through this weakness and suffering, not by means of his omnipotence, that Christ is with us and helps us (Bonhoeffer 1981: 129–30). In place of religion we should put the life of Jesus, which is a life *for others*. Bonhoeffer writes: 'Our relation to God is not a "religious" relationship to a highest, most powerful, and best Being imaginable—that is not authentic transcendence—but our relation to God is a new life in "being there for others", in participation in the being of Jesus' (Bonhoeffer 1981: 139). It is Christ's 'being there for others' even unto death that is the experience of transcendence. Faith is the participation in this being of Jesus in which human beings follow Christ in being there for others.

Important impulses for rethinking the incarnation in post-metaphysical terms have come from Heidegger's later thought and from thinkers such as Levinas, Derrida, and others. Heidegger looks to poetry, particularly that of Hölderlin, as a resource for posing the question of being in a non-ontotheological way. Drawing on Hölderlin's poem 'Friedensfeier' Heidegger speaks of the passing by of the last God whose touching of the dwellings of human beings only for a 'moment' constitutes an 'event' in which the divine flashes forth and whose effects reverberate through time (Heidegger 1989). Levinas's notion of our encountering a trace of the infinite in the face of the other and Derrida's notion of *Khora* (Derrida 1995) to denote an abysmal space in which the wholly other is encountered open up new possibilities for conceiving of the incarnation in a post-metaphysical context.

What links postmodernist thinkers' discourse about God is their insistence on taking leave of the metaphysical God so that we can encounter God anew in the void left by the death of the metaphysical God. The loss of the metaphysical God creates a space that elicits desire for the absent other God, whom we as hosts can welcome as our guest. The demise of the metaphysical God is a necessary prerequisite to a new encounter with God. God cannot come until we have bidden farewell to the omnipotent, omnipresent, omniscient God of metaphysics.

These notions of the post-metaphysical God have led to creative reworkings of the doctrine of the incarnation. Jean-Luc Marion (b. 1946) conceives of God as the *gift* who gives Being to beings and bestows himself in Christ. As the icon of the invisible God, Christ is the 'saturated phenomenon' par excellence, in whom God's self-giving love overflows our capacity to grasp it and the world's capacity to accept it (Marion 1995; 2002). René Girard (b. 1923) integrates Christ into his mimetic theory of desire and interprets the incarnation as the dissolution of the sacred as violence. As the Son of God, Jesus is 'the only one capable of revealing the true nature of violence to the utmost' (Girard 1987: 209). Through his innocent death Christ unmasks and undermines the violence of the sacrificial system by revealing that it is the perpetrators and not the victim who are guilty. Gianni Vattimo (b. 1936) 'rediscovers' Christianity through combining the notion of kenosis with his interpretation of Heidegger's thought as 'weak ontology' (Vattimo 1999). The secularization of the modern world is the continuation of the kenosis that began with the incarnation and which culminates in the dissolution of the sacred as the natural-violent and the arrival of an ethics of charity (Vattimo 1997: 51). John Milbank (b. 1952) provides a Christology based on Christ conceived as a linguistic and poetic reality which transfigures the human discourses which mediate it (Milbank 1997), while Graham Ward (b. 1955) develops a Christology in terms of embodiment, desire, and mimesis (Ward 1999, 2005).

X. CONCLUSION

The impact of modern European thought on the incarnation has been profound. It has both challenged the doctrine and provided resources for reconstituting it in the face of this challenge. The critique of metaphysics since the Enlightenment has exposed the inadequacy of the substance ontology upon which the classical doctrine was based. The search to fill the vacuum left by the slow withdrawal of the God of metaphysics has led to a creative engagement with new modes of thinking and has driven forward the quest for more adequate ways of understanding Jesus of Nazareth. The result has been the upsurge of new visions of Christ—ethical, experiential, idealist, kenotic, dialectical, existentialist, political, eschatological, and post-metaphysical—each of which captures an aspect of Christ's significance for us today, but none of which seems able to do justice to the character and significance of this enigmatic man.

References

Barth, Karl (1956). *Church Dogmatics*, vol. 4, Pt. 1. (Edinburgh: T. & T. Clark).

——(1958). *Church Dogmatics*, vol. 4, Pt. 2. (Edinburgh: T. & T. Clark).

——(1968). *The Epistle to the Romans*. (London, Oxford, and New York: Oxford University Press.

——(1975). *Church Dogmatics*, vol. 1, Pt. 1. (Edinburgh: T. & T. Clark).

Bartsch, Hans Werner (1953). *Kerygma and Myth*, vol. 1. (London: SPCK).

Boff, Leonardo (1980). *Jesus Christ Liberator: A Critical Christology for Our Time*. (London: SPCK).

Bonhoeffer, Dietrich (1981). *Letters and Papers from Prison*, abridged edn. (London: SCM).

Brunner, Emil (1952). *The Mediator: A Study of the Central Doctrine of the Christian Faith*. (London: Lutterworth).

Brunner, Emil, and Barth Karl (1946). *Natural Theology: Comprising 'Nature and Grace' by Emil Brunner and the Reply 'No' by Karl Barth*. (London: Geoffrey Bles).

Bultmann, Rudolf (1955). *Essays: Philosophical and Theological*. (London: SCM).

Chadwick, Henry (1956). *Lessing's Theological Writings*. (Stanford, CA: Stanford University Press).

Derrida, Jacque (1974). *Of Grammatology*. (Baltimore, MD: Johns Hopkins University Press).

——(1978). *Writing and Difference*. (Chicago: University of Chicago).

——(1995). *On the Name*. (Stanford, CA: Stanford University Press).

Dorner, Isaak August (1994). *Divine Immutability: A Critical Reconsideration*. (Minneapolis: Fortress Press).

Feuerbach, Ludwig (1854). *The Essence of Christianity*. (London: John Chapman).

Frank, F. H. R. (1885–6). *System der christlichen Wahrheit*, 2 vols, 2nd edn. (Erlangen: Andreas Deichert).

Girard, René (1987). *Things Hidden Since the Foundation of the World*. (Stanford, CA: Stanford University Press).

Gogarten, Friedrich (1970). *Christ the Crisis*. (London: SCM).

Hannay, Alistair (1982). *Kierkegaard*. (London, Boston, Melbourne, and Henley: Routledge & Kegan Paul).

Harnack, Adolf (1893). *Outlines of the History of Dogma*. (London: Hodder and Stoughton).

——(1901). *What is Christianity?* (London: Williams and Norgate).

Heidegger, Martin (1989). *Gesamtausgabe, vol. 65: Beiträge zur Philosophie. (Vom Ereignis)*. (Frankfurt am Main: Vittorio Klostermann).

Herrmann, Willibald (1895). *The Communion of the Christian with God: A Discussion in Agreement with the View of Luther*. (London: Williams and Norgate).

Heschel, Susannah (2008). *The Aryan Jesus. Christian Theologians and the Bible in Nazi Germany*. (Princeton, NJ: Princeton University Press).

Kant, Immanuel (1934). *Religion within the Limits of Reason Alone*. (London: Open Court).

——(1990). *Critique of Pure Reason*. (Basingstoke: Macmillan).

——(1997). *Critique of Practical Reason*. (Cambridge: Cambridge University Press).

Kierkegaard, Søren (1985). *Philosophical Fragments/Johannes Climacus*. (Princeton, NJ: Princeton University Press).

——(1991). *Practice in Christianity*. (Princeton, NJ: Princeton University Press).

——(1992). *Concluding Unscientific Postscript to Philosophical Fragments*, vol. 1. (Princeton, NJ: Princeton University Press).

König, Johann Ludwig (1844). *Die Menschwerdung Gottes als eine in Christus geschehene und in der christlichen Kirche noch geschehende.* (Mainz: Zabern).

Küng, Hans (1980). *Does God Exist?* (London: Collins).

——(1987). *The Incarnation of God: An Introduction to Hegel's Theological Thought as Prolegomena to a Future Christology.* (Edinburgh: T. & T. Clark).

Levinas, Emmanuel (1969). *Totality and Infinity: An Essay on Exteriority.* (Pittsburgh: Duquesne University Press).

Liebner, Karl Theodor Albert (1849). *Die christologische Dogmatik aus dem chistologischen Princip dargestellt.* (Göttingen: Vandenhoeck and Ruprecht).

Lyotard, Jean-François (1989). *The Postmodern Condition: A Report on Knowledge.* (Manchester: Manchester University Press).

——(1999). *Postmodern Fables.* (Minneapolis: University of Minnesota Press).

Macquarrie, John (1977). *Principles of Christian Theology.* (London: SCM).

Marion, Jean-Luc (1995). *God without Being: Hors-Texte.* (Chicago: University of Chicago Press).

——(2002). *In Excess: Studies of Saturated Phenomena.* (New York: Fordham University Press).

Metz, Johann Baptist (1981). *The Emergent Church: the Future of Christianity in a Postbourgeois World.* (New York: Crossroad).

——(2007). *Faith in History and Society: Toward a Practical Fundamental Theology.* (New York: Crossroad).

Milbank, John (1997). *The Word Made Strange: Theology, Language, Culture.* (Oxford: Blackwell).

Moltmann, Jürgen (1974). *The Crucified God.* (London: SCM).

——(1993). *Theology of Hope.* (Minneapolis: Fortress).

Pannenberg, Wolfhart (1968). *Jesus—God and Man.* (London: SCM).

——(1969). 'Dogmatic Theses on the Doctrine of Revelation', in Wolfhart Pannenberg (ed.), *Revelation as History.* (London: Sheed and Ward).

Rahner, Karl (1978). *Foundations of Christian Faith: An Introduction to the Idea of Christianity.* (London: Darton, Longman, and Todd).

Ritschl, Albrecht (1966). *The Christian Doctrine of Justification and Reconciliation: The Positive Development of the Doctrine.* (Clifton, NJ: Reference Book Publishers).

Schleiermacher, Friedrich (1988). *On Religion: Speeches to its Cultured Despisers.* (Cambridge: Cambridge University Press).

——(1989). *The Christian Faith.* (Edinburgh: T. & T. Clark).

Schweitzer, Albert (1914). *The Mystery of the Kingdom of God: the Secret of Jesus' Messiahship and Passion.* (New York: Dodd, Mead and Company).

——(2000). *The Quest of the Historical Jesus*, 1st complete edn. (London: SCM).

Sobrino, Jon (1978). *Christology at the Crossroads: A Latin American Approach.* (London: SCM).

Strauss, David Friedrich (1846). *The Life of Jesus, Critically Examined.* (London: Chapman Brothers).

Talbert, Charles H. (1971). *Reimarus, Fragments.* (London: SCM).

Teilhard de Chardin, Pierre (1965). *Hymn of the Universe.* (London: Collins).

Thomasius, Gottfried (1845). 'Ein Beitrag zur kirchlichen Christologie', *Zeitschrift für Protestantismus und Kirche*, new series, vol. 9: 1–30, 65–110, 218–58.

——(1856–63). *Christi Person und Werk. Darstellung der evangelisch-lutherischen Dogmatik vom Mittelpunkte der Christologie aus*, 3 vols, 2nd edn. (Erlangen: Theodor Bläsing).

Thurneysen, Eduard (2010). *Dostoevsky*. (Eugene, OR: Wipf & Stock).

Tillich, Paul (1953). *Systematic Theology*, vol. 1. (London: SCM).

——(1957). *Systematic Theology*, vol. 2. (London: SCM).

——(1959). *Theology of Culture*. (London, Oxford, and New York: Oxford University Press).

Tyrell, George (1913). *Christianity at the Crossroads*. (London: Longmans, Green and Co).

Vattimo, Gianni (1997). *Beyond Interpretation: The Meaning of Hermeneutics for Philosophy*. (Cambridge: Polity Press).

——(1999). *Belief*. (Cambridge: Polity Press).

Ward, Graham (1999). 'Bodies: The Displaced Body of Jesus Christ', in John Milbank, Catherine Pickstock, and Graham Ward (eds), *Radical Orthodoxy: A New Theology*. (London: Routledge).

——(2005). *Christ and Culture*. (Oxford: Blackwell).

Weiss, Johannes (1971). *Jesus' Proclamation of the Kingdom of God*, ed. and introd. Riachard Hyde Hiers and David Larrimore Holland (Philadelphia: Fortress Press).

SUGGESTED READING

Baillie, D. M. (1961). *God was in Christ*. (London: Faber and Faber).

McCarthy, Vincent (1986). *Quest for a Philosophical Jesus*. (Macon, GA: Mercer University Press).

McGrath, Alister (1986). *The Making of Modern German Christology*. (Oxford: Blackwell).

Macquarrie, John (1990). *Jesus Christ in Modern Thought*. (London: SCM).

Moltmann (1974).

O'Collins, Gerald (2009). *Christology: A Biblical, Historical, and Systematic Study*, 2nd rev. edn. (Oxford: Oxford University Press).

Pannenberg (1968).

Schweitzer (2000).

Spence, Alan (2008). *Christology. A Guide for the Perplexed*. (London: Continuum).

CHAPTER 29

SACRAMENTALITY

DAVID BROWN

READERS unfamiliar with the history of Christian theology might well expect this chapter to focus exclusively upon either the seven acknowledged sacraments of the Roman Catholic tradition, or else more narrowly on the two (Baptism and Eucharist) accepted by Protestant and Catholic alike. But that would be to ignore the wider context within which the term first arose and to which much post-Vatican II thinking has returned. In effect during the first millennium the term could be applied to almost any material reality that symbolically mediated the divine presence. It was only really the desire for philosophical precision and the rigorous requirements of canon law that led in the high Middle Ages to a much narrower usage, and even then wider applications are still occasionally found among theologians, as later with Luther (Brown 2004: 25–33).

In describing the recovery of the earlier usage the usual account attributes the change either exclusively (or almost so) to the work of a number of French theologians known collectively as the Nouvelle Théologie (discussed later). While not denying the importance of their contribution, I do think it important to acknowledge other earlier modern attempts to use the notion to ground a sense of divine presence in the world. As we shall see, sometimes the terminology is explicit and sometimes not and sometimes it is even borrowed for non-theistic purposes, but throughout what links all such usages is the view that material reality can point beyond itself to some kind of transcendent reality.

I. PLATONISM AND THE ROMANTIC MOVEMENT

How far Enlightenment thought of the seventeenth and eighteenth centuries should be explained in terms of its own historical context, and how far antecedent factors need to be taken into account, such as the Reformation and the revival of Aristotelian ideas in the Middle Ages, is too complex an issue to enter into here. Suffice it to say that, in so far as belief in God continued to be maintained, this was given such a strong transcendent emphasis that for many the deity seemed altogether too distant and no longer directly concerned with ordinary human life. That its successor, the Romantic Movement at the end of the eighteenth and beginning of the nineteenth century, should find its response in Platonism usually occasions surprise among those (including many contemporary theologians) who think of Platonism as essentially transcendent in its orientation but this is to ignore the richness of its metaphors. Because the highest form of reality is to be found elsewhere (in the world of Forms), it is easy to present Platonism as world-denying but that is to forget Plato's two primary metaphors for the relation: imitation and participation. As in Christianity's wider understanding of the sacramental and symbolic, material reality is thus also seen as constituting a bridge to another and higher reality. Indeed, precisely because of its ability to share to some degree in that other world, this world is seen as already valuable because of the transcendent light that is being cast upon it. In that context it becomes unsurprising to discover in the *Symposium* Plato's very positive evaluation of physical beauty as a bridge to higher forms of beauty or his frequent finely evocative descriptions of nature (as in *Phaedrus* 230B–C).

Of course, it would be possible to object that such an account fails to allow the world any autonomy or value in its own right. On purely Platonic principles that might well be so, but for Christian thinkers of the time any such disadvantage was outweighed by the ability of the imagery to overcome the wholly transcendent God of the Enlightenment on the one hand and on the other a wholly immanent account that would inevitably collapse into pantheism with the world and the divine simply identified as one. Indeed, Hegel (1770–1831), who knew the Platonic tradition extremely well, in his *Lectures on the Philosophy of Religion* suggests that Christianity constitutes the historical resolution of precisely these two extremes, the transcendence found in Judaism and the immanence of Greek religion. On the one hand, through the doctrine of *creatio ex nihilo* the world is given an independent and separate existence from God and divine transcendence thus preserved: on the other hand, features of the divine are still built into that creation, in humanity as the image of God, in the work of Holy Spirit helping to bring the cosmos to fulfilment, and pre-eminently in the doctrine of the incarnation, with God coming in the flesh.

Whereas in the 1821 and 1824 versions the two religions are treated as mutually complementary, by 1827 Hegel was prepared to treat Judaism as a definite advance on the Greek view. He even reverses the order in which the two religious approaches are discussed (Hegel 1988: 50–7). Even so, as a contrast it is undoubtedly overplayed. After all in Judaism there is the mystic immanence of much Kabbalistic writing, in part derived from Platonism and in turn itself influential on Christian writers such as Jacob Boehme (d. 1624). Equally, Greek imagery for the gods was at times not at all naturalistic. So, for example, early Greek images for the gods that were much less human than those created in the classical period continued to be prized, as with the *xoanon* carried in procession at the Panathenaea festival in Athens. Yet, that conceded, the presence of both aspects within Christianity allows us to see why its immanent aspect might find the divine not just active within the world but also mediated through the material itself. It is that notion of a more general material mediation which earlier notions of the sacramental tried to encapsulate, and which one finds reflected in a number of Romantic writers, not least in Coleridge and Hölderlin where the Platonic dimension is at its most explicit, even though their characteristic Romantic references to feeling and experience might scarcely suggest any natural Platonic affinities. What they shared with Plato was in effect a similar sacramental understanding of the world, with its symbols suggesting mystical participation in a larger reality.

In the case of Samuel Taylor Coleridge (1772–1834) his Platonism comes mediated through the understanding of symbol in the German philosopher Schelling as the stepping stone to the spiritual, but he gives the notion his own distinctive gloss by insisting on symbol as mediating between the literal and the metaphorical. Things in the world are thus rather more than just pointers or distant analogies for the divine; they participate in its very life:

> O! the one Life within us and abroad,
> Which meets all motion and becomes its soul.
>
> (*The Eolian Harp*, 26–7)

The lines were added in 1817 to an earlier version of 1796 and may possibly indicate some influence from Boehme (Jasper 1985: 35–40). Perhaps more clearly, such ideas also emerge in *The Statesman's Manual* of 1816 where he defines a symbol as 'not a metaphor or allegory or any other figure of speech or form of fancy, but an actual and essential part of that, the whole of which it represents', and so symbols are 'consubstantial with the truths of which they are the conductors' (Coleridge 1856: I, App. B, 436–7, 465). The result is that like the chariot wheels in Ezekiel's vision (ch.1) they can aid our ascent to God. Indeed, for Coleridge there is no essential difference between the Eucharist and other symbols that draw us into that more inclusive understanding of the world. As he observed in his *Marginalia*, 'as the Sacrament is the Epiphany for as many as receive it in faith, so the crucifixion, resurrection and ascension of Christ himself in the flesh were the Epiphanies, the sacramental acts and Phaenomena, . . . the visible Words of the invisible Word that was in the beginning' (Coleridge 1992: vol. XII, Pt. 2, 279).

For some such ideas may seem suspiciously close to pantheism, and it is indeed true that Coleridge spent much of his life trying to distinguish his own account from any such position (McFarland 1969). But there is in fact a clear distinction to be observed, which can be seen by considering why the most famous theologian of the period might more easily fit within such a framework, even though he too can be defended from any such charge. The reason why Schleiermacher (d. 1834) looks so much better a candidate is because in establishing his own account Schleiermacher shows no interest whatsoever in the details of the world. Its contingency, wherever experienced, helps to evoke a sense of our absolute dependence on the divine, but beyond that there are no symbolic correspondences that a sacramental attitude would require. In other words, whereas for Schleiermacher the world evokes a general sense of divine indwelling or support, for

Coleridge there is a whole communicative or revelatory structure in play correspond-ing, as in Augustine's earlier adaptation of Platonism, to a range of 'ideas' in the divine mind.

Such correspondences one certainly finds in Coleridge's friend and fellow poet, William Wordsworth (1770–1850). They are seen most clearly perhaps in his long poem, *The Prelude*. Ironically, William Blake (d. 1827) described Wordsworth in his notes on Wordsworth's poetry as 'a heathen philosopher', precisely because of his failure to proceed immediately beyond the veil, whereas for Wordsworth encounter with nature was already to experience God: 'Nature's self, which is the breath of God' (V.221). Each of its various forms could be seen as

> A type, for finite natures, of the one
> Supreme existence, the surpassing life.   (VI.133–4)

So the bringing of good out of evil is a recurrent theme (e.g. VI, 635–9; XII, 1–43), as is the sense of peace and timelessness (e.g. VI, 129–41; VII, 654–62), or the way in which

> The naked summit of a far-off hill
> . . . .
> Was like an invitation into space
> Boundless, or guide into eternity.   (XIII, 148–51)

Not that such experience is constant. Instead, Wordsworth speaks of 'spots of time' (XII, 208–15), decisive experiential moments that help shape our lives as a whole, though even then he also stresses the distancing that adulthood brings, expressed most famously in his poem *Intimations of Immortality*, especially stanza V. Although Wordsworth, unlike Coleridge, never explicitly applies sacramental terminology to such ideas, that this is what he intends is clear, and not just to theologians: for example in Theodore Roszak (1972: ch. 9) where the expression 'sacramentality of nature' is applied to Wordsworth several times. Perhaps it was the difficulty of integrating a key role for Christ within such a framework that held him back from more explicitly sacramental language (J. R. Barth 2003: e.g. 28).

Meanwhile in Germany Friedrich Hölderlin (1770–1843) offered a more pessimistic perspective, in finding intimations strongest not in the present but in humanity's past history and its longed for future. Born the same year as Wordsworth, he was a student at Tübingen where Hegel and Schelling were his contemporaries and friends, and it is there that his love of all things Greek became firmly established. Not only did he produce translations of Pindar and Sophocles, he knew Plato well, being especially fond of the *Phaedrus* and the *Symposium*. The result is that he uses the rivers and mountains of Greece to suggest a world infused with divine presence, though on occasion he also uses landscape nearer to hand, as when he describes Alpine peaks as God's throne (Constantine 1988: 157). While all this so far might suggest merely nostalgia for a vanished world, that rather more is at stake is indicated by his attitude to what he sees as the function of his poetry. Religion of its very essence he claims is poetic (*ihrem Wesen nach poëtisch*), since it is through this means that divinity comes to self-expression (Constantine 1988: 125). So for Hölderlin poetry is a way of momentarily allowing us to see the divine that is inherent in our world but which is usually hidden from view.

Of course, it would be possible to interpret such language as no more than the use of religious imagery for other purposes, aesthetic, moral, or political. But Hölderlin went to Tübingen to train for the Lutheran ministry, and he seems in fact never quite to have abandoned his Christian faith. Indeed, the last poems he wrote before the advent of his long insanity (from 1807) try hard to reconcile Christianity and his Greek ideals. In the first version of his unfinished tragedy, *Der Tod des Empedocles*, for example, Empedocles is made to resemble Christ in making atonement and so allowing the gods once more to draw close. Again, in *Brod und Wein* Christ and Dionysus virtually merge, but in a way that could be seen as enriching for Christianity, inasmuch as it is more a case of the significance of Christ being enlarged as his influence is found to extend into all material reality: itself an obvious sacramental expression of more traditional ideas. Hölderlin's imagery would be taken up in the following century by Paul Celan (d. 1970) in his poem *Die Winzer*, but in a way that is at once both sacramental and its subversion (Brown and Loades 1996: 18–19).

II. RUSKIN AND THE SYMBOLIST MOVEMENT

Developments in the later nineteenth century were to raise a number of new issues. One was the question of whether human creativity could also be seen as sacramental. While in Britain John Ruskin insisted that all great art and architecture somehow imitated the greater divine handwork in nature, Symbolists in France allowed a more innovative role to human artists, and one can see why. There was influence from the high Romantic doctrine of human creativity (that its originality approximated to what divinity itself achieved), and, more generally acceptable, the fact that artists could well succeed in more effectively highlighting features in nature that merely hinted at divine presence. A painter, for instance, might help us better appreciate a particular landscape (its order, fecundity, or sublimity, for example) or a poet or dramatist the transformative potential of some particular action. A second related issue was whether for such creativity to fulfil its sacramental role it necessarily needed an explicit religious motivation on the part of the artist. In this case even Ruskin thought not.

Admittedly, John Ruskin (1819–1900) as art critic might not seem at first sight a likely source for any such sacramental reflections given his own theological background. Brought up in a strictly Calvinist home, many of his key writings were first produced while he still espoused a similar religious position. Even after his fundamentalist leanings were shaken by Darwin and he had had some more positive experiences of Catholicism, he remained firmly a Protestant rather than Catholic agnostic, holding to what he now saw as an undogmatic kind of biblical Christianity (Hilton 2000: II, 549). Yet in *Modern Painters* the various volumes of which first appeared between 1843 and

1860, he advocates what is in effect a high sacramental account of how divinity can be mediated to us through our experience of the natural world. Probably borrowing from Wordsworth the terminology of types, he distinguished different 'types' of beauty, each of which has the capacity to mediate a particular divine attribute: infinity or incomprehensibility, unity or integration, repose or permanence, symmetry or justice, purity or energy, and moderation or restraint (Ruskin 1906: vol. II, Pt. III, chs v–x). Certainly, Calvin had spoken of God's disclosure through the natural world, and in this he was followed at much greater length by his American disciple, Jonathan Edwards. But Calvin insisted on the prior need for faith if such perceptions were to be had, while in any case what is experienced is analysed as divine effects rather than divinity itself (Calvin 1960: I, 16, esp. 2). So it is important to note that for Ruskin such aesthetic experiences did not merely have the potential to point elsewhere, but that God was somehow to be found in the very experience of the material world as such. That is what makes his position so firmly sacramental, and why the discoveries of Darwin came as such a shock.

As is made clear elsewhere in his defence of Gothic architecture, for Ruskin the structure of every leaf spoke of God, and so it was precisely because Gothic was seen to match better those natural structures that it should on his view hold pre-eminent place. So, for instance, in *Stones of Venice* he declares that 'to the Gothic workman the living foliage became a subject of intense affection'. He also argues that the Gothic pointed arch, so far from being unnatural, is more natural than either the Classical plinth or the Romanesque round arch, partly because of its relation to the roof pitch and partly because of the way in which it lends itself to foliated decoration (Ruskin 2001: 152, 160–70). So it is perhaps not altogether surprising to discover that comparisons are drawn between architecture and scripture or the Book of Common Prayer, or that in a striking parallel to Communion Ruskin talks of wanting to 'eat up' St Mark's Basilica in Venice with all his mind. Nor should it be thought that the weakening of his early rigid Evangelical position resulted in any hostility to former insights. Not only did he continue to allow the earlier works to be reprinted (admittedly, with some modifications), he also in some ways became more convinced of the value of religion, for example no longer underestimating the potential contribution of devout painters, as in *Mornings in Florence* (Ruskin 1912: XXIII, xlv). Equally, however, on the other hand even in his most Christian period he was insistent that the full sacramental potential of landscape should not necessarily be accorded to the most devout. Thus on his view the value of the work of John Constable (d. 1837) and Samuel Palmer (d. 1881) was to be firmly subordinated to that of the agnostic J. M. W. Turner (d. 1851).

Although Ruskin's influence on European thought was considerable, he was too much of an individualist to create a school, and so he stands in marked contrast to the other phenomenon of the later nineteenth century that I wish to mention here, Symbolism. Originating in France, the movement influenced both art and literature with related developments also in Germany and England. Essentially, it was a revolt against materialism and realism in favour of the 'spiritual', somewhat loosely understood since it was seen to include dreams and magic as well as religion. This meant that there was no necessary connection between its exponents and sacramentalism, but its contention that the aim of art was to bring to expression spiritual ideas did at least offer fruitful ground for the development of possible connections. 'Symbol' so understood was at the very least seen as a medium for linking two quite different realms, and so potentially at least might be viewed as allowing the possibility of material reality participating in a higher, heavenly order.

Admittedly, from a contemporary perspective it is quite hard to enter into such a thought-world as it applied itself to art. So far from revolting against the Realist Manifesto of Gustave Courbet (d. 1877) or the concerns of the Impressionists with immediate experience, modern viewers now flock in their tens of thousands to see each new exhibition, particularly of the latter. Yet such artists were precisely the intended targets of Jean Moréas in his *Symbolist Manifesto* of 1886 where it is stated that the essential aim of art is 'to clothe the idea in sensuous form'. While the way in which Odilon Redon's dream paintings anticipate Surrealism has helped to keep his name in view, the contributions of more religious figures have long since been effectively marginalized. Gustave Moreau (1826–1908) is one case in point, though his pupil Georges Rouault (1871–1958) continues to be highly esteemed, not least for the value he was able to communicate to those on the fringes of society such as clowns and prostitutes.

Maurice Denis (1870–1934) is also now less well known, despite the fact that he was the leader of the Nabis (the 'prophets'), a group that included Bonnard and Vuillard. While landscape was one element in his approach to sacramentality, as with Rouault it is perhaps his figures that impress most, with some comparing his treatment of the human form to that of Fra Angelico but there are also some very effective combinations of people and landscape as with his *Sacred Wood* of 1900 (now in the Musée de Petit-Palais in Paris). Although he was one of the main theorists of Symbolism with two major collections of essays on principles (*Théories* of 1912 and *Nouvelles Théories* of 1922) and also wrote an impressive history of religious art which appeared in 1939, his ultimate importance probably lies in his founding of the Ateliers d'art sacré, where his most famous pupil studied, Marie Alain Couturier (1897–1954). As well as eventually editing the influential journal *L'Art sacré*, Fr Couturier was responsible for commissioning Henri Matisse's work in the chapel at Vence and that of Braque, Chagall, Léger, and Rouault at Assy. Couturier was clear that God's spirit could not be narrowly confined to those of explicit Christian belief, and that it was the job of the Church to employ the best talent available. As with Ruskin, his contention was that the power of art to effect sacramental mediation was to be found well beyond the contours of the Christian Church. However, although in 1950 Pius XII appeared to take a similar view in his declaration that 'the purpose of all art is to break the narrow boundaries of the finite, and open windows onto the infinite' (Pius XII 1950), two years later a much more negative judgement was issued (Pius XII 1952: 542–5), and the Vatican has continued somewhat of a see-saw approach ever since.

Although Vincent van Gogh (1853–90) was to be dead within two years of the Symbolist Manifesto being launched, as many commentators have noticed, he and his friend Paul Gauguin (d. 1903) in fact share more with the Symbolists than they do with the Impressionists. A son of the manse, in his earlier years van Gogh had served as a missionary in the coalfields of Belgium. Although *The Potato Eaters* dates from four years after his loss of faith in 1880, it is possible to read the painting as continuing a traditional form of Christian sacramentalism, evoking as it does in some ways the Supper at Emmaus. For some, that rejection of orthodox Christianity led to the blossoming of a purely natural mysticism. But, as with *The Potato Eaters*, it is possible to point to larger continuities. Thus, his father actually belonged to the more liberal branch of the Dutch Church which was already seeking for new ways of negotiating a sense of divine presence in the world, partly under the influence of Schleiermacher's writings (Erickson 1998: 9–60). So when we find the figure of Christ replaced by a glowing sun in *The Raising of Lazarus* or a halo given to *The Sower* in the field, it is not necessary to jump immediately to the conclusion that pantheism has simply replaced his earlier Christian belief. Certainly, the specifics of Christian belief had gone but there is evidence to suggest that he continued to be closer to the sacramental idea of specific forms of mediation rather than the generalized pantheistic notion of presence everywhere. So, for instance, certain colours (in particular yellow and blue) were treated as especially indicative of divine presence (Brown 2004: 130–3).

On the literary side, Charles Baudelaire (1821–67) is often seen as a precursor, with Stéphane Mallarmé (1842–98), Paul Verlaine (1844–96), and Arthur Rimbaud (1854–91) poets at the movement's heart, while in the German-speaking world Stefan George (1868–1933) and Rainer Maria Rilke (1875–1926) provided obvious religious dimensions. Both the latter had been brought up as Roman Catholics, both use the image of an angel as intermediary, and both see their poetry in terms of a spiritual quest. How far the divine is for them an actual reality, however, remains much disputed. So, for example, while Rilke talks in a letter of 1923 of his poetry involving 'the ascent of God outside the living heart with which the sky covers itself, and its descent again in rain', elsewhere one finds the impermanence of all matter contrasted not with God but with its survival in our own souls: *Erde, ist est nicht dies, was du willst: unsichtbar in uns erstehn?* (*Duino Elegies* 9).

There are similar conflicting interpretations of the French poets. Undoubtedly, there are clear elements of decadence in Baudelaire, Verlaine, and Rimbaud, and it is possible to interpret that side as having its final triumph over Catholicism. So, for example, although Verlaine converted after his first period in prison, his poetry continued to pull in opposing directions: his great conversion poem *La sagesse* (1881) was continued in *Amour* (1888) and *Liturgies intimes* (1892) but opposed in the more earthy lyrics of *Parallèlement* (1889). Again, with Rimbaud we have only the word of his sister Isabelle to guarantee a deathbed conversion. But that is to look at matters altogether too narrowly. What gives their poetry such strength is in large part explained by such conflicts. Indeed, somewhat ironically it is here that we first find an element hitherto lacking in our account of sacramentality that some would deem essential, and that is the element of transformation or redemption. For instance, Anthony Kenny is adamant that lines such as those that open *God's Grandeur*, 'The world is charged with the grandeur of God', are insufficient to make Gerard Manley Hopkins a sacramental poet, since the sacramental must 'relate to God not as designer but as redeemer of the world' (Kenny 1988: 11–18 esp. 18) But even in terms of the traditional sacraments the point would seem misplaced since it is not on every occasion that the giving of communion or the anointing of the sick or dying need have such transformative effects. Sometimes, reassurance of the divine presence and aid is surely sufficient justification. Similarly, then, with the natural world: its symbols sometimes offer reassurance but at other times summon us to a different evaluation of our existence, as indeed some of Jesus' parables and analogies so finely demonstrate. Think, for instance, of the parable of the mustard seed or of the tares, or again of Jesus' comparison between lilies and Solomon arrayed in all his glory.

If we consider Baudelaire first, there is no doubt that he is prepared to describe all reality as coded for a higher existence, as in the opening lines of his sonnet *Correspondances*:

> *La Nature est un temple où des vivants piliers*
> *Laissent parfois sortir des confuses paroles.*

As his notorious collection *Les Fleurs du mal* (1857) makes clear, the difference for him is that all this is mediated through the conflict between good and evil (*spleen* and *idéal*); hence his willingness to extract truth from '*l'horreur et l'ecstase de la vie*', from the low life of Paris and what threatens damnation. Yet even so in the final sections he declares that nothing can defeat God, and so longs for death and the discovery of God at the heart of such conflict: '*Nous voulons . . . plonger au fond du gouffre, Enfer au Ciel, qu'importe? Au fond de l'Inconnu pour trouver du nouveau.*' Or at any rate that is how I interpret the text as a whole, though admittedly the concluding poems, in particular *Révolte* and *La Mort*, do easily admit of other interpretations. In the case of Rimbaud in what is perhaps his finest poem *Le Bateau ivre* (1871) he uses the image of himself adrift on a rudderless boat tossed by hurricanes across luminous seas to suggest his own confused state. But again, as with Baudelaire, opinion remains divided as to whether a work of two years later *Une Saison en enfer* is intended to represent his final submission to religious faith or its continued rejection.

Such ambiguities might seem inappropriate to mention in a chapter as short as this, were it not for the fact that this tradition and Rimbaud in particular (interpreted positively) led to the flowering of the most obviously sacramental writing of this redemptive kind in the poet and dramatist Paul Claudel (1865–1955). His mystical conversion may have been at an early age while listening to Vespers in Paris's Notre Dame Cathedral, but it is the Symbolist tradition that gave precise shape to his sensuous adaptation of biblical imagery and poetic forms in his own distinctive type of verse (the *verset claudelien*), consisting of long, unrhymed lines of free verse that he claimed were modelled on the Latin psalms of the Vulgate. Passionate, obsessive human love is used to convey the power of God's infinite love for humanity: as in his play *L'Annonce faite à Marie* (1910) that tells of sacrifice and sanctification in the life of a young medieval peasant woman who has contacted leprosy; or in the better known

Le Soulier de satin (1931) that recounts a Spanish nobleman's love for a married woman, his moral decline in one part of the empire and her growing sanctity in another, with his eventual transformation when they are finally reunited at her deathbed. The critic George Steiner ranks Claudel along with Brecht as the two greatest dramatists of the twentieth century, observing that Claudel's 'overwhelming plays are "sacramental mysteries" in the medieval and baroque sense. Suffering, waste, the frustration of love are the long prologue to transfiguration' (Steiner 1996: 138–9). If that sounds an all too familiar theme, there is considerable originality in how this is achieved, with elaborate symbolism, erotic imagery, and a surprising readiness to engage with the negative side of life: in his Foreword to *The Satin Slipper* he describes 'disorder' as 'the delight of the imagination'. Claudel also won the admiration of Hans Urs von Balthasar while he was studying as a young Jesuit at Lyons (1933–7). Indeed, so impressed was Balthasar by Claudel's 'celebration of the finite' that he himself organized the first performance of *The Satin Slipper* in the Zurich Playhouse, despite its notorious length of approximately eleven hours. In Claudel appreciation for the beauty of nature, Balthasar thought, was now nicely integrated with stories of redemption.

III. DISENCHANTMENT AND RESPONSES FROM SECULAR AND SACRED

However, in the eyes of some such more positive evaluations of divine presence in the world were but the last occasional sparks from the embers of a now dying attitude to the world, destined to disappear in much the same way as magic had already done. Although only mentioned by him in passing, such ideas were encapsulated in a much quoted phrase used by the sociologist Max Weber (1864–1920) that he seems to have borrowed from the dramatist and poet Friedrich Schiller (d. 1805): the *Entzauberung der Welt* or 'disenchantment of the world' (Weber 1948: 129–56, esp. 155). Although the process seemed to him virtually inevitable as rational, scientific approaches continued their advance, surprisingly it was not something that Weber himself welcomed, despite the absence in him of any religious belief. Instead, the result of such a disappearance was to imprison human beings 'in an iron cage', a phrase much debated in later sociological writing (e.g. Scaff 1989). Perhaps Weber's attitude was rather like the one-time ordinand Thomas Hardy who recounts in his poem *The Oxen* the legend of the animals kneeling at Christ's nativity yet ends despite his absence of belief: 'Hoping it might be so'. It is perhaps, therefore, not altogether surprising that, while some intellectuals responded by identifying signs of that divine 'magical' element still at work, others more pessimistically endorsed Weber's analysis though at the same time pleading for a weaker, non-theistic version of those transcendental moments.

One of the earliest and most significant responses of the latter kind is to be found in the Irish novelist James Joyce (1882–1941), in his use of the notion of an 'epiphany'. In

Christian liturgy the term is used to describe key moments of divine disclosure or revelation, in particular the worship of the infant Christ by the Wise Men, the miracle at Cana, and the voice and vision from heaven at Jesus' baptism. For Joyce, the erstwhile Catholic, it became any moment surrounded by a kind of magical aura that seemed to reveal the deeper significance of some otherwise ordinary object or person. The first appearance of the term in *Stephen Hero*, an earlier version of *Portrait of the Artist as a Young Man*, is clearly indebted both to St Thomas Aquinas's three criteria of beauty and to Gerard Manley Hopkins's notion of *haeccitas* ('thisness' or 'whatness'). Thus in chapter 25 after considering how Aquinas's criteria of integrity (or wholeness), symmetry (or harmony) and radiance might be applied to an overheard conversation or to the striking of a public clock, Joyce concludes: 'Its soul, its whatness, leaps to us from the vestment of its appearance. The soul of the commonest object, the structure of which is so adjusted, seems to us radiant. The object achieves its epiphany.' A little earlier Stephen had spoken of the need for 'the man of letters to record these epiphanies with extreme care' since each was 'a sudden spiritual manifestation . . . in "the most delicate and evanescent of moments"', and in fact forty such have been identified in Joyce's writings, including the later version of this discussion in *Portrait*, talk of 'epiphanies on green oval leaves' in *Ulysses* and indeed the penultimate entry in his journal. In *Portrait* he observes how 'the mind in that mysterious instant Shelley likened beautifully to a fading coal' (Joyce 1960: 211–13, esp. 213). What Joyce seems to be pleading for is the existence of ciphers that raise particular events or things beyond their purely temporal significance into a quasi-religious realm.

Much later in the century another lapsed Catholic, the philosopher Martin Heidegger, was to offer an analysis of human placement in the world that was to assume a similar divine absence, even as religious terminology continued to be accorded some legitimate place in his analysis of human experience. In a much quoted article *Bauen Wohnen Denken*, Heidegger argues against an instrumental analysis of building, with even the absence of commas between the nouns itself a deliberate ploy to emphasize the complete interdependence of the three ideas (Heidegger 1971: 145–61). Human beings, Heidegger suggests, do not 'build' in order to 'dwell'; rather, authentic building is to dwell, to bring the primitive 'fourfold' (earth and sky, divinities and mortals) into appropriate relation to one another. Hence instead of undifferentiated 'space' he wants us to recognize the indispensable character to human beings of 'location', the bounded area that gives a sense of presence (154–5). Although the word 'sacrament' is not used, both the way he presents his final example of a Black Forest farmhouse and his reference in another article to Hölderlin inevitably suggest parallels with a sacramental attitude to nature and the built environment's place within it. While Heidegger himself is clear that all we have of 'the divinities' are 'signs of their absence' it does not take much imagination to envisage a world differently perceived: instead of a sense of presence lost, one of presence felt and realized (150). Indeed, his first example of a bridge giving meaning to the river's banks rather than the other way round is very effectively echoed by the American poet Hart Crane in his masterpiece *The Bridge* (1930). In its proem the bridge effectively functions in just such a way, with the poet apostrophizing the bridge and requesting it to 'descend |And of the curveship lend a myth to God' (end of stanza 11).

Crane's poem was intended in part as a response to what he saw as the highly negative attitudes of his fellow American, T. S. Eliot, in *The Waste Land* (1922). Eliot's attitudes, however, were changing. In 1927, not only did he become a British citizen but also an active member of the Anglo-Catholic wing of the Church of England, significant because, along with its stress on the incarnation, a sacramental attitude to the world could be characterized as its other main focus. The result was literary criticism that saw the role of the poet's metaphors to interconnect what might otherwise seem an unintegrated, uncreated world and poetry that demonstrated a new positive value for images drawn from the world, not least a powerful sense of the hallowedness of place, as in *Little Gidding*, the final poem of his *Four Quartets* (1935–42). Indeed, as his essay on 'The Metaphysical Poets' well illustrates, such an integrated view was one to which he was already tending even prior to his explicit conversion (Eliot 1975: 59–67, esp. 64–5). Although so very different in many other ways, it was also an Anglo-Catholic version of Christianity that W. H. Auden (1907–73) would come to espouse, and so sacramental themes also likewise begin to appear in his poetry. For example, *Thanksgiving for a Habitat* (1963) finds God's presence in the activities of the home and not least in meals, as in 'Tonight at Seven-Thirty' (X).

Prior to the Second Vatican Council (1962–5) twentieth-century Roman Catholic writers and poets were on the whole quite conventional in their approach to the sacramental. So their tendency was to highlight the role of the seven sacraments rather than the sacramental more generally. This can be seen, for example, in the German writer Gertrud von Le Fort (1876–1971) in many of whose novels one or more of the sacraments appears quite prominently, or in the way in which G. C. Chesterton (1874–1936) allows sacramental confession to trump the gallows in one of his Father Brown detective stories ('The Queer Feet'), the cleric observing 'I caught him with an unseen hook and an invisible line' (Chesterton 1964: 70). Yet the most influential treatise of the time on the Eucharist, Maurice de la Taille's *Mysterium Fidei* (1924), had spoken of Christ at the Last Supper 'placing himself in the order of signs'. While the comment might have acted as an impetus to reflect more broadly, there is little evidence of this apart from in the writings of the Welsh painter and poet David Jones (1896–1976) where the phrase is used as an epigraph for his collection *Epoch and Artist* and also at the conclusion of one of its most important essays on 'Art and Sacrament'. For Jones part of the role of artists is to help the society in which they live to recover a tradition of symbols but also to inhabit them as gratuitous sign makers in their own right. Yet the obscurity of so many of Jones's own images was such that his theories had little impact. Indeed, for a strongly Christian sense of divine presence in the world of that time one might well turn instead to the one-time Methodist turned Anglican, Sir Stanley Spencer (1891–1959). Although without reinforcement from theory of any kind, the ordinary life of his native village of Cookham is repeatedly transfigured as settings for the life of Christ himself. House, brewery, and regatta alike all become symbolically charged with additional levels of meaning.

IV. Nouvelle Théologie

The change at the Second Vatican Council (1962–5) whereby Christ himself became the primordial sacrament and the Church 'like a sacrament' in helping to communicate his presence had been a long time in coming. In fact, it is part of a general *ressourcement* or return to sources that gave a new importance to ecclesiastical understandings of the first millennium as against the second. Theologians revolted against the neo-Thomism that had dominated Roman Catholic thinking since Leo XIII's encyclical *Aeterni Patris* (1879). According to this interpretation of Aquinas grace was seen as quite extrinsic to nature. Nature, it was believed, could of itself both prove God's existence and make revelation reasonable but grace then came as a further, quite distinct stage, rather than as human life's initial building blocks, as it were. Ironically, although a Frenchman, Réginald Garrigou-Lagrange (1877–1964), remains the best known representative of that earlier interpretation of Aquinas, it was also in France that the counter-movement first arose, in the Dominican centre of La Saulchoir with Marie-Dominique Chenu (d. 1990) and Georges-Yves Congar (d. 1995) and among the Jesuits of Lyons-Fourviere with Henri De Lubac (d. 1991) and Jean Daniélou (d. 1974). The initial title for the movement came from its detractors who drew comparisons with the Modernist heresy at the beginning of the century. So successful were their opponents that papal condemnation followed (in 1950), and their books were suppressed.

So it was no uniform advance. Inspiration came initially from the lay philosopher, Maurice Blondel (1861–1949). Blondel was as much opposed to the purely immanentist approach of Modernism as he was to the extrinsicism of neo-Thomism. So in contrast to neo-Thomism which denied any internal relationship between nature and grace, all the advocates of the new movement to varying degrees insisted that grace was already operative within nature itself. As De Lubac put it in his *Surnatural* of 1946, human beings had an inbuilt natural desire for some divinely given ('supernatural') goal. What made the approach inherently sacramental was thus the conviction that nature was in itself infused with the divine. At the same time there was considerable resistance to expressing this in any way that seemed to ape the rationalism of neo-Thomism. So such inbuilt grace was presented largely in terms of 'mystery', participation in what could never be fully explained. Nonetheless, sacramental language was applied not now just to the traditional sacraments but also to the world in general, to the Church and to scripture, where Daniélou in particular defended the patristic use of typology as one event participating in another.

Members of the group, however differed on the degree to which they thought it necessary to present revelation as subverting human expectations, and so a discontinuity between the two types of grace involved. One way in which the dispute manifested itself was through the two influential journals, *Concilium* and *Communio*. Like Congar, De Lubac had initially supported *Concilum* when it was founded in 1965 to further the reforms of Vatican II, but left in 1972 to join Hans Urs von Balthasar and Joseph Ratzinger in setting up the more conservative *Communio*. As his writings and actions as Pope Benedict XVI also indicate, the recovery of mystery in the liturgy has been one of Joseph Ratzinger's central concerns (Ratzinger 2000), whereas Balthasar's enthusiasm for the work of Karl Barth suggests a somewhat different emphasis, as does his fundamental disagreement with the German theologian, Karl Rahner (d. 1984). Although in his explicitly theological works his greatest philosophical debt is to Heidegger under whom he had studied at Freiburg, in his most philosophical work, *Geist in Welt* of 1939, Rahner had adopted the Kantian approach to interpreting Aquinas advocated by his fellow Jesuit, the Belgian philosopher Joseph Maréchal. According to this account, already embedded in human consciousness is a *Vorgriff* or basic pre-apprehension of God that makes human beings already inclined to respond to the infinite, whether this is found in the moral demands of conscience, in the aesthetic power of a landscape, or in numerous other ways. Balthasar like Barth, however, was insistent on an explicitly Christological connection.

The disagreements between Congar and the later De Lubac or between Rahner and Balthasar are also reflected in many another theologian. Two other French theologians may be used to illustrate how, while all were agreed that the term 'sacramental' had been used far too narrowly in the past, its precise range beyond the Church continues to be a subject of contention. Although the Jesuit Pierre Teilhard de Chardin (1881–1955) predates many of those discussed above, he is really a figure quite apart. Most of his life was devoted to scientific study, in particular palaeontology, and although he was engaged also with theology, none of these works appeared until after his death: *Le Phénomène humain* in 1955 and *Le Milieu divin* in 1957. His importance lies in his attempt to connect science and sacramentality. While *The Phenomenon of Man* interprets evolution as leading under the direction of God to the gathering of all things up into God, *Le Milieu Divin* expresses this advance in explicitly sacramental terms, as does his *Hymn of the Universe*. All matter is seen as sacramentally charged, with the Eucharistic consecration contributing, however attenuatedly, to the 'Christification' of the whole universe. Although some of his writings were censured by the Holy Office in 1962, Joseph Ratzinger seemed on the whole prepared to interpret him charitably despite the extent of the role now assigned to the sacramental (Ratzinger 2000: 29).

Even so, the approach of Louis-Marie Chauvet (b. 1942) in his influential *Symbole et Sacrement* of 1987 (significantly subtitled *une relecture sacramentalle de l'existence chrétienne*) is more obviously representative of where Roman Catholic thinking now stands. Rejecting what he calls 'ontotheology' and the causal theories that accompany such metaphysics which he traces back ultimately to Plato's *Philebus* (Chauvet 1987: 27–30), Chauvet suggests that we think instead in more personal and social terms of the symbolic language of the Church mediating God's new world and the values that go with it. Sacraments should therefore not be offered to nominal Catholics but only to those who take seriously not only the call to participate in a new way of viewing reality but also its ethical implications for transformative behaviour. The Church's sacraments are thus presented as necessary entry points for properly appreciating the much wider symbolic system that is found to exist. All these ideas are bolstered by a deep grounding in the philosophy of Heidegger which is seen as evoking mystery rather than actually denying God's existence (Chauvet 1987: 52–71, esp. 63–7).

V. THE WAY FORWARD

Given the continuing decline of religious practice in Europe, some readers might be inclined to support the direction suggested by writers such as James Joyce and Martin Heidegger, with 'sacramental' merely used as a term to indicate transcendental moments rather than any specific reference to a divine presence. If so, they would find support from some of the most influential writing in contemporary Britain. So, for example, the literary polymath George Steiner (b. 1929) argues in *Real Presences* (1989) that taking artistic creation seriously means acknowledging a transcendent element: that the act mimics the original divine act in creation (e.g. 215) and so is a kind of annunciation (143) or sacramental act (e.g. 149, 217), a disclosure or presence that cannot be exhausted simply by relating the work to its immediate context. Yet, while such a claim could be expressed in terms of a full sacramental theology, it seems that for Steiner the divine creative act is seen more as a helpful limiting case rather than to be treated as an actual reality as such. A similar point applies with the philosopher and novelist, Irish Murdoch (1919–99). While happy to use the language of sacrament for art (1970: 69), she makes her rejection of theistic belief quite explicit (75–6), and insists this applies to Plato also (Murdoch 1992: 38). Yet at the same time she laments the loss of ritual and the attentiveness that goes with it, for the way in which such absences reduce the capacity for the impact of any transcendent good in our lives (306–7).

Given the wider resonance of the term dominant in Roman Catholic theology for the past fifty years, one might have thought that more positive use of the theme could have been illustrated from Catholic novelists, but in general this has not been so. Heinrich Böll, Graham Greene and Muriel Spark, for instance, do of course raise religious issues, but not usually in this form, and so one needs to turn to the American writer Flannery O'Connor (1925–64) for a key case in point. Poetry in fact fares better, as, for example in the work of Elizabeth Jennings (d. 2001) or Kathleen Raine (d. 2003) (Brown and Fuller 1995: 4–5, 9–10, 96–7). Ironically, though, perhaps the best example of sacramentality mediated through literature comes not from a contemporary at all but in the newly rediscovered seventeenth-century writer, Thomas Traherne (e.g. Brown and Fuller 1995: 6–7). His *Centuries of Meditations* was first published only in 1903, *Select Meditations* in 1997 and the works in the Lambeth Manuscript finally in 2005.

One reason for such relative neglect of the notion may well be the retreat of so many Christians into more conservative attitudes. In other words, the wider use is still seen as 'trendy' rather than as a *ressourcement* or return to earlier ways of thinking. If so, that seems to me a pity. If Christians believe in a generous God, then they should expect his address to humanity everywhere and not just within the Church. None of this to deny the uniqueness of the contribution that the Christian revelation can make. But it is to challenge the notion that it must always impose a prior grid for experiences outside the Church to be taken seriously. Instead, there is the challenge to engage in creative dialogue not only with those who explicitly describe their experiences as religious but also with those who speak more vaguely like Joyce or Heidegger of moments of 'epiphany'. Indeed, one might argue that it is the Church and its theologians who have retreated from consideration of such experiences rather than society as such (Brown 2012). Numerous anthropologists and philosophers have spoken of humanity as essentially a *homo symbolicus*, as a being who necessarily operates with symbols, among them Mircea Eliade and Clifford Geertz, and Ernst Cassirer and Susanne Langer. If the range of those symbols were to be taken more seriously it is my view that current society would emerge as much more inherently religious or spiritually orientated than any church attendance figures might suggest; in other words, the implicit character of so much such belief would once more come to the fore.

REFERENCES

Barth, J. R. (2003). *Romanticism and Transcendence: Wordsworth, Coleridge and the Religious Imagination*. (Columbia: University of Missouri).

Brown, David (2004). *God and Enchantment of Place: Reclaiming Human Experience*. (Oxford: Oxford University Press).

—— (2012). 'Experience, Symbol and Revelation: Continuing the Conversation', in R. MacSwain and T. Worley (eds), *Theology, Aesthetics and Culture: Responses to David Brown*. (Oxford: Oxford University Press).

—— and Fuller, D. (1995). *Signs of Grace: Sacraments in Poetry and Prose*. (London: Continuum).

—— and Loades, Ann (eds) (1996). *The Sacramental Word*. (London: SPCK).

Calvin, John (1960). *Institutes of the Christian Religion*, ed. J. T. McNeill (Philadelphia: Westminster Press).

Chauvet, M. (1987). *Symbole et Sacrement*. (Paris: Les editions du Cerf).

Chesterton, G. K. (1964). 'The Queer Feet', *The Innocence of Father Brown*. (Harmondsworth: Penguin).

Coleridge (1856). *The Complete Works of Samuel Taylor Coleridge*, ed. W. G. T. Shedd (New York).

—— (1992). *The Collected Works of Samuel Taylor Coleridge*, ed. H. J. Jackson and G. Whalley (Princeton, NJ: Princeton University Press).

Constantine, David (1988). *Hölderlin*. (Oxford: Clarendon Press).

Eliot, T. S. (1975). *Selected Prose of T. S. Eliot*, ed. F. Kermode (London: Faber and Faber).

Erickson, K. P. (1998). *At Eternity's Gate: The Spiritual Vision of Vincent van Gogh*. (Grand Rapids, MI: Eerdmans).

Hegel, G. W. F. (1988). *Lectures in the Philosophy of Religion*, ed. P. C. Hodgson (Berkeley, CA: University of California Press).

Heidegger, Martin (1971). *Poetry, Language, Thought*. (New York: Harper & Row).

Hilton, T. (2000). *John Ruskin*. (New Haven, CT: Yale University Press).

Jasper, David (1985). *Coleridge as Poet and Religious Thinker*. (London: Macmillan).

Joyce, James (1960). *A Portrait of the Artist as a Young Man*. (Harmondsworth: Penguin).

Kenny, A. (1988). *God and Two Poets*. (London: Sidgwick and Jackson).

McFarland, T. (1969). *Coleridge and the Pantheist Tradition*. (Oxford: Clarendon Press).

Murdoch, Iris (1970). *The Sovereignty of the Good*. (London: Routledge & Kegan Paul).

—— (1992). *Metaphysics as a Guide to Morals*. (London: Chatto & Windus).

Pius XII (1950). 'Address to the First International Congress of Catholic Artists', *Liturgical Arts* 19.

—— (1952). *Acta Apostolicae Sedis* 44.

Ratzinger, J. (2000). *The Spirit of the Liturgy*. (San Francisco: Ignatius Press).

Roszak, Theodore (1972). *Where the Wasteland Ends: Politics and Transcendence in Post-industrial Society*. (New York: Doubleday).

Ruskin John (1906). *Modern Painters*. (London: George Allen).

—— (1912). *The Works of John Ruskin*, ed. E. T. Cook and A. Wedderburn (London: George Allen).

—— (2001). *The Stones of Venice*. (London: Pallas Athene).

Scaff, L. A. (1989). *Fleeing the Iron Cage*. (Berkeley, CA: University of California Press).

Steiner, G. (1989). *Real Presences*. (London: Faber and Faber).

Steiner, George (1996). *No Passion Spent*. (New Haven, CT: Yale University Press).

Weber, Max (1948). 'Science as a Vocation', in H. H. Gerth and C. Wright Mills (eds), *From Max Weber*. (London: Routledge & Kegan Paul).

Suggested Further Reading

Boersma, H. (2009). *Nouvelle Théologie & Sacramental Ontology*. (Oxford: Oxford University Press).

Brown, David (2004). *God and Grace of Body: Sacrament in Ordinary*. (Oxford: Oxford University Press).

Steiner, G. (1989). *Real Presences*. (London: Faber and Faber).

CHAPTER 30

....

ATONEMENT

....

SIMEON ZAHL

THE modern period has witnessed major shifts in the doctrine of the atonement in Europe and beyond, largely through the impact of ideas generated in disciplines outside of theology. These shifts stand in tension with the persistence of more traditional models among broad swaths of Christians.

In Christian theology, atonement refers to a fundamental reconciliation between God, humanity, and the world. This reconciliation is set in motion and achieved by God in Jesus Christ, through his incarnation, teaching, crucifixion, and resurrection, though different models of atonement emphasize different aspects. Doctrines of the atonement presuppose that evil, sin, and the 'brokenness' of the world have created a rift of some kind between God and his creatures, and that the coming and work of Christ serve to resolve this rift. Atonement is the particular mechanism or process by which this reconciliation occurs. Traditionally, reconciliation has meant salvation and eternal life for those reconciled, though more recent approaches have also emphasized its immanent aspects, in addressing contemporary social, political, and cultural concerns, as well as its cosmic implications for the whole of creation, rather than for particular individuals and groups only.

Developments in European thought in recent centuries have had a profound effect on the Christian concept of atonement. First, there has been the enormous impact of the Enlightenment, in particular what Charles Taylor has called its 'anthropocentric turn' (Taylor 2007: 221). This 'turn' included a new confidence in the powers of human reasoning, unaided by revelation or traditional theological confessions, to discern the nature of God and the universe. This went together with a profound questioning of the traditional views of humanity as tainted by original sin that had long undergirded the doctrine of the atonement.

Second, following the lead of Ludwig Feuerbach, a series of powerful reductive critiques of religion, including of atonement, were developed. These provided alternative explanations for religion as an artefact of human culture rather than of divine revelation. Significantly, several of these non-religious accounts of the world—most saliently that of psychologist Sigmund Freud—have led to alternative therapies for approaching many of the human problems traditionally addressed by atonement theology—the experience of guilt, in particular, but also anxiety, depression, and feelings of meaninglessness. This has further undermined some of the traditional force of the doctrine.

A third development has been closely intertwined with the first: sustained critiques of substitution and satisfaction-based models of the atonement (including retributive, sacrificial, and forensic models). Models of this type had come to the fore with Anselm in the eleventh century, were developed further by Aquinas, and became even more important as a result of the Reformation. By the seventeenth century in various forms they had become the dominant approach in European theology. Different thinkers in recent centuries have attacked such models as variously incoherent, primitive, immoral, unnecessary, and even as actively destructive of human flourishing.

In what follows, these three developments will be examined. While not exhaustive, together they provide a useful map of the doctrine over the past two centuries and beyond. This is particularly the case in the Protestant tradition, where atonement discussion has been most vigorous and most fraught. Each of these themes has retained a remarkable degree of interest and impact even after more than two centuries of discussion; they are selected here not least for their continuing relevance. Although there have been a number of important 'intra-Christian' debates on the atonement in recent centuries, the focus here will be on the ways in which developments outside of the Christian tradition have made an impact on thinking about the atonement.

A critical and often overlooked theme will emerge along the way: the unexpected persistence of the Protestant-Pietist synthesis in atonement theology, from the seventeenth century to the twenty-first, particularly outside of the halls of the academy.

A concluding section will offer a brief overview of trends in constructive accounts of the atonement from the nineteenth and twentieth centuries, including classic accounts by Schleiermacher and Barth, and the non-satisfaction-oriented alternatives that have been rehabilitated in light of the larger developments.

I. Background: The Dominance of Satisfaction Theories

The story of the atonement in Europe since 1800 is the continuation of a story that begins several centuries earlier, and it cannot be properly understood without this background. In Roman Catholic theology in this period, the dominant model remained that of Thomas Aquinas, who built on Anselm's non-penal satisfaction model as the mechanism for the removal of original sin, and further connected it to a soteriology of sacramental participation. In Protestant theology, the story begins with the consolidation and narrowing of the doctrine of justification by faith in the generations after Luther's death. As his thought developed, Philipp Melanchthon began to express justification increasingly through the lens of a single overriding metaphor: the *forensic* image of the law court. In this account, the mechanism of Christian salvation is above all one of God, in a sort of divine 'courtroom', passing judgement over sinful humanity. Christ, who is sinless, steps in, as a substitute, to be judged in place of the sinner. This substitution is understood primarily in terms of the satisfaction of God's justice through a transfer of merit: 'Christ's merits are given to us so that we might be reckoned righteous by our trust in the merits of Christ when we believe in him, as though we had merits of our own' (Melanchthon 2000 [1531]: 240). The result is that a person's sin is forgiven and the way to eternal life is opened.

The period after the death of the first generation Reformers, the age of Protestant Orthodoxy, continued for the most part in Melanchthon's forensic direction, with further emphasis on the 'penal' aspect of the atonement, which was an important theme in Calvin's account of the work of Christ. The argument behind the penal model is that because God is just and cannot but uphold his justice, a consequence of breaking divine law is that there is a *punishment* that must be meted out. Christ's death on the cross, then, is understood above all to be taking on the punishment sinners deserve rather than simply making a more general satisfaction to God on their behalf, as would be the case in Anselm or Aquinas. The focus in this the period is on what is happening *coram deo*, 'before God'—on the divine process by which God saves a particular person instead of judging them for their sin. This type of model is known as an 'objective' account of the atonement, in which what is decisive is the change in God and his view of particular people, rather than a change or transformation taking place in the person themselves, as it would be in a 'subjective' account.

By the end of the seventeenth century, the doctrine of the atonement had undergone an important further development. Starting in the Lutheran churches in the 1620s, there was an increasing reaction against the 'coldness' of Protestant Orthodoxy, particularly its perceived focus on the minutiae of correct doctrine at the expense of a lived Christian spirituality. The emphasis on what is happening *coram deo* was found to come at the expense of *experiencing* salvation in one's inner self and in the world, and to be abstract and cut off from living religion. To be converted, for a Pietist, is not merely for an abstract change of status before God to take place, but also to be filled with feelings of joy and freedom and a renewed sense of purpose. The Pietist impulse, then, was to restore to importance the 'subjective' aspect of the atonement—what it means for individuals in their day-to-day lives and practices.

Pietism spread rapidly, producing the culture of revivals and awakenings that characterized much of eighteenth century Christianity in Europe and beyond. For all its focus on individual piety, however, Pietism, and its Anglophone heir, Methodism, still affirmed, in its broad contours, the judicial and substitutionary model of the atonement worked out in Protestant orthodoxy. Salvation was still by faith, and Jesus' death on the cross remained the sole and necessary mechanism by which sins could be forgiven, God's favour restored, and the door to eternal life opened. Even as many Pietists began to emphasize the role of free will in accepting or rejecting salvation, and became more optimistic about sanctification, the atonement model at work remained in key respects that of the older Protestantism—and indeed, in so far as it was satisfaction-based, of the Catholic tradition since Anselm.

By the start of the eighteenth century, an important synthesis had been achieved in the doctrine of the atonement, between the substitutionary and forensic model of confessional Protestantism and the subjective, personalist orientation of Pietism. It is a synthesis to which more recent accounts of the atonement, especially those that criticize forensic models as a 'legal fiction' that fails to take adequate account of the subjective side, have often failed to do justice. The synthesis is illustrated in two of the most influential conversion narratives in an era famous for such narratives, those of August Hermann Francke (1663–1727), a key early Pietist leader, social activist, and theologian, and John Wesley (1703–91), the founder of Methodism. Because this synthesis is the foil for so many later developments, and especially critiques, it is worth looking at them more closely.

The Protestant-Pietist Synthesis on the Atonement

According to his widely read *Autobiography* of 1690, as a young man Francke 'fell into unrest and doubt', became increasingly convinced of a 'deep corruption' in his inner self, and began to feel 'constricted' in his internal 'state', 'as one who is in a deep quagmire' (Francke 1983 [1690]: 101, 104). His inner emotional turmoil and despondence, which lasted for some months, was closely bound up with a sense of sinfulness: 'And there my whole life and everything which I had done, said, and thought was presented before me as sin and a great abomination before God'. The 'chief source' of the problem, he came to believe, was not individual 'sins' but a very specific and fundamental sin: 'unbelief or mere false belief' (Francke 1983 [1690]: 103). Eventually, he 'went once more upon [his] knees' and 'cried to God'.

> [God] immediately heard me. My doubt vanished as quickly as one turns one's hand; I was assured in my heart of the grace of God in Christ Jesus and I knew God not only as God but as my Father. All sadness and unrest of my heart was taken away at once, and I was immediately overwhelmed as with a stream of joy so that with full joy I praised and gave honor to God who had shown me such great grace. I arose a completely different person from the one who had knelt down.... (Francke 1983 [1690]: 105)

Here we have the Protestant-Pietist synthesis on the atonement. Personal feelings of doubt, depression, anxiety, inner unrest, and rootlessness are understood to be closely connected to a sense of sin and guilt before God. A deeply emotional and individual conversion experience takes place which removes the negative affect and replaces it with powerful feelings of joy and purpose. The mechanism behind this event— described by Francke as the encounter of a disbelieving sinner with a gracious God who accepts him nevertheless—is the forgiveness of sins through the vicarious sacrifice of Jesus Christ. Importantly, however, the imputation of Christ's righteousness *coram deo*, and the non-imputation of sin, are utterly connected with particular inner feelings and a sensation of personal transformation at a particular time and place in Francke's life. Accompanying the 'forensic' event there is a concrete affective change: the eclipse of feelings of 'sadness and unrest' by an inner joy and the transformation of his desires and ambitions (Francke 1983 [1690]: 106). The experience was felt to have lifelong power: 'From this time on, my Christianity had a place to stand' (Francke 1983 [1690]: 106).

The same synthesis is illustrated in the most famous and influential Pietist conversion narrative of all, that of John Wesley at Aldersgate in 1738:

> About a quarter before nine, while the leader was describing the change which God works in the heart through faith in Christ, I felt my heart strangely warmed. I felt I did trust in Christ alone for salvation; and an assurance was given me that He had taken away my sins, even mine, and saved me from the law of sin and death. (Wesley 1987 [1738]: 34–5)

Wesley, too, takes for granted that the 'objective' element in atonement—the taking away of sin and sins, and salvation from the law of sin and death—is inseparable from the 'subjective' element—from the bodily and spiritual sensation, at 'about a quarter before nine', of his heart being strangely warmed.

The story of the atonement after 1690 is in an important sense the story of how the synthesis illustrated by Francke and Wesley came to be critiqued and undermined. At the same time, versions of their approach have demonstrated remarkable resilience in global Christianity, through to the twenty-first century, both in the confessional positions of many major denominations and in the continued success of evangelical and Pentecostal Christian expressions. This is due not least to the fact that their synthesis in fact succeeded remarkably well, in the initial experience, in holding together 'objective' and 'subjective' elements—in convincingly connecting the mechanism of atonement *coram deo* with particular day-to-day emotional states and desires. It is not the only approach in the Christian tradition to be successful at this connection, and it has a number of weaknesses, as we shall see. But the vehemence of reactions against substitutionary and forensic models over the centuries has often obscured recognition of their sheer effectiveness in a wide variety of contexts and over many centuries.

II. Reason and the 'Anthropocentric Shift'

At the same time as Francke was having his conversion experience, other thinkers in Europe were beginning to come to quite different conclusions about salvation, human nature, and the traditional theological confessions. Charles Taylor describes 'a striking anthropocentric shift' that occurs 'around the turn of the seventeenth/eighteenth centuries', as a consequence of various aspects of Enlightenment thought as well as the increasing explanatory power of science. In Taylor's view, this anthropocentric shift has several features, 'each one reducing the role and place of the transcendent' in favour of a greater role for humanity (Taylor 2007: 222).

The first shift, in Taylor's account, is the increasing sense that God's purpose for humanity and creation is nothing more than the flourishing of humanity on earth—a 'new ethic of purely immanent human good' (Taylor 2007: 263). The second is 'the eclipse of grace'. As he describes it, 'The order God had designed was there for all to see. By reason and discipline, humans could rise to the challenge and realize it' (Taylor 2007: 222). No further divine help is needed for humanity to thrive—God-given reason and innate human powers were for the first time seen as adequate to the task. Implicit here is a decline in belief in the innate fallenness of humanity—what Christian tradition in the west had called original sin. A third change is that 'the sense of mystery' in the universe 'fades' (Taylor 2007: 223). This shift is supported and catalysed by the scientific breakthroughs of the seventeenth century, above all the enormous power of Newtonian science to explain the motions and energies of the natural world with mathematical precision.

The broad accuracy of this characterization as it relates to theology is evident from the profusion of texts and thinkers in this period, both Deist and more traditional or orthodox Christian, who seek to identify a 'natural' religion that, while not necessarily at odds with Christianity, can be deduced by reason and empirical observation alone, without the aid of divine revelation. Examples include John Locke's *The Reasonableness of Christianity* in 1695, John Toland's *Christianity Not Mysterious* in 1696, and Matthew Tindal's *Christianity as Old as the Creation* in 1730 (Byrne 1996: 105–13). For Deists, reason is simply more true and reliable than the revelation-based alternative, and less subject to the sort of confessional disputes that had torn Europe apart in the Thirty Years' War earlier in the century. For more traditional Christian thinkers like Samuel Clarke (1675–1729), the argument from 'natural' religion had apologetic value in an age of Enlightenment: if the existence of God and other key tenets of Christianity could be deduced without recourse to revelation, this could be seen as a powerful argument in favour of the truth of the religion as a whole (Buckley 1987: 33, 73–7, 193). That is, truths discovered by reason could be seen as complementary to Christian orthodoxy and revelation rather than as competitive with them.

In Britain, one of the most important early Deist documents appeared in 1690, the same year as Francke's *Autobiography*: Charles Blount's controversial edited collection, *The Oracles of Reason*. Here Blount (together with the anonymous contributor 'A. W.') voices two of the chief arguments against traditional Christian conceptions of the atonement, both in the name of 'Reason'. The first is against 'Original Sin, which I must ingenuously confess was ever a difficult Pill with me to swallow, my Reason stopping it in my Throat, and not having Faith enough to wash it down' (Blount 1995 [1690]: 12). The fundamental issue with original sin, for Blount, is the sheer injustice of God condemning all of humanity on the basis of the sin of one particular ancestor: "tis altogether inconsistent with God's Attributes of Mercy and Justice, to punish all

Mankind for one single Person's sin, which we could no ways prevent or hinder . . . For how can another's sin, wherein we have no hand, be imputed to us?' (Blount 1995 [1690]: 14–15). Without the support of revelation, the doctrine of original sin must be evaluated on its own terms. Under the light of reason alone, the doctrine comes across to Blount as arbitrary and unfair, and cannot be consistent with a God of love and mercy.

The second problem with the traditional view of the atonement raised in *The Oracles of Reason* is related: that it is neither just nor fair for God to require infinite punishment or satisfaction from a finite creature. As 'A.W.' puts it, 'infinite Justice cannot be extended on a finite Creature infinitely, without a Contradiction to infinite Mercy'; otherwise, God's mercy would be less extensive than his justice. In other words, despite the claim of traditional Protestant and Catholic views to resolve, in the vicarious sacrifice of Christ, the competing demands of justice and love in God, they in fact prioritize justice over love. Blount goes one step further in his influential 'Summary Account of the Deists Religion', anticipating many later critiques of atonement theology: for the propitiation of human sin, he argues, no 'Mediator' is necessary, '*Misericordia dei* being *sufficiens justitiae suae*' (God's compassion being sufficient for his justice). Why should God's mercy not trump his justice? Indeed, might not the glory and power of divine justice be that it consists in the triumph of grace precisely over merely human, *quid pro quo* conceptions? While the first critique, of original sin, would apply to a variety of traditional Christian concepts of atonement in the Latin west, this latter is targeted more at penal and forensic models in particular.

It is important to recognize that at this early stage the Deist critiques of original sin and of propitiatory sacrifice as means of securing forgiveness do not yet arise from a general optimism about humanity and its capacities per se. Indeed, Blount viewed most Christians in his day as naïve about human nature and blind to their own hypocrisy (Redwood 1974: 493). What is new is the degree of trust specifically in the powers of *human reason*—which for Blount largely means simple logic shorn of dogmatic assumptions—to gain access to the truth of world and of God without divine aid. Revelation, which to many seemed since the Reformation to have produced little more than confessional squabbling and bloodshed, needed to be held to account to an alternative authority. In the seventeenth century, reason had begun to demonstrate extraordinary promise both for explaining the workings of the natural world and for providing new, more peaceful bases for human political community. Blount's primary difficulty with the concepts of original sin and vicarious satisfaction, then, was not the Christian idea that people are sinners; it was that in his view these concepts did not *make sense*. Before long, however, the optimism about one particular human faculty—reason—waxed for many European thinkers into an optimism about human capacities more broadly, and for many the doctrine of original sin increasingly lost plausibility.

III. Reductive Interpretations
of the Atonement

A heightened view of reason soon led to a new sort of critique of atonement: the reductive interpretation. Particularly problematic for traditional Christian doctrines in the long term has been the capacity for reason and scientific enquiry to provide persuasive alternative explanations for why human beings believe in God, and for the genesis and continuing appeal of particular Christian doctrines, including not least the concepts of alienation from God and its resolution through Christ.

Ludwig Feuerbach

The figure that towers over reductive accounts of religion is the nineteenth-century German philosopher Ludwig Feuerbach (1804–72). Although he was not the first European thinker to offer an alternative explanation for Christian belief (Buckley 1987: 291–6), Feuerbach provided the most influential theory, upon which later reductive accounts, such as those of Marx and Freud, were in different measures to rely. In the first instance, Feuerbach was not as concerned with atonement as he was with belief in God in general (especially in Christianity), but his powerful idea contained the seed of what remain perhaps the most effective critiques of traditional atonement theories.

Feuerbach's claim in *The Essence of Christianity* is that 'the true sense of Theology is Anthropology' (Feuerbach 1957 [1854]: p. xxxvii). Put a different way, 'The divine being is nothing else than the human being, or, rather, the human nature purified, freed from the limits of individual man, made objective—i.e., contemplated and revered as another, a distinct being' (Feuerbach 1957 [1854]: 14). The classic word for what Feuerbach is describing is *projection*. Humanity, in his view, has taken its own sense of self, stripped it of limitations and defects, and projected it out into the world. So attractive and fundamentally true does this picture feel, that we begin to worship it as a divine 'object', forgetting its source as an idealized version of our selves. In a significant sense Feuerbach actually affirms the projection, believing it to be a critical motor behind human achievement and aspiration. But he simultaneously reduces it to something within ourselves: 'this transcendentalism is an illusion' (Feuerbach 1957 [1854]: 16). There is not actually a living, independent divine agent 'out there'. Traditional religion, especially Christianity, is the victim of an innocent misunderstanding, a false attribution of metaphysical, extra-human reality to our own inner yearnings, hopes, and possibilities. '[M]etaphysics is resolvable into psychology' (Feuerbach 1957 [1854]: 40).

The implications for the doctrine of the atonement become clearer later in the book, where Feuerbach anticipates Freud in key respects. 'God', he claims, 'is the Love that satisfies our wishes, our emotional wants; he is himself the realized wish of the heart, the wish exalted to the certainty of its fulfillment, of its reality' (Feuerbach 1957 [1854]: 121). Our emotional needs and wants presuppose the idea of their satisfaction. If we are lonely, we can postulate, and hope for, companionship and love. If we are troubled or anxious, we can postulate lasting inner peace. God, for Feuerbach, is therefore more specifically the perfect form of these goods—peace, joy, fellowship, wholeness, love—projected into an enduring divine agent.

The Protestant-Pietist synthesis on the atonement is particularly vulnerable to this sort of critical interpretation. As we have seen above, Francke, in his 'deep quagmire' of 'unrest and doubt', wished to find peace and certainty, and relief from a potent inner suffering. He felt himself to find it in God, above all in a powerful conviction that his sins were forgiven through Christ. But what if this God, and this mechanism for the forgiveness of sins, were merely his own 'emotional wants . . . exalted to the certainty of [their] fulfilment, of [their] reality'? What if his cry on his knees to God was merely 'the wish of the heart expressed with confidence of its fulfilment' (Feuerbach 1957 [1854]: 122), and therefore the 'help [lay] in the prayer itself' (Feuerbach 1957 [1854]: 124), rather than in any divine agent? Feuerbach's approach takes what happened to Francke and offers a plausible alternative explanation. Pietist reference to God and to the atonement need not be anything more than a symbolic structure that makes sense of, and helps induce, a profound moment of psychological healing. The 'objective' element in the atonement here, God's forgiveness of sin, is a disguise or costume for a purely 'subjective' phenomenon.

Feuerbach opened the door for a wide variety of reductive interpretations of religion over the next century and a half. Karl Marx (1818–83) explained religion in economic terms, as a tool in class warfare between the weak and the powerful, 'the opiate of the masses'. Emile Durkheim (1858–1917) in his opus *The Elementary Forms of the Religious Life* interpreted and explained religion in terms of his new science of sociology—a ritualized product of human social needs. Charles Darwin's (1809–82) great insight into the development of life led eventually to accounts of religion as a byproduct of human development and evolution (e.g. Boyer 2001). But for atonement theology, perhaps the most significant figure among the reductive interpreters was Sigmund Freud (1856–1939), founder of psychotherapy and of the modern academic discipline of psychology. Freud's special significance here is due to his extended engagement with the psychology of *guilt*.

Sigmund Freud

Writing over half a century after Feuerbach, Freud, too, viewed religion as an understandable but ultimately problematic projection. 'Religious ideas', in Freud's view, 'are illusions, fulfillments of the oldest, strongest and most urgent wishes of mankind'. In particular, 'the terrifying impression of helplessness in childhood aroused the need for protection . . . provided by the father . . . Thus the benevolent rule of a divine Providence allays our fear of the dangers of life' (Freud, 1961c [1927]: 38–9). God is a deep unconscious desire for a protective parental figure, projected into the sky.

With regard to the atonement it is not the critique of religion as illusion, which we have already seen in Feuerbach, which is of greatest interest. It is rather Freud's general psycho-dynamic theory, with its explanations for the phenomenon of human guilt and for the existence of the 'conscience'. The ability to make sense of and to resolve guilt feelings has long been one of the great strengths of Christian atonement theologies, whether the resolution took place through penitential practices such as confession, through the inner 'experiences' of divine forgiveness reported by Protestants and Pietists, or in various other ways. The forgiveness of sins and a consequent feeling of inner relief and freedom is also an important biblical theme, particularly in the New Testament (e.g. Ps. 51, 130:3–4; Matt. 26:27–8; Acts 13:37–9; Eph. 1:7; etc.). Crucially, Freud's theory provided him with tools for developing a therapeutic method that not only explained, but could actually address and potentially ease the symptoms of guilt without any reference to religion, atonement, sin, blood, or forgiveness. In so far as atonement theory had always included what could be called a 'therapeutic' component, Freud set the stage for sophisticated alternative therapies for the same human problems.

In *The Ego and the Id*, the last of his major theoretical works, Freud describes the 'the ego-ideal' or 'super-ego', one of the three main divisions of the mind. The super-ego is the inner moral voice or conscience, which derives from an 'introjected' voice of parents and their authority. As Freud puts it, 'this ego-ideal or super-ego [is] the representative of our relation to our parents. When we were little children we knew these higher natures, we admired and feared them; and later we took them into ourselves' (Freud 1961b [1923]: 26). The super-ego is strengthened and maintained later in life by 'teachers and others in authority; their injunctions and prohibitions remain powerful in the ego ideal and continue, in the form of conscience, to exercise moral censorship' (Freud 1961b [1923]: 27). It is the inner voice that says 'You *ought to be like this* (like your father)' as well as 'You *may not be* like this (like your father)' (Freud 1957 [1923]: 24). Here then, is the psychological origin of guilt feelings: we often fail to live up to the standards set by the super-ego, and when this happens 'The tension between the demands of conscience and the actual performances of the ego is experienced as a sense of guilt' (Freud 1957 [1923]: 27).

It is difficult to understate the significance of guilt in Freud's theory. The thesis of perhaps his best-known work, *Civilization and Its Discontents*, is that 'the sense of guilt [is] the most important problem in the development of civilization and . . . that the price we pay for our advance in civilization is a loss of happiness through the heightening of the sense of guilt' (Freud 1957 [1930]: 97). Furthermore, through its role as the source of the inner concept of a judging authority and the consequent experience of guilt feelings, the super-ego 'contains the germ from which all religions have evolved' (Freud 1957 [1923]: 27). Religions 'claim to redeem mankind from this sense of guilt, which they call sin', and 'in Christianity . . . this redemption is achieved

... by the sacrificial death of a single person, who in this manner takes upon himself a guilt that is common to everyone' (Freud 1961a [1930]: 99).

Freud's psycho-analytic method prescribes various therapeutic tools for resolving pathologies, increasing happiness, and opposing the super-ego to 'lower its demands' (Freud 1961 [1930]: 108) (i.e. to minimize the debilitating experience of guilt feelings). As psychological science advanced in the twentieth century, the number of psychologists who adhered to Freud's particular therapeutic methods dwindled in the face of more developed and data-supported theories and methods. But the basic idea of guilt as a fundamentally immanent, psychological phenomenon, 'curable' to a significant degree through cutting-edge psychological therapies, has persisted.

Once again, Francke's conversion narrative is illustrative here. A psychotherapist in the early twenty-first century might propose that his 'doubt and unrest' could have been explained instead through attachment theory and current understanding of clinical depression, and could have been eased through, for example, a regime of cognitive behavioural or mindfulness therapy, or anti-depressant medication. Likewise, in the wake of Freud the possibility is opened for interpreting Wesley's Aldersgate experience, in which 'an assurance was given me that He had taken away my sins, even mine, and saved me from the law of sin', as nothing more divine than a psychological coming to terms with the 'introjected' voice of a judgmental father figure.

The consequences for guilt and forgiveness-oriented doctrines of the atonement are substantial. Western Christians have long sought and found peace and new beginnings in the vicarious sacrifice of Christ. Although traditional Christianity has never viewed the atonement as simply reducible to its immanent, therapeutic outworkings and consequences, neither has it tended to thrive when completely divorced from them. The more powerful psychological explanations and therapies have become, the more difficulties have been raised for upholding theories of the atonement and rendering them plausible as answers to particular human emotional and psychological problems. Even F. W. Dillistone's classic, generous study of the diversity of models of the atonement, *The Christian Understanding of Atonement*, grounds itself first and foremost in the doctrine's possibilities for resolving particular modern human problems and pathologies, namely, 'Alienation' and 'Estrangement' (Dillistone 1984: 2), and therefore remains part of the long tradition of viewing the implications of atonement to a significant degree in *therapeutic* terms.

What is the consequence for traditional views of the atonement when many people begin to find psychotherapy and pharmaceuticals to be more effective solutions to debilitating feelings of guilt, anxiety, depression, or alienation from society—the problems to which the atonement traditionally has provided robust and compelling answers? What is the role for talk of reconciliation between God and his creatures when the creatures no longer feel as strong a need for reconciliation, or when they can explain their feelings of alienation adequately without reference to God?

One answer is to point out that this view does not really take seriously the self-reporting of the many Christians down the centuries who have had experiences like Francke's. Another is to view the situation as part of a wider wake-up call to theories of atonement that emphasize the themes of guilt and judgement, and an impulse to retrieve alternative models from the long Christian tradition. It is to some of the primary critiques of substitutionary and sacrificial models, and the alternative soteriologies proposed in their place, that we now turn.

IV. Modern Critiques of Traditional Theories

Although classic Roman Catholic and Protestant accounts of the atonement have important differences, over which there has often been intense debate, some of the most fundamental features are shared. Protestant and Catholic accounts have tended to follow a broadly Anselmian pattern which (a) views Christ as standing *in some sense* in the place of sinners in the eyes of God, as a substitute, and (b) sees the brutal death of Jesus on the cross as having been necessary for the salvation of believers. Both also affirm in different ways the potentially 'therapeutic' character of atonement theology and its apparatus in the sense discussed in the previous section, as well as the Augustinian doctrine of original sin. Just how much they do share has been illustrated in the past two centuries by the fact that many of the strongest critiques of atonement theology that have developed apply more or less to classic positions in both traditions.

The Moral Critique Revisited

In the nineteenth century, two influential American thinkers continued along lines we have seen above in Blount and his fellow Deists. Both William Ellery Channing (1780–1842), the leading light of the early Unitarian movement, and Horace Bushnell (1802–76), a founder of American religious liberalism, put forth criticism of substitution and satisfaction-based atonement theories, with enormous impact on American religious life, especially in predominately Calvinist New England. Like Blount, they found views based on the need to appease God through the suffering and sacrifice of Christ to be both morally repugnant and philosophically questionable. In Bushnell's words, what is at work on the cross cannot be 'a literal substitution of places, by which Christ becomes a sinner for sinners', for 'That is a kind of substitution that offends every strongest sentiment of our nature', and 'all God's moral sentiments would be revolted by that' (Bushnell 1984 [1849, 1866]: 141).

Although his particular target is a Calvinist concept of penal substitution, the way Bushnell reinterprets the meaning of the term 'sacrifice' shows that his difficulty is really with any notion at all of God requiring satisfaction as a result of the sin of human beings. 'It is not that the suffering [of Christ on the cross] appeases God, but that it expresses God—displays, in open history, the unconquerable love of God's Heart' (Bushnell 1984 [1849, 1866]: 132). Bushnell's view is best described as a mystical approach to a 'moral' theory of the atonement, by which the crucifixion 'expresses' God's love for sinners and for the world and the power of this expression is seen as transformative. What is 'expressed', however, is not so much an idea—the *concept* that God must love humanity if he was willing to die to show it—as a sensual and deeply attractive divine reality. As he puts it, 'when God appears in His beauty, loving and lovely, the good, the glory, the sunlight of soul, the affections, previously dead, awake into life and joyful play, and ... an exulting spirit of liberty' (Bushnell 1984 [1849, 1866]: 130).

What separates Bushnell's arguments from those of a Deist like Blount, and shows him to be a thoroughly nineteenth-century figure, is his trust more in an inner human moral 'sentiment' (which in this instance secures the moral case against substitution) than in the capacities of reason per se. Indeed, his Romantic inclinations cause him to question the adequacy of any particular rational statement of a doctrine:

> [N]o dogmatic statement can adequately represent [Christ's] work; for the matter of it does not lie in formulas of reason, and cannot be comprehended in them. It is more a poem than a treatise ... It addresses the understanding, in great part, through the feeling or sensibility.   (Bushnell 1984 [1849, 1866]: 127)

On this last point, Bushnell was ahead of his time. For him, the multiple biblical metaphors for atonement and salvation are all attempting to communicate something that goes beyond any one metaphor or any particular doctrinal formulation. Initially unpopular, this is a view that found increasing traction in Christian theology by the end of the twentieth century (e.g. Gunton 1998). Additionally, Bushnell's sheer moral revolt against the implications of overdetermined satisfaction and retributive theories prefigured more specific and explicit worries in the following century, about the violence of the cross and its implicit affirmation of suffering.

Girard and Structural Violence

Few thinkers have drawn more attention to the violence inherent in concepts of sacrifice and atonement than René Girard (b. 1923). Girard's work uses a mix of anthropological, literary, and cultural analysis to identify an ancient human pattern of using 'sacrifice' as a means for redirecting violent impulses that threaten society onto a particular, representative object. In engaging in sacrificial ritual, 'society is seeking to deflect upon a relatively indifferent victim, a "sacrificeable" victim, the violence that would otherwise be vented on its own members, the people it most desires to protect' (Girard 1977: 4). In this way 'the sacrifice serves to protect the entire community from *its own* violence' (8) and to 'prevent conflicts from erupting' (14). Both religion and the concept of 'the sacred' are understood to be originally and fundamentally tied up with the management of violence in society (Girard 1977: 31). A particular controlled act of violence—a sacrifice—grounds and expends a society's violent energy, at least temporarily, and so preserves order.

In Christianity, for Girard, the violence inherent in sacrifice and in 'the sacred' is exposed and brought to an end. Jesus' teaching (in particular the command to love enemies) 'shows us a God who is alien to all violence and who wishes in consequence to abandon violence' (Girard 1987: 183). The crucifixion, too, should be understood not as an instance of sacrifice, as it has often been viewed, but as the end of it. The words from the cross 'My god, my god, why have you forsaken me?' are words of 'anguished impotence and final surrender'. They 'make quite clear that we are dealing with something entirely different from the sacred. Here life does not come directly out of the violence, as in primitive religions' (Girard 1987: 231). In the Girardian model, sacrificial theories of the atonement uphold the economy of violence rather than exposing and ending it, and in this they tragically misunderstand Jesus' intentions. Following this approach, Timothy Gorringe has even contended that there is a structural connection between 'satisfaction theory', criminal law, and publicly legitimated violent penal practice in Europe from the eleventh to the nineteenth century (Gorringe 1996: 12).

Stephen Finlan argues that even Girard's position may fail fully to escape the violent cycle of sacrifice and scapegoating, because Girard 'has God making use' (if only to reveal the truth that violence is a dead end) of at least one 'act of violence', 'that against Jesus' (Finlan 2005: 93). Building on arguments from historical criticism, psychology and anthropology, as well as theology, Finlan's polemical approach sums up many threads of atonement critique over the past two centuries. He argues that the sacrificial and scapegoat metaphors that appear in a number of biblical texts are both harmful and manipulative. They promote 'primitive' ideas: 'that innocent blood purifies, or that God is moved by our ritual actions, or that the killing of Jesus was accepted as a payment for sins, apparently arranged by God'. Finlan asks, 'Why could God not open up the way to salvation without a blood-rite? Is this not based on primitive beliefs about the polluting effect of sin and the magical cleansing power of lifeblood?' (Finlan 2005: 107) In the Middle Ages such beliefs worked themselves out in 'manipulative' strategies of 'punishment and pain', 'penances, self-flagellations, . . . and other attempts at negotiation with God'. Protestantism was no better: 'The intense Reformation focus on guilt followed by undeserved rescue from destruction leave a powerful and painful psychological legacy.' The consequence of belief in satisfaction and sacrifice for sin is a cruel 'pattern of shame, release, and submissive gratitude' (Finlan 2005: 82). After extended consideration of the biblical material, Finlan concludes that 'To really understand Christ's life mission it is necessary to discard sacrificial thinking' (Finlan 2005: 112)—although he admits that atonement doctrine in some form is critical in a range of biblical texts (Finlan 2005: 120). In line with many late twentieth- and early twenty-first-century thinkers, he proposes that

Christian theology should build its soteriology on the incarnation and participation in Christ, not on the atonement.

To return again to our touchstone for modern theories of atonement, in Finlan's approach Francke's fall into despair and doubt could be interpreted as itself the product of Christian social pressures, doctrines, and symbol structures, including especially satisfaction theories. Raised a Christian, Francke does report that he felt his greatest sin of all to be lack of faith (Francke 1983: 103–4)—a sin that makes little sense outside of a prior religious framework. It is perhaps not a great stretch, then, to see Francke's experience as more the result of socialization into a 'pattern of shame, release and submissive gratitude', through a 'manipulative' account of the atonement, than of a genuine divine experience. For Finlan, Pietist atonement theology actually created and exacerbated the very problems it claimed to solve.

Feminism and Non-Redemptive Suffering

In the twentieth century, the feminist movement inspired related concerns about traditional atonement theologies. Drawing on powerful accounts of the ways in which the less powerful and the voiceless are actively and also structurally oppressed in societies, including not least the oppression of women by cultures of patriarchy, the target here has been the implicit affirmation of suffering and victimhood implicit in classical Christian views of the crucifixion. Joanne Carlson Brown and Rebecca Parker summarize the view in no uncertain terms:

> Christianity has been a primary—in many women's lives, *the* primary, force in shaping our acceptance of abuse. The central image of Christ on the cross as the savior of the world communicates the message that suffering is redemptive. (Brown and Parker 1989: 2)

Although 'there is no classical theory of the atonement that questions the necessity of Jesus' suffering' (Brown and Parker 1989: 4), it is the satisfaction approach that is the worst offender, its legacy nothing more than the 'sanctioning of suffering' (Brown and Parker 1989: 8). For Brown and Parker, 'Suffering is never redemptive, and ... cannot be redeemed' (Brown and Parker 1989: 27), and Christian theories that argue otherwise are perverse. The traditional concept of God the Father deliberately sending his Son to die for the world's sin is morally revolting—'Divine child abuse' (Brown and Parker 1989: 2). As it currently exists, 'Christianity is an abusive theology that glorifies suffering ... We must do away with the atonement, this idea of a blood sin upon the whole human race which can be washed away only by the blood of the lamb. This bloodthirsty God is the God of the patriarchy' (Brown and Parker 1989: 26). For Brown and Parker, it is only when the cross is understood exclusively as a tragedy, which 'eternally remains and is eternally mourned' (Brown and Parker 1989: 27) that anything positive might be rescued from the Christian tradition.

V. TRENDS IN MODERN
CONSTRUCTIVE ACCOUNTS

Few Christian doctrines have inspired either as much anger or as much thoughtful critique in recent centuries as satisfaction and substitution-based theories of the atonement. As we have seen, a great many tools have been brought to bear in analysing and criticizing such doctrines, with many of the most insightful having sources outside of the Christian tradition, in psychology, philosophy, and critical and political theory (especially about structures of power). But the story has not all been negative. Modern developments have also stimulated a number of positive proposals on salvation and atonement. Two of the most formidable are those of Friedrich Schleiermacher and Karl Barth.

Schleiermacher and Barth: Two Ways of Being Modern

Friedrich Schleiermacher's influential approach in *The Christian Faith* is similar to Bushnell's, which it influenced. He accepts to a significant degree the rational and moral arguments that substitution and satisfaction do not necessarily make philosophical sense, and that some of the assumptions they traditionally make, like the necessity of divine punishment, are morally unacceptable (Schleiermacher 1999 [1830]: 460). Basing his exposition of the topic 'entirely on the inner experience of the believer' (Schleiermacher 1999 [1830]: 428), Schleiermacher is critical of any approach to redemption or reconciliation that is not dependent on natural and historical mediation of Christ's 'God-consciousness' and 'unclouded blessedness' through the community of believers in time. Traditional satisfaction views depend instead, he argues, on Christ's 'immediate influence upon the individual', which in his view amounts to 'magic' and 'divine arbitrariness' (Schleiermacher 1999 [1830]: 435). Additionally, unlike his own approach, such views are psychologically and pastorally inadequate to relieve the burdened conscience:

> In no less magical a way is the forgiveness of sins achieved, if the consciousness of deserving punishment is supposed to cease because the punishment has been borne by another. That in this way the expectation of punishment might be taken away is conceivable . . . [But] the consciousness of deserving punishment would still remain. (Schleiermacher 1999 [1830]: 435)

Schleiermacher's approach is sophisticated and complex, and not easily reducible to a particular position within the tradition. At the same time, he clearly disagrees with any view that conceives of the saving influence of Christ as supernaturally leaping over the course of time instead of being mediated naturally through it, and he unquestionably has moral difficulties with substitution and with the concept of necessary divine punishment. On the other hand, he also finds a constructive place for various satisfaction-oriented terms ('vicarious', 'satisfaction', 'High Priest', 'representative', etc. (Schleiermacher 1999 [1830]: 451, 460–3)), but only after redefining them substantially. The weight in his approach falls ultimately on the experienced transformation of believers through the historically-mediated influence of Christ, but it does so in a way that is richer and more multivalent than a simple 'moral influence' theory.

Karl Barth takes a very different approach to reconciliation, and his, too, defies over-simple critique. Barth draws particularly on Protestant forensic and substitutionary traditions, even as he reinterprets them. On the one hand, Barth's approach in *Church Dogmatics* does affirm the ideas that sin deserves God's wrath, that human guilt in God's eyes is real, that the wrath must be in some way appeased or redirected, and that Christ is the one who accomplishes this. '[T]he rejected man, who alone and truly takes and bears and bears away the wrath of God is called Jesus Christ' (Barth 1957: 348–9). His fundamental commitment to the Bible as a source for theology rules out the possibility of rejecting sacrifice or substitution as illogical, immoral, or irredeemably violent concepts. At the same time, Barth rigorously unites God's being and his action, with the result (among others) that the incarnation is made necessary to his system more naturally and organically than in many Protestant accounts. Likewise, Barth's organizes his treatment in such a way that the resurrection, 'the great verdict of God' (Barth 1956: 309) is if anything even more significant than the crucifixion itself, correcting a commonly criticized tendency in satisfaction and substitution-oriented models.

Barth's approach is intricate and multifaceted, encompassing discussions from across *Church Dogmatics*. In what is arguably the climactic section for the whole doctrine, Barth focuses not on substitution or satisfaction but on Jesus as 'Victor' over 'the surrounding world of darkness' (Barth 1961: 168, 180)—an image that is intentionally dynamic rather than static and cosmic rather than individualistic. Furthermore, in addition to substitution, the bearing of wrath, and the concept of victory, Barth's account makes extensive use of many further categories and metaphors from the Bible and the history of the Church, including covenant theology, the doctrine of election, various aspects of Christology, and eschatology.

If in the context of atonement theology we take 'modern' to mean engaging seriously with the problems posed by moral, philosophical, and reductive critiques in recent centuries, then Schleiermacher and Barth represent two different ways of being modern. Schleiermacher provides a robust account that avoids many of the problems of rational coherence and violence raised before and after him by thinkers like Blount, Girard, and feminist critics. But he does so largely at the expense of traditional—and, to some degree, biblical—concepts that view Jesus' death on the cross as a divine response to divine wrath. Although Schleiermacher does make a case for the significance of the cross, in the end 'The climax of [Jesus'] suffering . . . was sympathy with misery' (Schleiermacher 1999: 436). It is Jesus' 'God-consciousness' and his 'unclouded blessedness' that are salvific; the cross is a consequence of these, but, it is not strictly necessary to them. A critique is that this cannot be completely squared with the language of atonement as vicarious sacrifice that, while by no means the only biblical conception of salvation, is nevertheless 'central to the Pauline tradition, to First Peter, Hebrews, First John, and Revelation' (Finlan: 2005: 120), as well as the cultic and ransom imagery that appears in the gospels. For a scriptural religious tradition, this is a serious price to pay.

Barth's approach is 'modern' in a rather different way. He is much more aware than Schleiermacher of the key problem with 'subjective' accounts: that in anchoring the atonement to its subjective effects such models are vulnerable to being interpreted as finally reducible to those effects, and therefore as not actually theological but psychological or sociological. His concept of revelation can be seen as a sophisticated defensive strategy for outmaneuvering reductive critiques. But even Barth's approach does not completely succeed in this regard. Despite his protests to the contrary, his strategy can tend towards a dangerous sort of conceptual abstraction. While Schleiermacher learns about God's involvement in the world by drawing quite explicitly on Christian experience, in time, through a concrete chain of believers going back to the historical Christ, Barth is more conceptual, inferring about Christian experience from the revelation of Jesus Christ, who is for him always the 'true man' and therefore the only meaningful index of what it means to be human (§43 and §44 in *CD* III/2 (Barth 1960)). Barth's ceaseless reorientation of theology to his concept of 'Jesus Christ' risks making the latter a kind of 'object' in Feuerbach's sense—a theological cipher on which to project whatever your system needs it to be. An important question to be asked, then, is whether in certain respects even Barth's achievement might be, in Feuerbach's terms, a 'metaphysics' that is in part 'resolvable into psychology'.

Retrieving Alternative Models of Salvation

Two further plausible candidates have been discussed in recent years as alternatives to substitutionary and judicial approaches. In his classic early twentieth-century work *Christus Victor*, Gustaf Aulén proposes the retrieval of a third approach to the atonement (contrasted with 'satisfaction' and 'moral' models). This 'Christus Victor' model emphasizes biblical imagery of salvation as the 'victory' of Jesus over the many powers that oppose God, including sin, death, and the devil, and understands the cross as a key battleground in this victory. Aulén argues that this model in various forms was the dominant one in the patristic period, and that 'satisfaction' models should therefore be viewed as an innovation rather than as the traditional view (Aulén 2010: 6). Although his book overstates its historical case, there is no question that the 'victor' model has strong biblical and patristic support, at the very least as one of several key New Testament metaphors, and it has had a wide influence.

This model became all the more significant in the wake of the rise of Pentecostalism in global Christianity in the twentieth and twenty-first centuries, with its emphasis on physical healing and its serious consideration of supernatural powers and principalities as day-to-day forces in the world. Most Pentecostals and charismatics hold, either formally or informally, to a two-pronged soteriology that places emphasis both on the forgiveness of sins (satisfaction) and on the 'continuous' (Aulén 2010: 5) and eschato-logically-grounded power of Jesus, through the Holy Spirit, for victory over sin, sickness, and forces of supernatural evil.

The second development to note is the return to prominence of models that understand salvation as incorporation, through Christ, into the triune divine life, through a process described variously as 'participation', 'union with Christ', or, drawing on the Orthodox tradition, *theosis* or divinization. These approaches have a clear biblical pedigree, often overlooked in a Protestant-dominated European biblical studies tradition. They also overcome, it is argued, a number of the problems associated with forensic and substitutionary models, particularly the classic 'intra-Christian' critique that judicial models constitute a 'legal fiction', and the perennial challenge in Protestant theology in rendering a fully plausible account of sanctification in light of a radical concept of justification. Paul Fiddes has argued that, by the first decade of the twenty-first century, such models had taken 'a central place in all modern systematic theology', both eastern and western (Fiddes 2007: 176), and become the new baseline for accounts of salvation, at least in academic theology.

A particular strength of such models is their ecumenical character in a period exhausted by long-dominant Protestant forensic categories. Participation is an old theme in Catholic and Orthodox accounts of salvation, but can also be construed, it is argued, in a more or less 'Augustinian' fashion accessible to traditional Protestant concerns over semi-Pelagianism and the misleading connotations of terms like 'deification'. They also map particularly well on to catholic-oriented sacramentologies. At the same time, Andrew Louth has pointed out that the versions of *theosis* taken on by ecumenical Protestants are often somewhat anaemic and vague: true *theosis* in the Orthodox tradition is at one level 'something beyond our human powers', but 'on the other hand...involves the most profound commitment of human powers; it is not a change in which we will be passively put right...[I]t is a change that requires our utmost cooperation, that calls for truly ascetic struggle' (Louth 2007: 37).

The trend towards soteriologies of participation and divinization has often been beset by failures to define exactly what is meant by such wide-ranging terms (Hallonsten 2007: 281, 286). If they are to continue to prove productive in the long term for modern Christian atonement discussion, proponents will need to address more concretely their own 'Feuerbach' problem: that their vague and highly metaphysical character may make such approaches as vulnerable to reductive psychological critique as substitutionary and sacrificial models.

VI. CONCLUSION

Some observations can be made at this stage about the story of the atonement and modern European thought, and the ongoing creative tension it illustrates between the ancient Christian tradition and the insights of intellectual inquiry outside of it.

The first is to underline the substantial divide between much academic theology and the beliefs and practices of the world's lay Christians. It is remarkable that a huge number of the world's Christians, particularly in Protestant and charismatic traditions, continue to recognize themselves far more in the experiences of Francke and Wesley from the late seventeenth and early eighteenth centuries than in the accounts provided by mainstream academic theology, where there has long been widespread discomfort with retributive and forensic models.

The new wrinkle in the twenty-first century is that the majority of the world's Christians now live outside of Europe and the west, in areas where theological education is often still in its infancy. It is to be hoped that these new Christian expressions—in China, Africa, Latin America, and in charismatic and Pentecostal churches the world over—will contribute creatively to understanding of the atonement. But it may be that in the near term the shift of Christianity's centre of gravity away from Europe will only further widen the academic/lay divide.

The second observation has to do with the old problem of connecting the 'objective' and the 'subjective' in soteriology. This issue has been put on a new and stimulating, but also potentially explosive footing through the increasing sophistication of reductive and scientific accounts of religion. This is particularly true for the 'subjective' side of soteriology, with its therapeutic engagement with problems like guilt feelings, depression, and isolation from communities.

Catholic and Orthodox traditions have tended in their different ways to bridge the objective/subjective divide by emphasizing Christian *practice* (prayer, the sacraments, penitential and mystical practices, spiritual disciplines). This in turn is anchored in a powerful but flexible—even underdetermined—soteriological apparatus of participation and *theosis*. Their real success here helps explain recent Protestant renewal of interest in these themes.

Protestant traditions are often thought to be less successful at aligning what is happening *coram deo* and *coram hominibus*. As we have seen, this is only partly true—preaching of judicial models of the atonement in fact often maps quite closely to particular affective and embodied experiences, however temporary. The reason for Protestantism's reputation in this area has in part to do with the failure of the traditional categories to do full justice to the very experiences that gave rise to them. Dualisms like justification/sanctification and faith/works have proven somewhat limited in capturing the full range of what is happening in an experience like Francke's—or, indeed, Luther's. They need to be supplemented through further work on theological categories that can mediate between them, such as the doctrine of the Holy Spirit or the role of the affections in theological anthropology.

The increasing success of reductive interpretations raises new versions of old questions. Perhaps the most interesting is whether and to what degree it is possible to describe the 'subjective' consequences, whether of 'participation' or 'union with Christ' or 'conversion experiences', in terms of contemporary psychology or biology or neuroscience. Is it that particular emotions or emotional patterns are being changed? Are unhealthy childhood attachment schemas being refocused? Are cognitive structures and patterns being rewired, as they might be in cognitive behavioural therapy? Or, as in the Lutheran tradition, is very little long-term change in fact taking place after all? Finally, and crucially, to what degree and in what way are there metaphysical realities here that cannot be completely mapped in psychological or neuroscientific terms? What of the fact that reductive interpretations of experiences are almost never convincing to those actually experiencing them? If it does not wish to concede the field completely to Feuerbach, atonement theology will need to continue to provide constructive answers to these questions.

References

Aulén, Gustaf (2010). *Christus Victor: An Historical Study of the Three Main Types of the Idea of the Atonement.* (London: SPCK Classics).

Barth, Karl (1956). *Church Dogmatics,* IV:1. (Edinburgh: T & T Clark).

——(1957). *Church Dogmatics,* II:2. (Edinburgh: T. & T. Clark).

——(1960). *Church Dogmatics,* III:2. (Edinburgh: T. & T. Clark).

——(1961). *Church Dogmatics,* IV:3.1. (Edinburgh: T. & T. Clark).

Blount, Charles (1995). *The Oracles of Reason.* (London: Routledge/Thoemmes).

Boyer, Pascal (2001). *Religion Explained: The Evolutionary Origins of Religious Thought.* (New York: Basic Books).

Brown, Joanne Carlson, and Parker, Rebecca (1989). 'For God So Loved the World?', in Brown and Bohn (eds), *Christianity, Patriarchy and Abuse: A Feminist Critique.* (Cleveland: Pilgrim), 1–30.

Buckley, Michael J. (1987). *At the Origins of Modern Atheism.* (New Haven, CT: Yale University Press).

Bushnell, Horace (1984). *Horace Bushnell: Selected Writings on Language, Religion, and American Culture,* ed. David L. Smith (Chico, CA: Scholars Press).

Byrne, James (1996). *Glory, Jest and Riddle: Religious Thought in the Enlightenment.* (London: SCM Press).

Dillistone, F. W. (1984). *The Christian Understanding of Atonement.* (London: SCM Press).

Feuerbach, Ludwig (1957). *The Essence of Christianity.* (New York: Harper and Brothers).

Fiddes, Paul (2007). 'Salvation', in John Webster, Kathryn Tanner, and Iain Torrance (eds), *The Oxford Handbook of Systematic Theology.* (Oxford: Oxford University Press), 176–96.

Finlan, Stephen (2005). *Problems with Atonement: The Origins of, and Controversy about, the Atonement Doctrine.* (Collegeville, MN: Liturgical Press).

Francke, August Hermann (1983). 'Autobiography', in Peter C. Erb (ed.), *The Pietists: Selected Writings.* (New York: Paulist Press), 99–107.

Freud, Sigmund (1961a). *Civilization and Its Discontents.* (New York: W.W. Norton).

——(1961b). *The Ego and the Id.* (New York: W. W. Norton).

——(1961c). *The Future of an Illusion.* (New York: W.W. Norton).

Girard, René (1977). *Violence and the Sacred.* (Baltimore and London: Johns Hopkins University Press).

——(1987). *Things Hidden since the Foundation of the World.* (London: Athlone Press).

Gorringe, Timothy (1996). *God's Just Vengeance: Crime, Violence and the Rhetoric of Salvation.* (Cambridge: Cambridge University Press).

Gunton, Colin (1998). *The Actuality of Atonement: A Study of Metaphor, Rationality and the Christian Tradition.* (London: T. & T. Clark).

Hallonsten, Gösta (2007). 'Theosis in Recent Research: A Renewal of Interest and Need for Clarity', in Christensen and Wittung (eds), *Partakers of the Divine Nature.* (Grand Rapids, MI: Baker Academic), 281–93.

Louth, Andrew (2007). 'The Place of *Theosis* in Orthodox Theology', in Christensen and Wittung (eds), *Partakers of the Divine Nature.* (Grand Rapids, MI: Baker Academic), 32–44.

Melanchthon, Philipp (2000). 'Apology of the Augsburg Confession', in Robert Kolb and Timothy J. Wengert (eds), *The Book of Concord.* (Minneapolis: Fortress), 109–294.

Redwood, J. A. (1974). 'Charles Blount (1654–93), Deism, and English Free Thought', *Journal of the History of Ideas* 35: 490–8.

Schleiermacher, Friedrich (1999). *The Christian Faith.* (Edinburgh: T. & T. Clark).

Taylor, Charles (2007). *A Secular Age.* (Cambridge, MA: Harvard University Press).

Wesley, John (1987). *The Journal of John Wesley: A Selection*, ed. Elisabeth Jay (Oxford: Oxford University Press, 1987).

SUGGESTED READING

Aulén (2010 [1931]).

Balthasar, Hans Urs von (1990). *Mysterium Paschale: The Mystery of Easter.* (Edinburgh: T. & T. Clark).

Barth (1956).

Boyer (2001).

Christensen, Michael J. and Wittung, Jeffery A. (eds) (2007). *Partakers of the Divine Nature.* (Grand Rapids, MI: Baker Academic).

Davidson, Ivor J. and Rae, Murray A. (eds) (2011). *God of Salvation: Soteriology in Theological Perspective.* (Farnham: Ashgate).

Davis, Stephen T., Kendall, Daniel, and O'Collins, Gerald (eds) (2004). *The Redemption: An Interdisciplinary Symposium on Christ as Redeemer.* (Oxford: Oxford University Press).

Dillistone (1984).

Feuerbach (1957 [1854]).

Finlan (2005).

Weber, Otto (1983). 'Reconciliation', *Foundations of Dogmatics*, vol. 2. (Grand Rapids, MI: Eerdmans), 177–226.

CHAPTER 31

....

DIVINE PROVIDENCE

....

DAVID FERGUSSON

THIS chapter argues that the traditional Christian account of providence underwent significant modifications during the early modern period, particularly as a result of deism. The effect of this, however, was not its disappearance but its refraction in more secular contexts. Two of these are selected for attention—imperial expansion and market economics. Here we find the discourse of providence being utilized in ways that are significant yet problematic. These continue to owe a debt, even when undeclared, to the theological traditions of the Church but in important respects they have become detached from scriptural traditions. In conclusion, it will be claimed that the perceived misuses of the idea of providence in modernity has left its theological articulation today in need of more careful and modest reconstruction.

I. THE STORY OF PROVIDENCE IN MODERNITY
....

Writing on providence in the final edition of the *Institutes* (1559), Calvin insists that the will of God governs every single event in the cosmos (Calvin 1960: 1: 17). Active rather than passive, the divine rule superintends each outcome directing it towards a wise and fitting end. So he cites Proverbs 16:4. 'God has made everything for its purpose, even the wicked for the day of trouble.' Each event thus has a fittingness in relation both to its immediate environment and in the overall accomplishment of God's primal decree. Anything else would render God idle, disengaged, or lacking a definite purpose and appropriate control of the created order. These alternatives are pagan notions that have to be excluded in maintaining a faithful account of the God of the Bible. While this yielded a doctrine of providence that was typically Reformed, Calvin believed himself merely to be stating what had already been taught by the Catholic Church. In the following century, the Reformed orthodox would struggle with notions of creaturely freedom and causal integrity (van Asselt 2010). Many of them offered quite subtle proposals within the parameters of this doctrine of providence, these often resisting some of the lazy caricatures that have been depicted. Nevertheless, their conviction remained that a divine purpose specified not only the general framework of the world but each event that occurred.

It is worth comparing this account of providence with the one that emerges in the deist thinking of the early modern period. Here the world is ordered by its divine creator, but this tends to reduce to a general pattern that provides the setting for the exercise of creaturely freedom. The divine imprint is evident in the order of nature, in the exercise of reason, the discernment of moral principles, and in the awareness of God and the worship that is required of us. The more particular or immediate instances of divine rule, however, either disappear or undergo significant modifications. The causes of this intellectual shift are multiple and include a prioritizing of philosophical reason, a loss of confidence in scripture to provide clear and distinct knowledge of God, scepticism around miracles as offering proofs of divine revelation, a preference for the natural over against the historical and a representation of Jesus primarily as a moral teacher.

Deism has had a notoriously bad press in theological circles. It is used rhetorically as a broad-brush term to dismiss positions that threaten to make divine existence otiose. God creates the world, it is claimed, but after this initial act of origination is altogether absent, remote, and irrelevant to its subsequent direction. In the border country between deism and atheism, there may have been some who held this position. It has been argued that this is the final resting place of Hume's *Dialogues concerning Natural Religion*, a philosophical work that is often taken as the classical expression of agnosticism. Nevertheless, deism took many different forms. Representing more a family of views than one single established position, it included many who believed themselves to be part of a Christian mainstream.

Part of the difficulty in assessing deism is the absence of leading primary and secondary sources. There is no one deist writer or text which stands above the rest and provides a *locus classicus* for the movement. Similarly, the body of secondary literature that has emerged is less than impressive and surprisingly meagre given the current interest in the early modern period. E. C. Mossner once wrote that,

> The deists were long subjected to the *odium theologicum*, and the historians of the movement have almost without exception downgraded or slandered them socially as well as intellectually since the time of John Lelan in the mid-eighteenth century. . . . Rarely have the achievements of deism been acknowledged and appreciated, and then only in passing, in brief comments from specialized monographs, articles and encyclopedia entries. No really satisfactory, complete, impartial, and scholarly account of the significance of the movement has as yet appeared. (Mossner 1967: 325)

There is little to suggest that this has changed in the generation since Mossner.

We should view deism as including a spectrum of views, one end of which is quite close to classical Christianity whereas at the other end it verges on a practical atheism.

In the second series of his Boyle Lectures (1705), Samuel Clarke distinguished four kinds of deist. a) Those who believe in God as infinitely powerful, all-knowing and perfectly good, the creator of the world who exercises providential control. This God has created us with moral and religious duties, and will ensure a future life of rewards and punishments. This deist accepts these truths not through revelation but through reason. b) A second kind of deist holds to these views but denies immortality and the afterlife. c) A third type of deist believes in God as creating and controlling the natural operations of the world but as lacking moral attributes and therefore being indifferent to human welfare. d) A fourth and even more minimalist doctrine ascribes to God only a creative action in the beginning. God gives the world its first impulse but thereafter does nothing. God is only the name of a first cause. Clarke claims with some plausibility that these types of deism drift away from scriptural claims about miracles, revelation and redemption. The first is most proximate, the last most distant.

The first type of deist identified by Clarke retains a lively belief in providence. William Wollaston's *The Religion of Nature Delineated* (1722) might be a good example of this—he remains committed to both general and particular providence but defends these as tenets of a natural or philosophical religion (Wollaston 1722: section V, ch. XVIII). Indeed the absence of other key articles ensured that greater stress was now placed upon providentialist notions. These became central to the self-understanding of the believer who continued to think and act as under God's direction. Yet the result of its transposition to this different setting is a significant alteration in the forms taken by providence. Several of these merit comment. It is assumed by much of deist thought (and here of course the deists were not alone) that divine providence is displayed in the moral order of the creation as this is apprehended through a natural and innate ethical sense. Moreover, compliance with this moral order is held to produce human happiness and flourishing. This leads to what Charles Taylor has called an 'anthropocentric' turn in providentialist thinking (Taylor 2007: 221). Calvin had seen the function of providence as leading us into a truer obedience and a glorifying of God in the Christian life. We are called primarily to honour God rather than to secure our personal salvation, although these are not unrelated. In this sense, his thought is theocentric rather than anthropocentric. But now it is assumed that what providence offers us is simply our own happiness, if only we abide by the dictates of our moral sense. Toland seems to have believed that God could do without our servile glorification, being content merely that we should follow the laws of morality for our own wellbeing. Indeed, it was the adoption of this view into his moral philosophy that led the eighteenth-century philosopher Francis Hutcheson into difficulties with the courts of the Church of Scotland, while also contributing significantly to the *Zeitgeist* of the Scottish Enlightenment. A further and related feature of this deist take on providence is its stronger secularism. The service of God is not to be offered in the spiritual life of cloistered worship, intense devotion, or fervent prayer so much as in the fulfilling of our duties to God, self and neighbour. The honouring of the deity in acts of worship may have had its place, but the hand of providence is also evinced in worldly pursuits. Again, this can be traced back to the Reformation with Luther's secularization of vocations but it now becomes increasingly foregrounded in the different political and intellectual landscape of the eighteenth century.

As a result of these developments, providence assumed a more this-worldly character. The secular realm has its own laws. These can be discovered by the practice of the natural sciences. Economic and political activity can be successfully pursued. Progress in human affairs under divine rule is possible. The world has a harmony, order, and structure which, when properly discerned, lead to human flourishing. This is the staple diet of much natural theology from Newton onwards. The regular law-governed character of the world is a mark of divine design, this extending to constitutive features of human nature and society. What is missing here is the earlier scriptural stress on sin, grace, and redemption. There are fewer signs of apocalyptic disjunction or of the foolishness of the cross in the dominant theologies of the period. As it is presently constituted, the world is the field of human flourishing. It is not depraved or in need of drastic reordering, or if this is recognized then it is more often as a minor note in an otherwise harmonious world view. The work of Christ is almost redundant, except his moral teaching which articulates what our natural knowledge may already have intuited. So Joseph Priestley later believed that he could extract from the gospels the purest and most sublime precepts that had been known (Priestley 1804). To be fair, many of the deists maintained a lively belief in the afterlife where God would reward earthly virtue and punish vice—many seemed to retain this as a form of social control. Yet this eschatology was not so much one of transforming creation but of concluding unfinished business. Its practical function was to maintain focus on the fulfilment of our earthly duties and the proper pursuit of our happiness.

Not surprisingly, this led to greater degrees of theological minimalism, even outright scepticism and atheism. In launching a counter-attack, theologians increasingly turned their attention to apologetic strategies by employing the design argument, claims about the transcendent source of the moral sense, and appeals to the historicity of miracles. As Michael Buckley has claimed, this merely conceded ground to the forces of unbelief by abandoning advocacy of the distinctive tenets of the Church and the Christian life (Buckley 1987). Theology became absorbed with apologetics and turned away from the transforming power of Jesus in the Christian life.

These patterns of thought characterized much Enlightenment thinking of the eighteenth century. Its exponents believed that they had history on their side. The wars of religion had hindered the progress of civilized life in the previous century. Fanaticism had led to a disproportionate significance being attached to minor doctrinal differences between groups of believers, sometimes at the cost of violence. Historical study of the Bible demanded a more discerning approach to its contents—the critical challenge posed by Spinoza and others could not simply be ignored. There was much in scripture that seemed a declension from the purer moral religion of the deists. The relegation of revealed theology was not merely the result of scruples about the Bible. General providence had bestowed a natural religion and ethics upon the human race as a whole. Divine revelation could not therefore be confined to a single historical episode that made sense of everything else, access to which was limited to a few. This egregious favouritism was unworthy of providence (Byrne 1989). The scientific and economic benefits of the age suggested that a better way had been found and one that could unite people of different confessional allegiance in common political pursuits. Provided some commitment to the Church and to the teaching of Jesus could be elicited, this might be sufficient for social cohesion, moral order, and the advance of Christian society.

This providentialism dominated the thinking of the Scottish Enlightenment, some of whose leading figures were suspected of deism. The standard theology of the moderate intellectuals at this time tended to follow lines already apparent in thinkers such as Hutcheson. The role of God as creator and sustainer of the world is emphasized. The signs of the divine presence are evident in the natural world; in this respect, the design argument is widely assumed to be valid. The beneficial function of religion in civil society is stressed. Religion contributes to social order and harmony. When purged of irrational fanaticism and intolerance, faith exercises a cohesive function through the moral direction and focus it offers human life. As benevolent and wise, God has ordered the world so that its moral and scientific laws contribute to human welfare. The prospect of an eschatological state, in which virtue and felicity coincide, provides further moral motivation.

The moderates had little interest in revisiting the doctrinal controversies of the previous century. Concentrating on creation and providence, their theology was less specific on the tenets of revealed theology. A pragmatic religion emerged that was preoccupied with the business of living well here and now. The Stoics were more important than early Christian writers in providing useful source material. Indeed, as Alexander Broadie has shown, it may have been part of God's providential purpose that, for the sake of the practical concerns of life, human beings are given only such knowledge as is sufficient to that end. This appears to have been the default position of thinkers such as Thomas Reid (1710–96) and Hugh Blair (1718–1800), both ministers of the Kirk. Reid's philosophy is remarkable in that he says so little about theology, yet in his epistemology and moral theory the providential purposes of God are everywhere assumed. In his study of Reid, Nicholas Wolterstorff has pointed to the ways in which he stresses the epistemological restrictedness of our human condition (Wolterstorff 2001: 250ff.; see also Wolterstorff 2004). This awareness of the limits of knowledge produces a distinctive form of piety. By attending to what we can know, we are able to live 'wisely in the darkness'. For Reid, this is divinely ordered. We are enabled by the Creator to act in ways that lead fulfilled and useful lives. Blair's famous sermon on 'seeing through a glass darkly' makes a practical virtue out of an epistemological necessity. Although 'we are strangers in the universe of God', this is fitting. Had God equipped us with too keen a vision of transcendent realities, we would likely have been incapacitated for the tasks to which we are called here and now. While a characteristic moderate theme, this also resonates with the earlier Reformed theological stress on the limitations of human reason before the mystery of God (Broadie 2001: 146ff.). Blair's sermons ran to numerous editions throughout the nineteenth century and were translated into German by Schleiermacher.

Yet, despite its genuine piety, we can detect here a drift away from scriptural sources in the more rationalist type of theism that emerges after the early modern period. The providentialism that is presented seems more self-confident and complacent than anything we find in the Bible where a greater measure of patience and struggle are found alongside elements of surprise and grace. Themes of struggle, resistance, and covenant partnership are increasingly detached from the philosophical justification offered of evil. These tend to revolve around notions of pedagogical or instrumental efficacy in so far as evils are the necessary condition of human flourishing and progress. With the slippage from earlier scriptural and doctrinal themes, it is not surprising that ideas of providences undergo a secular replacement. These persist but are now located in altered contexts and put to different work. The following two examples illustrate this.

II. IMPERIAL EXPANSION

William Robertson (1721–93) was Principal of the University of Edinburgh and leader of the moderate party in the Church of Scotland. As an Enlightenment scholar, he ranks alongside Hume, Gibbon, and Voltaire as among the leading European historians of the eighteenth century. His first published work already reveals a strong providential narrative of history, a theme that is later developed in detail in his acclaimed *History of America* (1777). Writing at the outset of his scholarly career, he repeats the ancient argument of Augustine and others that the Christian revelation was given to the world at a providential time. Under the conditions of the Roman Empire, it was able to spread rapidly and to counteract negative aspects of Judaism and paganism. 'Favoured by the union and tranquillity of the Roman empire, the disciples of Christ executed their commission to great advantage' (Robertson 1755: 14). Robertson describes the Christian commitment to marriage as mutual friendship rather than patriarchal ownership, and he criticizes the brutality of slavery in the Roman Empire. This is mitigated and counteracted by the equality of personhood and mildness of spirit which are the genius of Christianity. Robertson goes on to claim that, in the part of the world where Christianity has been received most fully, we can see the benefits it brings to the sciences as well as other improvements of power and reputation. This is Europe, and Robertson believes that the spread of its commerce, customs and political power is a further mark of divine providence, not least as this will also be accompanied by the wider transmission of the Christian faith. 'And tho' hitherto subservient to the designs of interest or ambition, may we not flatter ourselves, that, at last, they should become noble instruments in the hand of God, for preparing the world to receive the gospel?' (Robertson 1755: 43).

Robertson reflects the spirit of the age. British imperial expansion is seen as an expression of divine providence, continuous with the rise and spread of Christianity in the ancient world. On the other hand, his vision is measured and subtle in places. He abhors slavery and offers an account of marriage which stresses the equality of women and men. In writing of the native Americans in his *History of America*, he deplores the cruelty and greed of the Spanish conquistadores. The humanity and suffering of the native population are defended. On the other hand, he continues to judge in favour of the benefits that are brought to the Americas by European agriculture and commerce (Robertson 1777).[1]

Robertson's theological views are notoriously elusive. Although the leading Presbyterian clergyman of his day, he was suspected by some of harbouring deist leanings. There is less about original sin, predestination, the atoning work of Christ, and the order of salvation in the life of the believer than one finds in the Reformed orthodoxy of the previous century. Nevertheless, he stays in touch with many important features of that tradition. The Church remains a powerful institution for Robertson and one that is vital to the moral fabric of society. Without its influence and restraining powers, civil society would quickly degenerate. Nevertheless, there may also be a revisionary quality to Robertson's work that adumbrates later theological developments. At the end of his life, he was working on a history of India. Its ancient civilization fascinated him and he expresses admiration for the scholarship and thought of the Brahmins, comparing them to the Stoics (Phillipson 1997). The capacity of Hindu polytheism and Islam to coexist likewise impressed him. He quotes a letter advocating an accommodation of Hindus, Christians, and Muslims as necessary to the future prosperity of India. Perhaps for this reason, his critics suspected that he was not fully committed to the evangelizing of that region. Discussing the reception of Robertson's history of India, Nicholas Phillipson has suggested that there may be 'hints here of the seeds of a new religion, pluralistic, united by a common stoic ethics and a belief in toleration, a religion absorbing all creeds and denominations' (Phillipson 1997: 73).

All this shows the subtlety and complexity of the leading Christian thinkers of the Enlightenment. Their work pulls in different directions and cannot easily be enlisted without caricature to one ideological perspective. Nevertheless, shorn of key classical elements, the theology of providential history in Robertson informs and constructs a narrative of progress that is very much to the advantage of the project of European expansion. It is neither unequivocally supportive nor lacking in moral discrimination, yet it invests European culture with a value by comparison with which other parts of the world are seen as backward, savage, and primitive, albeit with some qualification. In need of the enlightenment that has emerged in Europe, their societies will inevitably benefit from a process of colonization. Robertson of course remains alert to the older theological traditions and practices that he is self-consciously revising. Affirming the moral and social cohesion created by religion, he is a strong supporter of the establishment of the Church of Scotland while also in favour of extending greater toleration to Roman Catholics. The moral texture of society is given close attention (as it is in Adam Smith) and, like other moderate thinkers, Robertson is committed to a programme of

---

[1] For further discussion, see Brown 1997.

national virtue that is advanced not only by scholars and politicians but also by preachers. Richard Sher has pointed to the way in which the rhetorical device of the 'jeremiad' is brilliantly adapted by moderate preachers such as Blair and Carlyle (Sher 1985: 207–12). With echoes of the covenanting sermons of the seventeenth century, they castigate their congregations for moral laxity, greed, and selfishness. Fast days are called at times of national crisis, especially during the American War of Independence. Their sermons urge repentance and a return to the ways of true religion. Within this preaching, the discourse of 'providence' is again marked. There is a sense in which God has particularly blessed the people of Scotland (and Britain) although this is combined with a lament about backsliding and a call for acts of penance and reform. In all this, the secular and anthropocentric turn in the doctrine of providence remains allied to a strong moderate theology.[2]

Immanuel Kant's political writings provide further illustration of the refraction of providential themes. The 'Idea for a Universal History with a Cosmopolitan Aim' (1784) offers a philosophical account of history in which the base and selfish aims of human beings in society bring about a rational political constitution in which these are over-ruled. In this essay, he makes his famous remark about the 'crooked wood' of humanity from which nothing entirely straight can be made (Kant: 2007: 108–20). Yet the exhausting and destructive effects of conflict eventually persuade human persons of the worth of a better political order. Through suffering the ill effects of our 'unsociable sociability', we are constrained to acknowledge to assent to the rule of law. Similarly, even the just political state will find itself in conflict with rival states in the international arena. Yet although the selfish drives of individuals are writ large in competition and wars, in the course of time these too will yield to the establishment of a more just cosmopolitan order. One sentence of Kant will suffice here.

> Finally war itself will gradually become not only an enterprise so artificial, and its outcome on both sides so uncertain, but also the aftereffects which the state suffers through an ever-increasing burden of debt (a new invention), whose repayment becomes unending, will become so dubious an undertaking, and the influence of every shake-up in a state in our part of the world on all other states, all of whose trades are to very much chained together, will be so noticeable, that these states will be urged merely through danger to themselves to offer themselves, even without legal standing, as arbiters, and thus remotely prepare the way for a future large state body, of which the past world has no example to show.   (Kant: 2007: 117–18)

Kant's hope for a rational cosmopolitan order is based on a conviction that, despite the unsociable and selfish tendencies of human beings, there is a capacity latent within nature to produce a greater good. Although this emerges in spite of our individual

---

[2] This is evident, for example, in Blair's Fast Day Sermon at the outbreak of war in 1793. 'We have reason to respect those rulers, under whose administration the empire, though engaged in an expensive and hazardous war, has all along continued to hold a high rank among the nations of Europe, and has attained to that flourishing state of commerce, opulence and safety, in which we behold it at this day' (Blair 1808: 138).

actions, we are capable of assenting to it rationally. The traumas of war and the benefits of trade will tend to ensure that, through selfish means, a greater common good will naturally emerge. Kant's view of organic development appears indebted to Stoic notions of a natural law unfolding everywhere in the cosmos. This organic order manifests itself through the actions of individual agents, which from a more particular perspective would otherwise appear base and irrational. In describing how this occurs in world history, Kant seems to be distancing himself from Rousseau's account where individual goals have to be deliberately suppressed to achieve a common good.

Genevieve Lloyd regards Kant's vision of world history as a secularized version of Augustine's providential account of the city of God (Lloyd 2009). The principal difference is that the earthly city is the exclusive focus of Kant's attention—it is the only arena in which providence is now manifested. This providence, moreover, is the result of the outworking of natural laws rather than a future fashioned by the redeeming work of Christ. There are echoes of Leibniz and Rousseau in much of Kant's essay, although he seems more focused than either of his predecessors on the actual outcomes of world history. Whether Kant intended to present the cosmopolitan ideal as an imminent historical probability or a more regulative ideal is not entirely clear, but the redirection of the idea of providence to international relations governed by organic processes of development is evident.

The natural forces of human history lend themselves to the eventual establishment of a cosmopolitan world order. Under such a regime, our more rational and moral capacities will be developed. This is not to be equated so much with happiness as with the cultivation of what makes us distinctly personal. There are threads in Kant's writing which are also discernible in Robertson. The narrative of progress may be qualified in important respects—in particular, given the genuine openness of our free choices, the exact course of history appears to be indeterminate and unpredictable—but in general it seems to support some form of European expansionism. Here again Kant's position is ambivalent. He deplores conquest by force—the ends of civilization cannot justify the means of coercion—while his stress on the respect to be accorded each human person provides a powerful argument against enslavement. On the other hand, he maintains a troubling silence on the matter of chattel slavery despite having the resources to attack it. Moreover, in his writings on race, Kant assumes that in some racial groups the development of human potential has been greater than in others. This results in a privileging of white Europeans which is narrowed to further developments within Europe itself. Much of this is typical of Enlightenment thinkers, although no less objectionable for that reason. But what is significant in this context is the implicit notion that providence seems to have ordained the hegemony of a particular type of civilization in which distinctive human capacities have been developed. This is most evident in the notorious claim that there is a hierarchy of racial characteristics with the greatest perfections being confined to 'the white race'. Kant's account in his lectures on physical geography is typical: 'Humanity is at its greatest perfection in the race of the whites. The yellow Indians do have a meagre talent. The Negroes are far below them and at the lowest point are a part of the American peoples' (Eze 1997: 63). Kant's views on race have been interpreted in a variety of ways (Bernasconi 2002; Louden 2011: 131–5); it has even been argued that the racialized subject in Kant becomes a theological construct (Carter 2008: 8off.).

The dangers in this providential construction of political events and systems are manifold. The exceptionalism that often accompanies forms of civil religion (and not only in large nations and empires) can have the effect of over-riding the competing claims of other nations and political groups when these clash. There is little New Testament warrant for concluding that the gospel might be advanced by the peculiar singling out of one nation state, race, or empire as its vehicle. Yet many of the arguments advanced in favour of imperial expansion from the sixteenth century revolve around the notion that Europeans served a divinely ordained purpose by colonizing other parts of the world. Two arguments in particular recur in variant forms, particularly in the Americas. These appeal to the twin notions of the empty and the promised land. In the case of the former, the ancient Roman legal principle of *res nullius* was cited. Empty things may be considered common property. If a land is largely vacant or only sparsely populated, settlers from other parts have a right of occupation and a duty of development (Pagden 1995: 76ff.). This was reinforced by the further claim that if native inhabitants came into conflict with such occupation then they could be assimilated or improved. Since it would be in their interests to do so, one could even assume tacit assent on the (spurious) ground that if were they able to make an informed choice then they would surely choose to do so. This reasoning was buttressed by the further argument that in the event of outright opposition, enforced conquest might be justified by the precedent of the Israelite occupation of Canaan. While not forming a systematic corpus, these arguments recur in haphazard ways over several centuries and provide something like a Christian ideology for imperial expansion. At the same time, dissenting voices were also raised, most notably Bartholomé de las Casas who argued on theological grounds against the subjugation and slaughter of native Americans. But the drift of political ideologies drawing upon theological claims is clear.[3]

One might seek to overcome this sort of particularism and its attendant partiality, by viewing the whole of history as moving forwards under some divine influence. But this would be done in such a way that each of its constituent parts makes a contribution to the whole, so that none is selected at the expense of the other. The weak and the strong, the righteous and the unrighteous, the successful and the unlucky would all be gathered into a single movement which collectively leads to the realization of some overarching scheme. Divine providence would here over-rule all nations and empires in working out a single purpose. This might be a kind of historicized version of Leibniz's theodicy in which each particular make its distinctive contribution to an overall harmony and in which its identity is realized only in relation to everything else. It is of course in Hegel's philosophy of history that something resembling this appears. Here it is the global

---

[3] The fusion of empty land and promised land motifs in relation to the native Americans is expertly documented in Cave 1988.

function of providence that is set out. God's spirit directs the particular events and actors of history with an 'absolute cunning'. Each contributes in some way to an emergent whole which cannot be understood except, if at all, with the benefit of hindsight. It is not that this is a meaning imposed deterministically in a top-down manner. By contrast, it is a pattern that emerges on the 'slaughter bench of history' through the evils, self-interest, and violence of human affairs. Hegel employs a fabric metaphor by which the interweaving of the idea of God within the passions of history brings about a realization of divine consciousness in human freedom (Hodgson 1989: 118ff.). Although there are similarities with Kant's providentialism, Hegel is more cautious in one important respect. The idea of progress does not appear to have the same regulative function in his philosophy precisely because this is discernible only with the benefit of hindsight. It is backward rather than forward looking. An instant reading of meaning into history, whether of individuals or nations, is generally disparaged by Hegel. Only in retrospect can we discern a meaning amid the historical processes we inhabit. Progress is neither smooth nor unilateral.

> When philosophy paints its grey on grey, then has a shape of life grown old. By philosophy's grey on grey it cannot be rejuvenated but only understood. The owl of Minerva spreads its wings only with the falling of the dusk.   (Hegel 1952: 13.)

While Hegel's position has unfairly been castigated for the promotion of a bland optimism, nevertheless there remains the same sense of an immanent purpose within world history which closely resembles this secularizing or raising to a speculative register of older ideas of divine providence.

The writings of great historians and philosophers are usually nuanced and qualified, offering different strands of thought each of which can lead in a particular direction. Hence to claim that Robertson and Kant simply offered a carte blanche for European imperial expansion and the imposition of Enlightenment values would be to distort the subtlety of their thought and its capacity for self-criticism and the challenging of regnant assumptions. Nevertheless, there does seem to be a clear link between the providential historicism of Enlightenment thinkers and the imperial projects of the eighteenth and nineteenth centuries.

Much of the British imperial drive through the nineteenth century was fuelled by the conviction that this was a divinely-appointed mission and one which rendered an important service to other parts of the world. Religion not only promoted internal civic life but legitimized imperial expansion, much of the appeal being again to divine providence. Wilberforce, the evangelical reformer and leading abolitionist, argued that the opening of India to the imperial venture was itself providentially organized. The renewal of the East India Company charter in 1813 enabled Wilberforce and the Clapham sect to campaign for the insertion of the so-called 'pious clause' in the parliamentary act which required formal support for Christian mission in the sub-continent. Petitions were submitted to parliament. These had amassed almost half a million signatures, much of the supporting campaign drawing heavily upon notions of divine providence. Robert Hall, a Baptist minister, claimed that 'our acquisition of power has been so rapid, so extensive, and so disproportionate to the limits of our native empire, that there are few events in which the interposition of Providence may be more distinctly traced.' The *Evangelical Magazine* of May 1813 could even claim that 'in the course of Providence, Britain is become mistress of the East' (Brown 2008: 37).

III. FREE TRADE

Alongside arguments for imperial expansion in the eighteenth century, we can discern related but different claims for the value of trading under free market conditions. Here considerations were advanced that appealed to a similar 'cunning of reason'. By engaging for private ends in commercial transactions, individuals contributed unwittingly to a wider public good. This was already recognized by thinkers such as Mandeville and Butler but its classical expression is found in Adam Smith's notion of the 'invisible hand', an image evocative of providential themes once again transposed into a secular context.

Writing in *The Wealth of Nations* (1776), Smith notes the ways in which the pursuit of private commercial ends by a variety of individual agents can result in an overall benefit to the common good. Human acquisitiveness is thus turned to the advantage of all by the working of laws of economic generation. This is a sign of the operation of an 'invisible hand'.

> By preferring the support of domestic to that of foreign industry he intends only his own security; and by directing that industry in such a manner as its produce may be of greatest value, he intends only his own gain, and he is in this, as in many other cases, led by an invisible hand to promote an end which was no part of his intention . . . by pursuing his own interest he frequently promotes that of the society more effectually than when he really intends to promote it. I have never known much good to be done by those who affected to trade for the public good.[4]

Critics are divided over the extent to which Smith implies a theological context for this invisible hand. Secular commentators have tended to insist that it is merely a metaphor for the natural mechanism of equilibrium in competitive markets. All we have are efficient causes that happen to function in an orderly manner. In this way, Smith is closely aligned to the naturalism of Hume. Other critics see this as a modern eisegesis that fails to take sufficient account of the implicit theology of his *Theory of Moral Sentiments*. The removal of any hidden superintendence of economic processes is itself ideologically driven by the belief that the economy does best without external management.

---

[4] Adam Smith, *The Wealth of Nations*, 456.

There are varied and contradictory interpretations of the meaning of the 'invisible hand' (Martin 1990; Rothschild 1994; Smith 2006: 82–4). What is clear, however, is that the image of the invisible hand is redolent on theories of divine providence. This is entirely consistent with understanding that hand to work through the medium of natural economic forces. The philosophers of the Enlightenment typically saw the hand of providence in the arrangement of the natural world. In promoting our prosperity, the constitution of human nature and society could be seen as benevolently designed by God. Moreover, in deploying this Smithian notion, later thinkers were inclined to attribute to market forces a quasi-sacral function (Macleod 2007: 103–17). Given free rein, these could be relied upon to bring about beneficial outcomes. To interfere with them is to violate a natural order. In writings of early nineteenth-century political economists, these Smithian arguments were aligned with more distinctively theological commitments than we find in Smith himself. Thomas Chalmers, for example, believed that one beneficial effect of market forces was to promote self-reliance, improvement, and philanthropy in the social order. Writing in 1845, he states that 'in the philosophy of free trade, the essence of which consists in leaving this mechanism to its own spontaneous evolutions, (there is) a striking testimony to the superior intelligence of Him who is the author both of human nature and of human society' (Hilton 1985: 146).

This argument may be most cogent when directed against the inefficiencies and harmfulness of excessive state planning and control over the market. As it stands, however, it raises several problems about what is intended by self-interest and the good of society. Does it assume that economic agents will always narrowly pursue their selfish interests? How are these to be understood? And is the good of society to be measured in terms of total economic output, average incomes or levels of poverty? Aside from these questions, there are also important issues around the social, legal and moral conditions which are required for such transactions to take place in a transparent and equitable manner which commands the confidence of all parties.

A commitment to trading partnerships can conceivably be presented as an argument against the aforementioned project of imperial conquest. This is apparent from Hume's criticism of empires which overreach themselves, resulting in a multitude of deleterious consequences. A supporter of American independence, he deplores the conquest and colonial rule of overseas territories, perceiving these to contain the seeds of their own downfall. By contrast, he argues for free trade amongst peoples as the means to promote material prosperity and forms of peaceful interaction (Hume 1996: 301–14).

Smith's own position on these questions is not always clear. For example, in *The Theory of Moral Sentiments*, his use of the invisible hand image appears to be directed to the observation that human acquisitiveness and ambition lead naturally to greater wealth for the poorest in society. It is a means for the improvement of the whole social order. Why is this? The generation of wealth by the most industrious and ambitious persons in society is likely to exceed their appetites. But, rather than condemn the pursuit of luxury as early civic humanists had done, Smith (and Hume) celebrate it as contributing to the benefit to all sectors of society, including the poorest. However implausible, the following passage makes this clear.

(The rich) consume little more than the poor, and in spite of their natural selfishness and rapacity, though they mean only their own conveniency, though the sole end which they propose from the labours of all the thousands whom they employ, be the gratification of their own vain and insatiable desires, they divide with the poor the produce of their achievements. They are led by an invisible hand to make nearly the same distribution of the necessaries of life, which would have been made, had the earth been divided into equal portions among all its inhabitants, and thus without intending it, without knowing it, advance in the interest of the society, and afford means to the multiplication of the species. When Providence divided the earth among a few lordly masters, it neither forgot nor abandoned those who seemed to have been left out of the partition.   (Smith 2009: Part IV, ch. I, 215)

Smith's religious commitments seem minimal—biographers have struggled to discern where his true allegiance lies. Despite his early lectures on natural theology, he is reticent in his two principal publications about the resting place of his theological views. On the other hand, the Stoic influences upon his thought are unquestionable and much that appears in the *Theory of Moral Sentiments* has clear deist antecedents. Indeed it has recently been argued that there is a much greater theological influence upon Smith than has hitherto been recognized (Oslington 2011). What we are offered by Smith is something like a description of a world that is providentially ordered but without any sense of particular divine interpositions. Hence the onwards movement of human civilization is the outcome of laws of development that produce rising levels of prosperity and happiness, as well as the more increase of populations. This arises from many successful adaptations of nature in which particular actions or tendencies are harnessed in ways that serve the purpose of the whole. The phenomenon of sympathy moderates human interaction and yields beneficial levels of cooperation. The division of labour produces not just greater degrees of wealth but also contributes to technological development. 'The uncoordinated, self-regarding acts of individuals, ultimately form part of a wider beneficent pattern orchestrated by Providence and geared towards human happiness and material prosperity' (Hill 2001: 14).

What Smith shows by reference to this ordered pattern is that human moral and economic exchanges do not constitute a zero-sum game. The result of increased trading, manufacturing and the division of labour was not the wealth of a few but the wealth of nations. All the boats in the water can rise together as the tide flows. How far Smith actually perceived his theories to require a theology as their necessary condition is, for the moment, beside the point. What we see at work here is the socialization of a theory of general providence. There is an order to the moral and economic world that is beneficial. The intellectual antecedents of this view are in Reformed theology and its transposition in deism. Again this generates a further movement in which providentialist notions do not disappear but are increasingly refracted in a range of other disciplines. Smith's argument for the invisible hand is but one strand in his overall understanding of how society functions. What is sometimes missed is his recognition that economic transactions require relatively stable social and moral frameworks. These provide conditions of trust, honesty, and equity that ensure the regulation of economic relations. Our trading is facilitated by a social order than cannot be understand solely in terms of market relations between autonomous agents with acquisitive desires. Many exponents of Smith's economics in the nineteenth century recognized the importance of this wider context, particularly in relation to religious institutions and ends.

The clearest example of this is in the slogan 'commerce and Christianity' that was prominent from about 1840–60 (Stanley 1983: 71–94). It denoted the alliance between the interests of free trade and Christian mission which was justified in heavily providentialist language by exponents such as David Livingstone and Samuel Wilberforce. While the interests of free trade and Christian mission did not always coincide these were presented for a time as convergent, the latter capable of correcting the excesses of the former and investing it with great spiritual purpose. To justify this, the language of divine providence was once again invoked.

> Commerce . . . is a mighty machinery laid in the wants of man by the Almighty Creator of all things, to promote the intercourse and communion of one race with another, and especially of the more civilised races of the earth with the less civilised. . . . As this commerce must exist for the supply of the wants of man, it follows, I think, that Christian nations are bound to seek to impregnate commerce with their Christianity, and so to carry to the ends of the earth those blessings of religion which are the chiefest of all possessions.   (Wilberforce 1874: 176–7)

Several claims can be detected in passages such as this. God has not blessed the British Empire with such success for material ends alone. There is some greater purpose at work here. Christianity can most readily be communicated through the medium of other civilizing forces such as law, education, government, and free trade. Hence the promotion of free trade around the world will work in tandem with the spread of the gospel to other lands. These alliances may have proved temporary and not without their strains (Porter 1985). Sometimes the interests of commerce and Christianity could diverge, resulting in the former being viewed with suspicion by the latter. Yet the extension of a classical doctrine of providence to a secular context is again apparent as a key element of the ideological justification for spreading both commerce and Christianity at a time when these were seen as convergent ends. John Bowring, governor of Hong Kong, could even announce the startling equation that 'Jesus Christ is Free Trade and Free Trade is Jesus Christ' (Brown 2008: 145).

Much more recently, however, we have witnessed the secular isolation of 'invisible hand' arguments in which a surfeit of faith has been placed too exclusively on market forces, as if these possessed some quasi-magical function in producing widespread benefits for an entire society or international order. The theology of providence may have disappeared but a confidence in a spontaneous natural order appears to remain, as if it were a work of divine design. Such claims are a familiar element of current political discourse. Milton and Rose Friedman see Smith's 'flash of genius' as residing in his insight that economic order can emerge from the actions of many people seeking their own interest. Although unintended by individual agents, it is a natural outcome of their activity. Moreover, this pattern is extended from economics to other areas of human culture as part of a wider argument to restrict the role of government in interfering with these beneficial processes. 'A society's values, its culture, its social convention—all these develop in the same ways, through voluntary exchange, spontaneous cooperation, the evolution of a complex structure through trial and error, acceptance and rejection' (Friedman 1980: 26). This confidence in the market remains central to much political debate, particularly in the USA.

IV. Conclusion

Saint-Simon is said to have remarked on his deathbed that religion can never disappear from the world but only transform itself (Gentile 2001: 30). In terms of lending ideological support for imperialism and free market economics, the theology of providence has not so much disappeared as been transformed in secular contexts. Although one element only in the work of seminal thinkers, this has been privileged and even isolated in its subsequent reception, usually with damaging consequences. Nevertheless, it is not clear that there is a simple pathway of retrieval that can take us back to a purer account of providence. As we have seen, already in the early modern period arguments are being advanced for imperial conquest that anticipate later Enlightenment moves. Might the root of the problem already be latent within classical formulations of the theology of providence? As noted earlier, these attribute a divine control and wisdom to every single event in the cosmos, each lending itself indispensably to the outworking of a set of purposes. Every entity, force, and event has its purpose, these combining to achieve an overall *telos* which is divinely ordained. As scholars turned their attention to historiography and the social sciences, it is hardly surprising that providential notions would feature in more secular contexts. In seeking to understand progress in history and the laws governing social forces, writers were equally apt to discern divine foresight and design, just as they had done in the natural world. Arguments from design, which were so pervasive in the natural philosophy of the eighteenth and nineteenth centuries, had their inevitable counterparts in the fields of history and economics. There is a continuity of argument, theme, and conviction, which should caution us against a rewinding of the clock to an earlier century in order merely to rehabilitate the views of Augustine, Aquinas, or Calvin.

One theological lesson emerging from all this is the need for a more modest account of providence that neither overdetermines our capacity for discerning purpose and progress in history nor too readily identifies divine intention with historical and social forces which may be very ambivalent when ethically assessed. Hegel wrote with some scorn of 'peddling' views of providence that limited these to features of personal lives. But it may be time to revisit these and to learn again of the ways in which scripture attests a divine wrestling with a recalcitrant creation as well as the hiddenness of God's kingdom in quiet places and small beginnings. At the same time, the language of providence needs to be retained rather than discarded. Its misuses may have led to its demise from public discourse, and an over-reliance on general providence is to be avoided. Yet to discount the possibility of divine involvement in the secular might be at least as troublesome. We need to envisage possibilities within the socio-political realm for anticipating the reign of God attested by Jesus. Without this, the discourse of politics will itself became debased, theology having retreated altogether from the public domain. While providence should not too swiftly be read into or out of history, neither should it be eschewed altogether as a means of discerning divine involvement in the world.

References

Asselt, Willem J., van (ed.) (2010). *Reformed Thought on Freedom: The Concept of Free Choice in Early Modern Reformed Theology.*(Grand Rapids, MI: Baker).

Bernasconi, Robert (2002). 'Kant as an Unfamiliar Source of Racism', in Julie K. Ward and Tommy L. Lott (eds.), *Philosophers on Race: Critical Essays.* (Oxford: Blackwell), 145–66.

Blair, Hugh (1808). 'On the Love of our Country', *Sermons*, vol. v. (London: 1808).

Broadie, Alexander (2001). *The Scottish Enlightenment.* (Edinburgh: Birlinn).

Brown, Stewart J. (1997). 'William Robertson (1721–1793) and the Scottish Enlightenment', in Steward J. Brown (ed.), *William Robertson and the Expansion of Empire.* (Cambridge: Cambridge University Press), 7–35.

—— (ed.) (2008). *Providence and Empire 1815–1914.* (Harlow: Longman).

Buckley, Michael (1987). *At the Origins of Modern Atheism.* (New Haven, CT: Yale University Press).

Byrne, Peter (1989). *Natural Religion and the Nature of Religion.* (London: Routledge).

Calvin, Jean (1960). *Institutes of the Christian Religion*, ed. John T. McNeill (Philadelphia: Westminster).

Carter, J. Kameron (2008). *Race: A Theological Account.* (Oxford: Oxford University Press).

Cave, Alfred (1988). 'Canaanites in a Promised Land: The American Indian and the Providential Theory of Empire', *American Indian Quarterly* 12: 4, 277–97.

Eze, E. C (ed.) (1997). *Race and the Enlightenment: A Reader.* (Oxford: Blackwell).

Friedman, Milton and Rose (1980). *Free to Choose.* (London: Secker and Warburg).

Gentile, Emilio (2001). *Politics as Religion.* (Princeton, NJ: Princeton University Press).

Hegel, G. W. F. (1952). *Philosophy of Right*, trans. T. M. Knox (Oxford: Clarendon Press).

Hill, Lisa (2001). 'The Hidden Theology of Adam Smith', *European Journal of the History of Economic Thought* 8: 1, 1–29.

Hilton, Boyd (1985). 'Chalmers as Political Economist', in A. C. Cheyne (ed.), *The Practical and the Pious: Essays on Thomas Chalmers (1780–1847).* (Edinburgh: St Andrew Press), 141–56.

Hodgson, Peter (1989). *God in History: Shapes of Freedom.* (Nashville: Abingdon).

Hume, David (1996). 'The Idea of a Perfect Commonwealth', *Selected Essays.* (Oxford: Oxford University Press), 301–14.

Kant, Immanuel (2007). 'Idea for a Universal History with a Cosmopolitan Aim', *Anthropology, History and Education*, ed. Robert B. Louden and Guenther Zoeller (Cambridge: Cambridge University Press), 107–20.

Lloyd, Genevieve (2009). 'Providence as Progress: Kant's Variations on a Tale of Origins', in Amélie Oksenberg Rorty, and James Schmidts (eds), *Kant's Idea for a Universal History with a Cosmopolitan Aim: A Critical Guide*. (Cambridge: Cambridge University Press), 200–15.

Louden, Robert B. (2011). *Kant's Human Being: Essays on his Theory of Human Nature*. (Oxford: Oxford University Press).

Macleod, Alastair (2007). 'Invisible Hand Arguments: Milton Friedman and Adam Smith', *Journal of Scottish Philosophy* 5: 2, 103–17.

Martin, David (1990). 'Economics as Ideology: On Making "the Invisible Hand" Visible', *Review of Social Economy* 48: 1, 272–87.

Mossner, E. C. (1967). 'Deism,' in Paul Edwards (ed.), *Encyclopaedia of Philosophy*, Vols. 1–2. (New York: Macmillan), 326–36.

Oslington, Paul (2011). 'Divine Action, Providence and Adam Smith's Invisible Hand', in Paul Oslington (ed.), *Adam Smith as Theologian*. (London: Routledge), 61–76.

Pagden, Anthony (1995). *Lords of all the World: Ideologies of Empire in Spain, Britain and France c1500–c1800*. (New Haven, CT: Yale University Press).

Phillipson, Nicholas (1997). 'Providence and Progress: An Introduction to the Historical Thought of William Robertson', in Stewart J. Brown (ed.), *William Robertson and the Expansion of Empire*. (Cambridge: Cambridge University Press), 55–73.

Porter, Andrew (1985). 'Commerce and Christianity': The Rise and Fall of a Nineteenth-Century Missionary Slogan', *Historical Journal* 28: 3, 597–621.

Priestley, Joseph (1804). *The Life and Morals of Jesus.* (London).

Robertson, William (1755). *The Situation of the World at the Time of Christ's Appearance, and its Connexion with the Success of his Religion Considered*. (Edinburgh).

—— (1777). *History of America.* (Edinburgh).

Rothschild, Emma (1994). 'Adam Smith and the Invisible Hand', *The American Economic Review* 84: 2, 319–22.

Sher, Richard (1985). *Church and University in The Scottish Enlightenment: The Moderate Literati of Edinburgh*. (Edinburgh: Edinburgh University Press).

Smith, Adam (1999). *The Wealth of Nations*, Vol. II, Books IV–V. (London: Penguin).

—— (2009). *Theory of Moral Sentiments*, ed. R. P. Hawley (London: Penguin).

Smith, Craig (2006). *Adam Smith's Political Philosophy: The Invisible Hand and Spontaneous Order*. (London: Routledge).

Stanley, Brian (1983). 'Commerce and Christianity': Providence Theory, the Missionary Movement, and the Imperialism of Free Trade, 1842–1860', *Historical Journal* 26: 1, 71–94.

Taylor, Charles (2007). *A Secular Age.* (Boston: Harvard University Press).

Wilberforce, Samuel (1874). *Speeches on Missions.* (London).

Wollaston, William (1722). *The Religion of Nature Delineated.* (London: Knapton).

Wolterstorff, Nicholas (2001). *Thomas Reid and The Story of Epistemology.* (Cambridge: Cambridge University Press).

—— (2004). 'God and Darkness in Reid', in Joseph Houston (ed.), *Thomas Reid: Context, Influence, Significance*. (Edinburgh: Dunedin Academic Press), 77–102.

Suggested Reading

Asselt, van (2010).
Brown (2008).
Hodgson (1989).
Oslington (2011).
Sher (1985).

AFTERWORD

NICHOLAS ADAMS, GEORGE PATTISON, AND GRAHAM WARD

MODERNITY can be read in many different ways. Recently, the psychiatrist Iain McGilchrist has read modernity's project in terms of the dominance of the left hemisphere activity of the human brain.[1] While right hemisphere activity is closely associated with intuition, emotion, imagination, ambiguity, and believing, the left hemisphere is associated with reason, categorization, judgement, language, abstraction, and instrumentalization. It is a highly suggestive and much more subtle account of modernity than might appear from this all too brief sketch of its thesis. Nevertheless, the book points to the dangers of caricature that frequently beset synoptic accounts of modernity. Because this volume consists of a number of chapters by different authors and plots modernity thematically, then a rich and complex presentation of modernity and, in particular, the relationship between theology and modern thought, emerges. There is something highly consonant with modernity about this approach. In his extended 'Dedication' of *Minima Moralia: Reflections on Damaged Life*, Adorno extols the appropriateness of the fragment as a literary genre for modern thought as opposed to the system, even the book:

> the attempt to present aspects of our shared [Adorno and Horkheimer's] philosophy from the standpoint of subjective experience, necessitates that the parts do not altogether satisfy the demands of the philosophy of which they are nevertheless a part. The disconnected and non-binding character of the form, the renunciation of explicit theoretical cohesion, are meant as one expression of this.[2]

The experience of modernity demands appropriate forms: in literature, the essay and the aphorism; in art, cinema and the photograph. While not indulging in the aphoristic,

---

[1] (2010). *The Master and His Emissary: The Divided Brain and the Making of the Western World.* (New Haven: Yale University Press).

[2] Theodor Adorno (1974). *Minima Moralia: Reflections on Damaged Life*, trans. E. F. N. Jephcott (London: Verso), 18.

the essay form this volume adopts does share some continuity with its contents; if only because the *Handbook* as a genre requires it. As such, the book does much to make complex, and even discredit, characterizations of modernity in which the atomized individual is acclaimed above the corporate, reason above passion, mind above body, the instrumental above the ornamental, the mechanical above the organic, and the secular above the sacred. Modernity cannot be reduced to a set of hierarchically organised binarisms. That does indeed place a question mark at the end of Bruno Latour's polemic (mentioned in our Introduction) *We Have Never Been Modern*. But, in its turn, this raises even more profound questions about both 'modernity' as the characterization of a cultural epoch and the definition of cultural epochs as such.

The questions, put boldly, are: what is the degree of cohesion and distinctiveness necessary to characterize a cultural epoch and does 'modernity' display such a degree of cohesion and distinctiveness? In the Introduction we drew attention to the advent of discussion concerning both 'modernities' and 'postmodernity'. As late arrivals, these discourses open up the question of the future or even the end of 'modernity' as an adequate characterization of contemporary culture. Several of the chapters in this volume allude to different geographical, cultural, and linguistic inflexions of the modern. Other chapters also foreground the way in which modern thinkers, theologians, and artists made explicit reference to the past in ways that emphasized some continuity between, say, Hellenism and Romanticism, and the revival of the Gothic. Any number of cultural historians, working on the boundaries of what have been named distinctive cultural epochs prior to the modernity, the mediaeval and the Renaissance, have likewise emphasized intellectual continuities, influences, retrievals, and repristinations that run counter to the cohesive unity necessary to name a distinctive cultural epoch.[3]

And yet... this is a period in which three revolutions took place (the French, the Industrial, and the Russian); two major world wars were waged; empires waxed and waned (Napoleon's, the British, the Russian, and the American); colonies were seized and lost; cities were founded or considerably reshaped; a secularization of certain institutions and the public sphere more generally occurred; new technologies were invented; new scientific discoveries made; etc. Such events profoundly marked social experience and not just in Western Europe or fledgling North America. They fostered new philosophies and modes of thinking, new artistic movements, new forms of architecture and landscape, new figurations of the political, politics, and polity, new types of transport, and new opportunities for travel and communication. It is not difficult to point to what is new in modernities: the culture that produced Caravaggio and the culture that produced Cezanne are quite distinct in terms of the ways they thought about and experienced and constructed

---

[3] As only one example, see Suzannah Biernoff (2002). *Sight and Embodiment in the Middle Ages*. (Basingstoke: Palgrave Macmillan) who points to a continuity between the work of the mediaeval Franciscan, Roger Bacon, and the French phenomenologist, Maurice Merleau-Ponty. Scholars of Descartes have also been concerned to distinguish between the work of Descartes himself (which is not nearly as dualistic as it first appears) and the Cartesians.

their worlds. There cannot have been one aspect of life from an earlier period that did not have to die or adapt to the new social and cultural conditions of the modern era.

Perhaps it is only when a tide has turned and the circulations of those social and cultural energies that gave rise to a specific epoch have petered out or changed dramatically that we can appreciate, looking backward, the cohesiveness and distinctiveness of a specific period. Certainly, there remain far too many identifications with the various plots and subplots of modernity for our present cultural situation to claim it is something unique and distinctive. All today's multiculturalism, pluralism, glitz, glamour, internationalism, eclecticism, and hybridity are the late flowerings of modernity. But there are rumours of new currents that could see the end of the modernity and, therefore, provide historians with a space for looking back and assessing more clearly its cohesiveness and distinctiveness as a cultural era. Two are probably most prominent. The first concerns finance, particularly credit. One of the most decisive developments of modern capitalism came with the extensive employment of double-entry book-keeping, from the early sixteenth century onwards, among the merchant class. This made possible the compilation of precise records of capital and outlay that facilitated calculations of expendable wealth that could be used for speculation and credit.[4] Capitalism was the economic basis for modernity and all its failures (international warfare, genocide, deathcamps) and achievements. If capitalism were to collapse, and there are rumours today of the possibility of such a collapse, then it is likely that unprecedented levels of scarcity and austerity could inaugurate an epochal change. The second current is not unrelated to the first in so far as it announces a global shift of emphasis from the Atlantic to the Pacific seaboard. Modernity is a western cultural formation, however much its universal vision coincided with a burgeoning international relations that was economic, diplomatic, military, and cultural. Modernity's cosmopolitanism coincided with nascent and developing globalism. Its early manifestations were European and later North American. Hence there is a high degree of accuracy in mapping modernity on to those nations who comprise NATO (North Atlantic Treaty Organisation). Since the end of the First World War, the United States has been the economic and military powerhouse behind an alliance with Europe that is both historical and cultural. But there are rumours that this is changing; that the Orient is in the ascendant and the Occident on the wane; that the economic and growing military power of China, India, and Japan will eclipse the strengths of Europe and the North America. Once more, such an axial shift in the structures of global power would inaugurate an epochal change.

For the moment, modernity, however diverse its manifestations and values, remains an unfinished project. This volume draws together some of the most prominent aspects of that project and some of its major voices, organizing them along specific key trajectories. In this way it offers a statement, not simple, not singular, but many-faceted; a statement nevertheless of not just about where we have been but also where

---

[4] See Mary Poovey (1998). *A History of the Modern Fact: Problems of Knowledge in the Sciences of Wealth and Society.* (Chicago: University of Chicago Press), ch. 2, 29–91.

we still are. The statement is orientated around two disciplines, theology and philosophy, and an interrelationship between them that goes back to ancient times. It is the interrelationship that is most fascinating. Individually they show the creative urge to think again, to start anew and to cast off the vestiges of any dogmatic slumbering. Descartes, Kant, Nietzsche, and Wittgenstein have theological counterparts in Schleiermacher, Kierkegaard, Strauss, and Barth. At times both disciplines renounce metaphysics and at times they embrace it. At times both view anthropology as an enemy and at times they both view it as a friend. Frequently, they are fighting over the same terrain: epistemology, ethics, aesthetics, hermeneutics, and ontology. They draw together: Hegel, Dostoyevsky, Tillich, and Levinas. They draw apart: Marx, Heidegger, Sartre, and Barth. When they draw apart, it is notably the philosophers who inscribe the boundary. Theologically, the variety of confluence between both disciplines is as rich and complex as modernity itself. The chapters in the volume emphasize the variety of that confluence in cultural and geographical contexts, which evolve over almost four hundred years. Is there a lesson each can learn from this? Possibly only that they share too much in common in their pursuit of truth to ever be entirely free of each other. Even the current fashion of new atheism remains an appeal to the theisms and their histories which it rejects. The unfinished project of modernity, then, will require also the continuation of the relations between these two disciplines. There is also the unfinished project of the modern university at the heart of these issues, with its exaggerated distinctions between disciplines. The latter are especially significant and problematic for a discipline like theology. And it is possibly here that a further change will make itself evident. For under the secularization thesis, the discipline of philosophy took the cultural lead and theology was demoted; but under conditions in late modernity in which religion is once more coming to the fore as an important public phenomenon, then perhaps, it is the discipline of theology that will once more take the cultural lead. *Tempus edax rerum*? Possibly. Time has certainly been central to modernity's understanding of itself as concerned with the *modo*, the present.

Nicholas Adams
George Pattison
Graham Ward

INDEX

·····················

Footnotes are in bold subscript.

Printed and bound by CPI Group (UK) Ltd, Croydon, CR0 4YY

Printed and bound by CPI Group (UK) Ltd, Croydon, CR0 4YY